The New Guinness Book of Records 1996

Editor
Peter Matthews

Founding Editor
Norris D. McWhirter

GUINNESS PUBLISHING

Copyright

British Library Cataloguing in Publication Data
A catalogue record for this book is available from the British Library

ISBN 0-85112-646-4.
'Guinness' is a registered trade mark of Guinness Publishing Ltd.

Printed and bound in Spain by Printer Industria Gráfica S.A., Barcelona

Contents

Earth & Space   5

The Universe...5
    Carolyn's Comets...............................10
The Earth...11
Structure and Dimensions......................11
    In the Beginning was the Dreamtime........13
    Deepest Valley.................................19
Natural Phenomena................................20
Weather..22
Gems, Jewels and Precious Stones.................23

Living World   25

Animal Kingdom....................................25
    The Clouds That Crawled....................26
Mammals..27
Birds...32
    Watching the Birdie..........................34
Reptiles...35
    Goliath the Galapagos Tortoise.................36
Amphibians...37
Fish..37
    Perilous Piranhas.............................39
Crustaceans...39
Spiders..39
Insects..40
Earthworms...42
Molluscs..42
Jellyfish...43
Sponges..43
Endangered Species................................43
Prehistoric Animals................................44
    Which Way To Jurassic Park?.................45
Plant Kingdom......................................46
    Largest Fruits and Vegetables.................47
Microbes, Fungi.....................................52
Plants, Zoos, Aquaria..............................52

Human Being   53

Origins..53
Dimensions...54
Reproductivity.......................................57
Longevity..58
    The Life of Jeanne Calment...................59
Anatomy and Physiology.........................60

Science & Technology   67

Elements...67
Chemical Extremes.................................68
Physical Extremes...................................69
    Fermilab...71
Mathematics..72
    The Marginal Legacy.........................72
Computers...73
Power...73

Engineering...74
    The Case Against Working Weekends........76
Mining and Drilling...............................77
Time Pieces...79
Telephones and Facsimiles.......................79
Telescopes...80
    Starry-Eyed.....................................81
Rocketry...82
Space Flight...83

Buildings & Structures   85

Buildings for Living................................85
    House of Cards................................88
Buildings for Working.............................89
    The Lap of Luxury............................89
Buildings for Leisure...............................90
    On a Roll.......................................92
Towers and Masts...................................94
Bridges...95
Canals..97
Dams..98
Tunnels...99
Specialized Structures.............................99

Transport   105

Ships..105
    Mission Water Beatle.......................107
    A Remarkable Case of Riveting.............109
Coaching...113
Bicycles...113
Motorcycles...114
    Progression of World Speed Records........114
Motorcars..115
    What a Smash Up...........................120
Roads..120
Railways..122
Aviation..125
    Heavy Flying.................................127
    Busiest Airports..............................129

Arts & Entertainment   133

Art...133
Antiques..136
Language...136
    Drunk on Words.............................138
Literature..140
Music..144
Recorded Sound...................................149
    40 Years of Pop..............................150
Radio..152
Television...152
Photography...153
Cinema..154
    Horrors!.......................................156
Theatre..157
Dancing...159
    Lucky Dragons...............................158
Circus..160

Features shown in italics

Business World   161

Commerce..161
    Highest Office Rents........................163
Economics..164
Personal Wealth....................................165
    Dexterous Dean's Deeds....................168
Agriculture...170
    Fine Wines....................................171

Human World   175

Political and Social................................175
    Will the Flattest Country Disappear?........176
    Tornado Devastation........................178
Royalty and Heads of State.....................181
Legislatures..182
    The World's Most Popular Politician?........183
Judicial..186
    Off with his Head!..........................191
Honours, Decorations and Awards..............192
Military and Defence.............................194
Education...197
Religions..199

Human Achievements   201

Endurance and Endeavour......................201
    Around the World Together.................202
Miscellaneous Endeavours......................206
    Phenomenal Footbag Feat..................206
    Microwriting..................................208
    The Amazing Rope Trick....................209
Juggling...211
    Hurdling to Heaven?........................211
Food...211
    Popping to the Top..........................212
Drink...214
    Liquid Gold?..................................215
Manufactured Articles............................215
Collections...218

Sports & Games   219

Records for 117 Sports, Games and Pastimes, from Aerobatics to Yachting; including all the major sports such as Athletics, Cricket, Football and Tennis and lesser known ones like Curling, Harness Racing, Pétanque and Roller Hockey.

    Life Begins at 40............................239
    Cycling—The Hour..........................249
    Rugby Union World Cup....................282
    Olympic Games...............................306

Stop Press   309

Dear Guinness Book of Records   312

Index   314

Introduction

In this edition of the Guinness Book of Records we are not only recording the thousands of new records that have been set since our last edition, but also looking back at how records have changed in the 40 years since our first.

It is fascinating to note how the advance of science has brought fresh understanding of our world. For instance the very first record in the first Guinness Book of Records said that the remotest known heavenly bodies were at a distance of some 1,000 million light years. Now we locate them at some 13,200 million light years away. Indeed, all of man's penetration into space has occurred during the life cycle of our book.

The development of leisure activities since the 1950s has been enormous. In sport, the world records of those days for measurable activities in athletics, swimming and weightlifting often look ordinary now. Over this time span the number of participants throughout the world has grown very rapidly, as more and more people have been able to include sports and recreation as part of their life. There are many more competitive opportunities and improvements to equipment, facilities, technique and training have materially contributed to higher standards.

In our first edition the longest distance for a world running record for a woman was at 880 yards. Now women participate at the full range, and ideas that they should not participate at long distance events have long since been relegated to historical curiosities.

Cultural changes over the past 40 years have been enormous. In 1955 pop music was rarely mentioned in the newspapers, and the recently-introduced charts were only to be found in the trade press. There was no mention of them in the first Guinness Book of Records, although there was an entry for the best-selling gramophone records.

I am often asked whether I think that records can go on improving. Surely, some may say, there has to be an end to the merry-go-round of record breaking. Our experience at the Guinness Book of Records, however, is that if there is a target for mankind to aim at, then people will have a go at it, and I am sure that we are far from the limits in many activities.

Of course there are records that will remain for ever in our book. Mount Everest remains the world's highest mountain, records will remain for activities for which the conditions have changed, and surely nobody will ever challenge the pole sitting record of St Simeon the Younger, or 'Stylites'. Most records, however, do not come into such categories.

As ever, we at the Guinness Book of Records, have been delighted to record the changes in world and national records over the past year, and look forward to continuing to track the amazing achievements by people of all ages and all nations in the years ahead. We trust that you, the reader, will share our pleasure in these deeds.

The section at the end of the book "Dear Guinness Book of Records", which we introduced last year, gives some idea of the range of items submitted to the Guinness Book of Records team. We may not be able to include many such items on a permanent basis, through them being too specialised or lacking true international competitiveness, but we continue to admire the ingenuity and tenacity of would-be record-breakers. May I wish you all every success in meeting at least your own personal targets in the year ahead.

Peter Matthews, Editor

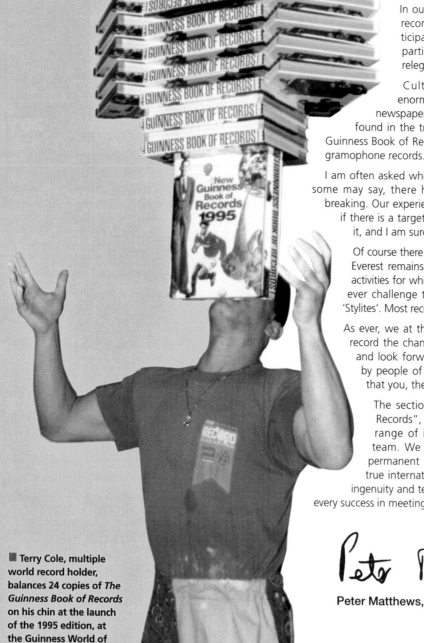

■ Terry Cole, multiple world record holder, balances 24 copies of *The Guinness Book of Records* on his chin at the launch of the 1995 edition, at the Guinness World of Records Exhibition in the Trocadero, London on 4 Oct 1994.

GUINNESS PUBLISHING LTD, 33 LONDON ROAD, ENFIELD, MIDDLESEX, EN2 6DJ, ENGLAND

The Universe

LIGHT YEAR—the distance travelled by light, the speed of which is 299,792.458 km/sec *186,282.397 miles/sec*, in one tropical year (365.24219878 mean solar days at January 0, 12 hours Ephemeris time in AD 1900). It is equivalent to 9,460,528,405,000 km *5,878,499,814,000 miles*.

Largest structure in the Universe The largest structure found to date in the universe is a cocoon-shaped shell of galaxies about 650 million light years across, surrounding the Local Supercluster (⟷ below). This discovery, by a team of French astronomers led by Georges Paturel, was announced in June 1994.

Galaxies The largest is the central galaxy of the Abell 2029 galaxy cluster, 1070 million light years distant in Virgo. Its discovery was announced in July 1990 by Juan M. Uson, Stephen P. Boughn and Jeffrey R. Kuhn (USA). It has a major diameter of 5,600,000 light years, which is eighty times the diameter of our own Milky Way galaxy, and has a light output equivalent to 2 trillion (2×10^{12}) Suns.

Our own galaxy is only one of 10 billion galaxies. It has a visible diameter of 75,000 light years but is detectable up to at least three times this value. It has a mass 4×10^{11} times that of the Sun, which is currently 26,100 light years from the centre. It is part of the so-called 'Local Group', which is being gravitationally attracted towards the centre of the Local Supercluster (⟷ above), which is dominated by the Virgo Cluster of galaxies. The closest extra-galactic object is the Sagittarius Dwarf galaxy, at a distance of 82,000 light years. The discovery by R.A. Ibata, G. Gilmore and M.J. Irwin (UK) was announced in April 1994.

The brightest galaxy (or galaxy in the process of forming) is IRAS F10214+4724, which was detected as a faint source by IRAS (Infra Red Astronomy Satellite) in 1983 and is 4.7×10^{14} times more luminous than the Sun. It has a red shift of 2.286, equivalent to a distance of 11,600 million light years, but the remotest galaxy is the radio galaxy 8C 1435+635, the discovery of which was announced by a joint Dutch, UK, and US team in May 1994. It has a red shift of 4.25, equivalent to a distance of 13,000 million light years.

Age of the Universe For the age of the Universe estimated values of 10 to 18 gigayears (a gigayear being a billion years) are obtained from various cosmological techniques. Current experimental values of the Hubble constant—named after Edwin Hubble (1889–1953)—at 50 to 90 km per sec per megaparsec are consistent with this range.

It was announced on 23 Apr 1992 that the COBE (Cosmic Background Explorer) satellite, launched by NASA on 18 Nov 1989, had detected minute fluctuations from the cosmic microwave background temperature of −270.424 °C *−454.763 °F*. This has been interpreted as evidence for the initial formation of galaxies within the Universe only a million years after the Big Bang (⟷ Stars, oldest).

Remotest object The interpretation of the red shifts of quasars in terms of distance is limited by a lack of knowledge of the Universal constants. The record red shift is 4.897 for the quasar PC 1247+3406 as determined by Donald P. Schneider, Maarten Schmidt and James E. Gunn and announced in May 1991, following spectroscopic and photometric observations made in February and April of the same year using the Hale Telescope at Palomar Observatory,

Guess What?

Q. What is Uluru usually known as?

A. See Page 13

In 1955 we recorded the remotest known heavenly body as being 1 billion light years away. Now we have the record as 13.2 billion.

California, USA. If it is assumed that there is an 'observable horizon', where the speed of recession is equal to the speed of light, i.e. at 14,000 million light years or 1.32×10^{23} km 8.23×10^{22} miles, then a simple interpretation would place this quasar at 94.4 per cent of this value or 13,200 million light years.

Farthest visible object The remotest heavenly body visible with the naked eye is the Great Galaxy in Andromeda (mag. 3.47), known as Messier 31. It was first noted from Germany by Simon Marius (1570–1624). It is a rotating nebula in spiral form at a distance from the Earth of about 2,310,000 light years, and our Galaxy is moving towards it. Under good conditions for observations, Messier 33, the Spiral in Triangulum (mag. 5.79), can be glimpsed by the naked eye at a distance of 2,530,000 light years.

Quasars Quasi-stellar radio sources (quasars or QSOs) are believed to be the active centres of distant galaxies and appear as highly luminous point-like sources. Over 7200 are known and include the most luminous object in the sky, the quasar HS 1946+7658, which is at least 1.5×10^{15} times more luminous than the Sun. Its discovery was announced in July 1991 following the Hamburg Survey of northern quasars. This quasar has a red shift of 3.02 and is therefore at a distance of 12,400 million light years.

The most violent outburst observed in a quasar was recorded on 13 Nov 1989 by a joint US-Japanese team who noted that the energy output of the quasar PKS 0558−504 (which is about 2000 million light years distant) increased by two thirds in three minutes, equivalent to all the energy released by the Sun in 340,000 years.

Stars

MAGNITUDE—a measure of stellar brightness such that the light of a star of any magnitude bears a ratio of 2.511886 to that of a star of the next magnitude. Thus a fifth-magnitude star is 2.511886 times brighter than a sixth-magnitude star whilst a first-magnitude star is 100 (or 2.511886^5) times brighter. Magnitude is expressed as a negative quantity for exceptionally bright bodies such as the Sun (apparent magnitude −26.78).

Nearest star Excepting the special case of our own Sun, the nearest is the very faint Proxima Centauri, discovered in 1915, which is 4.225 light years (4.00×10^{13} km 2.48×10^{13} miles) away.

The nearest 'star' visible to the naked eye is the southern-hemisphere binary alpha Centauri (4.35 light years distant), with an apparent magnitude of −0.27. By AD 30,000 this binary will reach a minimum distance from the Earth of 3.11 light years and should be the second-brightest 'star', with an apparent magnitude of −1.00.

Largest star The M-class supergiant Betelgeuse (alpha Orionis—the top left star of Orion), which is 310 light years distant, is the largest star. It has a diameter of 700 million km *400 million miles*, which is about 500 times greater than that of the Sun. It is surrounded by a dust 'shell' and also by an outer tenuous gas halo up to 8.5×10^{11} km 5.3×10^{11} miles in diameter.

Most massive star The variable eta Carinae, which is 9100 light years distant in the Carina Nebula, is estimated to be 150 to 200 times more massive than the Sun. However, the most massive stars whose masses have actually been determined are the two stars of the binary known as Plaskett's Star (discovered by K. Plaskett in 1922), which both have masses 60 to 100 times that of the Sun.

Most luminous star If all the stars could be viewed at the same distance, eta Carinae would also be the most luminous star, with a total luminosity 6,500,000 times that of the Sun. However, the *visually* brightest star is the hypergiant Cygnus OB2 No. 12, which is 5900 light years distant. It has an absolute visual magnitude of −9.9 and is therefore visually 810,000 times brighter than the Sun. This brightness may be matched by the supergiant IV b 59 in the nearby galaxy Messier 101. During 1843 the absolute luminosity and absolute visual brightness of eta Carinae temporarily increased to values 60 and 70 million times the corresponding values for the Sun.

Smallest star Neutron stars, which may have a mass up to three times that of the Sun, only have diameters of 10–30 km *6–19 miles*. Although black holes are point-like sources, their distortion of local space-time means that they appear as black stars, with a diameter of 59 km *37 miles* for one having a mass ten times that of the Sun.

Least massive star The white dwarf companion to the millisecond pulsar PSR B1957+20, the discovery of which was announced by A.S. Fruchter, D.R. Stinebring and J.H. Taylor in April 1988, has a mass only 0.02 that of the Sun and is being evaporated by the fast-spinning neutron star. Brown dwarves such as the candidate GD 165B (⇔ below) are expected to have a mass 0.05 that of the Sun whilst normal stars (those undergoing continuous fusion of hydrogen) cannot have a mass less than 0.08 that of the Sun.

Dimmest star GD 165B, the brown dwarf candidate companion to the white dwarf GD 165A which is 117 light years distant, is the dimmest star. It has a luminosity ten thousand times less than that of the Sun and a visual brightness eight million times less. Its discovery was announced by E.E. Becklin and B. Zuckerman in September 1988.

Brightest star (As seen from earth) Sirius A (alpha Canis Majoris), 8.64 light years distant, is the

■ Eta Carinae, the most massive star, was also around the middle of the last century among the brightest stars, although it has since faded and is no longer visible to the naked eye. Located at the centre of the Carina Nebula, it does, however, provides a dramatic sight (above). The picture on the left is an optical image of the nebula as seen by the Hubble Space Telescope after the servicing mission which took place in 1993, with eta Carinae itself again standing out in the centre. (Photos: Royal Observatory and Science Photo Library/Space Telescope Science Institute/NASA)

Torcularis Septentrionalis is the name applied to the star omicron Piscium in the constellation Pisces, and is not surprisingly the longest star name.

Guess What?
Q. Where is the world's largest planetarium?
A. See Page 81

brightest star in the sky with an apparent magnitude of −1.46 at present, but this will rise to a maximum of −1.67 by AD 61,000. It has a diameter of 2.33 million km *1.45 million miles*, a mass 2.14 times that of the Sun, and is visually 24 times brighter.

Youngest star Two protostars known collectively as IRAS–4, buried deep in dust clouds in the nebula NGC 1333, which is 1100 light years distant, appear to be the youngest stars. Announced in May 1991 by a combined British, German and American team, these protostars will not blaze forth as fully fledged stars for at least another 100,000 years.

Oldest star The oldest stars in the Galaxy have been detected in the halo, high above the disc of the Milky Way, by a group, led by Timothy Beers (USA), which discovered 70 such stars by January 1991 but eventually expect to detect 500. Such stars would have been formed c. 1 billion years after the Big Bang (⟺ Age of the Universe).

Pulsars For pulsars whose spin rates have been accurately measured, the fastest-spinning is PSR B1937+214, which was discovered by a group led by Donald C. Backer in November 1982. It is in the minor constellation Vulpecula (the Little Fox), 11,700 light years distant and has a pulse period of 1.5578064916 millisec, which is equivalent to a spin rate of 641.9282532 revolutions per sec. However, the pulsar which has the slowest spin-down rate, and is therefore the most accurate stellar clock, is PSR J0034−0534 (the discovery of which was announced in September 1993) at only 6.7×10^{-21} sec per sec.

Brightest supernova The brightest ever seen by historic man is believed to be SN 1006, noted in April 1006 near Beta Lupi, which flared for two years and attained a magnitude of −9 to −10. The remnant is believed to be the radio source G327.6+14.5, nearly 3000 light years distant. Others have occurred in 1054, 1604 and 1885 and most recently on 23 Feb 1987, when Ian Shelton sighted that now designated SN 1987A in the Large Magellanic Cloud 170,000 light years distant. This supernova was visible to the naked eye when at its brightest in May 1987.

Constellations The largest of the 88 constellations is Hydra (the Sea Serpent), which covers 1302.844 deg² or 3.16 per cent of the whole sky and contains at least 68 stars visible to the naked eye (to 5.5 magnitude). The constellation Centaurus (Centaur), ranking ninth in area, however, embraces at least 94 such stars.

The smallest constellation is Crux Australis (Southern Cross), with an area of only 0.16 per cent of the whole sky, viz. 68.477 deg² compared with the 41,252.96 deg² of the whole sky.

The Sun

ASTRONOMICAL UNIT—the mean distance from the centre of the Earth to the centre of the Sun as defined in 1938, equivalent to 149,597,871 km *92,955,807 miles*.

Distance extremes The true distance of the Earth from the Sun is 1.00000102 astronomical units or 149,598,023 km *92,955,902 miles*. Our orbit being elliptical, the distance of the Sun varies between a minimum (perihelion) of 147,098,200 km *91,402,600 miles* and a maximum (aphelion) of 152,097,900 km *94,509,200 miles*. Based on an orbital circumference of 939,886,500 km *584,018,400 miles* and an orbital period (sidereal year) of 365.256366 days, the average orbital velocity is 107,220 km/h *66,620 mph*, but this varies between a minimum of 105,450 km/h *65,520 mph* at aphelion and a maximum of 109,030 km/h *67,750 mph* at perihelion.

Temperature and dimensions The Sun has a stellar classification of a *yellow dwarf* type G2, although its mass at 1.9889×10^{27} tonnes is 332,946.04 times that of the Earth and represents over 99 per cent of the total mass of the Solar System. The solar diameter at 1,392,140 km *865,040 miles* leads to a density of 1.408 times that of water or a quarter that of the Earth.

The Sun has a central temperature of about 15,400,000 K and a core pressure of 25.4 PPa (2.54×10^{16} Pa *3.68×10^{12} lb force/in²*). It uses up about 4 million tonnes of hydrogen per sec, equal to an energy output of 3.85×10^{26} watts, although it will have taken 10,000 million years to exhaust its energy supply (about 5000 million years from the present). The luminous intensity of the Sun is 2.7×10^{27} candelas, which is equal to a luminance of 4.5×10^8 candelas/m² *290,000 candelas/in²* (⟺ also Sunspots).

Sunspots To be visible to the *protected* naked eye, a sunspot must cover about one two-thousandth part of the Sun's disc and thus have an area of about 1300 million km² *500 million miles²*. The largest sunspot ever noted was in the Sun's southern hemisphere on 8 Apr 1947. Its area was about 18,000 million km² *7000 million miles²*, with an extreme longitude of 300,000 km *187,000 miles* and an extreme latitude of 145,000 km *90,000 miles*. Sunspots appear darker because they are more than 1500°C *2700°F* cooler than the rest of the Sun's surface temperature of 5504°C *9939°F*.

In October 1957 a smoothed sunspot count showed 263, the highest recorded index since records started in 1755 (cf. the previous record of 239 in May 1778). In 1943 one sunspot lasted for 200 days, from June to December.

Planets

Largest planet The nine major planets (including the Earth) are bodies within the Solar System and revolve round the Sun in definite orbits.

Jupiter, with an equatorial diameter of 142,984 km *88,846 miles* and a polar diameter of 133,708 km *83,082 miles*, is the largest of the nine major planets, with a mass 317.828 times, and a volume 1323.3 times, that of the Earth. It also has the shortest period of rotation, resulting in a Jovian day of only 9 hr 50 min 30.003 sec in the equatorial zone.

Smallest and coldest planet The discovery of Pluto by Clyde William Tombaugh (US) at the Lowell Observatory, Flagstaff, Arizona, USA was announced on 13 Mar 1930. The planet has a diameter of 2320 km *1442 miles* and a mass 0.0021 that of the Earth. The discovery of Pluto's moon Charon was announced on 22 Jun 1978 from the US Naval Observatory, Flagstaff, Arizona. Although the surface temperature of Pluto is only approximately known, its surface composition suggests that it must be similar to the value of −235°C *−391°F* measured for Neptune's moon Triton, the lowest observed surface temperature of any natural body in the Solar System.

Outermost planet The Pluto–Charon system orbits at a mean distance from the Sun of 5914 million km *3674 million miles* in a period of 248.54 years, but because of the large orbital eccentricity they are closer to the Sun than Neptune between 23 Jan 1979 and 15 Mar 1999. However, Pluto lost its status as the outermost object with the discovery of the Kuiper belt object 1992 QB₁ by David Jewitt (UK) and Jane Luu (USA), announced on 14 Sep 1992. Based on the definition that the remotest Solar System object is that with the largest perihelion, this would be 1994 ES₂ (another Kuiper Belt object), discovered by Jewitt and Luu on 13 Mar 1994, which does not approach the Sun any closer than 6691 million km

■ The nearest star is the Sun. Its corona—the outermost region of its atmosphere—shows a range of colours, but is only visible to the naked eye during a total solar eclipse.
(Photo: Spectrum Colour Library)

Guess What?

Q. Which is the largest satellite?

A. See Page 8

Zodiac

The largest zodiacal constellation is Virgo, with an area of 1294.428 square degrees, and the smallest Capricornus (Capricorn) of area 413.947 square degrees. Taurus is the zodiacal constellation with the most bright stars, with 125 down to magnitude 6, whilst Aries, Capricornus and Libra have the fewest, with only 50 each.

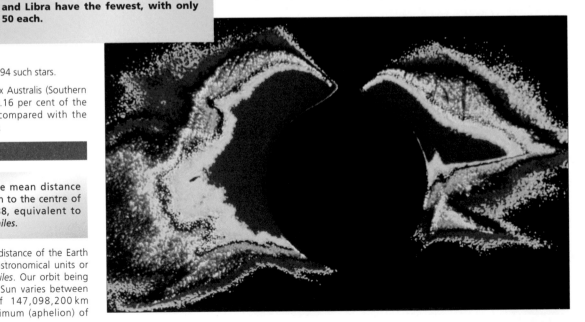

4157 *million miles* and has the largest non-cometary mean distance at 6772 million km *4208 million miles* (⇨ Asteroids, Number and distance extremes and Comets, Longest period).

Fastest planet Mercury, which orbits the Sun at an average distance of 57,909,200 km *35,983,100 miles*, has a period of revolution of 87.9686 days, so giving the highest average speed in orbit of 172,248 km/h *107,030 mph*.

Hottest planet For Venus a surface temperature of 462°C *864°F* has been estimated from measurements made from the Soviet *Venera* and American *Pioneer* surface probes.

In 1955 the hottest planet was thought to be Mercury (the nearest planet to the Sun). Its average temperature was reckoned to be 315°C *600°F*. Now we know that Venus is the hottest planet.

Nearest planet The fellow planet closest to the Earth is Venus, which is at times only 41,360,000 km *25,700,000 miles* inside the Earth's orbit, compared with Mars' closest approach of 55,680,000 km *34,600,000 miles* outside the Earth's orbit.

Densest and least dense planet Earth is the densest planet, with an average density of 5.515 times that of water, while Saturn has an average density only about one-eighth of this value or 0.685 times that of water.

Surface features By far the highest and most spectacular surface feature on any planet is the volcano Olympus Mons (formerly Nix Olympica) in the Tharsis region of Mars. It has a diameter of 500–600 km *310–370 miles* and an estimated height of 26 km *16 miles* above the surrounding plain.

Conjunctions The most dramatic recorded conjunction of the seven principal members of the Solar System besides the Earth (Sun, Moon, Mercury, Venus, Mars, Jupiter and Saturn) occurred on 5 Feb 1962, when 16° covered all seven during an eclipse in the Pacific area. It is possible that the sevenfold conjunction of September 1186 spanned only 12°. The next notable conjunction will take place on 5 May 2000.

Satellites

Most and least satellites The Solar System has a total of 61 satellites, with Saturn having the most at 18 whilst Earth and Pluto have only one satellite each and Mercury and Venus none. The most recently discovered, announced on 16 Jul 1990 by Mark R. Showalter (USA), is the Saturnian satellite Pan (Saturn XVIII), which was found on eleven *Voyager 2*

To Scale

Largest scale model The largest scale model of the solar system was developed by the Lakeview Museum of Arts and Sciences in Peoria, Illinois, USA and first displayed in April 1992. The Sun, with a diameter of 11 m *36 ft*, was painted on the exterior of the museum's planetarium, and the planets (spheres ranging in diameter from 2.5 cm *1 in* in the case of Pluto up to 1.1 m *3 ft 9 in* for Jupiter) were situated in appropriate locations in accordance with their distance from the Sun. This meant that the Earth was 1.2 km *¾ mile* away, with Pluto being in the town of Kewanee, some 64 km *40 miles* from the museum.

A smaller model of the solar system was created by Lars Broman and inaugurated by the Futures' Museum, Borlänge, Sweden on 29 Nov 1986. Its Sun had a diameter of 1.5 m *5 ft* and the planets ranged from 3.5 mm *⅛ in* to 140 mm *5½ in* in diameter, with the closest to the Sun being 60 m *200 ft* away and the furthest 6 km *3¾ miles* away. Unlike the American model, it also included the nearest star to the Sun, Proxima Centauri, which was sited to scale in the Museum of Victoria, Melbourne, Australia.

Bright & Faint

Brightest planet Viewed from Earth, the brightest of the five planets normally visible to the naked eye (Jupiter, Mars, Mercury, Saturn and Venus) is Venus, with a maximum magnitude of –4.4.

Faintest planet Uranus, with a magnitude of 5.5, can only be seen with the naked eye under certain conditions. The faintest of the nine planets as seen from Earth is Pluto (magnitude 15.0), which can only be viewed through a telescope.

■ Uranus is the faintest planet which has been seen without a telescope. This picture is an artist's impression from one of its 15 satellites, Miranda, and shows the rings around it, discovered on 10 Mar 1977.
(Photo: Spectrum Colour Library)

photographs taken during the close approach in August 1981. It has a diameter of only about 20 km *12 miles* and orbits within the Encke Division, which is 322 km *200 miles* wide, in the A ring. In 1994 highly tentative evidence was obtained from *Voyager* photographs for the possible existence of a further seven satellites in the Saturn system.

Distance extremes The distance of satellites from their parent planets varies from the 9377 km *5827 miles* of Phobos from the centre of Mars to the 23,700,000 km *14,700,000 miles* of Jupiter's outer satellite Sinope (Jupiter IX).

Largest and smallest satellite The largest and most massive satellite is Ganymede (Jupiter III), which is 2.017 times as heavy as the Earth's Moon and has a diameter of 5268 km *3273 miles*. Of satellites whose diameters have been measured the smallest is Deimos, the outer moon of Mars. Although irregularly shaped, it has an average diameter of 12.5 km *7.8 miles*.

Asteroids

Number and distance extremes There are an estimated 45,000 asteroids, but the orbits of only about 6500 have been computed. Whilst most orbit between Mars and Jupiter, distances from the Sun vary between 20,890,000 km *12,980,000 miles* for the Apollo asteroid 3200 Phaethon (discovered 11 Oct 1983) at perihelion and 7788 million km *4839 million miles* in the case of the Kuiper belt object 1993 SB, discovered on 16 Sep 1993, at aphelion (⇨ Planets, Outermost and Comets, Longest period).

Largest and smallest asteroid The largest asteroid is 1 Ceres (the first discovered, by G. Piazzi at Palermo, Sicily on 1 Jan 1801) with an equatorial diameter of 959 km *596 miles* and a polar diameter of 907 km *563 miles*. The smallest asteroid is 1993KA₂, discovered on 21 May 1993, with a diameter of c. 5 m *16 ft*.

Brightest and dimmest asteroid The brightest asteroid is 4 Vesta (discovered on 29 Mar 1807) with an absolute magnitude of 3.16. It is the only asteroid visible to the naked eye and attains a maximum apparent magnitude of 5.0 as viewed from the Earth. The dimmest asteroid is $1993KA_2$ ($\Leftrightarrow$ above), whose absolute magnitude of 29 makes it the faintest object ever detected.

Closest approach The asteroid $1994XM_1$ was discovered by James Scotti (USA) on 9 Dec 1994 only 14 hours before its record close approach to the Earth at 100,000 km *62,000 miles*. It is 10 m *33 ft* in diameter.

The Moon

The Earth's closest neighbour in space and its only natural satellite is the Moon, which has an average diameter of 3475.1 km *2159.3 miles* and a mass of 7.348×10^{19} tonnes, or 0.0123 Earth masses, so that its density is 3.344 times that of water.

The Moon orbits at a mean distance of 384,399.1 km *238,854.5 miles* centre-to-centre. In the present century the closest approach (smallest perigee) was 356,375 km *221,441 miles* centre-to-centre on 4 Jan 1912, and the farthest distance (largest apogee) was 406,711 km *252,718 miles* on 2 Mar 1984. The orbital period (sidereal month) is 27.321661 days, giving an average orbital velocity of 3683 km/h *2289 mph*.

Craters and 'seas' Only 59 per cent of the Moon's surface is directly visible from the Earth because it is in 'captured rotation', i.e. the period of rotation is equal to the period of orbit. The largest wholly visible crater is the walled plain Bailly, towards the Moon's South Pole, which is 295 km *183 miles* across, with walls rising to 4250 m *14,000 ft*. The largest impact basin on the Moon is the far-side South Pole-Aitken, which is 2500 km *1550 miles* in diameter and on average 12,000 m *39,000 ft* deep below its rim. This is the largest and deepest such crater known in the Solar System.

The largest regular 'sea' or 'mare' is the Mare Imbrium, which has a diameter of 1300 km *800 miles*.

Highest mountains In the absence of a sea level, lunar altitudes are measured relative to an adopted radius of 1738.000 km *1079.943 miles*. On this basis the highest elevation is 8000 m *26,000 ft* for the highlands north of the Korolev Basin on the lunar far-side.

Temperature extremes When the Sun is overhead, the temperature on the lunar equator reaches 117°C *243°F* (17 degC *31 degF* above the boiling point of water). By sunset the temperature is 14°C *58°F*, but after nightfall it sinks to −163°C *−261°F*.

Eclipses

Earliest recorded eclipse Although computer programs can calculate eclipses far back into history, there now appears to be no real evidence for ancient descriptions of eclipses prior to the partial eclipse observed in Nineveh in Assyria on 15 Jun 763 BC. The first definite evidence

for a total eclipse stems from Chu-fu, China, observed on 17 Jul 709 BC.

The first description of a solar eclipse in Britain is that of 15 Feb 538, described in the Anglo-Saxon Chronicle with the Sun being two-thirds eclipsed in London. No centre of path of totality for a solar eclipse crossed London for the 837 years from 2 Nov 878 to 3 May 1715. On 14 Jun 2151 an eclipse will be 99 per cent total in London but total for a path stretching from Dover, Kent to Belfast. The next total eclipse in London will not occur until 5 May 2600. The most recent occasion when a line of totality of a solar eclipse crossed Great Britain was on 29 Jun 1927, but totality lasted only for 40 seconds and most of the track over north Wales and northern England was covered by cloud. The next instance of such an eclipse will clip the coast of Cornwall at St. Just at 10:10 a.m. on 11 Aug 1999 with totality there lasting 2 min 2 sec.

Longest duration The maximum *possible* duration of an eclipse of the Sun is 7 min 31 sec. The longest of recent date was on 20 Jun 1955 (7 min 8 sec), west of the Philippines, although it was clouded out along most of its track. An eclipse of 7 min 29 sec should occur in the mid-Atlantic Ocean on 16 Jul 2186.

The longest possible eclipse in the British Isles is 5 min 30 sec. In recent times that of 3 May 1715 was 4 min 4 sec, but that of 22 Jul 2381, which will be observed in the Borders area, will last 5 min 10 sec.

Eclipse

Although normally the maximum possible duration of an eclipse of the Sun is 7 min 31 sec, durations can be 'extended' when observers are airborne. The total occultation of the Sun was extended to 74 minutes for observers aboard a Concorde which took off from Toulouse, France and stayed in the Moon's shadow from 10:51 to 12:05 GMT on 30 Jun 1973 over the Atlantic before landing in Chad.

The longest totality of any lunar eclipse is 107 minutes, as on 16 Jul 2000.

Most eclipses The highest number of eclipses possible in a year is seven, as in 1935, when there were five solar and two lunar eclipses. In 1982 there were four solar and three lunar eclipses. The lowest possible number in a year is two, both of which must be solar, as in 1944 and 1969.

The only recent example of three total solar eclipses occurring at a single location was at a point 44°N, 67°E in Kazakhstan, east of the Aral Sea. These took place on 21 Sep 1941, 9 Jul 1945 and 25 Feb 1952.

Comets

Earliest recorded comet Records date from the 7th century BC. The successive appearances of Halley's Comet can be traced back to 240 BC. The first prediction of its return by Edmund Halley (1656–1742) proved true on Christmas Day 1758, 16 years after his death.

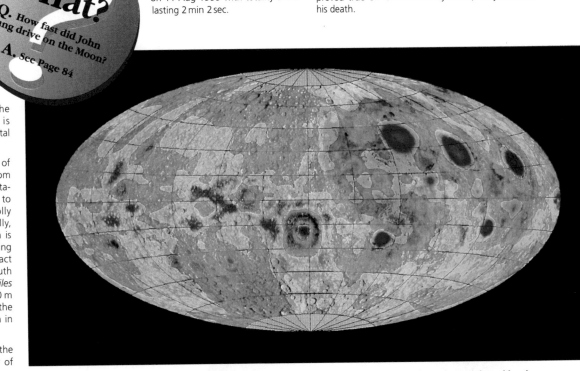

■ An unusual map showing gravity around the whole of the Moon, derived from data gathered by the Clementine spacecraft. The map shows differences between the gravity distribution predicted by a computer model and observed gravity. Yellow areas are where the model is correct. Red areas have more gravity than expected, whilst green, blue and purple areas have progressively less than predicted. The data comes from velocity deviations of the spacecraft owing to gravity. The large red areas near the top on the right are the great 'seas' of the near side of the Moon, including the Mare Imbrium (furthest to the left), the largest regular 'sea'.
(Photo: Science Photo Library/NASA)

Largest comet The object Chiron (number 2060), discovered by C.T. Kowal on 18 Oct 1977 and with a diameter of 182 km *113 miles*, is now considered to be the largest comet, but does not show spectacular cometary behaviour because it does not approach the Sun closer than 1273 million km *791 million miles*. The largest coma observed was that of the comet of 1811, which was about 2 million km *1.2 million miles* in diameter, whilst the tail of the brilliant Great Comet of 1843 trailed for 330 million km *205 million miles*.

Brightest comet The brightest comets are held to be either the Cruls Comet of 1862 or the Ikeya-Seki Comet of 1965.

Shortest period Encke's Comet has an orbital period of 1198 days (3.28 years) and has the closest approach to the Sun at 49,500,000 km *30,800,000 miles* at perihelion, at which time its speed is 254,000 km/h *158,000 mph*. First identified

Guess What?

Q. How fast did John Young drive on the Moon?

A. See Page 84

in 1786, it has been missed on only 8 of its 63 returns to perihelion, although with modern instruments it is now possible to track it over most of its orbit. Comets with low orbital eccentricity, such as the faint Schwassmann-Wachmann I which orbits between Jupiter and Saturn, can be observed continuously throughout their orbits.

Longest period The comet with the longest confirmed period, at 156 years, is Herschel-Rigollet, discovered by Caroline Herschel in 1788 and re-observed in 1939. The longest computed period is about 1550 years for Comet McNaught-Russell (1993v), discovered by Robert H. McNaught and Kenneth S. Russell on 17 Dec 1993. Its mean distance from the Sun at 20 billion km *12 billion miles* and aphelion distance at 40 billion km *25 billion miles* are the largest for any known Solar System object (⇨ Planets, Outermost and Asteroids, Number and distance extremes).

Closest approach On 1 Jul 1770, Lexell's Comet, travelling at 138,600 km/h *86,100 mph* (relative to the Sun), came to within 1,200,000 km *745,000 miles* of the Earth. However, more recently the Earth is believed to have passed through the tail of Halley's Comet on 19 May 1910.

Meteorites

When a *meteoroid* (consisting of broken fragments of cometary or asteroidal origin and ranging in size from fine dust to bodies several kilometres in diameter) penetrates to the Earth's surface, the remnant, which could be either aerolite (stony) or siderite (metallic), is described as a *meteorite*. Such events occur about 150 times per year over the whole land surface of the Earth.

Oldest meteorite A revision by T. Kirsten in 1981 of the age estimates of meteorites which have remained essentially undisturbed after their formation suggests that the oldest which has been accurately dated is the Krähenberg meteorite at 4600 ± 20 million years, which is just within the initial period of Solar System formation. It was reported in August 1978 that dust grains in the

Guess What?

Q. What was the cause of the huge explosion on 27 August 1883?

A. See Page 20

Murchison meteorite, which fell in Australia in September 1969, may be older than the Solar System.

Largest meteorite A block 2.7 m *9 ft* long by 2.4 m *8 ft* broad, estimated to weigh 59 tonnes, is the largest known meteorite. It was found in 1920 at Hoba West, near Grootfontein in Namibia. The largest meteorite exhibited by any museum is the *Cape York* meteorite, weighing 30,883 kg *68,085 lb*, found in 1897 near Cape York, on the west coast of Greenland, by the expedition of Commander (later Rear Admiral) Robert Edwin Peary (1856–1920). It was known to the Inuits as the Abnighito and is now exhibited in the Hayden Planetarium in New York City, USA. The largest piece of stony meteorite recovered is a piece weighing 1770 kg *3902 lb*, part of a 4 tonne shower which struck Jilin (formerly Kirin), China on 8 Mar 1976.

The heaviest of the 23 meteorites known to have fallen on the British Isles since 1623 was one weighing at least 46 kg *102 lb* (the largest known fragment being 7.88 kg *17 lb 6 oz*), which fell around 4:15 p.m. on 24 Dec 1965 at Barwell, Leics.

Greatest explosion The explosion of 10–15 megatons high-explosive equivalent which

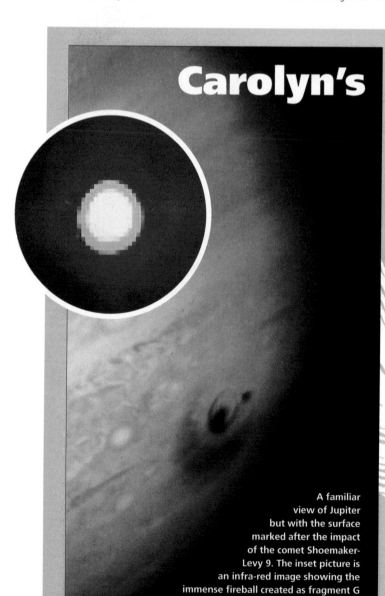

Carolyn's Comets

Carolyn Shoemaker holds the record for having discovered more comets than anyone alive, and has more comets bearing her name than any other astronomer, living or dead. Her total is an astounding 32 comets plus some 800 asteroids. Some of the most exciting moments of her life have taken place in the middle of the night while she sat on a dark, freezing-cold mountain top. Generally she didn't know it at the time, and it wasn't until later, while studying telescope photographs in a well-lit, warm lab, that she could say "I think I've got something here."

Her astronomy career took off after her children left home and she began assisting her husband, geological astronomer Eugene Shoemaker. Once a month, they'd drive all night to get to Palomar Mountain, 800 km *500 miles* from their Arizona home. They'd set up their telescope and pray for clear skies. Shoemaker soon realized she had a talent for seeing asteroids and comets. One fateful night, the photographs they and partner David Levy took were accidentally ruined, and they had no choice but to set up their equipment again under cloudy conditions. A rip in the clouds revealed Jupiter, and the picture that resulted showed something phenomenal — a comet like a string of pearls in the sky, on a collision course with the big planet.

Nowadays, a photograph of Comet Shoemaker-Levy 9 hangs over the Shoemakers' bed. Photographs of asteroids they've discovered and named after family members have been known to appear under the Christmas tree.

So how does she sum up her observations? "The universe is full of chaos, even if it looks peaceful to us."

Carolyn Shoemaker standing by one of the tools of her trade.
Photos: Terence Dickinson (above)
Ann Ronan/Image Select (left)
and Science Photo Library (inset)

A familiar view of Jupiter but with the surface marked after the impact of the comet Shoemaker-Levy 9. The inset picture is an infra-red image showing the immense fireball created as fragment G of the comet hit Jupiter on 18 Jul 1994.

occurred over the basin of the Podkamennaya Tunguska River on 30 Jun 1908 resulted in the devastation of an area of 3900 km² *1500 miles²*, with the shock wave being felt up to 1000 km *625 miles* away. The cause has most recently been thought to be the energy released following the total disintegration at an altitude of 10 km *33,000 ft* of a common type stony meteoroid 30 m *98 ft* in diameter travelling at hypersonic velocity at an incoming angle of 45 degrees.

Showers

The greatest meteor shower on record occurred on the night of 16–17 Nov 1966, when the Leonid meteors (which recur every 33¼ years) were visible between western North America and eastern Russia (then USSR). It was calculated that meteors passed over Arizona, USA at a rate of 2300 per minute for a period of 20 minutes from 5 a.m. on 17 Nov 1966.

Lunar meteorites Twelve known meteorites are believed to be of lunar origin, as distinguished by characteristic element and isotopic ratios. The first eleven were found in Antarctica, but the most recently discovered, which is only 3 cm *1 in* in diameter and weighs 19 g *0.67 oz*, was found at Calcalong Creek on the Nullarbor Plain to the north of the Great Australian Bight by D.H. Hill, W.V. Boynton and R.A. Haag (USA), with the discovery being announced in January 1991.

Craters It has been estimated that some 2000 asteroid-Earth collisions have occurred in the last 600 million years. One hundred and two collision sites or astroblemes have been identified. A crater 240 km *150 miles* in diameter and 800 m *½ mile* deep was attributed to a meteorite in 1962 in Wilkes Land, Antarctica. Such a crater could have been caused by a meteorite weighing 13 billion tonnes striking at 70,800 km/h *44,000 mph*.

Soviet scientists reported in December 1970 an astrobleme with a diameter of 95 km *60 miles* and a maximum depth of 400 m *1300 ft* in the basin of the River Popigai. There is a crater-like formation or astrobleme 442 km *275 miles* in diameter on the eastern shore of Hudson Bay, Canada, where the Nastapoka Islands are just off the coast. The largest and best-preserved crater which was definitely formed by a meteorite is Coon Butte (or Barringer Crater), discovered in 1891, near Winslow, Arizona, USA. It is 1265 m *4150 ft* in diameter and now about 175 m *575 ft* deep, with a parapet rising 40–48 m *130–155 ft* above the surrounding plain. It has been estimated that an iron-nickel mass of some 2 million tonnes and a diameter of 61–79 m *200–260 ft* gouged this crater in c. 25,000 BC

The Earth

The Earth is approximately 4540 million years old. It is not a true sphere but flattened at the poles and hence an oblate spheroid. The equatorial diameter (12,756.2726 km *7926.3803 miles*) is 42.7694 km *26.5757 miles* larger than the polar diameter of 12,713.5032 km *7899.8046 miles*.

The Earth has a pear-shaped asymmetry, with the north-pole radius being 44 m *144 ft* longer than the south-pole radius. There is also a slight ellipticity of the equator, with its major diameter at 14.95° W being 139 m *456 ft* longer than its minor axis. The greatest departures from the reference ellipsoid are a protuberance of 73 m *240 ft* in the area of Papua New Guinea and a depression of 105 m *344 ft* south of Sri Lanka, in the Indian Ocean.

In 1955 the Earth was thought to be around 3400 million years old. Now it is estimated to be 4540 million years old.

The greatest circumference of the Earth, at the equator, is 40,075.012 km *24,901.458 miles*, compared with 40,007.858 km *24,859.731 miles* for any meridian. The area of the surface is estimated to be 510,065,500 km² *196,937,400 miles²* and the volume 1,083,207,000,000 km³ *259,875,300,000 miles³*.

The mass of the Earth, which was first assessed by Dr Nevil Maskelyne (1732–1811) in Perthshire in 1774, is 5.974×10^{21} tonnes, and the density is 5.515 times that of water. The Earth picks up about 40,000 tonnes of cosmic dust a year. The true rotation period of the Earth, i.e. the mean sidereal day increased by 0.0084 sec to account for precession, is 23 hr 56 min 4.0989 sec mean solar time.

Structure and Dimensions

Oceans

The area of the Earth covered by oceans and seas (the hydrosphere) is estimated to be 362,033,000 km² *139,782,000 miles²* or 70.98 per cent of the total surface. The mean depth of the hydrosphere is 3729 m *12,234 ft* and the volume 1,349,930,000,000 km³ *323,870,000 miles³*, compared to 35,000,000,000 km³ *8,400,000 miles³* of fresh water. The total weight of the water is 1.41×10^{18} tonnes, or 0.024 per cent of the Earth's weight.

Largest ocean The Pacific is the largest ocean in the world. Excluding adjacent seas, it represents 45.9 per cent of the world's oceans and covers 166,241,700 km² *64,186,300 miles²* in area. The average depth is 3940 m *12,925 ft*.

The brightest fireball ever photographically recorded was photographed by Dr Zdeněk Ceplecha over Šumava, Czechoslovakia (now Czech Republic) on 4 Dec 1974. It had a momentary magnitude of –22 or 10,000 times brighter than a full Moon.

Smallest ocean The Arctic, with an area of 13,223,700 km² *5,105,700 miles²*, is the smallest ocean. It has an average depth of 1038 m *3407 ft*.

Deepest ocean The deepest part of the ocean was first pinpointed in 1951 by HM Survey Ship *Challenger* in the Marianas Trench in the Pacific Ocean. On 23 Jan 1960 the manned US Navy bathyscaphe *Trieste* descended to the bottom at 10,916 m *35,813 ft*. A more recent visit produced a figure of 10,924 m ± 10 m *35,839 ft ± 33 ft*, from data obtained by the survey vessel *Takuyo* of the Hydrographic Department, Japan Maritime Safety

Agency in 1984, using a narrow multi-beam echo sounder.

The deepest point in the territorial waters of the UK is an area 316 m *1037 ft* deep, 6 cables (*1100 m*) off the island of Raasay, near Skye, in the Inner Sound at Lat. 57° 30′ 33″ N, Long. 5° 57′ 27″ W.

Largest sea The largest of the world's seas is the South China Sea, with an area of 2,974,600 km² *1,148,500 miles²*.

Largest bay The largest bay in the world measured by shoreline length is Hudson Bay, Canada, with a shoreline of 12,268 km *7623 miles* and an area of 1,233,000 km² *476,000 miles²*. Measured by area, the Bay of Bengal, in the Indian Ocean, is larger, at 2,172,000 km² *839,000 miles²*.

Great Britain Great Britain's largest bay is Cardigan Bay, which has a shoreline 225 km *140 miles* long and measures 116 km *72 miles* across from the Lleyn Peninsula, Gwynedd to St David's Head, Dyfed.

Largest gulf The largest gulf in the world is the Gulf of Mexico, with an area of 1,544,000 km² *596,000 miles²* and a shoreline of 5000 km *3100 miles* from Cape Sable, Florida, USA, to Cabo Catoche, Mexico.

Longest fjord The world's longest fjord is the Nordvest Fjord arm of Scoresby Sund in eastern Greenland, which extends inland 313 km *195 miles* from the sea. The longest Norwegian fjord is the Sognefjord, which extends 204 km *127 miles* inland from the island of Sogneoksen to the head of the Lusterfjord arm at Skjolden. Its width ranges from 2.4 km *1½ miles* at its narrowest up to 5.1 km *3¼ miles* at its widest. It has a deepest point of 1308 m *4291 ft*.

Remote

The world's most distant point from land is a spot in the South Pacific, 47° 30′ S, 120° W, which is 2575 km *1600 miles* from the nearest points of land, namely Pitcairn Island, Ducie Island and Peter I Island. Centred on this spot is a circle of water with an area of 20,826,800 km² *8,041,200 miles²*—more than 3,000,000 km² or *1,000,000 miles²* larger than Russia, the world's largest country.

Longest sea loch Loch Fyne, Scotland, extends 60.5 km *37.6 miles* inland into Strathclyde.

Highest seamount The highest known submarine mountain, or seamount, is one discovered in 1953 near the Tonga Trench, between Samoa and New Zealand. It rises 8700 m *28,500 ft* from the seabed, with its summit 365 m *1200 ft* below the surface.

Most southerly ocean The most southerly part of the oceans is located at 87° S, 151° W, at the snout of the Scott Glacier, 320 km *200 miles* from the South Pole.

Sea temperature The temperature of the water at the surface of the sea varies greatly. It is as low as –2° C *28° F* in the White Sea and as high as 36° C *96° F* in the shallow areas of the Persian Gulf in summer.

The highest temperature recorded in the ocean is 404° C *759° F*, for a hot spring measured by an American research submarine some 480 km *300 miles* off the American west coast in 1985.

Waves, Currents, Rocks ▶▶ ▶▶

Clearest sea The Weddell Sea, 71°S, 15°W, off Antarctica, has the clearest water of any sea. A 'Secchi' disc 30cm *1ft* in diameter was visible to a depth of 80m *262ft* on 13 Oct 1986, as measured by Dutch researchers at the German Alfred Wegener Institute. Such clarity corresponds to what is attainable in distilled water.

Straits

Longest straits The Tatarskiy Proliv or Tartar Strait between Sakhalin Island and the Russian mainland is the longest strait in the world. They run from the Sea of Japan to Sakhalinsky Zaliv, a distance of 800km *500miles*, thus marginally longer than the Malacca Straits, between Malaysia and Sumatra.

Broadest straits The broadest *named* strait in the world is Davis Strait between Greenland and Baffin Island, Canada, with a minimum width of 338km *210miles*. The Drake Passage between the Diego Ramirez Islands, Chile and the South Shetland Islands is 1140km *710miles* across.

Narrowest straits The narrowest navigable straits are those between the Aegean island of Euboea and the mainland of Greece. The gap is only 40m *45yd* wide at Khalkis.

Waves

Highest waves The highest officially recorded sea wave was calculated at 34m *112ft* from trough to crest; it was measured by Lt Frederic Margraff, USN from the USS *Ramapo* proceeding from Manila, Philippines to San Diego, California, USA on the night of 6–7 Feb 1933, during a hurricane which reached 126km/h *68knots*. The highest instrumentally measured wave was one 26m *86ft* high, recorded by the British ship *Weather Reporter*, in the North Atlantic on 30 Dec 1972 at Lat. 59°N, Long. 19°W.

On 9 Jul 1958 a landslip caused a wave moving at 160km/h *100mph* to wash 524m *1720ft* high along the fjord-like Lituya Bay in Alaska, USA.

Guess What?

Q. Where did the largest shipwreck occur?

A. See Page 106

Currents

Greatest current The Antarctic Circumpolar Current or West Wind Drift Current is the greatest current in the oceans. On the basis of four measurements taken in 1982 in the Drake Passage, between South America and Antarctica, it was found to be flowing at a rate of 130,000,000m³ *4.3billion ft³* per sec. Results from computer modelling in 1990 estimate a higher figure of 195,000,000m³ *6.9billion ft³* per sec.

Strongest current The world's strongest currents are the Nakwakto Rapids, Slingsby Channel, British Columbia, Canada (Lat. 51°05'N, Long. 127°30'W), where the flow rate may reach 30km/h *16knots*.

Great Britain The fastest current in British territorial waters is 19.8km/h *10.7knots* in the Pentland Firth between the Orkney Islands and the Scottish mainland.

Tides

The greatest tides occur in the Bay of Fundy, which divides the peninsula of Nova Scotia, Canada from the United States' north-easternmost state of Maine and the Canadian

(Photo: Jacana/B Tollu)

Highest seismic waves The highest reported *tsunami* (often wrongly called a tidal wave) was one triggered by an underwater landslide which struck the island of Lanai in Hawaii c. 105,000 years ago and deposited sediment up to an altitude of approximately 375m *1230ft*. The highest known in modern times appeared off Ishigaki Island, Ryukyu island chain on 24 Apr 1771. It was possibly as high as 85m *278ft*, and tossed a 750-tonne block of coral more than 2.5km *1.3miles* inland.

province of New Brunswick. Burncoat Head in the Minas Basin, Nova Scotia, has the greatest mean spring range, with 14.5m *47ft 6in*. A range of 16.6m *54ft 6in* was recorded at springs in Leaf Basin, in Ungava Bay, Quebec, Canada in 1953. Tahiti, in the mid-Pacific Ocean, experiences virtually no tide.

Great Britain The place with the greatest mean spring range in Great Britain is Beachley, on the Severn, with a range of 12.40m *40ft 8½in*, compared with the British Isles' average of 4.6m *15ft*. Prior to 1933, tides as high as 8.80m *28ft 11in* above and 6.80m *22ft 3½in* below datum (total range 15.60m *51ft 2½in*) were recorded at Avonmouth, although an extreme range of 15.90m *52ft 2½in* for Beachley was officially accepted. In 1883 a freak tide of greater range was reported from Chepstow, Gwent.

The Centre

The land location remotest from open sea is at Lat. 46°16.8'N, Long. 86°40.2'E in the Dzungarian Basin, which is in the Xinjiang Uygur autonomous region, in the far north-west of China. It is at a great-circle distance of 2648km *1645miles* from the nearest open sea—Baydaratskaya Guba to the north (Arctic Ocean), Feni Point to the south (Indian Ocean) and Bohai Wan to the east (Yellow Sea).

The point furthest from the sea in Great Britain is near Meriden, W Mids, 117km *72½miles* equidistant from the Severn bridge, the Dee estuary and the Welland estuary.

Land

There is strong evidence that about 300 million years ago the Earth's land surface comprised a single primeval continent of 1.5 × 10⁸km² *60million miles²*, now termed Pangaea, and it is possible that even prior to its existence there had been other super-continents. Pangaea is believed to have split about 190 million years ago, during the Jurassic Period, into two super-continents. These are termed Laurasia (Eurasia, Greenland and North America) and Gondwana (Africa, Arabia, India, South America, Oceania and Antarctica).

Rocks

The age of the Earth is generally considered to be within the range of 4540 ± 40 million years. However, no rocks of this great age have yet been found on the Earth, since geological processes have presumably destroyed them.

Oldest rocks The greatest reported age for any scientifically dated rock is 3962 million years in the case of Acasta Gneisses found in May 1984. The rocks were discovered approximately 320km *200miles* north of Yellowknife, Northwest Territories, Canada by Dr Samuel Bowring (USA) as part of an ongoing Canadian geology survey mapping project.

Older minerals which are not rocks have also been identified. Some zircon crystals discovered by Bob Pidgeon and Simon Wilde in the Jack Hills, 700km *430miles* north of Perth, Western Australia in August 1984 were found to be 4276 million years old. These are the oldest fragments of the Earth's crust discovered so far.

Great Britain The oldest rocks in Great Britain were originally sediments and basic igneous rocks probably formed c. 2950 million years ago. They, and granitic rocks intruded into them, were metamorphosed c. 2500 million years ago to form the gneisses of the Scourian Complex of the north-west Highlands and the Western Isles of Scotland.

Largest rocks It was estimated in 1940 that La Gran Piedra, a volcanic plug located in the Sierra Maestra, Cuba, weighs 61,355 tonnes (⇨ also facing page).

Continents

Largest continent Of the Earth's surface 41.25 per cent, or 210,400,000km² *81,200,000miles²*, is covered by continental masses, of which only

Icebergs

Largest and tallest icebergs An antarctic tabular iceberg of over 31,000km² *12,000 miles²* is the largest on record. It was 335km *208miles* long and 97km *60miles* wide (and thus larger than Belgium) and was sighted 240km *150miles* west of Scott Island, in the South Pacific Ocean, by the USS *Glacier* on 12 Nov 1956. The tallest iceberg measured was one of 167m *550ft* reported off western Greenland by the US icebreaker *East Wind* in 1958.

Most southerly arctic iceberg A USN weather patrol sighted the most southerly arctic iceberg on record in the Atlantic at Lat. 28°44'N, Long. 48°42'W, in April 1935. The southernmost iceberg reported in British home waters was sighted 96km *60miles* from Smith's Knoll, on the Dogger Bank, in the North Sea.

Most northerly antarctic iceberg A remnant sighted in the Atlantic by the ship *Dochra* at Lat. 26°30'S, Long. 25°40'W on 30 Apr 1894 was the most northerly antarctic iceberg ever sighted.

In the beginning was the Dreamtime........

when the earth was flat and void without light or darkness. Then Nature waited for the coming of god-like heroes to give it form and life

Ayers Rock rises mysteriously out of the barren land, and standing on the summit, 348 m 1143 ft above the desert plain, it is not hard to see how this massive monolith came to play such a prominent part in aboriginal culture. To the Aborigines of the Pitjatjantjara and Yankunytjatjara tribes, each feature of Uluru, as it is known in their language, is the work or embodiment of one of the ten mythical beings who appeared at the end of the Dreamtime. Aborigines still gather in the caves at the base of the rock to hold their sacred ceremonies and paint their Dreamtime legends.

An aerial view shows Ayers Rock sprawling across the desert land (left).
(Photo: Spectrum Colour Library)

The Brain, as this feature is sometimes known, is the result of years of weathering. Legend has it that pock marks in the rock were made when enemy tribes threw spears at the tribes who lived there during the Dreamtime.
(Photo: Denise Duncan)

At 2.5 km 1.5 miles long and 1.6 km 1 mile wide, with a circumference of 9 km 5.6 miles, Uluru is the world's largest rock and an awe-inspiring sight. A mystical aura seems to surround the rock, and if you stay there long enough, you will see it change colour from vivid red to lilac, blue, pink, and brown, as the sun moves around it. Its smooth, steep walls rise at an angle of 80°, making it very difficult for vegetation to

Background Illustration: Frances Button © Guinness Publishing

take root; plaques on the rock commemorate tourists who have likewise failed to scale its mighty sides.

At the base of Uluru, however, life is abundant. When it rains, water cascades down the rock and lands in pools at the bottom. Here, dingos, kangaroos, birds, reptiles and other animals come to drink, and trees and shrubs thrive. A tiny fraction of water leaks through cracks in the hard sandstone on the way down, weakening the subsurface layer and gradually forcing the outer layers to peel off. As debris slides down the rock, it forms caves and crannies where animals find shelter. This slow process of weathering has resulted in strange formations, many of which feature in aboriginal legend. Thus, a boulder near the north-east face is a Mala, one of the Hare-Wallaby People who lived at Uluru but who were mostly destroyed by the devilish dingo, Kulpunya, himself represented by a slab of rock.

Uluru is in fact slowly decreasing in size as layers of the hard crust break off, although its form alters little, and its formidable beauty endures. To the Aborigines, to whom the rock belongs, Uluru is unlikely to diminish in importance; it will always symbolise the mystery of creation, life rising out of the desert land.

Blue in colour, the rock looms over desert oaks, which to the Aborigines represent an invading army of Poisonous Snake-People.
(Photo: Spectrum Colour Library)

A tourist with a head for heights surveys the scene from the summit of Ayers Rock.
(Photo: Gamma/ Kactus Foto)

148,021,000 km² *57,151,000 miles²* (about two-thirds, or 29.02 per cent, of the Earth's surface) is land above water, with a mean height of 756 m *2480 ft* above sea level. The Eurasian land mass is the largest, with an area (including islands) of 53,698,000 km² *20,733,000 miles²*. The Afro-Eurasian land mass, separated artificially only by the Suez Canal, covers an area of 84,702,000 km² *32,704,000 miles²* or 57.2 per cent of the Earth's land mass.

Smallest continent The Australian mainland, with an area of 7,614,500 km² *2,939,960 miles²*, is the smallest continent. Australia (including Tasmania), together with New Zealand, Papua New Guinea and the Pacific Islands, is sometimes described as Oceania.

Peninsula The world's largest peninsula is Arabia, which has an area of about 3,250,000 km² *1,250,000 miles²*.

Islands

Largest islands Discounting Australia, which is usually regarded as a continental land mass, the largest island in the world is Greenland, with an area of about 2,175,000 km² *840,000 miles²*. The largest sand island in the world is Fraser Island, Queensland, Australia with a sand dune 120 km *75 miles* long.

The largest island surrounded mostly by fresh water (48,000 km² *18,500 miles²*) is the Ilha de Marajó in the mouth of the Amazon River, Brazil. The world's largest inland island (i.e. land surrounded by rivers) is Ilha do Bananal, Brazil (20,000 km² *7700 miles²*). The largest island in a lake is Manitoulin Island (2766 km² *1068 miles²*) in the Canadian section of Lake Huron.

■ **Excluding Australia, which is normally classified as a continental land mass, Greenland is the world's largest island. With its ice, glaciers and fjords, it provides a spectacular view from space.**
(Photo: Ann Ronan/Image Select)

Great Britain The mainland of Great Britain is the eighth largest island in the world, with an area of 229,979 km² *88,795 miles²*. It stretches 971 km *603½ miles* from Dunnet Head in the north to Lizard Point in the south and 463 km *287½ miles* across from Porthaflod, Dyfed to Lowestoft, Suffolk.

The largest lake island in Great Britain is Inchmurrin, in Loch Lomond, Strathclyde/Central with an area of 115 ha *284 acres*.

Remotest island Bouvet Island (Bouvetøya), discovered in the South Atlantic by J.B.C. Bouvet de Lozier on 1 Jan 1739, is the remotest island in the world. Its position is 54°26' S, 3°24' E. This uninhabited Norwegian dependency is about 1700 km *1050 miles* north of the nearest land—the coast of Queen Maud Land, which is also uninhabited, in Antarctica.

The remotest inhabited island in the world is Tristan da Cunha, discovered in the South Atlantic by Tristão da Cunha, a Portuguese admiral, in March 1506. It has an area of 98 km² *38 miles²*. The nearest

> For two years nobody lived on Tristan da Cunha, as it had been evacuated in 1961 following volcanic activity. Eventually 198 islanders went back there in November 1963.

Newest

Pulau Batu Hairan ('Surprise Rock Island'), some 65 km *40 miles* to the north-east of Kudat, in Sabah, Malaysia, is the world's newest island. It was first sighted by three local fishermen on 14 Apr 1988. A week later it had doubled in height, and now has an area of 0.77 ha *1.9 acres* and a maximum height of 3.1 m *10 ft*.

inhabited land to the group is the island of St Helena, 2435 km *1315 nautical miles* to the north-east.

British Isles The remotest of the British islets is Rockall, 307 km *191 miles* west of St Kilda, Western Isles. This rock, measuring 21 m *70 ft* high and 25 m *83 ft* across, was not formally annexed until 18 Sep 1955.

The remotest British island which has ever been inhabited is North Rona, which is 71 km *44 miles* from the next nearest land at Cape Wrath and the Butt of Lewis. It was evacuated c. 1844. Currently the most remote inhabited British island is Fair Isle, 38.5 km *24 miles* to the south-west of Sumburgh Head, Shetland. It has a population of some 80 people.

Greatest archipelago The world's greatest archipelago is the crescent of more than 17,000 islands, 5600 km *3500 miles* long, which forms Indonesia.

Highest rock pinnacle The world's highest rock pinnacle is Ball's Pyramid near Lord Howe Island in the

Pacific, which is 561m *1843ft* high but has a base axis of only 200m *220yd*.

Northernmost land On 26 Jul 1978 Uffe Petersen of the Danish Geodetic Institute observed the islet of Odaaq Ø, 30m *100ft* across, 1.36km *1478yd* north of Kaffeklubben Ø off Pearyland, Greenland at Lat. 83°40'32.5" N, Long. 30°40'10.1" W. It is 706.4km *438.9miles* from the North Pole.

Southernmost land The South Pole, unlike the North Pole, is on land. At the South Pole the ice sheet is drifting 10m *33ft* per annum away from the geographic pole along the 40th meridian west of Greenwich. In 1956/7 the Amundsen–Scott South Pole station was built at an altitude of 2855m *9370ft*, but it could not withstand the conditions and was replaced by a new structure in 1975.

Largest atoll The world's largest atoll is Kwajalein in the Marshall Islands, in the central Pacific Ocean. Its slender coral reef 283km *176miles* long encloses a lagoon of 2850km^2 *1100miles^2*. The atoll with the largest land area is Christmas Atoll, in the Line Islands in the central Pacific Ocean. It has an area of 649km^2 *251miles^2*, of which 321km^2 *124miles^2* is land.

Longest reef The Great Barrier Reef off Queensland, north-eastern Australia is 2027km *1260miles* in length. It is not actually a single reef but consists of thousands of separate reefs. Between 1959 and 1971, and again between 1979 and 1991, corals on large areas of the central section of the reef — approximately between Cooktown and Proserpine — were devastated by the crown-of-thorns starfish (*Acanthaster planci*).

Depressions

Deepest depression The bedrock of the Bentley sub-glacial trench, Antarctica, at 2538m *8326ft* below sea level, is the deepest depression so far discovered. The greatest submarine depression is an area of the north-west Pacific floor which has an average depth of 4600m *15,000ft*. The deepest exposed depression on land is the shore surrounding the Dead Sea, now 400m *1310ft* below sea level. The deepest point on the bed of this saltiest of all lakes is 728m *2388ft* below sea level. The rate of fall in the lake surface since 1948 has been 350mm *13¾in* per annum. The deepest part of the bed of Lake Baikal in Russia is 1181m *3875ft* below sea level.

Great Britain The lowest-lying area in Great Britain is in the Holme Fen area of the Great Ouse, in Cambridgeshire at 2.7m *9ft* below sea level.

Largest depression The largest exposed depression in the world is the Caspian Sea basin in Azerbaijan, Russia, Kazakhstan, Turkmenistan and Iran. It is more than 518,000km^2 *200,000miles^2*, of which 371,800km^2 *143,550miles^2* is lake area. The preponderant land area of the depression is the Prikaspiyskaya Nizmennost, lying around the northern third of the lake and stretching inland for a distance of up to 450km *280miles*.

Caves

Longest cave The most extensive cave system in the world is that under Mammoth Cave National Park,

---

Kentucky, USA, first entered c. 4000 years ago. Explorations by many groups of cavers have revealed that interconnected cave passages beneath the Flint, Mammoth Cave and Toohey Ridges make up a system with a total mapped length which is now 560km *348miles*.

Great Britain The longest cave system in Great Britain is the Ease Gill system, W Yorks, which now has 70km *44miles* of explored passage.

Guess What?

Q. In which year did Roald Amundsen's expedition reach the South Pole?

A. See Page 203

Largest cave The world's largest cave chamber is the Sarawak Chamber, Lubang Nasib Bagus, in the Gunung Mulu National Park, Sarawak, discovered and surveyed by the 1980 British–Malaysian Mulu Expedition. Its length is 700m *2300ft*, its average width is 300m *980ft* and it is nowhere less than 70m *230ft* high. It is large enough to span the West End of London, reaching from Trafalgar Square to beyond Piccadilly Circus and Leicester Square.

Underwater cave The longest explored underwater cave is the Nohoch Nah Chich cave system in Quintana Roo, Mexico, with 39.48km *24.53miles* of mapped passages. Exploration of the system, which began in November 1987, has been carried out by the CEDAM Cave Diving Team under the leadership of Mike Madden (USA).

Deepest Caves by Countries

Depth			
m	ft	Location	
1602	5256	Réseau Jean Bernard	France
1508	4947	Shakta Pantjukhina	Georgia
1485	4872	Lamprechtsofen	Austria
1475	4839	Sistema Huautla	Mexico
1441	4728	Sistema del Trave	Spain
1415	4642	Boj Bulok	Uzbekistan
1392	4567	Lukina Jama	Croatia
1370	4495	Ceki 2	Slovenia
1324	4344	Siebenhengstehohlensystem	Switzerland
1249	4098	Abisso Paolo Roversi	Italy
1195	3920	Cukurpinar Dudeni	Turkey
1170	3838	Anou Ifflis	Algeria
308	1010	Ogof Ffynnon Ddu	Wales
214	702	Giant's Hole System	England
181	594	Poll na Gceim	Republic of Ireland
179	587	Reyfad Pot	Northern Ireland
76	249	Cnoc nan Uamh	Scotland

The longest dived traverse into a single flooded cave passage is one of 4055m *13,300ft* into the Doux de Coly, Dordogne, France by Olivier Issler (Switzerland) on 4 Apr 1991.

In 1955 the deepest ever cave descent was to a depth of 757m *2485ft*. Now the record stands at 1602m *5256ft*.

Greatest descent The world depth record was set by the Groupe Vulcain in the Gouffre Jean Bernard, France at 1602m *5256ft* in 1989. However, this cave, explored via multiple entrances, has never been entirely descended, so the 'sporting' record for the greatest descent into a cave is recognized as 1508m *4947ft* in Shakta Pantyukhina in the Caucasus Mountains of Georgia by a team of Ukrainian cavers in 1988.

Longest stalactite The longest known stalactite in the world is a wall-supported column extending 59m *195ft* from roof to floor in the Cueva de Nerja, near Málaga, in Spain. The longest free-hanging stalactites

---

in the world are believed to be some c. 10m *33ft* long in the Gruta do Janelão, in Minas Gerais, Brazil.

Tallest stalagmite The tallest known stalagmite in the world is one in the Krásnohorská cave, near Rožňava, Slovakia, which is generally accepted as being about 32m *105ft* tall. The tallest cave column is considered to be the Flying Dragon Pillar, 39m *128ft* high, in Daji Dong, Guizhou, China.

Mountains

Highest mountain An eastern Himalayan peak known as Peak XV on the Tibet–Nepal border was discovered to be the world's highest mountain in 1856 by the Survey Department of the Government of India, from theodolite readings taken in 1849 and 1850. Its height was calculated to be 8840m *29,002ft*. It was named Mt Everest after Col. Sir George Everest (1790–1866), formerly Surveyor-General of India, who pronounced his name 'Everest'. There have been a number of surveys since then, with 8848m *29,029ft* now being the most widely accepted height. (For details of ascents of Everest ⇨ Mountaineering)

The mountain whose summit is farthest from the Earth's centre is the Andean peak of Chimborazo (6267m *20,561ft*), 158km *98miles* south of the equator in Ecuador. Its summit is 2150m *7057ft* further from the Earth's centre than the summit of Mt Everest, since the Earth's radius in Ecuador is longer than the radius at the latitude of Mt Everest.

The highest mountain on the equator is the Cayambe volcano (5790m *18,996ft*), Ecuador, at Long. 77°58'W. A mountaineer on the summit would be moving at 1671km/h *1038mph* relative to the Earth's centre, due to the Earth's rotation.

The highest insular mountain in the world is Puncak Jaya in Irian Jaya, Indonesia. A survey by the Australian Universities' Expedition in 1973 yielded a height of 4884m *16,023ft*. Ngga Pulu (also in Irian Jaya), which is now 4861m *15,950ft*, was in 1936 possibly c. 4910m *16,110ft* before the melting of its snow cap.

United Kingdom The highest mountain in the UK is Ben Nevis (1343.6m *4408ft 1in* above sea level excluding the cairn, which is 3.65m *12ft* high), 6.85km *4¼miles* south-east of Fort William, Argyll, Highland. It was climbed before 1720, but though acclaimed the highest in 1790, was not officially recognized to be higher than Ben Macdhui (1310m *4300ft*) until 1870. In 1834 Ben Macdhui and Ben Nevis (Gaelic, *Beinn Nibheis*) (first reference, 1778) were respectively quoted as 4570ft *1393m* and 4370ft *1332m*.

Tallest mountain Mauna Kea (White Mountain) on the island of Hawaii is the world's tallest

Unconquered

The highest unclimbed mountain is Kankar Pünsum (7541m *24,741ft*), on the Bhutan/Tibet border. It is the 67th named mountain peak in order of height. The highest unclimbed summit is Lhotse Middle (8414m *27,605ft*), one of the peaks of Lhotse, in the Khumbu district of the Nepal Himalaya. It is the tenth highest individually recognized summit in the world, Lhotse being the fourth highest mountain.

■ Depending on what definition is used to measure the length of the Amazon, the Nile could be considered as the world's longest river. Above is a fairly familiar Nile scene, in Egypt, but the view on the right may surprise as it shows the Nile (Blue Nile) at Tissiat Falls in Ethiopia, a country renowned for its droughts and lack of water.
(Photos: Spectrum Colour Library)

50,000 m³/sec *1,750,000 cusec*. However, the closing of the Itaipú dam gates in 1982 ended this claim to fame.

Widest waterfall The Khône Falls (15–21 m *50–70 ft* high) in Laos is the widest waterfall in the world, with a width of 10.8 km *6.7 miles* and a flood flow of 42,500 m³/sec *1,500,000 cusec*.

Rivers

Longest river The two longest rivers in the world are the Nile, flowing into the Mediterranean, and the Amazon, flowing into the South Atlantic. Which is the longer is more a matter of definition than simple measurement.

Not until 1971 was the true source of the Amazon discovered, by Loren McIntyre (USA) in the snow-covered Andes of southern Peru. The Amazon begins with snowbound lakes and brooks—the actual source has been named Laguna McIntyre—which converge to form the Apurimac. This joins other streams to become the Ene, the Tambo and then the Ucayali. From the confluence of the Ucayali and the Marañón the river is called the Amazon for the final 3700 km *2300 miles* as it flows through Brazil into the Atlantic Ocean. The Amazon has several mouths, which widen towards the sea, so that the exact point where the river ends is uncertain. If the Pará estuary (the most distant mouth) is counted, its length is approximately 6750 km *4195 miles*.

The length of the Nile watercourse, as surveyed by M. Devroey (Belgium) before the loss of a few miles of meanders due to the formation of Lake Nasser, behind the Aswan High Dam, was 6670 km *4145 miles*. This course is unitary from a hydrological standpoint and runs from the source in Burundi of the Luvironza branch of the Kagera feeder of the Victoria Nyanza via the White Nile to the delta in the Mediterranean.

Great Britain The longest river in Great Britain is the Severn, which empties into the Bristol Channel and is 354 km *220 miles* long. Its basin extends over 11,419 km² *4409 miles²*. It rises in north-western Powys, Wales, and flows through Shropshire, Hereford and Worcester, Gloucestershire and Avon. With 17 tributaries, it has more than any other British river.

Shortest river As with the longest river, two rivers could also be considered to be the shortest river with a name. The Roe River, near Great Falls, Montana, USA, has two forks fed by a large fresh-water spring. These relatively constant forks measure 61 m *201 ft* (East Fork Roe River) and 17.7 m *58 ft* (North Fork Roe River) respectively. The Roe River flows into the larger Missouri River. The D River, located at Lincoln City, Oregon, USA, connects Devil's Lake to the Pacific Ocean. Its length is officially quoted as 37 ± 1.5 m *120 ± 5 ft*.

Largest basin The largest river basin in the world is that drained by the Amazon, which covers

mountain. Measured from its submarine base (6000 m *3280 fathoms*) in the Hawaiian Trough to its peak, it has a combined height of 10,205 m *33,480 ft*, of which 4205 m *13,796 ft* are above sea level.

Greatest ranges The greatest of all mountain ranges is the submarine Mid-Ocean Ridge, extending 65,000 km *40,000 miles* from the Arctic Ocean to the Atlantic Ocean, around Africa, Asia and Australia, and under the Pacific Ocean to the west coast of North America. It has a greatest height of 4200 m *13,800 ft* above the base ocean depth.

The world's greatest land mountain range is the Himalaya-Karakoram, which contains 96 of the world's 109 peaks of over 24,000 ft *7315 m*. The longest range is the Andes of South America, which is approximately 7600 km *4700 miles* in length.

Longest lines of sight Vatnajökull (2118 m *6952 ft*), Iceland has been seen by refracted light from the Faeroe Islands 550 km *340 miles* away. In Alaska, Mt McKinley (6193 m *20,320 ft*) has been sighted from Mt Sanford (4949 m *16,237 ft*)—a direct distance of 370 km *230 miles*.

Greatest plateau The most extensive high plateau in the world is the Tibetan Plateau in Central Asia. The average altitude is 4900 m *16,000 ft* and the area is 1,850,000 km² *715,000 miles²*.

Highest halites Along the northern shores of the Gulf of Mexico for 1160 km *725 miles* there exist 330 subterranean 'mountains' of salt, some of which rise more than 18,300 m *60,000 ft* from bedrock and appear as low salt domes first discovered in 1862.

Waterfalls

Highest waterfall The Salto Angel in Venezuela, on a branch of the Carrao River, an upper tributary of the Caroní, is the highest waterfall (as opposed to vaporized 'Bridal Veil') in the world. It has a total drop of 979 m *3212 ft*—the longest single drop being 807 m *2648 ft*. The 'Angel Falls' were named after the American pilot Jimmie Angel (died 8 Dec 1956), who recorded them in his log book on 16 Nov 1933. The falls, known by the Indians as Churun-Meru, had been reported by Ernesto Sánchez la Cruz in 1910.

The highest waterfall in the UK is Eas a'Chùal Aluinn, from Glas Bheinn (774 m *2541 ft*), Highland, with a drop of 201 m *658 ft*. The greatest single drop is one of 107 m *350 ft* in the case of An Steall Ban (Steall), near Glen Nevis, Highland.

Greatest waterfall On the basis of the average annual flow, the greatest waterfall in the world is the Boyoma Falls in Zaïre, with 17,000 m³/sec *600,000 cusec*. The flow of the Guaíra (Salto das Sete Quedas) on the Alto Paraná River between Brazil and Paraguay had on occasions in the past attained a rate of

Submarine

In 1952 a submarine river 300 km *190 miles* wide, known as the Cromwell Current, was discovered flowing eastward below the surface of the Pacific for 6500 km *4000 miles* along the equator. In places it flows at depths of up to 400 m *1300 ft*. Its volume is 1000 times that of the Mississippi.

Subterranean river
In August 1958 a concealed river, tracked by radioisotopes, was discovered flowing under the Nile, with six times its mean annual flow, or 500,000 million m³ *20 trillion ft³*.

about 7,045,000 km² *2,720,000 miles²*. It has countless tributaries, including the Madeira, which at 3380 km *2100 miles* is the longest tributary in the world, being surpassed by only 17 other rivers.

Longest estuary The world's longest estuary is that of the Ob', in the north of Russia, at 885 km *550 miles*. It is up to 80 km *50 miles* wide, and is also the widest river which freezes solid.

Largest delta The world's largest delta is that created by the Ganges and Brahmaputra in Bangladesh and West Bengal, India. It covers an area of 75,000 km² *30,000 miles²*.

Greatest flow The greatest flow of any river in the world is that of the Amazon, which discharges an average of 120,000 m³/sec *4,200,000 cusec* into the Atlantic Ocean, increasing to more than 200,000 m³/sec *7,000,000 cusec* in full flood. The lower 1450 km *900 miles* average 17 m *55 ft* in depth, but the river has a maximum depth of 124 m *407 ft*. The flow of the Amazon is 60 times greater than that of the Nile.

Largest swamp The world's largest tract of swamp is the Pantanal in the states of Mato Grosso and Mato Grosso do Sul in Brazil. It is about 109,000 km² *42,000 miles²* in area.

Waterway

The longest trans-continental waterway is 10,682 km *6637 miles* in length, and links the Beaufort Sea in northern Canada with the Gulf of Mexico in the south of the USA. It starts in the north at Tuktoyaktuk on the Mackenzie River, ending at Port Eads at the delta of the Mississippi. The final link was formed in 1976 with the completion of the South Bay Diversion Channel in Manitoba, Canada, joining the Churchill River system and the Nelson River system.

River Bores

The bore (abrupt rise of tidal water) on the Qiantong Jiang (Hangzhou He) in eastern China is the most remarkable of the 60 in the world. At spring tides the wave attains a height of up to 7.5 m *25 ft* and a speed of 24–27 km/h *13–15 knots*. It is heard advancing at a range of 22 km *14 miles*. The annual downstream flood wave on the Mekong, in south-east Asia, sometimes reaches a height of 14 m *46 ft*. The greatest volume of any tidal bore is that of the Furo do Guajarú, a shallow channel which splits Ilha Caviana in the mouth of the Amazon.

The most notable of the eight river bores in the UK is that on the Severn, which attained a

measured height of 2.8 m *9 ft 3 in* on 15 Oct 1966 downstream of Stonebench, and a speed of 20 km/h *13 mph*. It travels from Framilode towards Gloucester.

Lakes and Inland Seas

Largest lake The largest inland sea or lake in the world is the Caspian Sea (in Azerbaijan, Russia, Kazakhstan, Turkmenistan and Iran). It is 1225 km *760 miles* long and its area is 371,800 km² *143,550 miles²*. Of the total area, some 143,200 km² *55,280 miles²* (38.5 per cent) is in Iran. Its maximum depth is 1025 m *3360 ft*, and the surface is 28.5 m *93 ft* below sea level. Its estimated volume is 89,600 km³ *21,500 miles³* of saline water (⇔ also Depressions).

Deepest lake Lake Baikal in the southern part of eastern Siberia, Russia is the deepest lake in the world. It is 620 km *385 miles* long and 32–74 km *20–46 miles* wide. In 1974 the lake's Olkhon Crevice was measured by the Hydrographic Service of the Soviet Pacific Navy and found to be

1637 m *5371 ft* deep, of which 1181 m *3875 ft* is below sea level (⇔ also Depressions).

The deepest lake in Great Britain is Loch Morar, in Highland. Its surface is 9 m *30 ft* above sea level and its extreme depth 310 m *1017 ft*. It is 16.57 km *10.30 miles* long. The lake with the greatest mean depth is Loch Ness, with 130 m *427 ft*.

Highest lakes The highest navigable lake in the world is Lake Titicaca (maximum depth 370 m *1214 ft*, with an area of about 8290 km² *3200 miles²*) in South America (4790 km² *1850 miles²* in Peru and 3495 km² *1350 miles²* in Bolivia). It is 160 km *100 miles* long and is 3811 m *12,506 ft* above sea level. There are higher lakes in the Himalayas, but most are glacial and of a temporary nature only. A survey of the area carried out in 1984 showed a lake at a height of 5414 m *17,762 ft*, named Panch Pokhri, which was 1.6 km *1 mile* long.

The highest lake in the UK is Lochan Buidhe, at 1100 m *3600 ft* above sea level in the Cairngorms, Grampian. It covers an area of 0.76 ha *1.9 acres*.

Freshwater lake Lake Superior, one of the Great Lakes of North America, is the freshwater lake with the greatest surface area. The total area is 82,350 km² *31,800 miles²*, of which 53,600 km² *20,700 miles²* are in Minnesota, Wisconsin and Michigan, USA and 27,750 km² *11,100 miles²* in Ontario, Canada. It is 180 m *600 ft* above sea level. The freshwater lake with the greatest volume is Lake Baikal in Siberia, Russia, with an estimated volume of 23,000 km³ *5500 miles³*.

The largest lake in the UK is Lough Neagh (14.6 m *48 ft* above sea level) in Northern Ireland. It is 29 km *18 miles* long and 17.7 km *11 miles* wide and has an area of 381.73 km² *147.39 miles²*. Its extreme depth is 31 m *102 ft*.

Guess What?
Q. Where is the world's largest artificial lake?
A. See Page 98

■ Two views of the world's largest swamp, the Pantanal in Brazil. The shot on the right shows one of the swamp's many rivers with its pronounced meander. Not surprisingly the whole area is frequently flooded.
(Photos: Jacana/P Wild)

The largest lake in a lake is Manitou Lake (106.42 km² *41.09 miles²*) on the world's largest lake island, Manitoulin Island (2766 km² *1068 miles²*), in the Canadian part of Lake Huron. The lake itself contains a number of islands.

Freshwater loch The largest lake in Great Britain, and the largest inland loch in Scotland, is Loch Lomond, which is situated in the Strathclyde and Central regions at a height of 7 m *23 ft* above sea level. It is 36.44 km *22.64 miles* long and has a surface area of 70.04 km² *27.45 miles²*. Its greatest depth is 190 m *623 ft*. The lake or loch with the greatest volume is, however, Loch Ness, with 7,443,000,000 m³ *262,845,000,000 ft³*. The longest lake or loch is Loch Ness, which measures 38.99 km *24.23 miles*, although the three arms of the Y-shaped Loch Awe, Strathclyde aggregate 40.99 km *25.47 miles*.

Largest lagoon Lagoa dos Patos, located near the seashore in Rio Grande do Sul, southernmost Brazil, is 280 km *174 miles* long and extends over 9850 km² *3803 miles²*, separated from the Atlantic Ocean by long sand strips. It has a maximum width of 70 km *44 miles*.

Underground

The largest known underground lake is that in the Drachenhauchloch cave near Grootfontein, Namibia, discovered in 1986. When surveyed in April 1991 the surface area was found to be 2.61 ha *6.45 acres*. The surface of the lake is some 66 m *217 ft* underground, and its depth 84 m *276 ft*.

Other Features

Desert Nearly an eighth of the world's land surface is arid, with a rainfall of less than 25 cm *10 in* per annum. The Sahara in North Africa is the largest desert in the world. At its greatest length it is 5150 km *3200 miles* from east to west. From north to south it is between 1280 and 2250 km *800 and 1400 miles*. The area covered by the desert is about 9,269,000 km² *3,579,000 miles²*.

Sand dunes The world's highest measured sand dunes are those in the Saharan sand sea of Isaouane-N-Tifernine in east central Algeria, at Lat. 26°42'N, Long. 6°43'E. They have a wavelength of 5 km *3 miles* and attain a height of 465 m *1525 ft*.

Largest mirage The largest mirage on record was that sighted in the Arctic at 83°N, 103°W by Donald B. MacMillan in 1913. This type of mirage, known as the Fata Morgana, appeared as the same 'hills, valleys, snow-capped peaks extending through at least 120 degrees of the horizon' that Peary had misidentified as Crocker Land six years earlier. On 17 Jul 1939 a mirage of Snaefellsjökull (1446 m *4744 ft*) on Iceland was seen from the sea at a distance of 540–560 km *335–350 miles*.

The Fata Morgana is the Sicilian name for mirages seen in the Straits of Messina and is named after the Celtic fairy enchantress Morgan le Fay, the sister of King Arthur.

Largest gorge The largest land gorge in the world is the Grand Canyon on the Colorado River in north-central Arizona, USA. It extends from Marble Gorge to the Grand Wash Cliffs, over a distance of 446 km *277 miles*. It averages 16 km *10 miles* in width and 1.6 km *1 mile* in depth. The submarine Labrador Basin

■ **The largest desert in the world is the Sahara, which stretches into 11 countries. The vastness of the desert is typified by the shot below from Algeria, showing vehicles dwarfed by the surrounding features. Moving east one comes to Libya (inset pictures) where the temperature reached a world record 58°C *136°F* in the shade in 1922.**
(Photos: Gamma/E Bonnier and Gamma/Beziau-Boisberrange)

canyon, between Greenland and Labrador, Canada, is 3440 km *2140 miles* long.

Deepest canyon A canyon or gorge is generally regarded as a valley with steep rock walls and a considerable depth in relation to its width. The Grand Canyon (⇔ above) has the characteristic vertical sections of wall, but is much wider than its depth. The Vicos Gorge in the Pindus mountains of north-west Greece is 900 m *2950 ft* deep and only 1100 m *3600 ft* between its rims. Gorges in many countries have a higher depth/width ratio, but none is as deep.

The often cited Colca canyon in Peru has the cross-profile of a valley, but is neither as deep nor as steep-sided as the Yarlung Zangbo valley (⇔ right). The deepest submarine canyon yet discovered is one 40 km *25 miles* south of Esperance, Western Australia which is 1800 m *6000 ft* deep and 32 km *20 miles* wide.

Glaciers It is estimated that 13,600,000 km^2 *5,250,000 miles^2*, or 9.7 per cent of the Earth's land surface, is permanently covered by glacier ice. The Antarctic ice sheet accounts for 86 per cent of this, and the Greenland ice sheet 11 per cent. The world's longest glacier is the Lambert Glacier, discovered by an Australian aircraft crew in Australian Antarctic Territory in 1956/7. Draining about a fifth of the East Antarctic ice sheet, it is up to 64 km *40 miles* wide and, with its seaward extension (the Amery Ice Shelf) it measures at least 700 km *440 miles* in length.

> The fastest-moving major glacier is the Columbia Glacier, near Valdez, in Alaska, USA, which is flowing at an average of 20 m *65 ft* per day.

Cliffs The highest known sea cliffs in the world are those on the north coast of east Moloka'i, Hawaii, near Umilehi Point, which descend 1010 m *3300 ft* to the sea at an average angle of inclination of more than 55°, and an average gradient of more than 1.428.

The highest cliffs in the UK are the Conachair cliffs on St Kilda, Western Isles, which are 400 m *1300 ft* high. The highest sheer sea cliffs on the mainland of Great Britain are at Clo Mor, 5 km *3 miles* south-east of Cape Wrath, Sutherland, which drop 281 m *921 ft*.

Natural arches The longest natural arch in the world is the Landscape Arch in the Arches National Park, 40 km *25 miles* north of Moab in Utah, USA. This natural sandstone arch spans 88 m *291 ft* and is set about 30 m *100 ft* above the canyon floor. In one place erosion has narrowed its section to 1.8 m *6 ft*. Larger, however, is the Rainbow Bridge, Utah, USA, discovered on 14 Aug 1909, which, although only 82.3 m *270 ft* long, is more than 6.7 m *22 ft* wide and rises to a height of 88.4 m *290 ft*.

Deepest permafrost The deepest recorded permafrost is more than 1370 m *4500 ft*, reported from the upper reaches of the Viluy River, Siberia, Russia in February 1982.

Icy

The greatest recorded thickness of ice is 4.78 km *2.97 miles*, measured by radio echo soundings from a US Antarctic research aircraft at 69° 56' 17" S, 135° 12' 9" E, 440 km *270 miles* from the coast in Wilkes Land, Antarctica on 4 Jan 1975.

Photo: Richard D Fisher   Artwork: Peter Harper © Guinness Publishing

Deepest Valley

Namche Barwa 7753 m *25,436 ft*

21 km *13 miles*

Jala Peri 7282 m *23,891 ft*

2440 m *8000 ft* elevation

Yarlung Zangbo River

For years the Yarlung Zangbo valley in eastern Tibet was known to be among the deepest valleys in the world, if not *the* deepest, but its inaccesibility meant that it had never been documented—until 1993 when American explorer Richard Fisher was able to obtain the necessary permits to visit the area after ten years of trying.

A British botanist, Francis Kingdon Ward, had explored the area around the beginning of the century, but no other westerner had been able to do so again until Fisher led his expedition there. With fellow Americans, plus Chinese and Tibetan colleagues and Minba and Loba tribal co-explorers, the team set off into the unknown.

The result was clear-cut—the discovery of *the* deepest valley on earth. With soaring peaks either side of the Yarlung Zangbo a number of measurements were taken under extremely difficult conditions, resulting in the conclusion that the valley is 5075 m *16,650 ft* deep where the river almost turns back on itself in the Himalayas, not far from the Chinese (Tibetan)/Indian border. The peaks of Namche Barwa (7753 m *25,436 ft*) and Jala

Peri (7282 m *23,891 ft*) are just 21 km *13 miles* apart with the Yarlung Zangbo River between them, at an elevation of 2440 m *8000 ft*.

Richard Fisher summed up the expedition by saying that it is the only chasm he has encountered which compares with the Grand Canyon for sheer beauty. Having documented canyons in the USA, various parts of South America, China and Tibet he adds:– 'The Yarlung Zangbo is so vast and diverse that it must contain many mysteries yet to be discovered.' And maybe more world records too!

Natural Phenomena

Avalanches

Greatest avalanches The greatest natural avalanches, though rarely observed, occur in the Himalayas, but no estimates of their volume have been published. It was estimated that 3,500,000 m³ *120,000,000 ft³* of snow fell in an avalanche in the Italian Alps in 1885. The avalanche triggered by the Mount St Helens eruption in Washington State, USA on 18 May 1980 was estimated to measure 2800 million m³ *96,000 million ft³* and travelled at 400 km/h *250 mph* (⇨ Accidents and Disasters).

Earthquakes

Seismologists record all dates with the year *first*, based not on local time but on Universal Time/ Greenwich Mean Time.

It is estimated that each year there are some 500,000 detectable seismic or micro-seismic disturbances, of which 100,000 can be felt and 1000 cause damage. The deepest recorded hypocentres are of 720 km *447 miles* in Indonesia in 1933, 1934 and 1943.

Greatest earthquakes The most commonly used measure of the size (energy release) of an earthquake is its surface-wave magnitude (M_s). This scale was developed by the American seismologists Beno Gutenberg and Dr Charles Richter (1949). The largest reported magnitudes on this scale—commonly known as the Richter scale—are about 8.9, but the scale does not properly represent the size of the very largest earthquakes (those having an M_s of more than about 8), for which it is better to use the concept of seismic moment, M_o, developed by Kei Aki in 1966. Moment can be used to derive a 'moment magnitude', M_w, first used by Hiroo Kanamori in 1977. The largest recorded earthquake on the M_w scale is the Chilean shock of 22 May 1960, which had M_w=9.5 but measured only 8.3 on the M_s scale.

Worst death toll The greatest estimate for a death toll is the 830,000 fatalities in a prolonged earthquake (*dizhen*) in the Shaanxi, Shanxi and Henan provinces of China, of 2 Feb 1556 (new style) (23 Jan old style). The highest death toll in modern times has been in the Tangshan earthquake (Mag. M_s=7.9) in eastern China on 27 Jul 1976 (local time was 3 a.m. 28 July). The first figure published, on 4 Jan 1977, revealed 655,237 killed, later adjusted to 750,000. On 22 Nov 1979 the New China News Agency inexplicably reduced the death toll to 242,000. The figure of 1,100,000 sometimes attributed to the eastern Mediterranean earthquake of 20 May 1202 is a gross exaggeration, since it includes those dying in a famine the following year. A more plausible death toll is c. 30,000.

Guess What?

Q. How did the Kobe earthquake in January 1995 affect the Akashi-Kaikyo bridge?

A. See Page 95

Material damage The greatest physical devastation was in the earthquake on the Kanto plain, Japan, of 1 Sep 1923 (Mag. M_s=8.2, epicentre at Lat. 35°15′N, Long. 139°30′E). In Tokyo and Yokohama 575,000 dwellings were destroyed. The official total of persons killed and missing in this *Dai-Shinsai*, or great 'quake and resultant fires, was 142,807.

Great Britain The record undisputed death toll for Great Britain is two—an apprentice, Thomas Grey, struck by falling masonry from Christ's Hospital Church, near Newgate, London at 6 p.m. on 6 Apr 1580, and another young person, Mabel Everet, who died of injuries four days later. The shock was centred in the Strait of Dover.

The East Anglian or Colchester earthquake of 22 Apr 1884 (9:18 a.m.) (epicentre Lat. 51°49′N, Long. 0°54′E) caused damage estimated at more than £12,000 to 1250 buildings. Langenhoe Church was wrecked. Windows and doors were rattled over an area of 137,000 km² *53,000 miles²* and the shock was felt in Exeter, Devon and Ostend, Belgium. It is estimated that it would have been Mag. 4.4 on the Richter scale.

The highest instrumentally measured magnitude is 5.5 for the Dogger Bank event of 7 Jun 1931. The highest measured on land was 4.8 for the Swansea earthquake of 27 Jun 1906 and also for the Lleyn earthquake of 19 Jul 1984.

Volcanoes

The total number of volcanoes in the world which might be described as active (believed to have erupted in the past 10,000 years) is 1343, of which many are submarine. The name volcano derives from the now dormant Vulcano Island (from the god of fire Vulcanus) in the Mediterranean.

Greatest explosion The greatest explosion in historic times (possibly since Santorini in the Aegean Sea, 95 km *60 miles* north of Crete, in 1628 BC) occurred at c. 10 a.m. (local time), or 3.00 a.m. GMT, on 27 Aug 1883, with an eruption of Krakatoa, an island (then 47 km² *18 miles²*) in the Sunda Strait, between Sumatra and Java, in Indonesia. The wave which it caused wiped out 163 villages and killed 36,380 people. Pumice was thrown 55 km *34 miles* high, and dust fell 5330 km *3313 miles* away 10 days later. The explosion was recorded four hours later on the island of Rodrigues, 4776 km *2968 miles* away, as 'the roar of heavy guns' and was heard over one thirteenth of the surface of the globe. This explosion, estimated to have had about 26 times the power of the greatest H-bomb test (by the USSR), was still only one-third as powerful as the Santorini cataclysm.

Greatest eruption The total volume of matter discharged in the eruption of Tambora, a volcano on the Indonesian island of Sumbawa, from 5 to 10 Apr 1815, was 150–180 km³ *36–43 miles³*. This compares with a probable 60–65 km³ *14–16 miles³* ejected by Santorini (⇨ above)

and 20 km³ *5 miles³* ejected by Krakatoa (⇨ above). The energy of the Tambora eruption, which lowered the height of the island by 1250 m *4100 ft* from 4100 m *13,450 ft* to 2850 m *9350 ft*, was 8.4×10^{19} joules. A crater 8 km *5 miles* in diameter was formed. More than 90,000 were killed or died as a result of the subsequent famine.

The ejecta in the Taupo eruption in New Zealand c. AD 130 have been estimated at 30,000 million tonnes of pumice moving at one time at 700 km/h *400 mph*. It flattened 16,000 km² *6200 miles²*. Less than 20 per cent of the 14×10^9 tonnes of pumice carried up into the air in this most violent of all documented volcanic events fell within 200 km *125 miles* of the vent.

Longest lava flow The longest lava flow in historic times is a mixture of *pahoehoe* ropey lava (twisted cord-like solidifications) and *aa* blocky lava, resulting from the eruption of Laki in 1783 in south-east Iceland, which flowed 65–70 km *40½–43½ miles*. The largest known prehistoric flow is the Roza basalt flow in North America c. 15 million years ago, which had an unsurpassed length (300 km *190 miles*), area (40,000 km² *15,400 miles²*) and volume (1250 km³ *300 miles³*).

Largest active volcano Mauna Loa, on Hawaii, has the shape of a broad gentle dome 120 km *75 miles* long and 50 km *31 miles* wide (above sea level), with lava flows which occupy more than 5125 km² *1980 miles²* of the island. It has a total volume of 42,500 km³ *10,200 miles³*, of which 84.2 per cent is below sea level. Its caldera or volcano crater, Mokuaweoweo, measures 10.5 km² *4 miles²* and is 150–180 m *500–600 ft* deep. Mauna Loa rises 4170 m *13,680 ft* and has averaged one eruption every 4½ years since 1843, although none since 1984.

Highest active volcano The highest volcano regarded as active is Ojos del Salado (which has fumaroles), at a height of 6887 m *22,595 ft*, on the frontier between Chile and Argentina.

Northernmost and southernmost volcanoes The northernmost volcano is Mt Beerenberg (2276 m *7470 ft*) on the island of Jan Mayen (71°05′N) in the Greenland Sea. It erupted on 20 Sep 1970, and the island's 39 inhabitants (all male) had to be evacuated. The Ostenso seamount (1775 m *5825 ft*), 556 km *346 miles* from the North Pole at Lat. 85°10′N, Long. 133°W, was volcanic. The most southerly known active volcano is Mt Erebus (3794 m *12,447 ft*), on Ross Island (77°35′S) in Antarctica.

Largest crater The world's largest caldera or volcano crater is that of Toba, north-central Sumatra, Indonesia, covering 1775 km² *685 miles²*.

Geysers

Tallest geysers The Waimangu (Maori 'black water') geyser, in New Zealand, erupted to a height in excess of 460 m *1500 ft* in 1903, when it was erupting every 30–36 hours, but has not been active since late 1904. In August 1903 four people were killed during one of its violent eruptions. *(continued)*

In 1955 the record for the greatest material damage caused by an earthquake was 575,000 buildings destroyed in Japan in 1923. Fortunately today this is still the record.

Four people were killed in August 1903 during one of Waimangu's violent eruptions (⇨ below). They were standing 27 m 90 ft away, but their bodies were found up to 800 m ½ mile away. One was jammed between two rocks, one in a hole in the ground, one suspended in a tree and the fourth on flat ground.

World's Strongest Earthquakes

Progressive list of instrumentally recorded earthquakes

Kanamori Scale Magnitudes M_w	Richter Scale Magnitude M_s	Location	Date
8.8	8.6	Ecuador	31 Jan 1906
9.0	8¼	Kamchatka, Russia (then USSR)	4 Nov 1952
8.6–9.1	7¾	Andreanof Islands, Aleutian Islands, USA	9 Mar 1957
9.5	8.3	Chile	22 May 1960

Guess What?

Q. In which year did humans first cross the Antarctic Circle?

A. See Page 203

■ The southernmost active volcano is Mt Erebus, in Antarctica. At close quarters an erupting volcano can be highly dangerous and can cause widespread loss of life, but from afar it may be one of the most breathtaking sights which nature can offer.
(Photo: Jacana/J-P Ferrero)

Currently the world's tallest active geyser is Steamboat Geyser in Yellowstone National Park, Wyoming, USA. During the 1980s it erupted at intervals ranging from 19 days to more than four years, although there were occasions in the 1960s when it erupted as frequently as every 4–10 days. The maximum height ranges from 60 to 115 m *195 to 380 ft*. The greatest measured water discharge was an estimated 28,000–38,000 hl *616,000–836,000 gal* emitted by the Giant Geyser, also in Yellowstone National Park. However, this estimate, made in the 1950s, was only a rough calculation.

Weather

The meteorological records given below relate largely to the last 150–170 years, since data before that time are both sparse and often unreliable. Reliable registering thermometers were introduced as recently as c. 1820. The longest period of observations has been maintained at the Radcliffe Observatory, Oxford since 1767, and on a daily basis since 1814, though discontinuous records have enabled the Chinese to assert that 903 BC was a very bad winter.

Palaeo-entomological evidence is that there was a southern European climate in England c. 90,000 BC, while in c. 6000 BC the mean summer temperature reached 19°C *67°F*, or 3 degC *6 degF* higher than the present. It is believed that 1.2 million years ago the world's air temperature averaged 35°C *95°F*.

Ozone levels Ozone levels reached a record low between 9 and 14 Oct 1993 over the South Pole in Antarctica, when an average figure of 91 Dobson units (DU) was recorded. This compares to 300 DU as a figure considered adequate to shield the Earth from solar ultraviolet radiation and sustain biological systems as we know them. The largest ozone depletion takes place in spring in Antarctica (August and September), and as late as 23 Aug 1993 a figure of 276 DU had been measured, indicating a loss of about ⅔ of the ozone in under two months. The ozone hole was discovered in 1985, and a hole the size of North America was created as a result of the events of the spring of 1993.

Most equable temperature
The location with the most equable recorded temperature over a short period is Garapan, on Saipan in the Mariana Islands, Pacific Ocean. During the nine years from 1927 to 1935, inclusive, the lowest temperature recorded was 19.6°C *67.3°F* on 30 Jan 1934, and the highest was 31.4°C *88.5°F* on 9 Sep 1931, giving an extreme range of 11.8 deg C *21.2 degF*. Over a long period of time, between 1911 and 1990 the Brazilian offshore island of Fernando de Noronha had a minimum temperature of 17.7°C *63.9°F* on 27 Feb 1980 and a maximum of 32.2°C *90.0°F* on 3 Mar 1968, 25 Dec 1972 and 17 Apr 1973, giving an extreme range of 14.5 deg C *26.1 deg F*.

Greatest temperature ranges The greatest recorded temperature ranges in the world are around the Siberian 'cold pole' in the east of Russia. Temperatures in Verkhoyansk (67°33′N, 133°23′E) have ranged 105 degC *188 degF*, from –68°C *–90°F* to 37°C *98°F*. The greatest temperature variation recorded in a day is 56 degC *100 degF* (a fall from 7°C *44°F* to –49°C *–56°F*) at Browning, Montana, USA on 23–24 Jan 1916. The most freakish rise was 27 degC *49 degF* in 2 min at Spearfish, South Dakota, USA, from –20°C *–4°F* at 7:30 a.m. to 7°C *45°F* at 7:32 a.m. on 22 Jan 1943.

The British record is 29 degC *52.2 degF* (–7°C *19.4°F* to 22°C *71.6°F*) at Tummel Bridge, Tayside on 9 May 1978.

Highest shade temperature The highest shade temperature ever recorded is 58°C *136°F* at Al'Azīzīyah, Libya (alt. 111 m *367 ft*) on 13 Sep 1922.

The highest in Britain is 37.1°C *98.8°F* at Cheltenham (Glos) on 3 Aug 1990. The 38°C *100°F* which was once reported from Tonbridge (Kent) was a nonstandard exposure and is estimated to be equivalent to 36–37°C *97–98°F*.

Hottest place On an annual-mean basis, with readings taken over a six-year period from 1960 to 1966, the temperature at Dallol, in Ethiopia, was 34°C *94°F*. In Death Valley, California, USA, maximum temperatures of over 120°F *49°C* were recorded on 43 consecutive days, between 6 Jul and 17 Aug 1917. At Marble Bar, Western Australia (maximum 120.5°F *49.2°C*), 160 consecutive days with maximum temperatures of 100°F *37.8°C* or higher were recorded between 31 Oct 1923 and 7 Apr 1924. At Wyndham, also in Western Australia, the temperature reached 90°F *32.2°C* or more on 333 days in 1946.

In Britain, annual mean temperatures of 11.5°C *52.7°F* were recorded both at Penzance, in Cornwall, and in the Isles of Scilly in the period 1931 to 1960.

Driest place The annual mean rainfall on the Pacific coast of Chile between Arica and Antofagasta is less than 0.1 mm *0.004 in*.

In Britain, the lowest annual mean rainfall on record is at Lee Wick Farm, St Osyth, Essex, with 513 mm *20.2 in*, based on the period 1964 to 1982. The lowest rainfall recorded in a single year was 236 mm *9.3 in* at one station in Margate, Kent in 1921.

Longest drought The Atacama Desert, in northern Chile, experiences virtually no rain, although several times a century a squall may strike a small area of it.

Britain's longest drought lasted 73 days, from 4 Mar to 15 May 1893, at Mile End, Greater London.

Most sunshine The annual average at Yuma, Arizona, USA is 91 per cent of the possible hours of sunshine (a mean of 4055 hours out of 4456 possible hours in a year). St Petersburg, in Florida, USA recorded 768 consecutive sunny days from 9 Feb 1967 to 17 Mar 1969.

The best in Britain was 78.3 per cent of the maximum possible in one month (382 hours out of 488) at Pendennis Castle, Cornwall in June 1925.

Best and worst British summers According to Prof. Gordon Manley's survey over the period 1728–1978, the best (i.e. driest and hottest) British summer was that of 1976, and the worst (i.e. wettest and coldest) that of 1879. Temperatures of more than 32°C *90°F* were recorded on 13 consecutive days (25 Jun–7 Jul 1976) within Great Britain, peaking at 35.9°C *96.6°F* in Cheltenham on 3 July. In 1983 there were 40 days with temperatures above 80°F *27°C* in Britain between 3 July–31 August, including 17 consecutively (3–19 July).

Lowest screen temperature A record low of –89.2°C *–128.6°F* was registered at Vostok, Antarctica (alt. 3419 m *11,220 ft*) on 21 Jul 1983.

Britain's lowest was –27°C *–17°F* on 11 Feb 1895 and again on 10 Jan 1982, both times at Braemar, Grampian. The –31°C *–23°F* at Blackadder, Borders, on 4 Dec 1879, and the –29°C *–20°F* at Grantown-on-Spey on 24 Feb 1955, were not standard exposures. The lowest maximum temperature for a day was –19.1°C *–2.4°F* at Braemar, again on 10 Jan 1982.

Coldest place Polyus Nedostupnosti (Pole of Inaccessibility), in Antarctica, at 78°S, 96°E, is the coldest location in the world, with an extrapolated annual mean of –58°C *–72°F*. The coldest measured mean is –57°C *–70°F*, at Plateau Station, Antarctica.

For Britain, the coldest mean temperature recorded at a weather station is 6.3°C *43.4°F*, at Braemar, Grampian, based on readings taken between 1952 and 1981.

Longest freeze The longest recorded unremitting freeze in the British Isles was one of 40 days at the Great Dun Fell radio station, Appleby, Cumbria, from 23 Jan to 3 Mar 1986. Less rigorous early data include a frost from 5 Dec 1607 to 14 Feb 1608 and a 91-day frost on Dartmoor, Devon in 1854–5.

Most rainy days Mt Wai-'ale-'ale (1569 m *5148 ft*), Kauai, Hawaii has up to 350 rainy days per annum.

The place in the British Isles which has had the most rainy days in a calendar year is Ballynahinch, in Co. Galway, Republic of Ireland, with 309 in 1923.

Most intense rainfall Difficulties attend rainfall readings for very short periods, but the figure of 38.1 mm *1½ in* in one minute at Barst, Guadeloupe, in the Caribbean on 26 Nov 1970 is regarded as the most intense recorded by modern methods.

The cloudburst of 'near 2 ft *600 mm* in less than a quarter of half an hour' at Oxford on the afternoon of 31 May (old style) 1682 is regarded as unacademically recorded. The most intense rainfall in Britain recorded to modern standards has been 51 mm *2 in* in 12 minutes at Wisbech, Cambs on 27 Jun 1970.

Greatest rainfall A record 1870 mm *73.62 in* of rain fell in 24 hours in Cilaos (alt. 1200 m *3940 ft*), Réunion, Indian Ocean on 15 and 16 Mar 1952. This is equal to 7554 tonnes of rain per acre. For a calendar month the record is 9300 mm *366 in* at Cherrapunji, Meghalaya, India in July 1861, and the 12-month record was also set at Cherrapunji, with 26,461 mm *1041¾ in* between 1 Aug 1860 and 31 Jul 1861.

In Great Britain, the 24-hour record is 279 mm *11 in* at Martinstown, Dorset on 18 and 19 Jul 1955. At Llyn Llydau, Snowdon, Gwynedd 1436 mm *56½ in* fell in October 1909, and over a 12-month period, 6527 mm *257 in* fell at Sprinkling Tarn, Cumbria, in 1954.

Greatest flood Scientists reported the discovery of the largest fresh-water flood in history in January 1993. It occurred c. 18,000 years ago when an ancient ice-dammed lake in the Altay Mountains of Siberia, Russia broke, allowing the water to pour out. The lake

Lowest

The coldest permanently inhabited place is the Siberian village of Oymyakon (pop. 4000), 63° 16′ N, 143° 15′ E (700 m *2300 ft*), in Russia, where the temperature reached –68°C *–90°F* in 1933, and an unofficial –72°C *–98°F* has been published more recently.

Longest-lasting rainbow
A rainbow was visible for six hours continuously, from 9 a.m. to 3 p.m., over Sheffield, S Yorks on 14 Mar 1994.

Wettest

By average annual rainfall, the wettest place in the world is Mawsynram, in Meghalaya State, India, with 11,873 mm *467½ in* per annum.

Styhead Tarn (487 m *1600 ft*), in Cumbria, with 4391 mm *173 in*, is Britain's wettest place.

was estimated to be 120 km *75 miles* long and 760 m *2500 ft* deep. The main flow of water was reported to be 490 m *1600 ft* deep and travelling at 160 km/h *100 mph*.

Windiest place Commonwealth Bay, on George V Coast, Antarctica, where gales reach 320 km/h *200 mph*, is the world's windiest place.

In Britain, an average reading of 33.1 km/h *20.6 mph* was registered at Fair Isle in the period 1974–8.

Highest surface wind-speed A surface wind-speed of 371 km/h *231 mph* was recorded at Mt Washington (1916 m *6288 ft*), New Hampshire, USA on 12 Apr 1934. The highest speed at a low altitude was registered on 8 Mar 1972 at the USAF base at Thule (44 m *145 ft*), in Greenland, when a peak speed of 333 km/h *207 mph* was recorded. The highest speed measured to date in a tornado is 450 km/h *280 mph* at Wichita Falls, Texas, USA on 2 Apr 1958.

The record high surface wind-speed for Britain is 150 knots (278 km/h *172 mph*), on Cairn Gorm Summit (1245 m *4084 ft*), on 20 Mar 1986. A figure of 285.2 km/h *177.2 mph*, at RAF Saxa Vord, Unst, in the Shetlands on 16 Feb 1962, was not recorded with standard equipment. British tornadoes may reach 290 km/h *180 mph*.

Tornadoes (⇨ also Accidents and Disasters) Britain's strongest tornado was at Southsea, Portsmouth, Hants on 14 Dec 1810 (Force 8 on the Meaden-TORRO scale). On 23 Nov 1981, 58 tornadoes were reported in one day from Anglesey to eastern England.

Greatest snowfall Over a 12-month period from 19 Feb 1971 to 18 Feb 1972, 31,102 mm *1224½ in* of snow fell at Paradise, Mt Rainier, in Washington State, USA. The record for a single snowstorm is 4800 mm *189 in* at Mt Shasta Ski Bowl, California, USA from 13–19 Feb 1959, and for a 24-hour period it is 1930 mm *76 in* at Silver Lake, Colorado, USA on 14–15 Apr 1921.

Britain's 12-month record is the 1524 mm *60 in* which fell in Upper Teesdale and also in the Denbighshire Hills, Clwyd, in 1947. London's earliest recorded snow was on 25 Sep 1885, and the latest on 2 Jun 1975. Less reliable reports suggest snow on 12 Sep 1658 (old style) and on 12 Jun 1791.

White Christmases London has experienced eight 'white' or snowing Christmas Days since 1900. These have been 1906, 1917 (slight), 1923 (slight), 1927, 1938, 1956 (slight), 1970 and 1981. These were more frequent in the 19th century and even more so before the change of the calendar which by removing 3–13 September brought forward all dates subsequent to 2 Sep 1752 by 11 days.

Highest waterspout The highest waterspout of which there is a reliable record was one observed on 16 May 1898 off Eden, New South Wales, Australia. A theodolite reading from the shore gave its height as 1528 m *5014 ft*. It was about 3 m *10 ft* in diameter.

The Spithead waterspout off Ryde, Isle of Wight on 21 Aug 1878 was measured by sextant to be 1600 m or 'about a mile' in height. A more reliably estimated

St Swithin's

The legend that the weather on St Swithin's Day, celebrated on 15 July (old and new style) since AD 912, determines the rainfall for the next 40 days is one which has long persisted. There was a brilliant 13½ hours of sunshine in London on 15 Jul 1924, but 30 of the next 40 days were wet. On 15 Jul 1913 there was a downpour lasting 15 hours, yet it rained on only nine of the subsequent 40 days in London.

The heaviest hailstones in Britain fell on 5 Sep 1958 at Horsham, W Sussex, and weighed 142 g *5 oz*. Much heavier ones are sometimes reported, but usually these are coalesced rather than single stones.

Cloud extremes The highest standard cloud form is cirrus, averaging 9000 m *29,500 ft*, but the rare nacreous or mother-of-pearl formation may reach nearly 24,500 m *80,000 ft*. The lowest is stratus, below 460 m *1500 ft*.

Thunder-days In Tororo, Uganda an average of 251 days of thunder per annum was recorded for the 10-year period 1967–76.

The record number of thunder-days recorded in a specific place in a calendar year in Britain is 38, twice. The first time was in 1912, at Stonyhurst, in Lancashire, and the second was in 1967, at Huddersfield, in W Yorks.

The greatest depth of snow ever measured on the ground was 1146 cm *37 ft 7 in* at Tamarac, California, USA in March 1911.

Longest sea-level fogs Sea-level fogs, with visibility less than 900 m *1000 yd*, persist for weeks on the Grand Banks, Newfoundland, Canada, with the average being more than 120 days per year.

The duration record for Britain is 4 days 18 hours, twice, in both cases in London. The first time was from 26 Nov to 1 Dec 1948, and the second from 5 to 9 Dec 1952. Worse visibilities occur at higher altitudes. Ben Nevis is reputedly in cloud 300 days per year.

Barometric pressure The highest barometric pressure ever recorded was 1083.8 mb *32.0 in* at Agata, Siberia, Russia (alt. 262 m *862 ft*) on 31 Dec 1968. The highest in Britain was 1054.7 mb *31.15 in*, in Aberdeen on 31 Jan 1902.

The lowest sea-level pressure was 870 mb *25.69 in* in Typhoon Tip, 480 km *300 miles* west of Guam, Pacific Ocean, at Lat. 16° 44′ N, Long. 137° 46′ E, on 12 Oct 1979. Britain's lowest was 925.5 mb *27.33 in*, at Ochtertyre, near Crieff, Tayside on 26 Jan 1884.

waterspout was one which developed off Yarmouth, Isle of Wight on 6 Aug 1987. It was some 760 m *2500 ft* in height.

Heaviest hailstones The heaviest hailstones on record, weighing up to 1 kg *2¼ lb*, are reported to have killed 92 people in the Gopalganj district of Bangladesh on 14 Apr 1986.

Guess What?
Q. How did 81 people die through being struck by lightning?
A. See Page 179

Lightning!

The only man in the world to be struck by lightning seven times is ex-park ranger Roy C. Sullivan (US), the human lightning conductor of Virginia, USA. His attraction for lightning began in 1942 (lost big toe nail) and was resumed in July 1969 (lost eyebrows), in July 1970 (left shoulder seared) on 16 Apr 1972 (hair set on fire), on 7 Aug 1973 (new hair re-fired and legs seared) and on 5 Jun 1976 (ankle injured), and he was sent to Waynesboro Hospital with chest and stomach burns on 25 Jun 1977 after being struck while fishing. In September 1983 he died by his own hand, reportedly rejected in love.

■ The cloud form with the greatest vertical range is cumulonimbus, which has been observed to reach a height of nearly 20,000 m *68,000 ft* in the tropics. The bottom of cumulonimbus clouds is always dark, indicating rain, snow or hail, and they are often associated with thunder and lightning.
(Photo: Jacana/P Pilloud)

Gems, Jewels and Precious Stones

Diamond

Largest diamond 3106 carats. This was found on 26 Jan 1905 at the Premier Diamond Mine, near Pretoria, South Africa. It was named *The Cullinan* and was cut into 106 polished diamonds. It produced the largest cut fine-quality colourless diamond, which weighs 530.2 carats. Several large pieces of low-quality diamonds have been found, including a carbonado of 3167 carats discovered in Brazil in 1905. Currently the largest known single piece of rough diamond still in existence weighs 1462 carats and is retained by De Beers in London.

Largest cut diamond 545.67 carats, known as the *Unnamed Brown*. This was fashioned from a 755.50 carat rough into a fire rose cushion cut and acted as the forerunner to the *Centenary Diamond*, the world's largest flawless top-colour modern fancy cut diamond at 273.85 carats.

Smallest brilliant cut diamond 0.0000743 carats, fashioned by hand by Pauline Willemse, at Coster Diamonds B.V. in Amsterdam, Netherlands between 1991 and 1994. The stone is 0.16–0.17 mm *0.0063–0.0067 in* in diameter and 0.11 mm *0.0043 in* in height, and is smaller than the average grain of sand on a beach.

Highest-priced diamond $12,760,000 for a pear-shaped mixed-cut diamond of 101.84 carats. The stone was bought at Sotheby's, Geneva, Switzerland on 14 Nov 1990.

The highest price known to be paid for a rough diamond was £5.8 million for a 255.10-carat stone from Guinea, paid by the William Goldberg Diamond Corporation in partnership with the Chow Tai Fook Jewellery Co. Ltd of Hong Kong, in March 1989. *Many sales of polished diamonds are considered private transactions, and the prices paid are not disclosed.*

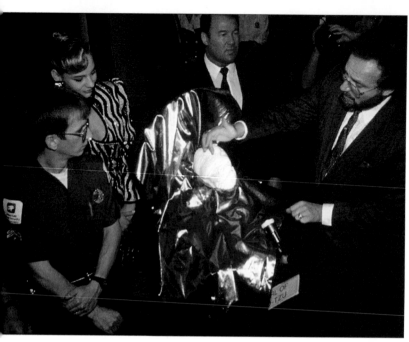

■ The world's largest pearl is the Pearl of Lao-tze. An appraisal by the San Francisco Gem Laboratory in 1984 concluded that its estimated retail replacement value would be between 40 and 42 million US dollars.
(Photo: Gamma/Sander/Liaison)

The record per carat is $926,315.79, for a 0.95-carat fancy purplish-red stone sold at Christie's, New York, USA on 28 Apr 1987.

Ruby

Largest star ruby 6465 carats. The *Eminent Star* ruby, believed to be of Indian origin, is owned by Kailash Rawat of Eminent Gems Inc. of New York, USA. It is an oval cabochon with a six-ray star and measures 109 × 90.5 × 58 mm *4¼ × 3⅝ × 2¼ in*.

Highest-priced ruby $4,620,000. A ruby and diamond ring made by Chaumet in Paris, France, weighing 32.08 carats, was sold at Sotheby's, New York, USA on 26 Oct 1989. The record per carat is $227,300 for a ruby ring with a stone weighing 15.97 carats, which was sold at Sotheby's, New York, USA on 18 Oct 1988.

Emerald

Largest cut emerald 86,136 carats. A natural beryl was found in Carnaiba, Brazil in August 1974. It was carved by Richard Chan in Hong Kong and valued at £718,000 in 1982.

Largest single crystal 7025 carats. The largest single emerald crystal of gem quality was found in 1969 at the Cruces Mine, near Gachala, Colombia and is owned by a private mining concern.

Highest priced emerald $3,080,000 (Single lot of emeralds). An emerald and diamond necklace made by Cartier, London in 1937 (a total of 12 stones weighing 108.74 carats) was sold at Sotheby's, New York, USA on 26 Oct 1989. The highest price for a single emerald is $2,126,646, for a 19.77 carat emerald and diamond ring made by Cartier in 1958, which was sold at Sotheby's, Geneva, Switzerland on 2 Apr 1987. This also represented the record price per carat for an emerald, at $107,569.

Sapphire

Largest star sapphire 9719.50 carats. A stone, cut in London in November 1989, has been named *The Lone Star* and is owned by Harold Roper.

Highest priced sapphire $2,791,723. A step-cut stone of 62.02 carats was sold as a sapphire and diamond ring at Sotheby's, St Moritz, Switzerland on 20 Feb 1988.

Opal

Largest opal 26,350 carats. The largest single piece of gem-quality white opal was found in July 1989 at the Jupiter Field at Coober Pedy in South Australia. It has been named *Jupiter-Five* and is in private ownership.

Largest black opal 1520 carats. A stone found on 4 Feb 1972 at Lightning Ridge, New South Wales, Australia produced this finished gem, called the *Empress of Glengarry*. It measures 121 × 80 × 15 mm *4¾ × 3⅛ × ⅝ in*, and is owned by Clive Heard of Sydney, Australia.

Largest rough black opal 1982.5 carats. The largest gem quality uncut black opal was also found at Lightning Ridge, on 3 Nov 1986. After cleaning, it measures 100 × 66 × 63 mm *4 × 2⅝ × 2½ in*. It has been named *Halley's Comet* and is owned by a team of opal miners known as The Lunatic Hill Syndicate.

Pearl

Largest pearl 6.37 kg *14 lb 1 oz*. The *Pearl of Lao-tze* (also known as the *Pearl of Allah*) was found at Palawan, Philippines on 7 May 1934 in the shell of a giant clam. It is 24 cm *9½ in* long and 14 cm *5½ in* in diameter.

Largest abalone pearl 469.13 carats. A baroque abalone pearl measuring 7 × 5 × 2.8 cm *2¾ × 2 × 1⅛ in* was found at Salt Point State Park, California, USA in May 1990. It is owned by Wesley Rankin and is called the *Big Pink*.

Largest cultured pearl 138.25 carats. A cultured pearl with a diameter of 40 mm *1½ in* and weighing 27.65 g *1 oz* was found near Samui Island, off Thailand, in January 1988. The stone is owned by the Mikimoto Pearl Island Company, Japan.

Highest-priced pearl $864,280. *La Régente*, an egg-shaped pearl weighing 15.13 g *302.68 grains* and formerly part of the French Crown Jewels, was sold at Christie's, Geneva, Switzerland on 12 May 1988.

Jade

Largest piece of jade 577 tonnes. A single lens of nephrite jade was found in the Yukon Territory of Canada by Max Rosequist in July 1992. It is owned by Yukon Jade Ltd.

> In 1955 the record for the largest mass of gold ever found was 214.32 kg *7560 oz* for the *Holtermann Nugget*. Forty years on this record still stands.

Amber

Largest amber 15.25 kg *33 lb 10 oz*. The *Burma Amber* is located in the Natural History Museum, London.

Gold

Largest mass of gold 214.32 kg *7560 oz*. The *Holtermann Nugget*, found on 19 Oct 1872 in the Beyers & Holtermann Star of Hope mine, Hill End, New South Wales, Australia, contained some 99.8 kg *220 lb* of gold in a 285.7 kg *630 lb* slab of slate.

Largest pure nugget 69.92 kg *2248 troy oz*. The *Welcome Stranger*, found at Moliagul, Victoria, Australia in 1869, yielded 69.92 kg *2248 troy oz* of pure gold from 70.92 kg *2280¼ oz*.

Platinum

Largest platinum nugget 9635 g *340 oz*. The largest platinum nugget ever found was discovered in the Ural Mountains in Russia in 1843 but was melted down shortly after its discovery.

Largest existing nugget 7860 g *277 oz*. The largest surviving platinum nugget is known as the *Ural Giant* and is currently in the custody of the Diamond Foundation in the Kremlin, Moscow, Russia.

■ The largest flawless fancy cut diamond is the Centenary Diamond (⇨ p. 23). The stone was found at the Premier Diamond Mine in South Africa and the Centenary Diamond itself was designed by master cutter Gabi Tolkowsky.
(Photo: De Beers)

Animal Kingdom

Unless otherwise stated, all measurements refer to adult specimens.

General Records

Oldest land animals Animals moved from the sea to the land at least 414 million years ago, according to discoveries made in 1990 near Ludlow, Shrops. The first known land animals included two kinds of centipede and a tiny spider found among plant debris. However, it is believed that all three species were fairly advanced predators—and therefore must have been preying on animals that lived on land even before they did.

Loudest animal sound The low-frequency pulses made by blue whales (*Balaenoptera musculus*) and fin whales (*B. physalus*) when communicating with each other have been measured at up to 188 decibels, making them the loudest sounds emitted by any living source. They have been detected, using specialist equipment, 850 km *530 miles* away.

Most fertile animal It has been calculated that with unlimited food and no predators, a single cabbage aphid (*Brevicoryne brassicae*) could *theoretically* give rise in a year to a mass of descendants weighing 822 million tonnes, or more than three times the total weight of the world's human population.

Strongest animal In proportion to their size, the strongest animals are the larger beetles of the family Scarabaeidae, which are found mainly in the tropics. In tests carried out on a rhinoceros beetle of the family Dynastinae, it was found to support 850 times its own weight on its back. As a comparison, in a trestle lift a human can support 17 times his own body weight.

Strongest animal bite Experiments carried out with a 'Snodgrass gnathodynamometer' (shark-bite meter) at the Lerner Marine Laboratory in Bimini, Bahamas revealed that a dusky shark (*Carcharhinus obscurus*) 2 m *6 ft 6¾ in* long could exert a force of 60 kg *132 lb* between its jaws. This is equivalent to a pressure of 3 tonnes/cm^2 or *19.6 tons/in^2* at the tips of the teeth. The bites of larger sharks, such as the great white (*Carcharodon carcharias*), must be considerably stronger, but have never been measured.

Most dangerous animal The malarial parasites of the genus *Plasmodium*, carried by mosquitoes of the genus *Anopheles*, have, excluding wars and accidents, probably been responsible for half of all human deaths since the Stone Age. According to 1993 World Health Organisation estimates, between 1.4 million and 2.8 million people die from malaria each year in sub-Saharan Africa alone.

Most poisonous animal The brightly-coloured poison-arrow frogs (*Dendrobates* and *Phyllobates*) of South and Central America secrete some of the most deadly biological toxins known to man. The skin secretion of the golden poison-arrow frog (*Phyllobates terribilis*) of western Colombia is the most poisonous; the species is so dangerous that scientists have to wear thick gloves to pick it up, in case they have cuts or scratches on their hands.

Animal reincarnation In 1846, two specimens of the desert snail *Eremina desertorum* were presented

Noisiest

The world's noisiest land animals are the howler monkeys (*Alouatta*) of Central and South America. The males have an enlarged bony structure at the top of the windpipe which enables the sound to reverberate, and their fearsome screams have been described as a cross between the bark of a dog and the bray of an ass increased a thousandfold. Once in full voice, they can be heard clearly up to 5 km *3.1 miles* away.

The Monarch is the largest butterfly found in Britain. It breeds in the southern United States and Central America. (Photo: Jacana/Varin/Visage)

THE CLOUDS THAT CRAWLED

Above: face-to-face with one of the locusts.

In July 1874, enormous swarms of Rocky Mountain locusts descended on Nebraska and the surrounding frontier settlements, causing inestimable agricultural damage and loss to the pioneers of the region. Many had only recently brought their families to settle there, and had already endured the effects of the persistently hostile climate, with raging storms in one season and intolerable drought in the next.

Newspapers and historical documents contain graphic descriptions of how the insects' unmitigated attack caused havoc amongst the communities of Nebraska. By destroying the crops, they destroyed the pioneers' livelihood. The locusts flew through the air in dense clouds and covered the ground with grey, oily clusters. Trains could not run on the clogged tracks, and volunteers would spend days shovelling them clear. After devouring all the vegetation they could, the insects would lay eggs in the ground which later hatched in droves, prolonging the suffering of the pioneers for years to come. According to the Nebraskan *Daily State Journal* of 30 Nov 1874, 10,000 inhabitants were destitute and $1.5 million was needed for them to survive for just one year.

They covered the ground almost like a blanket. They jumped to the right and left as you walked through them, opening a pathway and closing in behind you as you passed. I had some young celery plants in the garden that I was especially proud of and I covered them with some large pie-plant leaves in the morning. When I came home at noon the pie-plant leaves were eaten and the celery leaves were eaten; not a scrap of anything green remained. The grasshopper brigades also ate all the leaves on my little trees, leaving them as bare as in winter. Even the weeds were not spared by the destroying hosts.

These swarms passed over us often like vast flying squadrons. When they did not stop you could see them, as I have said before, only by looking towards the sun and shading your eyes when you could see their wings shining in the sunlight. Those were tragic days indeed. It became pathetic to see a man standing in that attitude by his little home watching the shining clouds above and waiting to see if a changing wind would send destruction from the air and leave him and his little household destitute.

Recollections of a Pioneer Lawyer, Othman A. Abbott; from the Nebraska History Magazine, Volume XI, July–September 1928.

The dishevelled tree, above left, shows the kind of damage that a swarm of locusts in search of sustenance can cause. The Nebraska swarm of 1874 destroyed vegetation in this way across thousands of miles.

The swarm covered an estimated 514,400 km² *198,600 m²* as it moved across Nebraska, and it was at its worst on 20–30 Jul 1874.

---

to the British Museum (Natural History) as dead exhibits. They were glued on a small tablet and placed on display. Four years later, in March 1850, the Museum staff, suspecting that one of the snails was still alive, removed it from the tablet and placed it in tepid water. The snail moved and later began to feed. This hardy little creature lived for a further two years before it fell into a torpor and died.

Animal regeneration The sponges (*Porifera*) have the most remarkable powers of regeneration of lost parts of any animal, and are capable of regrowing from tiny fragments of their former selves. If a sponge is forced through a fine-meshed silk gauze, the separate fragments can re-form into a full-size sponge.

Smell

Results of German experiments carried out in 1961 showed that the male emperor moth (*Eudia pavonia*) can detect the sex attractant of the virgin female at the range of 11km 6.8miles. This scent has been identified as one of the higher alcohols ($C_{16}H_{29}OH$), of which the female carries less than 0.0001mg. The chemoreceptors on the male moth's antennae are so sensitive that they can detect a single molecule of scent.

Largest eye The Atlantic giant squid (*Architeuthis dux*) has the largest eye of any animal—living or extinct. It has been estimated that the record example from Thimble Tickle Bay, Newfoundland, Canada, had eyes measuring 500mm *20in* in diameter, almost the width of this open book (↔ Molluscs).

Largest colony of mammals The black-tailed prairie dog (*Cynomys ludovicianus*), a rodent of the family Sciuridae found in the western USA and northern Mexico, builds large colonies. One single 'town' discovered in 1901 contained about 400 million individuals, and was estimated to cover 61,440 km² *24,000 miles²* (almost the size of the Republic of Ireland), making it the largest colony of mammals ever recorded.

Greatest concentration A huge swarm of Rocky Mountain locusts (*Melanoplus spretus*) flying over Nebraska, USA on 20–30 Jul 1874 covered an area estimated at 514,400km² *198,600miles²*. This swarm was thought to contain around 12.5 trillion (12.5×10^{12}) insects, weighing an estimated 25 million tonnes.

Greediest animal The larva of the polyphemus moth (*Antheraea polyphemus*) of North America consumes an amount equal to 86,000 times its own

birthweight in the first 56 days of its life. In human terms, this would be equivalent to a 3.17-kg *7-lb* baby taking in 273 tonnes of nourishment.

Greatest weight loss During the 7-month lactation period, a 120-tonne female blue whale (*Balaenoptera musculus*) can lose up to 25 per cent of her body-weight nursing her calf.

Gender difference The most striking difference in size between the sexes is in the marine worm *Bonellia viridis*. The females are 10–100 cm *4–40 in* long (including the extendable proboscis), compared with 1–3 mm *0.04–0.12 in* for the male, thus making the females thousands of times heavier than their mates.

Slowest growth The slowest growth rate in the Animal Kingdom is that of the deep-sea clam *Tindaria callistiformis*, which takes about 100 years to reach a length of 8 mm *⅓ in*. It is found in the North Atlantic.

Most valuable animal The most valuable animals are racehorses. The most paid for a yearling is $13.1 million on 23 Jul 1985 at Keeneland, Kentucky, USA by Robert Sangster and partners for *Seattle Dancer* (⇔ Horse Racing).

Mammals

Largest mammal The largest animal on earth is the blue whale (*Balaenoptera musculus*). Newborn calves are 6–8 m *20–26 ft* long and weigh up to 3 tonnes. The barely visible ovum of the blue-whale calf weighing a fraction of a milligram grows to a weight of c. 26 tonnes in 22¾ months, made up of 10¾ months' gestation and the first 12 months of life. This is equivalent to an increase of 3×10^{10} (⇔ General records).

Heaviest A female weighing 190 tonnes and measuring 27.6 m *90 ft 6 in* in length was caught in the Southern Ocean on 20 Mar 1947.

Longest mammal A female blue whale measuring 33.58 m *110 ft 2½ in* landed in 1909 at Grytviken, South Georgia in the South Atlantic.

Deepest dive by a mammal On 25 Aug 1969, a bull sperm whale (*Physeter macrocephalus*) was killed 160 km *100 miles* south of Durban, South Africa after it had surfaced from a dive lasting 1 hr 52 min, and inside its stomach were two small sharks which had been swallowed about an hour earlier. These were *Scymnodon*, a type found only on the sea floor. The water there exceeds a depth of 3193 m *10,473 ft* for a radius of 48–64 km *30–40 miles*, which suggests

that the sperm whale sometimes descends to over 3000 m *9840 ft* when seeking food and is limited by pressure of time rather than by pressure of pressure.

The deepest authenticated dive was made by a bull sperm whale off the coast of Dominica, in the Caribbean, in 1991. Scientists from the Woods Hole Oceanographic Institute recorded a dive of 2000 m *6560 ft*, lasting a total of 1 hr 13 min.

Largest mammal on land The average bull of the African bush elephant (*Loxodonta africana africana*), stands 3–3.7 m *9 ft 10 in–12 ft 2 in* at the shoulder and weighs 4–7 tonnes. The largest specimen ever recorded was a bull shot in Mucusso, Angola on 7 Nov 1974. Lying on its side, this elephant measured 4.16 m *13 ft 8 in* in a projected line from the highest point of the shoulder to the base of the forefoot, indicating a standing height of about 3.96 m *13 ft*. Its weight was computed to be 12.24 tonnes *12,240 kg*.

Tallest mammal on land The tallest elephants are those of the endangered desert race from Damaraland, Namibia, because they have proportionately longer legs than other elephants. The tallest recorded example was a bull shot near Sesfontein, Damaraland on 4 Apr 1978, after it had allegedly killed 11 people and caused widespread crop damage. Lying on its side, this mountain of flesh measured 4.42 m *14½ ft* in a projected line from the shoulder to the base of the forefoot, indicating a standing height of about 4.21 m *13 ft 10 in*. It weighed an estimated 8 tonnes.

UK Red deer (*Cervus elaphus*) stags are up to 1.22 m *4 ft* tall at the shoulder and weigh 104–113 kg *230–250 lb*. The heaviest ever recorded was a stag killed at Glenfiddich, Grampian in 1831, which weighed 238 kg *525 lb*.

Smallest mammal The smallest mammal in the world is the bumblebee or Kitti's hog-nosed bat (*Craseonycteris thonglongyai*), which is confined to about 21 limestone caves on the Kwae Roi River, Kanchanaburi Province, south-west Thailand. With a body no bigger than a large bumble-bee, it has a

head–body length of only 2.9–3.3 cm *1.14–1.30 in*, a wingspan of approximately 15–16 cm *5.9–6.3 in*, and a weight of 1.7–2.0 g *0.06–0.07 oz*.

The smallest non-flying mammal is Savi's white-toothed pygmy shrew, also called the Etruscan shrew (*Suncus etruscus*), which has a head and body length of 36–52 mm *1.32–2.04 in*, a tail length of 24–29 mm *0.94–1.14 in* and a weight of 1.5–2.5 g *0.05–0.09 oz*. It is found along the Mediterranean coast and southwards to Cape Province, South Africa.

Largest toothed mammal The lower jaw of a sperm whale or cachelot (*Physeter macrocephalus*), measuring 5 m *16 ft 5 in* long and exhibited in the British Museum (Natural History), belonged to a bull reputedly measuring nearly 25.6 m *84 ft*. However, the longest officially measured specimen was a male measuring 20.7 m *67 ft 11 in* long, captured in the summer of 1950 off the Kurile Islands, in the northwest Pacific.

British Isles A bull sperm whale measuring 19 m *61 ft 5 in* was washed ashore at Birchington, Kent on 18 Oct 1914. Another huge bull stranded at Derryloughan, Co. Galway, Republic of Ireland on 2 Jan 1952 reportedly measured 19.8 m *65 ft*, but the carcass was so decomposed that there must have been some length extension.

Tallest mammal The giraffe (*Giraffa camelopardalis*), is found in the dry savannah and open woodland areas of Africa, south of the Sahara. The tallest specimen ever recorded was a Masai bull (*G. c. tippelskirchi*) named George, received at Chester Zoo on 8 Jan 1959 from Kenya. His 'horns' almost grazed the roof of the 6.09 m *20 ft* high Giraffe House when he was nine years old. George died on 22 Jul 1969.

Fastest mammal on land Over a short distance (i.e. up to 550 m *1804 ft*), the cheetah (*Acinonyx jubatus*) of the open plains of East Africa, Iran, Turkmenistan and Afghanistan has a probable maximum speed of about 100 km/h *60 mph* on level ground.

The pronghorn antelope (*Antilocapra americana*), of the western United States, south-western Canada and parts of northern Mexico, is the fastest land

---

Structure

The largest structure ever built by living creatures is the 2027 km *1260 mile* long Great Barrier Reef, off Queensland, Australia, covering an area of 207,000 km^2 *80,000 miles^2*. It consists of countless billions of dead and living stony corals (order Madreporaria or Scleractinia). Over 350 species of coral are currently found there, and its accretion is estimated to have taken 600 million years.

Although animal records change more frequently that one might think, many have stayed the same since the first edition. The largest animal ever to have inhabited the earth is still the blue whale, the fastest mammal is still the cheetah, the tallest mammal is still the giraffe. While the giraffe has not grown taller, man has been leaping higher: in 1955, the world pole vault record was 4.77 m *15 ft 7 in*, and the record now stands at 6.15 m *20 ft 2¼ in* — thus progressing from well below the height of the giraffe to far above it.

■ **A cheetah showing off its penchant for speed—over a short distance, the cheetah is the fastest land mammal in world.**
(Photo left: Jacana/F. Polking)
(Photo centre: Jacana/Varin/Visage)
(Photo right: Jacana/Y. Arthus-Bertrand)

Carnivores, Primates, Pinnipeds ▶▶ ▶▶

Slowest mammal The three-toed sloth of tropical South America (*Bradypus tridactylus*), has an average ground speed of 1.8–2.4 m *6–8 ft* per minute (0.1–0.16 km/h *0.07–0.1 mph*), but in the trees it can accelerate to 4.6 m *15 ft* per minute (0.27 km/h *0.17 mph*).

animal over a long distance. It has been observed to travel at 56 km/h *35 mph* for 6 km *4 miles*, at 67 km/h *42 mph* for 1.6 km *1 mile* and 88.5 km/h *55 mph* for 0.8 km *½ mile*.

UK Over a sustained distance, the roe deer (*Capreolus capreolus*) can cruise at 40–48 km/h *25–30 mph* for more than 32 km *20 miles*, with occasional bursts of up to 64 km/h *40 mph*. On 19 Oct 1970, a frightened runaway red deer (*Cervus elaphus*) charging through a street in Stalybridge, Greater Manchester registered 67.5 km/h *42 mph* on a police radar speed trap.

Fastest marine mammal On 12 Oct 1958, a bull killer whale (*Orcinus orca*), measuring an estimated 6.1–7.6 m *20–25 ft* long, was timed at 55.5 km/h *34.5 mph* in the eastern North Pacific. Similar speeds have also been reported for Dall's porpoise (*Phocoenoides dalli*) in short bursts.

Sleepiest mammal Some armadillos (Dasypodidae), opossums (Didelphidae) and sloths (Bradypodidae and Megalonychidae) spend up to 80 per cent of their lives sleeping or dozing. The least active of all mammals are probably the three species of three-toed sloths in the genus *Bradypus*.

Oldest mammal No other land mammal can match the age attained by Man (*Homo sapiens*) (⇨ Human Being), but the Asiatic elephant (*Elephas maximus*) probably comes closest. There are a number of claims of animals reaching 80 years or more, but the greatest verified age is 78 years for a cow named Modoc, who died at Santa Clara, California, USA on 17 Jul 1975. Certain whale species are believed to live even longer, although little is known about this. The fin

■ Quintuplet bear cubs named Konrad, Paul, Christian, Johannes, and Günther were born at Haag Wildlife Park, Austria, on 6 January 1993. (Photo: Tierpark Haag)

whale (*Balaenoptera physalis*) is probably the longest lived, with a maximum attainable lifespan estimated at 90–100 years.

Highest mammal By a small margin, the highest-living mammal in the world is the large-eared pika (*Ochtona macrotis*), which has been recorded at a height of 6130 m *20,106 ft* in high-altitude mountain ranges in Asia. The yak (*Bos mutus*) of Tibet and the Sichuanese Alps, China climbs to an altitude of 6100 m *20,000 ft* when foraging.

Largest herd of mammals The largest herds on record were those of the springbok (*Antidorcas marsupialis*) during migration across the plains of the western parts of southern Africa in the 19th century. In 1849 John (later Sir John) Fraser observed a *trekbokken* that took three days to pass through the settlement of Beaufort West, Cape Province.

Longest gestation period of any mammal The Asiatic elephant (*Elephas maximus*) has an average gestation period of 609 days (over 20 months) and a maximum of 760 days—more than two and a half times that of humans.

Shortest gestation period of any mammal The shortest mammalian gestation period is 12–13 days, which is common in a number of species. These include the Virginia opossum (*Didelphis marsupialis*) of North America and the rare water opossum or yapok (*Chironectes minimus*) of central and northern South America. On rare occasions, gestation periods of as low as 8 days have been recorded for some of these species.

Youngest mammal breeder The female true lemming (*Lemmus lemmus*) of Scandinavia can become pregnant after 14 days. The gestation period is 16 to 23 days, and litter size varies from 1 to 13. They are

Smallest

Smallest carnivore The least or dwarf weasel (*Mustela nivalis*), has a head–body length of 110–260 mm *4–10 in*, a tail length of 13–87 mm *0.5–3.5 in*, and a weight of 30–200 g *1–7 oz*. This species varies in size more than any other mammal, with the smallest individuals being females living in the north of the range (especially Siberia), and in the Alps.

also prolific animals: one pair of lemmings was reported to have produced eight litters in 167 days, after which the male died.

Carnivores

Largest carnivore on land The largest of all the carnivores is the polar bear (*Ursus maritimus*). Adult males typically weigh 400–600 kg *880–1323 lb*, and have a nose-to-tail length of 2.4–2.6 m *95–102 in*. The male Kodiak bear (*Ursus arctos middendorffi*), a sub-species of brown bear found on Kodiak Island and the adjacent Afognak and Shuyak islands, in the Gulf of Alaska, USA, is usually smaller in length than the polar bear but more robustly built.

Heaviest In 1960 a polar bear estimated at around 2000 lb *907 kg* was shot at a frozen ice pack in the Chukchi Sea, west of Kotzebue, Alaska, USA. The bear was said to measure 3.5 m *11 ft 3 in* nose-to-tail over the contours of the body, 1.5 m *4 ft 10 in* around the body and 43 cm *17 in* around the paws. Although these figures have been disputed, this specimen is still the most likely candidate for the heaviest bear ever to have been taken in the wild.

A Kodiak bear named Goliath at the Space Farms Zoo in Sussex, New Jersey, reportedly exceeded 900 kg *2000 lb* in weight in the early 1980s. Owing to advanced arthritis, he was euthanatised in April 1991 aged 24 years, weighing about 750 kg *1650 lb*.

The greatest number of young born to a *wild* mammal at a single birth is 31 (30 of which survived) in the case of a tail-less tenrec (*Tenrec ecaudatus*), found in Madagascar and the Comoro Islands.

UK The largest land carnivore found in Britain is the badger (*Meles meles*). The average boar (sows are slightly smaller) is 90 cm *3 ft* long nose-to-tail and weighs 12.3 kg *27 lb* in the early spring and 14.5 kg *32 lb* at the end of the summer when it is in 'grease'. In December 1952, a boar weighing 27.2 kg *60 lb* was killed near Rotherham, S Yorks.

Largest feline carnivore The male Siberian tiger (*Panthera tigris altaica*), averages 3.15 m *10 ft 4 in* in length from the nose to the tip of the extended tail, stands 99–107 cm *39–42 in* at the shoulder and weighs about 265 kg *585 lb*. An Indian tiger (*P. t. tigris*) shot in northern Uttar Pradesh in November 1967 measured 3.22 m *10 ft 7 in* between pegs (3.37 m *11 ft 1 in* over the curves) and weighed 389 kg *857 lb* (cf. 2.82 m *9 ft 3 in* and 190 kg *420 lb* for an average male).

Lions The heaviest wild African lion (*Panthera leo leo*) on record weighed 313 kg *690 lb* and was shot near Hectorspruit, Transvaal, South Africa in 1936.

UK In July 1970, a weight of 375 kg *826 lb* and a shoulder height of 1.11 m *44 in* was reported for a black-maned lion named Simba at Colchester Zoo, Essex. He died on 16 Jan 1973, at the now defunct Knaresborough Zoo, N Yorks, aged 14.

Smallest feline carnivore The rusty-spotted cat (*Priongilurus rubiginosus*) of southern India and Sri Lanka, has a head–body length of 35–48 cm *13.8–18.9 in*, and an average weight of 1.1 kg *2 lb 7 oz* (female) and 1.5–1.6 kg *3 lb 5 oz–3 lb 8 oz* (male). The black-footed cat (*Felis nigripes*) of southern Africa is almost as small.

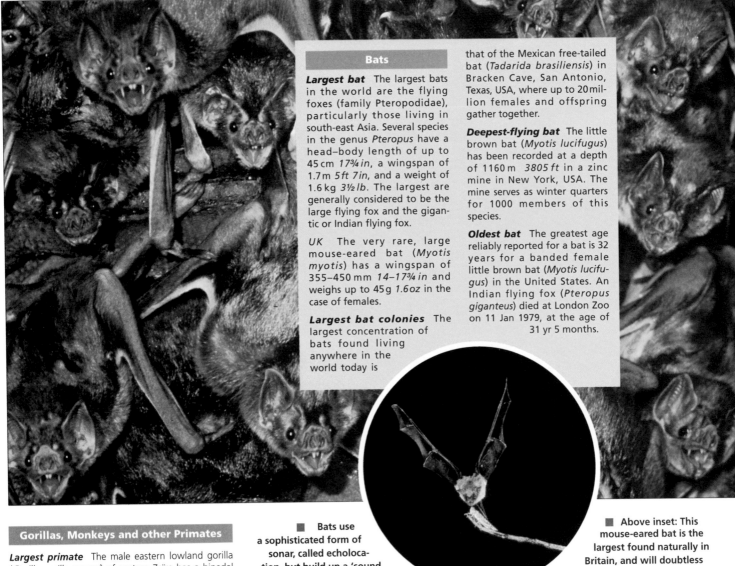

Bats

Largest bat The largest bats in the world are the flying foxes (family Pteropodidae), particularly those living in south-east Asia. Several species in the genus *Pteropus* have a head–body length of up to 45 cm *17¾ in*, a wingspan of 1.7 m *5 ft 7 in*, and a weight of 1.6 kg *3½ lb*. The largest are generally considered to be the large flying fox and the gigantic or Indian flying fox.

UK The very rare, large mouse-eared bat (*Myotis myotis*) has a wingspan of 355–450 mm *14–17¾ in* and weighs up to 45 g *1.6 oz* in the case of females.

Largest bat colonies The largest concentration of bats found living anywhere in the world today is that of the Mexican free-tailed bat (*Tadarida brasiliensis*) in Bracken Cave, San Antonio, Texas, USA, where up to 20 million females and offspring gather together.

Deepest-flying bat The little brown bat (*Myotis lucifugus*) has been recorded at a depth of 1160 m *3805 ft* in a zinc mine in New York, USA. The mine serves as winter quarters for 1000 members of this species.

Oldest bat The greatest age reliably reported for a bat is 32 years for a banded female little brown bat (*Myotis lucifugus*) in the United States. An Indian flying fox (*Pteropus giganteus*) died at London Zoo on 11 Jan 1979, at the age of 31 yr 5 months.

■ Bats use a sophisticated form of sonar, called echolocation, but build up a 'sound picture' of their surroundings and, consequently, have the most acute hearing of any terrestrial animal.
Most species use frequencies in the 20–80 kHz range, although some go as high as 120–250 kHz (the normal range of human hearing is 20 Hz to almost 20 kHz). The bats listen to the returning echoes of sounds they produce to locate objects in their path, enabling them to gather information on the distance, direction and relative velocity of their insect prey — in total darkness — as well as their shape, size and texture.
(Photo: Jacana/G. Ziesler)

■ Above inset: This mouse-eared bat is the largest found naturally in Britain, and will doubtless be even larger when it has devoured the hapless locust.
(Photo: Jacana/Axel)

Gorillas, Monkeys and other Primates

Largest primate The male eastern lowland gorilla (*Gorilla gorilla graueri*) of eastern Zaïre has a bipedal standing height of up to 1.8 m *5 ft 11 in* and weighs up to 175 kg *386 lb*.

Tallest The greatest height (top of crest to heel) recorded for a gorilla in the wild is 1.95 m *6 ft 5 in* for a mountain bull shot in the eastern Congo (Zaïre) on 16 May 1938.

Heaviest The heaviest gorilla ever kept in captivity was a male of the mountain race named N'gagi, who died in San Diego Zoo, California, USA on 12 Jan 1944, at the age of 18. He weighed 310 kg *683 lb* at his heaviest in 1943. He was 1.72 m *5 ft 7¾ in* tall and boasted a record chest measurement of 198 cm *78 in*.

Smallest primate The smallest true primate (excluding tree shrews, which are normally classified separately) is the western rufous mouse lemur (*Microcebus myoxinus*), which has recently been rediscovered in the deciduous forests of western Madagascar. It has a head–body length of about 6 cm *2.4 in*, and an average weight of 30.6 g *1.1 oz*.

Oldest primate The greatest irrefutable age recorded for a non-human primate is 59 yr 5 months for a chimpanzee (*Pan troglodytes*) named Gamma, who died at the Yerkes Primate Research Center in Atlanta, Georgia, USA on 19 Feb 1992. Gamma was born at the Florida branch of the Yerkes Center in September 1932.

> The world's oldest monkey, a male white-throated capuchin (*Cebus capucinus*) called Bobo, died on 10 Jul 1988 aged 53 years.

Seals, Sea-lions and Walrus

Largest pinniped The largest of the 34 known species of pinniped is the southern elephant seal (*Mirounga leonina*) of the sub-Antarctic islands. Bulls average 5 m *16½ ft* in length from the tip of the inflated snout to the tips of the outstretched tail flippers, have a maximum girth of 3.7 m *12 ft* and weigh about 2000–3500 kg *4400–7720 lb*. The largest accurately measured specimen of the elephant seal was a bull which weighed at least 4 tonnes and measured 6.5 m *21 ft 4 in* after flensing (stripping of the blubber or skin). Its original length was estimated to be about 6.85 m *22½ ft*. It was killed in the South Atlantic at Possession Bay, South Georgia on 28 Feb 1913.

Live The largest reported live specimen is a bull nicknamed Stalin from South Georgia at 2662 kg *5869 lb* and 5.10 m *16 ft 9 in*, recorded by members of the British Antarctic Survey on 14 Oct 1989.

Smallest pinniped The smallest pinniped, by a small margin, is the Galapagos fur seal (*Arctocephalus galapagoensis*). Adult females average 1.2 m *47 in* in length and weigh about 27 kg *60 lb*. Males are usually considerably larger, averaging 1.5 m *59 in* in length and weighing around 64 kg *141 lb*.

Oldest pinniped The greatest authenticated age for a pinniped was estimated by scientists at the Limnological Institute, Irkutsk, Russian Federation, to be 56 years for the female Baikal seal (*Phoca sibirica*) and 52 years for the male, based on cementum layers in the canine teeth.

UK A female grey seal (*Halichoerus grypus*) shot at Shunni Wick, Shetland on 23 Apr 1969 was estimated to be at least 46 years old, based on a count of dentine rings.

Fastest pinniped The highest swimming speed recorded for a pinniped is a short spurt of 40 km/h *25 mph* by a California sea-lion (*Zalophus californianus*).

Rodents, Horses and Ponies, Dogs ▶▶ ▶▶

Fastest on land The fastest pinniped on land is the crabeater seal (*Lobodon carcinophagus*), which has been timed at 19 km/h *12 mph*.

Deepest pinniped dive In May 1989, scientists testing the diving abilities of northern elephant seals (*Mirounga angustirostris*) off the coast of San Miguel Island, California, USA, documented an adult male which reached a maximum depth of 1529 m *5017 ft*.

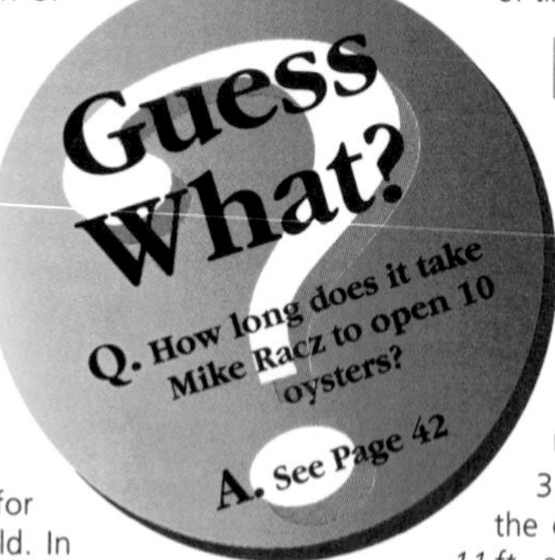

Rodents

Largest rodent The capybara (*Hydrochoerus hydrochaeris*), of northern South America, has a head and body length of 1.0–1.4 m *3¼–4½ ft* and can weigh up to 66 kg *145½ lb*—although one exceptional cage-fat specimen attained 113 kg *250 lb*.

Smallest rodent Several species vie for the title of smallest rodent in the world. In particular, the northern pygmy mouse (*Baiomys taylori*) of Mexico, Arizona and Texas, USA and the Baluchistan pygmy jerboa (*Salpingotus michaelis*) of Pakistan, both have a head–body length of as little as 3.6 cm *1.42 in*, and a tail length of 7.2 cm *2.84 in*.

Oldest rodent The greatest reliable age reported for a rodent is 27 yr 3 months for a Sumatran crested porcupine (*Hystrix brachyura*) which died in the National Zoological Park, Washington, DC, USA on 12 Jan 1965.

Longest hibernation by a rodent Arctic ground squirrels (*Spermophilus parryi*), living in northern Canada and Alaska, USA, hibernate for nine months of the year.

Highest density of rodents A population of house mice (*Mus musculus*) numbering 205,000/ha *83,000/acre* was found in the dry bed of Buena Vista Lake, Kern County, California, USA, in 1926–7.

Antelopes

Largest antelope The giant eland (*Tragelaphus derbianus*) of western and central Africa can attain a height of 1.83 m *6 ft* at the shoulder and weigh over 940 kg *2072 lb*.

Smallest antelope The royal antelope (*Neotragus pygmaeus*) of western Africa stands 25–31 cm *10–12 in* tall at the shoulder and weighs 3–3.6 kg *7–8 lb*, the size of a brown hare (*Lepus europaeus*).

Deer

Largest deer The largest deer is the Alaskan moose (*Alces alces gigas*). A bull standing 2.34 m *7 ft 8 in* between pegs and weighing an estimated 816 kg *1800 lb* was shot in the Yukon Territory of Canada in September 1897.

Oldest deer The world's oldest recorded deer was a Scottish red deer (*Cervus elaphus scoticus*) named Bambi (b. 8 Jun 1963), who died on 20 Jan 1995 at the advanced age of 31 yr 8 months. She was owned by the Fraser family of Kiltarlity, Beauly, Highland.

The smallest true deer (family Cervidae) is the southern pudu (*Pudu puda*), which is 33–38 cm *13–15 in* tall at the shoulder and weighs 6.3–8.2 kg *14–18 lb*. It is found in Chile and Argentina.

Kangaroos

Largest kangaroo The male red kangaroo (*Macropus rufus*) of central, southern and eastern Australia measures up to 1.8 m *5 ft 11 in* tall when standing in the normal position, and up to 2.85 m *9 ft 4 in* in total length (including the tail). It weighs up to 90 kg *198 lb* in exceptional cases.

Fastest kangaroo The highest speed recorded for a marsupial is 64 km/h *40 mph* for a mature female eastern grey kangaroo (*Macropus giganteus*). The highest sustained speed is 56 km/h *35 mph* recorded for a large male red kangaroo which died from its exertions after being paced for 1.6 km *1 mile*.

Highest jump by a kangaroo A captive eastern grey kangaroo once cleared a 2.44 m *8 ft* fence when a car backfired, and there is also a record of a hunted red kangaroo clearing a stack of timber 3.1 m *10 ft* high.

Guess What?
Q. How long does it take Mike Racz to open 10 oysters?
A. See Page 42

Tusks

Longest tusk The longest tusks (excluding prehistoric examples) are a pair from an African elephant (*Loxodonta africana*) taken from Zaïre and kept in the New York Zoological Society in Bronx Park, New York City, USA. The right tusk measures 3.49 m *11 ft 5½ in* along the outside curve, the left 3.35 m *11 ft* and their combined weight is 133 kg *293 lb*.

Heaviest tusk A pair of African elephant (*Loxodonta africana*) tusks in the British Museum (Natural History) from a bull shot in Kenya in 1897 weighed 109 kg *240 lb* (length 3.11 m *10 ft 2½ in*) and 102 kg *225 lb* (length 3.18 m *10 ft 5½ in*), giving a total weight of 211 kg *465 lb*. Their combined weight today is 200 kg *440½ lb*.

Horns

Longest horns The longest horns of any living animal are those of the water buffalo (*Bubalus arnee=B. bubalis*) of India, Nepal, Bhutan and Thailand. One bull shot in 1955 had horns measuring 4.24 m *13 ft 11 in* tip-to-tip along the outside curve across the forehead.

A record spread of 3.2 m *10 ft 6 in* was recorded for a Texas longhorn steer on exhibition at the Heritage Museum, Big Springs, Texas, USA.

Largest antlers The record antler spread or 'rack' of any living species is 1.99 m *6 ft 6½ in* from a moose (*Alces alces*) killed near the Stewart River, Yukon, Canada in October 1897 and now on display in the Field Museum, Chicago, Illinois, USA.

Horses and Ponies

(⇨ Agriculture for record prices)

Earliest domestication of a horse Evidence from the Ukraine indicates that horses may have been ridden earlier than 4000 BC (⇨ Agriculture).

Largest horse The tallest and heaviest documented horse was the shire gelding Sampson (later renamed Mammoth), bred by Thomas Cleaver of Toddington Mills, Beds. This horse (foaled 1846) measured 21.2½ hands (2.19 m *7 ft 2½ in*) in 1850, and was later said to have weighed 1524 kg *3360 lb*.

Smallest horse The smallest recorded horse was the stallion Little Pumpkin (foaled 15 Apr 1973), which stood 35.5 cm *14 in* and weighed 9 kg *20 lb* on 30 Nov 1975. It was owned by J.C.

Longest Jump

During a chase in New South Wales, Australia in January 1951, a female red kangaroo made a series of bounds which included one of 12.8 m *42 ft*. There is also an unconfirmed report of an eastern grey kangaroo jumping nearly 13.5 m *44½ ft* on the flat.

Williams Jr of Della Terra Mini Horse Farm, Inman, South Carolina, USA.

The smallest breed of horse is the Falabella of Argentina, developed by Julio Falabella of Recco de Roca. The smallest example was a mare which was 38 cm *15 in* tall and weighed 11.9 kg *26¼ lb*.

Oldest horse The greatest age reliably recorded for a horse is 62 years for Old Billy (foaled 1760), bred by Edward Robinson of Woolston, Lancs. Old Billy died on 27 Nov 1822.

Thoroughbred The oldest recorded thoroughbred racehorse was the 42-year-old chestnut gelding Tango Duke (foaled 1935), owned by Carmen J. Koper of Barongarook, Victoria, Australia. The horse died on 25 Jan 1978.

Oldest pony The greatest age reliably recorded for a pony is 54 years for a stallion (*fl.* 1919) owned by a farmer in central France.

UK A moorland pony called Joey, owned by June and Rosie Osborne of the Glebe Equestrian Centre, Wickham Bishop, Essex, died in May 1988 at the age of 44.

Mules The largest mules on record are Apollo (foaled 1977) and Anak (foaled 1976), owned by Herbert L. Mueller of Columbia, Illinois, USA. Apollo stands 19.1 hands (1.96 m *6 ft 5 in*) tall and weighs 998 kg *2200 lb*, with Anak at 18.3 hands (1.91 m *6 ft 3 in*) and 952.2 kg *2100 lb*. Both are the hybrid offspring of Belgian mares and mammoth jacks.

Dogs

Largest dog The heaviest breeds of domestic dog (*Canis familiaris*) are the Old English mastiff and the St Bernard, with males of both species regularly weighing 77–91 kg *170–200 lb*. The heaviest (and longest) dog ever recorded is Aicama Zorba of La-Susa (whelped 26 Sep 1981), an Old English mastiff owned by Chris Eraclides of London. 'Zorba' stands 94 cm *37 in* at the shoulder and weighed a peak 155.58 kg *343 lb* in November 1989.

Tallest The tallest dog ever recorded was Shamgret Danzas (whelped 1975), a great Dane owned by Wendy and Keith Comley of Milton Keynes, Bucks. This dog stood 105.4 cm *41½ in* tall (106.6 cm *42 in* with hackles raised) and weighed up to 108 kg *238 lb*. He died on 16 Oct 1984.

Smallest dog The smallest dog on record was a matchbox-sized Yorkshire terrier owned by Arthur Marples of Blackburn, Lancs, a former editor of *Our Dogs*. This tiny atom, which died in 1945 aged nearly two, stood 6.3 cm *2½ in* at the shoulder and measured 9.5 cm *3¾ in* from the tip of its nose to the root of its tail. It weighed just 113 g *4 oz*.

Oldest dog Most dogs live for 8–15 years, and authentic records of dogs living over 20 years are rare and generally involve the smaller breeds. The greatest reliable age recorded for a dog is 29 years 5 months for an Australian cattle-dog named Bluey, owned by Les Hall of Rochester, Victoria, Australia. Bluey was obtained as a puppy in 1910 and worked among cattle and sheep for nearly 20 years before being put to sleep on 14 Nov 1939.

Forty years ago, the heaviest horse on record was the Shire mare Erfyl Lady Grey, London show champion 1924–26. She weighed 25 cwt. Our first edition also reported the largest mane on record — one of 13 feet *4 m*, belonging to a Percheron from Dee in 1891. This horse also allegedly had a tail measuring 10 ft *3 m* long.

UK A Welsh collie named Taffy, owned by Evelyn Brown of Forge Farm, West Bromwich, W Mids, lived for 27 years and 313 days. He was whelped on 2 Apr 1952 and died on 9 Feb 1980.

Tracking In 1925 a Dobermann pinscher named Sauer, trained by Detective-Sergeant Herbert Kruger, tracked a stock-thief 160 km *100 miles* across the Great Karroo, South Africa by scent alone.

Ratting During the period 1820–24, a 11.8 kg *26 lb* 'bull and terrier' dog named Billy dispatched 4000 rats in 17 hours, a remarkable feat considering that he was blind in one eye. His most notable feat was the killing of 100 rats in 5 min 30 sec at the Cockpit in Tufton Street, Westminster, London on 23 Apr 1825. He died on 23 Feb 1829, at the age of 13. James Searle's famous 'bull and terrier' bitch Jenny Lind was another outstanding ratter. On 12 Jul 1853 she was backed to kill 500 rats in under 3 hr at The Beehive in Old Crosshall Street, Liverpool, and completed the job in 1 hr 36 min.

Guide dogs The longest period of active service reported for a guide dog is 14 yr 8 months (August 1972–March 1987) in the case of a labrador retriever bitch named Cindy-Cleo (whelped 20 Jan 1971), owned by Aron Barr of Tel Aviv, Israel. The dog died on 10 Apr 1987.

The largest legacy devoted to a dog was £15 million, bequeathed by Ella Wendel of New York, USA to her standard poodle Toby in 1931.

The most popular breed of dog has changed considerably over the last 40 years. Our first edition reported that the cocker spaniel had been the most popular breed in the British Isles since 1935. It reached a popularity peak in 1947 with 27,000 Kennel Club registrations and a total estimated population of over 450,000. The most Kennel Club registrations for the year 1955, however, were among miniature poodles.

Ten years later, in 1965, *The Guinness Book of Records* reported the most Kennel Club registrations to be for the Alsatian with 12,572. In 1975, the Yorkshire Terrier came through as most popular, with 14,640 registrations at the Kennel Club. Now, the most popular breed is the Labrador, with 29,118 registrations made in 1994.

Hearing Donna, a hearing guide dog owned by John Hogan of Pyrmont Point, Australia had completed ten years of active service in Australia to 1995 and eight years of service prior to that in New Zealand. Donna was also the first hearing dog to be licensed under Australian Dog Law in 1985.

Largest dog show
The centenary of the annual Crufts show, held outside London for the first time at the National Exhibition Centre, Birmingham, W Mids on 9–12 Jan 1991, attracted a record 22,993 entries.

■ **Zorba, the largest, longest and heaviest dog ever recorded, pictured here with his owner Chris Eraclides of London.**
(Photo: Chris Eraclides)

Highest jump by a dog The canine high jump record for a leap and scramble over a smooth wooden wall (without ribs or other aids) is 3.72 m *12 ft 2½ in* achieved by an 18-month-old lurcher dog named Stag, at the annual Cotswold Country Fair in Cirencester, Glos, on 27 Sep 1993. The dog was owned by Mr and Mrs P.R.Matthews of Redruth, Cornwall.

Duke, a three-year-old German shepherd dog handled by Corporal Graham Urry of RAF Newton, Notts, scaled a ribbed wall with regulation shallow slats to a height of 3.58 m *11 ft 9 in* on the BBC *Record Breakers* programme on 11 Nov 1986.

Longest dog jump A greyhound named Bang jumped 9.14 m *30 ft* while hare coursing at Brecon Lodge, Glos in 1849. He cleared a gate 1.4 m *4 ft 6 in* high and landed on a road, damaging his pastern bone.

Largest Pet Litters

Animal/Breed	No.	Owner	Date
CAT *Burmese/Siamese*	19[1]	V. Gane, Church Westcote, Kingham, Oxon	7 Aug 1970
DOG *American foxhound*	23	W. Ely, Ambler, Pennsylvania, USA	19 Jun 1944
St Bernard	23[3]	R. and A. Rodden, Lebanon, Missouri, USA	6–7 Feb 1975
Great Dane	23[3]	M. Harris, Little Hall, Essex	June 1987
FERRET *Domestic*	15	J. Cliff, Denstone, Uttoxeter, Staffs	1981
GERBIL *Mongolian*	14[4]	S. Kirkman, Bulwell, Notts	May 1983
GUINEA PIG	12	Laboratory specimen	1972
HAMSTER *Golden*	26[5]	L. and S. Miller, Baton Rouge, Louisiana, USA	28 Feb 1974
MOUSE *House*	34[6]	M. Ogilvie, Blackpool, Lancs	12 Feb 1982
RABBIT *New Zealand white*	24	J. Filek, Cape Breton, Nova Scotia, Canada	1978

[1] Four stillborn. [2] Fourteen survived. [3] Sixteen survived. [4] Litter of 15 recorded in 1960s by George Meares, geneticist-owner of gerbil-breeding farm in St Petersburg, Florida, USA using special food formula. [5] Eighteen killed by mother. [6] Thirty-three survived.

Guess What?
Q. For how long did the longest-lived goldfish live?
A. See Page 37

Cats, Rabbits and Hares, Birds ▶▶ ▶▶

Caged Pet Longevity

Animal/Species	Name, Owner, etc.	Yr	Months
BIRD *Parrot*	*Prudle* captured 1958, I. Frost, East Sussex	35	—
Budgerigar	*Charlie* April 1948–20 Jun 1977, J. Dinsey, Stonebridge, London	29	2
RABBIT *Wild*	*Flopsy* caught 6 Aug 1964, died 29 Jun 1983, L.B. Walker Longford, Tasmania, Australia	18	10¾
GUINEA PIG	*Snowball* died 14 Feb 1979, M. A. Wall, Bingham, Notts	14	10½
GERBIL *Mongolian*	*Sahara* May 1973–4 Oct 1981, Aaron Milstone, Lathrup Village, Michigan, USA	8	4½
MOUSE *House*	*Fritzy* 11 Sep 1977–24 April 1985, Bridget Beard West House School, Edgbaston, Birmingham, W Mids	7	7
RAT *Common*	*Rodney* January 1983–25 May 1990, Rodney Mitchell Tulsa, Oklahoma, USA	7	4

Top show dogs The greatest number of Challenge Certificates won by a dog is 78 by the chow chow named Ch. U'Kwong King Solomon (whelped 21 Jun 1968). Owned and bred by Joan Egerton of Bramhall, Cheshire, Solly won his first CC at the Cheshire Agricultural Society Championship Show on 4 Jun 1969, and his 78th CC was awarded at the City of Birmingham Championship Show on 4 Sep 1976. He died on 3 Apr 1978.

The greatest number of 'Best-in-Show' awards won by any dog in all-breed shows is 275, compiled by the German shepherd bitch Altana's Mystique (born in May 1987), formerly owned by Mrs Jane Firestone and now owned and trained by James A. Moses of Altharetta, Georgia, USA.

Drug sniffing Snag, a US customs labrador retriever trained and partnered by Jeff Weitzmann, has made 118 drug seizures worth a canine record $810 million (£580 million).

UK In October 1988 a German shepherd owned by the Essex Police sniffed out 2 tonnes of cannabis worth £6 million when sent into a remote cottage on the outskirts of Harlow, Essex.

Cats

Largest cat The heaviest reliably recorded domestic cat was a neutered male tabby named Himmy, which weighed 21.3 kg *46 lb 15¼ oz* (neck 38.1 cm *15 in*, waist 83.8 cm *33 in* and length 96.5 cm *38 in*) at the time of his death from respiratory failure on 12 Mar 1986. He was aged 10 yr 4 months. Himmy was owned by Thomas Vyse of Redlynch, Cairns, Queensland, Australia.

UK An 11-year-old male tabby called Poppa, owned by Gwladys Cooper of Newport, Gwent, weighed 20.19 kg *44½ lb* in November 1984. He died on 25 Jun 1985.

Smallest cat Tinker Toy, a male blue point Himalayan-Persian cat owned by Katrina and Scott Forbes of Taylorville, Illinois, USA, is just 7 cm 2 in tall and 19 cm 7½ in long.

Oldest cat The oldest reliably recorded cat was the female tabby Ma, which was put to sleep on 5 Nov 1957 at the age of 34. Her owner was Alice St George Moore of Drewsteignton, Devon.

A less well-documented record is of the tabby Puss, owned by Mrs T. Holway of Clayhidon, Devon, who celebrated his 36th birthday on 28 Nov 1939 and died the next day.

Most prolific cat A tabby named Dusty (b. 1935) of Bonham, Texas, USA produced 420 kittens during her breeding life. She gave birth to her last litter (a single kitten) on 12 Jun 1952.

Oldest feline mother In May 1987 Kitty, owned by George Johnstone of Croxton, Staffs, produced two kittens at the age of 30 years, making her the oldest feline mother on record. She died in June 1989, just short of her 32nd birthday, having given birth to a known total of 218 kittens.

Best climber On 6 Sep 1950, a 4-month-old kitten belonging to Josephine Aufdenblatten of Geneva, Switzerland followed a group of climbers to the top of the 4478-m *14,691-ft* Matterhorn in the Alps.

Mousing champion A female tortoiseshell cat named Towser (b. 21 Apr 1963), owned by Glenturret Distillery Ltd near Crieff, Tayside, notched up an estimated lifetime score of 28,899 mice. She averaged three mice per day until her death on 20 Mar 1987.

Rabbits and Hares

Largest rabbit In April 1980 a 5-month-old French lop doe weighing 12 kg *26 lb 7 oz* was exhibited at the Reus Fair in north-east Spain.

The world's largest wild rabbit or hare is the Alaskan hare (*Lethus othus*), which lives on the open tundra in west and south-west Alaska, and attains a maximum weight of about 6.5 kg *14¼ lb*. The European or brown hare (*Lepus europaeus*), also attains a large size: in November 1956, a brown hare weighing 6.83 kg *15 lb 1 oz* was shot near Welford, Northants. The average weight is 3.62 kg *8 lb*.

Smallest rabbit Both the Netherland dwarf and the Polish have a weight range of 0.9–1.13 kg *2–2½ lb*, but in 1975 Jacques Bouloc of Coulommière, France announced a new hybrid of these weighing 396 g *14 oz*.

Most prolific rabbit The most prolific domestic breeds produce 5–6 litters a year, each containing 8–12 kittens during their breeding life, compared with five litters and 3–7 young for the wild rabbit.

Longest ears Sweet Majestic Star, a champion black English lop owned and bred by Therese and Cheryl Seward of Exeter, Devon, had ears measuring 72.4 cm *28½ in* long and 18.4 cm *7¼ in* wide. He died on 6 Oct 1992. The ears of his grandson Sweet Regal Magic are also this length.

Guess What?
Q. What is the slowest mammal?
A. See Page 28

Birds

Heaviest flying bird The world's heaviest flying (carinate) birds are the Kori bustard or paauw (*Ardeotis kori*) of north-east and southern Africa and the great bustard (*Otis tarda*) of Europe and Asia. Weights of 19 kg *42 lb* have been reported for the former. The heaviest reliably recorded great bustard weighed 18 kg *39 lb 11 oz*, although there is an unconfirmed record of 21 kg *46 lb 4 oz* for a male great bustard shot in Manchuria which was too heavy to fly.

The mute swan (*Cygnus olor*), which is resident in Britain, can reach 18 kg *40 lb* on very rare occasions, and there is a record from Poland of a cob (male) weighing 22.5 kg *49 lb 10 oz* which had temporarily lost the power of flight. The largest nesting colony in Britain is the Abbotsbury Swannery at Chesil Beach, Dorset.

Largest

The largest living bird is the North African ostrich (*Struthio c. camelus*). Male examples (hens are smaller) of this flightless (ratite) sub-species have been recorded up to 2.74 m *9 ft* tall and weighing 156.5 kg *345 lb*.

Bird of prey The heaviest bird of prey is the Andean condor (*Vultur gryphus*), males of which average 9–12 kg *20–27 lb* and have a wingspan of 3 m *10 ft* or more. A weight of 14.1 kg *31 lb* has been claimed for a male California condor (*Gymnogyps californianus*) now preserved in the California Academy of Sciences at Los Angeles, USA, but this species is generally much smaller than the Andean condor and rarely exceeds 10.4 kg *23 lb*.

'Best talking bird' A number of birds are renowned for their talking ability (i.e. the reproduction of words) but the African grey parrot (*Psittacus erythacus*) excels in this ability. A female named Prudle, originally owned by Lyn Logue (died January 1988) and then residing in the care of Iris Frost of Seaford, E Sussex, won the 'Best talking parrot-like bird' title at the National Cage and Aviary Bird Show in London each December for 12

■ A Ruppell's vulture was discovered at an altitude of 11,277 m *37,000 ft*, when it collided with an aircraft.
(Photo: Jacana/Ferrero/Labat)

■ An ostrich demonstrating its remarkable athleticism. It can run at up to 72 km/h *45 mph* when necessary.
(Photo: Jacana/J-P Varin.)

Bird Flight

The greatest distance covered by a ringed bird is 22,530 km *14,000 miles* by an Arctic tern (*Sterna paradisaea*), banded as a nestling on 5 Jul 1955 in the Kandalaksha Sanctuary on the White Sea coast of Russia and captured alive by a fisherman 13 km *8 miles* south of Fremantle, Western Australia on 16 May 1956. The bird had probably flown south via the Atlantic Ocean and then circled Africa before crossing the Indian Ocean. It did not survive to make the return journey.

45°. There is still some controversy over the accuracy of these figures, but there is little doubt that the peregrine is able to reach a maximum speed of at least 200 km/h *124 mph*.

The fastest fliers in level flight are found among the ducks and geese (Anatidae). Some powerful species such as the red-breasted merganser (*Mergus serrator*), the eider (*Somateria mollissima*), the canvasback (*Aythya valisineria*) and the spur-winged goose (*Plectropterus gambiensis*) can probably reach 90–100 km/h *56–62 mph* on rare occasions.

Fastest wing-beat The wing-beat of the horned sungem (*Heliactin cornuta*), a hummingbird living in tropical South America, is 90 beats/sec. At this speed, the bird's wings make the strange humming sound that gives the hummingbirds their family name.

Slowest flying bird The slowest-flying birds are the American woodcock (*Scolopax minor*) and the Eurasian woodcock (*S. rusticola*), which have been timed during their courtship displays at 8 km/h *5 mph* without stalling.

Oldest bird An unconfirmed age of about 82 years was reported for a male Siberian white crane (*Crus leucogeranus*) named Wolf at the International Crane Foundation, Baraboo, Wisconsin, USA. Wolf died in late 1988 after breaking his bill while repelling a visitor near his pen.

consecutive years (1965–76), and retired undefeated. Prudle, who had a vocabulary of nearly 800 words, was taken from a nest at Jinja, Uganda in 1958. She died on 13 Jul 1994, but was still talking two days before her death.

Largest vocabulary Puck, a budgerigar owned by Camille Jordan of Petaluma, CA had a vocabulary estimated at 1728 words on 31 Jan 1994.

Highest flying birds Most migrating birds fly at relatively low altitudes (i.e. below 90 m *300 ft*), with only a few dozen species flying higher than 900 m *3000 ft*.

The highest confirmed altitude recorded for a bird is 11,277 m *37,000 ft* for a Ruppell's vulture (*Gyps rueppellii*), which collided with a commercial aircraft over Abidjan, Ivory Coast on 29 Nov 1973. The impact damaged one of the aircraft's engines, causing it to shut down, but the plane landed safely without further incident. Sufficient feather remains of the bird were recovered to allow the US Museum of Natural History to make a positive identification of this high-flier, which is rarely seen above 6000 m *20,000 ft*.

Fastest bird The fastest bird on land is the ostrich, which, despite its bulk, can run at up to 72 km/h *45 mph* when necessary.

Tallest bird The tallest of the flying birds are cranes, tall waders of the family Gruidae, some of which can stand almost 2 m *6 ft 6 in* high.

Largest wingspan The wandering albatross

(*Diomedea exulans*) of the southern oceans has the largest wingspan of any living bird. The largest was a very old male with a wingspan of 3.63 m *11 ft 11 in*, caught by members of the Antarctic research ship USNS *Eltanin* in the Tasman Sea on 18 Sep 1965.

Smallest bird The smallest is the bee hummingbird (*Mellisuga helenae*) of Cuba and the Isle of Pines. Males measure 57 mm *2¼ in* in total length, half of which is taken up by the bill and tail, and weigh 1.6 g *0.056 oz* (females are slightly larger) (⇨ Smallest nest).

UK The smallest regularly breeding British bird is the goldcrest (*Regulus regulus*), which is 85–90 mm *3.3–3½ in* long and weighs 3.8–4.5 g *0.13–0.16 oz*, half the weight of the common wren (*Troglodytes troglodytes*).

Bird of prey The smallest bird of prey in the world is a title held jointly by the black-legged falconet (*Microhierax fringillarius*) of south-east Asia and the white-fronted or Bornean falconet (*M. latifrons*) of north-western Borneo. Both species have an average length of 14–15 cm *5½–6 in* (including a 5-cm *2-in* tail) and a weight of about 35 g *1¼ oz*.

Fastest flying bird At least 50 per cent of the world's flying birds cannot exceed 64 km/h *40 mph* in level flight. The peregrine falcon (*Falco peregrinus*), however, is the fastest living creature, reaching record speed levels when stooping from great heights during territorial displays, or when catching prey birds in mid-air. In one series of German experiments, a velocity of 270 km/h *168 mph* was recorded at a 30° angle of stoop, rising to a maximum of 350 km/h *217 mph* at an angle of

Abundant

Most abundant bird The red-billed quelea (*Quelea quelea*), a seed-eating weaver of the drier parts of Africa south of the Sahara, has an estimated adult breeding population of 1.5 billion, and at least 200 million of these 'feathered locusts' are slaughtered annually without having any impact on this number.

UK The commonest of all the wild bird species found in Britain—more than 520 have been recorded this century—is now the blackbird (*Turdus merula*), with a breeding population of 5 million pairs. It is followed by the robin (*Erithacus rubecula*) and the blue tit (*Parus caeruleus*) with 4 million pairs each.

Talking birds have apparently become all the more talkative since 1955. Forty years ago, the talking bird with the greatest vocabulary in the world was Sandy Paul, a yellow brown-beaked budgerigar owned by Mrs Irene Pauls of Staines, Middlesex, England. This bird, hatched in 1952, believed to be a female, knew twelve nursery rhymes, and had a total vocabulary of over 300 words.

The greatest irrefutable age reported for any bird is over 80 years for a male sulphur-crested cockatoo (*Cacatua galerita*) named Cocky, who died at London Zoo in 1982.

Domestic Excluding the ostrich, which has been known to live up to 68 years, the longest-lived domesticated bird is the goose (*Anser a. domesticus*), which has a normal life-span of about 25 years. On 16 Dec 1976, a gander named George, owned by Florence Hull of Thornton, Lancs, died aged 49 years 8 months. He was hatched in April 1927.

Most airborne bird The most aerial of all birds is the sooty tern (*Sterna fuscata*), which, after leaving the nesting grounds as a youngster, remains aloft continuously for 3–10 years whilst maturing before returning to land to breed as an adult.

The most aerial land bird is the common swift (*Apus apus*), which remains airborne for 2–4 years, during which time it sleeps, drinks, eats and even mates on the wing. It has been calculated that a young swift completes a non-stop flight of 500,000 km *310,700 miles* between fledging and its first landing at a potential nesting site two years later.

On The Record

Watching the Birdie

■ Phoebe with companion Fern Piersol and a boatman in Papua New Guinea, August 1990.

Phoebe Snetsinger is the world's leading birdwatcher, and is renowned for her thorough approach to identifying birds. She has seen 80 per cent of the world's recognized species, or 90 per cent of the genera, and all the familes but one. She has heard evidence of 100 additional species, but only considers 'countable' those that she sees well enough to identify precisely.

"From the beginning I've been fascinated by the problems of identification, and it has always been a key ingredient of my birding style to learn in advance the important features of any birds—especially the new ones—that I might see on a trip. It's vitally important to me to be able to know and recognize what I'm seeing, which then enables me to amass and retain new information. I keep a card-file record system which gives me quick reference to my entire experience with any given species.

I didn't start watching birds until the age of 35, a married woman with four small children. Various factors combined to provide the vital trigger. The first 15 years of my birding career consisted of learning how to do it and acquiring the necessary skills and knowledge, all through local birding, first in Minnesota, and then in St Louis, Missouri, which has been my home for nearly 30 years. My horizons expanded gradually to include most of North America and a few foreign locations, as my family grew and we all gained independence.

From age 50 until my present 63, I've been threatened with periodic recurrences of malignant melanoma and consequent surgery, all of which has led me into a 'now or never' approach to international birding and an ongoing succession of short-term goals. I've had the good fortune to be able to pursue this to a degree I never dreamed possible.

Within the next year or so, I hope to have seen 8000 of the world's 9700 plus bird species, and to know something about the rest of them. Then I'll plan to continue birding at a less frantic pace and pursue especially some high-priority species. I prefer to be called a 'birder' or 'birdwatcher' rather than 'lister' or 'twitcher', because my main interest lies in observing, learning about and identifying birds, rather than the strictly numerical approach of 'ticking' or 'twitching' a large number of species."

■ Phoebe, left, with companions in Szechwan, China, May 1990

Fastest bird swimmer
The gentoo penguin (*Pygoscelis papua*) has a maximum burst of speed of about 27 km/h *17 mph.*

Deepest dive by a bird The deepest dive accurately measured for any bird is 483 m *1584 ft,* by an emperor penguin (*Aptenodytes forsteri*) in the Ross Sea, Antarctica, in 1990. The longest known dive is 18 minutes, made by an emperor penguin at Cape Crozier, Antarctica, in 1969.

Keenest vision by a bird It has been calculated that a large bird of prey can detect a target object at a distance 3 or more times greater than that achieved by humans, and thus a peregrine falcon (*Falco peregrinus*) can spot a pigeon at a range of over 8 km *5 miles* under ideal conditions.

The woodcock (*Scolopax rusticola*) has eyes set so far back on its head that it has a 360° field of vision, enabling it to see all round and even over the top of its head, without having to move.

Highest g force American experiments have shown that the beak of the red-headed woodpecker (*Melanerpes erythrocephalus*) hits the bark of a tree with an impact velocity of 20.9 km/h *13 mph,* subjecting the brain to a deceleration of about 10 g when the head snaps back. Little research has been done in this field and other woodpeckers may experience an even higher g-force.

The shortest bills in relation to body length belong to the smaller swifts (family Apodidae) and, in particular, to the glossy swiftlet (*Collocalia esculenta*), whose bill is almost non-existent.

Longest bills The bill of the Australian pelican (*Pelicanus conspicillatus*) is 34–47 cm *13–18½ in* long. The longest beak in relation to overall body length is that of the sword-billed hummingbird (*Ensifera ensifera*) of the Andes from Venezuela to Bolivia. The beak measures 10.2 cm *4 in,* making it longer than the bird's actual body if the tail is excluded.

Longest feathers The longest feathers grown by any bird are those of the Phoenix fowl or Yokohama chicken (a strain of red junglefowl *Gallus gallus*), which has been bred in south-western Japan for ornamental purposes since the mid-17th century. In 1972 a tail covert measuring 10.6 m *34 ft 9½ in* was reported for a rooster owned by Masasha Kubota of Kochi, Shikoku, Japan.

Largest bird egg The egg of an ostrich (*Struthio camelus*) normally measures 15–20 cm *6–8 in* long, 10–15 cm *4–6 in* in diameter and weighs 1.0–1.78 kg *2.2–3.9 lb* (around two dozen hens' eggs in volume). The shell, although only 1.5 mm *0.06 in* thick, can support the weight of an adult person. The largest egg on record weighed 2.3 kg *5.1 lb* and was laid on 28 Jun 1988 by a 2-year-old northern/southern hybrid (*Struthio c. camelus × S. c. australis*) at the Kibbutz Ha'on collective farm, Israel.

UK The largest egg laid by any bird on the British list is that of the mute swan (*Cygnus olor*) at 109–124 mm *4.3–4.9 in* long, 71–78.5 mm *2.8–3.1 in* in diameter and weighing 340–370 g *12–13 oz.*

Guess What?
Q. Who holds the record for milking the most venomous snakes?
A. see Page 37

Smallest bird egg Eggs emitted from the oviduct before maturity, known as 'sports', are not considered to be of significance. The smallest egg laid by any bird is that of the vervain hummingbird (*Mellisuga minima*) of Jamaica and two nearby islets. Two specimens measuring less than 10 mm *0.39 in* in length weighed 0.365 g *0.0128 oz* and 0.375 g *0.0132 oz* (⇔ Smallest nest).

UK The smallest egg laid by a bird on the British list is that of the goldcrest (*Regulus regulus*), which measures 12.2–14.5 mm *0.48–0.57 in* long, 9.4–9.9 mm *0.37–0.39 in* in diameter and weighs 0.6 g *0.021 oz*.

Guess What?

Q. Where are the largest bat colonies found?

A. See Page 29

known species since 1965, representing over 80 per cent of the available total.

UK The British life list record is 485 by Ron Johns (b. 1941) of Slough, Bucks, who started spotting in 1952. The British year list record is 359 by Lee Evans (b. 1960) of Little Chalfont, Bucks, who established it in 1990 after travelling over 123,916 km *77,000 miles*, compared with his average yearly total of 96,000 km *60,000 miles*.

24 hours The greatest number of species spotted in a 24-hour period is 342 by Kenyans Terry Stevenson, John Fanshawe and Andy Roberts on day two of the Bridwatch Kenya '86 event held on 29–30 November.

and 16 Aug 1964. The three largest females measured 18 mm *0.70 in* from snout to vent, with a tail of approximately the same length.

Fastest lizard The highest speed measured for any reptile on land is 34.9 km/h *21.7 mph* for a spiny-tailed iguana (*Ctenosaura*) from Costa Rica, in a series of experiments by Professor Raymond Huey from the University of Washington, USA, and colleagues at the University of California, Berkeley, USA.

Longest lizard
The slender Salvadorii or Papuan monitor (*Varanus salvadorii*) of Papua New Guinea has been reliably measured at up to 4.75 m *15 ft 7 in* in length, but nearly 70 per cent of its total length is taken up by the tail.

Reptiles

Incubation

The shortest incubation period for a bird is 10 days in the case of the shore lark (*Eremophila alpestris*), lesser whitethroat (*Sylvia curruca*) and a number of other small passerine species.

The youngest incubator is the female white-rumped swiftlet (*Aerodramus spodiopygius*), which lives in Australia, New Guinea and on several Pacific Islands, and lays two eggs several weeks apart. By the time she has laid the second one, the first has hatched and the young chick is old enough to do the incubating.

Longest incubation A very small number of birds incubate their eggs for longer than 70 days: the wandering albatross (*Diomedea exulans*), for 75–82 days; the royal albatross (*D. epomophora*), for 75–81 days; and the kiwis (family Apterygidae), for 71–84 days. There is an isolated case of an egg of the mallee fowl (*Leipoa ocellata*) of Australia taking 90 days to hatch, compared with its normal 62 days.

Largest bird's nest The incubation mounds built by the mallee fowl (*Leipoa ocellata*) of Australia measure up to 4.57 m *15 ft* in height and 10.6 m *35 ft* across, and it has been calculated that a nest site may involve the mounding of 250 m³ *8829 ft³* of material, weighing 300 tonnes.

A nest measuring 2.9 m *9½ ft* wide and 6 m *20 ft* deep was built by a pair of bald eagles (*Haliaeetus leucocephalus*), and possibly their successors, near St Petersburg, Florida, USA. It was examined in 1963 and was estimated to weigh more than 2 tonnes. The golden eagle (*Aquila chrysaetos*) also constructs huge nests, and one 4.57 m *15 ft* deep was reported from Scotland in 1954.

Bird-spotters The world's leading bird-spotter or 'twitcher' is Phoebe Snetsinger of Webster Groves, Missouri, USA, who has logged 7772 out of the 9700

The smallest nests are built by hummingbirds. That of the vervain hummingbird (*Mellisuga minima*) is about half the size of a walnut shell, while the deeper but narrower one of the bee hummingbird (*M. helenae*) is thimble-sized (⇔ Smallest bird, Smallest egg).

Crocodilians

Largest crocodilian The largest reptile in the world is the estuarine or saltwater crocodile (*Crocodylus porosus*), which ranges throughout the tropical regions of Asia and the Pacific. The Bhitarkanika Wildlife Sanctuary in Orissa State, India houses four protected estuarine crocodiles measuring more than 6 m *19 ft 8 in* in length, the largest being over 7 m *23 ft* long. There are several unauthenticated reports of specimens up to 10 m *33 ft* in length.

Smallest crocodilian The dwarf caiman (*Paleosuchus palpebrosus*) of northern South America is the smallest crocodilian in the world today. Females rarely exceed a length of 1.2 m *4 ft*, and males rarely grow to more than 1.5 m *4 ft 11 in*. The dwarf crocodile (*Osteolaemus tetraspis*) of west and central Africa is also very small, although a number of individuals reach a length of 2 m *6½ ft*, and a few grow even longer.

Oldest crocodilian The greatest authenticated age for a crocodilian is 66 years for a female American alligator (*Alligator mississippiensis*) which arrived at Adelaide Zoo, South Australia on 5 Jun 1914 as a 2-year-old, and died there on 26 Sep 1978.

Lizards

Largest lizard The largest lizard is the Komodo dragon (*Varanus komodoensis*), otherwise known as the Komodo monitor or ora, and found on the Indonesian islands of Komodo, Rintja, Padar and Flores. Males average 2.25 m *7 ft 5 in* in length and weigh about 59 kg *130 lb*. The largest accurately measured specimen was a male presented to an American zoologist in 1928 by the Sultan of Bima. In 1937 it was put on display in St Louis Zoological Gardens, Missouri, USA for a short period, by which time it was 3.10 m *10 ft 2 in* in long and weighed 166 kg *365 lb*.

Oldest lizard The greatest age recorded for a lizard is over 54 years for a male slow worm (*Anguis fragilis*) kept in the Zoological Museum in Copenhagen, Denmark from 1892 until 1946.

Smallest lizard *Sphaerodactylus parthenopion*, a tiny gecko indigenous to the island of Virgin Gorda, one of the British Virgin Islands, is the world's smallest lizard. It is known only from 15 specimens, including some pregnant females found between 10

Smallest

Smallest chelonian The stinkpot or common musk turtle (*Sternotherus odoratus*) has an average shell length of 7.62 cm *3 in* when fully grown and a weight of only 227 g *8 oz*. The smallest marine turtle in the world is the Atlantic ridley (*Lepidochelys kempii*), which has a shell length of 50–70 cm *20–28 in* and a maximum weight of 80 kg *176 lb*.

Tortoises and Turtles

Largest chelonian The largest living chelonian is the widely distributed leatherback turtle (*Dermochelys coriacea*), which averages 1.83–2.13 m *6–7 ft* from the tip of the beak to the end of the tail (carapace 1.52–1.67 m *5–5½ ft*), and about 2.13 m *7 ft* across the front flippers. It weighs up to 450 kg *1000 lb*.

The largest leatherback turtle ever recorded is a male, found dead on the beach at Harlech, Gwynedd on 23 Sep 1988. He measured 2.91 m *9 ft 5½ in* in total length over the carapace, 2.77 m *9 ft* across the front flippers and weighed 961.1 kg *2120 lb*. Although most museums refuse to exhibit large turtles because they can drip oil for up to 50 years, this specimen was put on display at the National Museum of Wales, Cardiff on 16 Feb 1990.

Largest tortoise The largest living specimen is a Galapagos tortoise (*Geochelone elephantopus elephantopus*) named Goliath, who has resided at the Life Fellowship Bird Sanctuary in Sessner, Florida, USA since 1960. He measures 135½ cm *53⅝ in* long, 102 cm *40½ in* wide, and 68½ cm *27 in* high, and weighs 385 kg *849 lb*.

Oldest chelonian The greatest authentic age recorded for a chelonian is over 152 years for a male Marion's tortoise (*Geochelone sumeirei*) brought from the Seychelles to Mauritius in 1766 by the Chevalier de Fresne, who presented it to the Port Louis army garrison. This specimen, which went blind in 1908, was accidentally killed in 1918.

When our first edition emerged in 1955, the greatest proven age of a tortoise was 116 years, for a Mediterranean spur-thighed tortoise (*Testude graeca*) at Paignton Zoological Gardens, Devon, England. The oldest chelonian is now known to have been a specimen of Marion's tortoise that reached the advanced age of 152 years.

Fastest chelonian The highest speed claimed for any reptile in water is 35 km/h *22 mph* by a frightened Pacific leatherback turtle (*Dermochelys coriacea*).

Deepest dive by a chelonian In May 1987 it was reported by Dr Scott Eckert that a leatherback turtle (*Dermochelys coriacea*) fitted with a pressure-sensitive recording device had reached a depth of 1200 m *3973 ft* off the Virgin Islands in the West Indies.

Snakes, General

Longest snake The reticulated python (*Python reticulatus*) of south-east Asia, Indonesia and the Philippines regularly exceeds 6.25 m *20 ft 6 in*, and the record length is 10 m *32 ft 9½ in* for a specimen shot in Celebes, Indonesia in 1912.

Shortest snake The world's shortest snake is the very rare thread snake (*Leptotyphlops bilineata*), known only from Martinique, Barbados and St Lucia. The longest known specimen measured 108 mm *4¼ in*, and had such a matchstick-thin body that it could have entered the hole left by the removal of the lead from a standard pencil.

UK The smallest native British snake is the smooth snake (*Coronella austriaca*), which averages up to 60 cm *23½ in in length*.

Heaviest snake The most massive snake is the anaconda (*Eunectes murinus*) of tropical South America and Trinidad. The average length is 5.5–6.1 m *18–20ft*. A female shot in Brazil c. 1960 was not weighed, but as it was 8.45 m *27 ft 9 in* long with a girth of 111 cm *44 in*, it must have weighed nearly 227 kg *500 lb*.

Venomous Snakes

Longest venomous snake The longest venomous snake is the king cobra (*Ophiophagus hannah*), also called the hamadryad, which averages 3.65–4.5 m *12–15 ft* in length and is found in south-east Asia and India. A specimen 5.54 m *18 ft 2 in* long captured alive near Fort Dickson in the state of Negri Sembilan, Malaysia in April 1937 later grew to 5.71 m *18 ft 9 in* in London Zoo. It was destroyed at the outbreak of war in 1939, to avoid the risk of escape.

GOLIATH
the Galapagos Tortoise

In 1960 two tiny Galapagos Tortoises *Geochelone elephantopus elephantopus,* were brought to the *Life Fellowship Bird Sanctuary* (then the *New Age Ranch*) in Sessner, Florida, USA by a UNESCO researcher who had collected them on southern Isabela. One of them, later named Goliath, weighed just two pounds. In the 34–5 years since then Goliath has grown to record-breaking proportions and is now the world's largest tortoise: in March 1988, when he was induced to walk onto the platform of a government-certified scale, he was found to weigh 356 kg *785 lb*; he weighed 385 kg *849 lb* in October 1994. By tortoise standards he is still quite young, and is continuing to grow each year. At his present weight he is likely to pass the 900-pound mark in a few years. He eats well, but not *too* well—his weight is in proportion with his size and he is in fact fit and lean.

According to Greg A. Moss, General Curator of *Life Fellowship*, Goliath shows superior intelligence and the kind of levels of comprehension a dog might display. He is affectionate towards workers at the Sanctuary, and when touched by someone he knows he rises on all four legs and extends his head to be petted. As autumn approaches Goliath is the first to use the heated winter house; others in his paddock have to become accustomed each year to being closed up overnight for the sake of warmth.

■ Just a few of the 94 Galapagos hatchlings produced at the Sanctuary in 1989.
(Photo: Life Fellowship Bird Sanctuary)

■ Ramon Noegel, Director of the *Life Fellowship Bird Sanctuary*, with six male Galapagos tortoises in 1989. He has his hand on Goliath's carapace; the others weigh 226.8–266 kg *500–590 lb*.
(Photo: Life Fellowship Bird Sanctuary)

The *Life Fellowship Bird Sanctuary* specializes in the captive breeding of endangered species. It has a herd of 44 *gigantea*, believed to be the largest in the Americas. In seven breeding seasons (1987–1993) *Life Fellowship* succeeded in hatching and keeping alive 411 Galapagos tortoises, an unparalleled achievement in any captive herd of these endangered giants outside their habitat in the Galapagos. In 1994 alone they hatched seventy-four Galapagos tortoises. Few kept in captivity ever breed.

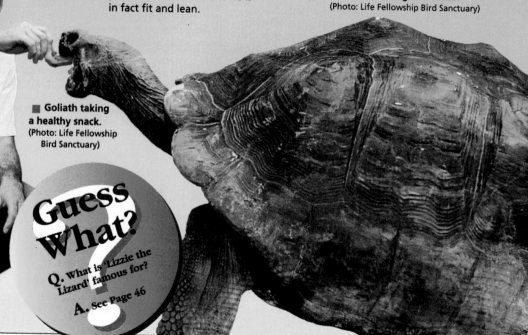

■ Goliath taking a healthy snack.
(Photo: Life Fellowship Bird Sanctuary)

Guess What?
Q. What is 'Lizzie the Lizard' famous for?
A. See Page 46

Shortest venomous snake The namaqua or spotted dwarf adder (*Bitis schneideri*) of Namibia, has an average length of 200 mm *8 in*.

Most venomous snake All sea snakes are venomous, and in particular, the species *Hydrophis belcheri* has a myotoxic venom many times more toxic than the venom of any land snake. However, fatalities are rare since the potency of the venom is matched only by the snake's friendly temperament. It abounds around Ashmore Reef in the Timor Sea, off north-west Australia.

The most venomous land snake is the small-scaled or fierce snake (*Oxyuranus microlepidotus*). Measuring around 1.7 m *5 ft 7 in* long, it is found mainly in the Diamantina River and Cooper's Creek drainage basins in Channel County, Queensland and western New South Wales, Australia. Its venom is several times more toxic than that of the feared tiger snake (*Notechis scutatus*) of South Australia and Tasmania. One specimen yielded 110 mg *0.00385 oz* of venom after milking—enough to kill 250,000 mice—but so far no human fatalities have been reported.

Longest fangs The longest fangs of any snake are those of the highly venomous gaboon viper (*Bitis gabonica*) of tropical Africa. In a specimen 1.83 m *6 ft* long they measured 50 mm *1.96 in*.

Oldest snake The greatest reliable age recorded for a snake is 40 yr 3 months 14 days for a male common boa (*Boa constrictor constrictor*) named Popeye, who died at Philadelphia Zoo, Pennsylvania, USA on 15 Apr 1977.

Fastest snake The fastest land snake is probably the aggressive black mamba (*Dendroaspis polylepis*), of the eastern part of tropical Africa. Top speeds of 16–19 km/h *10–12 mph* may be possible in short bursts over level ground.

Champion milker Over a 10-year period ending in December 1970, Bernard Keyler (b. 1918), a supervisor at the South African Institute for Medical Research in Johannesburg, South Africa, personally milked 780,000 venomous snakes and obtained 3960 litres *870 gallons* of venom. He was never bitten.

Heavy Snake

The heaviest venomous snake is probably the eastern diamondback rattlesnake (*Crotalus adamanteus*) of the south-eastern United States, which averages 5.5–7 kg *12–15 lb* (1.5–1.8 m *5–6 ft* in length). The heaviest on record weighed 15 kg *34 lb* and was 2.36 m *7 ft 9 in* long.

Snakebites

More people die of snakebites in Sri Lanka than any comparable area in the world. An average of 800 people are killed annually on the island by snakes, with over 95 per cent of the fatalities caused by the common krait (*Bungarus caeruleus*), the Sri Lankan cobra (*Naja n. naja*) and Russell's viper (*Vipera russelli pulchella*).

The saw-scaled or carpet viper (*Echis carinatus*), which ranges from West Africa to India, bites and kills more people in the world than any other species.

***UK* The only venomous snake in Britain is the adder, or viper, (*Vipera berus*), whose bite has caused ten human deaths since 1890, including six children. The most recent recorded death was on 1 Jul 1975 when a 5-year-old was bitten at Callander, Perthshire and died 44 hours later (⇨ Longest venomous).**

Amphibians

Frogs and Toads

Largest frog The largest known frog is the goliath frog (*Conraua goliath*). A specimen captured in April 1989 on the Sanaga River, Cameroon by Andy Koffman of Seattle, Washington, USA had a snout-to-vent length of 36.83 cm *14½ in* (87.63 cm *34½ in* overall with legs extended) and weighed 3.66 kg *8 lb 1 oz* on 30 Oct 1989.

Largest toad The largest known toad is the cane or marine toad (*Bufo marinus*) of tropical South America and Queensland, Australia (introduced). An average specimen weighs 450 g *1 lb* and the largest ever recorded was a male named *Prinsen* (The Prince), owned by Håkan Forsberg of Åkers Styckebruk, Sweden. It weighed 2.65 kg *5 lb 13½ oz* and measured 38 cm *15 in* from snout to vent (53.9 cm *21 1/5 in* when extended) in March 1991.

The largest toad and heaviest amphibian found in Britain is the common toad (*Bufo bufo*).

Smallest frog The world's smallest frog, and the smallest known amphibian, is *Sminthillus limbatus* of Cuba, which is 0.85–1.2 cm *0.34–0.5 in* long (snout-to-vent), when fully grown.

Toad The world's smallest toad is the sub-species *Bufo taitanus beiranus* of Africa, the largest specimen of which measured 24 mm *1 in* in length.

Longest jump by a frog *Competition frog jumps are invariably the aggregate of three consecutive leaps.*

The greatest distance covered by a frog in a triple jump is 10.3 m *33 ft 5½ in* by a South African sharp-nosed frog (*Ptychadena oxyrhynchus*) named Santjie at a frog Derby held at Lurula Natal Spa, Paulpietersburg, Natal, South Africa on 21 May 1977.

Newts and Salamanders

Largest amphibians The largest are the giant salamanders (family Cryptobranchidae), of which there are three species. The record-holder is the Chinese giant salamander (*Andrias davidianus*), which lives in mountain streams in north-eastern, central and southern China. One record-breaking specimen collected in Hunan measured 1.8 m *71 in* in length and weighed 65 kg *143 lb*.

Smallest The world's smallest newt or salamander is the Mexican lungless salamander (*Bolitoglossa mexicana*), which attains a maximum length of about 2.54 cm *1 in*, including the tail.

Fastest Fish

The cosmopolitan sailfish (*Istiophorus platypterus*) is considered to be the fastest species of fish over short distances, although practical difficulties make measurements extremely difficult to secure. In a series of speed trials carried out at the Long Key Fishing Camp, Florida, USA, one sailfish took out 91 m *300 ft* of line in 3 sec, which is equivalent to a velocity of 109 km/h *68 mph* (cf. 96 km/h *60 mph* for the cheetah).

Guess What?

Q. Which is longer, the longest prehistoric snake or the present-day longest snake?

A. See Page 46

Fish

(⇨ also Angling)

General Records

Largest fish The world's largest fish is the rare plankton-feeding whale shark (*Rhincodon typus*), which is found in the warmer areas of the Atlantic, Pacific and Indian Oceans. The largest scientifically recorded example was 12.65 m *41½ ft* long, measured 7 m *23 ft* around the thickest part of the body and weighed an estimated 15–21 tonnes. It was captured off Baba Island, near Karachi, Pakistan on 11 Nov 1949.

British Isles The largest fish recorded in British waters was a basking shark (*Cetorhinus maximus*), measuring 11.12 m *36 ft 6 in* and weighing an estimated 8 tonnes. It was washed ashore at Brighton, E Sussex in 1806.

Smallest fish The shortest recorded marine fish—and the shortest known vertebrate—is the dwarf goby (*Trimmatom nanus*) of the Chagos Archipelago in the Indian Ocean. Average lengths recorded for a series of specimens collected by the 1978/79 Joint Services Chagos Research Expedition of the British Armed Forces were 8.6 mm *0.34 in* for males and 8.9 mm *0.35 in* for females.

Lightest fish The lightest of all vertebrates and the smallest catch possible is the dwarf goby (*Schindleria praematurus*) which weighs only 2 mg (equivalent to 14,184 to the ounce) and is 12–19 mm *¼–¾ in* long. It is found in Samoa.

Oldest fish In 1948, the death was reported of an 88-year-old female European eel (*Anguilla anguilla*) named Putte, in the aquarium at Hälsingborg Museum, Sweden. She was allegedly born in 1860 in the Sargasso Sea, North Atlantic, and was caught in a river as a 3-year-old elver.

Most abundant fish The most abundant species of fish is probably the deep-sea bristlemouth (*Cyclothone elongata*), which has an almost worldwide distribution. It is around 76 mm *3 in* long, and it would take about 500 of them to weigh 0.45 kg *1 lb*.

Oldest goldfish Goldfish (*Carassius auratus*) have been reported to live for over 50 years in China, although there are few authenticated records.

A goldfish named Fred, owned by A.R. Wilson of Worthing, W Sussex, died on 1 Aug 1980 aged 41 years.

Shortest-lived fish The shortest-lived fish are probably certain species of the family Cyprinodontidae (Killifish), found in Africa, the Americas, Asia and the warmer parts of Europe, which normally live for about eight months.

Deepest fish Brotulids of the genus *Bassogigas* are generally regarded as the deepest-living vertebrates. The greatest depth from which one of these fish has been recovered is 8300 m *27,230 ft*, in the Puerto Rico Trench (8366 m *27,488 ft*) in the Atlantic, by Dr Gilbert L. Voss of the US research vessel *John Elliott*, who captured a *Bassogigas profundissimus* 16.5 cm *6½ in* long in April 1970. It was only the fifth such brotulid ever caught.

Electric!

The most powerful electric fish is the electric eel (*Electrophorus electricus*) from the rivers of Brazil, Colombia, Venezuela and Peru. An average-sized specimen can discharge 1 amp at 400 volts, but measurements up to 650 volts have been recorded.

Fewest fish eggs The mouth-brooding cichlid *Tropheus moorii* of Lake Tanganyika, East Africa produces seven eggs or fewer during normal reproduction.

Most valuable fish The world's most valuable fish is the Russian sturgeon (*Huso huso*). One 1227-kg *2706-lb* female caught in the Tikhaya Sosna River in 1924 yielded 245 kg *540 lb* of best-quality caviar, which would be worth £189,350 on today's market.

The ginrin showa koi, 76 cm *30 in* long, won supreme championship in nationwide Japanese koi shows in 1976, 1977, 1979 and 1980, and was sold two years later for 17 million yen (about £50,000). In March 1986, this ornamental carp was acquired by Derry Evans, owner of the Kent Koi Centre near Sevenoaks, Kent for an undisclosed sum, but the 15-year-old fish died five months later. It has since been stuffed and mounted to preserve its beauty.

■ A great white shark posing for the cameras. This creature is the world's largest carnivorous fish.
(Photo: Jacana/ K.Deacon/Auscape)

Most ferocious fish The razor-toothed piranhas of the genera *Serrasalmus*, *Pygocentrus* and *Pygopristis* are generally considered to be the most ferocious freshwater fish in the world. They live in the sluggish waters of the large rivers of South America, and will attack any creature, regardless of size, if it is injured or making a commotion in the water. On 19 Sep 1981, more than 300 people were reportedly killed and eaten when an overloaded passenger-cargo boat capsized and sank as it was docking at the Brazilian port of Obidos. According to one official, only 178 of the estimated number of people aboard the boat survived.

Most venomous fish The most venomous fish in the world are the stonefish (Synanceidae) of the tropical waters of the Indo-Pacific, and in particular *Synanceia horrida*, which has the largest venom glands of any known fish. Direct contact with the spines of its fins, which contain a strong neurotoxic poison, can prove fatal.

Freshwater Fish

Largest freshwater fish The largest fish which spends its whole life in fresh or brackish water is the rare pla buk or pa beuk (*Pangasianodon gigas*), found only in the Mekong River and its major tributaries in China, Laos, Cambodia and Thailand. The largest specimen, captured in the River Ban Mee Noi, Thailand, was reportedly 3 m *9 ft 10¼ in* long and weighed 242 kg *533½ lb*. This was exceeded by the European catfish or wels (*Silurus glanis*) in earlier times (in the 19th century lengths of 4.6 m *15 ft* and weights of 336 kg *720 lb* were reported for Russian specimens), but today anything over 1.83 m *6 ft* and 90 kg *200 lb* is considered large.

British Isles The largest fish ever caught in a British river was a common sturgeon (*Acipenser sturio*) weighing 230 kg *507½ lb*

Most fish eggs The ocean sunfish (*Mola mola*) produces up to 30 million eggs, each measuring about 1.3 mm *0.05 in* in diameter, at a single spawning.

and measuring 2.74 m *9 ft*, which was accidentally netted in the Severn at Lydney, Glos on 1 Jun 1937. Larger specimens have been taken at sea—notably one weighing 317 kg *700 lb* and 3.18 m *10 ft 5 in* in length, which was netted by the trawler *Ben Urie* off Orkney and landed on 18 Oct 1956.

Smallest freshwater fish The shortest and lightest freshwater fish is the dwarf pygmy goby (*Pandaka pygmaea*), a colourless and nearly transparent species found in the streams and lakes of Luzon in the Philippines. Males are only 7.5–9.9 mm *0.28–0.38 in* long and weigh 4–5 mg *0.00014–0.00018 oz*.

Commercial The world's smallest commercial fish is the now endangered sinarapan (*Mistichthys luzonensis*), a goby found only in Lake Buhi, Luzon, Philippines. Males are 10–13 mm *0.39–0.51 in* long, and a dried 454-g *1-lb* fish cake would contain about 70,000 of them.

Starfish

Largest starfish The largest of the 1600 known species of starfish is the very fragile brisingid *Midgardia xandaros*. A specimen collected by the Texas A&M University research vessel *Alaminos* in the Gulf of Mexico in 1968 measured 1.38 m *4½ ft* tip-to-tip, but its disc was only 26 mm *1.02 in* in diameter.

Deepest starfish The greatest depth from which a starfish has been recovered is 7584 m *24,881 ft*, for a specimen of *Porcellanaster ivanovi* collected by the Soviet research ship *Vityaz* in the Marianas Trench, west Pacific c. 1962.

The smallest known starfish is the asterinid sea star *Patiriella parvivipara* discovered by Wolfgang Zeidler on the west coast of the Eyre peninsula, South Australia in 1975. It has a maximum radius of only 4.7 mm *0.18 in* and a diameter of less than 9 mm *0.35 in*.

Predatory

The largest predatory fish is the rare great white shark (*Carcharodon carcharias*). Adult specimens average 4.3–4.6 m *14–15 ft* in length, and generally weigh 520–770 kg *1150–1700 lb*. There are many claims of huge specimens up to 10 m *33 ft* in length and, although few have been properly authenticated, there is plenty of circumstantial evidence to suggest that some great whites grow to more than 6 m *20 ft* in length.

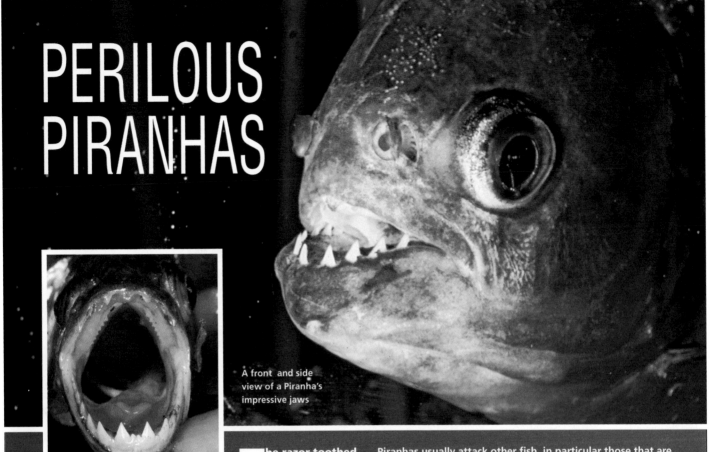

PERILOUS PIRANHAS

A front and side view of a Piranha's impressive jaws

The razor-toothed piranhas of the genera *Serrasalmus, and Pygocentrus* are the most ferocious freshwater fish in the world. They live in the sluggish waters of the large rivers of South America, and rarely exceed 60 cm *23.6 in* long. They congregate and attack any creature, regardless of size, if it is injured or making a commotion in the water. They attack in an increasingly frenzied manner as their victim bleeds into the water, and they even compete with each other to finish off the corpse first. Their teeth are so sharp that the Amazonian natives use them as scissors, and their jaws are so strong that they can snap off a human finger like a carrot. It is said that they can strip an alligator of all its flesh in under five minutes.

Piranhas usually attack other fish, in particular those that are wounded or diseased, although they have been known to attack much larger creatures that happen to be passing through the rivers. Luckily only a handful of the 20 species of piranha are considered dangerous to man, and the worst of these four is *Serrasalmus natterei*. In fact they seldom attack a human, unless he or she has an open wound exposed in the water. In general they avoid peopled areas. The piranha has a number of predators, including the Amazonian dolphin or boutu (*Inia geoffrensis*) and the giant Brazilian otter (*Pteronura brasiliensis*).

The largest piranha held in captivity was reportedly a specimen called Percy who lived at Marineland in Morecambe, Lancs. Percy was 13.25 in *337 mm* long and weighed 1.53 kg *3 lb 6 oz*. On 10 Apr 1980 he met an unhappy end when he was electrocuted after hungrily biting through the heating cable in his tank.

Crab, lobster and other crustaceans

Largest marine crustacean The largest of all crustaceans (although not the heaviest) is the taka-ashi-gani or giant spider crab (*Macrocheira kaempferi*). One particularly large specimen was found to have a claw-span of 3.7 m *12 ft 1½ in*, and a weight of 18.6 kg *41 lb*. The heaviest is the American or North Atlantic lobster (*Homarus americanus*). On 11 Feb 1987, a specimen weighing 20.14 kg *44 lb 6 oz* and measuring 1.06 m *3 ft 6 in* from the end of the tail-fan to the tip of the largest claw, was caught off Nova Scotia, Canada, and later sold to a New York restaurant owner.

Largest concentration of crustaceans The largest single concentration of crustaceans ever recorded was a swarm of krill (*Euphausia superba*), estimated to weigh 10 million tonnes, which was tracked by US scientists off Antarctica in March 1981.

Largest

The largest freshwater crustacean is the crayfish or crawfish (*Astacopsis gouldi*), found in the streams of Tasmania, Australia. It has been measured up to 61 cm *2 ft* in length and may weigh as much as 4.1 kg *9 lb*. In 1934, an unconfirmed weight of 6.35 kg *14 lb* (total length 73.6 cm *29 in*) was reported for one caught at Bridport.

Spiders

Largest spider The world's largest known spider is the goliath bird-eating spider (*Theraphosa leblondi*) of the coastal rainforests of Surinam, Guyana and French Guiana, but isolated specimens have also been reported from Venezuela and Brazil. A male collected by members of the Pablo San Martin Expedition at Rio Cavro, Venezuela in April 1965, had a record leg-span of 280 mm *11.02 in*—sufficient to cover a dinner plate.

UK Of the 617 known species of British spider, covering an estimated population of over 500 billion, the cardinal spider (*Tegenaria gigantea*) of southern England has the greatest average leg-span. In September 1994 Lynda & John Culley of Wantage, Oxon found a cardinal spider with a leg span of 5.8 in *14.9 cm* in their bathroom sink. The well-known 'daddy longlegs' spider (*Pholcus phalangioides*) rarely exceeds 114 mm *4½ in* in leg-span, but one specimen collected in England measured 15.2 cm *6 in* across.

Heaviest spider Female bird-eating spiders are more heavily built than males and in February 1985 Charles J. Seiderman of New York City, USA captured a female example near Paramaribo, Surinam which weighed a record peak 122.2 g *4.3 oz* before its death from moulting problems in January 1986. Other measurements included a maximum leg-span of 267 mm *10½ in*, a total body length of 102 mm *4 in* and 25 mm *1 in* long fangs.

UK The heaviest spider found in Britain is the orb weaver (*Araneus quadratus*). On 10 Sep 1979, a female weighing 2.25 g *0.08 oz* was collected at Lavington, W Sussex by J. R. Parker.

Smallest spider The smallest known spider is *Patu marplesi* (family Symphytognathidae) of Western Samoa. The type specimen (male) found in moss at c. 600 m *2000 ft* in Madolelei, Upolu in January 1965, measured 0.43 mm *0.017 in* overall—about the size of a full-stop on this page.

UK The extremely rare money spider *Glyphesis cottonae* is found only in a swamp near Beaulieu Road Station, Hants and on Thursley Common, Surrey. Both sexes have a body length of 1 mm *0.04 in*.

Oldest spider The longest-lived of all spiders are the tropical bird-eaters (famly Theraphosidae). One female collected in Mexico in 1935 lived for an estimated 26–28 years. It is believed that a 25-year lifespan is not unusual for bird-eating spiders, putting them among the longest-lived of all terrestrial invertebrates.

UK The longest-lived British spider is probably the purse web spider (*Atypus affinis*), one specimen of which was kept in a greenhouse for nine years.

Most venomous spider The world's most venomous spiders are the Brazilian wandering spiders of the genus *Phoneutria*, and particularly the Brazilian huntsman *P. fera*, which has the most active neurotoxic venom of any living spider. These large and highly aggressive creatures often enter human dwellings and hide in clothing or shoes. When disturbed, they bite furiously several times, and hundreds of accidents involving these species are reported annually. Fortunately, however, an effective antivenin is available, and when deaths do occur they are usually of children under the age of seven.

The smallest spider in Britain is now less than half the size it was believed to be 40 years ago. Then, the smallest was believed to be *Saloca diceros*, found among mosses in Dorsetshire and Staffordshire. It had a body length of less than 1.53 kg *0.1 in*. The smallest now is the elusive money spider, which has a body length of just 1 mm *0.04 in*.

Q. What does the true lemming hold the record for?

A. See Page 28

Guess What?

Scorpions

Largest scorpion The largest of the 800 or so species of scorpion is a species called *Heterometrus swannerderdami*, from southern India. Males frequently attain a length of more than 18 cm *7 in* from the tips of the pedipalps or 'pincers' to the end of the sting. The record-holder is a specimen that was found during the Second World War and measured 29.2 cm *11.5 in* in overall length. The tropical emperor or imperial scorpion (*Pandinus imperator*) of West Africa also grows to 18 cm *7 in*; the largest on record is a male from Sierra Leone which measured 22.9 cm *9.01 in*.

Smallest scorpion The world's smallest scorpion is *Microbothus pusillus*, which measures about 13 mm *½ in* in total length and is found on the Red Sea coast.

Most venomous scorpion The most venomous scorpion in the world is the Palestine yellow scorpion (*Leiurus quinquestriatus*), which ranges from the eastern part of North Africa through the Middle East to the Red Sea. Fortunately, the amount of venom it delivers is very small (0.255 mg *0.000009 oz*) and adult lives are seldom endangered, but it has been responsible for a number of fatalities among children under the age of five.

■ The 'emperor' scorpion measures a spine-chilling 18 cm *7 in* long, and is the largest in the world.
(Photo: Jacana/P. & C Vasselet)

Insects

It is estimated that there may be as many as 30 million species of insect—more than 90 per cent of all plant and animal species put together—but most have yet to be discovered and thousands are known only from a single type specimen.

Heaviest insect The heaviest insects are the Goliath beetles (family Scarabaeidae) of Equatorial Africa. The largest are *Goliathus regius*, *G. meleagris*, *G. goliathus* (=*G. giganteus*) and *G. druryi*, and in measurements of one series of males (females are smaller) the lengths from the tips of the small frontal horns to the end of the abdomen were up to 110 mm *4.33 in*, with weights of 70–100 g *2½–3½ oz*.

UK The heaviest insect found in Britain is the stag beetle (*Lucanus cervus*) which is widely distributed over southern England. The largest specimen on record was a male which was 87.4 mm *3.04 in* long (body plus mandibles) and probably weighed over 6 g *0.21 oz* when alive. it was collected at Sheerness, Kent in 1871 and is now in the British Museum (Natural History), London. On 2 Jun 1994 10-year-old Ryan Morris and friends James Simpson, Scott Cowan and Ross Cowan found a stag beetle near their homes in Sheppey, Kent which, at 8.9 cm *3.5 in* long was a larger example. It was later identified as *Odontolabis delessertii*, a strain of stag beetle that does not naturally occur in Britain.

Longest

The longest recorded insect in the world is *Pharnacia kirbyi*, a stick insect from the rainforests of Borneo. The longest-known specimen is in the British Museum (Natural History) in London, UK; it has a body length of 328 mm *12.9 in* and a total length, including the legs, of 546 mm *20 in*. In the wild this species is often found with some legs missing because they are so long and easily trapped when the insect sheds its skin.

Smallest insect The smallest recorded insects are the 'feather-winged' beetles of the family Ptiliidae (=Trichopterygidae) and the battledore-wing fairy flies (parasitic wasps) of the family Mymaridae, which are smaller than some species of protozoa (single-celled animals).

Lightest The male bloodsucking banded louse (*Enderleinellus zonatus*) and the parasitic wasp *Caraphractus cinctus* may each weigh as little as 0.005 mg, or *5,670,000 to an oz*. Eggs of the latter each weigh 0.0002 mg (*141,750,000 to an oz*).

Loudest insect At 7400 pulses/min the tymbal organs of the male cicada (family Cicadidae) produce a noise (officially described by the US Department of Agriculture as 'Tsh-ee-EEEE-e-ou') detectable more than 400 m *¼ mile* away. The only British species is the very rare mountain cicada (*Cicadetta montana*), which is confined to the New Forest area in Hampshire.

Largest grasshopper The largest known grasshopper in the world is an unidentified species from the border of Malaysia and Thailand measuring 25.4 cm *10 in* in length and capable of leaping 4.6 m *15 ft*.

Fastest flying insect Acceptable modern experiments have established that the highest maintainable airspeed of any insect, including the deer bot-fly (*Cephenemyia pratti*), hawk moths (Sphingidae), horse flies (*Tabanus bovinus*) and some tropical butterflies (Hesperiidae), is 39 km/h *24 mph*, rising to a maximum of 58 km/h *36 mph* for the Australian dragonfly *Austrophlebia costalis* for short bursts.

Fastest moving insect The fastest insects on land are certain large tropical cockroaches, and the record is 5.4 km/h *3.36 mph*, or 50 body lengths per second, registered by *Periplaneta americana* at the University of California at Berkeley, USA in 1991.

Highest g force endured by an insect The click beetle (*Athous haemorrhoidalis*) averages 400 g when 'jack-knifing' into the air to escape predators. One example measuring 12 mm *½ in* in length and weighing 40 mg *0.00014 oz* which jumped to a height of 30 cm *11¾ in* was calculated to have endured a peak brain deceleration of 2300 g by the end of the movement.

Oldest insect The longest-lived insects are the splendour beetles (Buprestidae). On 27 May 1983 a specimen of *Buprestis aurulenta* appeared from the staircase timber in the home of Mr W. Euston of Prittlewell, Southend-on-Sea, Essex after at least 47 years as a larva.

Fastest insect wing-beat The fastest wing-beat of any insect under natural conditions is 62,760 per min by a tiny midge of the genus *Forcipomyia*. The muscular contraction–expansion cycle in 0.00045 sec, necessary for such rapid wing beats, further represents the fastest muscle movement ever measured.

Largest cockroach The world's largest cockroach is *Megaloblatta longipennis* of Colombia. A preserved female in the collection of Akira Yokokura of Yamagata, Japan measures 97 mm *3.81 in* in length and 45 mm *1.77 in* across.

Mantle of bees Jed Shaner was covered by a mantle of an estimated 343,000 bees weighing 36.3 kg *80 lb* at Staunton, Virginia, USA, on 29 Jun 1991.

Dragonflies

Largest dragonfly *Megaloprepus caeruleata* of Central and South America has been measured up to 120 mm *4.72 in* in length, with a wingspan of up to 191 mm *7.52 in* .

Smallest dragonfly The world's smallest dragonfly is *Agriocnemis naia* of Myanmar (Burma). A specimen in the British Museum (Natural History) had a wingspan of 17.6 mm *0.69 in* and a body length of 18 mm *0.71 in*.

Fleas

Largest flea Siphonapterologists recognize 1830 varieties, of which the largest known is *Hystrichopsylla schefferi*, which was described from a single specimen taken from the nest of a mountain beaver (*Aplodontia rufa*) at Puyallup, Washington, USA in 1913. Females are up to 8 mm *0.3 in* long.

Longest jump by a flea The champion jumper among fleas is the cat flea (*Ctenocephalides felis*), which has been known to reach a height of 34 cm *13.4 in* in a single jump. The common flea (*Pulex irritans*) is capable of equivalent or similar feats. In one American experiment carried out in 1910 a specimen allowed to leap at will performed a long jump of 330 mm *13 in* and a high jump of 197 mm *7¾ in*. In jumping 130 times its own height, a flea subjects itself to a force of 200 g.

Butterflies

Largest butterfly The largest known butterfly is the Queen Alexandra's birdwing (*Ornithoptera alexandrae*) of Papua New Guinea. Females may have a wingspan exceeding 280 mm *11 in* and weigh over 25 g *0.9 oz*.

UK The largest butterfly found in Britain is the monarch or milkweed butterfly (*Danaus plexippus*), a rare vagrant from the other side of the Atlantic. It has a wingspan of up to 127 mm *5 in* (⇨ Migration). However, the largest resident butterfly is the swallowtail (*Papilio machaon britannicus*), a rare species resident only in the Norfolk Broads; it has a wingspan of up to 80 mm *3.2 in*.

Smallest butterfly The smallest of the 165,000 known species of Lepidoptera is a micro-moth called *Stigmella ridiculosa*, which has a wingspan of 2 mm *0.079 in* with a similar body length and is found in the Canary Islands.

Migration A tagged female monarch or milkweed butterfly (*Danaus plexippus*) released by Donald Davis at Presqu'ile Provincial Park near Brighton, Ontario, Canada on 6 Sep 1986 was recaptured 3432 km *2133 miles* away, on a mountain near Angangueo, Mexico, on 15 Jan 1987. This distance was obtained by measuring a line from the release site to the recapture site, but the actual distance travelled could be up to double this figure (⇨ Largest butterfly).

Largest Egg

The largest egg laid by an insect belongs to the 15-cm *6-in* Malaysian stick insect *Heteropteryx dilitata* and measures an immense 1.3 cm *0.5 in* in length; this makes it larger in size than a peanut. Some insects, notably mantids and cockroaches, lay egg cases which are much larger — but these contain as many as 200 individual eggs.

In 1955 there were reportedly 140,000 species of Lepidoptera, and now there are known to be at least 165,000. Forty years ago the smallest was believed to be *Nepticula microtheviella*, with a wingspan of 0.12 in *3 mm*. The micro-moth called *Stigmella ridiculosa* is now known to be even smaller, with a wingspan of just 0.079 in *2 mm*.

■ Migrating Monarch butterflies. The Monarch is the largest butterfly found in Britain; it breeds in the southern United States and Central America.
(Photo: Jacana/F. Gohier)

■ The largest *resident* butterfly is the swallowtail (inset).
(Photo: Jacana/P. Lorne)

Earthworms

Longest earthworm The longest is *Microchaetus rappi* (=*M. microchaetus*) of South Africa. In c. 1937 a giant measuring 6.7 m *22 ft* in length when naturally extended and 20 mm *0.8 in* in diameter was collected in the Transvaal.

UK The longest earthworm found in Britain is *Lumbricus terrestris*. Its normal range is 90–300 mm *3½–12 in* but this species has been reliably measured up to 350 mm *13¾ in* when naturally extended. Measurements of up to 508 mm *20 in* have been claimed, but in each case the body was probably first macerated or mistaken for the intestinal tract of some small buried mammal.

Shortest earthworm Chaetogaster annandalei measures less than 0.5 mm 0.02 in in length.

Worm charming At the first World Worm Charming Championship held at Willaston, near Nantwich, Cheshire on 5 Jul 1980 Tom Shufflebotham (b. 1960), charmed a record 511 worms out of the ground (a 3 m² *9.84 ft² plot*) in the allotted time of 30 minutes. Nobody since has been able to exceed this record at the championship. Garden forks or other implements are vibrated in the soil by competitors to coax up the worms, but water is banned.

Molluscs

Most venomous mollusc The two closely-related species of blue-ringed octopus *Hapalochlaena maculosa* and *H. lunulata*, found around the coasts of Australia, and parts of south-east Asia, carry a neurotoxic venom so potent that their relatively painless bite can kill in a matter of minutes. It has been estimated that each individual carries sufficient venom to cause the paralysis (or even death) of 10 adult

people. Fortunately, blue-ringed octopuses are not considered aggressive and normally bite only when they are taken out of the water and provoked. These molluscs have a radial spread of just 100–200 mm *4–8 in*.

The most venomous gastropods are cone shells in the genus *Conus*, all of which can deliver a fast-acting neurotoxic venom. Several species are capable of killing people, but the geographer cone (*Conus geographus*) of the Indo- Pacific is considered to be one of the most dangerous.

Largest invertebrate The Atlantic giant squid (*Architeuthis dux*) is the world's largest known invertebrate. The heaviest ever recorded ran aground in Thimble Tickle Bay, Newfoundland, Canada on 2 Nov 1878. Its body was 6.1 m *20 ft* long and one tentacle measured 10.7 m *35 ft* (↪General records, largest eye).

Oldest mollusc The longest-lived mollusc is the ocean quahog (*Arctica islandica*), a thick-shelled clam found on both sides of the Atlantic and in the North Sea. A specimen with 220 annual growth rings was collected in 1982. Although this implies an age of 220 years, not all biologists accept these growth rings as an accurate measure of age.

Oyster opening The record for opening oysters is 100 in 2 min 20.07 sec, by Mike Racz in Invercargill, New Zealand on 16 Jul 1990.

Largest snail (Gastropod) The largest known gastropod is the trumpet or baler conch (*Syrinx aruanus*) of Australia. One specimen collected off Western Australia in 1979 and now owned by Don Pisor of San Diego, California has a shell 77.2 cm *30.4 in* long with a maximum girth of 101 cm *39¾ in*. It weighed nearly 18 kg *40 lb* when alive.

The largest known land gastropod is the African giant snail *Achatina achatina*, the largest recorded specimen of which measured 39.3 cm *15½ in* from snout to tail when fully extended (shell length 27.3 cm *10¾ in*) in December 1978 and weighed exactly 900 g *2 lb*. Named Gee Geronimo, this snail was owned by Christopher Hudson (1955–79) of Hove, E Sussex and was collected in Sierra Leone in June 1976. *UK* The largest land snail found in Britain is the Roman or edible snail (*Helix pomatia*), with a body length of up to 10 cm *4 in* when fully extended and a shell length of 5 cm *2 in*. It weighs up to 85 g *3 oz*.

Clam

The largest of all existing bivalve shells is that of the marine giant clam *Tridacna gigas*, found on the Indo-Pacific coral reefs. One specimen measuring 115 cm *45¹/₅ in* in length and weighing 333 kg *734 lb* was collected off Ishigaki Island, Okinawa, Japan in 1956 but was not scientifically examined until August 1984. It probably weighed just over 340 kg *750 lb* when alive (the soft parts weigh up to 9.1 kg *20 lb*).

■ This oversized snail is the largest on land; it is found in Africa and has a shell length of 27.3 cm *10 in*. The largest gastropod of all, the trumpet or baler conch, is twice as large.
(Photo: Jacana/Mero)

Actual Size

Guess What?
Q. Have you ever heard of a snail with two lives?
A. See Page 26

Winkling Sheila Bance picked 50 shells (with a straight pin) in 1 min 30.55 sec at the European Food and Drink Fair at Rochester, Kent on 7 May 1993.

Racing

Snail racing On 20 Feb 1990 a garden snail named Vern, owned by Sally DeRoo of Canton, Michigan, completed a 31 cm *12.2 in* course at West Middle School in Plymouth, Michigan, USA in a record 2 min 13 sec at 0.233 cm/sec.

The British record was set on 20–21 Jul 1991 when a garden snail named Streaker reportedly completed the 33 cm *13 in* course at the World Snail Racing Championships in Congham, Norfolk in 2 min 22 sec. Life on a gastropod breeding farm awaited the winner.

Jellyfish

Largest jellyfish An Arctic giant (*Cyanea capillata arctica*) of the north-western Atlantic washed up in Massachusetts Bay, USA had a bell diameter of 2.28 m *7 ft 6 in* and tentacles stretching 36.5 m *120 ft*.

British Isles The largest cnidarian found in British waters is the now rare lion's mane jellyfish (*Cyanea capillata*), also known as the common sea blubber. One specimen measured at St Andrew's Marine Laboratory, Fife had a bell diameter of 91 cm *35.8 in* and tentacles stretching over 13.7 m *45 ft*.

Most venomous jellyfish The beautiful but deadly Australian sea wasp or box jellyfish (Chironex fleckeri) is the most venomous cnidarian in the world. Its cardiotoxic venom has caused the deaths of at least 70 people off the coast of Australia alone in the past century, with some victims dying within four minutes if medical aid is not available. One effective defence, however, is women's hosiery, outsize versions of which were once worn by Queensland lifesavers at surfing tournaments.

Sponges

Largest sponge The largest known sponge is the barrel-shaped loggerhead sponge (*Spheciospongia vesparium*), measuring up to 105 cm *3 ft 6 in* in height and 91 cm *3 ft* in diameter. It is found in the West Indies and the waters off Florida, USA.

Heaviest In 1909 a wool sponge (*Hippospongia canaliculatta*) measuring 183 cm *6 ft* in circumference was collected off the Bahamas. It initially weighed 36–41 kg *80–90 lb* but this fell to 5.44 kg *12 lb* after it had been dried and relieved of all excrescences. It is now preserved in the US National Museum, Washington, DC, USA.

Smallest sponge The widely distributed *Leucosolenia blanca* is just 3 mm *0.11 in* tall when fully grown.

Deepest sponge Sponges have been recovered from depths of 5637 m *18,500 ft*.

Rarest

Rarest land mammal The Javan rhinoceros (*Rhinoceros sondaicus*), a solitary, single-horned species, is considered to be the world's rarest large mammal. Once widely distributed in south-east Asia, its population has declined to an estimated 60 animals (some 50 on the remote western tip of Java, Indonesia, and about 10 in Vietnam). The decline is mainly due to the illegal hunting of its horns for use in traditional Oriental medicines, and, to a much lesser extent, the destruction of its habitats. There are none held in captivity.

Endangered Species

Many animals are only known from a single or type specimen, and the population sizes of others are unknown. This makes it very difficult to establish the identity of the world's rarest species and, consequently, this selection simply highlights some of the better known examples from the 5929 species currently listed by the World Conservation Union (IUCN) as known or suspected to be threatened with extinction.

Rarest marine mammal The baiji, or Yangtze river dolphin (*Lipotes vexillifer*) has an estimated population of only 150, and it is still falling due to competition with fisheries, incidental capture in fishing nets, hunting, pollution, disturbance and habitat destruction. The few survivors live mainly in the middle reaches of the Yangtze River, China.

Rarest bird In the wild, Spix's macaw (*Cyanopsitta spixii*) is as rare as it is possible to be without actually going extinct. Ornithologists searching for the bird in 1990 managed to locate only one survivor, believed to be a male, living in a remote corner of north-eastern Brazil. The only hope for its survival now lies in at least 31 individuals known to be kept in captivity.

Rarest reptile Assuming that the Round Island boa (*Bolyeria multocarinata*) is already extinct, the world's rarest snake—and one of the rarest reptiles—is probably the St. Lucia racer or couresse (*Liophis ornatus*). There are probably fewer than 100 survivors, with no specimens held in captivity.

Rarest amphibian The world's rarest amphibians include the Texas blind salamander (*Typhlomolge rathbuni*) of the USA, the Table Mountain ghost frog (*Heleophryne rosei*) of South Africa, and the spotted frog (*Litoria spenceri*) of Australia.

Rarest fish A coelacanth, a large, deepwater fish formerly known only from fossilized remains dating from 400–65 million years old, was landed at East London, South Africa on 22 Dec 1938 and only later identified as such and named *Latimeria chalumnae*. Following this discovery, a living coelacanth was observed 200 m *656 ft* below the waters off the Comoros in the Indian Ocean in the late 1980s, and nearly 200 other specimens have been found. Some scientists believe that its muscular, paddle-like fins may hold clues to the crucial stage of evolution when aquatic creatures first developed limbs and took to the land.

Prehistoric Animals

Dinosaurs

Part of the reptile class, dinosaurs are undoubtedly the best known group of extinct animals. The first dinosaur to be described scientifically was *Megalosaurus bucklandi* ('great fossil lizard') in 1824. Remains of this bipedal flesh-eater were found by workmen before 1818 in a slate quarry near Woodstock, Oxon and later placed in the University Museum at Oxford. The first fossil bone of *Megalosaurus* was actually illustrated in 1677, but its true nature was not realized until much later. It was not until 1841 that the name Dinosauria ('terrible lizards') was given to these newly-discovered giants.

Earliest dinosaur The most primitive dinosaur is *Eoraptor lunensis* ('dawn stealer'), named in 1993 from a skeleton found in the foothills of the Andes in Argentina in rocks dated as 228 million years old. This dinosaur was 1 m *39in* long and is classified as a theropod, a member of the group of meat-eating dinosaurs. It is the most primitive of the group since it lacks the dual-hinged jaw present in all other members.

Largest dinosaur The largest ever land animals were sauropod dinosaurs, a group of long-necked, long-tailed, four-legged plant-eaters that lumbered around most of the world during the Jurassic and Cretaceous periods 208–65 million years ago.

Heaviest dinosaur The largest known sauropods appear to have weighed around 50–80 tonnes, but this does not necessarily represent the ultimate weight limit for a land vertebrate. Theoretical calculations suggest that some dinosaurs approached the maximum body weight possible for a terrestrial animal, namely 120 tonnes. At weights greater than this, such massive legs would have been needed that the dinosaur could not have moved.

The main contenders for the heaviest dinosaur are probably the titanosaurid *Antarctosaurus giganteus* ('Antarctic lizard') from Argentina and India, at 40–80 tonnes; the brachiosaurid *Brachiosaurus altithorax* (45–55 tonnes); and the diplodocids *Seismosaurus halli* ('earthquake lizard') and *Supersaurus vivianae* (both over 50 tonnes, and estimated by some as weighing nearer 100 tonnes). A new titanosaurid from Argentina, *Argentinocaurus*, was estimated in 1994 to have weighed up to 100 tonnes, based on its vast vertebrae.

UK Britain's heaviest known dinosaur was the diplodocid *Cetiosaurus oxoniensis* ('whale lizard'), from southern England about 170 million years ago at about 45 tonnes based on estimates on part of a femur found in Clifton Regnes, Olney, Bucks.

Tallest dinosaur The tallest and largest dinosaur species known from a complete skeleton is *Brachiosaurus brancai* ('arm lizard') from the Tendaguru site in Tanzania, dated as Late Jurassic (150–144 million years ago). The site was excavated by German expeditions during the period 1909–11 and the bones prepared and assembled at the Humboldt Museum für Naturkunde in Berlin. A complete skeleton was constructed from the remains of several individuals and put on display in 1937. It is the world's largest and tallest mounted dinosaur skeleton, measuring 22.2 m *72 ft 9½ in* in overall length (height at shoulder 6 m *19 ft 8 in*) and has a raised head height of 14 m *46 ft*. A weight of 30–40 tonnes is likely. However, larger sizes are suggested by an isolated fibula from another *Brachiosaurus* in the same museum.

Longest dinosaur Based on the evidence of footprints, the brachiosaurid *Breviparopus* may have attained a length of 48 m *157 ft*, which would make it the longest vertebrate on record. However, a diplodocid from New Mexico, USA named *Seismosaurus halli* was estimated in 1994 to be 39–52 m *128– 170 ft* long based on comparisons of individual bones.

Complete The longest dinosaur known from a complete skeleton is the diplodocid *Diplodocus carnegii* ('double beam'), assembled at the Carnegie Museum in Pittsburgh, Pennsylvania, USA from remains found in Wyoming in 1899. *Diplodocus* was 26.6 m *87½ ft* long, with much of that length made up by a long neck and an extremely long whip-like tail, and probably weighed 5.8–18.5 tonnes, with an estimate of around 12 tonnes being the most likely. The mounted skeleton was so spectacular that casts were requested by other museums, and copies may be seen in London, La Plata, Washington, Frankfurt and Paris.

UK On the evidence of a haemal arch (the bone running beneath the vertebrae of the tail) found on the Isle of Wight, the brachiosaur *Pelorosaurus* ('monstrous lizard') may have reached 24 m *80 ft* in length. A more complete brachiosaurid was found on the island in 1993 and the jumbled bones, including much of the hips, ribs, shoulders and arms, indicated a 12 m *40 ft* long animal.

A composite skeleton of a slightly smaller specimen of this nightmarish beast can be seen in the American Museum of Natural History, New York, USA.

Smallest dinosaur The chicken-sized *Compsognathus* ('pretty jaw') of southern Germany and south-east France, and an undescribed plant-eating fabrosaurid from Colorado, USA measured 70–75 cm *27½–29½ in* from the snout to the tip of the tail and weighed about 3 kg *6lb 8oz* (*Compsognathus*) and 6.8 kg *15 lb* (fabrosaurid).

Fastest dinosaur Trackways can be used to estimate dinosaur speeds, and one from

Guess What?

Q. Which is known to be larger, the largest prehistoric fish or the largest fish in modern times?

A. See Page 46

Brainless!

Stegosaurus ('plated lizard'), which roamed across Colorado, Oklahoma, Utah and Wyoming about 150 million years ago, was up to 9 m *30 ft* long but had a walnut-sized brain weighing only 70 g *2½ oz*. This represented 0.0042 of 1 per cent of its computed bodyweight of 3.3 tonnes (cf. 0.06 of 1 per cent for an elephant and 1.88 per cent for a human).

Flesh-Eating

The largest flesh-eating dinosaur recorded so far is *Tyrannosaurus rex* ('king tyrant lizard'), which, *c.* 75 million years ago, reigned over parts of the USA and the provinces of Alberta and Saskatchewan, Canada. The largest and heaviest example, as suggested by a discovery in South Dakota, USA in 1991, was 5.9 m *19½ ft* tall, had a total length of 11.1 m *36½ ft* and weighed an estimated 6–7.4 tonnes.

---

the Late Morrison of Texas, USA discovered in 1981 indicated that a carnivorous dinosaur had been moving at 40 km/h *25 mph*. Some ornithomimids were even faster, and the large-brained, 100 kg *220 lb Dromiceiomimus* ('emu mimic lizard') of the Late Cretaceous of Alberta, Canada could probably outsprint an ostrich, which has a top speed in excess of 60 km/h *37.3 mph*.

Largest footprints In 1932 the gigantic footprints of a large bipedal hadrosaurid ('duckbill') measuring 1.36 m *53½ in* in length and 81 cm *32 in* wide were discovered in Salt Lake City, Utah, USA, and other reports from Colorado and Utah refer to footprints 95–100 cm *37–40 in* wide. Footprints attributed to the largest brachiosaurids also range up to 100 cm *40 in* wide for the hind feet.

Largest dinosaur skull The skulls of the long-frilled ceratopsids were the largest of all known land animals and culminated in the long-frilled *Torosaurus* ('piercing lizard'). This herbivore, which measured about 7.6 m *25 ft* in total length and weighed up to 8 tonnes, had a skull measuring up to 3 m *9 ft 10 in* in length (including fringe) and weighing up to 2 tonnes. It ranged from Montana to Texas, USA.

Largest dinosaur claws The therizinosaurids ('scythe lizards') from the Late Cretaceous of the Nemegt Basin, Mongolia had the largest claws of any known animal. In the case of *Therizinosaurus cheloniformis* they measured up to 91 cm *36 in* along the outer curve (cf. 20.3 cm *8 in* for *Tyrannosaurus rex*). It has been suggested that these talons were designed for grasping and tearing apart large victims, but this creature had a feeble skull partially or entirely lacking teeth and probably lived on termites.

UK In January 1983 a claw-bone measuring 30 cm *11.8 in* in length was found by amateur fossil collector William Walker near Dorking, Surrey. The claw was later identified as possibly belonging to a spinosaur measuring more than 9 m *29 ft 6 in* overall (estimated weight 2 tonnes), with a bipedal height of 3–4 m *9–13 ft*. It was also distinguished from other theropods by having 128 teeth instead of the usual 64. This enigma, said to be the most important dinosaur fossil found in Europe this century, was subsequently named *Baryonyx walkeri* ('heavy claw').

WHICH WAY TO JURASSIC PARK?

The oldest genetic material ever discovered was recently identified in ancient termites trapped in amber (see right). In the film *Jurassic Park*, the plot had scientists extract dinosaur DNA and create living dinosaurs. During 1994 and 1995, scientists have claimed that they have taken the first steps towards making this unbelievable story come true. Could we see living dinosaurs some day?

DNA, short for deoxyribonucleic acid, is a complex molecule that carries messages. Every cell in every plant or animal contains DNA, which is divided into units called genes, which give precise codes for every feature of the body and behaviour. Different species have different DNAs. The DNA code is passed on from parents to offspring in the egg and the sperm, and this is the way in which inheritance occurs.

Before 1990, ancient DNA had been extracted from some fossils, and many scientists hoped that this would open up a whole new area of research. However, problems soon arose. DNA is a very delicate molecule, and it breaks down very rapidly after a plant or animal dies. In many cases, the ancient DNA that had been extracted from fossils was not original: it was DNA from bacteria that were involved in the decay process. Clearly, ancient DNA could only be found when fossils had been preserved in very unusual ways.

Michael Crichton, in his book *Jurassic Park*, realised that one special kind of preservation was in amber, the ancient resin of conifer trees. Insects were often

trapped in the sticky resin, and they were preserved instantly, with no chance for decay. Crichton suggested that dinosaur DNA might be found in the guts of blood-sucking insects. Indeed, in 1993, when the film came out, DNA was reported for the first time from a dinosaur-age insect, a weevil that was dated as over 120 million years old.

The first reports of dinosaur DNA came in 1994 from two teams, Scott Woodward of Brigham Young University, Utah, USA and Jack Horner of Montana State University, USA. In both cases, the dinosaur bones were Late Cretaceous in age, perhaps 80 million years old, and they were preserved in lowland sediments, some of them in association with coals.

These reports have not been widely accepted, however, since neither team has been able to prove yet that the DNA they have found is entirely free from contamination. The search continues!

■ Left: A reconstructed diplodocus roaming through a lake. Is this the shape of things to come?

Dinosaur DNA was first reported in late 1994 from bones of a duckbilled dinosaur like this *Edmontosaurus*.
Artwork: Matthew Hillier © Guinness Publishing

Eggs

The largest known dinosaur eggs are those of *Hypselosaurus priscus* ('high ridge lizard'), a 12 m *40 ft* long titanosaurid which lived about 80 million years ago. Examples found in the Durance valley near Aix-en-Provence, France in October 1961 would have had, uncrushed, a length of 300 mm *12 in* (about the height of this page) and a diameter of 255 mm *10 in* (capacity 3.3 litres *5.8 pt*).

Other reptiles

Earliest fossil reptile The oldest reptile fossil, nicknamed 'Lizzie the Lizard', was found on a site in Scotland by palaeontologist Stan Wood in March 1988. The 20.3 cm *8 in* long reptile is estimated to be about 340 million years old, 40 million years older than previously discovered reptiles. 'Lizzie' was officially named *Westlothiana lizziae* in 1991.

Largest predator The largest ever land predator may have been an alligator found on the banks of the Amazon in rocks dated as 8 million years old. Estimates from a skull 1.5 m *5 ft* long (complete with 10 cm *4 in* long teeth) indicate a length of 12 m *40 ft* and a weight of about 18 tonnes, making it larger than the fearsome *Tyrannosaurus rex*. It was subsequently identified as a giant example of *Purussaurus brasiliensis*, a species named in 1892 on the basis of smaller specimens.

Largest flying creature The largest ever flying creature was the pterosaur *Quetzalcoatlus northropi* ('feathered serpent'). About 70 million years ago it soared over what is now Texas, Wyoming and New Jersey, USA, Alberta, Canada and Senegal and Jordan. Partial remains discovered in Big Bend National Park, Texas, USA in 1971 indicate that this reptile must have had a wing span of 11–12 m *36–39 ft* and weighed about 86–113 kg *190–250 lb*.

UK Ornithodesmus latidens, from the Wealden Shales of Atherfield, Isle of Wight about 120 million years ago, had a wing span of c. 5 m *16 ft 4¼ in*.

Mammals

Earliest mammal In 1991 a partial skull of a mammal named *Adelobasileus cromptoni* was reported from 225 million-year-old rocks in New Mexico, USA. The first true mammals, as represented by odd teeth, appeared about 220 million years ago during the Late Triassic. Modern mammals (therians) arose in the Mid-Cretaceous period, and the earliest representatives of modern orders, such as *Purgatorius*, the first primate, by the end of the Cretaceous period, 65 million years ago. This creature was similar in appearance to modern tree shrews of the order Scandentia.

Largest mammal The largest land mammal ever recorded was *Indricotherium* (=*Baluchitherium* or *Paraceratherium*), a long-necked, hornless rhinocerotid which roamed across western Asia and Europe about 35 million years ago and first known from bones discovered in the Bugti Hills of Baluchistan, Pakistan in 1907–8. A restoration in the American Museum of Natural History, New York City, USA measures 5.41 m *17 ft 9 in* to the top of the shoulder hump and 11.27 m *37 ft* in total length. The most likely maximum weight of this browser was revised in 1993 to 11–20 tonnes from earlier estimates of 34 tonnes.

Birds

Earliest bird The earliest fossil bird is known from two partial skeletons found in Texas, USA in rocks dating from 220 million years ago. Named *Protoavis texensis* in 1991, this pheasant-sized creature has caused much controversy by pushing the age of birds back many millions of years from the previous record, that of the more familiar *Archeopteryx lithographica* from Germany. It is still unclear whether *Protoavis* will be widely accepted as a true bird, making *Archaeopteryx* the earliest unambiguous fossil bird.

Largest prehistoric bird The largest prehistoric bird was the flightless *Dromornis stirtoni*, a huge emu-like creature which lived in central Australia between 15 million and 25,000 years ago. Fossil leg bones found near Alice Springs in 1974 indicate that the bird must have stood c. 3 m *10 ft* tall and weighed about 500 kg *1100 lb*.

The giant moa *Dinornis maximus* of New Zealand may have been even taller, possibly attaining a height of 3.7 m *12 ft*, t weighed about 227 kg *500 lb*.

Flying bird The largest known flying bird was the giant teratorn (*Argentavis magnificens*), which lived in Argentina about 6–8 million years ago. Fossil remains discovered at a site 160 km *100 miles* west of Buenos Aires, Argentina in 1979 indicate that this gigantic vulture-like bird had a wing span of over 6 m *19 ft 8 in* (possibly up to 7.6 m *25 ft*) and weighed about 80 kg *176 lb*.

Fish

Largest prehistoric fish No prehistoric fish larger than living species has yet been discovered. Modern estimates suggest that the largest in prehistoric times, however, was the great shark *Carcharodon megalodon*, which abounded in middle and late Tertiary seas, some 50–4.5 million years ago. Recent studies suggest that it attained a maximum length of 13.7 m *45 ft*, although its size has been a subject for debate since the first fossil teeth were found in the early 1800s. Many earlier estimates of lengths up to 30 m *98½ ft* are now known to have been in error.

Snake

The longest prehistoric snake was the python-like *Gigantophis garstini*, which inhabited what is now Egypt about 38 million years ago. Parts of a spinal column and a small piece of jaw discovered at Fayum in the Western Desert indicate a length of about 11 m *36 ft*. This is 1 m *3 ft 3 in* longer than the present-day longest snake.

Antlers

The extinct giant deer or Irish elk (*Megaloceros giganteus*), found in Continental Europe as recently as 10,000 years ago, had the longest antlers of any known animal. One specimen recovered from an Irish bog had greatly palmated antlers measuring 4.3 m *14 ft* across, which corresponds to a shoulder height of 1.83 m *6 ft* and a weight of 500 kg *1100 lb*.

Plant Kingdom

General Records

Oldest plant 'King Clone', the oldest known clone of the creosote plant (*Larrea tridentata*), of California, USA, was estimated in February 1980 by Prof. Frank C. Vasek to be 11,700 years old.

Most massive plant The most massive organism was reported in December 1992 to be a network of quaking aspen trees (*Populus tremuloides*) growing in the Wasatch Mountains, Utah, USA from a single root system, covering 43 ha *106 acres* and weighing an estimated 6000 tonnes. The clonal system is genetically uniform and acts as a single organism, with all the component trees, part of the willow family, changing colour or shedding leaves in unison.

> The greatest depth at which plant life has been found is 269 m *884 ft* for algae found by Mark and Diane Littler off San Salvadore Island, Bahamas in October 1984. These maroon-coloured plants survived although 99.9995 per cent of sunlight was filtered out.

Northernmost plant The yellow poppy (*Papaver radicatum*) and the Arctic willow (*Salix arctica*) survive at Lat. 83°N., although the latter exists there in an extremely stunted form.

Southernmost plant Lichens resembling *Rhinodina frigida* have been found in Moraine Canyon at Lat. 86°09'S, Long. 157°30'W in 1971 and in the Horlick Mountain area of Antarctica at Lat. 86°09'S, Long. 131°14'W in 1965.

The southernmost recorded flowering plant was the Antarctic hair grass (*Deschampsia antarctica*) found in Lat. 68°21'S on Refuge Island, Antarctica on 11 Mar 1981.

Highest plant The greatest certain altitude at which any flowering plants have been found is 6400 m *21,000 ft* on Mt Kamet (7756 m *25,447 ft*) in the Himalayas by N.D. Jayal in 1955. They were *Ermania himalayensis* and *Ranunculus lobatus*.

Roots The greatest reported depth to which roots have penetrated is a calculated 120 m *400 ft* for a wild fig tree at Echo Caves, near Ohrigstad, Transvaal, South Africa. A single winter rye plant (*Secale cereale*) has been shown to produce 622.8 km *387 miles* of roots in 0.051 m³ *1.801 ft³* of earth.

UK An elm tree root at least 110 m *360 ft* long was reported from Auchencraig, Largs, Strathclyde in about 1950.

Fastest growing plant Some species of the 45 genera of bamboo have been found to grow at up to 91 cm *3 ft* per day (0.00003 km/h *0.00002 mph*) (⇔ Grasses).

Flowers

Earliest flower A flower believed to be 120 million years old was identified in 1989 by Drs Leo Hickey and David Taylor of Yale University, Connecticut, USA from a fossil discovered near Melbourne, Victoria, Australia. The flowering angiosperm, which resembles a modern black pepper plant, had two leaves and one flower and is known as the Koonwarra plant.

Largest flower The mottled orange-brown and white parasite *Rafflesia arnoldi* has the largest of all blooms. These attach themselves to the cissus vines of the jungle in Southeast Asia. They measure up to 91 cm *3 ft* across and their petals are 1.9 cm *¾ in* thick, weighing up to 11 kg *36 lb*.

UK The largest bloom of any native British plant is that of the wild white water lily (*Nymphaea alba*), at 15 cm *6 in* across.

Tallest and Longest Flowering Plants

All plants should, where possible, be entered in official international, national or local garden and/or horticultural contests.

WORLD RECORDS

Type	Size		Grower	Location	Year
ASPIDISTRA	1.42 m	4 ft 8 in	C. Evans	Kiora, New South Wales, Australia	1989
CACTUS	10.7 m	35 ft 1 in	A. Kashi	Mysore, India	1992
CHRYSANTHEMUM	2.7 m	8 ft 10 in	M. Comer	Desford, Leics	1993
DAHLIA	7.8 m	25 ft 7 in	R. Blythe	Nannup, Western Australia	1990
FUSCHIA	4.2 m	13 ft 10 in	B. Lavery	Llanharry, Mid Glam	1995
PETUNIA	5.8 m	19 ft 1 in	B. Lavery	Llanharry, Mid Glam	1994
PHILODENDRON *Climbing*	339.55 m	1114 ft	F. Francis	University of Massachusetts, USA	1984
SUNFLOWER[1]	7.76 m tall	25 ft 5½ in	M. Heijms	Oirschot, Netherlands	1986

BRITISH ISLES RECORDS

Type	Size		Grower	Location	Year
AMARYLLIS	1.32 m	4 ft 4 in	Rev. and Mrs Miles	West Malling, Kent	1993
ASPIDISTRA	1.27 m	4 ft 2 in	G. James	Staveley, Chesterfield, Derbys	1979
BUSY LIZZIE	2.8 m	9 ft 6 in	V. & M. Clifford	Mayfield, Cork	1994
DAFFODIL	1.55 m	5 ft 1 in	M. Lowe	Chessell, Isle of Wight	1979
DAHLIA	3.3 m	10 ft 10 in	R. Lond	Diss, Norfolk	1989
GLADIOLUS	2.55 m	8 ft 4½ in	A. Breed	Melrose, Borders	1981
LUPIN	1.96 m	6 ft 5¼ in	A.H. Fennell	Palatine, Carlow, Ireland	1993
PETUNIA	2.53 m	8 ft 4 in	G. Warner	Dunfermline, Fife	1978
PHILODENDRON *Climbing*	224 m	735 ft	M.J. Linhart	Thornton, Leics	1990
Tree	11.7 m	38½ ft	B. Lavery	Llanharry, Mid Glam	1992
SUNFLOWER[1]	7.17 m	23 ft 6½ in	F. Kelland	Exeter, Devon	1976

[1] *A sunflower with a head diameter of 82 cm 32¼ in was grown by Emily Martin of Maple Ridge, British Columbia, Canada in Sep 1983. A fully mature sunflower measuring just 56 mm 2⅕ in was grown by Michael Lenke of Lake Oswego, Oregon, USA in 1985 using a patented bonsai technique.*

Inflorescence The largest known inflorescence (as distinct from bloom) is that of *Puya raimondii*, a rare Bolivian monocarpic member of the Bromeliaceae family. Its erect panicle (diameter 2.4 m *8 ft*) emerges to a height of 10.7 m *35 ft* and each of these bears up to 8000 white blooms (⟺ Slowest flowering plant).

Fastest growing flowering plant It was reported from Tresco Abbey, Isles of Scilly in July 1978 that a *Hesperoyucca whipplei* of the Liliaceae family had grown 3.65 m *12 ft* in 14 days, a rate of about 254 mm *10 in* per day.

Slowest flowering plant The slowest flowering plant is the rare *Puya raimondii*, the largest of all herbs, discovered at 3960 m *13,000 ft* in Bolivia in 1870. The panicle emerges after about 80–150 years of the plant's life. It then dies. One planted near sea level at the University of California's Botanical Garden, Berkeley, USA in 1958 grew to 7.6 m *25 ft* and bloomed as early as August 1986 after only 28 years (⟺ Largest blooms).

Longest daisy chain The longest daisy chain measured 2.12 km *6980 ft 7 in* and was made in 7 hr by villagers of Good Easter, Chelmsford, Essex on 27 May 1985. The teams are limited to 16.

Orchids *Tallest* The tallest of all orchids is *Grammatophyllum speciosum* from Malaysia, specimens of which have been recorded up to 7.6 m *25 ft* tall.

Smallest

Smallest flowering and fruiting plant The floating, flowering aquatic duckweed (*Wolffia angusta*) of Australia is only 0.6 mm *0.0236 in* long and 0.33 mm *0.0129 in* wide. It weighs about 0.00015 g *5.2 ×10⁻⁶ oz* and its fruit, which resembles a minuscule fig, weighs 0.00007 g *2.4 ×10⁻⁶ oz*.

UK The smallest land plant regularly flowering in Britain is the chaffweed (*Cetunculus minimus*), a single seed of which weighs 0.00003 g *1 ×10⁻⁷ oz*.

A height of 15 m *49 ft* has been recorded for *Galeola foliata*, a saprophyte of the vanilla family. It grows in the decaying rain forests of Queensland, Australia, but is not free-standing.

Largest flower The largest orchid flower is that of *Paphiopedilum sanderianum*, whose petals are reported to grow up to 90 cm *3 ft* long in the wild. It was discovered in 1886 in the Malay Archipelago. A plant of this variety grown in Somerset in 1991 had three flowers averaging 61 cm *2 ft* from the top of the dorsal sepal to the bottom of the ribbon petals, giving a record stretched length of 122 cm *4 ft*.

Largest cactus The largest of all cacti is the saguaro (*Cereus giganteus* or *Carnegiea gigantea*), found in Arizona and California, USA and Mexico. The green fluted column is surmounted by candelabra-like branches rising to a height of 17.67 m *57 ft 11¾ in* in a specimen discovered in the Maricopa Mountains, near Gila Bend, Arizona on 17 Jan 1988.

An armless 24 m *78 ft* tall cactus was measured in April 1978 by Hube Yates in Cave Creek, Arizona, USA. It was toppled in a windstorm in July 1986 at an estimated age of 150 years (⟺ also Table).

Largest rhododendron An example of the scarlet *Rhododendron arboreum* on Mt Japfu, Nagaland, India reportedly reached a height of 20 m *65 ft*.

The cross-section of a trunk of *Rhododendron giganteum* with a reputed height of 27.5 m *90 ft* from

■ The oversized saguaro cactus (pronounced sa-wah-ro) of the Arizona desert. It grows extremely slowly, sprouting less than one inch in its first 10 years of life and then growing by a further 10 cm *3.9 in* a year thereafter. It blooms for the first time when aged between 50 and 75 years. (Photo: Jacana/F. Gohier)

Guess What?
Q. What is the most number of leaves to have been found on a clover?
A. See Page 49

1. Mel Ednie and his world record onion.
(Garden News)

2. A new world record for beetroot was established in 1994; here it is proudly displayed by its grower, Ian Neale.
(Photo: Guinness Publishing/ M.Good)

Largest Fruits and Vegetables

In the interests of fairness and to minimize the risk of mistakes being made, all plants should, where possible, be entered in official international, national or local garden contests. Only produce grown primarily for human consumption will be considered for publication. The assistance of Garden News and the World Pumpkin Confederation is gratefully acknowledged.

WORLD RECORDS

Type	Size		Grower	Location	Year
APPLE	1.47 kg	3 lb 4 oz	The Hanners Family	Hood Rivers, Oregon, USA	1994
BEETROOT	18.37 kg	40 lb 8 oz	I. Neale	Newport, Gwent	1994
BROCCOLI	15.87 kg	35 lb	J & M Evans	Palmer, Alaska, USA	1993
CABBAGE	56.24 kg	124 lb	B. Lavery	Llanharry, Mid Glam	1989
CARROT[1]	7 kg	15 lb 7 oz	I. Scott	Nelson, New Zealand	1978
CELERY	20.89 kg	46 lb 1 oz	B. Lavery	Llanharry, Mid Glam	1990
CORN COB	92 cm	36 ¼ in	B.Lavery	Llanharry, Mid Glam	1994
COURGETTE	29.25 kg	64 lb 8 oz	B. Lavery	Llanharry, Mid Glam	1990
CUCUMBER[2]	9.1 kg	20 lb 1 oz	B. Lavery	Llanharry, Mid Glam	1991
GARLIC	1.19 kg	2 lb 10 oz	R. Kirkpatrick	Eureka, California, USA	1985
GRAPEFRUIT	2.97 kg	6 lb 8½ oz	J. and A. Sosnow	Tucson, Arizona, USA	1984
GRAPES (bunch)	9.4 kg	20 lb 11½ oz	Bozzolo y Perut Ltda	Santiago, Chile	1984
GREEN BEAN	121.9 cm	48 in	B. Rogerson	Robersonville, North Carolina, USA	1994
LEEK (pot)	5.5 kg	12 lb 2 oz	P. Harrigan	Linton, Northumberland	1987
LEMON	3.88 kg	8 lb 8 oz	C. and D. Knutzen	Whittier, California, USA	1983
MARROW	49.04 kg	108 lb 2 oz	B. Lavery	Llanharry, Mid Glam	1990
MELON (cantaloupe)	28.12 kg	62 lb	G. Daughtridge	Rocky Mount, North Carolina, USA	1991
ONION	5.55 kg	12 lb 4 oz	M. Ednie	Anstruther, Fife	1994
PARSNIP	4.36 m	171 ¾ in	B. Lavery	Llanharry, Mid Glam	1990
PINEAPPLE	8.06 kg	17 ¾ oz	E. Kamuk	Ais Village, WNBP, Papua New Guinea	1994
POTATO[3]	3.5 kg	7 lb 13 oz	K. Sloane	Patrick, Isle of Man	1994
PUMPKIN	449 kg	990 lb	H. Bax	Ashton, Ontario, Canada	1994
RADISH	17.2 kg	37 lb 15 oz	Litterini family	Tanunda, South Australia	1992
RHUBARB	2.67 kg	5 lb 14 oz	E. Stone	East Woodyates, Wilts	1985
SQUASH	408.6 kg	900 lb 12 oz	J. & C. Lyons	Baltimore, Ontario, Canada	1994
STRAWBERRY	231 g	8.17 oz	G. Andersen	Folkestone, Kent	1983
SWEDE	25.54 kg	56 lb 5 oz	N. Craven	Stouffville, Ontario, Canada	1995
TOMATO	3.51 kg	7 lb 12 oz	G. Graham	Edmond, Oklahoma, USA	1986
TOMATO PLANT	16.3 m	53 ft 6 in	G. Graham	Edmond, Oklahoma, USA	1985
WATERMELON	118.84 kg	262 lb	B. Carson	Arrington, Tennessee, USA	1990

UK NATIONAL RECORDS

Type	Size		Grower	Location	Year
CARROT	5.2 kg	11 lb 7½ oz	B. Lavery	Llanharry, Mid Glam	1993
GOOSEBERRY	61.04 g	2.18 oz	K. Archer	Scholar Green, Cheshire	1993
GRAPEFRUIT	1.67 kg	3 lb 11 oz	Willington G.C.	Willington, Beds	1986
LEMON	2.13 kg	4 lb 11 oz	Pershore College	Pershore, Hereford & Worcester	1986
MELON (cantaloupe)	8.33 kg	18 lb 5 ¾ oz	B. Lavery	Llanharry, Mid Glam	1991
PEACH	411 g	14 ½ oz	J. Bird	London	1984
PUMPKIN	351.3 kg	774 lb 8 oz	J. Perkins	Devizes, Wiltshire	1994
SQUASH	228.61 kg	504 lb	B. Lavery	Llanharry, Mid Glam	1991
TOMATO	2.54 kg	5 lb 9½ oz	R. Burrows	Huddersfield, W Yorks	1985
TOMATO PLANT	13.96 m	45 ft 9 ½ in	Chosen Hill School	Gloucester	1981
WATERMELON	16.33 kg	36 lb	B. Lavery	Llanharry, Mid Glam	1990

[1] A 5.14 m 16 ft 10 ½ in long carrot was grown by Bernard Lavery of Llanharry, Mid Glam in 1991. [2] A Vietnamese variety 1.83 m 6 ft long was reported by L. Szabó of Debrecen, Hungary in September 1976. A.C. Rayment of Chelmsford, Essex grew one measuring 1.10 m 43 ½ in in 1984–6. [3] One weighing 8.275 kg 18 lb 4 oz reported dug up by Thomas Siddal in his garden in Chester on 17 Feb 1795. A yield of 233.5 kg 515 lb was achieved from a 1.1 kg 2 ½ lb parent seed by Bowcock planted in April 1977.

WINNER

Yunnan, China is preserved at Inverewe Gardens, Highland.

British Isles The largest rhododendron in the British Isles is a specimen 11 m *36 ft* tall and 93.9 m *308 ft* in circumference, at Government House, Hillsborough, Co. Down.

Largest rose bush A 'Lady Banksia or Banks' rose bush at Tombstone, Arizona, USA has a trunk 409 cm *162 in* thick, stands 2.75 m *9 ft* high and covers an area of 742 m² *8000 ft²*. It is supported by 77 posts and several thousand feet of piping, which enables 250 people to be seated under the arbour. The cutting came from Scotland in 1885.

Largest bouquet A team of students and community helpers led by Susan Williams of Victoria, British Columbia, constructed a giant bouquet of 10,011 roses measuring 12.8 metres *41.9 ft* long in August 1994.

Basket

A giant hanging basket measuring 6.1m *20ft* in diameter and containing about 600 plants was created by Rogers of Exeter Garden Centre in 1987. Its volume was approximately 118m³ *4167ft³* and it weighed an estimated 4 tonnes. Another example from France with the same diameter but more conical in shape was smaller in terms of volume.

Fruits and Vegetables

Most nutritive fruit An analysis of 38 fruits commonly eaten raw (as opposed to dried) shows that the avocado (*Persea americana*) has the highest calorific value, with 163 kilocalories per edible 100g *741 kilocal/lb*; it also contains vitamins A, C and E and 2.2 per cent protein. Avocados originated in Central America.

Least nutritive fruit The fruit with the lowest calorific value is the cucumber (*Cucumis sativus*), with 16 kilocal/100 g *73 kilocal/lb*.

Grape catching The greatest distance at which a grape thrown from level ground has been caught in the mouth is 99.82 m *327 ft 6 in*, by Paul J. Tavilla at East Boston, Massachusetts,

USA on 27 May 1991. The grape was thrown by James Deady.

Most expensive fruit Anthony Baskeyfield purchased a grape for £700 from David Cinavas at the Helpston Garden Centre, Cambs on 28 Mar 1993. The sale was made in order to circumvent the Sunday Trading laws which applied at the time in Great Britain, and a statue of Apollo (valued at £700) was given away with the grape.

John Synnott of Ashford, Co. Wicklow, Republic of Ireland sold 453g *1 lb* of strawberries (a punnet of 30 berries) for £530 or £17.70 a berry on 5 Apr 1977. The buyer was restaurateur Leslie Cooke, at an auction by Walter L. Cole Ltd in the Dublin Fruit Market.

Potato peeling The greatest quantity of potatoes peeled by five people to an institutional cookery standard with standard kitchen knives in 45 min is 482.8 kg *1064 lb 6 oz* (net) by Marj Killian, Terry Anderson, Barbara Pearson, Marilyn Small and Janene Utkin at the 64th Annual Idaho Spud Day celebration, held at Shelley, Idaho, USA on 19 Sep 1992.

Apple peeling The longest single unbroken apple peel on record is one of 52.51 m *172 ft 4 in*, peeled by Kathy Wafler of Wolcott, New York, USA in 11 hr 30 min at Long Ridge Mall, Rochester, New York on 16 Oct 1976. The apple weighed 567 g *20 oz*.

Apple picking The greatest recorded performance is 7180.3 kg *15,830 lb* picked in 8 hr by George Adrian of Indianapolis, Indiana, USA on 23 Sep 1980.

Leaves

Largest leaves The largest leaves of any plant are those of the raffia palm (*Raffia farinifera* = *R. ruffia*) of the Mascarene Islands in the Indian

Ocean, and the Amazonian bamboo palm (*R. taedigera*) of South America and Africa, whose leaf blades may be up to 20 m *65 ft 6 in* long, with petioles measuring 3.96 m *13 ft.*

UK The largest leaves found on outdoor plants in Great Britain are those of *Gunnera manicata* from Columbia, with rhubarb-like leaves measuring up to 3 m *10 ft* in diameter on prickly stems up to 2.5 m *8 ft* tall.

Undivided The largest undivided leaf is that of *Alocasia macrorrhiza*, from Sabah, Malaysia. A specimen found in 1966 was 3.02 m *9 ft 11 in* long, 1.92 m *6 ft 3½ in* wide, and had a surface area of 3.17 m² *34.12 ft²*. A specimen of the water lily *Victoria amazonica* (Longwood hybrid) measuring 2.4 m *8 ft* in diameter was grown at the Stratford-upon-Avon Butterfly Farm, Warks in 1989.

Clovers A fourteen-leafed white clover (*Trifolium repens*) was found by Randy Farland near Sioux Falls, South Dakota, USA on 16 Jun 1975. A fourteen-leafed red clover (*Trifolium pratense*) was reported by Paul Haizlip at Bellevue, Washington, USA on 22 Jun 1987.

Seeds

Largest seed The largest seed in the world is that of the giant fan palm *Lodoicea maldivica* (= *L. callipyge, L. sechellarum*), commonly known as the double coconut or coco de mer, found wild only in the Seychelles. The single-seeded fruit weighs up to 20 kg *44 lb* and can take 10 years to develop.

Norman Johnson of Blackpool College, Lancs set a record of 13.4 sec for slicing a 30.5 cm *12 in* cucumber, 3.8 cm *1½ in* in diameter, at 22 slices to the inch (total 264 slices) at the studios of West Deutscher Rundfunk in Cologne, Germany on 3 Apr 1983.

■ Left and below: exhibits and exhibitors at the 1994 Baytree Giant Vegetable Show in Spalding, Lincs.
(Photo: Guinness Publishing/M. Good)

■ Right: Herman Bax and his record-breaking, 990-lb *449-kg* pumpkin. It took nine grown men just to move it on to the electronic scales.
(Photo: William Rankin)

Smallest seed The smallest seeds are those of epiphytic (non-parasitic plants growing on others) orchids, at 992.25 million seeds/g *28,129.81 million/oz* (cf. grass pollens at up to 170.1 billion grains/g *6 billion grains/oz*).

Most conquering conker The most victorious untreated conker—the fruit of the common horse-chestnut (*Aesculus hippocastanum*)—was a 'five thousander plus', which won the BBC Conker Conquest in 1954. However, a professor of botany believes that this heroic specimen might well have been a 'ringer', probably an ivory or tagua nut (*Phytelephas macrocarpa*). *The Guinness Book of Records* will not publish any category for the largest collection of conkers for fear that trees might suffer wholesale damage.

Weeds

Largest weed The largest weed is the giant hogweed (*Heracleum mantegazzianum*), originally from the Caucasus. It reaches 3.65m *12ft* tall and has leaves 91cm *3ft* long.

Most damaging weed The virulence of weeds tends to be measured by the number of crops they affect and the number of countries in which they occur. On this basis the worst would appear to be the purple nut sedge, nut-grass or nutsedge (*Cyperus rotundus*), a land weed native to India but which attacks 52 crops in 92 countries.

UK The most damaging and widespread cereal weeds in Britain are the wild oats *Avena fatua* and *A. ludoviciana*. Their seeds can withstand temperatures of 115.6°C *240°F* for 15 min and remain viable, and up to 50 per cent losses have been recorded in crops affected by them.

Most spreading weed The greatest area covered by a single clonal growth is that of the wild box huckleberry (*Gaylussacia brachycera*), a mat-forming evergreen shrub first reported in 1796. A colony covering about 40ha *100 acres* was found on 18 Jul 1920 near the Juniata River, Pennsylvania, USA. It has been estimated that this colony began 13,000 years ago.

Seaweed

Longest seaweed The longest species of seaweed is the Pacific giant kelp (*Macrocystis pyrifera*), which, although it does not exceed 60m *196ft* in length, can grow 45cm *18in* in a day.

UK The longest of the 700 species of British seaweed is the brown seaweed (*Chorda filum*), which grows to a length of 6.10m *20ft*. The Japanese species *Sargassum muticum*, introduced into Britain c. 1970, can reach 9.0m *30ft*.

Trees

Earliest tree The earliest surviving species of tree is the maidenhair (*Ginkgo biloba*) of Zhejiang, China, which first appeared about 160 million years ago during the Jurassic era. It was 'rediscovered' by Kaempfer (Netherlands) in 1690 and reached England c. 1754. It has been grown in Japan since c. 1100, where it was known as *ginkyō*('silver apricot') and is now known as *icho*.

Oldest tree Dendrochronologists estimate the *potential* life-span of a bristlecone pine (*Pinus longaeva*) to be nearly 5500 years, and that of a giant sequoia (*Sequoiadendron giganteum*) at perhaps 6000 years, although no single cell lives more than 30 years. The oldest recorded tree is the 'Eon Tree', a coast redwood (*Sequoia sempervirens*) in Humboldt County, California, USA, believed to be at least 6200 years old. It is understood to have grown to a height of around 250ft *76m*, and to have fallen in December 1977. It was discovered in January 1994.

Living The oldest recorded living tree is another bristlecone pine named 'Methuselah', growing at 3050m *10,000ft* on the California side of the White Mountains, USA and confirmed as 4700 years old. In March 1974 it was reported to have produced 48 live seedlings.

UK The longest-lived British tree is the yew (*Taxus baccata*), for which a maximum age of well over 1000 years is usually conceded. The oldest known is the Fortingall yew near Aberfeldy, Tayside, part of which still grows. In 1777 this tree was over 15m *50ft* in girth and it is estimated to be some 1500 years old.

The oldest dated coppice is a patch of 60 small-leaved lime trees at Silk Wood near Tetbury, Glos, estimated by DNA analysis to have derived from a tree living 2000 years ago.

Most massive tree The world's most massive single tree is 'General Sherman' the giant sequoia (*Sequoiadendron giganteum*) growing in the Sequoia National Park, California, USA. It stands 83.82m *275ft* tall, has a diameter of 11.1m *36.5ft* and a girth of 31.3m *102.6ft*. This tree is estimated to contain the equivalent of 606,100 board feet of timber, enough to make 5 billion matches, and its red-brown bark may be up to 61cm *24in* thick in parts. Its weight, including the root system, is estimated at 2000 tonnes (⇨ General Records).

Greatest spread The tree canopy covering the greatest area is that of the great banyan (*Ficus benghalensis*) in the Indian Botanical Garden, Calcutta, with 1775 prop or supporting roots and a circumference of 412m *1350ft*. It covers some 1.2ha *3acres* and dates from before 1787.

UK The greatest spread in Britain is a canopy circumference of 198m *649 ft* for an oriental plane at Corsham Court, Wiltshire.

Greatest girth A circumference of 57.9m *190ft* was recorded for the pollarded (trimmed to encourage a more bushy growth) European chestnut (*Castanea sativa*) known as the 'Tree of the Hundred Horses' (*Castagno di Cento Cavalli*) on Mt Etna, Sicily, Italy in 1770 and 1780. It is now in three parts, widely separated.

'El Arbol del Tule' in Oaxaca state, Mexico is a 41m *135ft* tall Montezuma cypress (*Taxodium mucronatum*) with a girth in 1982 of 35.8m *117½ft*, measured 1.52m *5ft* above the ground. Generally speaking, however, the largest girths are attributed to African baobab trees (*Adansonia digitata*), with measurements of 43.0m *141ft* recorded.

UK A sweet (Spanish) chestnut (*Castanea sativa*) in the grounds of Canford School, near Poole, Dorset has a trunk with a circumference of 13.33m *43ft 9in*.

Weedy

The worst aquatic weed of the tropics and subtropics is the water hyacinth (*Eichhornia crassipes*), a native of the Amazon Basin, but which extends from Lat. 40°N to 45°S. The intransigence of aquatic plants in man-made lakes is illustrated by the mat-forming water weed *Salvinia auriculata*, found in Africa. It was detected when Lake Kariba, which straddles the border of Zimbabwe and Zambia, was filled in May 1959 and within 13 months it had choked an area of 518km² *200miles²*, rising to 1002km² *387 miles²* by 1963.

Slow Grow

Excluding *bonsai*, the 14th century Oriental art of cultivating miniature trees, the extreme in slow growth is represented by the *Dioon edule* (Cycadaceae) measured in Mexico between 1981 and 1986 by Dr Charles M. Peters, who found the average annual growth rate to be 0.76mm *0.03 in*; a 120-year-old specimen was just 10cm *4in* tall.

Tallest tree A *Eucalyptus regnans* at Mt Baw Baw, Victoria, Australia is believed to have measured 143m *470ft* in 1885. According to the researches of Dr A.C. Carder, the tallest tree ever measured was another Australian eucalyptus at Watts River, Victoria, Australia, reported in 1872 by forester William Ferguson. It was 132.6m *435ft* tall and almost certainly measured over 150m *500ft* originally. However, the Dyerville Giant, which fell in March 1991, was proven to be 113.38m *372ft* high, not counting the 1.5m *5ft* of buried base. It grew in Humboldt Redwoods State Park, California, and was the tallest tree of modern times.

Living The tallest tree currently standing is the 'National Geographic Society' coast redwood (*Sequoia sempervirens*) in the Redwood National Park, California, USA. Its latest measurement was 111.4m *365ft 6 in* in May 1993, according to Ron Hildebrant of California. The 'Federation Giant' tree in Humboldt Redwoods State Park, California, is believed to be of a similar height, but has not yet been measured officially.

British Isles The best two claimants for Britain's tallest tree are two Douglas firs (*Pseudotsuga menziesii*), both standing 64.5m *212ft* in 1993: one at the Forestry Commission property at The Hermitage, Perthshire; and the other at Dunans in Strathclyde (⇨ Table).

Christmas tree The world's tallest cut Christmas tree was a 67.36m *221ft* Douglas fir (*Pseudotsuga menziesii*) erected at Northgate Shopping Center, Seattle, Washington, USA in December 1950.

UK A Norway spruce (*Picea abies*) 26.3m *86ft 5in* tall was grown on the Marquess of Bath's Longleat estate in Wiltshire and given to the King's College, Cambridge Choir School Development Appeal for Christmas 1989.

The record for the tallest tree in Britain is more than 35ft *10.6m* taller than it was in our first edition. The Sequoia (Wellingtonia) at Fonthill Abbey, Dorset, was found to be 165ft *50.3m* high when it was measured in 1954. Now the record for Britain's tallest tree is shared by two Douglas Firs, which both reach a height of 212ft *64.6m*.

Fastest growing tree Discounting bamboo, which is classified as a woody grass, the fastest recorded rate of growth is 10.74m *35ft 3in* in 13 months (about 28 mm *1¹¹/₁₀in* per day) by an *Albizzia falcata* planted on 17 Jun 1974 in Sabah, Malaysia.

Most leaves Little work has been done on the laborious task of establishing which species has the most leaves. A large oak has perhaps 250,000, but a cypress may have some 45–50 million leaf scales.

Remotest tree The most remote tree is believed to be a solitary Norwegian spruce on Campbell Island, Antarctica, whose nearest companion would be over 222km *120 nautical miles* away on the Auckland Islands.

Largest forest The largest afforested areas in the world are the vast coniferous forests of northern Russia, lying between Lat. 55°N and the Arctic Circle. The total wooded area covers 1.1 billion ha *2.7*

Tallest Trees in the British Isles

Species	Location	m	ft
ALDER (Italian)	Westonbirt, Glos	34	111
ASH	Rossie Priory, Tayside	38	124
BEECH	Tullynally Castle, Co. Westmeath	40	132
BIRCH (Silver)	Savill Gardens, Windsor, Berks	30	98
CEDAR (of Lebanon)	Leaton Knolls, Shrops	43	141
CHESTNUT (Horse)	Rectory, Much Hadham, Herts	36	118
CHESTNUT (Sweet)	Reigate Park, Surrey	39	128
CYPRESS (Lawson)	Balmacaan, Highlands	42	138
EUCALYPTUS (Blue gum)	Glencormack, Co. Wicklow	44	144
FIR (Douglas)	The Hermitage, Perth, Tayside	64.5	212
	Dunans, Argyll	64.5	212
FIR (Grand)	Strone, Strathclyde	63	206
GINKGO	Sezincote, Glos	26	98
GINKGO	Bitton, Glos	26	85
HEMLOCK (Western)	Benmore, Argyll, Strathclyde	51	167
HOLLY	Hallyburton, Tayside	23	75
LARCH (European)	Glenlee, Dumfries & Galloway	46	150
LIME	Duncombe Park, Helmsley, N Yorks	44	144
METSEQUOIA	Leonardslee, Sussex	28	92
MONKEY PUZZLE	Bicton, Devon	30	98
OAK (Turkey)	Knightshayes, Tiverton, Devon	40	132
OAK (Common)[1]	Abbotsbury, Dorset	40	132
PINE (Corsican)	Adhurst St. Mary, Petersfield, Hants	46	150
PLANE	Bryanston School, Blandford, Dorset	48	156
POPLAR (Black Italian)	Lincoln Arboretum, Lincoln	44	144
SEQUOIA (Wellingtonia)[2]	Castle Leod, Strathpeffer, Highland	53	174
SPRUCE (Sitka)	Strathearn, Tayside	61	200
SYCAMORE	Lennoxlove, Haddington, Lothian	40	132
WALNUT (Black)	Much Hadham Rectory, Herts	36	118
WILLOW (Weeping)	Radnor Gardens, London	25	82
YEW[3]	Belvoir Castle, Leics	29	95

[1] The largest English Oaks are both 384 cm in diameter at Bowthorpe in Lincs and Fredville in Kent.
[2] The largest Sequoia (Wellingtonia) is 345 cm in diameter and is at Clunie Gardens, Tayside.
[3] The largest Yew is 334 cm in diameter at Ulcombe Church, Kent

Source: The Tree Register of the British Isles

■ The maidenhair tree of Zhejiang, China, first appeared about 160 million years ago during the Jurassic era.
(Photo: Jacana/R. Durand)

Inset: a close-up of the maidenhair leaves.
(Photo: Jacana/D. Lecourt)

billion acres. In comparison, the largest area of tropical forest is the Amazon rainforest, covering some 330 million ha *815 million acres*.

UK The largest forest in Britain is the Kielder Forest District in Northumberland, covering 39,380 ha *97,309 acres*.

Largest hedges The world's tallest and longest hedge is the Meikleour beech hedge in Perthshire, planted in 1746 by Jean Mercer and her husband Robert Murray Nairne. Its tapered height when trimmed now varies from 24.4 m *80 ft* to 36.6 m *120 ft* along its length of 550 m *1804 ft*. Trimming takes place every 10 years or so and was last completed in six weeks in 1988.

A yew hedge planted in 1720 in Earl Bathurst's Park, Cirencester, Glos runs for 155.5 m *510 ft*, reaches 11 m *36 ft* in height and is 4.5 m *15 ft* thick at its base. The hedge is trimmed annually, in August, occupying two men for 12 days. The hedge trimmings are used in research work in the fight against cancer.

The tallest box hedge is 11 m *36 ft* high, and grows at Birr Castle, Co. Offaly, Republic of Ireland. It is at least three centuries old.

Longest avenue of trees The world's longest avenue is the Nikko Cryptomeria Avenue comprising three parts converging on Imaichi City in the Tochigi Prefecture of Japan, with a total length of 35.41 km

Hedge laying Steven Forsyth and Lewis Stephens of Sennybridge, Brecon, hedged by the 'stake and pleach' method a total of 280.7 m *920 ft 11 in* in 11 hr on 23 Apr 1994.

22 miles. Planted in 1628–48, over 13,500 of its original 200,000 Japanese cedar (*Cryptomeria japonica*) trees survive, at an average height of 27 m *88½ ft*.

UK The longest avenue of trees in Great Britain is the privately-owned stretch of 1750 beeches measuring 5.8 km *3.6 miles* in Savernake Forest, near Marlborough, Wilts.

Tree planting The most trees to have been planted in one day by an unlimited number of volunteers is 10,136. The trees were planted as part of a project called 'Pinte Bauru de Verde' (Paint Bauru Green) in Bauru, Sao Paulo, Brazil, on 15 Jun 1993.

During National Tree Week, between 25 Nov and 5 Dec 1993, 300 schoolchildren and adults from the Walsall area planted 1774 trees in 17 hr 20 min (over six days).

Tree sitting
The duration record for staying in a tree is more than 24 years, by Bungkas, who went up a palm tree in the Indonesian village of Bengkes in 1970 and has been there ever since. He lives in a nest which he made from branches and leaves. Repeated efforts have been made to persuade him to come down, but without success.

Tree climbing The fastest time up a 30.5 m *100 ft* fir spar pole and back down to the ground is 24.82 sec, by Guy German of Sitka, Alaska, USA on 3 Jul 1988 at the World Championship Timber Carnival in Albany, Oregon, USA. The fastest time up a 9 m *29 ft 6 in* coconut tree barefoot is 4.88 sec, by Fuatai Solo, 17, in Sukuna Park, Fiji on 22 Aug 1980.

Tree topping Guy German climbed a 30.5 m *100 ft* spar pole and sawed off the top (circumference of 100 cm *40 in*) in a record time of 53.35 sec at Albany, Oregon, USA on 3 Jul 1989.

Wood cutting The first recorded lumberjack sports competition was held in 1572 in the Basque region of Spain.

The following records were set at the Lumberjack World Championships at Hayward, Wisconsin, USA (founded 1960):

Power saw (three slices of a 51 cm *20 in* diameter white-pine log with a single-engine saw from dead start)—7.45 sec by Rick Halvorson (US) in 1994.

Bucking (one slice from a 51 cm *20 in* diameter white-pine log with a crosscut saw)—one-man, 16.05 sec by Melvin Lentz (US) in 1994; two-man, 6.67 sec by Mike Slingerland and Matt Bush (both US) in 1994.

Standing block chop (chopping through a vertical 35.5 cm *14 in* diameter white-pine log 76 cm *30 in* in length)—22.05 sec by Melvin Lentz (US) in 1988.

Underhand block chop (chopping through a horizontal 35.5 cm *14 in* diameter white-pine log 76 cm *30 in* in length)—17.84 sec by Laurence O'Toole (Australia) in 1985.

Springboard chopping (scaling a 2.7 m *9 ft* spar pole on springboards and chopping a 35.5 cm *14 in* diameter white-pine log)—1 min 18.45 sec by Bill Youd (Australia) in 1985.

Microbes

Microbes are measured in microns (μm), where 1 μm is one thousandth of a millimetre. A human hair is approximately 80 μm thick. A typical bacterium might measure about 5 μm × 1 μm.

Largest microbe The largest known protozoans in terms of volume are the extinct calcareous foraminifera (Foraminiferida) of the genus *Nummulites*. Individuals measuring up to 150 mm *6 in* wide were found in the Middle Eocene rocks of Turkey.

The largest existing protozoan, a species of the fan-shaped *Stannophyllum* (Xenophyophorida), can exceed this in length (25 cm *9¾ in* has been recorded), but not in volume.

Smallest free-living entity The smallest of all free-living organisms are pleuro-pneumonia-like organisms (PPLO) of the *Mycoplasma*. One of these, *Mycoplasma laidlawii*, first discovered in

sewage in 1936, has a diameter during its early existence of only 10^{-7} m. Examples of the strain known as H.39 have a maximum diameter of 3×10^{-7} m and weigh an estimated 10^{-16} g. Thus a 190-tonne blue whale would weigh 1.9×10^{24} times as much.

Highest microbe In April 1967 the US National Aeronautics and Space Administration (NASA) reported that bacteria had been discovered at an altitude of 41.13 km *25½ miles*.

Fastest microbe By means of a polar flagellum rotating 100 times/sec, the rod-shaped bacillus *Bdellovibrio bacteriovorus* can travel 50 times its own length of 2 μm per sec. This would be the equivalent of a human sprinter reaching 320 km/h *200 mph*, or a swimmer crossing the English Channel in 6 min.

Toughest

Toughest microbe The bacterium *Micrococcus radiodurans* can withstand atomic radiation of 6.5 million röntgens, or 10,000 times that fatal to the average human.

In March 1983 John Barras of the University of Oregon, USA reported bacteria from sulphurous seabed vents thriving at 306°C *583°F* in the East Pacific Rise at Lat. 21°N.

Fastest reproduction The protozoan *Glaucoma*, which reproduces by binary fission, divides as frequently as every three hours. Thus in the course of a day it could become a great-great-great-great-great-great grandparent and the progenitor of 512 descendants.

Fungi

Fungi were once classified in the subkingdom Protophyta of the kingdom Protista.

Largest fungi The world's largest fungus is a single living clonal growth of the underground fungus *Armillaria ostoyae*, reported in May 1992 as covering some 600 ha *1500 acres* in the forests of Washington state, USA. Estimates based on its size suggest that the fungus is 500–1000 years old, but no attempts have been made to estimate its weight. Also known as the honey or shoestring fungus, it fruits above ground as edible gilled mushrooms.

Heaviest A single living clonal growth of the fungus *Armillaria bulbosa*, reported on 2 Apr 1992 to be covering about 15 ha *37 acres* of forest in Michigan, USA, was calculated to weigh over 100 tonnes, which is comparable with blue whales. The organism is thought to have originated from a single fertilized spore at least 1500 years ago.

Largest edible fungi A giant puffball (*Calvatia gigantea*) measuring 2.64 m *8 ft 8 in* in circumference and weighing 22 kg *48½ lb* was found by Jean-Guy Richard of Montreal, Canada in 1987.

Heaviest An example of the edible chicken of the woods mushroom (*Laetiporus sulphureus*) weighing 45.4 kg *100 lb* was found in the New Forest, Hants by Giovanni Paba of Broadstone, Dorset on 15 Oct 1990.

■ *Nummulites laevigatus* from the Middle Eocene rocks of Turkey, an example of the largest known protozoans in terms of volume. (Photo: Jacana/N. Le Roy)

The largest recorded tree fungus is the bracket fungus *Rigidoporus ulmarius* growing from dead elm wood in the grounds of the International Mycological Institute at Kew, Surrey. It measured 150×144 cm *59×56¾ in* with a circumference of 454 cm *178¾ in*. In 1992 it was growing at a rate of 22.5 cm *9 in* per year but this has now slowed.

Most poisonous fungi The yellowish-olive death cap (*Amanita phalloides*), which can be found in Britain, is the world's most poisonous fungus, responsible for 90 per cent of fatal poisonings caused by fungi. Its total toxin content is 7–9 mg dry weight, whereas the estimated lethal amount of amatoxins for humans, depending on bodyweight, is only 5–7 mg—equivalent to less than 50 g *1¾ oz* of a fresh fungus. From 6–15 hours after eating, the effects are vomiting, delirium, collapse and death. Among its victims was Cardinal Giulio de' Medici, Pope Clement VII (b. 1478) on 25 Sep 1534.

Aeroflora The highest recorded total fungal spore count was 5,686,861/m³ *161,037/ft³* near Cardiff, S Glam on 21 Jul 1971. The lowest counts of airborne allergens are nil.

Parks, Zoos, Aquaria

Parks

Largest park The world's largest national park is the National Park of North-Eastern Greenland, covering 972,000 km² *375,289 miles²* and stretching from Liverpool Land in the south to the northernmost island, Odaaq Ø, off Pearyland. Established in 1974 and enlarged in 1988, much of the park is covered by ice and is home to a variety of protected flora and fauna, including polar bears, musk ox and birds of prey.

UK The Lake District National Park (designated as such in 1951) is the largest of the 11 National Parks in Great Britain. It covers 2243 km² *554,254.2 acres* and lies wholly in Cumbria. The largest private park is Woburn Park (1200 ha *3000 acres*), near Woburn Abbey, the seat of the Dukes of Bedford.

Largest game reserve The world's largest zoological reserve is the Etosha National Park in Namibia. Established in 1907, it now covers 99,525 km² *38,427 miles²*.

Zoos

Oldest zoo The earliest known collection of animals was established by Shulgi, a 3rd-dynasty ruler of Ur from 2097–2094 BC at Puzurish, Iraq.

Without bars The earliest zoo without bars was at Stellingen, near Hamburg, Germany. It was founded in 1907 by Carl Hagenbeck (1844–1913), who used deep pits and large pens instead of cages to separate the exhibits from the visitors.

Aquaria

Largest aquaria In terms of the volume of water held, the Living Seas main tank at the EPCOT Center's Living Seas Pavillion in Florida, USA is the world's largest, with a total capacity of 5.7 million gal *21.2 million litres*. The tank, opened to the public in 1986, is 3251.5 m² *35,000 ft²*, with walls measuring 14.6 m *48 ft* high. The tank contains nearly 8000 aquatic specimens, comprising approximately 85 different species of Caribbean reef fish.

The largest in terms of marine-life is the Monterey Bay Aquarium in California, USA, which houses 6500 specimens (525 species) of flora and fauna in its 86 tanks. The volume of water held is 3,785,000 litres *1 million gal*.

Origins

Earliest Man

If the age of the Earth-Moon system (latest estimate 4540 ± 40 million years) is likened to a single year, hominids appeared on the scene at about 3:35p.m. on 31 December. Britain's earliest traceable inhabitants arrived at about 10:50p.m. and the life span of a 120-year-old person would be 0.83 seconds.

Man (*Homo sapiens*) is a species in the sub-family Homininae of the family Hominidae of the super-family Hominoidea of the sub-order Simiae (or Anthropoidea) of the order Primates of the infra-class Eutheria of the sub-class Theria of the class Mammalia of the sub-phylum Vertebrata (Craniata) of the phylum Chordata of the sub-kingdom Metazoa of the animal kingdom.

Earliest Primates Primates appeared in the late Cretaceous epoch about 65 million years ago. The earliest members of the sub-order Anthropoidea are known from both Africa and South America in the early Oligocene era, 30–34 million years ago. Finds from Faiyûm, Egypt represent primates from the early Oligocene period, 37 million years.

Earliest hominoid A jaw-bone with three molars found in the Otavi Hills, Namibia on 4 Jun 1991, has been dated to 12–13 million years and named *Otavi pithecus namibiensis*.

Earliest hominid An Australopithecine jaw-bone, with two molars 5cm *2in* long was found near Lake Baringo, Kenya in February 1984. It has been dated to 4 million years ago by associated fossils and to 5.4–5.6 million years ago through rock correlation by potassium-argon dating.

Earliest genus Homo The earliest species of this genus is *Homo habilis*, or 'Handy Man', from Olduvai Gorge, Tanzania, named by Louis Leakey, Philip Tobias and John Napier in 1964 after a suggestion from Prof. Raymond Arthur Dart (1893–1988). The greatest age attributed to fossils of this genus is about 2.4 million years for a piece of cranium found in western Kenya in 1965.

Oldest mummy
Mummification dates from 2600 BC or the 4th dynasty of the Egyptian pharaohs. The oldest complete mummy is of Wati, a court musician of c. 2400 BC from the tomb of Nefer in Saqqàra, Egypt, found in 1944.

Earliest Homo erectus This species (upright man), the direct ancestor of *Homo sapiens*, was discovered by Eugène Dubois (Netherlands) (1858–1940) at Trinil, Java in 1891. Javan *H. erectus* were dated to 1.8 million years in 1994.

Earliest human presence in Great Britain Pieces of a brain case from a specimen of *Homo sapiens* were recovered in June 1935 and March 1936 from the Boyn Hill Terrace in the Barnfield Pit, near Swanscombe, Kent. The remains were associated with a Middle Acheulian tool culture and probably date from either the Hoxnian or an earlier Interglacial Stage. Amino-acid dates for the Swanscombe deposits suggest an age of 400,000 years.

Guess What?
Q. What was the world's tallest building until 1930?
A. See Page 59

■ **Jeanne Calment**
(Photo: Gamma/ Figaro Magazine/ N'Guyen)

Dimensions

However, Lower Palaeolithic hand-axes from the Waverley Wood Farm site, Warwicks and the hand-axe factory and occupation site at Boxgrove, W Sussex may date from more than 600,000 years ago. Sites showing evidence of Acheulian culture represent the earliest evidence of a human presence in Britain.

In 1988, radiocarbon dating showed a jaw-bone of *Homo sapiens sapiens* (i.e. anatomically modern man) from a cave near Torquay, Devon, to be 31,000 years old.

The tallest authenticated human being was Robert Wadlow, a record that stands to this day. It is likely that this will never be bettered due to advances in medical science which allow an individual's growth to be controlled to some extent. Consequently, a height approaching Wadlow's could, and most probably would, be avoided for health reasons.

■ In September 1991, the mummy of a Neolithic man was discovered in a melting glacier in the Tyrolean Alps on the Italian-Austrian border. Analysis of 'Ötzi' and his belongings have given a new insight into the technology and culture of central Europe some 5000 years ago. The discoveries have also confirmed a number of predictions and deductions archaeologists had made for this particular period. The picture shows the world's most accomplished mountaineer, Reinhold Messner, examining the body during thawing/extrication.
(Photo: Gamma/P. Hanny)

Giants

Introduction Growth of the body is determined by growth hormone. This is produced by the pituitary gland in the brain. Over-production in childhood produces abnormal growth and gigantism is the result. The true height of human giants is frequently obscured by exaggeration and commercial dishonesty. Giants exhibited in circuses and exhibitions are routinely under contract not to be measured and are, almost traditionally, billed by their promoters at heights up to 46cm *18in* in excess of their true heights. The only admissible evidence on the actual height of giants is that collected since 1870 under impartial medical supervision.

Tallest men The tallest man in medical history for whom there is irrefutable evidence is Robert Pershing Wadlow, born at 6:30a.m. at Alton, Illinois, USA on 22 Feb 1918. When he was last measured, on 27 Jun 1940, he was found to be 8ft 11.1in *272cm* tall (arm-span 9ft 5¾in *288cm*).

Wadlow died at 1:30 a.m. on 15 Jul 1940 in a hotel in Manistee, Michigan, as a result of a septic blister on his right ankle caused by a poorly fitting brace. He was still growing during his terminal illness and would probably have ultimately reached or just exceeded 9ft *274cm* in height if he had survived for another year.

His greatest recorded weight was 35st 1lb *222.7kg* on his 21st birthday and when he died he weighed 31st 5lb *199kg*. His shoes were size 37AA (18½in *47cm*) and his hands measured 12¾in *32.4cm* from the wrist to the tip of the middle finger.

Tallest in Great Britain William Bradley (1787–1820), born in Market Weighton, East Riding (now Humberside), stood 7ft 9in *236cm*.

John Middleton (1578–1623) of Hale, near Liverpool, was credited with a height of 9ft 3in *282cm* but a life-size impression of his right hand (length 11½in *29.2cm*, cf. Wadlow's 12¾in *32.4cm*) painted on a panel in Brasenose College, Oxford indicates that his true stature was nearer 7ft 9in *236cm*.

Ireland Patrick Cotter (O'Brien) (1760–1806), born in Kinsale, Co. Cork, was 8ft 1in *246cm* tall. He died at Hotwells, Bristol.

Tallest living person Haji Mohammad Alam Channa (Pakistan) (b. 1956) and the world's tallest living woman, Sandy Allen (USA) (b. 18 Jun 1955) (⇨Tallest women), are both around 7ft 7¼in *231.7cm* tall.

UK The tallest man living in the UK is Christopher Paul Greener (b. New Brighton, Merseyside, 21 Nov 1943) of Hayes, Kent, who measures 7ft 6¼in *229cm* (weight 26st *165kg*).

True Giant

The world's tallest recorded 'true' (non-pathological) giant was Angus Macaskill (1823–63), born on the island of Berneray in the Sound of Harris, Western Isles. He stood 7ft 9in *236cm* and died in St Ann's, Cape Breton Island, Nova Scotia, Canada. His grandfather, Angus, was also a giant.

Woman

The tallest living woman is Sandy Allen (USA) (b. 18 Jun 1955) who is currently 7ft 7¼in *231.7cm*. Her abnormal growth began soon after birth, she stood 6ft 3in *190.5cm* by the age of 10 and was 7ft 1in *216cm* by 16. She now weighs 33st *209.5kg* and takes a size 16 EEE American shoe (14½ UK).

Tallest woman Zeng Jinlian (b. 26 Jun 1964) of Yujiang village in the Bright Moon Commune, Hunan Province, central China, measured 8ft 1¾in *248cm* when she died on 13 Feb 1982. This figure represented her height with assumed normal spinal curvature because she suffered from severe scoliosis (curvature of the spine) and could not stand up straight. She began to grow abnormally from the age of four months and stood 5ft 1½in *156cm* before her fourth birthday and 7ft 1½in *217cm* when she was 13. Her hands

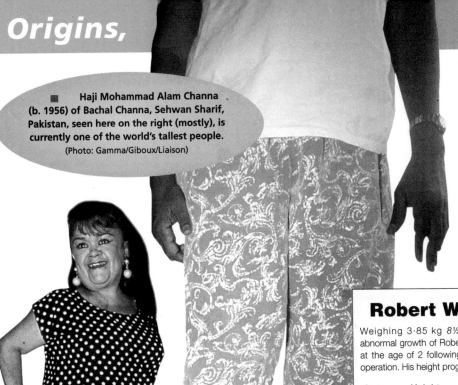

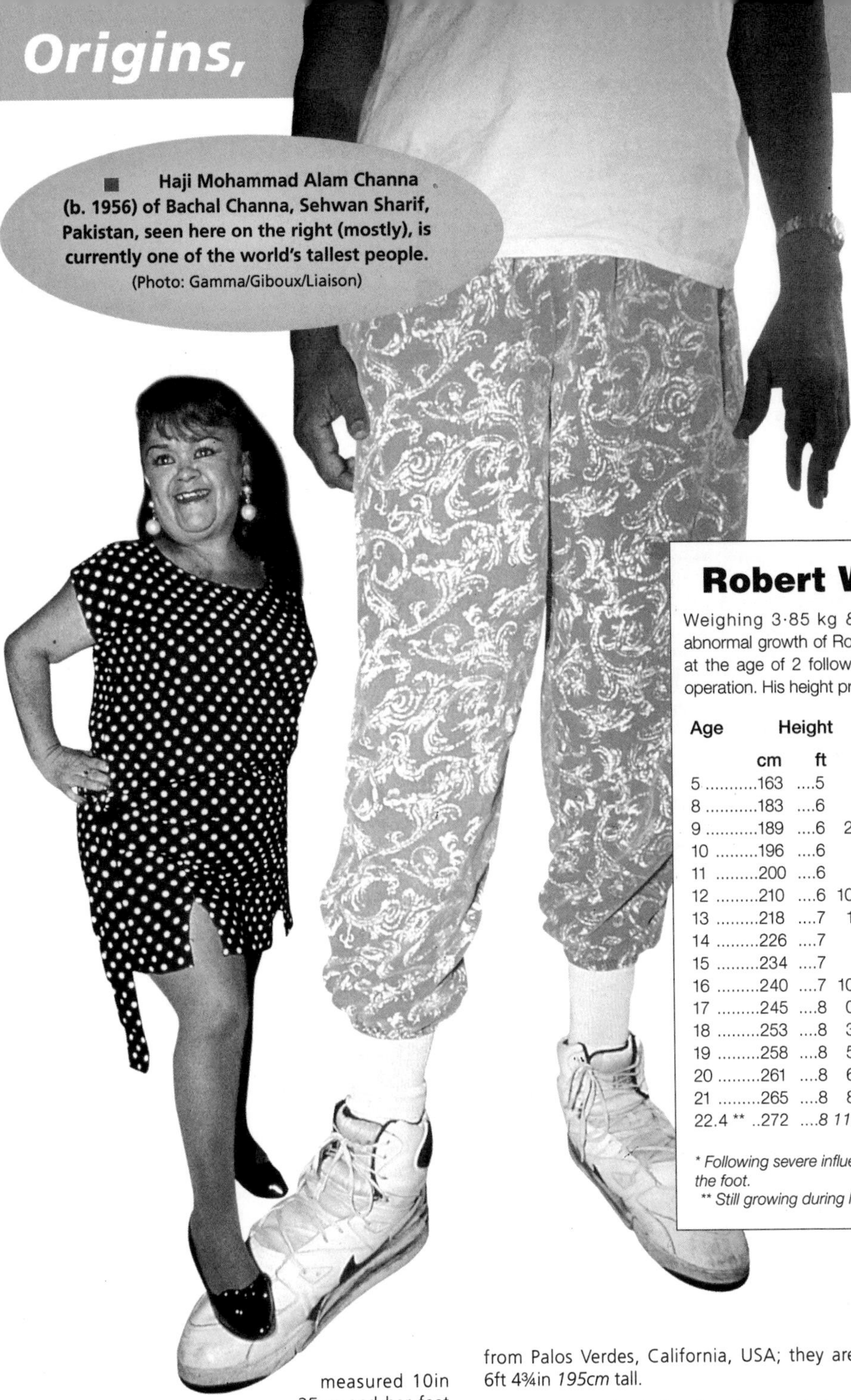

Haji Mohammad Alam Channa (b. 1956) of Bachal Channa, Sehwan Sharif, Pakistan, seen here on the right (mostly), is currently one of the world's tallest people.
(Photo: Gamma/Giboux/Liaison)

2½in *220cm*, making them the tallest married couple on record.

Most dissimilar married couple Fabien Pretou (b. 15 Jun 1968) (188.5cm *6ft 2in*) married Natalie Lucius (b. 19 Jan 1966) (94cm *3ft 1in*) at Seyssinet-Pariset, France on 14 Apr 1990, a height difference of 94.5cm *37in*.

Most variable stature Adam Rainer, born in Graz, Austria in 1899, measured 118cm *3ft 10½in* at the age of 21. He then suddenly started growing at a rapid rate and by 1931, he had reached 218cm *7ft 1¾in*. He became so weak as a result that he was bedridden for the rest of his life. At the time of his death on 4 Mar 1950, aged 51, he measured 234cm *7ft 8in* and was the only person in medical history to have been both a dwarf and a giant.

Robert Wadlow

Weighing 3·85 kg *8½lb* at birth, the abnormal growth of Robert Wadlow started at the age of 2 following a double hernia operation. His height progressed as follows:

Age	Height			Weight	
	cm	ft	in	kg	lb
5	163	5	4	48	105
8	183	6	0	77	169
9	189	6	2¼	82	180
10	196	6	5	95	210
11	200	6	7	–	–
12	210	6	10½	–	–
13	218	7	1¾	116	255
14	226	7	5	137	301
15	234	7	8	161	355
16	240	7	10¼	170	374
17	245	8	0½	*143	315
18	253	8	3½	–	–
19	258	8	5½	218	480
20	261	8	6¾	–	–
21	265	8	8¼	223	491
22.4 **	272	8	11¹⁄₁₀	199	439

* Following severe influenza and infection of the foot.
** Still growing during his terminal illness.

Dwarfs

Introduction The strictures that apply to giants apply equally to dwarfs—exaggeration gives way to understatement. In the same way as 9ft *274cm* is the limit towards which the tallest giants tend, so 22in *56cm* is the limit towards which the shortest adult dwarfs or midgets tend (cf. the average length of new-born babies is 18–20in *46–50cm*).

Shortest person The shortest mature human of whom there is independent evidence is Gul Mohammed (b. 15 Feb 1957) of New Delhi, India. On 19 Jul 1990 he was examined at Ram Manohar Hospital, New Delhi, and found to measure 22½in *57cm* in height (weight 37½lb *17kg*). The other members of his immediate family are of normal height.

The shortest ever female has been Pauline Musters, known as 'Princess Pauline'. She was born at Ossendrecht, Netherlands on 26 Feb 1876 and measured 12in *30cm* at birth. At nine years of age she was 21½in *55cm* tall and weighed only 3lb 5oz *1.5kg*. She died of pneumonia with meningitis on 1 Mar 1895 in New York City, USA at the age of 19. A post mortem examination showed her to be exactly 24in *61cm* (there was some elongation after death). Her mature weight varied from 7½–9lb *3.4–4kg* and her 'vital statistics' were 18½–19–17in *47–48–43cm*, which suggest she was overweight.

Great Britain The shortest mature human ever recorded in Britain was Joyce Carpenter (1929–73), of Charford, now Hereford & Worcester, who stood 29in *74cm* tall and weighed 30lb *13.6kg*. She suffered from Morquio's disease which causes deformities of the spine and shortening of the neck and trunk.

measured 10in *25cm* and her feet 14in *35.5cm* in length. Both her parents and her brother were of normal size.

GB The tallest woman in British medical history was Jane 'Ginny' Bunford, (b. 26 Jul 1895) of Bartley Green, Northfield, Birmingham. Her skeleton, now preserved in the Anatomical Museum in the Medical School at Birmingham University, measures 7ft 4in *223.5cm* high. Her abnormal growth started at the age of 11 following a head injury, and on her 13th birthday she measured 6ft 6in *198cm*. Shortly before her death on 1 Apr 1922 she stood 7ft 7in *231cm* tall, but she had severe kyphoscoliosis and would have measured at least 7ft 11in *241cm* if she had been able to stand fully erect.

Tallest twins *World* Michael and James Lanier (b. 27 Nov 1969) of Troy, Michigan, USA both stand 7ft 4in *223.5cm*. Their sister Jennifer is 5ft 2in *157cm* tall.

The world's tallest female twins are Heather and Heidi Burge (b. 11 Nov 1971)

from Palos Verdes, California, USA; they are both 6ft 4¾in *195cm* tall.

UK The tallest identical male twins recorded were the Knipe brothers (b. 1761) of Magherafelt, near Londonderry, who both measured 7ft 2in *218cm*.

The tallest living male twins are Andrew and Timothy Hull (b. 23 and 24 Oct 1968 respectively) of Redditch, Worcs, who are 6ft 9.3in *206.5cm* and 6ft 10.3in *209cm* respectively.

The tallest identical female twins are: Daphne Turner and Evelyn Staniford (*née* Gould) (b. 28 Apr 1931) both 6ft ½in *184cm* tall, and Nestor Long and Patricia Reed-Boswell (*née* Reed) (b. 11 Nov 1945) who measure 6ft ¾in *185cm* and 6ft ¼in *183cm*, respectively .

Tallest married couple Anna Hanen Swan (1846–88) of Nova Scotia, Canada was said to be 8ft 1in *246cm* but actually measured 7ft 5½in *227cm*. On 18 Jun 1871, she married Martin van Buren Bates (1845–1919) of Whitesburg, Letcher County, Kentucky, USA, who stood 7ft

Guess What?
Q. Who are the world's heaviest twins?
A. See Page 56

Oldest

There are only two centenarian dwarfs on record. The older was Hungarian-born Susanna Bokoyni (b. 6 Apr 1879), alias 'Princess Susanna', of Newton, New Jersey, USA, who died aged 105 years on 24 Aug 1984. She was 101.5cm *3ft 4in* tall.

The other was Miss Anne Clowes of Matlock, Derbys, who died on 5 Aug 1784 aged 103 years. She was 3ft 9in *114cm* tall.

■ **Madge Bester (far right) of Johannesburg, South Africa is the world's shortest living woman and is only 65cm 25.5in tall.**
(Photo: Gamma/D. Barrit)

Hopkins Hopkins (1737–54) of Llantrisant, Mid-Glamorgan, who suffered from progeria, was 31in *79cm* tall. He weighed 19lb *8.6kg* at the age of 7 and 13lb *6kg* at the time of his death.

Shortest living person *Female* Madge Bester (b. 26 Apr 1963) of Johannesburg, South Africa, is only 65cm 25.5in tall. However, she suffers from Osteogenesis imperfecta (characterized by brittle bones and other deformities of the skeleton) and is confined to a wheelchair. Her mother Winnie is not much taller, measuring 70cm *27½in*, and is also confined to a wheelchair.

UK The shortest living person in the UK is Michael Henbury-Ballan (b. 26 Nov 1958) of Bassett, Southampton, Hants who is 94cm *37in* tall and weighs 35kg *5½st*. He weighed 2.66kg *5lb 14oz* at birth and he stopped growing at the age of 13. His twin brother Malcolm is 175cm *5ft 9in* tall and weighs 73kg *11st 7lb*.

Patrick Scanlan (b. 1966) of Maida Vale, London stands 91cm *36in* tall and weighs only 19kg *42lb*, but he suffers from MPS, an enzyme disease that causes severe bone abnormalities, including curvature of the spine, and cannot stand erect. He stopped growing at the age of 4 years.

Shortest twins Matjus and Bela Matina (b. 1903–fl. 1935) of Budapest, Hungary, who later became naturalized American citizens, both measured 76cm *30in*.

Living John and Greg Rice (b. 3 Dec 1951) of West Palm Beach, Florida, USA, both measure 86.3cm *34in*.

The shortest identical twin sisters are Dorene Williams of Oakdale and Darlene McGregor of Almeda, California, USA (b. 1949), who each stand 124.4cm *4ft 1in*.

Weight

Heaviest person The heaviest person in medical history was Jon Brower Minnoch (1941–83) of Bainbridge Island, Washington State, USA, who had suffered from obesity since childhood. He was 6ft 1in *185cm* tall, and weighed 28st *178kg* in 1963, 50st *317kg* in 1966 and 69st 9lb *442kg* in September 1976.

In March 1978, Minnoch was rushed to University Hospital, Seattle, saturated with fluid and suffering from heart and respiratory failure. It took a dozen firemen and an improvized stretcher to move him from his home to a ferry-boat. When he arrived at the hospital he was put in two beds lashed together. It took 13 people just to roll him over. Consultant endocrinologist Dr Robert Schwartz calculated that Minnoch must have weighed more than 100st *635kg* when he was admitted, a great deal of which was water accumulation due to his congestive heart failure. After nearly two years on a diet of 1200 calories per day, he was discharged at 34st *216kg*. In October 1981 he had to be readmitted, after putting on over 14st *89kg*. When he died on 10 Sep 1983 he weighed more than 57st *362kg*.

Great Britain Peter Yarnall of East Ham, London weighed 58st *368kg* and was 5ft 10in *178cm* tall. He began putting on weight at a rapid rate in 1978 and for the last two years of his life he was bedridden. He died on 30 Mar 1984 aged 34 years and it took 10 firemen five hours to demolish the

wall of his bedroom and winch his body down to street level.

Heaviest living person The heaviest living man is T. J. Albert Jackson (b. 1941 as Kent Nicholson) of Canton, Mississippi, USA. He weighs 63st 9lb *404kg*, his chest measurement is 120in *305cm*, his waist 116in *294cm*, his thighs 70in *178cm*, and his neck 29½in *75cm*.

Great Britain The professional wrestler Martin Ruane, alias Luke McMasters ('Giant Haystacks'), who was born in Camberwell, London in 1946, once claimed to be 50st *317kg*. His weight fluctuates between 45st *286kg* and 46st *292kg* and he is 6ft 11in *211cm* tall.

Heaviest female Rosalie Bradford (USA) (b. 27 Aug 1943) is claimed to have registered a peak weight of 85st *544kg* in January 1987. In August of that year she developed congestive heart failure and was rushed to hospital. She was consequently put on a carefully controlled diet and by February 1994 weighed 20st 3lb *128kg* (⇨Weight loss). Her target weight is 10st 10lb *68kg*.

Great Britain The heaviest woman ever recorded was Mrs Muriel Hopkins (b. 1931) of Tipton, W Mids, who weighed 43st 11lb *278kg* (height 5ft 11in *180cm*) in 1978. Shortly before her death on 22 Apr 1979 she weighed 47st 7lb *301kg*.

Heaviest twins Billy Leon (1946–79) and Benny Loyd (b. 7 Dec 1946) McCrary, alias McGuire, of Hendersonville, North Carolina, USA were normal in size until the age of six. In November 1978, Billy and Benny weighed 53st 1lb *337kg* and 51st 9lb *328kg* respectively, and each had waists measuring 84in *213cm*. As professional tag wrestling performers they were billed at weights up to 55st *349kg*. Billy died at Niagara Falls, Ontario, Canada on 13 Jul 1979.

Greatest weight loss Jon Brower Minnoch (⇨ Heaviest male) who weighed 100st *635kg* had reduced to 34st *216kg* by July 1979, thus indicating a weight loss of at least 66st *419kg* in 16 months.

Female Rosalie Bradford (⇨ Heaviest female) went from a weight of 1200lb *544kg* in January 1987 to 283lb *128kg* in February 1994, a loss of a record 917lb *416kg*.

Great Britain Dolly Wager (b. 1933) of Charlton, London, between September 1971 and 22 May 1973 reduced her weight from 31st 7lb *200kg* to 11st *70kg*, so losing 20st 7lb *130kg*.

Sweating Ron Allen (b. 1947) sweated off 21½lb *9.7kg* of his weight of 17st 1lb *113kg* in Nashville, Tennessee, USA in 24 hours in August 1984.

Lightest person Lucia Xarate (1863–89) of San Carlos, Mexico, an emaciated ateleiotic dwarf of 26½in *67cm*, weighed 2.13kg *4.7lb* at the age of 17. She 'fattened up' to 13lb *5.9kg* by her 20th birthday. At birth she weighed 2½lb *1.1kg*.

Great Britain The lightest adult was Hopkins Hopkins (⇨ Dwarfs).

Net Gain

Jon Brower Minnoch (⇨ Heaviest male) gained 14st *89kg* in 7 days in October 1981 before readmittance to University of Washington Hospital, Seattle, USA. Arthur Knorr (USA) (1916–60) gained 21st *133kg* in the last six months of his life.

Miss Doris James of San Francisco, California, USA is alleged to have gained 23st 3lb *147kg* in the 12 months before her death in August 1965, aged 38, at a weight of 48st 3lb *306kg*. She was only 5ft 2in *157cm* tall.

Guess What?
Q. How much does the Earth weigh?
A. See Page 11

Reproductivity

Motherhood

Most children The greatest officially recorded number of children born to one mother is 69, to the wife of Feodor Vassilyev (b. 1707–*fl.*1782), a peasant from Shuya, Moscow, Russia. In 27 confinements she gave birth to 16 pairs of twins, seven sets of triplets and four sets of quadruplets. The case was reported to Moscow by the Monastery of Nikolskiy on 27 Feb 1782. Only two of the children who were born in the period c. 1725–65 failed to survive their infancy.

The world's most prolific mother is currently believed to be Leontina Albina (*née* Espinosa) (b. 1925) of San Antonio, Chile, who in 1981 produced her 55th and last child. Her husband, Gerardo Secunda Albina (variously Alvina) (b. 1921), states that they were married in Argentina in 1943 and had 5 sets of triplets (all boys) before coming to Chile.

UK Elizabeth, wife of John Mott whom she married in 1676, of Monks Kirby, Warks, had 42 children. She died in 1720.

Mrs Elizabeth Greenhille (died 1681) of Abbots Langley, Herts is alleged to have had 39 children (32 daughters, seven sons) in a record 38 confinements.

In this century, Margaret McNaught (b. 1923), of Balsall Heath, Birmingham, had 12 boys and 10 girls in single confinements; two boys died in infancy. Mabel Constable (b. 1920), of Long Itchington, Warwicks, also had 22 children, including a set of triplets and two sets of twins.

Ireland Mrs Kathleen Scott (b. 4 Jul 1914) of Dublin gave birth to her 24th child on 9 Aug 1958.

Oldest mother It was reported that Rossanna Dalla Corta (b. February 1931) of Viterbo, Italy gave birth to a baby boy on 18 Jul 1994. Menopause is the end of a women's reproductive life and occurs in the majority of women between the ages of 45 and 55 years. Recent hormonal techniques, however, have led to post-menopausal women becoming fertile. It is therefore now feasible for a women of *any* age to become pregnant.

> **Heaviest twins** The world's heaviest, weighing 27lb 12oz *12.6kg*, were born to Mrs J.P. Haskin, Fort Smith, Arkansas, USA on 20 Feb 1924.

■ **Mildred Widman Philippi and Mary Widman Franzini of St Louis, Missouri, USA, the oldest female twins, celebrated their 104th birthday on 17 Jun 1984. Mildred sadly died on 4 May 1985.**
(Photo: Gamma/Stricklin)

The only other reported birthweight in excess of 20lb *9kg* is 20lb 2oz *9.13kg* for a boy born to a 33-year-old schoolmistress in Crewe, Cheshire on 12 Nov 1884.

Guy Warwick Carr was born on 9 Mar 1992, the eighth child of Andrew and Nicola Carr (5ft 2in *157cm* tall) of Kirkby-in-Furness, Cumbria, weighing 15lb 8oz *7kg*. He was 25in *63cm* in length and midwives at the Maternity Unit had to raid the Children's Ward for nappies and clothes large enough to fit him.

Heaviest triplets The heaviest triplets in Great Britain, weighing 24lb *10.9kg*, were born to Mrs Mary McDermott of Bearpark, Co Durham on 18 Nov 1914.

Heaviest quadruplets The world's heaviest quadruplets (2 girls, 2 boys), weighing 10.426kg *22lb 15¾oz*, were born to Mrs Tina Saunders at St Peter's Hospital, Chertsey, Surrey on 7 Feb 1989.

Heaviest quintuplets Two cases have been recorded for heaviest quintuplets, with both recording a weight of 25lb *11.35kg*: on 7 Jun 1953 to Mrs Liu Saulian of Zhejiang, China, and on 30 Dec 1956 to Mrs Kamalammal of Pondicherry, India.

Lightest single births A premature baby girl weighing 280g *9.9oz* was reported to have been born on 27 Jun 1989 at the Loyola University Medical Center, Illinois, USA.

Great Britain The lowest birthweight recorded for a surviving infant, of which there is definite evidence, is 10oz *283g* in the case of Marian Taggart (*née* Chapman) (1938–83). She was born six weeks premature in South Shields, Tyne & Wear. She was born unattended (length 12in *30cm*) and was nursed by Dr D.A. Shearer, who fed her hourly for the first 30 hours with brandy, glucose and water through a fountain-pen filler. At three weeks she weighed 1lb 13oz *821g* and by her first birthday 13lb 14oz *6.3kg*. Her weight on her 21st birthday was 7st 8lb *48kg*.

Lightest twins Anne Faith Sarah (420g *14.8oz*) and John Alexander Morrison (440g *15.5oz*) were born to Wendy Kay Morrison at Ottawa General Hospital, Ontario, Canada on 14 Jan 1994.

UK Mary, 16oz *453g*, and Margaret, 19oz *538g*, were born on 16 Aug 1931 to Mrs Florence Stimson, Old Fletton, Peterborough, Cambs.

Longest separated twins Through the help of New Zealand's television programme *Missing* on 27 Apr 1989, Iris (*née* Haughie) Johns and Aro Campbell (b. 13 Jan 1914) were reunited after 75 years' separation.

> **Guess What?**
> Q. Which mammal can breed at the youngest age?
> A. See Page 28

Interval

Danny Petrungaro (*née* Berg) (b. 1953) of Rome, Italy, who had been on hormone treatment after suffering four miscarriages, gave birth normally to a baby girl, Diana, on 22 Dec 1987, but she was not delivered of the other twin, Monica, (by Caesarean section) until 27 Jan 1988, 36 days later.

Jackie Iverson of Saskatoon, Canada gave birth normally to a boy, Christopher, on 21 Nov 1993, a girl, Alexandra, on 29 Nov 1993, and was delivered of another boy and girl, Matthew and Sarah, (by Caesarean), on 30 Nov 1993, a total period of 10 days.

Babies

Heaviest single birth The heaviest baby born to a healthy mother was a boy weighing 10.2kg *22lb 8oz* who was born to Sig. Carmelina Fedele of Aversa, Italy in September 1955.

Mrs Anna Bates (*née* Swan) (Canada) (1846–88), who measured 7ft 5½in *227cm*, gave birth to a boy weighing 23lb 12oz *10.8kg* (length 30in *76cm*) at her home in Seville, Ohio, USA on 19 Jan 1879, but the baby died 11 hours later.

UK It was reported in a letter to the *British Medical Journal* (1 Feb 1879) from a doctor in Torpoint, Cornwall that a child born on Christmas Day 1852 weighed 21lb *9.5kg*.

Most premature baby James Elgin Gill was born to Brenda and James Gill, on 20 May 1987 in Ottawa, Ontario, Canada 128days premature, and weighing 624g 1lb 6oz.

UK Rukaya Bailey was born to Joanne Bailey 122 days premature on 26 Jun 1989 at Salford, Greater Manchester, and weighed 600g 1lb 3oz.

Most premature twins Joanna and Alexander Bagwell were born on 2 Jun 1993 at the John Radcliffe Hospital, Oxford, 114 days premature.

Most premature quadruplets Tina Piper of St Leonards-on-Sea, E Sussex, was delivered of quadruplets on 10 Apr. 1988, at exactly 26 weeks term. Oliver 2lb 9oz 1.16kg, (died February 1989), Francesca 2lb 2oz 0.96kg, Charlotte 2lb 4½oz 1.03kg and Georgina 2lb 5oz 1.05kg were all born at the Royal Sussex County Hospital, Brighton, Sussex.

Multiple Births

'Siamese' twins Conjoined twins derive the name 'Siamese' from the celebrated Chang and Eng Bunker ('Left' and 'Right' in Thai) born at Meklong on 11 May 1811 of Chinese parents. They were joined by a cartilaginous band at the chest. They married (in April 1843) the Misses Sarah and Adelaide Yates of Wilkes County, North Carolina, USA, and fathered 10 and 12 children respectively. They died within three hours of each other on 17 Jan 1874, aged 62.

Quindecaplets

It was announced by Dr Gennaro Montanino of Rome that he had removed, after four months of the pregnancy, the foetuses of ten girls and five boys from the womb of a 35-year-old housewife on 22 Jul 1971. A fertility drug was responsible for this unique instance of quindecaplets.

Rarest The most extreme form of conjoined twins is dicephales tetrabrachius dipus (two heads, four arms and two legs). The only fully reported example is Masha and Dasha Krivoshlyapovy, born in the USSR on 4 Jan 1950.

Earliest successful separation The earliest successful separation of Siamese twins was performed on xiphopagus (joined at the sternum) girls at Mount Sinai Hospital, Cleveland, Ohio, USA by Dr Jac S. Geller on 14 Dec 1952.

Highest number at a single birth Ten children (decaplets) (two males, eight females) were reported to have been born at Bacacay, Brazil on 22 Apr 1946. Reports were also received from Spain in 1924 and China on 12 May 1936.

The highest number medically recorded is nine (nonuplets) born to Mrs. Geraldine Brodrick at the Royal Hospital for Women, Sydney, Australia on 13 Jun 1971. None of the children (five boys [two stillborn] and four girls) lived for more than six days. The birth of nine

Deep-Rooted

The lineage (or family tree) of K'ung Ch'iu or Confucius (551–479BC) can be traced back further than that of any other family. His four greats grandfather K'ung Chia is known from the 8th century BC. K'ung Chia's 85th lineal descendants, Wei-yi (b. 1939) and Wei-ning (b. 1947), live today in Taiwan.

children has also been reported on at least two other occasions; Philadelphia, Pennsylvania, USA, 29 May 1971, and Bagerhat, Bangladesh, c. 11 May 1977; in both cases none survived.

Great Britain The greatest number recorded is seven (septuplets) (four boys, three girls) born to Mrs Susan Halton (b. 1960) at Liverpool Maternity Hospital on 15 Aug 1987—none of the children survived.

Most sets of multiple births in a family *Quintuplets* There is no recorded case of more than a single set.

Quadruplets Four sets to Mme Feodor Vassilyev, Shuya, Russia (died ante 1770) (⇔ Motherhood).

Triplets 15 sets to Maddalena Granata, Italy (b. 1839–fl. 1886).

Twins 16 sets to Mme Vassilyev (⇔ above). Mrs Barbara Zulu of Barberton, South Africa bore 3 sets of girls and 3 mixed sets in seven years (1967–73). Mrs Anna Steynvaait of Johannesburg, South Africa produced 2 sets within 10 months in 1960.

In Britain, Mrs Mary Jonas of Chester (died 4 Sep 1899) bore 15 sets, all mixed.

Descendants

Greatest number of descendants In polygamous countries, the number of a person's descendants can become incalculable. The last Sharifian Emperor of Morocco, Moulay Ismail (1672–1727), known as 'The Bloodthirsty', was reputed to have fathered a total of 525 sons and 342 daughters by 1703 and achieved a 700th son in 1721.

At the time of his death on 15 Oct 1992, Samuel S. Mast, aged 96, of Fryburg, Pennsylvania, USA, had 824 living descendants. The roll call comprised 11 children, 97 grandchildren, 634 great-grandchildren and 82 great-great-grandchildren.

Great Britain Mrs Sarah Crawshaw (died 25 Dec 1844) left 397 descendants according to her gravestone in Stones Church, Ripponden, Halifax, W Yorks.

Seven-generation family Augusta Bunge (née Pagel) (b. 13 Oct 1879) of Wisconsin, USA, learned that she had become a great-great-great-great-great-grandmother when her great-great-great-granddaughter gave birth to a son, Christopher John Bollig, on 21 Jan 1989.

Youngest living great-great-great grandmother Harriet Holmes of Newfoundland, Canada (b. 17 Jan 1899) was 88yr 50days old, when she became a great-great-great-grandmother on 8 Mar 1987.

Most living ascendants At her birth on 16 May 1982, Megan Sue Austin of Bar Harbor, Maine, USA had a full set of grandparents and great-grandparents and five great-great-grandparents, making 19 direct ascendants.

Q. Who are the world's tallest twins? **A.** See Page 55

Q. Who is the UK's oldest ever person? **A.** See Page 60

Longevity

Introduction Centenarians surviving beyond their 113th year are extremely rare and the present absolute proven limit of human longevity does not yet admit of anyone living to celebrate their 121st birthday.

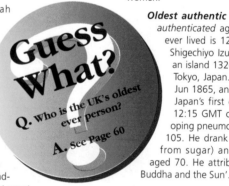

Since the book began, there have only been three people listed as the oldest ever human being, based on official authentication. The first such record holder was Canadian Pierre Joubert who died aged 113yr 124days in 1701. Research in the mid-70s threw light on Delina Felkins (USA) who died aged 113yr 214days in 1928. She remained the record holder until early in 1979 when she was surpassed by Shigechiyo Izumi (Japan). He added progressively to the record for seven years.

However, the next edition of the book may see the addition of a fourth holder of this record, Jeanne Calment. At the time of writing, she had celebrated her 120th birthday and survival to 17 October 1995 would claim the 'title'.

Data on documented centenarians has shown that only one 115-year life can be expected in 2.1 billion lives (cf. world population which was estimated to be c.5480 million by mid-1992).

The number of UK centenarians announced on 23 Dec 1992 comprised a total of 263 men and 2090 women.

Oldest authentic centenarian The greatest *authenticated* age to which any human has ever lived is 120yr 237days in the case of Shigechiyo Izumi of Isen on Tokunoshima, an island 1320km 820miles south-west of Tokyo, Japan. He was born at Isen on 29 Jun 1865, and recorded as a 6-year-old in Japan's first census of 1871. He died at 12:15 GMT on 21 Feb 1986 after developing pneumonia. He worked until he was 105. He drank sho-chu (firewater, distilled from sugar) and took up smoking when aged 70. He attributed his long life to 'God, Buddha and the Sun'.

Oldest living person The oldest living person in the world whose date of birth can be authenticated is Jeanne Louise Calment who was born in France on 21 Feb 1875. She now lives in a nursing home in Arles, southern France.

UK The oldest living person in Britain is Annie Isabella Scott (b. 15 Mar 1883), who lives in Thurso, Highland. The oldest living man is Vinson Gulliver (b. 28 Nov 1887), who lives in Altrincham, Cheshire.

Family centenarians The first recorded case in Great Britain of four siblings being centenarians occurred on 2 Apr 1984 when Mrs Lily Beatrice Parsons (née Andrews) reached her 100th birthday. Her three sisters were Mrs Florence Eliza White (1874–1979), Mrs Maud Annie Spencer (1876–1978), Mrs Eleanor Newton Webber (1880–1983). The family came from Teignmouth, Devon.

Oldest twins Eli Shadrack and John Meshak Phipps were born on 14 Feb 1803 at Affington, Virginia,

The life of Jeanne Calment

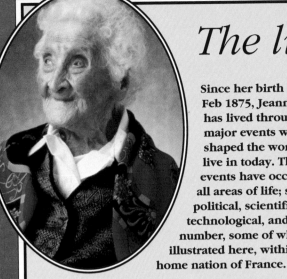

Since her birth on 21 Feb 1875, Jeanne Calment has lived through many major events which have shaped the world we live in today. These events have occurred in all areas of life; social, political, scientific and technological, and a number, some of which are illustrated here, within her home nation of France.

She has lived through the two World Wars, the development of television, the modern motor car, aeroplanes and numerous other items which today are taken for granted such as incandescent lighting.

Asked on her 120th birthday what she expected of the future, she replied, "a very short one".

Louis Blériot Successfully crossed the English Channel on 25 July 1909, the first ever over-the-ocean crossing by a heavier-than-air craft. The cover of *Le Petit Journal* (8 August 1909) shows him completing his crossing over the white cliffs of Dover.

Eiffel Tower Opened on 31 March 1889 as part of the Centennial Exposition to commemorate the French Revolution, it was originally viewed as a temporary structure and was to be dismantled in 1910. However, due to its usefulness in many scientific fields such as astronomy and meteorology, it was saved from destruction and remained the world's tallest building until 1930.

Louis Pasteur Made a wide and varied contribution to science most notably in the fields of chemistry and microbiology. Best known for the development of the pasteurization process, he also did important work with vaccines especially rabies and anthrax.

Tour de France

The world's premier cycling event was first held in July 1903. The winner was Maurice Garin, known as the "le ramoneur" (the chimney sweep, his original occupation), who won with ease. He also won the following year, as celebrated in this poster, but was disqualified four months later for having taken a lift in a car. Millions now watch the race every summer.

World War I Victorious French troops marching through Strasbourg on 22 Nov 1918. Strasbourg, in the Alsace region, was annexed by the Germans during the Franco-Prussian War (1870-71) but returned to France after the Treaty of Versailles. Germany occupied the city again in the Second World War.

Vincent van Gogh

Jeanne Calment recalls meeting the great Dutch artist in her father's shop in Arles and selling him coloured pencils although the memory is clouded by the fact he was scruffy and smelt of alcohol. This picture, *Sunflowers* (Les Tournesols), one of a series of seven on the subject which were painted during his stay in Arles in 1888, was sold at auction on 30 Mar 1987 for a then world record price of £22,500,000 (excluding buyer's premium).

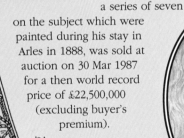

Authentic National Longevity Records

Country	Years	days	Name	Born	Died
Japan	120	237	Shigechiyo Izumi	29 Jun 1865	21 Feb 1986
France	120	40	Jeanne Louise Calment	21 Feb 1875	fl. April 1995
United States	116	88	Carrie White (Mrs) (née Joyner)	18 Nov 1874	14 Feb 1991
United Kingdom	115	229	Charlotte Hughes (Mrs) (née Milburn)	1 Aug 1877	17 Mar 1993
Canada	113	124	Pierre Joubert	15 Jul 1701	16 Nov 1814
Australia	112	330	Caroline Maud Mockridge	11 Dec 1874	6 Nov 1987
Wales	112	292	John Evans	19 Aug 1877	10 Jun 1990
Spain	112	228	Josefa Salas Mateo	14 Jul 1860	27 Feb 1973
Norway	112	61	Maren Bolette Torp	21 Dec 1876	20 Feb 1989
Morocco	112	+	El Hadj Mohammed el Mokri (Grand Vizier)	1844	16 Sep 1957
Poland	112	+	Roswlia Mielczarak (Mrs)	1868	7 Jan 1981
Netherlands	111	354	Thomas Peters	6 Apr 1745	26 Mar 1857
Ireland	111	327	The Hon. Katherine Plunket	22 Nov 1820	4 Oct 1932
Scotland	111	238	Kate Begbie (Mrs)	9 Jan 1877	5 Sep 1988
South Africa	111	151	Johanna Booyson	17 Jan 1857	16 Jun 1968
Sweden	111	350	Hulda Johansson	24 Feb 1882	fl. February 1994
Italy	111	60	Chelidonia Merosi	11 Oct 1883	fl. February 1995
Czechoslovakia	111	+	Marie Bernatková	22 Oct 1857	fl. October 1968
Germany	111	+	Maria Corba	15 Aug 1878	fl. March 1990
Finland	111	+	Fanny Matilda Nystrom	30 Sep 1878	1989
Northern Ireland	110	234	Elizabeth Watkins (Mrs)	10 Mar 1863	31 Oct 1973
Denmark	110	60	Anne Kathrine Matthiesen	26 Nov 1884	fl. February 1995
Yugoslavia	110	+	Demitrius Philipovitch	9 Mar 1818	fl. August 1928
Greece	110	+	Lambrini Tsiatoura (Mrs)	1870	19 Feb 1981
USSR	110	+	Khasako Dzugayev	7 Aug 1860	fl. August 1970
Superior claims but insufficient authentication					
Brazil	124	30	Maria do Como	6 Mar 1871	fl. April 1995
United States	121	+	Mark Thrash	December 1822	17 Dec 1943
Spain	114	335	Benita Medrana	29 Dec 1864	28 Jan 1979
South Africa	114	+	Susan Johanna Deporter	1840	4 Aug 1954

Note: fl. is the abbreviation for the Latin = floruit, he or she was living (at the relevant date).

Anatomy and Physiology

Of the 24 elements which constitute the human body, the commonest is hydrogen which accounts for 63 per cent.

Cells

Largest cell The megakaryocyte, a blood cell, measures 0.2mm. It is found in the bone marrow and produces the 'stickiest' particles in the body—the platelets, which play an important role in blood clotting.

Smallest cell The brain cells in the cerebellum measure about 0.005mm.

Longest cell Motor neurons are some 1.3m *4.26ft* long; they have cell bodies (grey matter) in the lower spinal cord with axons (white matter) that carry nerve impulses from the spinal cord down to the big toe. The cell systems which carry certain sensations (vibration and positional sense) back from the big toe to the brain are even longer. Their uninterrupted length, from the toe and up the posterior part of the spinal cord to the medulla of the brain, is about equal to the height of the body.

Most abundant cell
The body contains in the region of 30 billion red blood cells. The function of these cells is to carry oxygen around the body.

Fastest turnover of body cells The body cells with the shortest life are in the lining of the alimentary tract (gut) where the cells are shed every three days.

Longest life (of a cell) The brain cells last for life and can be three times as old as bone cells, which may live for 25–30 years.

Longest memory (of a cell) As successive generations of the lymphocyte (a type of white blood cell which is part of the body's immune defence system) are produced during one's life, they never forget an enemy.

USA. Eli died at Hennessey, Oklahoma on 23 Feb 1911 at the age of 108yr 9days.

On 17 Jun 1984, identical twin sisters Mildred Widman Philippi and Mary Widman Franzini of St Louis, Missouri, USA celebrated their 104th birthday. Mildred died on 4 May 1985, 44 days short of the twins' 105th birthday.

UK Identical twin sisters, Alice Maria and Emily Edith Weller were born within 15minutes of each other on 20 Apr 1888 in Epsom, Surrey. Alice died on 21 Feb 1991 when aged 102.

Oldest triplets The longest-lived triplets recorded were Faith, Hope and Charity Cardwell who were born on 18 May 1899 at Elm Mott, Texas, USA. Faith died on 2 Oct 1994, aged 95yr 137days.

GB The oldest were Faith Alice, Hope Fanny and Charity Sarah Stockdale of Cracoe, near Skipton, N Yorks, born on 28–29 Dec 1857. Charity was the first to die, on 30 Jul 1944, aged 86yr 213days.

Oldest quadruplets The Ottman quads of Munich, Germany—Adolf, Anne-Marie, Emma and Elisabeth—were born on 5 May 1912. Adolf was the first to die, on 17 Mar 1992, aged 79yr 316days.

Guess What?

Q. Where was the oldest mummy found?

A. See Page 53

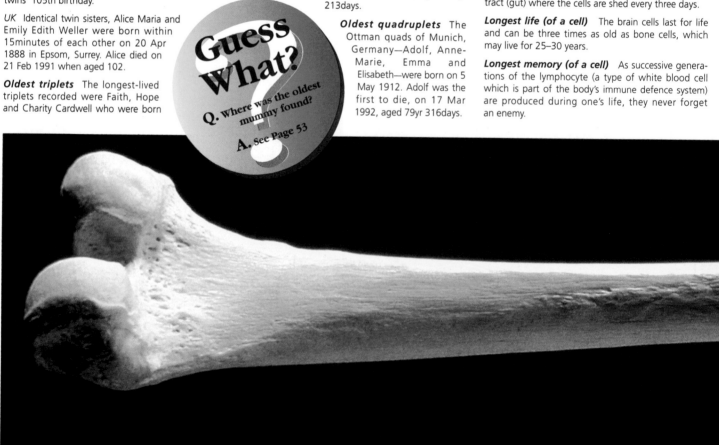

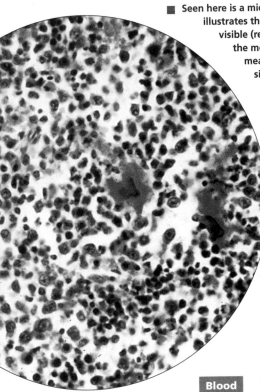

■ Seen here is a micrograph of human red bone marrow which illustrates the blood producing cells. Two examples are visible (red with large nuclei) of the body's largest cell, the megakaryocyte. This cell produces platelets and measures 0.2 mm which is approximately half the size of this full stop.
(Photo: Science Photo Library/ A. & Hanns-Frieder Michler)

surgery at the Michael Reese Hospital, Chicago, Illinois, USA in December 1970.

Largest artery The aorta is 3cm *1.18in* in diameter where it leaves the heart and by the time it ends at the level of the fourth lumbar vertebra, it is about 1.75cm *0.68in* in diameter.

Largest vein The largest is the inferior vena cava, which returns the blood from the lower half of the body to the heart and is slightly larger that the aorta.

Highest blood alcohol level The California University Medical School, Los Angeles, USA reported in December 1982 the case of a confused but conscious 24-year-old female, who was shown to have a blood alcohol level of 1510mg per 100ml—nearly 19 times the UK driving limit (80mg of alcohol per 100ml of blood) and triple the normally lethal limit. After two days she discharged herself.

sartorius

■ The longest muscle in the human body is the *sartorius* (arrowed) which is a narrow ribbon-like muscle running from the pelvis and across the front of the thigh to the top of the tibia below the knee. Its function is to draw the lower limb into the cross-legged position.
(Photo: Science Photo Library/J. Daugherty)

Blood

Commonest blood group On a world basis Group O is the most common (46 per cent), but in some areas, for example Norway, Group A predominates.

The full description of the commonest sub-group in Britain is O MsNs, P+, Rr, Lu(a–), K–, Le(a–b+), Fy(a+b+), Jk(a+b+), which occurs in one in every 270 people.

Rarest blood group The rarest in the world is a type of Bombay blood (sub-type h-h) found so far only in a Czechoslovak nurse in 1961, and in a brother (Rh positive) and sister (Rh negative) named Jalbert in Massachusetts, USA, reported in February 1968.

Using the ABO system, one of 14 systems, group AB occurs in less than 3 per cent of persons in the British Isles.

Recipient of most blood A 50-year-old haemophiliac, Warren C. Jyrich, required 2400 donor units of blood, equivalent to 1080litres, when undergoing open-heart

Bones

Longest bone Excluding a variable number of sesamoids (small rounded bones), there are 206 bones in the adult human body, compared with about 300 for children (as they grow, some bones fuse together). The thigh bone, or femur, is the longest. It constitutes 27.5 per cent of a person's stature normally, and may be expected to be 50cm *19¾in* long in a man measuring 180cm *6ft* tall. The longest recorded bone was a femur measuring 76cm *29.9in*, which belonged to Constantine, a German giant.

Smallest bone The stapes or stirrup bone, one of the three auditory ossicles in the middle ear, measures 2.6–3.4mm *0.10–0.13in* in length and weighs from 2.0 to 4.3mg *0.03– 0.066grains*.

Muscles

Largest muscle Muscles normally account for 40 per cent in men of human bodyweight and 35 per cent in women. The bulkiest of the 639 named muscles in

the human body is usually the *gluteus maximus* or buttock muscle, which extends the thigh. However, in pregnancy the uterus or womb can increase from about 30g *1oz* to over 1kg *2.2lb* in weight.

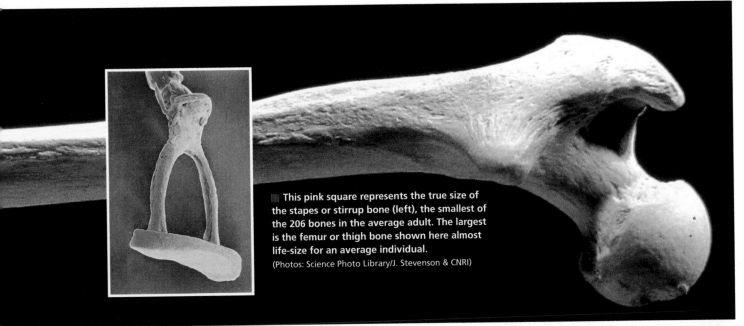

■ This pink square represents the true size of the stapes or stirrup bone (left), the smallest of the 206 bones in the average adult. The largest is the femur or thigh bone shown here almost life-size for an average individual.
(Photos: Science Photo Library/J. Stevenson & CNRI)

Most active muscle
It has been estimated that the eye muscles move more than 100,000 times a day. Many of these rapid eye movements take place during the dreaming phase of sleep. (⇨ Longest and shortest dreams)

Smallest muscle The stapedius, which controls the stapes in the ear (⇨ Smallest bone), is less than 0.127cm *0.05in* long.

Longest muscle The longest muscle in the human body is the *sartorius* which is a narrow ribbon-like muscle running from the pelvis and across the front of the thigh to the top of the tibia below the knee. Its action is to draw the lower limb into the cross-legged position

Strongest muscle The strongest muscle in the human body is the masseter (one on each side of the mouth) which is responsible for the action of biting. In August 1986, Richard Hofmann (b. 1949) of Lake City, Florida, USA, achieved a bite strength of 442kg *975lb* for approximately 2 seconds in a research test using a gnathodynamometer at the College of Dentistry, University of Florida, USA. This figure is more than six times the normal biting strength.

Largest chest measurements Robert Earl Hughes (USA) (1926–58) had a chest measurement of 124in *315cm*, and T. J. Albert Jackson, currently the heaviest living man (⇨ Heaviest men) has a chest measurement of 120in *305cm*.

The largest chest ever recorded in Britain was that of William Campbell (⇨ Heaviest men) which measured 96in *244cm*. Among muscular subjects (mesomorphs) of normal height, *expanded* chest measurements above 56in *142cm* are extremely rare.

The largest muscular chest measurement is that of Isaac Nesser of Greensburg, Pennsylvania, USA at 74¹⁄₁₆in *188cm*.

Largest bicep The right bicep of Denis Sester of Bloomington, Minnesota, USA right bicep measures 30⅝in *77.8cm* cold.

Body Temperature

The standard body temperature is 37°C *98.6°F* but there are small variations in this figure throughout the body. The coolest parts are the hands and feet whilst the hottest is the centre of the brain.

Highest body temperature Willie Jones, 52, was admitted to Grady Memorial Hospital, Atlanta, Georgia, USA on 10 Jul 1980 with heatstroke on a day when the temperature reached 32.2°C *90°F* with 44 per cent humidity. His temperature was found to be 46.5°C *115.7°F*. He was discharged after 24 days.

Lowest body temperature People may die of hypothermia with body temperatures of 35°C *95°F*. The lowest authenticated body temperature is 14.2°C *57.5°F* (rectal temperature) for Karlee Kosolofski, aged two, of Regina, Saskatchewan, Canada on 23 Feb 1994. She had accidentally been locked outside her home for

six hours in a temperature of –22°C *–8°F*. Despite severe frostbite, which meant the amputation of her left leg above the knee, she has made a full recovery.

Brains

Heaviest brain The heaviest brain ever recorded was that of a 30-year-old male, which weighed 2300g *5lb 1.1oz* and was reported by Dr T. Mandybur of the Department of Pathology and Laboratory Medicine at the University of Cincinnati, Ohio in December 1992.

Computation (human) Mrs Shakuntala Devi of India correctly multiplied two 13-digit numbers (7,686,369,774,870 × 2,465,099,745,779) which were randomly selected by the Computer Department of Imperial College, London, on 18 Jun 1980; the feat took 28 seconds and the answer was 18,947,668,177,995,426,462,773,730. Some experts on prodigies in calculation refuse to give credence to Mrs Devi on the grounds that her achievements are so vastly superior to the calculating feats of any other invigilated prodigy that the invigilation must have been defective.

Light-Headed

The lightest 'normal' or non-atrophied brain on record was one weighing 680g *1lb 8oz*. It belonged to Daniel Lyon (Ireland), who died aged 46, at New York, USA in 1907. He was just over 5ft *1.50m* in height and weighed 145lb *66kg*.

Memory skills Bhanddanta Vicittabi Vumsa (1911–93) recited 16,000 pages of Buddhist canonical texts in Yangon (Rangoon), Myanmar (Burma) in May 1974.

Card memorizing Dominic O'Brien (GB) memorized a random sequence of 40 separate packs of cards (2080) (with one error) all of which had been shuffled together on a single sighting, at the BBC Studios, Elstree, Herts on 26 Nov 1993. The fastest time to memorise a single pack of shuffled cards is 42.01 seconds by Tom Groves at Jesus College, Cambridge on 3 Nov 1994.

Memorizing π Hideaki Tomoyori (b. 30 Sep 1932) of Yokohama, Japan recited 'pi' from memory to 40,000 places in 17hr 21min, including breaks totalling 4hr 15min, on 9–10 Mar 1987 at the Tsukuba University Club House.

The British record is 20,013 by Creighton Herbert James Carvello (b. 19 Nov 1944) on 27 Jun 1980 in 9hr 10min at Saltscar Comprehensive School, Redcar, Cleveland.

Hair

Longest hair Human hair grows at the rate of about 1.2cm *0.5in* in a month. If left uncut it will usually grow to a maximum of 60–90cm *2–3ft*.

The longest documented length of hair belongs to Mata Jagdamba (b. 1917) of Ujjain, India. It measured 13ft 10½in *4.23m* on 21 Feb 1994.

Most valuable hair On 18 Feb 1988 a bookseller from Cirencester, Glos, paid £5575 for a lock of hair belonging to Vice Admiral Lord Nelson (1758–1805) at an auction held at Crewkerne, Somerset.

Hair splitting The greatest reported achievement in hair splitting has been that of Alfred West (GB) (1901–85), who succeeded in splitting a human hair 17 times into 18 parts on eight occasions.

Longest beard The beard of Hans N. Langseth (b. 1846 near Eidsroll, Norway) measured 533cm *17½ft* at the time of his burial at Kensett, Iowa in 1927 after 15 years residence in the United States. It was presented to the Smithsonian Institution, Washington, DC, in 1967.

The beard of the 'bearded lady' Janice Deveree (b. 1842) of Bracken County, Kentucky, USA was measured at 14in *36cm* in 1884.

Most expensive skull
The skull of Emanuel Swedenborg (1688–1772), the Swedish philosopher and theologian, was bought in London by the Royal Swedish Academy of Sciences for £5500 on 6 Mar 1978.

Longest moustache The moustache of Kalyan Ramji Sain of Sundargarth, India grown since 1976, reached a span of 339cm *133½in* (right side 172cm *67¾in* and left side 167cm *65¾in*) in July 1993.

The longest moustache in Great Britain was that of John Roy (1910–88), of Weeley, near Clacton, Essex. It attained a peak span of 6ft 2½in *189cm* on 2 Apr 1976 (began growing in 1939). He accidentally sat on it in the bath in 1984 and lost 16½in *42cm*. He then took off the same amount from the other side to even the moustache.

Guess What?
Q. What is 6500 times thinner than human hair?
A. See Page 70

Of the physiological records
listed in the first edition of the book, the one which has undergone the greatest change is the longest moustache. The first listed record was one which was 16½in long grown by John Roy and he progressed the record to 6ft 2½in. The current record of Kaylan Ramji Sain is over eight times longer than the 1955 record!

The current UK champion is Ted Sedman of St Albans, Herts whose handlebar moustache measures 63in *160cm*.

Shaving The fastest barbers on record are Denny Rowe and Tom Rodden. Denny Rowe shaved 1994 men in 60minutes with a retractor safety razor in Herne Bay, Kent on 19 Jun 1988, taking on average 1.8seconds per volunteer, and drawing blood four times. Tom Rodden of Chatham, Kent shaved 278 even braver volunteers in 60minutes with a cut-throat razor on 10 Nov 1993 for the BBC *Record Breakers* programme, averaging 12.9seconds per face. He drew blood seven times.

Optics

Highest hyperacuity The human eye is capable of judging relative position with remarkable accuracy, reaching limits of between 3 and 5seconds of arc.

In April 1984, Dr Dennis M. Levi of the College of Optometry, University of Houston, Texas, USA, repeatedly identified the relative position of a thin bright green line within 0.85seconds of arc. This is equivalent to a displacement of some 6mm *¼in* at a distance of 1.6km *1mile*.

Light sensitivity Working in Chicago, Illinois, USA in 1942, Maurice H. Pirenne detected a flash of blue light of 500nm in total darkness, when as few as five quanta or photons of light were available to be absorbed by the rod photoreceptors of the retina.

Dentition

Earliest teeth Tooth enamel is the only part of the human body which basically remains unchanged throughout life; it is also the hardest substance in the body. The first deciduous or milk teeth normally appear in infants at 5–8 months, these being the upper and lower jaw first incisors. There are many recorded examples of children born with teeth. Sean Keaney of Newbury, Berks was born on 10 Apr 1990 with 12 teeth. They were, however, extracted to prevent possible feeding problems. Molars usually appear at 24 months, but in Pindborg's case (published in Denmark in 1970), a 6-week premature baby was documented with eight teeth at birth with four in the molar region.

Most sets of teeth Cases of the growth in late life of a third set of teeth have been recorded several times. A reference to a case in France of a *fourth* dentition, known as Lison's case, was published in 1896.

Lifting and pulling with teeth Walter Arfeuille of Ieper-Vlamertinge, Belgium lifted weights totalling 281.5kg *621lb* a distance of 17cm *6¾in* off the ground with his teeth in Paris, France on 31 Mar 1990.

Earliest false teeth
From discoveries made in Etruscan tombs, partial dentures of bridge-work type were being worn in what is now Tuscany, Italy as early as 700 BC. Some were permanently attached to existing teeth and others were removable.

Robert Galstyan of Masis, Armenia pulled two railway wagons coupled together, weighing a total of 219,175kg *483,197lb*, a distance of 7m *23ft* along a railway track with his teeth at Shcherbinka, Moscow, Russia on 21 Jul 1992.

Guess What?
Q. Which snake has the longest fangs?
A. See Page 38

Most dedicated dentist Brother Giovanni Battista Orsenigo of the Ospedale Fatebenefratelli, Rome, a monk who was also a dentist, kept all the teeth he extracted during the time he exercised his profession from 1868 to 1904. In 1903, the number was counted and found to be 2,000,744 teeth, indicating an average of 185 teeth, or nearly six total extractions, a day.

Most valuable tooth In 1816, a tooth belonging to Sir Isaac Newton (1642–1727) was sold in London for £730. It was purchased by a nobleman who had it set in a ring.

Voice

Greatest range (voices) The normal intelligible outdoor range of the male human voice in still air is 180m *200yd*. The *silbo*, the whistled language of the Spanish-speaking Canary Island of La Gomera, is intelligible under ideal conditions at 8km *5miles*. There is a recorded case, under optimal acoustic conditions, of the human voice being detectable at a distance of 17km *10½miles* across still water at night.

Screaming The highest scientifically measured emission is 128dbA at 2½m *8ft 2in* by Simon Robinson of McLaren Vale, South Australia in 'The Guinness Challenge' at Adelaide, Australia on 11 Nov 1988.

Whistling Roy Lomas achieved 122.5 dbA at 2½m *8ft 2in* in the Deadroom at the BBC studios in Manchester on 19 Dec 1983.

Shouting Annalisa Wray (b. 21 Apr 1974) of Comber, Co. Down achieved a level of 121.7 dbA, shouting the word 'Quiet', at the Citybus Challenge, Belfast, Co. Antrim, Northern Ireland on 16 Apr 1994.

Town crier The greatest number of wins in the national Town Criers' Contest is 11 (between 1939–73) by Ben Johnson of Fowey, Cornwall.

Fastest talker Few people are able to speak *articulately* at a sustained speed above 300 words per minute.

Fastest yodel
Thomas Scholl of Munich, Germany achieved 22 tones (15 falsetto) in 1 second on 9 Feb 1992.

Steve Woodmore of Orpington, Kent spoke 595 words in a time of 56.01seconds or 637.4 words per minute on the ITV Programme *Motor Mouth* on 22 Sep 1990.

Hamlet's soliloquy Sean Shannon (Canada) recited Hamlet's soliloquy 'To be or not to be' (260 words) in a time of 24 seconds (650 words per minute) on BBC Radio Oxford on 26 Oct 1990.

Backwards talking Steve Briers of Kilgetty, Dyfed recited the entire lyrics of Queen's album *A Night at the Opera* at BBC North-West Radio 4's 'Cat's Whiskers' on 6 Feb 1990 in a time of 9min 58.44sec.

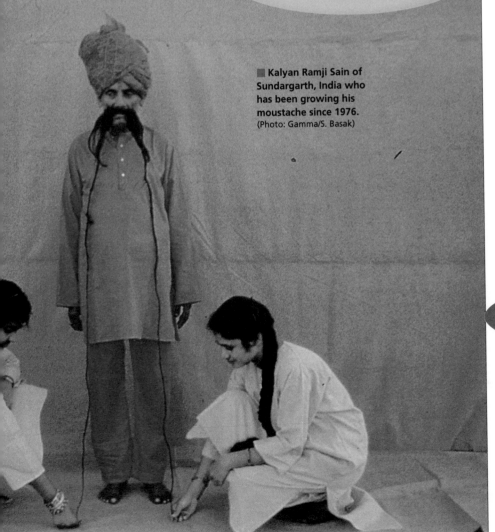

■ Kalyan Ramji Sain of Sundargarth, India who has been growing his moustache since 1976.
(Photo: Gamma/S. Basak)

■ Shridhar Chillal (India) (b. 18 Aug 1937) is the record holder for the longest fingernails. He last cut his nails in 1952 and if anybody is interesting in owning such a set of nails, they are for sale (protective large mitten optional).

Hands and Feet

Touch The extreme sensitivity of the fingers is such that a vibration with a movement of 0.02 of a micron can be detected.

Longest fingernails Fingernails grow about 0.05cm *0.02in* a week—four times faster than toenails. The aggregate measurement of the five nails of the left hand of Shridhar Chillal (India) (b. 18 Aug 1937) was 226in *574cm* on 25 Feb 1995 (thumb 52in *132cm*, first finger 40in *102cm*, second finger 43in *109cm*, third finger 46in *117cm*, and the fourth 45in *114cm*). He last cut his nails in 1952.

Most fingers and toes (polydactylism) At an inquest held on a baby boy at Shoreditch in the East End of London on 16 Sep 1921 it was reported that he had 14 fingers and 15 toes.

Necks

Longest neck The maximum measured extension of the neck by the successive fitting of copper coils, as practised by the women of the Padaung or Kareni tribe of Myanmar (Burma), is 40cm *15¾in*. When the rings are removed, the muscles supporting the head and neck shrink to their normal length.

Waists

Largest waist Walter Hudson (1944–91) of New York, USA measured 119in *302cm* at his peak weight of 85st 7lb *545kg*.

Smallest waist The smallest waist of a person with normal stature was that of Ethel Granger (1905–82) of Peterborough, Cambs. She reduced from a natural 22in *56cm* to 13in *33cm* over the period 1929–39. A measurement of 13in *33cm* was also claimed for the French actress Mlle Polaire (real name Emile Marie Bouchand) (1881–1939).

Largest feet If cases of elephantiasis are excluded, then the biggest feet currently known are those of Matthew McGrory (b. 17 May 1973) of Pennsylvania, USA, who wears size 26 US shoes.

The owner of Britain's largest feet is John Thrupp (b. 1964) of Stratford-upon-Avon, Warks, who wears a size 21 shoe. He is 2.11m *6ft 11in* tall.

Motionlessness António Gomes dos Santos of Zare, Portugal stood motionless for 15hr 2min 55sec on 30 Jul 1988 at the Amoreiras Shopping Centre, Lisbon.

Standing The longest period on record that anyone has stood continuously is more than 17 years in the case of Swami Maujgiri Maharaj when performing the *Tapasya* or penance from 1955 to 1973 in Shahjahanpur, Uttar Pradesh, India. When sleeping he would lean against a plank. He died in September 1980 at the age of 85.

> **Balancing on one foot**
> The longest recorded duration for balancing on one foot is 55hr 35min by Girish Sharma at Deori, India from 2–4 Oct 1992. The disengaged foot may not be rested on the standing foot nor may any object be used for support or balance.

Illness and Disease

Commonest disease *Non-contagious* Periodontal diseases, such as gingivitis (inflammation of the gums) are the most prevalent. In their lifetime few people used to escape the effects of tooth decay but the 1981 level of 93 per cent among UK schoolchildren had fallen to 55 per cent by 1992.

Contagious The commonest contagious disease in the world is coryza (acute nasopharyngitis), or the common cold.

Highest mortality There are a number of diseases which are generally considered to be universally fatal—AIDS (Acquired Immune Deficiency Syndrome) and rabies encephalitis, a virus infection of the central nervous system, are well known examples. The *disease* rabies, however, should not be confused with being bitten by a rabid animal. With immediate treatment the virus can be prevented from entering the nervous system and chances of survival are high.

Historically, the pneumonic form of plague (bacterial infection), as evidenced by the Black Death of 1347–51, killed everyone who caught it—a quarter of the then population of Europe and some 75 million worldwide.

Leading cause of death In industrialized countries diseases of the heart and of blood vessels account for more than 50 percent of deaths. The commonest of these are heart attacks and strokes, commonly due to atheroma (degeneration of the arterial walls) obstructing the flow of blood. Deaths from these diseases of the circulatory system totalled 283,459 in Great Britain in 1992.

Medical Extremes

Longest cardiac arrest The longest is four hours in the case of a Norwegian fisherman, Jan Egil Refsdahl (b. 1936), who fell overboard in the icy waters off Bergen on 7 Dec 1987. He was rushed to nearby Haukeland Hospital after his body temperature fell to 24°C *75°F* and his heart stopped beating, but he made a full recovery after he was connected to a heart-lung machine.

Guess What?
Q. Which dinosaur had the longest claws?
A. See Page 44

Cardiopulmonary resuscitation Brent Shelton and John Ash completed a CPR marathon (cardiopulmonary resuscitation—15 compressions alternating with two breaths) of 130hours from 28 Oct–2 Nov 1991 at Regina, Saskatchewan, Canada.

Longest coma
Elaine Esposito (b. 3 Dec 1934) of Tarpon Springs, Florida, USA, never stirred after an appendectomy on 6 Aug 1941, when aged 6. She died on 25 Nov 1978 aged 43yr 357 days, having been in a coma for 37yr 111 days.

Longest and shortest dreams Dreaming sleep is characterized by rapid eye movements known as REM. The longest recorded period of REM is one of 3hr 8min by David Powell at the Puget Sound Sleep Disorder Center, Seattle, Washington, USA on 29 Apr 1994. In July 1984, the Sleep Research Centre, Haifa, Israel recorded nil REM in a 33-year-old male who had a shrapnel brain injury.

Highest g forces Racing driver David Purley (1945–85) survived a deceleration from 173km/h *108mph* to zero in 66cm *26in* in a crash at Silverstone, Northants on 13 Jul 1977. The crash involved a force of 179.8g, and he suffered 29 fractures, three dislocations and six heart stoppages.

The highest g value voluntarily endured is 82.6g for 0.04 seconds by Eli L. Beeding Jr on a water-braked rocket sled at Holloman Air Force Base, New Mexico, USA on 16 May 1958. He was subsequently hospitalized for three days.

Hiccoughing Charles Osborne (1894–1991) of Anthon, Iowa, USA started hiccoughing in 1922 while attempting to weigh a hog before slaughtering it. He was unable to find a cure, but led a normal life in which he had two wives and fathered eight children. He continued until a morning in February 1990.

Hospital stay The longest stay was by Martha Nelson who was admitted to the Columbus State Institute for the Feeble-Minded in Ohio, USA in 1875. She died in January 1975 at the age of 103yr 6months in the Orient State Institution, Ohio after spending more than 99 years in hospitals.

Human salamanders The highest dry-air temperature endured by naked men in US Air Force experiments in 1960 was 205°C *400°F*, and for heavily clothed men 260°C *500°F*. Temperatures of 140°C *284°F* have been found quite bearable in saunas.

Most injections
Samuel L. Davidson (b. 30 Jul 1912) of Glasgow, has had a conservative estimate of 77,200 insulin injections since 1923.

Longest in iron lung Dorothy Stone (b. 2 Jun 1928) of Liss, Hants has been in a negative pressure respirator since 1947. John Prestwich (b. 24 Nov 1938) of Kings Langley, Herts has been dependent on a respirator since 24 Nov 1955.

Heaviest organ The skin is medically considered to be an organ and it weighs around 2.7kg *5.9lb* in an average adult. The heaviest internal organ is the liver at 1.5kg *3.3lb*. This is four times heavier than the heart.

Pill-taking The highest recorded total of pills swallowed by a patient is 565,939

between 9 Jun 1967 and 19 Jun 1988 by C.H.A. Kilner (1926–88) of Bindura, Zimbabwe.

Post mortem birth The longest gestation interval in a post mortem birth was one of 84 days in the case of a baby girl delivered of a brain-dead woman at Roanoke, Virginia, USA on 5 Jul 1983.

Sleeplessness Victims of the very rare condition of total insomnia have been known to go without definable sleep for many years.

Sneezing The longest sneezing fit ever recorded is that of Donna Griffiths (b. 1969) of Pershore, Hereford & Worcester. She started sneezing on 13 Jan 1981, sneezed an estimated million times in the first 365 days and achieved her first sneeze-free day on 16 Sep 1983—the 978th day.

The highest speed at which expelled particles have ever been measured to travel is 167km/h *103.6 mph.*

Snoring Kåre Walkert (b. 14 May 1949) of Kumala, Sweden, who suffers from the breathing disorder apnea, recorded peak levels of 93 dBA whilst sleeping at the Örebro Regional Hospital, Sweden on 24 May 1993.

Swallowing The worst reported case of compulsive swallowing involved an insane female, Mrs H., aged 42, who complained of a 'slight abdominal pain'. She proved to have 2533 objects, including 947 bent pins, in her stomach. These were removed by Drs Chalk and Foucar in June 1927 at the Ontario Hospital, Canada.

The heaviest object extracted from a human stomach was a ball of hair weighing 2.53kg *5lb 3oz* from a 20-year-old female compulsive swallower in the South Devon and East Cornwall Hospital on 30 Mar 1895.

Eating Michel Lotito (b. 15 Jun 1950) of Grenoble, France, known as Monsieur Mangetout, has been eating metal and glass since 1959. Gastroenterologists have X-rayed his stomach and have described his ability to consume 900g *2lb* of metal per day as unique. His diet since 1966 has included 18 bicycles, 15 supermarket

trolleys, 7 TV sets, 6 chandeliers, 2 beds, a pair of skis, a low-calorie Cessna light aircraft and a computer. He is said to have provided the only example in history of a coffin (handles and all) ending up inside a man.

Longest without food and water The longest recorded case of survival without food *and* water is 18 days by Andreas Mihavecz, then 18, of Bregenz, Austria. He was put into a holding cell on 1 Apr 1979 in a local government building in Höchst, but totally forgotten by the police. On 18 Apr 1979, he was discovered close to death. Mihavecz had been a passenger in a crashed car.

Underwater submergence In 1986, 2-year-old Michelle Funk of Salt Lake City, Utah, USA, made a full recovery after spending 66 minutes underwater having falling into a swollen creek.

Lung power The inflation of a standard meteorological balloon (1000g *35oz*) to a diameter of 2.44m *8ft* against time was achieved by Nicholas Mason of Cheadle, Greater Manchester in

Guess What?
Q. Where was the longest-lasting rainbow?
A. See Page 22

■ Nicholas Mason puffs away as he beats his own record for inflating a meteorological balloon, demonstrating his claim to have the world's most powerful lungs.
(Photos: BBC)

■ **The first successful heart transplant was performed by a team of 30 led by Dr Christiaan Barnard (above) in December 1967. Although the first recipient, Louis Washkansky, survived for only 18 days, a heart transplant recipient just 3½ years later survived for over 23 years, a record.**
(Photo: South African Embassy, London)

The greatest age in Britain for an operation was in the case of Miss Mary Wright (b. 28 Feb 1862) who died during a thigh operation at Boston, Lincs on 22 Apr 1971, aged 109yr 53days.

Earliest general anaesthesia Dr Crawford Williamson Long (1815–78) removed a cyst from the neck of James Venable, using diethyl ether ($C_2H_5)_2O$, in Jefferson, Georgia, USA on 30 Mar 1842.

Tracheostomy Winifred Campbell (1902–92) of Wanstead, London breathed through a silver tube in her throat for 88 years.

Haemodialysis Brian Wilson (b. 1940) of Edinburgh, Lothian, suffered from kidney failure from the age of 24, and began dialysis at the Royal Infirmary of Edinburgh on 30 May 1964. He averages three visits per week to the hospital.

Largest tumour The largest tumour ever reported was Dr Arthur Spohn's case of an ovarian cyst estimated to weigh 148.7kg *23st 6lb*. It was was drained during the week prior to surgical removal of the cyst shell, in Texas, USA in 1905. The patient made a full recovery.

Gallstones The largest gallstone reported in medical literature was one of 6.29kg *13lb 14oz* removed from an 80-year-old woman by Dr Humphrey Arthure at Charing Cross Hospital, London on 29 Dec 1952.

In August 1987 it was reported that 23,530 gallstones had been removed from an 85-year-old woman by Mr K. Whittle Martin at Worthing Hospital, W Sussex, after she complained of severe abdominal pain.

Transplants

Heart The first operation was performed on Louis Washkansky, aged 55, at the Groote Schuur Hospital, Cape Town, South Africa between 1a.m. and 6a.m., on 3 Dec 1967, by a team of 30 headed by Prof. Christiaan Neethling Barnard (b. 8 Oct 1922). The donor was Miss Denise Ann Darvall, aged 25. Washkansky lived for 18 days.

Britain's first heart transplant operation took place at the National Heart Hospital, London on 3 May 1968. The patient, Frederick West, survived for 46 days.

Heart, longest surviving Dirk van Zyl of Cape Town, South Africa (b. 10 Aug 1926) survived 23yr 57days having received an unnamed person's heart at the Grooe Schuur Hospital, University of Cape Town on 10 May 1971.

Heart, youngest Paul Holt of Vancouver, British Columbia, Canada underwent a heart transplant at Loma Linda Hospital in California, USA on 16 Oct 1987 at the age of 2hr 34min. He was born six weeks premature and weighed 2.9kg *6lb 6oz*.

The youngest in the UK was Hollie Roffey, who received a new heart when aged only 10 days at the National Heart Hospital in London on 29 Jul 1984. She survived for only 10 days.

Heart-lung-liver The first triple transplant took place on 17 Dec 1986 at Papworth Hospital, Cambridge, when Mrs Davina Thompson (b. 28 Feb 1951) of Rawmarsh, S Yorks, underwent surgery for seven hours by a team of 15 headed by chest surgeon Mr John Wallwork and Prof. Sir Roy Calne.

Kidney R.H. Lawler (b. 1895) (USA) performed the first transplant of the kidney in a human at Little Company of Mary Hospital, Chicago, Illinois, USA on 17 Jun 1950.

The longest surviving kidney transplant patient is Johanna Leonora Rempel (*née* Nightingale) (b. 24 Mar 1948) of Red Deer, Alberta, Canada who was given a kidney from her identical twin sister Lana Blatz on 28 Dec 1960. The operation was performed at the Peter Bent Brigham Hospital, Boston, Massachusett, USA. Both Johanna and her sister have continued to enjoy excellent health and both have had healthy children.

45min 2.5sec for the BBC *Record Breakers* television programme on 26 Sep 1994.

Most tattoos The ultimate in being tattooed is represented by Tom Leppard of the Isle of Skye. He has opted for a leopard skin design, with all the skin between the dark spots tattooed saffron yellow. The area of his body covered is approximately 99.2 per cent.

Bernard Moeller of Pennsylvania, USA has had 14,010 individual tattoos as of 5 Feb 1994.

The world's most decorated woman is strip artiste 'Krystyne Kolorful' (b. 5 Dec 1952, Alberta, Canada). Her 95 per cent body suit took 10 years to complete.

Britain's most decorated woman is Rusty Field (b. 1944) of Norfolk, who has 85 per cent of her body tattooed.

Operations

Longest operation The most protracted operation reported lasted for 96hours performed from 4–8 Feb 1951 in Chicago, Illinois, USA on Mrs Gertrude Levandowski for the removal of an ovarian cyst. During the operation her weight fell 280kg *44st* to 140kg *22st*.

Most operations performed Dr M.C. Modi, a pioneer of mass eye surgery in India since 1943, has performed as many as 833 cataract operations in one day. He had visited 46,120 villages and 12,118,630 patients, performing a total of 610,564 operations to February 1993.

Dr Robert B. McClure (b. 1901) of Toronto, Canada performed a career total of 20,423 major operations from 1924 to 1978.

Most operations endured From 22 Jul 1954 to the end of 1994, Charles Jensen of Chester, South Dakota, USA had 970 operations to remove the tumours associated with basal cell naevus syndrome.

Oldest patient The greatest recorded age at which anyone has undergone an operation is 111yr 105days for a hip operation on James Henry Brett, Jr (1849–1961) of Houston, Texas, USA on 7 Nov 1960.

Doctor, Doctor!

The most extreme recorded case of the rare and incurable condition known as 'Munchausen's syndrome' (a continual desire to have medical treatment) was William McIlroy (b. 1906), who cost the National Health Service an estimated £2.5 million during his 50-year career as a hospital patient. During that time he had 400 major and minor operations, and stayed at 100 different hospitals using 22 aliases. The longest period he was ever out of hospital was six months. In 1979, he hung up his bedpan for the last time, saying he was sick of hospitals, and retired to an old people's home in Birmingham, W Mids where he died in 1983.

The largest tumour ever removed intact was a multicystic mass of the right ovary weighing 137.6kg *303lb*. The operation, which took over six hours, was performed by Professor Katherine O'Hanlan of Stanford University Medical Center, California, USA. The growth had a diameter of 1m *3ft* and was removed in its entirety in October 1991 from the abdomen of an unnamed 35-year-old woman. The patient, who weighed 95kg *210lb* after the operation and has made a full recovery, left the operating theatre on one stretcher and the cyst on another.

Largest gall bladder On 15 Mar 1989, at the National Naval Medical Center in Bethesda, Maryland, USA, Prof. Bimal C. Ghosh removed a gall bladder weighing 10.4kg *23lb* from a 69-year-old woman. The patient had been complaining of increasing swelling around the abdomen, but after removing this enlarged gall bladder—which weighed more than three times the average new born baby—the patient made a full recovery.

First transplantee to give birth
Johanna Rempel gave birth to a baby boy, Kerry Melvin Ross 3.47kg *7lb 12oz* at Winnipeg General Hospital, Manitoba, Canada on 7 Sep 1967. She had received a donor kidney in December 1960 (see above).

Artificial heart On 1–2 Dec 1982 at the Utah Medical Center, Salt Lake City, Utah, USA Dr Barney B. Clark, 61, of Des Moines, Washington, was the first recipient of an artificial heart. The surgeon was Dr William C. DeVries and the heart was a Jarvik 7 designed by Dr Robert K. Jarvik (b. 11 May 1946). The patient died on 23 Mar 1983, 112 days later. The longest surviving recipient was William J. Schroeder who survived for 620 days at Louisville, Kentucky, USA from 25 Nov 1984 to 7 Aug 1986.

Britain's first artificial heart patient was Raymond Cook of Hucknall, Notts who temporarily received a Jarvik 7 on 2 Nov 1986 at Papworth Hospital, Cambridge, Cambs.

Science & Technology

Elements

Of the 111 known elements the first 94 exist naturally. At room temperature the elements consist of 2 liquids, 11 gases and 85 known solids (if they could be obtained in a coherent form elements 85, 87 and 101 to 111 would also prove to be solid at this temperature).

Sub-Atomic Particles

Electron volt (eV)—mass-energy unit equivalent to $1.7826627 \times 10^{-36}$ kg.

Quarks and leptons There are three tiers or 'families' of quarks and leptons with two of each in each family. The lightest quark is the up quark, with a short-range mass of 6 MeV, whilst the heaviest is the top quark—discovered at Fermilab, Batavia, Illinois, USA in February 1995 and announced on 2 March — with a mass of 170 GeV. The three neutrino leptons are predicted to have zero mass (the electron neutrino mass has been experimentally proved to be less than 10 eV), whilst the heaviest lepton is the tau (discovered 1975) with a mass of 1.777 GeV.

Quanta The photon (and the theoretically predicted graviton) are both expected to have zero mass, with current cosmological models placing upper limits on these values of 3×10^{-27} eV and 4.3×10^{-34} eV respectively.

Heaviest known The heaviest gauge boson and the heaviest particle known is the Z° (discovered 1983) of mass 91.19 GeV. It also has the shortest lifetime of any particle at 2.64×10^{-25} sec.

Hadrons *Lightest and heaviest* Of the 259 particles (and an equal number of anti-particles) predicted by the accepted existence of 80 meson multiplets and 62 baryon multiplets, the lightest is the neutral pion meson (discovered 1949) of mass 134.976 Mev, and the heaviest is the upsilon (11020) meson (discovered 1984) of mass 11.02 GeV.

Most and least stable The least stable hadron is the N (2600) baryon (discovered 1978–9), of lifetime 1.0×10^{-24} sec. The most stable is the proton, with a lifetime of at least 10^{25} years.

Isotopes

Most and least isotopes There are at least 2570 isotopes, and caesium (Cs) has the most with 37, whilst tin (Sn) has the most stable isotopes, with 10. Hydrogen (H) has the least number of accepted isotopes, with only three.

■ Apollo 11 rises to clear its mobile launcher on 16 Jul 1969 as it takes Neil Armstrong and Buzz Aldrin to the Moon. Michael Collins, the third member of the crew, remained in the command module whilst Armstrong and Aldrin were on the Moon (⇨ page 84).
(Photo: NASA/Image Select)

Of the 101 elements known forty years ago, 92 were known to occur naturally (elements 43 and 61 had not been found in natural sources at that time)

Guess What?

Q. What was the name of the lunar module which landed on the Moon on 20 Jul 1969?

A. See Page 84

■ Scientists recognise particles by their electronic signatures. These are shown graphically by computers in colour-enhanced displays, such as this photograph of the tracks of sub-atomic particles.
(Photo: Science Photo Library/P. Loiez, CERN)

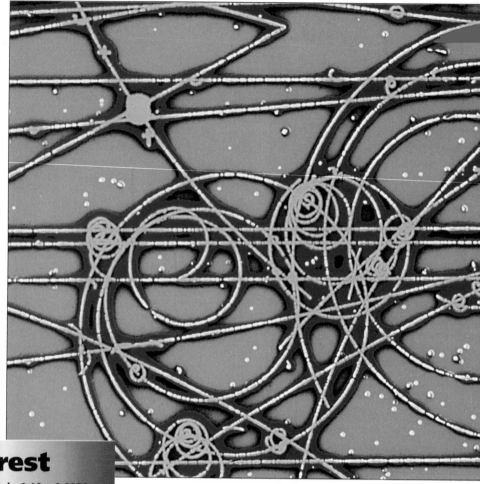

Lightest and heaviest isotopes   The lightest nuclide is hydrogen 1 (H 1) or protium (discovered 1920), whilst the heaviest is unununium 272 (Uuu 272), discovered in December 1994 (⇨Newest element).

Most and least stable isotopes   As far as it is known the most stable radioactive isotope is the double beta decaying tellurium 128 (Te-128; discovered 1924 and radioactivity proved 1968), with a half-life of 1.5×10^{24} years. The least stable nuclide is lithium 5 (Li 5; discovered 1950) with a lifetime of 4.4×10^{-22} sec.

The 111 Elements

Commonest element   Hydrogen is the commonest element in both the Universe (over 90%) and the Solar System (70.68%). Iron is the commonest element in the earth, accounting for 36% of the mass, whilst molecular nitrogen (N_2) is the commonest in the atmosphere at 78.08% by volume or 75.52% by mass.

Newest element   Element 111, provisional name unununium (literally one-one-one; Uuu), was discovered on a three-atom basis in December 1994 at the Gesellschaft für Schwerionenforschung, Darmstadt, Germany, by a joint German, Russian, Slovakian, and Finnish team. Element 110, provisional name ununnilium (Uun), was discovered only a month earlier in the same laboratory.

Density—solid   At room temperature the least dense metal is lithium (Li) at 0.5334 g/dm³ and the densest is osmium (Os), at 22.59 g/cm³ *0.8161 lb/in³*.

Density—gas   At NTP (normal temperature and pressure 0°C and one atmosphere), the lightest gas is hydrogen (H) at 0.00008989 g/cm³ *0.005612 lb/ft³* whilst the densest is radon (Rn) at 0.01005 g/cm³ *0.6274 lb/ft³*.

Melting and boiling points   *Highest*   Metallic tungsten or wolfram (W) melts at 3414°C *6177°F*. The graphite form of carbon sublimes directly to vapour at 3704°C *6699°F* and can only be obtained as a liquid from above a temperature of 4730°C *8546°F* and a pressure of 10 MPa *100 atmospheres*.

Lowest   Helium (He) cannot be obtained as a solid at atmospheric pressure, the minimum pressure being 2.532 MPa *24.985 atmospheres* at a temperature of −272.375°C *−458.275°F*. Helium also has the lowest boiling point at −268.928°C *−458.275°F*. For metallic elements mercury (Hg) has the lowest melting and boiling points, at −38.829°C *−37.892°F* and 356.62°C *673.92°F* respectively.

Purest element   In April 1978 P.V.E. McClintock of the University of Lancaster reported success in obtaining the isotope helium 4 (He-4) with impurity levels at less than two parts in 10^{15}.

Hardest element   The carbon (C) allotrope diamond has a Knoop value of 8400.

Rarest

Rarest element   Only 0.16 g *0.0056 oz* of astatine (At) is present in the Earth's crust, of which the isotope astatine 215 (At 215; discovered 1943) accounts for only 4.5 nanograms *1.6×10^{-10} oz*. Radon (Rn) is the rarest element in the atmosphere at only 6×10^{-18} parts by volume (equivalent to only 2.4 kg *5.3 lb* overall).

Thermal expansion   Caesium (Cs) has the highest thermal expansion of a metallic element, at 9.4×10^{-5} per deg C, while the diamond allotrope of carbon (C) has the lowest expansion at 1×10^{-6} per deg C.

Most ductile element   One gram of gold (Au) can be drawn to 2.4 km, or *1 oz* to *43 miles*.

Highest tensile strength   The strongest element is boron (B), with a tensile strength of 5.7 GPa (5.7×10^9 Pa or 8.3×10^5 lbf/in²).

Strongest pure metal   The strongest pure metal appears to be iridium (Ir), with a typical tensile strength of 550 MPa (5.5×10^8 Pa or 8.0×10^4 lbf/in²), although values as high as 2.5 GPa (2.5×10^9 Pa or 3.6×10^5 lbf/in²) have been reported for hot drawn wire.

> The compound 2, 3, 7, 8-tetrachlorodibenzo-p-dioxin), or TCDD, is the most deadly of the 75 known dioxins. It is 150,000 times more deadly than cyanide.

Liquid range   Based on the differences between melting and boiling points, the element with the shortest liquid range (on the Celsius scale) is the inert gas neon (Ne) at only 2.542 degrees (from −248.594 to −246.052°C *−415.469 to −410.894°F*). The radioactive element neptunium (Np) has the longest range, at 3453 degrees (from 637 to 4090°C *1179 to 7394°F*).

Toxicity   The severest restriction placed on any element in the form of a radioactive isotope is 2.4×10^{-16} g/m³ in air for thorium 228 (Th 228) or radiothorium, while for non-radioactive elements it is beryllium (Be), with a threshold limit in air of only 2×10^{-6} g/m³.

Chemical Extremes

Smelliest substance   The most evil of the 17,000 smells so far classified is obviously a matter of opinion, but ethyl mercaptan (C_2H_5SH) and butyl seleno-mercaptan (C_4H_9SeH) are pungent claimants, each with a smell reminiscent of a combination of rotting cabbage, garlic, onions, burnt toast and sewer gas.

Most powerful nerve gas   Ethyl S-2-diisopropylaminoethylmethyl phosphonothiolate, or VX, developed at the Chemical Defence Experimental Establishment, Porton Down, Wilts in 1952, is 300 times more powerful than the phosgene ($COCl_2$) used in World War I. A lethal dosage is 10 mg-minute/m³ airborne, or 0.3 mg orally.

Strongest acid and alkaline solutions   Normal solutions of strong acids and alkalis tend towards pH values of 0 and 14 respectively, but this scale is inadequate for describing the 'superacids'—the strongest of which is an 80% solution of antimony pentafluoride in hydrofluoric acid (fluoro-antimonic acid

---

Bitter

Bitterest substance   The bitterest-tasting substances are based on the denatonium cation and have been produced commercially as benzoate and saccharide. Taste detection levels are as low as one part in 500 million, and a dilution of one part in 100 million will leave a lingering taste.

Laboratory, California, USA. The main use will be in space to collect micrometeoroids and the debris present in comets' tails.

Highest superconducting temperature In April 1993, bulk superconductivity with a maximum transition temperature of $-140.7\,°C$ $-221.3\,°F$ was achieved at the Laboratorium für Festkörperphysik, Zurich, Switzerland, in a mixture of oxides of mercury, barium, calcium and copper, $HgBa_2Ca_2Cu_3O_{1+x}$ and $HgBa_2CaCu_2O_{6+x}$. Claims to have obtained higher temperatures have not been substantiated.

Most magnetic substance The most magnetic substance is neodymium iron boride $Nd_2Fe_{14}B$, with a maximum energy product (the highest energy that a magnet can supply when operating at a particular operating point) of up to $280\,kJ/m^3$.

Most expensive perfume Retail prices tend to be fixed with an eye to public relations rather than the market cost of ingredients and packaging. From March 1984 Jōvan, based in Chicago, Illinois, USA, marketed a cologne called Andron, containing a trace of the attractant pheromone androstenol, at a cost of $2750 per oz.

Guess What?

Q. What is a 'yocto'?

A. See Page 70

> The highest velocity at which any solid object has been projected is 150 km/sec *93 miles/sec* for a plastic disc at the Naval Research Laboratory, Washington, DC, USA, in August 1980.

The world's most efficient lubricant is *Tufoil*, manufactured by Fluoramics Inc of Mahwah, New Jersey, USA. Its coefficient of friction is .029.

In the centrifuge at the University of Virginia, USA a 13.6-kg *30-lb* rotor magnetically supported has been spun at 1000 rev/sec in a vacuum of $10^{-6}\,mm$ of mercury pressure. It loses only one revolution per second per day, thus spinning for years.

Most powerful electric current If fired simultaneously, the 4032 capacitors comprising the Zeus capacitor at the Los Alamos Scientific Laboratory, New Mexico, USA would produce, for a few microseconds, double the current generated elsewhere on Earth.

Hottest flame The hottest flame is produced by carbon subnitride (C_4N_2) which, at one atmosphere pressure, can generate a flame calculated to reach $4988\,°C$ *9010 °F*.

Highest frequency The highest frequency measured *directly* is a visible yellow-green light at 520.2068085 terahertz for the o-component of the 17–1 P (62) transition line of iodine-127.

The highest measured frequency determined by precision metrology is a green light at 582.491703 terahertz for the b_{21} component of the R (15) 43–0 transition line of iodine-127.

$HF:SbF_5$). The H_0 acidity function of this solution has not been measured, but even a weaker 50% solution is 10^{18} times stronger than concentrated sulphuric acid.

Sweetest substance Talin obtained from arils (appendages found on certain seeds) of the katemfe plant (*Thaumatococcus daniellii*) discovered in West Africa is 6150 times as sweet as a one per cent sucrose solution.

Most absorbent substance The US Department of Agriculture Research Service announced on 18 Aug 1974 that 'H-span' or Super Slurper—composed of one half starch derivative and one quarter each of acrylamide and acrylic acid—can, when treated with iron, retain water at 1300 times its own weight.

Most heat-resistance substance The existence of a complex material known as NFAAR, or Ultra Hightech Starlite was announced in April 1993. Invented by Maurice Ward (GB; b. 1932), it is apparent that it can temporarily resist plasma temperatures ($10,000\,°C$ *18,032 °F*).

Most refractory substance The most refractory compound is tantalum carbide $TaC_{0.88}$ which melts at $3990\,°C$ *7214 °F*.

Least dense solid The solid substances with the lowest density are silica aerogels in which tiny spheres of bonded silicon and oxygen atoms are joined into long strands separated by pockets of air. The lightest of these aerogels, with a density of only $0.005\,g/cm^3$ *5 oz/ft³* was produced at the Lawrence Livermore

Physical Extremes

Highest temperature The highest man-made temperature attained is $510,000,000\,°C$ *920,000,000 °F*, on 27 May 1994, at the Tokamak Fusion Test Reactor at the Princeton Plasma Physics Laboratory, New Jersey, USA, using a deuterium-tritium plasma mix ($\Leftrightarrow$Fusion Power).

Lowest temperature The absolute zero of temperature, 0 K on the Kelvin scale, corresponds to $-273.15\,°C$ *−459.67 °F*. The lowest temperature reached is 280 pK ($2.8 \times 10^{-10}\,K$), achieved in a nuclear demagnetization device at the Low Temperature Laboratory of the Helsinki University of Technology, Finland and announced in February 1993.

Highest pressures A sustained laboratory pressure of 170 GPa *11,000 tons force/in²* was reported from the giant hydraulic diamond-faced press at the Carnegie Institution's Geophysical Laboratory, Washington, DC, USA in June 1978.

Momentary pressures of 7000 GPa *498,000 tonnes/in²* were reported from the United States in 1958 using dynamic methods and impact speeds of up to 29,000 km/h *18,000 mph*.

Lowest friction The lowest coefficient of static and dynamic friction of any solid is 0.03. This result was achieved by sliding Hi-T-Lube on itself. The material is manufactured by General Magnaplate Corporation of Linden, New Jersey, USA.

> The record for the highest temperature is one that changes frequently; when our first edition was published, the highest known temperature was just 600,000°C, officially disclosed in a report of the Monte Bello Island Atom Bomb Test, of 3 Oct 1952. Compare this with the record today...

Longest echo The longest echo produced in any building is 15 seconds, following the closing of the door of the Chapel of the Mausoleum in Hamilton, Strathclyde, built 1840–55.

Brightest light The brightest artificial sources are laser pulses generated at the Los Alamos National Laboratory, New Mexico, USA announced in March 1987. An ultra-violet flash lasting 1 picosecond ($1 \times 10^{-12}\,sec$) is intensified to a power of $5 \times 10^{15}\,W$.

The most powerful searchlight ever was produced during World War II by The General Electric Company Ltd at the Hirst Research Centre, Wembley, London. It had a consumption of 600 kW and gave an arc luminance of 46,500 candelas/cm² *300,000 candelas/in²* and a maximum beam intensity of 2.7 billion candelas from its parabolic mirror of 3.04 m *10 ft* diameter.

Of continuously burning light sources, the most powerful is a 313 kW high-pressure argon arc lamp of

Longest Index

The 12th collective index of *Chemical Abstracts*, completed in December 1992, contains 35,137,626 entries in 215,880 pages and 115 volumes and weighs 246.7 kg *544 lb*. It provides references to 3,052,700 published documents in the field of chemistry.

Smallest Hole

Holes corresponding to a diameter of 3.16 Å ($3.16 \times 10^{-10}\,m$) were produced on the surface of molybdenum disulphide by Dr Wolfgang Heckl (University of Munich) and Dr John Maddocks (University of Sheffield) using a chemical method involving a mercury drill. The holes were drilled on 17 Jul 1992 at the University of Munich, Germany.

1,200,000 candelas, completed by Vortek Industries Ltd of Vancouver, British Columbia, Canada in March 1984.

Highest vacuum In January 1991 K. Odaka and S. Ueda of Japan reported having obtained a vacuum of 7×10^{-11} Pa 7×10^{-16} atmospheres in a stainless steel chamber.

Magnetic fields The strongest continuous field strength achieved was a total of 38.7 ±0.3 teslas at the Francis Bitter National Magnet Laboratory, Massachusetts Institute of Technology, USA on 25 May 1994 by a hybrid magnet with holmium pole pieces. These had the effect of enhancing the central magnetic field of 35.2±0.2 teslas generated by the hybrid magnet.

The weakest magnetic field measured is one of 8×10^{-15} teslas in the heavily shielded room at the same laboratory. It is used for research into the very weak magnetic fields generated in the heart and brain.

Highest voltage The highest-ever potential difference obtained in a laboratory has been 32±1.5 MV by the National Electrostatics Corporation at Oak Ridge, Tennessee, USA on 17 May 1979.

Scientific Instruments

Finest balance The Sartorius Microbalance Model 4108, manufactured in Göttingen, Germany, can weigh objects of up to 0.5 g *0.018 oz* to an accuracy of 0.01 μg, or 1×10^{-8} g *3.5x10⁻¹⁰ oz*, which is equivalent to little more than one sixtieth of the weight of the ink on this full stop.

Fastest centrifuge Ultra-centrifuges were invented by the Swedish Nobel prize-winning chemist Theodor Svedberg (1884–1971) in 1923. The highest man-made rotary speed ever achieved is 7250 km/h *4500 mph* by a tapered 15.2 cm *6 in* carbon fibre rod rotating in a vacuum at Birmingham University, reported on 24 Jan 1975.

Most powerful laser Albert Einstein (1879–1955) formulated the principle of light amplification by stimulated emissions of radiation in 1917, but the first practical device was a gas maser (microwave amplification by stimulated emissions of radiation) produced in 1954 by J. Gordon, H. Zeiger and C. Townes. The first laser (a term coined by Richard Gould) was constructed in 1960 by Theodore Maiman of the Hughes Research Laboratory in California, USA, with similar devices developed independently by Soviet physicists N. Bassov and A. Prokhorov.

The most powerful laser is the 'Nova' at the Lawrence Livermore National Laboratory, California, USA. Its 10 arms produce laser pulses capable of generating 100×10^{12} W of power, much of which is delivered to a target the size of a grain of sand in 1×10^{-9} sec. For this brief instance, that power is 200 times greater than the combined output of all the electrical generating plants in the US. Fitted with two target chambers, the laser itself is 91 m *300 ft* long and about three storeys high.

Heaviest magnet The heaviest magnet is in the Joint Institute for Nuclear Research at Dubna, near Moscow, Russia for the 10 GeV synchrophasotron.

Guess What?
Q. Which European country was the first to introduce phone cards?
A. See Page 79

It weighs 36,000 tonnes and is 60 m *196 ft* in diameter.

Largest electromagnet The world's largest electromagnet is part of the L3 detector experiment at LEP (⇨Largest Scientific Instrument). The octagonal magnet consists of 6400 tonnes of low carbon steel yoke and 1100 tons of aluminium coil and 300 amperes of current flowing through the aluminium coil is used to create a uniform magnet field of 5 kilogauss. The magnet is higher than a four-storey building of about 1728 m³ *59,320 ft³* volume. Its total weight, including the frame, coil and inner support tube, is 7810 tons and it is composed of more metal than the Eiffel Tower.

Most powerful particle accelerator The world's highest energy 'atomsmasher' is the proton synchrotron 'Tevatron' at the Fermi National Accelerator Laboratory (Fermilab) near Batavia, Illinois, USA. On 3 Jan 1987 a centre of mass energy of 1.8 TeV (1.8×10^{12} eV) was achieved by colliding beams of protons and antiprotons.

Thinnest glass Type D263 glass, made by Deutsche Spezialglas AG of Grünenplan, Germany for use in electronic and medical equipment, is the world's thinnest: it has a minimum thickness of 0.025 mm *0.00098 in* and a maximum thickness of 0.035 mm *0.00137 in*.

Instrument

The largest scientific instrument (and arguably the world's largest machine) is the Large Electron Positron (LEP) storage ring at CERN, Geneva, Switzerland which is 3.8 m *12½ ft* in diameter and 27 km *17 miles* in circumference. Over 60,000 tonnes of technical equipment have been installed in the tunnel and its eight underground working zones. (⇨ Heaviest particle)

Smallest thermometer Dr Frederich Sachs, a biophysicist at the State University of New York at Buffalo, USA, has developed an ultra-microthermometer for measuring the temperature of single living cells. The tip is one micrometer in diameter, about ¹/₅₀th of the diameter of a human hair.

Smallest microphone A microphone with a frequency response of 10 Hz–10 kHz and measuring 1.5×0.76 mm *0.06 x 0.03 in* was developed in 1967 by Prof. Ibrahim Kavrak of Bogazici University, Istanbul, Turkey as a new technique in measuring pressure in fluid flow.

Largest barometer An oil-filled barometer, of overall height 16.8 m *53.1 ft*, was constructed by Benny Dierckx, Jan Geerts and Marc Gommé of Stedelijk Lyceum Borgerhout in Belgium on 26 Mar 1994. It attained a *standard* height of 13.58 m *44.5 ft* (at which pressure mercury would stand at 0.76 m *2½ ft*).

The largest permanently-installed barometer has an overall height of 13 m *42 ft*, and was constructed by Alan Mills and John Pritchard of the Department of Physics and Astronomy, University of Leicester in 1991.

Slowest machine A nuclear environmental machine for testing stress corrosion that can be controlled at a speed as slow as one million millionth of a millimetre per minute (1 m *3.3 ft* in about 2000 million years) has been developed by Nene Instruments of Wellingborough, Northants.

Smallest prism A glass prism with sides measuring 0.01 mm *0.005 in*, barely visible to the naked eye, was

Sharpest

The sharpest manufactured objects are glass micro-pipette tubes whose bevelled tips have outer and inner diameters of 0.02 μm and 0.01 μm respectively, the latter being 6500 times thinner than a human hair. They are used in intracellular work on living cells in techniques developed in 1977.

created at the National Institute of Standards and Technology in Boulder, Colorado, USA in 1989.

Glass blowing A bottle standing 2.3 m *7 ft 8 in* tall with a capacity of about 712 litres *188 gal* was blown at Wheaton Village, Millville, New Jersey, USA on 26 Sep 1992 by a team led by glass artist Steve Tobin. The attempt was made during the 'South Jersey Glass Blast', part of a celebration of the local glassmaking heritage.

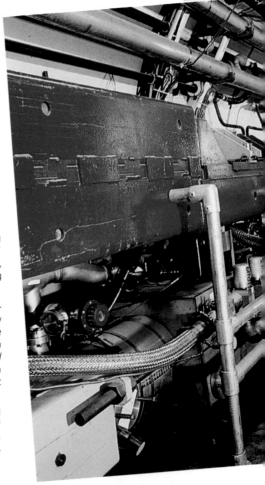

Finest cut The $13-million Large Optics Diamond turning Machine at the Lawrence Livermore National Laboratory in California, USA was reported in June 1983 to be able to sever a human hair 3000 times lengthways.

Fermilab
Home of the world's most powerful particle accelerator

■ Left: an aerial view of Fermilab (Fermi National Accelerator Laboratory) in Batavia, Illinois, USA, showing the 6.3-km *4-mile* circumference ring which houses the world's highest-energy particle accelerator—the Tevatron. Fixed-target experimental beam lines branch off from the Tevatron's circular tunnel, north of the 16-storey central laboratory building known as Wilson Hall.
(Photo: Fermilab Visual Media Services)

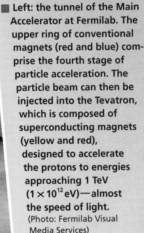

■ Left: the tunnel of the Main Accelerator at Fermilab. The upper ring of conventional magnets (red and blue) comprise the fourth stage of particle acceleration. The particle beam can then be injected into the Tevatron, which is composed of superconducting magnets (yellow and red), designed to accelerate the protons to energies approaching 1 TeV $(1 \times 10^{12}\,\text{eV})$—almost the speed of light.
(Photo: Fermilab Visual Media Services)

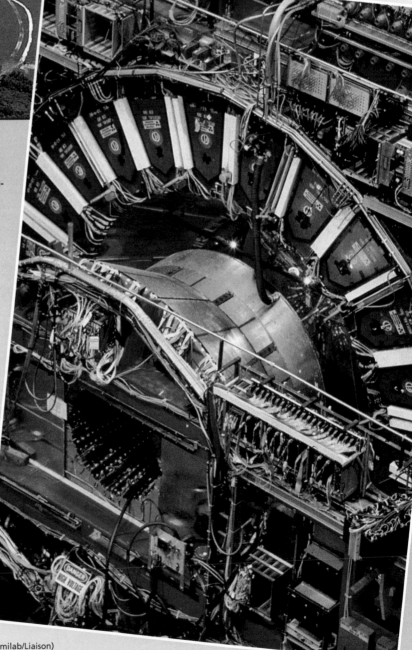

■ Right: the Collider Detector at Fermilab weighs approximately 5000 tons and stands more than three storeys tall. It is used to detect and measure the particles produced in collisions between protons and antiprotons; there are around 400,000 collisions each second. Physicists analyse the stored data from CDF and Fermilab's other detector, DZero, and are able to make fundamental studies about nature and energy. It was at Fermilab that scientists finally observed the long-awaited top quark in 1995 (⇨ Quarks and leptons).
(Photo: Gamma/Fermilab/Liaison)

Mathematics

In dealing with large numbers, the notation of 10 raised to various powers is used to eliminate a profusion of noughts. For example, 19,160,000,000,000 km would be expressed as 1.916×10^{13} km. Similarly, a very small number, for example 0.0000154324 g, would be written as a negative power, i.e 1.54324×10^{-5}. Of the prefixes used with numbers, the smallest is 'yocto' (y), of power 10^{-24} and the largest is 'yotta' (Y), of power 10^{24}. Both are based on the Greek octo, eight (for the eighth power of 10^3).

Largest number The largest lexicographically accepted named number in the system of successive powers of ten is the centillion, first recorded in 1852. It is the hundredth power of a million, or 1 followed by 600 noughts (although only in the UK and Germany).

Prime numbers A prime number is any positive integer (excluding unity 1) having no integral factors other than itself and unity, e.g. 2, 3, 5, 7 or 11. The lowest prime number is thus 2.

The highest *known* prime number was discovered by computer scientists David Slowinski and Paul Gage at Cray Research Inc, Eagan, Minnesota, USA in January 1994, while they were conducting tests on a CRAY C90 series supercomputer (⟺ Most powerful computer). The new prime number has 258,716 digits, enough to fill over 21 pages of *The Guinness Book of Records*. In mathematical notation it is expressed as $2^{859,433} - 1$, which denotes two, multiplied by itself 859,433 times, minus one. Numbers expressed in this form are known as 'Mersenne' prime numbers, named after Father Marin Mersenne, a French monk (1588–1648)

■ **Above: Pierre de Fermat, whose unsolved theorem inspired centuries of hopeless searching.**
(Photo: Ann Ronan Picture Library)

Below: Andrew J. Wiles, the Princeton University professor who claims to have brought an end to the search.
Photo: Gamma/Liaison)

who spent years searching for prime numbers of this type (⟺ Perfect numbers)

The largest known twin primes are $1,706,595 \times 2^{11,235} - 1$ and $1,706,595 \times 2^{11,235} + 1$, found on 6 Aug 1989 by a team in Santa Clara, California, USA using an Amdahl 1200 supercomputer.

Composite numbers The lowest of the non-prime, or composite, numbers (excluding 1) is 4.

Perfect numbers A number is said to be perfect if it is equal to the sum of all divisors of the number other than itself, for example 1+2+4+7+14 = 28. The lowest perfect number is 6, as in 1+2+3.

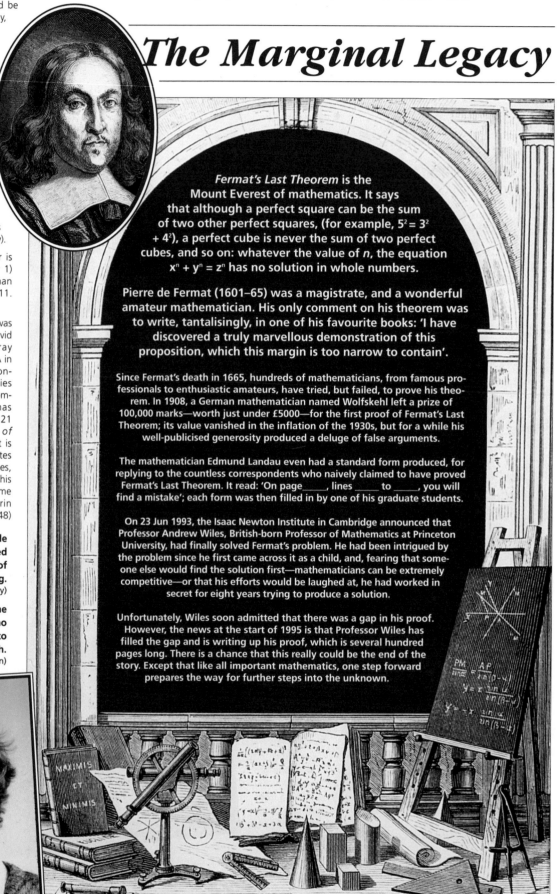

The Marginal Legacy

Fermat's Last Theorem is the Mount Everest of mathematics. It says that although a perfect square can be the sum of two other perfect squares, (for example, $5^2 = 3^2 + 4^2$), a perfect cube is never the sum of two perfect cubes, and so on: whatever the value of *n*, the equation $x^n + y^n = z^n$ has no solution in whole numbers.

Pierre de Fermat (1601–65) was a magistrate, and a wonderful amateur mathematician. His only comment on his theorem was to write, tantalisingly, in one of his favourite books: 'I have discovered a truly marvellous demonstration of this proposition, which this margin is too narrow to contain'.

Since Fermat's death in 1665, hundreds of mathematicians, from famous professionals to enthusiastic amateurs, have tried, but failed, to prove his theorem. In 1908, a German mathematician named Wolfskehl left a prize of 100,000 marks—worth just under £5000—for the first proof of Fermat's Last Theorem; its value vanished in the inflation of the 1930s, but for a while his well-publicised generosity produced a deluge of false arguments.

The mathematician Edmund Landau even had a standard form produced, for replying to the countless correspondents who naively claimed to have proved Fermat's Last Theorem. It read: 'On page_____, lines _____ to _____, you will find a mistake'; each form was then filled in by one of his graduate students.

On 23 Jun 1993, the Isaac Newton Institute in Cambridge announced that Professor Andrew Wiles, British-born Professor of Mathematics at Princeton University, had finally solved Fermat's problem. He had been intrigued by the problem since he first came across it as a child, and, fearing that someone else would find the solution first—mathematicians can be extremely competitive—or that his efforts would be laughed at, he had worked in secret for eight years trying to produce a solution.

Unfortunately, Wiles soon admitted that there was a gap in his proof. However, the news at the start of 1995 is that Professor Wiles has filled the gap and is writing up his proof, which is several hundred pages long. There is a chance that this really could be the end of the story. Except that like all important mathematics, one step forward prepares the way for further steps into the unknown.

All perfect numbers have a direct relationship to Mersenne primes. The highest known perfect number, therefore, and the 33rd so far discovered, is $(2^{859,433}-1) \times 2^{859,433}$. It has a total of 517,430 digits (enough to fill over 41 pages of *The Guinness Book of Records*) and it is derived from the largest known Mersenne prime (⟨⟩ Prime numbers).

Newest mathematical constant The study of turbulent water, the weather and other chaotic phenomena has revealed the existence of a new universal constant, the Feigenbaum number, first calculated by Mitchell J. Feigenbaum of the US. It is approximately equal to 4.669201609102990.

Most-proved theorem A book published in 1940 and entitled *The Pythagorean Proposition* contained 370 different proofs of Pythagoras' theorem, including one by American President James Garfield (1831–81).

Longest proof The proof of the classification of all finite simple groups is spread over more than 14,000 pages in nearly 500 papers in mathematical journals, contributed by more than 100 mathematicians over a period of more than 35 years.

Most prolific mathematician The prolific output of Swiss mathematician Leonhard Euler (1707–83) was such that his papers were still being published for the first time more than 50 years after his death. His collected works have been printed bit by bit since 1910 and will eventually occupy more than 75 large quarto volumes.

Oldest mathematical puzzle 'As I was going to St Ives, I met a man with seven wives. Every wife had seven sacks, and every sack had seven cats. Every cat had seven kits. Kits, cats, sacks and wives, how many were going to St Ives?'

Apart from slight differences in wording, this is identical to a puzzle found in the Rhind papyrus, an Egyptian scroll bearing mathematical tables and problems, copied by the scribe A'h-mosè c. 1650 BC.

Least numerate
The Nambiquara people of the north-west Matto Grosso in Brazil lack any system of numbers. They do, however, have a verb which means 'they are alike'.

Most accurate version of 'pi' The most decimal places to which pi (π) has been calculated is 2,260,321,336 by brothers Gregory Volfovich and David Volfovich Chudnovsky, on their homemade supercomputer m zero in New York City, USA in Summer 1991.

Most inaccurate In 1897 the General Assembly of Indiana, USA enacted in Bill No. 246 stating that *pi* was *de jure* 4, though the Bible manages to imply that *pi* equals 3.

Longest computer computation for a yes–no answer The 20th Fermat number, $2^{2^{20}}+1$, was tested on a CRAY–2 supercomputer in 1986 to see if it was a prime number. After 10 days of calculation the answer was no.

Smallest robot The world's smallest robot is the 'Monsieur' microbot, developed by the Seiko Epson Corporation of Japan in 1992. The light-sensitive

Earliest Weight

The earliest known measure of weight is the *beqa* of the Amratian period of Egyptian civilization c. 3800 BC, found at Naqada, Egypt. The weights are cylindrical, with rounded ends and weigh from 188.7–211.2 g *6.65–7.45 oz*.

The unit of length used by the megalithic tomb-builders in north-western Europe c. 3500 BC, and generally known as the megalithic yard, was deduced by Prof. Alexander Thom (1894–1985) in 1966 to have been 82.90 ± 0.09 cm *2.72 ± 0.003 ft*.

robot measures less than 1 cm³ *0.06 in³*, weighs 1.5 g *0.05 oz* and is made of 97 separate watch parts (equivalent to two ordinary watches). Capable of speeds of 11.3 mm/sec *0.4 in/sec* for about 5 min when charged, the 'Monsieur' has earned a design award at the International Contest for Hill-Climbing Micromechanisms.

Time measure The longest measure of time is the *para* in Hindu chronology. It is equivalent to the length of the complete life of Brahma, and is equivalent to 311,040,000,000,000 years (this is 68,500 times longer than the estimated age of the Earth). In astronomy a cosmic year is the period of rotation of the Sun around the centre of the Milky Way galaxy, i.e. 223 million years, assuming a circular orbit. In the Late Cretaceous Period of c. 85 million years ago the Earth rotated faster, resulting in 370.3 days per year, while in Cambrian times c. 600 million years ago there is evidence that the year comprised 425 days.

Computers

Earliest computer The earliest programmable electronic computer was the 1500-valve Colossus formulated by Prof. Max H.A. Newman (1897–1985) and built by T.H. Flowers. It was run in December 1943 at Bletchley Park, Bucks to break the German coding machine Enigma. It arose from a concept published in 1936 by Dr Alan Mathison Turing (1912–54) in his paper *On Computable Numbers with an Application to the* Entscheidungsproblem. Colossus was not declassified until 25 Oct 1975.

The world's first stored-programme computer was the Manchester University Mark I, which incorporated the Williams storage cathode ray tube (patented 11 Dec 1946). It ran its first program, by Prof. Tom Kilburn (b. 11 Aug 1921), for 52 min on 21 Jun 1948.

Computers were greatly advanced by the invention of the point-contact transistor by John Bardeen and Walter Brattain (announced in July 1948), and the junction transistor by R.L. Wallace, Morgan Sparks and Dr William Bradford Shockley (1910–89) in early 1951.

The concept of the integrated circuit, which has enabled micro-miniaturisation, was first published on 7 May 1952 by Geoffrey W.A. Dummer (GB; b. 1909) in Washington, DC, USA.

The invention of the microcomputer was attributed to a team led by M.E. Hoff, Jr of Intel Corporation with the production of the microprocessor chip '4004' in 1969–71. On 17 Jul 1990, however, priority was accorded to Gilbert Hyatt (b. 1938), who devised a single chip microcomputer at Micro Computer Inc. of Van Nuys, Los Angeles in 1968–71 with the award of US Patent No. 4942516.

Fastest computer The fastest general-purpose vector-parallel computer is the Cray Y-MP C90 supercomputer, with 2 gigabytes (gigabytes = one billion bytes) of central memory and with 16 CPUs (central processing units) giving a combined peak performance of 16 gigaflops (gigaflops = one billion flops/floating point operations/per second).

Several suppliers now market 'massively parallel' computers which, with enough processors, have a theoretical aggregate performance exceeding that of a C-90, though the performance on real-life applications can often be less. This is because it may be harder to harness effectively the power of a large number of small processors than a small number of large ones.

Largest computer network The network of computers collectively known as the Internet is easily the world's largest. At the beginning of 1995, the number of users was thought to be around 24 million; of those, around 17 million were based in the United States. The Internet has more than doubled in size each year since it began in 1988.

Power

Steam Engines

Oldest steam engine The oldest steam engine in working order is the Smethwick Engine dating from 1779. Designed by James Watt (1736–1819) and built by the Birmingham Canal Company at a cost of £2000, the pump—originally a 60-cm *24-in* bore with a stroke of 2.4 m *8 ft*—worked on the canal locks at Smethwick, W Mids until 1891. The engine was presented to the Birmingham Museum of Science and Industry in 1960 and is regularly steamed for the public.

The oldest engine working as such and on its original site is the 1812 Boulton & Watt 26-hp, 1066 mm *42 in* bore beam engine on the Kennet and Avon Canal at Great Bedwyn, Wilts. It was restored by the Crofton Society in 1971 and still runs periodically.

Steam Engine

The largest ever single-cylinder steam engine was designed by Matthew Loam of Cornwall and built by the Hayle Foundry Co. in 1849 for land draining at Haarlem, Netherlands. The cylinder was 3.65 m *12 ft* in diameter and each stroke, also of 3.65 m *12 ft*, lifted 61,096 litres *13,440 gal* of water.

Most efficient steam engine The most efficient steam engine recorded was Taylor's engine built by Michael Loam for United Mines of Gwennap, Cornwall in 1840. It registered only 0.8 kg *1.7 lb* of coal per horsepower per hour.

Windmills *Earliest* Although usually associated with the Netherlands, the earliest recorded windmills were used for grinding corn in Iran in the 7th century AD. The oldest Dutch mill is the tower-mill at Zeddam, Gelderland, built c. 1450.

UK The earliest authenticated windmills in England date back to the last quarter of the 12th century: 1185 at Amberley, Sussex, and 1185–1190 at Weedley near Hull. A windmill at

Fast Chips

The world's fastest microprocessor is the Alpha AXP 21164, developed by Digital Equipment Corporation of Maynard, Massachusetts, and unveiled in September 1994. It can run at speeds of 300 MHz (compared to 66 MHz for a modern personal computer).

Guess What?

Q. What is the most proven mathematical theorem?

A. See Page 73

Wigston Parva, Leics is claimed to date from 1137, but this has not been proven.

The oldest remains of a windmill in England is the stump, wrongly known as 'The Beacon', at Burton Dasset, Warks, which dates from the 14th century. The only windmill to remain in full commercial use since its construction in 1813 is the Subscription Mill at North Leverton, Notts.

Largest The tallest windmill in the world is the St Patrick's Distillery Mill in Dublin, now without sails. It is 150 ft *45.72 m* tall. The tallest working windmill in Europe is de Noord Molen at Schiedam, Netherlands, at 109 ft 4 in *33.33 m*, though there are other disused Dutch windmills that are taller.

The UK's tallest working windmill is the five-sailed Maud Foster windmill at Boston, Lincs, built in 1819, which is 80 ft *24.38 m* high.

Largest battery The 10 MW lead-acid battery at Chino, California, USA has a design capacity of 40 MWh. It is currently used at an electrical sub-station for levelling peak demand loads. This $13-million project is a co-operative effort by Southern California Edison Co. Electric Power Research Institute and International Lead Zinc Research Organization Inc.

Most durable The zinc foil and sulfur dry-pile batteries made by Watlin and Hill of London in 1840 have powered ceaseless tintinnabulation inside a bell jar at the Clarendon Laboratory, Oxford since that year.

Biggest black-out The greatest power failure in history struck seven north-eastern US states and Ontario, Canada on 9–10 Nov 1965. About 30 million people over an area of 207,200 km^2 *80,000 miles²* were plunged into darkness; only two were killed.

Fusion power Sustained fusion was first achieved in the Joint European Torus (JET) at Culham, Oxfordshire, on 9 Nov 1991, by tritium injection into a deuterium plasma.

Highest rating The highest power rating attained is 10.7 megawatts, in the Tokamak Fusion Test Reactor (TFTR), at the Princeton Plasma Physics Laboratory, New Jersey, USA on 2 Nov 1994 (⇨Highest temperature).

Transformers The world's largest single-phase transformers are rated at 1,500,000 kVA. Of the eight in service with the American Electric Power Service Corporation, five step down from 765 to 345 kV. Britain's largest transformers are rated at 1,000,000 kVA. Commissioned for the CEGB (Central Electric Generating Board) in October 1968, they were built by Hackbridge & Hewittic of Walton-on-Thames, Surrey.

Transmission lines The longest span of any power line between pylons is 5376 m *17,638 ft* across the Ameralik Fjord near Nuuk, Greenland. Built and erected by A.S. Betonmast of Oslo, Norway in 1991–2 as part of the 132 kV line serving the 45 MW Buksefjorden Hydro Power Station, the line weighs 38 tonnes.

The longest in Britain are the 1618 m *5310 ft* lines built by J.L. Eve across the Severn, with main towers each 148 m *488 ft* high.

Highest The world's highest power lines span 3627 m *11,900 ft* across the Straits of Messina,

Italy from towers at heights of 205 m *675 ft* (Sicily side) and 224 m *735 ft* (Calabria).

The highest lines in Britain are suspended from 192 m *630 ft* tall towers at a minimum height of 76 m *250 ft* across the Thames estuary. They are 1371 m *4500 ft* apart, have a breaking load of 130 tonnes and were made by BICC at West Thurrock, Essex.

Highest voltages The highest voltages carried on a DC (direct current) line are 1330 kV over a distance of 1224 miles *1970 km* on the DC Pacific Inter-Tie in the United States, which stretches from approximately 100 miles *160 km* east of Portland, Oregon, to a location east of Los Angeles, California.

The highest voltages carried on a three-phase AC (alternating current) line are 1200 kV in Russia over a distance greater than 1000 miles *1610 km*. The first section carries the current from Siberia to the province of North Kazakhstan, while the second section takes the current from Siberia to Ural.

Turbines The largest hydraulic turbines are rated at 815 MW. They are 9.7 m *32 ft* in diameter, have a 407-tonne runner, a 317.5-tonne shaft and were installed by Allis-Chalmers at the Grand Coulee Third Powerplant, Washington, USA.

Smallest A self-sustaining gas turbine with compressor and turbine wheels measuring just 5 cm *2 in* and an operating speed of 50,000 rev/min was built by Geoff Knights of London. The engine was completed and first ran on 4 Feb 1989.

Power Plants

Largest power plant The most powerful installed power station is the Itaipu hydro-electric plant on the Paraná River near the Brazil-Paraguay border. Opened in 1984, the station has now attained its ultimate rated capacity of 13,320 MW.

UK The power station with the greatest installed capacity in Great Britain is the Drax installation in North Yorkshire, with six 660-MW sets yielding 4000 MW.

Largest generator The largest operational is a turbo-generator of 1450 MW (net) under installation at the Ignalina atomic power station in Lithuania.

Nuclear reactors Work began on the 1455-MW planned net capacity CHOOZ-B1 reactor in France in July 1982, and the first reactor became operational in 1991. The USA has the most nuclear reactors (109), generating 98,729 megawatt hours or 29.8% of the world total of nuclear power.

UK The pressurised water reactor at Sizewell B, Leiston, Suffolk, completed in 1994, is the UK's most powerful reactor, with a net capacity of 1200 MW.

Solar power In terms of nominal capacity, the largest solar electric power facility in the world is the Harper Lake Site (LSP 8 & 9) in the Mojave Desert, California, USA operated by UC Operating Services. These two solar electric generating stations (SEGS)

have a nominal capacity of 160 MW (80 MW each). The station site covers 1280 acres.

Wind generator The largest operating wind generator is the $55-million Boeing Mod-5B wind generator in Oahu, Hawaii, USA. It has 97.5-m *320-ft* rotors, and produces 3200 kW when the wind reaches 32 mph.

Engineering

Strongest alloy Carbon-manganese steel music wire measuring 0.1 mm *0.004 in* wide, has a required tensile strength in the range of 3.40 to 3.78 GPa (3.40×10^9 to 3.78×10^9 Pa or 4.93×10^5 to 5.48×10^5 lbf/in²).

Smallest man-made object By using field ion microscopy the tips of probes of scanning tunnelling microscopes have been shaped to end in a single atom — the last three layers constituting the world's smallest man-made pyramid, consisting of 7, 3 and 1 atoms. Since the announcement in January 1990 that D.M. Eigler and E.K. Schweizer of the IBM Almaden Research Center, San Jose, California, USA had used an STM to move and reposition single atoms of xenon on a nickel surface in order to spell out the initials 'IBM', other laboratories around the world have used similar techniques on single atoms of other elements.

Most powerful diesel engines Five 12RTA84 type diesel engines each with a 12 cylinder power unit giving a maximum continuous output of 41,920 kW *57,000 bhp* at 95 rev/min were constructed by Sulzer Brothers of Winterthur, Switzerland for container ships built for the American President Lines. The first of these ships, the *President Truman*, was delivered in April 1988.

Nuts

The largest nuts ever made have an outer diameter of 132 cm *52 in*, a 63.5 cm *25 in* thread and weigh 4.74 tonnes. Known as 'Pilgrim Nuts', they are manufactured by Pilgrim Moorside Ltd of Oldham, Lancs for use on the columns of large forging presses.

The world's largest nuclear power station, consisting of 10 reactors giving a net output of 8814 MW, is in Fukushima, Japan.

Crackers

The world's largest catalytic cracker—a machine used to 'crack' heavy, long-chain hydrocarbon molecules into consumer products, such as gasoline, heating oil and diesel fuel—is at the Bayway Refinery plant at Linden, New Jersey, USA. It had a fresh feed rate of 19.8 million litres *5.25 million gal* per day in 1994. The Bayway Refining Company is a wholly-owned subsidiary of Tosco Corporation of Stamford, Connecticut, USA.

Largest radar installation The largest of the three installations in the US Ballistic Missile Early Warning System (BMEWS) is that near Thule, Kalaallit Nunaat (Greenland), 1498 km *931 miles* from the North Pole. It was completed in 1960 at a cost of $500 million.

Largest wind tunnel The world's largest wind tunnel is at the NASA Ames Research Center in Mountain View, Palo Alto, California, USA. The largest test section measures 36 × 24 m *118 × 79 ft* and is powered by six 22,500-horsepower motors (135,000 horsepower total), producing a top speed of 106,000 kW.

The oldest water mill in continuous commercial use is Priston Mill near Bath, Avon, first mentioned in AD 931 in a charter of King Athelstan (reigned 924/5–939). It is driven by the Conygre Brook.

Most powerful press The world's most powerful production machines are two forging presses in the USA. The Loewy closed-die forging press, owned and operated by the Wyman-Gordon Company at North Grafton, Massachusetts, weighs 10,438 tonnes and stands 33 m *108 ft 2½ in* high. It has a rated capacity of 50,000 tonnes and became operational in October 1955. A press of similar weight, height and rated capacity is in operation at the plant of the Aluminum Company of America in Cleveland, Ohio, USA.

Largest blast furnace The world's largest blast furnace, with a volume of 5500 m³, is the No. 5 furnace at the Cherepovets works in Russia.

Largest steel producer The world's largest steel producer is the Nippon Steel Corporation of Tokyo, Japan, which produced 25,123 thousand tonnes of steel for the year ending March 1994. The company currently has 50,458 employees.

Most powerful crane The 28.14 m *92.3 ft* wide Rahco (R.A. Hanson Disc Ltd) gantry crane at the Third Powerplant of the Grand Coulee Dam in Washington, D.C., USA was tested in 1975 to lift a load weighing 2232 tonnes. It lowered a 1789-tonne generator rotor with an accuracy of 0.8 mm *¹/₃₂ in*.

Tallest mobile crane The 810-tonne Rosenkranz K10001, with a lifting capacity of 1000 tonnes and a combined boom and jib height of 202 m *663 ft*, is carried on 10 trucks each limited to a length of 23.06 m

■ The production line at Nippon Steel Corporation in Tokyo, Japan, the world's largest steel producer.
(Photo: Gamma/K. Kurita)

75 ft 8 in and an axle weight of 118 tonnes. The crane can lift 30 tonnes to a height of 160 m *525 ft*.

Largest fork lift truck In 1991 Kalmar LMV of Lidhult, Sweden manufactured three counterbalanced fork lift trucks capable of lifting loads up to 90 tonnes at a load centre of 2400 mm *90.5 in*. They were built to handle the great manmade river project comprising two separate pipelines, one 998 km *620 miles* long running from Sarir to the Gulf of Sirte and the other 897 km *557 miles* from Tazirbu to Benghazi, Libya.

Largest earthmover
The largest is the L-1400 loader developed by Marathon LeTourneau. It is 17.22 m *56 ft 6 in* long, weighs 410,000 lb, and has a bucket capacity of 21.4 m³ *714 ft³*.

Greatest load raised The heaviest operation in engineering history was the raising of the entire 1.6 km *1 mile* long offshore Ekofisk complex in the North Sea on 17–18 Aug 1987 because of subsidence of the sea bed. The complex, consisting of eight platforms weighing some 40,000 tonnes, was raised 6.5 m *21 ft 4 in* by 122 hydraulic jacks run by a computer-controlled hydraulic system.

Largest snow-plough blade A snow-plough with a blade 15.3 m *50.25 ft* long, 1.24 m *4 ft* high and with a clearing capacity of 31 m³ *1095 ft³* in one pass was made by Aero Snow Removal Corporation of New York, USA in 1992 for operation at JFK International Airport.

Longest escalators The longest escalators in Britain are three flights at the Angel underground station, London, each measuring 60 m

197 ft. Built by French engineers and installed as part of a £70 million facelift at the station, they caused great embarrassment to the management but no real surprise to London's commuters by breaking down three days after being put into operation on 12 Aug 1992.

The world's longest *ride* is on the four-section outdoor escalator at Ocean Park, Hong Kong, which has an overall length of 227 m *745 ft* and a total vertical rise of 115 m *377 ft*.

Moving walkways The world's longest moving walkways (or Travelators) are those installed in 1970 in the Neue Messe Centre, Düsseldorf, Germany, which measure 225 m *738 ft* between comb plates.

Shortest escalators The moving walkway at *Okadaya More's* Shopping Mall at Kawasaki-shi, Japan, has a vertical height of 83.4 cm *32.83 in*. It was installed by Hitachi Ltd.

Escalator riding The record distance travelled on a pair of 'up' and 'down' escalators is 214.34 km *133.18 miles*, by David Beattie and Adrian Simons at Top Shop, Oxford Street, London from 17–21 Jul 1989. They each completed 7032 circuits.

Fastest lifts The world's fastest domestic passenger lifts are the express lifts in the 70-storey, 296 m *971 ft* tall Yokohama Landmark Tower in Yokohama, Japan, opened to the public on 16 Jul 1993.

Conveyor Belts

The world's longest single-flight conveyor belt stretches across 29 km *18 miles* in Western Australia and was installed by Cable Belt Ltd of Camberley, Surrey. Great Britain's longest, also installed by Cable Belt, runs for 8.9 km *5 ½ miles* underground at Longannet power station, Fife.

Guess What?
Q. Which country is the largest oil producer?
A. See Page 78

On The Record

The Case Against Working Weekends

When Graham Coates stepped into the lift at his work in Brighton, East Sussex one Saturday in 1986, he meant simply to travel to the second floor. He had no idea that he would not emerge for another three days. Nine years on, he can still recall the nightmarish episode that made him an involuntary record-breaker.

After the lift had ground to a halt and nothing had happened, he pressed the buttons to operate the door. He jumped up and down in the lift, but still nothing happened. Then he pressed the alarm button and heard the bell ringing out. Unfortunately no-one else heard it. Not only was the office empty as it was a weekend, but the alarm bell was located inside the building and so could not be heard outside.

He began shouting at intervals at the top of his voice in order to attract the attention of the people next door, only to realise the further irony of his fate: that his working neighbour was a radio station whose employees worked from soundproofed studios. 'I decided that I would have to live with it until it was over or go out of my mind. There was no way that anyone would have missed me; I was living with my parents at the time and they were used to me staying out for a weekend.

'I had a part-time job as a cellarman at a pub called *The Counting House*, and as the time passed I started thinking to myself what I would be doing if I were not in the lift—serving pints, and talking to the locals. I became terribly thirsty. I started to imagine that I had poured myself a lager. When it came to Sunday I thought about the marvellous lunch that the landlady would have laid on.

'It was in the early hours of Tuesday morning that I heard noises in the building. After shouting for about ten minutes, someone heard me. It was my M.D. He called the manufacturer and they explained to him over the telephone how to lower the lift manually. After 62 hours of incarceration I was cold, tired and weak. I had to have several weeks off work to recover and suffered from headaches for some time afterwards'.

Occasionally, he says, he gets flashbacks when getting into a lift. These days, he only travels in one when there is a phone installed.

Longest cable car The highest and longest passenger-carrying aerial ropeway in the world is the Teleférico Mérida in Venezuela, from Mérida City (1639.5 m *5379 ft*) to the summit of Pico Espejo (4763.7 m *15,629 ft*), a rise of 3124 m *10,250 ft*. The ropeway is in four sections, involving three car changes in the 12.8 km *8 mile* ascent in one hour. The fourth span is 3069 m *10,070 ft* in length. The cars have a maximum capacity of 45 people and travel at 5 km/h *3 mph*.

Largest ropes The largest rope ever made was a coir fibre launching rope with a diameter of 119 cm *47 in* made in 1858 for the British liner *Great Eastern* by John and Edwin Wright of Birmingham, W Mids. It consisted of four strands, each of 3780 yarns.

Wire ropes The world's longest wire ropes are four made at British Ropes Ltd, Wallsend, Tyne & Wear, each measuring 24 km *15 miles*. The ropes are 35 mm *1.3 in* in diameter, weigh 108.5 tonnes each and were ordered by the CEGB for use in the construction of the 2000 MW cross-Channel power cable.

The suspension cables on the Seto Grand Bridge, Japan, completed in 1988, are 104 cm *41 in* in diameter.

A cable-laid rope 56 cm *22 in* in diameter, with a calculated breaking strength of 11,000 tonnes, was manufactured for demonstration purposes only by Franklin Offshore Supply & Engineering PTE LTD of Singapore in 1992.

Designed and built by Mitsubishi Electric Corporation of Tokyo, the lifts operate at 45 km/h *28 mph*, taking passengers from the second floor to the 69th floor observatory in 40 sec.

Much higher speeds are achieved in the winding cages of mine shafts. A hoisting shaft 2072 m *6800 ft* deep, owned by Western Deep Levels Ltd in South Africa, winds at speeds of up to 65 km/h *41 mph*. Otitis media (popping of the ears) presents problems above even 16 km/h *10 mph*.

Longest incarceration in a lift Graham Coates of Brighton, East Sussex established an involuntary duration record when trapped in a lift for 62 hr in Brighton on 24–27 May 1986.

Guess What?

Q. Where are the fastest lifts found?

A. See Page 73

Mining and Drilling

Deepest mine Man's deepest penetration into the Earth's crust is a geological exploratory borehole near Zapolarny in the Kola peninsula of Arctic Russia, begun on 24 May 1970 and reported in April 1992 to have surpassed a depth of 12,262 m *40,230 ft*. The eventual target of 15,000 m *49,212 ft* is expected in 1995.

Coal cutting The individual coal cutting record using pick and shovel is 45.4 tonnes per person in one shift (six hours) by five Soviet miners under the leadership of Aleksey Stakhanov at the Tsentralnaya-Irmino mine, Donetsk region, Ukraine (then USSR) on 19 Sep 1935.

Using machinery the British record output for a single colliery in a year is 3,045,986 tonnes, from Riccall Mine in the Selby Complex, N Yorks between April 1993 and March 1994. The record output in a week is 173,156 tonnes, produced at Wistow, also in the Selby Complex, in the week ending 16 Jan 1993.

Coal shovelling The record for filling a ½ ton *508 kg* hopper with coal is 26.83 sec, by Brian McArdle at the Fingal Valley Festival in Fingal, Tasmania, Australia on 5 Mar 1994.

Guess What?
Q. In which British town was the busiest telephone exchange?
A. See Page 79

Mine Records

Earliest
World 100,000 BC—CHERT (silica) Nazlet Sabaha Garb, Egypt.
UK 3390 BC±150—FLINT, Church Hill, Findon, W. Sussex

Deepest
World [1] 3581 m *11,749 ft*—GOLD, Western Deep Levels, Carletonville, South Africa.
UK 1105.5 m *3627 ft*—COAL, No. 2 shaft, Boulby Mine of Cleveland Potash Ltd, Saltburn, Cleveland.

Coal
Oldest (UK) c. 1822, Wearmouth, Tyne and Wear.
Deepest (exploratory shaft) 2042 m *6700 ft*, Donbas field, Ukraine.
(open cast, lignite) 325 m *1066 ft*, near Bergheim, Germany.

Copper
Earliest (UK) 1700–2000 BC, Cwmystwyth, Dyfed.
Deepest (open pit) 800 m *2625 ft*, Bingham Canyon, near Salt Lake City, Utah, USA.
Longest (underground) 1600 km *994 miles*, Division El Teniente, Codelco, Chile.

Gold
Largest (world) [2] 27,903 ha *68,949 acres*, Free State Cons Gold Mines Ltd, Orange Free State, South Africa. *UK* 120000 fine oz (1854–1914), Clogau, St David's (discovered 1836), Gwynedd.

Iron
Largest 20,300 million tonnes (45–65% ore), Lebedinsky, Kursk region, Russia.

Lead
Largest >10 per cent of world output, Viburnum Trend, Missouri, USA.

Platinum
Earliest 2nd century BC, La Tolita, Ecuador.
Largest 28 tonnes per year, Rustenburg Platinum Mines Group, Transvaal, South Africa.

Quarry
Largest (world) 7·21 km[2] *2·81 miles[2]*, 3355 million tonnes (extracted), Bingham Canyon, Utah, USA.
UK 150 m *500 ft* deep, 2·6 km *1·6 miles* circumference, Old Delabole Slate Quarry (from c. 1570), Cornwall.

Spoil Dump
Largest (world) 7·4 billion ft[3] *210 million m[3]*, New Cornelia Tailings, Ten Mile Wash, Arizona, USA.
UK 141 ha *348 acres*, Allerton Tip, near Castleford, W Yorks.

Uranium[3]
Largest (in terms of world prod) 5380 tonnes uranium per year, Cameco's Lake mine in Saskatchewan, Canada, 15.5% of world production.

[1] Sinking began in July 1957 and 4267 m *14,000 ft* is regarded as the limit. Its No. 3 vertical ventilation shaft is the world's deepest shaft, at 2949 m *9675 ft*. This mine requires 128,050 tonnes of air per day and equivalent refrigeration energy for making 33,600 tonnes of ice. An underground shift comprises 11,150 men.

[2] The world's most productive gold mine may be Muruntau, Kyzyl Kum, Uzbekistan, with an estimated 80 tonnes per year. It has been estimated that South Africa has produced in 107 years (1886–1993) more than 39 per cent of all gold mined since 3900 BC. Over 34.4 per cent of the world's output is produced at the 31 mines of the Witwatersrand fields, South Africa, first discovered in 1886.

[3] This has been shut down, but remains on standby. The Gas Hills mine in Wyoming, USA, at 2540 tonnes per day, is currently the most productive.

The record by a team of two is 15.01 sec, by Brian McArdle and Rodney Spark, both of Middlemount, Queensland, Australia on the same occasion.

Fastest drilling
The most footage drilled in one month is 10,477 m *34,574 ft* in June 1988 by Harkins & Company Rig Number 13 during the drilling of four wells in McMullen County, Texas, USA.

Ocean drilling The deepest recorded drilling into the sea bed is 2111 m *6926 ft* by the Ocean Drilling Program's vessel *JOIDES Resolution*, in the eastern equatorial Pacific in 1993. The greatest amount of core recovered during a single leg of the Ocean Drilling Program was 5808 m *19,055 ft* in 1994. The sediment cores, composed of calcareous ooze and chalk, were recovered from the Ceara Rise in the western equatorial Atlantic on ODP Leg 154.

Ice-core drilling The deepest borehole in ice was reported in July 1993 to have reached the bottom of the Greenland ice sheet at a depth of 3053.51 m *10,018 ft* after five years' drilling by American researchers.

Greatest penetration into the earth The deepest penetration made into the ground by human beings is in the Western Deep Levels Mine at Carletonville, Transvaal, South Africa, where a record depth of 3581 m *11,749 ft* was attained on 12 Jul 1977.

Shaft-sinking record The one-month (31 days) world record is 381.3 m *1251 ft* for a standard shaft 7.9 m *26 ft* in diameter at Buffelsfontein Mine, Transvaal, South Africa, in March 1962.

■ The end of the line at the Teleférico Mérida in Venezuela—the highest and longest cable car in the world. Passengers travel from Mérida City to the summit of Pico Espejo, a rise of 3124 m *10,250 ft*.
(Photo: Spectrum Colour Library)

Oil, Natural Gas ▶▶ ▶▶

■ A section of the Trans-Alaskan oil pipeline, passing across the Arctic tundra. In its entirety, the pipeline runs 1284 km *798 miles* from Prudhoe Bay on the north coast to Valdez on the southern coast of Alaska, USA.
(Photo: Science Photo Library/W. Bacon)

Oil

Oil production The world's largest oil producer is Saudi Arabia, with production in 1994 estimated at 7.818 million barrels per day (b/d).

Oil consumption The largest is the USA with 17.2 million b/d consumed in 1993, 26 percent of the world's total. The UK consumed 1.8 million b/d in 1993.

Oil fields The world's largest oil field is the Ghawar field in Saudi Arabia, developed by Aramco, and measuring 240×35 km *150×22 miles*.

Oil refineries The oil refinery with the largest crude capacity in the world is Amoco's in Texas City, Texas, USA, with crude capacity of 433,000 b/d as of January 1995.

UK The largest oil refinery in the UK is the Esso Refinery at Fawley, near Southampton, Hants. Opened in 1921 and much expanded in 1951, it has a capacity of 15.6 million tonnes per year.

Oil platforms *Heaviest* The world's heaviest oil platform is the *Pampo* platform in the Campos Basin off Rio de Janeiro, Brazil, built and operated by the Petrobrás company. Opened in the 1970s, the platform weighs 24,100 tonnes, covers 3000 m² *32,292 ft²* and produces 30,000 barrels per day. It operates at a height of 115 m *377 ft* from the sea bed (⇨Tallest).

Tallest In December 1993 the 'Auger' tension leg platform was installed in the Gulf of Mexico. Designed and engineered by the Shell Oil Company, it set a new water-depth record for a drilling and production platform, extending 872 m *2860 ft* from seabed to surface.

Oil spills The world's worst oil spill occurred as a result of a marine blow-out beneath the drilling rig *Ixtoc I* in the Gulf of Campeche, Gulf of Mexico, on 3 Jun 1979. The slick reached 640 km *400 miles* by 5 Aug 1979. It was eventually capped on 24 Mar 1980 after an estimated loss of up to 500,000 tonnes.

The worst single assault ever made upon the ecosystem was released on 19 Jan 1991 by the Iraqi President Saddam Hussein, who ordered the pumping of Gulf crude from the Sea Island terminal, Kuwait, and from seven large tankers. Provisional estimates put the loss at 816,000 tonnes.

British Isles The worst spill in British waters was from the 118,285 dwt *Torrey Canyon* which struck the Pollard Rock off Land's End on 18 Mar 1967, resulting in the loss of up to 120,000 tonnes of oil.

Oil tanks The largest oil tanks ever constructed are the five Aramco 1½-million-barrel storage tanks at Ju'aymah, Saudi Arabia. They are 21.94 m *72 ft* tall with a diameter of 117.6 m *386 ft* and were completed in March 1980.

Oil gusher The greatest wildcat ever recorded blew at Alborz No. 5 well, near Qum, Iran on 26 Aug 1956. The uncontrolled oil gushed to a height of 52 m *170 ft* at 120,000 barrels per day at a pressure of 62,055 kPa *9000 lb/in²*. It was closed after 90 days' work by B. Mostofi and Myron Kinley of Texas, USA.

Pipelines

The world's longest crude oil pipeline is the Interprovincial Pipe Line Inc. installation, which spans the North American continent from Edmonton, Alberta, Canada through Chicago to Montreal: a distance of 3787.2 km *2367 miles*. Along the length of the pipe, 82 pumping stations maintain a flow of 6 million litres *1.6 million gal* a day.

The longest natural gas pipeline in the world is the TransCanada pipeline, which transported a record 62 million m³ *2.2 billion ft³* of gas over 13,843 km *8652 miles* of pipe in 1994.

The world's most expensive pipeline is the Alaska pipeline running 1287 km *800 miles* from Prudhoe Bay to Valdez. The total cost of the pipeline is $9 billion. The pipe is 1.21 m *48 in* in diameter and its capacity is now 2.1 million barrels per day.

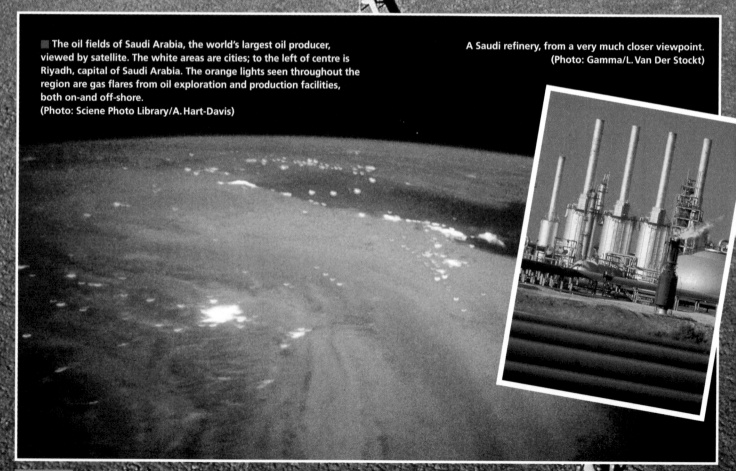

■ The oil fields of Saudi Arabia, the world's largest oil producer, viewed by satellite. The white areas are cities; to the left of centre is Riyadh, capital of Saudi Arabia. The orange lights seen throughout the region are gas flares from oil exploration and production facilities, both on-and off-shore.
(Photo: Sciene Photo Library/A. Hart-Davis)

A Saudi refinery, from a very much closer viewpoint.
(Photo: Gamma/L. Van Der Stockt)

Natural Gas

Natural gas production The world's largest producer of natural gas is the Commonwealth of Independent States (CIS), with 727 billion m^3 *25,673.8 billion ft^3*, produced in 1994. The USA was second, with production of 561.3 billion m^3 *19,822 billion ft^3*. The UK produced 72 billion m^3 *2,539 billion ft^3*.

Water wells The world's deepest water bore is the Stensvad Water Well 11-W1 of 2231 m *7320 ft* drilled by the Great Northern Drilling Co. Inc. in Rosebud County, Montana, USA in October–November 1961. The Thermal Power Co. geothermal steam well begun in Sonoma County, California, USA in 1955 is down to 2752 m *9029 ft*.

UK The deepest well in Great Britain is a water-table well 866 m *2842 ft* deep in the Staffordshire coal at Smestow, near Wolverhampton, W Mids.

Gas flare The greatest gas fire burnt at Gassi Touil in the Algerian Sahara from noon on 13 Nov 1961 to 9:30 a.m. on 28 Apr 1962. The pillar of flame rose 137 m *450 ft* and the smoke 182 m *600 ft*. It was eventually extinguished by Paul Neal ('Red') Adair (b. 1915) of Houston, Texas, USA, using 245 kg *540 lb* of dynamite, for a fee of about $1 million plus expenses.

Deposits

The largest gas deposit in the world is at Urengoi, Russia, with an eventual production of 200 billion m^3 *7062 billion ft^3* per year through six pipelines from proved reserves of 8 trillion m^3 *285.59 trillion ft^3*. The trillionth (10^{12}) m^3 was produced on the 23rd Apr 1986.

Telephones & Facsimiles

Telephones It has been estimated by the International Telecommunication Union that there were approximately 607 million telephone subscribers in the world by the end of 1993. The country with the greatest number was the United States, with 148,084,000. This compares with the United Kingdom figure of 27,380,000 (March 1994), or 470 per 1000 people. Monaco has the most per head of population, with 1994 per 1000. The greatest number of calls made in any country is in the United States, with 502.85 billion per annum (1992 figure).

Mobile phones The country with the greatest number of cellular telephone subscribers is the USA, with 24.1 million in early 1995. The United Kingdom total is 3,653,000. The country with the greatest penetration is Sweden, where there are 167 cellular telephone subscribers for every 1000 people, compared to the UK figure of 63 per 1000 people.

Busiest routes The busiest international telephone route is between the USA and Canada. In 1993 there were some 4.1 billion minutes of two-way traffic between the two countries. The country with which Britain has most telephone contact is the USA, with 1.3 billion minutes of two-way traffic in 1993.

Longest telephone cable The world's longest submarine telephone cable is ANZCAN, which

Time Pieces

Most accurate time-keeping device The most accurate time-keeping device is a commercially available atomic clock manufactured by Hewlett-Packard of Palo Alto, California, USA, unveiled in December 1991. Designated the HP 5071A primary frequency standard with caesium-2 technology, the device, costing $54,000 and about the size of a desktop computer, is accurate to one second in 1.6 million years.

Clocks

Oldest clock The world's oldest surviving working clock is the faceless clock dating from 1386, or possibly earlier, at Salisbury Cathedral, Wilts. It was restored in 1956, having struck the hours for 498 years and ticked more than 500 million times.

Largest clock The world's largest clock is the astronomical clock in the Cathedral of St Pierre, Beauvais, France, constructed between 1865 and 1868. It consists of 90,000 parts and is 12.1 m *40 ft* high, 6.09 m *20 ft* wide and 2.7 m *9 ft* deep.

Largest clock faces The world's largest clock face is that of the floral clock, which is 31 m *101 ft* in diameter. It was installed on 18 Jun 1991 at Matsubara Park, Toi, Japan.

Highest clock The world's highest two-sided clock is 177 m *580 ft* above street level on top of the Morton International Building, Chicago, Illinois, USA.

Largest sundial The world's largest sundial has a base diameter of 37.2 m *122 ft* and is 36.6 m *120 ft* high with a gnomon (projecting arm) of the same length. Designed by Arata Isozaki of Tokyo, Japan as the centre-piece of the Walt Disney World Co. headquarters in Orlando, Florida, USA, it was unveiled on 1 Mar 1991.

A sundial with a surface area of 3877.86 m^2 *41,741 ft^2*, designed by Shin Minohara of the Tadashi Minohara Design Studio, was built at the Keihanna Interaction Plaza, Kyoto, Japan in 1991.

Most expensive clock The highest price paid for any clock is £905,882 at Christie's, New York, USA on 24 Apr 1991 by a private bidder for a rare 'Egyptian Revival' clock made by Cartier in 1927. Designed as an ancient Egyptian temple gate, with figures and hieroglyphs, the clock is made of mother-of-pearl, coral and lapis lazuli.

The world's most accurate and complicated clock in 1955 was the Olsen clock, installed in the Copenhagen Town Hall. The clock, which had more than 14,000 units, took ten years to make, and the mechanism of the clock functioned in 570,000 different ways.

■ A jewelled wrist-watch by Jaeger le Coultre of Switzerland, makers of the world's smallest watches. (Photo: Gamma)

The world's longest pendulum measures 22.5 m *73 ft 9¾ in* and is part of the water-mill clock installed by the Hattori Tokeiten Co. in the Shinjuku NS building in Tokyo, Japan in 1983.

Watches

Largest watch The largest watch was a 'Swatch' 162 m *531 ft 6 in* long and 20 m *65 ft 7½ in* in diameter, made by D. Tomas Feliu, which was displayed on the Bank of Bilbao building, Madrid, Spain from 7–12 Dec 1985.

Heaviest watch The Eta 'watch' on the Swiss pavilion at Expo '86 in Vancouver, British Columbia, Canada from May to October weighed 35 tonnes and was 24.3 m *80 ft* high.

Smallest watch The smallest watches, measuring just over 12 mm *½ in* long and 4.76 cm *³⁄₁₆ in* wide, are produced by Jaeger le Coultre of Switzerland. They are equipped with a 15-jewelled movement and the movement and case weigh under 7 g *0.25 oz*.

Most expensive watch The record price paid for a watch is SwFr4.95 million (£1,864,304) at Habsburg Feldman, Geneva, Switzerland on 9 Apr 1989 for a Patek Philippe 'Calibre '89' with 1728 separate parts.

Longest stoppage of 'Big Ben' The longest stoppage of the clock in the House of Commons clock tower, London since the first tick on 31 May 1859 has been 13 days, from noon on 4 April to noon on 17 Apr 1977. In 1945 a host of starlings slowed the minute hand by five minutes.

In 1955 some 60 billion telephone calls were made in the USA. Now the annual figure is more than 500 billion.

The smallest operational telephone was created by Zbigniew Rózanek of Pleszew, Poland in September 1992. It measured just 6.7 × 1.9 × 2.8 cm *2⅝ × ¾ × 1⅛ in.*

runs for 15,151 km *9415 miles* (8181 nautical miles) from Port Alberni, Canada to Auckland, New Zealand and Sydney, Australia via Fiji and Norfolk Island. It cost some US $379 million and was inaugurated by HM Queen Elizabeth II in November 1984.

Largest telephone The world's largest operational telephone was exhibited at a festival on 16 Sep 1988 to celebrate the 80th birthday of Centraal Beheer, an insurance company based in Apeldoorn, Netherlands. It was 2.47 m *8 ft 1 in* high and 6.06 m *19 ft 11 in* long, and weighed 3.5 tonnes. The handset, being 7.14 m *23 ft 5 in* long, had to be lifted by crane in order to make a call.

Telescopes ▶▶ ▶▶

Telephone cards The first plastic phone cards issued were those in Rome in January 1976. The highest price paid for a phone card is believed to be for the first card issued in Japan, which changed hands in January 1992 for £28,000.

Busiest telephone exchange GPT (GEC Plessey Telecommunications Ltd) demonstrated the ability of the 'System X' telephone exchange to handle 1,558,000 calls in an hour through one exchange at Beeston, Nottingham on 27 Jun 1989.

Largest switchboard The world's biggest switchboard is that in the Pentagon, Washington, DC, USA, with 34,500 lines handling nearly 1 million calls per day through 322,000 km *200,000 miles* of telephone cable.

The Pentagon's busiest ever day was 6 Jun 1994—the 50th anniversary of D-Day—when there were 1,502,415 calls.

Largest and smallest fax machines The largest facsimile machine is manufactured by WideCom Group Inc of Ontario, Canada. 'WIDEfax 36' is able to transmit, print and copy documents up to 91 cm *36 in* in width.

The smallest is the Real Time Strategies Inc. hand-held device Pagentry, which combines various functions including the transmission of messages to facsimile machines. It measures just 7.6 × 12.7 × 1.9 cm *3 × 5 × ¾ in* and weighs 141.75 g *5 oz*.

Telegrams The highest price ever paid for a telegram is $68,500 (£45,900) by Alberto Bolaffi of Turin, Italy for the congratulatory telegram sent by Soviet premier Nikita Khrushchev to Yuri Gagarin on 12 Apr 1961 after he became the first man in space, at Sotheby's in New York, USA on 11 Dec 1993.

Telescopes

Earliest telescopes In October 1608 three Dutch spectacle-makers stated that they had each invented a telescope and actually produced refracting telescopes. Credit is usually given to one of these, Hans Lippershey (*c.* 1570–1619), but Galileo (1564–1642) brought the invention to the notice of the scientific world, first constructing and using telescopes in 1609. However, recent examination of evidence for the claims by Thomas Digges (*c.* 1547–95) that his father Leonard Digges (*c.* 1520–59) had invented both a refractor and, it seems, a reflector as well, strongly indicates that a refractor at least existed in Elizabethan times. The first successful reflector to be made was that by Sir Isaac Newton (1642–1727), constructed in 1668 or 1669. He presented it, or a copy of it, to the Royal Society in 1671.

Largest telescope The Keck telescope on Mauna Kea, Hawaii, USA has a 1000 cm *394 in* mirror, made up of 36 segments fitted together to produce the correct curve. The first image of the spiral galaxy NGC 1232 was obtained on 24 Nov 1990, when nine of the segments were in place. A twin Keck telescope is to be set up close to the first. When completed, Keck I and Keck II will be able to work together as an interferometer.

When Keck II is finished, the two Keck telescopes should theoretically be able to see a car's headlights separately from a distance of 25,000 km 15,500 miles.

Largest reflector The largest single-mirror telescope now in use is the 6 m *19 ft 8 in* reflector sited on Mount Semirodriki, near Zelenchukskaya in the Caucasus Mountains, Russia. It is at an altitude of 2080 m *6830 ft* and was completed in 1976. It has never come up to expectations, partly because it is not set up on a really good observing site. The largest satisfactory single-mirror telescope is the 508 cm *200 in* Hale reflector at Mount Palomar, California, USA.

The largest British reflector is the 420 cm *165 in* William Herschel completed in 1987, which is set up at the Los Muchachos Observatory on La Palma, Canary Isles. Also at La Palma is the 256 cm *101 in* Isaac Newton telescope, transferred there from its old site at Herstmonceux in Sussex.

Metal-mirror A 183 cm *72 in* reflector was made by the third Earl of Rosse (1800–67), and set up at Birr Castle, Republic of Ireland in 1845. The mirror was of speculum metal (an alloy of copper and tin). With it, Lord Rosse discovered the spiral forms of the galaxies. It was last used in 1909.

The Future

The largest telescope of the century should be the VLT (Very Large Telescope) being planned by the European Southern Observatory. It will be at Cerro Paranal, northern Chile, and will consist of four 8.2 m *26 ft 8 in* telescopes working together, providing a light-grasp equal to a single 16 m *52 ft 6 in* mirror. It is hoped to have the first units working in 1995, and the complete telescope by 2000.

Largest refractor A 101.6 cm *40 in* refractor 18.9 m *62 ft* in length completed in 1897 is situated at the Yerkes Observatory, Williams Bay, Wisconsin, USA and belongs to the University of Chicago, Illinois. Although nearly 100 years old, it is still in full use on clear nights. A larger refractor measuring 150 cm *59 in* was built in France and shown at the Paris Exhibition in 1900. It was a failure and was never used for scientific work.

Britain's largest refractor is the 71.1 cm *28 in* Great Equatorial Telescope of 1893 installed in the Old Royal Observatory, Greenwich, south-east London.

Largest infra-red telescope The largest infra-red telescope is the UKIRT (United Kingdom Infrared Telescope) on Mauna Kea, Hawaii, USA, which has a 374 cm *147 in* mirror. It is, however, so good that it can be used for visual work as well as infra-red.

Largest sub-millimetre telescope The James Clerk Maxwell telescope on Mauna Kea, Hawaii, USA has a 15 m *49 ft 3 in* paraboloid primary, and is used for studies of the sub-millimetre part of the electromagnetic spectrum (0.3–1.0 mm *0.01–0.03 in*). It does not produce a visual image.

In Space

The largest space telescope is the $2.1 billion (£1.4 billion) NASA Edwin P. Hubble Space Telescope of 11 tonnes and 13.1 m *43 ft* in overall length, with a 240 cm *94½ in* reflector. It was placed in orbit at 613 km *381 miles* altitude aboard a US space shuttle on 24 April 1990.

Largest solar telescope The McMath solar telescope at Kitt Peak, Arizona, USA has a 2.1 m *6 ft 11 in* primary mirror; the light is sent to it via a 32° inclined tunnel from a coelostat (rotatable mirror) at the top end. Extensive modifications to it are now being planned.

Largest Schmidt telescope A Schmidt telescope uses a spherical mirror with a correcting plate and can cover a very wide field with a single exposure. It is consequently invaluable in astronomy. The largest is the 2 m *6 ft 6¾ in* instrument at the Karl Schwarzschild Observatory at Tautenberg, Germany. It has a clear aperture of 134 cm *52¾ in* with a 200 cm *78¾ in* mirror and a focal length of 4 m *13 ft*. It was brought into use in 1960.

Largest radio dish Radio waves from the Milky Way were first detected by Karl Jansky of Bell Telephone Laboratories, Holmdel, New Jersey, USA in 1931 when he was investigating 'static' with an improvised 30.5 m *100 ft* aerial. The only purpose-built radio

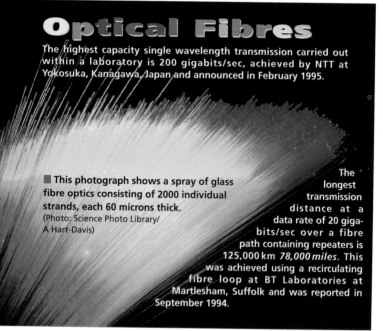

Optical Fibres

The highest capacity single wavelength transmission carried out within a laboratory is 200 gigabits/sec, achieved by NTT at Yokosuka, Kanagawa, Japan and announced in February 1995.

■ This photograph shows a spray of glass fibre optics consisting of 2000 individual strands, each 60 microns thick.
(Photo: Science Photo Library/ A Hart-Davis)

The longest transmission distance at a data rate of 20 gigabits/sec over a fibre path containing repeaters is 125,000 km *78,000 miles*. This was achieved using a recirculating fibre loop at BT Laboratories at Martlesham, Suffolk and was reported in September 1994.

Morse code The highest recorded speed at which anyone has received Morse code is 75.2 words per minute. This was achieved by Ted R. McElroy of the USA in a tournament at Asheville, North Carolina, USA on 2 Jul 1939.

The highest speed recorded for hand key transmitting is 175 symbols a minute (equivalent to 35 wpm) by Harry A. Turner of the US Army Signal Corps at Camp Crowder, Missouri, USA on 9 Nov 1942.

Thomas Morris, a GPO operator, is reputed to have been able to send at 39–40 wpm c. 1919, but this has not been verifiable.

Guess What?

Q. What does 'Mauna Kea' mean?

A. See Page 15

telescope built before the outbreak of the war in 1939 was made by an amateur, Grote Reber, who detected radio emissions from the Sun. The diameter of the dish was 9.5 m *31 ft 2 in*.

The pioneer large 'dish' was the 76 m *250 ft* telescope at Jodrell Bank, Cheshire, now known as the Lovell Telescope, completed in 1957. It is part of the MERLIN network, which includes other dishes in various parts of Britain.

The world's largest dish radio telescope is the partially-steerable ionospheric assembly built over a natural bowl at Arecibo, Puerto Rico, completed in November 1963. The dish has a diameter of 305 m *1000 ft* and covers 7.48 ha *18½ acres*.

The world's largest fully-steerable dish is the 100 m *328 ft* diameter assembly at the Max Planck Institute for Radio Astronomy of Bonn in the Effelsberger Valley, Germany. It was completed in 1971 and weighs 3048 tonnes.

Largest radio installation The largest radio installation is the Australia Telescope which includes dishes at Parkes (64 m *210 ft* in diameter), Siding Spring (22 m *72 ft*) and Culgoora (also 22 m *72 ft*). There are also links with tracking stations at Usuada and Kashima, Japan,

and with the TDRS (Tracking and Data Relay Satellite), which is in a geo-synchronous orbit. This is equivalent to a radio telescope with an effective diameter of 2.16 Earth diameters, or 27,523 km *17,102 miles*.

The VLA (Very Large Array) of the US National Science Foundation is Y-shaped, with each arm 20.9 km *13 miles* long and with 27 mobile antennae (each of 25 m *82 ft* diameter) on rails. It is 80 km *50 miles* west of Socorro in the Plains of San Augustin, New Mexico, USA and was completed on 10 Oct 1980.

Observatory *Oldest* The oldest building extant is the 'Tower of the Winds', used by Andronichus of Cyrrhus in Athens, Greece c. 100 BC and equipped with sundials and clepsydras (water clocks).

Highest The high-altitude observatory at Denver, Colorado, USA is at 4300 m *14,100 ft* and was opened in 1973. The main instrument is a 61 cm *24 in* reflector.

Lowest The lowest 'observatory' is at Homestake Mine, South Dakota, USA, where the 'Telescope' is a tank of cleaning fluid (perchloroethylene), which contains chlorine, and can trap neutrinos from the Sun. The installation is 1.7 km *1.1 miles* below ground level, in the shaft of a gold-mine.

Planetarium

The ancestor of the modern planetarium is the rotatable Gottorp Globe, built by Andreas Busch in Denmark about 1660. It was 10.54 m *34 ft 7 in* in circumference, weighed nearly 3½ tonnes and is now preserved in St Petersburg, Russia. The stars were painted on the inside.

Starry-eyed

The world's largest planetarium is in the Ehime Prefectural Science Museum, in Niihama City, Japan. It has a dome with a diameter of 30 m *98 ft 5 in*. Up to 25,000 stars can be displayed, and viewers can observe space as seen from other planets. It can seat 300 lucky people for one of its shows.

The huge museum, of which the planetarium is just one part, is on five storeys and cost 19 billion yen (£120 million) to build. It only opened its doors to the public on 11 Nov 1994, but is expecting some 300,000 visitors in its first year. Located just 200 km *125 miles* from Kobe, it was fortunately far enough away to escape damage as a result of the earthquake which struck Kobe and the surrounding area on 17 Jan 1995.

Osamu Seike, Vice Superintendent of the museum, spoke with pride about the facilities, saying:– 'The Ehime Prefectural Science Museum offers exhibits on nature, science and industry, as well as a planetarium, thereby satisfying a wide range of interests. We take pride in the fact that people can learn about all branches of science at the museum, an aspect which is shared by only a few facilities throughout the country. We hope our museum will be widely enjoyed and instrumental in the rejuvenation of the local culture'.

The enthusiasm was shared by youngsters who had visited the museum and the record-breaking planetarium in particular:– 'I was surprised by the vast spectacle of stars. I want to come again' and 'The stars were beautiful. The programme featuring astrological myths was inspiring' were just two of the many complimentary responses.

All in all, a spectacular new record providing a memorable experience for anyone who is able to visit the world's largest planetarium.

(Photos: Ehime Prefectural Science Museum/Hiroaki Nakazawa)

Rocketry

Guess What?

Q. How much was paid for the telegram sent to Yuri Gagarin by Nikita Khrushchev?
A. See Page 80

Earliest uses War 'flying fireworks', propelled by gunpowder (charcoal-saltpetre-sulfur), were described by Zeng Gongliang of China in 1042. War rockets originated in 1245 near Hangzhou, China.

The pioneer of military rocketry in Britain was Col. Sir William Congreve (1772–1828), Comptroller of the Royal Laboratory, Woolwich, London and Inspector of Military Machines. His '6 lb rocket' was developed to a range of 1800 m *2000 yd* by 1805 and first used by the Royal Navy against Boulogne, France on 8 Oct 1806.

The first launch of a liquid-fuelled rocket (patented 14 Jul 1914) was by Dr Robert Hutchings Goddard (1882–1945) of the USA, at Auburn, Massachusetts, USA on 16 Mar 1926, when his rocket reached an altitude of 12.5 m *41 ft* and travelled a distance of 56 m *184 ft*.

The earliest Soviet rocket was the semi-liquid-fuelled GIRD–R1 (object 09), begun in 1931 and tested on 17 Aug 1933. Their first fully liquid-fuelled rocket, GIRD–X, was launched on 25 Nov 1933.

Highest velocity The first space vehicle to achieve the Third Cosmic velocity sufficient to break out of the Solar System was *Pioneer 10*. The Atlas SLV–3C launcher with a modified Centaur D second stage and a Thiokol TE–364–4 third stage left the Earth at an unprecedented 51,682 km/h *32,114 mph* on 3 Mar 1972.

However, the fastest escape velocity from Earth was 54,614 km/h *34,134 mph*, achieved by the ESA

The first photographic images of the hidden side of the Moon were collected by the Soviet *Lunar III* from 6:30 a.m. on 7 Oct 1959 from a range of up to 70,400 km *43,750 miles*, and transmitted to the Earth from a distance of 470,000 km *292,000 miles*.

Ulysses spacecraft, powered by an IUS–PAM upper stage after deployment from the Space Shuttle *Discovery* on 7 Oct 1990, en route to an orbit around the poles of the Sun via a fly-by of Jupiter.

Mariner 10 reached a recorded speed of 211,126 km/h *131,954 mph* as it passed Mercury in September 1974, but the highest speed of approximately 252,800 km/h *158,000 mph* is recorded by the NASA–German *Helios A* and *B* solar probes each time they reach the perihelion of their solar orbits (⇔ Closest approach to the Sun by a rocket).

Most powerful rocket The NI booster of the former USSR (also known as the G–1 in the west), first launched from the Baikonur Cosmodrome at Tyuratam, Kazakhstan on 21 Feb 1969, had a thrust of 4620 tonnes, but exploded at takeoff + 70 sec. Three other launch attempts also failed.

Rocket engine The most powerful rocket engine was built in the former USSR by the Scientific Industrial Corporation of Power Engineering in 1980. The RD–170 has a thrust of 806 tonnes in open space and 740 tonnes at the Earth's surface. It also has a turbopump rated at 190 MW, and burns liquid oxygen and kerosene. The RD–170 powered the four strap-on boosters of the *Energiya* booster, launched in 1987 but now grounded by budget cuts.

Lunar records The first direct hit on the Moon was achieved at 2 min 24 sec after midnight (Moscow time) on 14 Sep 1959, by the Soviet space probe *Lunar II* near the Mare Serenitatis.

Closest approach to the Sun by a rocket The research spacecraft *Helios B* approached within 43.5 million km *27 million miles* of the Sun, carrying both US and West German instrumentation, on 16 Apr 1976 (⇔ Highest velocity).

Remotest man-made object *Pioneer 10*, launched from Cape Canaveral, Florida, USA, crossed the mean orbit of Pluto on 17 Oct 1986, being then at a distance of 5.91 billion km *3.67 billion miles*. *Voyager 1*, travelling faster, will have surpassed *Pioneer 10* in remoteness from the Earth by the end of the century. *Pioneer 11* and *Voyager 2* are also leaving the solar system.

■ Currently the most powerful rocket is *Energiya*, seen here in a hangar at Baikonur Cosmodrome in Kazakhstan with the space shuttle *Buran* on its back.
(Photo: Science Photo Library/Novosti Press Agency)

Progressive Rocket Altitude Records

Height Miles	Km	Rocket	Place	Launch Date
0.71	1.14	A 7.62 cm *3 in* rocket	Hackney, London, England	April 1750
1.25	2	Reinhold Tiling[1] (Germany) solid fuel rocket	Osnabrück, Germany	April 1931
1.9	3.1	'07' with liquid fuel engine '02' (USSR)	Nakhabino, Moscow region, USSR (now Russia)	16 Jul 1935
52.46	84.42	A4 rocket (Germany)[2]	Peenemünde, Germany	3 Oct 1942
c.85	c.136	A4 rocket (Germany)	Heidelager Blizna, Poland	early 1944
118	190	A4 rocket (Germany)	Heidelager Blizna, Poland	mid 1944
244	393	V2/WAC Corporal (2-stage) Bumper No. 5 (USA)	White Sands, New Mexico, USA[3]	24 Feb 1949
682	1097	Jupiter C (USA)	Cape Canaveral, Florida, USA	20 Sep 1956
>800	>1300	ICBM test flight R-7 (USSR)	Tyuratam, USSR (now Kazakhstan)	21 Aug 1957
>2700	>4345	Farside No. 5 (4-stage) (USA)	Eniwetok Atoll	20 Oct 1957
70,700	113,770	Pioneer 1-B Lunar Probe (USA)	Cape Canaveral, Florida, USA	11 Oct 1958
215,300,000*	346,480,000	Luna 1 or Mechtá (USSR)	Tyuratam, USSR (now Kazakhstan)	2 Jan 1959
242,000,000*	389,450,000	Mars 1 (USSR)	Tyuratam, USSR (now Kazakhstan)	1 Nov 1962
3,666,000,000[4]	5,900,000,000	Pioneer 10 (USA)	Cape Canaveral, Florida, USA	2 Mar 1972

*Apogee in solar orbit.

[1] There is some evidence that Tiling may shortly afterwards have reached 9.5 km *5.9 miles* with a solid-fuel rocket at Wangerooge, East Friesian Islands, Germany.
[2] The A4 was latterly referred to as the V2 rocket, an acronym for second revenge weapon (Vergeltungswaffe) following upon the V1 'flying bomb'.
[3] The V2/WAC height may have been exceeded during the period 1950–6 to the time of the Jupiter C flight, as the Soviets reported in 1954 that a rocket had reached 386 km *240 miles* at an unspecified date.
[4] Distance on crossing Pluto's orbit on 17 Oct 1986. Pioneer 11, Voyager 1 and Voyager 2 are also leaving the solar system.

◄◄ ◄◄ **Observatories, Planetaria**

Space Flight

The physical laws controlling the flight of artificial satellites were first propounded by Sir Isaac Newton (1642–1727) in his *Philosophiae Naturalis Principia Mathematica* ('Mathematical Principles of Natural Philosophy'), begun in March 1686 and first published in July 1687.

The first artificial satellite was successfully put into orbit by an inter-continental ballistic missile from the Baikonur Cosmodrome at Tyuratam, Kazakhstan, 275 km *170 miles* east of the Aral Sea and 250 km *155 miles* south of the town of Baikonur, on the night of 4 Oct 1957. It reached an altitude of between 228.5 km (perigee or nearest point to Earth) and 946 km (apogee or furthest point from Earth) *142 miles and 588 miles*, and a velocity of more than 28,565 km/h *17,750 mph*. This spherical satellite *Sputnik 1* ('Fellow Traveller'), officially designated 'Satellite 1957 Alpha 2', weighed 83.6 kg *184.3 lb*, with a diameter of 58 cm *22¾ in*. Its lifetime is believed to have been 92 days, ending on 4 Jan 1958. The 29.17 m *95 ft 8 in* tall SL–1 launcher was designed under the direction of former Gulag prisoner Dr Sergey Pavlovich Korolyov (1907–66).

In 1955 there were no records in The Guinness Book of Records for space travel. Now all sorts of spaceflight records exist.

Earliest manned satellite The earliest manned spaceflight ratified by the world governing body, the Fédération Aéronautique Internationale (FAI, founded 1905), was by Cosmonaut Flight Major (later Col.) Yuri Alekseyevich Gagarin (1934–68) in *Vostok 1* on 12 Apr 1961. The take-off was from the Baikonur Cosmodrome, Kazakhstan at 6:07 a.m. GMT and the landing near Smelovka, near Engels, in the Saratov region of Russia, 115 minutes later. Col. Gagarin landed separately from his spacecraft 118 minutes after the launch, by parachute after ejecting 108 minutes into the flight as planned.

The maximum altitude during the 40,868.6 km *25,394½ mile* flight of *Vostok 1* was listed at 327 km *203 miles*, with a maximum speed of 28,260 km/h *17,560 mph*. Col. Gagarin, invested a Hero of the Soviet Union and awarded the Order of Lenin and the Gold Star Medal, was killed in a jet plane crash near Moscow on 27 Mar 1968.

There had been 178 manned spaceflights to 3 Apr 1995, of which 98 were American and 80 Soviet or former Soviet Union, including 8 Russian.

First woman in space The first woman to orbit the Earth was Junior Lt (now Lt-Col. Eng.) Valentina Vladimirovna Tereshkova (b. 6 Mar 1937). She was launched in *Vostok 6* from the Baikonur Cosmodrome, Kazakhstan at 9:30 a.m. GMT on 16 Jun 1963. *Vostok 6* landed at 8:20 a.m. on 19 June, after a flight of 2 days 22 hr 50 min and 48 orbits (1,971,000 km *1,225,000 miles*). It passed momentarily to within 5 km *3 miles* of *Vostok 5*. Like Gagarin, Tereshkova ejected, after 2 days 22 hr 40 min and landed six minutes later. As at 3 Apr 1995 a total of 28 women had flown into space—22 Americans, two Soviets, one from Canada, one from Japan, one from Russia and one from the UK (⇨ below)—out of the total of 325 people who have been into space.

First Briton in space Helen Sharman (b. 30 May 1963) became the first Briton in space, in *Soyuz TM12* on 18 May 1991. She was the 15th woman in space, and the first non-Soviet, non-US woman. Britain became the 21st 'space nation' as a result.

Astronaut *Oldest* The oldest astronaut of the 325 people in space (to 3 Apr 1995) was Vance DeVoe Brand (USA) (b. 9 May 1931), aged 59, on 2 Dec 1990 while on the space shuttle mission aboard STS 35 *Columbia*. The oldest woman was Shannon Lucid (USA), aged 50 years, on space shuttle mission STS 58 *Columbia* in October 1993. She is also the first woman to make four spaceflights.

Youngest The youngest has been Major (later Lt-Gen.) Gherman Stepanovich Titov (b. 11 Sep 1935), who was aged 25 years 329 days when launched in *Vostok 2* on 6 Aug 1961. The youngest woman in space was Valentina Tereshkova, who was 26 (⇨ First woman in space).

Longest and shortest manned spaceflight For details of Valeriy Poliyakov's record-breaking spaceflight, ⇨ right.

The longest spaceflight by a woman was 169 days

space, and the first non-Soviet, non-US woman. Britain became the 21st 'space nation' as a result.

5 hr 21 min 20 sec by Yelena Kondakova (Russia), who was launched to the *Mir* space station aboard *Soyuz TM20* on 3 Oct 1994 and landed in the same spacecraft on 22 Mar 1995. She is also the woman with the most space experience, accumulated on the one spaceflight.

The shortest manned flight was made by Cdr Alan Bartlett Shepard (b. 18 Nov 1923), USN aboard *Mercury Redstone 3* on 5 May 1961. His sub-orbital mission lasted 15 min 28 sec.

Although not spaceflights, the space shuttle *Challenger* flew for 73 sec before being destroyed on 28 Jan 1986, while the launch escape system of *Soyuz T10A* took Vladimir Titov and Gennadiy Strekalov on a 17 g ride

A Year in Space

The longest manned flight was by Russian doctor Valeriy Poliyakov (b. 27 Apr 1942), who was launched to the *Mir* space station aboard *Soyuz TM18* on 8 Jan 1994 and landed in *Soyuz TM20* on 22 Mar 1995 after a spaceflight lasting 437 days 17 hr 58 min 16 sec.

■ **The most expensive space project is the US manned space programme. By the spring of 1995 its total cost is estimated to have exceeded $85 billion, with the NASA shuttle programme costing some $50 billion.**

The shuttle is normally associated with missions into space, but the dramatic 1982 photograph above right shows it in a very different setting.

The demands of space travel are such that huge amounts of training are required before undertaking a mission. The photograph on the right was taken in October 1993, during preparations for flight STS 61, which was to take place two months later.

Extravehicular activity, or walking in space, is one of the highlights of an astronaut's career. Gregory Harbaugh and Mario Runco Jr are seen outside Endeavour on 17 Jan 1993 (below) during shuttle flight STS 54.
(Photos: Gamma/Wells/Liaison, Gamma/NASA/ Liaison and NASA/Image Select)

lasting 5min 30sec after the *Soyuz* booster caught fire and eventually exploded before lift-off on 27 Sep 1983.

The most experienced space traveller is the Russian doctor Valeriy Poliyakov (⇨ above), who has clocked up 678days 16hr 33min 16sec on two spaceflights in 1988–9 and 1994–5.

The longest US-launched manned spaceflight, 84days 1hr 15min 31sec, was completed by *Skylab 4* astronauts Gerry Carr, Edward Gibson and Bill Pogue, in 1973–4. The longest flight by a US spaceperson, however, will be completed by Norman Thagard, who was launched to the *Mir* space station aboard *Soyuz TM21* on 14 Mar 1995 and was due to exceed the *Skylab 4* record on 6 June. A veteran of five spaceflights, Thagard was also due to become the most experienced US space traveller on 13 May, overtaking Carr, Gibson and Pogue. He was scheduled to land in mid-June.

Most journeys Capt. John Watts Young (b. 24 Sep 1930) (USN ret.) completed his sixth spaceflight on 8 Dec 1983, when he relinquished command of *Columbia* STS 9/Spacelab after a space career of 34days 19hr 41min 53sec. Young flew *Gemini 3*, *Gemini 10*, *Apollo 10*, *Apollo 16*, STS 1 and STS 9. The greatest number of flights by Soviet/Russian cosmonauts is five by Vladimir Dzhanibekov (between 1978 and 1985) and Gennadiy Strekalov (between 1980 and 1995). The most by a woman is four, by Shannon Lucid (STS 51G, 34, 43 and 58).

Largest crew The most crew on a single space mission is eight. This included one female and was launched on space shuttle STS 61A *Challenger* on 30 Oct 1985, carrying the West German Spacelab D1 laboratory. The flight (the 22nd shuttle mission) was commanded by Henry Warren 'Hank' Hartsfield and lasted 7days 44min 51sec. The most women in a space crew is three (of seven) during STS 40 *Columbia* in June 1991.

Most in space The greatest number of people in space at any one time has been 13. Seven Americans were aboard the space shuttle STS 67 *Endeavour*, three CIS cosmonauts aboard the *Mir* space station and two cosmonauts and a US astronaut aboard *Soyuz TM21* on 14 Mar 1995.

A record five countries had astronauts or cosmonauts in space at the same time on 31 Jul 1992 — CIS, France, Italy, Switzerland and USA — when four CIS cosmonauts and one Frenchman were aboard *Mir* at the same time as five US astronauts, one Swiss and one Italian were on STS 46 *Atlantis*.

Most isolated human being The farthest any human has been removed from his nearest living fellow human is 3596.4km *2233.2miles*, in the case of the command module pilot Alfred M. Worden on the US *Apollo 15* lunar mission of 30 Jul–1 Aug 1971, while David Scott and James Irwin (1930–91) were at Hadley Base exploring the surface.

Lunar conquest Neil Alden Armstrong (b. Wapakoneta, Ohio, USA of Scottish [via Ireland] and German ancestry, on 5 Aug 1930), command pilot of the *Apollo 11* mission, became the first man to set foot on the Moon, on the Sea of Tranquillity, at 02:56 and 15sec GMT on 21 Jul 1969 (22:56 and 15sec EDT—Eastern Daily Time—on 20 Jul 1969). He was followed out of the lunar module *Eagle* by Col. Edwin Eugene 'Buzz' Aldrin, Jr, USAF (b. Montclair, New Jersey, USA of Swedish, Dutch and British ancestry, on 20 Jan 1930), while the command module *Columbia* piloted by Lt-Col. Michael Collins, USAF (b. Rome, Italy, of Irish and pre-Revolutionary American ancestry, on 31 Oct 1930) orbited above.

Eagle landed at 20:17 and 42sec GMT (16:17 and 42sec EDT) on 20 July and lifted off at 17:54 GMT (13:54 EDT) on 21 July, after a stay of 21hr 36min. *Apollo 11* had blasted off from Cape Canaveral, Florida, USA at 13:32 GMT (09:32 EDT) on 16 July and was a culmination of the US space programme which at its peak employed 376,600 people and in 1966–7 attained a record budget of $5.9 billion.

Altitude The greatest altitude attained by man was when the crew of the *Apollo 13* were at apocynthion (i.e. their furthest point) 254km *158miles* from the lunar surface, and 400,171km *248,655miles* above the Earth's surface, at 1:21a.m. BST on 15 Apr 1970. The crew were Capt. James Arthur Lovell, Jr, USN (b. 25 Mar 1928), Fred Wallace Haise, Jr (b. 14 Nov 1933) and John L. Swigert (1931–82).

The greatest altitude attained by a woman is 600km *375miles*, by Kathryn Thornton (USA) (b. 17 Aug 1952) after an orbital engine burn on 10 Dec 1993 during the space shuttle STS 61 *Endeavour* mission.

Speed The fastest speed at which humans have travelled is 39,897 km/h *24,791 mph*. The command module of *Apollo 10*, carrying Col. (now Brig. Gen.) Thomas Patten Stafford, USAF (b. 17 Sep 1930), Cdr (now Capt.) Eugene Andrew Cernan (b. 14 Mar 1934) and Cdr (now Capt.) John Watts Young, USN (b. 24 Sep 1930), reached this maximum value at the 121.9km *75.7 mile* altitude interface on its trans-

Earth return flight on 26 May 1969, when travelling at 11.08km/sec *6.88miles/sec*.

The highest speed recorded by a woman is 28,582km/h *17,864mph*, by Kathryn Sullivan at the start of re-entry at the end of the STS 31 *Discovery* shuttle mission on 29 Apr 1990, although this may have been exceeded by Kathryn Thornton at the end of the STS 61 *Endeavour* mission on 13 Dec 1993. The highest recorded by a Soviet space traveller was 28,115km/h *17,470mph*, by Valentina Tereshkova of the USSR (⇨ First woman in space) in *Vostok 6* on 19 Jun 1963. However, because orbital injection of Soyuz spacecraft occurs at marginally lower altitude, it is probable that Tereshkova's speed was exceeded twice by Svetlana Savitskaya (b. 8 Aug 1948) aboard *Soyuz T7* and *Soyuz T12* on 27 Aug 1982 and 28 Jul 1984, and also by Helen Sharman aboard *Soyuz TM12* on 18 May 1991.

Duration record on the Moon The crew of *Apollo 17* collected a record 114.8kg *253lb* of rock and soil during their three EVAs of 22hr 5min. They were Capt. Eugene Cernan (⇨ Speed) and Dr Harrison Hagen 'Jack' Schmitt (b. 3 Jul 1935), who became the 12th man on the Moon. The crew were on the lunar surface for 74hr 59min during this longest of lunar missions, which took 12 days 13hr 51min on 7–19 Dec 1972.

Spacewalks Lt-Col. (now Maj. Gen.) Aleksey Arkhipovich Leonov (b. 20 May 1934) from *Voskhod 2* was the first person to engage in EVA 'extra-vehicular activity', on 18 Mar 1965. Capt. Bruce McCandless II, USN (b. 8 Jun 1937), from the space shuttle *Challenger*, was the first to engage in untethered EVA, at an altitude of 264km *164miles* above Hawaii, on 7 Feb 1984. His MMU (Manned Manoeuvering Unit) back-pack cost $15 million to develop. There had been 119 spacewalks to 3 Apr 1995, involving 93 people.

The first woman to perform an EVA was Svetlana Savitskaya from *Soyuz T12/Salyut 7* on 25 Jul 1984. The greatest number of spacewalks is ten, by Russian cosmonaut Aleksandr Serebrov (b. 15 Feb 1944) during two missions in 1990 and 1993.

The longest spacewalk ever undertaken was one of 8hr 29min, by Pierre Thuot, Rick Hieb and Tom Akers of STS 49 *Endeavour* on 13 May 1992. Anatoly Solovyov and Aleksandr Balandin of *Soyuz TM9* made a 7hr 16min EVA outside the Mir space station on 1 Jul 1990, which was the longest by Soviet cosmonauts.

Space fatalities The greatest published number to perish in any of the 179 attempted manned spaceflights to 3 Apr 1995 is seven (five men and two women) aboard the *Challenger* 51L on 28 Jan 1986, when an explosion occurred 73seconds after lift-off from the Kennedy Space Centre, Florida, at a height of 14,020m *46,000ft*. *Challenger* broke apart under extreme aerodynamic overpressure. Four people, all Soviet, have been killed during actual spaceflight—Vladimir Komarov of *Soyuz 1* which crashed on landing on 24 Apr 1967, and the un-spacesuited Georgi Dobrovolsky, Viktor Patsayev and Vladislav Volkov who died when their *Soyuz 11* spacecraft depressurized during the re-entry on 29 Jun 1971.

First extra-terrestrial vehicle The first wheeled vehicle landed on the Moon was the unmanned *Lunokhod 1* which began its Earth-controlled travels on 17 Nov 1970. It moved a total of 10.54 km *6.54miles* on gradients up to 30° in the Mare Imbrium and did not become non-functioning until 4 Oct 1971.

Most expensive suits
Suits for extra-vehicular activity worn by Space Shuttle crews from 1982 cost $3.4 million each.

Guess What?
Q. What are the maximum and minimum temperatures on the Moon?
A. See Page 9

■ A model of the eight-wheel drive *Lunokhod 1*, the first extra-terrestrial vehicle (⇨ right). (Photo: Science Photo Library/Novosti Press Agency)

The lunar speed and distance record was set by the manned *Apollo 16* Rover, driven by John Young, with 18km/h *11.2mph* downhill and 33.8km *22.4miles*.

Space Flight

Buildings & Structures

Buildings for Living

Habitations

Greatest altitude The highest inhabited buildings in the world are those in the Indo-Tibetan border fort of Bāsisi by the Māna Pass (Lat. 31°04'N, Long. 79°24'E) at c. 5990 m *19,700 ft*.

In April 1961, a three-room dwelling believed to date from the late pre-Columbian period c. 1480 was discovered at 6600 m *21,650 ft* on Cerro Llullaillaco (6723 m *22,057 ft*), on the Argentine–Chile border.

Northernmost habitation The Danish scientific station set up in 1952 in Pearyland, northern Greenland is over 1450 km *900 miles* north of the Arctic Circle and is manned every summer.

The former USSR's drifting research station 'North Pole 15' passed within 2.8 km *1¼ miles* of the North Pole in December 1967.

The most northerly continuously inhabited place is the Canadian Department of National Defence outpost at Alert on Ellesmere Island, Northwest Territories (Lat. 82°30'N, Long. 62°W), set up in 1950.

The most southerly permanent human habitation is the United States' Amundsen–Scott South Polar Station, completed in 1957 and replaced in 1975.

Castles

Earliest castle The castle at Gomdan, Yemen dates from before AD 100 and originally had 20 storeys.

Oldest castle The oldest stone castle in Great Britain is Chepstow Castle, Gwent, built c. 1067 on the west bank of the River Wye by William fitz Osbern.

Largest castle The largest ancient castle in the world is Hradčany Castle in Prague, Czech Republic, originating in the 9th century. It is an oblong irregular polygon with an axis of 570 m *1870 ft* and an average transverse diameter of 128 m *420 ft*, giving a surface area of 7.28 ha *18 acres*.

The world's largest inhabited castle is the royal residence of Windsor Castle at Windsor, Berks. Originally of 12th-century construction, it is in the form of a waisted parallelogram measuring 576 × 164 m *1890 × 540 ft*.

The largest castle in Scotland is Edinburgh Castle, Lothian, with a major axis of 402 m *1320 ft* and measuring 1025 m *3360 ft* along its perimeter wall, including the Esplanade.

Guess What?
Q. In which city would you find this tower?
A. See Page 94

Palaces, Housing, Flats ▶▶▶▶

Guess What?

Q. How tall was the tallest lego tower?

A. See Page 90

■ The Nara Todaiji temple in Japan, which, at around 1300 years old, is one of the oldest wooden buildings still standing.
(Photo: Spectrum Colour Library)

Largest moat
From plans drawn by French sources it appears that the moats surrounding the Imperial Palace in Beijing, China are 49 m *160 ft* wide and have a total length of 3290 m *3600 yd*. In all, the city's moats total 38 km *23½ miles* (⇨ Palaces).

Sand castle
The tallest sand castle on record, constructed only with hands, buckets and shovels, was 6.56 m *21 ft 6 in* high and was made by a team led by Joe Maize, George Pennock and Ted Siebert at Harrison Hot Springs, British Columbia, Canada on 26 Sep 1993.

The longest sand castle was 8.37 km *5.2 miles* long, made by staff and pupils of Ellon Academy, near Aberdeen, Grampian on 24 Mar 1988.

Largest fort Fort George in Ardersier, Highland, built in 1748–69, is 640 m *2100 ft* long and has an average width of 189 m *620 ft* on a site covering a total of 17.2 ha *42½ acres*.

Palaces

Largest palace The Imperial Palace in the centre of Beijing, China covers a rectangle measuring 960 × 750 m *3150 × 2460 ft* over an area of 72 ha *178 acres*. The outline survives from the construction of the third Ming Emperor, Yongle (1402–24), but owing to constant reconstruction work, most of the intra-mural buildings (five halls and 17 palaces) are from the 18th century.

The Palace of Versailles, 23 km *14 miles* south-west of Paris, is 580 m *1902 ft* long and has a façade with 375 windows. The building, completed in 1682 for Louis XIV, occupied over 30,000 workmen under Jules Hardouin-Mansart (1646–1708).

Residential The palace (Istana Nurul Iman) of HM the Sultan of Brunei in the capital Bandar Seri Begawan was completed in January 1984 at a reported cost of £300 million. It is the largest residence in the world, with 1788 rooms and 257 lavatories. The underground garage accommodates the Sultan's 153 cars.

UK The largest royal palace is Hampton Court, Greater London, acquired by Henry VIII from Cardinal Wolsey in 1525 and greatly enlarged by him and later by William III, Queen Anne and George I, whose son George II was its last resident monarch. It covers 1.6 ha *4 acres* on a site extending over 271 ha *669 acre*.

Roomy

The house with the most rooms is Knole, near Sevenoaks, Kent, believed to have had 365 rooms, one for each day of the year. Built round seven courtyards, its total depth from front to back is about 120 m *400 ft*. Building was begun in 1456 by Thomas Bourchier, Archbishop of Canterbury (1454–86), and the house was extended by Thomas Sackville, 1st Earl of Dorset, *c.* 1603–8. Knole is now administered by the National Trust.

The largest palace in the United Kingdom in royal use is Buckingham Palace, London, so named after its site, bought in 1703 by John Sheffield, the 1st Duke of Buckingham and Normanby (1648–1721). Buckingham House was reconstructed in the Palladian style between 1825 and 1836, following the design of John Nash (1752–1835). The East Front, 186 m *610 ft* long, was built in 1846 and refaced in 1912. The Palace, which stands in 15.8 ha *39 acres* of garden, has 600 rooms, including a ballroom measuring 34 m *111 ft* long used for investitures.

Camping out The silent Indian *fakir* Mastram Bapu ('contented father') remained on the same spot by the roadside in the village of Chitra for 22 years, from 1960 through to 1982.

Housing

Earliest housing Eastry Court near Sandwich, Kent includes part of a Saxon building said to have been built in AD 603 by King Ethelbert I of Kent (d. 616), possibly as a palace. The present building is, however, in a much altered form.

Oldest inhabited house Barton Manor in Pagham, W Sussex includes structures dating from Saxon times *c.* AD 800.

England's oldest inhabited house is reputed to be Little Dean Hall, Forest of Dean, Glos, dating from AD 1080. A Roman temple was found in its grounds in 1982.

Largest residence The largest non-palatial residence is St Emmeram Castle in Regensburg, Germany. It has 517 rooms and a floor area of 21,460 m² *231,000 ft²*. It was owned by the late Prince Johannes von Thurn und Taxis, whose family use only 95 of the rooms. The castle is valued at more than 336 million DM (£122 million).

UK The main part of Wentworth Woodhouse, near Rotherham, S Yorks, built over 300 years ago, has more than 240 rooms, and its principal façade is

183 m *600 ft* long. Formerly the seat of the Earls Fitzwilliam, the house is now privately owned by Wensley Haydon-Baillie.

Smallest house The 19th-century fisherman's cottage at The Quay, Conwy, Gwynedd, consists of two tiny rooms and a staircase. It has only 182 cm *72 in* of frontage, is 309 cm *122 in* high and measures 254 cm *100 in* from front to back.

The narrowest known house frontage is 119 cm *47 in* for 50 Stuart Street, Millport, on the island of Great Cumbrae, Strathclyde.

Most durable resident Virginia Hopkins Phillips of Onancock, Virginia, USA resided in the same house from the time of her birth in 1891 until shortly after her 102nd birthday in 1993.

Most expensive house The most expensive private house ever built is the Hearst Ranch at San Simeon, California, USA. It was built between 1922 and 1939 for William Randolph Hearst (1863–1951), at a total cost of more than $30 million. It has more than 100 rooms, a heated swimming pool 32 m *104 ft* long, an assembly hall 25 m *83 ft* long and a garage for 25 limousines. The house required 60 servants to maintain it.

Brick carrying The greatest distance achieved for carrying a brick weighing 9 lb *4.08 kg* in a nominated ungloved hand in an uncradled downward pincher grip is 104.6 km *65 miles*, by Paddy Doyle of Atherstone, Warks around Ballycotton, Co. Cork, Republic of Ireland on 3–4 Sep 1994.

Demolition work Fifteen members of the Aurora Karate Do demolished a seven-room house in Prince Albert, Saskatchewan, Canada in 3 hr 9 min 59 sec by foot and empty hand on 16 Apr 1994.

Bricks

Gary Lovegrove of Wisbech, Cambs laid 809 bricks, each weighing 2 kg *4 lb 7 oz*, in 60 minutes at the Buildex exhibition at Wembley, Greater London on 5 Dec 1994. This was achieved in accordance with the rules of the Brick Development Association and the Guild of Bricklayers.

The largest aggregation of private blocks is the one forming the Barbican Estate, designed by architects Chamberlin, Bon & Powell, in the City of London. The site occupies 16 ha *40 acres* and includes 2014 flats and parking for 1710 cars.

Buildings demolished by explosives The largest has been the 21-storey Traymore Hotel, Atlantic City, New Jersey, USA on 26 May 1972, by Controlled Demolition Inc. of Towson, Maryland. This 600-room hotel had a cubic capacity of 181,340 m³ *6,403,926 ft³*.

The tallest chimney ever demolished by explosives was the Matla Power Station chimney, Kriel, South Africa, on 19 Jul 1981. It stood 275 m *902 ft* and was brought down in a joint project between the Santon (Steeplejack) Co. Ltd of Greater Manchester and Dykon, Inc. of Tulsa, Oklahoma, USA.

In Great Britain, Controlled Demolition Group Ltd of Leeds successfully demolished eight blocks of high-rise flats at Kersal Vale, Salford, Manchester on 14 Oct 1990. The total cubic capacity of the tower blocks was 155,000 m³ *5,474,000 ft³*.

Largest estate The UK's largest housing estate is the 675-ha *1667-acre* Becontree Estate on a site covering 1214 ha *3000 acres* in Barking and Redbridge, London, built between 1921 and 1929. It contains a total of 26,822 homes, with an estimated population of nearly 90,000.

Flats

Tallest block of flats The John Hancock Center in Chicago, Illinois, USA is 343.5 m *1127 ft* and 100 storeys high; floors 44–92 are residential.

The tallest purely residential block of flats is the 70-storey Lake Point Tower in Chicago, Illinois, USA, which is 195 m *639 ft* high and has 879 apartments.

UK The tallest residential block in Great Britain is Shakespeare Tower, Barbican, City of London. The 44-storey block, topped out on 24 Mar 1969, is 127.77 m *419 ft 2½ in* high and contains 116 flats.

Pole sitting Modern records do not compare with that of St Simeon the Younger (c. AD 521–97), called Stylites, a monk who spent his last 45 years up a stone pillar on the Hill of Wonders, near Antioch, Syria.

St Simeon's pole-sitting feat is the longest-standing record chronicled in the *Guinness Book of Records*.

The 'standards of living' at the top of poles can vary widely. Mellissa Sanders lived in a shack measuring 1.8 × 2.1 m *6 × 7 ft* at the top of a pole in Indianapolis, Indiana, USA from 26 Oct 1986 to 24 Mar 1988, a total of 516 days.

Rob Colley stayed in a barrel (maximum capacity 150 gal *682 litres*) at the top of a pole 43 ft *13.1 m* high at Dartmoor Wildlife Park, near Plymouth, Devon for 42 days 35 min from 13 Aug to 24 Sep 1992.

Guess What?
Q. What site can you rent for $115 million a year?
A. See Page 90

■ **The Hearst Ranch at San Simeon, California, USA** cost more than $30 million to build during its 17-year construction in 1922–39, making it the world's most expensive private house.
(All photos: Spectrum Colour Library)

HOUSE OF CARDS

The greatest number of storeys ever achieved in building a free-standing house of standard playing cards is 83, to a height of 4.88m *16ft 0in*. It was built by Bryan Berg of Spirit Lake, Iowa, USA between 24 February and 3 March 1995, without the use of any sort of adhesives.

A lot of people who try to build a house of cards will be happy to manage two or three storeys. To the average person this is the extent of their ambition, but over the years record-breaking attempts have required not only skill, a steady hand and patience, but also a head for heights. Since the record first surpassed 60 storeys in 1978 when James Warnock of Cantley, Canada managed 61, there have been six improvements on the record.

Hotels

Oldest hotel The Hōshi Ryokan at the village of Awazu in Japan, dates back to A.D. 717, when Garyo Hōshi built an inn near a hot-water spring which was said to have miraculous healing powers. The waters are still celebrated for their recuperative effects, and the Ryokan now has 100 bedrooms (⇨Business World—Oldest family business).

Largest hotel The MGM Grand Hotel/Casino/Theme Park in Las Vegas, Nevada, USA consists of four 30-storey towers on a site covering 45.3ha *112acres*. The hotel has 5009 rooms, with suites of up to 557m² *6000ft²*, a 15,200-seat arena, and a 13.3-ha *33-acre* theme park.

UK Britain's largest hotel is the Grosvenor House Hotel in Park Lane, London, opened in 1929. It is eight storeys high, covers 1 ha *2½ acres* and caters for over 100,000 visitors per year in 470 rooms. The Great Room is the largest single hotel room measuring 55 × 40m *181 ×131ft*, with a height of 7m *23ft*. Banquets for 1500 can readily be held there.

The London Forum Hotel in Cromwell Road is Britain's most capacious, accommodating 1856 guests in 910 bedrooms. It employs 330 staff and was opened in 1973 (⇨ Tallest).

Tallest hotel Measured from the street level of its main entrance, the 73-storey Westin Stamford in Raffles City, Singapore is 226.1m *742ft* tall. The $235-million hotel is operated by Westin Hotel Co. and owned jointly by DBS Land and Overseas Chinese Banking Corporation. Measured from its rear entrance level, the Westin Stamford in Detroit Plaza, USA is 227.9m *748ft* tall. The incomplete Ryujyong Hotel, North Korea, has been under construction for 20 years, and is reportedly 105 storeys high.

UK The London Forum Hotel has 27 storeys and is 132m *380ft* tall (⇨ Largest).

Most expensive hotel room The Galactic Fantasy Suite in the Crystal Tower of the Crystal Palace Resort and Casino in Nassau, Bahamas costs $25,000 (£17,360) per night, but the casino's big spenders are likely to be accommodated on a complimentary basis.

UK The Presidential Suite of the Hotel Hyatt Carlton Tower, London costs £2000 plus VAT (£2,350 inc VAT).

Most remote hotel The Garvault Hotel in Kinbrace, Highland is claimed to be the most isolated hotel in mainland Britain, being some 26km *16miles* from its nearest competitor at Forsinard, also in Highland.

Largest casino
Foxwoods Resort Casino in Ledyard, Connecticut, USA includes a total gaming area of 193,000ft² *17,929m²*. There are 3854 slot machines, 234 table games and 3500 bingo seats.

■ The MGM lion heralds the entrance to the MGM Grand in Las Vegas, Nevada, USA, the world's largest hotel, which also encompasses a Theme Park and an expansive casino.
(Photos: Gamma/E. Sander/Liaison)

On The Record

What Bryan Berg says about his hobby:

❝ You have to be a little insane. A lot of people wouldn't have the patience or the time. I just like to build things. ❞

What a local said about him:

❝ It's exciting to see someone have such a passion to be creative. He's inspired many kids and adults. His excitement is contagious, and it's a lot of fun to see someone make it so much fun. ❞

■ Bryan Berg by his 81-storey house of cards, built in 1994.

HOW MANY STOREYS?	WHO?	WHEN?	WHERE?
62	Anthony de Bruxelles	1983	Weinheim, Germany
68	John Sain	1983	South Bend, Indiana, USA
75	Bryan Berg	1992	Spirit Lake, Iowa, USA
76	Dan Waters	1994	Hampton, New Jersey, USA
81	Bryan Berg	1994	Okoboji, Iowa, USA
83	Bryan Berg	1995	Boston, Massachusetts, USA

Guess What?
Q. Where is Britain's oldest castle?
A. See Page 85

The bi-level, 2-bed, 2-bath Galactic Fantasy suite is furnished in white, chrome, and silver, and is designed to create a '23rd Century Experience'. High-tech accessories like the crystal clear lucite grand piano, which creates moving art as the piano plays, and the thunder-and-lightning sound-and-light show are explained by obliging robot Ursula, who also hands guests a towel as they step out of the shower. In the living room, a tropical aquarium faces a dramatic ocean view. There is a choice of two beds: a huge, rotating one on the first-floor, or for the less queasy, a rhinestone-studded one on the second.

■ Main picture: some pampered guests taking a ride on the rotating sofa. Inset: Ursula stands to attention.
(Photos: DJS Marketing Group)

The Lap of Luxury

The Galactic Fantasy Suite at the Nassau Marriot Resort in the Bahamas is the world's most expensive hotel room, at $25,000 (£17,360) a night.

Largest hotel lobby The lobby at the Hyatt Regency in San Francisco, California, USA is 107 m *350 ft* long, 49 m *160 ft* wide, and at 52 m *170 ft* tall, is the height of a 17-storey building.

Hotel move The three-storey brick Hotel Fairmount (built 1906) in San Antonio, Texas, USA, which weighed 1451 tonnes, was moved on 36 dollies with pneumatic tyres over city streets approximately five blocks and over a bridge, which had to be reinforced. The move by Emmert International of Portland, took six days, 30 Mar–4 Apr 1985, and cost $650,000.

Forty years ago, the most expensive hotel in the world was the Fontainebleau, Miami Beach, Florida. The daily standard room rate for 11th to 14th floor rooms with terraces facing the ocean, during the peak season (January to March), was £16 8s. 0d., or £114 16s. 0d. per week. Nine 'presidential' suites were available at daily rates of £51 17s. 6d.

Buildings for Working

Urban regeneration project The world's largest is London Docklands, which covers 22 km² *8½ miles²*. Over 2.2 million m² *27 million ft²* of commercial-development space and over 19,000 new homes have been completed or are under construction, and following the completion of the Jubilee Line Underground extension in 1988, over £4 billion will have been invested in new public transport. By 1996, a total of £6.1 billion will have been invested by the private sector, together with a further £1.6 billion invested by the London Docklands Development Corporation, with more than 40,000 jobs created since 1981. The London Docklands Canary Wharf development is also the world's largest commercial development (⇨ also Tallest offices).

Industrial building The largest multi-level industrial building that is one discrete structure is the container freight station of Asia Terminals Ltd at Hong Kong's Kwai Chung container port. The 14-level building was completed in 1994 and has a total area of 865,937 m² *9,320,867 ft²*. It measures 276 × 292 m *906 × 958 ft* and is 109.5 m *359.25 ft* high. The entire area in each floor of the building is directly accessible by 13.7-m *45-ft* container trucks, and the building has 26.84 km *16.67 miles* of roadway and 2609 container-truck parking spaces.

Commercial building In terms of floor area, the world's largest commercial building under one roof is the flower-auction building Bloemenveiling Aalsmeer (VBA) in Aalsmeer, Netherlands. The floor surface of the building measures 710,000 m² *7.6 million ft²*.

Construction

The largest public-works project of modern times is the Madinat Al-Jubail Al-Sinaiyah project in Saudi Arabia, started in 1976 for the industrial city covering 1,014,600,000 m² *250,705 acres*. At the peak of construction, nearly 52,000 workers were employed, representing 62 nationalities, and a total volume of 270 million m³ *9535 million ft³* of earth has been dredged and moved, enough to construct a belt 1 m *3 ft 3 in* high around the Earth at the equator seven times.

The world's most capacious building is the Boeing Company's main assembly plant in Everett, Washington, USA, at 5,564,200 m³ *196,476,000 ft³* on completion in 1968. Subsequent expansion programmmes have increased the volume to 13.4 million m³ *472 million ft³*, with a further increase in volume of 50 per cent due for completion in 1993 in preparation for production of the new 777 airliner. The site covers some 410 ha *1025 acres*.

UK Britain's largest building is the Ford Parts Centre at Daventry, Northants, with an area of 142,674 m² *1.5 million ft²*. It was opened on 6 Sep 1972 at a cost of nearly £8 million and employs 1300 people.

Largest wooden building Between 1942 and 1943, 16 wooden blimp hangars for Navy airships were built at various locations throughout the USA. They are 317 m *1040 ft* long, 51.91 m *170 ft 4 in* high at the crown and 90.37 m *296 ft 6 in* wide at the base. There are only eight remaining, one each at Tillamook, Oregon and Elizabeth City, North Carolina; and two each at Moffett Field and Santa Ana, California, and Lakehurst, New Jersey.

Building contractor The largest construction group in the United Kingdom is Tarmac. The company had sales of £2.5 billion in 1994, and employed 18,270 staff. Peak sales turnover was £3.7 billion in 1990.

Highest rent In January 1994 it was announced that Russia was prepared to rent out the Baikonur space centre—launch site for several satellites—for $115 million (£76.9 million) a year for 20 years.

Offices

Largest office The largest rentable office complex is the World Trade Center in New York City, USA, with a total of 1,114,800 m² *12 million ft²* of rentable space available in the seven buildings, including 406,000 m² *4.37 million ft²* in each of the twin towers. There are 99 lifts in each tower and 43,600 windows comprising 182,880 m² *600,000 ft²* of glass. There are 50,000 people working in 350 firms and organisations in the complex, and 70,000 tourists visit daily.

UK The largest single open-plan office in the United Kingdom is that of British Gas West Midlands at Solihull, Warks, built by Spooners (Hull) Ltd in 1962. It now measures 230 × 49 m *753 × 160 ft* and can accommodate 2125 staff.

Tallest office The tallest office building in the world (although not as tall as the CN Tower—⇨ Tallest Towers) is the Sears Tower, national headquarters of Sears, Roebuck & Co. on Wacker Drive, Chicago, Illinois, USA. The building has 110 stories rising to 443 m *1454 ft*; the addition of two TV antennae

■ The translucent roof of the Pontiac Silverdome Stadium is supported by 34.4 kPa *5 lb/ft²* of air pressure.
(Photo: Gamma/Caputo/Liaison)

brought the total height to 520 m *1707 ft*. Construction was started in August 1970, and it was topped out on 4 May 1973. The building has a gross area of 1.4 million m² *4.5 million ft²*, and is served by 104 lifts and 16,100 windows.

UK The tallest office building in Britain is the Canary Wharf tower in London Docklands, at 243.8 m *800 ft*. The tallest of three towers at the development, the 50-storey building, resembling an obelisk, was designed by US architect Cesar Pelli and consists of nearly 16,000 pieces of steel. It overtook the National Westminster tower block by 61 m *200 ft* when it was topped out in November 1990.

Tallest lego tower A Lego tower measuring 22.13 m *72.6 ft* high was built at 'La Belle Etoile' shopping centre in Luxembourg on 4 Sep 1994, by the supermarket CACTUS SA.

The tallest Lego tower in Britain measured 20.86 m *68 ft 5 in* and was built by Lego UK Ltd at Earl's Court, London in March 1993 during the Daily Mail Ideal Home Exhibition.

Embassies The former Soviet (now Russian) embassy on Bei Xiao Jie, Beijing occupies the whole 18.2-ha *45-acre* site of the old Orthodox Church Mission (established 1728), now known as the *Beiguan*. The building was handed over to the USSR in 1949.

UK The largest embassy in Great Britain is that of the United States in Grosvenor Square, London. The Chancery Building alone, completed in 1960, has a usable floor area of 23,689 m² *255,000 ft²*, 600 rooms on nine floors, and can accommodate 700 staff.

Largest exhibition centre The International Exposition Center in Cleveland, Ohio, USA is situated

Administrative

The largest ground area covered by any office building is that of the Pentagon, in Arlington, Virginia, USA. Built to house the US Defense Department's offices, it was completed on 15 Jan 1943 and cost an estimated $83 million. Each of the outermost sides is 281 m *921 ft* long and the perimeter of the building is about 1405 m *4610 ft*. Its five storeys enclose a floor area of 604,000 m² *149.2 acres*, the corridors total 28 km *17.5 miles* in length, and there are 7754 windows to be cleaned. There are 23,000 military and civilian employees working in the building (⇨ Telephones and Facsimiles).

Largest Indoor stadium The $173-million Superdome in New Orleans, Louisiana, USA, is 83.2 m *273 ft* tall, and covers 5.26 ha *13 acres*. It was completed in May 1975. Its maximum seating capacity is 97,365 for conventions and 76,791 for American football. A gondola with six 8-m *26-ft* TV screens produces instant replays.

on a 76-ha *188-acre* site adjacent to Cleveland Hopkins International Airport, in a building measuring 232,250 m² *2.5 million ft²*. The Center accommodates 200 different events each year.

UK The National Exhibition Centre, Birmingham, W Mids, which opened in February 1976, consists of 15 halls covering 158,000 m² *1.7 million ft²*, a 12,000-seat arena, 2 hotels, car parking for 18,000, plus numerous restaurants and a lake on the 250-ha *618-acre* site.

Buildings for Leisure

Stadia

Largest stadium The open Strahov Stadium in Prague, Czech Republic, completed in 1934, could accommodate 240,000 spectators for mass displays of up to 40,000 Sokol gymnasts.

Covered The largest covered stadium is the Aztec Stadium in Mexico City, opened in 1968, which has a capacity of 107,000 for football, although a record attendance of 132,274 was achieved for boxing on 20 Feb 1993. Nearly all seats are under cover (⇨ Boxing).

The largest covered stadium in Great Britain is the Empire Stadium, Wembley, Middx, opened on 23 Apr 1923 and scene of the 1948 Olympic Games and the final of the 1966 World Cup. In 1962–3 the capacity under cover was increased to 100,000, with 45,000 seated, and the original cost was £1,250,000. However, following a refurbishment programme and new safety guidelines, the seating capacity has now been reduced to 81,500.

Largest roof The transparent acrylic glass 'tent' roof over the Munich Olympic Stadium, Germany measures 85,000 m² *914,940 ft²* in area and rests on a steel net supported by masts.

The longest roof span in the world is 240 m *787 ft 4 in* for the major axis of the elliptical Texas Stadium, completed in 1971 at Irving, Texas, USA.

Retractable roof The world's largest retractable roof covers the SkyDome, home of the Toronto Blue Jays baseball team, near the CN Tower in Toronto, Canada, completed in June 1989. The roof covers 3.2 ha *8 acres*, spans 209 m *674 ft* at its widest point and rises to 86 m *282 ft*. It takes 20 minutes to retract the roof fully. The stadium itself has a capacity of 67,000 for concerts, 53,000 for Canadian football and 50,600 for baseball (⟿ Baseball).

Largest air-supported building
The octagonal Pontiac Silverdome Stadium in Detroit, Michigan, USA is 220 m *722 ft* long and 159 m *522 ft* wide and has a capacity for 80,638. The air pressure is 34.4 kPa *5 lb/ft²* supporting the 4-ha *10-acre* translucent 'Fiberglas' roofing. The main floor measures 123 × 73 m *402 × 240 ft*, and the roof is 62 m *202 ft* high. The structural engineers were Geiger-Berger Associates of New York City, USA.

The largest standard-size airhall is 262 m *860 ft* long, 42.6 m *140 ft* wide and 19.8 m *65 ft* high, first sited at Lima, Ohio, USA and made by Irvin Industries of Stamford, Connecticut, USA.

Shopping Centres

The world's largest centre is the $1.1-billion West Edmonton Mall in Alberta, Canada, which was opened on 15 Sep 1981 and completed four years later. It covers 483,080 m² *5.2 million ft²* on a 49-ha *121-acre* site and encompasses over 800 stores and services, as well as 11 major department stores. Parking is provided for 20,000 vehicles for more than 500,000 shoppers per week (⟿ Car parks).

The world's largest wholesale merchandise mart is the Dallas Market Center on Stemmons Freeway, Dallas, Texas, USA, covering nearly 641,000 m² *6.9 million ft²* in five buildings. The whole complex covers 70 ha *175 acres* and houses some 2580 permanent showrooms displaying the merchandise of more than 30,000 manufacturers. The Center attracts 800,000 buyers each year to its 40 annual markets and trade shows.

Guess What?
Q. What is the name of the world's largest restaurant chain?
A. See Page 93

UK The largest shopping complex in Britain and Europe is the MetroCentre in Gateshead, Tyne & Wear. The site covers an area of 54.63 ha *135 acres* housing 350 retail units (including the largest single-storey branch of Marks and Spencer at 17,279 m² *186,000 ft²*), giving a gross selling area of 204,380 m² *2.2 million ft²*. The complex also includes a leisure centre, an 11-screen cinema, a 28-lane bowling centre, parking for 12,000 cars, a coach park and its own purpose-built British Rail station and bus station.

Football Stadia

The Maracanã Municipal Stadium in Rio de Janeiro, Brazil, has a normal capacity for 205,000, of whom 155,000 can be seated. A crowd of 199,854 was accommodated for the World Cup final between Brazil and Uruguay on 16 Jul 1950. A dry moat, 2.13 m *7 ft* wide and more than 1.5 m *5 ft* deep, protects players from spectators and vice versa.

Britain's most capacious football stadium was Hampden Park, Glasgow, Strathclyde, home of Queen's Park Football Club, opened on 31 Oct 1903. Its record attendance was 149,547 on 17 Apr 1937, but the current Ground Safety Certificate limits the seated capacity to 38,335.

■ Why not take a break from such onerous tasks as shopping and polish up your golf, or practise your breast-stroke? Apparently, anything is possible at West Edmonton Mall in Alberta, Canada, which contains no end of distraction to shoppers on its huge, 49-ha *121-acre* site. (Photo: West Edmonton Mall)

Resorts

Largest amusement resort Disney World is set in 12,140 ha *30,000 acres* of Orange and Osceola Counties, 32 km *20 miles* south-west of Orlando, Florida, USA. It was opened on 1 Oct 1971 after a $400 million investment.

Most attended Disneyland at Anaheim, California, USA (opened 1955) had received more than 350 million visitors by the end of 1994.

Amusement park The largest amusement park in the UK, and the most-visited tourist attraction, is Blackpool pleasure beach, Lancs, which received 7.2 million visitors in 1994. It will be 100 years old in 1996.

Pleasure piers *Earliest* The earliest date attributed to a seaside 'jetty' is 1560 at Great Yarmouth, Norfolk; it was replaced in 1808 by a new structure, which was washed away in 1953. The first conventional piers were constructed at Weymouth, Dorset in 1812 and Ryde, Isle of Wight in 1813–14. There is some doubt over the

Pleasure

Virginia Beach, Virginia, USA is the world's largest pleasure beach, with 45 km *28 miles* of beach front on the Atlantic and 16 km *10 miles* of estuary frontage on Chesapeake Bay. The city of Virginia Beach covers 803 km² *310 miles²*, with 147 hotel properties and 2323 campsites.

Weymouth date, though records show that a new reinforced-concrete pier (pleasure/commercial) replaced an old 274-m *900-ft* wooden pier in 1933. They both remain in situ today, although greatly altered over the years.

Longest The longest pleasure pier in the world is Southend Pier, Southend-on-Sea, Essex. The original wooden pier was opened in 1830 and extended in 1846. The present iron pier is 2.15 km *1.34 miles* long and was opened on 8 Jul 1889. In 1949–50 the pier had a peak 5.75 million visitors. The pier has been

The world's longest shopping mall measures 650 m *2133 ft* and is part of the £40-million shopping centre at Milton Keynes, Bucks.

Roller-coasters ▶▶ ▶▶

Naturists

The largest naturist site is Domaine de Lambeyran, near Lodève in southern France, at 340 ha *840 acres*. The Centre Hélio Marin at Cap d'Agde, also in southern France, is visited by around 250,000 people per annum. The largest naturist site in Great Britain is that of the Naturist Foundation in Orpington, Kent, at 20 ha *50 acres*.

breached by 14 vessels since 1830, and there have been 3 major fires.

Most The resort with the most piers was Atlantic City, New Jersey, USA with eight, although currently only five remain, dating from 1883 to 1912. Of British resorts, Blackpool, Lancs has three piers, the North, Central and South.

Largest spa Spas are named after the watering-place in the Liège province of Belgium, where hydropathy was developed from 1626. The largest spa in terms of available accommodation is Vichy, Allier, France, with 14,000 hotel rooms. The highest French spa is Barèges, Hautes-Pyrénées, at 1240 m *4068 ft* above sea level.

Fairs

Earliest fair The earliest major international fair was the Great Exhibition of 1851 in the Crystal Palace, Hyde Park, London, which in 141 days attracted 6,039,195 admissions.

Big wheels The original Ferris wheel, named after its constructor George W. Ferris (1859–96), was erected in 1893 at the Midway, Chicago, Illinois, USA at a cost of $385,000. It was 76 m *250 ft* in diameter and 240 m *790 ft* in circumference, weighed 1087 tonnes and had 36 cars each carrying 40 seated and 20 standing passengers, giving a record capacity of 2160. The structure was removed in 1904 to St Louis, Missouri, USA and was eventually sold as scrap for $1800.

In 1897 a Ferris wheel with a diameter of 86.5 m *284 ft* was erected for the Earl's Court Exhibition, London. It had ten 1st-class and 30 2nd-class cars each carrying 30 people.

The largest-diameter wheel now operating is the Cosmoclock 21 at Yokohama City, Japan. It is 105 m *344 ½ ft* high and 100 m *328 ft* in diameter, with 60 gondolas each with eight seats. There

are such features as illumination by laser beams and acoustic effects by sound synthesizers. Sixty arms hold the gondolas, each serving as a second hand for the electric clock mounted at the hub, which is 13 m *42.65 ft* wide.

Britain's largest is one 61 m *200 ft* in diameter, with a capacity for 240 people, at Margate, Kent.

Roller-coasters

The maximum speeds and dimensions claimed for gravity-based amusement devices have long been exaggerated for commercial reasons.

Oldest operating roller-coaster Rutschebahnen (Scenic Railway) Mk.2 was constructed at the Tivoli Gardens, Copenhagen, Denmark in 1913. This coaster opened to the public in 1914 and has remained open ever since.

UK The oldest operating roller-coaster in Britain is the *Scenic Railway* at Dreamland Amusement Park, Margate, Kent. This traditional wooden coaster has continued to operate since it opened to the public on 3 Jul 1920.

Longest roller-coaster The world's longest is *The Ultimate* at Lightwater Valley, Theme Park in Ripon, N Yorks.

The site of the Louisiana Purchase Exposition in St Louis, Missouri, USA in 1904 covered 514.66 ha *1271.76 acres*, and there was an attendance of 19,694,855. Events of the 1904 Olympic Games were staged in conjunction.

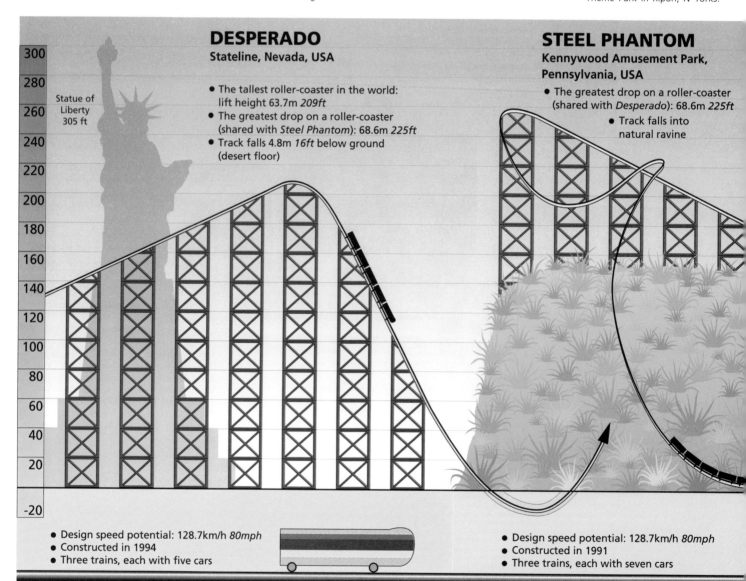

DESPERADO
Stateline, Nevada, USA

- The tallest roller-coaster in the world: lift height 63.7m *209ft*
- The greatest drop on a roller-coaster (shared with *Steel Phantom*): 68.6m *225ft*
- Track falls 4.8m *16ft* below ground (desert floor)

STEEL PHANTOM
Kennywood Amusement Park, Pennsylvania, USA

- The greatest drop on a roller-coaster (shared with *Desperado*): 68.6m *225ft*
- Track falls into natural ravine

Statue of Liberty 305 ft

- Design speed potential: 128.7km/h *80mph*
- Constructed in 1994
- Three trains, each with five cars

- Design speed potential: 128.7km/h *80mph*
- Constructed in 1991
- Three trains, each with seven cars

ALL ROLLER-COASTER DESIGNS BY ARROW DYNAMICS INC. UTAH, USA   (Illustration: Peter Harper © Guinness Publishing)

The tubular-steel track measures 2.29 km *1.42 miles*.

Greatest drop The four-inversion *Steel Phantom* roller-coaster at Kennywood Amusement Park, West Mifflin, Pennsylvania, USA has a second vertical drop of 68.6 m *225 ft* into a natural ravine, with a design speed of 128 km/h *80 mph*.

Sharing the record for the greatest drop is *Desperado*, a non-inversion coaster at Buffalo Bill's Resort and Casino, Primadonna Resorts Complex, Jean, Nevada, USA. Its first vertical drop plunges 68.6 m *225 ft*, and the ride also has a design speed of 128 km/h *80 mph* (⇨Tallest roller-coaster).

Tallest roller-coaster The tallest complete-circuit roller-coaster is *Desperado* (⇨ Greatest drop) at Buffalo Bill's Casino, Nevada, USA. It features a lift height of 63.7 m *209 ft*.

UK The tallest roller-coaster in the UK and Europe is the non-inversion *Pepsi-Max Big One* at Blackpool Pleasure Beach, Lancs. The ride has an actual lift height of 61.3 m *201.2 ft*, and a first vertical drop of 62.5 m *205.1 ft*.

> **The most roller-coasters at any amusement park is 11, at Cedar Point Amusement Park/Resort in Sandusky, Ohio, USA. There is a choice of 2 wooden-track and 9 steel-track coasters.**

Greatest number of loops/inversions The most for any complete-circuit multi-element coaster in the world is the *Dragon Khan* at Port Aventura, Salou, Spain. It is designed by Bolliger & Mabillard of Mothey, Switzerland. Riders are turned upside-down eight times over the steel track, which extends for 1269.8 m *4166.2 ft*.

Nightclubs and Restaurants

Nightclubs The earliest nightclub (*boîte de nuit*) was 'Le Bal des Anglais' at 6 rue des Anglais, Paris, France. Established in 1843, it closed c.1960.

Largest 'Gilley's Club' (formerly 'Shelly's'), built in 1955, was extended in 1971 on Spencer Highway, Houston, Texas, USA, with a seating capacity of 6000 under one roof covering 1.6 ha *4 acres*.

In the more classical sense the largest nightclub in the world is 'The Mikado' in the Akasaka district of Tokyo, Japan, with a seating capacity of 2000. Binoculars can be essential to an appreciation of the floor show.

Lowest The 'Minus 206' in Tiberias, Israel, on the shores of the Sea of Galilee is 206 m *676 ft* below sea level.

Restaurants *Earliest* The Casa Botín was opened in 1725 in Calle de Cuchilleros 17, Madrid, Spain.

Largest The Royal Dragon (Mang Gorn Luang) restaurant in Bangkok, Thailand, opened in October 1991, can seat 5000 customers served by 1200 staff. Because of the large service area (3.37 ha *8.35 acres*), the staff wear roller skates in order to speed the service.

Restaurateurs

The world's largest restaurant chain is operated by McDonald's Corporation of Oak Brook, Illinois, USA, founded in 1955 by Ray A. Kroc (1902–84) after buying out the brothers Dick and 'Mac' McDonald, pioneers of the fast-food drive-in. By the end of 1994, McDonald's licensed and owned 15,205 restaurants in 79 countries. Worldwide sales in 1994 were $26 billion.

Their most capacious outlet is the 700-seat restaurant in Beijing, China. It measures 2601 m² *28,000 ft²*, and employs 1,000 staff.

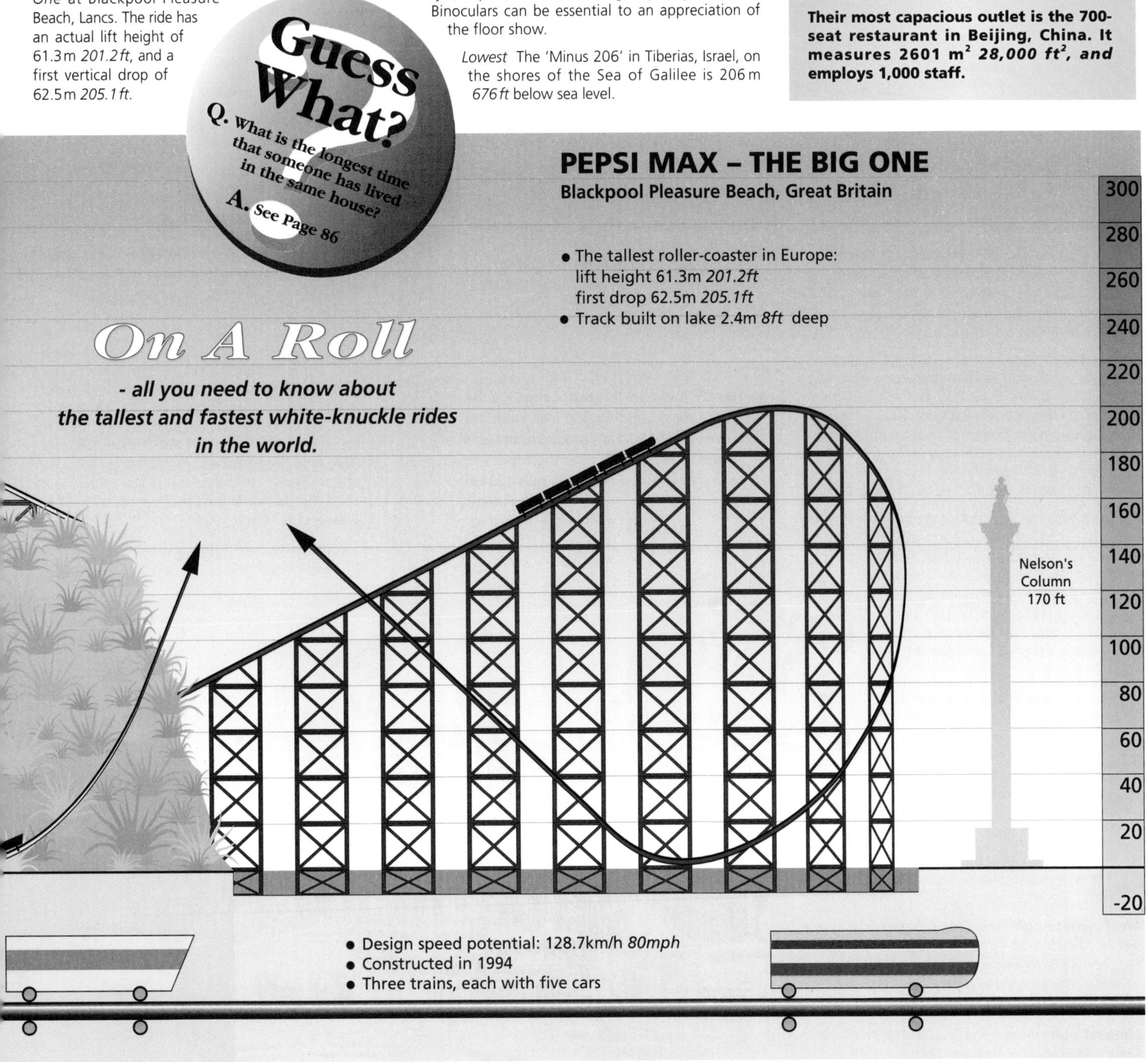

Guess What?

Q. What is the longest time that someone has lived in the same house?

A. See Page 86

On A Roll

- all you need to know about the tallest and fastest white-knuckle rides in the world.

PEPSI MAX – THE BIG ONE
Blackpool Pleasure Beach, Great Britain

- The tallest roller-coaster in Europe: lift height 61.3m *201.2ft* first drop 62.5m *205.1ft*
- Track built on lake 2.4m *8ft* deep

Nelson's Column 170 ft

- Design speed potential: 128.7km/h *80mph*
- Constructed in 1994
- Three trains, each with five cars

Highest The highest restaurant in the world is at the Chacaltaya ski resort, Bolivia, at 5340 m *17,519 ft.*

The highest in Great Britain is the Ptarmigan Observation Restaurant at 1112 m *3650 ft* above sea level on Cairngorm (1244 m *4084 ft*), near Aviemore, Highland.

Fish-and-chip restaurant The world's largest fish-and-chip shop is Harry Ramsden's at White Cross, Guiseley, W Yorks, with 140 staff serving 1 million customers per year, who consume 213 tonnes of fish and 356 tonnes of potatoes. The Glasgow Branch sold and served a record 11,964 portions of fish and chips on 17 May 1992.

Bars and Public Houses

Oldest pub There are various claimants to the title of Great Britain's oldest inn. A foremost claimant is 'The Fighting Cocks', at St Albans, Herts, an 11th-century structure on an eighth-century site. The timber frame of the Royalist Hotel, Digbeth Street, Stow-on-the-Wold, Glos has been dated to even earlier; it was 'The Eagle and the Child' in the 13th century and known to exist in AD 947. An origin as early as AD 560 has been claimed for 'Ye Olde Ferry Boat Inn' at Holywell, Cambs. There is some evidence that it antedates the local church, built in 980, but no documentation is available earlier than AD 1100. The 'Bingley Arms', Bardsey, near Leeds, W Yorks, restored and extended in 1738, existed as the 'Priest's Inn', according to Bardsey Church records of AD 905.

Largest pub The largest beer-selling establishment in the world is the 'Mathäser', Bayerstrasse 5, Munich, Germany, where the daily sale reaches 48,000 litres *84,470 pints*. It was established in 1829, demolished in World War II and rebuilt by 1955. It now seats 5500 people.

UK The largest public house in Great Britain is the 'Downham Tavern', Downham Way, Bromley, Kent, built in 1930. Two large bars (counter length 13.7 m *45 ft*) accommodate 1000 customers, and the pub employs 18–20 staff.

Tallest bar The bar at Humperdink's Seafood and Steakhouse in the Las Colinas business development in Irving, Texas, USA is 7.69 m *25 ft 3 in* high with two levels of shelving containing over 1000 bottles. The lower level has four rows of shelves approximately 12 m *40 ft* across and can be reached from floor level. If an order has to be met from the upper level, which has five rows of shelves, it is reached by climbing a ladder.

Longest bar The world's longest permanent continuous bar is the counter 123.7 m *405 ft 10 in* long in the Beer Barrel Saloon, which opened at Put-in-Bay, South Bass Island, Ohio, USA, in 1989. The bar is fitted with 56 beer taps and surrounded by 160 bar stools. Longer temporary bars have been erected, notably for beer festivals.

The longest bar in Great Britain with beer pumps is the Long Bar at the Cornwall Coliseum Auditorium at Carlyon Bay, St Austell, Cornwall. It measures 31.8 m *104¼ ft* and has 34 dispensers. The Grandstand Bar at Galway Racecourse, Republic of Ireland, completed in 1955, measures 64 m *210 ft.*

The longest pub bar is the counter 31.7 m *104⅓ ft* long at 'The Horse Shoe', Drury Street, Glasgow, Scotland.

Most remote pub The Old Forge public house at Inverie, Knoydart, Inverness-shire is 32 km *20 miles* by ferry and 38.6 km *24 miles* 'as the crow flies' from its nearest contender; there are no roads into or out of Knoydart.

Longest pub name 'The Old Thirteenth Cheshire Astley Volunteer Rifleman Corps Inn' in Astley

Smallest Pub

The ground floor of 'The Nutshell' in Bury St. Edmunds, Suffolk is 4.82 × 2.28 m *15 ft 10 in × 7 ft 6 in.* It was granted a licence personally by a thirsty King Charles II (1630–1685) when passing by. The 'Lakeside Inn', The Promenade, Southport, Merseyside has a floor area of 6.7 × 4.87 m *22 × 16 ft* and is 4.57 m *15 ft* in height.

'The Smiths Arms' in Godmanstone, Dorset has external dimensions of 12.04 × 3.5 m *39½ × 11½ ft* and is 3.65 m *12 ft* in height.

The pub with the smallest bar room is the 'Dove Inn', Upper Mall, Chiswick, London, measuring 127 × 239 cm *4 ft 2 in × 7 ft 10 in.*

Street, Stalybridge, Manchester has 55 letters. A very contrived name consisting of 12,822 letters and 1487 words was added to Bugsy's Amazin Downtown Diner/Bar at King's Stables Road, Edinburgh, Scotland.

Shortest pub name 'Q' in Stalybridge, Cheshire, owned by Julia and David Connor, has the shortest pub name in Britain.

Commonest pub name There are probably about 630 pubs in Britain called the 'Red Lion'. Arthur Amos of Bury St Edmunds, Suffolk, recorded 21,516 different pub names from 1938 to his death in June 1986. His son John took over the collection, which now numbers 25,545.

■ **The CN Tower in Toronto, Canada is the world's tallest building and free-standing tower. It is 553.34 m *1815 ft 5 in* tall and from its restaurant near the top it has been possible to see hills 120 km *75 miles* away.**
(Photo: Spectrum Colour Library)

Highest pub The 'Snowdon Summit' licensed bar and cafeteria is the highest, at 1085 m *3560 ft.* It is open only in summer due to the prevailing weather conditions. In Great Britain the 'Tan Hill Inn' (licensee Margaret Baines) is 528 m *1732 ft* above sea level. It is just in N Yorks on the moorland road between Reeth, N Yorks and Brough, Cumbria.

Most pub visits Bruce Masters of Flitwick, Beds has visited 27,897 pubs and a further 1369 other drinking establishments since 1960, partaking of the local brew in each case where available. There are a total of 77,000 pubs nationwide.

Towers and Masts

Tallest Structures

The all-time height record for any structure is the guyed Warszawa Radio mast at Konstantynow, 96 km *60 miles* north-west of the capital of Poland. Prior to its fall during renovation work on 10 Aug 1991 it was 646.38 m *2120 ft 8 in* tall. The mast was completed on 18 Jul 1974 and put into operation on 22 Jul 1974. It was designed by Jan Polak and weighed 550 tonnes. It recaptured for Europe, after 45 years, a record held in the USA since the Chrysler Building had surpassed the Eiffel Tower in 1929.

After the collapse of the world's tallest tower in Poland in 1991 the local people laid claim to a new record—the world's longest tower!

Currently, the tallest structure is a stayed television transmitting tower 629 m *2063 ft* tall, between Fargo and Blanchard, North Dakota, USA. It was built for Channel 11 of KTHI-TV in 30 days (2 Oct to 1 Nov 1963) by 11 men of Hamilton Erection, Inc. of York, South Carolina, USA. From then until the completion of the mast at Konstantynow it was the tallest structure in the world, and it remained the second tallest between 1974 and 1991.

Guess What?
Q. Which British football stadium can hold the most fans?
A. See Page 91

■ The Seto-Ohashi bridge is the world's longest road and rail bridge, with an overall length of 12,306 m *43,374 ft*. It links Honshu—Japan's main island—with the smaller island of Shikoku.
(Photo: Gamma/K. Kurita)

Forty years ago the longest bridge span was that of the Golden Gate Bridge, San Francisco, USA, at 1280 m *4200 ft*. The longest now is that of the Humber Estuary Bridge, Humberside, at 1410 m *4626 ft*, but the Golden Gate remains a world-famous landmark.

Great Britain The tallest structure in Britain is NTL's Belmont mast, north of Horncastle, Lincs, completed in 1965 to a height of 385.5 m *1265 ft*, with 2.13 m *7 ft* added by meteorological equipment installed in September 1967. It serves Yorkshire TV and weighs 210 tonnes.

Tallest Towers

The tallest building and free-standing tower (as opposed to a guyed mast) in the world is the $63-million CN Tower in Toronto, Canada, which rises to 553.34 m *1815 ft 5 in*. Excavation began on 12 Feb 1973 for the erection of the 130,000-tonne reinforced, post-tensioned concrete structure, which was 'topped out' on 2 Apr 1975. The 416-seat restaurant revolves in the Sky Pod at 351 m *1150 ft*, from which the visibility can extend to hills 120 km *75 miles* distant.

Great Britain The tallest self-supported tower in Britain is the NTL transmitter, 330.5 m *1084 ft* tall, at Emley Moor, W Yorks, completed in September 1971. The structure, which cost £900,000, has an enclosed room 264 m *865 ft* up, and weighs more than 15,000 tonnes, including its foundations.

Bridges

Oldest bridges Arch construction was understood by the Sumerians as early as 3200 BC, and there is a reference to the bridging of the Nile in 2650 BC.

The oldest datable bridge in the world still in use is the slab-stone single-arch bridge over the river Meles in Izmir (formerly Smyrna), Turkey, which dates from c. 850 BC. Remnants of Mycenaean bridges dated c. 1600 BC exist in the neighbourhood of Mycenae, Greece over the River Havos.

Great Britain The clapper bridges of Dartmoor and Exmoor (e.g. the Tarr Steps over the river Barle, Exmoor, Somerset) are thought to be of prehistoric types, although none of the existing examples can be certainly dated. They are made of large slabs of stone placed over boulders.

Remains of Roman stone bridges have been found at Corbridge, Northumberland, dating to the 2nd century AD, and at Chesters, Northumberland and Willowford, Cumbria. Remains of a very early wooden bridge have been found at Aldwinkle, Northants.

Longest cable-suspension bridges The world's longest bridge span is the main span of the Humber Estuary Bridge, Humberside, at 1410 m *4626 ft*. Work began on 27 Jul 1972 and was completed on 18 Jul 1980 at a cost of £96 million. The towers are 162.5 m *533 ft 1⅝ in* tall from datum and are 36 mm *1⅜ in* out of parallel to allow for the curvature of the Earth. Including the Hessle and the Barton side spans, the bridge stretches 2220 m *7284 ft or 1.38 miles*. The bridge was officially opened by HM the Queen on 17 Jul 1981.

The Akashi-Kaikyo road bridge linking Honshu and Shikoku, Japan was started in 1988, and completion is planned for 1998. The main span will be 1990.8 m *6531 ft 6 in or 1.24 miles* long, and the overall suspended length with side spans will total 3911.1 m *12,831 ft 8 in or 2.43 miles*. Two towers will rise 297 m *974 ft 5 in* above water level, and the two main supporting cables will be 112 cm *44 in* in diameter, making both tower height and cable diameter world records.

The main span of the Akashi-Kaikyo road bridge was scheduled to be 1990 m *6528 ft 10 in* in length, but the earthquake which hit Kobe on 17 Jan 1995 had an interesting side-effect—it made the bridge even longer than it was going to be (⇨ above).

Road and rail The Seto-Ohashi double-deck road and rail bridge linking Kojima, Honshu with Sakaide, Shikoku, Japan was opened on 10 Apr 1988. The overall length of the Seto-Ohashi Bridge is 12,306 m *43,374 ft or 8.28 miles*, making it the longest combined road/railway bridge in the world. It was built at a cost of £4.9 billion and 17 lives. The toll for cars is £33 each way.

The Tsing Ma Bridge in Hong Kong, due for completion in 1997, will have a main span of 1377 m *4518 ft*, making it the longest suspension-bridge span for combined road/railway traffic.

Longest cable-stayed bridges The Pont de Normandie, in Le Havre, France, has a cable-stayed main span of 856 m *2808 ft*. It was opened to traffic on 20 Jan 1995.

UK Currently the longest cable-stayed bridge in the UK is the £86-million Queen Elizabeth II Bridge on the M25 motorway over the river Thames at Dartford, Kent, with a span of 450 m *1476 ft*. It was opened to traffic in 1991.

The United Kingdom's longest-span cable-stayed bridge will be the second Severn Bridge, due for completion in 1996, with a main span of 456 m *1496 ft*. The overall length of the crossing structure will be 5168 m *16,955 ft or 3.21 miles*, making it the longest bridge in Britain. The bridge will join England with Wales.

Longest cantilever bridge The Quebec Bridge (Pont de Québec) over the St Lawrence River in Canada has the longest cantilever truss span of any in the world, measuring 549 m *1800 ft* between the piers and 987 m *3239 ft* overall. It carries a railway track and two carriageways. Work started in 1899, and it was finally opened to traffic on 3 Dec 1917, having cost $Can22.5 million and 87 lives.

Great Britain Great Britain's longest cantilever bridge is the Forth Bridge. Its two main spans are 521 m *1710 ft* long. It carries a double railway track over the Firth of Forth 47.5 m *156 ft* above the water level. Work began in November 1882, and the first test trains crossed on

Taking the high road

The Royal Gorge suspension bridge is a record 321 m *1053 ft* above water. Above is Donald Betty, whose hobby is walking over spectacular bridges all over the world. He always lies down in the middle of the bridge to take a vertical shot of the tower, and is used to people asking "What's that man doing lying there?".
(Photos: Spectrum Colour Library and Joan S. Betty)

22 Jan 1890 after an expenditure of £3 million. It was officially opened on 4 Mar 1890.

Longest floating bridge Second Lake Washington Bridge, Evergreen, Seattle, Washington State, USA has a total length of 3839 m *12,596 ft or 2.39 miles*, with its floating section measuring 2291 m *7518 ft or 1.42 miles*. The bridge was built at a total cost of $15 million and completed in August 1963.

Longest covered bridge The bridge at Hartland, New Brunswick, Canada, measures 390.8 m *1282 ft* overall and was completed in 1899.

Longest plastic bridge The longest span reinforced-plastic bridge is at the Aberfeldy Golf Club at Aberfeldy, Tayside. The main span is 63 m *206 ft 8 in* and the overall bridge length 113 m *370 ft 9 in*.

Longest railway bridge The world's longest rail/road bridge is the Seto-Ohashi Bridge (⇨ Longest Cable suspension bridges, above).

Great Britain Britain's longest is the second Tay Bridge, at 3552 m *11,653 ft or 2.21 miles*, across the Firth of Tay at Dundee, Scotland, opened on 20 Jun 1887. It has 85 spans, of which 74—with a length of 3136 m *10,289 ft or 1.95 miles*—are over the waterway.

The 878 brick arches of the former London–Greenwich Railway viaduct between London Bridge and Deptford Creek, built in 1836, extend for 6 km *3¾ miles*.

Longest steel arch bridge The New River Gorge bridge, near Fayetteville, West Virginia, USA was completed in 1977 and has a span of 518 m *1700 ft*.

Great Britain The Runcorn–Widnes bridge, Cheshire was opened on 21 Jul 1961, and has a span of 329.8 m *1082 ft*.

Longest stone arch bridge Rockville Bridge north of Harrisburg, Pennsylvania, USA was completed in 1901. It is 1161 m *3810 ft* long, and its 48 spans contain 196,000 tonnes of stone.

The longest stone arch span is the Wuchaohe Bridge at Fenghuang, Hunan Province, China, at 120 m *394 ft*. It was completed in 1990.

UK The longest in the United Kingdom is the Grosvenor Bridge at Chester, Cheshire (61 m *200 ft*) completed in 1830. At the time of its construction this was the longest such span in the world.

Longest bridging The Second Lake Pontchartrain Causeway was completed on 23 Mar 1969, joining Mandeville and Metairie, Louisiana, USA. It has a length of 38,422 m *126,055 ft or 23.87 miles*. It cost $29.9 million and is 69 m *228 ft* longer than the adjoining First Causeway, completed in 1956.

Widest bridge The widest long-span bridge is the 503 m *1650 ft* Sydney Harbour Bridge, Australia (48.8 m *160 ft* wide). It carries two electric overhead railway tracks, eight lanes of roadway and a cycle track and footway. It was officially opened on 19 Mar 1932.

The river Roch is bridged for a distance of 445 m *1460 ft* where the culvert passes through the centre of Rochdale, Greater Manchester, and this is sometimes therefore claimed to be its breadth rather than its length.

Tallest bridge The tallest bridge towers in the world are those of the Golden Gate Bridge, which connects San Francisco and Marin County, California, USA. The towers of this suspension bridge extend 227 m *745 ft* above the water. Completed in 1937, the bridge has an overall length of 2733 m *8966 ft*. The bridge will lose its status in 1998 to the Akashi-Kaikyo towers (⇨ Longest cable-suspension bridges).

Guess What?
Q. What is the difference between all of these bridges and the Rainbow Bridge?
A. See Page 19

Highest bridge The world's highest bridge is over the Royal Gorge of the Arkansas River in Colorado, USA, at 321 m *1053 ft* above the water level. It is a suspension bridge with a main span of 268 m *880 ft* and was constructed in six months, ending on 6 Dec 1929.

The tallest multispan cantilever-construction viaduct in the United Kingdom is over the Dee on the A483 Newbridge Bypass, Clwyd. It is 57.3 m *188 ft* high. The Crumlin viaduct in Gwent (61 m *200 ft*) had held the United Kingdom record from 1857 until its demolition in 1966.

Railway The highest railway bridge in the world is the Mala Reka viaduct of Yugoslav Railways at Kolašin on the Belgrade–Bar line. It is 198 m

650 ft high and was opened on 1 Jun 1976. It consists of steel spans mounted on concrete piers.

The highest railway bridge in Great Britain is the Ballochmyle viaduct over the river Ayr, Strathclyde, built 51.5 m *169 ft* over the river bed in 1846–8. At that time it had the world's longest masonry railway arch span of 55.2 m *181 ft*.

Road The road bridge at the highest altitude in the world, 5602 m *18,380 ft*, is a Bailey bridge 30 m *98 ft 5 in* long, designed and constructed by Lt Col. S.G. Vombatkere and an Indian Army team in August 1982 near Khardung-La, in Ladakh, India.

Cycleway bridge The longest cycleway bridge is over the 17 railway tracks of Cambridge Station, Cambs. It has a tower 35 m *115 ft* high and two approach ramps 50 m *164 ft* long and is 237.6 m *779 ft 6 in* in length.

Bridge sale The largest antique ever sold was London Bridge, in March 1968. Ivan F. Luckin of the Court of Common Council of the Corporation of London sold it to the McCulloch Oil Corporation of Los Angeles, California, USA for £1,029,000. The 10,000 tonnes of façade stonework were re-assembled at a cost of £3 million at Lake Havasu City, Arizona, USA and 're-dedicated' on 10 Oct 1971.

Bridge-building A team of British soldiers from 21 Engineer Regiment based at Nienburg, Germany constructed a bridge across a gap 8 m *26 ft* wide using a five-bay single-storey MGB (medium girder bridge) in a time of 7 min 12 sec at Hameln, Germany on 3 Nov 1992. Future timings will be slower, following the introduction of new rules.

Viaducts

The longest railway viaduct in the world is the rock-filled Great Salt Lake Railroad Trestle, carrying the Southern Pacific Railroad 19 km *11.85 miles* across the Great Salt Lake, Utah, USA. It was opened as a pile-and-trestle bridge on 8 Mar 1904 but converted to rock fill in 1955–60.

Aqueducts

Longest ancient aqueduct The greatest of ancient aqueducts was that of Carthage in Tunisia, which ran 141 km *87.6 miles* from the springs of Zaghouan to Djebel Djougar. It was built by the Romans during the reign of Publius Aelius Hadrianus, or Hadrian (AD 117–138). In 1895, 344 arches still survived. Its original capacity has been calculated at 31.8 million litres *7 million gal* per day.

Longest modern aqueduct The world's longest aqueduct, in the non-classical sense of water conduit, excluding irrigation canals, is the California State Water Project aqueduct, with a length of 1329 km *826 miles*, of which 619 km *385 miles* is canalized. It was completed in 1974.

The longest bridged aqueduct in Great Britain is the Pont Cysylltau in Clwyd on the Frankton to Llantisilio branch of the Shropshire Union Canal, generally known as the Llangollen or Welsh Canal. It is 307 m *1007 ft* long and has 19 arches up to 36 m *118 ft* high above low water on the Dee. Designed by Thomas Telford (1757–1834), it was opened in 1805. It is still in use today by pleasure craft.

Tallest aqueduct The tallest of the 109 arches of the Aguas Livres aqueduct, built in Lisbon, Portugal from 1729 to 1748, is 65 m *213 ft*.

■ **The St Lawrence Seaway is the world's longest artificial seaway, linking Montreal in Canada to Lake Ontario, 304 km *189 miles* away. This photograph shows the entrance to the seaway.**
(Photo: Spectrum Colour Library)

Canals

Earliest canals Relics of the oldest canals in the world, dated by archaeologists c. 4000 BC, were discovered near Mandali, Iraq early in 1968.

The earliest canals in Britain were first cut by the Romans. In the Midlands the 17 km *11 mile* long Fossdyke Canal between Lincoln and the River Trent at Torksey, Lincs was built c. AD 65 and was scoured in 1122. It is still in use today.

Although the Exeter Canal was cut as early as 1564–6, the first wholly artificial major navigation canal in the United Kingdom was the 29.7 km *18½ mile* long canal with 14 locks from Whitecoat Point to Newry, Northern Ireland, opened on 28 Mar 1742.

Longest canals The longest canal in the ancient world was the Grand Canal of China from Beijing to Hangzhou. It was begun in 540 BC and not completed until 1327, by which time it extended (including canalized river sections) for 1781 km *1107 miles*. Having been allowed by 1950 to silt up to the point that it was nowhere more than 1.8 m *6 ft* deep, it is now, however, plied by vessels of up to 2000 tonnes.

The Belomorsko-Baltiyskiy Canal from Belomorsk to Povenets, Russia is 227 km *141 miles* long and has 19 locks. It was completed with the use of forced labour in 1933. It cannot accommodate ships of more than 5 m *16 ft* in draught.

There are more than 16,000 transits of the Suez Canal annually, or some 44 per day.

The world's longest big-ship canal is the Suez Canal, linking the Red and Mediterranean Seas, opened on 17 Nov 1869. It took 10 years to build the canal, with a workforce of 1.5 million people, of whom 120,000 perished during the construction. It is 162.2 km *100.8 miles* in length from Port Said lighthouse to Suez Roads and has a minimum width of 300 m *984 ft* and a maximum width of 365 m *1198 ft*.

The largest vessel to transit the Suez Canal has been *Jahre Viking*, on 29 Jan 1995. It has a deadweight tonnage of 564,650 tonnes and is 485.5 m *1592 ft 10 in* long, with a beam of 68.8 m *225 ft 9 in*. The USS *Shreveport* transited southbound on 15–16 Aug 1984 in a record 7 hr 45 min.

Great Britain Canals and navigable stretches of river in Great Britain amount to approximately 5630 km *3500 miles*, with a further 290 km *180 miles* being restored. Of these, 4000 km *2500 miles* are interlinked.

Busiest canal The busiest ship canal is the Kiel Canal, linking the North Sea with the Baltic Sea in Germany. Over 40,000 transits are recorded annually. The busiest in terms of tonnage of shipping is the Suez Canal, with 423,723,000 grt in the fiscal year 1994.

Largest canal system The seawater cooling system associated with the Madinat Al-Jubail Al-Sinaiyah construction project in Saudi Arabia is believed to be the world's largest canal system. It currently brings 11 million m^3 *388 million ft^3* of seawater per day to cool the industrial establishments (⇔ Construction project).

Longest artificial seaway The St Lawrence Seaway is 304 km *189 miles* in length along the New York State–Ontario border from Montreal to Lake Ontario. It enables ships up to 222 m *728 ft* long and 8 m *26 ft 3 in* draught (some of which are of 26,400 tonnes) to sail 3769 km *2342 miles* from the North Atlantic up the St Lawrence estuary and across the Great Lakes to Duluth, Minnesota, USA. The project, begun in 1954, cost $470 million and was opened on 25 Apr 1959.

Longest irrigation The Karakumsky Canal stretches 1200 km *745 miles* from Haun-Khan to Ashkhabad, Turkmenistan. The course length is currently 800 km *500 miles*.

Locks

Largest lock The Berendrecht lock, which links the River Scheldt with docks of Antwerp, Belgium, is the largest sea lock in the world. First used in April 1989, it has a length of 500 m *1640 ft*, a width of 68 m *223 ft* and a sill level of 13.5 m *44 ft*. Each of its four sliding lock gates weighs 1500 tonnes.

The largest and deepest lock in the United Kingdom is the Royal Portbury Lock, Bristol, opened in 1977, which measures 366.7 × 43 m *1199.8 × 140 ft* and has a depth of 20.2 m *66 ft*.

Deepest lock The world's deepest lock, although no longer operational, is the Zaporozhe lock on the Dnieperbug Canal, Ukraine, which could once raise or lower barges 39.2 m *128 ft*.

Britain's lowest bridge over a public road is just 1.61 m *5 ft 3½ in* high. It is under a railway line and next to a level crossing at Hoddesdon, Herts.

Guess What?
Q. What is the world's largest ship?
A. See Page 108

Guess What?
Q. How long is the famous wall named after Hadrian?
A. See Page 104

Highest rise and longest flight The world's highest lock elevator overcomes a head of 68.6 m *225 ft* at Ronquières on the Charleroi–Brussels Canal, Belgium. Two 236-wheeled caissons are each able to carry 1370 tonnes and take 22 minutes to cover the inclined plane, which is 1432 m *4698 ft* long.

The longest flight of locks in the United Kingdom is on the Worcester and Birmingham Canal at Tardebigge, Hereford & Worcester, where in a stretch 4 km *2½ miles* long there are the Tardebigge (30 locks) and Stoke (six locks) flights, which together drop the canal 78.9 m *259 ft*.

In the stretch from Huddersfield to Marsden, W Yorks on the Huddersfield Narrow Canal (closed in 1944) there were a total of 42 locks in 11.6 km *7¼ miles*.

Largest cut The Corinth Canal, Greece, opened in 1893, is 6.33 km *3.93 miles* long, 8 m *26 ft* deep and 24.6 m *81 ft* wide at the surface and has an extreme depth of cutting of 79 m *259 ft*. It is still in use today. The Gaillard Cut (known as 'the Ditch') on the Panama Canal is 82 m *270 ft* deep between Gold Hill and Contractor's Hill, with a bottom width of 152 m *500 ft*.

Guess What?

Q. How much rain fell in a minute in Barst on 26 November 1970?

A. See Page 22

Dams

Most massive dam Measured by volume, the largest dam is New Cornelia Tailings on Ten Mile Wash, in Arizona, USA, with a volume of 209.5 million m³ *274.5 million yd³*. When completed, the Syncrude Tailings dam near Fort McMurray, in Alberta, Canada will be the largest, with a planned volume of 540 million m³ *706.3 million yd³*. Both are earth-fill dams.

The most massive dam in Britain is Gale Common Tailings Dam at Cridling Stubbs, N Yorks. It is an ash disposal scheme, and to date c. 15 million m³ *20 million yd³* of compacted fill has been put in place.

Highest dam The Nurek dam, 300 m *984 ft* high, on the river Vakhsh, Tajikistan is currently the highest dam, but this should be surpassed by the Rogunskaya dam, at 335 m *1098 ft*, also across the river Vakhsh. However, the break-up of the former Soviet Union has delayed its completion.

The rock-fill Llyn Brianne dam, Dyfed is Great Britain's highest dam, reaching 91 m *298 ft 6 in* in November 1971. It became operational on 20 Jul 1972.

Longest dam The Kiev dam across the Dniepr, Ukraine, completed in 1964, has a crest length of 41.2 km *25.6 miles*.

The Yacyretá dam across the River Paraná on the Argentinian/Paraguayan border, due for completion in 1998, is designed to be 69.6 km *43.2 miles* long.

Strongest dam Completed, but not operational, is the 245 m *803 ft* high Sayano-Shushenskaya dam on the river Yenisey, Russia, which is designed to bear a load of 18 million tonnes from a fully-filled reservoir of 31,300 million m³ *41,000 million yd³* capacity.

Largest concrete dam The Grand Coulee dam on the Columbia River, Washington State, USA was begun in 1933 and became operational on 22 Mar 1941. It was finally completed in 1942 at a cost of $56 million. It has a crest length of 1272 m *4173 ft*

The Grand Coulee Dam became even more famous in 1958, when Lonnie Donegan had a top 10 hit in Britain with a song about it. Record-breaking dams are not normally the subject of successful pop songs!

and is 167 m *550 ft* high. The volume of concrete poured was 8,092,000 m³ *10,585,000 yd³* to a weight of 19,595,000 tonnes.

Highest concrete dam Grande Dixence, on the river Dixence in Switzerland, is the highest concrete dam. It was built between 1953 and 1961 to a height of 285 m *935 ft*, with a crest length of 700 m 2297 ft, using 5,960,000 m³ *7,800,000 yd³* of concrete.

Largest reservoir The most voluminous man-made reservoir is the Kakhovskaya reservoir, on the river Dniepr in Ukraine, with a volume of 182.0 km³ *43.6 miles³* and an area of 2160 km² *834 miles²*. It was completed in 1955.

The world's largest artificial lake measured by surface area is Lake Volta, Ghana, formed by the Akosombo dam, completed in 1965. By 1969 the lake had filled to an area of 8482 km² *3275 miles²*, with a shoreline 7250 km *4500 miles* in length.

The completion in 1954 of the Owen Falls Dam near Jinja, Uganda, across the northern exit of the White

■ The largest levees (embankments built to prevent river floods) are those alongside the Mississippi in the USA. However, they could not cope with the heavy rainfall in the summer of 1993 which hit the area, causing widespread flooding and leaving a trail of destruction. (Photo: Gamma/Holbrooke/Liaison)

Levees

The most massive ever built were the Mississippi levees, begun in 1717 but vastly augmented by the US Federal Government after the disastrous floods of 1927. These extended for 2787 km *1732 miles* along the main river from Cape Girardeau, Missouri, USA to the Gulf of Mexico and comprised more than 765 million m³ *1000 million yd³* of earthworks, but the 1993 floods greatly reduced these impressive figures. Levees on the tributaries of the Mississippi comprised an additional 3200 km *2000 miles*.

Nile from the Victoria Nyanza, marginally raised the level of that *natural* lake by adding 204.8 km³ *49.1 miles³*, and technically turned it into a reservoir with a surface area of 69,484 km² *26,828 miles²* and a capacity of 2.7×10^{12} m³ *3.5×10^{12} yd³*.

UK The most capacious reservoir in Great Britain is Loch Quoich, Highland, which was filled to 382 billion litres *84 billion gal* between February 1954 and January 1957 and which acquired a surface area of 1922 ha *4750 acres* and a perimeter of 44.1 km *27.4 miles*.

Largest polder (reclaimed land) Of the five great polders in the old Zuider Zee, Netherlands, the largest will be the Markerwaard, if it is completed, at 60,000 ha *148,250 acres* (603 km² *231 miles²*). However, for the time being the project has been abandoned. Work on the surrounding dyke, 106 km *65 miles* long, began in 1957. The water area remaining after the erection of the dam (32 km *20 miles* in length), built between 1927 and 1932, is called IJsselmeer, which is due to have a final area of 1262.6 km² *487½ miles²*.

Tunnels

Water-supply tunnel The longest tunnel of any kind is the New York City West Delaware water-supply tunnel, begun in 1937 and completed in 1944. It has a diameter of 4.1 m *13 ft 6 in* and runs for 169 km *105 miles* from the Rondout reservoir into the Hillview reservoir, in Yonkers, New York, USA.

The United Kingdom's longest tunnel is the Thames Water Ring Main, completed in December 1994 to supply half of London's water needs. The tunnel, which is 80 km *50 miles* long, carries up to 1300 million litres *285 million gal* of drinking water a day to up to six million people.

Rail tunnel The Seikan rail tunnel, 53.85 km *33.46 miles* long, was bored to 240 m *787 ft* beneath sea level and 100 m *328 ft* below the seabed of the Tsugaru Strait between Tappi Saki, Honshū, and Fukushima, Hokkaidō, Japan. Tests started on the sub-aqueous section (23.3 km *14½ miles*) in 1964 and construction in June 1972. It was holed through on 27 Jan 1983 after a loss of 66 lives. The first test run took place on 13 Mar 1988.

Proposals for a Gotthard base tunnel between Erstfeld and Bodio, both in Switzerland, envisage a rail tunnel 57 km *35½ miles* long.

Great Britain's longest main-line railway tunnel is the Severn Tunnel, 7 km 4 miles long, linking Avon and Gwent, constructed with 76,400,000 bricks between 1873 and 1886.

Construction of the world's longest undersea tunnel—the £10-billion Channel Tunnel under the English Channel between Folkestone, Kent and Calais, France—began on 1 Dec 1987, and a link was created between Great Britain and France when the service tunnel drives met under the channel on 1 Dec 1990. The tunnel was officially opened by HM the Queen and President François Mitterrand of France on 6 May 1994. The length of each twin rail tunnel is 49.94 km *31.03 miles* and the diameter 7.6 m *24 ft 11 in*. The section under the sea is 14.7 km *9.1 miles* longer than the section under the sea of the Seikan rail tunnel (⇨ above), although the overall length of the Channel Tunnel is less.

Continuous subway The Moscow metro Kaluzhskaya underground railway line from Medvedkovo to Bittsevsky Park is c. 37.9 km *23½ miles* long

The completion of the Malpas tunnel (⇨ right column) enabled vessels to navigate from the Atlantic Ocean to the Mediterranean Sea via the river Garonne to Toulouse and the Canal du Midi to Sète.

Guess What?
Q. Which city has the busiest underground system?
A. See Page 124

and was completed in early 1990.

Road tunnel *Longest* The two-lane St Gotthard road tunnel from Göschenen to Airolo, Switzerland, 16.32 km *10.14 miles* long, was opened to traffic on 5 Sep 1980. Nineteen lives were lost during its construction, begun in autumn 1969, and costing 690 million Swiss francs (then £175 million).

The longest road tunnel in the United Kingdom is the Mersey (Queensway) Tunnel, joining Liverpool and Birkenhead, Merseyside. It is 3.43 km *2.13 miles* long, or 4.62 km *2.87 miles* including branch tunnels. Work began in December 1925, and it was opened by HM King George V on 18 Jul 1934. The four-lane roadway, 11 m *36 ft* wide, carries nearly 7½ million vehicles a year. The first tube of the second Mersey (Kingsway) Tunnel was opened on 24 Jun 1971, with the breakthrough of the second in 1972.

Largest The largest-diameter road tunnel in the world is that blasted through Yerba Buena Island, San Francisco, California, USA. It is 24 m *77 ft 10 in* wide, 17 m *56 ft* high and 165 m *540 ft* long. Around 250,000 vehicles pass through on its two decks every day.

Forty years ago the world's longest road tunnel was the Mersey (Queensway) Tunnel, linking Liverpool and Birkenhead, at 3.43 km 2.13 miles. Today it is still Britain's longest, but the world's longest is the St Gotthard Tunnel in Switzerland, at 16.32 km 10.14 miles.

Lowest The Hitra Tunnel in Norway, linking the mainland to the island of Hitra, reaches a depth of 264 m *866 ft* below sea level. It is 5.6 km *3½ miles* long, with three lanes, and was opened in December 1994.

Hydroelectric irrigation The 82.9 km *51½ mile* long Orange–Fish Rivers tunnel, South Africa, was bored between 1967 and 1973 at an estimated cost of £60 million. The lining to a minimum thickness of 23 cm *9 in* gave a completed diameter of 5.33 m *17 ft 6 in*.

The Majes dam project in Peru involves 98 km *60.9 miles* of tunnels for hydroelectric and water-supply purposes. The dam is at an altitude of 4200 m *13,780 ft*.

Longest and largest canal-tunnel The Rove tunnel on the Canal de Marseille au Rhône in the south of France was completed in 1927 and is 7120 m *23,359 ft* or *4.42 miles* long, 22 m *72 ft* wide and 11.4 m *37 ft* high. Built to be navigated by sea-going ships, it was closed in 1963 following a collapse of the structure and has not been re-opened.

Great Britain The longest canal-tunnel is the Standedge (more properly Standedge) Tunnel in W Yorks on the Huddersfield Narrow Canal, built from 1794 to 4 Apr 1811. It measures 5.1 km *3 miles* in length and was closed on 21 Dec 1944. However, there are plans for its restoration.

The British canal system contained 84 tunnels exceeding 30 yd *27.4 m*, of which 49 are open today. The longest of these is the Dudley Tunnel, 2.88 km *1.79 miles* in length, on the Birmingham & Black Country canals, although navigation is restricted.

Oldest navigable tunnel The Malpas tunnel on the Canal du Midi in south-west France was completed in 1681 and is 161 m *528 ft* long.

Tunnelling The longest unsupported example of a machine-bored tunnel is the Three Rivers water tunnel, 9.37 km *5.82 miles* long with a diameter of 3.2 m *10 ft 6 in*, constructed for the city of Atlanta, Georgia, USA from April 1980 to February 1982.

Sewage tunnels The Chicago TARP (Tunnels and Reservoir Plan) in Illinois, USA, when complete, will involve 211 km *131 miles* of machine-bored sewer tunnels 2.7–10 m *9–33 ft* in diameter. Phase I will comprise 175.4 km *109 miles*. As of March 1995, 121.3 km *75.4 miles* are operational, 29.0 km *18.0 miles* are under construction, and the remaining 25.1 km *15.6 miles* are unfunded. The system provides pollution control (Phase I) and flood control (Phase II) and will service 3.9 million people in 52 communities over an area of 971 km² *375 miles²*. The estimated cost for the project is $3.6 billion ($2.4 billion for Phase I, $1.2 billion for Phase II).

The Henriksdal plant in Stockholm, Sweden was the world's first major waste-water plant to be built underground. It was built between 1941 and 1971, and involved the excavation of nearly 1 million m³ *35,300,000 ft³* of rock. It is now being enlarged, with the extension due for completion in 1997.

Bridge-tunnel The Chesapeake Bay bridge-tunnel, opened to traffic on 15 Apr 1964, extends 28.40 km *17.65 miles* from the Eastern Shore region of the Virginia Peninsula to Virginia Beach, Virginia, USA. The longest bridged section is Trestle C (7.34 km *4.56 miles* long), and the longest tunnel is the Thimble Shoal Channel Tunnel (1.75 km *1.09 miles*).

Specialized Structures

Advertising signs The highest is the logo 'I' at the top of the First Interstate World Centre building, Los Angeles, California, USA, a 73-storey building 310 m *1017 ft* high.

The largest and tallest free-standing advertising sign is at the Hilton Hotel and Casino in Las Vegas, Nevada, USA and was completed in December 1993. Its two faces had a total area of 7648.5 m² *82,328 ft²* or *1.89 acres*, and it was 110.3 m *362 ft* high when completed, but it was damaged in a storm on 18 Jul 1994

Far away!

The most conspicuous sign ever erected was the electric Citroën sign on the Eiffel Tower, Paris. It was switched on on 4 Jul 1925 and could be seen 38 km *24 miles* away. It was in six colours, with 250,000 lamps and 90 km *56 miles* of electric cables. The letter 'N' which terminated the name 'Citroën' between the second and third levels measured 20.8 m *68 ft 5 in* in height. The whole apparatus was taken down in 1936.

and part of it fell down. Even after this it nonetheless remains both the largest and tallest sign.

The largest advertisement on a building measured 3879 m² *41,756 ft²* and was erected to promote Emirates, the international airline of the United Arab Emirates. It was located by the M4 motorway, near Chiswick, London, and was displayed from November 1992 to January 1993.

Airborne Reebok International Ltd of Massachusetts, USA flew from a single-seater plane a banner which read 'Reebok Totally Beachin'. The banner measured 15 m *50 ft* in height and 30 m *100 ft* in length and was flown from 13 to 16 and 20 to 23 Mar 1990 for four hours each day.

Hoarding The world's largest hoarding is that of the Bassat Ogilvy Promotional Campaign for Ford España, measuring 145 m *475 ft 9 in* in length and 15 m *49 ft 3 in* in height. It is sited at Plaza de Toros Monumental de Barcelona, Barcelona, Spain and was installed on 27 Apr 1989.

Illuminated The world's largest illuminated sign is that at the Hilton Hotel and Casino in Las Vegas, Nevada, USA (⇔ above). The longest such sign is 60 m *197 ft* in length. It is lit by 62,400 w metal-halide projectors and was erected by Abudi Signs Industry Ltd at Ramat Gan, Israel.

The UK's longest illuminated sign is that shared by P & O European Ferries and Stena Sealink at Dover Eastern Docks, Kent. It is 82 m *269 ft* long and 65 cm *25½ in* high, and was installed by Dover Sign Co. in August 1993.

Neon The longest neon sign is the letter 'M' installed on the Great Mississippi River Bridge in Memphis, Tennessee, USA. It is 550 m *1800 ft* long and comprises 200 high-intensity lamps.

> **Grave digging** It is recorded that Johann Heinrich Karl Thieme, sexton of Aldenburg, Germany, dug 23,311 graves during a 50-year career. In 1826 his understudy dug *his* grave.

The largest measures 111.4 × 19.05 m *365 ft 6 in × 62 ft 6 in* and was built to promote 999, a traditional Chinese medicine from the Nanfang Pharmaceutical Factory in China. It was erected between November 1992 and April 1993 on Hong Kong Island and contains 13.14 km *8.16 miles* of neon tubing.

Bonfire The largest bonfire was constructed at Workington, Cumbria by inhabitants of the town and off-duty firefighters. It was 37.33 m *122 ft 6 in* high, with an overall volume of 7100 m³ *250,700 ft³*, and was lit on 5 Nov 1993.

Breakwater The world's longest breakwater is that which protects the Port of Galveston, Texas, USA. The granite South Breakwater is 10.85 km *6.74 miles* in length.

Great Britain's longest is the North Breakwater at Holyhead, Anglesey, which is 2.39 km *1.49 miles* in length and was completed in 1873.

Cemeteries Largest Ohlsdorf Cemetery in Hamburg, Germany is the largest cemetery, covering an area of 400 ha *990 acres*, with 969,969 burials and 403,263 crema-

tions as at 31 Dec 1994. It has been in continuous use since 1877.

Great Britain's largest cemetery is Brookwood Cemetery, Brookwood, Surrey, owned by Mr Ramadan Güney. It is 200 ha *500 acres* in extent and has more than 231,000 interments.

Tallest The permanently illuminated Memorial Necrópole Ecumênica, in Santos, near São Paulo, Brazil, is 10 storeys high, occupying an area of 1.8 ha *4.4 acres*. Its construction started in March 1983 and the first burial was on 28 Jul 1984.

Chimneys Tallest The coal power-plant No. 2 stack at Ekibastuz, Kazakhstan, completed in 1987, is 420 m *1377 ft* tall. The diameter tapers from 44 m *144 ft* at the base to 14.2 m *46 ft 7 in* at the top, and it weighs 60,000 tonnes.

The tallest chimney in Great Britain is one of 259 m *850 ft* at Drax Power Station, N Yorks, completed in 1969. It has an untapered diameter of 26 m *85 ft* and also has the greatest capacity of any British chimney.

> In 1955 the tallest chimney was one in Anaconda, Montana, USA which was 178 m *585 ft* tall. The record today is one in Ekibastuz, Kazakhstan which is 420 m *1377 ft* tall.

Most massive The world's most massive chimney in terms of internal volume was built by M.W. Kellog Co. for Empresa Nacional de Electricidad S.A at Puentes de García Rodríguez, Spain. The chimney is 350 m *1148 ft* tall, contains 15,750 m³ *20,600 yd³* of concrete and 1315 tonnes of steel and has an internal volume of 189,720 m³ *248,100 yd³*.

Columns The tallest columns are the thirty-six 27.5 m *90 ft* tall fluted pillars of Vermont marble in the colonnade of the Education Building, Albany, New York State, USA. Their base diameter is 1.98 m *6 ft 6 in*.

The tallest load-bearing stone columns in the world are those measuring 21 m *69 ft* in the Hall of Columns of the Temple of Amun at Karnak, opposite Thebes on the Nile, the ancient capital of Upper Egypt. They were built in the 19th dynasty in the reign of Rameses II c. 1270 BC.

Cooling towers The largest cooling tower is 180 m *590 ft* tall and is adjacent to the nuclear power plant at Uentrop, Germany. It was completed in 1976.

UK The largest in the United Kingdom are at Drax Power Station, N Yorks. They are 115 m *377 ft* tall and 92.68 m *304 ft* in diameter at the base.

Crematorium The largest crematorium in the world is at the Nikolo-Arkhangelskiy Crematorium, east Moscow, Russia with seven twin cremators of British design, completed in March 1972. It covers an area of 210 ha *519 acres* and has six Halls of Farewell for atheists.

The oldest crematorium in Great Britain was built in 1879 at Woking, Surrey. The first cremation took place there on 26 Mar 1885.

Domes The largest is the Louisiana Superdome, New Orleans, USA, which has a diameter of 207.26 m *680 ft*.

> **Guess What?**
> Q. What speed did *The Blue Flame* reach on 23 October 1970?
> A. See Page 117

> The record-breaking bonfire built in Workington in 1993 beat the British record for the largest bonfire which had stood for 91 years!

■ The world's largest bonfire, built at Workington, Cumbria, is closely watched by fire-officers just in case anything goes wrong. Fortunately nothing did, and a new record was established without any accidents. The temperature at the heart of the bonfire was estimated to be 5500°C *9900 °F*

■ **The tallest lighting columns in the world are these four floodlights in Muscat, Oman. They are 63.5 m *208 ft 4 in* high.**
(Photo: Gamma/J-Claude Francolon)

Britain's largest is that of the Bell Sports Centre, Perth, Tayside with a diameter of 67 m *222 ft*. It was designed by D.B. Cockburn and constructed in Baltic whitewood by Muirhead & Sons Ltd of Grangemouth, Central.

Doors *Largest* The four doors in the Vehicle Assembly Building near Cape Canaveral, Florida, USA have a height of 140 m *460 ft*.

Great Britain's largest are those of the Britannia Assembly Hall, at Filton airfield, Avon. The doors are 315 m *1035 ft* in length and 20 m *67 ft* high, divided into three bays each 105 m *345 ft* across.

The largest simple hinged door in Great Britain is that of Ye Old Bull's Head, Beaumaris, Anglesey, which is 3.35 m *11 ft* wide and 3.96 m *13 ft* high.

Heaviest The heaviest door is that of the laser target room at Lawrence Livermore National Laboratory, California, USA. It weighs 326.5 tonnes, is up to 2.43 m *8 ft* thick and was installed by Overly Manufacturing Company.

Oldest Great Britain's oldest are those of Hadstock Church, near Saffron Walden, Essex, which date from c. 1040 AD and exhibit evidence of Danish workmanship.

Earthworks The longest and most extensive earthworks prior to the mechanical era were the Linear Earth Boundaries of the Benin Empire (c. 1300) and earlier in the Edo state (formerly Bendel) of Nigeria. In March 1993 it was estimated by Dr Patrick Darling that the total length of the earthworks was probably around 16,000 km *10,000 miles*, with the amount of earth moved estimated at 75 million m³ *100 million yd³*.

The greatest prehistoric earthwork in Britain is Wansdyke, originally Wodensdic, which ran 138 km *86 miles* from Portishead, Avon to Inkpen Beacon and Ludgershall, south of Hungerford, Berks. It was built by the Belgae (c. 150 BC) as their northern boundary.

Flagpoles The tallest flagpole is at Panmunjon, North Korea, near the border with South Korea. It is 160 m *525 ft* high and flies a flag 30 m *98 ft 6 in* long.

The tallest unsupported flagpole in the world is the steel pole, 86 m *282 ft* tall and weighing 54,400 kg *120,000 lb*, which was erected on 22 Aug 1985 at the Canadian Expo 86 exhibition in Vancouver, British Columbia. This supports a gigantic ice-hockey stick 62.5 m *205 ft* in length.

Great Britain's tallest flagpole is a Douglas-fir staff 68 m *225 ft* tall at Kew, Richmond-upon-Thames, Surrey. Cut in Canada, it was shipped across the Atlantic and towed up the river Thames on 7 May

Guess What?
Q. How many spectators could the Strahov Stadium in Prague accommodate?
A. See Page 90

1958, to replace the old staff, 65 m *214 ft* tall, erected in 1919.

Floodlights The tallest lighting columns are the four made by Petitjean & Cie of Troyes, France and installed by Taylor Woodrow at Sultan Qaboos Sports Complex, Muscat, Oman. They stand 63.5 m *208 ft 4 in* high.

Fountains The tallest fountain is the one at Fountain Hills, Arizona, USA, built at a cost of $1.5 million for McCulloch Properties Inc. At full pressure of 26.3 kg/cm² *375 lb/in²* and at a rate of 26,500 litres/min *5850 gal/min*, the column of water, 171.2 m *562 ft* tall, weighs more than 8 tonnes. If all three pumps are in use, it can reach 190 m *625 ft* in calm or windless conditions.

Britain's tallest is the Emperor Fountain at Chatsworth, Bakewell, Derbyshire. When first tested on 1 Jun 1844, it attained the then unprecedented height of 79 m *260 ft*. In recent years it has not been played to more than 76 m *250 ft* and rarely beyond 55 m *180 ft*.

Fumigation The largest fumigation carried out was during the restoration of the Mission Inn complex in Riverside, California, USA on 28 Jun–1 Jul 1987 to rid the buildings of termites. It was performed by Fume Masters Inc. of Riverside. Over 350 tarpaulins were used, each weighing up to 160 kg *350 lb*, and the operation involved completely covering the site—an area of 6500 m² *70,000 ft²*. The buildings which had to be covered included domes, minarets, chimneys and balconies, some of which exceeded 30 m *100 ft* in height.

Gasholders The largest gasholder was the one at Oberhausen, Germany. It had a height of 102 m *335 ft*, a diameter of 66 m *217 ft* and a working gas volume of 630,000 m³ *22,250,000 ft³* under standard conditions.

Currently the largest is at the Prosper coking plant of Ruhrkohle AG at Essen, Germany. It has a working

gas volume of 325,000 m³ *11,480,000 ft³* under standard conditions.

Great Britain's largest was at the East Greenwich Gas Works. The No. 2 holder was built in 1891 with an original capacity for 346,000 m³ *12,200,000 ft³*. It was later reconstructed with a capacity of 252,000 m³ *8.9 million ft³*, a water tank 92 m *303 ft* in diameter and a full inflated height of 45 m *148 ft*. However, it has been demolished in the meantime, and the record is now held by the No. 1 holder, built in 1885, also at Greenwich. It has a capacity of 229,000 m³ *8.1 million ft³* and a height of 61 m *200 ft*.

Globe The largest revolving globe is a sphere 10 m *33 ft* in diameter, weighing 30 tonnes. It is called 'Globe of Peace' and was built between 1982 and 1987 by Orfeo Bartolucci of Apecchio, Pesaro, Italy.

Grain elevators The largest grain elevator is a single-unit one operated by the C-G-F Grain Co. at Wichita, Kansas, USA and consists of a triple row of storage tanks, 123 on each side of the central loading tower or 'head house'. The unit is 828 m *2717 ft* long and 30.48 m *100 ft* wide. Each tank is 37 m *120 ft* high and has an internal diameter of 9.14 m *30 ft*, giving a total storage capacity of 7.3 million hl *20,000,000 bushels* of wheat.

Jetty The longest deep-water jetty is the Quai Hermann du Pasquier at Le Havre, France, with a length of 1520 m *5000 ft*. It is part of an enclosed basin and has a constant depth of water of 9.8 m *32 ft* on both sides.

An Indian government field kitchen set up in April 1973 at Ahmadnagar, Maharashtra, then a famine area, daily provided 1.2 million subsistence meals.

Lighthouses *Tallest* The steel tower near Yamashita Park in Yokohama, Japan is 106 m *348 ft* high. It has a power of 600,000 candelas and a visibility range of 32 km *20 miles*.

The tallest lighthouse in Great Britain is the Bishop Rock Lighthouse, 49 m *160 ft 9 in* tall, in the Isles of Scilly, 11.3 km *7 miles* south-west of Hugh Town, the capital of the Scillies. Established in 1858, it was converted to automatic operation on 21 Dec 1992.

Fencing

Longest The dingo-proof wire fence enclosing the main sheep areas of Australia is 1.8 m *6 ft* high, plus 30 cm *1 ft* underground and stretches for 5531 km *3437 miles*. The Queensland state government discontinued full maintenance in 1982.

Tallest The world's tallest fences are security screens 20 m *65 ft* high, erected by Harrop-Allin of Pretoria, South Africa in November 1981 to protect fuel depots and refineries at Sasolburg from terrorist rocket attack.

Guess What?

Q. Why is Ambrose light tower significant for Serge Madec and Laurent Bourgnon?

A. See Page 112

Most powerful The lighthouse in Great Britain with the most powerful light is Strumble Head Lighthouse on Ynysmeicl (St Michael's Island), 4.8km *3miles* west of Fishguard, Dyfed, Wales. Its intensity is 6,000,000 candelas and its range is 39km *24miles*, characterized by four white flashes every 15 seconds. Electrified in 1965, the lighthouse was converted to unmanned automatic operation in 1980.

Greatest range The lights with the greatest range are those 332m *1089ft* above the ground on the Empire State Building, New York City, USA. Each of the four-arc mercury bulbs is visible 130km *80miles* away on the ground and 490km *300miles* away from aircraft.

Marquees *Largest* A marquee covering an area of 17,500m² *188,350ft²* (1.75 ha *4.32acres*) was erected by the firm of Deuter from Augsburg, Germany for the 1958 'Welcome Expo' in Brussels, Belgium.

Britain's largest marquee in regular use is that made by Piggott Brothers of Stanford Rivers, Essex and used annually by the Royal Horticultural Society at their show at Chelsea,

■ The largest monolithic obelisk in the world, weighing 455tonnes, is the 'skewer' or 'spit' of Tuthmosis III in Rome, Italy. It was taken to Rome from Egypt in AD357.

London. It measures 94 × 146m *310 ×480ft*, covering a ground area of 13,820m² *148,800ft²* (1.38ha *3.42acres*), and the canvas weighs 19tonnes. It is replaced from time to time by a new marquee of the same dimensions.

The largest single-unit tent in Britain covers a ground area of *c.* 12,000m² *130,000ft²* (1.2ha *2.98acres*) and was manufactured by Clyde Canvas Ltd of Edinburgh, Lothian.

Maypole The tallest maypole erected in Britain was one of Sitka spruce 32.12m *105ft 7in* tall, put up in Pelynt, Cornwall on 1 May 1974.

Maze The oldest datable representation of a labyrinth is that on a clay tablet from Pylos, Greece *c.* 1220 BC.

Britain's oldest surviving hedge maze is at Hampton Court Palace, Greater London. It was designed by George London and Henry Wise in 1690 and measures 68×25m *222 ×82ft*.

The world's largest maze ever constructed was made in a cornfield at Lebanon Valley College, Pennsylvania, USA. Cut in the shape of a stegosaurus, it was 152m *500ft* long and covered an area of 11,700m² *126,000 ft²*, and was in existence for two months between September and November 1993.

The largest permanent maze is the hedge maze at Ruurlo, Netherlands, which has an area of 8740m² *94,080ft²*. It is made of beech hedges, and was created in 1891. The maze with the greatest path length is that at Longleat, near Warminster, Wilts, which has 2.72km *1.69miles* of paths flanked by 16,180 yew trees. It was opened in 1978.

Menhir The tallest known menhir is the Grand Menhir Brisé at Locmariaquer, Brittany, France, which was originally 18m *59ft* high and weighed *c.* 300tonnes but is now in four pieces.

Monuments *Tallest* The tallest monument is the stainless-steel Gateway to the West arch in St Louis, Missouri, USA, completed on 28 Oct 1965 to commemorate the westward expansion after the Louisiana Purchase of 1803. It is a sweeping arch spanning 192m *630ft* and rising to the same height. It cost $29 million and was designed in 1947 by the Finnish-American architect Eero Saarinen (1910–61).

The tallest monumental column is that commemorating the Battle of San Jacinto (21 Apr 1836), on the bank of the San Jacinto River near Houston, Texas, USA. Constructed from 1936 to 1939, the tapering column is 173m *570ft* tall, 14m *47ft* square at the base and 9m *30ft* square at the observation tower, which is surmounted by a star weighing 199.6 tonnes.

Obelisks

Largest (monolithic) The 'skewer' or 'spit' (from the Greek *obeliskos*) of Tuthmosis III brought from Aswan, Egypt by Emperor Constantius in the spring of AD 357 was repositioned in the Piazza San Giovanni in Laterano, Rome, Italy on 3 Aug 1588. Once 36m *118ft 1in* tall, it now stands 32.81m *107ft 7in* and weighs 455tonnes.

The unfinished obelisk, probably commissioned by Queen Hatshepsut *c.*1490BC and *in situ* at Aswan, Egypt, is 41.75m *136ft 10in* long and weighs 1168tonnes.

The record for the time that a raised obelisk has remained *in situ* is held by that at Heliopolis, near Cairo, erected by Senusret I *c.* 1750BC.

Great Britain's largest megalithic prehistoric monument and largest henge are the 11.5 ha *28½acre* earthworks and stone circles of Avebury, Wilts, 'rediscovered' in 1646. The earliest calibrated date in the area of this Neolithic site is *c.* 4200BC. The work is 365m *1200ft* in diameter with a ditch 12m *40ft* wide around the perimeter.

The henge of Durrington Walls, Wilts, obliterated by road-building, had a diameter of 472m *1550ft*. It was built *c.* 2500BC and required some 900,000 man-hours.

The largest trilithons are at Stonehenge, to the south of Salisbury Plain, Wilts, with single sarsen blocks weighing over 45tonnes and requiring over 550 men to drag them up a 9 degree gradient. The earliest stage of the construction of the ditch has been dated to 2800BC.

Seven Wonders of the World

The Seven Wonders of the World were first designated by Antipater of Sidon in the 2nd century BC. They were:– the Pyramids of Giza, the Hanging Gardens of Babylon, the Statue of Zeus at Olympia, the Temple of Artemis at Ephesus, the Tomb of King Mausolus, the Colossus of Rhodes and the Pharos of Alexandria.

Only the Pyramids of Giza still exist substantially today. They are to be found near El Giza (El Gizeh), southwest of El Qâhira (Cairo) in Egypt. They were built by three Fourth Dynasty Egyptian Pharaohs: Khwfw (Khufu or Cheops), Kha-f-Ra (Khafre, Khefren or Chepren) and Menkaure (Mycerinus). The great pyramid (The 'Horizon of Khufu') was built *c.*2550 BC. Its original height was 146.6m *481ft 0in* (now, since the loss of its topmost stones and the pyramidion, reduced to 137.5m *451ft 1in*) with a base line of 230.4m *755ft 10in*, thus covering slightly more than 5 ha *13acres*. It has been estimated that a permanent work force of 100,000 required 30 years to manoeuvre into position the 2,300,000 limestone blocks averaging 2½tonnes each, totalling about 5,840,000 tonnes

and a volume of 2,593,000 m³ *91,571,000ft³*. Some blocks weigh 15tonnes.

Of the other six wonders only fragments remain of the Temple of Artemis (Diana) of the Ephesians, built *c.*350BC at Ephesus, Turkey (destroyed by the Goths in AD262), and of the Tomb of King Mausolus of Caria, built at Halicarnassus, now Bodrum, Turkey, *c.*325BC.

No trace remains of:– the Hanging Gardens of Semiramis, at Babylon, Iraq *c.*600BC; the statue of Zeus (Jupiter), by Phidias (5th century BC) at Olympia, Greece (lost in a fire at Istanbul) in marble, gold and ivory and 12m *40ft* tall; the figure of the god Helios (Apollo), a 35m *117ft* tall statue sculptured 292–280BC, by Chares of Lindus (destroyed by an earthquake in 224BC); and the world's earliest lighthouse, 122m *400ft* tall built by Sostratus of Cnidus (*c.*270BC) as a pyramid shaped tower of white marble, on the island of Pharos (Greek, *pharos*=lighthouse), off the coast of El Iskandariya (Alexandria), Egypt (destroyed by earthquake in AD1375).

Guess What?

Q. How deep was the snow in Tamarac in March 1911?

A. See Page 23

■ The illuminated ice construction at St Paul, Minnesota, USA, which was the latest in a long line of record-breaking ice palaces in the city going back over a century.
(Photo: Gamma/B. Pugliano/Liaison)

Southwest Sewage Treatment Works) began operation in 1939 on a site covering 231 ha *570 acres* in suburban Chicago, Illinois and serves an area containing 2,193,000 people. A total of 651 staff are employed at the plant, which treated an average of 2926 million litres *644 million gal* of waste per day in 1994.

UK The largest full-treatment works in Britain and Europe is the Beckton Works, east London, which serves a population equivalent of 2,980,000 and handles an estimated daily flow of 955 million litres *210 million gal*. The total capacity of the tanks is 773,000 m³ *27,300,000 ft³*.

Snow and ice constructions A snow palace with a volume of 103,591.8 m³ *3,658,310.2 ft³* and 30.29 m *99 ft 5 in* in height was unveiled on 8 Feb 1994 at Asahikawa, Hokkaidō, Japan. It was made to resemble Suwon castle in South Korea.

The world's largest ice construction was the ice palace completed in January 1992, using 18,000 blocks of ice, at St Paul, Minnesota, USA during the Winter Carnival. Built by TMK Construction Specialties Inc., it was 50.8 m *166 ft 8 in* high and contained 4900 tonnes *10.8 million lb* of ice.

Snowman The tallest was 27.47 m *90 ft 1 in* high and was made by a team of eight local residents at Saas-Fee, Switzerland. It took 21 days to build the snowman, which was completed on 6 Nov 1993.

Stairway The longest stairway is the service staircase for the Niesenbahn funicular near Spiez, Switzerland, which rises to 2365 m *7759 ft*. It has 11,674 steps and a bannister.

The longest stairs in Great Britain are those from the transformer gallery to the surface, 324 m *1065 ft*, in the Cruachan Power Station, Argyll. They have 1420 steps, and the plant's work-study unit allows 27 min 41.4 sec for the ascent.

Spiral The tallest spiral staircase is on the outside of the Bòbila Almirall chimney at Tarrasa, Spain. Built by Mariano Masana Ribas in 1956, it is 63.2 m *207 ft* high and has 217 steps.

The longest spiral staircase is one 336 m *1103 ft* deep with 1520 steps, installed in the Mapco-White County Coal Mine, Carmi, Illinois, USA by Systems Control in May 1981.

Statues *Longest* Near Bamiyan, Afghanistan there are the remains of the recumbent Sakya Buddha, built of plastered rubble, which was 'about 305 m' *1000 ft* long and is believed to date from the 3rd or 4th century AD.

Tallest A bronze statue of Buddha 120 m *394 ft* high was completed in Tokyo, Japan in January 1993. It is 35 m *115 ft* wide and weighs 1000 tonnes. The statue took seven years to make and was a joint Japanese–Taiwanese project.

The statue of Maitreya, which stands 26 m *85 ft* high, is carved out of a single piece of white sandalwood tree. It is located at the Lama Temple (Yonghegong), in the north-east of Beijing. The Imperial Court

---

Oldest The oldest scheduled ancient monument is Kent's Cavern, near Torquay, Devon, which is a cave site containing deposits more than 300,000 years old dating from the Lower Palaeolithic period.

Youngest The youngest scheduled ancient monument consists of a hexagonal pillbox and 48 concrete tank-traps near Christchurch, Dorset, built in World War II and protected since 1973.

Mound The largest artificial mound is the gravel one built as a memorial to the Seleucid King Antiochus I (reigned 69–34 BC) which stands on the summit of Nemrud Daği (2494 m *8182 ft*), south-east of Malatya, Turkey. It is 59.8 m *197 ft* tall and covers 3 ha *7.5 acres*.

The largest in Great Britain is Silbury Hill, 9.7 km *6 miles* west of Marlborough, Wilts, which involved the moving of an estimated 680,000 tonnes of chalk, at a cost of 18 million man-hours to make a cone 39 m *130 ft* high with a base of 2 ha *5½ acres*. Prof. Richard Atkinson, who was in charge of the 1968 excavations, showed that it is based on an innermost central mound, similar to contemporary round barrows, and it is now dated to 2745 ± 185 BC.

Obelisk *Tallest* The world's tallest obelisk is the Washington Monument in Washington, DC, USA. Situated in a site covering 43 ha *106 acres* and standing 169.3 m *555 ft 5⅛ in* high, it was built to honour George Washington (1732–99), the first President of the United States.

The United Kingdom's tallest is Cleopatra's Needle on the Embankment, London, which at 20.88 m *68 ft 5 in* is the world's 11th tallest. Weighing 189.35 tonnes, it was towed up the Thames from Egypt on 21 Jan 1878 and positioned on 13 September.

Promenade The longest covered promenade is the Long Corridor in the Summer Palace in Beijing, China, running for 728 m *2388 ft*. It is built entirely of wood and divided by crossbeams into 273 sections. These crossbeams, as well as the ceiling and side pillars,

---

have over 10,000 paintings of famous Chinese landscapes, episodes from folk tales, flowers and birds.

Pyramids *Largest* The largest pyramid, and the largest monument ever constructed, is the Quetzalcóatl at Cholula de Rivadabia, 101 km *63 miles* south-east of Mexico City. It is 54 m *177 ft* tall, and its base covers an area of nearly 18.2 ha *45 acres*. Its total volume has been estimated at 3.3 million m³ *4.3 million yd³*, compared with the current volume of 2.4 million m³ *3.1 million yd³* for the Pyramid of Khufu or Cheops (⬦ Seven Wonders of the World).

Oldest The Djoser Step Pyramid at Saqqâra, Egypt was constructed by Imhotep (Djoser's royal architect) c. 2630 BC to a height of 62 m *204 ft*.

Refuse tip Reclamation Plant No. 1, in Staten Island, New York, USA, which opened in 1948, is the world's largest refuse tip. It is estimated to contain 100 million tonnes of rubbish and covers 1200 ha *3000 acres*. An average of 12,000 tonnes is processed every day.

Scaffolding The tallest scaffolding was erected by Regional Scaffolding & Hoisting Co., Inc. of the Bronx, New York, USA around the New York City Municipal Building and was in place from 1988 to 1992. Its total height was 198 m *650 ft* and its volume 135,900 m³ *4,800,000 ft³*. The work required 12,000 scaffold frames and 20,000 aluminium planks.

Scarecrow The tallest scarecrow was 'Stretch II', constructed by the Speers family of Paris, Ontario, Canada and a crew of 15 at the Paris Fall Fair on 2 Sep 1989. It measured 31.56 m *103 ft 6¾ in* in height.

Sewage works The Stickney Water Reclamation Plant, Stickney, Illinois, USA (formerly the West-

---

Forty years ago the longest staircase was one at a power station in Norway with a total height of 747 m *2450 ft* and 3715 steps. Today the longest is one in Switzerland with a total height of 2365 m *7759 ft* and 11,674 steps.

David McBride and Tom Stirling of Turner Plus Eight Ltd, Glasgow built a two-storey scaffold measuring 20 × 5 × 1 m *65 ft 7 in × 16 ft 5 in × 3 ft 3 in* in 25 min 53 sec on 31 Mar 1995.

TALLEST TOTEM POLE

Totem pole A totem pole 54.94 m *180 ft 3 in* tall, known as the *Spirit of Lekwammen* (Lekwammen = land of the winds), was raised on 4 Aug 1994 at Victoria, British Columbia, Canada prior to the Commonwealth Games taking place there. It was a Spirit of Nations project developed by Richard Krentz of Campbell River, also in British Columbia.

■ The tallest totem pole was carved over nine months in late 1993 and early 1994. It is an intricate work of art and needed precision to hoist it delicately into position.
(Photos: Paul Jonson and Barbara Brennan, Victoria, Canada)

Guess What?

Q. How tall was the record-breaking scarecrow, also made in Canada?

A. See Page 103

allowed two years for the carving of the statue and finished the project in 1750.

Swing A glider swing 9.1 m *30 ft* high was constructed by Kenneth R. Mack, Langenburg, Saskatchewan, Canada for Uncle Herb's Amusements in 1986. The swing is capable of taking its four riders to a height of 7.6 m *25 ft* off the ground.

Tidal river barrier The largest tidal river barrier is the Oosterscheldedam, a storm-surge barrier in the south-western corner of the Netherlands. It has 65 concrete piers and 62 steel gates and covers a total length of 9 km *5½ miles*. It was opened by HM Queen Beatrix on 4 Oct 1986.

Tombs The Mount Li tomb, the burial place of Qin Shi Huangdi, the 1st Emperor of Qin, was built during his reign from 221 to 210 BC and is situated 40 km *25 miles* east of Xianyang, China. The two walls surrounding the grave measure 2173 × 974 m *7129 × 3195 ft* and 685 × 578 m *2247 × 1896 ft*. Several pits in the tomb contained a vast army of an estimated 8000 terracotta soldiers and horses which are life-size and larger.

A tomb housing 180,000 World War II dead on Okinawa, Japan was enlarged in 1985 to accommodate another 9000 bodies thought to be buried on the island.

Vats *Largest* The largest wooden wine cask in the world is the Heidelberg Tun, completed in 1751, in the cellar of the Friedrichsbau, Heidelberg, Germany. Its capacity is 221,726 litres *48,773 gal*.

The vat named 'Strongbow', used by H.P. Bulmer Ltd, the English cider-makers of Hereford, measures 19.65 m *64½ ft* in height and 23 m *75½ ft* in diameter, with a capacity of 7.41 million litres *1.63 million gal*.

Oldest The world's oldest known vat is still in use at Hugel et Fils (founded 1639) in Riquewihr, Haut-Rhin, France. Twelve generations of the family have used it since 1715.

Walls *Longest* The Great Wall of China is the longest in the world and has a main-line length of 3460 km *2150 miles*—nearly three times the length of Britain. Completed during the reign of Qin Shi Huangdi (221–210 BC), it also has 3530 km *2195 miles* of branches and spurs. Its height varies from 4.5 to 12 m *15 to 39 ft* and it is up to 9.8 m *32 ft* thick. It runs from Shanhaiguan,

on the Gulf of Bohai, to Yumenguan and Yangguan and was kept in repair up to the 16th century. Some 51.5 km *32 miles* of the wall have been destroyed since 1966, and part of the wall was blown up to make way for a dam in July 1979.

The longest of the Roman walls in Britain was Hadrian's Wall, 4.5–6 m *15–20 ft* tall and built AD 122–6. It crossed the Tyne-Solway isthmus for 118 km *73½ miles* from Bowness-on-Solway, Cumbria, to Wallsend-on-Tyne, Tyne & Wear, and was abandoned in AD 383.

Thickest Ur-nammu's city walls at Ur (now Muqayyar, Iraq), destroyed by the Elamites in 2006 BC, were 27 m *88 ft* thick and made of mud brick.

The walls of the Great Tower or Donjon of Flint Castle, Clwyd, built in 1277–80, are 7 m *23 ft* thick.

Indoor waterfall The tallest indoor waterfall measures 34.75 m *114 ft* in height and is backed by 840 m² *9000 ft²* of marble. It is situated in the lobby of the International Center Building, Detroit, Michigan, USA.

Water tower The Waterspheroid at Edmond, Oklahoma, USA, built in 1986, rises to a height of 66.5 m *218 ft* and has a capacity of 1,893,000 litres *416,000 gal*. The tower was manufactured by Chicago Bridge and Iron Na-Con, Inc.

Waterwheel The Mohammadieh Noria wheel at Hamah, Syria has a diameter of 40 m *131 ft* and dates from Roman times.

The largest waterwheel in the British Isles is the Lady Isabella at Laxey, Isle of Man, with a diameter of 22 m *72 ft 2 in* and an axle weighing 10 tonnes. It was completed on 24 Sep 1854 for draining the local lead mine but has not been used commercially since 1929, although it is still in working order for tourists.

Windows The largest sheet of glass ever manufactured was one of 50 m² *540 ft²*, or 20 × 2.5 m *65 ft 7 in × 8 ft 2¼ in*, exhibited by the Saint Gobain Co. in France at the *Journées Internationales de Miroiterie* in March 1958.

The largest single windows in the world are those in the Palace of Industry and Technology at Rondpoint de la Défense, Paris, France, with an extreme width of 218 m *715 ft* and a maximum height of 50 m *164 ft*.

The United Kingdom record was a sheet made by Pilkington of St Helens, Merseyside for the Festival of Britain in 1951, measuring 2.5 × 15.2 m *8 ft 2¼ in × 49 ft 10½ in*.

Stained glass The tallest piece of stained glass is the 41.14 m *135 ft* high back-lit glass mural installed in 1979 in the atrium of the Ramada Hotel, Dubai (⇨ Religions, Stained glass).

The largest single stained-glass window in the UK is one with an area of 746.9 m² *8039 ft²*, designed by Brian Clarke and installed at the Victoria Quarter, Leeds, W Yorks in 1990 (⇨ Religions, Stained glass).

Ziggurat The largest ziggurat ever built was that of the Elamite King Untas, c. 1250 BC, known as the Ziggurat of Choga Zambil, 30 km *18.6 miles* from Haft Tepe, Iran. The outer base was 105 × 105 m *344 × 344 ft* and the fifth 'box' 28 × 28 m *92 × 92 ft*, nearly 50 m *164 ft* above.

The largest partially surviving ziggurat is the Ziggurat of Ur (now Muqayyar, Iraq) with a base 61 × 45.7 m *200 × 150 ft*, built to three storeys and surmounted by a summit temple. The first storey and part of the second storey now survive to a height of 18 m *60 ft*. It was built in the reign of Ur-nammu (c. 2250–2232 BC).

Transport

Ships

Earliest Boats

Earliest river or lake boats The earliest surviving vessel is a pine logboat or dugout found in Pesse, Netherlands and dated to *c.*6315 ± 275 BC. It is now in the Provincial Museum, Assen. A fleet of 12 funerary river boats discovered in 1991 at Abydos, Egypt have been tentatively dated to *c.* 3000 BC. The vessels are up to 18 m *60ft* long.

The oldest surviving prehistoric logboat in Britain was found in 1984 on Hasholme Hall Farm, Holme upon Spalding Moor, Humberside. The 2300-year-old boat, which is 13.71 m *45ft* long, will require special conservation until the late 1990s.

Oldest active paddle-steamer
The world's oldest active paddle steamer continuously operated as such is *Skibladner*, which has plied Lake Mjøsa, Norway since 1856. She was built in Motala, Sweden and has had two major refits.

Ocean-going The world's oldest active ocean-going ship is the *MV Doulos* (Greek for 'servant'), built in 1914 in the USA and first named *Medina*. She is currently operating as an international Educational and Christian service vessel with approximately 300 crew, staff and passengers on board from 30 different nations.

UK The oldest British vessel afloat is the *Foudroyant*, built of teak in Bombay in 1817 as HMS *Trincomalee*, and for many years a familiar sight moored in Portsmouth Harbour, Hants. Used as a training ship since 1897, the *Foudroyant* was moved from Portsmouth to Hartlepool, Cleveland in 1987 for repairs and restoration as a typical naval frigate of the Nelson era before eventually being displayed in a specially constructed dry-dock at Hartlepool.

Earliest powered vessels Marine propulsion by steam engine was first achieved in 1783 when the Marquis Jouffroy d'Abbans (1751–1832) ascended a reach of the river Saône near Lyon, France, in the 180-tonne paddle steamer *Pyroscaphe*.

The first successful power-driven vessel was the tug *Charlotte Dundas*, a stern paddle-wheel steamer built for the Forth and Clyde Canal in 1801–2 by Alexander Hart, using a double-acting condensing engine constructed by British pioneer of marine steam propulsion, William Symington .

Earliest turbine ship The *Turbinia* was designed by the Hon. Sir Charles Parsons (1854–1931) and built in 1894 at Wallsend-on-Tyne, Tyne & Wear. She was 30 m *100ft* long, had a displacement of 45.2 tonnes and was powered by three steam turbines totalling about 2000 shaft horsepower (shp). First publicly demonstrated in 1897, when a speed of 34.5 knots *64 km/h* was achieved, the ship is now preserved at Newcastle-upon-Tyne.

Wooden ships *Heaviest* The 8662-tonne *Richelieu*, measuring 101.7 m *333⅔ ft* long, was launched in Toulon, France on 3 Dec 1873.

Guess What?
Q. What is the highest recorded mileage for a car?
A. See Page 117

Aborigines are thought to have been able to cross the Torres Strait from New Guinea to Australia, then at least 70 km *43½ miles* across, as early as *c.* 55,000 BC. It is believed that they may have used sea-going rafts.

■ Licence plate No. 9 was sold at a Hong Kong government auction for HK$13 million on 19 Mar 1994 to Albert Yeung Sau-shing. 'Nine' sounds like the word 'dog' in Chinese and was considered lucky because 1994 was the Year of The Dog. The plate was worth over eight times the value of the Rolls-Royce it was assigned to. (Photo: Emperor Group)

Longest The longest wooden ship ever constructed was the *Rochambeau* formerly the *Dunderberg*, built in New York (1867–72). It was 115 *377 ft 4 in* long. By comparison, the biblical length of Noah's Ark was 300 cubits or, at 45.7 cm *18 in* to a cubit, 137 m *450 ft*.

Shipwrecks

Largest shipwreck The 321,186-tonne deadweight VLCC (very large crude carrier) *Energy Determination* blew up and broke in two in the Strait of Hormuz, Persian Gulf on 12 Dec 1979. The ship was in ballast at the time but its hull value was $58 million.

The largest wreck removal was carried out in 1979 by Smit Tak International, who removed the remains of the 120,000-ton French tanker *Betelgeuse* from Bantry Bay, Republic of Ireland within 20 months.

Most massive collision The closest approach to an irresistible force striking an immovable object occurred on 16 Dec 1977, 35 km *22 miles* off the coast of southern Africa, when the tanker *Venoil* (330,954 dwt) struck her sister ship *Venpet* (330,869 dwt).

Warships

Largest battleships The largest battleships ever commissioned were the Japanese vessels *Yamato* (completed on 16 Dec 1941 and sunk south-west of Kyūshū, Japan by US planes on 7 Apr 1945) and *Musashi* (sunk in the Philippine Sea by 11 bombs and 16 torpedoes on 24 Oct 1944). Both ships had a full load displacement of 69,988 tons, an overall length of 263 m *863 ft*, a beam of 38.7 m *127 ft* and a full load draught of 10.8 m *35½ ft*. They were armed with nine guns 460 mm *18.1 in* long, in three triple turrets. Each gun weighed 164.6 tonnes, was 22.8 m *75 ft* long and fired 1451-kg *3200-lb* projectiles.

The last battleships in active service were the USS *Missouri* and USS *Wisconsin*, 270 m *887 ft* long and with a full load displacement of 58,000 tonnes. Both were first commissioned in 1944 and later recommissioned in 1986 and 1988 respectively following major refits. Armaments included nine 16-inch guns used in the Gulf War in 1991 and capable of firing 1225-kg *2700-lb* projectiles a distance of 39 km *23 miles*. Both ships, together with two others of the same class, USS *New Jersey* and USS *Iowa*, have now been withdrawn from service.

UK Britain's largest and last battleship was HMS *Vanguard* (1944–60), which had a full load displacement of 52,245 tonnes, was 248.1 m *814 ft* long overall and was armed with eight 15-in guns, which were originally mounted in the battlecruisers *Courageous* and *Glorious* in 1917. *Vanguard* was completed too late for service in World War II, and spent much of her time in the Home Fleet's Training Squadron before being broken up at Faslane, Strathclyde in 1960.

Fastest destroyer The highest speed attained by a destroyer was 45.25 knots *83.42 km/h* by the 2830-tonne French ship *Le Terrible* in 1935. Built in Blainville, France and powered by four Yarrow small-tube boilers and two Rateau geared turbines, giving 100,000 shp, she was decommissioned at the end of 1957.

Largest aircraft carriers The warships with the largest full load displacement in the world are the Nimitz class US Navy aircraft carriers USS *Nimitz*, *Dwight D. Eisenhower*, *Carl Vinson*, *Theodore Roosevelt*, *Abraham Lincoln* and *George Washington*, the last two of which displace 102,000 tons. They are 332.9 m *1092 ft* long, have 1.82 ha *4½ acres* of flight deck and, driven by four nuclear-powered 260,000 shp geared steam turbines, can reach speeds of well over 30 knots *56 km/h*. Their complement is 5986. Two more ships of this class, *John C. Stennis* and *United States* are under construction, the former being due for delivery in December 1995.

UK The Royal Navy's largest fighting ships are the aircraft carriers HMS *Ark Royal*, commissioned on 1 Nov 1985, and her sister ships HMS *Invincible* and *Illustrious*. They have a flight deck 167.6 m *550 ft* long, are 209.3 m *685.8 ft* long overall and are powered by four Rolls-Royce Olympus TM3B gas turbines delivering 97,200 hp, giving a top speed of 28 knots *51.8 km/h*.

Most landings The greatest number on an aircraft carrier in one day was 602, achieved by Marine Air Group 6 of the United States Pacific Fleet Air Force aboard the USS *Matanikau* on 25 May 1945 between 8 a.m. and 5 p.m.

Guns and armour The largest guns ever mounted in any of HM ships had a calibre of 18 inches and were used in the light battle-cruiser (later aircraft carrier) HMS *Furious* in 1917. In 1918 they were transferred to the monitors HMS *Lord Clive* and *General Wolfe*.

The thickest armour ever carried was in HMS *Inflexible* (completed 1881), measuring 60 cm *24 in* backed by teak up to a maximum thickness of 107 cm *42 in*.

Longest submarine patrol The longest submerged and unsupported patrol made public is 111 days (57,085 km *30,804 nautical miles*) by HM Submarine *Warspite* (Cdr J.G.F. Cooke RN) in the South Atlantic from 25 Nov 1982 to 15 Mar 1983.

Submarines

Largest submarine The world's largest submarines are of the Russian Typhoon class. The launch of the first at the secret covered shipyard at Severodvinsk in the White Sea was announced by NATO on 23 Sep 1980. The vessels are believed to have a dived displacement of 26,500 tonnes, to measure 171.5 m *562.7 ft* overall and to be armed with 20 multiple warhead SS-NX-20 missiles with a range of 8895 km *4800 nautical miles*. Six of the class are now in service.

UK The largest submarines ever built for the Royal Navy are the four nuclear-powered vessels of the Vanguard class, the first three of which, *Vanguard*, *Victorious* and *Vigilant* were laid down in 1986–91, with HMS *Vanguard* commissioned in 1993, and *Victorious* in 1994. They are 150 m *491 ft 8 in* long, have a beam of 12.8 m *42 ft*, a draught of 12 m *39.4 ft* and have a dived displacement of 15,900 tonnes.

Smallest submarine William G. Smith of Bognor Regis, West Sussex, constructed a fully-functional submarine only 2.95 m *9 ft 8 in* long, 1.15 m *3 ft 9 in* wide and 1.42 m *4 ft 8 in* high in 1991.

Fastest submarine The Russian Alpha class nuclear-powered submarines had a reported maximum speed of over 83.4 km/h *45 knots*, and were believed capable of diving to 762 m *2500 ft*. It is believed that only one now remains in service, as a trials boat.

Fastest underwater human-powered vehicle The fastest speed attained by a human-powered propeller submarine is 5.94 ± 0.05 knots *3.06 m/sec* by *F.A. U-Boat*, designed and built by the Florida Atlantic University, Ocean Engineering Department, Boca Raton, Florida, USA, using a two-blade high aspect ratio propeller propulsion system, on 8 Mar 1994. It was crewed by Charles Callaway and William Fay, with team leader Karl Heeb.

The record by a human-powered non-propeller submarine is 2.9 ± 0.1 knots *1.49 m/sec* by *SubDUDE*, designed by the Scripps Institution of Oceanography, University of California, San Diego, USA using a horizontal oscillating foil propulsion system on 21 Aug 1992. It was crewed by Kimball Millikan and Ed Trevino, with team leader Kevin Hardy.

Fastest warship
On 25 Jan 1980 the 100-tonne test vehicle SES-100B, a US Navy hovercraft 23.7 m *78 ft* long, achieved a speed of 91.9 knots *170 km/h* (⇨ Hovercraft).

Old Wreck

The oldest shipwreck ever found at sea is one off Ulu Buren, near Kas, southern Turkey, which is dated to the 14th Century BC. It is not yet clear whether artefacts excavated from the sea off the isle of Dhókós, near the Greek island of Hydra and dated to 2450 BC ± 250 came from a wreck.

The largest propeller ever is the 11 m 36 ft 1 in diameter triple-bladed screw made by Kawasaki Heavy Industries of Japan and delivered on 17 Mar 1982 for the 208,739 dwt bulk carrier Hoei Maru (now New Harvest).

Deepest dive by a submarine
The 30-ton US Navy deep submergence vessel *Sea Cliff* (DSV 4), commissioned in 1973, reached a depth of 6000 m *20,000 ft* in March 1985.

Passenger Ships

Largest liners The RMS *Queen Elizabeth* (finally 82,998 but formerly 83,673 gross tons), of the Cunard fleet, was the largest passenger vessel ever built and had the largest displacement of any liner in the world. She had an overall length of 314 m *1031 ft*, was 36 m *118 ft 7 in* in breadth and was powered by steam turbines which developed 168,000 hp. Her last passenger voyage ended on 15 Nov 1968. In 1970 she was removed to Hong Kong to serve as a floating marine university and renamed *Seawise University*. She was burnt out on 9 Jan 1972 when three *simultaneous* outbreaks of fire strongly pointed to arson. The gutted hull had been cut up and removed by 1978. *Seawise* was a pun on the owner's initials, C.Y. Tung (1911–82).

The largest in current use and the longest ever is the *Norway* of 76,049 grt. She is 315.53 m *1035 ft 7½ in* in overall length, with a passenger capacity of 2022 and 900 crew, and was built as the SS *France* in 1960 and renamed after purchase in June 1979 by Knut Kloster of Norway. She is normally employed on cruises in the Caribbean and based at Miami, USA. Work undertaken during an extensive refit during the autumn of 1990 increased the number of passenger decks to 11. She draws 10.5 m *34½ ft*, has a beam of 33.5 m *110 ft* and cruises at 18 knots for the Norwegian Cruise Line.

Guess What?
Q. In which country is the world's leading shipbuilder?
A. See Page 110

Mission Water Beatle

■ **William Smith and his yellow submarine.**

In 1991, retired RAF officer William Smith set out to raise funds for St Richards Hospital, Chichester by building the world's smallest fully-functional submarine. He had considerable expertise on the subject: whilst serving in the RAF he had been Diving Officer of the RAF Locking Sub-Aqua Club for 18 years, and as Joint Services Diving Superviser had trained hundreds of airmen and led many major RAF diving expeditions. He spent two years constructing the submarine in his garage. All fundraising objectives were easily achieved.

Measuring just 2.95 m *9.6 ft* long, the yellow submarine — named *Water Beatle* — has gone from strength to strength. After initial trials at a local swimming pool, an 80-ft *24.4-m* dive was successfully achieved in June 1993, and a small 4.8-HP diesel engine was acquired a year later.

Following a stint on display at the Aviation museum in Shoreham, Mr Smith installed auxiliary pressure tanks. *Water Beatle* is now being used for locating aircraft wreckage off the Sussex coast.

WATER BEATLE: Performance figures

Power: 4.8 HP diesel engine (for surface propulsion)
1.25 HP Electric motor (when underwater)
Speed: Surface—5 knots*
Submerged—3 knots
Underwater duration: At least four hours using 3 HP air cyls (this can be increased by the use of 2 additional external cyls)
Max depth: As applicable to the Scuba Diver and subject to the same physiological considerations—but nominally 100 feet.

*conservative estimate.

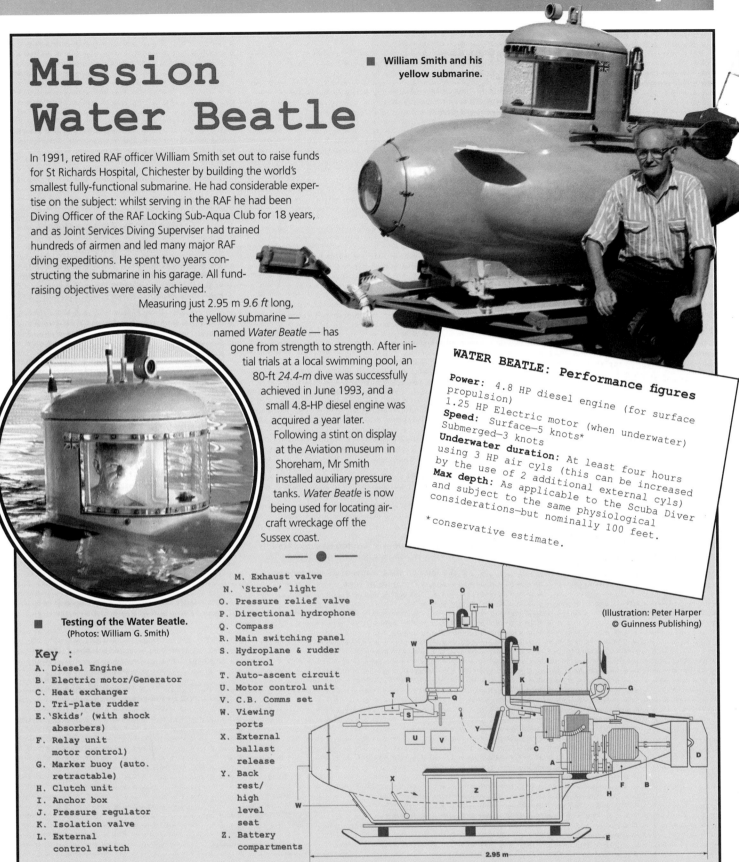

■ **Testing of the Water Beatle.**
(Photos: William G. Smith)

(Illustration: Peter Harper
© Guinness Publishing)

Key :

A. Diesel Engine
B. Electric motor/Generator
C. Heat exchanger
D. Tri-plate rudder
E. 'Skids' (with shock absorbers)
F. Relay unit motor control)
G. Marker buoy (auto. retractable)
H. Clutch unit
I. Anchor box
J. Pressure regulator
K. Isolation valve
L. External control switch
M. Exhaust valve
N. 'Strobe' light
O. Pressure relief valve
P. Directional hydrophone
Q. Compass
R. Main switching panel
S. Hydroplane & rudder control
T. Auto-ascent circuit
U. Motor control unit
V. C.B. Comms set
W. Viewing ports
X. External ballast release
Y. Back rest/ high level seat
Z. Battery compartments

2.95 m

Even bigger cruise-liners are under construction at the Fincantieri yard in Italy; the 77,000-ton *Sun Princess* is due to enter P&O service in December 1995, with a sister ship entering service two years later. Carnival Cruise Lines' *Carnival Destiny*, due in 1996, and P&O's *Grand Princess*, due in 1997, will both exceed 100,000 tons gross.

The largest liner under the British Flag is MV *Queen Elizabeth 2* of 69,053 grt and an overall length of 293 m *963 ft*. Her maiden vogage for the Cunard Line was on 2 May 1969 and she set a 'turn round' record of 3 hr 18 min at New York City, USA on 14 Dec 1993. Built by John Brown & Co. (Clydebank) Ltd, Scotland and refitted by Lloyd Werft, Bremerhaven, Germany with diesel electric engines in 1986–7 to give a maximum speed of 32½ knots. She had travelled a total distance of 3,736,141 miles *6,012,571 km* to May 1994, more than any other ship.

Yachts *Largest* The largest yacht is the Saudi Arabian royal yacht *Abdul Aziz*, which is 147 m *482 ft* long. Built in Denmark and completed on 22 Jun 1984 at Vospers Yard, Southampton, Hants, itwas estimated in September 1987 to be worth over $100 million.

Private The largest private (non-Royal) yacht is the *Alexander*, measuring 122 m *400ft*, long. She was converted from a ferry in 1986.

Hydrofoils The largest passenger hydrofoils are three 165-ton Supramar PTS 150 Mk IIIs, which carry 250 passengers at 40 knots *74 km/h* across the Öre Sound between Malmö, Sweden and Copenhagen, Denmark. They were built by Westermoen Hydrofoil Ltd of Mandal, Norway.

Longest canoe The 35.7 m *117 ft* long kauri wood Maori war canoe *Nga Toki Matawhaorua* of 20.3 tonnes was shaped with adzes at Kerikeri Inlet, New Zealand in 1940. The crew numbered 70 or more.

The 'Snake Boat' *Nadubhagóm* measuring 41.1 m *135 ft* long from Kerala, southern India has a crew of 109 rowers and nine 'encouragers'.

Cargo Vessels

Largest cargo vessel The world's largest ship of any kind is the oil tanker *Jahre Viking* (formerly the *Happy Giant* and *Seawise Giant*), at 564,763 tonnes deadweight. The tanker is 458.45 m *1504 ft* long overall, has a beam of 68.8 m *226 ft* and a draught of 24.61 m *80 ft 9 in*. Declared a total loss after being disabled by severe bombardment in 1987–8 during the Iran-Iraq war, the tanker underwent extensive renovation in Singapore and Dubai, United Arab Emirates costing some $60 million and was

Guess What?

Q. What made HMS *Inflexible* a record-breaker?

A. See Page 106

Barges

The world's largest RoRo (roll-on, roll-off) ships are four *El Rey* class barges of 16,700 tons and 176.78 m *580 ft* in length. They were built by the FMC Corp of Portland, Oregon, USA and are operated by Crowley Maritime Corp of San Francisco, USA between Florida, USA and Puerto Rico with tri-level lodging of up to 376 truck-trailers.

relaunched under its new name in November 1991.

The largest ship carrying dry cargo is the ore carrier *Berge Stahl* of 364,767 tonnes deadweight, built in South Korea for its Norwegian owner Sig Bergesen. The vessel is 343 m *1125 ft* long, has a beam of 63.5 m *208 ft* and was launched on 5 Nov 1986.

Car ferries *Fastest* The fastest car ferries are the twin-hulled, wave-piercing Sea Cats constructed of aluminium alloy by International Catamarans of Hobart, Tasmania which have a cruising speed of 35 knots and are capable of 42 knots. They are 74 m *242 ft 9 in* overall with a beam of 26 m *85 ft 3½ in*. The first was launched in 1990 with the name *Christopher Columbus*, but has since been renamed *Hoverspeed Great Britain*. Each can carry 432 passengers and 80 cars.

In 1995 a five-times larger and even faster vessel is due to enter service with Stena Line between Holyhead, Wales and Dun Laoghaire, Ireland. Stena AB of Sweden have ordered two HSS (Highspeed Sea Service) catamarans from a Finnish builder. Service speed will be 40 knots.

Most powerful dredger The 10,586-grt *Prins der Nederlanden*, at 142.7 m *468.4 ft* long, can dredge 20,000 tonnes of sand from a depth of 35 m *115 ft* via two suction tubes in less than an hour.

■ A Russian icebreaker forging its way through Antarctica. The most powerful icebreakers are three Russian sister ships of 23,460 tonnes, built in 1985.
(Photo: Gamma/F. Lochon)

Largest hydrofoil The 64.6 m *212 ft* long *Plainview* (314 tonnes full load) naval hydrofoil was launched by the Lockheed Shipbuilding and Construction Co. at Seattle, Washington, USA on 28 Jun 1965. She has a service speed of 92 km/h *57.2 mph*.

Most powerful icebreakers The most powerful purpose-built icebreakers are the *Rossiya* and her sister ships *Sovetskiy Soyuz* and *Oktyabryskaya Revolutsiya*. Built in Leningrad (now St. Petersburg), Russia and completed in 1985, *Rossiya* is of 23,460 tonnes, is 148 m *485 ft* long and is powered by 55.95 MW *75,000 hp* nuclear engines.

Containers

Earliest Shipborne containers, or 'lift vans', were used in conjunction with railway transport, usually on short-sea routes, from early this century. Containerization in the modern sense started in the 1950s, one of the first vessels being the tanker *Ideal X*, which was modified in 1955 to carry containers on deck over its tanks. Development accelerated with the adoption of standard sizes in 1961 and 1968, and the introduction of purpose-built ships.

Largest In terms of gross tonnage, the largest are the five ships built in Germany for American President Lines: *President Adams*, *President Jackson*, *President Kennedy*, *President Polk* and *President Truman*. These are termed post-Panamax, being the first container vessels too large to transit the Panama Canal. They are 275.12 m *902.69 ft* in length and 39.41 m *129.29 ft* in beam; the maximum beam for the Panama transit is 32.3 m *106 ft*. These vessels have a quoted capacity of 4340 TEU (standard length 20 ft—i.e. 6.096 m—Equivalent Unit containers).

Although of smaller registered tonnage, *Dresden Express*, built in South Korea in 1991 for the German Hapag-Lloyd company, is longer at 294 m *964 ft*, and has a quoted capacity of 4422 TEU. The greatest capacity is that of *NYK Altair* at 4812 TEU, delivered in December 1994, and that of *NYK Vega*, delivered in February 1995.

● ● A Remarkable Case of Riveting ● ● ● ●

During World War I, at the end of 1917 and the beginning of 1918, German submarines continued to sink an alarming number of British merchant ships, causing considerable anxiety in the government over the speed of British shipbuilding for defence. From this came the idea of a mutual competition for increasing production rates, and attempts were made in America, Glasgow, Barrow, London and Belfast in the yards of Harland & Wolff Ltd and Workman, Clark and Co Ltd to set the fastest rate of riveting in the world.

■ Right and below: rows of rivets at the shipbuilding yards where the competitions took place.

Inset: the board on which was recorded the official count of the rivets driven in by John Moir —note the record-breaking seventh hour.
(Photos: Ulster Folk & Transport Museum, Harland & Wolff Collection)

	NUMBER OF RIVETS	ACCUMULATING TOTALS
1ST HOUR	1167	1167
2ND ..	1101	2268
3RD ..	1071	3339
4TH ..	1187	4526
5TH ..	1267	5793
6TH ..	1328	7121
7TH ..	1409	8530
8TH ..	1276	9806
9TH ..	1403	11209
TOTAL		

Records were set and then broken. But at Messrs Workman, Clark and Co's shipbuilding yard in Belfast, on 5 Jun 1918, John W. Moir eclipsed the world's riveting record by driving in 11,209 ⅞-in rivets on the double-bottom floor of a standard ship in nine hours. In the seventh hour, Moir beat his own one-hour world record of the previous week by driving in 1409 rivets— that's an average of nearly 23½ per minute. In his best minute he drove in 26.

John Moir beat his nearest rival, John Lowry at Harland and Wolff, by over 4,000 rivets. His firm presented him with a cheque for £50 as a prize. His endeavours, which constituted a very real contribution to the war effort, earned him gratitude from all over the country and telegrams from the King and Prime Minister Lloyd George.

The largest *converted* icebreaker was the SS *Manhattan* (43,000 shp), 306.9 m *1007 ft* long, which was converted into a 152,407-tonne icebreaker by the Humble Oil Co. She made a double voyage through the North-West Passage in arctic Canada from 24 August to 12 November 1969.

The North-West Passage was first navigated by Roald Engebereth Gravning Amundsen of Norway (1872–1928) in the sealing sloop *Gjøa* in 1906.

Car Ferries

The world's largest car and passenger ferry in terms of tonnage is *Silja Europa* which entered service in 1993 between Stockholm, Sweden and Helsinki, Finland. Operated by the Silja Line, she is of 59,914 grt, with a length of 201.8 m *662 ft*, and a beam of 32.6 m *107 ft*. She can carry 3000 passengers, 350 cars and 60 lorries.

Rail ferries The largest international rail ferries are the *Klaipeda*, *Vilnius*, *Mukran* and *Greifswald*, operating in the Baltic sea between Klaipeda, Lithuania and Mukran, Germany. Built in Wismar, Germany, each ferry is 11,700 tons deadweight and has two decks measuring 190.5 m *625 ft* in length and 91.86 m *301.4 ft* wide. Each vessel can lift 103 standard 84-ton railcars 14.83 m *48.65 ft* long, and cover 506 km *273 nautical miles* in 17 hr.

Most powerful tugs The largest and most powerful tugs are the

Nikolay Chiker (SB 131) and *Fotiy Krylov* (SB 135), commissioned in 1989 and built by Hollming Ltd of Finland for the former USSR. Of 25,000 bhp and with a bollard pull in excess of 291 tons, they are 98.8 m *324 ft* long and 19.45 m *64 ft* wide. *Fotiy Krylov* is reported to be under charter to the Tsavliris Group of Companies of Piraeus, Greece, and may for a time have been named *Tsavliris Giant* and *Tsavliris Titan*.

Largest whale factory The Russian *Sovietskaya Ukraina* (32,034 gross tons) with a summer deadweight of 46,738 tonnes, was completed in October 1959. She is 217.8 m *714½ ft* in length and 25.8 m *84 ft 7 in* in the beam.

Riveting The world record for riveting is 11,209 in nine hours, by John Moir at the Workman Clark Ltd shipyard, Belfast in June 1918. His best hour was his 7th, with 1409 rivets — nearly 23½ per minute.

Sailing Ships

Oldest active sailing ship The oldest active square-rigged sailing vessel in the world is the restored SV *Maria Asumpta*, (formerly the *Ciudad de Inca*), built near Barcelona, Spain in 1858. She is 29.8m *98ft* overall of 127 gross registered tonnage. She was restored in 1981–2 and is used for film work, promotional appearances at regattas and sail training. She is operated by The Friends of *Maria Asumpta* of Lenham, Maidstone, Kent.

Largest sailing ship The largest vessel ever built in the era of sail was the *France II* (5806 gross tons), launched at Bordeaux, France in 1911. This was a steel-hulled, five-masted barque (square-rigged on four masts and fore and aft rigged on the aftermost mast). Her hull measured 127.4m *418ft* overall. Although principally designed as a sailing vessel with a stump top gallant rig, she was also fitted with two auxiliary engines; however these were removed in 1919 and she became a pure sailing vessel. She was wrecked off New Caledonia on 12 Jul 1922.

The only seven-masted sailing schooner ever built was the *Thomas W. Lawson* (5218 gross tons and 114.4m *375.6ft* long), built at Quincy, Massachusetts, USA in 1902 and wrecked off the Isles of Scilly, Cornwall on 15 Dec 1907 (⇔ Largest junks).

Largest sailing ship in service The world's only surviving First Rate Ship-of-the-Line is the Royal Navy's 104-gun battleship HMS *Victory*, laid down at Chatham, Kent on 23 Jul 1759 and constructed from the wood of some 2200 oak trees. She bore the body of Admiral Nelson from Gibraltar to Portsmouth, Hants arriving 44 days after serving as his victorious flagship at the Battle of Trafalgar on 21 Oct 1805. In 1922 she was moved to No. 2 dock at Portsmouth—site of the world's oldest graving dock.

The largest sailing ship now in service is the *Sedov* at 109m *357ft*, built in 1921 at Kiel, Germany and used for training by the Russians. She is 14.6m *48ft* in width, with a displacement of 6300 tonnes, 3556 grt and a sail area of 4192m^2 *45,123ft^2*.

Longest sailing ship The longest sailing ship is the 187-m *613-ft* French-built *Club Med 1*, with five aluminium masts and 2800 m^2 *30,139ft^2* of computer-controlled polyester sails. Operated as a Caribbean cruise vessel for 425 passengers for Club Med, with the small sail area and powerful engines she is really a motor-sailer. A sister-ship *Club Med II* has been commissioned.

Largest sails Sails are known to have been used for marine propulsion since 3500 BC. The largest spars ever carried were those in HM Battleship *Temeraire*, completed at Chatham, Kent, on 31 Aug 1877. She was broken up in 1921. The fore and main yards measured 35 m *115ft* in length. The foresail contained 1555 m *5100ft* of canvas, weighing 2.03 tonnes and the total sail area was 2322 m^2 *25,000ft^2*.

Model boats Members of the Lowestoft Model Boat Club crewed a radio-controlled scale model boat on 17–18 Aug 1991 at Dome Leisure Park, Doncaster to a 24-hour distance record of 178.92 km *111.18miles*.

David and Peter Holland of Doncaster, S. Yorks, members of the Conisbrough and District Modelling Association, crewed a 71-cm *28-in* scale model boat of the Bridlington trawler *Margaret H* continuously on one battery for 24 hours for a distance of 53.83km *33.45miles* at the Dome Leisure Complex, Doncaster on 15–16 Aug 1992.

Tallest Mast

The *Velsheda*, a J-class sailing vessel, is the tallest-known single-masted yacht in the world, at 51.6m *169¼ft* measured from heel fitting to mast truck. Built in 1933, the second of the four British J-class yachts, she is unusual in being the only one ever built that was not intended for the America's Cup race. With a displacement of 145 tonnes, she supports a sail area of 696.75 m^2 *7500ft^2*.

Junks

A river junk 110m *361ft* long, with treadmill-operated paddle-wheels, was recorded in AD 1161.

The largest on record was the sea-going *Zheng He*, flagship of Admiral Zheng He's 62 treasure ships, of c. 1420, with a displacement of 3150 tonnes and a length variously estimated up to 164m *538ft*. She is believed to have had nine masts. In c. AD 280 a floating fortress 183m *600ft* square, built by Wang Jun on the Yangzi river, took part in the Jin-Wu river war. Present-day junks do not, even in the case of the Jiangsu traders, exceed 52m *170ft* in length.

Merchant Shipping

Total merchant shipping The world total of merchant shipping, excluding vessels of less than 100 grt, non-propelled craft, naval auxiliaries, the US Reserve Fleet, and ships restricted to harbour or river/canal service, was 80,676 ships of 475,900,000 grt at 31 Dec 1994.

Shipbuilding Worldwide production of ships completed in 1994, with the same exclusions as above, was 19 million grt. The figures for Russia, Ukraine and the People's Republic of China are incomplete.

Japan completed 8.6 million grt (45 per cent of the world total) in 1994 and UK completions totalled 22 ships of 226,643 grt.

The world's leading shipbuilder in 1994 was Hyundai Heavy Industries Co Ltd of South Korea, which completed 34 ships of 2.21 million gross tons.

Biggest owner The largest ship owners are the Japanese NYK Group, whose fleet of owned vessels totalled 11,921,701 tons gross at 1 Feb 1995.

Largest fleet The largest merchant fleet in the world at the end of 1994 was that under the flag of Panama, totalling 64.2 million tons gross. The equivalent UK figure was 1481 ships of 4.4 million tons gross.

Building

The fastest times in which complete ships of more than 10,000 tons were ever built were achieved at Kaiser's Yard, Portland, Oregon, USA during the wartime programme for building 2742 Liberty ships in 18 shipyards from 27 Sep 1941. In 1942 No. 440, named *Robert E. Peary*, had her keel laid on 8 November, was launched on 12 November and was operational after 4 days 15½ hr on 15 November. She was broken up in 1963.

Hovercraft

Earliest hovercraft The ACV (air-cushion vehicle) was first made a practical proposition by Sir Christopher Sydney Cockerell (b. 4 Jun 1910), a British engineer who had the idea in 1954, published his Ripplecraft report 1/55 on 25 Oct 1955 and patented it on 12 Dec 1955.

The earliest patent relating to air-cushioned craft was applied for in 1877 by Sir John I. Thornycroft (1843–1928) of London, and the idea was developed by Toivo Kaario of Finland in 1935.

The first flight by a hovercraft was made by the 4-tonne Saunders-Roe SRN1 at Cowes, Isle of Wight on 30 May 1959. With a 680kg *1500lb* thrust Viper turbojet engine, this craft reached 68 knots *126km/h* in June 1961.

The first hovercraft public service was run across the Dee estuary between Rhyl, Clwyd and Wallasey, Merseyside by the 60-knot *111-km/h* 24-passenger Vickers-Armstrong VA-3 between 20 July and September 1962.

Largest hovercraft The SRN4 Mk III, a British-built civil hovercraft, weighs 305 tons and can accommodate 418 passengers and 60 cars. It is 56.38m *185ft* in length, and is powered by four Bristol Siddeley Marine Proteus engines, giving a maximum speed in excess of the scheduled permitted cross-Channel operating speed of 65 knots.

Fastest hovercraft The world's fastest warship is the 100-tonne US Navy test hovercraft SES-100B. She attained a world record 91.9 knots *170km/h* on 25 Jan 1980 on the Chesapeake Bay Test Range, Maryland, USA. As a result of the success of this test craft, a 3000-tonne US Navy Large Surface Effect Ship (LSES) was built by Bell Aerospace under contract from the Department of Defense in 1977–81 (⇔ Warships).

Cross-Channel The fastest scheduled crossing of the Channel by hovercraft was achieved by an SRN 4 Mark II Mountbatten class hovercraft operated by Hoverspeed, on 1 Sep 1984, when *The Swift* completed the Dover–Calais run in 24 min 8.4 sec to average more than 54½ knots.

Highest hovercraft The highest altitude reached by a hovercraft was on 11 Jun 1990 when *Neste Enterprise* and her crew of ten reached the navigable source of the Yangzi river, China at 4983m *16,050ft*.

The greatest altitude at which a hovercraft is operating is on Lake Titicaca, Peru, where since 1975 an HM2 Hoverferry has been hovering 3811m *12,506ft* above sea level.

Longest hovercraft journey The longest hovercraft journey was one of 8047km *5000miles*, by the British Trans-African Hovercraft Expedition, under the leadership of David Smithers, through eight West African countries in a Winchester class SRN6, between 15 Oct 1969 and 3 Jan 1970.

Ocean Crossings

Earliest Atlantic crossing The earliest crossing of the Atlantic by a power vessel, as opposed to an auxiliary-engined sailing ship, was a 22-day voyage begun in April 1827, from Rotterdam, Netherlands, to the West Indies, by the *Curaçao*. She was a wooden paddle boat of 438 tons and measuring 38.7m *127ft* long, built as the *Calpe* in Dover, Kent in 1826 and purchased by the Dutch Government for a West Indian mail service.

The earliest Atlantic crossing entirely under steam (with intervals for desalting the boilers) was by HMS *Rhadamanthus*, from Plymouth, Devon to Barbados, West Indies in 1832.

■ **Rows of containers awaiting their turn at Rotterdam, the world's busiest port.**
(Photo: Gamma/M. Deville)

The earliest crossing under continuous steam power was by the condenser-fitted packet ship *Sirius*, 714 tonnes from Queenstown (now Cóbh), Republic of Ireland to Sandy Hook, New Jersey, USA, in 18 days 10 hr from 4–22 Apr 1838.

Fastest Atlantic crossing The fastest crossing of the Atlantic is by the 68-m *222-ft* powerboat *Destriero* (⇨Marine Transatlantic record table).

The fastest regular commercial crossing and thus winner of the Hales Trophy or 'Blue Riband' is by the liner *United States* (then 51,988, now 38,216 gross tons), former flagship of the United States Lines. On her maiden voyage on 3–7 Jul 1952 from New York, USA to Le Havre, France and Southampton, Hants, she averaged 35.39 knots, *65.95 km/h* for three days 10 hr 40 min (6:36 p.m. GMT, 3 July to 5:16 a.m., 7 July) on a route of 5465 km *2949 nautical miles* from the Ambrose light vessel to the Bishop Rock lighthouse, Isles of Scilly, Cornwall. During this run, on 6–7 July, she steamed the greatest distance ever covered by any ship in a day's run (24 hr) — 1609 km *868 nautical miles*, averaging 36.17 knots *67.02 km/h*. The maximum speed attained from her 240,000 shaft horsepower engines was 38.32 knots *71.01 km/h* in trials on 9–10 Jun 1952.

Fastest Pacific crossing The fastest crossing from Yokohama, Japan to Long Beach, California, USA (4840 nautical miles *8960 km*) took 6 days 1 hr 27 min (30 Jun–6 Jul 1973) by the 50,315-ton container ship *Sea-Land Commerce*, at an average speed of 33.27 knots *61.65 km/h*.

Fastest Channel crossing The SeaCat catamaran ferry *Hoverspeed France* sailed from Dover to Calais in 34 min 23 sec on 15 Oct 1991, at an average speed of 37.87 knots *70 km/h*.

Speeds on Water

The highest speed ever achieved on water is an estimated 300 knots *555 km/h* by Kenneth Peter Warby (b. 9 May 1939) on the Blowering Dam Lake, New South Wales, Australia on 20 Nov 1977 in his unlimited hydroplane *Spirit of Australia*.

The official world water speed record is 275.8 knots *511.11 km/h* set on 8 Oct 1978 by Warby on Blowering Dam Lake.

Mary Rife of Flint, Texas, USA set a women's unofficial record of 332.6 km/h *206.72 mph* in her blown fuel hydro *Proud Mary* in Tulsa, Oklahoma, USA on 23 Jul 1977. Her official record is 317 km/h *197 mph*.

Message in a bottle
The longest recorded interval between drop and pick-up is 73 years in the case of a message thrown from the SS *Arawatta* out of Cairns, Queensland, Australia on 9 Jun 1910 in a lotion bottle and reported to be found on Moreton Island Queensland, on 6 Jun 1983.

Youngest and oldest solo transatlantic crossings
Youngest sailing:
17 yr 176 days, by David Sandeman (GB) 43 days, 1976
Oldest sailing:
76 yr 165 days, by Stefan Szwarnowski (GB) 72 days, 1989
Youngest rowing:
25 yr 306 days, by Sean Crowley (GB) 95 days 22 hr, 1988
Oldest rowing:
51 years, by Sidney Genders (GB) 160 days 8 hr, 1970

Guess What?
Q. Where was the oldest shipwreck found?
A. See Page 106

Ports

Largest port The Port of New York and New Jersey, USA has a navigable waterfront of 1215 km *755 miles* (474 km *295 miles* in New Jersey) stretching over 238 km² *92 miles²*. A total of 261 general cargo berths and 130 other piers give a total berthing capacity of 391 ships at one time. The total warehousing floor space is 170.9 ha *422.4 acres*.

The largest British port by tonnage is London (including Tilbury), which handles some 55 million tonnes each year. The largest container port is Felixstowe, Suffolk, which handled 1,746,653 TEUs and 22,110,092 tonnes of cargo in 1994.

Busiest port The world's busiest port and largest artificial harbour is Rotterdam, Netherlands, which covers 100 km² *38 miles²*, with 122.3 km *76 miles* of quays. It handled 294 million tonnes of sea-going cargo in 1994.

■ *Destriero*, the power-boat which crossed the Atlantic in record time.

Inset, above: the record-breakers themselves— Cesare Fiorio and his crew.
(Photos: Gamma Sport)

Transatlantic Rowing and Sailing Records

(More detailed marine tables compiled from information supplied by Nobby Clarke and Richard Boehmer can be found in earlier editions)

Category	Vessel	Skipper/Crew	Start	Finish	Duration
FIRST SOLO SAILING E–W	15 ton gaff sloop	Josiah Shackford (US)	Bordeaux, France 1786	Surinam (Guiana)	35 days
FIRST ROWING	Ship's boat c. 6.1m *20ft*	John Brown and five British deserters from garrison	St Helena 10 Jun 1799	Belmonte, Brazil (fastest-ever row)	28 days (83 mpd)
FIRST SOLO SAILING W–E	*Centennial* 6.1m *20ft*	Alfred Johnson (US)	Shag Harbor, Maine, USA 1876	Wales	46 days
FIRST SOLO ROWING E–W	*Britannia* 6.7m *22ft*	John Fairfax (GB)	Las Palmas, Canary Island 20 Jan 1969	Ft Lauderdale, Florida, USA, 19 Jul 1969	180 days
FIRST SOLO ROWING W–E	*Super Silver* 6.1m *20ft*	Tom McClean (Ireland)	St John's, Newfoundland, Canada 1969	Black Sod Bay, Republic of Ireland 27 Jul 1969	70.7 days
FIRST ROW *Both directions*	QE III 6.05m *19ft 10in*	Don Allum (GB)	Canary Islands 1986 St John's, Canada	Nevis, West Indies Ireland 1987	114 days 77 days
FASTEST SAIL W–E *Non-solo*	*Jet Services 5* 22.9 m *75ft* catamaran sloop	Serge Madec (France)	Ambrose Light Tower, USA 2 Jun 1990	Lizard Point, Cornwall 9 Jun 1990	6 days 13 hr 3 min *32 sec* (18.4 knots smg)
FASTEST SAIL W–E *Solo*	*Primagaz* 18.3m *60ft* trimaran	Laurent Bourgnon (France)	Ambrose Light Tower, USA 27 Jun 1994	Lizard Point, Cornwall 4 Jul 1994	7 days 2 hr 34 min 42 sec (17.15 knots)
FASTEST SAIL E–W *Solo*	*Fleury Michon (IX)* 18.3m *60ft* trimaran	Philippe Poupon (France)	Plymouth, Devon (STAR) 5 Jun 1988	Newport, Rhode Island 15 Jun 1988	10 days 9 hr (11.6 knots smg)
FASTEST SAIL E–W *Non-solo*	*Primagaz* 18.3 m *60 ft* trimaran	Laurent Bourgnon (France) and Cam Lewis (USA)	Plymouth, Devon (2-star event) 5 Jun 1994	Newport, Rhode Island 14 Jun 1994	9 days 8 hr 58 min 20 sec 12.49 knots

Transpacific Records

FIRST ROWING	*Britannia II* 10.7 m *35ft*	John Fairfax (GB) Sylvia Cook (GB)	San Francisco, USA 26 Apr 1971	Hayman Island, Australia 22 Apr 1972	362 days
FIRST SOLO ROWING E–W	*Hele-on-Britannia* 9.75 m *32ft*	Peter Bird (GB)	San Francisco, USA 23 Aug 1982	Gt Barrier Reef, Australia 14 Jun 1983	294 days 14,480 km *9000 miles*
FIRST SOLO ROWING W–E	*Sector* 8m *26ft*	Gérard d'Aboville (France)	Choshi, Japan 11 Jul 1991	Ilwaco, Washington, USA, 21 Nov 1991	133 days 10,150 km *6300 miles*
FASTEST SAIL *California–Japan*	*Aotea* 12.2 m *40 ft* trimaran	Peter Hogg (New Zealand)	San Francisco, USA 13 Apr 1992	Tokyo, Japan 18 May 1992	34 days 6 hr 26 min (4.66 knots smg)

N.B. The earliest single-handed Pacific crossings were achieved East–West by Bernard Gilboy (US) in 1882 in the 5.48-m 18-ft double-ender *Pacific* to Australia, and West–East by Fred Rebel (Latvia) in the 5.48 m 18ft *Elaine* (from Australia) and Edward Miles (US) in the 11.2 m 36¾ ft *Sturdy II* (from Japan), both in 1932, the latter via Hawaii. smg = speed made good.

Marine Circumnavigation Records

(More detailed marine tables compiled from information supplied by Nobby Clarke and Richard Boehmer can be found in earlier editions)
Strictly speaking, a circumnavigation involves passing through a pair of antipodal points and all the records listed below are known to have met this requirement unless marked with an asterisk. A non-stop circumnavigation is entirely self-maintained; no water supplies, provisions, equipment or replacements of any sort may be taken aboard en route. Vessels may anchor, but no physical help may be accepted apart from passing mail or messages. All distances refer to nautical miles.

Category	Vessel	Skipper	Start	Finish
FIRST	*Vittoria* Expedition of Fernão de Magalhães (Ferdinand Magellan)	Juan Sebastián de Elcano or del Cano (d. 1526) and 17 crew	Seville, Spain 20 Sep 1519	San Lucar, Spain 6 Sep 1522 93,573.6 km *30,700 miles*
FIRST SOLO	*Spray* 11.2m *36ft 9in* gaff yawl	Capt Joshua Slocum (US) (a non-swimmer)	Newport, RI, USA via Magellan Straits, Chile 24 Apr 1895	3 Jul 1898 140,028 km *46,000 miles*
FIRST NON-STOP SOLO W–E	*Suhaili* 9.87 m *32ft 4in* Bermudan ketch	Robin Knox-Johnston (GB)	Falmouth, Cornwall 14 Jun 1968	22 Apr 1969 312 days
FIRST NON-STOP SOLO E–W	*British Steel* 18 m *59 ft* ketch	Chay Blyth (GB)	Hamble River, Hants 18 Oct 1970	6 Aug 1971 292 days
FASTEST NON-STOP	*Enza* 28.0 m *92 ft* catamaran	Peter Blake (NZ) and Robin Knox-Johnston (GB)	Ushant, France 16 Jan 1994	Ushant, France 1 Apr 1994 Holder Jules Verne Trophy 74 days 22 hr 17 min
FASTEST SOLO NON-STOP	*Ecureil d'Aquitaine II* 18.3 m *60 ft* monohull	Titouan Lamazou (France)	Les Sables d'Olonne Nov 1989	Les Sables d'Olonne March 1990 109 days 8 hr 48 m

Eduard Roditi, author of Magellan of the Pacific, advances the view that Magellan's slave, Enrique, was the first circumnavigator. He had been purchased in Malacca and it was shown that he already understood the Filipino dialect Vizayan, when he reached the Philippines from the east. He 'tied the knot' off Limasawa on 28 Mar 1521.

British Isles Records

Category	Vessel	Skipper	Start	Finish	Duration
AROUND MAINLAND BRITAIN *Fastest power*	*Drambuie Tantalus* 15.3m *50ft* monohull	Dag Pike (GB)	Ramsgate 9 Jul 1992	Ramsgate 11 Jul 1992	1 day 20 hr 3 min (36.6 knots smg)
AROUND MAINLAND BRITAIN *Fastest power, under 50-ft vessel*	Rapier 29 8.8 m *29 ft* RIB	Steve Brownridge (GB)	Southampton 25 Jun 1993	Southampton 27 Jun 1993	1 day 39 hr 32 min (av. speed 21.4 knots)
AROUND BRITISH ISLES* *Fastest sailing vessel*	*Lakota* 18.29 m *60 ft* trimaran	Steve Fossett (USA)	Ventnor, Isle of Wight 21 Oct 1994	Ventnor, Isle of Wight 27 Oct 1994	5 days 21 hr 5 min
ENGLISH CHANNEL *both ways* *Fastest sailing multihull*	*Fleury Michon VIII* 22.9m *75ft* trimaran	Philippe Poupon (France)	Calais, France Dec 1986	Calais via Dover, Kent Dec 1986	2hr 21min 57sec (18.6 knots smg)

ULDB = Ultra-light displacement boat. RB & I = Round Britain & Ireland Race. smg = speed made good. All mileages are nautical miles.
* All islands and rocks of Britain and Ireland including St Kildare, but not Rockall or Channel Islands.

Other Marine Records

(More detailed marine tables compiled from information supplied by Richard Boehmer can be found in earlier editions) For speed records ⇨Yachting.

Category	Vessel	Skipper	Start	Finish	Duration
DURATION AND DISTANCE *Non-stop by sail*	*Parry Endeavour* 13.9m *44ft* Bermudan sloop	Jon Sanders (Australia)	Fremantle, W Australia 25 May 1986	Fremantle 13 Mar 1988	71,000 miles in 658 days (av. speed 4.5 knots)
BEST DAY'S RUN* *Under sail and solo*	*Primagaz* 18.29 m *60 ft* trimaran	Laurent Bourgnon (France)	North Atlantic 28 Jun 1994	North Atlantic 29 Jun 1994	540 miles in 24 hours (av. speed 22.5 knots)
BEST DAY'S RUN *Monohull fully crewed*	*Intrum Justitia* 19.51m *64ft* monohull	Lawrie Smith (GB)	Southern Ocean 20 Feb 1994	Southern Ocean 21 Feb 1994	428.1 miles in 24 hours (av. speed 17.8 knots)
BEST DAY'S RUN *Sailboard*	*Fanatic board* Gaastra sail	Françoise Canetos (France)	Sète, France 13 Jul 1988	Sète, France 14 Jul 1988	227 miles/24 hr (9.46 knots smg)

*Best day's run for any vessel under sail and solo. GCD = Great circle distance. smg = speed made good. All mileages are nautical miles.

Although the port of Hong Kong handles less tonnage in total seaborne cargo than Rotterdam, it is the world's leading container port, and is now handling one million TEUs per month.

Britain's busiest port in terms of ship movements is Dover, Kent which in 1994 handled 24,461 movements, including those of hovercraft. It also handled 19.12 million passengers, 3.2 million accompanies vehicles, 157,064 coaches and 1.16 million road haulage vehicles.

Dry dock With a maximum shipbuilding capacity of 1,200,000 tons dwt, the Daewoo Okpo No. 1 Dry Dock, Koje Island in South Korea measures 530 m *1740 ft* long by 131 m *430 ft* wide and was completed in 1979. The dock gates, 14 m *46 ft* high and 10 m *33 ft* thick at the base, are the world's most massive.

Britain's largest dry dock is the Harland & Wolff building dock, Queen's Island, Belfast. It was excavated by George Wimpey Ltd to a length of 556 m *1825 ft* and a width of 93 m *305 ft* and can accommodate tankers of 1 million tons dwt. Work was begun on 26 Jan 1968 and completed on 30 Nov 1969; this involved the excavation of 306,000 m³ *400,000 yd³* of soil.

Guess What? Q. What is the largest liner under the British flag called? A. See Page 107

Coaching

General records Before the widespread use of tarred road surfaces from 1845, coaching was slow and hazardous. The zenith was reached on 13 Jul 1888 when James William Selby drove the *Old Times* coach 108 miles *173 km* from London to Brighton and back with eight teams and 14 changes in 7 hr 50 min, to average 13.8 mph *22.2 km/h*. A four-horse carriage could maintain a speed of 21⅓ mph *34 km/h* for nearly an hour.

The *Border Union* stagecoach, built c. 1825, ran four in hand from Edinburgh to London (393 miles *632 km*). When it ceased in 1845, due to competition from railways, the allowed schedule was 42 hr 23 min to average better than 9¼ mph *14.9 km/h*.

The record for changing a team of four horses by 12 ostlers is 21.32 seconds, set by the Norwich Union Charity Mail Coach team led by driver John Parker, at Donington Race Circuit, Leics on 9 Aug 1990.

Carriage driving The only man to drive 48 horses in a single hitch is Dick Sparrow of Zearing, Iowa, USA, between 1972 and 1977. The lead horses were on reins 41 m *135 ft* long.

Floyd Zopfi of Stratford, Wisconsin, USA has driven 52 llamas in a hitch on several occasions since 1990, with the lead llamas (four abreast) on reins 46 m *150 ft* long.

Bicycles

Earliest bicycle The earliest machine propelled by cranks and pedals with connecting rods and which was actually built, was in 1839–40 by Kirkpatrick Macmillan (1810–78) of Dumfries, Scotland. A copy of the machine is now in the Science Museum, Kensington, London.

The continuous history of cycling began with the *vélocipède* built in March 1861 by Pierre Michaux and his son Ernest of Rue de Verneuil, Paris, France.

> The world's smallest wheeled rideable bicycle is one with wheels of 1.9 cm *0.76 in* in diameter which was ridden by its constructor Neville Patten of Gladstone, Queensland, Australia for a distance of 4.1 m *13 ft 5½ in* on 25 Mar 1988.

In 1870, James Starley of Coventry, W. Midlands constructed the first penny-farthing or Ordinary bicycle. It had wire-spoked wheels for lightness and was later available with an optional-speed gear.

Penny-farthing The record for riding an Ordinary bicycle (penny-farthing) from Land's End to John o' Groats is 5 days 1 hr 45 min by G. P. Mills of Anfield Bicycle Club, riding a 53 inch-Humber a distance of 861 miles, 4–9 Jul 1886.

Jacques Puyouu of Pau, Pyrénées-Atlantiques, France has built a tandem 36 cm *14 in* long, which has been ridden by him and Madame Puyoou.

Largest bicycle The largest bicycle, as measured by the wheel diameter, is 'Frankencycle', built by Dave Moore of Rosemead, California, USA and first ridden by Steve Gordon of Moorpark, California, on 4 Jun 1989. The wheel diameter is 3.05 m *10 ft* and it is 3.35 m *11 ft 2 in* high.

A tricycle with a larger wheel diameter was also constructed by Dave Moore. Designed by Arthur Dillon, the Dillon Colossal has a back wheel diameter of 11 ft *3.35 m*, a front wheel diameter of 5 ft 10 in *1.77 m* and was built in 1994.

Longest bicycle The longest true bicycle ever built (i.e. without a third stabilizing wheel) is one designed and built by Terry Thessman of Pahiatua, New Zealand. It measures 22.24 m *72.96 ft* in length and weighs 340 kg *750 lb*. It was ridden by four riders a distance of 246 m *807 ft* on 27 Feb 1988. Cornering remains a problem.

Bicycle wheelie A duration record for a bicycle wheelie is 5 hr 12 min 33 sec set by David Robilliard at the Beau Sejour Leisure Centre, St Peter Port, Guernsey, Channel Islands on 28 May 1990.

Human-powered vehicles (HPVs) *Fastest land* The world speed records for human-powered vehicles (HPVs) over a 200 m flying start are: 105.36 km/h *65.48 mph* (single rider) by Fred Markham at Mono Lake, California, USA on 11 May 1986; and 101.3 km/h *62.92 mph* (multiple riders) by Dave Grylls and Leigh Barczewski at the Ontario Speedway, California on 4 May 1980. The one-hour standing start (single rider) record is held by Pat Kinch, riding *Kingcycle Bean*, averaging a speed of 75.57 km/h *46.96 mph* at Millbrook Proving Ground, Bedford on 8 Sep 1990.

Water cycle The men's 2000 m record (single rider) is 20.66 km/h *12.84 mph* by Steve Hegg on *Flying Fish* at Long Beach, California, USA on 20 Jul 1987.

Unicycles

Tallest unicycle The tallest unicycle ever mastered is one 31.01 m *101 ft 9 in* tall ridden by Steve McPeak (with a safety wire suspended from an overhead crane) for a distance of 114.6 m *376 ft* in Las Vegas, USA in October 1980. The freestyle riding (i.e. without any safety harness) of ever taller unicycles must inevitably lead to serious injury or fatality.

Smallest unicycle Peter Rosendahl (Sweden) rode an 8 in *20 cm* high unicycle with a wheel diameter of 1 in *2.5 cm*, with no attachments or extensions fitted, a distance of 12 ft *3.6 m* at Las Vegas, Nevada, USA on 25 Mar 1994.

Fastest sprint Peter Rosendahl set a sprint record for 100 m from a standing start of 12.11 secs (29.72 km/h *18.47 mph*) at Las Vegas on 25 Mar 1994.

100 miles Takayuki Koike of Kanagawa, Japan set a record for 100 miles *160.9 km* of 6 hr 44 min 21.84 sec on 9 Aug 1987 (average speed 23.87 km/h *14.83 mph*).

Endurance Akira Matsushima (Japan) unicycled 5248 km *3260 miles* from Newport, Oregon to Washington DC, USA from 10 Jul–22 Aug 1992.

Land's End to John o' Groats Mike Day (b. 13 Mar 1965) of Southgate, London and Michel Arets (b. 9 Sep 1959) of Brussels, Belgium rode 1450 km *901 miles* from Land's End, Cornwall to John o' Groats, Highland, in 14 days 12 hr 41 min, 27 Aug–10 Sep 1986.

Backwards unicycling
Ashrita Furman (USA) rode backwards for a distance of 85.56 km *53.17 miles* at Forest Park, Queens, New York, USA on 16 Sep 1994.

Motorcycles

Earliest motorcycle The earliest internal combustion-engined motorized bicycle was a wooden-framed machine built at Bad Cannstatt, Germany between October–November 1885 by Gottlieb Daimler (1834–1900) and first ridden by Wilhelm Maybach (1846–1929). It had a top speed of 19 km/h *12 mph* and developed one-half of one horsepower from its single-cylinder 264cc four-stroke engine at 700 rpm. Known as the 'Einspur', it was lost in a fire in 1903.

The first motorcycles of entirely British production were the 1046cc Holden flat-four and the 2¾ hp Clyde single both produced in 1898.

The earliest factory which made motorcycles in large numbers was opened in 1894 by Heinrich and Wilhelm Hildebrand and Alois Wolfmüller at Munich, Germany. In its first two years this factory produced over 1000 machines, each having a water-cooled 1488cc twin-cylinder four-stroke engine developing about 2.5 bhp at 600 rpm—the highest capacity motorcycle engine ever put into production.

Highest motorcycle speeds Official world speed records must be set with two runs over a measured distance made in opposite directions within a time limit of 1 hour for FIM records and of 2 hours for AMA records.

Dave Campos (USA), riding a 23 ft *7 m* long stream-liner named *Easyriders*, powered by two 91 in³ Ruxton Harley-Davidson engines, set AMA and FIM absolute records with an overall average of 322.150 mph *518.450 km/h* and completed the faster run at an average of 322.870 mph *519.609 km/h*, at Bonneville Salt Flats, Utah, USA on 14 Jul 1990.

Guess What?

Q. what is Thrust 2?

A. See Page 117

THEN & NOW

Progression of World Speed Record for a Motorcycle

In 1920 after many years of wrangling about rules, the Fédération Internationale Motocycliste at last controlled all competitive aspects of two-wheelers on a world basis, including the ratification of the world speed record.

The following are the officially accepted records at five yearly intervals (unless otherwise stated the record was set in the actual year).

Year	mph		Rider	Machine	Venue
1920	104·19		Ernest Walker	Indian	Daytona Beach, USA
1925	119·05	(1924)	Herbert Le Vack	Brough Superior	Arpajon, France
1930	150·65		Joseph S. Wright	OEC Temple JAP	Cork, Ireland
1935	159·104		Ernst Henne	BMW	Frankfurt/Munich autobahn
1940	173·680	(1937)	Ernst Henne	BMW	Frankfurt/Munich autobahn
1945	''	''	''	''	''
1950	''	''	''	''	''
1955	184·950		Russell Wright	Vincent HRD	Christchurch, New Zealand
1960	210·081	(1956)	Wilhelm Herz	NSU	Bonneville, USA
1965	224·570	(1962)	William A. Johnson	Truimph	Bonneville, USA
1970	264·960		Calvin Rayborn	Harley Davidson	Bonneville, USA
1975	302·928		Don Vesco	Yamaha	Bonneville, USA
1980	318·598	(1978)	Don Vesco	Kawasaki	Bonneville, USA
1985	''	''	''	''	''
1990	322·150		Dave Campos	Harley Davidson	Bonneville, USA

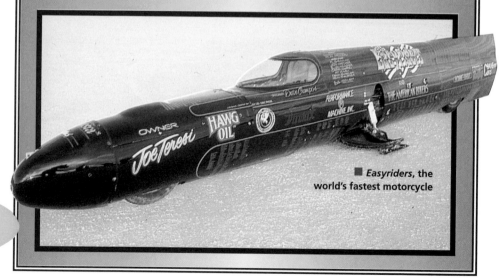

■ *Easyriders*, the world's fastest motorcycle

The highest speed achieved over two runs in the UK is 332.30 km/h *200.9 mph* by Michel Booys riding a streamliner motorcycle, built by Alexander Macfadzean and powered by a turbo-charged 588cc Norton rotary engine, at Bruntingthorpe Proving Ground, Leics on 24 Aug 1991.

The fastest time for a single run over 440 yd from a standing start is 6.19 sec by Tony Lang (USA) riding a super-charged Suzuki at Gainsville, Florida, USA in 1994.

The highest terminal velocity recorded at the end of a 440 yd run from a standing start is 372.16 km/h *231.24 mph* by Elmer Trett (USA) at Virginia Motorsports Park in 1994.

Longest motorcycle *World* Gregg Reid of Atlanta, Georgia, USA designed and built a 4.57 m *15 ft 6 in* long 250cc motorbike weighing 235 kg *520 lb*. It is street legal.

UK Les Nash of Coventry, W Mids constructed a 'self made' 3500cc machine with a Rover V-8 engine. It measures 3.81 × 1.22 m *12 ft 6 in x 4 ft* and weighs more than 220 kg *500 lb*.

Smallest motorcycle Simon Timperley and Clive Williams of Progressive Engineering Ltd, Ashton-under-Lyne, Greater Manchester designed and constructed a motorcycle with a wheel-base of 108 mm *4.25 in*, a seat height of 95 mm *3.75 in* and with a wheel diameter of 19 mm *0.75 in* for the front and 24 mm *0.95 in* for the back. The bike was ridden a distance of 1 m *3.2 ft*.

Magnor Mydland of Norway has constructed a motorcycle with a wheelbase of 120 mm *4.72 in*, a seat height of 148 mm *5.82 in* and with wheels 38 mm *1.49 in* for the front and 49 mm *1.92 in* for the back in diameter. He rode a distance of 570 m *1870 ft* reaching a speed of 11.6 km/h *7.2 mph*.

Motorcycle duration The longest time a motor scooter, a Kinetic Honda DX 100cc, has been kept in non-stop motion is 1001 hr when ridden by Har Parkash Rishi, Amarjeet Singh and Navjot Chadha of India. The team covered a distance of 30,965 km *19,241 miles* at Traffic Park, Pune, Maharashtra, India between 22 April and 3 Jun 1990.

Longest motorcycle ride Jari Saarelainen (b. 4 Apr 1959) of Finland riding his Honda Gold Wing 1500cc motorcycle travelled a distance of 108,000 km *67,109 miles* through 43 countries. He set off from Helsinki, Finland on 1 Dec 1989 and returned 742 days later on 12 Dec 1991.

The first woman to circumnavigate the world solo was Moniika Vega (b. 9 May 1962) of Rio de Janeiro, Brazil riding her Honda 125cc motorcycle. Her journey commenced at Milan, Italy on 7 Mar 1990 and she returned to Italy on 24 May 1991 having covered a distance of 83,500 km *51,885 miles* and visited 53 countries.

Jim Rogers and Tabitha Estabrook of New York, USA travelled a distance of 91,766 km *57,022 miles* on their motorcycles covering six continents. They set off from New York, USA in March 1990 and returned in November 1991.

Guess What?

Q. What is the world's smallest bicycle?

A. See Page 113

All Aboard!

The record for the most people on a single machine is all 46 members of the Illawarra Mini Bike Training Club, New South Wales, Australia. They rode on a 1000cc motorcycle and travelled a distance of 1 mile *1.609 km* on 11 Oct 1987.

Motorcycle pyramid The Army Service Corps, Indian Army, established a world record with a pyramid of 93 men on nine motorcycles. The pyramid which was held together by muscle and determination only, with no straps, harnesses or any other aids, travelled a distance of 600 m *328 yd* at Gill Stadium, Bangalore, India on 19 Jul 1994.

Ramp jumping (motorcycle) The longest distance ever achieved for motorcycle long-jumping is 76.5 m *251 ft*, by Doug Danger on a 1991 Honda CR500 at Loudon, New Hampshire, USA on 22 Jun 1991.

Motorcycle wheelie *Distance* Yasuyuki Kudō covered 331 km *205.7 miles* non-stop on the rear wheel of his Honda TLM220R motorcycle at the Japan Automobile Research Institute proving ground, Tsukuba, near Tsuchiura, Japan on 5 May 1991.

Speed The highest speed attained on a back wheel of a motorcycle is 254.07 km/h *157.87 mph* by Jacky Vranken (Belgium) on a Suzuki GSXR 1100 at St Truiden military airfield, Belgium on 8 Nov 1992.

Wall of death The greatest endurance feat on a 'wall of death' was 7 hr 0 min 13 sec, by Martin Blume at Berlin, Germany on 16 Apr 1983. He rode a Yamaha XS 400 over 12,000 laps on a wall which had a diameter of 10 m *33 ft*, averaging 45 km/h *30 mph* for the 292 km *181½ miles*.

Oldest motorcyclist Arthur Merrick Cook (b. 13 Jun 1895) of Exeter, Devon still regularly rides his Suzuki 125 GS Special motorcycle every day.

■ Simon Timperley and Clive Williams of Progressive Engineering Ltd, Ashton-under-Lyne, Greater Manchester designed and constructed the world's smallest motorcycle. The bike was ridden, with considerable skill, a distance of 1 m *3.2 ft*.

Motorcars

Earliest

Model The earliest automobile of which there is a record is a two-foot-long steam-powered model constructed by Ferdinand Verbiest (died 1687), a Belgian Jesuit priest, and described in his *Astronomia Europaea*. His model of 1668 was possibly inspired either by Giovanni Branca's description of a steam turbine, published in his *La Macchina* in 1629, or even by Nan Huairen (writings on 'fire carts') in the Chou dynasty (c. 800 BC).

Passenger-carrying motorcar The earliest full-scale automobile was the first of two military steam tractors, completed at the Paris Arsenal in October 1769 by Nicolas-Joseph Cugnot (1725–1804). This reached 3.6 km/h *2¼ mph*. Cugnot's second, larger tractor, completed in May 1771, today survives in the Conservatoire Nationale des Arts et Métiers in Paris.

Vehicle Production ▶▶ ▶▶

The world's first passenger-carrying automobile was a steam-powered road vehicle carrying eight passengers and built by Richard Trevithick (1771–1833). It first ran at Camborne, Cornwall on 24 Dec 1801.

Internal combustion Isaac de Rivaz (Switzerland) (died 1828) built a carriage powered by his 'explosion engine' in 1805. The first practical internal combustion engined vehicle was that built by the Londoner Samuel Brown (Brit. Pat. No. 5350, 25 Apr 1826), whose 4 hp two-cylinder 88 litre-engined carriage climbed Shooters Hill, Blackheath, Kent in May 1826.

The first successful petrol-driven car, the Motorwagen, built by Karl-Friedrich Benz (1844–1929) of Karlsruhe, Germany, ran at Mannheim, in late 1885. The three-wheeler weighed 254 kg *5 cwt* and could reach a speed of 13–16 km/h *8–10 mph*. Its single-cylinder engine (bore 91.4 mm *3.6 in*, stroke 160 mm *6.3 in*) delivered 0.85 hp at 400 rpm. It was patented on 29 Jan 1886. Its first 1 km *0.6 mile* road test was reported in the local newspaper, the *Neue Badische Landeszeitung*, of 4 Jun 1886, under the heading 'Miscellaneous'.

Britain's continuous motoring history started in November 1894 when Henry Hewetson drove his imported Benz Velo in the south-eastern suburbs of London.

Vehicle registrations The world's first plates were introduced by the Paris police in 1893 and in Britain in 1903.

The original A1 plate was secured by the 2nd Earl Russell (1865–1931) for his 12 hp Napier.

Licence plate No. 9 was sold at a Hong Kong government auction for HK$13 million on 19 Mar 1994 to Albert Yeung Sau-shing. 'Nine' sounds like the word 'dog' in Chinese and was considered lucky because 1994 was the Year of The Dog. The highest price paid for a British registration plate is £203,500 by an undisclosed buyer for K1 NGS at Christie's, London on 10 Dec 1993.

Guess What?
Q. Where is the world's leading shipbuilder?
A. See Page 110

Vehicle production

The number of vehicles constructed world-wide in 1992 was a record 47,955,000, of which 34,838,000 were motorcars. The peak year for motorcars only was 1990 when 35,277,986 were produced.

The UK production figure for 1994 was 1,694,638 vehicles of which 1,466,823 were cars. The peak year for production was 1964 when 2,332,376 vehicles (1,867,640 cars) were manufactured.

The world's largest manufacturer of motor vehicles and parts (and the largest manufacturing company) is

59 Not Out

The Morgan 4/4, the longest motorcar in production, celebrated its 59th birthday on 27 Dec 1994. Built by the Morgan Motor Car Co. of Malvern, Hereford & Worcester (founded 1910), there is still a six to eight-year waiting list for delivery.

■ The largest single automobile plant in the world is the Volkswagenwerk at Wolfsburg, Germany, with about 60,000 employees and a facility for producing 4000 vehicles every day. The factory buildings cover an area of 150 ha *371 acres* and the whole plant covers 760 ha *1878 acres*, with 74 km *46 miles* of rail sidings.
(Photos: Gamma/B. Edelhajt)

■ A total of approximately 21,220,000 Volkswagen 'Beetles' have been produced since 1937 when the Volkswagenwerk was established at Wolfsburg. The car continues to be produced at two production lines— Puebla, Mexico and São Paulo, Brazil.
(Photo: Gamma/J.L. Bulcao)

General Motors Corporation of Detroit, Michigan, USA. The company has on average 710,800 employees. A peak figure of 9,297,395 vehicles were produced in 1978 and the Company's highest yearly income was $138.2 billion in 1993.

The largest manufacturer in Britain is the Rover Group plc, which produced 486,828 vehicles in 1994. The company produced almost three out of every ten cars built in Britain and accounted for nearly one-third of the number of cars exported from the UK.

A total of approximately 21,220,000 Volkswagen 'Beetles' have been produced. Two production lines continue to produce the car—Puebla, Mexico and São Paulo, Brazil.

Britain's champion seller has been the Mini (5.3 million produced), designed by Sir Alec Issigonis (1906–88), which originally sold for £496 19s 2d in August 1959.

Largest car Of cars produced for private use, the largest was the Bugatti 'Royale' type 41, known in Britain as the 'Golden Bugatti', which was assembled at Molsheim, France by the Italian Ettore Bugatti (1882–1947). First built in 1927, this machine has an eight-cylinder engine of 12.7 litres capacity, and measures over 22 ft *6.7 m* in length. The bonnet is over 7 ft *2.13 m* long.

Largest car engine The greatest engine capacity of a production car was 13.5 litres, for the US Pierce-Arrow 6–66 Raceabout of 1912–18, the US Peerless 6–60 of 1912–14 and the Fageol of 1918.

Most powerful car The most powerful current production car is the McLaren F1 6.1 which develops in excess of 627 bhp.

Heaviest car The heaviest car recently in production (up to twenty-five were made annually) appears to be the Soviet-built Zil–41047 limousine with a 3.88 m *12.72 ft* wheel-base, weighing 3335 kg *7352 lb*. A 'stretched' Zil (two to three made annually) was used by former President Mikhail Gorbachev until December 1991. It weighed 6 tonnes and used 75 mm *3 in* armour-plated steel for protection in key areas. The eight-cylinder, 7-litre engine guzzled fuel at the rate of 9.6 km *6 miles* to the gallon.

Lightest car Louis Borsi of London has built and driven a 9.5 kg *21 lb* car with a 2.5cc engine. It is capable of 25 km/h *15 mph*.

Longest car A 30.5 m *100 ft* long 26-wheeled limo was designed by Jay Ohrberg of Burbank, California, USA. It has many features, including a swimming pool with diving board and a king-sized water bed. It is designed to drive as a rigid vehicle or it can be changed to bend in the middle. Its main purpose is for use in films and exhibitions.

Guess What?
Q. What is the highest speed achieved on water?
A. See Page 111

In 1955 the most expensive car available in the UK was the Pegaso type 102 Thrill Berlinetta which cost £9800. Today you would be able to buy over 64 Pegasos for the price of the current most expensive car, the McLaren F1. The least expensive car listed in the first edition was the Ford 'Popular' which cost including Purchase Tax, a total of £390 14s 2d. Interestingly, you could buy only 11 Populars for the price of the current least expensive car in the UK, the Lada Riva.

Most expensive car *Standard* The most expensive list-price British standard car is the McLaren F1 quoted at £634,500 plus tax.

Used The greatest confirmed price paid is $15 million for the 1931 Bugatti Type 41 Royale Sports Coupé by Kellner, sold by Nicholas Harley to the Meitec Corporation of Japan, completed on 12 Apr 1990.

Most inexpensive car The cheapest car of all time was the 1922 Red Bug Buckboard, built by the Briggs & Stratton Co. of Milwaukee, Wisconsin, USA, listed at $125–$150. It had a 1.57 m *62 in* wheel-base and weighed 111 kg *245 lb*. Early models of the King Midget cars were sold in kit form for self-assembly for as little as $100 in 1948.

In April 1995 the cheapest listed new car in Britain was the Lada Riva 1.5E at £4395.

Parade of Rolls-Royce A parade of 147 Rolls-Royces, organized by the Rolls-Royce Owners' Club of Australia, drove around Lake Wendouree, Ballarat, Victoria on 19 Sep 1992.

Fastest

Land speed (car) The *official* one-mile land-speed record is 1019.467 km/h *633.468 mph*, set by Richard Noble (b. 6 Mar 1946) on 4 Oct 1983 over the Black Rock Desert, Nevada, USA in his 17,000 lb thrust Rolls-Royce Avon 302 jet-powered *Thrust 2*, designed by John Ackroyd.

The highest speed attained in Britain is 444 km/h *276 mph* by Poutiaiten Risto (Finland) in a Top Fuel dragster on 27 May 1991 at the Santa Pod County Raceway, Beds.

Rocket-engined car The highest speed attained is 1016.086 km/h *631.367 mph* over the first measured kilometre by *The Blue Flame*, a rocket powered four-wheeled vehicle driven by Gary Gabelich (b. 23 Aug 1940) (USA) on the Bonneville Salt Flats, Utah, USA on 23 Oct 1970. Momentarily Gabelich exceeded 1046 km/h *650 mph*. The car was powered by a liquid natural gas/hydrogen peroxide rocket engine which could develop thrust up to 22,000 lb.

The highest reputed land speed figure in one direction is 1190.377 km/h *739.666 mph* or Mach 1.0106 by Stan Barrett (USA) in the *Budweiser Rocket*, a rocket-engined three-wheeled car, at Edwards Air Force Base, California, USA on 17 Dec 1979. *This published speed of Mach 1.0106 is not officially sanctioned by the USAF as the Digital Instrument Radar was not calibrated or certified. The radar information was not generated by the vehicle directly but by an operator aiming a dish by means of a TV screen.*

The highest land speed recorded by a woman is 843.323 km/h *524.016 mph* by Mrs Kitty Hambleton (*née* O'Neil) (USA) in the rocket-powered three-wheeled SM1 *Motivator* over the Alvard Desert, Oregon, USA on 6 Dec 1976. Her official two-way record was 825.126 km/h *512.710 mph* and she probably touched 965 km/h *600 mph* momentarily.

Piston-engined car The highest speed measured for a wheel-driven car is 696.331 km/h *432.692 mph* by Al Teague (USA) in *Speed-O-Motive/Spirit of 76* on Bonneville Salt Flats, Utah, USA on 21 Aug 1991 over the final 132 ft of a mile run (425.230 mph for the whole mile).

Diesel-engined car The prototype 3 litre Mercedes C 111/3 attained 327.3 km/h *203.3 mph* in tests on the Nardo Circuit, southern Italy on 5–15 Oct 1978, and in April 1978 averaged 314.5 km/h *195.4 mph* for 12 hours, so covering a world record 3773.5 km *2344.7 miles*.

Electric car *UK Land speed* On 22 Jun 1991 Max Rink (18) of Oundle School, Peterborough achieved a speed of 111.37 km/h *69.21 mph* over a one km flying start, at Bruntingthorpe Proving Ground, Leics. Over the two runs the average speed achieved was 106.43 km/h *66.14 mph*. The vehicle weighed only 60 kg *132 lb* and was built in 1986 by four 14-year-old pupils from Oundle School.

On 19 Aug 1985 Robert E. Barber broke the 79-year-old speed record for a steam car when *Steamin' Demon*, built by the Barber-Nichols Engineering Co., reached 234.33 km/h *145.607 mph* at Bonneville Salt Flats, Utah, USA.

Fastest road cars Various de-tuned track cars have been licensed for road use but are not normal production models.

The highest speed ever attained by a standard production car is 349.21 km/h *217.1 mph* for a Jaguar XJ220, driven by Martin Brundle at the Nardo test track, Italy on 21 Jun 1992.

The highest road-tested acceleration reported is 0–60 mph in 3.07 sec for a Ford RS200 Evolution, driven by Graham Hathaway at the Millbrook Proving Ground, Beds on 25 May 1994.

The fastest lap on a UK circuit by a production car was achieved in a Ferrari 512TR at an average speed of 282.2 km/h *175.4 mph*, and a peak speed over ½ mile of 285.2 km/h *177.3 mph* by Andrew Frankel of *Autocar & Motor* magazine at Millbrook, Beds on 10 Jun 1992.

Skid marks The longest recorded on a public road were 290 m *950 ft* long left by a Jaguar car involved in an accident on the M1 near Luton, Beds on 30 Jun 1960. Evidence given in the subsequent High Court case *Hurlock* v. *Inglis et al.* indicated a speed 'in excess of 100 mph before the application of the brakes'.

The skid marks made by the jet-powered *Spirit of America*, driven by Norman Craig Breedlove, after the car went out of control at Bonneville Salt Flats, Utah, USA on 15 Oct 1964, were nearly 6 miles *9.6 km* long.

Highest car mileage
The highest recorded mileage for a car is 1,563,278 miles *2,515,852 km* up to 15 Jan 1995 for a 1963 Volkswagen 'Beetle' owned by Albert Klein of Pasadena, California, USA.

Driving

Amphibious circumnavigation by car The only circumnavigation by an amphibious vehicle was by Ben Carlin (Australia) (died 7 Mar 1981) in the amphibious jeep, *Half-Safe*. He completed the last leg of the Atlantic crossing (the English Channel) on 24 Aug 1951. He arrived back in Montreal, Canada on 8 May 1958, having completed a circumnavigation of 39,000 miles *62,765 km* over land and 9600 miles *15,450 km* by sea and river. He was accompanied on the transatlantic stage by his ex-wife Elinore (USA) and on the long trans-Pacific stage (Tokyo to Anchorage, Alaska) by Boye Lafayette De Mente (USA) (b. 1928).

One-year driving duration record The greatest distance ever covered in one year is 573,029 km *354,257 miles* by two Opel Rekords, both of which covered this distance between 18 May 1988 and the same date in 1989 without any major mechanical breakdowns. The vehicles were manufactured by the Delta Motor Corporation, Port Elizabeth, South Africa, and were driven on tar and gravel roads in the Northern Cape by a team of company drivers from Delta.

Trans-Americas by car Garry Sowerby (Canada), with Tim Cahill (USA) as co-driver and navigator, drove a 1988 GMC Sierra K3500 from Ushuaia, Tierra del Fuego, Argentina to Prudhoe Bay, Alaska, USA, a distance of 23,720 km *14,739 miles*, in a total elapsed time of 23 days 22 hr 43 min from 29 September to 22 Oct 1987. The vehicle and team were surface freighted from Cartagena, Colombia to Balboa, Panama so as to by-pass the Darién Gap.

Round Britain car economy A Daihatsu Charade 1.0 turbo diesel driven by Helen Horwood, Joanne Swift and John Taylor around a 5827 km *3621 mile* course from 7–14 Oct 1991 returned a fuel consumption of 103.01 mpg.

The record for a petrol engined car is 85.96 mpg for a Honda Civic ETi driven by Team Mad Scientist & Crazy Guys + Naughty Ladies, led by Dr. Shigeru Miyano, from 18–25 Sep 1993.

Petrol consumption A 'car' specially designed by a team of students from Lycée St Joseph la Joliverie, St Sébastien sur Loire, France achieved a performance of 7591 mpg in the Shell Mileage Marathon at Silverstone, Northants on 17 Jul 1992.

Most economical car Amongst new production cars currently available in the United Kingdom, the Citroen AX Debut D could make this claim. The Department of Transport figures are 55.4 mpg (urban cycle), 78.5 mpg (steady 56 mph), 57.6 mpg (steady 75 mph).

On 9 Aug 1989 motoring writer Stuart Bladon drove a Citroen AX 14DTR a distance of 180.26 km *112.01 miles* using one gallon of fuel driving on the M11 Motorway in a test run arranged by Lucas Diesel Systems.

Longest fuel range The greatest distance driven without refuelling in a standard vehicle is 2724 km *1691.6 miles* by a 1991 Toyota LandCruiser diesel station wagon (factory optional twin fuel tanks, capacity 174 litres *38.2 gal*). The Toyota was driven by Ewan Kennedy with Ian Lee (observer) from Nyngan, New South Wales, Australia to Winton, Queensland and back between 18–21 May 1992. The average speed was 60 km/h *37 mph*.

The greatest distance travelled by a vehicle on the contents of a standard fuel tank is 2153.4 km *1338.1 miles* by an Audi 100 TDI diesel car (capacity 17.62 gal *80.1 litres*). Stuart Bladon, with RAC

observer Robert Proctor, drove from John o' Groats to Land's End and returned to Scotland between 26–28 Jul 1992.

Driving in reverse Charles Creighton (1908–70) and James Hargis of Maplewood, Missouri, USA drove their Model A Ford 1929 roadster in reverse from New York, USA 5375 km *3340 miles* to Los Angeles, California, from 26 Jul–13 Aug 1930 without once stopping the engine. They arrived back in New York in reverse on 5 September, so completing 11,555 km *7180 miles* in 42 days.

Brian 'Cub' Keene and James 'Wilbur' Wright drove their Chevrolet Blazer 14,533 km *9031 miles* in 37 days (1 August–6 Sep 1984) in reverse through 15 US states and Canada.

> Sven-Erik Söderman drove a Daf 2800 7.5 ton truck on two wheels for a distance of 10.83 km *6.73 miles* at Mora Siljan airport on 19 May 1991.

Layne Hall, the oldest known driver, holding his driving licence which lists his date of birth as 15 Mar 1880. He drove a 1962 Cadillac until his death in 1990.

Though it was prominently named 'Stuck in Reverse', law enforcement officers in Oklahoma refused to believe it and insisted they drove in reverse reverse, i.e. forwards, out of the state.

The highest average speed attained in any non-stop reverse drive exceeding 800 km *500 miles* was achieved by Gerald Hoagland, who drove a 1969 Chevrolet Impala 806.2 km *501 miles* in 17 hr 38 min at Chemung Speed Drome, New York, USA on 9–10 Jul 1976, to average 45.72 km/h *28.41 mph*.

Battery-powered vehicle David Turner and Tim Pickhard of Turners of Boscastle Ltd, Cornwall, trav-

elled 1408 km *875 miles* from Land's End to John o' Groats in 63 hr in a Freight Rover Leyland Sherpa powered by a Lucas electric motor from 21–23 Dec 1985.

Two-side-wheel driving *Car* Bengt Norberg (b. 23 Oct 1951) of Äppelbo, Sweden drove a Mitsubishi Colt GTi-16V on two side wheels non-stop for a distance of 310.391 km *192.873 miles* in a time of 7 hr 15 min 50 sec. He also achieved a distance of 44.808 km *27.842 miles* in 1 hr at Rattvik Horse Track, Sweden on 24 May 1989.

Sven-Erik Söderman (Sweden) (b. 26 Sep 1960) achieved a speed of 164.38 km/h *102.14 mph* over a 100 m flying start on the two wheels of an Opel Kadett at Mora Siljan airport, Mora, Sweden on 2 Aug 1990. Söderman achieved a record speed for the flying kilometre of 152.96 km/h *95.04 mph* at the same venue on 24 Aug 1990.

Ramp jumping (car) The longest ramp jump in a car, with the car landing on its wheels and being driven on, is 70.73 m *232 ft*, by Jacqueline De Creed (née Creedy) in a 1967 Ford Mustang at Santa Pod Raceway, Beds on 3 Apr 1983.

Most durable driver Goodyear Tire and Rubber Co. test driver Weldon C. Kocich drove 5,056,472 km *3,141,946 miles* from 5 Feb 1953 to 28 Feb 1986, so averaging 153,226 km *95,210 miles* per year.

Oldest driver Layne Hall (b. 24/25 Dec 1884 or 15 Mar 1880) of Silver Creek, NY, USA was issued with a New York State licence on 15 Jun 1989, valid until his birthday in 1993 when, based on his date of birth on the licence, he would have been aged 113. He died, however, on 20 Nov 1990, aged 105 (according to the death certificate).

Mrs Maude Tull of Inglewood, California, USA, who took to driving aged 91 after her husband died, was issued a renewal on 5 Feb 1976 when aged 104.

Britain's oldest known drivers have been Benjamin Kagan (1878–1988) of Leeds, Rev. Albert Thomas Humphrey (1886–1988) from Pawlett, near Bridgwater, Somerset and Kenneth Leech (1893–1995); who drove up to the age of 102.

The greatest age at which an individual has first passed the Department of Transport driving test has been 90 years 229 days by Mrs Gerty Edwards Land (b. 9 Sep 1897) on 27 Apr 1988 in Colne, Lancs. The oldest man to pass was David Coupar (b. 9 Feb 1898) on 4 Mar 1987 in Perth, Perthshire. He was aged 89 years 2 months.

Youngest driver Stephen Andrew Blackbourn of Lincoln having passed his driving test on his 17th birthday, went on to pass the advanced test less than five hours later on 20 Feb 1989. His brother Mark previously held the record.

Driving tests The record for persistence in taking the Department of Transport's driving test is held by Mrs Git Kaur Randhawa (b. 7 Feb 1937) of Hayes, Middlesex, who triumphed at her 48th attempt, after more than 330 lessons, on 19 Jun 1987.

The world's easiest tests have been those in Egypt, in which the ability to drive 6 m *19.6 ft* forward and the same in reverse has been deemed sufficient. In 1979 it was reported that accurate reversing between two

Guess What?

Q. Who is the oldest person to fly?

A. See Page 130

rubber traffic cones had been added. 'High cone attrition' soon led to the substitution of white lines.

Worst driver It was reported that a 75-year-old male driver received ten traffic tickets, drove on the wrong side of the road four times, committed four hit-and-run offences and caused six accidents, all within 20 minutes, in McKinney, Texas, USA on 15 Oct 1966.

The most comprehensively banned driver in Britain was John Hogg, 28, who, in the High Court, Edinburgh on 27 Nov 1975, received 5¾ years in gaol and his 3rd, 4th and 5th life bans for drunken driving in a stolen car while disqualified. For his previous 40 offences he had received bans of 71½ years plus two life bans.

Specialized Vehicles

Longest vehicle The Arctic Snow Train has 54 wheels and is 174.3m *572 ft* long. It was built by R.G. Le Tourneau Inc. of Longview, Texas, USA for the US Army. Its gross train weight is 400 tons, with a top speed of 32 km/h *20 mph*, and it was driven by a crew of six when used as an 'overland train' for the military. It generates 4680 shaft horsepower and has a fuel capacity of 29,648 litres *6522 gal*. It is owned by the world-famous wirewalker Steve McPeak (USA) who makes all repairs, including every punctured wheel, single-handed in often sub-zero temperatures in Alaska.

Largest ambulance The world's largest ambulances are the 18 m *59 ft* long articulated Alligator Jumbulances Marks VI, VII, VIII and IX, operated by the ACROSS Trust to convey the sick and handicapped on holidays and pilgrimages across Europe. They are built by Van Hool of Belgium with Fiat engines at a cost £200,000 and carry 44 patients and staff.

Buses *Earliest* The first municipal motor omnibus service in the world was inaugurated on 12 Apr 1903 and ran between Eastbourne railway station and Meads, E Sussex.

Longest The longest are the articulated DAF Super CityTrain buses of Zaïre, with 110 passenger seats and room for 140 'strap-hangers' in first trailer and 60 seated and 40 'strap-hangers' in the second, making a total of 350. Designed by the President of the Republic of Zaïre, Citoyen Mobutu Sese Seko Kuku Ngbendu wa za Banga (b. 14 Oct 1930), they are 32.20 m *105.64 ft* long and weigh 28 tonnes unladen.

The longest rigid single bus is 14.96 m *49 ft* long, carries 69 passengers and is built by Van Hool of Belgium.

Largest fleet The 10,895 single-decker buses in São Paulo, Brazil make up the world's largest bus fleet.

Longest route The longest regularly scheduled bus route is operated by Expreso Internacional Ormeño S.A. of Lima, Peru which runs a regular scheduled service between Caracas, Venezuela and Buenos Aires, Argentina. The route is 9660 km *6003 miles* long and takes 214 hours which includes a 12-hour stop in Santiago, Chile and 24-hour stop in Lima.

The longest route in Britain is route 806 between Penzance, Cornwall and Dundee, Tayside at 1102 km *685 miles*, operated by Western National Ltd and Tayside Travel Services Ltd, each company allocating coaches on alternate days.

Caravans *Largest* The largest two-wheeled five-storey caravan was built in 1990 for H.E Sheik Hamad Bin Hamdan Al Nahyan of Abu Dhabi, United Arab Emirates. It is 20m *66ft* long, 12m *39ft* wide and weighs 120 tons. There are eight bedrooms and bathrooms, four garages and water storage for 24,000 litres *5279 gal*.

Longest journey The continuous motor caravan journey of 231,288 km *143,716 miles* by Harry B. Coleman and Peggy Larson in a Volkswagen Camper from 20 Aug 1976 to 20 Apr 1978 took them through 113 countries.

Fastest The world speed record for a caravan tow is 204.02 km/h *126.77 mph* for a Roadstar caravan towed by a 1990 Ford EA Falcon saloon and driven by 'Charlie' Kovacs, at Mangalore Airfield, Seymour, Victoria, Australia on 18 Apr 1991.

Crawler The largest is the Marion eight-caterpillar crawler used originally for conveying Saturn V rockets, but now Shuttles, to their launch pads at Cape Canaveral, Florida, USA. The two built cost $12.3 million, each measuring 131 ft 4 in × 114 ft *40 × 34.7 m*. The loaded train weight is 8165 tonnes. The windscreen wiper blades are 106 cm *42 in* long and are the world's largest.

Dumper truck The world's largest is the Terex Titan 33–19 manufactured by General Motors Corporation and now in operation at Westar Mine, British Columbia, Canada. It has a loaded weight of 548.6 tonnes and a capacity of 317.5 tonnes. When tipping its height is 17 m *56 ft*. The 16-cylinder engine delivers 3300 hp. The fuel tank holds 5910 litres *1300 gal*.

Fire engines The fire appliance with the greatest pumping capacity is the 860 hp eight-wheel Oshkosh firetruck (manufactured by Oshkosh Truck Corporation, Oshkosh, Wisconsin, USA), weighing 60 tonnes and used for aircraft and runway fires. It can discharge 189,000 litres *41,600 gal* of foam through two turrets in just 150 seconds.

Fire pumping The greatest volume of water stirrup-pumped by a team of eight in 80 hours is 143,459 litres *31,557 gal*, by firefighters based at Knaresborough Fire Station, N Yorks, from 25–28 Jun 1992.

Go-Karting The highest mileage recorded in 24 hours on a outdoor circuit by a four-man team is 1664.7 km *1034.4 miles* on a 0.8 mile track at Brooklands, Weybridge, Surrey. The team drivers were Stefan Dennis, David Brabham, Russ and Steve Malkin on 24–25 Feb 1995.

The highest mileage recorded in 24 hours on an indoor track by a four-man team driving 160cc karts is 1422.6 km *883.9 miles* at the Welsh Karting Centre, Cardiff, S Glam. The drivers were Ian O'Sullivan, Paul Marram, Richard Jenkins and Michael Watts on 26 Nov 1993.

Lawn mowers The widest gang mower in the world is the 5 ton 60 ft *18 m* wide 27-unit 'Big Green Machine' used by the turf farmer Jay Edgar Frick of Monroe, Ohio, USA. It mows an acre in 60 seconds.

A 12-hour run-behind record of 169.1 km *105.1 miles* was set at Wisborough Green, W Sussex on 28–29 Jul 1990 by the 'Doctor's Flyers' team.

The greatest distance covered in the annual 12-hour Lawn Mower Race (under the rules of the British Lawn Mower Racing Association) is 468 km *291 miles* by John Gill, Robert Jones and Steve Richardson of Team Gilliams at Wisborough Green, W Sussex on 1 and 2 Aug 1992.

Rocket-powered sleds The highest speed recorded, unrailed, on ice is 399.00 km/h *247.93 mph* by *Oxygen*, driven by Sammy Miller (b. 15 Apr 1945) on Lake George, New York, USA on 15 Feb 1981.

Snowmobiles John Outzen, Andre, Carl and Denis Boucher drove snowmobiles a distance of 16,499.5 km *10,252.3 miles* in 56 riding days from Anchorage, Alaska, USA to Dartmouth, Nova Scotia, Canada from 2 Jan–3 Mar 1992.

Tony Lenzini of Duluth, Minnesota, USA drove his 1986 Arctic Cat Cougar snowmobile a total of 11,604.6 km *7211 miles* in 60 riding days between 28 Dec 1985 and 20 Mar 1986.

Solar powered vehicle The highest speed attained by a solely solar-powered land vehicle is 78.39 km/h *48.71 mph* by Molly Brennan driving the General Motors *Sunraycer* at Mesa, Arizona, USA on 24 Jun 1988. The highest speed of 135 km/h *83.88 mph* using solar/battery power was achieved by Star Micronics solar car *Solar Star* driven by Manfred Hermann on 5 Jan 1991 at Richmond RAAF Base, Richmond, NSW, Australia.

Taxis The largest taxi fleet is that in Mexico City, with 60,000 'normal' taxis, *pesaros* (communal fixed route taxis) and *settas* (airport taxis).

Currently there are 16,565 taxis and 20,220 taxi-drivers in London.

The longest fare on record is one of 23,196 km *14,413 miles* at a cost of 70,000 Finnmarks (approximately £9000). Mika Lehtonen and Juhani Saramies left Nokia, Finland on 2 May 1991 and travelled through Scandinavia down to Spain and arrived back in Nokia on 17 May 1991.

Charles Kerslake (b. 27 Jun 1895) held a London Metropolitan cab licence from February 1922 until his retirement in May 1988 aged 92 years 11 months.

Trams *Longest journey* The longest now possible is from Krefeld St Tönis to Witten Annen Nord, Germany. With luck at the eight inter-connections, the 105.5 km *65.5 mile* trip can be achieved in 5½ hours.

The city of St Petersburg, Russia has the most extensive tramway system with 2402 cars on 64 routes with 690.6 km *429.1 miles* of track.

Oldest The oldest trams in revenue service in the world are motorcars 1 and 2 of the Manx Electric Railway, dating from 1893. These run regularly on the 28.5 km *17¾ miles* railway between Douglas and Ramsey, Isle of Man.

The record for John o' Groats, Highland to Land's End, Cornwall by pedal car is 59 hr 21 min by a team of five from the Lea Manor High School and Community College, Luton on 30 May–1 June 1993.

Huge!

The most massive automotive land vehicle is 'Big Muskie' built by Bucyrus Erie. It is a walking dragline (a machine that removes dirt from coal) and weighs 13,200 tons. It is no longer in use because it is too expensive to run, but is to be found at Central Ohio Coal Co., Muskingham site, Ohio, USA.

The fastest fire engine on record is the Jaguar XJ12 'Chubb Firefighter', which on 2 Nov 1982 attained a speed of 210.13 km/h *130.57 mph* in tests when attending the *Thrust 2* land speed record trials. (⇨ Fastest cars, land speed)

Guess What?
Q. Where is the longest railway track?
A. See Page 122

Trolleybuses The last trolleybus in Britain, owned by Bradford Corporation, ran in 1972. Plans have been made to reintroduce trolleybuses by both West and South Yorks Passenger Transport Executives.

Truck Les Shockley of Galena, Kansas, USA drove his Jet Truck *ShockWave* powered by three Pratt & Whitney jet engines developing 36,000 hp to a record speed of 412 km/h *256 mph* in 6.36 sec over a quarter-mile standing start on 4 Jun 1989 at Autodrome de Monterrey Mexico. He set a further record for the standing mile at 605 km/h *376 mph* at Paine Field, Everett, Washington, USA on 18 Aug 1991.

Wrecker The world's most powerful wrecker is the Twin City Garage and Body Shop's 20.6 tonnes, 11 m *36 ft* long International M6-23 'Hulk' 1969 stationed at Scott City, Missouri, USA. It can lift in excess of 295 tonnes on its short boom.

Services

Car parks The world's largest is the West Edmonton Mall, Edmonton, Alberta, Canada, which can hold 20,000 vehicles. There are overflow facilities on an adjoining lot for 10,000 more cars.

The largest parking area in Great Britain is that for 15,000 cars and 200 coaches at the National Exhibition Centre, Birmingham, West Midlands (⇨ Buildings for Working, exhibition centres).

Britain's highest-capacity underground car park is at the Victoria Centre, Nottingham, with space for 1650 cars, opened in June 1972. The deepest underground car park in Britain and Europe is Aldersgate, City of London at 26 m *85 ft* below street level, comprising 14 split levels of parking and a capacity of 670 car parking spaces.

Parking meters The earliest were installed in the business district of Oklahoma City, Oklahoma, USA on 19 Jul 1935. They were invented by Carl C. Magee (USA) and reached London in 1958.

Guess What?

Q. Where is the world's largest park?

A. See Page 52

Traffic lights Semaphore-type traffic *signals* were set up in Parliament Square, London in 1868 with red and green gas lamps for night use. It was not an offence to disobey traffic signals until assent was given to the 1930 Road Traffic Act. Traffic *lights* were introduced in Great Britain with a one-day trial in Wolverhampton on 11 Feb 1928. They were first permanently operated in Leeds, W Yorks on 16 Mar 1928 and in Edinburgh, Scotland on 19 Mar 1928.

The first vehicle-actuated lights were installed by Plessey at the Cornhill–Gracechurch junction in the City of London in April 1932.

Filling stations The largest concentration of pumps are 204 — 96 of them Tokheim Unistar (electronic) and 108 Tokheim Explorer (mechanical) — in Jeddah, Saudi Arabia.

The highest filling station in the world is at Leh, Ladakh, India, at 3658 m *12,001 ft*, operated by the Indian Oil Corporation.

Garage The largest private garage is one of two storeys built outside Bombay for the private collection of 176 cars owned by Pranlal Bhogilal (b. 1939).

The KMB Overhaul Centre, operated by the Kowloon Motor Bus Co. (1933) Ltd, Hong Kong, is the world's largest multi-storey service centre. Purpose built for double decker buses, its four floors occupy in excess of 47,000 m² *11.6 acres*.

Tow The longest on record is one of 8038 km *4995 miles* from Ascot, Berks to Widmerpool, Notts conducted by the Automobile Association from 4–12 May 1993. They used a LandRover which towed a replica Model T Ford van.

Tyre supporting The greatest number of motor tyres supported in a free-standing 'lift' is 96, by Gary Windebank of Romsey, Hants in February 1984. The total weight was 653 kg *1440 lb*. The tyres used were Michelin XZX 155 × 13.

Loads

Heaviest load On 14–15 Jul 1984 John Brown Engineers & Contractors BV moved the Conoco Kotter Field production deck with a roll-out weight of 3805 tonnes for the Continental Netherlands Oil Co. of Leidsenhage, Netherlands.

The heaviest road load moved in the United Kingdom has been the 2045 tonnes, 79 m *259 ft* long Ingst motorway bridge on the M4 near Bristol. redundant after 26 years of use. The operation closed the Motorway from late on 28 Feb to 3 Mar 1992 and was conducted by Edmund Nuttall civil engineering firm and Econfreight, contractors.

Longest load The longest item moved by road was a high-pressure steel gas storage vessel 83.8 m *275 ft* long and weighing 233 tonnes transported to a new site at Beckton gasworks in east London on 10 Jul 1985. The overall train length was 99 m *325 ft*.

Model Cars

Non-stop model car duration A Scalextric Jaguar XJ8 ran non-stop for 866 hr 44 min 54 sec and covered a distance of 2850.39 km *1771.2 miles* from 2 May to 7 Jun 1989. The event was organized by the Rev. Bryan G. Apps, and church members of Southbourne, Bournemouth, Dorset.

Model car distance (24 hours) On 4–5 Sep 1994, H.O Racing and Hobbies of San Diego, California, USA achieved a distance of 603.631 km *375.079 miles* for a 1:64 scale car. On 5–6 Jul 1986 the North London Society of Model Engineers team at the ARRA club in Southport, Merseyside achieved a 24-hour distance record of 492.364 km *305.949 miles* for a 1:32 scale car, a Rondeau M482C Group C Sports car, built by Ian Fisher. This was under the rules of the B.S.C.R.A (British Slot Car Racing Association).

Longest slot car track The longest slot car track measured 377.4 m *1238 ft 4 in* and was built by Alan and David Brier at 1st West Byfleet Scout Centre, Surrey on 13–15 Apr 1995. One lap was successfully completed by a car.

On The Record

I'M GIVING UP THUMBING LIFTS!

2.R1 SKY

STUNTARAMA

What a smash up!

Over a period of more than 40 years up until his retirement in 1993 Dick Sheppard of Gloucester wrecked a total of 2003 cars, not because he was a bad driver but because it was his profession and hobby as a stuntman. The first one was in on a bomb site in 1951. In 1968 he formed the 'Disaster Squad', devoted entirely to car destruction. There were shows at home and abroad and perhaps the high point was being asked to appear in James Bond films.

So how did Dick become involved in this daring act with its ever-present risk of injury?

" 'From day one of the introduction of stock car racing in Great Britain in 1954 the sport became my hobby, and soon after that my occupation became auto stunt artist for films.'

His reputation blossomed and the demand was great. 'It was while I was gasping after a nine-day booking in Johannesburg, with two performances each day, and a pile of over 300 wrecked cars, that I realized that there could be no-one else doing this at the same rate!' Not bad going, 33 old cars smashed up every day for nine days.

'I don't know if the record will ever be surpassed, because during modern film making, with its demand for bigger and better crashes, most of the vehicles are projected driverless. But I would be happy to meet Mister or Miss 2004 plus and congratulate them.' He would also have lots of amusing anecdotes to tell them. Happy retirement Dick! "

Rubber

The world's largest tyres in production are manufactured by SAFE de Neumátios Michelin, Vitoria, Spain. They measure 3.723 m *12 ft 2½ in* in diameter, weigh 5782 kg *12,747 lb* and are used by the CAT 994 earthmover. A tyre 17 ft *5.2 m* in diameter is believed to be the largest practical.

Roads

Trackway *Oldest* The oldest known trackway in England is the Sweet Track in the Somerset Levels near Shapwick. Dendrochronologists in 1990 indicated that the road was built from trees felled in the winter of 3807–3806 BC.

The oldest in the Republic of Ireland are at Corlea and Derryoghil bogs near Lanesborough, Co. Roscommon, where prehistoric tracks made of oak and ash logs, radiocarbon dated to *c.* 2500–2300 BC, have been discovered.

Road mileages The country with the greatest length of road is the United States (all 50 states), with 6,244,497 km *3,880,151 miles* of graded roads.

Great Britain has 388,499 km *241,402 miles* of road, including 3255 km *2023 miles* of motorway.

Longest motorable road The Pan-American Highway, from north-west Alaska, USA to Santiago, Chile, thence eastward to Buenos Aires, Argentina

■ The picture shows just half of the Monumental Axis, the world's widest road, in Brasilia, the capital of Brazil. It runs for 2.4 km *1½ miles* from the Municipal Plaza to the Plaza of the Three Powers. The dual six-lane boulevard was opened in April 1960 and is 250 m *820.2 ft* wide.
(Photo: Gamma/E. Soderstrom)

Low Road

The lowest road in the world is to be found along the Israeli shores of the Dead Sea at 393 m *1290 ft* below sea level.

The lowest surface roads in Great Britain are just below sea level in the Holme Fen area of Cambridgeshire 2.75 m *9 ft* below sea level.

The greatest at any one point in Great Britain is at Hyde Park Corner, London. The peak flow (including the underpass) for 24 hours in 1990 was 240,000 vehicles.

Motorway Britain's busiest and most heavily travelled motorway is the M25; with the section between Junctions 13 (Staines) and 14 (Heathrow) having an average traffic flow of 168,000 vehicles over a 24 hour period.

Traffic density The territory with the highest traffic density in the world is Hong Kong. In 1993 there were 447 vehicles per mile of serviceable roads, i.e. a density of 3.59 m *3.93 yd* per vehicle.

The comparative figure for Great Britain was 15.4 m *16.9 yd* per vehicle in 1993.

Traffic jams The longest ever reported was that which stretched 176 km *109 miles* northwards from Lyon towards Paris, France on 16 Feb 1980. A record traffic jam was reported of 1½ million cars crawling bumper-to-bumper over the East-West German border on 12 Apr 1990.

The longest in Britain were two of 40 miles *64.3 km*: on the M1 from Junction 13 (Milton Keynes) to Junction 18 (Rugby) on 5 Apr 1985; and on the M6 between Charnock Richard and Carnforth, Lancs on 17 Apr 1987 involving 200,000 people and a tailback of 50,000 cars and coaches.

The longest of solid stationary traffic was 22 miles *35.40 km* on the M25 from midway between Junction 9 (Leatherhead) and Junction 8 (Reigate) on 17 Aug 1988.

Most complex interchange The most complex interchange on the British road system is that at Gravelly Hill, north of Birmingham on the Midland Link Motorway section of the M6, opened on 24 May 1972. Popularly known as 'Spaghetti Junction', it includes 18 routes on six levels (together with a diverted canal and river). Its construction consumed 26,000 tonnes of steel, 250,000 tonnes of concrete and 300,000 tonnes of earth, and cost £8.2 million.

Longest ring-road Work on the M25 London Orbital Motorway (mostly six lanes), 195.5 km *121½ miles* long commenced in 1972 and was completed on 29 Oct 1986 at an estimated cost of £909 million, or £7.5 million per mile.

Longest viaduct The longest elevated viaduct on the British road system is the 4.78 km *2.97 mile* Gravelly Hill to Castle Bromwich section of the M6 in the West Midlands. It was completed in May 1972 (⇔ Most complex interchange).

and terminating in Brasilia, Brazil is over 24,140 km *15,000 miles* in length. There is, however, a small incomplete section in Panama and Colombia known as the Darién Gap.

Great Britain The longest designated road in Great Britain is the A1 from London to Edinburgh, of 648 km *403 miles*.

The longest Roman roads were Watling Street, from Dubrae (Dover), 346 km *215 miles* through Londinium (London) to Viroconium (Wroxeter), and Fosse Way, which ran 350 km *218 miles* from Lindum (Lincoln) through Aquae Sulis (Bath) to Isca Dumnoniorum (Exeter), although a 16 km *10 mile* section near Ilchester remains indistinct.

Longest and shortest gaps The greatest error a motorway driver can make when missing an exit is travelling southbound on the M11 in Hertfordshire. The gap between junctions 10 (Duxford) and 8 (Bishop's Stortford) is 28.6 km *17.8 miles*. Junction 9 is open only to northbound drivers. The shortest gap between two exits is less than 160 m *174 yd*, between junctions 19 (Clydebank) and 18 (Charing Cross), on the eastbound M8 in central Glasgow.

Highest road The highest trail in the world is a 13 km *8 mile* stretch of the Gangdise, Tibet between Khaleb and Xinjifu, Tibet, which in two places exceeds 6080 m *20,000 ft*.

The highest road in the world is in Khardungla pass at an altitude of 5682 m *18,640 ft*. This is one of the three passes of the Leh–Manali road completed in 1976 by the Border Roads Organization, New Delhi, India; motor vehicles have been able to use it from 1988.

Europe The highest motor road is the Pico de Veleta in the Sierra Nevada, southern Spain. The shadeless climb of 36 km *22.4 miles* brings the motorist to

Guess What?

Q. Where is the world's widest railway gauge?
A. See Page 123

3469 m *11,384 ft* above sea level and became, on completion of a road on its southern side in 1974, arguably Europe's highest 'pass'.

Great Britain The highest unclassified road in the United Kingdom is the A6293 tarmaced private extension at Great Dun Fell, Cumbria (847 m *2780 ft*), leading to a Ministry of Defence and Air Traffic Control installation. A permit is required to use it.

The highest classified road in Britain is the A93 road over the Grampians through Cairnwell, a pass between Blairgowrie, Tayside and Braemar, Grampian, which reaches a height of 670 m *2199 ft*. An estate track exists to the summit of Ben a'Bhuird 1176 m *3860 ft* in Grampian.

Widest road The widest road in the world is the Monumental Axis, running for 2.4 km *1½ miles* from the Municipal Plaza to the Plaza of the Three Powers in Brasilia, the capital of Brazil. The dual six-lane boulevard was opened in April 1960 and is 250 m *820.2 ft* wide.

The San Francisco–Oakland Bay Bridge Toll Plaza has 23 lanes (17 westbound) serving the bridge in Oakland, California, USA.

The only instance of 17 carriageway lanes side by side in Britain occurs on the M61 at Linnyshaw Moss, Worsley, Greater Manchester.

Traffic volume The most heavily travelled stretch of road is Interstate 405 (San Diego Freeway) in Orange County, California, USA, which has a peak-hour volume of 25,500 vehicles. This volume occurs on a 0.9 mile stretch between Garden Grove Freeway and Seal Beach Boulevard.

The longest ford in any classified road in England is in Violet's Lane, north of Furneux Pelham, Herts, measuring 903 m *987½ yd* in length.

Streets *Longest* The longest designated street in the world is Yonge Street, running north and west from Toronto, Canada. The first stretch, completed on 16 Feb 1796, ran 55 km *34 miles*. Its official length, now extended to Rainy River on the Ontario–Minnesota border, is 1896.3 km *1178.3 miles*.

Narrowest The world's narrowest street is in the village of Ripatransone in the Marche region of Italy. It is called Vicolo della Virilita ('Virility Alley') and is 43 cm *16.9 in* wide.

Shortest The title of 'The Shortest Street in the World' is claimed by the town of Bacup in Lancashire, where Elgin Street, situated by the old market ground, measures just 17 ft *5.2 m*.

Steepest The steepest street in the world is Baldwin Street, Dunedin, New Zealand, which has a maximum gradient of 1 in 1.266.

Britain's steepest motorable road is the unclassified Chimney Bank at Rosedale Abbey, N Yorks which is signposted '1 in 3'. The county surveyor states it is 'not quite' a 33 per cent gradient. Unclassified road No. 149 at Ffordd Penllech, Harlech which is narrow and twisting, is at its steepest gradient 1 in 2.91.

Milestone Britain's oldest milestone *in situ* is a Roman stone dating from AD 150 on the Stanegate, at Chesterholme, near Bardon Mill, Northumberland.

Largest squares Tiananmen 'Gate of Heavenly Peace' Square in Beijing, described as the navel of China, covers 39.6 ha *98 acres*.

Great Britain The largest in Great Britain is the 2.82 ha *6.99 acre* Ladbroke Square (open to residents only), London, constructed in 1842–5, while Lincoln's Inn Fields covers 2.76 ha *6.84 acres*.

Railways

Trains

Earliest rail services Wagons running on wooden rails were used for mining as early as 1550 at Leberthal, Alsace, and in Britain for conveying coal from Strelley to Wollaton near Nottingham from 1604–15 and at Broseley Colliery, Shrops in October 1605.

Richard Trevithick built his first steam locomotive for the 914 mm *3 ft* gauge iron plateway at Coalbrookdale, Shrops in 1803, but there is no evidence that it ran. His second locomotive drew wagons in which men rode on a demonstration run at Penydarren, Mid Glamorgan on 22 Feb 1804, but it broke the plate rails.

The first permanent public railway to use steam traction from its opening, on 27 Sep 1825, was the Stockton & Darlington from Shildon to Stockton via Darlington, in Cleveland. The 7-tonne *Locomotion* could pull 48 tonnes at a speed of 24 km/h *15 mph*. It was designed and at times driven by George Stephenson (1781–1848).

The first regular steam passenger service was inaugurated over a one-mile section (between Bogshole Farm and South Street in Whitstable, Kent) on the 10.05 km *6¼ mile* Canterbury & Whitstable Railway on 3 May 1830, hauled by the engine *Invicta*.

Speeding

The highest speed attained by a railed vehicle is 9851 km/h *6121 mph*, or Mach 8, by an unmanned rocket sled over the 15.2 km *9½ mile* long rail track at White Sands Missile Range, New Mexico, USA on 5 Oct 1982.

The highest speed recorded on any national rail system is 515.3 km/h *320.2 mph* by the French SNCF high-speed train TGV (Train à Grande Vitesse) Atlantique between Courtalain and Tours on 18 May 1990. The TGV Sud-Est was brought into service on 27 Sep 1981. TGV Atlantique and Nord services now run at up to 300 km/h *186 mph*. The fastest point to point schedule is between Paris and St Pierre des

Corps, near Tours. The 232 km *144 miles* are covered in 55 minutes—an average of 253 km/h *157 mph*. The Eurostar service from London to Paris also runs at 300 km/h *186 mph*, on the French side of the Channel. New Series 500 trains for Japan's JR West rail system are likewise designed to run at 300 km/h *186 mph* in regular service.

The highest speed ever ratified for a steam locomotive was 201 km/h *125 mph* over 402 m *440 yd* by the LNER 4-6-2 No. 4468 *Mallard* (later numbered 60022), which hauled seven coaches weighing 243 tonnes gross down Stoke Bank, near Essendine, between Grantham, Lincs, and Peterborough, Cambs, on 3 Jul 1938. Driver Joseph Duddington was at the controls with Fireman Thomas Bray. The engine suffered damage to the middle big-end bearing.

Great Britain British Rail inaugurated their HST (High Speed Train) daily services between London–Bristol and South Wales on 4 Oct 1976. The electric British Rail APT-P (Advanced Passenger Train-Prototype) attained 261 km/h *162 mph* between Glasgow and Carlisle on its first revenue-earning run on 7 Dec 1981. It covered the 644 km *400 miles* from Glasgow to London in 4¼ hours, but was subsequently withdrawn from service because of technical problems.

The fastest trains in regular service run on the East Coast mainline between London King's Cross and Edinburgh. *The Scottish Pullman* is scheduled to cover the 633.2 km *393.5 miles* between the English and Scottish capitals in 245 minutes, with two stops, representing a start-to-stop average speed of 155.1 km/h *96.4 mph*. The same train covers the 302.8 km *188.2 miles* between London and York in 106 minutes, representing a start-to-stop average speed of 171.4 km/h *106.5 mph*.

Most powerful locomotives The world's most powerful steam locomotive, measured by tractive effort, was No. 700, a triple-articulated or triplex six-cylinder 2-8-8-8-4 engine built by the Baldwin Locomotive Works in 1916 for the Virginian Railway, USA. It had a tractive force of 75,434 kg *166,300 lb* when working compound and 90,520 kg *199,560 lb* when working simple.

The heaviest train ever hauled by a single engine is believed to be one of 15,545 tonnes made up of 250 freight cars stretching 2.5 km *1.6 miles* by the *Matt H. Shay* (No. 5014), a 2-8-8-8-2 engine, which ran on the Erie Railroad from May 1914 until 1929.

On 19 Jun 1990 a single locomotive hauled a 5226-tonne train with 50 wagons carrying limestone from Merehead Quarry, Somerset to Acton, Greater London—the heaviest on record in Britain (⇨ Freight trains).

Largest steam locomotive The largest operating steam locomotive is the Union Pacific RR *Challenger* type 4-6-6-4 No. 3985, built by the American Locomotive Co. in 1943. In working order, with tender, it weighs 485 tonnes. It is used on enthusiasts' specials in the USA.

Greatest load The world's strongest rail carrier, with a capacity of 807 tonnes, is the 336-tonne 36-axle 'Schnabel'. It is 92 m *301 ft 10 in* long and was

Guess What?

Q. How far did the model steam locomotive 'Peggy' travel in 24 hours?

A. See Page 125

built for a US railway by Krupp, Germany in March 1981.

The heaviest load carried in Britain was a boiler drum weighing 279 tonnes and 37.1 m *122 ft* long which was carried from Immingham Dock to Killingholme, Humberside in September 1968.

Freight trains The world's longest and heaviest freight train on record, with the largest number of wagons recorded, made a run on the 1065 mm *3 ft 6 in* gauge Sishen–Saldanha railway in South Africa on 26–27 Aug 1989. The train consisted of 660 wagons each loaded to 105 tons gross, a tank car and a caboose, moved by nine 50 kV electric and seven diesel-electric locomotives distributed along the train. The train was 7.3 km *4½ miles* long and weighed 69,393 tons excluding locomotives. It travelled a distance of 861 km *535 miles* in 22 hr 40 min.

Britain's heaviest freight train runs from Merehead Quarry, Somerset to Acton, Greater London, usually with 5100 tonnes of limestone in 50 wagons. The train is hauled by a single 'Class 59' Co-Co diesel-electric locomotive (⇨ Most powerful locomotives above).

Never-Ending

Longest passenger train The longest passenger train measured 1732.73 m *1895 yd*. Its 70 coaches were pulled by one electric locomotive, and the total weight was 2786 tonnes. This train of the National Belgian Railway Company took 1 hr 11 min 5 sec to complete the 62 km *38½ mile* journey from Ghent to Ostend on 27 Apr 1991.

The longest regular freight train journey in Britain is the china clay train from Burngullow, Cornwall to Irvine, Strathclyde covering a round trip of 1834 km *1140 miles*. It runs three times a week and is hauled by the same pair of diesel locomotives throughout.

Longest non-stop run The longest journey in Britain without any scheduled stop is the *Newcastle Pullman*, which covers the 374.1 km *232.5 miles* between Darlington and London in 2 hr 22 min.

Tracks

Longest tracks The world's longest run without changing trains is one of 9438 km *5864½ miles* on the Trans-Siberian line in Russia, from Moscow to Nakhodka on the Sea of Japan. There are 97 stops on the journey, which is scheduled to take 8 days 4 hr 25 min.

The longest cross-country railway in the world is the 3145 km *1954 mile* Baikal–Amur Mainline (BAM), begun in 1938, restarted in 1974 and put into service on 27 Oct 1984. It runs from Ust-Kut, Eastern Siberia to Komsomolsk on the Amur River in Russia.

Spike driving In the World Championship Professional Spike Driving Competition held at the Golden Spike National Historic Site in Utah, USA, Dale C. Jones, 49, of Lehi, Utah, USA drove six 17.8 cm *7 in* railroad spikes in a time of 26.4 sec on 11 Aug 1984. He incurred no penalty points under the official rules.

40 years ago the railway speed record was 330.9 km/h 205.6 mph, achieved in France. In 1955 the French still hold the record, but with 515.3 km/h 320.2 mph.

The heaviest load ever moved on rails is the 10,860-tonne Church of the Virgin Mary (built in 1548 in Most, now Czech Republic), in October–November 1975, because it was in the way of coal workings. It was moved 730 m 800 yd at 0.002 km/h 0.0013 mph over four weeks, at a cost of £9 million.

■ The longest railway in the world is the Trans-Siberian railway. This view shows typical scenery as one of the trains makes its way across Russia. (Photo: Gamma/Le Figaro Magazine)

Steep

The world's steepest railway is the Katoomba Scenic Railway in the Blue Mountains of NSW, Australia. It is 310m *1020ft* long with a gradient of 1 in 0.82. A 220hp electric winding machine hauls the car by twin steel cables 22mm diameter. The ride takes about 1min 40sec and carries around 420,000 passengers a year.

The lowest in Europe is the Channel Tunnel, where the rails are 127m *417ft* below mean sea level.

In Britain, the Severn Tunnel descends to 43.8m *144ft* below sea level.

Busiest system The railway carrying the largest number of passengers is the East Japan Railway Co., which in 1993 carried 16,700,000 daily, providing it with a revenue of \$19.5billion.

Greatest length of railway The country with the greatest length of railway is the United States with 271,921km *168,964miles* of track.

Train spotting Bill Curtis of Clacton-on-Sea, Essex is acknowledged as the world champion train spotter—or 'gricer' (after Richard Grice, the first champion, who held the title from 1896 to 1931). His totals include some 60,000 locomotives, 11,200 electric units and 8300 diesel units, clocked up over a period of 40 years in a number of different countries.

Longest straight The Australian National Railways Trans-Australian line over the Nullarbor Plain, from Mile 496 between Nurina and Loongana, Western Australia to Mile 793 between Ooldea and Watson, South Australia, is 478km *297miles* dead straight, although not level.

The longest straight in Britain is the 29km *18miles* between Barlby Junction and Brough, N Yorks on the 'down' line from Selby to Kingston-upon-Hull, Humberside.

Widest and narrowest gauge The widest in standard use is 1.676m *5ft 6in*, as used in Spain, Portugal, India, Pakistan, Bangladesh, Sri Lanka, Argentina and Chile.

The narrowest gauge on which public services are operated is 260mm *10¼in* on the Wells Harbour (1.12km *0.7mile*) and the Wells Walsingham Railways (6.5km *4miles*) in Norfolk.

Steepest gradient The world's steepest gradient worked by adhesion is 1 in 11, between Chedde and Servoz on the metre-gauge SNCF Chamonix line, France.

The steepest sustained adhesion-worked gradient on a main line in the United Kingdom is the 3.2km *2mile* Lickey incline of 1 in 37.7, just south-west of Birmingham, W Mids.

Highest line At 4818m *15,806ft* above sea level, the standard gauge (1435

mm *4ft 8½in*) track on the Morococha branch of the Peruvian State Railways at La Cima is the highest in the world.

The highest railway in Britain is the Snowdon Mountain Railway, which rises from Llanberis, Gwynedd to 1064m *3493ft* above sea-level, just below the summit of Snowdon (*Yr Wyddfa*). It has a gauge of 800mm *2ft 7½in*.

Lowest line The world's lowest line is in the Seikan Tunnel which crosses the Tsugaro Strait between Honshu and Hokkaido, Japan. It reaches a depth of 240m *786ft* below sea level. The tunnel was opened on 13 Mar 1988 and is 53.8km *33½miles* long.

Trains stop in the middle of the Seikan Tunnel for two minutes so that passengers can take pictures through the windows of panels on the walls of the tunnel.

Stations

Largest station The world's largest station is Grand Central Terminal, Park Avenue and 42nd Street, New York City, USA, built from 1903–13. It covers 19ha *48 acres* on two levels with 41 tracks on the upper level and 26 on the lower. On average more than 550 trains and 200,000 commuters use it every day.

The largest railway station in Britain is Waterloo, London (12.3ha *30½acres*). Following completion of five new platforms in 1993 for international trains

■ Grand Central Terminal is indeed an appropriate name for the world's largest railway station, in New York City. (Photo: Image Select)

Underground Railways, Rail Travel ▶▶ ▶▶

using the Channel Tunnel, its 24 platforms have a total length of 6194m *20,321ft or 3.85miles.*

Oldest station Liverpool Road Station, Manchester is the world's oldest station. It was first used on 15 Sep 1830 and was finally closed on 30 Sep 1975. Part of the original station is now a museum.

Highest station Condor station in Bolivia at 4786m *15,705ft* on the metre gauge Rio Mulato to Potosi line is the highest in the world.

> **The world's largest waiting rooms are the four in Beijing Station, Chang'an Boulevard, Beijing, China, opened in September 1959, with a total standing capacity of 14,000.**

The highest passenger station on the British main-line rail network is Corrour, Highland at an altitude of 410.5m *1347ft* above sea level.

Platforms The longest railway platform in the world is the Kharagpur platform, West Bengal, India, which measures 833m *2733ft* in length.

> **The largest goods yard is Bailey Yard at North Platte, Nebraska, USA, which covers 2850 acres *1153ha* and has 418km *260miles* of track. It handles an average of 108 trains and some 8500 wagons every day.**

The State Street Center subway platform on 'The Loop' in Chicago, Illinois, USA measures 1066m *3500 ft* in length.

The longest in Britain is the 602.7m *1977ft 4in* long platform at Gloucester.

Underground Railways

Most extensive systems The most extensive underground or rapid transit railway system in the world is the London Underground, with 408km *254miles* of route, of which 139km *86miles* is bored tunnel and 32km *20miles* is 'cut and cover'. The whole system is operated by a staff of 17,000 serving 270 stations. The 3955 cars form a fleet of 547 trains, with passengers making a total of 735 million journeys in 1993–4.

The underground system with the most stations in the world is the Metropolitan Transportation Authority/New York City Transportation Authority subway, USA (first section opened on 27 Oct 1904). There are 469 stations in a network which covers 383km *238miles.* It serves an estimated 7.1 million passengers per day.

Underground tour The record time for doing a tour of the London Underground taking in all of the 270 stations is 18hr 18min 9sec by Robert Robinson of Little Sandhurst, Surrey and Tom McLaughlin of Finchampstead, Berks on 4 Oct 1994.

Busiest system The world's busiest ever underground system has been the Greater Moscow Metro (opened 1935) in Russia. At its peak there were 3.3 billion passenger journeys in a year, although the figure has now declined to 2.6 billion. It has 3500 railcars and a workforce of 25,000. There are 149 stations (18 of which have more than one name, being transfer stations) and 242km *150miles* of track.

Rail Travel

Calling all stations Alan M. Witton of Chorlton, Manchester visited every open British Rail station (2362) in a continuous tour for charity of 26,703km *16,593miles* in 452hr 16min from 13 Jul–28 Aug 1980.

Colin M. Mulvany and Seth N. Vafiadis of west London visited every open British Rail station (2378) embracing also the Tyne & Wear, Glasgow and London underground systems (333 stations) for charity in 31 days 5hr 8min 58sec. They travelled over 24,989km *15,528miles* to average 61.2km/h *38.1mph* from 4 Jun–5 Jul 1984.

Four points of the compass Antony Davies of Stafford visited the northernmost, southernmost, westernmost and easternmost stations in Great Britain in a time of 37hr 34min from 14–15 Apr 1993. These are Thurso, Scotland (north), Lowestoft, Suffolk (east), Penzance, Cornwall (south) and Arisaig, Scotland (west).

Most miles in 7 days Andrew Kingsmell and Sean Andrews of Bromley, Kent together with Graham Bardouleau of Crawley, W Sussex travelled 21,090km *13,105miles* on the French national railway system in 6 days 22hr 38min from 28 Nov–5 Dec 1992.

> **Longest journey**
> **In the course of some 73 years commuting by British Rail from Kent to London, Ralph Ransome of Birchington travelled an equivalent of an estimated 39 times round the world. He retired at the age of 93 on 5 Feb 1986.**

Most miles in 24 hours The greatest distance travelled in Britiain in 24 hours (without duplicating any part of the journey) is 2842.5km *1766¼ miles* by Norma and Jonathan Carter, 15, from 3–4 Sep 1992.

Longest issued railway ticket A rail ticket measuring 34m *111ft 10½in* was issued to Ronald, Norma and Jonathan Carter for a series of journeys throughout England between 15–23 Feb 1992.

Suggestion boxes The most prolific example on record of the use of any suggestion box scheme is that of John Drayton (1907–87) of Newport, Gwent, who plied the British rail system with a total of 31,400 suggestions from 1924 to August 1987. More than one in seven were adopted and 100 were accepted by London Transport.

Most countries travelled through in 24 hours The record number of countries travelled through entirely by train in 24 hours is eleven, by Alison Bailey, Ian Bailey, John English and David Kellie on 1–2 May 1993. Their journey started in Hungary and continued through Slovakia, the Czech Republic, Austria, Germany, back into Austria, Liechtenstein, Switzerland, France, Luxembourg, Belgium and the Netherlands, where they arrived 22hr 10min after setting off.

Handpumped railcars A five-man team (one pusher, four pumpers) achieved a speed of 33.12km/h *20.58mph* in moving a handpumped railcar over a 300m *984ft* course at Rolvenden, Kent on 21 Aug 1989, recording a time of 32.61sec.

Model railway A standard 'Life-Like' BL2 HO scale electric train pulled six eight-wheel coaches for 1207½hr from 4 Aug–23 Sep 1990 covering a distance of 1463.65km *909½ miles*. The event was organized by Ike Cottingham

Guess What?
Q. Which city has the longest underground railway tunnel?
A. See Page 99

■ **Another day and another station on the New York subway. It has a record 469 altogether, 277 of which are actually underground.**
(Photo: Gamma/
C. Edinger/Liaison)

and Mark Hamrick of Mainline Modelers of Akron, Ohio, USA.

The greatest distance covered by a model steam locomotive in 24 hours is 269.9 km *167.7 miles* by the 18.4 cm *7¼ in* gauge 'Peggy', with ten drivers working in shifts, at Weston Park Railway, Weston Park, Shrops on 17–18 Jun 1994.

The most miniature model railway ever built is one of 1:1400 scale by Bob Henderson of Gravenhurst, Ontario, Canada. The engine measures 5 mm *³/₁₆ in* overall.

Aviation

Earliest Flights

The first controlled and sustained power-driven flight occurred near the Kill Devil Hill, Kitty Hawk, North Carolina, USA at 10:35 a.m. on 17 Dec 1903, when Orville Wright (1871–1948) flew the 9 kW *12-hp* chain-driven *Flyer I* for a distance of 36.5 m *120 ft* at an airspeed of 48 km/h *30 mph*, a ground speed of 10.9 km/h *6.8 mph* and an altitude of 2.5–3.5 m *8–12 ft* for about 12 seconds, watched by his brother Wilbur (1867–1912), four men and a boy. The *Flyer I* is now exhibited in the National Air and Space Museum at the Smithsonian Institution, Washington, DC, USA.

Cross-Channel The earliest crossing of the English channel was made on 25 Jul 1909 when Louis Blériot (1872–1936) of France flew his Blériot XI monoplane, powered by a 17.25 kW *23-hp* Anzani engine, 41.8 km *26 miles* from Les Barraques, France to Northfall Meadow, near Dover Castle, Kent in 36½ minutes, after taking off at 4:41 a.m.

Jet-engined flight Proposals for jet propulsion date back to Capt. Marconnet of France in 1909.

The earliest test run was that of British Power Jets' experimental WU1 (Whittle Unit No. 1) at Rugby on 12 Apr 1937, invented by Flying Officer (later Air Commodore Sir) Frank Whittle (b. 1 Jun 1907), who had applied for a patent on jet propulsion in 1930.

The first flight by an aeroplane powered by a turbojet engine was made by the Heinkel He 178, piloted by Flugkapitän Erich Warsitz, at Marienehe, Germany on 27 Aug 1939. It was powered by a Heinkel He S3b engine weighing 378 kg *834 lb* (as installed with long tailpipe) designed by Dr Hans Pabst von Ohain.

Transatlantic flight The first crossing of the North Atlantic by air was made by Lt Cdr (later Rear Admiral) Albert Cushion Read (1887–1967) and his crew (Stone, Hinton, Rodd, Rhoads and Breese) in the 84-knot *155 km/h* US Navy/Curtiss flying-boat NC-4 from Trepassey Harbor, Newfoundland, Canada via the Azores, to Lisbon, Portugal from 16–27 May 1919. The whole flight of 7591 km *4717 miles*, originating from Rockaway Air Station, Long Island, New York, USA on 8 May, required 53 hr 58 min, terminating at Plymouth, Devon on 31 May.

Non-stop The first non-stop transatlantic flight was achieved 18 days later. The pilot, Capt. John Williams Alcock (1892–1919), and navigator, Lt Arthur

Guess What? Q. How did John Brown cross the Atlantic in 1799? A. See Page 112

Whitton Brown (1886–1948) left Lester's Field, St John's, Newfoundland, Canada at 4:13 p.m. GMT on 14 Jun 1919, and landed at Derrygimla bog near Clifden, Co. Galway, Republic of Ireland at 8:40 a.m. GMT, 15 June, having covered 3154 km *1960 miles* in their Vickers Vimy, powered by two 270 kW *360-hp* Rolls-Royce Eagle VIII engines.

Solo The first solo transatlantic flight was achieved by Capt. (later Brig. Gen.) Charles Augustus Lindbergh (1902–74) who took off in his 165 kW *220-hp* Ryan monoplane *Spirit of St Louis* at 12:52 p.m. GMT on 20 May 1927 from Roosevelt Field, Long Island, New York, USA. He landed at 10:21 p.m. GMT on 21 May 1927 at Le Bourget Airfield, Paris, France. His flight of 5810 km *3610 miles* lasted 33 hr 29½ min, so winning a prize of $25,000. The aircraft is in the Smithsonian Institution, Washington, DC, USA.

Transpacific flight The first non-stop flight was by Major Clyde Pangborn and Hugh Herndon in the Bellanca cabin monoplane *Miss Veedol*. They took off from Sabishiro Beach, Japan and covered the distance of 7335 km *4558 miles* to Wenatchee, Washington State, USA in 41 hr 13 min from 3–5 Oct 1931.

Supersonic flight The first was achieved on 14 Oct 1947 by Capt. (later Brig. Gen.) Charles ('Chuck') Elwood Yeager (b. 13 Feb 1923), over Lake Muroc, California, USA in a Bell XS-1 rocket aircraft at Mach 1.015 (1078 km/h *670 mph*) at an altitude of 12,800 m *42,000 ft*. The XS-1 is in the Smithsonian Institution, Washington, DC, USA.

The former Soviet Tupolev Tu-144, first flown on 31 Dec 1968 and therefore the first supersonic airliner to fly, entered service initially carrying cargo only.

Circumnavigational flights Strict circumnavigation of the globe requires the aircraft to pass through two antipodal points, thus covering a minimum distance of 40,007.86 km *24,859.73 miles*.

Earliest The earliest such flight, of 42,398 km *26,345 miles*, was by two US Army Douglas DWC seaplanes in 57 'hops' between 6 April and 28 Sep 1924, beginning and ending at Seattle, Washington State, USA. The *Chicago* was

Fast

The fastest time to travel the 344 km *214 miles* from central Paris, France, to central London (BBC TV centre) is 38 min 58 sec by David Boyce of Stewart Wrightson (Aviation) Ltd on 24 Sep 1983. He travelled by motorcycle and helicopter to Le Bourget; Hawker Hunter jet (piloted by the late Michael Carlton) to Biggin Hill, Kent; and by helicopter to the TV centre car park.

Speed Scale

The use of the Mach scale for aircraft speeds was introduced by Prof. Ackeret of Zürich, Switzerland. The Mach number is the ratio of the velocity of a moving body to the local velocity of sound. This ratio was first employed by Dr Ernst Mach (1838–1916) of Vienna, Austria in 1887. Thus Mach 1.0 equals 1224.67 km/h *760.98 mph* at sea level at 15°C *59°F*, and is assumed, for convenience, to fall to a constant 1061.81 km/h *659.78 mph* in the stratosphere, i.e. above 11,000 m *36,089 ft*.

piloted by Lt Lowell H. Smith and Lt Leslie P. Arnold, and the *New Orleans* by Lt Erik H. Nelson and Lt John Harding. Their flying time was 371 hr 11 min.

Fastest The fastest flight under the FAI (Fédération Aéronautique Internationale) rules, which permit flights that exceed the length of the Tropic of Cancer or Capricorn (36,787.6 km *22,858.8 miles*), was that of 32 hr 49 min 3 sec by an Air France Concorde (Capts. Claude Delorme and Jean Boyé) westabout from Lisbon, Portugal via Santo Domingo, Acapulco, Honolulu, Guam, Bangkok and Bahrain on 12–13 Oct 1992. Flight AF1492 was undertaken to celebrate the 500th anniversary of Christopher Columbus' discovery of the New World.

First without refuelling Richard G. 'Dick' Rutan and Jeana Yeager, in their specially constructed aircraft *Voyager*, designed by Dick's brother Burt Rutan, flew westabout from Edwards Air Force Base, California, USA between 14–23 Dec 1986. Their flight took 9 days 3 min 44 sec and they covered a distance of 40,212 km *24,987 miles* averaging 186.11 km/h *115.65 mph*. The aircraft, with a wing span of 33.77 m *110 ft 10 in*, was capable of carrying 5636 litres *1240 gal* of fuel weighing 4052 kg *8934 lb*.

First circum-polar Capt. Elgen M. Long, 44, achieved the first circum-polar flight in a twin-engined Piper PA-31 Navajo from 5 Nov–3 Dec 1971. He covered 62,597 km *38,896 miles* in 215 flying hours.

Guess What? Q. How long did Robert Timm and John Cook spend in the air without landing? A. See Page 128

Oldest Fred Lasby (b. 28 May 1912) completed a solo round the world flight at the age of 82 in his single-engined Piper Comanche. Leaving Fort Myers, Florida, USA on 30 Jun 1994 he flew 37,366 km *23,218 miles* westabout with 21 stops, arriving back at Fort Myers on 20 Aug 1994.

Aircraft

Largest wing span The aircraft with the largest wing span ever constructed is the $40-million Hughes H4 Hercules flying-boat, usually dubbed the *Spruce Goose*. The eight-engined 193-tonne aircraft has a wing span of 97.51 m *319 ft 11 in* and a length of 66.64 m *218 ft 8 in*. It was raised 70 ft *21.3 m* into the air in a test run of 1000 yd *914 m*, piloted by Howard Hughes (1905–76), off Long Beach Harbor, California, USA on 2 Nov 1947, but never flew again.

Among current aircraft, the Ukrainian Antonov An-124 has a wing span of 73.3 m *240 ft 5¾ in*, and the Boeing 747-400 one of 64.92 m *213 ft*.

A modified six-engine version of the An-124, known as An-225 which was built to carry the former Soviet space shuttle *Buran*, has a wing span of 88.4 m *290 ft* (↔ Heaviest below).

The $34-million Piasecki Heli-Stat, comprising a framework of light-alloy and composite materials, to mount four Sikorsky SH-34J helicopters and the envelope of a Goodyear ZPG-2 patrol airship, was exhibited on 26 Jan 1984 at Lakehurst, New Jersey, USA. Designed for US Forest Service use and designated Model 94-37J Logger, it had an overall length of 104.55 m *343 ft* and was intended to carry a payload of 21.4 tons. It crashed on 1 Jul 1986.

Wing walking Roy Castle (1932–94), host of the BBC TV *Record Breakers* programme from 1972 to 1993, flew on the wing of a Boeing Stearman biplane for 3 hr 23 min on 2 Aug 1990, taking off from Gatwick, W Sussex and landing at Le Bourget, near Paris, France.

Pull

David Huxley single-handedly pulled a British Airways Concorde weighing 105 tonnes a distance of 143 m *469 ft 2 in* across the tarmac at Sydney Airport, Australia on 20 Oct 1994.

A team of 59 Qantas personnel pulled a Boeing 747 weighing 205 tonnes a distance of 100 metres in 62.1 sec at Perth airport, Australia on 22 Oct 1988.

Heaviest aircraft The aircraft with the highest standard maximum take-off weight is the Antonov An-225 *Mriya* (Dream) of 600 tonnes *1,322,750 lb*. Such an aircraft lifted a payload of 156,300 kg *344,579 lb* to a height of 12,410 m *40,715 ft* on 22 Mar 1989. The flight was made by Capt. Aleksandr Galunenko with his crew of seven pilots and covered a distance of 2100 km *1305 miles* in 3 hr 47 min (⇨ Most capacious).

Smallest aircraft The smallest biplane ever flown was *Bumble Bee Two*, built by Robert H. Starr of Tempe, Arizona, USA and capable of carrying one person. It was 2.64 m *8 ft 10 in* long, with a wing span of 1.68 m *5 ft 6 in*, and weighed 179.6 kg *396 lb* empty. The highest speed attained was 306 km/h *190 mph*. On 8 May 1988 after flying to a height of 120 m *400 ft* it crashed, and was totally destroyed.

The smallest monoplane ever flown is the *Baby Bird*, designed and built by Donald R. Stits. It is 3.35 m *11 ft* long, with a wing span of 1.91 m *6 ft 3 in* and weighs 114.3 kg *252 lb* empty. It is powered by a 41.25 kW *55-hp* two-cylinder Hirth engine, giving a top speed of 177 km/h *110 mph*. It was first flown by Harold Nemer on 4 Aug 1984 at Camarillo, California, USA.

The smallest twin-engined aircraft is believed to be the Colomban MGI5 Cricri (first flown 19 Jul 1973), which has a wing span of 4.9 m *16 ft* and measures 3.91 m *12 ft 10 in* long overall. It is powered by two 11.25 kW *15 hp* JPX PUL engines.

Bombers *Heaviest* The former Soviet four-jet Tupolev Tu-160 bomber has a maximum take-off weight of 275 tonnes *606,270 lb*.

The ten-engined Convair B-36J, weighing 185 tonnes, had the greatest wing span at 70.1 m *230 ft*, but it is no longer in service. Its top speed was 700 km/h *435 mph*.

Fastest The world's fastest operational bombers include the French Dassault Mirage IV, which can fly at Mach 2.2 (2333 km/h *1450 mph*) at 11,000 m *36,000 ft*.

The American variable-geometry or 'swing-wing' General Dynamics FB-111A has a maximum speed of Mach 2.5, and the former Soviet swing-wing Tupolev Tu-22M, known to NATO as 'Backfire', has an estimated over-target speed of Mach 2.0 but could be as fast as Mach 2.5.

Largest airliner The highest capacity jet airliner is the Boeing 747-400, which entered service with Northwest Airlines on 26 Jan 1989. It has a wing span of 64.4 m *211 ft 5 in*, a range exceeding 12,500 km *8000 miles* and can carry up to 567 passengers. The original Boeing 747 'Jumbo Jet' was first flown on 9 Feb 1969. It can carry from 385 to more than 560 passengers and has a maximum speed of 969 km/h *602 mph*. Its wing span is 59.6 m *195 ft 8 in* and its length 70.7 m *231 ft 10 in*. It entered service on 22 Jan 1970.

The largest-span British aircraft was the Bristol Type 167 Brabazon, which had a maximum take-off weight of 131.4 tonnes, a wing span of 70.10 m *230 ft* and a length of 53.94 m *177 ft*. This eight-engined transport first flew on 4 Sep 1949 but did not enter series production. The largest production aircraft was the four-jet Super VC10, the last design constructed by Vickers, which weighed 149.5 tons and had a wing span of 44.55 m *146 ft 10 in*.

Fastest airliner The Tupolev Tu-144, first flown on 31 Dec 1968, was reported to have reached Mach 2.4 (2587 km/h *1600 mph*), but normal cruising speed was Mach 2.2. It flew at Mach 1 for the first time on 5 Jun 1969 and exceeded Mach 2 on 26 May 1970, the first commercial transport to do so. Scheduled services began on 26 Dec 1975, flying freight and mail.

The BAC/Aérospatiale Concorde, first flown on 2 Mar 1969, cruises at up to Mach 2.2 (2333 km/h *1450 mph*) and became the first supersonic airliner used on passenger services on 21 Jan 1976. The New York–London record is 2 hr 54 min 30 sec, set on 14 Apr 1990.

Fastest time to refuel The record time for refuelling an aeroplane (with 388.8 litres *85.5 gal* of 100 octane avgas) is 3 min 42 sec, for a 1975 Cessna 310 (N92HH), by the Sky Harbor Air Service line crew. It had landed at Cheyenne airport, Wyoming, USA on 5 Jul 1992 during an around the world air race.

Most capacious airliner The Airbus Super Transporter A300-600ST *Beluga* has a main cargo compartment volume of 1400 m³ *49,441 ft³* and a maximum take-off weight of 150 tonnes. Its wing span is 44.84 m *147 ft 1 in*, its overall length 56.16 m *184 ft 3 in* and the usable length of its cargo compartment 37.70 m *123 ft 8 in*. Four identical aircraft are to built altogether.

The Ukrainian Antonov An-124 *Ruslan* has a cargo hold with a usable volume of 1014 m³ *35,800 ft³* and a maximum take-off weight of 405 tonnes, making it the most capacious production airliner. A special-purpose heavy-lift version of the An-124, known as An-225 *Mriya* (Dream), has been developed with a stretched fuselage providing as much as 1190 m³ *42,000 ft³* usable volume. Its cargo compartment includes an unobstructed 43 m *141 ft* hold length, with maximum width and height of 6.4 m *21 ft* and 4.4 m *14 ft 5 in* respectively.

Largest propeller The largest aeroplane propeller ever used was the 6.9 m *22 ft 7½ in* diameter Garuda propeller, fitted to the Linke-Hofmann R II built in Breslau, Germany (now Wroclaw, Poland) which flew in 1919. It was driven by four 195 kW *260-hp* Mercedes engines and turned at only 545 rpm.

Most flights by propeller-driven airliner General Dynamics (formerly Convair) reported in March 1994 that some of its CV-580 turboprop airliners had logged over 150,000 flights, many typically averaging no more than 20 minutes in short-haul operations.

Most flights by a jet airliner A survey of ageing airliners or so-called 'geriatric jets' published in April 1994 in the weekly *Flight International* magazine reported a McDonnell Douglas DC-9 still in service which had logged 95,939 flights in under 28 years.

The most hours recorded by a jet airliner still in service is the 94,804 hours in under 25 years reported for a Boeing 747 in the same issue of *Flight International* (⇨ above).

Oldest jet airliner According to the London-based aviation information and consultancy company Airclaims, a first-generation airliner built in January 1959—a Douglas DC-8—had been still in service in May 1994 as a flying operating theatre.

Scheduled flights *Longest* The longest non-stop scheduled flight is currently one of 12,825 km *7969 miles*, by joint operation between South African Airways and American Airlines for their flight from New York, USA to Johannesburg, South Africa. In terms of time taken, the longest is 15 hr 30 min, for Los Angeles, USA to Hong Kong with Delta Air Lines.

The longest non-stop flight by a commercial airliner was one of 18,545 km *10,008 nautical miles* from Auckland, New Zealand to Le Bourget, Paris, France in 21 hr 46 min on 17–18 Jun 1993 by the Airbus

Packed

Passenger load The greatest passenger load carried by any single commercial airliner was 1088 during *Operation Solomon* which began on 24 May 1991 when Ethiopian Jews were evacuated from Addis Ababa to Israel on a Boeing 747 of El Al airlines. The figure included two babies born during the flight.

■ Robert H. Starr sitting in *Bumble Bee Two*, the record-breaking biplane which he designed, built and flew. A fighter pilot in World War II, he had also held the previous record for the smallest biplane with *Bumble Bee One*.
(Photo: R.H. Starr)

In 1955 the heaviest single piece of cargo ever carried by air weighed just over 6 tonnes. Forty years on the record is 124 tonnes (⇨ right).

Q. How did Charlotte Hughes celebrate her 110th birthday?

A. See Page 130

Guess What?

Heavy *flying*

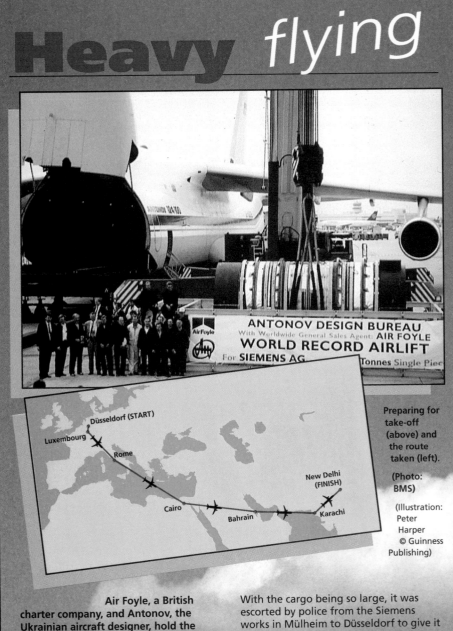

ANTONOV DESIGN BUREAU
With Worldwide General Sales Agents AIR FOYLE
WORLD RECORD AIRLIFT
For **SIEMENS AG**
Tonnes Single Piece

Düsseldorf (START)
Luxembourg
Rome
Cairo
Bahrain
Karachi
New Delhi (FINISH)

Preparing for take-off (above) and the route taken (left).

(Photo: BMS)

(Illustration: Peter Harper © Guinness Publishing)

Air Foyle, a British charter company, and Antonov, the Ukrainian aircraft designer, hold the record for carrying the heaviest single piece of cargo by air, taking a 124-tonne power plant generator from Düsseldorf, Germany to New Delhi, India on 22 Sep 1993. The aircraft used was the Ukrainian An-124 *Ruslan*, which is designed exclusively for heavy duty and outsize cargo. In fact it is the largest commercially available aircraft in the world. So how did this record come about? Air Foyle explained the background:–

'The generator was urgently needed at Dadri Combined Cycle Power Plant, the largest such plant in India, due to a fault in the generator of one of the gas turbines. Siemens, one of the world's leading electrical and electronic engineering companies, was asked to provide the generator, but time was of the essence. A sea voyage would have taken too long and would be followed by a lengthy overland transit into the heart of India.

With the cargo being so large, it was escorted by police from the Siemens works in Mülheim to Düsseldorf to give it free passage. The journey started at 11 p.m., as in some places the cargo took up most of the road. It then took over 10 hours to complete the whole loading operation. Owing to the huge weight carried, five refuelling stops were needed during the flight.

Once in India there were still further problems to be overcome. An alternative route had to be found from that which had been planned as there were numerous bridges which could not support the weight of both the load and the truck.'

Not surprisingly Air Foyle also felt that they had set a world record for technical dificulty! But they are well used to this type of challenge. With Antonov they held the previous record, and also hold the record for the greatest overall cargo consignment in one plane, set in 1991 when they took three transformers and other equipment, weighing a total of 140 tonnes, in the *Ruslan* from Spain to New Caledonia.

Industrie A340-200. It was the return leg of a flight which had started at Le Bourget the previous day.

A Boeing 767-200ER Royal Brunei Airlines flight from Seattle, Washington, USA to Nairobi, Kenya on 8–9 Jun 1990 set a new speed and endurance record for the longest delivery flight by a twin-engined commercial jet. A great-circle distance of 14,890 km *8040 nautical miles* was covered in 18 hr 29 min, consuming 75.4 tonnes of fuel.

Short

The shortest scheduled flight is by Loganair between the Orkney Islands of Westray and Papa Westray which has been flown with Britten-Norman BN-2 Islander twin-engined 10-seat transports since September 1967. Though scheduled for two minutes, in favourable wind conditions it was once accomplished in 58 seconds by Capt. Andrew D. Alsop. The check-in time for the flght is 20 minutes.

Round the world The fastest time for a circumnavigation under FAI regulations using scheduled flights is 44 hr 6 min by David J. Springbett (b. 2 May 1938) of Taplow, Bucks. His route took him from Los Angeles, California, USA eastabout via London, Bahrain, Singapore, Bangkok, Manila, Tokyo and Honolulu from 8–10 Jan 1980 over a course of 37,124 km *23,068 miles*.

Round the world—antipodal points Brother Michael Bartlett of Balham, London, an 'Eccentric Globetrotter', travelled round the world on scheduled flights, taking in exact antipodal points, in a time of 66 hr 38 min from 10–13 Jun 1993. Leaving from London he flew via Tokyo, Japan and Auckland, New Zealand to Palmerston, also in New Zealand, and then by car to Ti Tree Point, on Highway 52. He later changed aircraft at Madrid airport, Spain (the point exactly opposite Ti Tree Point on the other side of the world). His journey took him a total distance of 41,619 km *25,861 miles*.

He also achieved a record time for flying round the world on scheduled flights, but just taking in the airports closest to antipodal points, when he flew via Shanghai, China and Buenos Aires, Argentina in a time of 58 hr 44 min. On this trip he started and finished at Zürich, Switzerland, and travelled a distance of 41,547 km *25,816 miles* between 13–16 Feb 1995.

Longest air ticket A 12 m *39 ft 4½ in* single air ticket was issued to Bruno Leunen of Brussels, Belgium in December 1984 for a 85,623 km *53,203 mile* round trip on 80 airlines with 109 stopovers.

Brother Michael Bartlett of London used a monthly Skypass issued by the Belgian national airline Sabena to fly between London and Brussels 128 times between 18 Oct and 17 Nov 1993. He had the individual tickets stapled together to form a 25.3 m *83 ft* long ticket, and covered a total of 41,771 km *25,956 miles* during the month.

John o' Groats–Land's End The record time for an 'End to End' flight over Great Britain where supersonic overflying is banned is 46 min 44 sec by a McDonnell F-4K Phantom (Wing Cdr John Brady and Flt Lt Mike Pugh) on 24 Feb 1988.

Highest Speed

Official record The airspeed record is 3529.56 km/h *2193.17 mph*, by Capt. Eldon W. Joersz and Major George T. Morgan, Jr, in a Lockheed SR-71A 'Blackbird' near Beale Air Force Base, California, USA over a 25 km *15½ mile* course on 28 Jul 1976.

Air-launched records The fastest fixed-wing aircraft was the US North American Aviation X-15A-2, which flew for the first time (after modification from the X-15A) on 25 Jun 1964, powered by a liquid oxygen and ammonia rocket propulsion system. The landing speed was 389.1 km/h *242 mph*. The highest speed attained was 7274 km/h *4520 mph* (Mach 6.7) when piloted by Major William J. Knight, USAF (b. 1930), on 3 Oct 1967. An earlier version piloted by Joseph A. Walker (1920–66) reached 107,960 m *354,200 ft* over Edwards Air Force Base, California, USA on 22 Aug 1963.

United States NASA Rockwell International space shuttle orbiter *Columbia*, commanded by Capt. John W. Young, USN and piloted by Capt. Robert L. Crippen, USN, was launched from the Kennedy Space Center, Cape Canaveral, Florida, USA on 12 Apr 1981. *Columbia* broke all records in space by a fixed-wing craft, with 26,715 km/h *16,600 mph* at main engine cut-off. After re-entry from 122 km *400,000 ft* she glided home weighing 97 tonnes, and with a landing speed of 347 km/h *216 mph*, on Rogers Dry Lake, California, USA on 14 Apr 1981. The fastest space shuttle landing speed was 407 km/h *253 mph* by STS 3 *Columbia* on 30 Mar 1982.

Under the FAI (Fédération Aéronautique Internationale) regulations for Category P for aerospacecraft, *Endeavour* is holder of the current world record for duration—16 days 15 hr 8 min 47 sec to main gear touchdown. It was launched on its 18th mission, STS 67, with a crew of seven (five men and two women) on 2 Mar 1995.

Fastest jet The USAF Lockheed SR-71, a reconnaissance aircraft, has been the world's fastest jet (⇨ official record, above). First flown in its definitive form on 22 Dec 1964, it was reportedly capable of attaining an altitude of close to 100,000 ft *30,000 m*. It had a wing span of 16.94 m *55 ft 7 in* and a length of 32.73 m *107 ft 5 in* and weighed 77.1 tonnes *170,000 lb* at take-off. Its reported range at Mach 3 was 4800 km *3000 miles* at 24,000 m *79,000 ft*.

Fastest combat jet The fastest combat jet is the former Soviet Mikoyan MiG-25 fighter (NATO code name 'Foxbat'). The single-seat 'Foxbat-A' has a wing span of 13.95 m *45 ft 9 in*, is 23.82 m *78 ft 2 in* long and has an estimated maximum take-off weight of 37.4 tonnes *82,500 lb*. The reconnaissance 'Foxbat-B' has been tracked by radar at about Mach 3.2 (3395 km/h *2110 mph*).

Visiting 15 EU countries by scheduled flights
David Beaumont of Wimbledon, London visited the 15 European Union countries as a passenger on 15 different scheduled flights in a time of 35 hr 18 min on 2–3 May 1995.

Fastest biplane
The fastest was the Italian Fiat CR42B, with a 753 kW *1010 hp* Daimler-Benz DB601A engine, which attained 520 km/h *323 mph* in 1941. Only one was built.

Fastest piston-engined aircraft On 21 Aug 1989, in Las Vegas, Nevada, USA, the *Rare Bear*, a modified Grumman F8F Bearcat piloted by Lyle Shelton, set the FAI approved world record for a 3 km *1⅞ mile* course of 850.24 km/h *528.33 mph*.

Fastest propeller-driven aircraft The fastest propeller-driven aircraft in use is the former Soviet Tu-

Guess What?
Q. How did Lt Cdr Albert Read make history in May 1919?
A. See Page 125

95/142 (NATO code-name *Bear*) with four 14,795 hp *11,033 kW* engines driving eight-blade contra-rotating propellers with a maximum level speed of Mach 0.82 or 925 km/h *575 mph*.

The turboprop-powered Republic XF-84H experimental US fighter which flew on 22 Jul 1955 had a top *design* speed of 1078 km/h *670 mph*, but was abandoned.

Fastest transatlantic flight The flight record is 1 hr 54 min 56.4 sec by Major James V. Sullivan, 37, and Major Noel F. Widdifield, 33, flying a Lockheed SR-71A 'Blackbird' eastwards on 1 Sep 1974. The average speed, reduced by refuelling from a Boeing KC-135 tanker aircraft, for the New York–London stage of 5570.80 km *3461.53 miles* was 2908.3 km/h *1806.96 mph*.

The solo record (Gander, Newfoundland, Canada to Gatwick, W Sussex) is 8 hr 47 min 32 sec, an average speed of 426.7 km/h *265.1 mph*, by Capt. John J.A. Smith in a Rockwell Commander 685 twin-turboprop on 12 Mar 1978.

London-New York The record from central London to downtown New York City, New York, USA—by helicopter and Concorde—is 3 hr 59 min 44 sec and the return 3 hr 40 min 40 sec, set by David J. Springbett and David Boyce on 8–9 Feb 1982.

Most scheduled flights as a passenger in 24 hours Brother Michael Bartlett of London made 42 scheduled passenger flights with Heli Transport of Nice, southern France between Nice, Sophia Antipolis, Monaco and Cannes in 13 hr 33 min on 13 Jun 1990.

Airports

Busiest airports O'Hare International Airport, near Chicago, Illinois, USA, had a total of 66,488,269 passengers and 883,062 aircraft movements in the year 1994. This represents on average a take-off or landing every 36 seconds around the clock.

Heathrow Airport, London, handles more international traffic than any other, with 44,250,000 international passengers in 1994, but is only the fourth busiest including domestic flights (⇨ also Largest airports, below).

The busiest landing area ever has been Bien Hoa Air Base, South Vietnam, which handled 1,019,437 take-offs and landings in 1970.

Heliport The heliport at Morgan City, Louisiana, USA, owned and operated by Petroleum Helicopter, Inc. for energy-related offshore operations into the Gulf of Mexico, has pads for 48 helicopters. The world's largest heliport has been An Khe, South Vietnam, during the Vietnam War, which had an area of 2×3 km *1¼ ×1¾ miles* and could accommodate 434 helicopters.

Largest airports The £2.1 billion King Khalid international airport outside Riyadh, Saudi Arabia covers an area of 225 km² *55,040 acres*. It was opened on 14 Nov 1983.

64 Days
The duration record is 64 days 22 hr 19 min 5 sec, set by Robert Timm and John Cook in the Cessna 172 *Hacienda*. They took off from McCarran Airfield, Las Vegas, Nevada, USA just before 3:53 p.m. local time on 4 Dec 1958 and landed at the same airfield just before 2:12 p.m. on 7 Feb 1959. They covered a distance equivalent to six times round the world, being refuelled without any landings.

The Hajj Terminal at the £2.8 billion King Abdul-Aziz airport near Jeddah, Saudi Arabia is the world's largest roofed structure, covering 1.5 km² *370 acres*.

The world's largest airport terminal is at Hartsfield International Airport, Atlanta, Georgia, USA, opened on 21 Sep 1980, with floor space covering 53 ha *131 acres* and still expanding. In 1994 the terminal handled 54,093,051 passengers, although it has a capacity for 70 million.

UK Some 95 airline companies from 85 countries operate scheduled services into Heathrow airport, London (1197 ha *2958 acres*). Between 1 Jan–31 Dec 1994 there were 409,400 air transport movements, handled by a staff of 53,000 employed by the various companies, government departments and Heathrow Airport Limited, a subsidiary of BAA plc. The total number of passengers, both incoming and outgoing, was 51,360,000 including transit passengers.

One day records at Heathrow were set on 6 Jul 1990 with 1232 flights handled and on 29 Jul 1994 with 183,600 passengers. The airport's busiest single hour of two-way passenger flow was recorded on 27 Aug 1994 when 14,164 passengers travelled through the four terminals.

Largest hangars Hangar 375 ('Big Texas') at Kelly Air Force Base, San Antonio, Texas, USA, completed on 15 Feb 1956, has four doors each 76 m *250 ft* wide, 18.3 m *60 ft* high, and weighing 608 tonnes. The high bay is 610×90×27.5 m *2000 ×300 ×90 ft* in area and is surrounded by a 17.8 ha *44 acre* concrete apron. It is the largest free-standing hangar in the world.

Landing fields *Highest* The highest is La Sa (Lhasa) airport, Tibet, People's Republic of China, at 4363 m *14,315 ft*.

Lowest The lowest landing field is El Lisan on the east shore of the Dead Sea, 360 m *1180 ft* below sea level, but during World War II BOAC Short C-class flying boats operated from the surface of the Dead Sea at 394 m *1292 ft* below sea level.

The lowest international airport is Schiphol, Amsterdam, Netherlands at 4.5 m *15 ft* below sea level.

Longest runways The longest runway is at Edwards Air Force Base on the west side of Rogers dry lakebed at Muroc, California, USA, and is 11.92 km *7.41 miles* in length. The *Voyager* aircraft, taking off for its round-the-world unrefuelled flight (⇨ Circumnavigational flights), used 4.3 km *14,200 ft* of the 4.6 km *15,000 ft* long main base concrete runway.

The world's longest civil airport runway is one of 4.89 km *3.04 miles* at Pierre van Ryneveld airport, Upington, South Africa, built between August 1975 and January 1976.

A paved runway 6.24 km *3.88 miles* long appears on maps of Jordan at Abu Husayn.

The most northerly major runway (2 km *1¼ miles* in length) in the world is at Barrow, Alaska, USA (Lat 71°16′ N), which has scheduled flights the whole year round to ten other places in Alaska.

The most southerly major runway (1.6 km *1 mile* in length) in the world is at Ushuaia, Argentina (Lat 54°48′ S), which has scheduled flights the whole year round to four other places in Argentina including the capital city, Buenos Aires.

Busiest Airports — THEN & NOW

With its 66.5 million passengers in 1994, O'Hare International Airport near Chicago is the world's busiest airport. Heathrow, the main London airport, which is the fourth busiest in the world overall, has the most international passengers, with 44.3 million in 1994 out of a total of 51.4 million.

When The Guinness Book of Records first appeared in 1955 air travel was very different from today. Chicago's airport was already the busiest, but with only 7.9 million passengers in 1954 (at Midway airport—O'Hare only opened shortly after the first edition was published). Heathrow had already established itself as the busiest international airport, but with just 1.3 million international passengers, out of an overall total of 1.7 million.

Some other statistics make interesting reading. In 1954 Midway handled under 350,000 arriving and departing aeroplanes. O'Hare handled more than 880,000 in 1994. Heathrow's figure for 1954 was just over 63,000. By 1994 it was nearly 410,000. In 1954 there were 28 airlines using Heathrow. Now there are 95.

HEATHROW THEN

(Photos: Popperfoto and Peter Schulz, Chicago Department of Aviation)

Guess What?

Q. How far did David Huxley pull Concorde in October 1994?

A. See Page 126

Both airports have clearly changed radically over the past 40 years, so who better to ask for some recollections than a couple of employees who have seen the developments first hand?

Joan Winters, who worked as a secretary at O'Hare from 1957 to 1994, says:- 'When I first started at O'Hare there were lots of farms all around the airport. Next to us was the Old Orchard golf course, which I remember because I used to play golf there. Of course it's all been replaced by terminals and runways now.' And the equipment? 'We only had one telephone in the office and we only used manual typewriters. Today, with modern technology, it's all changed to computers.'

Peter Edmunds was at Heathrow from 1958 until 1993, first of all as a British Overseas Airways Corporation Station Officer and later as Airport Duty Manager. He looked back to those early days too:– 'Air travel from London Airport in the 1950s still retained some of the comforts associated with sea travel. Generally the passengers expected and received individual service—some even asking to sit at the Captain's table! They were subjected to no queuing in the departure formalities and no search. After passing through outbound customs they were escorted across the tarmac. The duty officer saluted the aircraft when it departed.'

Chicago and London may still be record holders as they were 40 years ago, but otherwise there are very few links to those days.

CHICAGO NOW

Delta Air Lines' jet base on a 56.6ha *175acre* site at Hartsfield International Airport, Atlanta, Georgia, USA has 14.5ha *36acres* roof area. A recent addition to the hangar gives it a high-bay area of 317 × 74 × 27 m *1041 × 242 × 90ft*.

> **Chalk's International Airline has flown amphibious aircraft from Miami, Florida, USA to the Bahamas since July 1919. Albert 'Pappy' Chalk flew from 1911–75.**

> **Edwin Shackleton of Bristol, Avon has flown as a passenger in 538 different types of aircraft. His first flight was in March 1943 in D.H. Dominie R9548, and other aircraft have included helicopters, gliders, microlights and balloons. Here he admires the hot-air balloon in which he made flight number 459.**
> (Photo: Charles Breton)

Airlines

Busiest airline The country with the busiest airlines system is the United States, where the total number of passengers for air carriers in scheduled domestic operations exceeded 481.3 million in 1994.

On 31 Dec 1994 British Airways operated a fleet of 253 aircraft. It employed an average of 51,164 staff, and 30,595,000 passengers were carried in 1993–4 on 644,000 km *400,000 miles* of unduplicated routes.

Busiest international route The city-pair with the highest international scheduled passenger traffic is London/Paris. More than 3.4 million passengers flew between the two cities in 1992, or nearly 4700 each way each day (although London-bound traffic is higher than that bound for Paris). The busiest intercontinental route is London/New York, with 2.3 million passengers flying between the two cities in 1992.

Largest airline The former Soviet Union's state airline Aeroflot, so named since 1932, was instituted on 9 Feb 1923 and has been the largest airline of all-time. In its last complete year of formal existence (1990) it employed 600,000—more than the top 18 US airlines put together—and flew 139 million passengers with 20,000 pilots, along 1,000,000 km *620,000 miles* of domestic routes across 11 time zones.

Following the break-up of the Soviet Union, the company which now carries the greatest number of passengers is Delta Air Lines, with 89,053,640 in 1994. The airline with the longest route network is the German airline Lufthansa, which covers 879,303 km *546,373 miles*.

Oldest airline Aircraft Transport & Travel was founded in 1916 and began regular scheduled flights from London to Paris on 25 Aug 1919, although it was swallowed up with several other airlines in 1924 to form Imperial Airways, the forerunner of British Overseas Airways Corporation, which with British European Airways later became British Airways. Of current airlines, the oldest is Koninklijke-Luchtvaart-Maatschappij NV (KLM), the national airline of the Netherlands. It was established in October 1919 and opened its first scheduled service (Amsterdam–London) on 17 May 1920.

Delag (Deutsche Luftschiffahrt AG) was founded at Frankfurt am Main, Germany on 16 Nov 1909 and started a scheduled airship service on 17 Jun 1910.

> **Most transatlantic flights**
> **Between March 1948 and his retirement on 1 Sep 1984 Charles M. Schimpf, a flight service manager with Trans World Airlines, logged a total of 2880 Atlantic crossings—a rate of 6.4 per month.**

Personal Aviation Records

Oldest and youngest passengers Airborne births are reported every year.

The oldest person to fly has been Mrs Jessica S. Swift (b. Anna Stewart, 17 Sep 1871), aged 110 years 3 months, from Vermont to Florida, USA in Dec 1981.

The oldest Briton to fly is Charlotte Hughes of Redcar, Cleveland (1877–1993). She was given a flight on Concorde from London to New York as a 110th birthday present on 4 Aug 1987, returning four days later. In February 1992 she became the oldest Briton of all-time (⇨ Longevity).

Pilots *Oldest* Stanley Wood (1896–1994) of Shoreham-by-Sea, W Sussex, was still taking the controls of aircraft at the age of 96, the last occasion being when he flew a Piper Cherokee Warrior on 7 Jun 1993. His first solo flight had been an unofficial one during World War I, which means that his flying career spanned more than 80 per cent of the history of aviation.

Hilda Wallace (b. 26 Nov 1908) of West Vancouver, British Columbia, Canada is the oldest person to qualify as a pilot, obtaining her licence on 15 Mar 1989 at the age of 80 years 109 days.

Longest serving military pilot
Squadron Leader Norman E. Rose, AFC and bar, AMN (RAF Retd) (b. 30 May 1924) flew military aircraft without a break in service for 47 years from 1942 to 1989 achieving 11,539 hours of flying in 54 different categories of aircraft. He learnt to fly in a de Havilland Tiger Moth in Southern Rhodesia, and then flew Hawker Hurricanes in World War II.

Most flying hours *Pilot* John Edward Long (b. 10 Nov 1915) (USA) has logged a total of 60,269 hr of flying as a pilot between May 1933 and April 1995—cumulatively nearly 7 years airborne.

Passenger The record as a supersonic passenger is held by Fred Finn, who has made 707 Atlantic crossings on Concorde. He commutes regularly between London and New Jersey, USA and had flown a total distance of 17,739,800 km *11,023,000 miles* by the end of March 1995.

Up to her retirement in 1988 Maisie Muir of Orkney, Scotland flew over 8400 times with Loganair in connection with business duties for the Royal Bank of Scotland.

Most aeroplanes flown James B. Taylor, Jr (1897–1942) flew 461 different types of powered aircraft during his 25 years as an active experimental test and demonstration pilot for the US Navy and a number of American aircraft manufacturing companies. He was one of the few pilots of the 1920s and 1930s qualified to perform terminal-velocity dives.

Human-powered flight Kanellos Kanellopoulos (b. 25 Apr 1957) averaged 30.3 km/h *18.8 mph* in his 34.1 m *112 ft* wing span machine flying from Crete to the island of Santoríni on 23 Apr 1988, covering 119 km *74 miles* in 3 hr 56 min.

Helicopters

Earliest helicopters Leonardo da Vinci (1452–1519) proposed the idea of a helicopter-type craft, although the Chinese had built helicopter-like toys as early as the 4th century BC.

Fastest helicopter Under FAI rules, the world's speed record for helicopters was set by John Trevor Eggington with co-pilot Derek J. Clews, who averaged 400.87 km/h *249.09 mph* over Glastonbury, Somerset on 11 Aug 1986 in a Westland Lynx demonstrator.

■ **Fred Finn, Rolls Royce and Concorde. An appropriate photograph for the man who has flown a record 707 times on Concorde. He is a frequent spokesman for the air traveller and has appeared on a number of television programmes on both sides of the Atlantic, discussing various aspects of executive travel.**

Largest helicopters The Russian Mil Mi-12 was powered by four 6500 hp *4847 kW* turboshaft engines and had a rotor diameter of 67 m *219 ft 10 in*, with a length of 37 m *121 ft 4½ in* and a weight of 103.3 tonnes. It was demonstrated in prototype form at the Paris Air Show in 1971 but never entered service.

The largest rotorcraft was the Piasecki Heli-Stat, which used four Sikorsky S-58 airframes attached to a surplus Goodyear ZPG-2 airship. Powered by four 1525 hp piston engines and 104.5 m *343 ft* long, 33.8 m *111 ft* high, and 45.4 m *149 ft* wide, it first flew in October 1985 at Lakehurst, New Jersey, USA but was destroyed in a crash on 1 Jul 1986.

> Doug Daigle, Brian Watts and Dave Meyer of Tridair Helicopters, and Rod Anderson of Helistream, Inc. of California, USA maintained a continuous helicopter hover in a 1947 Bell 47B model for 50 hr 50 sec from 13–15 Dec 1989.

Smallest helicopter The single-seat Seremet WS-8 ultra-light helicopter was built in Denmark in 1976 with a 35 hp engine and an empty weight of 53 kg *117 lb*. The rotor diameter was 4.5 m *14 ft 9 in*.

Longest flight Under FAI rules the world record for the longest unrefuelled non-stop flight was set by Robert Ferry, flying a Hughes YOH-6A over a distance of 3561.6 km *2213.1 miles* from Culver City, California to Ormond Beach, Florida, USA on 6 Apr 1966.

Highest altitude The record for helicopters is 12,442 m *40,820 ft* by an Aérospatiale SA315B Lama, flown by Jean Boulet over Istres, France on 21 Jun 1972.

The highest recorded landing has been at 7500 m *24,600 ft* during SA315B demonstrations in the Himalayas in 1969.

Airships

Earliest airship The earliest flight in an airship was by Henri Giffard from Paris to Trappes—a distance of 27 km *17 miles*—in his steam-powered coal-gas airship 2500 m³ *88,300 ft³* in volume and 43.8 m *144 ft* long, on 24 Sep 1852.

Largest airships The largest were the 213.9-tonne German *Hindenburg* (LZ 129) and *Graf Zeppelin II* (LZ 130), which each had a length of 245 m *803 ft 10 in* and a capacity of 200,000 m³ *7,062,100 ft³*. The *Hindenburg* first flew in 1936 and the *Graf Zeppelin II* in 1938.

The largest airship currently certificated for the public transport of passengers is the Sentinel 1000, which has a length of 67.5 m *221 ft 5 in* and a capacity of 10,000 m³ *353,100 ft³*. It was built by Westinghouse Airships, Inc. of Elizabeth City, North Carolina, USA and made its maiden flight on 26 Jun 1991.

Distance records The FAI accredited straight-line distance record for airships is 6384.5 km *3967.1 miles*, set up by the German *Graf Zeppelin*, captained by Dr Hugo Eckener, between 29 Oct–1 Nov 1928.

> The most people ever carried in an airship was 207, in the US Navy *Akron* in 1931. The transatlantic record is 117, by the German *Hindenburg* in 1937. It exploded at Lakehurst, New Jersey, USA on 6 May 1937.

From 21–25 Nov 1917 the German Zeppelin (L59) flew from Yambol, Bulgaria to south of Khartoum, Sudan, and returned to cover a minimum of 7250 km *4500 miles*.

Duration record The longest recorded flight by a non-rigid airship (without refuelling) is 264 hr 12 min by a US Navy Goodyear-built ZPG-2 class ship (Commander J.R. Hunt, USN) from South Weymouth Naval Air Station, Massachusetts, USA from 4–15 Mar 1957, landing back at Key West, Florida, USA after having flown 15,205 km *9448 miles*.

Autogyros

Earliest autogyro The autogyro or gyroplane, a rotorcraft with an unpowered rotor turned by the airflow in flight, preceded any practical helicopter with its engine-driven rotor.

Juan de la Cierva (Spain) designed the first successful gyroplane with his model C.4 (commercially named an 'Autogiro') which flew at Getafe, Spain on 9 Jan 1923. More recently, the principal development has concerned the gyrocopter, which derives all of its lift from the unpowered rotor, unlike de la Cierva's designs which incorporated wings.

Speed, altitude and distance records Wing Cdr Kenneth H. Wallis (GB) holds the straight-line distance record of 874.32 km *543.27 miles* set in his WA-116/F gyrocopter on 28 Sep 1975 with a non-stop flight from Lydd, Kent to Wick, Highland.

On 20 Jul 1982, flying from Boscombe Down, Wilts, he set a new altitude record of 5643.7 m *18,516 ft* in his WA-121/Mc gyrocopter.

Wing Cdr Wallis flew his WA-116/F/S gyrocopter, with a 45 kW *60-hp* Franklin aero-engine, to a record speed of 193.6 km/h *120.3 mph* over a 3 km *1⅞ mile* straight course at Marham, Norfolk on 18 Sep 1986.

Ballooning

Earliest balloon flight The earliest recorded ascent was by a model hot-air balloon invented by Father Bartolomeu de Gusmão (né Lourenço) (1685–1724), which was flown indoors at the Casa da India, Terreiro do Paço, Portugal on 8 Aug 1709.

Distance record The record distance travelled by a balloon is 8382.54 km *5208.68 miles*, by the Raven experimental helium-filled balloon *Double Eagle V* (capacity 11,300 m³ *399,100 ft³*) from 9–12 Nov 1981. The journey started from Nagashima, Japan and ended at Covello, California, USA. The crew for this first manned balloon crossing of the Pacific Ocean were Ben L. Abruzzo, 51, Rocky Aoki, 43 (Japan), Ron Clark, 41, and Larry M. Newman, 34.

Duration record Richard Abruzzo, 29, together with Troy Bradley, 28, set a duration record of 144 hr 16 min in *Team USA* in crossing the Atlantic Ocean from Bangor, Maine, USA to Ben Slimane, Morocco from 16 to 22 Sep 1992. The previous record had been set by Richard's father, Ben, in *Double Eagle II* in 1978.

Atlantic crossing Col. Joe Kittinger, USAF (⇨ Parachuting) became the first man to complete a solo transatlantic crossing by balloon. In the 2850 m³ *101,000 ft³* helium-filled balloon *Rosie O'Grady*, Kittinger lifted off from Caribou, Maine, USA on 14 Sep 1984 and completed a distance of 5701 km *3543 miles* before landing at Montenotte, near Savona, Italy 86 hours later on 18 Sep 1984.

Largest balloon The largest balloon ever made had an inflatable volume of 2 million m³ *70 million ft³* and was 300 m *1000 ft* in height. The unmanned balloon,

manufactured by Winzen Research, Inc. (now Winzen Engineering, Inc.) of South St Paul, Minnesota, USA, did not get off the ground and was destroyed at launch on 8 Jul 1975.

Highest altitude *Unmanned* The greatest altitude attained by an unmanned balloon was 51,800 m *170,000 ft* by a Winzen balloon of 1.35 million m³ *47.8 million ft³* launched at Chico, California, USA on 27 Oct 1972.

Manned The greatest altitude reached in a manned balloon is an unofficial 37,750 m *123,800 ft* by Nicholas Piantanida (1933–66) of Bricktown, New Jersey, USA, from Sioux Falls, South Dakota on 1 Feb 1966. He landed in Iowa but did not survive.

The official record (closed gondola) is 34,668 m *113,740 ft* by Commander Malcolm D. Ross, USNR and the late Lt Cdr. Victor A. Prother, USN in an ascent from USS *Antietam* over the Gulf of Mexico on 4 May 1961 in a 339,800 m³ *12 million ft³* balloon.

Hot-air ballooning This form of ballooning was revived in the USA in 1961, and the first World Championships were held in Albuquerque, New Mexico, USA from 10–17 Feb 1973.

Altitude Per Lindstrand achieved the altitude record of 19,811 m *64,997 ft* in a Colt 600 hot-air balloon over Laredo, Texas, USA on 6 Jun 1988.

Atlantic crossing Richard Branson (GB) with his pilot Per Lindstrand (GB) were the first to cross the Atlantic in a hot-air balloon, from 2–3 Jul 1987. They ascended from Sugarloaf, Maine, USA and covered the distance of 4947 km *3075 miles*, to Limavady, Co. Londonderry in 31 hr 41 min.

Pacific crossing Richard Branson and Per Lindstrand crossed the Pacific in the *Virgin Otsuka Pacific Flyer* from the southern tip of Japan to Lac la Matre, Yukon, north-western Canada on 15–17 Jan 1991 in a 73,600 m³ *2.6 million ft³* hot-air balloon (the largest ever flown) to set FAI records for duration (46 hr 15 min) and distance (great circle 7671.9 km *4768 miles*).

Mount Everest Two balloons achieved the first overflight of the summit of Mount Everest at the same time on 21 Oct 1991. They were *Star Flyer 1*, piloted by Chris Dewhirst (Australia) with cameraman Leo Dickinson, and *Star Flyer 2*, piloted by Andy Elson and cameraman Eric Jones (all British). The two 6800 m³ *240,000 ft³* balloons set hot-air balloon records for the highest launch at 4735 m *15,536 ft* and touch-down at 4940 m *16,200 ft*.

Gas The FAI endurance and distance record for a gas and hot-air balloon is 144 hr 16 min and 5340.2 km *3318.2 miles* by *Team USA*, crewed by Richard Abruzzo and Troy Bradley on 16–22 Sep 1992 (⇨ above).

Most passengers in a balloon A balloon of 73,600 m³ *2.6 million ft³* capacity named *Super Maine* was built by Tom Handcock of Portland, Maine, USA. Tethered, it rose to a height of 12.25 m *50 ft* with 61 passengers on board on 19 Feb 1988.

The Dutch balloonist Henk Brink made an untethered flight of 200 m *656 ft* in the 24,000 m³ *850,000 ft³* balloon *Nashua Number One* carrying a total of 50 passengers and crew. The flight, on 17 Aug 1988, lasted 25 minutes, started from Lelystad airport, Netherlands, and reached an altitude of 100 m *328 ft*.

Ballooning mass ascent The greatest mass ascent from a single site took place when 128 hot-air

> # Help
>
> Owing to an oversight, Keith Lang and Harold Froelich, scientists from Minneapolis, USA, ascended in an open gondola and without the protection of pressure suits to an altitude of 12,840 m *42,126 ft*, on 26 Sep 1956. During their 6½-hour flight, at maximum altitude and without goggles, they observed the Earth and measured a temperature of –58°C *–72°F*.

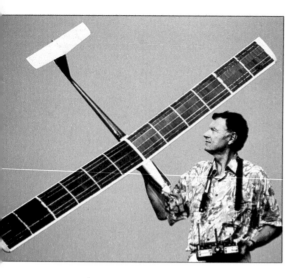

■ **Jean-Pierre Schiltknecht with his record-breaking solar driven model aircraft.**

Distance Gianmaria Aghem (Italy) holds the closed-circuit distance record, with 1239 km *769.9 miles*, set on 26 Jul 1986. The longest flight in a straight line to a nominated landing point was one of 493.17 km *306.44 miles*, by Peter Garoni (Australia) from Balladonia to Border Village, Western Australia, in 6 hr 30 min on 18 May 1994.

Speed The overall speed record is 395.64 km/h *245.84 mph*, with a model flown on control lines by Leonid Lipinski (USSR) on 6 Dec 1971. The record for a radio-controlled model is 390.92 km/h *242.91 mph*, by Walter Sitar (Austria) on 10 Jun 1977.

Duration The record duration is 33 hr 39 min 15 sec by Maynard Hill (⇔ above), with a powered model on 1–2 Oct 1992.

An indoor model with a wound rubber motor designed by Robert Randolph (USA) set a duration record of 55 min 6 sec on 5 Dec 1993.

Jean-Pierre Schiltknecht flew a solar driven model airplane for a duration record of 10 hr 43 min 51 sec at Wetzlar, Germany on 10 Jul 1991.

Largest model glider In January 1990 *Eagle III*, a radio-controlled glider weighing 6.5 kg *14 lb 8 oz* with a wing span of 9.80 m *32 ft 6 in*, was designed and constructed by Carlos René Tschen and Carlos René Tschen Jr of Colonia San Lázaro, Guatemala.

Smallest model aircraft The smallest to fly is one weighing 0.1 g *0.004 oz* powered by an attached horsefly and designed by insectonaut Don Emmick of Seattle, Washington State, USA. On 24 Jul 1977 it flew for five minutes at Kirkland, Washington State, USA.

balloons took off within one hour at the Ninth Bristol International Balloon Festival at Ashton Court, Bristol, Avon on 15 Aug 1987.

Most to jump from a balloon On 12 Sep 1992 a record fifteen people (a group of Royal Marines plus friends) all parachuted from a hot air balloon over the Somerset/Devon county boundary. The same group made a similar ascent on 1 Oct 1992 and this time a record ten people jumped *simultaneously*, from a height of 1800 m *6000 ft*.

Model Aircraft

Altitude Maynard L. Hill (USA), flying a radio-controlled model, established the world record for altitude, reaching a height of 8205 m *26,919 ft* on 6 Sep 1970.

Paper Aircraft

Duration The level flight duration record for a hand-launched paper aircraft is 18.80 sec by Ken Blackburn in a hangar at JFK airport, New York, USA on 17 Feb 1994.

Distance An indoor distance of 58.82 m *193 ft* was recorded by Tony Felch at the La Crosse Center, Wisconsin, USA on 21 May 1985.

> **Don Emmick, who constructed the smallest model aeroplane to fly, said about his plane:– 'You have to be careful not to blow on it or you'll blow a hole through the wing'.**

A paper plane was seen to fly 2 km *1¼ miles* by 'Chick' C.O. Reinhart from a tenth-storey office window at 60 Beaver Street, New York City, USA across the East River to Brooklyn in August 1933, helped by a thermal from a coffee-roasting plant.

Largest paper aircraft The largest flying paper aeroplane, with a wing span of 12.34 m *40 ft 6 in*, was constructed by a team of engineers from BP Chemicals Ltd and flown at Filton, Avon on 24 Jun 1994. It was launched indoors and was flown for a distance of 23.57 m *77 ft 4 in*.

> **In 1955 the record for the number of parachute jumps in a 24-hour period stood at 50. This has now been improved to 301, representing approximately one every 4¾ minutes.**

Parachuting Records

It is estimated that the human body reaches 99 per cent of its low-level terminal velocity after falling 573 m 1880 ft, which takes 13–14 sec. This is 188–201 km/h 117–125 mph at normal atmospheric pressure in a random posture, but up to 298 km/h 185 mph in a head-down position.

FIRST[1] Louis-Sébastien Lenormand (1757–1839), quasi-parachute, from tower, Montpellier, France, 1783.

LONGEST DURATION FALL Lt Col. Wm H. Rankin, USMC, 40 min due to thermals, North Carolina, USA, 26 Jul 1956.

LONGEST DELAYED DROP *World Man:* Capt. Joseph W. Kittinger[2], 25,820 m *84,700 ft* or *16.04 miles*, from balloon at 31,330 m *102,800 ft*, Tularosa, New Mexico, USA, 16 Aug 1960. *Woman:* Elvira Fomitcheva (USSR) 14,800 m *48,556 ft*, over Odessa, USSR, 26 Oct 1977.
Over UK *Man (Civilian):* M. Child, R. McCarthy, 10,180 m *33,400 ft* from balloon at 10,850 m *35,600 ft*, Kings Lynn, Norfolk, 18 Sep 1986. *Woman (Civilian):* Francesca Gannon and Valerie Slattery, 6520 m *21,391 ft* from aircraft at 7600 m *24,900 ft*, Netheravon, Wilts, 11 Mar 1987. *Group:* S/Ldr J. Thirtle, Fl. Sgt A.K. Kidd, Sgts L. Hicks (died 1971), P.P. Keane, K.J. Teesdale, 11,943 m *39,183 ft* from aircraft at 12,613 m *41,383 ft*, Boscombe Down, Wilts, 16 Jun 1967.

BASE JUMP Highest Nicholas Feteris and Dr Glenn Singleman from a ledge (the 'Great Trango Tower') at 5880 m *19,300 ft* in the Karakoram, Pakistan, 26 Aug 1992. *Jumps from buildings and claims for lowest base jumps will not be accepted.*

MID-AIR RESCUE Earliest Miss Dolly Shepherd (1886–1983) brought down Miss Louie May on her single 'chute from balloon at 3350 m *11,000 ft*, Longton, Staffs, 9 Jun 1908.
Lowest Eddie Turner saved Frank Farnan (unconscious), who had been injured in a collision after jumping out of an aircraft at 3950 m *13,000 ft*. He pulled his ripcord at 550 m *1800 ft*—less than 10 seconds from impact—over Clewiston, Florida, USA on 16 Oct 1988.

HIGHEST ESCAPE Flt Lt J. de Salis, RAF and Fg Off. P. Lowe, RAF, 17,100 m *56,000 ft*, Monyash, Derby, 9 Apr 1958.
Lowest S/Ldr Terence Spencer, RAF, 9–12 m *30–40 ft*, Wismar Bay, Baltic, 19 Apr 1945.

CROSS-CHANNEL (LATERAL FALL) Sgt Bob Walters with three soldiers and two Royal Marines, 35.4 km *22 miles* from 7600 m *25,000 ft*, Dover, Kent to Sangatte, France, 31 Aug 1980.

TOTAL SPORT PARACHUTING DESCENTS *Man:* Don Kellner (USA), 21,000, various locations in the USA up to 2 Oct 1994. *Woman:* Valentina Zakoretskaya (USSR), 8000, over USSR, 1964–80.

24-HOUR TOTAL *Man:* Dale Nelson (USA), 301 (in accordance with United States Parachute Association rules), Pennsylvania, USA, 26–27 May 1988. *Woman:* Cheryl Stearns (USA), 255 at Lodi, California, USA 26–27 Nov 1987.

LARGEST CANOPY STACK 46, by an international team at Davis, California, USA; held for 37.54 seconds on 12 Oct 1994.

LARGEST FREE FALL FORMATION 216, from 23 countries, held for 8.21 seconds, from 6400 m *21,000 ft*, over Bratislava, Slovakia, 19 Aug 1994 (unofficial). 200, from 10 countries held for 6.47 seconds, from 5030 m *16,500 ft*, over Myrtle Beach, South Carolina, USA, 23 Oct 1992 (record recognized by FAI). *Women:* 100, from 20 countries held for 5.97 seconds, from 5200 m *17,000 ft*, Aéreodrome du Cannet des Maures, France, 14 Aug 1992.
UK 60, held for 4 seconds, from 4600 m *15,000 ft*, Peterborough, Cambs, 8 Jun 1989.

OLDEST *Man:* Edwin C. Townsend (died 7 Nov 1987), 89 years, Vermillion Bay, Louisiana, USA, 5 Feb 1986. *Woman:* Sylvia Brett (GB), 80 years 166 days, Cranfield, Beds, 23 Aug 1986.
Tandem, *Man:* Edward Royds-Jones, 95 years 170 days, Dunkeswell, Devon, 2 Jul 1994. *Woman:* Corena Leslie (USA), 89 years 326 days, Buckeye airport, Arizona, USA, 8 Jun 1992.

SURVIVAL FROM LONGEST FALL WITHOUT PARACHUTE World Vesna Vulovic (Yugoslavia), air hostess in DC-9 which blew up at 10,160 m *33,330 ft* over Srbská Kamenice, Czechoslovakia (now Czech Republic), 26 Jan 1972.
UK Flt-Sgt Nicholas Stephen Alkemade (died 22 Jun 1987), from blazing RAF Lancaster bomber, at 5500 m *18,000 ft* over Germany (near Oberkürchen), 23 Mar 1944.

[1] *In 1687 the king of Ayutthaya, Siam was reported to have been diverted by an ingenious athlete parachuting with two large umbrellas. Faustus Verancsis is reputed to have descended in Hungary with a framed canopy in 1617.*
[2] *Maximum speed in rarefied air was 1006 km/h 625¼ mph at 90,000 ft 27,400 m—hence marginally supersonic.*

Art

Painting

Largest The largest painting measures 6727.56 m² *72,437 ft²* after allowing for shrinkage of the canvas. It is made up of brightly-coloured squares upon which a 'Smiley' face was displayed, and was painted by students of Robb College at Armidale, New South Wales, Australia, aided by local schoolchildren and students from neighbouring colleges. The canvas was completed by its designer, Australian artist Ken Done, and unveiled at the University of New England, Armidale on 10 May 1990.

UK The oval painting *Triumph of Peace and Liberty* by Sir James Thornhill (1676–1734) on the ceiling of the Painted Hall in the Royal Naval College, Greenwich measures 32.3×15.4 m *106 x51 ft* and took 20 years (1707–27) to complete.

Most valuable The 'Mona Lisa' (*La Gioconda*) by Leonardo da Vinci (1452–1519) in the Louvre, Paris, France was assessed for insurance purposes at $100 million for its move to Washington, DC, USA and New York City for exhibition from 14 Dec 1962 to 12 Mar 1963. However, insurance was not concluded because the cost of the closest security precautions was less than that of the premiums. It was painted c. 1503–07 and measures 77×53 cm *30.5 x20.9 in.* It is believed to portray either Mona (short for Madonna) Lisa Gherardini, the wife of Francesco del Giocondo of Florence, or Constanza d'Avalos, coincidentally nicknamed La Gioconda, mistress of Giuliano de Medici. King Francis I of France bought the painting for his bathroom in 1517 for 4000 gold florins, or 13.94 kg *30.75 lb* of gold. The equivalent today (May 1995) would be £120,800.

Most prolific painter Pablo Diego José Francisco de Paula Juan Nepomuceno Crispin Crispiano de la Santisima Trinidad Ruiz y Picasso (1881–1973) of Spain was the most prolific of all painters in a career which lasted 78 years. It has been estimated that Picasso produced about 13,500 paintings or designs, 100,000 prints or engravings, 34,000 book illustrations and 300 sculptures or ceramics. His *oeuvre* has been valued at £500 million.

Oldest RA The oldest Royal Academician was (Thomas) Sidney Cooper, who died on 8 Feb 1902 aged 98 yr 136 days having exhibited 266 paintings over the record span of 69 consecutive years (1833–1902).

The highest price ever fetched by a painting in public auction 40 years ago was a mere $360,000 (£128,570), for Gainsborough's *Harvest Wagon*, on 20 Apr 1928 in New York.

Q. What is the world's best-selling British single?

A. See Page 149

Guess What?

■ *La Gioconda* or the 'Mona Lisa', is too valuable to make insurance practical; it is also arguably the most expensive object ever stolen (⇨Human World). (Photo: AKG London)

Youngest RA Mary Moser (later Lloyd, 1744–1819) was elected on the foundation of the Royal Academy in 1768 when aged 24.

Youngest exhibitor The youngest exhibitor at the Royal Academy of Arts Annual Summer Exhibition was Lewis Melville 'Gino' Lyons (b. 30 Apr 1962). His *Trees and Monkeys* was painted on 4 Jun 1965, submitted on 17 Mar 1967 and exhibited on 29 Apr 1967, the day before his fifth birthday.

Largest gallery The world's largest art gallery is the Winter Palace and the neighbouring Hermitage in St Petersburg, Russia. One has to walk 24 km *15 miles* to visit each of the 322 galleries, which house nearly three million works of art and objects of archaeological interest.

Most heavily endowed The J. Paul Getty Museum at Malibu, California, USA was established with an initial £700 million budget in January 1974, and now has an annual budget well in excess of $100 million for acquisitions to stock its 38 galleries.

The finest standard brush sold is the 000 in Series 7 by Winsor and Newton known as a 'triple goose'. It is made of 150–200 Kolinsky sable hairs weighing 15 mg *0.00053 oz*.

Highest Prices

Sales were at auction unless stated otherwise and include the buyer's premium.

Item	Sold by	Price *m denotes millions*
Painting *Portrait of Dr Gachet*, Vincent van Gogh (1853–90)[1]	Christie's, New York, 15 May 1990	$82.5m (£49.1m)
UK Turner's *Van Tromp Going About to Please His Masters*	The University of London, Feb 1993 (private sale)	£11m
20th-century *Yo Picasso* (1901), self-portrait by Pablo Picasso	Sotheby's, New York, 9 May 1989	$47.8m (£28.3m)
Living artist *Interchange*, Willem de Kooning (USA; b. Rotterdam, 1904)	Sotheby's, New York, 8 Nov 1989	$20.68m (£13m)
UK *Triptych May–June*, Francis Bacon (1909–92)[2]	Sotheby's, New York, 2 May 1989	$6.27m (£3.71m)
Print 1655 etching *Christ Presented to the People*, Rembrandt (1606–69)	Christie's, London, December 1985	£561,600
Drawing *Jardin de Fleurs (1888)*, Vincent Van Gogh	Christie's, New York, 14 Nov 1990	$8.36m (£4.27m)
Poster by Charles R Mackintosh (1868–1928)	Christie's, London, Feb 1993	£68,200
Sculpture *The Dancing Faun*, by Adrien de Vries (1545/6–1626)[3]	Sotheby's, London, 7 Dec 1989	£6.82 m
Living Sculptor 190.5-cm *75-in-long* elmwood *Reclining figure*, Henry Moore (1898–1986)	Sotheby's, New York, 21 May 1982	$1.265m

[1] *The painting depicts Van Gogh's physician and was completed only weeks before the artist's suicide in 1890. It was sold within three minutes.* [2] *An advertisement for the 1895 exhibition of contemporary art at the Glasgow Institute of Fine Arts.* [3] *London dealer Cyril Humpris bought the figure from an unnamed Brighton, W Sussex couple who had paid £100 for it in the 1950s and in whose garden it had stood unremarked upon for 40 years.*

Largest poster A poster measuring 21,936 m² *236,119 ft²* was made by the Community Youth Club of Hong Kong on 26 Oct 1993. The poster followed the theme of the international year of the family, and was displayed at Victoria Park, Hong Kong.

Murals

Largest *Planet Ocean*, a mural by the American artist Wyland is the largest in the world, measuring 32 m *105 ft* high and 378.8 m *1220 ft* long. It is painted on the Long Beach Arena in California, USA and was completed on 4 May 1992.

Britain's largest mural covers 1709 m² *18,396 ft²*, the size of nearly eight tennis courts, and is painted on the Stage V wall of BBC Television Centre, London. Commissioned as the result of a competition run by the *Going Live* programme, the mural was painted in September 1991 by the Scenic Set company to a design by Vicky Askew.

Sculpture

Hill figures In August 1968, a figure 100 m *330 ft* tall was found on a hill above Tarapacá, Chile.

UK The largest permanent human hill carving in Britain is

■ The Hermitage in St. Petersburg, Russia, which, along with the neighbouring Winter Palace, houses nearly 3 million works of art and archaeological finds. (Photo: Gamma/Shone)

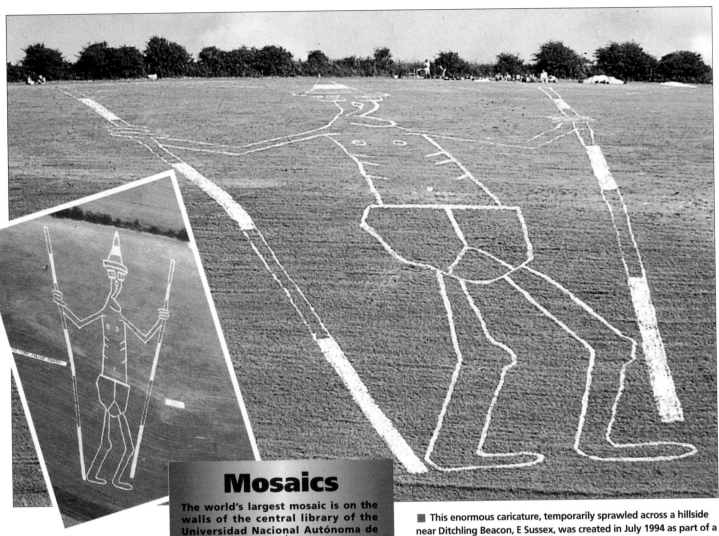

Mosaics

The world's largest mosaic is on the walls of the central library of the Universidad Nacional Autónoma de Mexico in Mexico City. Of the four walls, the two largest measure 1203m² *12,949ft²*, and the scenes on each represent the pre-Hispanic past.

UK The largest Roman mosaic in Britain is the Woodchester Pavement in Gloucester of c. AD 325. It measures 14.3m² *47ft²* and comprises 1.6 million tesserae (tiles).

■ This enormous caricature, temporarily sprawled across a hillside near Ditchling Beacon, E Sussex, was created in July 1994 as part of a protest against the Government's proposed Dover–Southampton expressway. It measured 150 m *492 ft* tall, and was made from 10 tonnes of chalk and several cans of whitewash. Dubbed the 'Grey Man' of Ditchling, after the 'Long Man' of Wilmington (⇨Hill figures), it drew its inspiration from the Prime Minister, John Major.
(Photo: Spectrum Colour Library)

the 'Long Man' of Wilmington, E Sussex, at 68 m *226 ft* in length.

The oldest of Britain's 'White Horses' is the Uffington horse in Oxfordshire. It was originally dated to the late Iron Age (c. 150 BC), although recent reports (February 1995) have suggested that it is as much as 3000 years old. It measures 114 m *374 ft* nose-to-tail and is 36 m *120 ft* high.

Largest The mounted figures of Jefferson Davis (1808–89), Gen. Robert Edward Lee (1807–70) and Gen. Thomas Jonathan (Stonewall) Jackson (1824–63) are 27.4 m *90 ft* high and cover 0.5 ha *1.33 acres* on the face of Stone Mountain, near Atlanta, Georgia, USA. Roy Faulkner was on the mountain face for 8 yr 174 days with a thermo-jet torch, working with the sculptor Walker Kirtland Hancock and other helpers, from 12 Sep 1963 to 3 Mar 1972.

The largest scrap-metal sculpture was built by Sudhir Deshpande of Nashik, India. Named *Powerful*, the colossus weighs 27 tonnes and stands 17 m *55¾ ft* tall.

Sand sculpture The longest sand sculpture ever made was the sculpture 26,375.9 m *86,535 ft* long named 'The GTE Directories Ultimate Sand Castle', built by more than 10,000 volunteers at Myrtle Beach, South Carolina, USA on 31 May 1991.

The tallest was the 'Invitation to Fairyland', which was 17.12 m *56 ft 2 in* high, and was built by 2000 local volunteers at Kaseda, Japan on 26 Jul 1989 under the supervision of Gerry Kirk of Sand Sculptors International of San Diego and Shogo Tashiro of Sand Sculptors International of Japan.

■ A classical exhibit at the J. Paul Getty Museum in California, USA, which has the largest budget for acquisitions of any museum.
(Photo: Gamma/ J. C. Francolon)

Guess What?

Q. What is the longest palindrome in the English language?

A. See Page 138

Antiques

All prices quoted are inclusive of the buyer's premium and all records were set at public auction unless stated otherwise.

Carpets The most valuable carpet ever made was the Spring carpet of Khusraw made for the audience hall of the Sassanian palace at Ctesiphon, Iraq. It consisted of about 650 m² *7000 ft²* of silk and gold thread encrusted with emeralds. The carpet was cut up as booty by looters in AD 635 and, from the known realization value of the pieces, must have had an original value of some £100 million.

Highest price On 9 Jun 1994, a Louis XV Savonnerie carpet 5.4 m × 5.8 m *18 ft × 19 ft*, probably made for Louis XV's Chateau de la Mouette in the 1740s, fetched a record £1,321,000 at Christie's, London. The buyer was M Djanhanguir Riahi, a Paris-based Iranian owner of a notable collection of 18th-century French art.

Furniture The highest price ever paid for a single piece of furniture is £8.58 million ($15.1 million) at Christie's, London on 5 Jul 1990 for the 18th-century Italian 'Badminton Cabinet' owned by the Duke of Beaufort. It was bought by Barbara Piasecka Johnson of Princeton, New Jersey, USA.

Jewellery The world's largest jewellery auction, which included a Van Cleef and Arpels 1939 ruby and diamond necklace, realized £31,380,197 when the collection belonging to the Duchess of Windsor (1896–1986) was sold at Sotheby's, Geneva, Switzerland on 3 Apr 1987.

The record for individual items of jewellery is £3.1 million for two pear-shaped diamond drop earrings of 58.6 and 61 carats bought and sold anonymously at Sotheby's, Geneva on 14 Nov 1980.

Playing cards The highest price for a deck of playing cards is $143,352 (£99,000) paid by the Metropolitan Museum of Art, New York City, USA at Sotheby's, London on 6 Dec 1983. The cards, dating from c. 1470–85, constituted the oldest known *complete* hand-painted set.

The highest price paid for a single card was £5000 for a card dated 1717, which was used as currency in Canada. It was sold by the dealer Yasha Beresiner to Lars Karlson (Sweden) in October 1990.

Shoes The red slippers worn by Judy Garland in the film *The Wizard of Oz* sold at Christie's, New York on 2 Jun 1988 for $165,000 (£90,000).

Toys The most expensive antique toy was sold for $231,000 (£128,333) to a telephone bidder at Christie's, New York City, USA on 14 Dec 1991. The work is a hand-painted tin plate replica of the 'Charles' hose reel, a piece of fire-fighting equipment, measuring 38.1 × 58.4 cm *15 × 23 in* and built c. 1870 by George Brown & Co. of Forestville, Connecticut, USA.

> The record for a thimble is £18,000 at Phillips' Midland branch on 13 Dec 1992 for a late 16th-century gold jewelled thimble reputed to have belonged to Queen Elizabeth I. It was bought by Asprey's on behalf of a client.

Auctioneers

The oldest firm of art auctioneers in the world is the Stockholms Auktionsverk of Sweden, which was established on 27 Feb 1674. The largest firm is the Sotheby Group of London and New York, founded in 1744. Sotheby's turnover was a record $2.9 billion in 1989 and their New York sales set a single series record of $360.4 million in May 1990.

The highest price paid for a single toy soldier is £3375 for a uniformed scale figure of Hitler's deputy, Rudolf Hess, made by the Lineol company of Brandenburg, Germany. The figure was among several sold by the Danish auction house Boyes, London on 23 Apr 1991.

Language

Earliest language The ability to articulate is believed to be dependent upon physiological changes in the height of the larynx between *Homo erectus* and *Homo sapiens sapiens* which occurred c. 45,000 BC. The discovery of a hyoid bone (from the base of the tongue) from a cave site on Mt Carmel, Israel shows that Neanderthal man may have been capable of speech 60,000 years ago, but the usual dating is 50,000–30,000 BC.

Oldest English words English is a branch of the Western group of Germanic languages brought to Britain by Germanic invaders c. 390 AD. The earlier Celts spoke an Indo-European language preserved in a few river and place names. Words in English which appear to go back to the old stages of Indo-European (from the North Caucasus and the Lower Volga) are those referring to family relationships such as 'father', 'mother' and 'son' and those for the numbers one to five.

There are eight indigenous languages older than English still in use in the British Isles. These are: Welsh, Cornish, Scots, Irish, Manx, Channel Isles patois, Sheldru or Shelta and Romani.

Commonest language The most common first language is Chinese, spoken by more than a billion people. The so-called 'common speech' (*pǔtōnghuà*) is the stan-

■ This Steiff bear named Teddy Girl was sold for £110,000, more than 18 times the estimate and twice the previous world record, by Christie's, London on 5 Dec 1994 to Japanese businessman Yoshihiro Sekiguchi. The bear was made in 1904, only a year after Steiff made the first jointed plush teddy bear, and was still in excellent condition. Teddy Girl had a particularly well-documented history; she belonged to a prominent collector, Colonel Bob Henderson, who took her everywhere with him—even to his landing on the D-Day beaches, where he was a small-arms adviser to Field Marshal Montgomery. Pictured far left is the future Colonel Henderson with his brother Charles and Teddy Girl in 1910.
(Photos: Gamma)

◀◀ ◀◀ **Murals, Sculpture**

■ Jubilee day in Papua New Guinea, the territory with the greatest concentration of separate languages in the world.
(Photo: Spectrum Colour Library)

Switzerland and converse with every delegate in his or her own language.

The greatest living linguist is Ziad Fazah (b. 10 Jul 1954), originally from Liberia but now a naturalized Brazilian citizen, who speaks and writes 58 languages. He was tested in a live interview in Athens, Greece on 30 Jul 1991, when he surprised members of the audience by talking to them in their various native tongues. He is currently a private language teacher.

Alphabets

Earliest alphabet The earliest example of alphabetic writing, clay tablets showing the 32 cuneiform letters of the Ugaritic alphabet, were found in 1929 at Ugarit (now Ras Shamra), Syria and dated to c. 1450 BC.

Oldest letter The letter 'O' is unchanged in shape since its adoption in the Phoenician alphabet c. 1300 BC.

Newest letters Until about 1600, there was no clear distinction in the English alphabet between the letters 'i' and 'j', or 'u' and 'v'. After 1600, 'i' and 'u' came to represent vowels only, while 'j' and 'v' became consonants. Even as recently as the 19th century, some dictionaries did not distinguish between 'i' and 'j' and in Alexander Cruden's *Concordance to the Holy Scriptures* (1815), the next word after *I* is *Jacinth*, while *Joyous* is followed by *Iron*.

Most and fewest consonants The language with the largest number of distinct consonantal sounds was that of the Ubykhs in the Caucasus, with 80–85. Ubykh speakers migrated from the Caucasus to Turkey in the nineteenth century, and the last fully competent speaker, Tevfik Esenç, died in October 1992. The language with the fewest consonants is Rotokas, which has only six.

Most and fewest vowels The language with the most vowels is Sedang, a central Vietnamese language with 55 distinguishable vowel sounds, and that with the fewest is the Caucasian language Abkhazian with two.

Most Languages

About 845 of the world's 3950 languages and dialects are spoken in India. Owing to its many isolated valleys, the former Australian territory of Papua New Guinea has the greatest concentration of separate languages in the world, with an estimated 869, i.e. each language has about 4000 speakers.

dard form of Chinese, with a pronunciation based on that of Beijing.

The most widespread and the second most-commonly spoken language is English, with a conservative estimate of 800 million speakers, rising to a liberal 1.5 billion. Of these, some 350 million are native speakers, mainly in the US (about 220 million), the UK (55 million), Canada (17 million) and Australia (15 million).

Most complex language The Amele language of Papua New Guinea has the most verb forms, with over 69,000 finite forms and 860 infinitive forms of the verb. Haida, the North American Indian language, has the most prefixes (70), and Tabassaran, a language of southeast Daghestan, uses the most noun cases (48). The Eskimo language used by the Inuit has 63 forms of the present tense, and simple nouns have as many as 252 inflections.

Rarest sounds The rarest speech sound is probably that written 'ř' in Czech and termed a 'rolled post-alveolar fricative'. It occurs in very few languages and is the last sound mastered by Czech children. In the southern Bushman language !xo there is a click articulated with both lips, which is written ʘ. This character is usually referred to as a 'bull's-eye' and the sound, essentially a kiss, is termed a 'velaric ingressive bilabial stop'. In some contexts the 'l' sound in the Arabic word *Allah* is pronounced uniquely in that language.

Commonest sound No language is known to be without the vowel 'a' (as in the English 'father').

Debating Students of St Andrews Presbyterian College in Laurinburg, North Carolina, USA, together with staff and friends, debated the motion 'There's No Place Like Home' for 21 days 13 hr 45 min from 4 to 26 Apr 1992. The aim of the debate was to increase awareness of the problems of being homeless.

Most synonyms The condition of being inebriated has more synonyms than any other condition or object. Paul Dickson of Garrett Park, Maryland, USA has compiled and published a list of 2660 words and phrases in his book *Word Treasury*.

Greatest linguist The world's greatest linguist is believed to be have been Dr Harold Williams of New Zealand (1876–1928), a journalist and one-time foreign editor of *The Times*. Self-taught in Latin, Greek, Hebrew and many of the European and Pacific-island languages as a boy, Dr Williams spoke 58 languages and many dialects fluently. He was the only person to attend meetings of the League of Nations in Geneva,

Guess What?

Q. Who is the highest-paid chat-show host?

A. See Page 153

Alphabets

The language with the most letters is Khmer (Cambodian), with 74 (including some without any current use).

Rotokas of central Bougainville Island, Papua New Guinea has fewest letters, with 11 (a, b, e, g, i, k, o, p, r, t and u).

Words

Longest words Lengthy concatenations and some compound, agglutinative and nonce words can be written in the closed-up style of a single word. The longest known example is a compound 'word' of 195 Sanskrit characters (transliterating to 428 letters in the Roman alphabet) describing the region near Kanci, Tamil Nadu, India, which appears in a 16th-century work by Tirumalāmbā, Queen of Vijayanagara.

English The longest word in the *Oxford English Dictionary* is *pneumonoultramicroscopicsilicovolcanoconiosis (-koniosis)*, which has 45 letters and describes 'a lung disease caused by the inhalation of very fine silica dust'. It is described as 'factitious' by the editors of the dictionary. Chemical names, if spelt out as opposed to being listed by their formulae, may run to thousands of letters.

Most succinct word The most challenging word for any lexicographer to define briefly is the Fuegian

Verbosity

Fewest irregular verbs The artificial language Esperanto has no irregular verbs. It was first published by its inventor Dr Ludwig Zamenhof (1859–1917) of Warsaw in 1887, and is now estimated (by textbook sales) to have a million speakers. The even earlier interlanguage Volapük, invented by Johann Martin Schleyer (1831–1912), also has absolutely regular configuration.

Most irregular verbs According to *The Morphology and Syntax of Present-day English* by Prof. Olu Tomori, English has 283 irregular verbs, 30 of which are formed simply by adding a prefix.

On The Record

D R U N K

Drenched Roasted Upsey tipped Keyed

Zozzled. Looped. Beerified. Lit. You can't reasonably describe Paul Dickson (photo right) as any of those, but you might say, to quote another old verbophile, that he's 'inebriated with the exuberance of his own verbosity' — that is to say, drunk on words.

"'The point is not to celebrate drunkenness, which is a social evil,' states Dickson. 'The idea is to show how the English language is versatile, flexible, phenomenal, gleeful.' He's done that all right, by finding a record number of synonyms for a word — 2660, for 'drunk'. And the record grows each time Dickson talks to another person on the subject, researches another era of history, or quizzes another bartender.

'Through the years many people have made their own 'drunk' lists. Benjamin Franklin, Edmund Wilson and H.L.Mencken all had lists. I collected those and added many more to them. It's almost a tradition. And every generation adds new words. It's like a huge snowball rolling down a hill.'

So what word, or group of words, is second place? Synonyms for 'crazy', Dickson claims: 'My favourite ones come out of a belt of the USA from West Virginia to Texas. They don't always make sense, but they sound nice.'

When we left him, Dickson was still running through his favourites: 'Crooked as a West Virginia mountain goat. One taco short of a combination platter. One sandwich shy of a picnic...'"

On Words!

(Photo: Russell Mott)

Longest scientific name
The systematic name for the *deoxyribonucleic acid* (DNA) of the human mitochondria contains 16,569 nucleotide residues and is thus *c.* 207,000 letters long. It was published in key form in *Nature* on 9 Apr 1981.

(southernmost Argentina and Chile) word *mamihlapinatapai*, meaning 'looking at each other hoping that either will offer to do something which both parties desire but are unwilling to do'.

Longest palindromes The longest known palindromic word is *saippuakivikauppias* (19 letters), which is Finnish for 'a dealer in lye'. The longest in English is *tattarrattat* (12 letters), a nonce word meaning rat-a-tat appearing in the *Oxford English Dictionary*.

Some baptismal fonts in Greece and Turkey bear the circular 25-letter inscription ΝΙΨΟΝ ΑΝΟΜΗΜΑΤΑ ΜΗ ΜΟΝΑΝ ΟΨΙΝ, meaning 'wash (my) sins, not only (my) face'. This appears at St Mary's Church, Nottingham, at St Paul's, Woldingham, Surrey and at other churches.

Longest anagrams The longest non-scientific English words which can form anagrams are the 17-letter transpositions *representationism* and *misrepresentation*. The longest scientific transposals are *hydroxydesoxycorticosterone* and *hydroxydeoxycorticosterones*, with 27 letters.

Longest abbreviations The initials of the Syarikat Kerjasama Orang-orang Melayu Kerajaan Hilir Perak Kerana Jimat Cermat Dan Pinjam-meminjam Wang Berhad compose the longest abbreviation: S.K.O.M.K.H.P.K.J.C.D.P.W.B.. This is the Malay name for The Cooperative Company of the Lower State of Perak Government's Malay People for Money Savings

Shortest abbreviation
The 55-letter full name of Los Angeles (El Pueblo de Nuestra Señora la Reina de los Angeles de Porciúncula) is abbreviated to L.A., or 3.63 per cent of its full length.

Common

The most frequently used words in written English are, in descending order of frequency: the, of, and, to, a, in, that, is, I, it, for and as. The most commonly used in conversation is 'I'. The commonest letter is 'e'. More words begin with the letter 's' than any other, but the most commonly used initial letter is 't' as in 'the', 'to', 'that' or 'there'.

and Loans Ltd, in Teluk Anson, Perak, West Malaysia (formerly Malaya). The abbreviation for this abbreviation is Skomk.

Longest acronym The longest acronym is NIIOMT-PLABOPARMBETZHEBETRABSBOMONIMONKON-OTDTEKHSTROMONT with 56 letters (54 in Cyrillic) in the *Concise Dictionary of Soviet Terminology, Institutions and Abbreviations* (1969), meaning: the laboratory for reinforcement, concrete and ferro-concrete operations, for composite-mono-lithic and monolithic constructions, of the Department of the Technology of Building-assembly operations, of the Scientific Research Institute of the Organization for mechanization and technical aid. This organization was employed for building the Academy of Building and Architecture of the USSR.

Most meanings The most overworked word in English is 'set', for which Dr Charles Onions (1873–1965) of Oxford University Press gave 58 noun uses, 126 verbal uses and 10 as a participial adjective.

Personal Names

Longest personal name The longest name appearing on a birth certificate is that of Rhoshandiatellyneshiaunneveshenk Koyaanfsquatsiuty Williams, born to Mr and Mrs James Williams in Beaumont, Texas, USA on 12 Sep 1984. On 5 Oct 1984, the father filed an amendment which expanded his daughter's first name to 1019 letters and the middle name to 36 letters.

Longest Place-names

In its most scholarly transliteration, Krungthep Mahanakhon, the 167-letter official name for Bangkok, the capital of Thailand, has 175 letters. The official short version (without capital letters which are not used in Thai) is included below.

World
krungthephphramahanakhon bowonratanakosin mahintharayuthaya mahadilokphiphobnovpharad radchataniburirom udomsantisug (111 letters)

Longest in use
Taumatawhakatangihangakoauauotamateaturipukakapikimaungahoronukupokaiwhenuakitanatahu (85 letters, Southern Hawke's Bay, New Zealand)[1]

British Isles
Gorsafawddachaidraigddanheddogleddollônpenrhynareurdraethceredigion (67 letters, Fairbourne Steam Railway, near Barmouth, Gwynedd)[2]
Llanfairpwllgwyngyllgogerychwyrndrobwllllantysiliogogogoch (58 letters, Anglesea, Gwynedd)[3]
Lower Llanfihangel-y-Creuddyn (26 letters, near Aberystwyth, Dyfed)[4]

[1] Unofficial name of a hill, the Maori translation meaning 'The place where Tamatea, the man with the big knees, who slid, climbed and swallowed mountains, known as landeater, played his flute to his loved one'. [2] Commercially-motivated creation on a station board 19.5m 64ft long. [3] Concocted version of a name translated as 'St Mary's Church by the pool of the white hazel trees, near the rapid whirlpool, by the red cave of the Church of St Tysilio'. This is the name used for the reopened (April 1973) village railway station in Anglesey, Gwynedd and was coined by a local bard, Y Bardd Cocos (John Evans, 1827–95) as a hoax. The official name consists of the first 20 letters. [4] The longest Welsh place-name in the Ordnance Survey Gazetteer.

Guess What?

Q. Which country produces the most films for the cinema

A. See Page 154

Most Christian names Mr A. Lindup-Badarou of Truro, Cornwall, formerly known as A. Hicks, has a total of 3530 Christian names as of March 1995.

Shortest surnames The commonest single-letter surname is 'O', prevalent in Korea.

British Isles Among the 47 million names on the Department of Social Security index, there are six examples of a one-letter surname—'A', 'B', 'J', 'N', 'O' and 'X'. The Christian name 'A' has been used for five generations in the Lincoln Taber family of Fingringhoe, Essex.

Tollemache (1884– 1917). At school he was known as Tolly. Of non-repetitious surnames, the last example of a five-part one was that of the Lady Caroline Jemima Temple-Nugent-Chandos-Brydges-Grenville (1858–1946).

The longest single English surname is Featherstone-haugh (17 letters), variously pronounced Feather-stonehaw or Festonhaw or Fessonhay or Freestonhugh or Feerstonhaw or Fanshaw. In Scotland the surname Nin (feminine of Mac) Achin-macdholicachinskerray (29 letters) was recorded in an 18th-century parish register.

'Macs' There are estimated to be some 1.6 million people in Britain with M', Mc or Mac (Gaelic genitive of 'son') as part of their surnames. The commonest of these is Macdonald, which accounts for about 55,000 of the Scottish population.

Place-Names

Earliest place-names The earliest recorded British place-name is Belerion, the Penwith peninsula of Cornwall, referred to by Pytheas of Massilia c. 308 BC. The earliest distinctive name for what is now Great Britain was Albion, used by Himilco c. 500 BC.

Longest Words

DANISH	speciallægepraksisplanlægningsstabiliseringsperiode (51)
	the stabilization period of the planning of a medical specialist's practices
DUTCH	kindercarnavalsoptochtvoorbereidingswerkzaamheden (49)
	preparation activities for a children's carnival procession
FINNISH	lentokonesuihkuturbiinimoottoriapumekaanikko aliupseerioppilas (61)
	apprentice non-commissioned officer, working as assistant-mechanic in charge of aeroplane jet-turbine engines
FRENCH	anticonstitutionnellement (25)
	anticonstitutionally
GERMAN	Rechtsschutzversicherungsgesellschaften (39)
	insurance companies which provide legal protection (This is the longest dictionary-defined word in everyday usage)
HUNGARIAN	megszentségteleníthetetlenségeskedéseitekért (44)
	for the times when you (pl.) acted as if you were unprofanable
ICELANDIC	hæstaréttarmálaflutningsmaður (29)
	supreme court barrister
ITALIAN	precipitevolissimevolmente (26)
	as fast as possible
PORTUGUESE	inconstitucionalissimamente (27)
	with the highest degree of unconstitutionality
RUSSIAN	ryentgyenoelyektrokardiografichyeskogo (33 Cyrillic letters, transliterating as 38)
	of the X-ray electrocardiographic
SPANISH	superextraordinarísimo (22)
	extraordinary to the highest degree possible
SWEDISH	Nordöstersjökustartilleriflygspaningssimulatoranläggning smateriel-underhållsuppföljningssystemdiskussionsinläggsför beredelse-arbetena (131)
	the preparatory work on the contribution to the discussion on the follow-up system of support of the material of the aviation survey simulator device within the coast artillery of the northern Baltic

[1] Agglutinative words are limited only by imagination and are not found in standard dictionaries. The first 100-letter such word was published in 1975 in Afrikaans.

Long Pedigree

It is claimed on behalf of the Clan Mackay that their clan can be traced to Loarn, the Irish invader of south-west Pictland, now Argyll, c. AD 501. The only non-royal English pedigree that can show with certainty a clear pre-Conquest descent is that of the Arden family, which includes Mary Arden, Shakespeare's mother.

Commonest surname The commonest surname in the English-speaking world is Smith. The most recent published count showed 659,050 nationally insured Smiths in Great Britain, of whom 10,102 were John Smith and another 19,502 were John (plus one or more names) Smith. Including uninsured persons there were over 800,000 Smiths in England and Wales alone, of whom 81,493 were called A. Smith.

Most surnames A six-part surname was borne by Major L.S.D.O.F. (Leone Sextus Denys Oswolf Fraudatifilius) Tollemache-Tollemache de Orellana-Plantagenet-Tollemache-

Most spellings
The spelling of the Dutch town of Leeuwarden has been recorded in 225 versions since AD 1046. Bromsberrow, Glos is recorded in 161 spellings since the 10th century, as reported by local historian Lester Steynor.

Shortest place-names Examples of single-letter place-names can be found in various countries around the world, including the villages of Y in France, Å in Denmark, Norway and Sweden and the River E, Highland.

Most common place-name Newton, meaning 'new settlement', occurs 467 times in Great Britain: 151 times in its simple form and 316 as part of a compound place-name. Of those towns with the name in its simple form, 90 are in Scotland, and 40 in the Grampian region alone.

Literature

Oldest book The oldest handwritten book, still intact, is a Coptic Psalter dated to about 1600 years ago, found in 1984 at Beni Suef, Eygpt.

UK The earliest known manuscript written in Britain is a bifolium of Eusebius' *Historia Ecclesiastica* from c. AD 625, possibly from the Jarrow library. Fragments of Roman wooden writing tablets found in the 1970s at Vindolanda (Chesterholme), Northumberland have been shown to make up the earliest known substantial written records in British history. These contain letters and a quotation from the Roman poet Virgil (70–19 BC) and are dated to c. AD 100.

Oldest

It is widely accepted that the earliest mechanically printed full-length book was the Gutenberg Bible, printed in Mainz, Germany, c. 1454 by Johann Henne zum Gensfleisch zur Laden, called 'zu Gutenberg' (c. 1398–1468).

Smallest book The smallest marketed, bound and printed book is printed on 22-gsm paper and measures 1 mm^2 *½s in^2*. It comprises the children's story *Old King Cole!* and 85 copies of it were published in March 1985 by The Gleniffer Press of Paisley, Strathclyde. The pages can be turned (with care) only by the use of a needle.

Largest publications The largest publication ever compiled was the *Yongle Dadian* (the great thesaurus of the Yongle reign) of 22,937 manuscript chapters (370 still survive) in 11,095 volumes. It was written by 2000 Chinese scholars in 1403–08. The entire Buddhist scriptures are inscribed on 729 marble slabs measuring 1.5×1 m *5 x 3½ ft* housed in 729 stupas in the Kuthodaw Pagoda, south of Mandalay, Myanmar (Burma). They were incised in 1860–68.

UK The 1112-volume set of *British Parliamentary Papers* was published by the Irish University Press in 1968–72. A complete set weighs 3.3 tonnes and would take six years to read at 10 hours per day. The production involved the skins of 34,000 Indian goats and the use of £15,000 worth of gold ingots.

CD-ROM In 1990, The British Library published its *General Catalogue of Printed Books to 1975* on a set of three CD-ROMs, priced at £9000. Alternatively, readers can spend six months scanning 178,000 catalogue pages in 360 volumes.

Dictionaries *Deutsches Wörterbuch*, started by Jacob and Wilhelm Grimm in 1854, was completed in 1971 and consists of 34,519 pages and 33 volumes (↔Longest literary gestation).

The largest English language dictionary is the 20-volume *Oxford English Dictionary*, with 21,728 pages. The longest entry is for the verb *set*, with over 75,000 words of text. The greatest outside contributor was Marghanita Laski (1915–88), with a reputed 250,000 quotations from 1958 until her death.

Encyclopedias The largest encyclopedia in current use is *La Enciclopedia Universal Ilustrada Europeo-Americana* (J. Espasa & Sons, Madrid and Barcelona), which comprises a total of 105,000 pages and an annual supplement of 165.2 million words.

The most comprehensive English-language encyclopedia is *The New Encyclopaedia Britannica*, the current 15th edition of which consists of 32 volumes, over 32,000 pages and more than 44 million words.

Fiction The novel *Tokuga-Wa Ieyasu* by Sohachi Yamaoka has been serialized in Japanese daily newspapers since 1951. If published in its entirety, it would require nearly 40 volumes.

Gestation

Longest literary gestation The standard German dictionary *Deutsches Wörterbuch* was begun by the brothers Grimm (Jacob and Wilhelm, 1785–1863 and 1786–1859 respectively) in 1854 and finished in 1971.

In 1629, the ecclesiastical historian Jean Bolland (1596–1665) began a chronicle of saints' lives called *Acta Sanctorum*, following an original idea by the priest Héribert Rosweyde. It was arranged according the saints' feast days; during his lifetime Bolland completed the first two parts, *January* and *February*. The work was later taken up by a group of Belgian Jesuits known as Bollandists, and additions were made periodically over the next three centuries. An introduction for December was published in 1940, and there are now 67 folio volumes of the completed *Acta Sanctorum*.

Oxford University Press received back their proofs of *Constable's Presentments* from the Dugdale Society in December 1984. They had been sent out for correction 35 years earlier in December 1949.

Who's Who Founded in 1848 and first published in 1849, *Who's Who* was the first biographical reference book in which all the entries were compiled by the biographees themselves, and were therefore *autobiographical*.

The longest entry in *Who's Who* was that of the Rt Hon. Sir Winston Leonard Spencer Churchill (1874–1965), who appeared in 67 editions from 1899 (18 lines) and had 211 lines by the 1965 edition. The longest entry in the book's current wider format is that of Dame Barbara Cartland, who was allocated 199 lines in the 1993 edition. Apart from those who qualify for inclusion by hereditary title, the youngest entrant was Yehudi Menuhin (Now Lord Menuhin; b. New York City, USA, 22 Apr 1916), the concert violinist, who first appeared in the 1932 edition at the age of 15.

Maps

Largest maps The largest permanent, 2-dimensional map measures 4552 m^2 *49,000 ft^2* and was painted by students of O'Hara Park School, Oakley, California, USA in the summer of 1992.

The Challenger relief map of British Columbia, Canada, measuring 575 m^2 *6080 ft^2*, was designed and built in the period 1945–52 by the late George Challenger and his son Robert. It is now on display at

Guess What?
Q. How old was the youngest bell-ringer?
A. See Page 145

■ The Mappae Mundi, dating from as early as the 10th century, are the earliest evidence of English map-making.
(Photo: E.T. Archive)

the Pacific National Exhibition in Vancouver, British Columbia.

Most expensive atlas The highest price paid for an atlas is $1,925,000, for a copy of Ptolemy's *Cosmographia* at Sotheby's, New York City, USA on 31 Jan 1990.

Smallest map In 1992, Dr Jonathon Mamin of IBM's Zurich laboratory used sudden electrical pulses to create a map of the Western Hemisphere from atoms. The map has a scale of one trillion to one, and has a diameter of about one micron (one millionth of a meter), which is about one hundredth of the diameter of a human hair (⇨ Science & Technology—Smallest man-made object).

Highest Prices

Books The highest price paid for any book is £8.14 million for the 226-leaf manuscript *The Gospel Book of Henry the Lion, Duke of Saxony* at Sotheby's, London on 6 Dec 1983. The book, which measures 34.3×25.4 cm *13½×10 in*, was illuminated *c.*1170 by the monk Herimann at Helmershansen Abbey, Germany with 41 full-page illustrations and was bought by Hans Kraus for the Hermann Abs consortium.

The record for a *printed* book is $5.39 million for an Old Testament (Genesis to Psalms) of the Gutenberg Bible printed in 1455 in Mainz, Germany. It was bought by Tokyo booksellers Maruzen Co. Ltd at Christie's, New York, USA on 22 Oct 1987.

Manuscripts An illustrated manuscript by Leonardo Da Vinci known as the 'Codex Hammer', in which Da Vinci predicted the invention of the submarine and the steam engine, was sold for a record $30.8 million at Christie's, New York on 11 Nov 1994. The buyer was Bill Gates (⇨Richest men). It is the only Leonardo manuscript in private hands.

Musical The auction record for a musical manuscript is £2,585,000 paid by London dealer James Kirkman at Sotheby's, London on 22 May 1987 for a 508-page bound volume of nine complete symphonies in Mozart's hand. The record for a single musical manuscript is £1.1 million paid at Sotheby's, London on 6 Dec 1991 for the autograph copy of the Piano Sonata in E minor, opus 90 by Ludwig van Beethoven (1770–1827).

Diaries and Letters

Longest-kept diary Col. Ernest Loftus of Harare, Zimbabwe began his daily diary on 4 May 1896 at the age of 12 and continued it until his death on 7 Jul 1987 aged 103 years 178 days, a total of 91 years.

UK T.C. Baskerville of Thornton Cleveleys, Blackpool has written an entry in his diary of international and home affairs every day since 1939. It consists of an estimated 7.25 million words in 42,340 pages, and includes signatures

Guess What?

Q. How many seats has the smallest theatre?

A. See Page 157

of all the Prime Ministers from Sir Winston Churchill to John Major.

Longest letter to an editor The *Upper Dauphin Sentinel* of Pennsylvania, USA published a letter of 25,513 words over eight issues from August to November 1979, written by John Sultzbaugh of Lykens, Pennsylvania.

Most letters to an editor David Green, author and solicitor of Castle Morris, Dyfed, had his 135th letter published in the main correspondence columns of *The Times* on 9 Aug 1994, more than any other correspondent. His record year was 1972 with 12; his shortest was 'Sir, "Yes".', on 31 May 1993.

Shortest letter to The Times The shortest letter to *The Times* comprised the single abbreviated symbol 'Dr²?' R. S. Cookson of London NW11 on 30 Jul 1984 in a correspondence on the correct form of recording a plurality of academic doctorates. On 8 Jan 1986, a letter was sent to *The Times* by a 7-year-old girl from the Isle of Man. It read 'Sir, Yours faithfully Caroline Sophia Kerenhappuch Parkes'. The brief epistle was intended to inform readers of her unusual name, Kerenhappuch, mentioned in a letter the previous week from Rev. John Ticehurst on the subject of uncommon 19th-century names.

Shortest letter The shortest correspondence on record was between Victor Marie Hugo (1802–85) and his publisher, Hurst and Blackett, in 1862. The author was on holiday and anxious to know how his new novel *Les Misérables* was selling. He wrote '?' and received the reply '!'.

Christmas cards The first Christmas card is thought to have been sent out by Sir Henry Cole (1808–82) in 1843 but this practice did not become an annual ritual until 1862.

The greatest number of personal Christmas cards sent out is believed to be 62,824 by Werner Erhard of San Francisco, California, USA in December 1975. Many must have been to unilateral acquaintances.

Most expensive letters The highest price ever paid on the open market for a single signed letter was $748,000 on 5 Dec 1991 at Christie's, New York, USA for a letter written by Abraham Lincoln on 8 Jan 1863 defending criticism of the Emancipation Proclamation. It was sold to Profiles in History of Beverly Hills, CA (⇨ Science & Technology, Telegrams).

The highest price paid for a letter signed by a living person is $12,500 at the Hamilton Galleries on 22 Jan 1981 for a letter from President Ronald Reagan praising Frank Sinatra.

Broadsheet

The highest price ever paid for a printed page was $2,420,000 for one of the 24 known copies of *The Declaration of Independence*, printed by John Dunlap in Philadelphia, Pennsylvania, USA in 1776. It was sold by Samuel T. Freeman & Co. to Donald Scheer of Atlanta, Georgia on 13 Jun 1991.

Letter-Writing

Uichi Noda, former Vice Minister of Treasury and Minister of Construction in Japan, wrote 1307 letters to his bedridden wife Mitsu during his overseas trips from July 1961 until her death in March 1985. These letters have been published in 25 volumes, totalling 12,404 pages and more than 5 million characters.

Britain's most successful writer of text books

Britain's most successful writer of text books is ex-schoolmaster Ronald Ridout (b. 23 Jul 1916) who has had 515 titles published since 1958, with sales of 91.35 million. His *The First English Workbook* has sold 5.6 million copies.

Authors

Most prolific author A lifetime output of 72–75 million words has been calculated for Charles Harold St John Hamilton, alias Frank Richards (1876–1961), the creator of Billy Bunter. In his peak years (1915–26) he wrote up to 80,000 words a week for the boys' school weeklies *Gem* (1907–39), *Magnet* (1908–40) and *Boys' Friend* (1895–1927).

Most prolific novelist The greatest number of novels published by one author is 1020 by Brazilian novelist José Carlos Ryoki de Alpoim Inoue (b. 22 Jul 1946). He writes science fiction, westerns and thrillers.

UK The most prolific author is currently Dame Barbara Cartland, with 583 titles published in 30 languages to date. She has averaged 23 titles per year for the last 19 years and was made a Dame of the Order of the British Empire by HM The Queen in the 1991 New Year's Honours List for services to literature and the community.

Although it is difficult to put precise figures to the output of Enid Mary Blyton (1897–1968) she is thought to have completed no less than 600 books in all; some sources believe her complete works to be in excess of 700. Her books have been translated into 165 languages.

Most pseudonyms The writer with the greatest number of pseudonyms is the minor Russian humorist Konstantin Arsenievich Mikhailov (b. 1868), whose 325 pen names are listed in the *Dictionary of Pseudonyms* by I.F. Masanov, published in Moscow in 1960. The names, ranging from Ab. to Z, were mostly abbreviations of his real name.

Greatest advance It was reported in August 1992, that Berkeley Putnam paid $14 million (£7.3 million) for the North American rights to *Without Remorse* by Tom Clancy, representing the greatest advance for a single book. On 9 Feb 1989, the American horror writer Stephen King (b. 21 Sep 1947) was reported to have scooped an advance of £26 million for his following four books.

On 6 May 1992, the British journalist and author Barbara Taylor Bradford (b. 10 May 1933) concluded a deal with HarperCollins for £17 million (over some five years) for three novels.

Rarest signature

Only one example of the signature of Christopher Marlowe (1564–93) is known. It is in the Kent County Archives on a will of 1583.

Top-selling authors The world's top-selling fiction writer is Dame Agatha Christie (née Miller, later Lady Mallowan, 1890–1976), whose 78 crime novels have sold an estimated 2 billion copies in 44 languages. Agatha Christie also wrote 19 plays and six romantic novels under the pseudonym Mary Westmacott. Royalty earnings are estimated to be worth £2.5 million per year.

The top-selling living author is Dame Barbara Cartland with global sales of over 650 million for her 583 titles published (⇨ Most prolific author).

Brazilian author Jorge Amado (b. 10 Aug 1912) has had his 32 novels published in 48 different languages in 60 countries. His first book *O Pai's do Carnaval* was published in 1931 and the most recent *A Descoberta da América pelos Turcos* in 1994.

Non-fiction It has been reported that 800 million copies of the red-covered booklet *Quotations from the Works of Mao Zedong (Tse-tung)* were sold or distributed between June 1966, when possession became virtually mandatory in China, and September 1971, when its promoter Marshal Lin Biao died in an air crash.

Highest-paid author In 1958, Deborah Schneider of Minneapolis, Minnesota, USA wrote 25 words to complete a sentence in a competition for the best blurb for Plymouth cars. She beat about 1.4 million entrants to claim a prize of $500 every month for life. On normal life expectations she should collect $12,000 per word. The winning phrase is in a deed box at her bank 'Only to be opened after death'. She passed $9000 a word in 1995.

Biography The longest in publishing history is the ongoing biography of Sir Winston Churchill, co-authored by his son Randolph and Martin Gilbert. The book currently comprises 22 volumes and 9,694,000 words.

Slowest-selling book The accolade for the world's slowest-selling book (known in US publishing as slooow sellers) probably belongs to David Wilkins' translation of the New Testament from Coptic into Latin, published by Oxford University Press (OUP) in 1716 in 500 copies. Selling an average of one each 20 weeks, it remained in print for 191 years.

Oldest author Alice Pollock (*née* Wykeham-Martin, 1868–1971) of Haslemere, Surrey, had her first book *Portrait of My Victorian Youth* (Johnson Publications) published in March 1971 when she was aged 102 years 8 months.

Youngest Poet Laureate Laurence Eusden (1688– 1730) 'received the bays' on 24 Dec 1718 at the age of 30 years and 3 months.

Oldest Poet Laureate

The greatest age at which a poet has succeeded is 73 in the case of William Wordsworth (1770–1850) on 6 Apr 1843. The longest-lived Laureate was John Masefield, who died on 12 May 1967 aged 88 years 345 days. The longest any poet has worn the laurel is 41 years 322 days in the case of Alfred (later the 1st Lord) Tennyson (1809–92), who was appointed on 19 Nov 1850 and died in office on 6 Oct 1892.

Longest poem The lengthiest poem ever published is the Kirghiz folk epic *Manas*, which appeared in printed form in 1958 but which has never been translated into English. According to the *Dictionary of Oriental Literatures*, this 3-part epic runs to about 500,000 lines. Short translated passages appear in *The Elek Book of Oriental Verse*.

The longest poem in English is one on the life of King Alfred by John Fitchett (1766–1838) of Liverpool, Merseyside, which ran to 129,807 lines and took 40 years to write. His editor, Robert Riscoe, added the concluding 2585 lines.

Best-Selling Books

The world's best-selling and most widely distributed book is the Bible, with an estimated 2.5 billion copies sold between 1815 and 1975. Since 1976, combined global sales of Today's English Version (*Good News*) New Testament and Bible (which is copyright of the Bible Societies) have exceeded 122 million copies. By the end of 1993, the whole bible had been translated into 337 languages; 2062 languages have at least one book of the bible in that language. The oldest publisher of bibles is the Cambridge University Press, which began with the Geneva version in 1591 (⇨ Oldest publisher).

■ Studying the bible, one of the world's best-selling and most widely-distributed books. (Photo: Gamma/R. Gaillarde)

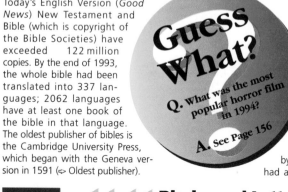

Q. What was the most popular horror film in 1994?

A. see Page 156

Lunches

Literary luncheons were inaugurated in October 1930 by Christina Foyle at the Old Holborn Restaurant, London. Attendances were over 1500 at Grosvenor House, Park Lane, London at lunches for Mistinguett (1873–1956) and Dr Edvard Benes (1884–1948), both in 1938.

Excluding non-copyright works such as the Bible and the Koran, the world's all-time best-selling book is *The Guinness Book of Records*, first published in October 1955 by Guinness Superlatives, a subsidiary of Arthur Guinness Son & Co. (Park Royal) Ltd, and edited by Norris Dewar McWhirter (b. 12 Aug 1925) and his twin brother Alan Ross McWhirter (killed 27 Nov 1975). Global sales in some 37 languages have passed 77 million to April 1995.

Fiction Due to a lack of audited figures, it is impossible to state which single work of fiction has the highest sales. Three novels have been credited with sales of around 30 million: *Valley of the Dolls* (1966) by Jacqueline Susann (1921–74), which sold 6.8 million copies in just the first six months, although it is now out of print; *To Kill a Mockingbird* (1960) by Harper Lee and *Gone With the Wind* by Margaret Mitchell.

Alistair Stuart MacLean (1922–87) wrote 30 books, 28 of which sold over a million copies each in the UK alone. His books have been translated into 28 languages and 13 have been filmed. It has been estimated that a 'MacLean' novel is purchased every 18 seconds.

Most weeks on a best-seller list The longest duration on the *New York Times* best-seller list (founded 1935) is for *The Road Less Traveled* by M. Scott Peck, which on 14 Apr 1995 had its 598th week on the lists. Over 5 million copies of the book, which is published by Touchstone (a division of Simon & Schuster), have been sold.

UK The hardback edition of *A Brief History of Time* (Transworld/Bantam Press) by Prof. Stephen Hawking (b. 8 Jan 1942), had appeared in *The Sunday Times* best-seller

The principle book publishing country in the world was the United Kingdom at the time of our first edition. During 1953, it reported, 18,257 titles were produced, including 12,734 first editions. In 1994, over 82,000 books were produced.

list (which excludes books published annually) for a record 237 weeks as of May 1995. The paperback, released on 9 April 1995, entered the list at number one the following week. *The Country Diary of an Edwardian Lady* (Michael Joseph, Webb & Bower) by Edith Holden (1871–1920) held the No. 1 position for 64 weeks.

Publishers and Printers

Oldest publisher Cambridge University Press has a continuous history of printing and publishing since 1584. The University received Royal Letters Patent 'to print and sell all manner of books' on 20 Jul 1534.

In 1978, the Oxford University Press (OUP) celebrated the 500th anniversary of the printing of the first book in the City of Oxford in 1478. This was before OUP itself was in existence.

Most prolific publisher At its peak in 1989, Progress Publishers (founded 1931 as the Publishing Association of Foreign Workers in the USSR) of Moscow, USSR printed over 750 titles in 50 languages annually.

Fastest

Two thousand bound copies of *The Book Fair Book*, published by the Zimbabwe International Book Fair Trust and printed by Print Holdings (Pvt) Ltd, were produced from raw disk in 5 hr 23 min at the Zimbabwe International Book Fair in Harare on 5 Aug 1993. The time for 1000 copies was 4 hr 50 min and Braille, large print, CD-ROM and audio-tape formats were produced simultaneously.

Largest publisher The world's largest publisher of books is Viacom Communications, based in New York, USA, with a total of $1.79 billion generated from books at year end June 1994. The largest publisher of UK-generated books is the Pearson Group based in Millbank, London, whose subsidiaries include Penguin, Longman and Westminster Press, and whose income generated from books in 1993 was £320 million.

Largest printer The largest printer is Bertelsmann in Germany. The company had 1993 sales of $10,956 million with profits of $289 million. It employs 14,696 people.

Highest Printings

It is believed that in the USA, Van Antwerp Bragg and Co. printed some 60 million copies of the 1879 edition of *The McGuffey Reader*, compiled by Henry Vail in the pre-copyright era for distribution to public schools.

The initial print order for the new postcode directory produced by Deutsche Bundespost for United Germany was 42,300,000 copies. Issued on 1 Jul 1993, the print run took 59,220 tons of paper and 2,480 trucks to transport. The publications were distributed to 36,300,000 homes and businesses.

The aggregate print of *The Highway Code* (instituted 1931) has reached 111 million, with 2 million copies of the new edition sold in three months to April 1993.

Fiction The highest print order for a work of fiction in the UK was 3 million by Penguin Books Ltd for their paperback edition of *Lady Chatterley's Lover*, by D.H. (David Herbert) Lawrence (1885–1930). Total worldwide sales to April 1995 were in excess of 4,900,000 copies.

Bookshops The bookshop with most titles and the longest shelving (48 km *30 miles*) is W.&G. Foyle Ltd of London. Established in 1904 in a small shop in Islington, the company is now at 113–119 Charing Cross Road in premises measuring 7044 m² *75,825 ft²*. The most capacious individual bookstore in the world measured by square footage is the Barnes & Noble Bookstore of New York City, USA. It covers 14,330 m² *154,250 ft²* and has 20.71 km *12.87 miles* of shelving.

Libraries and Museums

Largest library The United States Library of Congress in Washington, DC contains 107,824,509 items, including 16,448,469 books in the classified collections and 91,376,040 items in non-classified. The library occupies about 265,000 m² *2.85 million ft²* in the Capitol Hill buildings, with additional offices and branches world-wide. It has 925 km *532 miles* of shelving and 4701 employees.

UK The largest library in the United Kingdom is the British Library. It comprises 19 buildings in London, a site of 24.3 ha *60 acre* site at Boston Spa, W Yorks, and employs a total staff of some 2500. The Library contains over 18 million volumes. Stock increases involve over 12.8 km *8 miles* of new shelving annually.

The Newspaper Library at Colindale, north London, opened in 1932, has 583,000 volumes and parcels comprising 70,000 different titles on 35.4 km *22 miles* of shelving. The Document Supply Centre in West Yorks (shelf capacity 157.7 km *98 miles*) runs the largest library inter-lending operation in the world;

each year, the library handles over 3 million requests from other libraries (UK and overseas) for items they do not themselves hold in stock.

The National Sound Archive holds 1 million discs and 62,000 hours of recorded tape.

Oldest museum The Ashmolean in Oxford was built between 1679 and 1683, and was named after the collector Elias Ashmole (1617–92). Since 1924, it has housed an exhibition of historic scientific instruments.

Largest museum The Smithsonian Institution comprises 16 museums and the National Zoological Park in Washington, DC, USA. It contains over 140 million items and has over 6000 employees (↪Most popular).

The American Museum of Natural History in New York City, USA, founded in 1869, comprises 23 interconnected buildings. The buildings of the Museum and the Planetarium contain 11,148 m² *1.2 million ft²* of floor space, accommodating more than 30 million artifacts and specimens and the museum attracts over 3 million visitors each year.

Most popular museum The highest attendance for any museum is over 118,437 (with the doors temporarily closed) on 14 Apr 1984 at the Smithsonian's National Air and Space Museum, Washington, DC, USA, opened in July 1976.

Overdue books The record for an unreturned and overdue library book was set when a book in German on the Archbishop of Bremen, published in 1609, was borrowed from Sidney Sussex College, Cambridge by Colonel Robert Walpole in 1667–68. It was found by Prof. Sir John Plumb in the library of the then Marquess of Cholmondeley at Houghton Hall, Norfolk and returned 288 years later. No fine was exacted.

Newspapers

Oldest newspapers A copy has survived of a news pamphlet published in Cologne, Germany in 1470. The oldest newspaper still in existence is the Swedish official journal *Post och Inrikes Tidningar*, founded in 1645 and published by the Royal Swedish Academy of Letters.

UK The *London Gazette* (originally the *Oxford Gazette*) was first published on 16 Nov 1665. The newspaper with the earliest origins which is still published is *Berrow's Worcester Journal* (originally the *Worcester Post Man*), published in Worcester. It was traditionally founded in 1690 and has appeared weekly since June 1709. No complete file exists. The earliest foundation date for any British newspaper published under the same title is the *Stamford Mercury*, printed since 1712.

The oldest Sunday newspaper is *The Observer*, first issued on 4 Dec 1791.

Largest newspaper The 14 Jun 1993 edition of the daily newspaper 'Het Volk', published in Gent, Belgium, had a page size of 142 × 99.5 cm *55.9 × 39.2 in*. It sold 50,000 copies.

UK The *Worcestershire Chronicle* was the largest British newspaper, and a surviving issue of 16 Feb 1859 measures 82 × 57 cm *32¼ × 22½ in*.

Heaviest newspaper The most massive single issue of a newspaper was the 14 Sep 1987 edition of the Sunday *New York Times*, which weighed more than 5.4 kg *12 lb* and contained 1612 pages.

Smallest newspaper The smallest original page size was 7.6 × 9.5 cm *3 × 3¾ in* for the *Daily Banner* (25 cents per month) of Roseberg, Oregon, USA. Issues dated 1 and 2 Feb 1876 survive. The British Library Newspaper Library contains the *Watford News and Advertiser* of 1 Apr 1899, which measures 7.5 × 10 cm *2.9 × 3.9 in*.

Longest editorship Sir Etienne Dupuch (1899–1991) of Nassau, Bahamas was editor-in-chief of *The Tribune* from 1 Apr 1919 to 1972, and contributing editor until his death on 23 Aug 1991, a total of 72 years. The longest editorship of any UK national newspaper was 57 years by C.P. (Charles Prestwich) Scott (1846–1932) of the *Manchester Guardian* (the *Guardian* from 1959), who occupied the post from the age of 26 in 1872 until his retirement in 1929.

Most durable feature Mary MacArthur of Port Appin, Strathclyde has contributed a regular feature to *The Oban Times and West Highland Times* since 1926.

Most misprints The most in *The Times* was on 22 Aug 1978 when on page 19 there were 97 in 5½ single-column inches. The passage concerned 'Pop' (Pope) Paul VI.

Most durable advertiser The Jos Neel Co., a clothing store in Macon, Georgia, USA (founded 1880) ran an 'ad' in *The Macon Telegraph* every day in the top left-hand corner of page 2A from 22 Feb 1889 to 16 Aug 1987 — a total of 35,291 consecutive advertisements.

Most advertising pages The greatest number of pages of advertisements sold in a single issue of a periodical is 829.54 by the October 1989 edition of *Business Week*.

Cartoon strips The earliest cartoon is 'The Yellow Kid', which first appeared in the *New York Journal* on 18 Oct 1896.

The longest-lived newspaper comic strip is the 'Katzenjammer Kids' (Hans and Fritz), created by Rudolph Dirks and first published in the *New York Journal* on 12 Dec 1897. The strip was still running as of 13 April 1995, and is currently drawn by cartoonist Hy Eisman. It is now syndicated by King Features Syndicate to approximately 50 newspapers.

The most syndicated strip is 'Peanuts' by Charles Schulz of Santa Rosa, California, USA. First published in October 1950, it currently appears in 2300 newspapers in 68 countries and 26 languages.

Most syndicated columnist Ann Landers (née Eppie Lederer, b. 4 Jul 1918) appears in over 1200 newspapers with an estimated readership of 90 mil-

CD-ROM library MicroPatent of East Haven, Connecticut, USA, the commercial publisher of patent information, has a collection of 1580 discs containing almost 20 million pages of every US utility patent from 1976 to the present day. It is the largest CD-ROM library in the world.

Guess What?
Q. What was the world's best-selling video in 1994?
A. See Page 152

The British Library, which has not been challenged as the UK's largest library since our first edition, has tripled its collection of books and manuscripts in the last forty years.

Museum

The largest and most visited museum in the United Kingdom is the British Museum (founded in 1753), which was opened to the public in 1759. The main building in Bloomsbury, London was begun in 1823 and has a total floor area of 8.7 ha *21.5 acres*. In 1994, 6,286,838 people passed through its doors.

lion. Her only serious rival is 'Dear Abby' (Mrs Pauline Phillips), her identical twin sister based in Beverly Hills, California, USA.

Circulation

Highest circulation *Komsomolskaya Pravda* (founded 1925), the youth paper of the former Soviet Communist Party, reached a peak daily circulation of 21,975,000 copies in May 1990. The 8-page weekly newspaper *Argumenty i Fakty* (founded 1978) of Moscow, USSR attained a figure of 33,431,100 copies in May 1990, when it had an estimated readership of over 100 million.

The highest circulation for any *currently* published newspaper is that of *The Yomiuri Shimbun*, founded 1874, which publishes morning and evening editions in Tokyo, Japan, and had a combined daily circulation of 14.567 million in January 1995.

UK The *News of the World* (founded 1 Oct 1843) attained peak sales of 8,480,878 copies in April 1951 and had an estimated readership of over 19 million. Sales in March 1995 were 4,716,868, with an estimated daily readership of 12,230,000 between September 1994 and February 1995. The highest net sale of any daily newspaper is *The Sun*, with sales of 4,134,571 in March 1995.

> The first newspaper to achieve a circulation of 1 million copies was *Le Petit Journal*, published in Paris, France, which reached this figure in 1886, when selling at 5 centimes. Sales of the *Daily Mail* first reached a million on 2 Mar 1900.

Magazines

Oldest magazines The oldest existing magazine is *Philosophical Transactions of the Royal Society*, published in London, which first appeared on 6 Mar 1665. Britain's oldest weekly periodical is *The Lancet*, first published in 1823.

Annual The most durable annual is *Old Moore's Almanack*, published since 1697, when it appeared as a broadsheet produced by Dr Francis Moore (1657–1715) of Southwark, London to advertise his 'physiks'. Published by W. Foulsham & Co. Ltd of Slough, Berks, aggregate sales to date are over 113 million.

Largest circulations Total sales through non-commercial channels by Jehovah's Witnesses of *The Truth that Leads to Eternal Life*, published by the Watchtower Bible and Tract Society of New York City, USA on 8 May 1968, reached 107,651,627 in 117 languages by April 1995.

The peak circulation of any weekly magazine was achieved by the US *TV Guide* which, in 1974, became the first magazine to sell a billion copies in a year. In its 46 basic international editions, *Reader's Digest* (established February 1922) circulates more than 28 million copies monthly in 18 languages, including a US edition of more than 15 million copies and a UK edition (established 1939) of nearly 1.7 million copies. Readership in the UK alone was estimated at 6,418,000 between April and September 1993.

> **Guess What?**
> Q. How many letters has the world's shortest alphabet?
> A. See Page 137

Parade, the US syndicated colour magazine, is distributed with 352 newspapers every Sunday and as of 17 Apr 1995 had a peak circulation of 37.614 million, the highest in the world for any magazine. At $585,600 for a 4-colour page, it is also the most expensive magazine in which to advertise.

UK Before deregulation of the listings market in March 1991, the highest circulation of any periodical in Britain was that of the *Radio Times* (instituted on 28 Sep 1923). Average weekly sales for July–December 1989 was 3,037,129 copies, with a readership of 9,031,000. The highest sales figure for any issue was 11,037,139 copies for the 1989 Christmas edition.

Largest The bulkiest consumer magazine ever published was the 10 Jan 1990 issue of *Shukan Jutaku Joho* (Weekly Housing Information), running to 1940 pages. Published in Japan by the Recruit Company Ltd, it retailed for 350 yen.

Crosswords

Fastest solution The fastest recorded time for completing *The Times* crossword under test conditions is 3 min 45 sec by Roy Dean of Bromley, Kent in the BBC *Today* radio studio on 19 Dec 1970. Dr John Sykes (1929–93) won *The Times/Collins Dictionaries* championship 10 times between 1972 and 1990, when he solved each of the four puzzles in an average time of eight minutes and beat the field by a record margin of 9½ minutes on 8 Sep 1991 at the Hilton hotel, London. He set a championship best time of 4 min 28 sec in 1989.

> **Largest published crossword** In July 1982, Robert Turcot of Québec, Canada compiled a crossword comprising 82,951 squares. It contained 12,489 clues across, 13,125 down and covered $3.55 m^2$ $38.21 ft^2$.

Most prolific compiler Roger F. Squires of Ironbridge, Shrops compiles 38 puzzles single-handedly each week. His total output to September 1995 was over 46,000 crosswords and his millionth clue was published in the Daily Telegraph on 6 Sep 1989. He is one of only three compilers ever to have had puzzles published in all five broadsheet newspapers.

Music

The human voice Before this century the extremes were a staccato E in *alt altissimo* (eiv) by Ellen Beach Yaw (USA) (1869–1947) in Carnegie Hall, New York, USA on 19 Jan 1896, and an A_1 (55 Hz) by Kasper Foster (1617–73).

Madeleine Marie Robin (1918–60), the French operatic coloratura, could produce and sustain the B above high C in the Lucia mad scene in Donizetti's *Lucia di Lammermoor*. Since 1950, singers have achieved high and low notes far beyond the hitherto accepted extremes. However, notes at the bass and treble extremities of the register tend to lack harmonics and are of little musical value. Dan Britton of Branson, Missouri, USA can produce the note E-0 (18.84 Hz).

Ivan Rebroff, the Russian bass, has a voice extending easily over four octaves from low F to high F, 1¼ octaves above C.

The highest note put into song is Giv first occurring in Mozart's *Popoli di Tessaglia*.

The lowest vocal note in the classical repertoire is in Mozart's *Die Entführung aus dem Serail* in Osmin's aria, which calls for a low D (73.4 Hz).

Songs

Oldest songs The *shaduf* chant has been sung since time immemorial by workers on the Nile water mills (or *saqiyas*) in Egypt. An Assyrian love song to an Ugaritic god, c. 1800 BC, was reconstructed from a tablet of notation for an 11-string lyre, at the University of California, Berkeley, USA on 6 Mar 1974.

The oldest known harmonized music performed today is the English song *Sumer is icumen in*, which dates from c. 1240.

National anthems The oldest national anthem is the *Kimigayo* of Japan, the words of which date from the 9th century, whilst the oldest music belongs to the anthem of the Netherlands. The shortest anthems are those of Japan, Jordan and San Marino, each with only four lines. Of the 11 wordless national anthems, the oldest is that of Spain, dating from 1770.

Longest rendering of national anthem 'God Save the King' was played non-stop 16 or 17 times by a German military band on the platform of Rathenau railway station, Brandenburg, Germany on the morning of 9 Feb 1909. The reason was that King Edward VII was struggling to don the uniform of a German field-marshal before he could emerge from the train.

Songwriters The most successful songwriters in terms of number one singles are John Lennon (1940–80) and Paul McCartney (b. 18 Jun 1942). McCartney is credited as writer on 32 number one hits in the US to Lennon's 26 (with 23 co-written), whereas Lennon authored 29 UK number ones to McCartney's 28 (25 co-written).

Singer's pulling power In 1850, up to $653 was paid for a single seat at the US concerts of Johanna ('Jenny') Maria Lind (1820–87), the 'Swedish nightingale'. She had a vocal range from g to e[111], the middle register of which is still regarded as unrivalled.

Earliest hymn There are more than 950,000 Christian hymns in existence. The music and parts of the text of a hymn in the *Oxyrhynchus Papyri* from the 2nd century are the earliest known hymnody. The earliest exactly datable hymn is the *Heyr Himna Smiôur* (*Hear, the Maker of Heaven*) from 1208 by the Icelandic bard and chieftain Kolbeinn Tumason (1173–1208).

Longest published hymn *Sing God's Song*, a hymn by Carolyn Ann Aish of Inglewood, New Zealand, is 754 verses or 3016 lines long, with an additional 4-line refrain to each verse.

> ## Top Songs
> The most frequently sung songs in English are *Happy Birthday to You* (based on the original *Good Morning to All*), by Kentucky Sunday School teachers Mildred Hill and Patty Smith Hill of New York, USA (written in 1893 and under copyright from 1935 to 2010); *For He's a Jolly Good Fellow* (originally the French *Malbrouk*), known at least as early as 1781, and *Auld Lang Syne* (originally the Strathspey *I Fee'd a Lad at Michaelmass*), some words of which were written by Robert Burns (1759–96).

> **Most prolific hymnists** Frances (Fanny) Jane van Alstyne (1820–1915) of the US wrote 8500 hymns, and is reputed to have finished one hymn in 15 minutes. Charles Wesley (1707–88) wrote about 6000 hymns.

Bells

Oldest bell The tintinnabulum, found in the Babylonian Palace of Nimrod in 1849 by Austen (later Sir) Henry Layard (1817–94), dates from c. 1100 BC. The oldest known tower bell is one in St Benedict Church, Rome, Italy dated 'anno domini millesimo sexagesimo IX' (1069).

UK The fragile hand bell known as the Black or Iron Bell of St Patrick is dated c. AD 450. The oldest tower bell in Great Britain is dated *ante* 1100. It weighs 50 kg *1 cwt* and is still in use at St Botolph, Hardham, Sussex.

Heaviest bell The Tsar Kolokol, cast by Russian brothers I.F. and M.I. Motorin on 25 Nov 1735 in Moscow, weighs 202 tonnes and measures 6.6 m *22 ft* in diameter, 6.14 m *20 ft* high and 60 cm *24 in* at its thickest point. The bell was cracked in a fire in 1737 and a fragment, weighing about 11.5 tonnes, was broken off. The bell has stood, unrung, on a platform in the Kremlin in Moscow since 1836 with the broken section alongside.

The heaviest bell still in use is the Mingun bell, weighing 92 tonnes with a diameter of 5.09 m *16 ft 8½ in* at the lip, in Mandalay, Myanmar (Burma). The bell is struck by a teak boom from the outside. It was cast at Mingun late in the reign of King Bodawpaya (1782–1819).

UK The heaviest bell hung in Great Britain is 'Great Paul' in the south-west tower of St Paul's Cathedral, London. Cast in 1881, it weighs 17 tonnes, has a diameter of 2.9 m *9 ft 6½ in* and sounds the note E-flat.

Most broadcast bell 'Big Ben', the hour bell in the clock tower of the House of Commons, was cast in 1858 and weighs 13.8 tonnes. It plays the note E natural.

Bell-ringing Eight bells have been rung to their full 'extent' (40,320 unrepeated changes of Plain Bob Major) only once without relays. This took place in a bell foundry at Loughborough, Leics, beginning at 6:52 a.m. on 27 Jul 1963 and ending at 12:50 a.m. on 28 July, after 17 hr 58 min. The peal was composed by Kenneth Lewis of Altrincham, Manchester and the eight ringers were conducted by Robert B. Smith of Marple, Manchester. Theoretically, it would take 37 years 355 days to ring 12 bells (maximus) to their full extent of 479,001,600 changes.

Largest carillon The largest carillon (minimum of 23 bells) in the world is the Laura Spelman Rockefeller Memorial Carillon in Riverside Church, New York, USA, with 74 bells weighing 114 tons. The bourdon, giving the note lower C, weighs 20.5 tons and is the largest tuned bell in the world.

Oldest and youngest bell-ringers George Symonds (1875–1974) of Ipswich, Suffolk was a regular bell-ringer for 89 years. He conducted a peal at the age of 97 and rang his last peal in 1973 at the age of 98. He is thus the oldest ringer ever to have conducted and rung a peal, and also the longest-serving ringer.

The youngest is Jonathan Carpenter of Warfield Berks, who rang his first peal at Warfield Church on 19 Jun 1982 at the age of 7 yr 299 days.

Instruments

Grandest piano The grandest grand piano weighed 1.25 tonnes, measured 3.55 m *11 ft*

8 in long, and was made by Chas H. Challen & Son Ltd of London in 1935. The longest bass string measured 3.02 m *9 ft 11 in*, with a tensile strength of 30 tonnes.

Most expensive piano The highest price ever paid for a piano was $390,000 at Sotheby Parke Bernet, New York, USA on 26 Mar 1980 for a Steinway grand of c. 1888 sold by the Martin Beck Theater. It was bought by a non-pianist.

Largest organ The largest and loudest musical instrument ever constructed is the now only partially functional Auditorium Organ in Atlantic City, New Jersey, USA. Completed in 1930, it had two consoles (one with seven manuals and another movable one with five), 1477 stop controls and 33,112 pipes, ranging in tone from 4.7 mm *1/5 in* to 19.5 m *64 ft*. It had the volume of 25 brass bands, with a range of seven octaves.

Fully-functional The 6-manual Grand Court Organ in the Wanamaker Store, Philadelphia, Pennsylvania, USA has 30,067 pipes; the tone gravissima pipe is 19.5 m *64 ft* long. The organ was installed in 1911 and enlarged between then and 1930.

UK The largest organ in Great Britain is that completed in Liverpool Anglican Cathedral on 18 Oct 1926, with two 5-manual consoles and 9704 speaking pipes (originally 10,936) ranging from tones 1.9 cm *¾ in* to 9.75 m *32 ft*.

Most durable musicians The Romanian pianist Cella Delavrancea (1887–1991) gave her last public recital, receiving six encores, at the age of 103. Yiannis Pipis (b. 25 Nov 1889) of Nicosia, Cyprus has been a professional Folkloric violinist since 1912.

The world's oldest active musician is Jennie Newhouse (b. 12 Jul 1889) of High Bentham, N Yorks,

Most Peals

The greatest number of peals (minimum of 5000 changes, all in tower bells) rung in a year is 303, by Colin Turner of Abingdon, Oxon in 1989.

As of 1 May 1995, John Mayne of St Albans, Herts had rung in 3288 peals, more than any other bell-ringer.

Loudest organ stop
The Ophicleide stop of the Grand Great in the Solo Organ in the Atlantic City Auditorium (see above) is operated by a pressure of water 24 kPa *3½ lb/in²* and has a pure trumpet note of ear-splitting volume, more than six times the volume of the loudest locomotive whistles.

■ This sizeable cello stands 7.44 m *24.4 ft* high and 2.7 m *8.8 ft* wide, and took one thousand hours of work to complete at the Saint-Eloi carpentry in Toulouse, France. Made by master violin-maker Christian Urbista of Cordes, France, it is constructed of pinewood, maplewood, beechwood and planewood, and is potentially playable by someone with a suitably record-breaking reach.
(Photo: Gamma/J.Laberine)

(Photo: Gamma/G.Charneau)

who has been the regular organist at the church of St Boniface in Bentham since 1920.

Largest stringed instrument The largest movable stringed instrument ever constructed was a pantaleon with 270 strings stretched over 4.6 m² *50 ft²* used by George Noel in 1767. The greatest number of musicians required to operate a single instrument was the six required to play the gigantic orchestrion, known as the Apollonican, built in 1816 and played until 1840.

Largest double bass A double bass 4.26 m *14 ft* tall was built in 1924 in Ironia, New Jersey, USA by Arthur K. Ferris, reportedly on orders from the Archangel Gabriel. It weighed 590 kg *1301 lb* with a sound box 2.43 m *8 ft* across, and had leather strings totalling 31.7 m *104 ft*. Its low notes could be felt rather than heard.

Eighteen musicians played a double bass simultaneously (eight bowing, five fingering and five plucking) in a rendition of Strauss'

Big Brass

Largest brass instrument The contrabass tuba stands 2.28 m *7½ ft* tall, with 11.8 m *39 ft* of tubing and a bell measuring 1 m *3 ft 4 in* across. It was constructed for a world tour by the band of American composer John Philip Sousa (1854–1932), *c.* 1896–98, and is now owned by a circus promoter in South Africa.

Perpetuum Mobile at the studio of BBC *Record Breakers* on 28 Sep 1991.

Largest guitar The largest (and possibly the loudest) playable guitar in the world is 11.63 m *38 ft 2 in* tall, 4.87 m *16 ft* wide and weighs 446 kg *1865 lb*. Modelled on the Gibson 'Flying V', it was made by students of Shakamak High School in Jasonville, Indiana, USA. The instrument was unveiled on 17 May 1991 when, powered by six amplifiers, it was played simultaneously by six members of the school.

Acoustic guitar A fully-functional acoustic guitar measuring 8.66 m *28 ft 5 in* long and 0.972 m *3 ft 2 in* deep is exhibited at the Stradivarium exhibition in The Exploratory, Bristol. The dimensions were enlarged from the proportions of the classical guitar made by Antonius Stradivarius in the Ashmolean Museum, Oxford.

Largest guitar band On 7 May 1994, a gathering of 1322 guitarists played *Taking Care of Business* in unison for 68 min 40 sec, in an event organised by Music West of Vancouver, Canada.

Most valuable violin The highest price paid at auction for a violin, or any instrument, is £902,000 ($1.7 million) for the 1720 'Mendelssohn' Stradivarius, named after the German banking family who were descendants of the composer. It was sold to a mystery buyer at Christie's, London on 21 Nov 1990.

Q. Who was number one in the singles chart at week end 27 Aug 1955?

A. See Page 150

Guess What?

Most expensive guitar
A Fender Stratocaster belonging to Jimi Hendrix (1942–70) was sold by his former drummer 'Mitch' Mitchell for £198,000 at Sotheby's, London on 25 Apr 1990.

■ Eighteen performers huddle and stretch around a single double bass, in their attempt to break the record for the most number of simultaneous players. Flying in on a wire is former *Record Breakers* presenter Roy Castle.
(Photo: B.B.C.)

Drum Set

A drum set consisting of 308 pieces—153 drums, 77 cymbals, 33 cowbells, 12 hi-hats, 8 tambourines, 6 wood blocks, 3 gongs, 3 bell trees, 2 maracas, 2 triangles, 2 rain sticks, 2 bells, 1 ratchet, 1 set of chimes, 1 xylophone, 1 afuche, 1 doorbell—was built by Dan McCourt of Pontiac, Michigan, USA in 1994. A full demonstration takes 20 minutes.

Most valuable 'cello The highest ever auction price for a violoncello is £682,000 paid at Sotheby's, London on 22 Jun 1988 for a Stradivarius known as ' The Cholmondeley', which was made in Cremona, Italy c. 1698.

Largest drum A drum with a diameter of 3.96 m *13 ft* was built by the Supreme Drum Co., London and played at the Royal Festival Hall, London on 31 May 1987.

Fastest drumming Four hundred separate drums were played in 20.5 seconds by Carl Williams at the Alexander Stadium, Birmingham, W Mids on 4 Oct 1992.

Largest recorder A fully-functional recorder constructed of specially-treated stone pine and measuring 5 m *16.4 ft* long was made in Iceland by Stefán Geir Karlsson in 1994. Each hole is 8.5 cm *3.3 in* in diameter.

Orchestras

Largest orchestra On 17 Jun 1872, Johann Strauss the younger (1825–99) conducted an orchestra of 987 pieces supported by a choir of 20,000, at the World Peace Jubilee in Boston, Massachusetts, USA. The number of first-violinists was 400.

On 14 Dec 1991, the 2000-piece 'Young People's Orchestra and Chorus of Mexico', consisting of 53 youth orchestras from Mexico plus musicians from Venezuela and the former USSR, gave a full classical concert conducted by Fernando Lozano and others at the Magdalena Mixhiuca Sports Centre, Mexico City.

Bottle orchestra In an extraordinary display of oral campanology, the Brighton Bottle Orchestra—Terry Garoghan and Peter Miller—performed a musical

■ Just some of the strummers participating in the world's biggest guitar band, which took place in Vancouver, Canada in 1994.
(Photo: Music West)

medley on 444 miniature Gordon's gin bottles at the Brighton International Festival, E Sussex on 21 May 1991. It took 18 hours to tune the bottles, and about 10 times the normal rate of puff (90 breaths/min) to play them. There was no risk of intoxication, as the bottles were filled with water.

Largest band The most massive band ever assembled was one of 20,100 bandsmen at the Ullevaal Stadium, Oslo, Norway from Norges Musikkorps Forbund bands on 28 Jun 1964.

One-man Rory Blackwell, aided by his double left-footed perpendicular percussion-pounder, plus his three-tier right-footed horizontal 22-pronged differential beater, and his 12-outlet bellow-powered horn-blower, played 108 different instruments (19 melody and 89 percussion) simultaneously in Dawlish, Devon on 29 May 1989. He also played 314 instruments in a single rendition in 1 min 23.07 sec, again at Dawlish, on 27 May 1985.

Marching band The largest was one of 6017 players—including 927 majorettes and standard-bearers—on 27 Jun 1993. They marched for 940 m *3084 ft* at Stafsberg Airport in Hamar, Norway, under the direction of Odd Aspli, chairman of Hamar County Council.

Most prolific conductor Herbert von Karajan (Austria; 1908–89), made over 800 recordings encompassing all the major works. During his career, he conducted the London Philharmonic Orchestra, the Vienna State Opera and La Scala Opera of Milan, and founded the Salzburg Festival in 1967. He was principal conductor of the Berlin Philharmonic Orchestra for 35 years before his retirement, which was shortly before his death in 1989.

Largest choir Excluding 'sing-alongs' by stadium crowds, the greatest choir is one of 60,000, which sang in unison as the finale to a choral contest held among 160,000 participants in Breslau, Germany on 2 Aug 1937.

Concert Attendances

Estimating the size of audiences at open-air events where no admission is paid is often left to the police, media reporters, promoters and publicity agents. Estimates therefore vary widely and it is very difficult to check the accuracy of claims.

Rock/pop festival attendance The best claim is believed to be 725,000 for Steve Wozniak's 1983 US Festival in San Bernardino, California. The Woodstock Music and Art Fair held on 15–17 Aug 1969 at Bethel, New York, USA is thought to have attracted an audience of 300–500,000. The attendance at the 3rd Pop Festival at East Afton Farm, Freshwater, Isle of Wight on 30 Aug 1970 was claimed by its promoters, Fiery Creations, to be 400,000.

Rock concert attendance An estimated 195,000 people paid £10 each to attend A-ha's show at the Rock In Rio festival, at the Maracanã Stadium in Brazil in April 1990.

Solo performers The largest *paying* audience ever attracted by a solo performer was an estimated 180–184,000, also in the Maracanã Stadium, Rio de Janeiro, Brazil to hear Paul McCartney on 21 Apr 1990. A figure of 180,000 has also been quoted for the audience of Tina Turner's (b. Nutbush, Tennessee, USA; 26 Nov 1938) concert there in 1988.

Rod Stewart's concert at Copacabana Beach, Rio de Janeiro, Brazil on New Year's Eve, 1994, reportedly attracted an audience of 3.5 million. The concert was free.

Wembley Stadium Michael Jackson sold out seven nights at Wembley Stadium, performing to a total audience of 504,000 on 14, 15, 16, 22, 23 Jul and 26, 27 Aug 1988.

Largest concert On 21 Jul 1990, Potsdamer Platz, straddling East and West Berlin, was the site of the largest single rock concert in terms of participants and organisation ever staged. Roger Waters' production of Pink Floyd's *The Wall* involved 600 people performing on a stage measuring 168 m *551 ft* long and 25 m *82 ft* wide at its highest point. An estimated 200,000 people gathered for the building and demolition of a wall made of 2500 styrofoam blocks symbolising the demise of the Berlin Wall.

Classic

Classical concert attendance An estimated record 800,000 attended a free open-air concert by the New York Philharmonic conducted by Zubin Mehta, on the Great Lawn of Central Park, New York, USA on 5 Jul 1986, as part of the Statue of Liberty Weekend.

Most successful tour The Rolling Stones 1989 'Steel Wheels' North American tour earned an estimated £185 million ($310 million) and was attended by 3.2 million people in 30 cities.

Composers

Most prolific The most prolific composer was Georg Philipp Telemann (1681–1767) of Germany. He wrote 12 complete sets of services (one cantata every Sunday) for a year, 78 services for special occasions, 40 operas, 600 to 700 orchestral suites, 44 passions, plus concertos, sonatas and other chamber music. The most prolific symphonist was Johann Melchior Molter (c. 1695–1765) of Germany with over 170. Franz Joseph Haydn (1732–1809) of Austria wrote 108 numbered symphonies, many of which are regularly played today.

Longest symphony The symphony *Victory at Sea*, written by Richard Rodgers for the documentary film of the same name and arranged by Robert Russell Bennett for NBC TV in 1952, lasted 13 hours.

Longest solo piano composition The longest continuous non-repetitive piano piece ever published is *The Well-Tuned Piano* by La Monte Young, first presented by the Dia Art Foundation at the Concert Hall, Harrison St, New York, USA on 28 Feb 1980. The piece lasted 4 hr 12 min 10 sec.

Longest silence The longest interval between the known composition of a major composer and its per-

Oldest

The first modern symphony orchestra—basically four sections consisting of woodwind, brass, percussion and bowed string instruments—was founded at the court of Duke Karl Theodor at Mannheim, Germany in 1743. The oldest existing symphony orchestra, the Gewandhaus Orchestra of Leipzig, Germany, was also established in 1743. Originally known as the Grosses Concert and later as the Musikübende Gesellschaft, its current name dates from 1781.

■ Paul McCartney attracted record-breaking numbers to his concert at the Maracanã Stadium in Rio de Janeiro on 21 April 1990.
(Photo: Gamma/A. Sassaki)

Guess What?
Q. How would you turn the pages of the smallest book?
A. See Page 140

Opera, The UK Charts ▶▶ ▶▶

■ The Three Tenors—José Carreras, Placido Domingo and Luciano Pavarotti—received widespread acclaim for their performance at the World Cup Finals in Rome, Italy in 1990. Their subsequent *In Concert* album became the best-selling classical album ever and is now quintuple platinum. Four years after *In Concert*, their album *3 Tenors in Concert* brought them another number one in the album chart in September 1994. Both achievements also made them the oldest 'group' ever to have a number one, with an average age of 48 for *In Concert* and 52 for *3 Tenors in Concert 1994*. The record had briefly been captured by the Rolling Stones (average age 50) in July 1994.

Luciano Pavarotti has had more curtain calls than any other artist at one concert, with 165 on 24 Feb 1988 (⇨Most curtain calls).

Shortest

The shortest opera published is *The Sands of Time* by Simon Rees and Peter Reynolds, first performed by Rhian Owen and Dominic Burns on 27 Mar 1993 at The Hayes, Cardiff, S Glam and lasting for 4 min 9 sec. A shorter performance, lasting only 3 min 34 sec, was then achieved under the direction of Peter Reynolds at BBC Television Centre, London, on 14 Sep 1993.

formance in the manner intended is from 3 Mar 1791 until 9 Oct 1982 (over 191 years), in the case of Mozart's *Organ Piece for a Clock*, a fugue fantasy in F minor (K 608), arranged by the organ builders Wm Hill & Son and Norman & Beard Ltd at Glyndebourne, E Sussex.

Opera

Longest opera The longest of commonly performed operas is *Die Meistersinger von Nürnberg* by Wilhelm Richard Wagner (1813–83) of Germany. A normal uncut version as performed by the Sadler's Wells company between 24 Aug and 19 Sep 1968 entailed 5 hr 15 min of music.

Longest operatic encore The longest encore listed in the *Concise Oxford Dictionary of Opera* was of the entire opera Cimarosa's *Il Matrimonio Segreto* at its première in 1792. This was at the command of the Austro-Hungarian Emperor Leopold II (reigned 1790–92).

Oldest opera singer The tenor Hugues Cuénod (b. 26 Jun 1902) sang the part of Emperor Altoum in *Turandot* at the Metropolitan Opera House, New York, USA on 10 Mar 1988 at the age of 85.

Longest operatic career Danshi Toyotake (b. Yoshie Yokota, 1891–1989) of Hyogo, Japan sang *Musume Gidayu* (traditional Japanese narrative) for 91 years from the age of seven. Her professional career spanned 81 years.

Longest applause Placido Domingo (b. 21 Jan 1941) was applauded for 1 hr 20 min through 101 curtain calls after a performance of *Otello* at the Vienna Staatsoper on 30 Jul 1991.

Largest opera house The Metropolitan Opera House at the Lincoln Center, New York City, USA, completed in September 1966 at a cost of $45.7 million. It has a seating and standing room capacity of 4065; the auditorium, which is 137 m *451 ft* deep, seats 3800. The stage is 70 m *230 ft* wide and 45 m *148 ft* deep.

Most curtain calls On 24 Feb 1988, Luciano Pavarotti (b. 12 Oct 1935) received 165 curtain calls and was applauded for 1 hr 7 min after singing the part of Nemorino in Gaetano Donizetti's *L'elisir d'amore* at the Deutsche Oper in Berlin, Germany.

Youngest opera singer Ginetta Gloria La Bianca, born in Buffalo, New York, USA on 12 May 1934, sang Rosina in *The Barber of Seville* at the Teatro dell'Opera, Rome, Italy on 8 May 1950 aged 15 years 361 days, having appeared as Gilda in *Rigoletto* at Velletri 45 days earlier on 24 March.

The greatest recorded number of curtain calls ever received at a ballet is 89 by Dame Margot Fonteyn de Arias (*née* Margaret Evelyn Hookham (1919–91) and Rudolf Hametovich Nureyev (1938–93) after a performance of *Swan Lake* at the Vienna Staatsoper, Austria in October 1964.

Ballet

Fastest 'entrechat douze' In the *entrechat* (a vertical spring from the fifth position with the legs extended criss-crossing at the lower calf), the starting and finishing position each count as one, such that in an *entrechat douze* there are 5 crossings and uncrossings. This was performed by Wayne Sleep (b. 17 Jul 1948) for the BBC *Record Breakers* programme on 7 Jan 1973. He was in the air for 0.71 sec.

Grands jetés On 28 Nov 1988, Wayne Sleep completed 158 *grands jetés* along the length of Dunston Staiths, Gateshead, Tyne & Wear in two minutes.

Largest cast The largest number of ballet dancers used in a production in Britain was 2000 in the London Coster Ballet of 1962, directed by Lillian Rowley, at the Royal Albert Hall, London.

Turns

The greatest number of spins called for in classical ballet choreography is 32 *fouettés rond de jambe en tournant* in *Swan Lake* by Pyotr Ilyich Chaykovskiy (Tchaikovsky) (1840–93). Delia Gray (b. 30 Oct 1975) of Bishop's Stortford, Herts achieved 166 such turns during the Harlow Ballet School's summer workshop at The Playhouse, Harlow, Essex on 2 Jun 1991.

Recorded Sound

Smallest cassette The NT digital cassette made by the Sony Corporation of Japan for use in dictating machines measures just $30 \times 21 \times 5$ mm $1^1/_5 \times ^4/_5 \times ^1/_5$ in.

Smallest functional record Six titles of 33.3 mm $1^5/_{16}$ in diameter were recorded by HMV's studio at Hayes, Middx on 26 Jan 1923 for Queen Mary's Dolls' House. Some 92,000 of these miniature records were pressed including 35,000 of *God Save The King* (Bb 2439).

Most successful solo recording-artist Both Elvis Aron Presley (1935–77) and Harry Lillis (alias Bing) Crosby Jr (1904–77) could be considered for this title. Elvis Presley has had 109 UK hit singles and 96 top-selling albums in the UK since 1956. He holds the record for the most number one hits jointly with the Beatles, with 17, and his music has spent a record total of 1145 weeks on the UK singles chart.

Bing Crosby made more recordings than Presley, with 2600 singles and 125 albums cut in his lifetime. On 9 Jun 1960, the Hollywood Chamber of Commerce presented him with a platinum disc to commemorate the sale of 200 million records; on 15 Sep 1970, he received a second platinum disc when Decca claimed sales of 300,650,000 discs.

Most successful group The Beatles have amassed the greatest sales for any group. The band, from Liverpool, Merseyside, comprised George Harrison (b. 25 Feb 1943), John Ono (formerly John Winston) Lennon (b. 9 Oct 1940– killed 8 Dec 1980), James Paul McCartney (b. 18 Jun 1942) and Richard Starkey, *alias* Ringo Starr (b. 7 Jul 1940). All-time sales have been estimated by EMI at over 1 billion discs and tapes. Their latest album *Live At The BBC*, released on 29 Nov 1994, reached number one for one week in December of that year. The release in 1995 of the single *Baby It's You*, recorded 32 years ago and taken from the album *Live At The BBC*, brought them their 26th Top 10 hit—and their first since 1982.

Most recordings In the largest ever recording project, 180 compact discs containing the complete set of authenticated works by Mozart were released by Philips Classics in 1990–91 to commemorate the bicentenary of the composer's death. The complete set comprises over 200 hours of music and would occupy 2 m 6½ ft of shelving.

Most gold, platinum and multiplatinum discs The only *audited* measure of gold, platinum and multiplatinum singles and albums within the United States is certification by the Recording Industry Association of America (RIAA), introduced on 14 Mar 1958.

Elvis Presley's estate was presented with 60 gold and 50 platinum discs in August 1992, making him the most certified recording artist ever. The Rolling Stones have the most certified gold discs for any group, with 39 (34 albums, 5 singles). The female solo artist to receive the most gold discs is Barbra Streisand, with 43 (36 albums, 7 singles) (⇔Most Number Ones—US Albums).

The group Chicago have 17 platinum albums, more than any other group; Barbra Streisand holds the record for the most platinum albums awarded to a solo artist, with 23; Paul McCartney has more platinum discs than any other male artist, with 13. The group with the most multiplatinum albums is the Beatles, with 12. The solo artist with the most is Billy Joel, who has 11.

Most Grammy Awards An all-time record 31 awards to an individual (including a special Trustees' award presented in 1967) have been won since 1958 by the Hungarian-born British conductor, Sir Georg Solti (b. Budapest, Hungary, 12 Oct 1912).

The most won by a solo pop performer is 17, by Stevie Wonder. The most won by a pop group is eight, by the 5th Dimension. The largest shared Grammy Award is 46, by the Chicago Symphony. The greatest number won in a year is eight, by Michael Jackson, in 1984.

Biggest-selling single
UK The top-selling British single is *I Want to Hold Your Hand* by the Beatles, released in 1963, with world sales of over 13 million. The top-selling single in the UK is *Do They Know It's Christmas*, written and produced by Bob Geldof and Midge Ure and recorded by Band Aid in 1984, with sales of 3.6 million by May 1987. The profits went to the Ethiopian Famine Relief Fund.

Biggest sellers (albums) The best-selling album of all time is *Thriller* by Michael Jackson (b. 29 Aug 1958), with global sales of over 47 million copies to date. The best-selling album by a group is Fleetwood Mac's *Rumours* with over 21 million sales (⇔Most weeks on chart—UK Albums).

The best-selling album by a British group is *Dark Side of the Moon* by Pink Floyd, with sales audited at 19.5 million to December 1986. The best-selling album in Britain is *Sgt Pepper's Lonely Hearts Club Band* by the Beatles, with a reported 4.25 million sales since its release in June 1967.

Whitney Houston by Whitney Houston, released in 1985 and with sales of over 14 million copies (including over 9 million in the US, 1 million in the UK and a further million in Canada), is the best-selling debut album of all time.

Soundtrack The best-selling movie soundtrack is *Saturday Night Fever*, with sales of over 26.5 million to May 1987.

Best-selling classical album The best-selling classical album is *In Concert*, with global sales of 5 million copies to date. It was recorded by José Carreras, Placido Domingo and Luciano Pavarotti at the 1990 World Cup Finals in Rome, Italy.

Phonographic identification Dr Arthur B. Lintgen (b. 1932) of Rydal, Pennsylvania, USA, has a proven, and as yet unique, ability to identify the music on phonograph records purely by visual inspection without hearing a note.

Fastest rapper Rebel X.D. of Chicago, Illinois, USA rapped 674 syllables in 54.9 seconds at the Hair Bear Recording Studio, Alsip, Illinois on 27 Aug 1992. This represents 12.2 syllables per second.

Advance sales The greatest advance sale for a single worldwide is 2.1 million for *Can't Buy Me Love* by the Beatles, released on 21 Mar 1964. The UK record for advance sales of an album is 1.1 million for *Welcome to the Pleasure Dome*, the debut album by Frankie Goes To Hollywood, released in 1984.

Most song titles—DJ challenge Disc-jockey John Murray of Kirkcaldy, Fife played 37 song titles from two decks in two minutes on the BBC *Record Breakers* programme broadcast on 16 Nov 1990.

Most charted artist Elvis Presley's records spent a cumulative total of 1145 weeks on on the UK singles charts (⇔ Most successful recording artist).

The UK charts

Most weeks on singles chart The longest stay for a single is 124 weeks for *My Way* by Francis Albert Sinatra (b. 12 Dec 1915), in ten separate runs from 2 Apr 1969 to 1995. The record for most consecutive weeks on the chart is 56 weeks for Engelbert Humperdinck's *Release Me*, from 26 Jan 1967.

Most weeks on album chart The first No. 1 LP was the film soundtrack *South Pacific*, which held the position for a record 70 consecutive weeks, eventually totalling a record 115 weeks at No. 1.

The album with the most total weeks on the chart is *Bat Out of Hell* by Meatloaf with 471 weeks to April 1994.

Classical The recording of Vivaldi's *Four Seasons* by the English Chamber Orchestra directed by Nigel Kennedy has appeared in the UK album chart for 81 weeks to December 1993.

Most number one singles The Beatles and Elvis Presley hold the record for the most No. 1 hit singles, with 17 each.

Most consecutive The record for the most consecutive number ones is held by the Beatles, who had 11 in a row between 1963 and 1966 (from *From Me to You* through to *Yellow Submarine*). The Beatles also hold second place, with a separate run of six.

Most weeks at number one Singles record charts were first published in Britain on 14 Nov 1952 by *New Musical Express*. *I Believe* by Frankie Laine (b. 30 Mar 1913) held the No. 1 position for 18 weeks (non-consecutive) from April 1953. Bryan Adams (b. 5 Nov 1959) spent a record 16 consecutive weeks at No. 1 from July to October 1991 with *(Everything I Do) I Do It For You*, taken from the film *Robin Hood: Prince of Thieves*.

Fast Seller

The fastest-selling non-pop record of all time is *John Fitzgerald Kennedy—A Memorial Album* (Premium Albums), recorded on 22 Nov 1963, the day of President Kennedy's assassination, which sold 4 million at 99 cents in six days (7–12 Dec 1963). The fastest-selling British record is the Beatles' double album *The Beatles* (Apple) with 'nearly 2 million' sold in its first week in November 1968.

Big Seller

The biggest-selling single to date is *White Christmas* written by Irving Berlin (b. Israel Baline, 1888-1989) and recorded by Bing Crosby on 29 May 1942. It was announced on Christmas Eve 1987 that North American sales alone reached 170,884,207 copies by 30 June 1987 (⇔Most weeks on chart — US singles). The highest claim for any 'pop' record is an unaudited 25 million for *Rock Around the Clock*, copyright in 1953 by James E. Myers under the name Jimmy DeKnight and the late Max C. Freedman and recorded on 12 Apr 1954 by Bill Haley (1927–1981) and his Comets.

Most number one albums
The Beatles have had the most No.1 albums with 13, and Elvis Presley the most hit albums, a total of 96 to March 1995.

40 Years of Pop

1950s

27 August 1955: first copy of The Guinness Book of Records bound. The charts on that day:

■ Bill Haley.
(Photo: London Features International)

Week ending 27 Aug 1955

1. *ROSE MARIE* . . . . Slim Whitman
2. *LEARNIN' THE BLUES* . . . . Frank Sinatra
3. *COOL WATER* . . . . Frankie Laine
4. *EVE'RYWHERE* . . . . David Whitfield
5. *EVERMORE* . . . . Ruby Murray
6. *EVERY DAY OF MY LIFE* . . . . Malcolm Vaughan
7. *INDIAN LOVE CALL* . . . . Slim Whitman
8. *THE BREEZE AND I* . . . . Caterina Valente
9. *DREAMBOAT* . . . . Alma Cogan
10. *STRANGE LADY IN TOWN* . . . . Frankie Laine

■ Elvis Presley.
(Photo: London Features International)

1954: The first internationally-known pioneers of rock and roll, Bill Haley and the Comets, recorded *Rock Around the Clock* on 12 April. It still has the best claim for most sales of a pop record, with an estimated 25 million copies sold.

1956: On 11 May Elvis Presley's first single, *Heartbreak Hotel*, enters the charts at the start of a 21-week residency.

1959: Cliff Richard has his first number one hit, with *Livin' Doll*. Today he holds the record for the most hit singles achieved by any artist, with 115.

1960s

Week ending 2 Sep 1965

1. *I GOT YOU BABE* . . . . Sonny and Cher
2. *HELP!* . . . . The Beatles
3. *(I CAN'T GET NO) SATISFACTION* . . . . Rolling Stones
4. *ALL I REALLY WANT TO DO*. . . . . Byrds
5. *WALK IN THE BLACK FOREST* . . . . Horst Jankowski
6. *ZORBA'S DANCE* . . . . Marcello Minerbi
7. *EVERYONE'S GONE TO THE MOON*. . . . . . Jonathan King
8. *MAKE IT EASY ON YOURSELF*. . . Walker Brothers
9. *LIKE A ROLLING STONE* . . . . Bob Dylan
10. *SEE MY FRIEND* . . . . Kinks

■ The Beatles.
(Photo: London Features International)

1963: *I Want to Hold Your Hand* is released by the Beatles. It goes on to sell 13 million copies, more than any other British single.

1964: *Can't Buy Me Love* by the Beatles, released on 21 March, has record advance sales of 2.1 million.

1973: Pink Floyd release their ninth album, *Dark Side of the Moon*, which is to become the best-selling album ever by a British group.

1976: The Eagles are awarded the first ever platinum album with *Greatest Hits, 1971–75*.

1977: Elvis Presley dies. As well as sharing the record with The Beatles for the most number ones he had an overall record of 109 hits and a cumulative total of 1145 weeks on the UK singles chart from May 1956 to date.

1970s

Week ending 30 Aug 1975

1. *I Can't Give You Anything (But My Love)* . . . . Stylistics
2. *Sailing* . . . . Rod Stewart
3. *The Last Farewell* . . . . Roger Whittaker
4. *It's Been So Long* . . . . George McCrae
5. *That's The Way (I Like It)* . . . . K.C. And The Sunshine Band
6. *Blanket On The Ground* . . . . Billie Jo Spears
7. *Best Thing That Ever Happened* . . . . . Gladys Knight & The Pips
8. *Barbados* . . . . Typically Tropical
9. *Summertime City* . . . . Mike Batt
10. *If You Think You Know How To Love Me* . . . . Smokie

■ **Gary Glitter, who had eleven top ten hits in the 70s.** (Photo: London Features International)

1982: *Thriller* by Michael Jackson is released, and will achieve global sales of over 47 million, more than any other album before or since.

1984: Frankie Goes to Hollywood's debut album, *Welcome to the Pleasure Dome*, is released this year, with record advance sales for a UK album of 1.1 million. Bob Geldof and Midge Ure write and produce *Do They Know its Christmas* in aid of Ethiopian Famine Relief. The single was recorded by Band Aid, and had reached sales of 3.6 million in the UK by May 1987, with a further 8.1 million sold worldwide.

1985: *Whitney* by Whitney Houston breaks all records for sales of a debut album.

1987: The soundtrack to *Saturday Night Fever* becomes the best-selling movie soundtrack, with sales of over 26.5 million to May 1987.

1988: Kylie Minogue matures from soap star to pop star and proceeds to obtain the best-ever start to a singles chart career, with her first 10 releases reaching the top 5.

1989: The Rolling Stones perform their record-breaking tour.

1990: Pink Floyd hold the largest concert ever on 21 June.

1991: Largest-ever recording contract awarded to Michael Jackson by Sony in March, reportedly totalling $890 million and promising earnings of $1 billion. Bryan Adams breaks the record for most consecutive weeks at number one, following the release of *(Everything I Do) I Do It For You*.

July 1993 to April 1994: Take That have four consecutive hits debut at number one in a year.

September 1994: 24-year-old Whigfield — born Sannia Charlotte Carlson in Skarlskar, Denmark — became the first artist to enter the chart at number one with her debut hit, *Saturday Night*. After selling 150,000 copies of the single in just one week, she toppled Wet Wet Wet's hit *Love is All Around* from the number one position after its 15-week residency.

■ **Whigfield.** (Photo: London Features International)

1980s

■ **Tina Turner.** (Photo: London Features International)

Week ending 31 Aug 1985

1. *I Got You Babe* . . . . UB40 with Chrissie Hynde
2. *Into The Groove* . . . . Madonna
3. *Running Up That Hill* . . . . Kate Bush
4. *Drive* . . . . Cars
5. *Tarzan Boy* . . . . Baltimora
6. *Holiday* . . . . Madonna
7. *Say I'm Your Number One* . . . . Princess
8. *Money For Nothing* . . . . Dire Straits
9. *Alone Without You* . . . . King
10. *We Don't Need Another Hero* . . . Tina Turner

Most hit singles Cliff Richard (b. 14 Oct 1940) holds the record for the most hit singles, with 115 to December 1994.

Most successful debuts Kylie Minogue (b. 28 May 1968), whose debut album *Kylie* topped the chart in July 1988, had her first 10 singles reach the Top 5. In September 1994, *Saturday Night*, sung by Whigfield, entered the chart at number one, making the singer the first ever act to have her first ever hit come onto the chart at number one (⇔Biggest sellers—albums).

The US Charts

Most weeks on singles chart Bing Crosby's *White Christmas* spent a total of 77 weeks on the chart between 1942 and 1962, while *Tainted Love* by Soft Cell stayed on the chart for 43 *consecutive* weeks from January 1982.

Most weeks on album chart *Dark Side of the Moon* by Pink Floyd enjoyed 741 weeks on the *Billboard* charts to December 1992.

Most number one singles The Beatles have had the most No. 1 hits, with 20. Elvis Presley has had the most hit singles on *Billboard* Hot 100, namely 149 from 1956 to May 1990.

Most number one albums The Beatles had the most No. 1s (15), while Elvis Presley was the most successful soloist, with nine No. 1 albums. Elvis Presley also had the most hit albums (92 from 1956 to August 1992). The best-selling female singer of all time, with the most No. 1 albums (6), and most hit albums (42 between 1963 and October 1991), is Barbra Streisand (⇔ Most golden discs).

Most weeks at number one *Near You* by Francis Craig topped the chart for 17 weeks in 1947. Since 1955, the longest chart-toppers have been *I Will Always Love You* by Whitney Houston (1992), and *I'll Make Love To You* by Boyz II Men (1994), both of which were number one for 14 weeks.

Album The soundtrack *South Pacific* was No. 1 for 69 weeks (non-consecutive) from May 1949 (⇔Most weeks on UK album chart).

Radio

Earliest broadcast The world's first advertised broadcast was made on 24 Dec 1906 by the Canadian-born Prof. Reginald Aubrey Fessenden (1868–1932) from the mast of the National Electric Signalling Company at Brant Rock, Massachusetts, USA. The transmission included Handel's *Largo*. Fessenden had achieved the broadcast of speech as early as November 1900 but this was highly distorted.

UK The first experimental broadcasting transmitter in Great Britain was set up at the Marconi Works in Chelmsford, Essex in December 1919, and broadcast a news service in February 1920. The earliest regular broadcast was made from the Marconi transmitter '2MT' at Writtle, Essex on 14 Feb 1922.

Most durable radio programmes *Rambling with Gambling*, an early morning programme on WOR radio in New York City, USA, began in March 1925 and has been continued by three generations of the Gambling family. As of 30 Apr 1995, there had been 21,881 shows. The programme is currently broadcast six days a week, year round.

UK The longest-running BBC radio series is *The Week's Good Cause*, which began on 24 Jan 1926. The St Martin-in-the-Fields Christmas appeal by Canon Geoffrey Brown on 14 Dec 1986 raised a record £138,039.

The longest-running music programme is *Desert Island Discs*

which began on 29 Jan 1942. It was originally presented by its creator Roy Plomley, who died on 28 May 1985 having presented 1791 editions. It is now hosted by Sue Lawley. The record number of appearances is four by Arthur Askey (1900–82), the last time being on the 1572nd show on 20 Dec 1980. The most popular piece of music chosen by the guests is Beethoven's 'O Freude, nicht diese Töne' (Ode to Joy), which has been requested 60 times.

The longest-running solo radio feature is *Letter from America* by (Alfred) Alistair Cooke (b. 20 Nov 1908), first broadcast on 24 Mar 1946. The longest-running radio serial is *The Archers*, created by Godfrey Baseley and first broadcast on 1 Jan 1951. The only role played without interruption from the start is that of Philip Archer by Norman Painting (b. 23 Apr 1924).

Most radio stations The United States had 11,801 authorized radio stations as of 8 May 1995, more than any other country.

Highest listening Surveys carried out in over 100 countries show that the global estimated audience for the BBC World Service in 1994 was 133 million regular listeners—greater than any other international broadcaster. This is a conservative estimate, as listenership figures for several countries such as China, Cuba, Myanmar (Burma) and Iran, are not available due to restrictions on audience research. The World Service is now broadcast in 41 languages.

The peak recorded listenership on BBC Radio was 30 million on 6 Jun

Response

Highest response to a radio show On 21–27 Jun 1993, *FM Osaka 85.1* in Osaka, Japan received a total of 8,091,309 calls in response to a phone-in lottery. The prize was 100,000 yen (around £920), and the lines were open for twenty minutes at a time, 10 times a day. The maximum call-count in one day of phone-ins (3 hours 20 minutes) was 1,540,793, on 23 Jun 1993.

1950 for the boxing match between Lee Savold (US) and Bruce Woodcock (GB; b. 1921).

Brain of Britain quiz The youngest person to become 'Brain of Britain' on BBC radio was Anthony Carr of Anglesey, Gwynedd in 1956 at the age of 16. The oldest contestant has been the author and translator Hugh Merrick (1898–1980) in his 80th year in August 1977.

Topmost radio prize Mary Buchanan, 15, on WKRQ, Cincinnati, USA, won a prize of $25,000 a year for 40 years on 21 Nov 1980.

The record score is 35 by the 1981 winner Peter Barlow of Richmond, Surrey and Peter Bates of Taunton, Somerset who won the title in 1984.

Television

Earliest service John Logie Baird launched his first television 'service' via a BBC transmitter on 30 Sep 1929 and marketed the first sets, Baird Televisors, at 26 guineas (£27.30) in May 1930. The world's first high-definition (i.e. 405 lines) television broadcasting service was opened from Alexandra Palace, London on 2 Nov 1936, when there were about 100 sets in the United Kingdom.

Fastest video production Tapes of the Royal Wedding of HRH Prince Andrew and Miss Sarah Ferguson on 23 Jul 1986 were produced by Thames Video Collection. Live filming ended with the departure of the honeymoon couple from Chelsea Hospital by helicopter at 4:42 p.m., and the first fully-edited and packaged VHS tapes were purchased at 10:23 p.m., 5 hr

Guess What?
Q. Which film was awarded the most Oscars in 1995?
A. See Page 157

■ **Oprah Winfrey's inimitable chat-show style earned her the highest salary of any TV entertainer in 1994.**
(Photo: Stephen Green © 1994, Harpo Productions, Inc)

41 min later, from the Virgin Megastore in Oxford Street, London.

Best-selling video The world's best-selling video is Walt Disney's animated feature *Aladdin*, which was released in the United States in October 1993 and in the UK in August 1994, and which has sold more than 41 million copies worldwide to 1 May 1995.

Most films seen Gwilym Hughes of Dolgellau, Gwynedd had seen 22,118 films on video by 29 Mar 1995. He saw his first film in 1953 whilst in hospital.

Most durable TV shows NBC's *Meet the Press* was first transmitted on 6 Nov 1947 and was then shown weekly from 12 Sep 1948. It was originated by Lawrence E. Spivak, who appeared on each show as either moderator or panel member until 1975. As of 17 Apr 1995, 2391 shows had been aired.

UK Britain's most durable surviving television programme is the seasonal ballroom dancing show *Come Dancing*, first transmitted on 29 Sep 1950. The children's programme *Sooty* was first presented on the BBC by its deviser Harry Corbett (1918–89) in 1952. In 1968, *Sooty* moved to Thames Television and when Harry retired in 1975, the show was continued by his son Matthew (b. 28 Mar 1948), who still handles the puppets today.

The *BBC News* was inaugurated in vision on 5 Jul 1954. Richard Baker read the news for a record 28 years from 1954 to Christmas 1982. The most durable current affairs programme in the UK is BBC's *Panorama*, first transmitted on 11 Nov 1953 and broadcast weekly thereafter, but with summer breaks. The monthly *Sky at Night* has been presented by Patrick Moore CBE without a break or a miss since 24 Apr 1957. The 500th edition was broadcast on 3 April 1995.

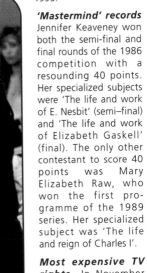

'Mastermind' records Jennifer Keaveney won both the semi-final and final rounds of the 1986 competition with a resounding 40 points. Her specialized subjects were 'The life and work of E. Nesbit' (semi–final) and 'The life and work of Elizabeth Gaskell' (final). The only other contestant to score 40 points was Mary Elizabeth Raw, who won the first programme of the 1989 series. Her specialized subject was 'The life and reign of Charles I'.

Most expensive TV rights In November 1991 it was reported that a group of US and European investors, led by American television network CBS, had paid $8 million for the television rights to *Scarlett*, the sequel to Margaret Mitchell's *Gone With the Wind*, written by Alexandra Ripley. The 8-hour mini-series was screened in November 1994.

Greatest TV audience The highest ever audience for a single programme was 133.4 million viewers watching the NBC transmission of Super Bowl XXVII on 31 Jan 1993. The *Muppet Show* is the most widely viewed programme in the world, with an estimated audience of 235 million in 106 countries at August 1989.

UK The biggest audience for a single broadcast on British television is 25.21 million for the England v. West Germany World Cup semi-final match on 4 Jul 1990. An aggregate audience of 39 million was estimated to have watched the wedding of TRH the Prince and Princess of Wales in London on 29 July 1981.

Most expensive TV production *War and Remembrance* was the most expensive television production ever, costing $110 million. This TV mini-series lasted for 14 episodes and was aired on American television by ABC in 2 parts in November 1988 and March 1989. It won the 1989 Emmy Award for best

Quizzes

Quizzes **The greatest number of participants was 80,799 in the All-Japan High School Quiz Championship televised by NTV on 31 Dec 1983.**

A record 41,599 questions were answered correctly in a quiz held at the Oak 'n' Ash pub at Walmley, W Mids from 9–15 Jun 1994. The final scores were 20,245 for Team A and 21,354 for Team B, with 10,366 wrong answers.

mini-series. Shooting of the series took three years to complete.

Largest TV contracts Oprah Winfrey (b. Kosclusko, Mississippi, USA; 29 Jun 1954) reportedly signed a contract with the King World Corporation through her own company Harpo in mid-March 1994 which guarantees Harpo $300 million by 31 Dec 2000, or $46,150,000 per annum for 6½ years.

UK The largest contract in British television was one of a reported £9 million, inclusive of production expenses, signed by Tom Jones (b. Thomas Jones Woodward, 7 Jun 1940) of Treforest, Mid Glam in June 1968 with ABC-TV of the United States and ATV in London for 17 one-hour shows per annum from January 1969 to January 1974.

Highest-paid TV entertainer The highest-paid television performer is chat-show host Oprah Winfrey, who reportedly earned $53 million in 1994.

Biggest TV sale The greatest number of episodes of any TV programme ever sold was 1144 episodes of *Coronation Street* by Granada Television to CBKST Saskatoon, Saskatchewan, Canada on 31 May 1971. This constituted 20 days 15 hr 44 min of continuous viewing.

Most prolific scriptwriter The most prolific television writer in the world was the Rt Hon. Lord Willis (1918–92), whose total output since 1942 is estimated to be 20 million words. From 1949 until his death he wrote 41 TV series, including the first seven years and 2.25 million words of *Dixon of Dock Green*, which ran on BBC television from 1955 to 1976. He also wrote 37 stage plays and 39 feature films.

Smallest TV set The Seiko TV-Wrist Watch, launched on 23 Dec 1982 in Japan, has a screen measuring 30.5 mm *1.2 in* wide. Together with the receiver unit and headphones, the entire black-and-white system, costing 108,000 yen, weighs only 320 g *11.3 oz*.

The smallest single-piece set is the Casio-Keisanki TV-10, weighing 338 g *11.9 oz* with a screen 6.85 cm *2.7 in* wide. It was launched in Tokyo in July 1983.

The smallest and lightest colour set, measuring 60 × 24 × 91 mm *2.4 × 0.9 × 3.6 in* and weighing 168.5 g *6 oz* with battery, is the Casio CV-1, launched by the Casio Computer Co. Ltd of Japan in July 1992.

TV drama serial
The longest-running domestic drama serial is Granada's *Coronation Street* which ran twice weekly from 9 Dec 1960 until 20 Oct 1989, after which viewers were treated to a third weekly episode. William Roache has played Ken Barlow without a break since the outset.

It has a screen size of 35 mm *1.4 in* and retails in Japan for 40,000 yen (about £200).

Highest advertising rates The highest TV advertising rate is $2.2 million per minute for ABC network prime-time during the transmission of Super Bowl XXIX, on 29 Jan 1995.

UK The maximum cost of a peak-time (8–11:30 p.m.) weekday 60-second slot on Thames Television was £110,000 + VAT in May 1992.

Fastest advertisement A TV advertisement for Reebok's InstaPUMP shoes was created, filmed, and aired during SuperBowl XXVII at the Atlanta Georgia Dome, USA. Filming continued up until the beginning of the fourth quarter of play; editing began in the middle of the third quarter and the finished product was aired during the advertisement break at the two minute warning of the fourth quarter. It starred Emmitt Smith of the Dallas Cowboys and lasted 30 seconds.

Longest advertisement The longest advertisement broadcast on British television was 7 min 10 sec by Great Universal Stores on TV-AM's *Good Morning Britain* on 20 Jan 1985, at a cost of £100,000.

Shortest advertisement An advertisement lasting only four frames (there are 30 frames in a second) was aired on KING-TV's *Evening Magazine* on 29 Nov 1993. The ad was for Bon Marche's Frango candies, and cost $3,780.

UK An advertisement for the 1993 Guinness Book of Records lasting just 3 seconds was devised by agency Leo Burnett and broadcast on UK satellite stations up to Christmas 1992.

Largest TV

The world's largest TV set is the Sony Jumbo Tron colour TV screen used at the Tsukuba International Exposition '85 near Tokyo, Japan in March 1985. It measured 24.3 × 45.7 m *80 × 150 ft*. The largest cathode ray tubes for colour sets are 94-cm *37-in* models manufactured by Mitsubishi Electric of Japan.

Photography

Earliest photographs The earliest known surviving photograph is by Joseph Niépce (1765–1833), and was taken in 1827 using a camera obscura; it shows the view from the window of his home. Rediscovered by Helmut Gernsheim in 1952, it is now in the Gernsheim Collection at the University of Texas, Austin, USA.

UK The oldest surviving photograph taken in England is a negative image of a window in Lacock Abbey, Wilts, taken in August 1835 by William Henry Fox Talbot (1800–77), inventor of the negative-positive process. Donated to the Science Museum, London, it is now at the National Museum of Photography, Film and Television, Bradford, W Yorks.

Most expensive photograph A photograph by Alfred Stieglitz of the hands of his wife, Georgia O'Keeffe, called *Georgia O'Keeffe—A Portrait with Symbol*, was sold at Christie's, New York, on 8 Oct 1993 for a record $398,500 (£260,458).

Largest camera The largest and most expensive industrial camera ever built is the 27-tonne Rolls-Royce camera commissioned in 1956 and now owned by BDC Holdings Ltd of Derby. It is 2.69 m *8 ft*

10in high, 2.51 m 8¼ ft wide and 14.02 m 46 ft long. The f16 Cooke Apochromatic lens measures 160 cm 63 in.

A pinhole camera was created from a Portakabin unit measuring 10.4 × 2.9 × 2.64 m 34 x9½ x9ft by photographers John Kippen and Chris Wainwright at the National Museum of Photography, Film and Television in Bradford, W Yorks on 25 Mar 1990. The unit produced a direct positive measuring 10.2 × 1.8 m 33 x6ft.

■ The largest camera lens, on display at the National Museum of Photography Film & Television, Bradford.
(Photo: N.M.P.F.T.)

Fastest camera A camera built for research into high-power lasers by The Blackett Laboratory of the Imperial College of Science and Technology, London registers images at a rate of 33 billion frames per second.

The fastest production camera is currently the Imacon 675, made by Hadland Photonics Ltd of Bovington, Herts, operating at up to 600 million frames per second.

Longest negative On 6 May 1992 Thomas Bleich of Austin, Texas, USA produced a negative measuring 712.47 × 25.4 cm 23ft 4½ x10½ in using a 26.67 cm 10½ in focal length Turner-Reich lens and Kodak No. 10 Cirkut Camera. The photograph was a portrait of about 3500 attendants at a concert in Austin.

Largest camera auction The record total for any camera auction is £296,043 for a collection of 'spy', subminiature and detective cameras sold at Christie's, London on 9 Dec 1991.

The highest auction price for any camera is £39,600, at Christie's, London on 25 Nov 1993. The camera was custom-made for the Sultan Abdel Aziz of Morocco in 1901, when each of its metal components was removed by the manufacturer and replaced with parts of gold. The sultan originally paid £2,100 for this piece of renovation; in trade magazines of the time it was condemned as 'wanton squandering'.

Guess What?
Q. What is the world's best-selling classical album?
A. See Page 149

Louis Nicholas (1862–1954) and Louis Jean (1864–1948).

Earliest feature film The world's first full-length feature film was *The Story of the Kelly Gang*, made in Melbourne, Victoria, Australia in 1906. Produced on a budget of £450, this biopic of the notorious armoured bushranger Ned Kelly (1855–80) ran for 60–70 minutes and opened at the Melbourne Town Hall on 26 Dec 1906. It was produced by the local theatrical company J. and N. Tait.

Earliest 'talkie' The earliest sound-on-film motion picture was achieved by Eugene Augustin Lauste (1857– 1935), who patented his process on 11 Aug 1906 and produced a workable system using a string galvanometer in 1910 at Benedict Road, Stockwell, London. The earliest public presentation of sound-on-film was by the Tri-Ergon process at the Alhambra cinema, Berlin, Germany on 17 Sep 1922.

Largest output India produces more feature-length films than any other country, with an average of 930 produced every year, and more than 26,000 produced altogether since 1913. The best year for UK film production was 1936, with 193 features released; the worst year was 1988, with just 27.

Least expensive full-length feature film The total cost of producing the 1927 Australian film *The Shattered Illusion* by Victorian Film Productions, was £300. It took 12 months to complete and included spectacular scenes of a ship being overwhelmed by a storm.

Most expensive film rights The highest price ever paid for film rights was $9.5 million announced on 20 Jan 1978 by Columbia for *Annie*, the Broadway musical by Charles Strouse starring Andrea McCardle, Dorothy Loudon and Reid Shelton.

A contract worth $4 million plus profit-sharing was signed by New Line on 20 Jul 93 for the psycho-thriller *The Long Kiss Goodnight* (USA i.p.) by Shane Black.

Longest film The longest film commercially released in its entirety was Edgar Reitz's *Die Zweite Heimat* (Germany 1992), which lasted 25 hr 32 min, and was premièred in Munich on 5–9 Sep 1992.

UK The longest commercially-released British film was Christine Edzard's screen adaptation of Charles Dickens's *Little Dorrit* (UK 87), with a total running time of 5 hr 57 min. The film was released in two parts, playing on alternate days.

Highest box office gross The film with the highest earnings was Universal's *Jurassic Park* (US 93), which had earned $912.8 million up to 21 Apr 1995 ($356.8 million in North America; $556 million elsewhere).

Cinema

Films

The earliest motion pictures were made by Louis Aimé Augustin Le Prince (1842–90). The earliest surviving film is a sensitized paper roll measuring 53.9 mm 2⅛ in wide. It is from Le Prince's camera, patented in Britain on 16 Nov 1888, and is of the garden of his father-in-law, Joseph Whitley, in Roundhay, Leeds, W Yorks at 10–12 frames/sec. It dates from early October 1988.

The first commercial presentation of motion pictures was at Holland Bros' Kinetoscope Parlor at 1155 Broadway, New York City, USA on 14 Apr 1894. Viewers could see five films for 25 cents or 10 for 50 cents from a double row of Kinetoscopes developed by William Kennedy Laurie Dickson (1860–1935), assistant to Thomas Edison (1847–1931), in 1889–91.

The earliest publicly presented film on a screen was La Sortie des Ouvriers de L'Usine Lumière, probably shot in August or September 1894 in Lyon, France. It was exhibited at 44 rue de Rennes, Paris, France on 22 Mar 1895 by the Lumière brothers, Auguste Marie

Largest lens The National Museum of Photography, Film and Television in Bradford, W Yorks currently displays the largest lens, made by Pilkington Special Glass Ltd of St Asaph, Clwyd. Its dimensions are: focal length 8.45 m 333in, diameter 1.372 m 54in, weight 215 kg 474 lb. Its focal length enables writing on the museum's walls to be read from a distance of 12.19 m 40ft.

Smallest camera Excluding those built for intra-cardiac surgery and espionage, the smallest marketed camera has been the circular Japanese 'Petal' camera, with a diameter of 2.9 cm 1.14in and a thickness of 1.65 cm 0.65in. It has a focal length of 12 mm 0.47in.

Expensive

The first film to have a budget over $100 million was *True Lies* (USA 94), starring Arnold Schwarzenegger and Jamie Lee Curtis, which cost around $115 million. The most expensive film ever produced was Universal's *Waterworld* (USA 95), starring Kevin Costner and Dennis Hopper, which cost an estimated $160 million. Extraordinary special effects and an overrunning schedule were two contributing factors to the huge costs. In terms of real costs adjusted for inflation, the most expensive film ever made was *Cleopatra* (USA 63), whose $44-million budget would be equivalent to over $200 million in 1995.

India produces more feature-length films than any other country. This cluster of billboards is in a Bombay street.
(Photo: Gamma/Bartholomew/Liaison)

Highest earnings Jack Nicholson stood to receive up to $60 million for playing 'The Joker' in Warner Brothers' $50 million *Batman*, through a percentage of the film's receipts in lieu of salary.

The highest paid child performer is Macaulay Culkin (b. 26 Aug 1980), who, at the age of 11, was paid $1 million for *My Girl* (1991). This was followed by a contract for $5 million (plus 5 per cent of gross) for *Home Alone II: Lost in New York* (1992), the sequel to his 1990 box-office hit. Culkin's fee for *Richie Rich* (USA 94) is said to have been $8 million.

Most durable series The longest series of films is the 103 features made in Hong Kong about the 19th century martial arts hero Huang Fei-Hong, starting with *The True Story of Huang Fei-Hong* (1949) and continuing to the latest production, *Once Upon a Time in China 5* (1995). The most durable continuing series with the same star is Shochiku Studios of Japan's 46 *Tora-San* comedy films, featuring Kiyoshi Atsumi (b. 1929) in a 'Chaplinesque' rôle from August 1969 to December 1995.

UK The longest British series was the 'Carry On' films, starting with *Carry On Sergeant* (1958) and continuing to *Carry On Columbus* (1992), which featured some survivors of the earlier films. Kenneth Williams (1926–88) appeared in 25 of the 30 films.

Largest studios The largest film studio complex in the world is at Universal City, Los Angeles, California, USA. The site, called the Back Lot, measures 170 ha *420 acres*, and comprises 561 buildings, and 34 sound stages. The largest studio in Britain is Pinewood Studios in Iver, Bucks, covering 36.8 ha *91 acres*. Built in 1936, it includes 75 buildings and 18 stages.

> The film which had made the most money at the time of our first edition was *Gone With The Wind*, which was reputed to have earned £12 million gross. Compare this with the average *budgets* of Hollywood films today.

Largest film set The largest-ever film set, measuring 400 × 230 m *1312 × 754 ft*, was the Roman Forum, designed by Veniero Colosanti and John Moore for Samuel Bronston's production of *The Fall of the Roman Empire* (1964). It was built on a 22.25 ha *55 acre* site outside Madrid, Spain. 1100 workmen spent seven months laying the surface of the Forum with 170,000 cement blocks, erecting 6705 m *22,000 ft* of concrete stairways, 601 columns and 350 statues, and constructing 27 full-size buildings.

Most expensive prop The highest price paid at auction for a film prop is $275,000 at Sotheby's, New York City, USA on 28 Jun 1986 for James Bond's Aston Martin DB5 from *Goldfinger* (UK, 1964).

Most portrayed character The character most frequently recurring on the screen is Sherlock Holmes, created by Sir Arthur Conan Doyle (1859–1930). The Baker Street sleuth has been portrayed by some 75 actors in over 211 films since 1900.

> **Largest loss** Columbia's *Last Action Hero* (USA 93), starring Arnold Schwarzenegger, costs $124,053,994 to produce, promote and distribute; it earned an estimated $44 million worldwide, creating a resounding loss of some $80 million.

Longest directorial career The directorial career of King Vidor (1894–1982) lasted for 67 years, beginning with *Hurricane in Galvaston* (1913) and culminating in a documentary called *The Metaphor* (1980).

Oldest director The Dutch director Joris Ivens (1898–1989) directed the Franco-Italian co-production *Une Histoire de Vent* in 1988 at the age of 89. He made his directorial debut with the Dutch film *De Brug* in 1928. Hollywood's oldest director was George Cukor (1899–1983), who made his 50th and final film, MGM's *Rich and Famous*, in 1981 at the age of 81.

Youngest director *Lex the Wonderdog*, a thriller of canine detection, was written, produced, and directed by Sydney Ling (b. 1959) when he was 13 years old. He was the youngest-ever director of a professionally-made, feature-length film.

Oldest performer The oldest screen performer in a speaking rôle was Jeanne Louise Calment (b. 21 Feb 1875), who portrayed herself at the age of 114 in the 1990 Canadian film *Vincent and Me*—a modern-day fantasy about a young girl who travels through time to meet Van Gogh. Ms Calment is the last living person to have known Vincent van Gogh (⇔ Human Being).

UK The oldest British film performer was Dame Gwen Ffrancon-Davies (1891–1992), who appeared in the Sherlock Holmes TV movie *The Master Blackmailer* (GB, 1991) at the age of 100. She died one month after the film was screened.

Most durable performers The record for the longest screen career is 80 years by German actor Curt Bois (1900–91), who made his debut in *Der Fidele Bauer* (1908) at the age of eight and whose last film was *Wings of Desire* (1988). The most enduring star of the big screen was Lillian Gish (1893–1993). She made her debut in *An Unseen Enemy* (1912) and her last film in a career spanning 75 years was *The Whales of August* (1987).

> **Most film extras** it is believed that over 300,000 extras appeared in the funeral scene of *Gandhi*, the 1982 epic directed by Lord Richard Attenborough CBE (b. 29 Aug 1923).

Costumes The largest number of costumes used for any one film was 32,000 for the 1951 film *Quo Vadis*.

Most changes Elizabeth Taylor changed costume 65 times in *Cleopatra* (1963). The costumes were designed by Irene Sharaff and cost $130,000.

Most expensive Constance Bennett's sable coat in *Madam X* (1965) was valued at $50,000. The most expensive costume designed and made specially for a

Studio Stage

The world's largest studio stage is the 007 stage at Pinewood Studios, designed by Michael Brown for producer Albert R. Broccoli and set creator Ken Adam and built in 1976 for the James Bond film *The Spy Who Loved Me*. The set measures 102 × 42 × 12 m *336 × 139 × 41 ft* and accommodated 4.54 million litres *1.2 million gal* of water, a full-scale section of a 600,000-ton supertanker and three scaled-down nuclear submarines.

HORRORS!

Psycho, 1960.
(Photo: Kobal Collection)

Winona Ryder in Bram Stoker's *Dracula*, 1994.
(Photo: Kobal Collection)

The first influential horror films were produced in Germany, shortly before World War I. In the 1920s, the US was making films with such well-known titles as *Dr. Jekyll and Mr. Hyde*, *The Hunchback of Notre Dame*, and *The Phantom of the Opera*. A decade later, *Dracula*, *Frankenstein* and *King Kong* were terrifying cinema audiences around the world. The peak year for horror film production was 1972, when 189 films were made, 83 of them US productions.

Max Von Sydow in *The Exorcist*, 1973.
(Photo: Kobal Collection)

Bela Lugosi in *Dracula*, 1931.
(Photo: Kobal Collection)

Brad Pitt flexing his muscles in *Interview with the Vampire*, 1994.
(Photo: Kobal Collection)

Most successful horror films

Year	Film
1974	The Exorcist
1975	Jaws
1976	The Omen
1977	King Kong
1978	Jaws II
1979	Alien/Amityville Horror
1980	The Shining
1981	An American Werewolf in London
1982	Poltergeist
1983	Jaws 3-D
1984	Gremlins
1985	Teen Wolf
1986	Aliens
1987	Witches of Eastwick/Predator
1988	A Nightmare on Elm Street 4
1989	Pet Sematory
1990	Arachnaphobia
1991	Terminator 2
1992	Alien 3
1993	Bram Stoker's Dracula
1994	Interview with the Vampire

Source: Movie Facts and Feats (Patrick Robertson)

William Peter Blatty, author of *The Exorcist* (1973), has grossed more than any other novelist in film history. The total amount received by Blatty is not known, but he received 40 per cent of the gross profits — in North American rentals alone, *The Exorcist* has grossed over $89 million.

Created by the Irish writer, Bram Stoker (1847-1912), Dracula is the of the Count, or his near relatives, outnumber those of his closest rival, Frankenstein, by 161 to 117.

The shower scene in *Psycho*, and the accompanying music, is probably one of the most memorable in horror film history. The scene involved 70 camera set-ups for 45 seconds of edited footage, and took seven days to shoot. *Psycho* is among the films for which the largest number of camera set-ups have ever been used for a single scene. It is also the only film to have used an orchestra composed entirely of strings for its musical film was Edith Head's mink and sequins dance costume worn by Ginger Rogers (1911–1995) in *Lady in the Dark* (1944), which cost Paramount $35,000 (⇨ Oscar winners).

Oscar winners Walter (Walt) Elias Disney (1901–66) has won more 'Oscars'—the awards of the United States Academy of Motion Picture Arts and Sciences, instituted on 16 May 1929 and named after Oscar Pierce of Texas, USA—than any other person. The count comprises 20 statuettes and 12 other plaques and certificates, including posthumous awards.

The artist to have won the most Oscars in a starring role is Katharine Hepburn (b. USA, b. 12 May 1907), with four, for *Morning Glory* (1932–3), *Guess Who's Coming to Dinner* (1967), *The Lion in Winter* (1968) and *On Golden Pond* (1981). She has been nominated 12 times. Edith Head (1907–81) won eight individual awards for costume design.

The film with most awards is *Ben Hur* (1959) with 11. The film receiving the highest number of nominations is *All About Eve* (1950) with 14.

Youngest winners The youngest winner in competition is Tatum O'Neal (b. 5 Nov 1963), who was aged 10 when she received the award in 1974 for Best Supporting Actress in *Paper Moon* (1973). Shirley Temple (b. 23 Apr 1928) was awarded an honorary Oscar at the age of five for achievements in 1934.

Oldest winner The oldest recipient of an Oscar was Jessica Tandy (1909–94), who won the award for Best Actress for *Driving Miss Daisy* in 1990 at the age of 80 years.

Most versatile personalities Three performers have won Oscar, Emmy, Tony and Grammy awards: actress Helen Hayes (b. 1900); composer Richard Rodgers (1902–1979) and actress/-singer/dancer Rita Moreno (b. 1931). Barbra Streisand has received Oscar, Grammy and Emmy awards in addition to a special 'Star of the Decade' Tony award.

Cinemas

Largest The largest cinema in the world is the Radio City Music Hall, New York City, USA, opened on 27 Dec 1932 with 5945 (now 5874) seats. Kinepolis, the first eight screens of which opened in Brussels, Belgium in 1988, is the world's largest cinema complex. It has 24 theatres with seating for between 160 and 700, and one other IMAX theatre seating 450 people, with a screen measuring 20 × 30 m *65.6 ft ×98.4 ft* . The total seating capacity of the complex is around 8000. The Odeon, Leicester Square, London—the biggest in the UK—has 1983 seats.

Highest cinema-going The country with the largest cinema audience is China, with mainland attendance figures of 14 billion in 1991, compared with a peak 21.8 billion in 1988. The year with the highest cinema attendance in the UK was 1946 with a weekly average of 31.4 million viewers.

■ The film to win the most Oscars in 1995 was *Forrest Gump*, with six awards out of 13 nominations: best picture; best director (Robert Zemeckis); best actor (Tom Hanks); best adapted screenplay; best editing and best visual effects. It was the second best actor award for Tom Hanks in successive years; the only other actor to have achieved this was Spencer Tracy in 1937–8.
(Photo: London Features International/Gregg De Guire)

■ **Right: Tom Hanks with his Oscar.**
(Photo: London Features International)

The largest permanently-installed cinema screen measures 33.3 × 24.7 m *109.25 ×81.04 ft* and is in the Ssangyong Earthscape Pavilion in the Science Park, Taejon, Korea. A temporary screen measuring 90.5×10 m *297 ×33 ft* was used at the 1937 Paris Exposition.

Theatre

Oldest indoor theatre The oldest indoor theatre in the world is the Teatro Olimpico in Vicenza, Italy. Designed in the Roman style by Andrea di Pietro, alias Palladio (1508–80), it was begun three months before his death and finished by his pupil Vicenzo Scamozzi (1552–1616) in 1583. It is preserved today in its original form.

Guess What?
Q. What is the most expensive film ever made?
A. See Page 154

UK The oldest theatre still in use in Great Britain is The Royal in Bristol, Avon. The foundation stone was laid on 30 Nov 1764, and the theatre was opened on 30 May 1766 with a 'Concert of Musick and a Specimen of Rhetorick'. The City Varieties Music Hall in Leeds, W Yorks was a singing room in 1762 and so claims to outdate the Theatre Royal. Actors had the legal status of rogues and vagabonds until the passing of the Vagrancy Act in 1824.

Largest theatre The world's largest building used for theatre is the National People's Congress Building (*Ren min da hui tang*) on the west side of Tiananmen Square, Beijing, China. It was completed in 1959 and covers an area of 5.2 ha *12.9 acres*. when used as a theatre, te building seats 10,000, as in 1964 for the play *The East is Red*. The most capacious purpose-built theatre is the Perth Entertainment Centre, Western Australia, with 8500 seats and a main stage area measuring 21.3 × 13.7 m *70 ×45 ft*. It was opened on 26 Dec 1974.

Smallest theatre The Piccolo in Juliusstrasse, Hamburg, Germany is the world's smallest regularly operated professional theatre. It was founded in 1970

Honoured

The world's most honoured entertainer is Bob Hope (*né Leslie Townes Hope*, London, 29 May 1903). He has been uniquely awarded the USA's highest civilian honours—the Medal of Freedom (1969); the Congressional Gold Medal (1963); the Medal of Merit (1966); the Distinguished Public Service Medal (1973); and the Distinguished Service Gold Medal (1971). Awarded a CBE in 1976 and appointed Honorary Brigadier of the US Marine Corps, he also has 44 honorary degrees.

and has a maximum capacity of 30 seats.

Largest stage The world's largest stage is the Hilton Theatre at the Reno Hilton, Reno, Nevada, USA. It measures 53.3 m × 73.4 m *175 × 241 ft*. The stage has three main lifts, each capable of raising 1200 performers (40 tons), and two turntables each with a circumference of 19.1 m *62½ ft*. The stage is lit by 800 spotlights.

Longest theatrical runs The longest continuous run of any show in the world is *The Mousetrap* by Dame Agatha Christie (1890–1976), which opened on 25 Nov 1952 at the Ambassadors Theatre, London (capacity 453) and moved after 8862 performances to the St Martin's Theatre next door on 25 Mar 1974. The 17,256th performance was on 9 May 1994, and the box office has grossed £20 million from more than nine million visitors.

Revue The greatest number of performances of any theatrical presentation is 47,250 (to April 1986) for *The Golden Horseshoe Revue*, a show staged at Disneyland Park, Anaheim, California, USA from 16 Jul 1955 to 12 Oct 1986. It was seen by 16 million people.

Largest amphitheatre .
The Flavian amphitheatre or Colosseum of Rome, Italy, completed in AD 80, covers 2 ha *5 acres* and has a capacity of 87,000. It has a maximum length of 187 m *612 ft* and a maximum width of 175 m *515 ft*.

Dancing ▶▶ ▶▶

Lucky Dragons

The longest dancing dragon on record measured 1559m *5114ft 10in* from the end of its nose to the tip of its tail. A total of 2180 people brought the dragon to life on 17 Apr 1994, making it dance for 30minutes on a newly-opened bridge which links Macau on the southern coast of China with the island of Taipa. According to Chinese folklore, dragons are supposed to bring good luck, and this is one of the reasons why a snake-like dancing dragon was chosen to mark the official opening of the bridge. It was such a dramatic sight that the South China Morning Post proclaimed that 'this massive dragon was just as impressive as the enormity of the structure it had come to celebrate'.

Always a popular record as it involves large numbers of people in a fun project, it also requires a good level of individual fitness when the time comes for the dragon to dance its way across a bridge, through streets or round a stadium. Records have been set in various countries, and not just ones where the Chinese culture is pre-dominant. The common link has been the goal of bringing a community together to work on a dramatic spectacle.

The head of the current record dancing dragon (inset) and the whole of the dragon on the bridge.
(Photos: Macau Government Information Service)

The progress of the record over the past few years is shown below.

St Helens, Lancs	300.23m *985ft*	1989
Hong Kong	921.41m *3023ft*	1991
Sheffield, S Yorks	1061m *3481ft*	1992
Havelte, Netherlands	1483.83m *4868ft 2in*	1993
Macau	1559m *5114ft 10in*	1994

Short by today's standards, but a record at the time, the dragon makes its way through the streets of St Helens in 1989.

A summer dragon on the track at the Don Valley Stadium in Sheffield in 1992.
(Photo: Jamie Corker © Diana Corker on behalf of South Yorkshire Cubscouts)

Hong Kong in 1991 and a record set at night.

A menacing looking dragon which snakes its way around a field at Havelte in 1993.

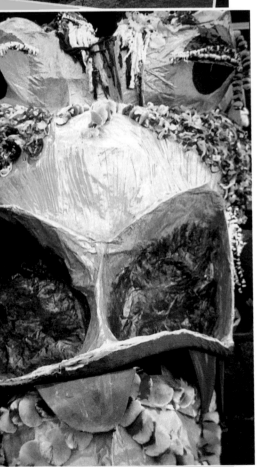

Broadway The musical *A Chorus Line* opened on 25 Jul 1975 and closed on 28 Apr 1990 after a record run of almost 15 years and 6137 performances. It was created by Michael Bennet (1943–87).

Musicals The off-Broadway musical *The Fantasticks* by Tom Jones and Harvey Schmidt opened on 3 May 1960. It celebrated its 35th anniversary on 3 May 1995, by which date the show had been performed a record 14,488 times at the Sullivan Street Playhouse, Greenwich Village, New York, USA.

UK The longest-running musical show performed in Britain was *The Black and White Minstrel Show*, later *Magic of the Minstrels*. The aggregate but discontinuous number of performances was 6464 with a total attendance of 7,794,552. The show opened at the Victoria Palace, London on 25 May 1962 and closed on 4 Nov 1972. It reopened for a season in June 1973 at the New Victoria and finally closed on 8 Dec 1973.

The longest running West End musical is *Cats* which has been playing at the New London Theatre, Drury Lane since 12 May 1981. The aggregate box office gross is estimated at over £250 million.

Comedy The longest-running comedy in Britain was *No Sex Please We're British*, written by Anthony Marriott and Alistair Foot and presented by John Gale. It opened at the Strand Theatre on 3 Jun 1971, transferred to the Duchess Theatre on 2 Aug 1986 and finally ended on 5 Sep 1987 after 16¼ years and 6761 performances. It was directed by Allan Davis throughout its run.

Shortest runs The shortest theatrical run on record was of *The Intimate Revue* at the Duchess Theatre, London, on 11 Mar 1930. Anything which could go wrong did. With scene changes taking up to 20 minutes apiece, the management scrapped seven scenes to get the finale on before midnight. The run was described as 'half a performance'.

Greatest theatrical loss The largest loss sustained by a theatrical show was borne by the American producers of the Royal Shakespeare Company's musical *Carrie*, which closed after five performances on Broadway on 17 May 1988 at a cost of $7 million. *King*, the musical about Martin Luther King, lost £3 million in a 6-week run ending on 2 Jun 1990, equalling the London record losses of *Ziegfeld* in 1988.

Most ardent theatre-goers Dr H. Howard Hughes (b. 1902), Prof. Emeritus of Texas Wesleyan College, Fort Worth, Texas, USA attended 6136 shows in the period 1956–87.

Britain's leading 'first nighter' Edward Sutro (1900–78) saw 3000 first-night productions from 1916–56 and possibly more than 5000 shows in his 60 years of theatre-going. The highest precisely recorded number of theatre attendances in Britain is 3687 shows in 33 years from 28 Mar 1953 until his death on 10 Sep 1986 by John Iles of Salisbury, Wilts.

Most durable performers Kanmi Fujiyama (b. 1929) played the lead role in 10,288 performances by the comedy company Sochiku Shikigeki from November 1966 to June 1983.

UK David Raven played Major Metcalfe in *The Mousetrap* on 4575 occasions between 22 Jul 1957 and 23 Nov 1968. Dame Anna Neagle (1904–86) played the lead role in *Charlie Girl* at the Adelphi Theatre, London for 2062 of 2202 performances between 15 Dec 1965 and 27 Mar 1971. She played the role a further 327 times in 327 performances in Australasia.

Jack Howarth (1896–1984) was an actor on the stage and later in television for 76 years from 1907 until his last appearance after 23 years as Albert Tatlock in *Coronation Street* on 25 Jan 1984. Frances Etheridge has played Lizzie, the housekeeper, in *Gold in the Hills* more than 660 times over a span of 47 years since 1936 (⇔ Longest runs).

Most durable understudy On 12 Mar 1994, Nancy Seabrooke, 79, retired from the Company of *The Mousetrap* after having understudied the part of 'Mrs Boyle' for 15 years and 6240 performances. She performed the part on 72 occasions.

Advance sales The musical *Miss Saigon*, produced by Cameron Mackintosh and starring Jonathan Pryce and Lea Salonga, opened on Broadway in April 1991 after generating record advance sales of $36 million.

Most acting roles The greatest recorded number of theatrical, film and television roles is 3389 since 1951 by Jan Leighton of New York City, USA.

Theatrical roles Kanzaburo Nakamura (b. July 1909) has performed in 806 Kabuki titles from November 1926 to January 1987. As each title in this classical Japanese theatrical form lasts 25 days, he has played 20,150 performances.

Longest chorus line The longest chorus line in performing history numbered up to 120 in some of the early Ziegfeld's Follies. In the finale of *A Chorus Line* on the night of 29 Sep 1983, when it broke the record as the longest-running Broadway show ever, 332 top-hatted 'strutters' performed on stage.

On 28 Mar 1992, 543 members of the cast of *Showtime News*, a major production by Hampshire West Guides, performed a routine choreographed by professional dancer Sally Horsley at the Swan Centre, Eastleigh.

Fashion shows The greatest distance covered by a model on a catwalk is 133.7 km *83.1 miles* by Eddie Warke at Parke's Hotel, Dublin, Republic of Ireland from 19–21 Sep 1983. The record by female models is 114.4 km *71.1 miles*, by Roberta Brown and Lorraine McCourt on the same occasion. The compère at this marathon fashion event was Marty Whelan of the Irish radio station Radio 2.

> **Forty years ago, the world's longest chorus line was that of the New York Radio City Music Hall's Rockettes. Thirty-six dancers performed precision routines across the 144-ft-wide stage. The whole troupe, which won the Grand Prix in Paris in July 1937, was forty-six strong, although ten girls were always on alternating vacation. In 1983, the finale of *A Chorus Line* had nearly nine times as many 'strutters'.**

> **Lowest theatre attendance** The ultimate in low attendances was achieved on 24 Nov 1983, when the comedy *Bag*, written by Bryony Lavery and directed by Michele Frankel, opened to a nil attendance at Grantham Leisure Centre, Lincs.

Dancing

Marathon dancing must be distinguished from dancing mania, or tarantism, which is a pathological condition. The worst outbreak of this was at Aachen, Germany in July 1374, when hordes of men and women broke into a frenzied and compulsive choreomania in the streets. It lasted for many hours until injury or complete exhaustion ensued.

Largest and longest dances An estimated 48,000 people took part in a Birdie Dance held during the 1994 Oktoberfest-Zinzinnati in Cincinnati, Ohio, USA on 17 Sep 1994.

The most taxing marathon dance staged as a public spectacle was one by Mike Ritof and Edith Boudreaux, who logged 5148hr 28½min to win $2000 at Chicago's Merry Garden Ballroom, Belmont and Sheffield, Illinois, USA from 29 Aug 1930 to 1 Apr 1931. Rest periods were progressively cut from 20 to 10 to 5 to nil minutes per hour, with 10-inch steps and a maximum of 15 seconds for closure of eyes.

The longest distance ever danced by one person was 21.1 km *13.1 miles*, by Elizabeth Ursic who tap-danced the Arizona Half Marathon at Tempe, Arizona, USA on 10 Jan 1993.

Rosie Radiator led an ensemble of 12 tap dancers through the streets of San Francisco, California, USA in a choreographed routine, covering a distance of 15.47km *9.61 miles* on 11 Jul 1994.

Ballroom The world's most successful professional ballroom dancing champions have been Bill and Bobbie Irvine, who won 13 world titles between 1960 and 1968. The oldest competitive ballroom dancer was Albert J. Sylvester (1889–1989) of Corsham, Wilts, who retired at the age of 94.

> In addition to being a record-breaking ballroom dancer, Albert Sylvester was the personal secretary to Prime Minister David Lloyd-George.

Conga The longest recorded conga was the Miami Super Conga, held in conjunction with Calle Ocho—a party to which Cuban-Americans invite the rest of Miami for a celebration of life together. Held on 13 Mar 1988, the conga consisted of 119,986 people.

The longest in Britain comprised a 'snake' of 8659 people from the South-Eastern Region of the Camping and Caravanning Club of Great Britain and Ireland. It took place on 4 Sep 1982 at Brands Hatch, Kent.

Country dancing The largest genuine Scottish country dance ever staged was a 512-some reel, held in Toronto, Canada on 17 Aug 1991 and organized by the Toronto branch of the Royal Scottish Country Dance Society.

> Ian Ashpole, having performed his trapeze act at 5005m *16,420 ft*, said:– 'Apart from the cold and oxygen problems, it was no different to doing it at 20 feet.'

Flamenco The fastest flamenco dancer ever measured is Solero de Jerez, aged 17, who in Brisbane, Australia in September 1967 attained 16 heel taps per second, in an electrifying routine.

Limbo The lowest height for a bar (flaming) under which a limbo dancer has passed is 15.25cm *6in* off the floor, by Dennis Walston, alias King Limbo, at Kent, Washington State, USA on 2 Mar 1991.

The record for a performer on roller skates is 11.94cm *4 7/10 in*, achieved by Syamala Gowri (b. 31 Oct 1988), at Hyderabad, Andhra Pradesh, India on 10 May 1993.

Tap The fastest *rate* ever measured for tap dancing is 32 taps per second by Stephen Gare of Sutton Coldfield, W Mids, at the Grand Hotel, Birmingham, W Mids on 28 Mar 1990. Roy Castle (1932–94), host of the BBC TV *Record Breakers* programme from 1972 to 1993, achieved one million taps in 23hr 44min at the Guinness World of Records exhibition, Piccadilly, London on 31 Oct–1 Nov 1985. The greatest-ever assemblage of tap dancers in a single routine numbered 6252 outside Macy's Store in New York City, USA on 21 Aug 1994.

> **Guess What?**
> Q. Apart from tap dancing, which other record does Roy Castle hold?
> A. see Page 125

Circus

The oldest permanent circus building is Cirque d'Hiver (originally Cirque Napoléon), which opened in Paris, France on 11 Dec 1852. The largest travelling circus tent belonged to Ringling Bros and Barnum & Bailey, and was used on USA tours from 1921 to 1924. It covered 8492m² *2.10acres*, consisting of a round top 61m *200ft* in diameter with five middle sections each 18m *60ft* wide.

The greatest number of performers in a circus act was 263 plus c. 175 animals, in the 1890 Barnum & Bailey Circus cast during its tour of the USA. The record for an animal-free circus is 60, for Cirque du Soleil's production of *Mystere* in Las Vegas, Nevada, USA in 1995.

The largest audience for a circus was 52,385 for Ringling Bros and Barnum & Bailey, at the Superdome, New Orleans, Louisiana, USA on 14 Sep 1975. The largest circus audience in a tent was 16,702 (15,686 paid), also for Ringling Bros and Barnum & Bailey, at Concordia, Kansas, USA on 13 Sep 1924.

Aerial acts The highest trapeze act was performed by Ian Ashpole (Great Britain) at a height of 5005m *16,420 ft*, suspended from a hot-air balloon between St. Neots, Cambs and Newmarket, Suffolk on 16 May 1986. Janet May Klemke (USA) performed a record 305 one-arm planges at Medina Shrine Circus, Chicago, Illinois, USA on 21 Jan 1938. A single-heel hang on a swinging bar was first performed by Angela Revelle in Australia in 1977.

Flying return trapeze A flying return trapeze act was first performed by Jules Léotard (France) at Cirque Napoléon, Paris, France on 12 Nov 1859. A triple back somersault on the flying trapeze was first performed by Lena Jordan (Latvia) to Lewis Jordan (USA) in Sydney, Australia in April 1897. The back somersault record is a quadruple back, by Miguel Vasquez (Mexico) to Juan Vasquez at Ringling Bros and Barnum & Bailey Circus, Tucson, Arizona, USA on 10 Jul 1982. The greatest number of consecutive triple back somersaults successfully carried out is 135, by Jamie Ibarra (Mexico) to Alejandro Ibarra, between 23 July and 12 Oct 1989, at various locations in the USA.

Flexible pole The first publicly performed quadruple back somersault on the flexible pole was accomplished by Maksim Dobrovitsky (USSR) of the Yegorov Troupe at the International Circus Festival of Monte Carlo in Monaco on 4 Feb 1989. Corina Colonelu Mosoianu (Romania) is the only person to have performed a triple full twisting somersault, on 17 Apr 1984 at Madison Square Garden, New York City, USA.

> Philippe Petit was arrested following his high-wire stunt in 1974. The New York policeman who took him into custody said 'A guy who does that cannot be right in the head'.

High wire A 7-person pyramid (three layers) was achieved by the Great Wallendas (Germany) at Wallenda Circus, USA in 1947. The highest high-wire feat (ground supported) was at a height of 411m

1350ft by Philippe Petit (France) between the towers of the World Trade Center, New York City, USA on 7 Aug 1974.

Horseback riding The record for consecutive somersaults on horseback is 23, by James Robinson (USA) at Spalding & Rogers Circus, Pittsburgh, Pennsylvania, USA in 1856. Willy, Beby and Rene Fredianis (Italy) performed a three high column at Nouveau Cirque, Paris, France in 1908, a feat not since emulated. 'Poodles' Hanneford (Ireland; b. England) holds the record for running leaps on and off, with 26 at Barnum & Bailey Circus, New York, USA in 1915.

Human cannonball The first human cannonball was Eddie Rivers (USA) billed as 'Lulu', from a Farini cannon at Royal Cremorne Music Hall, London in 1871. The record distance a human has been fired from a cannon is 53.4m *175ft* in the case of Emanuel Zacchini (Italy) in the USA in 1940.

Human pyramid The weight record is 771 kg *1700 lbs*, when Tahar Douis supported twelve members of the Hassani Troupe (three levels in height) at the BBC TV studios, Birmingham, W Mids on 17 Dec 1979. The height record is 12 m *39ft*, when Josep-Joan Martinez Lozano of the Colla Vella dels Xiquets mounted a 9-high pyramid at Valls, Spain on 25 Oct 1981.

Skipping Julian Albulet (USA) achieved 358 consecutive turns skipping on a tightrope at Las Vegas, Nevada, USA, 2 Jul 1990.

In a Spin

Plate spinning The greatest number of plates spun simultaneously is 108, by Dave Spathaky of London for the *Tarm Pai Du* television programme in Thailand on 23 Nov 1992.

Stilt-walking Even with a safety or Kirby wire, very high stilts are *extremely* dangerous—25 steps are deemed to constitiute 'mastery'. The tallest stilts ever mastered measured 12.36m *40ft 9½in* from ground to ankle. Eddy Wolf ('Steady Eddy') of Loyal, Wisconsin, USA walked a distance of 25 steps without touching his safety handrail wires on 3 Aug 1988 using aluminium stilts of this length. The heaviest stilts ever mastered weighed 25.9kg *57lb* each, and were the ones used by Eddy Wolf in his successful attempt on the height record.

Teeter board The Shanghai Acrobats achieved a 6-person high unaided column (with only one person on each level) at Shanghai, China in 1993.

Trampoline Marco Canestrelli (USA) performed a septuple twisting back somersault to bed at Ringling Bros and Barnum & Bailey Circus, St Petersburg, Florida, USA on 5 Jan 1979. He also achieved a quintuple twisting back somersault to a two high column, to Belmonte Canestrelli at Ringling Bros and Barnum & Bailey Circus, New York City, USA on 28 Mar 1979. Richard Tisson (France) achieved a triple twisting triple back somersault at Berchtesgaden, Germany on 30 Jun 1981.

Wild animal presentations Willy Hagenbeck (Germany) worked with 70 polar bears in a presentation at the Paul Busch Circus, Berlin, Germany in 1904.

The greatest number of lions mastered and fed in a cage by an unaided lion-tamer was 40, by 'Captain' Alfred Schneider in 1925.

Clyde Raymond Beatty (USA) handled 43 'mixed cats' (lions and tigers) simultaneously in 1938. Beatty was the featured attraction at every show he appeared in for more than 40 years. He insisted on being called a lion-trainer—as opposed to a lion-tamer.

Business World

Commerce

Oldest industry The oldest known industry is flint knapping, involving the production of chopping tools and hand axes, dating from 2.5 million years ago in Ethiopia. The earliest evidence of trading in exotic stone and amber dates from c. 28,000 BC in Europe.

Oldest company Although not strictly a company, the Royal Mint has origins dating back to AD 287. It is now based in Llantrisant, Pontyclun, Mid-Glamorgan.

The oldest existing documented company is Stora Kopparbergs Bergslags of Falun, which has been in continuous operation since the 11th century. It is first mentioned in historical records in the year 1288, when a Swedish bishop bartered an eighth share in the enterprise, and it was granted a charter in 1347.

Family business The Hōshi Ryokan in Japan, dates back to A.D. 717 and is a family business spanning 46 generations (↔ Hotels, Oldest).

The oldest family business in the UK is John Brooke & Sons Holdings Ltd, spinners and clothiers of Huddersfield, W Yorks, which was founded in 1541. The present directors, brothers E.L.M. and M.R.H. Brooke, are of the 16th generation.

Largest companies The largest manufacturing company in the world in terms of revenue and employees is General Motors Corporation of Detroit, Michigan, USA, with operations throughout the world and a workforce of 692,800. Revenues in 1994 totalled $154,951.2 million, with assets of $198,598.7 million. The company announced profits of $4.9 billion for the year.

UK The net assets of Shell Transport and Trading Co. plc at 31 Dec 1994 were £14.5 billion, mainly comprising its 40 per cent share in the net assets of the Royal Dutch Shell Group of companies, which stood at £35.98 billion. Group companies employ some 106,000 staff.

Smallest company equity Britain's smallest-ever company was Frank Davies Ltd, incorporated on 22 Aug 1924 with a ½d share capital divided into two ¼d shares. Converting to decimal coinage (£0.002 divided into two shares of £0.001), it was finally dissolved in 1978 without ever having increased its share capital.

Largest employer The world's largest commercial or utility employer is Indian Railways, with 1,623,158 staff in 1994. The largest employer in the UK is the National Health Service, with 1,238,000 staff (excluding general practitioners) at 30 Sep 1993.

Greatest sales General Motors Corporation of Detroit, Michigan, USA, had sales of $133.6 billion

Guess What?

Q. How old was Millicent Barclay when she first drew her pension?

A. See Page 164

Directors

The all-time record for directorships was set by Hugh T. Nicholson (1914–85), formerly senior partner of Harmood Banner & Sons of London, who, as a liquidating chartered accountant, became director of all 451 companies of the Jasper group in 1961 and had seven other directorships. The director with the most listings in the 1995 *Directory of Directors* is Mr Reginald Frank, with 252.

The largest farms in the world are the *kolkhozy* collective farms in Russia—some units cover as much as 25,000 ha 60,000 acres.
(Photo: Rex Features/Sipa Press/Laski)

for 1993. The first company to surpass the $1 billion mark in annual sales was the United States Steel (now USX) Corporation of Pittsburgh, Pennsylvania in 1917.

Sales per unit area Richer Sounds plc, the hi-fi retail chain, had sales at their London Bridge Walk outlet reaching a peak of £17,553 per square foot for the year ending 31 Jan 1994.

The greatest net profit ever by a corporation in 12 months is $7.6 billion, made by American Telephone and Telegraph Company (now AT&T Corp) from 1 Oct 1981 to 30 Sep 1982.

Greatest loss The world's worst annual net trading loss is $23.5 billion (£15.5 billion), reported for 1992 by General Motors. The bulk of this figure was, however, due to a single charge of some $21 billion for employees' health costs and pensions, disclosed because of new US accountancy regulations (⇨ Largest companies).

UK The greatest annual loss for a British company is £3.91 billion, made by the National Coal Board (now British Coal) in the year ending 31 Mar 1984.

Take-overs The highest bid in a corporate take-over was $21 billion for RJR Nabisco Inc., the tobacco, food and beverage company, made by the Wall Street leveraged-buyout firm Kohlberg Kravis Roberts, which offered $90 a share on 24 Oct 1988. By 1 Dec 1988 the bid, led by Henry Kravis, had reached $109 per share to aggregate $25 billion. A proposed bid of $22.8 billion for Chrysler by Tracinda Corporation was announced on 12 Apr 1995, although it was withdrawn on 1 Jun 1995.

UK The largest successful takeover bid in British history was the offer of almost £9 billion by Glaxo plc for Wellcome, the rival drugs company, on 23 Jan 1995 (⇨Largest cheque). The largest bid ever for a British company was £13 billion for BAT Industries on 11 Jul 1989, made by Hoylake, and led by Sir James Goldsmith, Jacob Rothschild and Kerry Packer.

Bankruptcies *Corporate* The biggest corporate bankruptcy in terms of assets amounted to $35.9 billion, filed by Texaco in 1987.

Banks The world's largest multilateral development bank is the International Bank for Reconstruction and Development, generally known as the World Bank. Based in Washington, DC, USA, the bank had total assets of $170 billion for the 1994 fiscal year.

According to *The Banker* magazine the world's biggest commercial bank measured by capital is the Sumitomo Bank of Japan, with $22,120 million at 31

The man with the most director-ships as listed in the *Directory of Directors* in 1955 was George Maurice Wright, Chairman of Debenhams Ltd, with 67 companies.

Mar 1994 and a 4.44 percent capital-assets ratio. The bank with most branches is the State Bank of India, which had 12,704 outlets at 1 Apr 1994 and assets of $36 billion.

UK The largest bank in the United Kingdom in terms of assets is Barclays plc, with consolidated total assets of £162.4 billion in 1994.

Oldest The UK's oldest independent bank is C. Hoare & Co., founded in 1672 by Richard Hoare, a goldsmith, in London. Child & Co. of Fleet St, although now part of the Royal Bank of Scotland, can trace its origins back to 1584, when its founder, William Wheeler, became formally apprenticed as a goldsmith.

Largest building societies The biggest lender in the world is the Japanese government-controlled House Loan Corporation. The biggest building society is the Halifax Building Society of Halifax, W Yorks with assets of £72.2 billion in 1994 and lending in that year of £9.6 billion. The Society has 22,110 employees and over 700 branches.

Surveyors The world's largest firm of surveyors and real-estate consultants is Jones, Lang Wootton of London, with 70 offices in 27 countries and a staff of 3800. Valuations completed in 1994 amounted to $160 billion, and capital transactions amounted to $12.9 billion, resulting in a worldwide fee income of over $350 million.

Chemists The largest chain of chemists in the world is Rite Aid Corporation of Camp Hill, Pennsylvania, USA which had 2834 branches throughout the US in 1994. The Walgreen Co. of Deerfield, Illinois, USA has fewer shops but greater sales, totalling $9.2 billion in 1994.

UK Britain's largest chain of pharmacies is Boots The Chemists, which had 1164 retail stores at March 1995. The firm was founded by Jesse Boot (1850–1931), later the 1st Baron Trent.

Department stores The largest department store in the United Kingdom is Harrods Ltd of Knightsbridge, London, named after Henry Charles Harrod (1800–85), who opened a grocery in Knightsbridge in 1849. It now has a total selling floor space of 10.5 ha *25 acres*, with 50 lifts and 36 flights of stairs and escalators, employs 3500– 4000 people, depending on the time of year, and achieved record sales of over £425 million in the year ending 30 Jan 1995.

The record for one day of business is nearly £13 million in the January 1995 sale, with over £24 million taken in the first four days and over £58 million taken during the month.

Toyshop The world's largest toyshop chain is Toys 'R' Us (head office Paramus, New Jersey, USA), with 911 stores and 3.8 million m² *41 million ft²* of

Jumble

The Cleveland Convention Center, Ohio, USA White Elephant Sale (instituted 1933) on 18–19 Oct 1983 raised $427,935.21. The greatest amount of money raised at a one-day sale is $214,085.99 at the 62nd one-day rummage sale organized by the Winnetka Congregational Church, Winnetka, Illinois, USA on 12 May 1994.

Britain's largest jumble sale was Jumbly '79, sponsored by *Woman's Own*, at Alexandra Palace, London from 5–7 May 1979 in aid of the Save the Children Fund. The attendance was 60,000 and the gross takings in excess of £60,000.

Bankruptcies On 3 Sep 1992 Kevin Maxwell (b. 20 Feb 1959), son of the former press magnate Robert Maxwell (1923–91), became the world's biggest bankrupt, with reported debts of £406.8 million.

retail space worldwide. The largest single store is the branch in Birmingham, Great Britain, at 6038.5 m² 65,000 ft².

Retailers The world's largest retailing firm is Wal-Mart Inc of Bentonville, Arizona, USA, founded by Sam Walton (1920–92) in 1962, with unaudited sales of $82.5 billion and an unaudited net income of $2.7 billion at 31 Jan 1994. At 1 May 1995, Wal-Mart had 2648 retail locations and employed 600,000 people.

Most outlets At 28 Jan 1995, Woolworth Corporation of New York City, USA operated 8629 retail stores worldwide. Frank Winfield Woolworth opened his first store in Utica, New York on 22 Feb 1879.

In our first edition, the Halifax building society was the largest building society in the world, and still is; although its assets have increased from £237.7 million to £72.2 billion.

Insurance

Largest insurance companies The world's largest single insurance association is the Blue Cross and Blue Shield Association of Chicago, Illinois, USA. At 31 Dec 1994, it had membership of 65.2 million and had paid out benefits totalling $71.4 billion.

The company with the highest volume of insurance in force in the world is the Metropolitan Life Insurance Co. of New York City, USA, with $1.27 trillion at year-end 1993. The Prudential Insurance Company of America, with headquarters at Newark, New Jersey, has the greatest volume of consolidated assets, with a total of $212 billion in 1994.

UK The Prudential Corporation plc had total assets at 1 Jan 1995 of £62.7 billion.

Largest policy The largest life-assurance policy ever issued was for $100 million, bought by a major US entertainment corporation on the life of a leading US entertainment-industry figure. The policy was sold in July 1990 by Peter Rosengard of London and was placed by Shel Bachrach of Albert G. Ruben & Co. Inc. of Beverly Hills, California, USA and Richard Feldman of the Feldman Agency, East Liverpool, Ohio with nine insurance companies to spread the risk.

Biggest payout The highest payout on a single life was reported on 14 Nov 1970 to be some $18 million to Linda Mullendore, widow of an Oklahoma, USA rancher. Her murdered husband had paid $300,000 in premiums in 1969.

Marine insurance The largest-ever marine insurance loss was $836 million for the Piper Alpha Oil Field in the North Sea. On 6 Jul 1988 a leak from a

Accountants Arthur Andersen & Co, SC has the largest worldwide fee income, with $6.738 billion at August 1994. The company has 72,722 employees and 358 offices.

gas compression chamber underneath the living quarters ignited and triggered a series of explosions which blew Piper Alpha apart. Of the 232 people on board, only 65 survived.

Property

Most expensive offices According to *World Rental Levels* by Richard Ellis of London, the highest rents in the world for prime offices are in Tokyo, Japan at £91.91 per ft² per annum (December 1994), compared with a peak of £127.20 ($206.68) in June 1991. Added service charges and rates raise the price for the same period to £105.21 per ft².

The UK equivalent at December 1994 was £42.50 per ft² per annum for offices in London's West End, rising to £71.21 with service charges included.

Highest Office Rents

If you've ever wondered about the costs of hiring a high-rise you need look no further. The table below gives a run-down of the twenty locations where you will pay most dearly for the privilege of working. Property is priciest in Tokyo, where it costs nearly three times as much to rent an office as it does in midtown New York City.

Right: inner central Tokyo—top of the list.
(Photo: Spectrum Colour Library)

New York midtown to downtown—14th and 28th on the list respectively.
(Photo: Image Select)

Above: Ho Chi Minh City, Vietnam; 18th on the list, above Rome, Sydney and downtown New York.
(Photo: Spectrum Colour Library)

Congestion on Dadabhoy Naoroji Road, Bombay./(Photo: Spectrum Colour Library)

Above: Exchange Square, home of the Hong Kong Stock Exchange.
(Photo: Spectrum Colour Library)

Location of offices	Rent as quoted locally Dec 1994 p.m.=per month p.a.= per annum	Equivalent net rent in £ per sq.ft.p.a.	Service charge	Rates/ Property tax	Total occupation cost £ sq.ft. p.a.	Exchange rate to £ 15 Dec 1994
1. Tokyo — Inner Central	¥ 40,000 tsubo[1] p.m.	£91.91	15%	N/A	**£105.21**	¥ 156.63
2. Hong Kong	HK$88.64 sq.ft. p.m.	£88.04	6%	6%	**£97.76**	HK$ 12.08
3. Bombay	US$960 sq.m. p.a.	£93.19	4%	N/A	**£97.10**	US$1.56
4. London — West End	£42.50 sq.ft. p.a.	£42.50	15%	52%	**£71.21**	-
5. London — City	£32.50 sq.ft. p.a.	£32.50	20%	78%	**£64.38**	-
6. Beijing	US$950 sq.m. p.a.	£56.52	6%	1%	**£60.59**	US$1.56
7. Shanghai	US$864 sq.m. p.a.	£51.40	6%	1%	**£55.10**	US$1.56
8. Tokyo — Outer Central	¥ 17,400 tsubo[1] p.a.	£39.37	22%	N/A	**£48.00**	¥ 156.63
9. Paris	FF 3300 sq.m. p.a.	£38.95	12%	8%	**£46.62**	FF 8.46
10. New Delhi	US$460 sq.m. p.a.	£44.65	4%	N/A	**£46.61**	US$1.56
11. Singapore	S$7.48 sq.ft. p.m.	£28.86	18%	18%	**£39.18**	S$2.29
12. Guangzhou	US$590 sq.m. p.a.	£35.10	9%	1%	**£38.51**	US$1.56
13. Mexico City	US$45 sq.m. p.m.	£35.70	7%	N/A	**£38.20**	US$1.56
14. New York — midtown	US$47.25 sq.ft. p.a.	£25.02	22%	29%	**£37.82**	US$1.56
15. Hanoi	US$45 sq.m. p.a.	£32.13	16%	N/A	**£37.12**	US$1.56
16. Frankfurt	DM 62.50 sq.m. p.a.	£30.53	13%	1%	**£34.92**	DM 2.45
17. Taipei	NT$2300 ping p.m.	£28.43	13%	2%	**£32.78**	NT$41.22
18. Ho Chi Minh City	US$38 sq.m. p.a.	£27.13	16%	N/A	**£32.13**	US$1.56
19. Prague	DM 55 sq.m. p.a.	£27.76	9%	N/A	**£30.28**	DM 2.45
20. Rome	Lit 600,000 sq.m. p.a.	£24.01	20%	N/A	**£28.82**	LIT 2551

[1] Japanese unit of measurement equivalent to 3.3 m^2 35.5 ft^2

Source: **Richard Ellis** *of London.*

Left: offices to rent in the West End of London.
(Photo: Spectrum Colour Library)

Economics ▶ ▶ ▶

Largest landowner The world's largest landowner is the United States Government, with a holding of 294.5 million ha *727.8 million acres*. It has been suggested that the former Soviet Government constitutionally owned all the land in the entire country, with the exception, perhaps, of that on which foreign embassies stand—a total of 22.4 million km^2 *8.6 million miles^2*.

British Isles The largest landowner is the Forestry Commission (instituted 1919), with 1,127,594 ha *2,786,285 acres* throughout England, Scotland and Wales. The largest non-governmental custodian of land is the National Trust, with 238,989 ha *590,555 acres* throughout England, Wales and Northern Ireland.

The UK's greatest-ever private landowner was George Granville Sutherland-Leveson-Gower, 3rd Duke of Sutherland (1828–92), who owned 550,000 ha *1.4 million acres* in 1883. The individual with the largest acreage is currently the 9th Duke of Buccleuch (b. 28 Sep 1923), who owns 136,035 ha *336,000 acres*.

Longest accepted land tenure St Paul's Cathedral, London holds land at Tillingham, Essex, which was given by Ethelbert, King of Kent no later than AD 616.

Smallest holding The Electricity Trust of South Australia are the proprietors of a registered and separately-delineated piece of land in Adelaide measuring just 25.4 mm *1 in* on all four sides, i.e. one square inch.

Employment

Working careers The longest working life has been the 98 years worked by Mr Izumi (<> Oldest authentic centenarian), who began work goading draught animals at a sugar mill at Isen, Tokunoshima, Japan in 1872. He retired as a sugarcane farmer in 1970 aged 105.

UK The longest working career was that of Susan O'Hagan (1802–1909) who was in domestic service with three generations of the Hall family of Lisburn, near Belfast, Co. Antrim for 97 years from the age of 10 to light duties at 107.

Longest in one job The longest recorded industrial career in one job in Britain was that of Miss Polly Gadsby, who started work with Archibald Turner & Co. of Leicester at the age of nine. In 1932, after 86 years' service, she was still at her bench wrapping elastic at the age of 95. Theodore C. Taylor (1850–1952) also served a total of 86 years with J.T. & J. Taylor of Batley, W Yorks, including 56 years as chairman.

Edward William Beard (1878–1982), a builder of Swindon, Wilts, retired in October 1981 after 85 years with the firm he had founded in 1896.

Longest pension Miss Millicent Barclay was born on 10 Jul 1872, three months after the death of her father, Col. William Barclay, and became eligible for a Madras Military Fund pension to continue until her marriage. She died unmarried on 26

Oct 1969, having drawn the pension for every day of her life of 97 years 3 months.

Unemployment *Highest* The highest percentage unemployment in Great Britain was recorded on 23 Jan 1933, when the total of unemployed persons on the Employment Exchange registers was 2,979,400, representing 23.0 per cent of the insured working population. The peak figure for the post-war period in the UK has been 12.3 per cent of the workforce (3,407,729 unemployed) on 9 Jan 1986.

Lowest In December 1973 in Switzerland the total number of unemployed was reported to be 81 from a population of 6.6 million. The lowest recorded peacetime level of unemployment in Britain was 0.9 per cent on 11 Jul 1955, when 184,929 persons were registered. The peak figure for the employed labour force in the UK has been 26,917,000 in December 1989.

Strikes *Earliest* The earliest recorded strike was one by an orchestra leader named Aristos from Greece, in Rome c. 309 BC. The dispute concerned meal breaks.

Largest The most serious single labour dispute in Britain was the General Strike of 4–12 May 1926, called by the Trades Union Congress in support of the Miners' Federation. During the nine days of the strike, 1,580,000 people were involved and 14,220,000 working days were lost. In the year 1926 as a whole, a total of 2,750,000 people were involved in 323 different labour disputes, and the working days lost during the year amounted to 162,300,000, the highest figure ever recorded.

Longest strike The world's longest recorded strike ended on 4 Jan 1961, after 33 years. It concerned the employment of barbers' assistants in Copenhagen, Denmark. The strike that caused most disruption was that at the plumbing-fixtures factory of the Kohler Co. in Sheboygan, Wisconsin, USA between April 1954 and October 1962. The strike is alleged to have cost the United Automobile Workers' Union about $12 million to sustain.

UK The longest industrial dispute in Britain lasted 8½ years, ending on 31 Dec 1994. It began when 38 men were sacked by Sheffield engineering works Keeton Sons and Co., in July 1986; during the course of the dispute several strikers reached retirement age, some found new employment, and one died.

Britain's most protracted national strike was called by the National Union of Mineworkers from 8 Mar 1984 to 5 Mar 1985. HM Treasury estimated the cost to be £2,625 million or £118.93 per household.

Trade unions *Largest* The world's largest union is the Profession-

alnyi Soyuz Rabotnikov Agro-Promyshlennogo Kompleksa (Agro-Industrial Complex Workers' Union) in Russia, with 15.2 million members in January 1993.

The largest union in the UK is UNISON, with 1.45 million members, formed on 1 Jul 1993 from the merger between NALGO, NUPE and COHSE. This compares with a peak membership of 2,086,281 in 1979 for the Transport and General Workers' Union (TGWU).

Smallest The ultimate in small unions was the Jewelcase and Jewellery Display Makers Union (JJDMU), founded in 1894. It was dissolved on 31 Dec 1986 by its general secretary, Charles Evans. The motion was seconded by Fergus McCormack, its only surviving member.

The smallest union is currently the 13-member Sheffield Wool Shear Workers.

Longest name The union with the longest name is the International Association of Marble, Slate and Stone Polishers, Rubbers and Sawyers, Tile and Marble Setters' Helpers and Marble Mosaic and Terrazzo Workers' Helpers, or the IAMSSPRSTMSH-MMTWH of Washington, DC, USA.

> The world's largest employment services group is Manpower, with world-wide sales of all their brand units of $5.6 billion in 1994.

Expensive

The most expensive piece of property ever recorded is the land around the Meijiya Building, the central Tokyo retail food store in the Ginza district, which was quoted in October 1988 by the Japanese National Land Agency at a peak 33.3 million yen per m^2 (then equivalent to $248,000).

Economics

National Economies

Richest country The richest territory as listed in the 1994 *World Bank Atlas* is Switzerland, with a gross national product (GNP) per capita of $36,410 for 1993. The GNP per capita for the United Kingdom in 1993 was $17,970.

Poorest country According to the same source, Mozambique had the lowest GNP per capita in 1992, with only $60, but figures were unavailable for several countries.

National debt The largest national debt of any country in the world is that of the United States. During fiscal year 1994 it was $4.848 trillion, and the gross interest paid on the debt was $296.278 billion. The net interest was $202.957 billion.

UK The national debt in Great Britain was less than £1 million during the reign of James II in 1687; at the end of March 1993 it amounted to some £248,600 million, of which around £20,200 million was in currencies other than sterling.

Largest GNP The country with the largest gross national product is the United States, with a record $6.726 trillion for the year ending 31 Dec 1994.

Most overseas debt The country most heavily in overseas debt at fiscal year-end 1994 was the United States, with over $654 billion. Among developing countries, Brazil has the highest foreign debt, with $116.5 billion at the end of 1992.

Foreign aid The greatest donor of foreign aid is the United States government, which has given a net total of $436.9 billion from 1 Jul 1994 to 1 May 1995. US foreign aid began with $50,000 to Venezuela for earthquake relief in 1812.

Balance of payments The record deficit for any country for a calendar year was $167.1 billion reported by the US in 1987. The record surplus was Japan's $117.64 billion (the equivalent of 149 trillion yen) for 1992.

> The US national debt, the world's largest, has grown since our first edition from $271,259 million, or $1660 per head, to the $4.848 trillion for fiscal year 1994.

Working

Longest working week A case of a working week of 142 hours (with an average each day of 3 hr 42 min 51 sec for sleep) was recorded in June 1980 by Dr Paul Ashton, 32, the anaesthetics registrar at Birkenhead General Hospital, Merseyside. He described the week in question as 'particularly bad but not untypical'. Some non-consultant doctors are contracted to work 110 hours a week or be available for 148 hours.

■ Kenneth Clarke, the chancellor, with his wife Gillian at Downing Street in November 1993. Governmental expenditure was at its highest ever in 1993/4, at £286.6 billion.
(Photo: Rex Features)

UK The most favourable yearly current balance-of-payments figure has been a surplus of £6748 million in 1981. The worst figure was a deficit of £21,726 million in 1989.

Worst inflation The world's worst inflation occurred in Hungary in June 1946, when the 1931 gold pengö was valued at 130 million trillion (1.3×10^{20}) paper pengös. Notes were issued for 'Egymillárd billió' (1000 trillion or 10^{21}) pengös on 3 Jun and withdrawn on 11 Jul 1946. Vouchers for 1 billion trillion (10^{27}) pengös were issued for taxation payment only.

The best-known and most frequently analysed hyperinflationary episode occurred in Germany in 1923. The circulation of the Reichsbank mark on 6 Nov 1923 reached 400,338,326,350,700,000,000, and inflation was 755,700 million-fold on 1913 levels.

The highest inflation rate in the world in 1994 was that of Brazil at 1120.4 per cent.

UK The worst rate in a year was for August 1974 to August 1975, when inflation ran at a rate of 26.9 per cent. The increase in the Tax and Price Index (allowing for tax reliefs) was 8.1 per cent for the 12 months to June 1990. The largest 12-month increase in the TPI (extrapolated) was 31.9 per cent, also recorded in August 1975.

Least inflation The country with the least inflation in 1994 was Canada, with 0.2 per cent.

Largest budget The greatest governmental expenditure of any country was $1.461 trillion, made by the US government for the fiscal year 1994. The highest-ever revenue figure was $1.258 trillion, made by the US in the same year.

The greatest fiscal surplus ever was $11.796 billion in the United States in 1947/48. The worst deficit was $290 billion in the US fiscal year 1992.

UK The greatest general UK government expenditure is £286.6 billion projected for the fiscal year 1993/4. The highest general government receipts are expected to be £223.1 billion for the same fiscal year. The public-sector borrowing requirement was at a peak of £45 billion (excluding privatisation proceeds) in 1993/4 compared with a debt repayment of £7,588 million in 1988/89.

Highest taxation The country with the highest effective corporate tax in May 1995 was Libya, with a rate of 64%. This includes a 4% contribution to the Jihad (Holy War) fund.

The country with the highest rate of income tax in 1992 was Norway, with 65 per cent, although additional personal taxes made it possible to be charged in excess of 100 per cent.

UK In the UK until 1979 the former top earned and unearned rates were 83 per cent and 98 per cent. The standard rate of tax was reduced to 25 per cent and the higher rate to 40 per cent in the 1988 Budget. The all-time record was set in 1967/68, when a 'special charge' of up to 9s (45p) in the £ additional to surtax brought the top rate to 27s 3d in the £ (or 136 per cent) on investment income.

Least taxed The sovereign countries with the least income tax are Bahrain and Qatar, where the rate, regardless of income, is nil.

UK No tax is levied on the Sarkese (inhabitants of Sark) in the Channel Islands.

Lowest rates of taxation (UK) Income tax was first introduced in Great Britain in 1799 for incomes above £60 per annum. It was discontinued in 1815, only to be reintroduced in 1842 at the rate of 7d (2.92p) in the £. It was at its lowest at 2d (0.83p) in the £ in 1875, gradually climbing to 1s 3d (6.25p) by 1913. From April 1941 until 1946 the record peak of 10s (50p) in the £ was maintained to assist in the financing of the war effort.

Minimum lending rate The highest-ever figure for the British bank rate (since 13 Oct 1972, the minimum lending rate) was 17 per cent from 15 Nov 1979 to 3 Jul 1980.

The longest period without a change in the lending rate was the 12 years 13 days from 26 Oct 1939 to 7 Nov 1951, during which time the rate stayed at 2 per cent. This lowest-ever rate had been first attained on 22 Apr 1852.

Gold reserves The world's greatest monetary gold reserves are those of the United States Treasury at 261.79 million fine oz at the end of 1993, equivalent to $92.961 billion at the current price of $355.10 per fine oz. The United States Bullion Depository at Fort Knox, 48 km *30 miles* south-west of Louisville, Kentucky, USA, has been the principal federal depository of US gold since December 1936. Gold is stored in 446,000 standard mint bars of 12.4414 kg *400 troy oz* measuring 17.7 × 9.2 × 4.1 cm *7 x 3⅝ x 1⅝ in*. Gold's peak price was $850 on 21 Jan 1980.

UK The UK's gold reserves totalled 18.45 million fine oz at September 1993.

Guess What?
Q. What is the UK's largest company by assets?
A. See Page 161

Personal Wealth

The comparison and estimation of extreme personal wealth are beset with intractable difficulties. Quite apart from reticence and the element of approximation in the valuation of assets, as Jean Paul Getty (1892–1976) once said: 'If you can count your millions, you are not a billionaire.' The term millionaire was coined c. 1740 and billionaire (in the original American sense of one thousand million) in 1861. The earliest dollar centi-millionaire was Cornelius Vanderbilt (1794–1877), who left $100 million in 1877. The first billionaires were John Davison Rockefeller (1839–1937) and Andrew William Mellon (1855–1937), with Rockefeller believed to be the first to accumulate a billion dollars.

The longest budget speech was that of the Rt Hon. David (later Earl) Lloyd George (1863–1945) on 29 Apr 1909. It lasted 4 hr 51 min, although with a 30 minute tea-break. He was later to be Prime Minister, from 7 Dec 1916 to 19 Oct 1922.

Richest men Much of the wealth of the world's monarchs represents national rather than personal assets. The richest person in the world is HM Sir Muda Hassanal Bolkiah Mu'izzaddin Waddaulah (b. 15 Jul 1946) of Brunei, self-appointed Prime Minister and Finance and Home Affairs Minister, who has a fortune estimated at $37 billion.

UK Britain's richest men at May 1995 were Hans and Gad Rausing, controllers of Tetra Laval, the manufacturer of TetraPak plastic and aluminium-laminated containers for milk and fruit juices. The brothers left their home in Sweden to live in Britain in the 1980s, and retired from daily involvement with the business in 1993. They are believed to be worth £4 billion.

Richest women HM the Queen is asserted by most to be the wealthiest woman, although the exact amount of her fortune has always been the subject of controversy. *The Sunday Times* estimated her personal fortune at £450 million in May 1995. This excludes her art collection, worth at least £4 billion, which is now controlled by the Royal Collection, a charitable trust. It also takes into account the fact that she is now paying tax to the tune of at least £1 million a year.

Millionaires

Youngest millionaires The youngest person ever to accumulate a million dollars was the American child film actor Jackie Coogan (1914–84), co-star with Sir Charles Chaplin (1889–1977) in *The Kid*, made in 1921.

The youngest of the 101 dollar billionaires reported in the US in 1992 was William Gates, 36, co-founder of software house Microsoft of Seattle, Washington. Gates was 20 when he set up his company in 1976 and was a billionaire in 11 years (⇨ Computers).

The youngest millionairess was Shirley Temple (b. USA, 23 Apr 1928), now Mrs Charles Black, who accumulated wealth exceeding $1 million before she was 10. Her childhood acting career lasted from 1934 to 1939.

The cosmetician Madame C.J. Walker (*née* Sarah Breedlove) (1857–1919) of Delta, Louisiana, USA is reputed to have become the first self-made millionairess. She was an uneducated Negro orphan whose fortune was founded on a hair straightener.

Richest families It was tentatively estimated in 1974 that the combined value of the assets nominally controlled by the Du Pont family of some 1600 members may be of the order of $150,000 million. The family arrived in the USA from France on 1 Jan 1800. Capital from Pierre Du Pont (1730–1817) enabled his son Eleuthère Irénée Du Pont to start his explosives company in the United States.

A more conclusive estimate for an individual family is the Walton retailing family, worth an estimated $24 billion, compared with Britain's retailing giants, the Sainsbury family, with an estimated $5.2 billion.

Highest incomes The largest incomes derive from the collection of royalties per barrel by rulers of oil-rich sheikhdoms who have not formally revoked personal entitlement. Shaikh Zayid ibn Sultan an-Nuhayan (b. 1918), Head of State of the United Arab Emirates, arguably has title to some $9 billion of the country's annual gross national product.

Guess What?
Q. What country has the largest stock of cattle?
A. See Page 171

> **The highest disclosed UK personal-income-tax demand raised is one for £5,371,220 for 1981 against merchant banker Nicholas van Hoogstraten.**

Greatest wills The will of the largest value ever proved in the UK was that of the 6th Marquess of Bute, who left an estate worth £130,062,015 at his death in 1994.

On 29 Apr 1985 the estate of Sir Charles Clore (1904–79) was agreed by a court hearing at £123 million. The Inland Revenue initially claimed £84 million in duties but settled for £67 million.

The largest fortune proved in the will of a woman in the UK was £92,814,057 net, left by Dorothy de Rothschild (1895–1988), matriarch of the leading family in world Jewry.

Greatest miser If meanness is measurable as a ratio between expendable assets and expenditure then Henrietta Howland Green (Hetty Green; *née* Robinson) (1835–1916), who kept a balance of over $31,400,000 in one bank alone, was the all-time world champion. Her son had to have his leg amputated because of her delays in finding a *free* medical clinic. She herself ate cold porridge because she was too thrifty to heat it. Her estate proved to be worth $95 million (equivalent to $1725 million in 1993).

Largest dowry The largest recorded dowry was that of Elena Patiño, daughter of Don Simón Iturbi Patiño (1861–1947), the Bolivian tin millionaire, who in 1929 bestowed £8 million (equivalent to £230 million in 1993) from a fortune at one time estimated to be worth £125 million.

Greatest bequests The largest single bequest in the history of philanthropy was the $1-billion art collection of the American publisher Walter Annenberg, who, on 12 Mar 1991, announced his intention to leave the collection to the Metropolitan Museum of Art in New York City, USA.

The largest single cash bequest was $500-million (equivalent in 1993 to $6 billion), made to 4157 educational and other institutions and announced on 12 Dec 1955 by the Ford Foundation (established 1936) of New York City, USA.

UK The greatest benefactions of a British millionaire were those of William Richard Morris, later Viscount Nuffield (1877–1963), which totalled more than £30 million between 1926 and his death on 22 Aug 1963.

Highest salary Fund manager George Soros earned at least $1.1 billion in 1993, according to *Financial World*'s list of the highest-paid individuals on Wall Street.

Highest fees The highest-paid investment consultant in the world is Harry D. Schultz, who lives in Monte Carlo and Zurich, Switzerland. His standard consultation fee for 60 minutes is $2400 on weekdays and $3400 at weekends. Most popular are the five-minute phone consultations at $200 (i.e. $40 a minute). His 'International Harry Schultz Letter', instituted in 1964, sells at $50 per copy. A life subscription costs $2400.

Lecture fees Dr Ronald Dante was paid $3,080,000 for lecturing students on hypnotherapy at a two-day course held in Chicago, Illinois, USA on 1–2 Jun 1986. He was teaching for 8 hours each day and thus earned $192,500 per hour.

Return of Cash

In May 1994 Howard Jenkins of Tampa, Florida, USA, a 31-year-old roofing company employee, discovered that $88 million had been transferred mistakenly into his bank account. Although he initially withdrew $4 million, his conscience got the better of him shortly afterwards and he returned the $88 million in full.

Stock Exchanges

Oldest The oldest of the world's Stock Exchanges is that of Amsterdam, Netherlands, founded in 1602 with dealings in printed shares of the United East India Company of the Netherlands in the Oude Zijds

■ Fund manager George Soros earned at least **$1.1 billion in 1993, according to** *Financial World***'s list of the highest-paid individuals on Wall Street.**
(Photo: Rex Feature/The Times)

Handshake

The largest golden handshake ever was one of $53.8 million, given to F. Ross Johnson, who left RJR Nabisco as chairman in February 1989.

In the UK, Dr Ernest Mario (b. 12 Jun 1938) was reported to have received a pay-off of at least £2.7 million after he resigned in March 1993 from his position as chief executive of Glaxo, following boardroom disagreements over future policy.

Kapel. The largest trading volume in 1994 was the New York Stock Exchange, with $2454.2 billion, ahead of London with £1045 billion and the Federation of Germany Stock Exchanges with £891 billion.

London Stock Exchange *Most bargains* The highest number of equity bargains in one day was 114,973 on 22 Oct 1987. The record for a year is 13,557,455 bargains in 1987. There were 7367 securities listed at 31 Dec 1992 (cf. the 9749 peak in June 1973). Their total nominal value was £511.6 billion (gilt-edged £172 billion), with a market value of £2579.3 billion (gilt-edged £186.5 billion).

Trading volume The busiest session on the London market was on 28 Jan 1993, when 1.3 billion shares were traded.

FT-SE 100 share index *Closing prices* The FT-SE 100 index reached an all-time intraday peak of 3539.2 on 3 Feb 1994 and a closing high of 3520.3 on 2 Feb 1994. The lowest closing figure was 986.9 on 23 Jul 1984.

Greatest rise and fall The greatest rise in a day has been 142.2 points to 1943.8 on 21 Oct 1987, and the greatest fall in a day's trading was 250.7 points to 1801.6 on 20 Oct 1987.

New York Stock Exchange The market value of stocks listed on the New York Stock Exchange reached an all-time high of $55 trillion at 4 May 1995. The record day's trading was 608,148,710 shares on 20 Oct 1987, compared with 16,410,030 shares traded on 29 Oct 1929, the 'Black Tuesday' of the famous 'crash', a record unsurpassed until April 1968.

The largest stock trade in the history of the NYSE took place on 10 Apr 1986 and involved a 48,788,800-share block of Navistar International Corporation stock sold at $10 per share on 10 Apr 1986.

The highest price paid for a seat on the New York Stock Exchange was $1.15 million in 1987. The lowest 20th-century price was $17,000, set in 1942.

Closing prices The highest closing figure on the Dow Jones Industrial average (instituted 8 Oct 1896) of selected stocks was 4465.14 on 31 May 1995.

The Depression caused the Dow Jones average to plunge from 381.71 on 3 Sep 1929 to its lowest-ever closing figure of 41.22 on 8 Jul 1932.

> The highest recorded personal paper losses on stock values were incurred by Ray A. Kroc (1902–84), former chairman of McDonald's Corporation, amounting to $65 million on 8 Jul 1974 (⇨ Restaurateurs).

Greatest rise and fall The record daily rise is 186.84 points, to 2027.85, achieved on 21 Oct 1987. The largest decline in a day's trading was 508 points (22.6 per cent) on 19 Oct 1987 (Black Monday). The total lost in security values from 1 Sep 1929 to 30 Jun 1932 was $74 billion. The greatest paper loss in a year was $210 billion in 1974.

Most valued companies The greatest market value of any corporation in May 1995 was £92.3 billion for General Electric of Fairfield, Connecticut, USA.

UK The largest British company in terms of market capitalization is Shell Transport and Trading Co. plc, valued at £25.8 billion at 2 Jun 1995.

Company names *Longest* The longest company name on the Index registered under the Companies Acts is 'Albion Highland All Tartans by metre in wool silk other Tweeds Velvet Stock & Bespoke Kilts Trews Clothes Highland Dress Jewellery Furnishing Presents Express Mail Order & London Appt Ltd', company number 3047127.

Shortest The shortest names on the Index are C Ltd, E Ltd, H Ltd, I Ltd, K Ltd, L Ltd, P Ltd, Q Ltd, R Ltd, W Ltd, X Ltd, Y Ltd and Z Ltd.

Largest flotation The flotation of British Gas plc had an equity offer which produced the record sum of £7.75 billion, to 4.5 million shareholders. Allotment letters were dispatched on 15 Dec 1986.

The record number of investors for a single issue is 5.9 million in the Mastergain '92 equity fund floated by the Unit Trust of India, Bombay, in April and May 1992.

Rights issue The largest recorded rights issue in Britain was one of £1,350 million by Zeneca, announced on 1 Jun 1993.

Highest share value The highest denomination of any share quoted in the world was a single share in Moeara Enim Petroleum Corporation, worth £50,586 (165,000 Dutch florins) on 22 Apr 1992.

AGM attendance A world record total of 20,109 shareholders attended the AGM in April 1961 of American Telephone and Telegraph Company (now AT&T Corp) (⇨Greatest profit).

Q. Where in the world would you pay the highest rent for an office?
A. See Page 163

Paper Money

Earliest Paper money was an invention of the Chinese, first tried in AD 812 and prevalent by AD 970. The world's earliest banknotes (*banco-sedlar*) were issued in Stockholm, Sweden in July 1661, the oldest survivor being one of five dalers dated 6 Dec 1662. The oldest surviving printed Bank of England note is one for £555 to bearer, dated 19 Dec 1699, measuring 11.4 × 19.1 cm *4½ × 7½ in*.

Smallest The smallest national note ever issued was the 10-bani note of the Ministry of Finance of Romania in 1917. It measured (printed area) 27.5 × 38 mm *1¹/₁₆ × 1½ in*. Of German *Notgeld*, the smallest were the ¹/₃ pfg notes of Passau (1920–21), measuring 18 × 18.5 mm *¹¹/₁₆ × ³/₄ in*.

> The largest paper money ever issued was the one-guan (one thousand cash) note of the Chinese Ming Dynasty issue of 1368–99, which measured 22.8 × 33.0 cm *9 × 13 in*. In October 1983 one sold for £340.

Highest values The highest-value notes in circulation are US Federal Reserve $10,000 banknotes, bearing the head of Salmon P. Chase (1808–73). It was announced in 1969 that no further notes higher than $100 would be issued, and only 345 $10,000 bills remain in circulation or unretired. The highest value ever issued by the US Federal Reserve System is a note for $100,000, bearing the head of Woodrow Wilson (1856–1924), which is used only for transactions between the Federal Reserve and the Treasury Department.

Two Bank of England notes for £1 million still exist, dated before 1812, but these were used only for internal accounting. There are also two Treasury £1-million notes dating from 1948 in existence, one of which was sold to dealer Brian Dawson for £23,100 at Christie's, London on 9 Oct 1990.

The highest-value notes in Great Britain which have been *issued* are £1000 notes, first printed in 1725, discontinued on 22 Apr 1943 and withdrawn on 30 Apr 1945. Just over 100 of these notes were still unretired up to April 1993.

Lowest values The lowest-value (and the lowest-denomination) legal tender banknote is the one-sen (or 1/100th of a rupiah) Indonesian note. Its exchange value in early 1993 was 327,170 to the £.

The lowest-denomination Bank of England notes ever printed were the black on pale blue half-crown (now 12½ p) notes

in 1941, signed by the late Sir Kenneth Peppiatt. Very few examples survive, and they are valued at not less than £1500.

Highest circulation The highest-ever Bank of England note circulation in the UK was £20,345 million worth on 24 Dec 1993—equivalent to a pile over 380 km *237 miles* high in new £5 notes.

Most expensive The record price achieved at auction for a single lot of banknotes was £240,350 (including buyer's premium), paid by Richard Lobel on behalf of a consortium, at Phillips, London on 14 Feb 1991. The lot consisted of a cache of British military notes which were found in a vault in Berlin, Germany and contained more than 17 million notes.

Banknote collection Israel Gerber of Ashdod, Israel has accumulated banknotes from 214 different countries since he started collecting in 1962.

Cheques and Coins

Largest The greatest amount paid by a single cheque in the history of banking was £2,474,655,000. Issued on 30 Mar 1995 and signed by Nicholas Morris, Company Secretary of Glaxo plc, the cheque represented a payment by Glaxo plc to Wellcome Trust Nominees Limited in respect of the Trust's share in Wellcome plc. The Lloyds Bank

---

Coins

Oldest
World: c. 630 BC electrum staters of King Gyges of Lydia, Turkey[1]. *British: c.* 90 BC Westerham-type gold stater[2].

Earliest Dated
World: Samian silver tetradrachm struck in Zankle (now Messina), Sicily, dated year 1, viz 494 BC—shown as 'A'. *Christian Era:* MCCXXXIIII (1234) Bishop of Roskilde coins, Denmark (6 known). *British:* 1539 James V of Scotland gold 'bonnet piece'. *Earliest English:* 1548 Edward VI gold ten shillings (MDXLVIII).

Heaviest
World: 19·71 kg *43 lb 7¼ oz* Swedish 10-daler copper plate 1644[3]. *British:* 121·1 g *4¼ oz* Shrewsbury silver pound of 1644, the heaviest of the Charles I silver pounds from the English Civil War[4].

Lightest
World: 0·002 g *14000 to the oz* Nepalese silver ¼ jawa *c.* 1740. *British:* 2·66 grains *180 to the oz* Henry VIII 2nd coinage silver farthings (1526–42).

Most Expensive
World: $3190000 for the King of Siam Proof Set, a set of 1804 and 1834 US coins which had once been given to the King of Siam, purchased by Iraj Sayah and Terry Brand at Superior Galleries, Beverly Hills, California, USA on 28 May 1990. Included in the set of nine coins was the 1804 silver dollar, which had an estimated value of about $2000000. The record price paid for an individual coin is $1500000, for the US 1907 Double Eagle Ultra High Relief $20 gold coin, sold by MTB Banking Corporation of New York, USA to a private investor on 9 Jul 1990. *British:* £124300 (including buyer's premium) bid for a Victoria gothic crown in gold (2 known), at a joint auction between Spink & Son, London and the Taisei Stamp and Coin Co., in Tokyo, Japan on 3 Jul 1988.

Footnotes
[1] *Chinese uninscribed 'spade' money of the Zhou Dynasty has been dated to c. 550 BC.*
[2] *Bellovaci-type gold staters, which were struck in northern France and not in Britain, circulated as early as c. 130 BC.*
[3] *The largest coin-like medallion was completed on 21 Mar 1986 for the World Exposition in Vancouver, British Columbia, Canada, Expo 86—a $1000000 gold piece. Its dimensions were 95·25 cm 37½ in diameter and 19·05 mm ¾ in thick, and it weighed 166 kg 365 lb 15 oz or 5337 oz (troy) of gold.*
[4] *The heaviest current British coin is the 39·94 g 1⅜ oz gold £5 piece.*

■ The Westerham-type gold stater is the oldest known British coin, dating from around 90 B.C. (Photo: Ashmolean Museum)

Registrar's computer system could not generate a cheque this large and so it was completed by a Lloyds employee using a typewriter. The typist was so overawed by the responsibility that she took three attempts to produce the cheque, numbered 020503.

A cheque for $4,176,969,623.57 was drawn on 30 Jun 1954, although this was an internal US Treasury cheque.

Piggy bank A giant pink piggy bank measuring 2.31 × 3.61 m *7½ × 12 ft* with a capacity of 7.2 m³ *254.25 ft³* was made by Mercian Housing Association Ltd of Birmingham in May 1990.

Hoards The most valuable hoard of coins was one of about 80,000 aurei in Brescello near Modena, Italy in 1714, believed to have been deposited c. 37 BC. The largest deliberately buried hoard ever found was the Brussels hoard of 1908 containing c. 150,000 coins.

The largest hoard of English coins was the Tutbury (Staffs) hoard of 1831 containing over 20,000 silver coins, the majority of which were pence of Edward I (1272–1307).

The largest accidental hoard on record was from the 1715 Spanish Plate Fleet, which sank off the coast of Florida, USA. A rea-sonable estimate of its contents would be some 60 million coins, about half of which were recovered by Spanish authorities shortly after the event. Of the remaining 30 million pieces, perhaps 500,000 have been recovered by modern salvors, presumably leaving the other 29½ million coins still awaiting recovery.

The record in terms of weight is 43 tonnes of gold, from the White Star Liner HMS *Laurentic*, which was mined in 40.2 m *132 ft* of water off Fanad Head, Donegal,

Ireland in 1917. Of the 3211 gold ingots, 3191 have been recovered since then by the Royal Navy, Cossum Diving Syndicate and Consortium Recovery Ltd.

Coin balancing Mohammad Irshadullah Hamidi of Muzaffarpur, India stacked a pyramid of 870 coins on the edge of a coin free-standing vertically on the base of a coin which was on a table on 16 Mar 1993.

The tallest single column of coins ever stacked on the edge of a coin was made up of 253 Indian one-rupee pieces on top of a vertical five-rupee coin, by Dipak Syal of Yamuna Nagar, India on 3 May 1991. He also balanced 10 one-rupee coins and 10 ten-paise coins alternately horizontally and vertically in a single column on 1 May 1991.

Mints *Largest* The largest mint in the world is that of the US Treasury. It was built from 1965 to 1969 on Independence Mall, Philadelphia, Pennsylvania, covers 4.7 ha *11.5 acres* and has an annual production capacity of 12 billion coins (down from 15 billion). One high-speed stamping machine called Graebner Press can produce coins at a rate of 42,000 per hour, and the record production was 19.5 billion coins produced between the Philadelphia and Denver mints in 1982.

Smallest The smallest issuing mint in the world belongs to the Sovereign Military Order of Malta, in the City of Rome. Its single-press mint is housed

Collection

The highest price ever paid for a coin collection was $25,235,360 for the Garrett family collection of US and colonial coins collected between 1860 and 1942, which had been donated to Johns Hopkins University, Baltimore, Maryland, USA. The sales were made at four auctions held on 28–29 Nov 1979 and 25–26 Mar 1981 at the Bowers & Ruddy Galleries in Wolfeboro, New Hampshire, USA.

The most valuable column of coins was worth 39,458 Irish pounds (then £37,458) and was 1.88 m *6 ft 2 in* high. It was built by St Brigid's Family and Community Centre at Waterford, Republic of Ireland on 20 Nov 1993.

Coin snatching is a skill which requires great patience, perfect balance, strength in an arm, fast hands and big hands! Build a stack of coins on your forearm near your elbow, bring your hand forward quickly and catch as many of the coins as you can in the same hand. Not easy is it?

Dean Gould of Felixstowe, Suffolk has caught 328 10p coins in this way, out of 482 placed on his forearm, setting his most recent record on 6 Apr 1993. After facing rivalry for the title of champion coin snatcher over a period of many years, he regained the record in 1991 and has held it ever since.

But why? 'It was an ambition of mine to get into The Guinness Book of Records. I chose coin snatching because it was something I was good at as a boy. I always wanted to be the best at something.'

Over the years different contenders have used different methods, from a single column in the early 1970s to Dean's highly intricate interlocking method now. This consists of 13 columns all linked to form one single stack. 'The interlocking stacking method which came about during the mid 1980s was the turning point for the high catches. It makes the coins keep together better.'

Dean goes on to say 'The technique has to be perfect, from the way the coins balance to how I stand and the speed of the snatch. Stacking the coins takes twenty minutes. The wider the stack the better, providing it is within your hand span.'

With his main rivals from the past now seemingly unable to take him on, is there anyone Dean knows of who could potentially threaten his record? 'I am only hoping Chris Greener doesn't have a go.' Chris Greener is Britain's tallest man, and Dean has seen his hands!

Dexterous Dean's Deeds

■ Dean Gould stacks his coins (far left) and catches as many as he can (left).

in one small room and has issued proof coins since 1961.

Line of coins The most valuable line of coins was made up of 1,724,000 US quarters to a value of $431,000. It was 41.68km *25.9 miles* long and was laid at the Atlanta Marriott Marquis Hotel, Atlanta, Georgia, USA by members of the National Exchange Club on 25 Jul 1992. The most valuable line of coins in Britain was the 'Golden Mile' of £1 coins with a value of £71,652, laid at the Town Hall at Romford, Essex on 22 Apr 1990. The attempt was carried out under the supervision of Pauline Obee, assisted by volunteers from Havering-atte-Bower, Essex.

The longest line of coins on record had a total length of 48.89km *30.38 miles* and was made using 1,886,975 2p coins. It was laid by the Friends of the Samaritans at the Great Park, Windsor, Berks on 16 Aug 1992.

Guess What?
Q. In 1946 which country experienced the worst inflation the world has ever known?
A. See Page 165

Pile of coins The most valuable pile of coins had a total value of $126,463.61 and consisted of 1,000,298 American coins of various denominations. It was constructed by the YWCA of Seattle-King County, Washington, USA at Redmond, Washington on 28 May 1992.

Charity fund-raising The greatest recorded amount raised by a charity walk or run is $Can 24.7 million by Terry Fox (1958–81) of Canada, who, with an artificial leg, ran from St John's, Newfoundland to Thunder Bay, Ontario in 143 days from 12 April to 2 Sep 1980. He covered 5373km *3339 miles*.

■ **The Swedish 3 skilling-banco yellow colour error of 1855, of which there is only one remaining example. It is one of the world's rarest stamps.**
(Photo: David Feldman SA—Geneva)

Postal Services

Largest mail The country with the largest volume of mail in the world is the United States, whose population posted 177.1 billion letters and packages in the fiscal year 1994. The US Postal Service now employs 728,944 people and had the world's largest civilian vehicle fleet of 200,000 cars and trucks. The average number of letters and packages per capita was 675.

The UK total was 16,364 million letters and 183.6 million parcels in the year ending 31 Mar 1992. The record day was 16 Dec 1991 with 121.1 million items, when Christmas cards coincided with share certificates following the privatization of BT.

The practice of numbering houses began on the Pont Notre-Dame, Paris, France in 1463. The highest-numbered house in Britain is No. 2679 Stratford Road, Hockley Heath, W Mids, owned since 1977 by Mr and Mrs Malcolm Aldridge.

Oldest pillar-boxes The first orthodox system of roadside posting-boxes was established in 1653 in Paris, France to facilitate the interchange of correspondence in the city. They were erected at the intersection of main thoroughfares and were emptied three times a day.

A cast-iron posting box dating from c. 1690 was found at the White Hart coaching inn, Spilsby, Lincs in January 1988. The oldest pillar-box still in service in the British Isles is one dating from 8 Feb

1853 in Union Street, St Peter Port, Guernsey, Channel Islands. Cast by John Vaudin in Jersey, it was restored to its original maroon livery in October 1981.

Post offices The country with the greatest number of post offices is India, with 150,346 in 1995. At 1 April 1995 there were 19,603 post offices in the UK. The oldest is at Sanquhar, Dumfries & Galloway, and was first referred to in 1763. The northernmost post office in the British Isles is at Haroldswick, Unst, Shetland Islands and the most southerly is at Samarès, Jersey, Channel Islands, although it is not run by the British Post Office. The most southerly in mainland Britain is the Lizard sub-post-office, Cornwall. The highest post office in England is at Quarnford, Buxton, Derbys at 359.9m *1181 ft*.

The post office with the greatest number of positions is the Trafalgar Square post office, with 22 excluding two parcel hatches.

Stamp-licking John Kenmuir of Hamilton, Strathclyde licked and affixed 393 stamps in 4 minutes at the BBC TV studios on 26 Sep 1990, later shown on the *Record Breakers* programme.

Stamp

The record price paid at auction in the UK for a single stamp is £203,500 (including buyer's premium) for a Bermuda 1854 Perot Postmaster's stamp (1d red on bluish wove paper on an 1855 letter) sold by Christie's Robson Lowe, London on 13 Jun 1991.

Postage Stamps
(Auction records unless stated otherwise and all prices include buyer's premium)

Earliest
Penny Black 1d of Great Britain, Queen Victoria, 68158080 printed. The Penny Black stamps were available from some of the main post offices in Great Britain from 1 May 1840, though were not valid for postage payment until 6 May 1840.

Highest Price (World)
Sw.Fr.5,750,000 (£2,590,090). Mauritius 'Bordeaux Cover'; an 1847 letter to wine merchants in Bordeaux, franked with the 1-penny and 2d first issues of Mauritius. It was bought by an anonymous buyer in less than a minute, at a sale at the Hotel International In Zurich on 3 Nov 1993.

Highest Price (UK)
£374000. China 1878 5 candarins 'wide spacing' unique mint sheet of 25, sold at Sotheby's, London on 11 Sep 1991 and bought by a Hong Kong collector. *Single stamp.* The Swedish 3 skilling-banco was sold in May 1990 for S.Fr.1,877,500 (approx £850,000).

Highest Total (World)
Sw.Fr. 15,000,000 (£6,756,756). The Mauritius auction of 3 Nov 1993, conducted by Geneva-based auctioneer David Feldman. The collection comprised 183 pages of the classic issues of Mauritius, owned by Japanese engineer-industrialist Hiroyuki Kanai.

Highest Total (UK)
£2,201,463. The Major James Starr collection of Chinese stamps on 11–13 Sep 1991, with all 993 lots sold.

Largest Purchase
$11 million. Marc Haas collection of 3000 US postal and pre-postal covers to 1869, bought by Stanley Gibbons Ltd, London in August 1979.

Largest (Special Purpose)
247.7 x 69.8mm 9¾ x 2¾ in. China 1913. 10 cent letter stamp.

Largest (Standard Postage)
160 x110mm 6⁵⁄₁₆ x 4⁵⁄₁₆ in. Marshall Islands 75 cents issued 30 Oct 1979.

Smallest
8 x9.5mm ⁵⁄₁₆ x ⅜ in. Colombian State of Bolivar, 1863–6. 10 cent and 1 peso value.

Highest Denomination (World)
£100. Red and black, Kenya, Uganda and Tanganyika 1925.

Highest Denomination (UK)
£10. Grey-white, issued 2 Feb 1993, depicting Britannia and embossed with Braille markings for the first time.

Lowest Denomination
3000 pengö of Hungary. Issued 1946 when 150 million million pengö=1p.

Rarest (World)
Unique examples include: British Guiana 1 cent black on magenta of 1856 (last on the market in 1980), and the Swedish 3 skilling-banco yellow colour error of 1855.

Largest Issue (UK)
A total of 751.25 million of the 1929 1½d Postal Union Congress commemorative stamps were sold.

Agriculture

Farms

Earliest The earliest mainland site in Britain is at Freshwater West, Dyfed, dated 5000–4680 BC.

Largest The largest farms in the world are *kolkhozy* (collective farms) in the former USSR. These were reduced in number from 235,500 in 1940 to 26,900 in 1988 and represented a total cultivated area of 169.2 million ha *417.6 million acres*. Units of over 25,000 ha *60,000 acres* were not uncommon.

The pioneer farm owned by Laucídio Coelho near Campo Grande, Mato Grosso, Brazil c.1901 covered 8700 km² *3358 miles²* and supported 250,000 head of cattle at the time of the owner's death in 1975.

British Isles The UK has about 18.5 million ha *45.7 million acres* of farmland on 241,400 holdings, the largest of which are the Scottish hill farms in the Grampians. The largest arable holding is farmed by Elveden Farms Ltd at Elveden, Suffolk, where 4081 ha *10,084 acres* are farmed on an estate covering 9148 ha *22,603 acres*. Production in 1994 included 9084 tonnes of combinable crops and 49,129 tonnes of sugar

(Photo: Jacana/P. Pilloud)

Largest crop producers

China is the largest overall crop producer, commanding 19% of world production

Crop	Producer	Amount in 1993 (million tons)
Maize	USA	160,954,000
Oats	Russian Federation	11,556,000
Seed Cotton	China (Mainland)	7,478,000
Wheat	China (Mainland)	106,390,000
Rice, Paddy	China (Mainland)	177,700,000
Barley	Russian Federation	26,843,008

Source: Food and Agriculture Organization of the United Nations

beet. Other vegetable crops, including potatoes, onions, carrots and parsnips, yielded 29,374 tonnes. The livestock includes 1200 lambs and 15,101 pigs.

Egg farm The Agrigeneral Company L.P. in Croton, Ohio, USA has 4.8 million hens laying some 3.7 million eggs daily.

Cattle station Until 1915 the Victoria River Downs Station in Northern Territory, Australia covered an area of 90,650 km² *35,000 miles²*, which is equivalent to the combined area of England's 20 largest counties. The world's largest cattle station is currently the Anna Creek station of South Australia, owned by the Kidman family. It covers 30,000 km² *11,600 miles²*, or 23 per cent the size of England, with the biggest component being Strangway at 14,000 km² *5500 miles²*.

Cowshed The longest cowshed in Britain is that of the Yorkshire Agricultural Society at Harrogate, N Yorks. It is 139 m *456 ft* long and can cater for 686 cows. The National Agricultural Centre at Kenilworth, Warks, completed in 1967, can house 782 animals.

Community garden The largest such project is that operated by the City Beautiful Council and the Benjamin Wegerzyn Garden Center at Dayton, Ohio, USA. It comprises 1173 allotments, each measuring 74.5 m² *812 ft²*.

Hop farm The world's leading private hop growers are John I. Haas, Inc., with farms in Oregon and Washington, USA, Tasmania and Victoria, Australia, covering a net area of 2403 ha *5940 acres*. The UK has 3527 ha *8715 acres* under hop production.

Mushroom farm The world's largest mushroom farm is owned by Moonlight Mushrooms Inc. and was founded in 1937 in a disused limestone mine near Worthington, Pennsylvania, USA. The farm employs 1106 people who work in a maze of underground galleries 251 km *156 miles* long, producing 24,500 tonnes of mushrooms per year. The French annual consumption is unrivalled at 3.17 kg *7 lb* per person.

Vineyards

Largest vineyard The world's largest vineyard extends over the Mediterranean slopes between the Pyrenees and the Rhône in the *départements* Gard, Hérault, Aude and Pyrénées-Orientales. It covers an area of 840,000 ha *2,075,685 acres*, 52.3 per cent of which is *monoculture viticole*.

UK The largest vineyard in the UK is Denbies Wine Estate in Dorking, Surrey, covering 101 ha *250 acres*. Planting began in 1986, and the 276,000 vines planted so far have a projected annual production capacity of 500,000 bottles.

Most northerly vineyard The most northerly commercial vineyard in Britain and probably in the world is at Whitworth Hall, owned by Derek Parnaby at Sherrymoor, County Durham on Lat. 54°42′N.

Most southerly vineyard The most southerly commercial vineyards are found in central Otago, South Island, New Zealand south of Lat. 45°S.

Largest vine This was planted in 1842 at Carpinteria, California, USA. By 1900 it was yielding more than 9 tonnes of grapes in some years, and averaged 7 tonnes per year until it died in 1920.

UK Britain's largest vine is the Great Vine at Hampton Court, Greater London, planted in 1768. It has a circumference of 2.16 m *7 ft 1 in* and branches up to 34.7 m *114 ft* long, and produces an average yield of 318.8 kg *703 lb*.

In 1990 Leslie Stringer of Dartford, Kent obtained a yield of over 2300 kg *5071 lb* from the Dartford Wondervine, planted in 1979. The plant was grown from a cutting taken from a vine planted in Banstead, Surrey in 1962.

Guess What?

Q. How old was Big Bertha when she died in 1993?

A. See Page 172

Piggery The world's largest piggery is the COMTIM unit near Timișoara, Romania. It has around 70,000 sows producing around 1,200,000 pigs per year.

Sheep station The largest sheep station in the world is Commonwealth Hill, in the north-west of South Australia. It grazes between 50,000 and 70,000 sheep, along with 24,000 uninvited kangaroos, in an area of 10,567 km² *4080 miles²* enclosed by 221 km *138 miles* of dog-proof fencing. The head count on Sir William Stevenson's 16,579-ha *40,970-acre* Lochinver station in New Zealand was 127,406 sheep on 1 Jan 1993.

The largest sheep drive on record involved the movement of 43,000 sheep from Barcaldine to Beaconsfield station, Queensland, Australia (a distance of 64 km *40 miles*) by 27 horsemen in 1886.

Livestock Prices

Some exceptionally high livestock auction prices are believed to result from collusion between buyer and seller to raise the ostensible price levels of the breed concerned. Others are marketing and publicity exercises with little relation to true market prices.

Cattle The highest price ever paid was $2.5 million for the beefalo (a ⅜ bison, ⅜ Charolais, ¼ Hereford) Joe's Pride, sold by D. C. Basalo of Burlingame, California to the Beefalo Cattle Co. of Calgary, Alberta, Canada on 9 Sep 1974.

UK A 14-month-old Canadian Holstein bull, Pickland Elevation B. ET, was bought by Premier Breeders of Stamfordham, Northumberland for £233,000 in September 1982.

The highest price paid for any farm animal at auction in the UK is 65,000 guineas (£68,250) for Grantchester Heather VIII, a Friesian cow sold to Brian Draper of Shrewsbury, Shrops by John Suenson-Taylor of Audlem, Cheshire at the Grantchester sale on 12 Aug 1992.

> The highest price paid for a cow is $1.3 million for a Friesan at auction in East Montpelier, Vermont, USA in 1985. The British record is £68,250, also for a Friesian (⇨ above).

Goat On 25 Jan 1985 an Angora buck bred by Waitangi Angoras of Waitangi, New Zealand was sold to Elliott Brown Ltd of Waipu, New Zealand for NZ $140,000.

Horse The highest price achieved for a draught horse is $47,000, paid by C.G. Good of Ogden, Iowa, USA for the seven-year-old Belgian stallion Farceur at Cedar Falls, Iowa on 16 Oct 1917.

A Welsh mountain pony stallion named Coed Cock Bari was sold to an Australian bidder in Wales in September 1978 for 21,000 guineas (£22,050).

Pig The highest price ever paid for a pig is $56,000 for a cross-bred barrow named Bud, owned by Jeffrey Roemisch of Hermleigh, Texas, USA and bought by E.A. Bud Olson and Phil Bonzio on 5 Mar 1983. The British record is 3300 guineas (£3465) paid by Malvern Farms for a Swedish Landrace gilt, Bluegate Ally 33rd, owned by the Davidson Trust, in a draft sale at Reading, Berks on 2 Mar 1955.

Sheep The highest price ever achieved for a sheep is $A450,000 (£205,000), paid by Willogoleche Pty Ltd for the Collinsville stud JC&S 43

> Forty years ago the record auction price for any breed of sheep was 5500 guineas (£5775) for a Kent ram at Fielding, New Zealand in January 1951.

Q. How much was paid for a glass of Beaujolais Nouveau in November 1993?
A. See Page 215

Guess What?

Fine wines

Photos: KWV

The world's largest wine cellars are those of the Ko-operatieve Wijnbouwers Vereniging, known as KWV, at Paarl, in Cape Province, in the centre of the wine-growing district of South Africa. They cover an area of 22 ha *54 acres* and have a capacity of 121 million litres *27 million gal*. More than 100 different natural wines, as well as a wide range of brandies and fortified wines, are produced here for the world market.

The historical and spiritual home of KWV wines is the famous Cathedral Cellar (above). For it is in this cool, peaceful sanctuary with its soaring barrel-vaulted roof, exquisite chandeliers and imposing row of huge wooden vats that KWV honours the long tradition of the making of fine wines. The cellar was given its name by the Dutch poet Antonie Donkersloot, who on seeing it exclaimed 'This is indeed a cathedral of wine!'

In an adjoining cellar are five huge vats under one roof—the largest collection of such massive vats in one place (below). A human being is dwarfed by these monsters.

Wine connoisseurs will be pleased to know that guided tours are available, but you do not have to be a wine lover to appreciate the beauty and sanctuary of the largest wine cellars in the world.

at the 1989 Adelaide Ram Sales, South Australia. The British record is £32,000 for a Scottish Blackface ram lamb named Old Sandy, sold by Michael Scott at Lanark, Strathclyde on 14 Oct 1988.

Lowest price The lowest price ever realized for livestock was at a sale at Kuruman, Cape Province, South Africa in 1934, where donkeys were sold for less than 2p each.

Cattle

The country with the largest stock of cattle in 1993 is India, with an estimated 192.7 million head out of a world total of 1.05 billion head. The leading producer of milk in 1993 was the US, with 68,303,008 million tonnes (⇨ Milk yields).

Largest The heaviest breed of cattle is the Chianini, which was brought to the Chiana Valley in Italy from the Middle East in pre-Roman times. Four types of the

■ India has the world's largest stock of cattle, with an estimated 192.7 million head in 1993—more than a third of the world total.
(Photo: Rex Features)

Guess What?
Q. In which country are the largest farms?
A. See Page 170

breed exist, the largest of which is the Val di Chianini, found on the plains and low hills of Arezzo and Siena. Bulls average 1.73 m *5 ft 8 in* at the shoulder and weigh 1300 kg *2865 lb*, but Chianini oxen have been known to attain heights of 1.9 m *6 ft 2¾ in*. The sheer expense of feeding such huge cattle has put the breed under threat of extinction in Italy, but farmers in North America, Mexico and Brazil are still enthusiastic buyers.

The heaviest cow on record was a Friesian–Durham cross named Mount Katahdin, which, from 1906 to 1910, frequently weighed 2267 kg *5000 lb*. He stood 1.88 m *6 ft 2 in* at the shoulder and had a girth measuring 3.96 m *13 ft*. The cow was exhibited by A.S. Rand of Maine, USA and died in a barn fire c. 1923.

UK Britain's largest breed of cattle is the South Devon, bulls of which measure up to 1.55 m *5 ft 1 in* at the shoulder and weigh about 1250 kg *2755 lb*. The heaviest example on record weighed 1678 kg *3700 lb*.

The British record for any breed is 2032 kg *4480 lb* recorded for The Bradwell Ox, owned by William Spurgin of Orpland Farm, Bradwell-on-Sea, Essex. In 1830, when six years old, this bull measured 4.57 m *15 ft* nose-to-tail and had a maximum girth of 3.35 m *11 ft*.

Smallest The smallest breed of domestic cattle is the Ovambo of Namibia, with bulls and cows averaging 225 kg *496 lb* and 160 kg *353 lb* respectively.

UK The smallest British breed is the miniature Dexter, bulls of which weigh 450 kg *992 lb* and stand 1.1 m *3 ft 3⅓ in* at the shoulder. In May 1984 a height of just 86.3 cm *34 in* was reported for an adult Dexter cow named Mayberry, owned by R. Hillier of Church Farm, South Littleton, Evesham, Worcs.

Oldest Big Bertha (1944–1993), a Dremon owned by Jerome O'Leary of Blackwatersbridge, Co. Kerry, Republic of Ireland, died less than three months short of her 49th birthday (⇔ Most prolific).

Most prolific On 25 Apr 1964 it was reported that a cow named Lyubik had given birth to seven calves in Mogilev, Belarus. A case of five live calves at one birth was reported in 1928 by T.G. Yarwood of Manchester.

The lifetime breeding record is 39 in the case of Big Bertha (⇔ Oldest).

Sires Soender Jyllands Jens, a Danish black-and-white bull, left 220,000 surviving progeny by artificial insemination when he was put down at the age of 11 in Copenhagen in September 1978. Bendalls Adema, a Friesian bull, died at the age of 14 in Clondalkin, Dublin, Republic of Ireland on 8 Nov 1978, having sired an estimated 212,000 progeny by artificial insemination.

Milk yields The highest recorded world lifetime yield of milk is 211,025 kg *465,224 lb* to 1 May 1984 from the unglamorously named cow No. 289, owned by M.G. Maciel & Son of Hanford, California, USA. The greatest yield from any British cow was 165,000 kg *363,759 lb* by Winton Pel Eva 2, owned by John Waring of Glebe House, Kilnwick, near Pocklington, Humberside.

The greatest recorded yield for one lactation (maximum 365 days) is 26,897 kg *59,298 lb* in 1993 by the Friesian cow Robthom Suzet Paddy, owned by Mark Thomson of Springfield, Missouri, USA. Suzet also has the world record for protein yield for 365 days, at 924 kg *2038 lb*.

British Isles Oriel Freda 10 (b. 21 Feb 1978), a Friesian owned by the Mellifont Abbey Trust of Collon, Co. Louth, Republic of Ireland, produced 21,513 kg *47,427½ lb* in 305 days in 1986. The British lactation record (305 days)

Birthweights

On 28 May 1986 a Friesian cow owned by Sherlene O'Brien of Simitar Farms, Henryetta, Oklahoma, USA gave birth to a perfectly formed stillborn calf weighing 122.4 kg *270 lb*. The sire was an Aberdeen-Angus bull which had 'jumped the fence'. The heaviest recorded live birthweight for a calf is 102 kg *225 lb* from a Friesian cow at Rockhouse Farm, Bishopston, Swansea, W Glam in 1961.

Lightest **The lowest live birthweight accurately recorded for a calf is 4.1 kg *9 lb* for a Friesian heifer called Christmas born on 25 Dec 1993 on the farm of Mark and Wendy Theuringer in Hutchinson, Minnesota, USA. Sadly she died of scours at five weeks.**

is 19,400 kg *42,769 lb*, produced in 1984–5 by Michaelwood Holm Emoselle 25 (b. 1 Aug 1973), a Friesian owned by Mr and Mrs M.T. Holder of Aylesmore Farm, Newent, Glos (⇔ also Butterfat yields).

The highest reported milk yield in a day is 109.3 kg *241 lb* by Urbe Blanca in Cuba on or about 23 Jun 1982.

Butterfat yields The world record for a lifetime is 7425 kg *16,370 lb*, yielded by the US Friesian Breezewood Patsy Bar Pontiac in 3979 days. The British record butterfat yield in a lifetime is 5518 kg *12,166 lb* (from 123,865 kg *273,072 lb* at 4.45 per cent), achieved by the Ayrshire cow Craighead Welma, owned by W. Watson Steele.

The world record for 365 days is 1418 kg *3126 lb*, yielded by Roybrook High Ellen, a Friesian owned by Yoshuhiro Tanaka of Tottori, Japan.

The British record for 365 days is 852 kg *1878 lb*, yielded by the Friesian Michaelwood Holm Emoselle 25. This cow went on to milk for a total of 395 days in her eighth lactation, producing 1012 kg *2231 lb* of butterfat. She also holds the British record for butterfat yield in one day, at 4.53 kg *10 lb* (⇔ also Milk yields).

> **Cow-milking by hand**
> Joseph Love of Kilifi Plantations Ltd, Kenya milked 531 litres *117 gal* from 30 cows on 25 Aug 1992.

Cheese The world's biggest producer is the US with a total of 2,961,000 million tonnes of cheese (by whole cow milk) produced in 1993. The most popular cheese in Britain is Cheddar, accounting for about 60 per cent of total consumption.

Goats

Largest The largest goat ever recorded was a British Saanen named Mostyn Moorcock, owned by Pat Robinson of Ewyas Harold, Hereford & Worcester, which reached a weight of 181.4 kg *400 lb* (shoulder height 111.7 cm *44 in* and overall length of 167.6 cm *66 in*). He died in 1977 at the age of four.

Smallest Some pygmy goats weigh only 15–20 kg *33–44 lb*.

Oldest The oldest goat on record was a Golden Guernsey-Anglo Nubian cross named Naturemade Aphrodite (15 Jul 1975–23 Aug 1993), belonging to Katherine Whitwell of Moulton, Newmarket, Suffolk, who died aged 18 years and 1 month. 'Aphrodite' bred for ten consecutive years, during which time she reared 26 kids, including five sets of triplets and one set of quads.

Most prolific According to the British Goat Society, at least one or two cases of quintuplets are recorded annually out of the 10,000 goats registered, but some breeders record only the females born. On 14 Jan 1980 a nanny named Julie, owned by Galen Cowper of Nampah, Idaho, USA, gave birth to septuplets, but they all died, including the mother.

Pigs

China was the world's leading hog-farming nation in 1993, with an estimated 384.2 million head out of a worldwide total of 754.3 million head.

Largest The heaviest pig ever recorded was a Poland–China hog named Big Bill, weighing 1157.5 kg *2552 lb* just before being put down after accidentally breaking a leg en route to the Chicago World's Fair for exhibition in 1933. Other statistics included a height of 1.52 m *5 ft* at the shoulder and a length of 2.74 m *9 ft*. At the request of his owner, W.J. Chappall, 'Bill' was mounted and displayed in Weekly County, Tennessee, USA until his acquisition in 1946 by a travelling carnival. On the death of the carnival's proprietor his family allegedly donated Big Bill to a museum, but no trace of him has been found since.

UK The British Gloucester Old Spot breed is known to have exceeded 635 kg *1400 lb* in weight. The heaviest on record was a boar bred by Joseph Lawton of Astbury, Cheshire (and possibly owned by Joseph Bradbury of Little Hay Wood, Staffs), which weighed 639.5 kg *1410 lb*, stood 1.43 m *4 ft 8¼ in* at the shoulder and was 2.94 m *9 ft 8 in* long.

Smallest The smallest breed of pig is the Mini Maialino, developed by Stefano Morini of San Golo d'Enza, Italy after 10 years' experimentation with Vietnamese pot-bellied pigs. The piglets weigh 400 g *14 oz* at birth and 9 kg *20 lb* at maturity.

Most prolific A Large White owned by H.S. Pedlingham farrowed 385 pigs in 22 litters from December 1923 to September 1934. During the period 1940–52 a Large Black sow belonging to A.M. Harris of Lapworth, Warks farrowed 26 litters. A Newsham Large White × Landrace sow from Meeting House Farm, Staintondale, near Scarborough, N Yorks farrowed 189 piglets (seven stillborn) in nine litters up to 22 Mar 1988. Between 6 May 1987 and 9 Feb 1988 she gave birth to 70 piglets.

Birth weights A Hampshire × Yorkshire sow belonging to Rev. John Schroeder of Mountain Grove, Missouri, USA farrowed a litter of 18 on 26 Aug 1979. Five were stillborn, including one male weighing 2.38 kg *5 lb 4 oz*, compared with the average birth weight of 1.36 kg *3 lb*.

The highest recorded weight for a piglet at weaning (eight weeks) is 36.7 kg *81 lb* for a boar, one of a litter of nine farrowed on 6 Jul 1962 by the Landrace gilt Manorport Ballerina 53rd ('Mary') and sired by a Large White named Johnny at Kettle Lane Farm, West Ashton, Trowbridge, Wilts.

In Nov 1957 a total weight of 514.3 kg *1134 lb* was reported at weaning for a litter of 18 farrowed by an Essex sow owned by B. Ravell of Seaton House, Thorugumbald, Hull, Humberside.

Milk

The highest recorded milk yield for any goat is 3499 kg *7714 lb* in 365 days, achieved by Osory Snow-Goose, owned by Mr and Mrs G. Jameson of Leppington, New South Wales, Australia, in 1977.

Cynthia-Jean ('Baba'), owned by Carolyn Freund-Nelson of Northport, New York, USA, has lactated continuously since June 1980.

Poultry

The United States is the world's leading producer of chicken meat, or broiler, with more than 15 million tons produced in 1993. The world's leading egg producer, however, is mainland China, where 9,438,000 million tonnes of hens eggs were laid in 1993.

Chickens *Largest* The heaviest breed of chicken is the White Sully, a hybrid of large Rhode Island Reds and other varieties developed by Grant Sullens of West Point, California, USA. The largest, a rooster named Weirdo, reportedly weighed 10 kg *22 lb* in January 1973 and was so aggressive that he killed two cats and maimed a dog which ventured too close. The largest recorded chicken is Big Snow, a rooster weighing 10.51 kg *23 lb 3 oz* on 12 Jun 1992, with a chest girth of 84 cm *2 ft 9 in* and standing 43.2 cm *1 ft 5 in* at the shoulder. Owned and bred by Ronald Alldridge of Deuchar,

Queensland, Australia, Big Snow died of natural causes on 6 Sep 1992.

Most prolific The highest authenticated rate of egg-laying is 371 in 364 days, laid by a White Leghorn (No. 2988) in an official test conducted by Prof. Harold V. Biellier ending on 29 Aug 1979 at the College of Agriculture, University of Missouri, USA. The British record is 353 eggs in 365 days in a national laying test at Milford, Surrey in 1957. The eggs were laid by a Rhode Island Red named Wonderful Lady, owned by W. Lawson of Welham Grange, Retford, Notts.

Guess What?

Q. Which country gives the most in foreign aid?

A. See Page 164

The highest annual average per bird for a flock is 322 eggs in 52 weeks in 1993 from 1400 ISA Brown birds owned by Jim and Erica Short of Withybush Farm, Surrey.

Largest egg The heaviest egg reported is one of 454 g *16 oz*, with a double yolk and double shell, laid by a White Leghorn at Vineland, New Jersey, USA on 25 Feb 1956. The largest recorded was a five-yolked egg measuring 31 cm *12¼ in* around the long axis, 22.8 cm *9 in* around the short and weighing nearly 12 oz, laid by a Black Minorca at Mr Stafford's Damsteads Farm, Mellor, Lancs in 1896.

Flying Sheena, a barnyard bantam owned by Bill and Bob Knox, flew 192.07 m *630 ft 2 in* at Parkesburg, Pennsylvania, USA on 31 May 1985.

Poultry-plucking *Chicken* Ernest Hausen (1877–1955) of Fort Atkinson, Wisconsin, USA died undefeated after 33 years as champion. On 19 Jan 1939 he was timed at 4.4 sec for plucking a chicken.

Turkey Vincent Pilkington of Cootehill, Co. Cavan, Republic of Ireland killed and plucked 100 turkeys in 7 hr 32 min on 15 Dec 1978. His record for a single turkey is 1 min 30 sec, set on RTE Television in Dublin on 17 Nov 1980.

> **The highest claim for the number of yolks in a hen's egg is nine, reported by Diane Hainsworth of Hainsworth Poultry Farms, Mount Morris, New York, USA in July 1971, and also from a hen in Kyrgyzstan in August 1977.**

Egg dropping The greatest height from which fresh eggs have been dropped (to earth) and remained intact is 213 m *700 ft*, by David Donoghue from a helicopter on 22 Aug 1994 onto a golf course at Blackpool, Lancs.

Egg shelling Two kitchen hands, Harold Witcomb and Gerald Harding, shelled 1050 dozen eggs in a 7¼-hr shift at Bowyers, Trowbridge, Wilts on 23 Apr 1971. Both men were blind.

Goose The heaviest goose egg weighed 680 g *24 oz*, measured 34 cm *13½ in* round the long axis and a maximum of 24 cm *9½ in* around the short axis. It was laid on 3 May 1977 by a white goose named Speckle, owned by Donny Brandenberg of Goshen, Ohio, USA. The average weight is 283–340 g *10–12 oz*.

Turkey The greatest dressed weight recorded for a turkey is 39.09 kg *86 lb* for a stag named Tyson reared by Philip Cook of Leacroft Turkeys Ltd, Peterborough, Cambs. It won the last annual 'heaviest turkey' competition, held in London on 12 Dec 1989, and was auctioned for charity for a record £4400. Stags of this size have been so overdeveloped for meat production that they are unable to mate because of their shape and the hens have to be artificially inseminated.

Sheep

The world's leading producer of sheep is Australia, with an estimated total of 147.1 million head in 1993.

Largest The largest sheep ever recorded was a Suffolk ram named Stratford Whisper 23H, which weighed 247.2 kg *545 lb* and stood 1.09 m *43 in* tall in March 1991. It is owned by Joseph and Susan Schallberger of Boring, Oregon, USA.

Smallest The smallest breed of sheep is the Ouessant, from the Ile d'Ouessant, Brittany, France at 13–16 kg *29–35 lb* in weight and standing 45–50 cm *18–20 in* at the withers. The species was saved from extinction by breeding programmes.

Most prolific On 4 Sep 1991 a Finnish Landrace ewe owned by the D.M.C. Partnership (comprising Trevor and Diane Cooke, Stephen and Mary Moss and Ken and Carole Mihaere) of Feilding, Manawatu, New Zealand gave birth to eight healthy lambs. On 19 Apr 1994 the record was equalled by 6-year-old Ewe 835 Ylva, owned by Birgitta and Kent Mossby of Halsarp Farm, Falköping, Sweden.

Birth weights The highest recorded birth weight for a lamb is 17.2 kg *38 lb* at Clearwater, Sedgwick County, Kansas, USA in 1975, but neither lamb nor ewe survived. Another lamb of the same weight was born on 7 Apr 1975 on the Gerald Neises Farm, Howard, South Dakota, USA but died soon afterwards.

UK On 13 Apr 1990 it was reported that a Kent ewe had given birth to a live lamb weighing 12.7 kg *28 lb* on the Belton estate, near Grantham, Lincs, farmed by Les Baker. A crossbred Suffolk lamb of the same weight was delivered on 22 Jan 1992 at Stoupergate Farm, owned by D. and E. Brooke, in Hatfield, S Yorks.

Combined weight A four-year-old Suffolk ewe owned by Gerry H. Watson of Augusta, Kansas, USA gave birth to two live sets of triplets on 30–31 Jan 1982. The total weight of the lambs was 22.4 kg *49½ lb*. The greatest combined birthweight for lambs in Britain is 21.1 kg *43½ lb* for live quadruplets produced on 20 Feb 1990 by a Friesian × Exmoor Horn owned by John and Margaret Sillick of South Stursdon Farm, Bude, Cornwall.

Lightest The lowest live birthweight recorded for a lamb is 900 g *1 lb 15¾ oz* for a female Texel (one of twins), born on 28 Mar

---

Ducks

Most prolific An Aylesbury duck belonging to Annette and Angela Butler of Princes Risborough, Bucks laid 457 eggs in 463 days, including an unbroken run of 375 in as many days. The duck died on 7 Feb 1986. Another duck of the same breed owned by Edmond Walsh of Gormanstown, Co. Kildare, Republic of Ireland laid eggs every year until her 25th birthday. She died on 3 Dec 1978 aged 28 yr 6 months.

1991 at the farm owned by Verner and Esther Jensen in Rødekro, Denmark.

Oldest A crossbred sheep owned by Griffiths & Davies of Dolclettwr Hall, Taliesin, near Aberystwyth, Dyfed gave birth to a healthy lamb in 1988 at the age of 28, after lambing successfully more than 40 times. She died on 24 Jan 1989 just one week before her 29th birthday.

Shearing The highest speed for sheep-shearing in a working day was recorded by Alan McDonald, who machine-sheared 805 lambs in nine hours (an average of 89.4 per hour) at Waitnaguru, New Zealand on 20 Dec 1990. Peter Casserly of Christchurch, New Zealand achieved a solo-blade (i.e. hand-shearing) record of 353 lambs in nine hours on 13 Feb 1976. The women's record is 390 lambs in eight hours, performed by Deanne Sarre of Pingrup at Yealering, Western Australia on 1 Oct 1989.

UK The British record set under National Shearing Competitions Committee rules is 1869, performed by the team of William Workman, Ian Matthews, Howell Havard and Philip Evans at Pant Farm, Merthyr Cynog, Powys on 30 Jun 1990. The solo record is 654 sheep, achieved by Wyn Jones of Welshpool, Powys on 9 Jul 1994 at Canon Farm, near Carno, Powys.

Robert Bull and Barry Godsell at Winchelsea Beach, E Sussex, sheared 973 lambs on 17 Jun 1989. A solo record of 817 was set by Philip Evans at Pant Farm, Merthyr Cynog, Powys on 20 Jul 1991. Although this exceeds the world record set in New Zealand, the attempts are not directly comparable because of differing rules.

Survival

On 24 Mar 1978 Alex Maclennan found one ewe still alive after he had dug out 16 sheep buried in a snowdrift for 50 days near the river Skinsdale on Mrs Tyser's Gordonbush Estate in Sutherland, Highland after the great January blizzard. The sheep's hot breath creates air-holes in the snow, and the animals gnaw their own wool for protein.

In a 24-hour shearing marathon, Alan MacDonald and Keith Wilson machine-sheared 2220 sheep at Warkworth, Auckland Province, New Zealand on 26 Jun 1988. Godfrey Bowen of New Zealand sheared a Cheviot ewe in 46 sec at the Royal Highland Show in Dundee, Tayside in June 1957.

Sheep to shoulder At the International Wool Secretariat Development Centre, Ilkley, W Yorks a team of eight using commercial machinery produced a jumper—from shearing sheep to the finished article—in 2 hr 28 min 32 sec on 3 Sep 1986.

Tailoring The highest speed at which the manufacture of a three-piece suit has been executed from sheep to finished article is 1 hr 34 min 33.42 sec, achieved by 65 members of the Melbourne College of Textiles, Pascoe Vale, Victoria, Australia on 24 Jun 1982. Catching and fleecing took 2 min 21 sec, and carding, spinning, weaving and tailoring occupied the remaining time.

Knitting The Exeter Spinners—Audrey Felton, Christine Heap, Eileen Lancaster, Marjorie Mellis, Ann Sandercock and Maria Scott—produced a jumper by hand from raw fleece in 1 hr 55 min 50.2 sec on 25 Sep 1983 at BBC Television Centre, London.

Fine spinning The longest thread of wool, hand-spun and plied to weigh 10 g *0.35 oz*, was one with a length of 553.03 m *1815 ft 3 in*, achieved by Julitha Barber of Bull Creek, Western Australia, Australia at the International Highland Spin-In, Bothwell, Tasmania on 1 Mar 1989.

Crochet Barbara Jean Sonntag (b. 1938) of Craig, Colorado, USA crocheted 330 shells plus five stitches (equivalent to 4412 stitches) in 30 min at a rate of 147 stitches per min on 13 Jan 1981.

Ria van der Honing of Wormerveer, Netherlands completed a crochet chain 62.50 km *38.83 miles* in length on 14 Jul 1986.

Most expensive wool The highest price ever paid for wool is A$ 10,300 per kg on 11 Jan 1995, when Aoki International Co Ltd bought a bale of extra superfine wool with an average fibre diameter of 13.8 microns.

Guess What?

Q. Who was the youngest person ever to become a millionaire?

A. See Page 165

■ The eight lambs of the world's largest litter, owned by the DMC Partnership in Feilding, Manawatu, New Zealand (Trevor and Diane Cooke, Stephen and Mary Moss and Ken and Carole Mihaere), and born on 4 Sep 1991 from a Finnish Land race ewe. The are pictured here in December 1991, at 12 weeks.
(Photo: Ken Mihaere)

Political and Social

Human World

The world comprises 192 sovereign countries and 65 non-sovereign or other territories (dependencies of sovereign states, territories claimed in Antarctica, disputed and other territories), making a total of 257 as at November 1994.

Largest country Russia has a total area of 17,075,400 km^2 *6,592,800 miles^2*, or 11.5 per cent of the world's total land area. It is 70 times larger than the UK, but at 148,174,000 in 1994 is only 2.54 times more populous than the UK.

The UK covers 244,100 km^2 *94,247 miles^2* (including 3218 km^2 *1242 miles^2* of inland water), or 0.16 per cent of the total land area of the world. Great Britain is the world's eighth largest island, with an area of 229,979 km^2 *88,795 miles^2* and a coastline 7930 km *4928 miles* long, of which Scotland accounts for 4141 km *2573 miles*, England 3104 km *1929 miles* and Wales 685 km *426 miles*.

Smallest country The smallest independent country in the world is the State of the Vatican City or Holy See (Stato della Città del Vaticano), which was made an enclave within the city of Rome, Italy on 11 Feb 1929. The enclave has an area of 44 ha *108.7 acres*. The world's smallest republic is Nauru, in the Pacific Ocean. It has an area of 2129 ha *5263 acres* and a population of 10,200 (1994 estimate).

The smallest colony in the world is Gibraltar (since 1969, the City of Gibraltar), with an area of 5.8 km^2 *1440 acres/2¼ miles^2*. However, Pitcairn Island, the only inhabited island (55 people in late 1993) of a group of four (total area 48 km^2 *18½ miles^2*), has an area of 388 ha *960 acres/1½ miles^2*.

Largest political division The Commonwealth, a free association of 51 independent states and their dependencies, covers an area of 30,554,762 km^2 *11,797,193 miles^2* with a population of some 1.5 billion. Almost all member countries once belonged to the former British Empire. They believe in democracy and equal rights for all men and women regardless of race, colour, religion or politics. The Commonwealth promotes world peace, international understanding and an end to poverty and racism.

National boundaries There are 306 national land boundaries in the world. The continent with the greatest number is Africa, with 112. Of the estimated 420 maritime boundaries, only 140 have so far been ratified. The ratio of boundaries to area of land is greatest in Europe.

The frontier which is crossed most frequently is that between the United States and Mexico. It extends for 3110 km *1933 miles* and in the year to 30 Sep 1993 there were 475,489,103 crossings.

Longest boundary The longest *continuous* boundary in the world is that between Canada and the United States, which (including the Great Lakes boundaries) extends for 6416 km *3987 miles* (excluding the frontier of 2547 km *1538 miles* with Alaska). If the Great Lakes boundary is excluded, the longest land boundary is that between Chile and Argentina, which is 5255 km *3265 miles* in length.

Guess What?

Q. Which is the largest freshwater lake in the world based on surface area?

A. See Page 17

The UK's boundary with the Republic of Ireland measures 358km *223miles*.

Shortest boundary The 'frontier' of the Holy See in Rome measures 4.07km *2.53miles*. The land frontier between Gibraltar and Spain at La Linea, closed between June 1969 and February 1985, measures 1.53km *1672yd*. Zambia, Zimbabwe, Botswana and Namibia almost meet at a single point on the Zambezi river in Africa.

Most boundaries The country with the most land boundaries is China, with 16—Mongolia, Russia, North Korea, Hong Kong, Macau, Vietnam, Laos, Myanmar (Burma), India, Bhutan, Nepal, Pakistan, Afghanistan, Tajikistan, Kyrgyzstan and Kazakhstan. These extend for 24,000 km *14,900 miles*. The country with the largest number of maritime boundaries is Indonesia, with 19. The longest maritime boundary is that between Greenland and Canada at 2697km *1676miles*.

In 1955 the largest country was the Union of Soviet Socialist Republics (the Soviet Union), with an area of 22,553,278km^2 *8,707,870 miles^2*. The largest country forty years on is smaller. Russia is now the largest, but with 'only' 17,075,400km^2 *6,592,800miles^2*.

Coastlines Canada has the longest coastline of any country in the world, with 243,798 km *151,489 miles* including islands. The sovereign country with the shortest coastline is Monaco, with 5.61km *3½ miles*, excluding piers and breakwaters.

Capital cities The nearest capitals of two neighbouring countries are the Vatican City and Rome (Italy), as the Vatican is actually surrounded by Rome. The greatest distance between the capitals of countries which share a common border is 4200km *2600miles*, in the case of Moscow (Russia) and Pyongyang (Democratic People's Republic of Korea).

Guess What?

Q. Which country has the largest army?

A. See Page 195

Populations

World population The current (1995) population of the world is estimated to be 5716 million. At the beginning of the century it was just 1633 milllion, and in the year 2000 it is expected to be 6159 million.

The all-time peak annual increase of 2.06 per cent in the period 1965–70 had declined to 1.74 per cent by 1985–90. In spite of the reduced percentage increase, world population is currently growing by more than 86 million people every year. Projections issued by the United nations have estimated that the population should stabilize at around 11,500 million c. 2150.

The average daily increase in the world's population is approximately 236,000 or an average of some 164 per minute.

Most populous country The most populated country is China, which in *pinyin* is written Zhongguo (meaning 'central kingdom'). It had an estimated population of 1,192,300,000 in mid-1994 and has a rate of natural increase of over 12.8 million per year or more than 35,000 a day. Its population is more than that of the whole world 150 years ago.

Least populous country The independent state with the smallest population is the Vatican City or the Holy See (⇔ Smallest country above), with 1000 inhabitants in 1994.

Will the flattest country *disappear?*

Lesotho's highest point 3491m *11,452ft*

Everyone needs rain, but too much causes flooding. If you lived in the Maldives, the complete country would be in danger of being submerged if it experienced the same conditions as parts of the USA did in the summer of 1993 when the Mississippi burst its banks.

The Maldives are located in the Indian Ocean to the south-west of India, and consists of some 1800 islands, of which around 200 are inhabited. They cover an area of 298km^2 *115 miles^2*, but no point in the country is higher than 2.4m *8ft* above sea level, giving it the record for having the lowest 'high point' of any country in the world.

Lesotho would not have this problem, being the country with the highest 'low point'. Nowhere is it lower than 1381m *4530ft* above sea level, so the rain of 1993 would certainly not make it disappear!

Lowest High Point **Maldives** 2.4m *8ft*	Highest Low Point **Lesotho** 1381m *4530ft*

Artwork: Peter Harper © Guinness Publishing

Dense

The most densely populated territory in the world is the Portuguese province of Macau, on the southern coast of China. It has an estimated population of 416,000 (1994) in an area of 18.0km^2 *6.9miles^2*, giving a density of 23,111/km^2 *60,290/mile^2*.

The principality of Monaco, on the south coast of France, has a population of 30,300 (1994) in an area of just 1.95km^2 *0.75miles^2*, a density equal to 15,538/km^2 *40,400/mile^2*.

Of territories with an area of more than 1000km^2, Hong Kong (1075km^2 *415miles^2*) contains an estimated 5,979,000 people (1994), giving the territory a density of 5562/km^2 *14,407/mile^2*. Hong Kong is the most populous of all colonies. The 1976 by-census showed that the West Area of the urban district of Mong Kok on the Kowloon Peninsula had a density of 252,090/km^2 *652,910/mile^2*.

Of countries over 2500km^2 or *1000miles^2* the most densely populated is Bangladesh, with a population of 117,404,000 (1994) living in 148,383 km^2 *57,295miles^2* at a density of 791/km^2 *2049/mile^2*. The Indonesian island of Java (with an area of 132,186km^2 *51,037miles^2*) had a population of 112,159,200 in 1993, giving a density of 848/km^2 *2198/mile^2*.

United Kingdom The UK (241,752 km^2 *93,316 miles^2*) had an estimated population of 58,540,000 in early 1995, giving a density of 242/km^2 *627/mile^2*. The 1994 population density for the Borough of Islington, London was 11,709/km^2 *30,327/mile^2*.

Most sparsely populated country Antarctica became permanently occupied by relays of scientists from 1943. The population varies seasonally and reaches 2000 at times.

The lowest rate of natural increase in any independent country in recent times was in Hungary, which actually experienced a decline in 1985–90, with a figure of –1.7 per 1000 (11.9 births and 13.6 deaths).

■ Tiny countries and territories such as Monaco apart, the most densely populated is Hong Kong, where skyscrapers and more skyscrapers is the order of the day. In 1959 it was reported that in one house designed for 12 people there were 459 occupants.
(Photo: Popperfoto)

The least populated territory, apart from Antarctica, is Greenland, with a population of 55,500 (1994) in an area of 2,175,600 km^2 *840,000 miles^2*, giving a density of one person to every 39.2 km^2 *15.1 miles^2*.

United Kingdom The lowest population density for any administrative area in the UK is that of Highland, Scotland with 8.1/km^2 *21.1/mile^2*.

Emigration More people emigrate from Mexico than from any other country, mainly to the USA. The Soviet invasion of Afghanistan in December 1979 caused an influx of 2.9 million Afghan refugees into Pakistan and a further 2.2 million into Iran.

A total of 126,000 British citizens emigrated from the United Kingdom in 1993. The largest number of emigrants from the UK in any one year was 360,000 in 1852 (at which time it comprised both Great Britain and the whole of Ireland), mainly from Ireland.

Immigration The country which regularly receives the most legal immigrants is the United States. It has been estimated that between 1820 and 1993 the USA received 60,699,450 *official* immigrants. One in 76 of the US population is, however, an *illegal* immigrant. In the fiscal year to September 1986, a record 1,615,854 people were arrested by US patrols on the Mexican border.

The peak year for immigration into the UK was the 12 months from 1 Jul 1961 to 30 Jun 1962, when about 430,000 Commonwealth citizens arrived. The number of foreign immigrants in the year 1993 was 120,000.

Tourism The World Tourism Organization reports that the most popular destination is France, which in 1994 received 60,639,000 foreign tourists. The country with the greatest receipts from tourism is the United States, with $60.0 billion in 1994. The biggest spenders on foreign tourism are Americans, who in the same year spent $43.1 billion abroad.

A record 20.6 million foreign tourists visited the United Kingdom in 1994. The highest level of expenditure was also in 1994, with £9.8 billion.

Birth rate *Highest and lowest* The crude birth rate—the number of births per 1000 population—for the whole world was estimated to be 27.0 per 1000 in 1985–90. The highest rate estimated by the United Nations for 1985–90 was 55.6 per 1000 for Malawi. Excluding the Vatican City, where the rate is negligible, the lowest recorded rate was 9.5 per 1000 for San Marino for the same period.

The crude birth rate for the UK was 13.1 registered live births per 1000 population in 1993. There were 761,700 live births altogether (on average 2087 per day or 87 per hour), of which 241,800 were outside marriage.

Death rate The crude death rate—the number of deaths per 1000 population of all ages—for the whole world was an estimated 9.7 per 1000 in 1985–90. East Timor had a rate of 45.0 per 1000 from 1975–80, although this had subsided to 21.5 in 1985–90. The highest estimated rate in the same period was 23.4 for Sierra Leone. The lowest estimated rate for 1985–90 was 3.5 deaths per 1000 for Bahrain.

The crude death rate for the UK was 11.3 in 1993. There were 657,700 deaths altogether (on average 1802 per day or 75 per hour).

Natural increase The rate of natural increase for the whole world was estimated to be 17.3 (27.0 births less 9.7 deaths) per 1000 in 1985–90 compared with a peak 20.6 per 1000 in 1965–70. The highest of the latest available

In early 1995 there were some 59 million refugees worldwide. In addition there may be as many as 120 million economic migrants who are drawn by economic opportunity.

Q. Which airline carries the most passengers?
A. See Page 130
Guess What?

recorded rates was 37.4 (43.0 less 5.6) for Oman in 1985–90.

The 1993 rate for the UK was 1.8 (13.1 births less 11.3 deaths). In 1976 the population actually decreased, with a rate of –0.1 (12.1 births less 12.2 deaths).

Suicide The daily rate of suicides throughout the world is estimated to be more than 2700. The country with the highest rate is Sri Lanka, with 47 per 100,000 population in 1991. The country with the lowest recorded rate is Jordan, with just a single case in 1970 and hence a rate of 0.04 per 100,000.

In the United Kingdom there were 4628 suicides in 1992 (on average 12.6 every day), giving a rate of 8.0 per 100,000 population.

Marriage and divorce The marriage rate for the Northern Mariana Islands, in the Pacific Ocean, is 31.2 per 1000 population. In the UK there were 356,013 marriages in 1992—a rate of 6.2 per 1000 population. The average (mean) age for first marriages in England and Wales in 1992 was 27.9 years (men) and 25.9 years (women).

The country with most divorces is the United States, with a total of 1,187,000 in 1993—a rate of 4.6 per thousand population. The all-time high rate was 5.4 per thousand in 1979. There were 175,500 divorces in 1992 in the UK.

Sex ratio There are estimated to be 1015 males in the world for every 1000 females. The country with the largest recorded shortage of women is the United Arab Emirates, which has an estimated 566 to every 1000 males. The country with the largest recorded shortage of males is Latvia, with an estimated 1167 females to every 1000 males.

The ratio in the UK, which was 1069 females to every 1000 males in 1961, had become 1044 to every 1000 males by 1993, and is expected to be 1034 per 1000 by the turn of the century.

Infant mortality The world infant mortality rate—the number of deaths at ages under one year per 1000 live births—was 68 per 1000 for 1985–90. The lowest of the latest recorded rates is 5 per 1000 in Japan for the period 1985–90.

In Ethiopia the infant mortality rate was unofficially estimated to be nearly 550 per 1000 live births in 1969.

The highest rate recently estimated is 172 per 1000 in Afghanistan (1985–90).

The rate of infant mortality for the UK was a record low of 6.6 in 1992.

Forty years ago the lowest infant mortality rate was nearly 19 deaths before one year of age for every 1000 live births, in Sweden. The lowest rate now is only 5 deaths before one year of age for every 1000 live births, in Japan.

Expectation of life at birth
World expectation of life has risen from 46.4 years

Doctors ▶▶ ▶▶

■ A wedding provides the opportunity for a rare gathering of the Waldron family, with their record number of doctors. In addition to Dr and Mrs Waldron's ten record-breaking children, their two other daughters are in the photograph, as is Mrs Waldron herself.
(Photo: Courtesy of the Waldron family)

The country with the greatest number of dwelling units is China, with 276,947,962 in 1990.

Great Britain had an estimated stock of 23,470,000 dwellings at the end of 1993, of which 66.4 per cent were owner-occupied. The record number of permanent houses built in a year was 425,835 in 1968.

Physicians The country with the greatest number of physicians is China, which had 1,808,000 in 1992, including those practising dentistry and those of traditional Chinese medicine. Niger has the highest number of people per physician, with 54,472.

UK There were 153,394 doctors on the General Medical Council's Principal List, and therefore entitled to practise in the UK, as at 1 Jan 1995, giving one doctor to every 381 people.

Medical families The eight sons and two daughters of Dr William and Beryl Waldron of Knocknacarra, Co. Galway, Republic of Ireland all qualified as doctors from University College Galway during the period 1976–90. The Barcia family of Valencia, Spain have

> The country with the greatest number of hospitals is China, with 63,101 in 1991. Nauru has the most hospital beds per person (250 for every 10,000 people), and Nepal and Bangladesh the fewest (3 per 10,000).

(1950–5) towards 63.3 years (1985–1990). There is evidence that expectation of life in Britain in the 5th century AD was 33 years for males and 27 years for females. In the decade 1890–1900 the expectation of life among the population of India was 23.7 years.

The highest average expectation of life at birth is in Japan, with 83.0 years for women and 76.3 years for men in 1992. The lowest estimated for the period 1985–90 is 39.4 years for males in Sierra Leone and 42.0 years for females in Afghanistan.

The latest available figures for the UK (1990–2) are 73.2 years for males and 78.8 years for females, putting it in 17th position in the world rankings. The British figures for 1901 were 45.5 years for males and 49.0 years for females.

Housing For comparison, dwelling units are defined as a structurally separated room or rooms occupied by private households of one or more people and having separate access or a common passageway to the street.

The world's worst tornado disaster occurred on 26 Apr 1989 when the town of Shaturia in Bangladesh was wiped out, with the loss of 1300 lives. Mankind can use its knowledge to reduce the likelihood of disaster striking, but when nature takes over with such force there is little that can be done.

The devastation came just a day after President Ershad had led national prayers for rain to end a four-month drought. The tornado naturally brought the much-needed rain as well as the winds, but left a trail of destruction. As one official put it:– 'For some time we thought hell was let loose on us'. Some 50,000 people were left homeless and survivors said thatched huts were blown away like bits of paper.

As is so often the case after a major disaster, violent scenes followed, with desperate people in remote villages besieging government relief workers for food. And of course the vultures got in on the act too.

Tornado Devastation

(Photo: Jacana/Image Select) (Map: Peter Harper © Guinness Publishing)

Worst Disasters in the World

Disaster	Number killed	Location	Date
Pandemic	75,000,000	Eurasia: The Black Death (bubonic, pneumonic and septicaemic plague)	1347–51
Famine	c. 40,000,000[1]	Northern China	1959–61
Genocide	c. 35,000,000	Mongol extermination of Chinese peasantry	1311–40
Influenza	21,640,000	World-wide	1918–19
Circular Storm[2]	1,000,000	Ganges Delta Islands, Bangladesh	12–13 Nov 1970
Flood	900,000	Huang He River, China	Oct 1887
Earthquake	830,000	Shaanxi, Shanxi and Henan provinces, China	2 Feb 1556
Dam Burst	c. 230,000[3]	Banqiao and Shimantan Dams, Henan province, China (near simultaneous dam bursts)	August 1975
Landslides (Triggered off by single earthquake)	180,000	Gansu Province, China	16 Dec 1920
Atomic Bomb	155,200	Hiroshima, Japan (including radiation deaths within a year)	6 Aug 1945
Conventional Bombing[4]	c. 140,000	Tokyo, Japan	10 Mar 1945
Volcanic Eruption	92,000	Tambora, Sumbawa, Indonesia	5–10 Apr 1815
Avalanches	c. 18,000[5]	Yungay, Huascarán, Peru	31 May 1970
Marine (Single ship)	c. 7700	Wilhelm Gustloff (25,484 tons) German liner torpedoed off Danzig by Soviet submarine S-13 (only 903 survivors)	30 Jan 1945
Panic	c. 4000	Chongqing, China, air raid shelter	6 Jun 1941
Smog	3500–4000	London fog, England	4–9 Dec 1952
Industrial (Chemical)	3350	Union Carbide methylisocyanate plant, Bhopal, India	2–3 Dec 1984
Tunnelling (Silicosis)	c. 2500	Hawk's Nest hydroelectric tunnel, West Virginia, USA	1931–35
Fire[6] (Single building)	1670	The Theatre, Guangdong (Canton), China	May 1845
Explosion	1635[7]	Halifax, Nova Scotia, Canada	6 Dec 1917
Mining[8]	1549	Honkeiko (Benxihu) Colliery, China (coal dust explosion)	26 Apr 1942
Riot	c. 1400	Riots following arrest of woman selling contraband cigarettes, Taiwan	March 1947
Tornado	c. 1300	Shaturia, Bangladesh	26 Apr 1989
Mass Suicide[9]	960	Jewish Zealots, Masada, Israel	73
Railway	>800	Bagmati River, Bihar, India	6 Jun 1981
Fireworks	>800	Dauphin's wedding, Seine, Paris, France	16 May 1770
Aircraft (Civil)[10]	583	KLM-Pan Am Boeing 747 ground crash, Tenerife	27 Mar 1977
Man-eating Animal	436	Champawat district, India, tigress shot by Col. Jim Corbett (1875–1955)	1902–7
Terrorism	329	Bomb aboard Air-India Boeing 747, crashed into Atlantic south-west of Ireland. Sikh extremists suspected	23 Jun 1985
Hail	246	Moradabad, Uttar Pradesh, India	20 Apr 1888
Road[11]	176	Petrol tanker explosion inside Salang Tunnel, Afghanistan	3 Nov 1982
Offshore Oil Platform	167	Piper Alpha oil production platform, North Sea	6 Jul 1988
Submarine	130	Le Surcouf rammed by US merchantman Thompson Lykes in Caribbean	18 Feb 1942
Elevator (Lift)	105	Gold mine lift at Vaal Reefs, South Africa fell 490m 1600 ft	11 May 1995
Lightning	81	Boeing 707 jet airliner, struck by lightning near Elkton, Maryland, USA	8 Dec 1963
Helicopter	61	Russian military helicopter carrying refugees shot down near Lata, Georgia	14 Dec 1992
Mountaineering	43	Lenin Peak, Tajikistan/Kyrgyzstan border (then USSR)	13 Jul 1990
Ski Lift (Cable car)	42	Cavalese resort, northern Italy	9 Mar 1976
Nuclear Reactor	31[12]	Chernobyl No. 4, Ukraine (then USSR)	26 Apr 1986
Yacht Racing	19	28th Fastnet Race—23 boats sank or abandoned in Force 11 gale	13–15 Aug 1979
Space Exploration	7[13]	US Challenger 51L Shuttle, Cape Canaveral, Florida, USA	28 Jan 1986
Nuclear Waste Accident	high but undisclosed[14]	Venting of plutonium extraction wastes, Kyshtym, Russia (then USSR)	c. Dec 1957

[1] It has been estimated that more than 5 million died in the post-World War I famine of 1920–1 in the USSR. The Soviet government informed Mr (later President) Herbert Hoover in July 1923 that the ARA (American Relief Administration) had since August 1921 saved 20 million lives from famine and famine-related diseases.

[2] This figure published in 1972 for the Bangladeshi disaster was from Dr Afzal, Principal Scientific Officer of the Atomic Energy Authority Centre, Dacca. One report asserted that less than half of the population of the four islands of Bhola, Charjabbar, Hatia and Ramagati (1961 Census 1.4 million) survived. The most damaging hurricane recorded was Hurricane Andrew from 23–26 Aug 1992, which was estimated to have done c. $22 billion worth of damage.

[3] The dynamiting of a Yangzi Jiang dam at Huayuan Kou by Guomindang (GMD) forces in April 1938 during the Sino-Japanese war is reputed to have resulted in 890,000 deaths.

[4] The number of civilians killed by the bombing of Germany has been put variously at 593,000 and 'over 635,000', including some 35,000 deaths in the raids on Dresden, Germany from 13–15 Feb 1945. Total Japanese fatalities were 600,000 (conventional) and 220,000 (nuclear).

[5] A total of 18,000 Austrian and Italian troops were reported to have been lost in the Dolomite valleys of northern Italy on 13 Dec 1916 in more than 100 snow avalanches. Some of the avalanches were triggered by gunfire.

[6] >200,000 killed in the sack of Moscow, as a result of fires started by the invading Tatars in May 1571. Worst-ever hotel fire, 162 killed, Hotel Daeyungak, Seoul, South Korea 25 Dec 1971. Worst circus fire, 168 killed, Hartford, Connecticut, USA 6 Jul 1944.

[7] Some sources maintain that the final death toll was over 3000 on 6–7 December. Published estimates of the 11,000 killed at the BASF chemical plant explosion at Oppau, Germany on 21 Sep 1921 were exaggerated. The most reliable estimate is 561 killed.

[8] The worst gold-mining disaster in South Africa was when 182 were killed in Kinross gold mine on 16 Sep 1986.

[9] As reported by the historian Flavius Josephus (c. 37–100). In modern times, the greatest mass suicide was on 18 Nov 1978 when 913 members of the People's Temple cult died of mass cyanide poisoning near Port Kaituma, Guyana. Some 7000 Japanese committed suicide, many of them jumping off cliffs to their deaths, in July 1944 during the US Marines' assault of the island of Saipan.

[10] The crash of JAL's Boeing 747, flight 123, near Tokyo on 12 Aug 1985, in which 520 passengers and crew perished, was the worst single plane crash in aviation history.

[11] Western estimates gave the number of deaths at c. 1100. Latvia has the highest fatality rate in road accidents, with 34.7 deaths per 100,000 population, and Malta the lowest, with 1.6 per 100,000.

[12] Explosion at 0123 hrs local time. Thirty-one was the official Soviet total of immediate deaths. It is not known how many of the c. 200,000 people involved in the clean-up operation died in the five-year period following the disaster since no systematic records were kept. The senior scientific officer Vladimir Chernousenko, who gave himself two to four years to live owing to his exposure to radiation, put the death toll as between 7000 and 10,000 in a statement on 13 Apr 1991.

[13] In the greatest space disaster on the ground 91 people were killed when an R-16 rocket exploded during fuelling at the Baikonur Space Center, Kazakhstan on 24 Oct 1960.

[14] More than 30 small communities in a 1200km² 460mile² area were eliminated from maps of the USSR in the years after the accident, with 17,000 people evacuated. It was possibly an ammonium nitrate-hexone explosion. A report released in 1992 indicated that 8015 people had died over a 32-year period of observation as a direct result of discharges from the complex.

---

had the same medical practice for seven generations since 1792.

Dentists The country with the most dentists is the United States, where 139,404 were registered members of the American Dental Association at the end of 1993.

The number of dentists registered in the UK as at 1 Jan 1995 was 27,472.

Mental health The country with the most psychologists and psychiatrists is the United States. The registered membership of the American Psychological Association (instituted in 1892) was 132,000 in 1995, and the membership of the American Psychiatric Association (instituted in 1844) was 39,450.

Political Unrest

Protest

Biggest demonstration A figure of 2.7 million was reported from China for a demonstration against the USSR in Shanghai on 3–4 Mar 1969 following border clashes.

Saving of life The greatest number of people saved from extinction by one man is estimated to be nearly 100,000 Jews in Budapest, Hungary from July 1944 to January 1945 by the Swedish diplomat Raoul Wallenberg (b. 4 Aug 1912). After escaping an assassination attempt by the Nazis, he was imprisoned without trial in the Soviet Union. On 6 Feb 1957 Andrey Gromyko, Deputy Foreign Minister, said prisoner 'Walenberg' had died in a cell in Lubyanka Jail, Moscow on 16 Jul 1947. Sighting reports within the Gulag system persisted for years after his disappearance.

Mass killings China The greatest massacre ever imputed by the government of one sovereign nation against the government of another is that of 26.3 million Chinese between 1949 and May 1965, during the regime of Mao Zedong (Mao Tse-tung, 1893–1976). This accusation was made by an agency of the Soviet government in a radio broadcast on 7 Apr 1969. The broadcast broke down the figure into four periods: 2.8 million (1949–52),

Q. How many people were killed by Behram?

A. See Page 188

Worst Disasters in the British Isles

Disaster	Number killed	Location	Date
Famine	1,500,000[1]	Ireland (famine and typhus)	1846–51
Pandemic (the Black Death)	800,000		1347–50
Influenza	225,000		Sep–Nov 1918
Circular Storm	c. 8000	'The Channel Storm'	26 Nov 1703
Smog	3500–4000	London fog	4–9 Dec 1952
Flood	c. 2000[2]	Severn Estuary	20 Jan 1606
Bombing	1436	London	10–11 May 1941
Marine (single ship)	c. 800[3]	HMS Royal George off Spithead, Hants	29 Aug 1782
Riot	565 (min)	London anti-Catholic Gordon riots	2–13 Jun 1780
Mining	439	Universal Colliery, Senghenydd, Mid Glam	14 Oct 1913
Terrorism (aircraft)	270[4]	Bomb aboard Pan Am Boeing 747, crashed over Lockerbie, Dumfries & Galloway	21 Dec 1988
Dam Burst	250	Bradfield Reservoir, Dale Dyke, near Sheffield, S Yorks (embankment burst)	12 Mar 1864
Railway	227[5]	Triple collision, Quintinshill, Dumfries & Galloway	22 May 1915
Fire (single building)	188[6]	Theatre Royal, Exeter	5 Sep 1887
Panic	183	Victoria Hall, Sunderland, Tyne and Wear	16 Jun 1883
Offshore Oil Platform	167	Piper Alpha oil production platform, North Sea	6 Jul 1988
Landslide	144	Pantglas coal tip No. 7, Aberfan, Mid Glam	21 Oct 1966
Explosion	134[7]	Chilwell, Notts (explosives factory)	1 Jul 1918
Nuclear Reactor	footnote[8]	Cancer deaths; Windscale (now Sellafield), Cumbria	10 Oct 1957
Submarine	99	HMS Thetis, during trials, Liverpool Bay	1 Jun 1939
Tornado	75	Tay Bridge collapsed under impact of 2 tornadic vortices	28 Dec 1879
Helicopter	45	Chinook, off Sumburgh, Shetland Islands	6 Nov 1986
Road	33[9]	Coach crash, River Dibb, near Grassington, N Yorks	27 May 1975
Lightning	31	(Annual total) Worst year on record	1914
Yacht Racing	19	28th Fastnet Race—23 boats sank or abandoned in Force 11 gale. Of 316 starters only 128 finished	13–15 Aug 1979
Avalanches	8	Lewes, E Sussex	27 Dec 1836
Mountaineering	6	On Cairn Gorm, near Aviemore (1245m 4084ft)	21 Nov 1971
Earthquake	2	London earthquake, Christ's Hospital (Newgate)	6 Apr 1580

FOOTNOTES

[1] Based on the net rate of natural increase between 1841 and 1851, a supportable case for a loss of population of 3 million can be made out if rates of under-enumeration of 25 per cent (1841) and 10 per cent (1851) are accepted. Potato rot (Phytophthora infestans) was first reported on 13 Sep 1845.

[2] Death tolls of 100,000 were reputed in England and Holland in the floods of 1099, 1421 and 1446.

[3] c. 4000 were lost on HM troopship Lancastria, 16,243 grt, off St Nazaire, France on 17 Jun 1940.

[4] The worst crash by a UK operated aircraft was that of a Dan-Air Boeing 727 from Manchester which crashed into a mountain on the Canary Islands on 25 Apr 1980, killing 146 people. There were no survivors.

[5] The 194.7m 213yd long troop train was telescoped to 61.2m 67yd. Signalmen Meakin and Tinsley were sentenced for manslaughter. Britain's worst underground train disaster was the Moorgate Tube disaster of 28 Feb 1975, when 43 persons were killed.

[6] In July 1212, 3000 were killed in the crush, burned or drowned when London Bridge caught fire at both ends. Britain's most destructive fire was that leading to a £165 million loss at the Army Ordnance depot, Donnington, Shrops on 24 Jun 1983.

[7] HM armed cruiser Natal blew up off Invergordon, Highland on 30 Dec 1915, killing 428. The biggest explosion in Britain occurred on 27 Nov 1944, when 3500 tonnes of bombs exploded at an underground bomb store at Hanbury, Staffs.

[8] There were no deaths as a direct result of the fire, but the number of cancer deaths that might be attributed to it was estimated by the National Radiological Protection Board in 1989 to be 100.

[9] The greatest pile-up on British roads was on the M6 near Lymm Interchange, near Thelwall, Cheshire on 13 Sep 1971. Two hundred vehicles were involved, with 10 dead and 61 injured. The worst year for road deaths in Great Britain was 1941, with 9161 deaths.

Guess What?

Q. When did the famous Long March take place in China?

A. See Page 196

3.5 million (1953–7), 6.7 million (1958–60) and 13.3 million (1961–May 1965).

The Walker Report, published by the US Senate Committee of the Judiciary in July 1971, placed the parameters of the total death toll within China since 1949 between 32.25 and 61.7 million. An estimate of 63.7 million was published by Jean-Pierre Dujardin in Figaro magazine of 19–25 Nov 1978.

In the 13th–17th centuries there were three periods of wholesale massacre in China. The numbers of victims attributed to these events are assertions rather than reliable estimates. The figure put on the Mongolian invasions of northern China from 1210–19 and from 1311–40 are both of the order of 35 million, while the number of victims of the bandit leader Zhang Xianzhong (c. 1605–47), known as the 'Yellow Tiger', from 1643–7 in the Sichuan province has been put at 40 million.

USSR Scholarly estimates for the number of human casualties of Soviet communism focus on some 40 million, excluding those killed in the 'Great Patriotic War'. Larger figures are claimed in Moscow today but these are not necessarily more authoritative. Nobel prizewinner Aleksandr Solzhenitsyn (b. 11 Dec 1918) put the total as high as 66,700,000 for the period between October 1917 and December 1959.

Nazi Germany The most extreme extermination campaign against a people was the Holocaust or the genocidal 'Final Solution' (Endlösung) ordered by Adolf Hitler, before or at the latest by autumn 1941 and continuing into May 1945. Reliable estimates of the number of victims range from 5.1 to 6 million Jews.

Cambodia As a percentage of a nation's total population the worst genocide appears to have been that in Cambodia (formerly Kampuchea). According to the Khmer Rouge Foreign Minister, Ieng Sary, more than a third of the 8 million Khmers were killed between 17 Apr 1975, when the Khmer Rouge captured Phnom Penh, and January 1979, when they were overthrown. Under the rule of Saloth Sar, alias Pol Pot, a founder member of the CPK (Communist Party of Kampuchea, formed in September 1960), towns, money and property were abolished and economical execution by bayonet and club introduced. Deaths at the Tuol Sleng interrogation centre reached 582 in a day.

Towns and Cities

Oldest town The oldest known walled town in the world is Arihā (Jericho). The radiocarbon dating on specimens from the lowest levels reached by archaeologists indicates habitation there by perhaps 2700 people as early as 7800 BC. The settlement of Dolní Věstonice, Czech Republic has been dated to the Gravettian culture c. 27,000 BC.

Great Britain Towns and villages The oldest town in Great Britain is often cited as Colchester, the old British Camulodunum, headquarters of Belgic chiefs in the first century BC. However, the name of the tin trading post Salakee, St Mary's, Isles of Scilly is derived from pre-Celtic roots and hence ante 550 BC.

The smallest place with a town council is Fordwich, in Kent (population 249). England's largest village is Lancing, W Sussex, with an estimated population of 18,100. The most remote village on mainland Great Britain is Inverie, Highland, which is a walk of 43.5km 27 miles from Arnisdale, also in Highland, its nearest village.

New towns Of the 32 set up in Great Britain, that with the largest eventual planned population is Milton Keynes, Bucks, with a current population of 181,000 and a projected 210,000 people for the end of the century.

Most populous cities The most populous urban agglomeration in the world as listed in the United Nations' 1992 publication World Urbanization Prospects is Tokyo, with a population of 25,000,000 in 1990. By the end of the century this is expected to have increased to 28,000,000.

Great Britain The most populous conurbation in Britain is Greater London, with an estimated 6,928,000 people (1994), compared to its peak figure of 8,615,050 in 1939. The residential population of the City of London (315ha 778acres) is 4037 (1994) compared with 129,000 in 1851. The daytime figure is 320,000.

Highest towns and cities The highest capital in the world, before the domination of Tibet by China, was Lhasa, at an elevation of 3684m 12,087ft above sea level. La Paz, administrative and de facto capital of Bolivia, stands at an altitude of 3631m 11,916ft above sea level. Its airport, El Alto, is at 4080m 13,385ft. Sucre, the legal capital of Bolivia, stands at 2834m 9301ft above sea level. Wenchuan, founded

> The oldest capital city in the world is Dimashq (Damascus), Syria. It has been continuously inhabited since c. 2500 BC.

in 1955 on the Qinghai–Tibet road north of the Tangla range in China, is the highest town in the world at 5100m *16,730ft* above sea level. A settlement on the T'e-li-mo trail in southern Tibet is sited at an altitude of 6019m *19,800ft*.

Great Britain The highest village in Britain is Flash, Staffs at 462.7m *1518ft* above sea level.

Lowest towns and cities The Israeli settlement of Ein Bokek, which has a synagogue, on the shores of the Dead Sea is the lowest in the world, at 393.5m *1291ft* below sea level.

Northernmost towns and cities The northernmost village is Ny-Ålesund (78°55'N), a coalmining settlement on King's Bay, Vest Spitsbergen, in the Norwegian territory of Svalbard. The northernmost capital is Reykjavík, Iceland (64°08'N). Its population was 100,855 in 1993.

Southernmost towns and cities The world's southernmost village is Puerto Williams (population about 1000) on the north coast of Isla Navarino, in Tierra del Fuego, Chile, 1090km *680miles* north of Antarctica. Wellington, North Island, New Zealand, with a population of 325,700, is the southernmost capital city (41°17'S). The world's southernmost administrative centre is Port Stanley, Falkland Islands (51°43'S), with a current population of 1643.

Guess What?
Q. Which mammal is found at the highest altitude?
A. See Page 28

No Sea

The large town most remote from the sea is Urumqi (Wu-lu-mu-ch'i) in Xinjiang, the capital of China's Xinjiang Uygur autonomous region, at a distance of about 2500km *1500miles* from the nearest coastline. Its population was estimated to be 1,379,000 in late 1993.

Royalty and Heads of State

Oldest ruling house The Emperor of Japan, Akihito (b. 23 Dec 1933), is the 125th in line from the first Emperor, Jimmu Tenno or Zinmu, whose reign was traditionally from 660 to 581 BC, but more probably dates from c. 40 BC to c. 10 BC.

Her Majesty Queen Elizabeth II (b. 21 Apr 1926) represents dynasties historically traceable back at least 54 generations to the 4th century AD in the case of Tegid, great grandfather of Cunedda, founder of the House of Gwynedd in Wales. If the historicity of some early Scoto-Irish and Pictish kings were acceptable, the lineage could be extended to about 70 generations.

Reigns Longest all-time Minhti, King of Arakan, which is now part of Myanmar (Burma), is reputed to have reigned for 95 years between 1279 and 1374, but the longest well documented reign of any monarch is that of Phiops II (also known as Pepi II), or Neferkare, a Sixth

The World

The world—republics rule Of the world's 192 sovereign states, 146 are republics. The other 46 are headed by 1 emperor, 14 kings, 3 queens, 2 sultans, 1 grand duke, 2 princes, 3 amirs, an elected monarch, the Pope, a president chosen from and by 7 hereditary sheiks, a head of state currently similar to a constitutional monarch, and 2 nominal non- hereditary 'princes' in one country. Queen Elizabeth II is head of state of 15 Commonwealth countries in addition to the UK.

Musoma Kanijo, although not a monarch, was chief of the Nzega district of western Tanganyika (now part of Tanzania), and reputedly reigned for more than 98 years from 1864, when aged 8, until his death on 2 Feb 1963.

Dynasty pharaoh of ancient Egypt. His reign began c. 2281 BC, when he was 6 years of age, and is believed to have lasted c. 94 years.

Longest current The King of Thailand, Bhumibol Adulyadej (Rama IX) (b. 5 Dec 1927), is currently the world's longest-reigning monarch, having succeeded to the throne following the death of his older brother on 9 Jun 1946. The most durable monarch is the King of Cambodia, Norodom Sihanouk (b. 31 Oct 1922), who first became King on 16 Apr 1941 but abdicated on 2 Mar 1955, and then returned to the throne on 24 Sep 1993. The longest-reigning queen is HM Queen Elizabeth II (⇔ above), who succeeded to the throne on 6 Feb 1952 on the death of her father.

Shortest The Crown Prince Luis Filipe of Portugal was mortally wounded at the same time that his father was killed by a bullet which severed his carotid artery, in the streets of Lisbon on 1 Feb 1908. He was thus technically King of Portugal (Dom Luis III) for about 20 minutes.

Highest post-nominal numbers The highest post-nominal number ever used to designate a member of a royal house was 75, briefly enjoyed by Count Heinrich LXXV Reuss zu Schleiz (1800–01). All male members of this branch of the German family are called Heinrich and are successively numbered from I upwards in three sequences. The first began in 1695 (and ended with Heinrich LXXV), the second began in 1803 (and ended with Heinrich XLVII) and the third began in 1910. These are purely *personal* numbers and should not be confused with *regnal* numbers.

Longest-lived 'royals' The longest life among the blood royal of Europe was that of the Princess Pauline Marie Madeleine of Croy (1887–1987), who celebrated her 100th birthday in her birthplace of Le Roeulx, Belgium on 11 Jan 1987.

■ **The reign of the King of Cambodia, Norodom Sihanouk, has spanned a current record 54 years, although with a break of more than 38 years from 1955 to 1993. During this time he filled various posts including Prime Minister and Foreign Minister and spent many years in exile in China. The photographs show him in France in 1946 and greeting supporters in Cambodia in 1993.**
(Photos: Popperfoto and Popperfoto/Romeo Gacao/AFP)

British Monarchy Records

Longest Reign or Tenure

Kings: 59 years 96 days[1] George III, from 1760–1820
Queens Regnant: 63 years 216 days Victoria, from 1837–1901
Queens Consort: 57 years 70 days Charlotte, from 1761–1818
(Consort of George III)

Shortest Reign or Tenure

Kings: 77 days[2] Edward V, in 1483
Queens Regnant: 13 days[3] Jane, from 6–19 Jul 1553
Queens Consort: 154 days Yoleta, from 1285–6
(Second Consort of Alexander III)

Longest Lived

Kings: 81 years 239 days[4] George III (1738–1820)
Queens Regnant: 81 years 243 days Victoria (1819–1901)
Queens Consort: 94 years Lady Elizabeth Bowes Lyon, Queen Elizabeth, the Queen Mother (b. 4 Aug 1900)

Oldest to Start Reign or Consortship

Kings: 64 years 10 months William IV (reigned 1830–7)
Queens Regnant: 37 years 5 months Mary I (reigned 1553–8)
Queens Consort: 56 years 53 days Alexandra (1844–1925)
(Consort of Edward VII, reigned 1901–10)

Youngest to Start Reign or Consortship

Kings: 269 days Henry VI in 1422
Queens Regnant: 6 or 7 days Mary, Queen of Scots in 1542
Queens Consort: 6 years 11 months Isabella (Second Consort of Richard II) in 1396

FOOTNOTES
[1] *James Francis Edward, the Old Pretender, known to his supporters as James III, styled his reign from 16 Sep 1701 until his death on 1 Jan 1766 (i.e. 64 years 109 days).*

[2] *There is a strong probability that in pre-Conquest times Sweyn 'Forkbeard', the Danish King of England, reigned for only 40 days in 1013–14.*

[3] *She accepted the allegiance of the Lords of the Council (9 July) and was proclaimed on 10 July so is often referred to as the 'Nine-day Queen'.*

[4] *Richard Cromwell (b. 4 Oct 1626), the 2nd Lord Protector from 3 Sep 1658 until his abdication on 24 May 1659, lived under the alias John Clarke until 12 Jul 1712, aged 85 years 9 months and was thus the longest-lived head of state.*

Guess What?

Q. How long did Dom Luis III reign as King of Portugal?

A. See Page 181

HRH Princess Alice (b. 25 Feb 1883), a granddaughter of Queen Victoria, became the longest-lived British royal ever on 15 Jul 1977 and died aged 97 years 313 days on 3 Jan 1981. She fulfilled 20,000 engagements, including the funerals of five British monarchs.

Heaviest monarch The world's heaviest monarch is the 1.90 m *6 ft 3 in* tall King Taufa'ahau of Tonga, who in September 1976 was weighed on the only adequate scales in the country, at the airport, recording 209.5 kg *33 st*. By 1985 he was reported to have slimmed down to 139.7 kg *22 st* and in early 1993 he was 127.0 kg *20 st*. The Tongan High Commissioner's embassy car in London has the number plate '1 TON', although this is an abbreviated reference to his status rather than any allusion to his monarch's weight.

Most prolific royal The most prolific monogamous 'royal' was Prince Hartmann of Liechtenstein (1613–86), who had 24 children, of whom 21 were born live, by Countess Elisabeth zu Salm-Reifferscheidt (1623–88). HRH Duke Roberto I of Parma (1848–1907) also had 24 children, but by two wives.

Heads of State *Oldest and youngest* The oldest head of state in the world is Joaquín Balaguer, President of the Dominican Republic (b. 1 Sep 1907). The oldest monarch is King Taufa'ahau of Tonga (b. 4 Jul 1918), who is also the heaviest (⇨ above). The youngest is King Mswati III of Swaziland (b. 19 Apr 1968) (⇨ above).

Meeting The summit segment of the United Nations Conference on Environment and Development, on 12–13 Jun 1992, was attended by 92 heads of state and heads of government—the largest gathering of world leaders. The summit had 103 participants altogether and was one of the meetings at the 'Earth Summit', which was held in Rio de Janeiro, Brazil from 3–14 Jun 1992.

■ Britain's longest-lived Queen Consort (wife of a King) is Queen Elizabeth, the Queen Mother. Equally at home in formal or informal settings, this photograph shows her with the Irish Guards at London's Chelsea Barracks.
(Photo: Gamma/J Hodson/Spooner)

Legislatures

Parliaments—World

Earliest and oldest parliaments The earliest known legislative assembly or *ukkim* was a bicameral one in Erech, Iraq c. 2800 BC. The oldest recorded legislative body is the Icelandic *Althing*, founded in AD 930. This body, which originally comprised 39 local chieftains at Thingvellir, was abolished in 1800, but restored by Denmark to a consultative status in 1843 and a legislative status in 1874. The legislative assembly with the oldest *continuous* history is the Isle of Man Tynwald which may have its origins in the late ninth century and hence possibly pre-date the *Althing*.

Largest parliament The largest legislative assembly in the world is the National People's Congress of the People's Republic of China. The Eighth National People's Congress, the first session of which was convened in March 1993, is composed of 2978 deputies indirectly elected from 22 provinces, five autonomous regions and three municipalities directly under the Central Government, and from the Chinese People's Liberation Army, representing the Communist Party of China, eight democratic parties and people without any political affiliations. The Congress is elected for a term of five years.

Young Ones

Youngest king and queen The country with the youngest king is Swaziland, where King Mswati III (⇨ below) was crowned on 25 Apr 1986 aged 18 years 6 days. He was born Makhosetive, the 67th son of King Subhusa II. The country with the youngest queen is Denmark, with Queen Margrethe II (b. 16 Apr 1940).

Rich

The most highly paid of the world's legislators are the Japanese. The Prime Minister has an annual salary of 38,463,360 yen (£232,000) including monthly allowances and bonuses, whilst members of both the House of Representatives and the House of Councillors have annual salaries of 23,633,565 yen (£142,000) including bonuses.

Greatest petitions The greatest petition on record was signed by 21,202,192 people, mainly from South Korea, between 1 Jun 1993 and 31 Oct 1994. They were protesting against the forced separation of families since the Korean war and the division of the country into North and South Korea.

In Great Britain the largest theoretically has been the Great Chartist Petition of 1848, but of the 5,706,000 'signatures' only 1,975,496 were valid. Otherwise the largest in Britain was in support of ambulance workers in their pay dispute, when a national petition containing 4,680,727 signatures was delivered to the House of Commons on 14 Dec 1989. Since 1974, the signatures on petitions which have been presented have not been counted at the House of Commons.

Today the highest paid legislators are the Japanese. Their Prime Minister has an annual salary equivalent to £232,000. Forty years ago the highest paid were members of the United States Congress. They had an annual salary equivalent to £8760.

Longest membership The longest span as a legislator was 83 years, by József Madarász (1814–1915). He first attended the Hungarian Parliament from 1832–86 as *oblegatus absentium* (i.e. on behalf of an absent deputy). He was a full member from 1848–50 and from 1861 until his death on 31 Jan 1915.

Longest speeches The longest speech made was one by Chief Mangosuthu Buthelezi, the Zulu leader, when he gave an address to the KwaZulu legislative assembly between 12 and 29 Mar 1993. He spoke on 11 of the 18 days, averaging nearly 2½ hours on each of the 11 days.

United Nations The longest speech made in the United Nations has been one of 4 hr 29 min on 26 Sep 1960 by President Fidel Castro Ruz (b. 13 Aug 1927) of Cuba.

Women's suffrage As far back as 1838 the Pitcairn Islands incorporated female suffrage in its constitution, although this was only *de facto* and not legally binding. The earliest legislature with female voters was the Territory of Wyoming, USA in 1869, followed by the Isle of Man in 1881. The earliest country to have universal suffrage was New Zealand in 1893.

Parliaments—

United Kingdom

Earliest parliament The earliest known use of the term 'parliament' is in an official royal document, in the meaning of a summons to the King's (Henry III's) Council, dating from 19 Dec 1241. The Houses of Parliament of the United Kingdom in the Palace of Westminster, London had 1848 members (House of Lords 1199, of whom *c.* 800 are active; House of Commons 649) in April 1995.

Longest parliament The longest English Parliament was the 'Pensioners' Parliament of Charles II, which lasted from 8 May 1661 to 24 Jan 1679, a period of 17 years 8 months and 16 days. The longest United Kingdom Parliament was that of George V, Edward VIII and George VI, lasting from 26 Nov 1935 to 15 Jun 1945, a span of 9 years 6 months and 20 days.

Shortest parliament The parliament of Edward I, summoned to Westminster for 30 May 1306, lasted only 1 day. That of Charles II at Oxford lasted 7 days, from 21–28 Mar 1681. The shortest United Kingdom Parliament was that of George III, lasting from 15 Dec 1806 to 29 Apr 1807, a period of only 4 months and 14 days.

Longest sittings The longest sitting in the House of Commons was one of 41½ hr from 4 p.m. on 31 Jan 1881 to 9:30 a.m. on 2 Feb 1881, on the question of better Protection of Person and Property in Ireland. The longest sitting of the Lords has been 19 hr 16 min from 2:30 p.m. on 29 Feb to 9:46 a.m. on 1 Mar 1968 on the Commonwealth Immigrants Bill (committee stage).

Longest speeches The longest recorded continuous speech in the Chamber of the House of Commons was that of Rt Hon Henry Peter Brougham (1778–1868) on 7 Feb 1828, when he spoke for 6 hours on Law Reform. Brougham, created the 1st

Peace

The oldest treaty still in force is the Anglo-Portuguese Treaty, which was signed in London over 622 years ago on 16 Jun 1373, making Portugal the UK's oldest ally. The text was confirmed 'with my usual flourish' by John de Banketre, Clerk.

Lord Brougham and Vaux on 22 Nov 1830, then set the House of Lords record, also with 6 hours, on 7 Oct 1831, when speaking on the second reading of the Reform Bill, 'fortified by 3 tumblers of spiced wine'.

The longest back-bench speech under present, much stricter standing orders has been one of 4 hr 23 min by Sir Ivan Lawrence (b. 24 Dec 1936), Conservative Member for Burton, opposing the Water (Fluoridation) Bill on 6 Mar 1985. John Golding (b. 9 Mar 1931) (then Labour, Newcastle-under-Lyme) spoke for 11 hr 15 min in committee on small amendments to the British Telecommunications Bill on 8–9 Feb 1983.

Divisions The record number of divisions in a House of Commons day is 64 on 23–24 Mar 1971, including 57 in succession between midnight and noon. The greatest number of votes in a division was 660, with a majority of 40 (350–310) against the government of the Marquess of Salisbury on the vote of no confidence on 11 Aug 1892.

Elections—World

Largest elections The elections beginning on 20 May 1991 for the Indian *Lok Sabha* (Lower House), which has 543 elective seats, were the largest elections ever to have taken place. A total of 315,439,908 people cast their votes in the 511 constituencies where the seats were being contested, out of an eligible electorate of 488,678,993. The elections were contested by 359 parties, and there were nearly 565,000 polling stations manned by 3 million staff. As a result of the election a new government was formed under the leadership of P. V. Narasimha Rao of the Congress (I) Party.

Closest elections The ultimate in close general elections occurred in Zanzibar (now part of Tanzania) on 18 Jan 1961, when the Afro-Shirazi Party won by a single seat, after the seat of Chake-Chake on Pemba Island had been gained by a single vote.

Highest personal majority The highest ever personal majority for any politician has been 4,726,112 in the case of Boris Nikolayevich Yeltsin (b. 1 Feb 1931), the people's deputy candidate for Moscow, in the parliamentary elections held in the former Soviet Union on 26 Mar 1989. Yeltsin received 5,118,745 votes out of the 5,722,937 which were cast in the Moscow constituency, his closest rival obtaining 392,633 votes.

Guess What?
Q. How do the Houses of Parliament help to keep Brian Davis fit?
A. See Page 210

(Photo: Rex Features/Alfred)

The world's most popular politician?

When election time comes around in the Larkana-III constituency in Pakistan, it is generally accepted that it is the safest seat in the country. For Larkana-III is the constituency of Benazir Bhutto, Pakistan's 43-year-old Prime Minister.

In December 1988 this remarkable woman had become the first ever female Prime Minister in a modern Islamic nation, receiving 96.71 per cent of the votes cast in her constituency. With 82,229 votes she had a majority of 80,250, her nearest rival obtaining just 1979 votes. After she was dismissed on corruption charges in August 1990, a general election was held on 24 October that year—and she achieved an even more staggering 98.48 per cent of the poll in her constituency, obtaining 94,462 votes. For the second time in two years she had set a record for the greatest percentage of the vote in a free election. A total of 95,919 votes were cast and this time the next highest candidate obtained only 718 votes, giving her a majority of 93,744. All this in a male-dominated nation. What made her achievement all the more remarkable was that her party actually lost the election. In October 1993 she became Prime Minister again (although without beating the record), after another general election.

Educated at Harvard and Oxford, Benazir Bhutto has wealth, celebrity and aristocratic status. She has been in exile, has led her country back to democracy following a period of military dictatorship, and has always had to be vigilant. She believes that in 1981, whilst undergoing an operation, the military may have tried to have her killed. She was also the target of death threats after she declared a war on drugs.

Benazir Bhutto does have her enemies but she also has her very loyal followers. None more so than in her own constituency.

Most decisive elections North Korea recorded a 100 per cent turn-out of electors and a 100 per cent vote for the Workers' Party of Korea in the general election of 8 Oct 1962. The next closest approach was in Albania on 14 Nov 1982, when a single voter spoiled national unanimity for the official (and only) Communist candidates, who consequently obtained 99.99993 per cent of the poll in a reported 100 per cent turn-out of 1,627,968.

Most bent elections In the Liberian presidential election of 1927 President Charles D.B. King (1875–1961) was returned with a majority over his opponent, Thomas J.R. Faulkner of the People's Party, officially announced as 234,000. President King thereby claimed a 'majority' more than 15½ times greater than the entire electorate.

Largest party The largest political party is the Chinese Communist Party, formed in 1920, which has an estimated membership of 50.3 million.

Largest ballot paper For the municipal elections in Prague, Czech Republic on 18–19 Nov 1994 there were 1187 candidates for the one constituency covering the whole of the city. The ballot paper measuring 101.5 cm × 71.5 cm *3 ft 4 in × 2 ft 4 in* was delivered to all 1,018,527 registered voters, who could nominate up to 55 candidates for the 55 available seats.

Political instability El Salvador has averaged one government every eighteen months since it obtained its independence in 1821, whilst Syria had 17 governments in the space of just 33 months between March 1949 and December

> In Mongolia the Communists (Mongolian People's Revolutionary Party) have been in power since 1924, although only since 1990 within a multi-party system. In February 1992 the term 'People's Republic' was dropped from the name.

1951, thus averaging a change every other month. Some statisticians contend that Bolivia, since it became a sovereign country in 1825, has had a record 191 attempted coups. Only 23 of these, however, have been successful.

Prime Ministers and Statesmen

Longest term of office The longest-serving Prime Minister of a sovereign state is currently Khalifa bin Sulman al-Khalifa (b. 3 Jul 1933) of Bahrain, who has held office since Bahrain became independent in August 1971. By then he had already been in office for 1½ years.

Marshal Kim Il Sung (*né* Kim Sung Chu) (1912–94) was head of government or head of state of the Democratic People's Republic of Korea for nearly 46 years, from 25 Aug 1948 until his death on 8 Jul 1994.

Pyotr Lomako (1904–90) served in the government of the former USSR as Minister for Non-Ferrous Metallurgy from 1940 to 1986. He was relieved of his post after 46 years on 1 Nov 1986, aged 82, having served on the Central Committee of the CPSU since 1952.

Oldest Prime Minister The longest-lived Prime Minister of any country was Antoine Pinay (France), who was born on 30 Dec 1891 and died on 13 Dec 1994, aged 102 years 348 days. He was his country's Prime Minister from March to December 1952.

> The oldest age at which anyone has *first* been appointed Prime Minister has been 81, in the case of Morarji Ranchhodji Desai of India (1896–1995) in March 1977.

El Hadji Muhammad el Mokri, Grand Vizier of Morocco, died on 16 Sep 1957 at a reputed age of 116 Muslim years, equivalent to 112½ Gregorian years (⇔ also Longevity — Authentic National Longevity Records table).

Philippe Pétain (1856–1951), although not 'Prime Minister', became 'Chief of State' of the French State on 10 Jul 1940 at the age of 84.

Youngest Prime Minister Currently the youngest head of government is Dr Mario Frick (b. 8 May 1965), who became Prime Minister of Liechtenstein at the age of 28 on 15 Dec 1993.

Women Prime Ministers Indira Gandhi (1917–84) of India was Prime Minister for a record 15 years in two spells, from 1966 to 1977 and 1980 to 1984. Eugenia Charles (b. 15 May 1919) of Dominica is the current record-holder for longevity in

office, having taken office when her Dominica Freedom Party won the elections in July 1980.

European Parliament election records Germany has most representatives in the 626-member parliament, with 99, and Luxembourg the fewest, with 6. The largest political grouping following the June 1994 elections is the Group of the Party of European Socialists, with 221 members, whilst the two smallest are the European Radical Alliance and Europe of Nations with 19 each. The best turnout has been in Belgium in 1989, when 93 per cent of the electorate voted (although voting is compulsory there).

> The lowest turnout in a European Parliament election has been in the United Kingdom in 1984, when just 32.5 per cent of the electorate cast their votes.

Handshaking The record number of hands shaken by a public figure at an official function was 8513 by President Theodore Roosevelt (1858–1919) at a New Year's Day White House presentation in Washington, DC, USA on 1 Jan 1907.

Kang Ho Dong, a Korean wrestler, shook hands with 28,233 different people in eight hours during Expo 93 in Taejon, South Korea on 22 Aug 1993.

Majorities — United Kingdom

Largest majority In 1931 the coalition of Conservatives, Liberals and National Labour achieved the largest majority, with 491 seats and 60.5 per cent of the vote. The largest majority in the era before universal suffrage was 288 by a 'Liberal' alliance of Whigs, Radicals and Irish supporters of O'Connell in 1832.

Smallest majority The narrowest majority has been that of Labour in 1964, with four over the Conservatives and Liberals combined. In the two elections of 1910 the Liberals had a majority of two in February and there was a dead heat in December, but in both cases they had the support of the Irish Nationalists and Labour, which gave them in practice majorities of 122 and 126.

Division The largest majority on a division in the House of Commons was one of 547 (556 for and 9 against), on a procedural motion relating to the European Communities (Amendment) Bill on 15 Apr 1994.

House of Lords

Oldest member The oldest member ever recorded was the Rt Hon. Lord Shinwell (1884–1986), who first sat in the Lower House in November 1922 and lived to be 101 years 202 days (⇔ Peerage). The oldest peer to make a maiden speech was Lord Maenan (1854–1951) at the age of 94 years 123 days (⇔ Most durable judges).

Youngest member The youngest current member of the House of Lords to have taken his seat is the Earl of Hardwicke (b. 3 Feb 1971).

Political Office Holders

Party The longest period of party ascendancy in British political and parliamentary history is definitional. The Whig Ascendancy ran from 17 Mar 1715 to the death of King George II on 25 Oct 1760, and followed until the assuming of office of the Earl of Bute on 26 May 1762 — 47 years 2 months, in which time there were eight general elections. The Tory Ascendancy ran from the appointment of William Pitt (the Younger) on 19 Dec

Five Votes

The narrowest recorded percentage win in an election was for the office of Southern District Highway Commissioner in Mississippi, USA on 7 Aug 1979. Robert E. Joiner was declared the winner over W. H. Pyron, with 133,587 votes to 133,582. The loser thus obtained more than 49.999 per cent of the votes.

■ The world's first woman prime minister was Sirimavo Bandaranaike, who became Prime Minister of what was then called Ceylon (now Sri Lanka) in 1960. In 1994 she became the country's prime minister again, appointed by the president—her daughter. Sirimavo Bandaranaike is on the left in the photograph, with the president, Chandrikar Bandaranaike Kumaratunga, on the right.
(Photo: Gamma/Bartholomew/Liaison)

> The greatest representation of women in a cabinet is in Sweden, where following a general election in September 1994 a new cabinet was formed containing 11 women out of 22 ministers.

Prime Ministerial Records

Though given legal warrant in the instrument of the Congress of Berlin in 1878 and awarded official recognition in a Royal Warrant of 1905, the first statutory mention of the title of Prime Minister was only in 1917. All previous acknowledged First Ministers had tenure as First Lords of the Treasury with the exception of No. 11, William Pitt, Earl of Chatham, who controlled his ministers as Secretary of State of the Southern Department or as Lord Privy Seal. The first to preside over his fellow King's ministers was Sir Robert Walpole. His ministry began in 1721, although it was not until 15 May 1730, when Viscount Townshend resigned from his position as Secretary of State, that Walpole gained absolute control of the Cabinet.

LONGEST SERVING	20 years 315 days	1st	Sir Robert Walpole (1676–1745)	3 Apr 1721–11 Feb 1742
MOST MINISTRIES	5	40th	Stanley (later Earl) Baldwin (1867–1947)	22 May 1923–28 May 1937
SHORTEST SERVICE IN OFFICE	120 days	21st	George Canning (1770–1827)	10 Apr–8 Aug 1827
YOUNGEST TO ASSUME OFFICE	24 years 205 days	16th	Hon. William Pitt (1759–1806)	19 Dec 1783 (declined when 23 years 275 days)
OLDEST FIRST TO ASSUME OFFICE	70 years 109 days	30th	Viscount Palmerston (1784–1865)	6 Feb 1855
GREATEST AGE IN OFFICE	84 years 64 days	32nd	William Gladstone (1809–98)	3 Mar 1894 (elected at 82 years 171 days)
SHORTEST MINISTRY	22 days	23rd	Duke of Wellington (1769–1852)	17 Nov–9 Dec 1834
MOST LIVING SIMULTANEOUSLY	19	8th, 11–26th, 29–30th	from birth of Peel (26th) to death of Chatham (11th)	5 Feb–11 May 1788
	19	12th, 14th–31st	from birth of Disraeli (31st) to death of Shelburne (14th)	21 Dec 1804–7 May 1805
MOST LIVING EX-PRIME MINISTERS	6	8th, 11–15th	Bute, Chatham, Grafton, North, Shelburne, Portland (Pitt) till Chatham died	19 Dec 1783–11 May 1788
	6	34–35th, 37–38th, 40th–41st	Rosebery, Balfour, Asquith, Lloyd-George, Baldwin, Macdonald (Baldwin's second term) till Asquith died	4 Nov 1924–15 Feb 1928

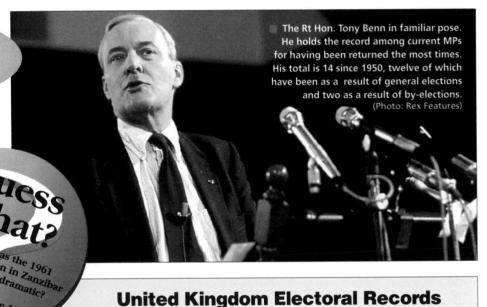

Lowest election expenses
When Paul Coulam stood as an Anti-Federalist League candidate for the Lewisham West constituency in the 1992 general election, his expenses totalled just £30.96.

The Rt Hon. Tony Benn in familiar pose. He holds the record among current MPs for having been returned the most times. His total is 14 since 1950, twelve of which have been as a result of general elections and two as a result of by-elections.
(Photo: Rex Features)

1783, as confirmed by the general election of March–May 1784, until the fall of the Duke of Wellington's second administration on 21 Nov 1830 — 46 years 11 months, during which time there were seven general elections.

Prime Ministers The only Prime Minister to retain power for four successive general elections was Lord Liverpool, in 1812 (30 Sep–24 Nov), 1818 (11 Jun–4 Aug), 1820 (1 Mar–21 Apr) and 1826 (3 Jun–23 Jul). Since the reduction of the term of Parliaments from seven years to five years in 1911, the only Prime Minister to have been returned to power in three successive general elections is Margaret Thatcher, now Baroness Thatcher of Kesteven (b. 13 Oct 1925), on 3 May 1979, 9 Jun 1983 and 11 Jun 1987. She is also the longest-serving Prime Minister this century, at 11 years 208 days, from 4 May 1979–28 Nov 1990.

Guess What?
Q. Why was the 1961 general election in Zanzibar particularly dramatic?
A. See Page 183

Fastest election result
In the 1959 general election, the result from Billericay, Essex was announced 57 minutes after the polls closed, at 9:57 p.m.

MPs *Youngest* Henry Long (1420–90) was returned for an Old Sarum seat at the age of 15. His precise date of birth is unknown. Minors were debarred in law in 1695 and in fact in 1832.

The youngest ever woman MP has been Josephine Bernadette Devlin, now Mrs McAliskey (b. 23 Apr 1947), elected for Mid Ulster (Independent Unity) aged 21 years 359 days on 17 Apr 1969.

The youngest current member is Matthew Taylor, MP (Liberal Democrat) for Truro (b. 3 Jan 1963).

Oldest Sir Francis Knollys (c. 1550–1648), 'the ancientest Parliament man in England', was re-elected for Reading in 1640 when apparently aged 90, and was probably 97 or 98 at the time of his death (⟺ below).

United Kingdom Electoral Records

Votes (electorate)
HIGHEST: 33,610,399, general election 9 Apr 1992.
HIGHEST (party): 14,094,116 (Con.), general election 9 Apr 1992.

Votes (individual)
MOST: 75,205, Sir Cooper Rawson (Con.), Brighton, Sussex, 1931.
LEAST: Nil, F.R. Lees (Temperance Chartist), Ripon, Yorks, Dec 1860.
LEAST SINCE UNIVERSAL FRANCHISE: 5, Lt. Cdr W. Boaks (Public Safety Democratic Monarchist White Resident), Glasgow, Hillhead, 25 Mar 1982; Dr Kailish Trivedi (Independent Janata), Kensington by-election, 14 Jul 1988.
LEAST SINCE UNIVERSAL FRANCHISE IN GENERAL ELECTION: 13, B.C. Wedmore (Belgrano), Finchley, 9 Jun 1983.

Majority
HIGHEST: Man: 62,253, Sir Cooper Rawson (Con.), Brighton, Sussex, 1931. Woman: 38,823, Countess of Iveagh (Con.), Southend, Essex, 1931.
HIGHEST (current): 36,230 by Rt Hon. John Major (Con., Huntingdon).
NARROWEST: 1 vote, Matthew Fowler (Lib.), Durham, 1895; 1 vote, H.E. Duke (Unionist), Exeter, Devon, Dec 1910. Since Universal Franchise: 2 votes, A.J. Flint (National Labour), Ilkeston, Derbyshire, 1931.

NARROWEST (current): 19 by Walter Sweeney (Con., Vale of Glamorgan).

Most Recounts
7: Brighton, Kemptown 1964 and Peterborough 1966.

General Election Turnout
HIGHEST: 93.42%, Fermanagh & S Tyrone, 1951.
LOWEST: 29.7%, Kennington, London, 1918.

Largest Electorate
217,900, Hendon (Barnet), 1941.

Smallest Electorate
10,851, City of London, 1945.

Most By-Election Candidates
19: Newbury, 6 May 1993, won by David Rendel (Lib. Dem.).

Most Elections Contested
Screaming Lord Sutch of the Official Monster Raving Loony Party has contested 36 elections or by-elections, losing his deposit on each occasion.

Longest Gap Between By-Elections
There were no by-elections between those at Hemsworth, Kincardine & Deeside and Langbaurgh on 7 Nov 1991 and that at Newbury on 6 May 1993 — 1 year 181 days later.

The oldest of 20th-century members has been Samuel Young (b. 14 Feb 1822), Nationalist MP for East Cavan (1892 to 1918), who died on 18 Apr 1918, aged 96 years 63 days.

Father of the House The title is nowadays bestowed on the Member who has the longest unbroken service in the Commons. The earliest occurrence of the phrase dates from 1816. The oldest Father was the Rt Hon. Charles Pelham Villiers (Wolverhampton South) when he died on 16 Jan 1898, aged 96 years 13 days. The current Father is the Rt Hon. Sir Edward Heath, MP (Old Bexley and Sidcup), who took the oath as MP on 2 Mar 1950.

Longest span Sir Francis Knollys (⇔ above) was elected for Oxford in 1575 and died a sitting member for Reading 73 years later in 1648.

The longest span of service of any 20th-century MP is 63 years 360 days (1 Oct 1900 to 25 Sep 1964) by the Rt Hon. Sir Winston Leonard Spencer Churchill (1874–1965), with breaks only in 1908 and from 1922–4. The record for a woman is 42 years 4 months (27 Oct 1931 to 28 Feb 1974) by Dame Irene Ward, who was MP for Wallsend from 1931 to 1945 and Tynemouth from 1950 to 1974.

The longest continuous span was that of C.P. Villiers (⇔ above), who was a member for 63 years 6 days, having been returned at 17 elections. The longest living of all parliamentarians was Theodore Cooke Taylor (1850–1952), Liberal MP for Batley from 1910–18.

Briefest span There are two 18th-century examples of posthumous elections. Capt. the Hon. Edward Legge, RN (1710–47) was returned unopposed for Portsmouth on 15 Dec 1747. News came later that he had died in the West Indies 87 days before polling. In 1780 John Kirkman, standing for the City of London, expired before polling had ended but was nonetheless duly returned. A.J. Dobbs (Lab, Smethwick), elected on 5 Jul 1945, was killed in a motor accident on the way to take his seat.

Women MPs The first woman to be elected to the House of Commons was Mme Constance Georgine Markievicz (*née* Gore Booth). She was elected as member (Sinn Fein) for St Patrick's Dublin on 28 Dec 1918. The first woman to take her seat was the Viscountess Astor (1879–1964) (*née* Nancy Witcher Langhorne at Danville, Virginia, USA; formerly Mrs Robert Gould Shaw), who was elected Unionist member for the Sutton division of Plymouth, Devon on 28 Nov 1919, and took her seat 3 days later.

Heaviest and tallest MPs The heaviest MP of all time is believed to be Sir Cyril Smith, Liberal member for Rochdale from October 1972 to April 1992, when in January 1976 his peak reported weight was 189.6 kg *29 st 12 lb*.

Sir Louis Gluckstein (1897–1979), Conservative member for East Nottingham (1931–45), was an unrivalled 2.02 m *6 ft 7½ in*. Currently the tallest is the The Hon. Sir Archie Hamilton (b. 30 Dec 1941), Conservative member for Epsom and Ewell, at 1.98 m *6 ft 6 in*.

Local government service duration records Major Sir Philip Barber (1876–1961) served as county councillor for Nottinghamshire for 63 years 41 days, from 8 Mar 1898 to 18 Apr 1961. Matthew Anderson was a member of the Borough Council of Abingdon, Oxon for 69 years 4 months, from April 1709 until August 1778. Henry Winn (1816–1914) served as parish clerk for Fulletby, near Horncastle, Lincs for 76 years.

Judicial

Legislation
and Litigation

Statutes *Oldest* The earliest surviving judicial code was that of King Ur-Nammu during the third dynasty of Ur, Iraq, c. 2250 BC. The oldest English statute in the Statute Book is a section of the Statute of Marlborough of 18 Nov 1267, re-entitled in 1948 'The Distress Act 1267' and most recently cited in the High Court in 1986. Some statutes enacted by Henry II (died 1189) and earlier kings are even more durable as they have been assimilated into the Common Law.

Longest in the UK The weightiest piece of legislation ever written is the Income and Corporation Taxes Act 1988 of more than 1000 pages and weighing 2.5 kg *5½ lb*. Lord Houghton of Sowerby appealed to fellow peers in November 1987 'not to walk about with it' for fear of ruptures.

Shortest The shortest statute is the Parliament (Qualification of Women) Act 1918, which runs to 27 operative words: 'A woman shall not be disqualified by sex or marriage from being elected to or sitting or voting as a Member of the Commons House of Parliament.' Section 2 contains a further 14 words giving the short title.

Patents The earliest of all known English patents was that granted by Henry VI in 1449 to Flemish-born John of Utyman for making coloured glass for the windows of Eton College. The peak number of applications for patents filed in the UK in any one year was 63,614 in 1969. The shortest patent is one of 48 words filed on 14 May 1956, concerning a harrow attachment. The longest, comprising 2290 pages of text and 495 sheets of drawings, was filed on 31 Mar 1965 by IBM to cover a computer.

Most protracted litigation A controversy over the claim of the Prior and Convent (now the Dean and Chapter) of Durham Cathedral to administer the spiritualities of the diocese during a vacancy in the See grew fierce in 1283. The dispute, with the Archbishop of York, flared up again in 1672 and 1890; an attempt in November 1975 to settle the issue, then 692 years old, was unsuccessful. Neither side admits the legitimacy of writs of appointment issued by the other even though identical persons are named.

Gaddam Hanumantha Reddy, a civil servant, brought a series of legal actions against the Hyderabad state government and the Indian government covering a total period of 44 years 9 months and 8 days from April 1945 through to January 1990. The litigation outlasted the entire period of his employment in the Indian Administrative Service. He complained that his results in the entrance examination for the Hyderabad Civil Service entitled him to greater seniority and higher pay. After winning the legal battle he did indeed receive his promotion.

Longest hearings The longest civil case heard before a jury is *Kemner v. Monsanto Co.*, which concerned an alleged toxic chemical spill in Sturgeon, Missouri, USA in 1979. The trial started on 6 Feb 1984, at St Clair County Court House, Belleville, Illinois, USA before Circuit Judge Richard P. Goldenhersh, and ended on 22 Oct 1987. The testimony lasted 657 days, following which the jury deliberated for two months. The residents of Sturgeon were awarded $1 million nominal compensatory damages and $16,280,000 punitive damages, but these awards were overturned by the Illinois Appellate Court on 11 Jun 1991 because the jury in the original trial had not found that any damage had resulted from the spill.

The Supreme Court of Sri Lanka spent a record 527 days hearing a challenge to the election of President Ranasinghe Premadasa as head of state in 1988. A total of 977 witnesses gave evidence over a three year period, from 19 Jun 1989 to 30 Jun 1992. The challenge, brought by the opposition leader Sirimavo Bandaranaike, was rejected by the court on 1 Sep 1992.

Longest British hearings The longest trial in the annals of British justice was the Tichborne personation case. The civil trial began on 11 May 1871, lasted 103 days and collapsed on 6 Mar 1872. The criminal trial went on for 188 days, resulting in a sentence on 28 Feb 1874 for two counts of perjury (two 7-year consecutive terms of imprisonment with hard labour) on London-born Arthur Orton, alias Thomas Castro (1834–98), who claimed to be Roger Charles Tichborne (1829–54), the elder brother of Sir Alfred Joseph Doughty-Tichborne, 11th Bt (1839–66). The whole case thus spanned 1025 days. The jury were out for only 30 minutes.

The impeachment of Warren Hastings (1732–1818), which began in 1788, dragged on for 7 years until 23 Apr 1795, but

■ The election of Ranasinghe Premadasa to the office of President of Sri Lanka in 1988 led to a trial lasting 527 days in the Supreme Court of Sri Lanka. The opposition leader, Sirimavo Bandaranaike, had challenged the result of the election, claiming that it had not been properly conducted.
(Photo: Rex Features/P Frilet)

Mayors

The longest recorded mayoralty was that of Edmond Mathis (1852–1953), *maire* of Ehuns, Haute-Saône, France for 75 years (1878–1953). Anthony Jennings served as Mayor of Fordwich, Kent for 45 consecutive years from 1785–1830.

Thomas Alva Edison (1847–1931) has had the most patents, with 1093 either on his own or jointly. They included the microphone, the motion-picture projector and the incandescent electric lamp.

Guess What?

Q. How many words are there in the longest will on record?

A. See Page 188

the trial lasted only 149 days. Hastings was appointed a member of the Privy Council in 1814.

The longest single fraud trial was the Britannia Park trial, which began on 10 Sep 1990 and ended on 4 Feb 1992 after 252 working days. The case centred on the collapse of the Britannia theme park near Heanor, Derbys in 1985. The fraud case *R. v. Bouzaglo and Others* ended before Judge Brian Gibbens (1912–85) on 1 May 1981 having lasted 274 days, but with two separate trials. They appealed on 10 Dec 1981.

Murder The longest murder trial in Britain was that at the Old Bailey, London of Reginald Dudley, 51, and Robert Maynard, 38, in the Torso Murder of Billy Moseley and Micky Cornwall which ran before Mr Justice Swanwick from 11 Nov 1976 to 17 Jun 1977 with 136 trial days. Both men were sentenced to life imprisonment (minimum 15 years).

> **The shortest recorded British murder hearings were *R. v. Murray* on 28 Feb 1957 and *R. v. Cawley* at Winchester assizes on 14 Dec 1959. Proceedings occupied only 30 seconds on each occasion.**

The case of Stephen Miller, Yusef Abdullahi and Tony Paris lasted longer, but there were two hearings. They were accused of murdering Lynette White, a Cardiff prostitute, on 14 Feb 1988. The first hearing in 1989 lasted 82 days, but ended with the death of the judge, Mr Justice McNeill. The second one lasted 115 days, ending on 20 Nov 1990. The three men were found guilty and sentenced to life imprisonment, but were cleared by the Court of Appeal on 10 Dec 1992.

Highest bail The highest bail set by a British court was £10 million. On 24 Mar 1994 Leonard Bartlett and Iain Mackintosh, both of London, were bailed on fraud charges by Bow Street Magistrates' Court subject to the condition that they each provided sureties worth that sum. The figure was later reduced to £1 million on appeal.

The highest bail figure on which a defendant was released by a British court is £3.5 million, which was set for Asil Nadir, the chairman of Polly Peck International, on 17 Dec 1990. He had developed the company over 20 years from a small clothing concern into an international group, but it collapsed in September 1990 and he subsequently faced 18 charges of theft and false accounting amounting to £25 million. He jumped bail on 4 May 1993, fleeing to Cyprus.

Best-attended trial The greatest attendance at any trial was at that of Major Jesús Sosa Blanco, aged 51, for an alleged 108 murders. At one point in the 12½ hour trial (5:30 p.m. to 6 a.m., 22–23 Jan 1959), 17,000 people were present in the Havana Sports Palace, Cuba. He was executed on 18 Feb 1959.

Greatest damages *Civil damages* The largest damages awarded in legal history were $11.12 billion to Pennzoil Co. against Texaco Inc. concerning the latter's allegedly unethical tactics in January 1984 to break up a merger between Pennzoil and Getty Oil Co., by Judge Solomon Casseb, Jr in Houston, Texas, USA on 10 Dec 1985. An out-of-court settlement of

$5500 million was reached after a 48-hour negotiation on 19 Dec 1987.

The largest damages awarded against an individual were $2.1 billion. On 10 Jul 1992 Charles H Keating Jr, the former owner of Lincoln Savings and Loan of Los Angeles, California, USA, was ordered by a federal jury to pay this sum to 23,000 small investors who were defrauded by his company. The figure was subject to final approval by the judge.

Personal injury The greatest personal injury damages awarded to an individual were $163,882,660, awarded by a jury to Shiyamala Thirunayagam, aged 27, in the Supreme Court of the State of New York on 27 Jul 1993. She was almost completely paralysed after the car in which she was travelling hit a truck which had broken down in the fast lane of the New Jersey Turnpike on 4 Oct 1987. Because the defendants would have challenged the jury's verdict in a higher court Mrs Thirunagayam agreed to accept a lump sum of $8,230,000 for her pain and suffering, and a guarantee that the defendants would pay up to $55,000,000 for her future medical expenses.

The compensation for the disaster at the Union Carbide Corporation plant in Bhopal, India on 2–3 Dec 1984 was agreed at $470 million. The

O.J.

Between 24 Jan and 31 May 1995, a daily average of 5.5 million Americans watched live coverage of the O.J. Simpson trial on three major cable television networks. Simpson, an American footballer and actor, was on trial for the murder, on 12 Jun 1994, of his ex-wife, Nicole, and a waiter, Ronald Goldman.

■ **The trial of O.J. Simpson has fascinated a record number of television viewers who have followed every development. For Simpson himself it just seems too much.**
(Photo: AP/WorldWide Photos)

Supreme Court of India passed the order for payment on 14 Feb 1989 after a settlement between the corporation and the Indian government, which represented the interests of more than 500,000 claimants including the families of 3350 people who died.

Sexual harassment The record award in a sexual harassment case was $7.1 million (£4.7 million) to Rena Weeks, a former secretary at the law firm Baker

& McKenzie in Palo Alto, California, USA, against Martin Greenstein, a partner in the firm, on 2 Sep 1994. The firm said that it would appeal.

Defamation The record award in a libel case is $58 million, to Vic Feazell, a former district attorney, on 20 Apr 1991 at Waco, Texas, USA. He claimed that he had been libelled by a Dallas-based television station and one of its reporters in 1985, and that this had ruined his reputation. The parties reached a settlement on 29 Jun 1991, but neither side would disclose the amount.

> **At the time of the first edition of *The Guinness Book of Records* the record for defamation was £25,000. Forty years on the record award is $58 million.**

The record damages for libel in Great Britain was the £1.5 million award to Lord Aldington, a former brigadier and former chairman of the Sun Alliance insurance company, against Count Nikolai Tolstoy, a historian, and Nigel Watts, a property developer. The award was made by a High Court jury on 30 Nov 1989 following accusations that Lord Aldington had been a war criminal. However, he did not receive any of the damages which he was awarded.

Guess What?
Q. How long did Paul Geidel spend in prison?
A. See Page 192

Greatest compensation for wrongful imprisonment Robert McLaughlin, 29, was awarded $1,935,000 in October 1989 for wrongful imprisonment as a result of a murder in New York City, USA in 1979 which he did not commit. He had been sentenced to 15 years in prison and actually served six years, from 1980 to 1986, when he was released after his foster father succeeded in showing the authorities that he had nothing to do with the crime.

Greatest divorce settlement The largest publicly declared settlement was that achieved in 1982 by the lawyers of Soraya Khashóggi from her husband Adnan—£500 million plus property. Mrs Anne Bass, former wife of Sid Bass of Texas, USA, was reported to have rejected $535 million as inadequate to live in the style to which she had been made accustomed.

The highest divorce award in Great Britain was one of £1,295,000 (£1,000,000 in cash plus a £295,000 maisonette), made to Yugoslavian-born Radojka Gojkovic against her former husband in the High Court Family Division on 17 Feb 1989. The settlement was upheld by the Court of Appeal on 12 Oct 1989.

Patent case Litton Industries Inc. was awarded $1.2 billion in Los Angeles, California, USA on 31 Aug 1993 in damages from Honeywell Inc. after a jury had decided that Honeywell had violated a Litton patent covering airline-navigation systems. Litton had filed a law suit in March 1990, which was followed by a counterclaim from Honeywell nine months later.

Expensive

The Blue Arrow trial, involving the illegal support of the company's shares during a rights issue in 1987, is estimated to have cost approximately £35 million. The trial at the Old Bailey, London lasted a year and ended on 14 Feb 1992 with four of the defendants being convicted. Although they received suspended prison sentences, they were later cleared on appeal.

Wills The shortest valid will in the world is that of Bimla Rishi of Delhi, India. It consists of four characters in Hindi, meaning 'All to son', and is dated 9 Feb 1995.

The shortest will contested but subsequently admitted to probate in English law was the case of *Thorne* v. *Dickens* in 1906. It consisted of the three words 'All for mother' in which 'mother' was not his mother but his wife. The smallest will preserved by the Record Keeper is an identity disc 3.8 cm 1½ in in diameter belonging to A.B. William Skinner, killed aboard HMS *Indefatigable* at Jutland in 1916. It had 40 words engraved on it including the signatures of two witnesses and was proved on 24 Jun 1922.

> **The longest will on record was that of Mrs Frederica Evelyn Stilwell Cook (b. USA), proved at Somerset House, London on 2 Nov 1925. It consisted of four bound volumes containing 95,940 words, primarily concerning some $100,000 worth of property.**

The oldest written will dates from 2061 BC, and is that of Nek'ure, the son of the Egyptian pharaoh Khafre. The will was carved onto the walls of his tomb, and indicated that he would bequeath 14 towns, 2 estates and other property to his wife, another woman and three children.

Longest lease There is a lease concerning a plot for a sewage tank adjoining Columb Barracks, Mullingar, Co. Westmeath, Republic of Ireland, which was signed on 3 Dec 1868 for 10 million years. Leases in Ireland lasting 'for ever' are quite common.

Most durable judges The oldest recorded active judge was Judge Albert R. Alexander (1859–1966) of Plattsburg, Missouri, USA. He was enrolled as a member of the Clinton County Bar in 1926, and was later the magistrate and probate judge of Clinton County until his retirement aged 105 years 8 months on 9 Jul 1965.

The greatest recorded age at which any British judge has sat on a bench was 93 years 9 months in the case of Sir William Francis Kyffin Taylor (later Lord Maenan), who was born on 9 Jul 1854 and retired as presiding judge of the Liverpool Court of Passage in April 1948, having held that position since 1903. Sir Salathiel Lovell (1619–1713) was still sitting when he died on 3 May 1713 in his 94th or 95th year.

Youngest judge John Payton was elected as a Justice of the Peace in Plano, Texas, USA and took office at the age of 18 years 11 months in January 1991. David Elmer Ward had to await the legal age of 21 before taking office after nomination in 1932 as Judge of the County Court (a higher level) at Fort Myers, Florida, USA.

Muhammad Ilyas passed the examination enabling him to become a Civil Judge in July 1952 at the age of 20 years 9 months, although formalities such as medicals meant that it was not until eight months later that he started work as a Civil Judge in Lahore, Pakistan.

The youngest certain age at which any English judge has been appointed is 28, for Sir Ernest Wild KC (1869–1934), when he was appointed Judge of the Norwich Guildhall Court of Record in 1897.

Most judges Lord Balmerino was found guilty of treason by 137 of his peers on 28 Jul 1746. In the 20th century, 26 judges of the European Court of Human Rights in Strasbourg, France gave judgment in *Brannigan and McBride* v. *United Kingdom* on 26 May 1993. The court rejected the applicants' challenge to their detention in Northern Ireland under the Prevention of Terrorism Act.

> **Most successful lawyer** Sir Lionel Luckhoo, senior partner of Luckhoo and Luckhoo of Georgetown, Guyana, succeeded in getting 245 successive murder charge acquittals between 1940 and 1985.

Most durable solicitors William George (1865–1967), brother of Prime Minister David Lloyd George, passed his preliminary law examination in May 1880 and was practising until December 1966 at the age of 101 years 9 months. The most durable firm is Pickering Kenyon of London, which was founded by William Umfreville (otherwise Umbervyle) in 1561.

Law firms The largest law firm is Baker & McKenzie, employing 1739 lawyers, 519 of whom are partners, in 33 countries in February 1995. It also has the highest revenues, with $512 million in 1993. The firm was founded in Chicago, Illinois, USA in 1949.

Crime

Largest criminal organizations In terms of profit, the largest syndicate of organized crime is believed to be the Mafia, which has its origins in Sicily and dates from the 13th century, and which has infiltrated the executive, judiciary and legislature of the United States. It consists of some 3000 to 5000 individuals in 25 'families' federated under 'The Commission', with an annual turnover in vice, gambling, protection rackets, tobacco, bootlegging, hijacking, narcotics, loan-sharking and prostitution which was estimated by *US News & World Report* in December 1982 at $200 billion, with a profit estimated in March 1986 by the Attorney Rudolph Giuliani at $75 billion.

Guess What?
Q. How long was the prison sentence given to Chamoy Thipyaso?
A. See Page 191

In terms of numbers, the Yamaguchi-gumi gang of the *yakuza* in Japan has 30,000 members. There are some 90,000 *yakuza* or gangsters altogether, in more than 3000 groups. They go about their business openly and even advertize for recruits. On 1 Mar 1992 new laws were brought in to combat their activities, which include drug trafficking, smuggling, prostitution and gambling.

Assassinations The most frequently assassinated heads of state in modern times have been the Tsars of Russia. In the two hundred years from 1718 to 1918 four Tsars and two heirs apparent were assassinated, and there were many other unsuccessful attempts.

The target of the highest number of *failed* assassination attempts on an individual head of state in modern times was Charles de Gaulle (1890–1970), President of France from 1958 to 1969. He was reputed to have survived no fewer than 31 plots against his life between 1944, when the shadow government which he had formed returned to Paris from Algeria, and 1966 (although some plots were foiled before culminating in actual physical attacks).

Most prolific murderers It was established at the trial of Behram, the Indian Thug, that he had strangled at least 931 victims with his yellow and white cloth strip or *ruhmal* in the Oudh district between 1790 and 1840. It has been estimated that at least 2,000,000 Indians were strangled by Thugs (*burtotes*) during the reign of the Thugee (pronounced tugee) cult from 1550 until its final suppression by the British raj in 1853.

20th century A total of 592 deaths was attributed to one Colombian bandit leader, Teófilo ('Sparks') Rojas, between 1948 and his death in an ambush near Armenia, Colombia on 22 Jan 1963. Some sources attribute 3500 slayings to him during *La Violencia* of 1945–62.

In a drunken rampage lasting 8 hours on 26–27 Apr 1982, policeman Wou Bom-kon, 27, killed 57 people and wounded 35 with 176 rounds of rifle ammunition and hand grenades in the Kyong Sang-namdo province of South Korea. He blew himself up with a grenade.

United Kingdom The biggest murder in the UK this century was committed by the unknown person or people who planted the bomb on Pan Am flight PA103, which crashed over Lockerbie, Dumfries & Galloway on 21 Dec 1988, killing a total of 270 people (259 in the aeroplane and 11 on the ground).

Mary Ann Cotton (*née* Robson) (b. 1832 at East Rainton, Co. Durham), hanged in Durham Jail on 24 Mar 1873, is believed to have poisoned 14, possibly 20, people with arsenic, including her husbands and her children. She was, however, only convicted of one murder.

> **The most prolific substantiated serial killers in the UK were William Burke and William Hare, who murdered 16 people in Edinburgh in 1827–8 in order to sell their bodies to the anatomist Dr Robert Knox.**

Dennis Andrew Nilsen (b. 1948), then of 23 Cranley Gardens, Muswell Hill, north London, admitted to 15 one-at-a-time murders between December 1978 and February 1983. He was sentenced to life imprisonment, with a 25-year minimum, on 4 Nov 1983 at the Old Bailey by Mr Justice Croom-Johnson for six murders and two attempted murders.

Dominic 'Mad Dog' McGlinchey (1955–94) admitted in a press interview in November 1983 to at least 30 killings in Northern Ireland. He was jailed for 10 years at Dublin's Special Criminal Court on 11 Mar 1986 for shooting with intent to resist arrest in Co. Clare, Republic of Ireland on 17 Mar 1984, but was released on 5 Mar 1993 having served just under seven years.

> **There are believed to be more than 250,000 members of Chinese triad societies worldwide, but they are fragmented into many groups which often fight each other and compete in disputed areas. Hong Kong alone has some 100,000 members.**

On 7 May 1981 John Thompson of Hackney, London was found guilty at the Old Bailey of the

'specimen' murder by arson of Archibald Campbell and jailed for life. There were 36 other victims at the Spanish Club, Denmark Street, London.

Thomas Cooper, who was born in London on 29 Aug 1919 and joined the *Waffen-SS* in Germany in 1939, once boasted to another British SS member that he had personally 'shot over 200 Poles and 80 Jews in one day'. However, no records were kept and his involvement in crimes against humanity have never been officially investigated.

Robbery The greatest robbery on record was that of the Reichsbank following Germany's collapse in April–May 1945. The Pentagon in Washington described the event, first published in *The Guinness Book of Records* in 1957, as 'an unverified allegation'. However *Nazi Gold* by Ian Sayer and Douglas Botting, published in 1984, finally revealed full details and estimated that the total haul would have been equivalent to £2.5 billion at 1984 values.

The government of the Philippines announced on 23 Apr 1986 that it had succeeded in identifying $860.8 million 'salted' by the former President Ferdinand Edralin Marcos (1917–89) and his wife Imelda. The total national loss from November 1965 was believed to be $5–10 billion.

Poison

On 1 May 1981 an 8-year-old boy became the first of more than 600 victims of the Spanish cooking oil scandal. On 12 June it was discovered that his cause of death was the use of 'denatured' industrial colza from rape seed. The trial of 38 defendants, including the manufacturers Ramón and Elías Ferrero, lasted from 30 Mar 1987 to 28 Jun 1988. The 586 counts on which the prosecution demanded jail sentences totalled 60,000 years.

Treasury Bills and certificates of deposit worth £292 million were stolen when a mugger attacked a money-broker's messenger in the City of London on 2 May 1990. As details of the documents stolen were quickly flashed on the City's market dealing screens and given to central banks world-wide, the chances of anyone being able to benefit from the theft were considered to be very remote.

The robbery in the Knightsbridge Safety Deposit Centre, London on 12 Jul 1987 was estimated at £30 million by the Metropolitan Police and has been said to be nearer to £60 million by the robbers themselves. Of the 126 boxes broken into, property was stolen from 113. The managing director Parvez Latif, 30, was among those charged on 17 Aug 1987.

It is arguable that the Mona Lisa, though never valued, is the most valuable object ever stolen. It disappeared from the Louvre, Paris on 21 Aug 1911. It was recovered in Italy in 1913, when Vincenzo Perugia was charged with its theft.

On 24 Dec 1985 a total of 140 'priceless' gold, jade and obsidian artifacts were stolen from the National Museum of Anthropology, Mexico City. The majority of the stolen objects were recovered in June 1989 from the Mexico City home of a man described by officials as the mastermind of the theft.

Bank During the extreme civil disorder prior to 22 Jan 1976 in Beirut, Lebanon, a guerrilla force blasted the vaults of the British Bank of the Middle East in Bab Idriss and cleared out safe deposit boxes with contents valued by former Finance Minister Lucien Dahdah at $50 million and by another source at an 'absolute minimum' of $20 million.

Train The greatest recorded train robbery occurred between 3:03 a.m. and 3:27 a.m. on 8 Aug 1963, when a General Post Office mail train from Glasgow, Strathclyde was ambushed at Sears Crossing and robbed at Bridego Bridge near Mentmore, Bucks. The gang escaped with about 120 mailbags containing £2,631,784 worth of banknotes being taken to London for destruction. Only £343,448 was recovered.

Jewels The greatest recorded theft of jewels was from the Carlton Hotel in Cannes, France, when gems with an estimated value of FF 250 million (£30 million) were stolen from the jewellery shop by a three-man gang on 11 Aug 1994. A security guard was seriously injured in the raid.

Largest object stolen by a single man On a moonless night at dead calm high water on 5 Jun 1966, armed with only a sharp axe, N. William Kennedy slashed free the mooring lines of the 10,639-dwt SS *Orient Trader*, owned by Steel Factors Ltd of Ontario, at Wolfe's Cove, St Lawrence Seaway, Canada. The vessel drifted to a waiting blacked-out tug, thus evading a ban on any shipping movements during a violent wildcat waterfront strike. It then sailed for Spain.

Evening Standard

WEST END FINAL

£2,525,100! AND IT'S STILL GOING UP

The soaring total of the stolen notes would tower above the Vickers skyscraper

Rewards: £260,000 — and they're breaking all records too

THE DUKE OF ARGYLL MARRIES IN SECRET

Art On 14 Apr 1991 twenty paintings, estimated to be worth $500 million, were stolen from the Van Gogh Museum in Amsterdam, Netherlands. However, only 35 minutes later they were found in an abandoned car not far from the museum. Just over a year earlier, on 18 Mar 1990, eleven paintings by Rembrandt, Vermeer, Degas, Manet and Flinck, plus a Chinese bronze beaker of about 1200 BC and a finial in the form of an eagle, worth in total an estimated $200 million, had been stolen from the Isabella Stewart Gardner Museum in Boston, Massachusetts, USA. Unlike the Van Gogh paintings, these have not been recovered in the meantime.

■ London's Evening Standard updates readers on the greatest train robbery ever committed. The total amount stolen was actually over £100,000 more than was thought at the time.

(Photo: Courtesy of Evening Standard)

Kidnapped!

Greatest kidnapping ransom Historically the greatest ransom paid was that for Atahualpa by the Incas to Francisco Pizarro in 1532–3 at Cajamarca, Peru, which constituted a hall full of gold and silver, worth in modern money some $1.5 billion.

The greatest ransom ever reported in modern times is 1500 million pesos ($60 million) for the release of the brothers Jorge Born, 40, and Juan Born, 39, of the family firm Bunge and Born, paid to the left-wing urban guerrilla group Montoneros in Buenos Aires, Argentina on 20 Jun 1975.

Crime prevention
A team of ten, consisting of representatives from Lancashire Constabulary, a local cycle shop and local schools, succeeded in postcoding 841 bicycles in four hours at Beaumont College, Lancaster on 16 Apr 1994.

Largest narcotics haul The greatest drug haul in terms of value was achieved on 28 Sep 1989, when cocaine with an estimated street value of $6–7 billion was seized in a raid on a warehouse in Los Angeles, California, USA. The haul of 20 tonnes was prompted by a tip-off from a local resident who had complained about heavy lorry traffic and people leaving the warehouse 'at odd hours and in a suspicious manner'.

The greatest haul in terms of weight was by the authorities in Bilo, Pakistan on 23 Oct 1991. The seizure comprised 38.9 tonnes *85,846 lb* of hashish and 3.23 tonnes *7128 lb* of heroin.

In Britain, cocaine with a value of £250 million and weighing 1.3 tonnes was seized at Birkenhead, Merseyside on 24 Jan 1994 after a Polish-American ship, the *Jurata*, arrived there on its way from Venezuela to Poland. The cocaine was hidden in a consignment of bitumen.

The largest quantity of drugs seized in one operation by weight was from the *Britannia Gazelle*, a British-registered oil rig support ship. The vessel had been boarded in the North Sea on 20 Nov 1992 and brought back to Hull, Humberside where more than 1000 sacks containing a total of 20 tonnes of cannabis were recovered the next day.

Largest narcotics operation The bulkiest drugs seizure was 2903 tonnes of Colombian marijuana in a 14-month-long project codenamed 'Operation Tiburon', carried out by the Drug Enforcement Administration and Colombian authorities. The arrest of 495 people and the seizure of 95 vessels was announced on 5 Feb 1982.

Fingerprints The first effective system of identification by fingerprints—the science of dactylography—was instituted in 1896 by Edward Henry, an inspector-general of police in British India, who eventually became Commissioner of Metropolitan Police in London. The first large scale murder hunt relying on fingerprints was carried out in 1948, when more than 46,000 sets of prints—those of almost the entire adult male population of Blackburn, Lancs—were examined in tracing Peter Griffiths as the killer of 3-year-old June Devaney, whom he had abducted from Queen's Park Hospital after leaving his prints on a bottle beside the child's hospital cot.

Biggest bank fraud The Banca Nazionale del Lavoro, Italy's leading bank, admitted on 6 Sep 1989 that it had been defrauded of a huge amount of funds, subsequently estimated to be in the region of $5 billion, with the disclosure that its branch in Atlanta, Georgia, USA had made unauthorized loan commitments to Iraq. Both the bank's chairman, Nerio Nesi, and its director general, Giacomo Pedde, resigned following the revelation.

Guess What?

Q. Why might it have been appropriate for Snag to be in Bilo in October 1991?

A. See Page 32

Forged

Greatest banknote forgery The greatest forgery was the German Third Reich's forging operation, code name 'Operation Bernhard', run by Major Bernhard Krüger during World War II. It involved more than £130 million worth of British notes in denominations of £5, £10, £20 and £50. They were produced by 140 Jewish prisoners at Sachsenhausen concentration camp.

Fines

Heaviest fines The largest fine ever was one of $650 million, which was imposed on the US securities house Drexel Burnham Lambert in December 1988 for insider trading. This figure represented $300 million in direct fines, with the balance to be put into an account to satisfy claims of parties that could prove they were defrauded by Drexel's actions.

The record for an individual is $200 million, which Michael Milken agreed to pay on 24 Apr 1990. In addition, he agreed to settle civil charges filed by the Securities and Exchange Commission. The payments were in settlement of a criminal racketeering and securities fraud suit brought by the US government. He was released from a 10-year prison sentence in January 1993.

United Kingdom The heaviest fine ever imposed in the UK was £5 million on Gerald Ronson (b. 26 May 1939), the head of Heron International, announced on 28 Aug 1990 at Southwark Crown Court, London. Ronson was one of four defendants in the Guinness case concerning the company's takeover bid for Distillers.

The highest fine ever imposed on a UK company was 32 million ECUs (equivalent to £24.3 million) on British Steel by the European Commission on 16 Feb 1994 for colluding in price-fixing in the 1980s.

Capital Punishment

The discovery of Tollund man in a bog near Silkeborg, Denmark in 1950 showed that capital punishment dates at least from the Iron Age. The countries in which capital punishment is still prevalent include China, Iran, Iraq, Saudi Arabia, Malaysia, USA (36 states) and some of the independent countries which were formerly in the USSR. Capital punishment was first abolished *de facto* in 1798 in Liechtenstein.

Capital punishment in the British Isles had been widely practised up until the reign of William I (1066–87), but was virtually abolished by him. It was then brought back for murder and a growing number of other crimes by Henry I in the next century. It reached a peak in the reign of Edward VI (1547–53), when an average of 560 persons were executed annually at Tyburn (near the point where Marble Arch now stands, in London) alone. It has been estimated that as many as 50,000 people may have been done to death at Tyburn by the time the last execution took place there in 1783.

Largest hanging The most people hanged from one gallows were 38 Sioux Indians by William J. Duly outside Mankato, Minnesota, USA on 26 Dec 1862 for the murder of a number of unarmed citizens. The Nazi Feldkommandant simultaneously hanged 50 Greek resistance men as a reprisal measure in Athens on 22 Jul 1944.

Last hangings The last public execution in England took place outside Newgate Prison, London at 8 a.m. on 26 May 1868, when Michael Barrett was hanged for his part in the Fenian bomb outrage on 13 Dec 1867, when 12 were killed outside the Clerkenwell House of Detention, London.

The last executions in the UK were those of Peter Anthony Allen (b. 4 Apr 1943), hanged at Walton Prison, Liverpool by Robert L. Stewart, and of John Robson Walby (b. 1 Apr 1940), alias Gwynne Owen Evans, by Harry B. Allen at Strangeways Gaol, Manchester, both on 13 Aug 1964. They had been found guilty of the capital murder of John Alan West on 7 April 1964.

The last public hanging in the United States occurred at Owensboro, Kentucky on 14 Aug 1936, when Rainey Bethea was executed in the presence of a crowd of more than 10,000. The following year a 'private' hanging was performed which was actually witnessed by some 500 people although the number

of official witnesses was limited to just 12—Roscoe 'Red' Jackson was hanged on 21 May 1937 at Galena, Missouri.

Youngest people hanged The lowest reliably recorded age was of a girl aged seven, hanged at King's Lynn, Norfolk in 1808. In Britain the death penalty for persons under 16 was excluded in the Children Act of 1908, although no person under that age had been executed for many years prior to this.

Oldest people hanged In 1843 Allan Mair was executed at Stirling, Central for murder. He was 82, and was hanged sitting in a chair as he was incapable of standing up. The oldest person hanged in the UK this century was a man of 71 named Charles Frembd (*sic*) at Chelmsford Gaol on 4 Nov 1914, for the murder of his wife at Leytonstone, London.

Hanging in chains The last recorded use of a gibbet occurred at Leicester in August 1832, when a local bookbinder, James Cook, was hanged for murder, and his corpse suspended in iron hoops, 10 m *33 ft* above the ground, with the head shaved and tarred.

Witchcraft The last legal execution of a witch was that of Anna Göldi at Glarus, Switzerland on 18 Jun 1782. It is estimated that at least 200,000 witches were executed during the European witchcraze of the 16th and 17th centuries.

> The last person executed in Britain for witchcraft was Jenny Horn, burned alive at Dornoch, Highland in 1722.

Burning The last case of execution by burning in Britain occurred in March 1789, when a woman named Murphy was 'burnt with fire until she was dead' outside Newgate Prison, London. This punishment, reserved for women convicted of coining or petit treason (murder of a husband), was abolished in the following year.

Boiling to death In 1530, John Roose, a cook, became the first person to be executed in England under a new law of Henry VIII whereby any person convicted of poisoning was to be judged guilty of high treason and executed in this cruel manner. Roose had killed two members of the Bishop of Rochester's household by poison.

Last death sentences The last person to be sentenced to death in the British Isles was Tony Teare, 22, who was convicted at Douglas, Isle of Man of murdering a 22-year-old woman, Corinne Bentley, and sentenced on 10 Jul 1992 to be hanged. The sentence was duly commuted to life imprisonment, and later that year the Manx parliament formally abolished the death penalty on the island, the last part of the British Isles to do so.

Last beheadings The last person to be publicly guillotined in France was the murderer Eugen Weidmann, before a large crowd at Versailles, near Paris at 4:50 a.m. on 17 Jun 1939. The last use of the guillotine before abolition on 9 Sep 1981 was on 10 Sep 1977 at Baumettes Prison, Marseille, for torturer and murderer Hamida Djandoubi, aged 28.

Death Row

The longest sojourn on Death Row was the 39 years of Sadamichi Hirasawa (1893–1987) in Sendai Jail, Japan. He was convicted in 1948 of poisoning 12 bank employees with potassium cyanide to effect a theft of £100, and died aged 94. On 31 Oct 1987 Liong Wie Tong, 52, and Tan Tian Tjoen, 62, were executed for robbery and murder by firing squad in Jakarta, Indonesia after 25 years on Death Row.

The last man to be executed by beheading in Britain was Simon Fraser, Lord Lovat, who was beheaded in his eightieth year on Tower Hill, London on 7 Apr 1747, for his part in the Jacobite rebellion.

Busiest prison The prison in which most death sentences have been carried out in Britain is Wandsworth, London. Between 1878, when Wandsworth became the hanging prison for London south of the Thames, and 1965, when the death penalty was abolished, 134 executions took place there.

Executioners For 55 years from 1901 to the resignation of Albert Pierrepoint in February 1956, the Pierrepoint family largely monopolized the task of executing murderers in Britain. Henry Albert Pierrepoint officiated from 1901 to 1910. The longest-serving of the Pierrepoints was his elder brother Thomas, who was in action from 1906 to 1946. Albert (1905–92), son of Henry, himself claimed to have officiated at the hanging of 550 men and women in several countries, including a record 27 war criminals in one day in Germany.

The longest period of office of a public executioner was that of William Calcraft (1800–79), who was in action from 1829 to 25 May 1874 and officiated at nearly every hanging outside and later inside Newgate Prison, London.

The oldest active executioner in British history was John Murdoch, who was already 64 when he was retained as an assistant hangman in Scotland in 1831. He carried out his last execution in Glasgow twenty years later, aged 84, and was able to mount the scaffold only with the aid of a staff.

> A sentence of 384,912 years was *demanded* at the prosecution of Gabriel March Grandos, 22, at Palma de Mallorca, Spain on 11 Mar 1972 for failing to deliver 42,768 letters, or 9 years per letter.

Prison Sentences

Longest sentences Chamoy Thipyaso, a Thai woman known as the queen of underground investing, and seven of her associates were each jailed for 141,078 years by the Bangkok Criminal Court, Thailand on 27 Jul 1989 for swindling the public through a multi-million dollar deposit-taking business.

The longest sentence imposed on a mass murderer was 21 consecutive life sentences and 12 death sentences in the case of John Gacy, who killed 33 boys and young men between 1972 and 1978 in Illinois, USA. He was sentenced by a jury in Chicago, Illinois on 13 Mar 1980, and was eventually executed on 10 May 1994.

Charles-Henri Sanson, known as *Monsieur de Paris*, has the unhappy distinction of having executed more people than anyone else in history, his total number of victims being more than 3000. Born in 1739, he was the son, grandson and great-grandson of executioners, and when he was as young as 15 he assisted his father, eventually taking over from him as chief executioner on his death in 1778.

When the guillotine was introduced to replace the sword as the method of beheading people, it was Sanson who performed the first execution with it on 25 Apr 1792 at the Place de Grève in Paris.

As the French Revolution developed and the period known as *The Terror* emerged, Sanson became such an expert with the guillotine—or *National Razor* as it became popularly known—that he could execute his victims at the rate of one a minute. He kept records of the numbers he dealt with: 'Seventeen persons were sentenced to death yesterday. I executed them this morning... The women were in a majority. Several of these women had their children in the carts.' Another entry simply said 'Fifty-four victims'.

Sanson's victims included the queen, Marie Antoinette, and the king, Louis XVI. It is also said that Napoleon once asked Sanson if he would be prepared to execute him if necessary. His reply was 'Sire, *I* executed Louis XVI!'

Before his victims were buried, Sanson made the severed heads of some of them available to a young sculptress by the name of Marie Grozholtz. She made effigies of famous people and became, on her marriage in 1795, Madame Tussaud. Who at the time could have imagined how famous her name would be 200 years later?

Off *with his head!*

Guess What?

Q. When Sylvain Dornon left Paris walking on stilts, what was his destination?

A. See Page 210

(Photo: AKG London)

Kevin Mulgrew from the Ardoyne district of Belfast was sentenced on 5 Aug 1983 to life imprisonment for the murder of Sergeant Julian Connolley of the Ulster Defence Regiment. In addition he was given a further 963 years to be served concurrently on 84 other serious charges, including 13 conspiracies to murder and 8 attempted murders.

The longest single period served by a reprieved murderer in Great Britain this century is 42 years 9 months up to 30 Apr 1995, by John Thomas Straffen, who was convicted at Winchester on 25 Jul 1952 of the murder of Linda Bowyer, aged 5, and sentenced to death. Straffen had escaped from Broadmoor, and was reprieved on account of his mental abnormality, but was not judged insane, and has been in prison ever since.

Longest time served Paul Geidel (1894–1987) was convicted of second-degree murder on 5 Sep 1911 when a 17-year-old porter in a hotel in New York, USA. He was released from the Fishkill Correctional Facility, Beacon, New York aged 85 on 7 May 1980, having served 68 years 8 months and 2 days—the longest recorded term in US history. He first refused parole in 1974.

Oldest prisoner Bill Wallace (1881–1989) was the oldest prisoner on record, spending the last 63 years of his life in Aradale Psychiatric Hospital, at Ararat, Victoria, Australia. He had shot and killed a man at a restaurant in Melbourne, Victoria in December 1925, and having been found unfit to plead, was transferred to the responsibility of the Mental Health Department in February 1926. He remained at Aradale until his death on 17 Jul 1989, shortly before his 108th birthday.

Bill Wallace, the oldest prisoner on record, when asked why he was in prison, responded:– 'There was a man... Well, to tell you the truth, I don't know'.

Blasphemy The last persons imprisoned for blasphemy in Great Britain were G.W. Foote, H.A. Kemp and W.J. Ramsey, the editor, printer and sales manager of *The Freethinker*, who were sentenced to one year, three months and nine months respectively in 1883, for publishing a cartoon of the Hebrew deity 'to the scandal of the Christian religion, and the high displeasure of Almighty God'.

Arresting

A record for arrests was set by Tommy Johns (1922–88) in Brisbane, Queensland, Australia on 9 Sep 1982 when he faced his 2000th conviction for drunkenness since 1957. His total at the time of his last drink on 30 Apr 1988 was 'nearly 3000'.

Greatest mass arrests The greatest mass arrest reported in a democratic country was of 15,617 demonstrators on 11 Jul 1988, rounded up by South Korean police to ensure security in advance of the 1988 Olympic Games in Seoul.

The largest in the UK occurred on 17 Sep 1961, when 1314 demonstrators supporting unilateral nuclear disarmament were arrested for obstructing highways leading to Parliament Square, London by sitting down. As a consequence of the 1926 General Strike there were 3149 prosecutions, for incitement (1760) and violence (1389).

Prisons

Largest prisons The largest prison ever built in Britain, and the first to be built and run by the state instead of local authorities, was Millbank Penitentiary in London. Completed in 1821, it covered 3 ha 7 acres

of ground and had 5 km *3 miles* of passages. It was closed in 1890 as an expensive failure, and demolished in 1903. The site is now partly occupied by the Tate Gallery. The most capacious prison in Great Britain is Wandsworth, south London, with a certified normal accommodation of 1216. A peak occupancy of 1556 was reached on 17 Aug 1990.

Highest population Some human rights organizations have estimated that there are 20 million prisoners in China, which would be equal to 1677 per 100,000 population, although this figure is not officially acknowledged. Among countries for which statistics are available, that with the highest per capita prison population is the USA, with 389 prisoners per 100,000 people.

Prison fatalities The largest number of prison fatalities in one incident occurred at Fort William, Calcutta, India, on the night of 20 Jun 1756, when 146 people—145 men and 1 woman—were locked in a military prison cell measuring 5.5 × 4.25 m *18 × 14 ft* by order of Surajah Dowlah, Nawab of Bengal. By 6 a.m. next morning, when the cell was opened, only 22 men and the woman were left alive, leaving 123 dead. Most of the victims died from suffocation or by being crushed to death.

Most expensive prison Spandau Prison, in Berlin, Germany originally built in 1887 for 600 prisoners, was used solely for the Nazi war criminal Rudolf Hess (1894–1987) for the last twenty years of his life. The cost of maintenance of the staff of 105—from the four occupying powers, namely France, the United Kingdom, the USA and the USSR—was estimated in 1976 to be $415,000 per annum. On 19 Aug 1987 it was announced that Hess had strangled himself two days earlier with a piece of electrical flex and that he had left a note in old German script. Shortly afterwards the prison was demolished.

Longest prison escape The longest recorded escape by a recaptured prisoner was that of Leonard T. Fristoe, 77, who escaped from Nevada State Prison, USA on 15 Dec 1923 and was turned in by his son on 15 Nov 1969 at Compton, California. He had had 46 years of freedom under the name of Claude R. Willis. He had killed two sheriff's deputies in 1920.

Most labour camp escapes A former Soviet citizen Tatyana Mikhailovna Russanova, now living in Haifa, Israel, escaped from various Stalin labour camps in the former Soviet Union on 15 occasions between 1943 and 1954, being recaptured and sentenced 14 times. All of the escapes are judicially recognized by independent Russian lawyers, although only nine are recognized by Soviet Supreme Court officials.

Greatest gaol break On 11 Feb 1979 an Iranian employee of the Electronic Data Systems Corporation led a mob into Gasr prison, Tehran, Iran in an effort to rescue two Americans colleagues, although the rest of the mob were not looking for the Americans. Some 11,000 other prisoners took advantage of this and the Islamic revolution in what became history's largest ever gaol break. Although it was the Iranian whose actions actually enabled the gaol break to happen, the plan to get the Americans out was masterminded by H. Ross Perot, their employer. Over 10 years later he was to make the news again when he stood for US president in 1992.

The greatest gaol break in the UK was that from the Maze Prison on 25 Sep 1983, when 38 IRA prisoners escaped from Block H-7.

In September 1971 Raúl Sendic and 105 other Tupamaro guerillas, plus five non-political prisoners, escaped from a Uruguayan prison through a tunnel 91 m 298 ft long.

Honours, Decorations and Awards

Oldest order The earliest honour known was the 'Gold of Honour' for extraordinary valour awarded in the 18th Dynasty c. 1440–1400 BC. A statuette was found at Qan-el-Kebri, Egypt. The oldest true order was the Order of St John of Jerusalem (the direct descendant of which is the Sovereign Military Order of Malta), legitimized in 1113.

Victoria Cross *Double awards* The only three men ever to have been awarded a bar to the Victoria Cross (instituted 29 Jan 1856) are:

Surg.-Capt. (later Lt-Col.) Arthur Martin-Leake VC*, VD, RAMC (1874–1953) (1902 and bar 1914).

Capt. Noel Godfrey Chavasse VC*, MC, RAMC (1884–1917) (1916 and bar posthumously 1917).

Second-Lt. (later Capt.) Charles Hazlitt Upham VC*, NZMF (1908–94) (1941 and bar 1942).

The most VCs awarded in a war were the 634 in World War I (1914–18). The greatest number gained exclusively in a single action was 11 at Rorke's Drift in the Zulu War on 22–23 Jan 1879.

Youngest The earliest established age for a VC is 15 years 100 days for hospital apprentice Andrew (wrongly gazetted as Arthur) Fitzgibbon (b. 13 May 1845 at Peteragurh, northern India) of the Indian Medical Services for bravery at the Taku Forts in northern China on 21 Aug 1860. The youngest living VC is Capt. Rambahadur Limbu (b. 1 Nov 1939 at Chyangthapu, Nepal) of the 10th Princess Mary's Own Gurkha Rifles. The award was for his courage as a Lance Corporal while fighting in Indonesian Borneo on 21 Nov 1965.

Oldest Capt. William Raynor was the oldest person to receive the medal. It was awarded when he was 62, for the part he played in blowing up an arms store besieged by insurgents on 11 May 1857, the second day of the Indian Mutiny.

Longest-lived The longest-lived of all the 1351 recipients of the Victoria Cross has been Lt-Col. Harcus Strachan. He was born in Bo'ness, West Lothian on 7 Nov 1884 and died in Vancouver, British Columbia, Canada on 1 May 1982 aged 97 years 175 days.

Record price The highest price ever paid for a Victoria Cross was £132,000 for the VC—and other medals—awarded to Major Edward 'Mick' Mannock (⇔ Top-scoring air aces) posthumously in 1919, in recognition of bravery of the first order in aerial combat. It was sold to a private collector at Billingshurst, W Sussex on 19 Sep 1992.

In 1955 the highest price ever paid for a medal group (primarily the Victoria Cross) was £300. The record now is £132,000, again for a VC plus other medals.

The record for a George Cross is £20,250 at Christie's on 14 Mar 1985, for that of Sgt Michael Willets (3rd Battalion Parachute Regiment), killed by an IRA bomb in Ulster in 1971.

Youngest awards Kristina Stragauskaite of Skirmantiskes, Lithuania was awarded a medal 'For Courage in Fire' when she was just 4 years 252 days old. She had saved the lives of her younger brother and sister

■ Charles Upham is one of only three double Victoria Cross holders, and the only fighting soldier. In this photograph he is seen at Kreikouki, Crete after receiving his first VC in 1941. The second award was for bravery in Egypt in 1942. Upham maintained that his VCs were a recognition of the achievements of all his fellow New Zealanders who had fought in the conflict.
(Photo: Courtesy of the High Commissioner of New Zealand)

Order of Merit The Order of Merit (instituted on 23 Jun 1902) is limited to 24 members at any one time. The longest-lived of the 162 holders has been the Rt Hon. Bertrand Arthur William Russell, 3rd Earl Russell, who died on 2 Feb 1970 aged 97 years 260 days. The oldest recipient was Dame Ninette de Valois (b. 6 Jun 1898), who received the Order at the age of 94 years 179 days on 2 Dec 1992. The youngest recipient has been HRH the Duke of Edinburgh, who was appointed on his 47th birthday on 10 Jun 1968.

Most valuable annual prize The most valuable annual prize is the Louis Jeantet Prize for Medicine, which in 1995 was worth SFr 2,100,000 (equivalent to approximately £1,150,000). It was first awarded in 1986 and is intended to 'provide substantial funds for the support of biomedical research projects'.

(Stalin Peak), although it was renamed in 1962. In addition numerous enterprises, schools, institutes and theatres were named after him, as were 15 Soviet towns or cities. The last statue of Stalin was demolished in 1992 in Ulan Bator, the capital of Mongolia.

Most honorary degrees The greatest number of honorary degrees awarded to any individual is 130, given to Rev. Father Theodore M. Hesburgh (b. 25 May 1917), president of the University of Notre Dame, Indiana, USA. These have been accumulated since 1954.

The Royal Society The longest term as a Fellow of the Royal Society (founded 1660) has been 68 years in the case of Sir Hans Sloane (1660–1753), who was elected in 1685. The longest-lived Fellow was Sir Rickard Christophers (1873–1978), who died aged 104 years 84 days. The youngest Fellow is believed to have been Sir Joseph Hodges, who was born c. 1704 and elected on 5 Apr 1716 at about 12 years of age. The oldest person to have been elected as a Fellow was Sir Rupert Edward Cecil Lee Guinness, the 2nd Earl of Iveagh (1874–1967), who was elected in 1964 at the age of 90.

Erasmus Darwin was elected on 9 Apr 1761 and was followed by his son Robert (1788 to 1848), *his* son Charles (1839 to 1882), his sons Sir George (1879 to 1912), Francis (1882 to 1925) and Horace (1903 to 1928) and Sir George's son Sir Charles (1922 to 1962), so spanning over 200 years with five generations.

when a fire had broken out on 7 April 1989 in the family's home while her parents were out. The award was decreed by the Presidium of the then Lithuanian Soviet Socialist Republic.

The youngest person to have received an official gallantry award is Julius Rosenberg of Winnipeg, Canada, who was given the Medal of Bravery on 30 Mar 1994 for foiling a black bear which had attacked his 3-year-old sister on 20 Sep 1992. Aged five at the time of the incident, he managed to save his sister by growling at the bear.

Most lifeboat medals Sir William Hillary (1771–1847), founder of the Royal National Lifeboat Institution in 1824, was personally and uniquely awarded four RNLI Gold Medals, in 1825, 1828 and 1830 (twice).

Lifesaving The greatest rescue in Britain was on 17 Mar 1907, when four lifeboats lifted 456 shipwreck survivors to safety off the Lizard, Cornwall.

> The greatest number of awards gained by a member of the Royal Life Saving Society is 224 by Eric Deakin of Hightown, Lancs since 1960.

Most post-nominal letters HRH the Duke of Windsor (1894–1972) when Prince of Wales had 10 sets and was also a privy counsellor, viz. KG, PC, KT, KP, GCB, GCSI, GCMG, GCIE, GCVO, GBE, MC. He later appended the ISO but never did so in the cases of the OM, CH or DSO, of which orders he had also been sovereign. Lord Roberts, who was also a privy counsellor, was the only non-royal holder of eight sets of *official* post-nominal letters.

Civilian gallantry Reginald H. Blanchford of Guernsey has received the following awards for life saving on land and at sea: MBE for gallantry in 1950; Queen's Commendation in 1957; Life Saving Medal of The Order of St John in Gold in 1957 with gold bar in 1963; George Medal in 1958; Carnegie Hero Fund's Bronze Medallion in 1959; OBE 1961. He was made a Knight of Grace of The Order of St John in 1970 and most recently received the American Biographical Institute's Silver Shield of Valor in 1992.

Nobel Prizes

Earliest 1901 for Physics, Chemistry, Physiology or Medicine, Literature and Peace.

Most Prizes USA has won 220, outright or shared, including most for Physiology or Medicine (72); Physics (58); Chemistry (39), Peace (18); Economics (22). France has most for Literature (12). The United Kingdom total is 90, outright or shared, comprising Chemistry (23); Physiology or Medicine (23); Physics (20); Peace (10); Literature (8); Economics (6).

Oldest Laureate Professor Francis Peyton Rous (US) (1879–1970) in 1966 shared in the Physiology or Medicine prize at the age of 87.

Youngest Laureates *At time of award:* Professor Sir Lawrence Bragg (1890–1971) 1915 Physics prize at 25. *At time of work:* Bragg, and Theodore W. Richards (US) (1868–1928), 1914 Chemistry prize for work done when 23.

Most 3 Awards: International Committee of the Red Cross, Geneva (founded 1863) Peace 1917, 1944 and 1963 (shared); 2 Awards: Dr Linus Carl Pauling (US) (1901–94) Chemistry 1954 and Peace 1962; Mme Marja Sklodowska Curie (Polish-French) (1867–1934) Physics 1903 (shared) and Chemistry 1911; Professor John Bardeen (US) (1908–91) Physics 1956 (shared) and 1972 (shared); Professor Frederick Sanger (b. 13 Aug 1918) Chemistry 1958 and 1980 (shared); Office of the United Nations' High Commissioner for Refugees, Geneva (founded 1951) Peace 1954 and 1981.

Highest Prize Swedish Krona 7,200,000 (for 1995), equivalent to £603,000.

Lowest Prize Swedish Krona 115,000 (for 1923), equivalent to £6620.

Peerage

Longest-lived peer The longest-lived peer ever recorded was the Rt Hon. Emanuel Shinwell (1884–1986), who was created a life baron in 1970 and died on 8 May 1986 aged 101 years 202 days. The oldest peeress recorded was the Countess Desmond, who was alleged to be 140 when she died in 1604. This claim is patently exaggerated but it is accepted that she may have been 104. Currently the oldest peer is the Rt Hon. Jeffery Amherst, 5th Earl Amherst (b. 13 Dec 1896).

Youngest peers Twelve Dukes of Cornwall became (in accordance with the grant by the Crown in Parliament) peers at birth as the eldest sons of a sovereign; and the 9th Earl of Chichester inherited his earldom at his birth on 14 Apr 1944, 54 days after his father's death. The youngest age at which a person has had a peerage conferred on him is 7 days old in the case of the Earldom of Chester on HRH the Prince George (later George IV) on 19 Aug 1762.

Longest peerage The longest tenure of a peerage has been 87 years 10 days in the case of Charles St Clair, Lord Sinclair, born 30 Jul 1768, succeeded 16 Dec 1775 and died aged 94 years 243 days on 30 Mar 1863.

The shortest enjoyment of a peerage was the 'split second' by which the law assumes that the Hon. Wilfrid Carlyl Stamp), the 2nd Baron Stamp, survived his father, Josiah Charles Stamp, the 1st Baron Stamp, when both were killed as a result of German bombing of London on 16 Apr 1941. Apart from this legal fiction, the shortest recorded peerage was one of 30 minutes in the case of Charles Brandon, the 3rd Duke of Suffolk, who died aged 13 or 14 just after succeeding his brother Henry, when both were suffering a fatal illness, at Buckden, Cambs on 14 Jul 1551.

Most statues The world record for raising statues to oneself was set by Joseph Vissarionovich Dzhugashvili, alias Stalin (1879–1953), the leader of the Soviet Union from 1924–53. It is estimated that at the time of his death there were c. 6000 statues to him throughout the USSR and in many cities in eastern Europe. The country's highest mountain was named Pik Stalina

> The man to whom most statues have been raised is Buddha. The 20th-century champion is Vladimir Ilyich Ulyanov, alias Lenin (1870–1924), busts of whom have been mass-produced, as also has been the case with Mao Zedong (Mao Tse-tung) (1893–1976) and Ho Chi Minh (1890–1969).

War ▶▶ ▶▶

Knights *Youngest and oldest* The youngest age for the conferment of a knighthood is 29 days for HRH the Prince George (b. 12 Aug 1762) (later George IV) by virtue of his *ex officio* membership of the Order of the Garter consequent upon his creation as Prince of Wales on 17 or 19 Aug 1762. The greatest age for the conferment of a knighthood is on a 100th birthday, in the case of the Knight Bachelor Sir Robert Mayer (1879–1985), who was also made a KCVO by the Queen at the Royal Festival Hall, London on 5 Jun 1979.

Most brothers George and Elizabeth Coles of Australia had four sons knighted — Sir George (1885–1977); Sir Arthur (1892–1982); Sir Kenneth (1896–1985) and Sir Edgar (1899–1981). George re-married and had a fifth son who was also knighted— Sir Norman (1907–89).

Military and Defence

War

Earliest conflict The oldest known offensive weapon is a broken wooden spear found in April 1911 at Clacton-on-Sea, Essex by S. Hazzledine Warren. This is much beyond the limit of radiocarbon dating but is estimated to have been fashioned before 200,000 BC.

Longest wars The longest war which could be described as continuous was the Thirty Years War, between various European countries from 1618 to 1648. As a result the map of Europe was radically changed. The so-called 'Hundred Years' War' between England and France, which lasted from 1338 to 1453 (115 years), was in fact an irregular succession of wars rather than a single one. The *Reconquista*—the series of campaigns in the Iberian Peninsula to recover the region from the Islamic Moors—began in 718 and continued intermittently for 774 years until 1492, when Granada, the last Moorish stronghold, was finally conquered.

Shortest war The shortest war on record was that between the UK and Zanzibar (now part of Tanzania), which lasted from 9:00 to 9:45a.m. on 27 Aug 1896. The UK battle fleet under Rear Admiral (later Admiral Sir) Harry Rawson (1843–1910) delivered an ultimatum to the self-appointed Sultan, Seyyid Khalid bin Bargash, to evacuate his palace and surrender. This was not forthcoming until after 45 minutes of bombardment. Admiral Rawson received the Order of the Brilliant Star of Zanzibar (first class) from Seyyid Hamoud bin Mohammed, the new Sultan.

Bloodiest wars By far the most costly war in terms of human life was World War II (1939–45), in which the total number of fatalities, including battle deaths and civilians of all countries, is estimated to have been 56.4 million, assuming 26.6 million Soviet fatalities and 7.8 million Chinese civilians killed. The country which suffered most was Poland, with 6,028,000 or 17.2 per cent of its population of 35,100,000 killed.

In the Paraguayan war of 1864–70 against Brazil, Argentina and Uruguay, Paraguay's population was reduced from 1,400,000 to 220,000 survivors, of whom only 30,000 were adult males.

Most costly war The material cost of World War II far transcended that of the rest of history's wars put together and has been estimated at $1.5 trillion. The total cost to the Soviet Union was estimated in May 1959 at 2.5 trillion roubles, while a figure of $530 billion has been estimated for the USA.

In the case of the UK the cost of £34,423 million was over five times as great as that of World War I (£6700 million) and 158.6 times that of the Boer War of 1899–1902 (£217 million).

Bloodiest battle *Modern* It is difficult to compare the major battles of World Wars I and II because of the timescales. The 142-day long first battle of the Somme, France (1 Jul–19 Nov 1916) produced an estimated total number of casualties of over 1.22 million, of which 398,671 were British (57,470 on the first day) and more than 600,000 German. The losses of the German Army Group Centre on the Eastern Front between 22 Jun and 8 Jul 1944 (17 days) totalled 350,000. The greatest death toll in a battle has been estimated at c. 1,109,000 in the Battle of Stalingrad, USSR (now Volgograd, Russia), ending with the German surrender on 31 Jan 1943 by Field Marshal Friedrich von Paulus (1890–1957). The Soviet army also lost c. 650,800 soldiers who were injured but survived. Additionally, only 1515 civilians from a pre-war population of more than 500,000 were found alive after the battle. The final drive on Berlin, Germany by the Soviet Army and the battle for the city which followed, from 16 Apr–2 May 1945, involved 3.5 million men, 52,000 guns and mortars, 7750 tanks and 11,000 aircraft on both sides.

Ancient Modern historians give no credence, on logistic grounds, to the casualty figures attached to ancient battles, such as the 250,000 reputedly killed at Plataea (Greeks *v.* Persians) in 479 BC or the 200,000 allegedly killed in a single day at Châlons-sur-Marne, France (Huns *v.* Romans) in AD 451. More reliably the Romans estimated the number of their own dead at the Battle of Cannae in 216 BC at 48,200, with the best estimate for the losses amongst the opposing forces under Hannibal being 5700.

British The bloodiest battle fought on British soil was the battle of Towton, near Tadcaster, N Yorks on 29 Mar 1461, when 36,000 Yorkists defeated 40,000 Lancastrians. The total loss has been estimated at between 28,000 and 38,000 killed. A figure of 80,000 British dead was attributed by Tacitus to the battle of AD 61 between Queen Boudicca (Boadicea) of the Iceni and the Roman Governor of Britain Suetonius Paulinus, for the reputed loss of only 400 Romans in an army of 10,000. Curiously the site of the battle remains undetermined but may have been near Borough Hill, Daventry, Northants, or more probably near Hampstead Heath, London.

Greatest naval battle The greatest number of ships and aircraft ever involved in a sea–air action was 231 ships and 1996 aircraft in the Battle of Leyte Gulf, in the Philippines. It raged from 22–27 Oct 1944, with 166 Allied and 65 Japanese warships engaged, of which 26 Japanese and six US ships were sunk. In addition, 1280 US and 716 Japanese aircraft were engaged. The greatest purely naval battle of modern times was the Battle of Jutland on 31 May 1916, in which 151 Royal Navy warships were involved against 101 German warships. The Royal Navy lost 14 ships and 6097 men and the German fleet 11 ships and 2545 men. The greatest of ancient naval battles was the Battle of Salamis, Greece in September 480 BC. There were an estimated 800 vessels in the defeated Persian fleet and 380 in the victorious fleet of the Athenians and their allies, with a possible involvement of 200,000 men. The death toll at the Battle of Lepanto on 7 Oct 1571 has been estimated at 33,000.

Greatest invasion *Seaborne* The greatest invasion in military history was the Allied land, air and sea operation against the Normandy coasts of France on D-Day, 6 Jun 1944. On the first three days 38 convoys of 745 ships moved in, supported by 4066 landing craft, carrying 185,000 men, 20,000 vehicles and 347 minesweepers. The air assault comprised 18,000 paratroopers from 1087 aircraft. The 42 available divisions had air support from 13,175 aircraft. Within a month 1,100,000 troops, 200,000 vehicles and 750,000 tons of stores were landed.

Airborne The largest airborne invasion was the Anglo-American assault of three divisions (34,000 men), with 2800 aircraft and 1600 gliders, near Arnhem, in the Netherlands, on 17 Sep 1944.

Last on the soil of Great Britain The last invasion of Great Britain occurred on 12 Feb 1797, when the Irish-American adventurer General Tate landed at Carreg Wastad Point, Pembroke (now Dyfed) with 1400 French troops. They surrendered outside Fishguard, a few miles away, to Lord Cawdor's force of the Castlemartin Yeomanry and some local inhabitants armed with pitchforks.

Greatest evacuation The greatest evacuation in military history was that carried out by 1200 Allied naval and civil craft from the beach-head at Dunkerque (Dunkirk), France between 27 May and 4 Jun 1940. A total of 338,226 British and French troops were taken off.

Forty years ago the record for the bloodiest war in terms of loss of life was World War II. Thankfully this record still stands in 1995.

Armour

The highest auction price paid for a suit of armour was £1,925,000, by B.H. Trupin (US) on 5 May 1983 at Sotheby's, London for a suit made in Milan by Giovanni Negroli in 1545 for Henri II of France. It came from the Hever Castle Collection in Kent.

Military feast
It was estimated that some 30,000 guests attended a military feast given at Radewitz, Poland on 25 Jun 1730 by King August II (1709–33).

Dr William Brydon (1811–73) and two natives were the sole survivors of a seven-day retreat of 13,000 soldiers and camp-followers from Kabul, Afghanistan. Dr Brydon's horse died 2 days after his arrival at Jellalabad, some 115km *70 miles* to the east on the route to the Khyber Pass, on 13 Jan 1842.

Evacuated

Largest civilian evacuation Following the Iraqi invasion of Kuwait in August 1990, Air India evacuated 111,711 of its nationals who were working in Kuwait. Beginning on 13 August, 488 flights took the ex-patriates back to India over a two-month period.

Youngest soldiers

Luís Alves de Lima e Silva, Marshal Duke of Caxias (1803–80), Brazilian military hero and statesman, entered his infantry regiment at the age of five in 1808. He was promoted to Captain in 1824 and made Duke in 1869. Fernando Inchauste Montalvo (b. 18 Jun 1930), the son of a major in the Bolivian air force, went to the front with his father on his 5th birthday during the war between Bolivia and Paraguay (1932–5). He had received military training and was also subject to military discipline.

■ Fernando Inchauste Montalvo was only five years old when he went to war with his father in 1935. The picture at the bottom of the collection of photographs shows him as a boy. In 1964 he was to experience dramatic events of a happier nature, representing Bolivia in the 1964 Olympic Games in canoeing and having the honour of carrying his country's flag.

Worst sieges The worst siege in history was the 880-day siege of Leningrad, USSR (now St Petersburg, Russia), by the German Army from 30 Aug 1941 until 27 Jan 1944. The best estimate is that between 1.3 and 1.5 million defenders and citizens died. This included 641,000 people who died of hunger in the city and 17,000 civilians killed by shelling. More than 150,000 shells and 100,000 bombs were dropped on the city. The longest recorded siege was that of Azotus (now Ashdod), Israel which according to Herodotus was besieged by Psamtik I of Egypt for 29 years in the period 664–610 BC.

Chemical warfare The greatest number of people killed through chemical warfare were the estimated 4000 Kurds who died at Halabja, Iraq in March 1988 when President Saddam Hussein used chemical weapons against Iraq's Kurdish minority for the support it had given to Iran in the Iran–Iraq war.

Defence Spending

In 1993 it was estimated that the world's spending on defence was running at an annual rate of some $823 billion. In 1993 there were 23,530,000 full-time armed forces regulars or conscripts plus 36,130,000 reservists, totalling 59,660,000. The budgeted expenditure on defence by the US government for the fiscal year 1994 was $262.2 billion. The defence budget of Russia was given as 40,626 billion roubles in 1994. The UK defence budget for 1994/5 is £22.51 billion.

Armed Forces

Largest armed forces China's People's Liberation Army's strength in 1994 was estimated to be 2,930,000 (comprising land, sea and air forces), with reductions continuing. Her reserves which can be mobilized number around 1.2 million plus many more for local militia duty. Numerically, the world's largest army is also that of the People's Republic of China, with a total strength of some 2.2 million in mid-1994.

Guess What?

Q. Which country's army used the heaviest operational tank?

A. See Page 196

Army drill

On 8–9 Jul 1987 a 90-man squad of the Queen's Colour Squadron, RAF performed a total of 2,722,662 drill movements (2,001,384 rifle and 721,278 foot) at RAF Uxbridge, Middx from memory and without a word of command in 23 hr 55 min.

Prior to its break-up, the USSR had the largest regular armed force in the world, with 3,400,000 personnel in 1991. The latest figure for the Russian armed forces is c. 1,714,000.

The UK's military manpower is 254,000 (1994), of which the army has the most, with 123,000. The highest ever strength of the army was 3.8 million, in March 1918.

Armies *Oldest* The oldest army in the world is the 80–90 strong Pontifical Swiss Guard in the Vatican City, with a regular foundation dating back to 21 Jan 1506. Its origins, however, predate 1400. (For details of largest armies ⇨ above)

Navies *Largest* The largest navy in the world in terms of manpower is the United States Navy, with 510,600 plus 183,000 Marines in mid-1994.

The strength of the Royal Navy in mid-1994 was 55,600, including The Fleet Air Arm and Royal Marines (7300). In 1914 the Royal Navy had 542 warships including 72 capital ships, making it the largest navy in the world at the time.

Air forces *Oldest* The earliest autonomous air force is the Royal Air Force, which can be traced back to 1878, when the War Office commissioned the building of a military balloon. Balloons had been used for

---

Mutiny

In World War I, 56 French divisions comprising some 650,000 men and their officers, refused orders on the Western Front sector of General Robert Nivelle in April 1917 after the failure of his offensive.

---

military observation by both sides during the American Civil War (1861–5).

Largest The greatest air force of all time was the United States Army Air Corps (now the US Air Force), which had 79,908 aircraft in July 1944 and 2,411,294 personnel in March 1944. The US Air Force, including strategic missile forces, had 433,800 personnel and 5900 (plus more in store) aircraft in mid-1994.

The strength of the Royal Air Force in 1994 was 75,700, with 39 operational squadrons.

Oldest soldiers The oldest 'old soldier' of all time is thought to be John B. Salling of the army of the Confederate States of America and the last accepted survivor of the US Civil War (1861–5). He died in Kingsport, Tennessee, USA on 16 Mar 1959, aged 113 years 1 day.

The oldest Chelsea pensioner, based *only* on the evidence of his tombstone, was 111-year-old William Hiseland (6 Aug 1620–7 Feb 1732). George Ives (b. Brighton, E. Sussex, 17 Nov 1881, d. 12 Apr 1993) of the 1st Imperial Yeomanry fought in the Boer War, and also lived to the age of 111. After the war ended he emigrated to Canada, where he lived for some 90 years. The longest-serving British soldier has been Field Marshal Sir William Gomm (1784–1875), who was an ensign in 1794 and Constable of the Tower of London over 80 years later at his death aged 91.

Youngest conscripts President Francisco Macias Nguema of Equatorial Guinea (deposed in August 1979) decreed in March 1976 compulsory military service for all boys aged between seven and 14. The edict stated that any parent refusing to hand over his or her son 'will be imprisoned or shot'.

Conscientious objector *Most obdurate* The only conscientious objector to be six times court-martialled in World War II was Gilbert Lane of Wallington,

Surrey. He served 31 months' detention and 183 days' imprisonment.

Longest march The longest march in military history was the famous Long March by the Chinese Communists in 1934–5. In 368 days, of which 268 days were days of movement, from October to October, their force of some 100,000 covered 9700 km *6000 miles* from Ruijin, in Jiangxi, to Yan'an, in Shaanxi. They crossed 18 mountain ranges and 24 rivers, and eventually reached Yan'an with only about 8000 survivors following continual rearguard actions against nationalist Guomindang (GMD) forces.

Top jet ace The greatest number of kills claimed in jet-to-jet battles is 21, by Capt. Nikolai Vasilevich Sutyagin (USSR) in the Korean war (1950–3).

Anti-submarine successes The highest number of U-boat kills attributed to one ship in World War II was 15, to HMS *Starling* (Capt. Frederic John Walker DSO***, RN, CB). Captain Walker was in command at the sinking of a total of 25 U-boats between 1941 and the time of his death on 9 Jul 1944. The US Destroyer Escort *England* sank six Japanese submarines in the Pacific between 18 and 30 May 1944.

Most successful submarine captains The most successful of all World War II submarine commanders was Leutnant Otto Kretschmer, captain of the U.23 and U.99, who up to March 1941 sank one destroyer and 44 Allied merchantmen totalling 266,629 gross registered tons.

In World War I Kapitänleutnant (later Vizeadmiral) Lothar von Arnauld de la Périère, in the U.35 and U.139, sank 195 Allied ships totalling 458,856 gross registered tons.

Speed March

A team of nine representing II Squadron RAF Regiment from RAF Hullavington, Wilts, each man carrying a pack weighing at least 40 lb *18.1 kg*, including a rifle, completed the London marathon in 4 hr 33 min 58 sec on 21 Apr 1991.

Flt Sgt Chris Chandler set an individual record in the RAF Swinderby Marathon at Swinderby, Lincs on 25 Sep 1992, with a pack weighing 40 lb *18.1 kg*. His time was 3 hr 56 min 10 sec.

Guess What?

Q. How long was the smallest submarine ever built?

A. See Page 107

The shock-wave circled the world three times, taking 36 hr 27 min for the first circuit. Some estimates put the power of this device at between 62 and 90 megatons. On 9 Aug 1961, Nikita Khrushchev, then the Chairman of the Council of Ministers of the USSR, declared that the Soviet Union was capable of constructing a 100-megaton bomb, and announced the possession of one during a visit to what was then East Berlin, East Germany on 16 Jan 1963.

Largest nuclear weapons The most powerful ICBM (inter-continental ballistic missile) is the former USSR's SS-18 (Model 5), officially called the RS-20, which is believed to be armed with 10 MIRVs (multiple independently targetable re-entry vehicles), each of 750-kilotons. SS-18 ICBMs are located on the territories of both Russia and Kazakhstan, although the dismantlement of those in Kazakhstan has begun. Earlier models had a single 20-megaton warhead. START 2 (START = Strategic Arms Reduction Talks) requires all SS-18, and all other ICBMs with more than one warhead, to be eliminated. The US Titan II carrying a W-53 warhead was rated at 9 megatons but was withdrawn, leaving the 1.2 megaton W-56 as the most powerful US weapon.

Tanks

Earliest tank The first tank was *No. 1 Lincoln*, modified to become *Little Willie*, built by William Foster & Co. Ltd of Lincoln. It first ran on 6 Sep 1915. Tanks first saw action with the Heavy Section, Machine Gun Corps, later the Tank Corps, at the Battle of Flers-Courcelette, France on 15 Sep 1916. The Mark I 'Male' tank, armed with a pair of 6-pounder guns and three machine guns, weighed 28.4 tonnes and was powered by a 105 hp motor, giving a maximum road speed of 4.8–6.4 km/h *3–4 mph*.

Heaviest tanks The heaviest tank ever constructed was the German Panzer Kampfwagen Maus II, which weighed 192 tonnes. By 1945 it had reached only the experimental stage and was abandoned. The heaviest operational tank used by any army was the 75.2 tonne 13-man French Char de Rupture 2C bis of 1922. It carried a 15.5 cm *6⅛ in* howitzer and was powered by two 250 hp engines giving a maximum speed of 12 km/h *8 mph*. The heaviest British tank was the Experimental Heavy Tank TOG 2 built in 1941. It weighed 80 tonnes, was 10.13 m *33 ft 3 in* long, had a crew of six and a top speed of 13.7 km/h *8½ mph*. It is on permanent display at the Tank Museum, Bovington, Dorset. The heaviest British tank to enter service was *Conqueror*, at 66 tonnes.

The most heavily armed tank in recent times has been the Russian T-72, which has a 12.5 cm *4⅞ in* high-velocity gun and is the only rocket-gun tank with explosive reactive armour. The American Sheridan light tank mounts a 15.2 cm *6 in* weapon which is both a gun and a missile launcher combined but this is not a long barrelled, high-velocity gun of the conventional type. The British AVRE *Centurion* had a 16.5 cm *6½ in* low-velocity demolition gun.

Fastest tanks The fastest tracked armoured reconnaissance vehicle is the British *Scorpion*, which can touch 80 km/h *50 mph* with a 75 per cent payload. The American experimental tank M1936 built by J.

Longest range attacks

Preparations are made on a B-52G bomber before embarking for the Gulf in one of the record-breaking long-range attacks in January 1991.
(Photo: Rex Features/J M Guhl)

The longest range attacks in air history were those undertaken by seven B-52G bombers, which took off from Barksdale air force base, Louisiana, USA on 16 Jan 1991 to deliver air-launched cruise missiles against targets in Iraq shortly after the start of the Gulf War. Each flew a distance of 22,500 km *14,000 miles*, refuelling four times in flight, with the round-trip mission lasting some 35 hours.

The largest target ever sunk by a submarine was the Japanese aircraft carrier *Shinano* (59,994 tonnes) by USS *Archerfish* (Cdr Joseph F. Enright, USN) on 29 Nov 1944.

Bombs

Heaviest bombs The heaviest conventional bomb ever used operationally was the Royal Air Force's *Grand Slam*, weighing 9980 kg *22,000 lb* and 7.74 m *25 ft 5 in* long, dropped on Bielefeld railway viaduct, Germany on 14 Mar 1945. In 1949 the United States Air Force tested a bomb weighing 19,050 kg *42,000 lb* at Muroc Dry Lake, California, USA. The heaviest known nuclear bomb was the MK 17 carried by US B-36 bombers in the mid-1950s. It weighed 19,050 kg *42,000 lb* and was 7.47 m *24 ft 6 in* long.

Atomic bombs The first atom bomb dropped on Hiroshima, Japan by the United States at 8:16 a.m. on 6 Aug 1945 had an explosive power equivalent to that of 12.5 kilotons of trinitrotoluene ($C_7H_5O_6N_3$), called TNT. Code-named *Little Boy*, it was 3.04 m *10 ft* long and weighed 4080 kg *9000 lb*. It burst 565 m *1850 ft* above the city centre. The most powerful thermonuclear device so far tested is one with a power equivalent to that of 57 megatons of TNT, detonated by the former USSR in the Novaya Zemlya area at 8:33 a.m. GMT on 30 Oct 1961.

Most prolific tank
The greatest production of any tank was that of the Soviet T-54/55 series, of which more than 50,000 were built between 1954 and 1980 in the USSR alone, with further production in the one-time Warsaw Pact countries and China.

Walter Christie was clocked at 103.4 km/h *64.3 mph* during official trials in Britain in 1938.

Guns

Earliest guns Although it cannot be accepted as proven, it is believed that the earliest guns were constructed in both China and in north Africa in c. 1250. The earliest representation of an English gun is contained in an illustrated manuscript dated 1326, now at Oxford.

Largest gun In the siege of Sevastopol, USSR (now Russia) in July 1942 the Germans used a gun of a calibre of 80 cm *31 in* with a barrel 28.87 m *94 ft 8½ in* long. Internally it was named *Schwerer Gustav*, and was one of three guns which were given the general name of *Dora*, although the other two were not finished and so were not used in action. It was built by Krupp, and its remains were discovered near Metzenhof, Bavaria in August 1945. The whole assembly of the gun was 42.9 m *141 ft* long and weighed 1344 tonnes, with a crew of 1500. The range for an 8.1 tonne projectile was 46.67 km *29 miles*.

During World War I the British Army used a gun of 45.7 cm *18 in* calibre. The barrel alone weighed 127 tonnes. In World War II the *Bochebuster*, a train-mounted howitzer with a calibre of 457 mm *18 in* firing a 1130 kg *2500 lb* shell to a maximum range of 20,850 m *22,800 yd*, was used from 1940 onwards as part of the Kent coast defences.

Greatest altitude and range The greatest altitude ever attained by a gun was achieved by the HARP (High Altitude Research Project) gun, consisting of two 42 cm *16½ in* calibre barrels fused in tandem into a single barrel 36.4 m *119 ft 5 in* long and weighing 150 tonnes, at Yuma, Arizona, USA. On 19 Nov 1966 an 84 kg *185 lb* projectile was fired to an altitude of 180 km *112 miles*.

The famous long-range gun which shelled Paris in World War I was the *Paris-Geschütz* (Paris Gun), with a calibre of 21 cm *8¼ in*, a designed range of 127.9 km *79½ miles* and an achieved range of 122 km *76 miles* from the Forest of Crépy in March 1918.

> **Field gun pull**
> Three teams of eight members from 72 Ordnance Company (V) RAOC pulled a 25-pounder field gun over a distance of 177.98 km *110.6 miles* in 24 hours at Donnington, Shrops on 2–3 Apr 1993.

Mortars The largest mortars ever constructed were Mallet's mortar (Woolwich Arsenal, London, 1857) and the *Little David* of World War II, made in the USA. Each had a calibre of 91.4 cm *36 in*, but neither was ever used in action. The heaviest mortar employed was the tracked German 60 cm *23½ in* siege piece *Karl*, of which there were seven such mortars built. Only six of these were actually used in action, although never all at the same time, at Sevastopol, USSR in 1942, at Warsaw, Poland in 1944, and at Budapest, Hungary, also in 1944.

Largest cannon The highest-calibre cannon ever constructed is the *Tsar Pushka* (*King of Cannons*), now housed in the Kremlin, Moscow, Russia. It was built in the 16th century with a bore of 89 cm *35 in* and a barrel 5.34 m *17 ft 6 in* long. It weighs 39.3 tonnes or 2400 *poods* (*sic*). The Turks fired up to seven shots per day from a bombard 7.92 m *26 ft* long, with an internal calibre of 106.6 cm *42 in*, against the walls of Constantinople (now Istanbul)

from 12 Apr–29 May 1453. The cannon was dragged by 60 oxen and 200 men and fired a 540 kg *1200 lb* stone ball.

The heaviest cannon was built in 1868 at Perm, Russia and weighs 144.1 tonnes, although it has a bore of only 50.8 cm *20 in* and a barrel 4.6 m *15 ft 1 in* long. It fired 300 shots in tests, using iron balls weighing nearly ½ tonne.

Education

Compulsory education was first introduced in 1819 in Prussia. It became compulsory in the UK in 1870.

University *Oldest* The Sumerians had scribal schools or *É-Dub-ba* soon after 3500 BC. The oldest existing educational institution in the world is the University of Karueein, founded in AD 859 in Fez, Morocco. The University of Bologna, the oldest in Europe, was founded in 1088.

The oldest university in the UK is the University of Oxford, which came into being c. 1167. The oldest of the existing colleges is probably University College (1249), though its foundation is less well documented than that of Merton in 1264.

Greatest enrolment The university with the greatest enrolment in the world is the State University of New York, USA, which had 393,228 students at 64 campuses throughout the state in late 1994. The greatest enrolment for a university centred in one city is at the City University of New York, USA, which had 213,000 students in late 1994. It has several campuses throughout the city.

> **The static V3**
> underground firing tubes built in 50° shafts during World War II near Mimoyècques, not far from Calais, France, to bombard London were never operative, but this would have been a distance of some 150 km *95 miles*.

Britain's largest university is the University of London, with 67,567 internal students and 21,754 external students in 1993/4, totalling 89,321. The Open University at Walton Hall near Milton Keynes, Bucks was first called the University of the Air and was granted a Royal Charter on 30 May 1969. In 1994 it had 143,173 registered students, of which 132,834 were undergraduates and 10,339 postgraduates.

Largest The largest existing university building in the world is the M.V. Lomonosov State University on the Lenin Hills, south of Moscow, Russia. It stands 240 m *787 ft 5 in* tall, and has 32 storeys and 40,000 rooms. It was constructed from 1949–53.

> In 1955 the University of London was Britain's largest university, with 41,148 students. It still is the largest, but now with more than twice as many students.

Professor *Youngest* The youngest at which anybody has been elected to a chair in a university is 19 years in the case of Colin MacLaurin (1698–1746), who was elected to Marischal College, Aberdeen as Professor of Mathematics on 30 Sep 1717. In 1725 he was made Professor of Mathematics at Edinburgh University on the recommendation of Sir Isaac Newton (1642–1727), who was a professor at Cambridge at the age of 26. Henry Phillpotts (1778–1869) became a don at Magdalen College, Oxford on 25 Jul 1795 aged 17 years 80 days.

> **Higher education**
> India has the greatest number of institutions, with 6600, whilst the USA has both the greatest number of students (13,711,000) and the highest ratio, at 5596 tertiary level students per 100,000 population.

Most durable Dr Joel Hildebrand (1881–1983), Professor Emeritus of Physical Chemistry at the University of California, Berkeley, USA, first became an assistant professor in 1913 and published his 275th research paper 68 years later in 1981. The longest period for which any professorship has been held in Britain is 63 years in the case of Thomas Martyn (1735–1825), Professor of Botany at Cambridge University from 1762 until his death. The last professor-for-life was the pathologist Prof. Henry Roy Dean (1879–1961) for his last 39 years at Cambridge.

> # Proud
> **Most graduates in family** Mr and Mrs Harold Erickson of Naples, Florida, USA saw all of their 14 children—11 sons and 3 daughters—obtain university or college degrees between 1962 and 1978. All 14 children—10 sons and 4 daughters—of Mr and Mrs Robert Johnson of Edwards, Mississippi, USA also obtained degrees, between 1959 and 1983.

Youngest undergraduate and graduate Michael Kearney (↔ p. 198) started studying for an Associate of Science degree at Santa Rosa Junior College, California, USA in September 1990 at the age of 6 years 7 months. He became the youngest graduate in June 1994, at the age of 10 years 4 months, when he obtained his BA in anthropology from the University of South Alabama.

In Britain, the most extreme recorded cases of undergraduate juvenility were those of Alexander Hill (1785–1867), who entered St Andrews University at the age of 10 years 4 months in November 1795, and William Thomson (1824–1907), later Lord Kelvin, who entered Glasgow University also at the age of 10 years 4 months, in October 1834.

Matthew Trout (b. 30 Mar 1983) of Upholland, Lancs became Britain's youngest undergraduate this century when he began an Open University mathematics course leading to a degree in mathematics at the age of 10 years 10 months in February 1994. Ganesh Sittampalam (b. 11 Feb 1979) of Surbiton, Surrey became Britain's youngest graduate this century in July 1992, obtaining a mathematics degree at the age of 13 years 5 months from the University of Surrey (↔ Youngest A level pass below).

Youngest doctorate On 13 Apr 1814 the mathematician Carl Witte of Lochau was made a Doctor of Philosophy of the University of Giessen, Germany when aged 12.

School *Oldest* The title of the oldest existing school in Britain is contested. It is claimed that King's School in Canterbury, Kent was a foundation of St Augustine, some time between his arrival in Kent in AD 597 and his death c. 604. Cor Tewdws (College of Theodosius) at Llantwit Major, South Glamorgan, reputedly burnt down in AD 446, was refounded, after a lapse of 62 years, by St Illtyd in 508, and flourished into the 13th century. Winchester College was founded in 1382. Lanark Grammar School claims to have been referred to in a papal bull drawn up in 1183 by Lucius III.

Most expensive Excluding schools catering for specialist needs, the most expensive school in Great Britain is Carmel College, Wallingford, Oxon

A Levels, Teachers ▶▶ ▶▶

(headmaster P.D. Skelker). The maximum annual fee for boarders in 1994/5 is £13,065.

The most expensive school which is a member of the Girls' School Association is Roedean School, Brighton, East Sussex (head-mistress Mrs A.R. Longley), with annual fees in 1994/5 of £12,405 for boarders.

In the academic year 1994/5 Bartholomews Tutorial College, Brighton, E Sussex (principal W. Duncombe) charges up to £15,837.75 for A level science courses (including accommodation).

Largest In 1994/5 Rizal High School, Pasig, Manila, Philippines had a record enrolment of 18,141 pupils.

The school with the most pupils in Great Britain was Banbury Comprehensive, Oxon with 2767 in the 1975 summer term. The highest enrolment in 1994/5 was 2308 at St Louise's Comprehensive College, Belfast.

Most schools The greatest documented number of schools attended by a pupil is 265, by Wilma Williams, now Mrs R.J. Horton, from 1933–43 when her parents were in show business in the USA.

Most O and A levels Since 1965 Dr Francis L. Thomason of Hammersmith, London has accumulated 70 O and O/A levels, 16 A levels and 1 S level, making a total of 87, of which 36 have been in the top grade.

The highest number of top-grade A levels attained at one sitting is seven, by Matthew James of Mortimer Wilson School, Alfreton, Derbys in June 1993, by Stephen Murrell—who also obtained an eighth pass at grade B—of Crown Woods School,

Michael Kearney (b. 18 Jan 1984) of Mobile, Alabama, USA received his high school diploma—equivalent to A levels in the UK—in June 1990 at the age of 6 years 5 months (⇨ Youngest undergraduate and graduate above).

Eltham, London in June 1978 and Ben Woolley of Lancing College, West Sussex in June 1994. Robert Pidgeon (b. 7 Feb 1959) of St Peter's School, Bournemouth, Dorset secured 13 O level passes at grade A at one sitting in the summer of 1975, and subsequently passed three A levels at grade A and two S levels with firsts. Nicholas Barberis achieved a total of 27 top grades while at Eltham College, London, passing 20 O/AO levels and 7 A levels, all at grade A, between 1984 and 1988.

Youngest A level pass Ganesh Sittampalam of Surbiton, Surrey is the youngest person to have passed an A level, achieving grade A in both Mathematics and Further Mathematics in June 1988, when aged 9 years 4 months (⇨ Youngest undergraduate and graduate above).

Terry Tyacke of Trowbridge, Wilts has passed a total of 20 A levels since 1973.

Youngest GCSE pass Sonali Pandya (b. 9 Apr 1985) of Edgware, London obtained a grade E in her GCSE Computer Studies examination in June 1993 at the age of 8 years 2 months.

Oldest A level pass George Lush of Hatfield, Herts passed A level Italian in 1969, obtaining a grade D, just a few months before his 89th birthday.

Youngest headmaster The youngest headmaster of a major public school in Great Britain was Henry Montagu Butler (b. 2 Jul 1833), appointed Headmaster of Harrow School on 16 Nov 1859, when aged 26

years 137 days. His first term in office began in January 1860.

Rev. G. S. Evans (b. 3 Jun 1802), was younger when he became headmaster of North End Academy, Hampstead (later known as Mill Hill School) in 1828, but only held the post for six months.

Most durable teachers Medarda de Jesús León de Uzcátegui, alias La Maestra Chucha, has been teaching in Caracas, Venezuela for a total of 84 years. In 1911, at the age of 12, she and her two sisters set up a school there which they named *Modelo de Aplicación*. Since marrying in 1942, she has run her own school, which she calls the *Escuela Uzcátegui*, from her home in Caracas.

David Rhys Davies (1835–1928) taught as a pupil teacher and subsequently a teacher and headmaster for a total of 76 years. Most of his teaching was done at Talybont-on-Usk School, near Brecon, Powys (1856–79) and at Dame Anna Child's School, Whitton, Powys. Elsie Marguerite Touzel (1889–1984) of Jersey, Channel Islands began her teaching career aged 16 in 1905 and taught at various schools in Jersey until her retirement 75 years later on 30 Sep 1980.

Highest endowment The greatest single gift in the history of education has been $500 million, to the US public education system by Walter H. Annenberg (1908–94) in December 1993. The gift was intended to help fight violence in American schools.

Walter Annenberg, who donated $500 million to public education, said:– 'I keep reading about so many youngsters with knives and revolvers and threatening the lives of teachers. I felt I had to drop a bomb to show the public what needs to be done'.

Guess What?

Q. What record did Jennifer Keaveney set in the 1986 Mastermind competition?
A. See Page 153

Schools

The country with the greatest number of primary schools is China, with 885,479 in 1992. San Marino has the lowest pupil to teacher ratio, with 5.3 children per teacher.

At general secondary level India has the most schools, with 235,793 in 1993, whilst San Marino has the best ratio— 5.8 pupils per teacher.

■ The country with the most primary schools is China. Looking smart and learning to write on the school blackboard is part of the way of life for these youngsters. (Photo: Gamma)

Religions

Earliest religion Human burial, which has religious connotations, is known from c. 60,000 BC among *Homo sapiens neanderthalensis* in the Shanidar cave, northern Iraq.

Largest religions Religious statistics are necessarily only tentative, since the test of adherence to a religion varies widely in rigour, while many individuals, particularly in the East, belong to two or more religions.

Christianity is the world's prevailing religion, with some 1.90 billion adherents in 1994, or 33.7 per cent of the world's population. There were 1.06 billion Roman Catholics in the same year. The largest non-Christian religion is Islam (Muslim), with some 1.03 billion followers in 1994.

In the UK the Roman Catholic population is 5,815,000, while the Anglicans have an actual membership (a different measure) of 1,855,000. They comprise members of the Established Church of England, the Dis-established Church in Wales, the Scottish Episcopal Church and the Church of Ireland. The Church of England has 2 provinces (Canterbury and York), 44 dioceses, 10,514 full-time diocesan clergy, including 848 women, and 13,067 parishes as at 31 Dec 1994. In Scotland the largest membership is that of the Church of Scotland (46 presbyteries), which had 715,571 members at the end of 1994.

Places of Worship

Earliest places of worship Many archaeologists are of the opinion that the decorated Upper Palaeolithic caves of Europe (c. 30,000–10,000 BC) were used as places of worship or religious ritual. The oldest surviving Christian church in the world is a converted house in Qal'at es Salihiye (formerly Douro-Europos) in eastern Syria, dating from AD 232.

Great Britain The oldest places of worship are the enigmatic stone circles or henges of the Neolithic period, for example Avebury, Wilts, dating from c. 3000–2800 BC. The earliest Christian church in the UK was at Colchester, Essex and was built c. AD 320. Its ruins can still be seen next to the modern police station. The oldest surviving ecclesiastical building in the UK is a 6th-century cell built by St Brendan in AD 542 on Eileachan Naoimh (pronounced 'Noo'), Garvelloch Islands, Strathclyde.

Temples *Largest* The largest religious structure ever built is Angkor Wat ('City Temple'), enclosing 162.6 ha *402 acres* in Cambodia (formerly Kampuchea). It was built to the Hindu god Vishnu by the Khmer King Suryavarman II in the period 1113–50. Its curtain wall measures 1280 × 1280 m *4199 × 4199 ft* and its population, before it was abandoned in 1432, was 80,000. The whole complex of 72 major monuments, begun c. AD 900, extends over 24 × 8 km *15 × 5 miles*.

The largest Buddhist temple in the world is Borobudur, near Jogjakarta, Indonesia, built in the 8th century. It is 31.5 m *103 ft* tall and 123 m *403 ft* square.

The largest Mormon temple is the Salt Lake Temple, Utah, USA, dedicated on 6 Apr 1893, with a floor area of 23,505 m^2 *253,015 ft^2* or 5.8 acres.

Cathedrals *Largest* The world's largest cathedral is the Gothic cathedral church of the Diocese of New York, St John the Divine, with a floor area of 11,240 m^2 *121,000 ft^2* and a volume of 476,350 m^3 *16,822,000 ft^3*. The cor-

■ St John the Divine, despite being unfinished, is the world's largest cathedral. Its interior clearly shows just how vast it is.
(Photos: Alex Goldberg for Image Select)

The world's smallest church is the chapel of Santa Isabel de Hungría, in Colomares, a monument to Christopher Columbus at Benalmádena, Málaga, Spain. It is an irregular shape and has a total floor area of 1.96 m^2 *21⅛ ft^2*.

nerstone was laid on 27 Dec 1892, but work on the building was stopped in 1941. Work restarted in earnest in July 1979. The nave is the longest in the world at 183.2 m *601 ft* in length, with a vaulting 37.8 m *124 ft* in height.

The cathedral covering the largest area is that of Santa Mariá de la Sede in Seville, Spain. It was built in Spanish Gothic style between 1402 and 1519, and is 126.2 m *414 ft* long, 82.6 m *271 ft* wide and 30.5 m *100 ft* high to the vault of the nave.

The largest cathedral in the British Isles is the Cathedral Church of Christ in Liverpool. It was built in modernized Gothic style, and work was begun on 18 Jul 1904; it was finally consecrated on 25 Oct 1978 after 74 years (cf. Exeter Cathedral, 95 years). The building encloses 9687 m^2 *104,275 ft^2* and has an overall length of 193.9 m *636 ft*. The Vestey Tower is 100.9 m *331 ft* high. It contains the highest vaulting in the world—53.3 m *175 ft* maximum at under-tower, and the highest Gothic arches ever built, being 32.6 m *107 ft* at apexes.

Smallest The smallest church in the world designated as a cathedral—the seat of a diocesan bishop—is that of the Christ Catholic Church, Highlandville, Missouri, USA. It was consecrated in July 1983. It measures 4.3 × 5.2 m *14 × 17 ft* and has seating for 18 people.

The smallest cathedral in use in the UK is Cumbrae Cathedral (the Cathedral of the diocese of the Isles) at Millport on the isle of Cumbrae, Strathclyde, which was built in 1849–51. The nave measures only 12.2 × 6.1 m *40 × 20 ft* and the total floor area is 197.3 m^2 *2124 ft^2*.

Largest church The largest church in the world is the Basilica of Our Lady of Peace (Notre Dame de la Paix) at Yamoussoukro, Ivory Coast, completed in 1989 at a cost of £100 million. It has a total area of 30,000 m^2 *100,000 ft^2* with seating for 7000 people. Including its golden cross, it is 158 m *519 ft* high.

The elliptical basilica of St Pie X at Lourdes, France, completed in 1957 at a cost of £2 million, has a capacity of 20,000 under its giant span arches and a length of 200 m *660 ft*.

The largest church in the UK is the Collegiate Church of St Peter in Westminster, generally referred to as Westminster Abbey, which was built between AD 1050–1745. Its maximum length is 161.5 m *530 ft*, the breadth across the transept 61.9 m *203 ft* and the internal height 30.98 m *101 ft 8 in*.

Longest The crypt of the underground Civil War Memorial Church in the Guadarrama Mountains, 45 km *28 miles* from Madrid, Spain, is 260 m *853 ft* in length. It took 21 years (1937–58) to build, at a reported cost of £140 million, and is surmounted by a cross 150 m *492 ft* tall.

Largest synagogue The largest synagogue in the world is Temple Emanu-El on Fifth Avenue at 65th Street, New York City, USA. The temple, completed in September 1929, has a frontage of 45.7 m *150 ft* on Fifth Avenue and 77.1 m *253 ft* on 65th Street. The sanctuary proper can accommodate 2500 people, and the adjoining Beth-El Chapel seats 350. When all the facilities are in use, more than 6000 people can be accommodated.

Highest

The Rongbu temple, between Tingri and Shigatse in Tibet, is at an altitude of c. 5100 m *16,750 ft*, just 40 km *25 miles* from Mt Everest. It contains nine chapels, and a number of lamas and nuns live there.

Guess What?

Q. What was unusual about the church built by Joseph Sciberras?

A. See Page 217

The largest synagogue in Great Britain is the Edgware Synagogue, in Greater London, completed in 1959, with seating for 1630. That with the highest registered membership is Stanmore and Canons Park Synagogue, in Greater London with 2435 members.

Largest mosque The largest mosque is Shah Faisal Mosque, near Islamabad, Pakistan. The total area of the complex is 18.97 ha *46.87 acres*, with the covered area of the prayer hall being 0.48 ha *1.19 acres*. It can accommodate 100,000 worshippers in the prayer hall and the courtyard, and a further 200,000 people in the adjacent grounds.

Tallest minaret The tallest minaret in the world is that of the Great Hassan II Mosque, Casablanca, Morocco, measuring 200 m *656 ft*. The cost of construction of the mosque was 5 billion dirhams (£360 million). Of ancient minarets the tallest is the Qutb Minar, south of New Delhi, India, built in 1194 to a height of 72.54 m *238 ft*.

Tallest and oldest stupa The now largely ruined Jetavanarama dagoba in the ancient city of Anuradhapura, Sri Lanka, is some 120 m *400 ft* in height. The 99.3 m *326 ft* tall Shwedagon pagoda, in Yangon (Rangoon), Myanmar (Burma), is built on the site of a pagoda dating from 585 BC which was 8.2 m *27 ft* tall.

Tallest spire The tallest cathedral spire in the world is that of the Protestant Cathedral of Ulm in Germany. The building is early Gothic and was begun in 1377. The tower, in the centre of the west façade, was not finally completed until 1890 and is 160.9 m *528 ft* high. The world's tallest church spire is that of the Chicago Temple of the First Methodist Church on Clark Street, Chicago, Illinois, USA. The building consists of a 22-storey skyscraper (erected in 1924) surmounted by a parsonage at 100.5 m *330 ft*, a 'Sky Chapel' at 121.9 m *400 ft* and a steeple cross at 173.1 m *568 ft* above street level.

Stained glass *Oldest* Pieces of stained glass dated before AD 850, some possibly even to the 7th century, excavated by Prof. Rosemary Cramp, were set into a window of that date in the nearby St Paul's Church, Jarrow, Co. Durham. The oldest complete stained glass in the world represents the Prophets in a window of the Cathedral of Augsburg, Germany, dating from the second half of the 11th century.

Largest The largest stained-glass window is that of the Resurrection Mausoleum in Justice, Illinois, USA, measuring 2079 m² *22,381 ft²* in 2448 panels, completed in 1971. Although not one continuous window, the Basilica of Our Lady of Peace (Notre Dame de la Paix) at Yamoussoukro, Ivory Coast contains a number of stained-glass windows covering a total area of 7430 m² *80,000 ft²*.

The largest single ecclesiastical stained-glass window in Great Britain is the east window in Gloucester Cathedral measuring 21.9 × 11.6 m *72 × 38 ft* and hence with an area of 254 m² *2736 ft²* (⟨> Largest window), set up to commemorate the Battle of Crécy (1346), while the largest area of stained glass comprises the 128 lights, totalling 2320 m² *25,000 ft²*, in York Minster.

Brasses The world's oldest monumental brass is that commemorating Bishop Yso von Wölpe in the Andreaskirche, Verden, near Hanover, Germany, dating from 1231. An engraved coffin plate of St

Ulrich (died 973), laid in 1187, was found buried in the Church of SS Ulrich and Afra, Augsburg, Germany in 1979.

The oldest brass in Great Britain is of Sir John D'Abernon (died 1277) at Stoke D'Abernon, near Leatherhead, Surrey, dating from c. 1320. A dedication brass dated 24 Apr 1241 in Ashbourne Church, Derbys has been cited as the earliest surviving arabic writing in Britain.

Church Personnel

Canonization The shortest interval that has elapsed between the death of a saint and his or her canonization was in the case of St Peter of Verona, Italy, who died on 6 Apr 1252 and was canonized 337 days later on 9 Mar 1253. The longest interval is 857 years, in the case of St Leo III, who died in 816 and was not canonized until 1673.

Bishops *Longest-serving* Bishop Louis François de la Baume de Suze (1603–90) was a bishop for a record 76 years 273 days from 6 Dec 1613.

The longest tenure of any Church of England bishopric is 57 years in the case of the Rt Rev. Thomas Wilson, who was consecrated Bishop of Sodar and Man on 16 Jan 1698 and died in office on 7 Mar 1755. Of English bishoprics, the longest tenures—if one excludes the unsubstantiated case of Aethelwulf, reputedly Bishop of Hereford from 937 to 1012—are those of 47 years by Jocelin de Bohun of Salisbury (1142–89) and Nathaniel Crew or Crewe of Durham (1674–1721).

Oldest The oldest serving diocesan bishop (excluding suffragans and assistants) in the Church of England as at April 1994 was the Rt Rev. Eric Kemp, Bishop of Chichester, who was born on 27 Apr 1915.

The oldest Roman Catholic bishop in recent times has been Archbishop Edward Howard, formerly Archbishop of Portland-in-Oregon, USA (b. 5 Nov 1877), who died aged 105 years 58 days on 2 Jan 1983. He had celebrated mass about 27,800 times. Bishop Herbert Welch of the United Methodist Church, who was elected a Bishop for Japan and Korea in 1916, died on 4 Apr 1969 aged 106.

Youngest The youngest serving diocesan bishop (excluding suffragans and assistants) in the Church of England is the Rt Rev. John Hind, Bishop of Gibraltar in Europe, who was born on 19 Jun 1945.

Oldest parish priest Father Alvaro Fernandez (1880–1988) served as a parish priest at Santiago de Abres, Spain from 1919 until he was 107 years old. The oldest Anglican clergyman, Rev. Clement Williams (b. 30 Oct 1879), died aged 106 years 3 months on 3 Feb 1986. He lined the route at Queen Victoria's funeral and was ordained in 1904.

Longest service Rev. K.M. Jacob (b. 10 Jul 1880) was made a deacon in the Marthoma Syrian Church of Malabar in Kerala, southern India in 1897. He served his church until his death on 28 Mar 1984, 87 years later.

The longest Church of England incumbency on record is one of 75 years 357 days by Rev. Bartholomew Edwards, Rector of St Nicholas, Ashill, Norfolk from 1813 to 1889. There is some doubt as to whether Rev. Richard Sherinton was installed at Folkestone from 1524 or 1529 to 1601. If the former is correct it would

Millions

The sacred object with the highest intrinsic value is the 15th-century gold Buddha in Wat Trimitr Temple in Bangkok, Thailand. It is 3 m *10 ft* tall and weighs an estimated 5½ tonnes. At the May 1995 price of £245 per fine ounce, its intrinsic worth was £30.9 million. The gold under the plaster exterior was found only in 1954.

There are more than 2000 'registered' saints, of whom around two-thirds are either Italian or French. The first Christian martyr was St Stephen, executed c. AD 36. Britain's first was St Alban, executed c. AD 209.

Papal Records

Longest Papal Reign
Pius IX—Giovanni Maria Mastai-Ferretti (1846–78). 31 years 236 days

Shortest Papal Reign
Stephen II (died 752). 2 days

Longest-Lived Popes
St Agatho (died 681) (probably exaggerated) ?106 years. Leo XIII—Gioacchino Pecci (1810–1903). 93 years 140 days

Youngest Elected Pope
John XII—Ottaviano (c. 937–64) in 955. 18 years old

Last Briton
Adrian IV—Nicholas Breakspear (c. 1100–59) (b. Abbots Langley, Herts). Elected 4 Dec 1154

Youngest

The youngest bishop of all time was HRH the Duke of York and Albany, the second son of George III, who was elected Bishop of Osnabrück, through his father's influence as Elector of Hanover, at the age of 196 days on 27 Feb 1764. He resigned 39 years later.

surpass the Edwards record (⟨> above). The parish of Farrington, Hants had only two incumbents in a period of 122 years: Rev. J. Benn (28 Mar 1797 to 1857) and Rev. T.H. Massey (1857 to 5 Apr 1919). From 1675 to 1948 the incumbents of Rose Ash, Devon were from eight generations of the family of Southcomb.

Sunday school F. Otto Brechel (1890–1990) of Mars, Pennsylvania, USA completed 88 years (4576 Sundays) of perfect attendance at church school at three different churches in Pennsylvania—the first from 1902 to 1931, the second from 1931 to 1954, and the third from 1954 onwards.

Oldest parish register The oldest part of any parish register surviving in England contains entries from the summer of 1538. There is a sheet from that of Alfriston, E Sussex recording a marriage on 10 Jul 1504, but it is thought that this is possibly a reference to 1544 as it is among entries from 1547. The original register for Great Bricett, Suffolk contained two burial entries dated 1525. A nineteenth century survey refers to Tonsor, Northants having register entries dated 1440.

Largest crowds The greatest recorded number of human beings assembled with a common purpose was an estimated 15 million at the Hindu festival of Kumbh mela, which was held at the confluence of the Yamuna (formerly the Jumna), the Ganges and the invisible 'Saraswathi' at Allahabad, Uttar Pradesh, India on 6 Feb 1989 (⟨> also Largest funerals).

Largest funerals The funeral of the charismatic C.N. Annadurai (died 3 Feb 1969), Madras Chief Minister, was attended by 15 million people, according to a police estimate. The queue at the grave of the Russian singer and guitarist Vladimir Visotsky (died 28 Jul 1980), stretched for 10 km *6 miles*.

Singing

Longest-serving chorister John Love Vokins (1890–1989) was a chorister for 92 years. He joined the choir of Christ Church, Heeley, Sheffield, S Yorks in 1895 and that of St Michael's, Hathersage, Derbys, 35 years later, and was still singing in 1987.

Human
Achievements

Endurance and Endeavour

Most travelled The world's most travelled man is John D. Clouse from Evansville, Indiana, USA, who has visited all of the sovereign countries and all but six of the non-sovereign or other territories which existed in early 1995 (↔ Countries).

The most travelled couple are Dr Robert and Carmen Becker of East Northport, New York, USA, both of whom have visited all of the sovereign countries and all but nine of the non-sovereign or other territories.

The most travelled man in the horseback era was believed to be the Methodist preacher Bishop Francis Asbury (b. Handsworth, W Mids, 1745), who travelled 425,000 km *264,000 miles* in North America between 1771 and 1815. During this time he preached some 16,000 sermons and ordained nearly 3000 ministers.

Longest walks The first person reputed to have 'walked round the world' is George Matthew Schilling (USA) from 3 Aug 1897 to 1904, but the first verified achievement was by David Kunst (b. 1939, USA) from 20 Jun 1970 to 5 Oct 1974, who walked 23,250 km *14,450 miles* through four continents.

The greatest distance claimed for a 'round the world walker' is 49,117 km *30,520 miles*, by Arthur Blessitt of North Fort Meyers, Florida, USA, in more than 25 years since 25 Dec 1969. He has been to all seven continents, including Antarctica, carrying a 3.7 m *12 ft* cross and preaching throughout his walk. Steven Newman of Bethel, Ohio, USA spent four years, from 1 Apr 1983 to 1 Apr 1987, walking 36,200 km *22,500 miles* around the world (thus going at a far faster rate than Schilling, Kunst and Blessitt), covering 20 countries and five continents.

The longest walk by a woman was one of 31,521 km *19,586 miles* by Ffyona Campbell of Dartmouth, Devon, who in five phases walked round the world covering four continents and 20 countries, leaving John o' Groats, Highland on 16 Aug 1983 and returning there on 14 Oct 1994.

Rick Hansen (b. Canada, 1957), who was paralysed from the waist down in 1973 as a result of a motor accident, wheeled his wheelchair 40,074.06 km *24,901.55 miles* through four continents and 34 countries. He started his journey from Vancouver on 21 Mar 1985 and arrived back there on 22 May 1987.

George Meegan (b. 2 Oct 1952) from Rainham, Kent walked 30,431 km *19,019 miles* from Ushuaia, the southern tip of South America, to Prudhoe Bay in northern Alaska, taking 2426 days from 26 Jan 1977

Q. In which country did this record attempt take place?
A. See Page 209

...Around the world together

The most travelled couple are Dr Robert and Carmen Becker of East Northport, New York, USA, both of whom have visited all 192 sovereign countries and all but 10 of the 65 non-sovereign or other territories.

They met in her home town in France during World War II, when he was serving in the US army. He went on to Germany, and when the war ended he came back to marry her. Bob and Carmen Becker have been running around together ever since.

The Beckers can reel off fascinating stories galore. Imelda Marcos sang for them, and they were once introduced to Japanese royalty. "We both travelled as kids," says Carmen Becker. "We had to go back to some places after we were married so we could say we'd been there as a couple."

Both groan when asked to recall how many trips they've taken. "We have no idea" Mrs. Becker says. Now retired, they spend a lot of time in their Florida home, sticking pins in their latest world map ("It all keeps changing!") and reminiscing. "I am so glad we did certain things when the world was more primitive. It's not as safe any more."

Of all the places she's been to, Mrs. Becker figures she could happily take up residence in French Polynesia, as a second choice to the USA. An archaeology enthusiast, her husband remembers Australia most fondly, especially Ayers Rock. "Everywhere we go, everybody is hospitable, everybody likes us. If you're nice to people, they're nice to you."

So, how many times have the world's most travelled couple lost their luggage? Only once!

■ Robert and Carmen Becker's travels together have taken them to an exciting range of countries, where they have seen all sorts of contrasts—great sights in cities and idyllic peaceful scenery in places as diverse as Thailand and Guadeloupe sum up the exciting life which they lead. The inset photograph shows them with the globe which is such a feature of their plans.
(Photos: Courtesy of Dr and Mrs R. Becker, Images and Spectrum/HOA-QUI)

to 18 Sep 1983. He thus completed the first traverse of the Americas and the western hemisphere.

Sean Eugene McGuire (USA; b. 15 Sep 1956) walked 11,791 km *7327 miles* from the Yukon River, north of Livengood, Alaska to Key West, Florida in 307 days, from 6 Jun 1978 to 9 Apr 1979. The trans-Canada (Halifax to Vancouver) record walk of 6057 km *3764 miles* is 96 days by Clyde McRae, aged 23, from 1 May to 4 Aug 1973. John Lees (b. 23 Feb 1945) of Brighton, E Sussex walked 4628 km *2876 miles* across the USA from City Hall, Los Angeles, California to City Hall, New York in 53 days 12 hr 15 min (averaging 86.49 km *53.75 miles* a day) between 11 April and 3 Jun 1972.

British Isles The longest walk round the coast of the British Isles was one of 15,239 km *9469 miles* by John Westley of Cheshunt, Herts from 5 Aug 1990 to 20 Sep 1991. His walk began and ended at Tower Bridge, London. Vera Andrews set a record for the longest walk in mainland Britain, when she covered a total distance of 11,777 km *7318 miles* between 2 Jan and 24 Dec 1990, taking in all of the British Gas showrooms. She started and finished at her home town of Clacton-on-Sea, Essex.

North Pole conquest The claims of the two Arctic explorers Dr Frederick Albert Cook (1865–1940) and Cdr (later Rear-Ad.) Robert Edwin Peary (1856–1920),

Guess What?
Q. What is the nationality of the person who has won most Olympic gold medals for walking?
A. See Page 230

of the US Naval Civil Engineering branch, to have reached the North Pole lack irrefutable proof, and several recent surveys have produced conflicting conclusions. On excellent pack ice and modern sledges, Wally Herbert's 1968–9 expedition (⇨ Arctic crossing, below) attained a best day's route mileage of 37 km *23 miles* in 15 hours. Cook (⇨ above) claimed 42 km *26 miles* twice, while Peary claimed an average of 61 km *38 miles* over eight consecutive days, which many glaciologists regard as quite unsustainable.

The first people indisputably to have reached the North Pole at ground level—the exact point Lat. 90°00'00" N (± 300 metres)—were Pavel Afanasyevich Geordiyenko, Pavel Kononovich Sen'ko, Mikhail Mikhaylovich Somov and Mikhail Yemel'yenovich Ostrekin (all of the former USSR), on 23 Apr 1948.

The earliest indisputable attainment of the North Pole by surface travel over the sea-ice took place at 3 p.m. (Central Standard Time) on 19 Apr 1968, when expedition leader Ralph Plaisted (USA), accompanied by Walter Pederson, Gerald Pitzl and Jean Luc Bombardier, reached the pole after a 42-day trek in four skidoos (snowmobiles).

Naomi Uemura (1941–84), the Japanese explorer and mountaineer, became the first person to reach the North Pole in a solo trek across the Arctic sea-ice at 4:45 a.m. GMT on 1 May 1978. He had travelled 725 km *450 miles*, setting out on 7 Mar from Cape Edward, Ellesmere Island in northern Canada.

The first people to ski to the North Pole were the seven members of a Soviet expedition, led by Dmitry Shparo. They reached the pole on 31 May 1979 after a trek of 1500 km *900 miles* which took them 77 days.

South Pole conquest The first men to cross the Antarctic Circle (Lat. 66°33'S) were the 193 crew members of the *Resolution* (462 tons) (Capt. James Cook, RN, 1728–79) and *Adventure* (336 tons) (Lt Tobias Furneaux, RN) on 17 Jan 1773 at 39°E. The first person known to have sighted the Antarctic ice shelf was Capt. Fabian Gottlieb Benjamin von Bellingshausen (Russia) (1778–1852) on 27 Jan 1820 from the vessel *Vostok* accompanied by *Mirnyy*.

> **The first person to reach the South Pole solo and unsupported was Erling Kagge, aged 29 (Norway), on 7 Jan 1993 after a 50-day trek of 1400 km *870 miles* from Berkner Island.**

The South Pole (alt. 2779 m *9186 ft* on ice and 102 m *336 ft* bedrock) was first reached at 11 a.m. on 14 Dec 1911 by a Norwegian party of five men led by Capt. Roald Engebereth Gravning Amundsen (1872–1928), after a 53-day march with dog sledges from the Bay of Whales, into which he had penetrated in the vessel *Fram*.

The longest unsupported trek in Antarctica was by team-leader Sir Ranulph Fiennes Bt, 48, with Dr Michael Stroud, 37, who set off from Gould Bay on 9 Nov 1992, reached the South Pole on 16 Jan 1993 and finally abandoned their walk on the Ross ice shelf on 11 February. They covered a distance of 2170 km *1350 miles* during their 94-day trek (⇨ Longest sledge journeys).

First to see both poles The first people to see both poles were Amundsen (⇨ above) and Oskar Wisting when they flew aboard the airship *Norge* over the North Pole on 12 May 1926, having previously been to the South Pole on 14 Dec 1911.

First to visit both poles Dr Albert Paddock Crary (USA) (1911–87) reached the North Pole in a Dakota aircraft on 3 May 1952. On 12 Feb 1961 he arrived at the South Pole by Sno Cat on a scientific traverse party from the McMurdo Station.

Pole to pole circumnavigation The first pole to pole circumnavigation was achieved by Sir Ranulph Fiennes and Charles Burton of the British Trans-Globe Expedition, who travelled south from Greenwich (2 Sep 1979), via the South Pole (15 Dec 1980) and the North Pole (10 Apr 1982), and back to Greenwich, arriving on 29 Aug 1982 after a 56,000 km *35,000 mile* trek (⇨ Arctic crossing and Antarctic crossing).

First to walk to both poles The first man to walk to both the North and the South Pole was Robert Swan (b. 28 Jul 1956). He led the three-man Footsteps of Scott expedition, which reached the South Pole on 11 Jan 1986, and three years later headed the eight-man Icewalk expedition, which arrived at the North Pole on 14 May 1989.

Arctic crossing The first crossing of the Arctic sea-ice was achieved by the British Trans-Arctic Expedition, which left Point Barrow, Alaska on 21 Feb 1968 and arrived at the Seven Island archipelago north-east of Spitzbergen 464 days later, on 29 May 1969. This involved a haul of 4699 km *2920 miles* with a drift of 1100 km *700 miles*, compared with the straight-line distance of 2674 km *1662 miles*. The team comprised Wally Herbert (leader), 34, Major Ken Hedges, RAMC, 34, Allan Gill, 38, and Dr Roy Koerner (glaciologist), 36, and 40 huskies.

> **Dr Jean-Louis Etienne, aged 39 (France), was the first person to reach the pole solo and without dogs, on 11 May 1986 after 63 days.**

The only crossing achieved in a single season was that by Fiennes and Burton (⇨ Pole to pole circumnavigation and Antarctic crossing) from Alert via the North Pole to the Greenland Sea in open snowmobiles.

Antarctic crossing The first surface crossing of the Antarctic continent was completed at 1:47 p.m. on 2 Mar 1958, after a trek of 3473 km *2158 miles* lasting 99 days from 24 Nov 1957, from Shackleton Base to Scott Base via the pole. The crossing party of 12 was led by Dr (now Sir) Vivian Ernest Fuchs (b. 11 Feb 1908).

The 4185 km *2600 mile* trans-Antarctic leg from Sanae to Scott Base of the 1980–2 Trans-Globe Expedition was achieved in 67 days, from 28 Oct 1980 to 11 Jan 1981, having reached the South Pole on 15 Dec 1980. The three-man party on snowmobiles comprised Sir Ranulph Fiennes Bt, Oliver Shepard and Charles Burton (⇨ Pole to pole circumnavigation and Arctic crossing).

Longest sledge journeys The longest polar sledge journey was that undertaken by the International Trans-Antarctica Expedition (six members), who sledged a distance of some 6040 km *3750 miles* in 220 days from 27 Jul 1989 (Seal Nunataks) to 3 Mar 1990 (Mirnyy). The expedition was accompanied by a team of 40 dogs, but a number of them were flown out from one of the staging posts for a period of rest before returning to the Antarctic. The expedition was supported by aircraft throughout its duration.

The longest *totally self-supporting* polar sledge journey ever made was one of 2170 km *1350 miles* from Gould Bay to the Ross ice shelf by Sir Ranulph Fiennes and Dr Michael Stroud (⇨ South Pole conquest).

Longest on a raft The longest recorded survival alone on a raft is 133 days (4½ months) by Second Steward Poon Lim (b. Hong Kong) of the UK Merchant Navy, whose ship, the SS *Ben Lomond*, was torpedoed in the Atlantic 910 km *565 miles* west of St Paul's Rocks in Lat. 00°30'N, Long. 38°45'W at 11:45 a.m. on 23 Nov 1942. He was picked up by a Brazilian fishing boat off Salinópolis, Brazil on 5 Apr 1943 and was able to walk ashore.

> **Guess What?**
> Q. How long did it take John Fairfax to row across the Atlantic Ocean in 1969?
> A. See Page 112

Tabwai Mikaie and Arenta Tebeitabu, two fishermen from the island of Nikunau in Kiribati, survived for 177 days adrift at sea in their fishing boat—a 4 m *13 ft* open dinghy. They were caught in a cyclone shortly after setting out on a trip on 17 Nov 1991 and were found washed ashore in Western Samoa, 1800 km *1100 miles* away, on 11 May 1992. A third man had left with them but died a few days before they reached Western Samoa.

Greatest ocean descent The record ocean descent was achieved in the Challenger Deep of the Marianas Trench, 400 km *250 miles* south-west of Guam in the Pacific Ocean, when the Swiss-built US Navy bathyscaphe *Trieste*, manned by Dr Jacques Piccard (Switzerland) (b. 28 Jul 1922) and Lt Donald Walsh, USN reached a depth of 10,916 m *35,813 ft* at 1:10 p.m. on 23 Jan 1960 (⇨ Oceans deepest).

Under Water

Submergence The **continuous** duration record (i.e. no rest breaks) for scuba (i.e. self-contained underwater breathing apparatus, used without surface air hoses) is 212 hr 30 min, by Michael Stevens of Birmingham in a Royal Navy tank at the National Exhibition Centre, Birmingham from 14–23 Feb 1986.

Deep-diving records The record depth for the *ill-advised* and dangerous activity of breath-held diving is 125 m *410 ft* by Francisco 'Pipin' Ferreras (Cuba) off Grand Bahama Island on 14 Nov 1993. He was under water for 2 min 9 sec.

The record dive with scuba (self-contained underwater breathing apparatus) is 133 m *437 ft* by John J. Gruener and R. Neal Watson (US) off Freeport, Grand Bahama on 14 Oct 1968.

> **Currently the overall underwater duration record is 212 hours 30 minutes, set by Michael Stevens in February 1986. Forty years ago the record was just 25 hours, set by Guy Cadieux in March 1955.**

The record dive utilizing gas mixtures was a simulated dive to a depth of 701 m *2300 ft* of sea-water by Théo Mavrostomos as part of the HYDRA 10 operation at the Hyperbaric Center of Comex in Marseilles, France on 20 Nov 1992, during a 43-day dive. He was breathing 'hydreliox' (hydrogen, oxygen and helium).

Arnaud de Nechaud de Feral performed a saturation dive of 73 days from 9 Oct–21 Dec 1989 in a hyperbaric chamber simulating a depth of 300 m *985 ft*, as part of the HYDRA 9 operation carried out by Comex at Marseilles, France. He was breathing 'hydrox', a mixture of hydrogen and oxygen.

Marriage ▶▶ ▶▶

Richard Presley spent 69 days 19 min in a module underwater at a lagoon in Key Largo, Florida, USA from 6 May to 14 Jul 1992. The test was carried out as part of a mission entitled Project Atlantis which had as its aim to explore the human factors of living in an undersea environment.

High altitude diving The record for high altitude diving is 5900 m *19,357 ft*, in a lagoon in the crater of Licancabur, a volcano on the border between Chile and Bolivia. Henri García of the Chilean *Expedición America* team spent 1 hr 8 min exploring the lake between depths of 5 m *16 ft* and 7 m *23 ft* on 16 Jan 1995.

Deepest underwater escapes The deepest underwater rescue ever achieved was of the *Pisces III*, in which Roger R. Chapman (28), and Roger Mallinson (35), were trapped for 76 hours when it sank to 480 m *1575 ft*, 240 km *150 miles* south-east of Cork, Republic of Ireland on 29 Aug 1973. It was hauled to the surface on 1 September by the cable ship *John Cabot* after work by *Pisces V*, *Pisces II* and the remote-control recovery vessel *Curv* (Controlled Underwater Recovery Vehicle).

The greatest depth from which an unaided escape without any equipment has been made is 68.6 m *225 ft*, by Richard A. Slater from the rammed submersible *Nekton Beta* off Catalina Island, California, USA on 28 Sep 1970.

The record for an escape with equipment was by Norman Cooke and Hamish Jones on 22 Jul 1987. During a naval exercise they escaped from a depth of 183 m *601 ft* from the submarine HMS *Otus* in Bjornefjorden, off Bergen, Norway. They were wearing standard suits with a built-in lifejacket, from which air expanding during the ascent passes into a hood over the escaper's head.

Deepest salvage The greatest depth at which salvage has been successfully carried out is 5258 m *17,251 ft*, in the case of a helicopter which had crashed into the Pacific Ocean in August 1991 with the loss of four lives. Crew of the USS *Salvor* and personnel from Eastport International managed to raise the wreckage

to the surface on 27 Feb 1992 so that the authorities could try to determine the cause of the accident.

The deepest salvage operation ever achieved with divers was on the wreck of HM cruiser *Edinburgh*, sunk on 2 May 1942 in the Barents Sea off northern Norway, inside the Arctic Circle, in 245 m *803 ft* of water. Over 31 days (from 7 Sep–7 Oct 1981), 12 divers worked on the wreck in pairs. A total of 460 gold ingots (the only 100 per cent salvage to date) was recovered.

Guess What?

Q. What is particularly unusual about Fabien Pretou and his wife Natalie?

A. See Page 55

Marriage

Most marriages The greatest number of marriages contracted by one person in the monogamous world is 28, by former Baptist minister Glynn 'Scotty' Wolfe (b. 1908) of Blythe, California, USA, who first married in 1927. He is currently separated from his 28th wife and hoping to marry again. He thinks that he has a total of 41 children.

The greatest number of monogamous marriages by a woman is 22, by Linda Essex of Anderson, Indiana, USA. She has had 15 different husbands since 1957, her most recent marriage being in October 1991. However, that also ended in a divorce.

> **Youngest married**
> It was reported in 1986 that an 11-month-old boy was married to a 3-month-old girl at Aminpur, near Pabna, Bangladesh to end a 20-year feud between two families over a disputed farm.

The record for bigamous marriages is 104, by Giovanni Vigliotto, one of many aliases used by either Fred Jipp (b. New York City, 3 Apr 1936) or Nikolai Peruskov (b. Siracusa, Sicily, 3 Apr 1929) between 1949 and 1981 in 27 US states and 14 other countries. On 28 Mar 1983 in Phoenix, Arizona, USA he received 28 years for fraud and six for bigamy, and was fined $336,000. He died in February 1991.

In Britain, the only woman to contract eight legal marriages is Olive Joyce Wilson of Marston Green, Birmingham, W Mids. She has consecutively been Mrs John Bickley, Mrs Don Trethowan, Mrs George

> In 1955 the record for monogamous marriages was 14 by Beverly O'Malley from Los Angeles, California. Forty years later Glynn 'Scotty' Wolfe of Blythe—also in California—holds the record, but with 28 marriages.

Hundley, Mrs Raymond Ward, Mrs Harry Latrobe, Mrs Leslie Harris, Mrs Ray Richards, and now Mrs John Grassick. All were divorced except Mr Hundley, who died.

Pat Hinton of Burton-on-Trent, Staffs has been married ten times since 1971, although four of these have been bigamous. She married her 10th husband in 1991.

Most married Richard and Carole Roble of South Hempstead, New York, USA have married each other 55 times, with their first wedding being in 1969. They have chosen a different location each time, including having ceremonies in all of the states of the USA.

Oldest bride and bridegroom The oldest recorded bridegroom has been Harry Stevens, aged 103, who married Thelma Lucas, 84, at the Caravilla Retirement Home, Wisconsin, USA on 3 Dec 1984. The oldest recorded bride is Minnie Munro, aged 102, who married Dudley Reid, 83, at Point Clare, New South Wales, Australia on 31 May 1991.

The British record was set by George Jameson (b. 19 Dec 1892), who married Julie Robinson, 53, at Honiton, Devon on 10 Mar 1995 when aged 102 years. Mrs Winifred Clark (b. 13 Nov 1871) became Britain's oldest recorded bride when she married 80-year-old Albert Smith at St Hugh's Church, Cantley, S Yorks the day before her 100th birthday.

Longest marriage The longest recorded marriages were both of 86 years. Sir Temulji Bhicaji Nariman and Lady Nariman, who were married from 1853 to 1940, were cousins and the marriage took place when both were aged five. Sir Temulji (b. 3 Sep 1848) died, aged 91 years 11 months, in August 1940 at Bombay, India. Lazarus Rowe (b. Greenland, New Hampshire, USA in 1725) and Molly Webber were recorded as marrying in 1743. He died first, in 1829, also after 86 years of marriage.

Next Year!

The longest engagement on record was between Octavio Guillen and Adriana Martinez. They finally took the plunge after 67 years in June 1969 in Mexico City. Both were then aged 82.

The longest marriage in Britain has been one of 82 years between James Frederick Burgess (b. 3 Mar 1861, died 27 Nov 1966) and his wife Sarah Ann, *née* Gregory (b. 11 Jul 1865, died 22 Jun 1965). They were married on 21 Jun 1883 at St James's, Bermondsey, London.

Golden weddings The greatest number of golden weddings in a family is 10, the six sons and four daughters of Joseph and Sophia Gresl of Manitowoc, Wisconsin, USA all celebrating golden weddings between April 1962 and September 1988, and the six sons and four daughters of George and Eleonora Hopkins of Patrick County, Virginia, USA all celebrating

■ Glynn 'Scotty' Wolfe with his 28th wife, Evia, after their wedding on 27 Jun 1994. Unfortunately the marriage did not last, and before long he was engaged and making plans to marry again.
(Photo: Courtesy of Glynn 'Scotty' Wolfe)

their golden weddings between November 1961 and October 1988.

The British record is seven, the three sons and four daughters of Mr and Mrs F. Stredwick of East Sussex all celebrating their golden weddings between May 1971 and April 1981.

Wedding cere-monies The largest mass wedding cere-mony was one of 20,825 couples officiated over by Sun Myung Moon (b. 1920) of the Holy Spirit Association for the Unification of World Christianity in the Olympic Stadium in Seoul, South Korea on 25 Aug 1992. In addition a further 9800 couples around the world took part in the ceremony through a satellite link.

Most expensive The wedding of Mohammed, son of Shaik Rashid Bin Saeed Al Maktoum, to Princess Salama in Dubai in May 1981 lasted seven days and cost an estimated £22 million. It was held in a pur-pose-built stadium for 20,000 people.

Greatest attendance An esti-mated 30,000 guests from the Belz Hasidic community attended the wedding of Aharon Mordechai Rokeah and Sara Lea Lemberger in Jerusalem, Israel on 4 Aug 1993.

Oldest divorced The oldest aggregate age for a couple to be divorced is 188. On 2 Feb 1984 a divorce was granted in Milwaukee, Wisconsin, USA to Ida Stern, aged 91, and her husband Simon,

97. The British record is 166, Harry Bidwell of Brighton, E Sussex, who was 101, divorcing his 65-year-old wife on 21 Nov 1980.

Feasts and Celebrations

Banquets The most lavish menu ever served was for the main banquet at the Imperial Iranian 2500th Anniversary gathering at Persepolis in October 1971. The feast comprised quails' eggs stuffed with Iranian caviar, a mousse of crayfish tails in Nantua sauce, stuffed rack of roast lamb, a main course of roast peacock stuffed with *foie gras*, fig rings and raspberry sweet champagne sherbet—and the very best wines.

The largest feast was attended by 150,000 guests on the occasion of the renunciation ceremony of Atul Dalpatlal Shah, when he became a monk, at Ahmedabad, India on 2 Jun 1991.

Dining out The world champion for eating out was Fred E. Magel of Chicago, Illinois, USA, who over a period of 50 years dined out 46,000 times in 60 countries as a restaurant grader. His favourite dishes were South African rock lobster and mousse of fresh English strawberries.

The greatest altitude at which a formal meal has been held is 6768 m *22,205 ft*, at the top of Mt Huascaran, Peru, when nine members of the Ansett Social

■ A spectacular mass of colour dominates the scene as a new mass balloon release record is set at Longleat, Wiltshire on 27 Aug 1994 (⇨ p. 206). (Photo: Mike Robertson © HCA Integrated Marketing)

Climbers from Sydney, Australia scaled the mountain on 28 Jun 1989 with a dining table, chairs, wine and three-course meal. At the summit they put on top hats, thermal black ties and balldresses for their dinner party, which was marred only by the fact that the wine froze.

Party-giving The International Year of the Child children's party in Hyde Park, London on 30–31 May 1979 was attended by the royal family and 160,000 children.

The world's biggest birthday party was attended by an estimated 100,000 people in the centre of Aberdeen, Grampian on 24 Jul 1994 to celebrate the 200th birthday of Union Street, the main street in the city.

The largest birthday party actually for someone who attended the party was attended by an estimated 35,000 people at Louisville, Kentucky, USA on 8 Sep 1979 to celebrate the 89th birthday of Col. Harland Sanders, the founder of Kentucky Fried Chicken. The largest in Britain was attended by an estimated 10,000 people on 5 Aug 1989 at Douglas, Isle of Man. The party was held to mark the 50th birthday of Trevor Baines, a well-known local businessman.

On 30 Sep 1994 a total of 433,544 people attended 12,067 coffee mornings held simultaneously through-out Great Britain as part of the Macmillan Nurse Appeal, raising £1 million in the process.

Best man
The world champion 'best man' is Ting Ming Siong, from Sibu, Sarawak, in Malaysia, who officiated at a wedding for the 964th time since 1976 in March 1995.

The largest teddy bears' picnic ever staged was attended by 18,116 bears together with their owners at Selsdon Park Hotel, Croydon, Greater London on 7 Aug 1994.

Guess What?
Q. Where is the largest restaurant in the world?
A. See Page 93

THE GUINNESS TIMES
10 April 1994

Phenomenal footbag feat

A new footbag record was achieved yesterday when Americans Andy Linder and Ted Martin set a doubles record of 100,001 consecutive kicks at Mount Prospect, Illinois. Keeping a footbag aloft is like doing ball control with a football, but with a soft object usually made of leather which does not bounce and is only 5 cm (2 in) in diameter. Additionally no part of the body above the waist may be used.

When they first met in 1988, the doubles record was 33,000 kicks. "We had each done higher than that individually," recalls Linder, so they teamed up and the rest is history. Linder and Martin set a record of 64,792 kicks in 1989. Together and separately they dominate the sport, with six men's records between them.

To train, Martin kicks the footbag 10,000 times a day. Certainly part of his talent is for concentration. "You have to be flexible, quick. One miss and it's over." Fortunately neither of them missed yesterday.

Andy Linder (left) and Ted Martin
(Photo: Hans T Martin)

Trevor Bradley, Colin Barnes and Ray Glover of Haunchwood Collieries Institute and Social Club, Nuneaton, Warks on 15 Aug 1982. A team of 10 rolled a 63.5kg *140lb* barrel 241 km *150 miles* in 30 hr 31 min in Chlumčany, Czech Republic on 27–28 Oct 1982.

Barrow pushing The heaviest loaded one-wheeled barrow pushed for a minimum 200 level feet *61 level metres* was one loaded with bricks weighing a gross 3.75 tonnes *8275 lb*. It was pushed a distance of 74.1 m *243 ft* by John Sarich at London, Ontario, Canada on 19 Feb 1987.

crossing the River Nidd by the Vibroplant team on 9 Jun 1990.

Beer keg lifting George Olesen raised a keg of beer weighing 62.9 kg *138 lb 11 oz* above his head 737 times in the space of six hours (on average more than twice every minute) at Horsens, Denmark on 1 May 1994.

Beer mat flipping Dean Gould of Felixstowe, Suffolk flipped a pile of 111 mats (1.2 mm thick 490 gsm wood pulp board) through 180 degrees and caught them at Edinburgh, Lothian on 13 Jan 1993.

Beer stein carrying Duane Osborn covered a distance of 15 m *49 ft 2½ in* in 3.65 seconds with five full steins in each hand in a contest at Cadillac, Michigan, USA on 10 Jul 1992.

Brick balancing John Evans of Marlpool, Derbys balanced 66 bricks (weighing a total of 134.4 kg *296 lb 4 oz*) on his head for 10 seconds at Cannock, Staffs on 12 Feb 1994.

Brick lifting Russell Bradley of Worcester lifted 31 bricks laid side by side off a table, raising them to chest height and holding them there for two seconds on 14 Jun 1992. The greatest weight of bricks lifted was by Fred Burton of Cheadle, Staffs, who held 20 far heavier bricks weighing a total of 89.65 kg *197 lb 10¼ oz* for more than four seconds on 17 Jul 1994.

Bubble David Stein of New York City, USA created a 15.2 m *50 ft* long bubble on 6 Jun 1988. He made the bubble using a bubble wand, washing-up liquid and water.

Bubble-gum blowing The greatest reported diameter for a bubble-gum bubble under the strict rules of this highly competitive activity is 58.4 cm *23 in*, by Susan Montgomery Williams of Fresno, California, USA at the ABC-TV studios in New York City, USA on 19 Jul 1994.

Bucket chain The longest fire service bucket chain stretched over 3496.4 m *11,471 ft*, with 2271 people passing 50 buckets along the complete course at the Centennial Parade and Muster held at Hudson, New York, USA on 11 Jul 1992.

Catapulting The greatest recorded distance for a catapult shot is 415 m *1362 ft* by James M. Pfotenhauer, using a patented 5.22 m *17 ft 1½ in* Monarch IV Supershot and a 53-calibre lead musket ball on Ski Hill Road, Escanaba, Michigan, USA on 10 Sep 1977.

Cigar box balancing Terry Cole of Walthamstow, London balanced 220 unmodified cigar boxes on his chin for nine seconds on 24 Apr 1992.

Clapping The duration record for continuous clapping (sustaining an average of 160 claps per minute, audible at 110 m *120 yd*) is 58 hr 9 min by V. Jeyaraman of Tamil Nadu, India from 12–15 Feb 1988.

Coal carrying Brian Newton of Leicester covered the marathon distance of 42.195 km *26 miles 385 yd* whilst carrying 1 cwt *50.8 kg* of household coal in an open bag in a time of 8 hr 26 min on 27 May 1983.

David Jones of Huddersfield, W Yorks holds the record for the annual race at Gawthorpe, W Yorks,

> **Beer tankard**
> The largest tankard was made by the Selangor Pewter Co. (now known as Royal Selangor International Sdn Bhd) of Kuala Lumpur, Malaysia and unveiled on 30 Nov 1985. It measures 1.99 m *6 ft 6 in* in height and has a capacity of 2796 litres *615 gal*.

Miscellaneous Endeavours

We are excluding records in the 'Human Achievements' area where the duration of the event is the only criterion for inclusion in favour of records which include a greater skill element.

Ball spinning François Chotard of Murs Erigné, France has on various occasions demonstrated the ability to spin nine balls on one hand simultaneously.

Balloon release The largest mass balloon release ever staged was one of 1,592,744 balloons by Disney Home Video at Longleat House, Wilts on 27 Aug 1994.

Balloon sculpture The largest balloon sculpture was a reproduction of Van Gogh's *Fishing Boats on the Beach of Les Saintes Maries*, made out of 25,344 coloured balloons on 28 Jun 1992. Students from Haarlem Business School created the picture at a harbour in Ouddorp in the Netherlands.

Barrel rolling The record for rolling a full 36 gal *1.64 hl* metal beer barrel over a measured mile is 8 min 7.2 sec, by Phillip Randle, Steve Hewitt, John Round,

Barrow racing The fastest time attained in a 1 mile *1.609 km* wheelbarrow race is 4 min 48.51 sec, by Piet Pitzer and Jaco Erasmus at the Transvalia High School, Vanderbijlpark, South Africa on 3 Oct 1987.

Bath tub racing The record for a 36 mile *57.9 km* bath tub race is 1 hr 22 min 27 sec, by Greg Mutton at the Grafton Jacaranda Festival, New South Wales, Australia on 8 Nov 1987. Tubs are limited to 75 in *1.90 m* and 6 hp *4.5 kW* motors. The greatest distance for paddling a hand-propelled bath tub in still water for 24 hours is 145.6 km *90½ miles*, by 13 members of Aldington Prison Officers Social Club, near Ashford, Kent on 28–29 May 1983.

Baton twirling The greatest number of complete spins done between tossing a baton into the air and catching it is 10 by Donald Garcia, on the BBC *Record Breakers* programme on 9 Dec 1986.

Bed making The pair record for making a bed with 1 blanket, 2 sheets, an undersheet, an uncased pillow, 1 counterpane and 'hospital' corners is 14.0 seconds, by Sister Sharon Stringer and Nurse Michelle Benkel of the Royal Masonic Hospital, London at the launch of the 1994 edition of *The Guinness Book of Records*, held at Canary Wharf, London on 26 Nov 1993.

The record time for one person to make a bed is 28.2 seconds, by Wendy Wall, 34, of Hebersham, Sydney, Australia on 30 Nov 1978.

Bed pushing The record distance is 5204 km *3233.65 miles*, in the case of a wheeled hospital bed by a team of nine employees of Bruntsfield Bedding Centre, Edinburgh from 21 Jun–26 Jul 1979.

Bed race The record time for the annual Knaresborough Bed Race (established 1966) in N Yorks is 12 min 9 sec for the 3.27 km *2.04 miles* course

Guess What?
Q. How many bricks did Gary Lovegrove lay in an hour?
A. See Page 87

Guess What?
Q. How high was the largest balloon ever made?
A. See Page 131

carrying a 50 kg *110 lb* bag over the 1012.5 m *1107.2 yd* course in 4 min 6 sec on 1 Apr 1991.

Crate climbing Philip Bruce stacked 38 beer crates in a single column and climbed up them to a height of 9.65 m *31 ft 8 in* at Sowerby Bridge, West Yorks on 26 Aug 1991.

Crawling The longest continuous voluntary crawl (progression with one or other knee in unbroken contact with the ground) is 50.6 km *31½ miles*, by Peter McKinlay and John Murrie, who covered 115 laps of an athletics track at Falkirk, Central on 28–29 Mar 1992. Over a space of 15 months ending on 9 Mar 1985, Jagdish Chander, 32, crawled 1400 km *870 miles* from Aligarh to Jamma, India to appease his revered Hindu goddess, Mata.

Egg and spoon racing Dale Lyons of Meriden, W Mids ran the London marathon (42.195 km *26 miles 385 yd*) while carrying a dessert spoon with a fresh egg on it in 3 hr 47 min on 23 Apr 1990.

Escapology Nick Janson of Benfleet, Essex has escaped from handcuffs locked on him by more than 1500 different police officers during the period since 1954.

Footbag The world record for keeping a footbag airborne is 51,155 consecutive kicks by Ted Martin (USA) at Mount Prospect, Illinois, USA on 29 May 1993. The greatest number of kicks in five minutes is 912 by Kenny Shults (USA) at Golden, Colorado on 30 Jul 1991.

French knitting Ted Hannaford of Sittingbourne, Kent has produced a piece of French knitting 9.03 km *5.61 miles* long since he started work on it in 1989.

Glass balancing Terry Cole of Walthamstow, London succeeded in balancing 50 pint glasses on his chin for 14 seconds on *The Big Breakfast* television programme on 6 Oct 1994.

Gurning The only gurner—someone who excels in the art of pulling grotesque faces—to have won eight national titles is Ron Looney of Egremont, Cumbria, from 1978–83 and 1990–1.

High diving Col. Harry A. Froboess (Switzerland) jumped 120 m *394 ft* into the Bodensee from the airship *Graf Hindenburg* on 22 Jun 1936.

The greatest height reported for a dive into an air bag is 99.4 m *326 ft* by stuntman Dan Koko, who jumped from the top of Vegas World Hotel and Casino on to a 6.1 × 12.2 × 4.2 m *20 × 40 × 14 ft* target on 13 Aug 1984. His impact speed was 141 km/h *88 mph*.

Hitch-hiking The title of world champion hitch-hiker is claimed by Stephan Schlei of Ratingen, Germany, who since 1960 has obtained free rides totalling 726,117 km *451,188 miles*.

Hod carrying Russell Bradley of Worcester carried bricks weighing 164 kg *361 lb 9 oz* up a ladder of the minimum specified length of 12 ft *3.65 m* on 28 Jan 1991 at Worcester City Football Club. The hod weighed 43 kg *94 lb 13 oz* and he was thus carrying a total weight of 207 kg *456 lb 6 oz*.

He also carried bricks weighing 264 kg *582 lb* in a hod weighing 48 kg *105 lb 13 oz* a distance of 5 m *16 ft 5 in* on the flat, before ascending a runged ramp to a height of 2.49 m *8 ft 2 in* at Worcester on 20 Nov 1993. This gave a total weight of 312 kg *687 lb 13 oz*.

Hop-scotch The greatest number of games of hopscotch successfully completed in 24 hours is 390, by Ashrita Furman of Jamaica, New York, USA on 2–3 Apr 1995.

Human centipede The largest 'human centipede' to move 30 m *98 ft 5 in* (with ankles firmly tied together) consisted of 1537 pupils from Great Barr School, Birmingham, W Mids on 11 Mar 1994. Nobody fell over in the course of the walk.

Human logos The largest human logo ever made was the Human US Shield, consisting of 30,000 officers and men at Camp Custer, Battlecreek, Michigan, USA on 10 Nov 1918.

Guess What?
Q. In which city is the world's largest beer-selling establishment?
A. See Page 94

Ha! Ha!

What constitutes a joke? How much does the audience need to laugh, if at all? Unfortunately the more the audience laughs, the more difficult it is to tell jokes quickly—a comedian would not want to carry on if his audience cannot hear what he is saying. Working on the basis that a joke must have a beginning, a middle and an end, Felipe Carbonell of Lima, Peru told 345 jokes in one hour on 29 Jul 1993, whilst Mike Hessman of Columbus, Ohio, USA has claimed 12,682 in 24 hours on 16–17 Nov 1992.

■ The largest human logo ever formed was this **Human US Shield**, consisting of 30,000 officers and men. Put together by Arthur S. Mole and John D. Thomas, the skill involved in organising everyone so that the perspective was exactly right resulted in a near-perfect photograph.
(Photo: Mole & Thomas/Chicago Historical Society)

Kissing Alfred A.E. Wolfram of New Brighton, Minnesota, USA kissed 8001 people in 8 hours at the Minnesota Renaissance Festival on 15 Sep 1990—one every 3.6 seconds.

Kite flying The following records are all recognized by *Kite Lines* magazine:–

A record height of 9740 m *31,955 ft* was reached by a train of eight kites over Lindenberg, Germany on 1 Aug 1919.

The altitude record for a single kite is 3801 m *12,471 ft*, in the case of a kite flown by Henry Helm Clayton and A.E. Sweetland at the Blue Hill Weather Station, Milton, Massachusetts, USA on 28 Feb 1898.

The longest kite flown was 1034.45 m *3394 ft* in length. It was made and flown by Michel Trouillet and a team of helpers at Nîmes, France on 18 Nov 1990.

The largest kite flown was one of 553 m² *5952 ft²*. It was first flown by a Dutch team on the beach at Scheveningen, Netherlands on 8 Aug 1981.

The fastest speed attained by a kite was 193 km/h *120 mph* flown by Pete DiGiacomo at Ocean City, Maryland, USA on 22 Sep 1989.

The greatest number of figure-of-eights achieved with a kite in an hour is 2911, by Stu Cohen at Ocean City, Maryland, USA on 25 Sep 1988.

The greatest number of kites flown on a single line is 11,284 by Sadao Harada and a team of helpers at Sakurajima, Kagoshima, Japan on 18 Oct 1990.

40 years ago the kite-flying altitude record for a single kite was 3801 m 12,471 ft, achieved in 1898. In 1995 it still is the record, and has now stood for nearly a century.

The longest recorded flight is one of 180 hr 17 min by the Edmonds Community College team at Long Beach, Washington State, USA from 21–29 Aug 1982. Managing the flight of this J-25 parafoil was Harry N. Osborne.

Knitting The world's fastest hand-knitter of all time has been Gwen Matthewman of Featherstone, W Yorks. She attained a speed of 111 stitches per minute in a test at Phildar's Wool Shop, Central Street, Leeds, W Yorks on 29 Sep 1980. Her technique has been filmed by the world's only Professor of Knitting—a Japanese.

Knot-tying The fastest recorded time for tying the six Boy Scout Handbook Knots (square knot, sheet bend, sheep shank, clove hitch, round turn and two half hitches, and bowline) on individual ropes is 8.1 seconds by Clinton R. Bailey, Sr, 52, of Pacific City, Oregon, USA on 13 Apr 1977.

Ladder climbing A team of 10 firefighters from Royal Berkshire Fire & Rescue Service climbed a vertical height of 76.56 km *47.58 miles* up a standard fire-service ladder in 24 hours at Reading, Berks on 28–29 Apr 1995.

Land rowing The greatest distance covered by someone on a land rowing machine is 5278.5 km *3280 miles*, by Rob Bryant of Fort Worth, Texas, USA, who 'rowed' across the USA. He left Los Angeles, California on 2 Apr 1990, reaching Washington, DC on 30 July.

Leap-frogging The greatest distance covered was 1603.2 km *996.2 miles*, by 14 students from Stanford University, California, USA, who started leap-frogging on 16 May 1991 and stopped 244 hr 43 min later on 26 May.

Litter collection The greatest number of volunteers involved in collecting litter in one location on one day is 50,405, along the coastline of California, USA on 2 Oct 1993 in conjunction with the International Coastal Cleanup.

Log rolling The record number of International Championships won is 10, by Jubiel Wickheim of Shawnigan Lake, British Columbia, Canada, between 1956 and 1969.

Fastest magician Eldon D. Wigton, alias Dr Eldoonie, performed 225 different tricks in two minutes at Kilbourne, Ohio, USA on 21 Apr 1991.

Milk bottle balancing The greatest distance walked by a person continuously balancing a milk bottle on the head is 113.76 km *70.16 miles* by Ashrita Furman at Jamaica, New York, USA on 1–2 Aug 1993. It took him 18 hr 46 min to complete the walk.

Milk crate balancing Terry Cole of Walthamstow, London managed to balance 29 crates on his chin for the minimum specified 10 seconds on 16 May 1994.

John Evans of Marlpool, Derbys balanced 91 crates (each weighing 1.36 kg *3 lb*) on his head for 10 seconds at Guernsey, Channel Islands on 9 May 1995.

Musical chairs The largest game on record was one starting with 8238 participants, ending with Xu Chong Wei on the last chair, which was held at the Anglo-Chinese School, Singapore on 5 Aug 1989.

Needle threading The record number of times that a strand of cotton has been threaded through a number 13 needle (eye 12.7 × 1.6 mm *½ × 1/16 in*) in two hours is 20,675, achieved by Om Prakash Singh of Allahabad, India on 25 Jul 1993.

Noodle making Simon Sang Koon Sung of Singapore made 8192 noodle strings (i.e 2^{13}, in thirteen movements) from a single piece of noodle dough in 59.29 seconds during the Singapore Food Festival on 31 Jul 1994. This is more than 138 noodles per second.

Paper chain A paper chain 59.05 km *36.69 miles* long was made by 60 students from University College Dublin as part of UCD Science Day in Dublin, Republic of Ireland on 11–12 Feb 1993. The chain consisted of nearly 400,000 links and was made over a period of 24 hours.

Pass the parcel The largest game of pass the parcel involved 3464 people who removed 2000 wrappers in two hours from a parcel measuring 1.5 × 0.9 × 0.9 m *5 × 3 × 3 ft* at Alton Towers, Staffs on 8 Nov 1992. The event was organized by Parcelforce International and the final present was an electronic keyboard, won by Sylvia Wilshaw.

Pedal-boating Kenichi Horie of Kobe, Japan set a pedal-boating distance record of 7500 km *4660 miles*, leaving Honolulu, Hawaii, USA on 30 Oct 1992 and arriving at Naha, Okinawa, Japan on 17 Feb 1993.

Pogo stick jumping The greatest number of jumps achieved is 177,737, by Gary Stewart at Huntington Beach, California, USA on 25–26 May 1990. Ashrita Furman of Jamaica, New York, USA set a distance record of 25.75 km *16.00 miles* in 6 hr 40 min on 8 Oct 1993 at Gotemba, Japan.

Pram pushing The greatest distance covered in pushing a pram in 24 hours is 563.62 km *350.23 miles* by 60 members of the Oost-Vlanderen branch of Amnesty International at Lede, Belgium on 15 Oct

Microwriting

The Guinness Book of Records has received a number of claims for miniature writing over the years. Brian J. Ford, an expert microscopist and a Guinness Book of Records adviser, was not impressed with many of the results.

'Unfortunately, as size decreases, so does legibility,' he says. 'Some of them look like scribble when magnified. In some cases we have been sent clear copies of what people said they wrote—but you would never guess that from looking through the microscope!'

The best recent claims come from India and China. Surendra Apharya of Jaipur, India, wrote 1749 characters (names of various countries, towns and regions) on a single grain of rice in May 1991. Xie Shui Lin of Jiangxi, China wrote 11,660 characters (speeches by Sir Winston Churchill) within the size of a definitive postage stamp, measuring 19.69 × 17.82 mm *0.78 × 0.70 in* In October 1993. Finally Pan Xixing of Wuxi, China wrote 395 characters, namely 'True friendship is like sound health, the value of which is seldom known until it be lost (Proverb)' on a human hair 2cm *8/10 in* long in April 1995.

Writing by hand is a painstaking process which rarely gives good results. To inscribe clear characters requires the use of a pantograph, which uses a series of levers to reduce the movement of the hand down to minuscule proportions.

Brian adds: 'The greatest micro-writer of all was the late Horace Dall of Luton, Beds. In the mid 1950s he constructed a pantograph with a writing stylus made from a diamond fragment. With this he was able to engrave writing which gave him 140 Bibles to the square inch—an entire Bible would fit onto a pin-head. This remains the world record for mechanical writing.

In 1985 Thomas Newman used a film of silicon nitride to record text in the form of a dot-matrix pattern, each dot only 60 atoms in width. The letters were printed at the rate of 3500 characters in a space measuring 5.8 μm square. On this scale you could write the Lord's Prayer several times on a single bacterium. Most recently the scanning tunnel microscope has allowed us to reduce the size further, since single atoms can now be moved at will. It is now possible to print text only five atoms tall.'

Guess What?

Q. How many pages were there in the heaviest newspaper ever produced?

A. See Page 143

The amazing rope trick

The greatest distance recorded in a rope slide, or death slide as it is also known, is 1746.5m *5730ft* by L/Cpl Peter Baldwin of the Royal Marines based at Plymouth, Devon and Stu Leggett of the Canadian School of Rescue Training, from the top of Mount Gibraltar, near Calgary, Canada on 31 Aug 1994. The descent took 36 seconds, some of which was done at speeds in excess of 160km/h *100mph*, but that only tells part of the story.

The whole event was a mammoth logistical exercise and there were many problems which had to be overcome. Bad weather meant that the attempt had to be put back by three days from the original proposed date, and it took two days to get all the supplies required to the base camp, which was a 1½ hour walk from the nearest road. A helicopter had to be used to take the specially made rope to the start point at the top of Mount Gibraltar, 2582m *8470ft* above sea level. The setting-up period took longer than planned as the rope kept getting caught on trees and the weather fluctuated from snow to extreme heat. It was four hours to the nearest hospital, so a helicopter had to be on standby just in case anything went wrong. As if this was not enough a grizzly bear was seen not far away standing on its hind legs—a further unwanted worry that everyone could do without!

Eventually everything was ready and the all-clear was given. Baldwin and Leggett hurled themselves off the mountain and just over half a minute later after a bumpy ride they were on *terra firma* again, albeit after hitting a tree and taking out its top branches near the end. The previous record of 366.4m *1202ft*, set by some of L/Cpl Baldwin's colleagues at Blackpool, Lancs, had been smashed out of sight and it is no surprise that the BBC *Record Breakers* decided to feature the spectacular record on a complete television programme.

Background picture:
Finishing touches to the rope at the summit

Above: Last pose for camera before the descent

Right: Positioning the rope ready to be uncoiled

Bringing in stores to base camp

Preparing to drop a weight to the ground after a test run

Former athlete Kriss Akabusi, now co-presenter of *Record Breakers*, attends to camp duties

(Photos: Steve Lewis RN © Crown Copyright Department)

1988. A ten-man team from the Royal Marines School of Music, Deal, Kent, with an adult 'baby', covered a distance of 437.2 km *271.7 miles* in 24 hours from 22–23 Nov 1990.

Riding in armour The longest recorded ride in armour is one of 334.7 km *208 miles* by Dick Brown, who left Edinburgh, Lothian on 10 Jun 1989 and arrived in his home town of Dumfries four days later. His total riding time was 35 hr 25 min.

Shorthand The highest recorded speeds ever attained under championship conditions are 300 words per minute (99.64 per cent accuracy) for five minutes and 350 wpm (99.72 per cent accuracy, that is, two insignificant errors) for two minutes, by Nathan Behrin (US) in tests in New York in December 1922. Behrin used the Pitman system, invented in 1837. Arnold Bradley achieved a speed of 309 wpm without error using the Sloan-Duployan system, with 1545 words in five minutes in a test in Walsall, W Mids on 9 Nov 1920.

Slinging The greatest distance achieved for a sling-shot is 477.10 m *1565 ft 4 in* using a 127 cm *50 in* long sling and a 62 g *2¼ oz* dart, by David P. Engvall at Baldwin Lake, California, USA on 13 Sep 1992.

Spear throwing The record distance achieved throwing a spear (using an atlatl or hand-held device which fits onto it) is 201.24 m *660 ft 3 in* by Wayne Brian at Rexberg, Idaho, USA on 16 Sep 1993.

Spitting The greatest recorded distance for a cherry stone is 26.96 m *88 ft 5½ in*, by Horst Ortmann at Langenthal, Germany on 29 Aug 1992. The record for projecting a water-melon seed is 20.96 m *68 ft 9⅛ in* by Lee Wheelis at Luling, Texas, USA on 24 Jun 1989. David O'Dell of Apple Valley, California, USA spat a tobacco wad 15.07 m *49 ft 5½ in* at the 19th World Tobacco Spitting Championships held at Calico Ghost Town, California on 26 Mar 1994.

Stair climbing The 100-storey record for stair climbing was set by Dennis W. Martz in the Detroit Plaza Hotel, Detroit, Michigan, USA on 26 Jun 1978 at 11 min 23.8 sec.

Brian McCauliff ran a vertical mile (ascending and descending eight times) on the stairs of the Westin Hotel, Detroit, Michigan, USA in 1 hr 38 min 5 sec on 2 Feb 1992.

In the line of duty, Brian Davis has mounted 334 of the 364 steps of the tower in the Houses of Parliament 5337 times in eleven years to 30 Apr 1995—equivalent to 33 ascents of Mt Everest.

Russell Gill climbed the 835 steps of the Rhodes State Office Tower in Columbus, Ohio, USA 53 times (a total of 44,255 steps and a vertical height of 8141.8 m *26,712 ft*) in 9 hr 16 min 24 sec on 20 Feb 1994. He went down by lift each time.

The record for the 1760 steps (vertical height 342 m *1122 ft*) in the world's tallest free-standing structure, Toronto's CN Tower, Canada, is 7 min 52 sec by Brendan Keenoy on 29 Oct 1989.

The record for the 1336 stairs of the world's tallest hotel, the Westin Stamford Hotel, Singapore, is 6 min 55 sec by Balvinder Singh, in their 3rd Annual Vertical Marathon on 4 Jun 1989.

Sunil Tamang of the 7th Gurkha Rifles climbed up the 50 storeys of Canary Wharf, Britain's tallest building, in a time of 7 min 3.44 sec on 22 Aug 1992.

Step-ups Terry Cole of Walthamstow, London completed 2362 step-ups in an hour on 5 Apr 1995 using a 38.1 cm *15 in* high exercise bench.

Stilt-walking The fastest stilt-walker on record is Roy Luiking, who covered 100 m *328 ft* on 30.5 cm *1 ft* high stilts in 13.01 seconds at Didam, Netherlands on 28 May 1992. Over a long distance, the fastest was M. Garisoain of Bayonne, France, who in 1892 walked the 8 km *4.97 miles* from Bayonne to Biarritz on stilts in 42 minutes, an average speed of 11.42 km/h *7.10 mph*.

The greatest distance ever walked on stilts is 4804 km *3008 miles*, from Los Angeles, California, USA to Bowen, Kentucky, USA by Joe Bowen from 20 Feb–26 Jul 1980. In 1891 Sylvain Dornon stilt-walked from Paris, France to Moscow, Russia in 50 stages, covering 2945 km *1830 miles*. Another source gives his time as 58 days. Either way, although Bowen's distance was greater, Dornon walked at a much higher speed.

Stone skipping (Ducks and drakes) The video-verified stone skipping record is 38 skips, achieved by Jerdone at Wimberley, Texas, USA on 20 Oct 1991.

Stretcher bearing The longest distance a stretcher with a 63.5 kg *10 st* 'body' has been carried is 270.15 km *167.86 miles*, in 49 hr 2 min from 29 Apr–1 May 1993. This was achieved by two teams of four from CFB (Canadian Forces Base) Trenton in and around Trenton, Ontario, Canada.

Les Stewart of Mudjimba Beach, Queensland, Australia has typed the numbers 1 to 860,000 in *words* on 17,090 quarto sheets as of 30 Apr 1995. His target is to become a 'millionaire'.

String ball, largest The largest ball of string on record is one 4.03 m *13 ft 2½ in* in diameter and 12.65 m *41 ft 6 in* in circumference, amassed by J.C. Payne of Valley View, Texas, USA between 1989 and 1992.

Tightrope walking The world tightrope endurance record is 205 days, by Jorge Ojeda-Guzman of Orlando, Florida, USA, on a wire 11 m *36 ft* long, which was 10.7 m *35 ft* above the ground. He was there from 1 Jan–25 Jul 1993 and entertained the crowds by walking, balancing on a chair and dancing. His main luxury was a wooden cabin measuring 91 × 91 cm *3 × 3 ft* at one end of the tightrope.

Ashley Brophy of Neilborough, Victoria, Australia walked 11.57 km *7.18 miles* on a wire 45 m *147 ft 8 in* long and 10 m *32 ft 10 in* above the ground at the Adelaide Grand Prix, Australia on 1 Nov 1985 in 3½ hours.

Steve McPeak (b. 21 Apr 1945) of Las Vegas, Nevada, USA ascended the 46.6 mm *1⅞ in* diameter Zugspitzbahn cable on the Zugspitze, Germany for a vertical height of 705 m *2313 ft* in three stints aggregating 5 hr 4 min on 24, 25 and 28 Jun 1981. The maximum gradient over the stretch of 2282 m *7485 ft* was more than 30 degrees.

The greatest drop over which anyone has walked on a tightrope is 3150 m *10,335 ft*, above the French countryside, by Michel Menin of Lons-le-Saunier, France, on 4 Aug 1989.

The oldest tightrope-walker was 'Professor' William Ivy Baldwin (1866–1953), who crossed the South Boulder Canyon, Colorado, USA on a 97.5 m *320 ft* wire with a 38.1 m *125 ft* drop on his 82nd birthday on 31 Jul 1948.

Top spinning A team of 25 from the Mizushima Plant of Kawasaki Steel Works in Okayama, Japan spun a giant top 2 m *6 ft 6¾ in* tall and 2.6 m *8 ft 6¼ in* in diameter, weighing 360 kg *793.6 lb*, for 1 hr 21 min 35 sec on 3 Nov 1986.

Typewriting The highest recorded speeds attained with a ten-word penalty per error on a manual machine are: five minutes— 176 wpm net Mrs Carole Forristall Waldschlager Bechen at Dixon, Illinois, USA on 2 Apr 1959; and one hour—147 wpm net Albert Tangora (US) (Underwood Standard), 22 Oct 1923.

The official hour record on an electric typewriter is 9316 words (40 errors) on an IBM machine, giving a net rate of 149 words per minute, by Margaret Hamma, now Mrs Dilmore (US), in Brooklyn, New York, USA on 20 Jun 1941. In an official test in 1946, Stella Pajunas, now Mrs Garnand, attained a rate of 216 words in a minute on an IBM machine.

Gregory Arakelian of Herndon, Virginia, USA set a speed record of 158 wpm, with two errors, on a personal computer in the Key Tronic World Invitational Type-Off, which attracted some 10,000 entrants worldwide. He recorded this speed in the semi-final, in a three-minute test, on 24 Sep 1991.

Mikhail Shestov set a numerical record by typing spaced *numbers* from 1 to 795 on a PC without any errors in 5 minutes at BBC Television Centre, London for the *Record Breakers* programme on 14 Oct 1993.

Unsupported circle The highest recorded number of people who have demonstrated the physical paradox of all being seated without a chair is an unsupported circle of 10,323 employees of the Nissan Motor Co. at Komazawa Stadium, Tokyo, Japan on 23 Oct 1982. The British record is 7402 participants at Goodwood Airfield, W Sussex on 25 May 1986, as part of a Sport Aid event.

Whip cracking The longest whip ever 'cracked' (i.e. the end made to travel above the speed of sound) is one of 56.24 m *184 ft 6 in* excluding the handle, wielded by Krist King of Pettisville, Ohio, USA on 17 Sep 1991.

Window cleaning Gerald Follis of Lurgan, Co. Armagh cleaned three standard 1079 × 1194 mm *42½ × 47 in* office windows with a 300 mm *11¾ in* long squeegee and 9 litres *2 gal* of water in 9.1 seconds on 16 Apr 1994. The record was achieved at the Citybus Guinness World of Records Weekend in Belfast.

Yo-yo 'Fast' Eddy McDonald of Toronto, Canada completed 21,663 loops with a yo-yo in three hours on 14 Oct 1990 at Boston, Massachusetts, USA, having previously set a one hour speed record of 8437 loops at Cavendish, Prince Edward Island, Canada on 14 Jul 1990.

The fastest typing speed kept up over a full hour is the equivalent of 149 words per minute, by Margaret Hamma (US). This is one of the records which has remained intact since *The Guinness Book of Records* first came out in 1955.

Guess What?
Q. How high were the tallest stilts ever mastered?
A. See Page 160

Guess What?
Q. In which city was someone arrested following a record-breaking high-wire performance?
A. See Page 160

Hurdling to heaven?

(Photo: Don Bennett)

Being able to run the 110 metre hurdles in 18.9 seconds is not bad for the average person although of course slow for top athletes. Doing so whilst juggling three balls, however, is something very different, and it is in fact the current world record.

The record holder is Michael Hout of Kettering, Ohio, in the USA and he achieved this time, beating his own record of 20.0 seconds, on 24 Jun 1993. But what does Michael Hout do when he isn't 'joggling' (running while juggling)? He might be dressing up as a clown on stilts, or riding his unicycle in a parade while strumming a guitar. Just as likely, he might be writing a sermon, working with a youth group, or carrying out some of the many responsibilities of a Lutheran pastor, husband, and father of three.

Like other record holders, Hout had to overcome a lot to get the record, previously held by Albert Lucas, who holds several other juggling and joggling records. "At first I just wanted exercise. The joggling was something to motivate me. I wanted just to be able to do the hurdles without dropping the balls."

One hurdle Hout didn't face was convincing his congregation at Good Shepherd Church in Kettering, Ohio, to support him. Nowadays, he'd be preaching to the converted:- "There are 60 or 70 people in our congregation who juggle. We have a great time at church picnics."

What does his superior think? "I can't quote what the bishop said," Hout says. "He kind of looks at me and says, 'Staying out of trouble?'"

Juggling

'Juggled' means the number of catches made equals twice the number of objects.

'Flashed' means the number of catches made equals at least the number of objects used but not twice as many.

*This historically accepted record is reported to have been achieved, but there is no existing proof which makes it clear whether the plates were only flashed or actually juggled.

12 rings (flashed) Albert Lucas (US), 1985; Anthony Gatto (US), 1993.

8 clubs (flashed) Anthony Gatto (US), 1989.

11 balls (flashed) Bruce Sarafian (US), 1992.

10 balls (bounce juggled) Tim Nolan (US), 1988.

8 plates (flashed) Enrico Rastelli* (Italy), 1920s; Albert Lucas (US), 1984.

7 flaming torches (juggled) Anthony Gatto (US), 1989.

Most objects aloft
826 jugglers kept 2478 objects in the air simultaneously, each person juggling at least three objects at Glastonbury, Somerset on 26 Jun 1994.

Duration: 5 clubs without a drop 45 min 2 sec, Anthony Gatto (US), 1989.

Duration: 3 objects without a drop Terry Cole (GB), 11 hr 4 min 22 sec, 1995.

5 balls inverted Bobby May (US), 1953.

3 objects while running (Joggling) Owen Morse (US), 100 m in 11.68 sec, 1989 and 400 m in 57.32 sec, 1990; Kirk Swenson (US), 1 mile 1.6 km in 4 min 43 sec, 1986 and 5000 m 3.1 miles in 16 min 55 sec, 1986; Ashrita Furman (US), marathon—42.195 km 26 miles 385 yd—in 3 hr 22 min 32.5 sec, 1988 and 50 miles 80.5 km in 8 hr 52 min 7 sec, 1989; Albert Lucas (US), 400 m hurdles in 1 min 7 sec, 1993; Owen Morse, Albert Lucas, Tuey

Wilson and John Wee (all US), 1 mile relay in 3 min 57.38 sec, 1990.

5 objects while running (Joggling) Owen Morse (US), 100 m in 13.8 sec, 1988. Bill Gillen (US), 1 mile in 7 min 41.01 sec, 1989 and 5000 m 3.1 miles in 28 min 11 sec, 1989.

Food

Apple pie The largest apple pie ever baked was that made by ITV chef Glynn Christian in a 12 × 7 m 40 × 23 ft dish at Hewitts Farm, Chelsfield, Kent from 25–27 Aug 1982. Over 600 bushels of apples were included in the pie, which weighed 13.66 tonnes 30,115 lb.

Banana split The longest banana split ever created measured 7.32 km 4.55 miles in length, and was made by residents of Selinsgrove, Pennsylvania, USA on 30 Apr 1988.

Barbecue The record attendance at a one-day barbecue was 44,158, at Warwick Farm Racecourse, Sydney, Australia on 10 Oct 1993. The greatest meat consumption ever recorded at a barbecue was at the Lancaster Sertoma Club's Chicken Bar-B-Que at

■ Smiles all-round as the attempt to make the world's largest Christmas pudding results in success for the people of Aughton. The recipe is a secret, known only to two residents of the village (<=> p. 212).
(Photo: Jon Sparks)

Guess What?
Q. How many balls can François Chotard spin simultaneously in one hand?
A. See Page 206

Lancaster, Pennsylvania, USA on 21 May 1994 — 19.96 tonnes *44,010 lb* or 31,500 chicken halves in eight hours.

Biscuit The largest biscuit ever made was a chocolate chip cookie with an area of 93 m² *1001 ft²*, made at Santa Anita Fashion Park in Arcadia, California, USA on 15 Oct 1993. It was 10.67 × 8.72 m *35 ft × 28 ft 7 in* and contained more than 3 million chocolate chips.

Cakes The largest cake ever created weighed 58.08 tonnes *128,238 lb 8 oz*, including 7.35 tonnes *16,209 lb* of icing. It was made to celebrate the 100th birthday of Fort Payne, Alabama, USA, and was in the shape of Alabama. The cake was prepared by a local bakery, EarthGrains, the first cut being made by 100-year-old resident Ed Henderson on 18 Oct 1989.

The tallest cake was 30.85 m *101 ft 2½ in* high, created by Beth Cornell Trevorrow and her team of helpers at the Shiawassee County Fairgrounds, Michigan, USA. It consisted of 100 tiers and was completed on 5 Aug 1990.

The Alimentarium Food Museum in Vevey, Switzerland has on display the world's oldest cake, which was sealed and 'vacuum-packed' in the grave of Pepionkh, who lived in Ancient Egypt around 2200 BC. The 11 cm *4¼ in* wide cake has sesame on it and honey inside, and was possibly made with milk.

Cheese The largest cheese ever created was a cheddar of 18.17 tonnes *40,060 lb*, made on 13–14 Mar 1988 at Simon's Specialty Cheese, Little Chute, Wisconsin, USA. It was subsequently taken on tour in a specially designed, refrigerated 'Cheesemobile'.

Cherry pie The largest cherry pie on record weighed 17.11 tonnes *37,740 lb 10 oz* and contained 16.69 tonnes *36,800 lb* of cherry filling. It measured 6.1 m *20 ft* in diameter, and was baked by members of the Oliver Rotary Club at Oliver, British Columbia, Canada on 14 Jul 1990.

Chocolate model The largest chocolate model was one weighing 4 tonnes *8818 lb*, in the shape of a traditional Spanish

sailing ship. It was made by Gremi Provincial de Pastissería, Confitería i Bollería school, Barcelona, Spain in February 1991 and measured 13 × 8.5 × 2.5 m *42 ft 8 in × 27 ft 10½ in × 8 ft 2½ in*.

Christmas pudding The largest was one of 3.28 tonnes *7231 lb 1 oz*, made by the villagers of Aughton, Lancs and officially unveiled at the Famous Aughton Pudding Festival held on 11 Jul 1992. Work on the pudding had started on 3 July and it was ready the day before the festival.

Doughnut The largest ever made was an American-style jelly doughnut weighing 1.7 tonnes *3739 lb*, which was 4.9 m *16 ft* in diameter and 40.6 cm *16 in* high in the centre. It was made by representatives from Hemstrought's Bakeries, Donato's Bakery and the radio station WKLL-FM at Utica, New York, USA on 21 Jan 1993.

Easter eggs The heaviest Easter egg on record, and also the tallest, was one weighing 4.76 tonnes *10,482 lb 14 oz*, 7.1 m *23 ft 3 in* high, made by staff of Cadbury Red Tulip at their factory at Ringwood,

Popping
to the top

The greatest amount of popped corn ever put in a container occupied 187.45 m³ *6619.76 ft³* of a box measuring 12.18 m *39 ft 11½ in* long, 6.31 m *20 ft 8½ in* wide and 2.44 m *8 ft 0 in* high. This was filled at Beauclerc Elementary School in Jacksonville, Florida, USA over six days from 6 to 11 Oct 1994.

It had been a huge task, but well worth it. Headmistress Montelle A. Trammell recalls "There was a hot air popper in every classroom. We had them piled in the hallways. Anywhere we could find an outlet we plugged in a popper. We even had to have school board electricians come in to do heavy rewiring so we wouldn't break the circuits."

As the school in Florida popped to the top of the record, a new precedent may have been set for having fun while learning. "This was also an educational experiment," Ms Trammell explains, "Every class was responsible for tying the popcorn popping to the curriculum."

(Photos: Beauclerc Elementary School/Theresa Walsh)

WORLD'S LARGEST BOX OF POPCORN

Eleven-year-old William Howard wrote a story about the experience, and Timmy Arvanetes (left) said, "In Maths I learned dividing and multiplication by figuring out how much the box was full and how much came up the sides."

However, the pupils hardly ate any of the leftover popcorn, since most of it was donated to charities. But combining a successful record attempt with education can't be a bad thing!

Victoria, Australia. It was completed on 9 Apr 1992.

Food company The world's leading food company is the Swiss-based Nestlé, with sales in 1994 totalling 56.9 billion Swiss francs (£27.8 billion). The biggest seller among their famous confectionery products is KitKat, 12.7 billion fingers of which were sold worldwide during the year. Every second 401 KitKat fingers are consumed throughout the world.

Haggis The largest haggis on record weighed 303.2 kg *668 lb 7 oz* and was made using 80 ox stomachs by the Troon Round Table, Burns Country Foods and a team of chefs at the Hilton Hotel in Glasgow, Strathclyde on 24 May 1993.

Hamburger The largest hamburger on record was one of 2.50 tonnes *5520 lb*, made at the Outagamie County Fairgrounds, Seymour, Wisconsin, USA on 5 Aug 1989.

Ice-cream sundae The largest ice-cream sundae was one weighing 24.91 tonnes *54,914 lb 13 oz*, made by Palm Dairies Ltd under the supervision of Mike Rogiani in Edmonton, Alberta, Canada on 24 Jul 1988. It consisted of 20.27 tonnes *44,689 lb 8 oz* of ice-cream, 4.39 tonnes *9688 lb 2 oz* of syrup and 243.7 kg *537 lb 3 oz* of topping.

Jelly The world's largest jelly, a 35,000 litre *7700 gal* water-melon flavoured pink jelly made by Paul Squires and Geoff Ross, was set at Roma Street Forum, Brisbane, Queensland, Australia on 5 Feb 1981 in a tank supplied by Pool Fab.

Kebab The longest kebab was one 880.6 m *2889 ft 3 in* long, made by the West Yorkshire Family Service Units, Trade Association of Asian Restaurant Owners and National Power at Bradford, W Yorks on 19 Jun 1994.

Lasagne The largest lasagne was one weighing 3.71 tonnes *8188 lb 8 oz* and measuring 21.33 × 2.13 m *70 × 7 ft*. It was made by the Food Bank for Monterey County at Salinas, California, USA on 14 Oct 1993.

Loaf The longest loaf on record was a Rosca de Reyes 1064 m *3491 ft 9 in* long, baked at the Hyatt Regency Hotel in Guadalajara, Mexico on 6 Jan 1991. If a consumer of a 'Rosca', or twisted loaf, finds the embedded doll, that person has to host the Rosca party (held annually at Epiphany) the following year.

The largest pan loaf ever baked, by staff of Sasko in Johannesburg, South Africa on 18 Mar 1988, weighed 1.43 tonnes *3163 lb 10 oz* and measured 3 × 1.25 × 1.1 m *9 ft 10 in × 4 ft 1 in × 3 ft 7 in*.

Lollipop The world's largest ice lolly was a vanilla, chocolate and nut one of 8.78 tonnes *19,357 lb*, made by staff of Augusto Ltd at Kalisz, Poland between 18 and 29 Sep 1994. The largest 'regular' lollipop was a peppermint-flavoured one weighing 1.37 tonnes *3011 lb 5 oz*, made by staff of BonBon at Holme Olstrup, Denmark on 22 Apr 1994.

Meat pie The largest meat pie on record weighed 9.03 tonnes *19,908 lb* and was the ninth in the series of Denby Dale, W Yorks pies. It was baked on 3 Sep 1988 to mark the bicentenary of Denby Dale pie-

Guess What?
Q. How many times did Fred Magel eat at restaurants in 50 years?
A. See Page 205

making, the first one in 1788 having been made to celebrate King George III's return to sanity.

Mince pie The largest mince pie recorded was one of 1.02 tonnes *2260 lb*, measuring 6.1 × 1.5 m *20 × 5 ft*, baked at Ashby-de-la-Zouch, Leics on 15 Oct 1932.

Omelette The largest omelette in the world had an area of 128.5 m² *1383 ft²* and contained 160,000 eggs. It was cooked by representatives of Swatch at Yokohama, Japan on 19 Mar 1994.

■ Frank Garcia of GNS Spices has developed the hottest spice — the Red 'Savina' Habanero. His company now grows it commercially, but back in 1989 he discovered its existence almost by accident.
(Photo: GNS Spices Inc.)

Omelette making
The greatest number of two-egg omelettes made in 30 minutes is 427, by Howard Helmer at the International Poultry Trade Show held at Atlanta, Georgia, USA on 2 Feb 1990.

Paella The largest paella measured 20 m *65 ft 7 in* in diameter and was made by Juan Carlos Galbis and a team of helpers in Valencia, Spain on 8 Mar 1992. It was eaten by 100,000 people.

Pancake The largest pancake was 15.01 m *49 ft 3 in* in diameter and 2.5 cm *1 in* deep, and weighed 3.00 tonnes *6614 lb*. It was made and flipped at Rochdale, Greater Manchester on 13 Aug 1994 as part of the celebrations to mark the 150th anniversary of the Co-operative movement.

Pastry The longest pastry was a mille-feuille (cream puff pastry) 1037.25 m *3403 ft* in length, made by employees of Pidy, a company based in Ypres, Belgium on 4–5 Sep 1992.

The fourth Denby Dale meat pie (Queen Victoria's Jubilee, 1887) went a bit 'off' and had to be buried.

Pizza The largest pizza ever baked was one measuring 37.4 m *122 ft 8 in* in diameter, made at Norwood Hypermarket, Norwood, South Africa on 8 Dec 1990.

Salami The longest salami on record was one 20.95 m *68 ft 9 in* long with a circumference of 63.4 cm *25 in*, weighing 676.9 kg *1492 lb 5 oz*, made by staff of A/S Svindlands Pølsefabrikk at Flekkefjord, Norway from 6–16 Jul 1992.

Sausage The longest continuous sausage on record was one of 46.30 km *28.77 miles*, made by M & M Meat Shops in partnership with J.M. Schneider Inc., at Kitchener, Ontario, Canada on 28–29 Apr 1995.

Spice, most expensive Prices for wild ginseng (root of *Panax quinque-folium*) from the Chan Pak Mountain area of China, thought to have aphrodisiac qualities, were reported in November 1979 to be as high as $23,000 per ounce in Hong Kong. Total annual shipments from Jilin Province do not exceed 4 kg *140 oz* a year.

Spice, hottest The hottest of all spices is believed to be Red 'Savina' Habanero, belonging to the genus *capsicum*, developed by GNS Spices of Walnut, California, USA. A single dried gram will produce detectable 'heat' in 326 kg *719 lb* of bland sauce.

Stick of rock The largest stick of rock was one weighing 413.6 kg *911 lb 13 oz*. It was 5.03 m *16 ft 6 in* long and 43.2 cm *17 in* thick, and was made by the Coronation Rock Company of Blackpool, Lancs on 20 Jul 1991.

Strawberry bowl The largest bowl of strawberries had a net weight of 2.39 tonnes *5266 lb*. The strawberries were picked at Joe Moss Farms near Embro, Ontario, Canada and the bowl was filled at the Kitchener-Waterloo Hospital, also in Ontario, on 29 Jun 1993.

Sweets The largest sweet on record was a marzipan chocolate weighing 1.85 tonnes *4078 lb 8 oz*, made at the Ven International Fresh Market, Diemen, Netherlands on 11–13 May 1990.

Trifle The largest sherry trifle on record was one weighing 3.13 tonnes *6896 lb*, including 91 litres *20 gal* of sherry, made on 26 Sep 1990 by students of Clarendon College of Further Education, Nottingham.

Yorkshire pudding The largest Yorkshire pudding was one with an area of 42.04 m² *452.2 ft²*, measuring 9.18 × 4.58 m *30 ft 1¼ in × 15 ft 0¼ in*. It was made by staff from the catering department of Rotherham Council at Rotherham, S Yorks on 1 Aug 1991 to celebrate Yorkshire Day.

Pancake tossing
The greatest number of times a pancake has been tossed in two minutes is 349, by Dean Gould at Felixstowe, Suffolk on 14 Jan 1995.

Drink ▶▶ ▶▶

Drink

Alcohol consumption Russia has the highest consumption of spirits per person, with 3.8 litres *6.7 pints* of pure alcohol in 1993. The Czech Republic is the leading beer consumer, with 140.0 litres *246.4 pints* per person, also in 1993, and France heads the list for wine, with 63.5 litres *111.7 pints* per person, again based on 1993 figures. The UK ranks 28th, 12th and 24th in the three lists.

Beer *Oldest* Written references to beer have been found dating from as far back as *c.* 5000 BC, as part of the daily wages of workers at the Temple of Erech in Mesopotamia. Physical evidence of beer dating from *c.* 3500 BC has been detected in remains of a jug found at Godin Tepe, Iran in 1973 during a Royal Ontario Museum expedition. It was only in 1991 that analysis of the remains was carried out, which established that residues in deep grooves in the jug were calcium oxalate, also known as beerstone and still created in barley-based beers.

> **Strongest**
> Baz's Super Brew, brewed by Barrie Parish and on sale at The Parish Brewery at Somerby, Leics, has an alcohol volume of 23.0 per cent. It is only sold in ⅓ measures.

Bottles *Largest* A bottle 3.11 m *10 ft 2 in* tall and 3.5 m *11 ft 6 in* in circumference was filled with 2250 litres *495 gal* of Schweppes Lemonade in Melbourne, Victoria, Australia on 17 Mar 1994 to celebrate 200 years of Schweppes.

The largest bottle of beer was 2.54 m *8 ft 4 in* tall and 2.17 m *7 ft 1½ in* in circumference, and was unveiled at the Shepherd Neame Brewery at Faversham, Kent on 27 Jan 1993. It took 13 minutes to fill the bottle, with 625.5 litres *137½ gal* of Kingfisher beer, the leading Indian lager.

Smallest The smallest bottles of liquor now sold are of White Horse Scotch Whisky, which stand just over 5 cm *2 in* high and contain 1.3 ml *22 minims*. A mini case of 12 bottles costs about £8.00, and measures 5.3 × 4.8 × 3.4 cm *2¹/₁₆ × 1⅞ × 1¹/₁₆ in*. The distributors are Cumbrae Supply Co., Linwood, Strathclyde.

> **Cocktail**
> The largest cocktail on record was a Finlandia Sea Breeze of 11,102.6 litres *2442.2 gal* made at Maui Entertainment Center in Philadelphia, Pennsylvania, USA on 5 Aug 1994. It consisted of Finlandia vodka, cranberry juice, grapefruit juice and ice.

Brewers The oldest brewery in the world is the Weihenstephan Brewery, Freising, near Munich, Germany, founded in AD 1040.

The largest single brewing organization in the world is Anheuser-Busch Inc. of St Louis, Missouri, USA, with 13 breweries in the United States. In 1993 the company sold 10.23 billion litres *2.25 billion gal*, the greatest annual volume ever produced by any brewing company in a year. This included the world's top-selling brand, Budweiser, at 4.82 billion litres *1.06 billion gal*.

> **Yard of ale**
> Peter Dowdeswell of Earls Barton, Northants drank a yard of ale (1.42 litres *2½ pints*) in 5.0 sec at RAF Upper Heyford, Oxon on 4 May 1975.

The largest brewery on a single site is that of the Coors Brewing Co. at Golden, Colorado, USA, where 2.22 billion litres *488.8 million gal* were produced in 1994. At the same location is the world's largest aluminium can manufacturing plant, with a capacity of more than 4 billion cans annually.

Distillers The world's most profitable spirits producer is United Distillers, the spirits company of Guinness plc, having made a profit of £915 million in 1994. The largest blender and bottler of Scotch whisky is also United Distillers, whose Shieldhall plant in Glasgow, Strathclyde has the capacity to fill an estimated 144 million bottles of Scotch a year. This is equivalent to approximately 109 million litres *24 million gal*, most of which is exported. The world's best-selling brands of Scotch and gin, Johnnie Walker Red Label and Gordon's, are both products of United Distillers.

Old Bushmills Distillery, Co. Antrim, licensed in 1608, claims to have been in production in 1276.

Most alcoholic drinks When Estonia was independent between the two world wars, the Estonian Liquor Monopoly marketed 98 per cent alcohol distilled from potatoes (196 per cent US proof).

Spirits *Most expensive* A bottle of 50-year-old Glenfiddich whisky was sold for a record price of 99,999,999 lire (approx. £45,200) to an anonymous Italian businessman at a charity auction in Milan, Italy. The postal auction was held over a two-month period from October to December 1992. The most expensive spirit on sale is Springbank 1919 Malt Whisky, a bottle of which costs £6750 (including VAT) at Fortnum & Mason in London.

Vintners The world's oldest champagne firm is Ruinart Père et Fils, founded in 1729. The oldest cognac firm is Augier Frères & Cie, established in 1643.

Champagne cork flight The longest flight of a cork from an untreated and unheated champagne bottle 1.22 m *4 ft* from level ground is 54.18 m *177 ft 9 in*, reached by Prof. Emeritus Heinrich Medicus at the Woodbury Vineyards Winery, New York, USA on 5 Jun 1988.

Fountain

The greatest number of storeys achieved in a champagne fountain, successfully filled from the top and using traditional long-stem glasses, is 47 (height 7.85 m *25 ft 9 in*), achieved by Moet & Chandon Champagne with 23,642 glasses at Caesars Palace in Las Vegas, Nevada, USA from 19–23 Jul 1993.

Wine *Oldest* It is thought that Stone Age man may have been cultivating wine as early as *c.* 8000 BC. Physical evidence of wine dating from as far back as *c.* 3500 BC has been detected in remains of a Sumerian jar found at Godin Tepe, Iran in 1973 during a Royal Ontario Museum expedition. It was only in 1989 that analysis of the remains was carried out, which established that a large red stain showed the presence of tartaric acid, a chemical naturally abundant in grapes. The oldest bottle of wine to have been sold at auction was a bottle of 1646 Imperial Tokay, which was bought by John A. Chunko of Princeton, New Jersey, USA and Jay Walker of Ridgefield, Connecticut, USA for SFr 1250 (including buyer's premium) at Sotheby's, Geneva, Switzerland on 16 Nov 1984. At the time the sum paid was equivalent to £405.

Most expensive A record £105,000 was paid for a bottle of 1787 Château Lafite claret, sold to Christopher Forbes (US) at Christie's, London on 5 Dec 1985. The bottle was engraved with the initials of Thomas Jefferson (1743–1826), 3rd President of the United States — 'Th J' — a factor which greatly affected the bidding. In November 1986 its cork, dried out by exhibition lights, slipped, making the wine undrinkable.

Tasting The largest ever reported was that sponsored by WQED, a San Francisco television station, in San Francisco, California, USA on 22 Nov 1986. Some 4000 tasters consumed 9360 bottles of wine.

■ Work is under way on mixing the world's largest cocktail. It took ten hours to make the record-breaking Finlandia Sea Breeze. And the comment afterwards? 'Everyone was pretty impressed with it. Now they're just trying to drink it.'
(Photo: Scott Weiner/Retna © Ricky Blatstein)

Liquid gold?

THE GUINNESS TIMES   19 Nov 1993

A new record was set in the early hours of yesterday morning for the highest price ever paid for a glass of wine. It was of course Beaujolais Nouveau 1993 day, and as in previous years the crowds had gathered at Pickwick's, a British pub in Beaune in the wine region of Burgundy. The amount paid? 8600 francs, or £982!

The excitement rose as the bidding got under way for the first glass released in the town. As always, knowing that charities would be benefiting, the difficult economic climate was forgotten as everyone got into the spirit of the auction and the old record set a year ago, also at Pickwick's, was beaten. Appropriately enough for a British pub, the

(Photo: Thierry Gaudillère)

record price was paid by a visitor from Britain, Robert Denby, who proudly shows his purchase to the press above.

Bottle-cap pyramid A pyramid consisting of 362,194 bottle caps was constructed by a team of 11 led by Yevgeniy Lepechov at Chernigov, Kiev, Ukraine from 17–22 Nov 1990.

Can construction A 1:4 scale-model of the Basilica di Sant'Antonio di Padova was built from 3,245,000 empty beverage cans in Padova (Padua), Italy by the charities AMNIUP, AIDO, AVIS and GPDS. The model, measuring 29.15 × 23 × 17.05 m *96 × 75 × 56 ft*, was completed on 20 Dec 1992 after 20,000 hours.

Basket The world's largest hand-woven basket measures 14.63 × 7.01 × 5.79 m *48 × 23 × 19 ft* and was made by the Longaberger Company of Dresden, Ohio, USA in 1990.

pulled in the car park at Westfield Shopping Town, Chatswood, Sydney, Australia on 9 Nov 1991.

Cigars The largest cigar ever made is 5.1 m *16 ft 8½ in* long and weighs 262 kg *577 lb 9 oz* (over ¼ ton). It was constructed in 243 hours using 3330 full tobacco leaves by Tinus Vinke and Jan Weijmer in February 1983 and is on display at the Tobacco Museum in Kampen, Netherlands.

The largest marketed cigar in the world is the 35.5-cm *14-in* Valdez Emperador made by Fábrica de Puros Santa Clara of San Andrés Tuxtla, Veracruz, Mexico and distributed exclusively by Tabacos San Andrés.

Dress A wedding outfit created by Parisian designer Hélène Gainville using jewels by Alexander Reza is estimated to be worth $7,301,587.20. The dress is embroidered with diamonds mounted on platinum and was unveiled in Paris, France on 23 Mar 1989.

The world's longest wedding dress train measured 157 m *515 ft* and was made by the Hansel and Gretel bridal outfitters of Gunskirchen, Germany in 1992. Britain's longest wedding dress train measured 29.8 m *97 ft 7¾ in* and was made by Margaret Riley of Thurnby Lodge, Leics for the blessing of the marriage of Diane and Steven Reid in Thurmaston, Leics on 6 May 1990.

■ **This diamond-encrusted wedding-dress by Hélène Gainville is the most expensive in the world**
(Photo: Gamma/F. Darmigny)

Guess What?
Q. How much are the most expensive shoes you can buy?
A. See Page 217

Auction The largest single sale of wine was conducted by Christie's of London on 10–11 Jul 1974 at Quaglino's Ballroom, London, when 2325 lots comprising 432,000 bottles realized £962,190.

Soft drinks PepsiCo of Purchase, New York, USA topped the *Fortune 500* table for beverage companies in May 1995, with total sales for 1994 of $28.5 billion, compared with $16.2 billion for the Coca-Cola Company of Atlanta, Georgia. Coca-Cola is, however, the world's most popular soft drink, with sales in 1994 of 540 million drinks per day, representing an estimated 46 per cent of the world market.

Milk shake The largest milk shake was a chocolate one of 7400.4 litres *1627.9 gal*, made by the Nelspruit and District Child Welfare Society and the Fundraising Five at Nelspruit, South Africa on 5 Mar 1994.

Manufactured Articles

Axe A steel axe 18.28 m *60 ft* long, 7 m *23 ft* wide and weighing 7 tonnes was designed and built by BID Ltd of Woodstock, New Brunswick, Canada. The axe was presented to the town of Nackawic, New Brunswick, on 11 May 1991 to commemorate the town's selection as Forestry Capital of Canada for 1991. Calculations suggested it would take a 140-tonne lumberjack to swing the axe, but a crane was used to lift it into its concrete 'stump'.

Blanket A hand-knitted, machine-knitted and crocheted blanket measuring a world record 17,289 m^2 *186,107.8 ft^2* was made by members of the Knitting and Crochet Guild world-wide, co-ordinated by Gloria Buckley of Bradford, W Yorks, and assembled at Dishforth Airfield, Thirsk, N Yorks on 30 May 1993.

Can pyramid Five adults and five children from Dunhurst School, Petersfield, Hants, built a record-breaking pyramid of 4900 cans in 25 mins 54 sec (time limit — 30 minutes) on 30 May 1994.

Chandeliers The world's largest set of chandeliers was created by the Kookje Lighting Co. Ltd of Seoul, South Korea. It is 12 m *39 ft* high, weighs 10.67 tonnes and has 700 bulbs. Completed in November 1988, it occupies three floors of the Lotte Chamshil Department Store in Seoul.

Britain's largest chandelier measures 9.1 m *30 ft* and is in the Chinese Room at the Royal Pavilion, Brighton, E Sussex. It was made in 1818 and weighs one ton.

Cheque The world's physically largest cheque measured 21.36 × 9.58 m *70 × 31 ft*. It was presented by InterMortgage of Leeds, W Yorks to Yorkshire Television's 1992 Telethon Appeal on 4 Sep 1992 to the value of £10,000 (⇔Business World—Largest cheque).

Christmas cracker The largest functional cracker ever constructed was 45.72 m *150 ft* long and 3.04 m *10 ft* in diameter. It was made by the international rugby league footballer, Ray Price for Markson Sparks! of New South Wales, Australia and

■ The Meisterstück Solitaire Royal fountain pen can be made to order by Mont Blanc for just £75,000. Included in the price are 4810 diamonds.
(Photo: Mont Blanc)

Fan A hand-painted fan made of fabric and wood measuring 5.5 m *18 ft 5½ in* when unfolded and 2.9 m *9 ft 6 in* high was completed by Brajesh Shrivastava of Bhopal, India in 1994.

Catherine Wheel A self-propelled vertical fire-work wheel 19.3 m *63 ft 6 in* in diameter was designed by Tom Archer and built by Essex Pyrotechnics Ltd of Saffron Walden, Essex. It was fired for 8 revolutions at a mean speed in excess of 5 rpm on 9 Jul 1994.

Flags The world's largest flag, measuring 154 × 78 m *505 × 255 ft* and weighing 1.36 tonnes, is the American 'Superflag' owned by 'Ski' Demski of Long Beach, California, USA. It was made by Humphrey's Flag Co. of Pottstown, Pennsylvania and unfurled on 14 Jun 1992.

The largest Union Flag (or Union Jack) measured 73.15 × 32.91 m *240 × 108 ft* and was displayed at the Royal Tournament, Earl's Court, London in July 1976. It weighed more than a ton and was made by Form 4Y of Bradley Rowe School, Exeter, Devon.

The largest flag *flown* from a flagstaff is a Brazilian national flag measuring 70 × 100 m *229 ft 8 × 328 ft 1 in* in Brasilia.

Jigsaw puzzles The earliest jigsaws were made as 'dissected maps' by John Spilsbury (1739–69) in Russell Court off Drury Lane, London c.1762. Enthusiasts call themselves dissectologists.

The world's largest jigsaw puzzle measured 4783 m² *51,484 ft²* and consisted of 43,924 pieces. Assembled on 8 Jul 1992, it was devised by Centre Socio-Culturel d'Endoume in Marseille, France and was designed on the theme of the environment.

A puzzle consisting of 204,484 pieces was made by BCF Holland b.v. of Almelo, Netherlands and assembled by students of the local Gravenvoorde School on 25 May–1 June 1991. The completed puzzle measured 96.25 m² *1036 ft²*.

Custom-made Stave puzzles of 2640 pieces, created by Steve Richardson of Norwich, Vermont, USA, cost $8680 in June 1992.

Kettle The largest antique copper kettle stood 0.9 m *3 ft* high with a girth of 1.8 m *6 ft* and a capacity of 90 litre *20 gal*, built in Taunton, Somerset, for the hardware merchants Fisher and Son in around 1800.

Fireworks

The largest firework ever produced was *Universe I Part II*, exploded for the Lake Toya Festival, Hokkaido, Japan on 15 Jul 1988. The 700 kg *1543 lb* shell was 139 cm *54.7 in* in diameter and burst to a diameter of 1.2 km *0.75 miles*.

Guess What?
Q. What is the world's best-selling pen?
A. See Page 217

■ This flower-pot—pictured here with its green-fingered creator, Peter Start—measures 1.95 m **6.4 ft** tall.
(Photo: P. Goff)

Knife The penknife with the greatest number of blades is the Year Knife made by cutlers Joseph Rodgers & Sons, of Sheffield, S Yorks, whose trademark was granted in 1682. The knife was made in 1822 with 1822 blades and a blade was added every year until 1973 when there was no further space. It was acquired by Britain's largest hand tool manufacturers, Stanley Works (Great Britain) Ltd of Sheffield, S Yorks, in 1970.

Litter bin The world's largest litter bin was made by Natsales of Durban, South Africa for 'Keep Durban Beautiful Association Week' from 16–22 Sep 1991. The fibre-glass bin, 6.01 m *19ft 9in* tall, is a replica of the standard Natsales make and has a capacity of 43,507 litres *9570gal*.

Pencil A fully-functional pencil measuring 2.74 m *8.9 ft* long and weighing 24 kg *53 lb* was constructed by students at Huddersfield Technical College for Cliffe Hill School, Lightcliffe, Halifax, in 1995.

Pens The most expensive writing pen is the Meisterstück Solitaire Royal fountain pen by Montblanc. It is made of solid gold and is encased with 4810 diamonds—the height in metres of the Mont Blanc mountain. The pen can be made to order for £75,000, and takes a painstaking 6 months to make.

The highest price ever achieved for a single pen was 1.3 million French francs, paid by a Japanese collector in February 1988 for the 'Anémone' fountain pen made by Réden, France. It was encrusted with 600 precious stones, including emeralds, amethysts, rubies, sapphires and onyx, and took skilled craftsmen over a year to complete.

The world's best-selling pen is the BiC Crystal made by the BiC organization, with daily global sales of over 15 million. Sales in the UK are over 600,000 daily, containing enough ink to draw a line around the Earth 37 times.

Pottery The largest thrown vase on record is one measuring 5.34 m *17½ ft* in height (including a lid 1.30 m *4¾ ft* tall), weighing 600 kg *1322 lb 12 oz*. It was completed on 1 Jun 1991 by Faiarte Ceramics of Rustenberg, South Africa.

Terracotta flower-pot The world's largest flower-pot measures 1.95 m *6ft 5in* tall with a circumference of 5.23 m *17ft 1in*. It was hand-built by Peter Start and Albert Robinson at The Plant Pottery, Barby, Northants, in May 1985.

Quilt The world's largest quilt was made by The Saskatchewan Seniors' Association of Saskatchewan, Canada. It measured 47.36 × 25.20 m *155⅓ ft × 82⅔ ft*, and was constructed on 13 Jun 1994.

The largest patchwork quilt made in the UK measures 15.24 × 28.3 m *50ft × 92ft 10in* and was completed on 14 Aug 1990 by residents of Anchor Housing Association sheltered schemes throughout the country.

> **Largest matchstick model** Joseph Sciberras of Malta constructed an exact replica, including the interior, of St. Publius Parish Church, Floriana, Malta consisting of over 3 million matchsticks. Made to scale, the model measures 2 × 2 × 1.5 m *6½ × 6½ × 5ft*.

■ **The record for the most expensive pair of shoes was set when Emperor Field Marshal Jean Fedor Bokassa of the Central African Empire (now Republic) commissioned pearl-studded shoes at a cost of $85,000 from the House of Berluti, Paris, France for his self-coronation at Bangui on 4 Dec 1977.** (Photo: Gamma/Abbas)

Scarf The longest was 32 km *20 miles* long, made by residents of Abbeyfield Houses for the Abbeyfield Society of Potters Bar, Herts and was completed on 29 May 1988.

Shoes The most expensive marketed shoes are mink-lined golf shoes with 18-carat gold embellishments and ruby-tipped spikes costing £13,600 a pair, made by Stylo Matchmakers Ltd of Northampton, Northants.

Sofa A red leather sofa 7.32 m *24 ft* long was made by Art Forma (Furniture) Ltd of Castle Donington, near Derby, for the Swiss company Spuhl AG in May 1995. The sofa, which seats 17 people, was then displayed at the Interzum Exhibition in Cologne, Germany on 19–23 May 1995.

Longest stuffed toy Pupils of Veien School in Hønefoss, Norway created a stuffed snake 419.7 m *1376.9 ft* long in June 1994.

Table cloth The world's largest measures 457.81 m *1502 ft* long and 1.37 m *4½ ft* wide. It was made by the Sportex division of Artex International in Highland, Illinois, USA on 17 Oct 1990.

UK A damask tablecloth 300.5 m *985⅔ ft* long and 1.83 m *6ft* wide was made by Tonrose Ltd of Manchester in June 1988. It had an ivy-leaf design woven into the cloth, which included a total of 134,000 leaves.

> **Guess What?**
> Q. Who is 'Mr Plastic Fantastic'?
> A. See Page 218

Wallet The world's most expensive wallet is a platinum-cornered diamond-studded creation of crocodile skin, made by Louis Quatorze of Paris and Mikimoto of Tokyo which sold in September 1984 for £56,000.

Yo-yo A yo-yo measuring 3.17 m *10⅓ ft* in diameter and weighing 407 kg *897 lb* was devised by J.N. Nichols (Vimto) Ltd and made by engineering students at Stockport College. It was launched by crane from 57.5 m *187 ft* at Wythenshawe, Manchester on 1 Aug 1993 and yo-yoed about four times.

Silver Pieces

The largest single pieces of silver are a pair of water jugs of 242.7 kg *10,408 troy oz (4.77 cwt)* made by Gorind Narain in 1902 for the Maharaja of Jaipur (1861–1922). They are 1.6 m *5¼ ft* tall, 2.48 m *8ft 1½in* in circumference and have a capacity of 8182 litres *1800 gal*. They are now in the City Palace, Jaipur, India.

> **Zip-fastener** The world's longest zip-fastener was laid around the centre of Sneek, Netherlands on 5 Sep 1989. The brass zipper, made by Yoshida (Netherlands) Ltd, is 2851 m *9353.56 ft* long and consists of 2,565,900 teeth.

Collections

Bags Heinz Schmidt-Bachem of Düren, Germany, has collected 60,000 plastic and paper bags since 1975.

Beer cans William B. Christensen of Madison, New Jersey, USA has a collection of over 75,000 different beer cans from some 125 different countries, colonies and territories.

A Rosalie Pilsner can sold for $6000 in the USA in April 1981. A collection of 2502 unopened bottles and cans of beer from 103 countries was bought for $25,000 by the Downer Club ACT of Australia at the Australian Associated Press Financial Markets Annual Charity Golf Tournament on 23 Mar 1990.

Beer labels (Labology) Jan Solberg of Oslo, Norway has amassed 353,500 different beer labels from around the world to May 1992.

Beer mats (Tegestology) The world's largest collection of beer mats is owned by Leo Pisker of Langenzersdorf, Austria, who has collected 145,430 different mats from 160 countries to date. The largest in his collection is 760 mm × 760 mm, and the smallest measures just 25 mm × 25 mm; both of these originate from Great Britain.

The largest collection of British mats to date is 71,450, owned by Timothy Stannard of Birmingham, W Mids.

Bottle caps Poul Høegh Poulsen (b. 1944) of Rødovre, Denmark, has amassed 82,169 different bottle caps from 179 countries since 1956.

Bottle collections George E. Terren of Southboro, Massachusetts, USA had a collection of 31,804 bottles (miniatures) of distilled spirit and liquor.

Beer Peter Broeker of Geesthacht, Germany, has a collection of 8131 unduplicated full beer bottles from 110 countries.

Whisky David L. Maund has a collection of 11,041 miniature Scotch whisky bottles and 323 miniature Guinness bottles at May 1995.

Edoardo Giaccone of Gardone Riviera, Broseia, Italy, has a total of 5348 unduplicated full-sized whisky bottles in his bottle collection, which is housed at his specially-built *whiskyteca*.

Cigarettes The world's largest collection of cigarettes was amassed by Robert E. Kaufman, of New York, USA and consisted of 8390 different cigarettes from 173 countries and territories. Upon his death in March 1992 his wife Naida took over the collection. The oldest brand represented is *Lone Jack* of c. 1885 and both the longest and shortest are represented (<> above).

Cigarette cards The largest known cigarette card collection is that of Edward Wharton-Tigar (b. 1913) of London with over 1 million cigarette and trade cards in some 45,000 sets. This collection has been bequeathed to the British Museum, who have agreed to make it available for public study.

Cigarette lighters Frans van der Heijden of Vlijmen, Netherlands has collected a total of 52,116 different lighters to May 1995.

Cigarette packets The largest verified private collection consists of 125,678 packets from 267 countries and territories, accumulated by Claudio Rebecchi of Modena, Italy since 1962. The most represented country in the collection is Japan, with 13,941 packets.

Earrings Carol McFadden of Oil City, Pennsylvania, USA has collected 18,750 different pairs of earrings to January 1995. She had her ears pierced in 1992.

Matchbox labels Teiichi Yoshizawa (b. 1904) of Chiba-Ken, Japan has amassed 743,512 different matchbox labels (including advertising labels) from over 130 countries since 1925. Phillumenist Robert Jones of Indianapolis, USA has a collection of some 280,000 (excluding advertising labels).

Matchbook covers Ed Brassard of Del Mar, California, USA had a collection of 3,159,119 matchbook covers at March 1995.

Parking meters Lotta Sjölin of Solna, Sweden, has a collection of 276 different parking meters as of May 1995. She has been collecting since 1989 and has obtained disused ones from local authorities all over the world.

Ties (Grabatology) A collection of 10,453 ties accumulated by Bill McDaniel of Santa Maria, California, USA was sold to a museum in St Augustine, Florida in 1992.

UK The champion grabatologist is Tom Holmes of Walsall, W Mids, who has collected 8421 different ties to May 1995. The term 'grabatologist' was coined specially for him in 1993 by the Guild of British Tie Makers.

■ You have to hand it to Carol McFadden of Oil City, Pennsylvania, USA (inset and left), who amassed several thousand earrings before even getting her ears pierced.

Her collection, mounted on display boards in her home, now totals 18,750.

Guess What?

Q. Which is the world's largest beverage company?

A. See Page 214

Sports and Games

Guess What?

Q. What is the men's javelin world record?

A. See Page 224

General Records

Fastest The fastest projectile speed in any moving ball game is c. 302 km/h *188 mph* in pelota. This compares with 273 km/h *170 mph* (electronically timed) for a golf ball driven off a tee.

Largest playing field For any ball game, the largest playing field is 12.4 acres *5 ha* for polo, or a maximum length of 300 yd *274 m* and a width, without side boards, of 200 yd *182 m*. With boards the width is 160 yd *146 m*.

Twice a year in the Parish of St Columb Major, Cornwall, a game called hurling (not to be confused with the Irish game) is played on a 'pitch', which consists of the entire parish, approximately 25 square miles *64.7 km²*.

World record breakers *Youngest* The youngest at which anybody has broken a non-mechanical world record is 12 years 298 days for Gertrude Caroline Ederle (USA) (b. 23 Oct 1906) with 13 min 19.0 sec for women's 880 yd freestyle swimming at Indianapolis, USA on 17 Aug 1919.

Oldest Gerhard Weidner (West Germany) (b. 15 Mar 1933) set a 20-mile walk record on 25 May 1974, aged 41 yr 71 days, the oldest to set an official world record, open to all ages, recognized by an international governing body.

Champion *Youngest* The youngest successful competitor in a world title event was a French boy, whose name is not recorded, who coxed the Netherlands' Olympic pair at Paris on 26 Aug 1900. He was not more than ten and may have been as young as seven.

Fu Mingxia (China) (b. 16 Aug 1978) won the women's world title for platform diving at Perth, Australia on 4 Jan 1991, at the age of 12 yr 141 days.

The youngest individual Olympic winner was Marjorie Gestring (USA) (b. 18 Nov 1922), who took the springboard diving title at the age of 13 yr 268 days at the Olympic Games in Berlin on 12 Aug 1936.

Oldest Fred Davis (b. 14 Feb 1913) won (and retained) the world professional billiards title in 1980, aged 67.

Youngest international The youngest at which any person has won international honours is aged eight in the case of Joy Foster, the Jamaican singles and mixed doubles table tennis champion in 1958.

Between 24 Jan 1970 and 1 Nov 1977 Vasiliy Alekseyev (USSR) (b. 7 Jan 1942) broke 80 official world records in weightlifting.

The youngest British international was diver Beverley Williams (b. 5 Jan 1957) who was 10 years 268 days old when she competed against the USA at Crystal Palace, London on 30 Sep 1967.

Oldest competitor at major games William Edward Pattimore (b. 1 Mar 1892) competed for Wales at bowls at the 1970 Commonwealth Games in Edinburgh at the age of 78, the oldest competitor at such an international event open to competitors of all ages.

Britain's oldest Olympian was Hilda Lorna Johnstone (1902–90) who was 70 years 5 days when she was placed twelfth in the Dressage competition at the 1972 Olympic Games.

Most versatile Charlotte 'Lottie' Dod (1871–1960) won the Wimbledon singles tennis title five times between 1887 and 1893, the British Ladies' Golf Championship in 1904, an Olympic silver medal for archery in 1908, and represented England at hockey in 1899. She also excelled at skating and tobogganing.

Longest Reign

Jacques Edmond Barre (France) (1802–73) was a world champion for 33 years (1829–62) at real tennis. Although archer Alice Blanche Legh (1855–1948) did not compete every year, she was a British champion for a span of 41 years (1881–1922), during which she won 23 national titles, the last when she was aged 67.

Mildred 'Babe' Zaharias (née Didrikson) (1911–56) (USA) won two gold medals (80 m hurdles and javelin) and a silver (high jump) at the 1932 Olympic Games. She set world records at those three events in 1930–2. She was an All-American basketball player for three years and set the world record for throwing the baseball 90.22 m *296 ft*. Switching to golf she won the US Women's Amateur title in 1946 and the US Women's Open in 1948, 1950 and 1954. She also excelled at several other sports.

Charles Burgess Fry (GB) (1872–1956) was perhaps the most versatile male sportsman at the highest level. On 4 Mar 1893 he equalled the world long jump record of 7.17 m *23 ft 6½ in*. He represented England v. Ireland at soccer (1901) and played first-class rugby for the Barbarians. His greatest achievements, however, were at cricket, where he headed the English batting averages in six seasons and captained England in 1912. He was also an excellent angler and tennis player.

Heaviest sportsman Professional wrestler William J. Cobb of Macon, Georgia, USA, who in 1962 was billed as 'Happy Humphrey', weighed 364 kg *802 lb*. The heaviest player of a ball-game was Bob Pointer, the 221 kg *487 lb* US Football tackle formerly on the 1967 Santa Barbara High School Team, California, USA.

Largest crowd *Stadium* A crowd of 199,854 attended the Brazil v. Uruguay soccer match, in the Maracanã Municipal Stadium, Rio de Janeiro, Brazil on 16 Jul 1950.

Most participants On 15 May 1988 an estimated 110,000 runners (including unregistered athletes) ran in the Examiner Bay to Breakers 12.2 km *7.6 mile* race in San Francisco, California, USA.

Crowded

The greatest number of live spectators for any sporting spectacle is the estimated 2,500,000 who have lined the route of the New York Marathon. However, spread over three weeks, it is estimated that more than 10,000,000 see the annual *Tour de France* cycling race.

The 1988 Women's International Bowling Congress Championship tournament attracted 77,735 bowlers for the 96-day event held 31 March–4 July at Reno/Carson City, Nevada, USA.

Worst disasters In recent history, the stands at the Hong Kong Jockey Club racecourse collapsed and caught fire on 26 Feb 1918, killing an estimated 604 people.

During the reign of Antoninus Pius (AD 138–161), 1112 spectators were quoted as being killed when the upper wooden tiers in the Circus Maximus, Rome collapsed during a gladiatorial combat.

Britain As a result of overcrowding just after the start of the FA Cup semi-final between Liverpool and Nottingham Forest at the Leppings Lane end of Hillsborough Stadium, Sheffield, S Yorks on 15 Apr 1989, 96 people were killed and 170 injured.

Aerobatics

World Championships Held biennially since 1960 (except 1974), scoring is based on a system originally devised by Col. José Aresti of Spain. The competition consists of a known and unknown compulsory and a free programme.

The men's team competition has been won a record six times by the USSR. Petr Jirmus (Czechoslovakia) is the only man to become world champion twice, in 1984 and 1986. Betty Stewart (USA) won the women's competition in 1980 and 1982.

Lyubov Nemkova (USSR) won a record five medals: first in 1986, second in 1982 and 1984 and third in 1976 and 1978. The oldest ever world champion has been Henry Haigh (USA) (b. 12 Dec 1924), aged 63 in 1988.

British The only medal achieved by Britain has been a bronze in the team event in 1976. The highest individual placing by a Briton is fourth by Neil Williams (1935–77) in 1976.

Inverted flight The duration record is 4 hr 38 min 10 sec by Joann Osterud from Vancouver to Vanderhoof, Canada on 24 Jul 1991.

Loops Joann Osterud achieved 208 outside loops in a 'Supernova' Hyperbipe over North Bend, Oregon, USA on 13 Jul 1989. On 9 Aug 1986, David Childs performed

Guess What?
Q. Where are the most loops on a rollercoaster ride?
A. See Page 93

2368 inside loops in a Bellanca Decathalon over North Pole, Alaska.

Brian Lecomber completed 180 consecutive inside loops in a Jaguar Extra 230 on 29 Jul 1988 over Plymouth, Devon.

American Football

NFL Records

Championships The Green Bay Packers won a record 11 NFL titles, 1929–31, 1936, 1939, 1944, 1961–2, 1965–7.

Most consecutive wins The record is 18 by: the Chicago Bears (twice), 1933–4 and 1941–2; the Miami Dolphins, 1972–3; and the San Francisco 49ers, 1988–9. The most consecutive games without defeat is 25 by Canton (22 wins and 3 ties) in 1921–3.

Most games played George Blanda (b. 17 Sep 1927) played in a record 340 games in a record 26 seasons in the NFL (Chicago Bears 1949–58, Baltimore Colts 1950, Houston Oilers 1960–66 and Oakland Raiders 1967–75). The most consecutive games played is 282 by Jim Marshall (Cleveland Browns 1960 and Minnesota Vikings 1961–79).

NFL Records

Most Points
Career	2002	George Blanda (Chicago Bears, Baltimore Colts, Houston Oilers, Oakland Raiders), 1949–75
Season	176	Paul Hornung (Green Bay Packers), 1960
Game	40	Ernie Nevers (Chicago Cardinals) v. Chicago Bears, 28 Nov 1929

Most Touchdowns
Career	139	Jerry Rice (San Francisco 49ers), 1985–94
Season	24	John Riggins (Washington Redskins), 1983
Game	6	Ernie Nevers (Chicago Cardinals) v. Chicago Bears, 28 Nov 1929
		William Jones (Cleveland Browns) v. Chicago Bears, 25 Nov 1951
		Gale Sayers (Chicago Bears) v. San Francisco 49ers, 12 Dec 1965

Most Yards Gained Rushing
Career	16,726	Walter Payton (Chicago Bears), 1975–88
Season	2105	Eric Dickerson (Los Angeles Rams), 1984
Game	275	Walter Payton (Chicago Bears) v. Minnesota Vikings, 20 Nov 1977

Most Yards Gained Receiving
Career	13,821	James Lofton (Green Bay Packers, Los Angeles Raiders, Buffalo Bills), 1978–92
Season	1746	Charley Hennigan (Houston Oilers), 1961
Game	336	Willie Anderson (Los Angeles Rams), v. New Orleans Saints, 26 Nov 1989

Most Yards Gained Passing
Career	47,003	Fran Tarkenton (Minnesota Vikings, New York Giants), 1961–78
Season	5084	Dan Marino (Miami Dolphins), 1984
Game	554	Norm Van Brocklin (Los Angeles Rams) v. New York Yanks, 28 Sep 1951

Most Passes Completed
Career	3686	Fran Tarkenton (Minnesota Vikings, New York Giants), 1961–78
Season	404	Warren Moon (Houston Oilers), 1991
Game	45	Drew Bledsoe (New England Patriots) v. Minnesota Vikings, 13 Nov 1994

Pass Receptions
Career	934	Art Monk (Washington Redskins, New York Jets), 1980–94
Season	112	Sterling Sharp (Green Bay Packers), 1993
Game	18	Tom Fears (Los Angeles Rams) v. Green Bay Packers, 3 Dec 1950

Field Goals
Career	373	Jan Stenerud (Kansas City Chiefs, Green Bay Packers, Minnesota Vikings), 1967–85
Season	35	Ali Haji-Sheikh (New York Giants), 1983
Game	7	Jim Bakken (St Louis Cardinals), v. Pittsburgh Steelers, 24 Sep 1967
		Rich Karlis (Minnesota Vikings) v. Los Angeles Rams, 5 Nov 1989
Longest	63	Tom Dempsey (New Orleans Saints) v. Detroit Lions, 8 Nov 1970

Super Bowl Game & Career Records

POINTS	18	Roger Craig (San Francisco 49ers)	1985
		Jerry Rice (San Francisco 49ers)	1990 & 1995
		Ricky Watters (San Francisco 49ers)	1995
Career	42	Jerry Rice	1989–90, 1995
TOUCHDOWNS	3	Roger Craig	1985
		Jerry Rice	1990 & 1995
		Ricky Watters	1990
Career	7	Jerry Rice	1989–90, 1995
TOUCHDOWN PASSES	6	Steve Young (San Francisco 49ers)	1990
Career	11	Joe Montana (San Francisco 49ers)	1982, 1985, 1989–90
YDS GAINED PASSING	357	Joe Montana	1989
Career	1142	Joe Montana	1982, 1985, 1989–90
YDS GAINED RECEIVING	215	Jerry Rice	1989
Career	512	Jerry Rice	1989–90, 1995
YDS GAINED RUSHING	204	Timmy Smith (Washington Redskins)	1988
Career	354	Franco Harris	1975–6, 1979–80
PASSES COMPLETED	31	Jim Kelly (Buffalo Bills)	1994
Career	83	Joe Montana	1982, 1985, 1989–90
PASS RECEPTIONS	11	Dan Ross (Cincinnati Bengals)	1982
		Jerry Rice	1989
Career	28	Jerry Rice	1989–90, 1995
FIELD GOALS	4	Don Chandler (Green Bay Packers)	1968
		Ray Wersching (San Francisco 49ers)	1982
Career	5	Ray Wersching	1982, 1985
MOST VALUABLE PLAYER	3	Joe Montana	1982, 1985, 1990

■ **During the 1994 season, Jerry Rice (80) of the San Francisco 49ers surpassed the record of most touchdowns held by Jim Brown, when he scored his 127th touchdown. He ended the season having scored 139 in total and his record-breaking feats continued to the Super Bowl. Here, with the assistance of MVP Steve Young (left), Rice set a number of game and career records. Young, himself had a superlative game, including throwing the fastest touchdown in Super Bowl history, 1 min 24 sec, to Jerry Rice of course.**

Longest run from scrimmage Tony Dorsett (b. 7 Apr 1954) scored on a touchdown run of 99 yd for the Dallas Cowboys *v.* the Minnesota Vikings on 3 Jan 1983.

Longest pass completion A pass completion of 99 yd has been achieved on seven occasions and has always resulted in a touchdown. The most recent was a pass from Stan Humphries to Tony Martin of the San Diego Chargers against the Seattle Seahawks on 18 Sep 1994.

Super Bowl

First held in 1967 between the winners of the NFL and the AFL. Since 1970 it has been contested by the winners of the National and American Conferences of the NFL.

The most wins is five the San Francisco 49ers, 1982, 1985, 1989–90, 1995.

The highest team score and record victory margin was when the San Francisco 49ers beat the Denver Broncos 55–10 at New Orleans, Louisiana on 28 Jan 1990. The highest aggregate score was in 1995 when the San Francisco 49ers beat the San Diego Chargers 49–26. In their 42–10 victory over the Denver Broncos on 31 Jan 1988, the Washington Redskins scored a record 35 points in the second quarter.

Other Records

Highest team score Georgia Tech, Atlanta, Georgia scored 222 points, including a record 32 touchdowns, against Cumberland University, Lebanon, Tennessee (nil) on 7 Oct 1916.

Angling

Oldest existing club The Ellem fishing club was formed by a number of Edinburgh and Berwickshire gentlemen in Scotland in 1829. Its first annual general meeting was held on 29 Apr 1830.

Fisheries The record for a single trawler is £278,798 from a 37,897-tonne catch by the Icelandic vessel *Videy* at Hull, Humberside on 11 Aug 1987. The greatest catch ever recorded from a single throw is 2471 tonnes by the purse seine-net boat M/S *Flømann* from Hareide, Norway in the Barents Sea on 28 Aug 1986. It was estimated that more than 120 million fish were caught in this shoal.

Guess What?

Q. What is the longest throw of a cricket ball?

A. See Page 246

Archery ▶▶ ▶▶

Largest single catch The largest officially ratified fish ever caught on a rod was a man-eating great white shark (*Carcharodon carcharias*) weighing 1208 kg *2664 lb* and measuring 5.13 m *16 ft 10 in* long, caught on a 59 kg *130 lb* test line by Alf Dean at Denial Bay, near Ceduna, South Australia on 21 Apr 1959. A great white shark weighing 1537 kg *3388 lb* was caught by Clive Green off Albany, Western Australia on 26 Apr 1976 but will remain unratified as whale meat was used as bait.

The biggest ever rod-caught fish by a British angler is a 620 kg *1366 lb* great white shark, by Vic Samson at The Pales, South Australia on 8 Apr 1989.

In June 1978 a great white shark measuring 6.2 m *20 ft 4 in* in length and weighing over 2268 kg *5000 lb* was harpooned and landed by fishermen in the harbour of San Miguel, Azores.

IGFA world records
The International Game Fish Association (IGFA) recognizes world records for a large number of species of game fish (both freshwater and saltwater). Their thousands of categories include all-tackle, various line classes and tippet classes for fly fishing. New records recognized by the IGFA reached an annual peak of 1074 in 1984.

The heaviest freshwater category recognized is for the sturgeon—record weight of 212.28 kg *468 lb* caught by Joey Pallotta on 9 Jul 1983 off Benicia, California, USA.

World Freshwater Championship The *Confédération Internationale de la Pêche Sportive* (CIPS) championships were inaugurated as European championships in 1953 and recognized as World championships in 1957.

France won the European title in 1956 and 12 world titles between 1959 and 1990. The individual title has been won a record three times by: Robert Tesse (France), 1959–60, 1965; and Bob Nudd (England), 1990–91, 1994.

The record weight (team) is 34.71 kg *76.52 lb* in 3 hr by West Germany on the Neckar at Mannheim, Germany on 21 Sep 1980. The individual record is 16.99 kg *37.45 lb* by Wolf-Rüdiger Kremkus (West Germany) at Mannheim on 20 Sep 1980. The most fish caught is 652 by Jacques Isenbaert (Belgium) at Dunaújváros, Hungary on 27 Aug 1967.

Casting The longest freshwater cast ratified under ICF (International Casting Federation) rules is 175.01 m *574 ft 2 in* by Walter Kummerow (West Germany), for the Bait Distance Double-Handed 30 g event held at Lenzerheide, Switzerland in the 1968 Championships. The British national record is 148.78 m *488 ft 1 in* by Andy Dickison on the same occasion.

At the currently contested weight of 17.7 g, known as 18 g Bait Distance, the longest Double-Handed cast is 139.31 m *457 ft ½ in* by Kevin Carriero (USA) at Toronto, Canada on 24 Jul 1984. The British national records are: Fixed spool reel, 138.79 m *455 ft 3 in* by Hugh Newton at Peterborough, Cambs on 21 Sep 1985; and Multiplier reel, 108.97 m *357 ft 6 in* by James Tomlinson at Torrington, Devon on 27 Apr 1985.

The longest Fly Distance Double-Handed cast is 97.28 m *319 ft 1 in* by Wolfgang Feige (West Germany) at Toronto, Canada on 23 Jul 1984. Hywel Morgan set a British national record of 91.22 m *299 ft 2 in* at Torrington, Devon on 27 Apr 1985.

The UK Surfcasting Federation record (150 g *5¼ oz* weight) is 257.32 m *844 ft 3 in* by Neil Mackellow at Peterborough, Cambs on 1 Sep 1985.

World fly fishing championships were inaugurated by the CIPS in 1981. The most team titles is five by Italy, 1982–4, 1986, 1992. The most individual titles is two by Brian Leadbetter (GB), 1987 and 1991.

Guess What? Q. What is the world's largest freshwater fish? A. See Page 38

World Angling Records; Freshwater and Saltwater

A selection of All-Tackle records ratified by the International Game Fish Association as at November 1994

Species	lb	Weight oz	kg	Name	Location	Date
Barracuda, Great	85	0	38.55	John W. Helfrich	Christmas Island, Kiribati	11 Apr 1992
Bass, Striped	78	8	35.60	Albert R. McReynolds	Atlantic City, New Jersey, USA	21 Sep 1982
Catfish, Flathead	91	4	41.39	Mike Rogers	Lake Lewisville, Texas, USA	28 Mar 1982
Cod, Atlantic	98	12	44.79	Alphonse J. Bielevich	Isle of Shoals, New Hampshire, USA	8 Jun 1969
Halibut, Pacific	368	0	166.92	Celia H. Dueitt	Gustavus, Alaska, USA	5 Jul 1991
Mackerel, King	90	0	40.82	Norton I. Thomton	Key West, Florida, USA	16 Feb 1976
Marlin, Black	1560	0	707.61	Alfred C. Glassell Jr	Cabo Blanco, Peru	4 Aug 1953
Pike, Northern	55	1	25.00	Lothar Louis	Lake of Grefeern, Germany	16 Oct 1986
Sailfish (Pacific)	221	0	100.24	C. W. Stewart	Santa Cruz Island, Ecuador	12 Feb 1947
Salmon, Atlantic	79	2	35.89	Henrik Henriksen	Tana River, Norway	1928
Shark, Hammerhead	991	0	449.50	Allen Ogle	Sarasota, Florida, USA	30 May 1982
Shark, Porbeagle	507	0	230.00	Christopher Bennett	Pentland Firth, Caithness	9 Mar 1993
Shark, Thresher	802	0	363.80	Dianne North	Tutukaka, New Zealand	8 Feb 1981
Shark, White	2664	0	1208.38	Alfred Dean	Ceduna, South Australia	21 Apr 1959
Snook	53	10	24.32	Gilbert Ponzi	Parasmina Ranch, Costa Rica	18 Oct 1978
Sturgeon, White	468	0	212.28	Joey Pallotta III	Benicia, California, USA	9 Jul 1983
Swordfish	1182	0	536.15	L. Marron	Iquique, Chile	17 May 1953
Trout, Brook	14	8	6.57	Dr W. J. Cook	Nipigon River, Ontario, Canada	July 1916
Trout, Brown	40	4	18.25	Howard L. Collins	Heber Springs, Arkansas, USA	9 May 1992
Trout, Lake	66	8	30.16	Rodney Harback	Great Bear Lake, NWT, Canada	19 Jul 1991
Trout, Rainbow	42	2	19.10	David Robert White	Bell Island, Alaska, USA	22 Jun 1970
Tuna, Bluefin	1496	0	679.00	Ken Fraser	Aulds Cove, Nova Scotia, Canada	26 Oct 1979
Tuna, Yellowfin	388	12	176.35	Curt Wiesenhutter	San Benedicto Island, Mexico	1 Apr 1977
Wahoo	155	8	70.53	William Bourne	San Salvador, Bahamas	3 Apr 1990

British Angling Records

COARSE FISH: A selection of those fish recognized by the National Association of Specialist Anglers

Species	lb	Weight oz	dr	kg	Name of Angler	Location	Date
Barbel	16	2	–	7.314	P. Woodhouse	River Medway, Keny	1994
Bleak		4	4	0.120	B. Derrington	River Monnow, Wye Mouth	1982
Bream (Common, Bronze)	16	9	–	7.512	M. McKeown	Southern water	1991
Bream, Silver		15	–	0.425	D. E. Flack	Grime Spring, Lakenheath, Suffolk	1988
Carp	51	8	–	23.358	C. Yates	Redmire Pool, Herefordshire	1980
Carp, Crucian	5	11	8	2.593	D. Lewis	Surrey water	1994
Carp, Grass	25	4	–	11.453	D. Buck	Honeycroft Fisheries, Canterbury, Kent	1993
Catfish (Wells)	49	14	–	22.623	S. Poyntz	Homersfield Lake, Norwich, Norfolk	1993
Chub	8	10	–	3.912	P. Smith	River Tees	1994
Dace	1	4	4	0.574	J. L. Gasson	Little Ouse, Thetford, Norfolk	1960
Eel	11	2	–	5.046	S. Terry	Kingfisher Lake, Ringwood, Hants	1978
Gudgeon		5	–	0.141	D. Hall	River Nadder, Salisbury, Wilts	1990
Orfe, Golden	6	11	–	3.033	B. Crawford	Lymmvale	1994
Perch	5	9	–	2.523	J. Shayler	Private water, Kent	1985
Pike	46	13	–	21.236	R. Lewis	Llandefgfedd Reservoir, Pontypool, Gwent	1992
Roach	4	3	–	1.899	R. N. Clarke	Dorset Stour	1990
Tench	14	7	–	6.548	G. Bevan	Southern stillwater	1993
Zander (Pikeperch)	18	10	–	8.448	D. Litton	Cambridge stillwater	1988

FRESHWATER GAME FISH:

Species	lb	Weight oz	dr	kg	Name of Angler	Location	Date
Salmon	64	–	–	29.03	Miss G. W. Ballantine	River Tay, Scotland	1922
Trout, American Brook	5	13	8	2.65	A. Pearson	Avington Fishery, Hants	1981
Trout, Brown	19	10	6	8.91	A. Thorne	Loch Awe, Strathclyde	1993
Trout, Rainbow	24	2	13	10.96	J. Moore	Pennine Trout Fishery, Littleborough, Lancs	1990
Trout, Sea	22	8	–	10.20	S. Burgoyne	River Leven	1989

Archery

Oldest club The oldest archery body in the British Isles is the Society of Archers in Yorkshire, formed on 14 May 1673, though the Society of Kilwinning Archers, in Scotland, has contested the Pa-pingo Shoot since 1488.

World Championships The most titles won by a man is four by Hans Deutgen (Sweden) (1917–89) in 1947–50, and the most by a woman is seven by Janina Spychajowa-Kurkowska (Poland) (1901–79) in 1931–4, 1936, 1939 and 1947. The USA has a record 14 men's and 8 women's team titles.

Olympic Games Hubert van Innis (Belgium) (1866–1961) won six gold and three silver medals at the 1900 and 1920 Olympic Games.

British Championships The most titles is 12 by Horace Alfred Ford (1822–80) in 1849–59 and 1867, and 23 by Alice Blanche Legh (1855–1948) in 1881, 1886–92, 1895, 1898–1900, 1902–9, 1913 and 1921–2. Miss Legh was inhibited from winning from 1882 to 1885 – because her mother was champion – and for four further years 1915–18 because there were no Championships during World War I.

British records York round – possible 1296 pts: Single round, 1192 and Double round, 2356 by Steven Hallard (b. 22 Feb 1965) at Lichfield, Staffs on 13–14 Aug 1994.

Hereford (Women) – possible 1296 pts: Single round, 1208 Pauline Edwards (b. 23 Apr 1949) on 30 Jun 1994; Double round, 2380 Joanne Franks (later Edens) (b. 1 Oct 1967) at the British Target Championships on 8 Sep 1987.

FITA round (Men): Single round, 1318 Steven Hallard on 22 May 1994; Double round, 2616 Steven Hallard at Lausanne, Switzerland in July 1989.

FITA round (Women): Single round, 1323 Alison Williamson (b. 3 Nov 1971) at the Olympics at Barcelona, Spain in August 1992; Double round, 2591 Alison Williamson at Belgian FITA Star on 5 Jun 1989.

Flight shooting The greatest distance that an arrow has been shot is 1871.84m *6141ft 2in* by Harry Drake (USA) using a crossbow at the 'Smith Creek' Flight Range near Austin, Nevada, USA on 30 Jul 1988.

■ April Moon holds a number records in the field of flight shooting, the object of which is to fire an arrow as far as possible. On 13 Sep 1981 at Wendover, Utah using a recurve bow, she fired an arrow an amazing 1039yd 1ft 1in *950.391m.*

Guess What?
Q. What is the longest inverted flight?
A. See Page 220

World Archery Records

MEN (Single FITA rounds)

Event	Pts	Poss	Name and Country	Year
FITA	1354	1440	Han Seuong-hoon (South Korea)	1994
90m	330	360	Vladimir Yesheyev (USSR)	1990
70m	344	360	Hiroshi Yamamoto (Japan)	1990
50m	345	360	Richard McKinney (USA)	1982
30m	360	360	Han Seuong-hoon (South Korea)	1994
Team	4035	4320	South Korea (Kim Kyeng-ho, Han Seong-nam, Park Kyeng-moo)	1993

WOMEN (Single FITA rounds)

Event	Pts	Poss	Name and Country	Year
FITA	1375	1440	Cho Youn-jeong (South Korea)	1992
70m	*341	360	Kim Soo-nyung (South Korea)	1990
	338	360	Cho Youn-jeong (South Korea)	1992
60m	347	360	Kim Soo-nyung (South Korea)	1989
50m	340	360	Lim Jung (South Korea)	1994
30m	357	360	Joanne Edens (GB)	1990
Team	4094	4320	South Korea (Kim Soo-nyung, Lee Eun-kyung, Cho Yuon-jeong)	1992

*unofficial

Indoor Compound (25m)

	Pts	Poss	Name and Country	Year
Men	577	600	Tom Henrikson (Denmark)	1994
Women	556	600	Annette Frederiksen (Sweden)	1994

Indoor Compound (18m)

	Pts	Poss	Name and Country	Year
Men	596	600	Magnus Pattersson (Sweden)	1995
Women	590	600	Natalya Valeyeva (Moldova)	1995

Greatest draw Gary Sentman, of Roseberg, Oregon, USA drew a longbow weighing a record 79.83kg *176 lb* to the maximum draw on the arrow of 72cm *28¼in* at Forksville, Pennsylvania, USA on 20 Sep 1975.

Bullseye

The highest recorded score over 24 hours by a pair of archers is 76,158 during 70 Portsmouth Rounds (60 arrows per round at 20yd at 60cm FITA targets) by Simon Tarplee and David Hathaway at Evesham, Worcs on 1 Apr 1991. During this attempt Simon Tarplee set an individual record of 38,500.

Athletics

Fastest speed An analysis of split times at each 10 metres in the 1988 Olympic Games 100m final in Seoul on 24 Sep 1988 won by Ben Johnson (Canada) in 9.79sec (average speed 36.77km/h *22.85mph* but later disallowed as a world record due to his positive drugs test for steroids) from Carl Lewis (USA) 9.92, showed that both Johnson and Lewis reached a peak speed (40m–50m and 80m–90m respectively) of 0.83sec for 10m, i.e. 43.37km/h *26.95mph*. In the women's final Florence Griffith-Joyner was timed at 0.91sec for each 10m from 60m to 90m, i.e. 39.56km/h *24.58mph*.

Most Olympic titles The most Olympic gold medals won is ten (an absolute Olympic record) by Raymond Clarence Ewry (USA) (1873–1937) in the standing high, long and triple jumps in 1900, 1904, 1906 and 1908.

Women The most gold medals won by a woman is four shared by: Francina 'Fanny' Elsje Blankers-Koen (Netherlands) (b. 26 Apr 1918) 100m, 200m, 80m hurdles and 4 × 100m relay, 1948; Elizabeth 'Betty' Cuthbert (Australia) (b. 20 Apr 1938) 100m, 200m, 4 × 100m relay, 1956 and 400m, 1964; Bärbel Wöckel (*née* Eckert) (GDR) (b. 21 Mar 1955) 200m and 4 × 100m relay in 1976 and 1980; and Evelyn Ashford (USA) (b. 15 Apr 1957) 100m and 4 × 100m relay in 1984, 1988 and 1992.

Heads Up

The greatest height cleared above an athlete's own head is 59cm *23¼in* by Franklin Jacobs (USA) (b. 31 Dec 1957), 1.73m *5ft 8in* tall, who jumped 2.32m *7ft 7¼in* at New York, USA, on 27 Jan 1978. The greatest height cleared by a woman above her own head is 32cm *12¾in* by Yolanda Henry (USA) (b. 2 Dec 1964), 1.68m *5ft 6in* tall, who jumped 2.00m *6ft 6¾in* at Seville, Spain on 30 May 1990.

Most wins at one Games The most gold medals at one celebration is five by Paavo Johannes Nurmi (Finland) (1897–1973) in 1924; 1500m, 5000m, 10,000m cross-country, 3000m team and cross-country team. The most at individual events is four by Alvin Christian Kraenzlein (USA) (1876–1928) in 1900: 60m, 110m hurdles, 200m hurdles and long jump.

Most Olympic medals The most medals won is 12 (nine gold and three silver) by Paavo Nurmi (Finland) in the Games of 1920, 1924 and 1928.

Sports and Games

Women The most medals won by a woman athlete is seven by Shirley Barbara de la Hunty (*née* Strickland) (Australia) (b. 18 Jul 1925) with three gold, one silver and three bronze in the 1948, 1952 and 1956 Games. A re-read of the photo-finish indicates that she finished third, not fourth, in the 1948 200 metres event, thus unofficially increasing her medal haul to eight. Irena Szewinska (*née* Kirszenstein) (Poland) (b. 24 May 1946) won three gold, two silver and two bronze in 1964, 1968, 1972 and 1976, and is the only woman athlete to win a medal in four successive Games.

Most Olympic titles *British* The most gold medals won by a British athlete (excluding tug of war and walking, *q.v.*) is two by: Charles Bennett (1871–1949) (1500 m and 5000 m team, 1900); Alfred Edward Tysoe (1874–1901) (800 m and 5000 m team, 1900); John Thomas Rimmer (1879–1962) (4000 m steeplechase and 5000 m team, 1900); Albert George Hill (1889–1969) (800 m and 1500 m, 1920); Douglas Gordon Arthur Lowe (1902–81) (800 m 1924 and 1928); Sebastian Newbold Coe (b. 29 Sep 1956) (1500 m 1980 and 1984) and Francis Morgan 'Daley' Thompson (b. 30 Jul 1958) (decathlon 1980 and 1984). Daley Thompson was also world champion at the decathlon in 1983.

■ **Noureddine Morceli has been the world's top middle distance runner of the early 1990s. Current holder of the mile, 1500 m and 3000 m, his stated aim is to hold all distance records from 800 m to 10,000 m.**
(Photo: Allsport/Vandystadt/R. Martin)

Most Olympic medals *British* The most medals won by a British athlete is four by Guy Montagu Butler (1899–1981) gold for the 4 × 400 m relay and silver for 400 m in 1920 and bronze for each of these events in 1924, and by Sebastian Coe, who also won silver medals at 800 m in 1980 and 1984. Three British women athletes have won three medals: Dorothy Hyman (b. 9 May 1941) with a silver (100 m, 1960) and two bronze (200 m, 1960 and 4 × 100 m relay, 1964), Mary

Guess What?

Q. Who is the youngest person to win an Olympic title?

A. See Page 219

World Records *Men*

World outdoor records for the men's events scheduled by the International Amateur Athletic Federation. Fully automatic electric timing is mandatory for events up to 400 metres.

Running	min:sec	Name and Country	Venue	Date
100 m	9.85*	Leroy Russell Burrell (USA) (b. 21 Feb 1967)	Lausanne, Switzerland	6 Jul 1994
200 m	19.72A	Pietro Paolo Mennea (Italy) (b. 28 Jun 1952)	Mexico City, Mexico	12 Sep 1979
400 m	43.29	Harry Lee 'Butch' Reynolds Jr (USA) (b. 8 Aug 1964)	Zürich, Switzerland	17 Aug 1988
800 m	1:41.73	Sebastian Newbold Coe (GB) (b. 29 Sep 1956)	Florence, Italy	10 Jun 1981
1000 m	2:12.18	Sebastian Newbold Coe (GB)	Oslo, Norway	11 Jul 1981
1500 m	3:28.86	Noureddine Morceli (Algeria) (b. 20 Feb 1970)	Rieti, Itlay	6 Sep 1992
1 mile	3:44.39	Noureddine Morceli (Algeria)	Rieti, Italy	5 Sep 1993
2000 m	4:50.81	Said Aouita (Morocco) (b. 2 Nov 1959)	Paris, France	16 Jul 1987
3000 m	7:25.11	Noureddine Morceli (Algeria)	Monte Carlo, Monaco	2 Aug 1994
5000 m	12:55.30	Moses Kiptanui (Kenya) (b. 10 Oct 1971)	Rome, Italy	8 Jun 1995
10,000 m	26:43.53	Haile Gebrselassie (Ethiopia) (b. 18 Apr 1973)	Hengelo, Netherlands	5 Jun 1995
20,000 m	56:55.6	Arturo Barrios (Mexico, now USA) (b. 12 Dec 1963)	La Flèche, France	30 Mar 1991
25,000 m	1 hr 13:55.8	Toshihiko Seko (Japan) (b. 15 Jul 1956)	Christchurch, New Zealand	22 Mar 1981
30,000 m	1 hr 29:18.8	Toshihiko Seko (Japan)	Christchurch, New Zealand	22 Mar 1981
1 hour	21,101 m	Arturo Barrios (Mexico, now USA)	La Flèche, France	30 Mar 1991
110 m hurdles	12.91	Colin Ray Jackson (GB) (b. 18 Feb 1967)	Stuttgart, Germany	20 Aug 1993
400 m hurdles	46.78	Kevin Curtis Young (USA) (b. 6 Sep 1966)	Barcelona, Spain	6 Aug 1992
3000 m s'chase	8:02.08	Moses Kiptanui (Kenya)	Zürich, Switzerland	19 Aug 1992
4×100 m	37.40	USA	Barcelona, Spain	8 Aug 1992
		(Michael Marsh, Leroy Burrell, Dennis A Mitchell, Frederick Carleton 'Carl' Lewis)		
	37.40	USA	Stuttgart, Germany	21 Aug 1993
		(John A Drummond Jr, Andre Cason, Dennis A Mitchell, Leroy Burrell)		
4×200 m	1:18.68	Santa Monica Track Club (USA)	Walnut, California, USA	17 Apr 1994
		(Michael Marsh, Leroy Burrell, Floyd Wayne Heard, Carl Lewis)		
4×400 m	2:54.29	USA	Stuttgart, Germany	21 Aug 1993
		(Andrew Valmon, Quincy Watts, Harry Reynolds, Michael Duane Johnson)		
4×800 m	7:03.89	Great Britain	Crystal Palace, London	30 Aug 1982
		(Peter Elliott, Garry Peter Cook, Stephen Cram, Sebastian Coe)		
4×1500 m	14:38.8	West Germany	Cologne, Germany	17 Aug 1977
		(Thomas Wessinghage, Harald Hudak, Michael Lederer, Karl Fleschen)		

* Ben Johnson (Canada) (b. 30 Dec 1961) ran 100 m in 9.79 sec at Seoul, South Korea on 24 Sep 1988, but was subsequently disqualified on a positive drugs test for steroids. He later admitted to having taken drugs over many years, and this invalidated his ratified 9.83 sec at Rome, Italy on 30 Aug 1987.
A This record was set at high altitude, best mark at low altitude: 19.73 sec by Michael Lawrence Marsh (USA) (b. 4 Aug 1967) at Barcelona, Spain on 5 Aug 1992.

Field Events	m	ft	in			
High Jump	2.45	8	0½	Javier Sotomayor (Cuba) (b. 13 Oct 1967)	Salamanca, Spain	27 Jul 1993
Pole Vault	6.14A	20	1¾	Sergey Nazarovich Bubka (Ukraine) (b. 4 Dec 1963)	Setriere, Italy	31 Jul 1994
Long Jump	8.95	29	4½	Michael Anthony 'Mike' Powell (USA) (b. 10 Nov 1963)	Tokyo, Japan	30 Aug 1991
Triple Jump	17.97	58	11½	William Augustus 'Willie' Banks (USA) (b. 11 Mar 1956)	Indianapolis, USA	16 Jun 1985
Shot	23.12	75	10¼	Eric Randolph 'Randy' Barnes (USA) (b. 16 Jun 1966)	Los Angeles, California, USA	20 May 1990
Discus	74.08	243	0	Jürgen Schult (GDR) (b. 11 May 1960)	Neubrandenburg, Germany	6 Jun 1986
Hammer	86.74	284	7	Yuriy Georgiyevich Sedykh (USSR) (b. 11 Jun 1955)	Stuttgart, Germany	30 Aug 1986
Javelin	95.66	318	10	Jan Zelezny (Czech Republic) (b. 16 Jun 1966)	Sheffield, S Yorks	29 Aug 1993

A This record was set at high altitude, best mark at low altitude: 6.13 m 20 ft 1¼ in by Sergey Bubka at Tokyo, Japan on 19 Sep 1992.

Decathlon 8891 points Dan Dion O'Brien (USA) (b. 18 Jul 1966) Talence, France 4-5 Sep 1992
Day 1: 100 m 10.43 sec, LJ 8.08 m *26 ft 6¼ in*, SP 16.69 m *54 ft 9¼ in*, HJ 2.07 m *6 ft 9½ in*, 400 m 48.51 sec,
Day 2: 110 m H 13.98 sec, D 2.07 m *159 ft 4 in*, PV 5.00 m *16 ft 4¼ in*, J 62.58 m *205 ft 4 in*, 1500 m 4:42.10 sec

World Records *Women*

World outdoor records for the women's events scheduled by the International Amateur Athletic Federation. Fully automatic electric timing is mandatory for all events up to 400 metres.

Running	min:sec	Name and Country	Venue	Date
100 m	10.49	Delorez Florence Griffith Joyner (USA) (b. 21 Dec 1959)	Indianapolis, Indiana, USA	16 Jul 1988
200 m	21.34	Delorez Florence Griffith Joyner (USA)	Seoul, South Korea	29 Sep 1988
400 m	47.60	Marita Koch (GDR) (b. 18 Feb 1957)	Canberra, Australia	6 Oct 1985
800 m	1:53.28	Jarmila Kratochvílová (Czechoslovakia) (b. 26 Jan 1951)	Münich, Germany	26 Jul 1983
1000 m	2:30.6	Tatyana Providokhina (USSR) (b. 26 Mar 1953)	Podolsk, USSR	20 Aug 1978
	2:30.67	Christine Wachtel (GDR) (b. 6 Jan 1965)	Berlin, Germany	17 Aug 1990
1500 m	3:50.46	Qu Yunxia (China) (b. 25 Dec 1972)	Beijing, China	11 Sep 1993
1 mile	4:15.61	Paula Ivan (Romania) (b. 20 Jul 1963)	Nice, France	10 Jul 1989
2000 m	5:25.36	Sonia O'Sullivan (Ireland) (b. 28 Nov 1969)	Edinburgh, Lothian	8 Jul 1994
3000 m	8:06.11	Wang Junxia (China) (b. 9 Jan 1973)	Beijing, China	13 Sep 1993
5000 m	14:37.33	Ingrid Kristiansen (*née* Christensen) (Norway) (b. 21 Mar 1956)	Stockholm, Sweden	5 Aug 1986
10,000 m	29:31.78	Wang Junxia (China)	Beijing, China	8 Sep 1993
20,000 m	1hr 06:48.8	Isumi Maki (Japan) (b. 10 Dec 1968)	Amagasaki, Japan	20 Sep 1993
25,000 m	1hr 29:29.2	Karolina Szabo (Hungary)	Budapest, Hungary	23 Apr 1988
30,000 m	1hr 47:05.6	Karolina Szabo (Hungary)	Budapest, Hungary	23 Apr 1988
1 hour	18,084 m	Silvana Cruciata (Italy)	Rome, Italy	4 May 1981
100 m hurdles	12.21	Yordanka Donkova (Bulgaria) (b. 28 Sep 1961)	Stara Zagora, Bulgaria	20 Aug 1988
400 m hurdles	52.74	Sally Jane Janet Gunnell (GB) (b. 29 Jul 1966)	Stuttgart, Germany	19 Aug 1993
4×100 m	41.37	GDR	Canberra, Australia	6 Oct 1985
		(Silke Gladisch (now Möller), Sabine Rieger (now Günther), Ingrid Auerswald (*née* Brestrich), Marlies Göhr (*née* Oelsner))		
4×200 m	1:28.15	GDR	Jena, Germany	9 Aug 1980
		(Marlies Göhr (*née* Oelsner), Romy Müller (*née* Schneider), Bärbel Wöckel (*née* Eckert), Marita Koch)		
4×400 m	3:15.17	USSR	Seoul, South Korea	1 Oct 1988
		(Tatyana Ledovskaya, Olga Nazarova (*née* Grigoryeva), Maria Pinigina (*née* Kulchunova), Olga Bryzgina (*née* Vladykina))		
4×800 m	7:50.17	USSR	Moscow, USSR	5 Aug 1984
		(Nadezhda Olizarenko (*née* Mushta), Lyubov Gurina, Lyudmila Borisova, Irina Podyalovskaya)		

Field Events	m	ft	in			
High Jump	2.09	6	10¼	Stefka Kostadinova (Bulgaria) (b. 25 Mar 1965)	Rome, Italy	30 Aug 1987
Pole Vault	4.13	13	6½	Daniela Bártová (Czech Republic) (b. 6 May 1974)	Wesel, Germany	24 Jun 1995
Long Jump	7.52	24	8¼	Galina Chistyakova (USSR) (b. 26 Jul 1962)	Leningrad, USSR	11 Jun 1988
Triple Jump	15.09	49	6	Ana Biryukova (Russia) (*née* Dereyankina) (b. 27 Sep 1967)	Stuttgart, Germany	21 Aug 1993
Shot	22.63	74	3	Natalya Venedictovna Lisovskaya (USSR) (b. 16 Jul 1962)	Moscow, USSR	7 Jun 1987
Discus	76.80	252	0	Gabriele Reinsch (GDR) (b. 23 Sep 1963)	Neubrandenburg, Germany	9 Jul 1988
Hammer	68.16	223	8	Olga Kuzenkova (Russia) (b. 4 Oct 1970)	Moscow, Russia	17 Jun 1995
Javelin	80.00	262	5	Petra Felke (now Meier) (GDR) (b. 30 Jul 1959)	Potsdam, Germany	9 Sep 1988

Heptathlon	**7291 points**	Jacqueline Joyner-Kersee (USA) (b. 3 Mar 1962)	Seoul, South Korea	23–24 Sep 1988

100 m hurdles 12.69 sec; High Jump 1.86 m *6ft 1¼ in*; Shot Put 15.80 m *51 ft 10 in*; 200 m 22.56 sec;
Long Jump 7.27 m *23 ft 10¼ in*; Javelin 45.66 m *149 ft 10 in*; 800 m 2 min 08.51 sec

■ **Jan Zelezny sends the javelin on its way to the world record distance of 95.66 m at Sheffield, S Yorks.**
(Photo: Allsport/G. Mortimore)

Denise Rand (*née* Bignal), (b. 10 Feb 1940) with a gold (long jump), a silver (pentathlon) and a bronze (4 × 100 m relay), all in 1964 and Kathryn Jane Cook (*née* Smallwood) (b. 3 May 1960), all bronze—at 4 × 100 m relay 1980 and 1984, and at 400 m in 1984.

Olympic champions *Oldest and youngest* The oldest athlete to win an Olympic title was Irish-born Patrick Joseph 'Babe' McDonald (*né* McDonnell) (USA) (1878–1954) who was aged 42 years 26 days when he won the 25.4 kg *56 lb* weight throw at Antwerp, Belgium on 21 Aug 1920. The oldest female champion was Lia Manoliu (Romania) (b. 25 Apr 1932) aged 36 yr 176 days when she won the discus at Mexico City on 18 Oct 1968. The youngest gold medallist was Barbara Pearl Jones (USA) (b. 26 Mar 1937) who at 15 yr 123 days was a member of the winning 4 × 100 m relay team, at Helsinki, Finland on 27 Jul 1952. The youngest male champion was Robert Bruce Mathias (USA) (b. 17 Nov 1930) aged 17 yr 263 days when he won the decathlon at the London Games on 5–6 Aug 1948.

The oldest Olympic medallist was Tebbs Lloyd Johnson (GB) (1900–84), aged 48 yr 115 days when he was third in the 1948 50,000 m walk. The oldest woman medallist was Dana Zátopková (Czechoslovakia) (b. 19 Sep 1922) aged 37 yr 348 days when she was second in the javelin in 1960.

Guess What?
Q. Who is the oldest world champion in sport?
A. See Page 219

World Championships World Championships, distinct from the Olympic Games, were inaugurated in 1983, when they were held in Helsinki, Finland. The most medals won is ten by Frederick Carleton 'Carl' Lewis (b. 1 Jul 1961), a record eight gold, 100 m, long jump and 4 × 100 m relay 1983; 100 m, long jump and 4 × 100 m relay 1987; 100 m and 4 × 100 m relay 1991; silver at long jump 1991 and bronze at 200 m 1993. Lewis has also won eight Olympic golds, 1984–92. The most medals by a women is ten by Merlene Ottey (Jamaica) (b. 10 May 1960) two gold, two silver, six bronze, 1983–93. The most gold medals won by a woman is four by Jackie Joyner-Kersee (USA) (b. 3 Mar 1962) long jump 1987, 1991, heptathlon 1987, 1993.

Indoor First held as the World Indoor Games in 1985, they are now staged biennially. The most individual titles is four by: Stefka Kostadinova (Bulgaria) (b. 25 Mar 1965) high jump 1985, 1987, 1989, 1993; Mikhail Shchennikov (Russia) (b. 24 Dec 1967) 5000 m walk 1987, 1989, 1991, 1993 and Sergey Bubka (Ukraine) pole vault 1985, 1987, 1991, 1995.

World Indoor Records

Track performances around a turn must be made on a track of circumference no longer than 200 metres.

MEN

Running	min:sec	Name and Country	Venue	Date
50 m	5.61*	Manfred Kokot (GDR) (b. 3 Jan 1948)	Berlin, Germany	4 Feb 1973
	5.61*	James Sanford (USA) (b. 27 Dec 1957)	San Diego, CA, USA	20 Feb 1981
60 m	6.41*	Andre Cason (USA) (b. 13 Jan 1969)	Madrid, Spain	14 Feb 1992
200 m	20.25	Linford Christie (GB) (b. 10 Apr 1960)	Liévin, France	19 Feb 1995
400 m	44.63	Michael Johnson (USA) (b. 13 Sep 1967)	Atlanta, GA, USA	4 Mar 1995
800 m	1:44.84	Paul Ereng (Kenya) (b. 22 Aug 1967)	Budapest, Hungary	4 Mar 1989
1000 m	2:15.26	Noureddine Morceli (Algeria) (b. 20 Feb 1970)	Birmingham, W Mids	22 Feb 1992
1500 m	3:34.16	Noureddine Morceli (Algeria)	Seville, Spain	28 Feb 1991
1 mile	3:49.78	Eamonn Coghlan (Ireland) (b. 21 Nov 1952)	East Rutherford, NJ, USA	27 Feb 1983
3000 m	7:35.15	Moses Kiptanui (Kenya) (b. 1 Sep 1971)	Ghent, Belgium	12 Feb 1995
5000 m	13:20.4	Suleiman Nyambui (Tanzania) (b. 13 Feb 1953)	New York, USA	6 Feb 1983
50 m hurdles	6.25	Mark McKoy (Canada) (b. 10 Dec 1961)	Kobe, Japan	5 Mar 1986
60 m hurdles	7.30	Colin Jackson (GB) (b. 18 Feb 1967)	Sindelfingen, Germany	6 Mar 1994
4×200 m	1:22.11	United Kingdom	Glasgow, Strathclyde	3 Mar 1991
		(Linford Christie, Darren Braithwaite, Ade Mafe, John Regis)		
4×400 m	3:03.05	Germany	Seville, Spain	10 Mar 1991
		(Rico Lieder, Jens Carlowitz, Karsten Just, Thomas Schönlebe)		
5000 m walk	18:07.08	Mikhail Schennikov (Russia) (b. 24 Dec 1967)	Moscow, Russia	14 Feb 1995

* Ben Johnson (Canada) (b. 30 Dec 1961) ran 50m in 5.55sec at Ottawa, Cananda on 31 Jan 1987 and 60m in 6.41sec at Indianapolis, USA on 7 Mar 1987, but these were invalidated due to his admission of having taken drugs, following his disqualification at the 1988 Olympics.

Field Events

	m	ft	in		Venue	Date
High Jump	2.43	7	11½	Javier Sotomayor (Cuba) (b. 13 Oct 1967)	Budapest, Hungary	4 Mar 1989
Pole Vault	6.15	20	2¼	Sergey Nazarovich Bubka (Ukraine) (b. 4 Dec 1963)	Donetsk, Ukraine	21 Feb 1993
Long Jump	8.79	28	10¼	Frederick Carleton 'Carl' Lewis (USA) (b. 1 Jul 1961)	New York, USA	27 Jan 1984
Triple Jump	17.77	58	3½	Leonid Voloshin (Russia) (b. 30 Mar 1966)	Grenoble, France	6 Feb 1994
Shot	22.66	74	4¼	Eric Randolph 'Randy' Barnes (USA) (b. 16 Jun 1966)	Los Angeles, CA, USA	20 Jan 1989

Heptathlon

6476 points ... Dan Dion O'Brien (USA) (b. 18 Jul 1966) ... Toronto, Canada ... 13–14 Mar 1993
(60m 6.67sec; LJ, 7.84m; SP, 16.02m; HJ, 2.13m; 60m hurdles, 7.85sec; PV, 5.20m; 1000m 2:57.96)

WOMEN

Running	min:sec	Name and Country	Venue	Date
50 m	5.96	Irina Privalova (Russia) (b. 12 Nov 1968)	Madrid, Spain	9 Feb 1995
60 m	6.92	Irina Privalova (Russia)	Madrid, Spain	11 Feb 1993
	6.92	Irina Privalova (Russia)	Madrid, Spain	9 Feb 1995
200 m	21.87	Merlene Ottey (Jamaica) (b. 10 May 1960)	Liévin, France	13 Feb 1993
400 m	49.59	Jarmila Kratochvílová (Czechoslovakia) (b. 26 Jan 1951)	Milan, Italy	7 Mar 1982
800 m	1:56.40	Christine Wachtel (GDR) (b. 6 Jan 1965)	Vienna, Austria	13 Feb 1988
1000 m	2:33.93u	Inna Yevseyeva (Ukraine) (b. 14 Aug 1964)	Moscow, Russia	7 Feb 1992
1500 m	4:00.27	Doina Melinte (Romania) (b. 27 Dec 1956)	East Rutherford, NJ, USA	9 Feb 1990
1 mile	4:17.14	Doina Melinte (Romania)	East Rutherford, NJ, USA	9 Feb 1990
3000 m	8:33.82	Elly van Hulst (Netherlands) (b. 9 Jun 1957)	Budapest, Hungary	4 Mar 1989
5000 m	15:03.17	Elizabeth McColgan (GB) (b. 24 May 1964)	Birmingham, W Midls	22 Feb 1992
50 m hurdles	6.58	Cornelia Oschkenat (GDR) (b. 29 Oct 1961)	Berlin, Germany	20 Feb 1988
60 m hurdles	7.69*	Lyudmila Narozhilenko (Russia) (b. 21 Apr 1964)	Chelyabinsk, Russia	4 Feb 1993
4×200 m	1:32.55	S. C. Eintracht Hamm (West Germany)	Dortmund, Germany	19 Feb 1988
		(Helga Arendt, Silke-Beate Knoll, Mechthild Kluth, Gisela Kinzel)		
4×400 m	3:27.22	Germany	Seville, Spain	10 Mar 1991
		(Sandra Seuser, Katrin Schreiter, Annett Hesselbarth, Grit Breuer)		
3000 m walk	11:44.00	Alina Ivanova (Ukraine) (b. 25 Jun 1969)	Moscow, Russia	7 Feb 1992

Field Events

	m	ft	in		Venue	Date
High jump	2.07	6	9½	Heike Henkel (Germany) (b. 5 May 1964)	Karlsruhe, Germany	9 Feb 1992
Pole vault	4.15	13	5¼	Sun Caiyun (China) (b. 21 Mar 1973)	Erfurt, Germany	15 Feb 1995
Long jump	7.37	24	2¼	Heike Drechsler (GDR) (b. 16 Dec 1964)	Vienna, Austria	13 Feb 1988
Triple jump	15.03	49	3½	Yolanda Chen (Russia) (b. 26 Jul 1961)	Barcelona, Spain	11 Mar 1995
Shot	22.50	73	10	Helena Fibingerová (Czechoslovakia) (b. 13 Jul 1959)	Jablonec, Czechoslovakia	19 Feb 1977

Pentathlon

4991 points ... Irina Belova (Russia) (b. 27 Mar 1968) ... Berlin, Germany ... 14–15 Feb .1992
(60m hurdles 8.22sec; HJ 1.93m; SP 13.25m; LJ 6.67m; 800m 2:10.26)

* Narozhilenko recorded a time of 7.63 at Seville, Spain on 4 Nov 1993, but was disqualified on a positive drugs test. u=unratified

Yolanda Chen was the first woman to triple jump 15 metres indoors when she won the 1995 World Championships at Barcelona, Spain.
(Photo: Allsport/G. Mortimore)

■ Javier Sotomayor holds both the indoor and outdoor high jump world records and was the first man to clear 8 ft.
(Photo: Allsport/G. Mortimore)

World record breakers *Oldest and youngest* For the greatest age at which anyone has broken a world record under IAAF jurisdiction (⇔ General Records). The female record is 36 years 139 days for Marina Styepanova (*née* Makeyeva) (USSR) (b. 1 May 1950) with 52.94 sec for the 400 m hurdles at Tashkent, USSR on 17 Sep 1986. The youngest individual record breaker is Wang Yan (China) (b. 9 Apr 1971) who set a women's 5000 m walk record at age 14 yr 334 days with 21 min 33.8 sec at Jian, China on 9 Mar 1986. The youngest male is 17 yr 198 days Thomas Ray (GB) (1862–1904) when he pole-vaulted 3.42 m *11 ft 2¾ in* on 19 Sep 1879 (prior to IAAF ratification).

It is only since 1994 that the IAAF, athletics' governing body, has officially recognised the women's pole vault. The records are constantly changing and Britain's top vaulter is Kate Staples (25 national records indoors and out), better known as Zodiac from the Gladiators TV pro- gramme. (Photo: Allsport/J. Gichigi)

Guess What?

Q. Who has had the most Number One records?

A. See Page 145

Most records in a day Jesse Owens (USA) (1913–80) set six world records in 45 min at Ann Arbor, Michigan on 25 May 1935 with a 9.4 sec 100 yd at 3:15 p.m., a 8.13 m *26 ft 8¼ in* long jump at 3:25 p.m., a 20.3 sec 220 yd (and 200 m) at 3:45 p.m. and a 22.6 sec 220 yd low hurdles (and 200 m) at 4 p.m.

Most national titles *Great Britain* The most national senior titles won by an ath- lete is 34 by Judith Miriam Oakes (b. 14 Feb 1958) at the shot with 12 WAAA or AAA outdoor, 13 WAAA indoor and nine UK titles, 1977–95. The men's record for senior AAA titles (excluding those in tug of war events) won by one athlete is 14 individual and one relay title by Emmanuel McDonald Bailey (Trinidad) (b. 8 Dec 1920), between 1946 and 1953. The most won outdoors in a single event is 13 by Denis Horgan (Ireland) (1871–1922) in the shot put between 1893 and 1912. Thirteen senior AAA titles were also won by: Michael Anthony Bull (b. 11 Sep 1946) at pole vault, eight indoor and five out, and by Geoffrey Lewis Capes (b. 23 Aug 1949) at shot, six indoor and seven out.

The greatest number of WAAA outdoor titles won by one athlete is 14 by Suzanne Allday (*née* Farmer) (b. 26 Nov 1934) with seven each at shot and discus between 1952 and 1962. She also won two WAAA indoor shot titles.

Most international appearances The greatest number of international matches contested for any nation is 89 by shot-putter Bjørn Bang Andersen (b. 14 Nov 1937) for Norway, 1960–81.

The greatest number of full Great Britain international appearances (outdoors and indoors) is 73 by Verona Marolin Elder (*née* Bernard) (b. 5 Apr 1953), mostly at 400 m, from 1971 to 1983. The men's record is 67 by shot-putter Geoff Capes, 1969–80. At pole vault and

United Kingdom (National) Records *Men*

Running	min:sec	Name	Venue	Date
100 m	9.87	Linford Christie (b. 10 Apr 1960)	Stuttgart, Germany	15 Aug 1993
200 m	19.87A	John Paul Lyndon Regis (b. 13 Oct 1966)	Sestriere, Italy	31 Jul 1994
400 m	44.47	David Grindley (b. 3 Sep 1965)	Barcelona, Spain	3 Aug 1992
800 m	1:41.73	Sebastian Newbold Coe (b. 29 Sep 1956)	Florence, Italy	10 Jun 1981
1000 m	2:12.18	Sebastian Newbold Coe	Oslo, Norway	11 Jul 1981
1500 m	3:29.67	Stephen Cram (b. 14 Oct 1960)	Nice, France	16 Jul 1985
1 mile	3:46.32	Stephen Cram	Oslo, Norway	27 Jul 1985
2000 m	4:51.39	Stephen Cram	Budapest, Hungary	4 Aug 1985
3000 m	7:32.79	David Robert Moorcroft (b. 10 Apr 1953)	Crystal Palace, London	17 Jul 1982
5000 m	13:00.41	David Robert Moorcroft	Oslo, Norway	7 Jul 1982
10,000 m	27:23.06	Eamonn Thomas Martin (b. 9 Oct 1958)	Oslo, Norway	2 Jul 1988
20,000 m	57:28.7	Carl Edward Thackery (b. 14 Oct 1962)	La Flèche, France	31 Mar 1990
25,000 m	1hr 15:22.6	Ronald Hill	Bolton, Lancashire	21 Jul 1965
30,000 m	1hr 31:30.4	James Noel Carroll Alder (b. 10 Jun 1940)	Crystal Palace, London	5 Sep 1970
1 hour	20,855 m	Carl Edward Thackery	La Flèche, France	31 Mar 1990
110 m hurdles	12.91	Colin Ray Jackson (b. 18 Feb 1967)	Stuttgart, Germany	20 Aug 1993
400 m hurdles	47.82	Kriss Kezie Uche Chukwu Duru Akabusi (b. 28 Nov 1958)	Barcelona, Spain	6 Aug 1991
3000 m s'chase	8:07.96	Mark Robert Rowland (b. 7 Mar 1963)	Seoul, South Korea	30 Sep 1988
4×100 m	37.77	National Team: Colin Jackson, Anthony Alexander Jarrett, John Regis, Linford Christie	Stuttgart, Germany	22 Aug 1993
4×200 m	1:21.29	National Team: Marcus Adam, Adeoye Mafe, Linford Christie, John Regis	Birmingham	23 Jun 1989
4×400 m	2:57.53	National Team: Roger Anthony Black, Derek Redmond, John Regis, Kriss Akabusi	Tokyo, Japan	1 Sep 1991
4×800 m	7:03.89	National Team: Peter Elliott, Garry Peter Cook, Stephen Cram, Sebastian Coe	Crystal Palace, London	30 Aug 1982
4×1500 m	14:56.8	National Team: Alan David Mottershead, Geoffrey Michael Cooper, Stephen John Emson, Roy Wood	Bourges, France	24 Jun 1979

A Record set at high altitude, best at low altitude: 19.94 sec by John Regis at Stuttgart, Germany on 20 Aug 1993.

Field Events	m	ft in	Name	Venue	Date
High Jump	2.37	7 9¼	Stephen James Smith (b. 29 Mar 1973)	Seoul, South Korea	20 Sep 1992
	2.37	7 9¼	Stephen James Smith	Stuttgart, Germany	22 Aug 1993
(indoors)	2.38	7 9¾	Stephen James Smith	Wuppertal, Germany	4 Feb 1994
Pole Vault	5.65	18 6½	Keith Frank Stock (b. 18 Mar 1957)	Stockholm, Sweden	7 Jul 1981
Long Jump	8.23	27 0	Lynn Davies (b. 20 May 1942)	Berne, Switzerland	30 Jun 1968
Triple Jump	17.72	58 1¾	Jonathon David Edwards (b. 10 May 1966)	Villeneuve d'Ascq, France	25 Jun 1995
Shot	21.68	71 1½	Geoffrey Lewis Capes (b. 23 Aug 1949)	Cwmbrân, Gwent	18 May 1980
Discus	64.32*	211 0	William Raymond Tancred (b. 6 Aug 1942)	Woodford, Essex	10 Aug 1974
Hammer	77.54	254 5	Martin Girvan (b. 17 Apr 1960)	Wolverhampton, W Mids	12 May 1984
Javelin	91.46	300 1	Stephen James Backley (GB) (b. 12 Feb 1969)	Auckland, New Zealand	25 Jan 1992

* *William Raymond Tancred threw 64.94 m 213 ft 1 in at Loughborough, Leicestershire on 21 Jul 1974 and Richard Charles Slaney (b. 16 May 1956) threw 65.16 m 213 ft 9 in at Eugene, Oregon, USA on 1 Jul 1985 but these were not ratified.*

Decathlon		Name	Venue	Date
Decathlon	8847 points	Francis Morgan 'Daley' Thompson (b. 30 Jul 1958)	Los Angeles, USA	8–9 Aug 1984

1st day: 100 m 10.44 sec, LJ 8.01 m *26 ft 3½ in*, SP 15.72 m *51 ft 7 in*, HJ 2.03 m *6 ft 8 in*, 400 m 46.97 sec
2nd day: 110 m H 14.33 sec, D 46.56 m *152 ft 9 in*, PV 5.00 m *16 ft 4¾ in*, J 65.24 m *214 ft 0 in*, 1500 m 4:35.00 sec

United Kingdom (National) Records *Women*

Running	min:sec	Name	Venue	Date
100 m	11.10	Kathryn Jane Smallwood (now Cook) (b. 3 May 1960)	Rome, Italy	5 Sep 1981
200 m	22.10	Kathryn Jane Cook (*née* Smallwood)	Los Angeles, California, USA	9 Aug 1984
400 m	49.43	Kathryn Jane Cook (*née* Smallwood)	Los Angeles, California, USA	6 Aug 1984
800 m	1:57.42	Kirsty Margaret McDermott (now Wade) (b. 6 Aug 1962)	Belfast, Northern Ireland	24 Jun 1985
1000 m	2:33.70	Kirsty Margaret McDermott (now Wade)	Gateshead, Tyne and Wear	9 Jul 1985
1500 m	3:59.96	Zola Budd (now Pieterse) (b. 26 May 1966)	Brussels, Belgium	30 Aug 1985
1 mile	4:17.57	Zola Budd (now Pieterse)	Zürich, Switzerland	21 Aug 1985
2000 m	5:26.93	Yvonne Carol Grace Murray (b. 4 Oct 1964)	Edinburgh, Lothian	8 Jul 1994
3000 m	8:28.83	Zola Budd (now Pieterse)	Rome, Italy	7 Sep 1985
5000 m	14:48.07	Zola Budd (now Pieterse)	Crystal Palace, London	26 Aug 1985
10,000 m	30:57.07	Elizabeth McColgan (*née* Lynch) (b. 24 May 1964)	Hengelo, Netherlands	25 Jun 1991
100 m hurdles	12.82	Sally Jane Janet Gunnell (b. 29 Jul 1966)	Zürich, Switzerland	17 Aug 1988
400 m hurdles	52.74	Sally Jane Janet Gunnell	Stuttgart, Germany	19 Aug 1993
4×100 m	42.43	National Team: Heather Regina Hunte (now Oakes), Kathryn Jane Smallwood (now Cook), Beverley Lanita Goddard (now Callender), Sonia May Lannaman	Moscow, USSR	1 Aug 1980
4×200 m	1:31.57	National Team; Donna-Marie Louise Hartley (*née* Murray), Verona Marolin Elder (*née* Bernard), Sharon Colyear (now Danville), Sonia May Lannaman	Crystal Palace, London	20 Aug 1977
4×400 m	3:22.01	National Team: Phyllis Smith (*née* Watt), Lorraine I Hanson, Linda Keough, Sally Janet Jane Gunnell	Tokyo, Japan	1 Sep 1991
4×800 m	8:19.9	National Team: Ann Margaret Williams, Paula Tracy Fryer, Yvonne Murray, Diane Delores Edwards	Sheffield, S Yorks	5 Jun 1992

Field Events	m	ft	in	Name	Venue	Date
High Jump	1.95	6	4¾	Diana Clare Elliot (now Davies) (b. 7 May 1961)	Oslo, Norway	26 Jun 1982
Pole Vault	3.75	12	3½	Katherine 'Kate' Staples (b. 2 Nov 1965)	Haringey, Greater London	25 Jun 1995
(indoors)	3.80	12	5½	Katherine 'Kate' Staples	Birmingham, W Mids	4 Feb 1995
Long Jump	6.90	22	7¾	Beverly Kinch (b. 14 Jan 1964)	Helsinki, Finland	14 Aug 1983
Triple Jump	14.37	47	1¾	Ashia Hansen (b. 5 Dec 1971)	Villeneuve d'Ascq, France	24 Jun 1995
Shot	19.36	63	6¼	Judith Miriam Oakes (b. 14 Feb 1958)	Gateshead, Tyne and Wear	14 Aug 1988
Hammer	64.90	212	11	Lorraine Anne Shaw (b. 2 Apr 1968)	Bedford	10 Jun 1995
Discus	67.48	221	5	Margaret Elizabeth Ritchie (b. 6 Jul 1952)	Walnut, California, USA	26 Apr 1981
Javelin	77.44	254	1	Fatima Whitbread (b. 3 Mar 1961)	Stuttgart, Germany	28 Aug 1986

Heptathlon ... 6623 points ... Judy Earline Veronica Simpson (*née* Livermore) (b. 14 Nov 1960) ... Stuttgart, Germany ... 29-30 Aug 1986
100 m hurdles 13.05 sec; High Jump 1.92 m *6 ft 3½ in*; Shot 14.75 m *48 ft 4 in*; 200 m 25.09 sec;
Long Jump 6.56 m *21 ft 6¼ in*; Javelin 40.92 m *134 ft 3 in*; 800 m 2 min 11.70 sec

decathlon Mike Bull had 66 full internationals or 69 including the European Indoor Games, before these were official internationals. The most outdoors is 61 by hammer thrower Andrew Howard Payne (b. South Africa, 17 Apr 1931) from 1960 to 1974.

Oldest and youngest internationals The oldest full Great Britain international was Donald James Thompson (b. 20 Jan 1933), aged 58 years 89 days, at 200 km walk at Bazencourt, France on 20–21 Apr 1991. In the same race Edmund Harold Shillabeer (b. 2 Aug 1939) became the oldest international débutant, aged 51 yr 260 days. The oldest woman was Christine Rosemary Payne (*née* Charters, now Chimes) (b. 19 May 1933) at discus in the Great Britain *v.* Finland match on 26 Sep 1974, aged 41 yr 130 days. The youngest man was high jumper Ross Hepburn (b. 14 Oct 1961) *v.* the USSR on 26 Aug 1977, aged 15 yr 316 days, and the youngest woman was Janis Walsh (now Cue) (b. 28 Mar 1960) *v.* Belgium (indoor) at 60 m and 4×200 m relay on 15 Feb 1975, aged 14 yr 324 days.

Longest winning sequence Iolanda Balas (Romania) (b. 12 Dec 1936) won a record 150 consecutive competitions at high jump from 1956 to 1967. The record at a track event is 122 at 400 metres hurdles by Edwin Corley Moses (USA) (b. 31 Jul 1955) between his loss to Harald Schmid (West Germany) (b. 29 Sep 1957) at Berlin, Germany on 26 Aug 1977 and that to Danny Lee Harris (USA) (b. 7 Sep 1965) at Madrid, Spain on 4 Jun 1987.

Longest running race The longest race ever staged was the 1929 trans-continental races from New York City to Los Angeles, California, USA of 5898 km *3665 miles*. The Finnish-born Johnny Salo (1893–1931) was the winner in 1929 in 79 days, from 31 March to 18 June. His elapsed time of 525 hr

'End to End'

The fastest confirmed run from John o' Groats to Land's End is 10 days 15 hr 27 min by Donald Alexander Ritchie (GB) (b. 6 Jul 1944) from 1–12 Apr 1989. A faster 10 days 3 hr 30 min was claimed by Fred Hicks (GB) for 1410 km *876 miles* on 20–30 May 1977. The fastest by a women is 13 days 17 hr 42 min by walker Ann Sayer (⇨ Walking). A relay team of 10 from Vauxhall Motors A.C. covered the distance in 76 hr 58 min 29 sec from 31 May–3 Jun 1990.

57 min 20 sec (averaging 11.21 km/h *6.97 mph*) left him only 2 min 47 sec ahead of Englishman Pietro 'Peter' Gavuzzi (1905–81).

The longest race staged annually is the New York 1300 Mile race, held since 1987, at Flushing Meadow-Corona Park, Queens, New York. The fastest time to complete the race is 16 days 17 hr 36 min 14 sec by Istvan Sidos (Hungary) from 15 Sep–2 Oct 1993.

Longest runs Al Howie (GB) ran across Canada, from St Johns to Victoria, a distance of 7295.5 km *4533.2 miles*, in 72 days 10 hr 23 min, 21 Jun–1 Sep 1991. Robert J Sweetgall (USA) (b. 8 Dec 1947) ran 17,071 km *10,608 miles* around the perimeter of the USA starting and finishing in Washington, DC, 9 Oct 1982–15 Jul 1983. Ron Grant (Australia) (b. 15 Feb 1943) ran around Australia, 13,383 km *8316 miles* in 217 days 3 hr 45 min, 28 Mar–31 Oct 1983. Max Telford (New Zealand) (b. Hawick, 2 Feb 1955) ran 8224 km *5110 miles* from Anchorage, Alaska to Halifax, Nova Scotia, in 106 days 18 hr 45 min from 25 Jul to 9 Nov 1977.

The fastest time for the cross-America run is 46 days 8 hr 36 min by Frank Giannino Jr (USA) (b. 1952) for the 4989 km *3100 miles* from San Francisco to New York from 1 Sep–17 Oct 1980. The women's trans-America record is 69 days 2 hr 40 min by Mavis Hutchinson (South Africa) (b. 25 Nov 1942) from 12 Mar–21 May 1978.

Greatest mileage Douglas Alistair Gordon Pirie (GB) (1931–91), who set five world records in the 1950s, estimated that he had run a total distance of 347,600 km *216,000 miles* in 40 years to 1981.

Dr Ron Hill (b. 21 Sep 1938), the 1969 European and 1970 Commonwealth marathon champion, has not missed a day's training since 20 Dec 1964. His meticulously compiled training log shows a total of 206,039 km *128,027 miles* from 3 Sep 1956 to 19 May 1994. He has finished 114 marathons, all sub 2:52 and has raced in 55 nations.

Mass relay records The record for 100 miles *160.9 km* by 100 runners from one club is 7 hr 53 min 52.1 sec by Baltimore

Guess What?

Q. what is the highest mileage for a car?

A. See Page 117

Road Runners Club, Towson, Maryland, USA on 17 May 1981. The women's record is 10 hr 33 min 38.81 sec by the Syracuse Chargers Running Club, New York, USA on 10 Aug 1994. The record for 100 × 100 m is 19 min 14.19 sec by a team from Antwerp at Merksem, Belgium on 23 Sep 1989.

The longest relay ever run was 17,391 km *10,806 miles* by 23 runners of the Melbourne Fire Brigade, around Australia on Highway No. 1, in 50 days 43 min, 6 Aug–25 Sep 1991. The most participants is 6500, 260 teams of 25, for the Batavierenrace from Nijmegen to Enschede, Netherlands on 25 Apr 1992. The greatest distance covered in 24 hours by a team of ten is 487.343 km *302.281 miles* by Puma Tyneside RC at Monkton Stadium, Jarrow on 10–11 Sep 1994.

Marathon

The Boston marathon, the world's longest-lasting major marathon, was first held on 19 Apr 1897 and covered 39 km *24 miles 1232 yd.*

Fastest It should be noted that courses may vary in severity. The following are the best times recorded, all on courses whose distance has been verified.

The world records are: (men) 2 hr 6 min 50 sec by Belayneh Dinsamo (Ethiopia) (b. 28 Jun 1965) at Rotterdam, Netherlands on 17 Apr 1988 and (women) 2 hr 21 min 6 sec by Ingrid Kristiansen (*née* Christensen) (Norway) (b. 21 Mar 1956) at London on 21 Apr 1985.

The British records are: (men) 2 hr 7 min 13 sec by Stephen Henry Jones (b. 4 Aug 1955) at Chicago, Illinois, USA on 20 Oct 1985 and (women) 2 hr 25 min 56 sec by Véronique Marot (b. 16 Sep 1955) at London on 23 Apr 1989.

Most competitors The record number of confirmed finishers in a marathon is 29,543 in the New York City on 6 Nov 1994. A record 105 men ran under 2 hr 20 min and 46 under 2 hr 15 min in the World Cup marathon at London on 21 Apr 1991, and a record 11 men ran under 2 hr 10 min at Boston on 18 Apr 1994, although the course is overall downhill and there was a strong following wind on the point-to-point course. A record 9 women ran under 2 hr 30 min in the first Olympic marathon for women at Los Angeles, USA on 5 Aug 1984.

Most run by an individual Norm Frank has run 525 marathons of 26 miles 385 yd or longer from 1967–95. Henri Girault (France) has run over 300 100 km races (an IAAF recognised distance) since 1979 and has completed a run on every continent except Antartica.

John A. Kelley (USA) (b. 6 Sep 1907) has finished the Boston Marathon 61 times, winning in 1933 and 1945, to 1992.

Not Finished

The oldest man to complete a marathon was Dimitrion Yordanidis (Greece), aged 98, in Athens, Greece on 10 Oct 1976. He finished in 7 hr 33 min. Thelma Pitt-Turner (New Zealand) set the women's record in August 1985, completing the Hastings, New Zealand marathon in 7 hr 58 min at the age of 82.

Three in three days The fastest combined time for three marathons in three days is 8 hr 22 min 31 sec by Raymond Hubbard (Belfast 2 hr 45 min 55 sec, London 2 hr 48 min 45 sec and Boston 2 hr 47 min 51 sec) on 16–18 Apr 1988.

Highest altitude The highest start to a marathon is for the biennially-held Everest Marathon, first run on 27 Nov 1987. It begins at Gorak Shep, 5212 m *17,100 ft* and ends at Namche Bazar, 3444 m *11,300 ft*. The fastest times to complete this race are, men 3 hr 59 min 4 sec by Jack Maitland in 1989, and women 5 hr 32 min 43 sec by Cath Proctor in 1993.

Half marathon The distance of a half the full marathon has become established in recent years as one of the most popular for road races. In 1992 the

Guess What?
Q. How high is Mt Everest?
A. See Page 15

IAAF held the first official world championships at this distance.

The world best time on a properly measured course is 59 min 47 sec by Moses Tanui (Kenya) (b. 20 Aug 1965) at Milan, Italy on 3 Apr 1993. The British best is 60 min 9 sec by Paul Evans (b. 13 Apr 1961) at Marrakech, Morocco on 15 Jan 1995.

Ingrid Kristiansen (Norway) ran 66 min 40 sec at Sandes, Norway on 5 Apr 1987, but the measurement of the course has not been confirmed. Liz McColgan ran 67 min 11 sec at Tokyo, Japan on 26 Jan 1992, but the course was

Ultra Long Distance World Records

MEN

Track	hr:min:sec	Name	Venue	Date
50 km	2:48:06	Jeff Norman (GB)	Timperley, Manchester	7 Jun 1980
50 miles	4:51:49	Don Ritchie (GB)	Hendon, London	12 Mar 1983
100 km	6:10:20	Don Ritchie (GB)	Crystal Palace, London	28 Oct 1978
100 miles	11:30:51	Don Ritchie (GB)	Crystal Palace, London	15 Oct 1977
200 km	15:11:10**	Yiannis Kouros (Greece)	Montauban, France	15–16 Mar 1985
200 miles	27:48:35	Yiannis Kouros (Greece)	Montauban, France	15–16 Mar 1985
500 km	60:23:00	Yiannis Kouros (Greece)	Colac, Australia	26–29 Nov 1984
500 miles	105:42:09	Yiannis Kouros (Greece)	Colac, Australia	26–30 Nov 1984
1000 km	136:17:00	Yiannis Kouros (Greece)	Colac, Australia	26 Nov–1 Dec 1984

kilometres

24 hours	285.362	Yiannis Kouros (Greece)	Surgères, France	6–7 May 1995
48 hours	470.781	Yiannis Kouros (Greece)	Surgères, France	6–8 May 1995
6 days	1023.200	Yiannis Kouros (Greece)	Colac, Australia	26 Nov–1 Dec 1984
(indoors)	1030.000	Jean-Gilles Bossiquet (France)	La Rochelle, France	16–23 Nov 1992

Road*	hr:min:sec			
50 km	2:43:38	Thompson Magawana (South Africa)	Claremont–Kirstenbosch	12 Apr 1988
50 miles	4:50:21	Bruce Fordyce (South Africa)	London–Brighton	25 Sep 1983
1000 miles	10d 10:30:35	Yiannis Kouros (Greece)	New York, USA	21–30 May 1988

kilometres

24 hours	286.463	Yiannis Kouros (Greece)	New York, USA	28–29 Sep 1985
6 days	1028.370	Yiannis Kouros (Greece)	New York, USA	21–26 May 1988

WOMEN

Track	hr:min:sec		Venue	Date
50 km	3:20:23	Ann Trason (USA)	Santa Rosa, California, USA	18 Mar 1995
50 miles	6:07:58	Linda Meadows (Australia)	Burwood, Australia	18 Jun 1994
100 km	7:50:09	Ann Trason (USA)	Hayward, California, USA	3–4 Aug 1991
100 miles	14:29:44	Ann Trason (USA)	Santa Rosa, California, USA	18–19 Mar 1989
200 km	19:28:48**	Eleanor Adams (GB)	Melbourne, Australia	19–20 Aug 1989
200 miles	39:09:03	Hilary Walker (GB)	Blackpool, Lancashire	5–6 Nov 1988
500 km	77:53:46	Eleanor Adams (GB)	Colac, Australia	13–15 Nov 1989
500 miles	130:59:58	Sandra Barwick (New Zealand)	Campbelltown, Australia	18–23 Nov 1990

kilometres

1 hour	18.084	Silvana Cruciata (Italy)	Rome, Italy	4 May 1981
24 hours	240.169	Eleanor Adams (GB)	Melbourne, Australia	19–20 Aug 1989
48 hours	366.512	Hilary Walker (GB)	Blackpool, Lancashire	5–7 Nov 1988
6 days	883.631	Sandra Barwick (New Zealand)	Campbelltown, Australia	18–24 Nov 1990

Road*	hr:min:sec			
30 km	1:38:27	Ingrid Kristiansen (Norway)	London	10 May 1987
50 km	3:08:13	Frith van der Merwe (South Africa)	Claremont-Kirstenbosch	25 Mar 1989
50 miles	5:40:18	Ann Trason (USA)	Houston, Texas, USA	23 Feb 1991
100 km	7:09:44	Ann Trason (USA)	Amiens, France	27 Sep 1993
100 miles	13:47:41	Ann Trason (USA)	Queens, New York	4 May 1991
200 km	19:08:21	Sigrid Lomsky (Germany)	Basel, Switzerland	1–2 May 1993
(indoors)	19:00:31	Eleanor Adams (GB)	Milton Keynes	3–4 Feb 1990
1000 km	7d 1:11:00	Sandra Barwick (New Zealand)	Queens, New York	16–23 Sep 1991
1000 miles	12d 14:38:40	Sandra Barwick (New Zealand)	Queens, New York	16–29 Sep 1991

*Where superior to track bests and run on properly measured road courses. It should be noted that road times must be assessed with care as course conditions can vary considerably. ** No stopped time known.*

33 m downhill, a little more than the allowable 1 in 1000 drop; she also ran a British best of 68min 42sec at Dundee, Tayside on 11 Oct 1992.

Pram-pushing Priscilla Margaret 'Tabby' Puzey, 38, pushed a pram while running the Abingdon half marathon on 13 Apr 1986 in 2 hr 4 min 9 sec.

Backwards running Timothy 'Bud' Badyna (USA) ran the fastest marathon in 3 hr 53 min 17 sec at Toledo, Ohio, USA on 24 Apr 1994. He also ran 10 km in 45 min 37 sec at Toledo on 13 Jul 1991. Donald Davis (USA) (b. 10 Feb 1960) ran 1 mile in 6 min 7.1 sec at the University of Hawaii on 21 Feb 1983. Ferdie Ato Adoboe (Ghana) ran 100 yd in 12.7 sec (100 m in 13.6 sec) at Smith's College, Northampton, Massachusetts, USA on 25 Jul 1991.

Arvind Pandya of India ran backwards across America, Los Angeles to New York, in 107 days, 18 Aug–3 Dec 1984. He also ran backwards from John o' Groats to Land's End, *940 miles* in 26 days 7 hr, 6 Apr–2 May 1990.

Three-legged Dale Lyons and David Pettifer (GB) set a three-legged running record in the London marathon with a time of 3 hr 58 min 33 sec on 2 Apr 1995. They were tied together both at ankle and wrist.

Walking

Most Olympic medals The only walker to win three gold medals has been Ugo Frigerio (Italy) (1901–68) with the 3000 m in 1920, and 10,000 m in 1920 and 1924. He also holds the record of most medals with four (he won the bronze medal at 50,000 m in 1932), a total shared with Vladimir Stepanovich Golubnichiy (USSR) (b. 2 Jun 1936), who won gold medals for the 20 km in 1960 and 1968, the silver in 1972 and the bronze in 1964.

The best British performance has been two gold medals by George Edward Larner (1875–1949) for the 3500 m and the 10 miles in 1908, but Ernest James Webb (1872–1937) won three medals, being twice 'walker up' to Larner and finishing second in the 10,000 m in 1912.

Most titles Four-time Olympian, Ronald Owen Laird (b. 31 May 1938) of the New York AC, won a total

Walking

It should be noted that severity of road race courses and the accuracy of their measurement may vary, sometimes making comparisons of times unreliable.

WORLD BESTS

MEN

20km: 1hr 17min 25.6sec (track), Bernardo Segura (Mexico) at Fana, Norway on 7 May 1994.
30km: 2hr 2min 41sec, Andrey Perlov (USSR) (b. 12 Dec 1961) at Sochi on 19 Feb 1989.
50km: 3hr 37min 41sec, Andrey Perlov (USSR) at Leningrad, USSR on 5 Aug 1989.

WOMEN

10km: 41min 29sec, Larisa Ramazonova (Russia) (b. 23 Sep 1971) at Izhevsk, Russia on 8 Jun 1995.
20km: 1hr 29min 40sec, Kerry Ann Saxby (Australia) (b. 2 Jun 1961) at Värnamo, Sweden on 13 May 1988.

BRITISH BESTS

MEN

20km: 1hr 22min 03sec, Ian Peter McCombie (b. 11 Jan 1961) at Seoul, South Korea on 23 Sep 1988.
30km: 2hr 7min 56sec, Ian Peter McCombie at Edinburgh, Lothian on 27 Apr 1986.
50km: 3hr 51min 37 sec, Christopher Lloyd Maddocks (b. 28 Mar 1957) at Burrator, Devon on 28 Oct 1990.

WOMEN

10km: 45min 28sec, Victoria Anne Lupton (b. 17 Apr 1972) at Livorno, Italy on 10 Jul 1993.
20km: 1hr 40 min 45sec, Irene Bateman at Basildon, Essex on 9 Apr 1983.

of 65 US national titles from 1958 to 1976, plus four Canadian Championships.

The greatest number of UK national titles won by a British walker is 27 by Vincent Paul Nihill (b. 5 Sep 1939) from 1963 to 1975.

'End to end' The fastest Land's End to John o' Groats walk is 12 days 3 hr 45 min for 1426.4 km *886.3 miles* by WO2 Malcolm Barnish of the 19th Regiment, Royal Artillery from 9–21 May 1986. The women's record is 13 days 17 hr 42 min by Ann Sayer (b. 16 Oct 1936), 20 Sep–3 Oct 1980. The Irish 'end to end' record over the 644 km *400.2 miles* from Malin Head, Donegal to Mizen Head, Cork is 5 days 22 hr 30 min, set by John 'Paddy' Dowling (b. 15 Jun 1929) on 18–24 Mar 1982.

24 hours The greatest distance walked in 24 hours is 228.930 km *142 miles 440 yd* by Jesse Castenada (USA) at Albuquerque, New

Mexico, USA on 18–19 Sep 1976. The best by a woman is 211.25 km *131.27 miles* by Annie van der Meer-Timmermann (Netherlands) at Rouen, France on 10 Apr–11 May 1986.

Backwards walking The greatest ever exponent of reverse pedestrianism has been Plennie L. Wingo (b. 24 Jan 1895) then of Abilene, Texas, USA who completed his 12,875 km *8000 mile* trans-continental walk from Santa Monica, California, USA to Istanbul, Turkey from 15 Apr 1931 to 24 Oct 1932. The longest distance recorded for walking backwards in 24 hr is 153.52 km *95.40 miles* by Anthony Thornton (USA) in Minneapolis, Minnesota, USA on 31 Dec 1988–1 Jan 1989.

Badminton

World championships Individual (instituted 1977) A record five titles have been won by Park Joo-bong (South Korea) (b. 5 Dec 1964), men's doubles 1985 and 1991 and mixed doubles 1985, 1989 and 1991. Three Chinese players have won two individual world titles: men's singles: Yang Yang (b. 8 Dec 1963) 1987 and 1989; women's singles: Li Lingwei 1983 and 1989; Han Aiping (b. 22 Apr 1962) 1985 and 1987.

Team The most wins at the men's World Team Badminton Championships for the Thomas Cup (instituted 1948) is nine by Indonesia (1958, 1961, 1964, 1970, 1973, 1976, 1979, 1984 and 1994). The most wins at the women's World Team Badminton Championships for the Uber Cup (instituted 1956) is five by: Japan (1966, 1969, 1972, 1978 and 1981); and China (1984, 1986, 1988, 1990 and 1992).

All-England Championships For long the most prestigious championships, they were institiuted in 1899. A record eight men's singles were won by Rudy Hartono Kurniawan (Indonesia) (b. 18 Aug 1948), in 1968–74 and 1976. The greatest number of titles won (including doubles) is 21 by George Alan Thomas (1881–1972) between 1903 and 1928. The most by a woman is 17 by: Muriel Lucas (later Mrs King Adams), 1899–1910; and Judith Margaret 'Judy' Hashman (*née* Devlin) (USA) (b. 22 Oct 1935) including a record ten singles, 1954, 1957–8, 1960–4, 1966–7.

Shortest game Christine Magnusson (Sweden) beat Martine de Souza (Mauritius) 11–1, 11–0 in 8 min 30 sec at the 1992 Olympics at Barcelona, Spain.

Longest rallies In the men's singles final of the 1987 All-England Championships between Morten Frost (Denmark) and Icuk Sugiarto (Indonesia) there were two successive rallies of over 90 strokes.

Handy

Walking on hands The distance record for walking on hands is 1400 km *870 miles*, by Johann Hurlinger of Austria, who in 55 daily 10-hr stints walked from Vienna to Paris in 1900, averaging 2.54 km/h *1.58 mph*. Mark Kenny of Norwood, Massachusetts, USA completed a 50 m inverted sprint in 16.93 sec on 19 Feb 1994. A four-man relay team of David Lutterman, Brendan Price, Philip Savage and Danny Scannell covered 1 mile *1.6 km* in 24 min 48 sec on 15 Mar 1987 at Knoxville, Tennessee, USA.

Guess What?
Q. Robert Wadlow's hands were how long?
A. See Page 54

Track Walking World Records

The International Amateur Athletic Federation recognises men's records at 20km, 30km, 50km and 2hours, and women's at 5km and 10km.

MEN

Event	hr:min:sec	Name, Country and Date of Birth	Venue	Date
10 km	38:02.60	Jozef Pribilinec (Czechoslovakia) (b. 6 Jul 1960)	Banská Bystrica, Czechoslovakia	30 Aug 1985
20 km	1:17:25.6	Bernardo Segura (Mexico) (b. 11 Feb 1970)	Fana, Norway	7 May 1994
30 km	2:01:44.1	Maurizio Damilano (Italy) (b. 6 Apr 1957)	Cuneo, Italy	4 Oct 1992
50 km	3:41:28.2	René Piller (France) (b. 23 Apr 1965)	Fana, Norway	7 May 1994
1 hour	15,577 m	Bernardo Segura (Mexico)	Fana, Norway	7 May 1994
2 hours	29,572 m	Maurizio Damilano (Italy)	Cuneo, Italy	4 Oct 1992

WOMEN

Event	hr:min:sec	Name, Country and Date of Birth	Venue	Date
3 km	11:48.24	Ileana Salvador (Italy) (b. 16 Jan 1962)	Padua, Italy	19 Aug 1993
5 km	20:07.52	Beate Anders (GDR) (b. 4 Feb 1968)	Rostock, Germany	23 Jun 1990
10 km	41:56.23	Nadezhda Ryashkina (USSR) (b. 1967)	Seattle, Washington, USA	24 Jul 1990

Baseball

US Major League Baseball Records

Batting

AVERAGE, Career, .366 Tyrus Raymond 'Ty' Cobb (Detroit AL, Philadelphia AL) 1905–28. **Season**, .440 Hugh Duffy (Boston NL) 1894.

RUNS, Career, 2245 Tyrus Raymond Cobb 1905–28. **Season**, 192 William Robert Hamilton (Phildelphia NL) 1894.

HOME RUNS, Career[*1], 755 Henry 'Hank' Aaron (Milwaukee NL, Atlanta NL, Milwaukee AL) 1954–76. **Season**, 61 Roger Eugene Maris (New York AL) 1961.

RUNS BATTED IN, Career, 2297 Henry 'Hank' Aaron 1954–76. **Season**, 190 Lewis Rober 'Hack' Wilson (Chicago NL) 1930. **Game**, 12 James LeRoy Bottomley (St Louis NL) 16 Sep 1924; Mark Whiten (St Louis NL) 7 Sep 1993. **Innings**, 7 Edward Cartwright (St Louis AL) 23 Sep 1890.

BASE HITS, Career, 4256 Peter Edward Rose (Cincinnati NL, Philadelphia NL, Montreal NL, Cincinnati NL) 1963–86. **Season**, 257 George Harold Sisler (St Louis AL) 1920.

TOTAL BASES, Career, 6856 Henry 'Hank' Aaron 1954–76. **Season**, 457 George Herman 'Babe' Ruth (New York AL) 1921.

HITS, Consecutive, 12 Michael Franklin 'Pinky' Higgins (Boston AL) 19–21 Jun 1938; Walter 'Moose' Dropo (Detroit AL) 14–15 Jul 1952.

CONSECUTIVE GAMES BATTED SAFELY, 56 Joseph Paul DiMaggio (New York AL) 15 May–16 Jul 1941.

STOLEN BASES, Career, 1117 Rickey Henley Henderson (Oakland AL, New York AL, Oakland AL, Toronto AL, Oakland AL) 1979–94. **Season**, 130 Rickey Henderson 1982.

CONSECUTIVE GAMES PLAYED[*2], 2130 Henry Louis 'Lou' Gehrig (New York AL) 1 Jun 1925–30 Apr 1939.

Pitching

GAMES WON, Career, 511 Denton True 'Cy' Young (Cleveland NL, St Louis NL, Boston AL, Cleveland AL, Boston NL) 1890–1911. **Season**, 60 Charles Gardner Radbourn (Providence NL) 1884.

CONSECUTIVE GAMES WON, 24 Carl Owen Hubbell (New York NL) 1936–7.

SHUTOUTS, Career, 113 Walter Perry Johnson (Washington AL) 1907–27. **Season**, 16 George Washington Bradley (St Louis NL) 1876; Grover Cleveland Alexander (Philadelphia NL) 1916.

STRIKEOUTS, Career, 5714 Lynn Nolan Ryan (New York NL, California AL, Houston NL, Texas AL) 1966–93. **Season**, 383 Lynn Nolan Ryan (California AL) 1973. (513 Matthew Aloysius Kilroy (Baltimore AA) 1886). **Game** (9 innings), 20 Roger Clemens (Boston AL) v. Seattle 29 Apr 1986.

NO-HIT GAMES, Career, 7 Lynn Nolan Ryan 1973–91.

EARNED RUN AVERAGE, Season, 0.90 Ferdinand Schupp (140 inns) (New York NL) 1916; 0.96 Hubert 'Dutch' Leonard (222 inns) (Boston AL) 1914; 1.12 Robert Gibson (305 inns) (St Louis NL) 1968.

Note: AL - American League
NL - National League
* Japanese League records that are superior to those in the US major leagues;
[1] 868 Sadaharu Oh (Yomiuri) 1959–80.
[2] 2215 Sachio Kinugasa (Hiroshima) 1970–87.

Origins Played annually betwen the winners of the National League and the American League, the World Series was first staged unofficially in 1903, and officially from 1905. The most wins is 22 by the New York Yankees between 1923 and 1978 from a record 33 series appearances for winning the American League titles between 1921 and 1981. The most National League titles is 19 by the Dodgers—Brooklyn 1890–1957, Los Angeles 1958–88.

Most valuable player The only men to have won this award twice are: Sanford 'Sandy' Koufax (b. 30 Dec 1935) (Los Angeles, NL 1963, 1965), Robert 'Bob' Gibson (b. 9 Nov 1935) (St. Louis NL, 1964, 1967) and Reginald Martinez 'Reggie' Jackson (b. 18 May 1946) (Oakland AL 1973, New York AL, 1977).

Attendance The record attendance for a series is 420,784 for the six games when the Los Angeles Dodgers beat the Chicago White Sox 4–2 between 1 and 8 Oct 1959. The single game record is 92,706 for the fifth game of this series at the Memorial Coliseum, Los Angeles on 6 Oct 1959.

Major League

Most games played Peter Edward 'Pete' Rose (b. 14 Apr 1941) played in a record 3562 games with a record 14,053 at bats for Cincinnati NL 1963–78 and 1984–6, Philadelphia NL 1979–83, Montreal NL 1984. Henry Louis 'Lou' Gehrig (1903–41) played in 2130 successive games for the New York Yankees (AL) from 1 Jun 1925 to 30 Apr 1939.

Most home runs *Career* Henry Louis 'Hank' Aaron (b. 5 Feb 1934) holds the major league career record with 755 home runs; 733 for the Milwaukee (1954–65) and Atlanta (1966–74) Braves in the National League and 22 for the Milwaukee Brewers (AL) 1975–6. On 8 Apr 1974 he had bettered the previous record of 714 by George Herman 'Babe' Ruth (1895–1948). Ruth hit his home runs from 8399 times at bat, the highest home run percentage of 8.5%. Joshua Gibson (1911–47) of Homestead Grays and Pittsburgh Crawfords, Negro League clubs, achieved a career total of nearly 900 homers including an unofficial record season's total of 84 in 1931.

Season The US major league record for home runs in a season is 61 by Roger Eugene Maris (1934–85) for New York Yankees in 162 games in 1961. 'Babe' Ruth hit 60 in 154 games in 1927 for the New York Yankees. The most official home runs in a minor league season is 72 by Joe Bauman of Roswell Rockets, New Mexico in 1954.

Game The most home runs in a major league game is four, first achieved by Robert Lincoln 'Bobby' Lowe (1868–1951) for Boston v. Cinncinnati on 30 May 1894. The feat had been achieved a further 11 times since then.

Consecutive games The most consecutive games hitting home runs is eight by Richard Dale Long (b. 6 Feb 1926) for Pittsburgh (NL), 19–28 May 1956; Donald Arthur Mattingly (b. 21 Apr 1961) for New York (AL), July 1987 and by Ken Griffey Jr for Seattle Mariners (AL), July 1993.

Most games won by a pitcher Denton True 'Cy' Young (1867–1955) had a record 511 wins and a record 750 complete games from a total of 906 games and 815 starts in his career for Cleveland NL 1890–98, St Louis NL 1899–1900, Boston AL 1901–08, Cleveland AL 1909–11 and Boston NL 1911. He pitched a record total of 7356 innings. The career record of most games pitching is 1070 by

Guess What?
Q. What is the most expensive cigarette card?
A. See Page 232

■ Perhaps the most notable record in baseball is that held by Lou Gehrig of the New York Yankees, for the most consecutive games played, 2130. On 2 Aug 1994, Cal Ripken, shortstop of the Baltimore Orioles, played his 2000th consecutive game. He has continued his 'streak' in the 1995 season and should pass the record by the end of August 1995, if he remains healthy.
(Photo: Allsport (USA)/J. Rettaliata)

World Series Records

Most series played 14	Lawrence Peter 'Yogi' Berra (New York, AL) 1947–63	
Most series played by pitcher ..11	Edward Charles 'Whitey' Ford (New York, AL) 1950–64	
Most home runs in a game 3	George Herman 'Babe' Ruth (New York, AL) ......6 Oct 1926	
3	George Herman 'Babe' Ruth (New York, AL) ......9 Oct 1928	
3	Reginald Martinez Jackson (New York, AL) ....18 Oct 1977	
Runs batted in 6	Robert C. Richardson (New York, AL) ....8 Oct 1960	
Strikeouts 17	Robert Gibson (St Louis, NL) ....2 Oct 1968	
Perfect game (9 innings)	Donald James Larson (New York, AL) v Brooklyn 8 Oct 1956	

Note: AL - American League   *NL - National League*

James Hoyt Wilhelm (b. 26 Jul 1923) for a total of nine teams between 1952 and 1972; he set the career record with 143 wins by a relief pitcher. The season's record is 106 games pitched by Michael Grant Marshall (b. 15 Jan 1943) for Los Angeles (NL) in 1974.

Most consecutive hits Michael Franklin 'Pinky' Higgins (1909–69) had 12 consecutive hits for Boston (AL) 19–21 Jun 1938. This was equalled by Walter 'Moose' Droppo (b. 30 Jan 1923) for Detroit (AL) 14–15 Jul 1952. Joseph Paul DiMaggio (b. 25 Nov 1914) hit in a record 56 consecutive games for New York in 1941; he was 223 times at bat, with 91 hits, scoring 16 doubles, 4 triples and 15 home runs.

Perfect game A perfect nine innings game, in which the pitcher allows the opposition no hits, no runs and does not allow a man to reach first base, was first achieved by John Lee Richmond (1857–1929) for Worcester against Cleveland in the NL on 12 Jun 1880. There have been 14 subsequent perfect games over nine innings, but no pitcher has achieved this feat more than once. On 26 May 1959 Harvey Haddix Jr. (b. 18 Sep 1925) for Pittsburgh pitched perfect game for 12 innings against Milwaukee in the National League, but lost in the 13th.

> The most consecutive games won by a pitcher is 24 by Carl Owen Hubbell (1903–88) of the New York Giants, 16 in 1936 and 8 in 1937.

Cy Young award Awarded annually from 1956 to the outstanding pitcher on the major leagues, the most wins is four by Stephen Norman Carlton (b. 22 Dec 1944) (Philadelphia, NL) 1972, 1977, 1980, 1982.

Youngest player Frederick Joseph Chapman (1872–1957) pitched for Philadelphia in the American Association at 14 years 239 days on 22 Jul 1887, but did not play again.

The youngest major league player of all time was the Cincinnati pitcher Joseph Henry Nuxhall (b. 30 Jul 1928), who played one game in June 1944, aged 15 yr 314 days. He did not play again in the NL until 1952. The youngest player to play in a minor league game was Joe Louis Reliford (b. 29 Nov 1939) who played for the Fitzgerald Pioneers against Statesboro Pilots in the Georgia State League, aged 12 yr 234 days on 19 Jul 1952.

Record attendances The all-time season record for attendances for both leagues is 70,257,938 in 1993. The record for an individual league is 36,924,573 for the National League in 1993. The record for an individual team is 4,483,350 for the home games of the Colorado Rockies at Mile High Stadium, Denver in 1993.

An estimated 114,000 spectators watched a game between Australia and an American Services team in a demonstration event during the Olympic Games at Melbourne on 1 Dec 1956.

Longest throw Glen Edward Gorbous (b. Canada, 8 Jul 1930) threw 135.88 m *445 ft 10 in* on 1 Aug 1957.

Women Mildred Ella 'Babe' Didrikson (later Mrs Zaharias) (USA) (1911–56) threw 90.2 m *296 ft* at Jersey City, New Jersey, USA on 25 Jul 1931.

Fastest base runner The fastest time for circling bases is 13.3 sec by Ernest Evar Swanson (1902–73) at Columbus, Ohio, USA in 1932, at an average speed of 29.70 km/h *18.45 mph*.

Fastest pitcher Lynn Nolan Ryan (then of the California Angels) (b. 31 Jan 1947) was measured to pitch at 162.3 km/h *100.9 mph* at Anaheim Stadium, California, USA on 20 Aug 1974.

Cigarette card The most valuable card is one of the six known baseball series cards of Honus Wagner, who was a non-smoker, which was sold at Sotheby's, New York, USA for $451,000 on 22 Mar 1991. The buyers were Bruce McNall, owner of the Los Angeles Kings ice hockey club, and team member Wayne Gretzky, (⇦ Ice Hockey).

Long Gone

The longest measured home run in a major league game is 634 ft by Mickey Mantle (b. 20 Oct 1931) for the New York Yankees against the Detroit Tigers at Briggs Stadium Detroit on 10 Sep 1960.

> Orel Leonard Hershiser IV (b. 16 Sep 1958) pitched a record 59 consecutive shutout innings for the Los Angeles Dodgers from 30 Aug to 28 Sep 1988.

Guess What?

Q. What is the furthest an egg has been thrown?

A. See Page 278

> The oldest player in the major league is Leroy Robert 'Satchel' Paige (1906–82) who pitched for Kansas City A's (AL) at 59 years 80 days on 25 Sep 1965.

■ Greg Maddux of the Atlanta Braves is the first major league pitcher to win the coveted Cy Young award three years in succession, 1992–4. His first success was with the Chicago Cubs.
(Photo: Allsport (USA)/S. Dunn)

Basketball

Most titles *Olympic* The USA has won ten men's Olympic titles. From the time the sport was introduced to the Games in 1936 to 1972, they won 63 consecutive matches until they lost 50–51 to the USSR in the disputed Final in Munich. Since then they have won a further 29 matches and had another loss to the USSR (in 1988).

The women's title has been won a record three times by the USSR in 1976, 1980 and 1992 (by the Unified team from the republics of the ex-USSR).

World The USSR has won most titles at both the men's World Championships (instituted 1950) with three (1967, 1974 and 1982) and women's (instituted 1953) with six (1959, 1964, 1967, 1971, 1975 and 1983). Three men's world titles have also been won by Yugoslavia, 1970, 1978 and 1990 and the USA 1954, 1986 and 1994.

European The most wins in the European Championships for men is 14 by the USSR, and in the women's event 21 also by the USSR, winning all but the 1958 championship since 1950, in this biennial contest.

The most European Champions Cup (instituted 1957) wins is eight by Real Madrid, Spain 1964–5, 1967–8, 1974, 1978, 1980 and 1995.

The women's title has been won 18 times by Daugava, Riga, Latvia between 1960 and 1982.

English The most English National Championship titles (instituted 1936) have been won by London Central YMCA, with eight wins in 1957–8, 1960, 1962–4, 1967 and 1969.

The English National League title has been won seven times by Crystal Palace 1974, 1976–8, 1980 and 1982–3. In the 1989/90 season Kingston won all five domestic trophies; the National League and Championship play-offs, the National Cup, League Cup and WIBC. The English Women's Cup (instituted 1965) has been won a record eight times by the Tigers, 1972–3, 1976–80 and 1982.

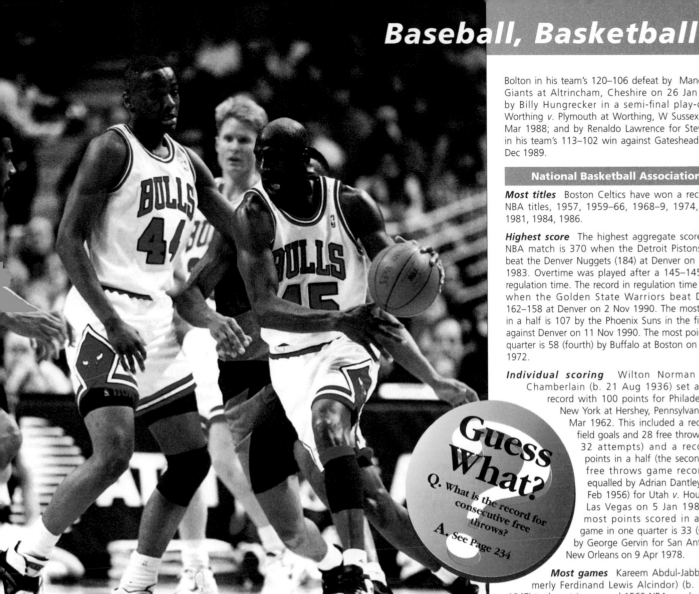

Bolton in his team's 120–106 defeat by Manchester Giants at Altrincham, Cheshire on 26 Jan 1985; by Billy Hungrecker in a semi-final play-off for Worthing v. Plymouth at Worthing, W Sussex on 20 Mar 1988; and by Renaldo Lawrence for Stevenage in his team's 113–102 win against Gateshead on 30 Dec 1989.

National Basketball Association

Most titles Boston Celtics have won a record 16 NBA titles, 1957, 1959–66, 1968–9, 1974, 1976, 1981, 1984, 1986.

Highest score The highest aggregate score in an NBA match is 370 when the Detroit Pistons (186) beat the Denver Nuggets (184) at Denver on 13 Dec 1983. Overtime was played after a 145–145 tie in regulation time. The record in regulation time is 320, when the Golden State Warriors beat Denver 162–158 at Denver on 2 Nov 1990. The most points in a half is 107 by the Phoenix Suns in the first half against Denver on 11 Nov 1990. The most points in a quarter is 58 (fourth) by Buffalo at Boston on 20 Oct 1972.

Individual scoring Wilton Norman 'Wilt' Chamberlain (b. 21 Aug 1936) set an NBA record with 100 points for Philadelphia v New York at Hershey, Pennsylvania on 2 Mar 1962. This included a record 36 field goals and 28 free throws (from 32 attempts) and a record 59 points in a half (the second). The free throws game record was equalled by Adrian Dantley (b. 28 Feb 1956) for Utah v. Houston at Las Vegas on 5 Jan 1984. The most points scored in an NBA game in one quarter is 33 (second) by George Gervin for San Antonio v. New Orleans on 9 Apr 1978.

Guess What?
Q. What is the record for consecutive free throws?
A. See Page 234

Most games Kareem Abdul-Jabbar (formerly Ferdinand Lewis Alcindor) (b. 16 Apr 1947) took part in a record 1560 NBA regular season games over 20 seasons, totalling 57,446 minutes played, for the Milwaukee Bucks, 1969–75, and the Los Angeles Lakers, 1975–89. He also played a record 237 play-off games. The most successive games is 906 by Randy Smith for Buffalo, San Diego, Cleveland and New York from 18 Feb 1972 to 13 Mar 1983. The record for complete games played in one season is 79 by Wilt Chamberlain for Philadelphia in 1962, when he was on court for a record 3882 minutes. Chamberlain went through his entire career of 1045 games without fouling out.

Most points Kareem Abdul-Jabbar set NBA career records with 38,387 points (average 24.6 points per game), including 15,837 field goals in regular season games, and 5762 points, including 2356 field goals in play-off games. The previous record holder, Wilt Chamberlain, had an average of 30.1 points per game for his total of 31,419 for Philadelphia 1959–62, San Francisco 1962–5, Philadelphia 1964–8 and Los Angeles 1968–73. He scored 50 or more points in 118 games, including 45 in 1961/2 and 30 in 1962/3 to the next best career total of 17. He set season's records for points and scoring average with 4029 at 50.4 per game, and also for field goals, 1597, for Philadelphia in 1961/2. The highest career average for players exceeding 10,000 points is 32.2 by Michael Jordan (b. 17 Feb 1963), 21,998 points in 684 games for the Chicago Bulls, 1984–95. Jordan also holds the career scoring average record for play-offs at 34.4 for 4165 points in 121 games, 1984–95.

Winning margin The greatest winning margin in an NBA game is 68 points when the Cleveland Cavaliers beat the Miami Heat, 148–80 on 17 Dec 1991.

■ Despite retiring at the end of the 1993 season, Michael Jordan, the most prolific scorer of modern times, returned to the NBA during the 1994/5 season after playing minor league baseball. He returned to the Chicago Bulls and once again maintained an average of over 30 points per game.
(Photo: Allsport (USA)/J. Daniel)

Los Angeles Lakers won a record 33 NBA games in succession from 5 Nov 1971 to 7 Jan 1972, and during the 1971/2 season they won a record 69 games with 13 losses.

Highest score In a senior international match Iraq scored 251 against Yemen (33) at New Delhi in November 1982 at the Asian Games.

The highest in a British Championship is 125 by England v. Wales (54) on 1 Sep 1978. England beat Gibraltar 130–45 on 31 Aug 1978.

US College The NCAA aggregate record is 399 when Troy State (258) beat De Vry Institute, Atlanta (141) at Troy, Alabama on 12 Jan 1992. Troy's total is the highest individual team score in a match.

United Kingdom The highest score recorded in a match is 250 by the Nottingham YMCA Falcons v. Mansfield Pirates at Nottingham on 18 Jun 1974. It was a handicap competition and Mansfield received 120 points towards their total of 145.

The highest score in a senior National League match is 174 by Chiltern Fast Break v. Swindon Rakers (40) on 13 Oct 1990.

The highest in the National Cup is 157 by Solent Stars v. Corby (57) on 6 Jan 1991.

Individual Mats Wermelin (Sweden), age 13, scored all 272 points in a 272–0 win in a regional boys' tournament in Stockholm, Sweden on 5 Feb 1974.

The record score by a woman is 156 points by Marie Boyd (now Eichler) of Central HS, Lonaconing, Maryland, USA in a 163–3 defeat of Ursaline Academy, Cumbria on 25 Feb 1924.

The highest score by a British player is 124 points by Paul Ogden for St Albans School, Oldham (226) v. South Chadderton (82) on 9 Mar 1982.

The highest individual score in a league match in Britain is 108 by Lewis Young for Forth Steel in his team's 154–74 win over Stirling in the Scottish League Division One at Stirling on 2 Mar 1985.

The record in an English National League (Div. One) or Cup match is 73 points by Terry Crosby (USA) for

Youngest and oldest player The youngest NBA player has been Bill Willoughby (b. 20 May 1957), who made his début for Atlanta Hawks on 23 Oct 1975 at 18 years 156 days. The oldest NBA regular player was Kareem Abdul-Jabbar, who made his last appearance for the Los Angeles Lakers at 42 yr 59 days in 1989.

Tallest player The tallest in NBA history has been Gheorge Muresan (Romania) of the Washington Bullets at 7 ft 7 in *2.31 m*. He made his pro début in 1994.

Other records

Most points The records for the most points scored in a college career are (women): 4061, Pearl Moore of Francis Marion College, Florence, South Carolina, USA, 1975–9; (men): 4045 by Travis Grant for Kentucky State, USA in 1969–72.

In the English National League, Russ Saunders (b. 25 Nov 1957) has scored 7141 points, 1982–95, and the most appearances is 432 by Ken Nottage (b. 2 Sep 1959), 1977–95.

Tallest players Suleiman 'Ali Nashnush (1943–91) was reputed to be 2.45 m *8 ft ¼ in* when he played for the Libyan team in 1962.

British Christopher Greener of London Latvians was 2.29 m *7 ft 6¼ in* and made his international début for England *v.* France on 17 Dec 1969.

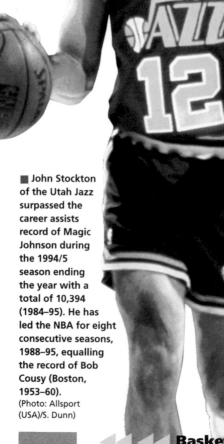

■ John Stockton of the Utah Jazz surpassed the career assists record of Magic Johnson during the 1994/5 season ending the year with a total of 10,394 (1984–95). He has led the NBA for eight consecutive seasons, 1988–95, equalling the record of Bob Cousy (Boston, 1953–60).
(Photo: Allsport (USA)/S. Dunn)

Shooting speed The greatest goal-shooting demonstration has been by Thomas Amberry (USA), who scored 2750 consecutive free throws at Seal Beach, California, USA on 15 November 1993. On 11 Jun 1992 Jeff Liles scored 231 out of 240 attempts in 10 minutes at Southern Nazarene University, Bethany, Oklahoma, USA. He repeated this total of 231 (241 attempts) on 16 June. This speed record is achieved using one ball and one rebounder. In one minute from seven scoring positions Jeff Liles scored 25 of 29 attempts at Bethany on 18 Sep 1994.

In 24 hours Fred Newman scored 20,371 free throws from a total of 22,049 taken (92.39 per cent) at Caltech, Pasadena, California, USA on 29–30 Sep 1990.

Longest goal Christopher Eddy (b. 13 Jul 1971) scored a field goal, measured at 27.49 m *90 ft 2¼ in*, for Fairview High School *v.* Iroquois High School at Erie, Pennsylvania, USA on 25 Feb 1989. The shot was made as time expired in overtime and it won the game for Fairview, 51–50.

Attendance

Largest attendance **The largest crowd for a basketball match is 80,000 for the final of the European Cup Winners' Cup between AEK Athens (89) and Slavia Prague (82) at the Olympic stadium, Athens, Greece on 4 Apr 1968.**

British A distance of 23.10 m *75 ft 9½ in* is claimed by David Tarbatt (b. 23 Jan 1949) of Altofts Aces *v.* Harrogate Demons at Featherstone, W Yorks on 27 Jan 1980.

Dribbling Ashrita Furman (USA) dribbled a basketball without 'travelling' 83 miles *133.5 km* in 24 hours at the National Stadium, Suva, Fiji on 6–7 Jan 1994.

Bob Nickerson of Gallitzin, Pennsylvania, Dave Davlin of Garland, Texas and Jeremy Kable of Highspire, Pennsylvania, all USA, have each successfully demonstrated the ability to dribble four basketballs simultaneously.

Spinning Bruce Crevier (USA) span 18 basketballs at the ABC-TV studios in New York City, USA on 18 Jul 1994.

Billiards

Most titles *World* The greatest number of World Championships (instituted 1870) won by one player is eight by John Roberts Jr (GB) (1847–1919) in 1870 (twice), 1871, 1875 (twice), 1877 and 1885 (twice). The record for world amateur titles is four by Robert James Percival Marshall (Australia) (b. 10 Apr 1910) in 1936, 1938, 1951 and 1962.

Britain The greatest number of United Kingdom professional titles (instituted 1934) won is seven (1934–9 and 1947) by Joe Davis (1901–78), who

also won four world titles (1928–30 and 1932). The greatest number of English Amateur Championships (instituted 1888) won is 15 by Norman Dagley (b. 27 Jun 1930) in 1965–6, 1970–5, 1978–84. The record number of women's titles is nine by Vera Selby (b. 13 Mar 1930), 1970–78. Uniquely, Norman Dagley has won the English Amateur Championships (as above), World Amateur Championships (1971, 1975), United Kingdom Professional Championship (1987) and World Professional Championship (1987).

> **The youngest winner of the world professional billiards title is Mike Russell (b. 3 Jun 1969), aged 20 years 49 days, when he won at Leura, Australia on 23 Jul 1989.**

Highest breaks Tom Reece (1873–1953) made an unfinished break of 499,135, including 249,152 cradle cannons (two points each) in 85 hr 49 min against Joe Chapman at Burroughes' Hall, Soho Square, London between 3 Jun and 6 Jul 1907. This was not recognized because press and public were not continuously present.

The highest certified break made by the anchor cannon is 42,746 by William Cook (England) from 29 May to 7 Jun 1907.

The official world record under the then baulk-line rule is 1784 by Joe Davis in the United Kingdom Championship on 29 May 1936.

Walter Albert Lindrum (Australia) (1898–1960) made an official break of 4137 in 2 hr 55 min against Joe Davis at Thurston's on 19–20 Jan 1932, before the baulk-line rule was in force. Geet Sethi (India) made a break of 1276 in the World Professional Championship in Bombay, India on 1 Oct 1992.

The highest break recorded in amateur competition is 1149 by Michael Ferreira (India) at Calcutta, India on 15 Dec 1978. Under the more stringent 'two pot' rule, restored on 1 Jan 1983, the highest break is Ferreira's 962 unfinished in a tournament at Bombay, India on 29 Apr 1986.

Fastest century Walter Lindrum made an unofficial 100 break in 27.5 sec in Australia on 10 Oct 1952. His official record is 100 in 46.0 sec set in Sydney, Australia in 1941.

3 Cushion

Most titles William F. Hoppe (USA) (1887–1959) won 51 billiards championships in all forms spanning the pre- and post-international era from 1906 to 1952.

UMB Raymond Ceulemans (Belgium) (b. 12 Jul 1935) has won 20 world three-cushion championships (1963–73, 1975–80, 1983, 1985, 1990).

Bar billiards Keith Sheard scored 28,530 in 19 min 5 sec in a league game at the Crown and Thistle, Headington, Oxford on 9 Jul 1984. Sheard scored 1500 points in a minute on BBC TV's *Record Breakers* on 23 Sep 1986.

The highest score in 24 hours by a team of five is 1,754,730 by Les Green, Ricard Powell, Kevin Clark, Mick Lingham and Curt Driver of The Shipwrights Arms, Chatham, Kent on 26–27 May 1990.

Guess What?
Q. What is the record for golf ball balancing?
A. See Page 261

Board Games

Chess

World Championships World champions have been officially recognized since 1886. The longest undisputed tenure was 26 years 337 days by Dr Emanuel Lasker (1868–1941) of Germany, from 1894 to 1921.

The women's world championship title was held by Vera Francevna Stevenson-Menchik (USSR, later GB) (1906–44) from 1927 until her death, and was successfully defended a record seven times.

Team The USSR has won the biennial men's team title (Olympiad) a record 18 times between 1952 and 1990, and the women's title 11 times from its introduction in 1957 to 1986. Since the dissolution of the USSR, Russia have won two men's and Georgia two women's titles, both 1992 and 1994.

Youngest Gary Kimovich Kasparov (USSR) (b. 13 Apr 1963) won the title on 9 Nov 1985 at 22 yr 210 days.

Maya Grigoryevna Chiburdanidze (USSR) (b. 17 Jan 1961) won the women's title in 1978 when only 17.

Oldest Wilhelm Steinitz (Austria, later USA) (1836–1900) was 58 years 10 days when he lost his title to Lasker on 26 May 1894.

Most active Anatoliy Yevgenyevich Karpov (USSR) (b. 23 May 1951) in his tenure as champion, 1975–85, averaged 45.2 competitive games per year, played in 32 tournaments and finished first in 26.

Most British titles The most British titles have been won by Dr Jonathan Penrose (b. 7 Oct 1933) with ten titles in 1958–63, 1966–9. Rowena Mary Bruce (née Dew) (b. 15 May 1919) won 11 women's titles between 1937 and 1969.

Grand Masters The youngest individual to qualify as an International Grand Master is Peter Leko (Hungary) (b. 8 Sep 1979), aged 14 yr 145 days on 30 Jan 1994.

The youngest Briton to qualify is Michael Adams (b. 17 Nov 1971), aged 17 yr 216 days on 21 Jul 1989.

Highest rating The highest rating ever attained on the officially adopted Elo System (devised by Arpad E. Elo (1903–92)) is 2805 by Gary Kasparov (USSR) at the end of 1992. The highest-rated woman player is Judit Polgar (Hungary), who achieved a peak rating of 2630 at the end of 1993.

The top British player on the Elo list has been Nigel David Short (b. 14 Jun 1965) who reached a peak rating of 2685 at the end of 1991. The top British woman is Susan Kathryn Arkell (née Walker) (b. 28 Oct 1965) who reached a peak of 2355 on 1 Jul 1988.

Fewest games lost by a world champion José Raúl Capablanca (Cuba) (1888–1942) lost only 34 games (out of 571) in his adult career, 1909–39. He was unbeaten from 10 Feb 1916 to 21 Mar 1924 (63 games) and was world champion 1921–7.

Most opponents The record for most consecutive games played is 663 by Vlastimil Hort (Czechoslovakia, later Germany) (b. 12 Jan 1944) over 32½ hours at Porz, Germany on 5–6 Oct 1984. He played 60–120 opponents at a time, scoring over 80 per cent wins and averaging 30 moves per game. He also holds the record for most games simultaneously, 201 during 550 consecutive games of which he only lost ten, in Seltjarnes, Iceland on 23–24 Apr 1977.

Slowest moves The slowest reported moving (before time clocks were used) in an official event is reputed to have been by Louis Paulsen (Germany)

■ Top woman player Judit Polgar (right) was just 15 years 150 days old when she qualified as the youngest ever Grandmaster on 20 Dec 1991, a record taken by compatriot, Peter Leko (14 years 145 days) in January 1994.
(Photo: Gamma/Gifford-Liaison)

Guess What?

Q. What is the fastest time to complete a game of solitaire?
A. See page 236

(1833–91) against Paul Charles Morphy (USA) (1837–84) at the first American Chess Congress, New York on 29 Oct 1857. The game ended in a draw on move 56 after 15 hours of play of which Paulsen used c. 11 hours.

Grand Master Friedrich Sämisch (Germany) (1896–1975) ran out of the allotted time (2 hr 30 min for 45 moves) after only 12 moves, in Prague, Czechoslovakia, in 1938.

The slowest move played, since time clocks were introduced, was at Vigo, Spain in 1980 when Francisco R. Torres Trois (b. 3 Sep 1946) took 2 hr 20 min for his seventh move v. Luis M. C. P. Santos (b. 30 Jun 1955).

The Master game with most moves on record was one of 269 moves, when Ivan Nikolić drew with Goran Arsović in a Belgrade, Yugoslavia tournament, on 17 Feb 1989. It took a total of 20 hr 15 min.

Oldest pieces The oldest pieces identified as chess pieces were found at Nashipur, datable to c.AD 900.

Domino stacking Edwin Sirko successfully stacked 401 dominoes on a single supporting domino on 4 Aug 1994 at Irvine, California, USA.

Domino toppling The greatest number set up single-handed and toppled is 281,581 out of 320,236

by Klaus Friedrich, 22, at Fürth, Germany on 27 Jan 1984. The dominoes fell within 12 min 57.3 sec, having taken 31 days (10 hours daily) to set up.

Thirty students at Delft, Eindhoven and Twente Technical Universities in the Netherlands set up 1,500,000 dominoes representing all of the European Community member countries. Of these, 1,382,101 were toppled by one push on 2 Jan 1988.

Draughts

World champions Walter Hellman (USA) (1916–75) won a record eight world titles during his tenure as world champion 1948–75.

The youngest winner of a world title is Patricia Breen of Co Carlow, Republic of Ireland, who won the Women's World Draughts Championship at Weston-super-Mare, Avon on 1 Apr 1993, aged 16.

British titles The British Championship (biennial) was inaugurated in 1886 and has been won six times by Samuel Cohen (London) (1905–72), 1924, 1927, 1929, 1933, 1937 and 1939. John McGill (Kilbride) (b. 1936) won six Scottish titles between 1959 and 1974.

Most opponents Charles Walker played a record 306 games simultaneously, winning 300, drawing 5 and losing 1, at Dollywood, Pigeon Force, Tennessee, USA on 22 Oct 1994.

The largest number of opponents played without a defeat or draw is 172 by Nate Cohen of Portland, Maine, USA at Portland on 26 Jul 1981. This was not a simultaneous attempt, but consecutive play over a period of four hours.

Scrabble (Crossword Game)

Highest scores The highest competitive game score is 1049 by Phil Appleby (b. 9 Dec 1957) in June 1989. His opponent scored 253 and the margin of victory, 796 points, is also a record.

Young & Old

Asa A. Long (b. 20 Aug 1904) became the youngest US national champion, aged 18 years 64 days, when he won in Boston, Massachusetts, USA on 23 Oct 1922. He became the oldest, aged 79 yr 334 days, when he won his sixth title in Tupelo, Mississippi, USA on 21 Jul 1984. He was also world champion 1934–8.

His score included a single turn of 374 for the word 'OXIDIZERS'. The highest competitive single turn score recorded, however, is 392 by Dr Saladin Karl Khoshnaw (of Kurdish origin) in Manchester in April 1982. He laid down 'CAZIQUES', which means 'native chiefs of West Indian aborigines'.

Most titles British National Championships were instituted in 1971. Philip Nelkon (b. 21 Jul 1956) has won a record four times, 1978, 1981, 1990 and 1992. The youngest winner was Allan Saldanha (b. 31 Oct 1966), aged 15 years 239 days in 1993.

World Championship The first world championship was held in London in 1991 and was played in English. The winner was Peter Morris (USA) (b. 1962) who collected a first prize of $10,000. The youngest winner is Mark Nyman (GB) (b. 14 Oct 1966), aged 26 years 320 days in 1993.

Most points in 24 hours The most points scored in 24 hours by two players is 111,154 by Paul Golder (b. 20 Sep 1968) and John Howell (b. 11 Jun 1965) at BBC Essex, Chelmsford on 4–5 Mar 1995.

> **Solitaire The shortest time taken to complete the game is 10.0 sec by Stephen Twigge at Scissett Baths, W Yorks on 2 Aug 1991.**

Biggest board game The world's biggest commercially available board game is *Galaxion*, created by Cerebe Design International of Hong Kong. The board measures 33 × 33 in *83.8 × 83.8 cm*.

Most expensive The most expensive commercially available board game is the deluxe version of *Outrage!* produced by Imperial Games of Southport, Merseyside. The game which is based on stealing the Crown Jewels from the Tower of London retails at £3995.

Bobsleigh and Tobogganing

Bobsledding

Most titles *World and Olympic* The world four-man bob title (instituted 1924) has been won 20 times by Switzerland (1924, 1936, 1939, 1947, 1954–7, 1971–3, 1975, 1982–3, 1986–90, 1993) including a record five Olympic victories (1924, 1936, 1956, 1972 and 1988).

Switzerland have won the two-man title 17 times (1935, 1947–50, 1953, 1955, 1977–80, 1982–3, 1987, 1990, 1992 and 1994) including a record four Olympic successes (1948, 1980, 1992 and 1994).

Eugenio Monti (Italy) (b. 23 Jan 1928) was a member of eleven world championship crews, eight two-man and three four-man in 1957–68.

The most Olympic gold medals won by an individual is three by Meinhard Nehmer (GDR) (b. 13 Jun 1941) and Bernhard Germeshausen (GDR) (b. 21 Aug 1951) in the 1976 two-man, 1976 and 1980 four-man events. The most medals won is seven (1 gold, 5 silver, 1 bronze) by Bogdan Musiol (GDR/Germany) (b. 25 Jul 1957) 1980–92.

The only British victory was at two-man bob in 1964 by the Hon. Thomas Robin Valerian Dixon (b. 21 Apr 1935) and Anthony James Dillon Nash (b. 18 Mar 1936).

Tobogganing

Oldest club The St Moritz Tobogganing Club, Switzerland, founded in 1887, is the oldest toboggan club in the world. It is notable for being the home of the Cresta Run, which dates from 1884.

Cresta Run The course is 1212 m *3977 ft* long with a drop of 157 m *514 ft* and the record is 50.41 sec (av. 86.56 km/h *53.79 mph*) by Christian Bertschinger (Switzerland) (b. 8 Feb 1964) on 23 Feb 1992. On 15 Jan 1995 Johannes Badrutt (Switzerland) (b. 16 Dec 1964) set a record from Junction (890 m *2920 ft*) of 41.27 sec.

> **The oldest person to have ridden the Cresta Run successfully is Robin Todhunter (GB) (b. 10 Mar 1903), aged 83 years 329 days on 2 Feb 1987.**

The greatest number of wins in the Grand National (instituted 1885) is eight by the 1948 Olympic champion Nino Bibbia (Italy) (b. 15 Mar 1922) in 1960–64, 1966, 1968 and 1973; and by Franco Gassner (Switzerland) (b. 2 May 1945) in 1981, 1983–6, 1988–9 and 1991. The greatest number of wins in the Curzon Cup (instituted 1910) is eight by Bibbia in 1950, 1957–8, 1960, 1962–4, and 1969.

Lugeing

Most titles The most successful riders in the World Championships (instituted 1953) have been Thomas Köhler (GDR) (b. 25 Jun 1940), who won the single-seater title in 1962, 1964 (Olympic) and 1967 and shared the two-seater title in 1965, 1967 and 1968 (Olympic). Georg Hackl (GDR/Germany) (b. 9 Sep 1966) has won four single-seater titles, 1989, 1990, 1992 (Olympic) and 1994 (Olympic).

Margit Schumann (GDR) (b. 14 Sep 1952) has won five women's titles, 1973–5, 1976 (Olympic) and 1977. Steffi Walter (*née* Martin) (GDR) (b. 17 Sep 1962) became the first rider to win two Olympic single-seater luge titles, with victories at the women's event in 1984 and 1988.

Fastest speed The highest recorded, photo-timed speed is 137.4 km/h *85.38 mph* by Asle Strand (Norway) at Tandådalens Linbana, Sälen, Sweden on 1 May 1982.

Bowling (Tenpin)

Highest scores The highest individual score for three sanctioned games (possible 900) is 899 by Thomas Jordan (USA) (b. 27 Oct 1966) at Union, New Jersey, USA on 7 Mar 1989. The record by a woman is 864 by Jeanne Maiden (b. 10 Nov 1957) of Tacoma, Washington at Solon, Ohio, USA on 23 Nov 1986. This series included a record 40 consecutive strikes.

The maximum 900 for a three-game series was achieved by Glenn Richard Allison (b. 22 May 1930) at the La Habra Bowl in Los Angeles, California, USA on 1 Jul 1982, but this was not recognized by the ABC due to the oiling patterns on the boards. It has been recorded five times in unsanctioned games – by Leon Bentley at Lorain, Ohio, USA on 26 Mar 1931; by Joe Sargent at Rochester, New York, USA in 1934; by Jim Murgie in Philadelphia, Pennsylvania, USA on 4 Feb 1937; by Bob Brown at Roseville Bowl, California, USA on 12 Apr 1980 and by John Strausbaugh at York, Pennsylvania, USA on 11 Jul 1987. Such series must have consisted of 36 consecutive strikes (i.e. all pins down with one ball).

The highest average for a season attained in sanctioned competition is 245.63 by Doug Vergouven of Harrisonville, Missouri, USA in 1989/90. The women's record is 232 by Patty Ann of Appleton, Wisconsin, USA in 1983/4.

Great Britain The British record for a three-game series is 847 by Lawrence William Ellis (b. 7 Dec 1950) at Airport Bowl, Hounslow, Greater London on 30 Aug 1992.

■ **Although there are a number of claims for a perfect three-game score of 900, the highest sanctioned score is 899 by Tom Jordan at Union, New Jersey in 1989.**

Guess What? Q. What is the world record for the men's shot? A. See Page 224

The three-game series record for a woman player is 740 by Emma Barlow at the Airport Bowl, Hounslow, Greater London on 24 Nov 1994.

The maximum score for a single game of 300 has been achieved on several occasions. The first man to do so was Albert Kirkham (b. 1931) of Burslem, Staffs on 5 Dec 1965. The first woman was Georgina Wardle (b. 24 Jul 1948) at the Sheffield Bowl, S Yorks on 20 Jan 1985. The first person to achieve the feat twice is Patrick Duggan (b. 26 May 1944), in 1972 and 1986, both at Bexleyheath Bowl, Kent.

PBA records Earl Roderick Anthony (b. 27 Apr 1938) was the first to win $1 million and won a record 41 PBA titles in his career.

The season's record earnings is $298,237 by Mike Aulby (b. 25 Mar 1960) in 1989. The career record is $1,711,971 by Peter Weber to 1 May 1995.

Highest score–24 hours A team of six scored 242,665 at Dover Bowl, Dover, Delaware, USA on 18–19 Mar 1995. During this record attempt a member of the team, Richard Ranshaw (USA), set an individual record of 51,064.

Bowls

Outdoor

World Championships (instituted 1966) The only man to win two or more singles titles is David John Bryant (England) (b. 27 Oct 1931), who won in 1966, 1980 and 1988. With the triples 1980, and the Leonard Trophy 1980 and 1988, he has won six World Championship gold medals.

The Leonard Trophy has been won three times by Scotland, 1972, 1984 and 1992.

Elsie Wilke (New Zealand) won two women's singles titles, 1969 and 1974. Three women have won three gold medals: Merle Richardson (Australia) fours 1977, singles and pairs 1985; Dorothy Roche (Australia) triples 1985 and 1988, fours 1988; and Margaret Johnston (Ireland) singles 1992 and pairs 1988 and 1992.

English and British Championships The record number of English Bowls Association (founded 8 Jun 1903) championships is 16 won or shared by David Bryant, including six singles (1960, 1966, 1971–3, 1975), three pairs (1965, 1969, 1974), three triples (1966, 1977, 1985) and four fours championships (1957, 1968, 1969 and 1971). He has also won seven British Isles titles (four singles, one pairs, one triple, one fours) in the period 1957–86. 1987.

The youngest ever EBA singles champion was David A. Holt (b. 9 Sep 1966) at 20 years 346 days in 1987.

Highest score In an international bowls match, Swaziland beat Japan by 63–1 during the World Championships at Melbourne, Australia on 16 Jan 1980.

Most eights Freda Ehlers and Linda Bertram uniquely scored three consecutive eights in the Southern Transvaal pairs event at Johannesburg, South Africa on 30 Jan 1978.

■ Tony Allcock, winner of a record six indoor world pairs titles with David Bryant, gets into the swing of things. Allcock has also won both the indoor and outdoor world singles titles, a feat only equalled by his pairs partner, Bryant.
(Photo: Allsport/M. Cooper)

Indoor

World Championships (instituted 1979) The most singles titles is three by: David Bryant, 1979–81 and Richard Corsie (GB), 1989, 1991 and 1993. Bryant with Tony Allcock (b. 11 Jun 1955) has won the pairs (instituted 1986) six times, 1986–7, 1989–92.

English Nationals (instituted 1960) The EIBA Singles Championship has been won most often by David Bryant with nine wins between 1964 and 1983. The youngest EIBA singles champion, John Dunn (b. 6 Oct 1963), was 17 years 117 days when he won in 1981.

Highest score The highest total in fours is 59 by Eastbourne & District Indoor Bowls Club against Egerton Park, at Eastbourne, E Sussex on 7 Feb 1989. The greatest 'whitewash' is 55–0 by C. Hammond and B. Funnell against A. Wise and C. Lock in the second round of the EIBA National Pairs Championships on 17 Oct 1983 at The Angel, Tonbridge, Kent.

Guess What?
Q. What is the record for balancing on one foot?
A. See Page 64

Boxing

Longest fights The longest recorded fight with gloves was between Andy Bowen of New Orleans (1867–94) and Jack Burke at New Orleans, Louisiana, USA on 6–7 Apr 1893. It lasted 110 rounds, 7 hr 19 min (9:15 p.m.–4:34 a.m.), and was declared a no contest (later changed to a draw). Bowen won an 85-round bout on 31 May 1893.

The longest bare-knuckle fight was 6 hr 15 min between James Kelly and Jack Smith at Fiery Creek, Dalesford, Victoria, Australia on 3 Dec 1855.

The greatest number of rounds was 276 in 4 hr 30 min when Jack Jones beat Patsy Tunney in Cheshire in 1825.

Shortest fights There is a distinction between the quickest knock-out and the shortest fight. A knock-out in 10½ seconds (including a 10 second count) occurred on 23 Sep 1946, when Al Couture struck Ralph Walton while the latter was adjusting a gum shield in his corner at Lewiston, Maine, USA. If the time was accurately taken it is clear that Couture must have been more than half-way across the ring from his own corner at the opening bell.

The shortest fight on record appears to be one in a Golden Gloves tournament at Minneapolis, Minnesota, USA on 4 Nov 1947, when Mike Collins floored Pat Brownson with the first punch and the contest was stopped, without a count, 4 seconds after the bell.

The shortest world title fight was 20 seconds, when Gerald McClellan (USA) beat Jay Bell in an WBC middleweight bout at Puerto Rico on 7 Aug 1993.

The shortest ever heavyweight world title fight was the James J. Jeffries (1875–1953)–Jack Finnegan bout at Detroit, USA on 6 Apr 1900, won by Jeffries in 55 seconds.

The shortest ever British title fight was one of 40 seconds (including the count), when Dave Charnley knocked out David 'Darkie' Hughes in a lightweight championship defence in Nottingham on 20 Nov 1961.

Eugene Brown, on his professional debut, knocked out Ian Bockes of Hull at Leicester on 13 Mar 1989. The fight was officially stopped after '10 seconds of the first round'. Bockes got up after a count of six but the referee stopped the contest.

Most British titles The most defences of a British heavyweight title is 14 by 'Bombardier' Billy Wells (1889–1967) from 1911 to 1919.

The only British boxer to win three Lonsdale Belts outright was heavyweight Henry William Cooper (b. 3 May 1934). He retired after losing to Joe Bugner (b. Hungary, 13 Mar 1950), having held the British heavyweight title from 12 Jan 1959 to 28 May 1969 and from 24 Mar 1970 to 16 Mar 1971.

Belter

The fastest time to win a Lonsdale Belt, for three successive championship wins, is 95 days by Michael Ayers at lightweight, 18 Feb–24 May 1995.

The longest time for winning a Lonsdale Belt outright is 8 years 236 days by Kirkland Laing (b. 20 Jun 1954), 4 Apr 1979–26 Nov 1987.

Tallest The tallest boxer to fight professionally was Gogea Mitu (b. 1914) of Romania in 1935. He was 2.23 m *7 ft 4 in* and weighed 148 kg *327 lb*. John Rankin, who won a fight in New Orleans, Louisiana, USA in November 1967, was reputedly also 2.23 m *7 ft 4 in*. Jim Culley, 'The Tipperary Giant', who fought as a boxer and wrestled in the 1940s is also reputed to have been 2.23 m *7 ft 4 in*.

Most fights without loss Edward Henry (Harry) Greb (USA) (1894–1926) was unbeaten in a sequence of 178 bouts, but these included 117 'no decision', of which five were unofficial losses, in 1916–23.

Of boxers with complete records, Packey McFarland (USA) (1888–1936) had 97 fights (5 draws) in 1905–15 without a defeat.

Pedro Carrasco (Spain) (b. 7 Nov 1943) won 83 consecutive fights from 22 April 1964 to 3 Sep 1970, drew once and had a further nine wins before his loss to Armando Ramos in a WBC lightweight contest on 18 Feb 1972.

Most knock-outs The greatest number of finishes classed as 'knock-outs' in a career (1936–63) is 145 (129 in professional bouts) by Archie Moore (USA) (b. Archibald Lee Wright, 13 Dec 1913 or 1916).

The record for consecutive KO's is 44 by Lamar Clark (USA) (b. 1 Dec 1934) from 1958 to 11 Jan 1960. He knocked out six in one night (five in the first round) at Bingham, Utah, USA on 1 Dec 1958.

Attendances *Highest* The greatest paid attendance at any boxing match is 132,274 for four world title fights at the Aztec Stadium, Mexico City on 20 Feb 1993, headed by the successful WBC super lightweight defence by Julio César Chávez (Mexico) over Greg Haugen (USA).

The indoor record is 63,350 at the Ali v. Leon Spinks (b. 11 Jul 1953) fight in the Superdome, New Orleans, Louisiana, USA on 15 Sep 1978.

The British attendance record is 82,000 at the Len Harvey v. Jock McAvoy fight at White City, London on 10 Jul 1939.

The highest non-paying attendance is 135,132 at the Tony Zale v. Billy Pryor fight at Juneau Park, Milwaukee, Wisconsin, USA on 16 Aug 1941.

Lowest The smallest attendance at a world heavyweight title fight was 2434, at the Cassius (Muhammad Ali) Clay v Sonny Liston fight at Lewiston, Maine, USA on 25 May 1965.

Long Career

Bob Fitzsimmons had a career of over 31 years from 1883 to 1914. He had his last world title bout on 20 Dec 1905 at the age of 42 years 208 days. Jack Johnson (USA) (1878–1946) also had a career of over 31 years, 1897–1928.

World Heavyweight

Reign *Longest* Joe Louis (USA) (b. Joseph Louis Barrow, 1914–81) was champion for 11 years 252 days, from 22 Jun 1937, when he knocked out James Joseph Braddock in the eighth round at Chicago, Illinois, USA, until announcing his retirement on 1 Mar 1949. During his reign Louis made a record 25 defences of his title.

Shortest Tony Tucker (USA) (b. 28 Dec 1958) was IBF champion for 64 days, 30 May–2 Aug 1987, the shortest duration for a title won and lost in the ring.

Most recaptures Muhammad Ali is the only man to regain the heavyweight championship twice. Ali first won the title on 25 Feb 1964, defeating Sonny Liston. He defeated George Foreman on 30 Oct 1974, having been stripped of the title by the world boxing authorities on 28 Apr 1967. He won the WBA title from Leon Spinks on 15 Sep 1978, having previously lost to him on 15 Feb 1978.

Undefeated Rocky Marciano (USA) (b. Rocco Francis Marchegiano) (1923–69) is the only world champion at *any weight* to have won every fight of his entire completed professional career, from 17 Mar 1947–21 Sep 1955 (he announced his retirement on 27 Apr 1956); 43 of his 49 fights were by knock-outs or stoppages.

Heaviest Primo Carnera (Italy) (1906–67), the 'Ambling Alp', who won the title from Jack Sharkey in New York City, USA on 29 Jun 1933, scaled 118 kg *260 lb* for this fight but his peak weight was 122 kg *269 lb*. He had an expanded chest measurement of 137 cm *54 in* and the longest reach at 217 cm *85½ in* (fingertip to fingertip).

Lightest Robert James 'Bob' Fitzsimmons (1863–1917), from Helston, Cornwall weighed 75 kg *165 lb*, when he won the title by knocking out James J. Corbett at Carson City, Nevada, USA on 17 Mar 1897.

Youngest Mike Tyson (USA) was 20 years 144 days when he beat Trevor Berbick (USA) to win the WBC

version at Las Vegas, Nevada, USA on 22 Nov 1986. He added the WBA title when he beat James 'Bonecrusher' Smith on 7 Mar 1987 at 20 yr 249 days. He became universal champion on 2 Aug 1987 when he beat Tony Tucker (USA) for the IBF title.

Oldest George Foreman (USA) (b. 22 Jan 1949) was 45 years 287 days, when he knocked out Michael Moorer (USA) at Las Vegas, Nevada, USA on 5 Nov 1994 and he defended the IBF version on 22 Apr 1995.

Longest-lived Jack Sharkey (b. Joseph Paul Zukauskas, 26 Oct 1902), champion from 21 Jun 1932 to 29 Jun 1933, surpassed the previous record of 87 years 341 days held by Jack Dempsey (1895–1983) on 3 Oct 1990.

World Champions Any weight

Reign *Longest* The Joe Louis heavyweight duration record of 11 years 252 days stands for all divisions.

Shortest Tony Canzoneri (USA) (1908–59) was world light-welterweight champion for 33 days, 21 May to 23 Jun 1933, the shortest period for a boxer to have won and lost the world title in the ring.

Youngest Wilfred Benitez (b. New York, 12 Sep 1958) of Puerto Rico, was 17 years 176 days when he won the WBA light welterweight title in San Juan, Puerto Rico on 6 Mar 1976.

Oldest Archie Moore, who was recognized as a light heavyweight champion up to 10 Feb 1962 when his title was removed, was then believed to be between 45 and 48.

Longest fight The longest world title fight (under Queensberry Rules) was that between the lightweights Joe Gans (1874–1910), of the USA, and Oscar Matthew 'Battling' Nelson (1882–1954), the 'Durable Dane', at Goldfield, Nevada, USA on 3 Sep 1906. It was terminated in the 42nd round when Gans was declared the winner on a foul.

Most different weights The first boxer to have won world titles at four weight categories was Thomas Hearns (USA) (b. 18 Oct 1958), WBA welterweight in 1980, WBC super welterweight in 1982, WBC light heavyweight in 1987 and WBC middleweight in 1987. He added a fifth weight division when he won the super middleweight title recognized by the newly created World Boxing Organization (WBO) on 4 Nov 1988, and he won the WBA light heavyweight title on 3 Jun 1991.

Sugar Ray Leonard (USA) (b. 17 May 1956) has also claimed world titles in five weight categories. Having previously won the WBC welterweight in 1979 and 1980, WBA junior middleweight in 1981 and WBC middleweight in 1987, he beat Donny Lalonde (Canada) on 7 Nov 1988, for both the WBC light heavyweight and super middleweight titles. However, despite the fact that the WBC sanctioned the fight, it is contrary to their rules to contest two divisions in the one fight. Consequently, although Leonard won, he had to relinquish one of the titles.

The feat of holding world titles at three weights *simultaneously* was achieved by Henry 'Homicide Hank' Armstrong (USA) (1912–88), at featherweight, lightweight and welterweight from August to December 1938. It is argued, however, that Barney Ross (b. Barnet David Rosofsky, USA) (1909–67) held

Guess What?

Q. What is the greatest weight difference in a title fight?

A. See Page 240

You're never too old to be the best there is...
or life begins at 40 !

The end of 1994 saw the remarkable success of George Foreman in winning the World Heavyweight boxing title at the tender age of 45 years 287 days. His boxing success began when he won the 1968 Olympic title and he turned professional the next year. He won the World Heavyweight title in 1973, defeating Joe Frazier and he made two successful defences before losing to Muhammed Ali in 1974.

He retired three years later to became a preacher but returned to boxing in 1987. Following two unsuccessful attempts to win the title in '91 and '93, losing both on points, he knocked out Michael Moorer in the 10th to reclaim the title (wearing the same shorts he had worn during his fight with Ali over twenty years earlier!).

The following brings together other people who have set records as 'the oldest', illustrating that success at the highest level is achievable when many are considered over the hill!

■ George Foreman lands a heavy right on Michael Moorer, on his way to winning the world heavyweight title.
(Photo: Allsport (USA)/H. Stein)

■ Fred Davis, world billiards champion in 1980 at the age of 67.
(Photo: Allsport)

The oldest competitor at a major games is William Edward Pattimore (b. 1 Mar 1892) who competed for Wales at bowls at the 1970 Commonwealth Games in Edinburgh at the age of 78, the oldest competitor at such an international event open to competitors of all ages.

Name	Age	Sport/Event - Date
Bertram Clifford Batt	*67 years 241days*	Channel swimmer - 1987
Fred Davis	*67 years*	World champion, any sport - 1980
Oscar Swahn	*64 years 258 days*	Olympic gold medallist - 1912
Henry Haigh	*63 years*	Aerobatics world champion - 1988
Ramon Blanco	*60 years 160 days*	Climbed Everest - 1993
Wilhelm Steinitz	*58 years 10 days*	Chess world champion - 1894
Wilfred Rhodes	*52 years 165 days*	Test cricketer - 1930
George Foreman *46 years 160 days* Boxing world champion - June 1995		
'Old Tom' Morris	*46 years 99 days*	Golf Major winner - 1867
Juan-Manuel Fangio	*46 years 41 day*	Motor racing world champion - 1957
Hermann-Peter Müller	*46 years*	Motorcycling world champion - 1955
Billy Meredith	*45 years 229 days*	Football international - 1920
Patrick 'Babe' McDonald	*42 years 26 days*	Athletics Olympic gold - 1920
Arthur Gore	*41 years 182 days*	Tennis, Singles title Grand Slam event - 1909

80
70
68
66
64
62
60
58
56
54
52
50
48
46
44
42
40

the lightweight, junior-welterweight and welterweight, simultaneously, from 28 May to 17 Sep 1934 (although there is some dispute as to when he relinquished his lightweight title).

In recent years there has been a proliferation of weight categories and governing bodies but Armstrong was undisputed world champion at widely differing weights which makes his achievement all the more remarkable.

Most recaptures The only boxer to win a world title five times at one weight is 'Sugar' Ray Robinson (USA) (b. Walker Smith Jr, 1921–89), who beat Carmen Basilio (USA) in the Chicago Stadium on 25 Mar 1958, to regain the world middleweight title for the fourth time.

Dennis Andries (b. Guyana, 5 Nov 1953) became the first British boxer to regain a world title twice. He had initially won the WBC light-heavyweight title on 30 Apr 1986 and first regained the title on 22 Feb 1989 after being beaten in 1987. He regained the title for a second time on 28 Jul 1990.

Most title bouts The record number of title bouts in a career is 37, of which 18 ended in 'no decision', by three-time world welterweight champion Jack Britton (USA) (1885–1962) in 1915–22. The record containing no 'no decision' contests is 29 including a record 28 wins by Julio César Chávez (Mexico), 1984–94.

Little & Large

When Primo Carnera (Italy) 122 kg *269 lb* fought Tommy Loughran (USA) 83 kg *183 lb* for the world heavyweight title at Miami, Florida, USA on 1 Mar 1934, there was a weight difference of 39 kg *86 lb* between the two fighters. Carnera won on points.

Greatest 'tonnage' The greatest 'tonnage' recorded in any fight is 317 kg *699 lb* when Claude 'Humphrey' McBride (Oklahoma), 154 kg *339½ lb*, knocked out Jimmy Black (Houston), who weighed 163 kg *359½ lb* in the third round at Oklahoma City on 1 Jun 1971.

The greatest 'tonnage' in a world title fight was 221.5 kg *488¼ lb*, when Carnera, then 117.5 kg *259 lb* fought Paolino Uzcudun (Spain) 104 kg *229¼ lb* in Rome, Italy on 22 Oct 1933.

Most knock-downs in title fights Vic Toweel (South Africa) (b. 12 Jan 1929) knocked down Danny O'Sullivan of London 14 times in ten rounds in their world bantamweight fight at Johannesburg on 2 Dec 1950, before the latter retired.

Amateur

Most Olympic titles Only two boxers have won three Olympic gold medals: southpaw László Papp (Hungary) (b. 25 Mar 1926), middleweight 1948, light-middleweight 1952 and 1956; and Teofilo Stevenson (Cuba) (b. 23 Mar 1952), heavyweight 1972, 1976 and 1980.

The only man to win two titles in one celebration was Oliver L. Kirk (USA), who won both bantam and featherweight titles in St Louis, Missouri, USA in 1904, but he needed only one bout in each class.

Another record that will stand forever is that of the youngest Olympic boxing champion: Jackie Fields (né Finkelstein) (USA) (b. 9 Feb 1908) who won the 1924 featherweight title at 16 years 162 days. The minimum age for Olympic boxing competitors is now 17.

World Championships A record number of five world titles (instituted 1974) have been won by Félix Savon (Cuba) heavyweight 1986, 1989, 1991 and 91 kg 1993, 1995.

Most British titles The greatest number of ABA titles won by any boxer is eight by John Lyon (b. 9 Mar 1962) at light-flyweight 1981–4 and at flyweight 1986–9.

Alex 'Bud' Watson (b. 27 May 1914) of Leith, Scotland won the Scottish heavyweight title in 1938, 1942–3, and the light-heavyweight championship 1937–9, 1943–5 and 1947, making ten in all. He also won the ABA light-heavyweight title in 1945 and 1947.

Longest span The greatest span of ABA title-winning performances is that of the heavyweight Hugh 'Pat' Floyd (b. 23 Aug 1910), who won in 1929 and gained his fourth title 17 years later in 1946.

Canoeing

Most titles *Olympic* Gert Fredriksson (Sweden) (b. 21 Nov 1919) won a record six Olympic gold medals, 1948–60. He added a silver and a bronze for a record eight medals.

The most by a woman is four by Birgit Schmidt (*née* Fischer) (GDR) (b. 25 Feb 1962), 1980–92.

The most gold medals at one Games is three by Vladimir Parfenovich (USSR) (b. 2 Dec 1958) in 1980 and by Ian Ferguson (New Zealand) (b. 20 Jul 1952) in 1984.

World Including the Olympic Games a record 24 titles have been won by Birgit Schmidt, 1979–93.

The men's record is 13 by Gert Fredriksson, 1948–60, Rüdiger Helm (GDR) (b. 6 Oct 1956), 1976–83, and Ivan Patzaichin (Romania) (b. 26 Nov 1949), 1968–84.

The most individual titles by a British canoeist is five by Richard Fox (b. 5 Jun 1960) at K1 slalom in 1981, 1983, 1985, 1989 and 1993. Fox also won five gold medals at K1 team, between 1981 and 1993. Ivan Lawler (b. 19 Nov 1966) has won world titles in both sprint (1990 K2 10,000m) and marathon (1992 K1, 1994 K2) disciplines.

Highest speed The German four-man kayak Olympic champions in 1992 at Barcelona, Spain covered 1000 m in 2 min 52.17 sec in a heat on 4 August. This represents an average speed of 20.90 km/h *12.98 mph*.

At the 1988 Olympics, the Norwegian four achieved a 250 m split of 42.08 sec between 500 m and 750 m in a heat, for a speed of 21.39 km/h *13.29 mph*.

Longest race The Canadian Government Centennial Voyageur Canoe Pageant and Race from Rocky Mountain House, Alberta to the Expo 67 site at Montreal, Quebec was 5283 km *3283 miles*. Ten canoes represented Canadian provinces and territories. The winner of the race, which took from 24 May to 4 Sep 1967, was the Province of Manitoba canoe *Radisson*.

Longest journey Father and son Dana and Donald Starkell paddled from Winnipeg, Manitoba, Canada

Guess What?

Q. Who was the first person to row across the Atlantic?

A. See Page 112

by ocean and river to Belem, Brazil, a distance of 19,603 km *12,181 miles* from 1 Jun 1980 to 1 May 1982. All portages were human powered.

Without portages or aid of any kind the longest is one of 9820 km *6102 miles* by Richard H. Grant and Ernest 'Moose' Lassy circumnavigating the eastern USA via Chicago, New Orleans, Miami, New York and the Great Lakes from 22 Sep 1930 to 15 Aug 1931.

North Sea On 17–18 May 1989, Kevin Danforth and Franco Ferrero completed the Felixstowe to Zeebrugge route in 27 hr 10 min in a double sea kayak. The open crossing, over 177 km *110 miles*, was self-contained and unsupported.

River Rhine The fastest time, solo and supported, is 7 days 13 hr 56 min by Roel Kimpe (Netherlands), 22–29 May 1993. The fastest woman, solo and supported, is Tracy Anderson (GB) who completed the journey in 12 days 15 hr 10 min, 17–29 May 1993. The 'Rhine Challenge', as organized by the International Long River Canoeists Club, begins from an official marker post in Chur, Switzerland and ends at Willemstad, Netherlands, a distance of approximately 1130 km *702 miles*.

24 hours Zdzislaw Szubski paddled 252.9 km *157.1 miles* in a Jaguar K1 canoe on the Vistula River, Wlocklawek to Gdansk, Poland on 11–12 Sep 1987.

Flat water Marinda Hartzenberg (South Africa) paddled, without benefit of current, 220.69 km *137.13 miles* on Loch Logan, Bloemfontein, South Africa on 31 Dec 1990–1 Jan 1991.

Open sea Randy Fine (USA) paddled 194.1 km *120.6 miles* along the Florida coast on 26–27 Jun 1986.

Greatest lifetime distance Fritz Lindner of Berlin, Germany, totalled 103,444 km *64,277 miles* from 1928 to 1987.

Eskimo rolls Ray Hudspith (b. 18 Apr 1960) achieved 1000 rolls in 34 min 43 sec at the Elswick Pool, Newcastle upon Tyne on 20 Mar 1987. He completed 100 rolls in 3 min 7.25 sec at Killingworth Leisure Centre, Tyne and Wear on 3 Mar 1991. The women's record is 3 min 47.54 sec by Helen Barnes at Crystal Palace, Greater London on 18 Feb 1995. Randy Fine (USA) completed 1796 continuous rolls at Biscayne Bay, Florida, USA on 8 Jun 1991.

'Hand rolls' Colin Brian Hill (b. 16 Aug 1970) achieved 1000 rolls in 31 minutes 55.62 sec at Consett, Co. Durham on 12 Mar 1987. He also achieved 100 rolls in 2 min 39.2 sec at Crystal Palace, London on 22 Feb 1987. He completed 3700 continuous rolls at Durham City Swimming Baths, Co. Durham on 1 May 1989.

Canoe Raft

A raft of 568 kayaks and canoes, organized by the Notts County Scout Council with the assistance of scouts from Derbys, Leics and Lincs, was held together by hands only, while free floating for 30 seconds, on the River Trent, Nottingham on 30 Jun 1991.

> The oldest Olympic gold medallist is Richard Kenneth Gunn (GB) (1871–1961) who won the featherweight title on 27 Oct 1908 in London aged 37 years 254 days.

Guess What?

Q. What is the record for walking on hands?

A. See Page 230

Card Games

Contract Bridge

Biggest tournament The Epson World Bridge Championship, held on 20–21 Jun 1992, was contested by more than 102,000 players playing the same hands, at over 2000 centres worldwide.

Most world titles The World Championship (Bermuda Bowl) has been won a record 13 times by Italy's Blue Team (*Squadra Azzura*), 1957–59, 1961–63, 1965–67, 1969, 1973–75 and by the USA, 1950–51, 1953–54, 1970–71, 1976–77, 1979, 1981, 1983, 1985, 1987. Italy also won the team Olympiad in 1964, 1968 and 1972. Giorgio Belladonna (b. 7 Jun 1923) was in all the Italian winning teams.

The USA have a record six wins in the women's world championship for the Venice Trophy: 1974, 1976, 1978, 1987, 1989 and 1991, and three women's wins at the World Team Olympiad: 1976, 1980 and 1984.

Most hands In the 1989 Bermuda Bowl in Perth, Australia, Marcel Branco (b. 1945) and Gabriel Chagas (b. 1944) (both Brazil) played a record 752 out of a possible 784 boards.

Cribbage

Rare hands Five maximum 29 point hands have been achieved Sean Daniels of Astoria, Oregon, USA, 1989–92. Paul Nault of Athol, Massachusetts, USA had two such hands within eight games in a tournament on 19 Mar 1977.

Card holding Ralf Laue held 326 standard playing cards in a fan in one hand, so that the value and colour of each one was visible, at Leipzig, Germany on 18 Mar 1994.

Card throwing Jim Karol of North Catasauqua, Pennsylvania, USA threw a standard playing card 61.26 m *201 ft 0in* at Mount Ida College, Newton Centre, Massachusetts, USA on 18 Oct 1992.

The most points scored by a team of four, playing singles in two pairs, is 126,414 by Mark Fitzwater, Eddie Pepper, Mark Perry and Gary Watson at The Green Man, Potton, Beds on 8–9 May 1993.

Cricket

Batting Records, Teams

Highest innings Victoria scored 1107 runs in 10hr 30 min against New South Wales in an Australian Sheffield Shield match at Melbourne on 27–28 Dec 1926.

Test England scored 903 runs for seven wickets declared in 15hr 17min, *v.* Australia at The Oval, London on 20, 22 and 23 Aug 1938.

County Championship Yorkshire scored 887 in 10hr 50 min, *v.* Warwickshire at Edgbaston, Birmingham on 7–8 May 1896.

Lowest innings The traditional first-class record is 12 by Oxford University (who batted a man short) *v.* the Marylebone Cricket Club (MCC) at Cowley Marsh, Oxford on 24 May 1877, and by

Northamptonshire *v.* Gloucestershire at Gloucester on 11 Jun 1907. However, 'The Bs' scored 6 in their second innings *v.* England at Lord's, London on 12–14 Jun 1810 in one of the major matches of that era.

Test 26 by New Zealand *v.* England at Auckland on 28 Mar 1955.

Aggregate for two innings 34 (16 and 18) by Border *v.* Natal in the South African Currie Cup at East London on 19 and 21 Dec 1959. In an early match, Leicestershire totalled 23 (15 and 8) *v.* Nottinghamshire (61) at Leicester on 25 Aug 1800.

Greatest victory A margin of an innings and 851 runs was recorded, when Pakistan Railways (910 for 6 wickets declared) beat Dera Ismail Khan (32 and 27) at Lahore on 2–4 Dec 1964.

Perfect Deals

The mathematical odds against dealing 13 cards of one suit are 158,753,389,899 to 1, while the odds against a named player receiving all 13 spades, a 'perfect hand', are 635,013,559,599 to 1. The odds against each of the four players receiving a complete suit (a 'perfect deal') are 2,235,197,406,895,366,368,301,599,999 to 1.

In England England won by an innings and 579 runs (also the record for a Test) against Australia at The Oval on 20–24 Aug 1938 when Australia scored 201 and 123 with two men short in both innings. The most one-sided county match was when Surrey (698) defeated Sussex (114 and 99) by an innings and 485 runs at The Oval on 9–11 Aug 1888.

Batting Records, Individuals

Highest innings Brian Charles Lara (b. 2 May 1969) scored 501 not out in 7hr 54min for Warwickshire *v.* Durham at Edgbaston on 3 and 6 Jun 1994. His innings included the most runs in a day (390 on 6 June) and the most runs from strokes worth four or more (308, 62 fours and 10 sixes). The highest by an English player is 424 in 7hr 50min by Archibald Campbell Maclaren (1871–1944) for Lancashire *v.* Somerset at Taunton, Somerset on 15–16 Jul 1895.

Test Brian Lara scored 375 in 12hr 46min for West Indies *v.* England at Recreation Ground, St John's, Antigua on 16–18 Apr 1994. The English Test record is 364 by Sir Leonard Hutton (1916–90) against Australia at The Oval on 20, 22 and 23 Aug 1938.

Longest innings Hanif Mohammad (Pakistan) (b. 21 Dec 1934) batted for 16hr 10min for 337 runs

■ Harold 'Dickie' Bird has stood as umpire in a record 62 Tests, his first Test being England v. New Zealand at Headingley in July 1973, to June 1995. Here, he signals four, wearing a sunhat as opposed to the usual distinctive white flat cap, in the First Test between Pakistan and Australia at Karachi in 1994.
(Photo: Allsport/S. Botterill)

Run Together

Most runs in a day Australia scored 721 all out (ten wickets) in 5hr 48min against Essex at Southchurch Park, Southend-on-Sea on 15 May 1948.

The most in a Test match is 588 at Old Trafford, Manchester on 27 Jul 1936 when England added 398 and India were 190 for 0 in their second innings by the close.

against the West Indies at Bridgetown, Barbados on 20–23 Jan 1958. The English record is 13hr 17min by Len Hutton in his record Test score of 364.

Most runs off an over The first batsman to score 36 runs off a six ball over was Sir Garfield St Aubrun Sobers (b. 28 Jul 1936) off Malcolm Andrew Nash (b. 9 May 1945) for Nottinghamshire *v.* Glamorgan at Swansea on 31 Aug 1968. His feat was emulated by Ravishankar Jayadritha Shastri (b. 27 May 1962) for Bombay *v.* Baroda at Bombay, India on 10 Jan 1985 off the bowling of Tilak Raj Sharma (b. 15 Jan 1960).

Playing in a Shell Trophy match for Wellington *v.* Canterbury at Christchurch on 20 Feb 1990, in a deliberate attempt to give away runs, Robert Howard

Individual Cricket Records

FIRST-CLASS (FC) AND TEST CAREER

Batting			Name	Team	Date
Most runs	FC	61,237	Sir John Berry 'Jack' Hobbs (1882–1963) (av. 50.65)	Surrey/England	1905–34
	Test	11,174	Allan Robert Border (b. 27 Jul 1955) (av. 50.56)	Australia (156 Tests)	1978–94
Most centuries	FC	197	Sir Jack Hobbs (in 1315 innings)	Surrey/England	1905–34
	Test	34	Sunil Gavaskar (in 214 innings)	India	1971–87
Highest average	FC	95.14	Sir Donald George Bradman (b. 28 Aug 1908)	NSW/South Australia/Australia	1927–49
			(28 067 runs in 338 innings, including 43 not outs)		
	Test	99.94	Sir Donald Bradman (6996 runs in 80 innings)	Australia (52 Tests)	1928–4

Bowling					
Most wickets	FC	4187	Wilfred Rhodes (1877–1973) (av. 16.71)	Yorkshire/England	1898–1930
	Test	434	Kapil Dev Nikhanj (b. 6 Jan 1959) (av. 29.62)	India (131 Tests)	1978–94
Lowest average	Test	10.75	George Alfred Lohmann (1865–1901) (112 wkts)	England (18 Tests)	1886–96
(min 25 wkts)					

Wicket-Keeping					
Most dismissals	FC	1649	Robert William Taylor (b. 17 Jul 1941)	Derbyshire/England	1960–88
	Test	355	Rodney William Marsh (b. 11 Nov 1947)	Australia (96 Tests)	1970–84
Most catches	FC	1473	Robert Taylor	Derbyshire/England	1960–88
	Test	343	Rodney Marsh	Australia	1970–84
Most stumpings	FC	418	Leslie Ethelbert George Ames (1905–90)	Kent/England	1926–51
	Test	52	William Albert Stanley Oldfield (1894–1976)	Australia (54 Tests)	1920–37

Fielding					
Most catches	FC	1018	Frank Edward Woolley (1887–1978)	Kent/England	1906–38
	Test	156	Allan Robert Border	Australia (156 Tests)	1978–94

IN A TEST SERIES

Batting		Name	Teams (No. of Tests)	Season
Most runs	974	Sir Donald Bradman (av. 139.14)	Australia v. England (5)	1930
Most centuries	5	Sir Clyde Leopold Walcott (b. 17 Jan 1926)	West Indies v. Australia (5)	1954/5
Highest average	563.00	Walter Reginald Hammond	England v. New Zealand (2)	1932/3
		(563 runs, 2 inns, 1 not out)		

Bowling				
Most wickets	49	Sydney Francis Barnes (1873–1967) (av. 10.93)	England v. South Africa (4)	1913/14
Lowest average	5.80	George Alfred Lohmann (35 wkts)	England v. South Africa (3)	1895/6
(min 20 wkts)				

Wicket-Keeping				
Most dismissals	28	Rodney Marsh (all caught)	Australia v. England (5)	1982/3
Most stumpings	9	Percy William Sherwell (1880–1948)	South Africa v. Australia (5)	1910/11

Fielding				
Most catches	15	Jack Morrison Gregory (1895–1973)	Australia v. England (5)	1920/21

All-Round				
400 runs/30 wkts	475/34	George Giffen (1859–1927)	Australia v. England (5)	1894/5

IN A FIRST-CLASS SEASON IN ENGLAND

Batting		Name (Team)	Year
Most runs	3816	Denis Charles Scott Compton (b. 23 May 1918) (av. 90.85) (Middlesex & England)	1947
Most centuries	18	Denis Compton (in 50 innings with 8 not outs) (Middlesex & England)	1947
Highest average	115.66	Sir Donald Bradman (2429 runs, 26 innings, 5 not outs) (Australians)	1938

Bowling			
Most wickets	304	Alfred Percy 'Tich' Freeman (1888–1965) (1976.1 o, av. 18.05) (Kent & England)	1928
Lowest average	8.54	Alfred Shaw (1842–1907) (186 wkts) (Nottinghamshire & England)	1880
(min 100 wkts)			

Wicket-Keeping			
Most dismissals	128	Leslie Ames (79 caught, 49 stumped) (Kent & England)	1929
Most catches	96	James Graham Binks (b. 5 Oct 1935) (Yorkshire)	1960
Most stumpings	64	Leslie Ames (Kent)	1932

Fielding			
Most catches	78	Walter Reginald Hammond (1903–65) (Gloucestershire & England)	1928

in the first innings on 26–27 July and 123 in the second on 30 July for a record Test aggregate 456 runs.

Fastest scoring Cedric Ivan James 'Jim' Smith (1906–79) scored 50 in 11 minutes for Middlesex v. Gloucestershire at Bristol on 16 Jun 1938. He went on to score 66. A faster 50 was completed off 13 balls in 8 minutes (1:22 to 1:30 p.m.) in 11 scoring strokes by Clive Clay Inman (b. 29 Jan 1936) in an innings of 57 not out for Leicestershire v. Nottinghamshire at Trent Bridge, Nottingham on 20 Aug 1965 but full tosses were bowled to expedite a declaration.

Fastest 100 The fastest against genuine bowling was completed in 35 minutes off between 40 and 46 balls by Percy George Herbert Fender (1892–1985), in his 113 not out for Surrey v. Northamptonshire at Northampton on 26 Aug 1920. Glen Chapple (b. 23 Jan 1974) completed a century in an estimated 21 minutes off 27 balls for Lancashire v. Glamorgan at Old Trafford on 19 Jul 1993.

The fastest hundred in a major one-day competition was by Graham David Rose (b. 12 Apr 1964) off 36

Guess What?

Q. What is the record for most runs off one ball?

A. See Page 246

Most Runs

Albert Neilson Hornby (1847–1925) scored ten off James Street (1839–1906) for Lancashire v. Surrey at The Oval on 14 Jul 1873, a feat equalled by Samuel Hill Wood (later Sir Samuel Hill Hill-Wood) (1872–1949) off Cuthbert James Burnup (1875–1960) for Derbyshire v. MCC at Lord's on 26 May 1900.

Vance (b. 31 Mar 1955) bowled an over containing 22 balls, 17 of which were deliberate no-balls (the umpire losing count and declaring over one ball early!). From this over Lee Kenneth Germon (b. 4 Nov 1968) of Canterbury hit 70 runs, including eight sixes and five fours, Richard George Petrie (b. 23 Aug 1967) scored five runs including one four, and with two runs from no-balls off which no runs were hit, a total of 77 runs was conceded.

Most sixes in an innings John Richard Reid (b. 3 Jun 1928) hit 15 in an innings of 296, lasting 3 hr 40 min, for Wellington v. Northern Districts in a Plunket Shield match at Wellington, New Zealand on 14–15 Jan 1963.

Test Walter Hammond hit ten sixes in his 336 not out for England v. New Zealand at Auckland on 31 Mar and 1 Apr 1933.

Triple hundred and hundred The only batsman to have scored a triple hundred and a hundred in the same match is Graham Alan Gooch (b. 23 Jul 1953) for England v. India at Lord's in 1990. He scored 333

balls for Somerset against Devon in the NatWest Trophy first round at Torquay on 27 Jun 1990.

The fastest Test hundred was completed in 70 minutes off 67 balls by Jack Morrison Gregory (1895–1973), in his 119 for Australia v. South Africa at Johannesburg on 12 Nov 1921. The fastest in terms of fewest balls received was one off 56 balls by Isaac Vivian Alexander Richards (b. 7 Mar 1952) for the West Indies v. England at St John's, Antigua on 15 Apr 1986. His final score was 110 not out in 81 minutes.

Edwin Boaler Alletson (1884–1963) scored 189 runs in 90 minutes for Nottinghamshire v. Sussex at Hove on 20 May 1911. The most prolific scorer of hundreds in an hour or less was Gilbert Laird Jessop (1874–1955), with 14 between 1897 and 1913.

Fastest 200 Scored in 113 minutes by Ravi Shastri off 123 balls for Bombay v. Baroda at Bombay on 10 Jan 1985 (⇔ Most runs off an over). Clive Hubert Lloyd (b. 31 Aug 1944), for West Indians v. Glamorgan at Swansea on 9 Aug 1976, and Gilbert Jessop (286), for Gloucestershire v. Sussex at Hove on 1 Jun 1903, both scored 200 in 120 minutes. Lloyd received 121 balls, but the figure for Jessop is not known.

Fastest 300 Completed in 181 minutes by Denis Compton, who scored 300 for the MCC v. North-Eastern Transvaal at Benoni, South Africa on 3–4 Dec 1948.

Slowest scoring The longest time a batsman has ever taken to score his first run is 1 hr 37 min by Thomas Godfrey Evans (b. 18 Aug 1920), before he scored 10 not out for England v. Australia at Adelaide on 5–6 Feb 1947. The longest innings without scoring is 87 min by Vincent Richard Hogg (b. 3 Jul 1952) for Zimbabwe–Rhodesia 'B' v. Natal 'B' at Pietermaritzburg in the South African Castle Bowl competition on 20 Jan 1980.

The slowest hundred on record is by Mudassar Nazar (b. 6 Apr 1956) for Pakistan v. England at Lahore on 14–15 Dec 1977. He required 9 hr 51 min for 114, reaching the 100 in 9 hr 17 min. The slowest double hundred is one of 12 hr 57 min (548 balls) by Don Sardha Brendon Priyantha Kuruppu (b. 5 Jan 1962) during an innings of 201 not out for Sri Lanka v. New Zealand at Colombo on 16–19 Apr 1987.

Highest partnership For any wicket is the fourth–wicket stand of 577 by Gulzar Mahomed (1921–92), 319, and Vijay Samuel Hazare (b. 11 Mar 1915), 288, for Baroda v. Holkar at Baroda, India on 8–10 Mar 1947.

In England 555, for the first-wicket by Percy Holmes (1886–1971) (224 not out) and Herbert Sutcliffe (1894–1978) (313) for Yorkshire v. Essex at Leyton, Essex on 15–16 Jun 1932.

Test 467, for the third wicket by Martin David Crowe (b. 22 Sep 1962) (299) and Andrew Howard Jones (b. 9 May 1959) (186) for New Zealand v. Sri Lanka at Wellington on 3–4 Feb 1991.

Double 100s

The only batsman to score double hundreds in both innings is Arthur Edward Fagg (1915–77), who made 244 and 202 not out for Kent v. Essex at Colchester, Essex from 13–15 Jul 1938. Sir Donald Bradman scored a career record 37 double hundreds, 1927–49.

Balls

The most balls bowled in a match is 917 by Cottari Subbanna Nayudu (b. 18 Apr 1914), 6–153 and 5–275, for Holkar v. Bombay at Bombay on 4–9 Mar 1945. The most balls bowled in a Test match is 774 by Sonny Ramadhin (b. 1 May 1929) for the West Indies v. England, 7–49 and 2–179, at Edgbaston on 29 May–4 Jun 1957. In the second innings he bowled a world record 588 balls (98 overs).

Bowling

Most wickets *In an innings* Only one bowler has taken all ten wickets in an innings on three occasions—Alfred 'Tich' Freeman of Kent, 1929–31. The fewest runs scored off a bowler taking all ten wickets is ten, off Hedley Verity (1905–43) for Yorkshire v. Nottinghamshire at Leeds on 12 Jul 1932 though the full analyses for some early performances of the feat are unknown. The only bowler to bowl out all ten was John Wisden (1826–84) for North v. South at Lord's in 1850.

In a match James Charles 'Jim' Laker (1922–86) took 19 wickets for 90 runs (9–37 and 10–53) for England v. Australia at Old Trafford from 27–31 Jul 1956.

Most consecutive wickets No bowler in first-class cricket has yet achieved five wickets with five consecutive balls. The nearest approach was that of Charles Warrington Leonard Parker (1882–1959) (Gloucestershire) in his own benefit match against Yorkshire at Bristol on 10 Aug 1922, when he struck the stumps with five successive balls but the second was called as a no-ball. The only man to have taken four wickets with consecutive balls more than once is Robert James Crisp (1911–94) for Western Province v. Griqualand West at Johannesburg, South Africa on 24 Dec 1931 and against Natal at Durban, South Africa on 3 Mar 1934.

Patrick Ian Pocock (b. 24 Sep 1946) took five wickets in six balls, six in nine balls and seven in eleven balls for Surrey v. Sussex at Eastbourne, E Sussex on 15 Aug 1972. In his own benefit match at Lord's on 22 May 1907, Albert Edwin Trott (1873–1914) of Middlesex took four Somerset wickets with four consecutive balls and then later in the same innings achieved a 'hat trick'.

Most consecutive maidens Hugh Joseph Tayfield (1929–94) bowled 16 consecutive eight-ball maiden overs (137 balls without conceding a run) for South Africa v. England at Durban on 25–26 Jan 1957. The greatest number of consecutive six-ball maiden overs bowled is 21 (131 balls) by Rameshchandra Gangaram 'Bapu' Nadkarni (b. 4 Apr 1932) for India v. England at Madras on 12 Jan 1964. Alfred Shaw (1842–1907) of Nottinghamshire bowled 23 consecutive 4-ball maiden overs (92 balls) for North v. South at Trent Bridge, Nottingham on 17 Jul 1876.

Most expensive bowling The most runs conceded by a bowler in a match is 428 by Cottari Nayudu in the Holkar v. Bombay match above. The greatest number of runs hit off one bowler in an innings is 362, off Arthur Alfred Mailey (1886–1967) of New South Wales by Victoria at Melbourne on 24–28 Dec 1926. The most runs conceded in a Test innings is 298 by Leslie O'Brien 'Chuck' Fleetwood-Smith (1908–71) for Australia v. England at The Oval on 20–23 Aug 1938.

Fastest The highest electronically measured speed for a ball bowled by any bowler is 160.45 km/h 99.7 mph by Jeffrey Robert Thomson (Australia) (b. 16 Aug 1950) against the West Indies in December 1975.

Guess What?

Q. What is the speed record for pitching in baseball?

A. See Page 232

All-Rounders

The double The 'double' of 1000 runs and 100 wickets in the same season was performed a record number of 16 times by Wilfred Rhodes between 1903 and 1926. The greatest number of consecutive seasons in which a player has performed the 'double' is

■ Sachin Tendulkar is the youngest player to captain the winning side in India's premier competition, the Ranji Trophy. He was aged just 21 when Bombay beat Punjab to win in 1995. (Photo: Allsport/B. Radford)

11 (1903–13) by George Herbert Hirst (1871–1954), of Yorkshire and England. Hirst is also the only player to score 2000 runs (2385) and take 200 wickets (208) in the same season (1906).

Test cricket *Career* The best all-round record is Kapil Dev Nikhanj (India) (b. 6 Jan 1959) who scored 5248 runs (av. 31.05), took 434 wickets (av. 29.64) and held 64 catches in 131 matches, 1978–94. England's best is Ian Terence Botham (England) (b. 24 Nov 1955) with 5200 runs (av. 33.54), 383 wickets (av. 28.40) and 120 catches in 102 matches, 1977–92.

Match and innings Botham is the only player to score a hundred and take eight wickets in an innings in the same Test, with 108 and 8–34 for England v. Pakistan at Lord's on 15–19 Jun 1978. He scored a hundred (114) and took more than ten wickets (6–58 and 7–48) in a Test, for England v. India in the Golden Jubilee Test at Bombay on 15–19 Feb 1980. This feat was emulated by Imran Khan Niazi (b. 25 Nov 1952) with 117, 6–98 and 5–82 for Pakistan v. India at Faisalabad on 3–8 Jan 1983.

Century on début and wicket with first ball Frederick Wilfred Stocks (b. 6 Nov 1918) of Nottinghamshire achieved the unique feat of scoring a century on his first-class début, v. Kent at Trent Bridge on 13 May 1946, and of taking a wicket with his first ball in first-class cricket, v. Lancashire at Old Trafford on 26 Jun 1946.

Wicket-Keeping

Most dismissals *Innings* The most dismissals is nine (eight catches and a stumping) by Tahir Rashid (b. 21 Nov 1960) for Habib Bank v. Pakistan Automobile Corporation at Gujranwala, Pakistan on 29 Nov 1992. Three other players have taken eight catches in an innings: Arthur Theodore Wallace 'Wally' Grout (1927–68) for Queensland v. Western Australia at Brisbane on 15 Feb 1960; David Edward East (b. 27 Jul 1959) for Essex v. Somerset at Taunton on 27 Jul 1985; and Stephen Andrew Marsh (b. 27 Jan 1961) for Kent v. Middlesex on 31 May and 1 Jun 1991. The most stumpings in an innings is six by Henry 'Hugo' Yarnold (1917–74) for Worcestershire v. Scotland at Broughty Ferry, Dundee, Tayside on 2 Jul 1951.

Match The most dismissals is 12 by: Edward Pooley (1838–1907), eight caught, four stumped, for Surrey v. Sussex at The Oval on 6–7 Jul 1868; nine caught, three stumped by both Donald Tallon (1916–84) for Queensland v. New South Wales at Sydney, Australia on 2–4 Jan 1939, and by Hedley Brian Taber (b. 29 Apr 1940) for New South Wales v. South Australia at Adelaide on 13–17 Dec 1968. The record for catches is 11 by: Arnold Long (b. 18 Dec 1940), for Surrey v. Sussex at Hove on 18 and 21 Jul 1964, by Rodney Marsh for Western Australia v. Victoria at Perth on 15–17 Nov 1975; by David Leslie Bairstow (b. 1 Sep 1951) for Yorkshire v. Derbyshire at Scarborough on 8–10 Sep 1982; by Warren Kevin Hegg (b. 23 Feb 1968) for Lancashire v. Derbyshire at Chesterfield on 9–11 Aug 1989; by Alec James

Stewart (b. 8 Apr 1963) for Surrey v. Leicestershire at Leicester on 19–22 Aug 1989; and by Timothy John Neilsen (b. 5 May 1968) for South Australia v. Western Australia at Perth on 15–18 Mar 1991. The most stumpings in a match is nine by Frederick Henry Huish (1869–1957) for Kent v. Surrey at The Oval on 21–23 Aug 1911.

Most dismissals in Tests *Innings* The record is seven (all caught) by Wasim Bari (b. 23 Mar 1948) for Pakistan v. New Zealand at Auckland on 23 Feb 1979, by Bob Taylor for England v. India at Bombay on 15 Feb 1980, and by Ian David Stockley Smith (b. 28 Feb 1957) for New Zealand v. Sri Lanka at Hamilton on 23–24 Feb 1991.

Guess What?
Q. Who has scored the most runs in Test cricket?
A. See Page 242

■ During the Ashes series in Australia 1993/4, Graham Gooch made a record 118th Test appearance for England.
(Photo: Allsport/B. Radford)

Match The record is ten, all caught, by Bob Taylor for England v. India at Bombay, 15–19 Feb 1980.

Fielding

Most catches *Innings* The greatest number of catches in an innings is seven, by Michael James Stewart (b. 16 Sep 1932) for Surrey v. Northamptonshire at Northampton on 7 Jun 1957; and by Anthony Stephen Brown (b. 24 Jun 1936) for Gloucestershire v. Nottinghamshire at Trent Bridge on 26 Jul 1966.

Match Walter Hammond held ten catches (four in the first innings, six in the second) for Gloucestershire v. Surrey at Cheltenham on 16–17 Aug 1928.

The most catches in a Test match is seven by: Greg Chappell for Australia v. England at Perth on 13–17 Dec 1974; Yajurvindra Singh (b. 1 Aug 1952) for India v. England at Bangalore on 28 Jan–2 Feb 1977 and Hashan Prasantha Tillekeratne (b. 14 Jul 1967) for Sri Lanka v. New Zealand at Colombo on 7–9 Dec 1992.

Test Records

Test appearances The most Test matches played is 156 by Allan Robert Border (Australia) (b. 27 Jul 1955), 1979–94. Border's total includes a record 153 consecutive Tests and a record 93 as captain. The English record for most Tests is 118 by Graham Alan Gooch (b. 23 Jul 1953), 1975–95; and for consecutive Tests is 65 by Alan Philip Eric Knott (b. 9 Apr 1946), 1971–7 and Ian Botham, 1978–84.

Largest crowds The greatest attendance at a cricket match is about 394,000 for the Test between India and England at Eden Gardens, Calcutta on 1–6 Jan 1982. The record for a Test series is 933,513 for Australia v. England (five matches) in 1936/7. The greatest recorded attendance at a cricket match on one day was 90,800 on the second day of the Test between Australia and the West Indies at Melbourne on 11 Feb 1961. The English match record is 159,000 for England v. Australia at Headingley, Leeds on 22–27 Jul 1948, and the record for one day probably a capacity of 46,000 for Lancashire v. Yorkshire at Old Trafford on 2 Aug 1926. The English record for a Test series is 549,650 for the series against Australia in 1953. The highest attendance for a limited-overs game is an estimated 90,450 at Eden Gardens to see India play South Africa on the latter's return to official international cricket, on 10 Nov 1991.

Most successful Test captain Clive Hubert Lloyd (b. 31 Aug 1944) led the West Indies in 74 Test matches from 22 Nov 1974 to 2 Jan 1985. Of these, 36

Long Match

The lengthiest recorded cricket match was the 'timeless' Test between England and South Africa at Durban on 3–14 Mar 1939. It was abandoned after ten days (eighth day rained off) because the ship taking the England team home was due to leave. The total playing time was 43 hr 16 min and a record Test match aggregate of 1981 runs was scored.

English One–Day Cricket Records

	NatWest Trophy (1981) (formerly Gillette Cup (1960–80))	Sunday League (1969)	Benson & Hedges (1972)
Total (highest)	413–4 Somerset v. Devon, Torquay, 1990	375–4 Surrey v. Yorkshire, Scarborough, 1994	388–7 Essex v. Scotland, Chelmsford, 1992
Total (lowest)	39 ......Ireland v. Sussex, Hove, 1985	23 ......Middlesex v. Yorkshire, Headingley, 1974	50......Hampshire v. Yorkshire, Headingley, 1991
Highest innings	206 ....Alvin Isaac Kallicharran (b. 21 Mar 1949), Warwickshire v. Oxon, Edgbaston, 1984	176 ....Graham Alan Gooch (b. 23 Jul 1953), Essex v. Glamorgan, Southend, 1983	198*...Graham Gooch, Essex v. Sussex, Hove, 1982
Best Bowling	8–21...Michael Anthony Holding (b. 16 Feb 1954), Derbyshire v. Sussex, Hove, 1988	8–26..Keith David Boyce (b. 11 Oct 1943), Essex v. Lancashire, Old Trafford, 1971**	7–12 ..Wayne Wendell Daniel (b. 16 Jan 1956), Middlesex v.Minor Counties (East), Ipswich, 1978
Most dismissals	7 ....Alec James Stewart (b. 8 Apr 1963), Surrey v. Glamorgan, Swansea, 1994	7 ....Robert William Taylor (b. 17 Jul 1941), Derbyshire v. Lancashire, Old Trafford, 1975	8........Derek John Somerset Taylor (b. 12 Nov 1942), Somerset v. Combined Universities, Taunton, 1982
Career - runs	2383 Graham Gooch, Essex 1973–94	7906 Graham Gooch, Essex 1973–94	4934 Graham Gooch, Essex 1973–95
- wickets	81.......Geoffrey Graham Arnold (b. 3 Sep 1944), Surrey, Sussex 1963–80	386 ....John Kenneth Lever (b. 24 Feb 1949), Essex 1969–89	149 ....John Lever, Essex 1972–89
- dismissals	66 ......Bob Taylor, Derbyshire 1963–84	257 ....David Bairstow, Yorkshire 1970–90	122 ....David Bairstow, Yorkshire 1972–90
Most wins	5 ....Lancashire 1970–2, 1975, 1990	3........Kent 1972–3, 1976 3........Essex 1981, 1984–5 3........Lancashire 1969–70, 1989 3........Worcestershire 1971, 1987–8	3........Kent 1973, 1976, 1978 3........Leicestershire 1972, 1975, 1985

*Not out   ** Alan Ward (b. 10 Aug 1947) took 4 wickets in 4 balls, Derbyshire v. Sussex, Derby, 1970.

■ Warwickshire's Tim Munton and Dermot Reeve celebrate having won an unprecedented three of the four trophies available in an English cricket season. They won, from left to right, the Sunday League, Benson and Hedges Cup and County Championship. They also reached the final of the fourth competition, the Nat West Trophy, but were beaten by their West Midlands rivals, Worcestershire.
(Photo: Allsport/C. Mason)

were won, 12 lost and 26 were drawn. His team set records for most successive Test wins, 11 in 1984, and most Tests without defeat, 27, between losses to Australia in December 1981 and January 1985 (through injury Lloyd missed one of those matches, when the West Indies were captained by Vivian Richards).

Most extras The West Indies hold the record for having conceded the most extras in both a Test innings and a one-day international. The Test record is 71 in Pakistan's 1st innings at Georgetown, Guyana on 3–4 Apr 1988. The figure consisted of 21 byes, 8 leg byes, 4 wides and 38 no-balls. The limited-overs record is 59 (8 byes, 10 leg byes, 4-no balls and 37 wides) also against Pakistan at Brisbane on 7 Jan 1989.

One-Day Internationals

World Cup The West Indies are the only double winners in 1975 and 1979.

One-day international records *Team* The highest innings score by a team is 363–7 (55 overs) by England v. Pakistan at Trent Bridge on 20 Aug 1992. The lowest completed innings total is 43 by Pakistan v. the West Indies at Newlands,

Cape Town, South Africa on 25 Feb 1993. The largest victory margin is 232 runs by Australia v. Sri Lanka (323–2 to 91), at Adelaide, Australia on 28 Jan 1985.

Individual The highest individual score is 189 not out by Isaac Vivian Alexander Richards (b. 7 Mar 1952) for the West Indies v. England at Old Trafford on 31 May 1984. The best bowling analysis is 7–37 by Aqib Javed (b. 5 Aug 1972) for Pakistan v. India at Sharjah on 25 Oct 1991. The best partnership is 263 by Aamir Sohail (b. 14 Sep 1966) (134) and Inzamam-ul-Haq (b. 3 Mar 1970) (137 not out) for Pakistan v. New Zealand at Sharjah, UAE on 20 Apr 1994.

Career The most matches played is 273 by Allan Border

Guess What?
Q. Who has won football's World Cup most often?
A. See Page 253

(Australia), 1979–94. The most runs scored is 8648 (av. 41.37) by Desmond Leo Haynes (West Indies) (b. 15 Feb 1956) in 238 matches, 1977–94; this total includes a record 17 centuries. The most wickets taken is 273 (av. 22.57) by Wasim Akram (Pakistan) (b. 3 Jun 1966) in 189 matches, 1985–95. The most dismissals is 204 (183 ct, 21 st) by Peter Jeffrey Leroy Dujon (West Indies) (b. 28 Mar 1956) in 169 matches, 1981–91. The most catches by a fielder is 127 by Border.

English County Championship The greatest number of victories since 1890, when the Championship was officially constituted, has been by Yorkshire with 29 outright wins (the last in 1968), and one shared (1949). The record number of consecutive title wins is seven by Surrey from 1952 to 1958. The greatest number of appearances in County Championship matches is 762 by Wilfred Rhodes for Yorkshire between 1898 and 1930, and the greatest number of consecutive appearances is 423 by Kenneth George Suttle (b. 25 Aug 1928) of Sussex between 1954 and 1969. James Graham 'Jimmy' Binks (b. 5 Oct 1935) played in all 412 County

Championship matches for Yorkshire between his début in 1955 and his retirement in 1969.

Oldest and Youngest

First-class The oldest player in first-class cricket was the Governor of Bombay, Raja Maharaj Singh (India) (1878–1959), aged 72 years 192 days, when he batted, scoring 4, on the opening day of the match played on 25–27 Nov 1950 at Bombay for his XI v. Commonwealth XI. The youngest is reputed to be Esmail Ahmed Baporia (India) (b. 24 Apr 1939) for Gujarat v. Baroda at Ahmedabad, India on 10 Jan 1951, aged 11 yr 261 days. The oldest Englishman was Benjamin Aislabie (1774–1842) for MCC (of whom he was the secretary) v. Cambridge University at Lord's on 1 and 2 Jul 1841, when he was aged 67 yr 169 days. The youngest English first-class player was Charles Robertson Young (1852–?) for Hampshire v. Kent at Gravesend on 13 Jun 1867, aged 15 yr 131 days.

Test The oldest man to play in a Test match was Wilfred Rhodes, aged 52 yr 165 days, for England v. West Indies at Kingston, Jamaica on 12 April 1930. Rhodes made his Test début in the last Test of William Gilbert Grace (1848–1915), who at 50 yr 320 days on 3 Jun 1899 was the oldest ever Test captain. The youngest Test captain was the Nawab of Pataudi (later Mansur Ali Khan) at 21 yr 77 days on 23 Mar 1962 for India v. West Indies at Bridgetown, Barbados. The youngest Test player was Mushtaq Mohammad (b. 22 Nov 1943), aged 15 yr 124 days, for Pakistan v. West Indies at Lahore on 26 March 1959. England's youngest player was Dennis Brian Close (b. 24 Feb 1931) aged 18 yr 149 days v. New Zealand at Old Trafford on 23 Jul 1949.

Women's Cricket

Batting *Individual* The highest individual innings recorded is 224 not out by Mabel Bryant for Visitors v. Residents at Eastbourne, E Sussex in August 1901. The highest innings in a Test match is 193 by Denise Audrey Annetts (now Anderson) (b. 30 Jan 1964), in 381 minutes, for Australia v. England at Collingham, Notts on 23–24 Aug 1987 in a four-day Test. With Lindsay Reeler (b. 18 Mar 1961), 110 not out, she added 309 for the third wicket, the highest Test partnership. The highest in a three-day Test is 189 (in 222 minutes) by Elizabeth Alexandra 'Betty' Snowball (1907–88) for England v. New Zealand at Christchurch, New Zealand on 16 Feb 1935.

Rachael Flint (*née* Heyhoe) (b. 11 Jun 1939) has scored the most runs in Test cricket with 1594 (av. 45.54) in 22 matches from December 1960 to July 1979, 1814 (av. 49.02) including three unofficial Tests v. Jamaica in 1991.

Team The highest innings score by any team is 567 by Tarana v. Rockley, at Rockley, New South Wales, Australia in 1896. The highest Test innings is 525 by Australia v. India at Ahmedabad on 4 Feb 1984. The highest score by England is 503 for five wickets declared by England v. New Zealand at Christchurch, New Zealand on 16 and 18 Feb 1935. The most in a Test in England is 426 by India at Stanley Park, Blackpool, Lancs on 3–7 Jul 1986.

The lowest innings in a Test is 35 by England v. Australia at St Kilda, Melbourne, Australia on 22 Feb 1958. The lowest in a Test in England is 63 by New Zealand at Worcester on 5 Jul 1954.

Bowling Mary Beatrice Duggan (England) (1925–73) took a record 77 wickets (av. 13.49) in 17 Tests from 1949 to 1963. She recorded the best Test analysis with seven wickets for six runs for England v. Australia at St Kilda, Melbourne on 22 Feb 1958.

Rubina Winifred Humphries (b. 19 Aug 1915), for Dalton Ladies v. Woodfield SC, at Huddersfield, W Yorks on 26 Jun 1931, took all ten wickets for no runs. (She also scored all her team's runs.) This bowling feat was equalled by Rosemary White (b. 22 Jan 1938) for Wallington LCC v. Beaconsfield LCC in July 1962.

All-round Elizabeth Rebecca 'Betty' Wilson (Australia) (b. 21 Nov 1921) was the first Test player, man or woman, to score a century and take ten wickets in a Test match. She took 7–7, including a hat-trick, and 4–9 and scored exactly 100 in the second innings against England at St Kilda on 21–24 Feb 1958. Enid Bakewell (b. 18 Dec 1940) was the first English Test player, man or woman, to achieve this Test Match double. Playing against the West Indies at Edgbaston on 1–3 Jul 1979, she scored 112 not out and had match figures of 10–75.

Wicketkeeping Lisa Nye (b. 24 Oct 1966) claimed a Test record eight dismissals (six caught, two stumpings) in an innings for England v. New Zealand at New Plymouth on 12–15 Feb 1992. Christina Matthews (Australia) (b. 1959) has taken a record 53 dismissals (43 catches, 10 stumpings) in 19 Tests.

World Cup Five women's World Cups have been staged. Australia won in 1978, 1982 and 1988, and England in 1973 and 1993. The highest individual score in this series is 143 not out by Lindsay Reeler for Australia v. Netherlands at Perth, Australia on 29 Nov 1988. The highest by an England player is 138 not out by Janette Ann Brittin (b. 4 Jul 1959) v. International XI at Hamilton, New Zealand on 14 Jan 1982. Brittin has scored a record 1007 runs in all World Cup matches.

Keep Running

Garry Chapman (partnered by Chris Veal) scored 17 (all run, with no overthrows) off a single delivery for Banyule against Macleod at Windsor Reserve, Victoria, Australia on 13 Oct 1990. Chapman had pulled the ball to mid-wicket where it disappeared into 25 cm *10 in* high grass.

Minor Cricket Records

Highest individual innings In a Junior House match between Clarke's House (now Poole's) and North Town, at Clifton College, Bristol, 22–23, 26–28 Jun 1899, Arthur Edward Jeune Collins (1885–1914) scored an unprecedented 628 not out in 6 hr 50 min, over five afternoons' batting, carrying his bat through the innings of 836. The scorer, E. W. Pegler, gave the score as '628–plus or minus 20, shall we say'.

Highest partnership During a Harris Shield match in 1988 at Sassanian Ground, Bombay, India, Vinod Kambli (b. 18 Jan 1972) (349 not out) and Sachin Tendulkar (b. 24 Apr 1973) (326 not out) put on an unbeaten partnership of 664 runs for the third wicket for Sharadashram Vidyamandir v. St Xavier's High School.

Fastest individual scoring Stanley Keppel 'Shunter' Coen (South Africa) (1902–67) scored 50 runs (11 fours and one six) in 7 minutes for Gezira v. the RAF in 1942. The fastest hundred by a prominent player in a minor match was by Vivian Frank Shergold Crawford (1879–1922) in 19 min at Cane Hill, Surrey on 16 Sep 1899. Lindsay Martin scored 100 off 20 deliveries (13 sixes, 5 fours and 2 singles) for Rosewater v. Warradale on 19 Dec 1987. David Michael Roberts Whatmore (b. 6 Apr 1949) scored 210 (including 25 sixes and 12 fours) off 61 balls for Alderney v. Sun Alliance at Alderney, Channel Islands on 19 Jun 1983. His first 100 came off 33 balls and his second off 25 balls.

Most runs off an over H. Morley scored 62, nine sixes and two fours, off an eight-ball over from R. Grubb which had four no-balls, in a Queensland country match in 1968/9.

Successive sixes Cedric Ivan James Smith (1906–79) hit nine successive sixes for a Middlesex XI v. Harrow and District at Rayner's Lane, Harrow in 1935. This feat was repeated by Arthur Dudley Nourse (1910–81) in a South African XI v. Military Police match at Cairo, Egypt in 1942/3. Nourse's feat included six sixes in one over.

Bowling Nine wickets with nine consecutive balls were taken by: Stephen Fleming, for Marlborough College 'A' XI v. Bohally Intermediate at Blenheim, New Zealand in December 1967; and by Paul Hugo for Smithfield School v. Aliwal North, South Africa in February 1931. In the Inter-Divisional Ships Shield at Purfleet, Essex on 17 May 1924, Joseph William Brockley (b. 9 Apr 1907) took all ten wickets, clean bowled, for two runs in 11 balls–including a triple hat trick. Bowling figures of 10 for 0 has been achieved on five occasions by: Jennings Tune, all bowled, in five overs for Cliffe v. Eastrington in the Howden and District League at Cliffe, Yorkshire on 6 May 1922; Alan Emery (26 balls) for Bowdon Vale against Heaton Mersey Parish at Bowdon Vale, Cheshire on 7 Sep 1947; Wynton Edwards of Queen's College (10 overs) against Selborne College at Queenstown, South Africa on 25 Mar 1950; Errol Hall (27 balls) for Australian v. Tannymorel at Warwick, Queensland on 2 Nov 1986; and Alex Kelly (27 balls) for Bishop Auckland v. Newton Aycliffe in the Milburngate Durham County Junior League at Bishop Auckland, Durham in June 1994.

In 1881 Frederick Robert Spofforth (1853–1926) at Bendemeer, New South Wales, Australia clean bowled all ten wickets in *both* innings (final figures 20 for 48). J. Bryant for Erskine v. Deaf Mutes in Melbourne on 15 and 22 Oct 1887, and Albert Rimmer for Linwood School v. Cathedral GS at Canterbury, New Zealand in December 1925, repeated the feat. In the 1910 season, H. Hopkinson, of Mildmay CC, London, took 99 wickets for 147 runs.

Longest throw A cricket ball (155 g 5½ oz) was reputedly thrown 128.6 m *140 yd 2 ft* by Robert Percival, a left-hander, on Durham Sands racecourse on Easter Monday, 18 Apr 1882.

Wicket-keeping Welihinda Badalge Bennett (b. 25 Jan 1933) caught four and stumped six batsmen in one innings, on 1 March 1953 for Mahinda College v. Galle CC, at the Galle Esplanade, Sri Lanka.

Fielding In a Wellington, New Zealand secondary schools 11-a-side match on 16 Mar 1974, Stephen Lane, 13, held 14 catches in the field (seven in each innings) for St Patrick's College, Silverstream v. St Bernard's College, Lower Hutt.

Guess What?
Q. What is the record for most most sixes in a first-class innings?
A. See Page 242

Guess What?
Q. What is the highest partnership in Test cricket?
A. See Page 243

Croquet

Most championships The greatest number of victories in the Open Croquet Championships (instituted at Evesham, Worcestershire, 1867) is ten by John William Solomon (b. 22 Nov 1931) (1953, 1956, 1959, 1961, 1963–8). He also won ten Men's Championships (1951, 1953, 1958–60, 1962, 1964–5, 1971–2), ten Open Doubles (with Edmond Patrick Charles Cotter (b. 24 Sep 1904)) (1954–5, 1958–9, 1961–5 and 1969) and one Mixed Doubles (with Freda Oddie) in 1954, making a total of 31 titles. Solomon has also won the President's Cup (instituted 1934, an invitation event for the best eight players) on nine occasions (1955, 1957–9, 1962–4, 1968 and 1971), and was Champion of Champions on all four occasions that that competition was run (1967–70).

George Nigel Aspinall (b. 29 Jul 1946) has won the President's Cup a record 11 times, 1969–70, 1973–6, 1978, 1980, 1982, 1984–5.

Dorothy Dyne Steel (1884–1965), fifteen times winner of the Women's Championship (1919–39), won the Open Croquet Championship four times (1925, 1933, 1935–6). She had also five Doubles and seven Mixed Doubles for a total of 31 titles.

World championships The first World Championships were held at the Hurlingham Club, London in 1989 and have been held annually since. The most wins is three by Robert Fulford (GB) (b. 1970), 1990, 1992 and 1994.

International trophy The MacRobertson Shield (instituted 1925) has been won a record nine times by Great Britain, 1925, 1937, 1956, 1963, 1969, 1974, 1982, 1990 and 1993.

A record seven appearances have been made by John G. Prince (New Zealand) (b. 23 Jul 1945) in 1963, 1969, 1975, 1979, 1982, 1986 and 1990; on his debut he was the youngest ever international at 17 years 190 days.

Cross-country Running

World Championships The inaugural International Cross-Country Championships took place at the Hamilton Park Racecourse, Scotland on 28 Mar 1903.

Since 1973 the events have been official world championships under the auspices of the International Amateur Athletic Federation.

The greatest margin of victory is 56 seconds or 356 m *390 yd* by John 'Jack' Thomas Holden (England) (b. 13 Mar 1907) at Ayr Racecourse, Strathclyde on 24 Mar 1934.

Most wins The greatest number of team victories has been by England with 45 for men, 11 for junior men and seven for women. The USA and USSR each has a record eight women's team victories. The greatest team domination was by Kenya at Auckland, New Zealand on 26 March 1988. Their senior men's team finished eight men in the first nine, with a low score of 23 (six to score) and their junior men's team set a record low score, 11 (four to score) with six in the first seven.

The greatest number of men's individual victories is five by John Ngugi (Kenya) (b. 10 May 1962),

Guess What?
Q. What is the record for the men's marathon?
A. See Page 229

1986–89 and 1992. The women's race has been won five times by: Doris Brown-Heritage (USA) (b. 17 Sep 1942), 1967–71; and by Grete Waitz (*née* Andersen) (Norway) (b. 1 Oct 1953), 1978–81 and 1983.

Most appearances Marcel van de Wattyne (Belgium) (b. 7 Jul 1924) ran in a record 20 races, 1946–65. The women's record is 16 by Jean Lochhead (Wales) (b. 24 Dec 1946), 1967–79, 1981, 1983–84.

English Championship The National Cross-Country Championship was inaugurated at Roehampton, London in 1877.

The most individual titles won is four by Percy Haines Stenning (1854–92) (Thames Hare and Hounds) in 1877–80 and Alfred E. Shrubb (1878–1964) (South London Harriers) in 1901–4. The most successful club in the team race has been Birchfield Harriers from Birmingham with 28 wins and one tie between 1880 and 1988.

The most individual wins in the English women's championships is six by Lillian Styles, 1928–30, 1933–4 and 1937; the most successful team is Birchfield Harriers with 13 titles.

The largest field was the 2195 finishers in the senior race in 1990 at Leeds, W Yorks on 24 February. In this race, a record 250 clubs scored (by having six runners finish).

Largest field The largest recorded field in any cross-country race was 11,763 starters (10,810 finished) in the 30 km *18.6 miles* Lidingöloppet, near Stockholm, Sweden on 3 Oct 1982.

■ At the 1995 World Cross-country Championships Kenya won the men's senior team title for a record 10th time in succession. Here, the Kenyan team group together at the front including the eventual winner of the individual title, Paul Tergat (9).
(Photo: Allsport/C. Mason)

Curling

Most titles Canada has won the men's World Championships (instituted 1959) 23 times, 1959–64, 1966, 1968–72, 1980, 1982–3, 1985–7, 1989–90, 1993–5.

The most Strathcona Cup (instituted 1903) wins is seven by Canada (1903, 1909, 1912, 1923, 1938, 1957, 1965) against Scotland.

The most women's World Championships (instituted 1979) is eight by Canada (1980, 1984–7, 1989, 1993–4).

The largest bonspiel in the world is the Manitoba Curling Association Bonspiel held annually in Winnipeg, Canada. In 1988 there were 1424 teams of four men, a total of 5696 curlers, using 187 sheets of curling ice.

Fastest game Eight curlers from the Burlington Golf and Country Club curled an eight-end game in 47 min 24 sec, with time penalties of 5 min 30 sec, at Burlington, Ontario, Canada on 4 Apr 1986, following rules agreed with the Ontario Curling Association. The time is taken from when the first rock crosses the near hogline until the game's last rock comes to a complete stop.

Largest rink The world's largest curling rink was the Big Four Curling Rink, Calgary, Alberta, Canada, opened in 1959 and closed in 1989. Ninety-six teams and 384 players were accommodated on two floors each with 24 sheets of ice.

Longest throw The longest throw of a curling stone was a distance of 175.66 m *576 ft 4 in* by Eddie Kulbacki (Canada) at Park Lake, Neepawa, Manitoba, Canada on 29 Jan 1989. The attempt took place on a specially prepared sheet of curling ice on frozen Park Lake, a record 1200 ft *365.76 m* long.

Cycling

Highest speed The highest speed ever achieved on a bicycle is 245.077 km/h *152.284 mph* by John Howard (USA) behind a wind-shield at Bonneville Salt Flats, Utah, USA on 20 Jul 1985. It should be noted that considerable help was provided by the slip-streaming effect of the lead vehicle.

The British speed record is 158.05 km/h *98.21 mph* over 200 metres by David Le Grys (b. 10 Aug 1955) on a closed section of the M42 at Alvechurch, Warks on 28 Aug 1985.

The 24 hour record behind pace is 1958.196 km *1216.8 miles* by Michael Secrest at Phoenix International Raceway, Arizona on 26–27 Apr 1990.

Roller cycling James Baker (USA) achieved a record speed of 246.5 km/h *153.2 mph* at El Con Mall, Tucson, Arizona, USA on 28 Jan 1989.

Most titles *Olympic* The most gold medals won is three by Paul Masson (France) (1874–1945) in 1896, Francisco Verri (Italy) (1885–1945) in 1906 and Robert Charpentier (France) (1916–66) in 1936. Daniel Morelon (France) (b. 28 Jul 1944) won two in 1968 and a third in 1972; he also won a silver in 1976 and a bronze medal in 1964. In the 'unofficial' 1904 cycling programme, Marcus Latimer Hurley (USA) (1885–1941) won four events.

World World Championships are contested annually. They were first staged for amateurs in 1893 and for professionals in 1895.

The fastest average speed in the Tour de France is 39.504 km/h *24.547 mph* by Miguel Induráin (Spain) (b. 16 Jul 1964) in 1992.

The most wins at a particular event is ten by Koichi Nakano (Japan) (b. 14 Nov 1955), professional sprint 1977–86.

The most wins at a men's amateur event is seven by Daniel Morelon (France), sprint 1966–7, 1969–71, 1973, 1975; and Leon Meredith (GB) (1882–1930), 100 km motor paced 1904–5, 1907–9, 1911, 1913.

The most women's titles is eight by Jeannie Longo (France) (b. 31 Oct 1958), pursuit 1986 and 1988–9; road 1985–7 and 1989 and points 1989.

British Beryl Burton (b. 12 May 1937), 25 times British all-round time trial champion (1959–83), won 72 individual road TT titles, 14 track pursuit titles and 12 road race titles to 1986. Ian Hallam (b. 24 Nov 1948) won a record 25 men's titles, 1969–82.

Tour de France (instituted 1903) The greatest number of wins in the *Tour de France* is five by Jacques Anquetil (France) (1934–1987), 1957, 1961–4; Eddy Merckx (Belgium) (b. 17 Jun 1945), 1969–72 and 1974; and Bernard Hinault (France) (b. 14 Nov 1954), 1978–9, 1981–2 and 1985.

The closest race ever was in 1989 when after 3267 km *2030 miles* over 23 days (1–23 Jul) Greg LeMond (USA) (b. 26 Jun 1960), who completed the Tour in 87 hr 38 min 35 sec, beat Laurent Fignon (France) (b. 12 Aug 1960) in Paris by only 8 seconds.

Tour of Britain (Open) Four riders have won the Tour of Britain twice each — Bill Bradley (GB) (1959–60), Leslie George West (GB) (1965, 1967), Fedor den Hertog (Netherlands) (1969, 1971) and Yuriy Kashurin (USSR) (1979, 1982).

The closest race ever was in 1976 when after 1665.67 km *1035 miles* over 14 days (30 May–12 Jun) Bill Nickson (GB) (b. 30 Jan 1953) beat Joe Waugh (GB) by 5 sec.

The fastest average speed is 42.185 km/h *26.213 mph* by Joey McLoughlin (GB) (b. 3 Dec 1964) in the 1986 race (1714 km *1065 miles*).

Guess What?
Q. What is the record for running across America?
A. See Page 228

British Road Records

Type	Time (hr:min:sec)	Name	Date
100 Miles			
Men's bike	3:11:11	Ian Cammish (b. 1 Oct 1956)	10 Aug 1993
Men's trike	3:39:51	Dave Pitt (b. 3 Mar 1950)	18 Oct 1991
Women's bike	3:49:42	Pauline Strong (b. 19 Mar 1956)	18 Oct 1991
London to Brighton and Back			
Men's bike	4:15:08	Phil Griffiths (b. 18 Mar 1949)	20 Jul 1977
Men's trike	4:51:07	Dave Pitt	25 Jul 1979
Women's bike	4:55:28	Gill Clapton (b. 25 Sep 1942)	15 Jul 1972
London to Bath and Back			
Men's bike	9:03:07	John Woodburn (b. 22 Dec 1936)	13 Jun 1981
Men's trike	10:19:00	Ralph Dadswell (b. 28 Jul 1964)	22 Jun 1991
Women's bike	10:41:22	Eileen Sheridan (b. 18 Oct 1923)	22 Aug 1952
Land's End to John O' Groats			
Men's bike	1 day 21:02:18	Andy Wilkinson (b. 22 Aug 1963)	29 Sep–1 Oct 1990
Men's trike	2 days 5:29:01	Ralph Dadswell	10–12 Aug 1992
Women's bike	2 days 6:49:45	Pauline Strong	28–30 Jul 1990

The longest ever Tour was in 1953 (2624.84 km *1631 miles* starting and finishing in London).

Six-day races The most wins in six-day races is 88 out of 233 events by Patrick Sercu (b. 27 Jun 1944), of Belgium, 1964–83.

Longest one-day race The longest single-day 'massed start' road race is the 551–620 km *342–385 miles* Bordeaux–Paris, France event. Paced over all or part of the route, the highest average speed was in 1981 with 47.186 km/h *29.32 mph* by Herman van Springel (Belgium) (b. 14 Aug 1943) for 584.5 km *363.1 miles* in 13 hr 35 min 18 sec.

Cross-America The trans-America solo records recognized by the Ultra-Marathon Cycling Association are: men, Paul Selon 8 days 8 hr 45 min; women, Susan Notorangelo 9 days 9 hr 9 min, both in the Race Across America, Costa Mesa, California to New York, 5000 km *3107 miles* in August 1989.

The trans-Canada record is 13 days 9 hr 6 min by Bill Narasnek of Lively, Ontario, 6037 km *3751 miles* from Vancouver, BC to Halifax, Nova Scotia on 5–18 Jul 1991.

Daniel Buettner, Bret Anderson, Martin Engel and Anne Knabe cycled the length of the Americas, from Prudhoe Bay, Alaska, USA to the Beagle Channel, Ushuaia, Argentina from 8 Aug 1986–13 Jun 1987. They cycled a total distance of 24,568 km *15,266 miles.*

Endurance Thomas Edward Godwin (GB) (1912–75) in the 365 days of 1939 covered 120,805 km *75,065 miles* or an average of 330.96 km *205.65 miles* per day. He then completed 160,934 km *100,000 miles* in 500 days to 14 May 1940.

Jay Aldous and Matt DeWaal cycled 22,997 km *14,290 miles* on a round-the-world trip from This is the Place Monument, Salt Lake City, Utah, USA in 106 days, 2 Apr–16 Jul 1984.

Tal Burt (Israel) circumnavigated the world (21,329 km *13,253 road miles*) from Place du Trocadero, Paris, France in 77 days 14 hr, from 1 Jun–17 Aug 1992.

Nick Sanders cycled 7728 km *4802 miles* around Britain in 22 days, 10 Jun–1 Jul 1984.

Since leaving his home country of Germany in November 1962, Heinz Stucke has travelled over 365,000 km *226,800 miles* and visited 211 countries

World Cycling Records

These records are those recognized by the Union Cycliste Internationale (UCI). From 1 Jan 1993 their severely reduced list no longer distinguished between those set by professionals and amateurs, indoor and outdoor, or at altitude and sea level.

MEN

Distance	min:sec	Name and Country	Venue	Date
Unpaced Standing Start				
1 km	1:02.091	Maic Malchow (GDR)	Colorado Springs, USA	28 Aug 1986
4 km	4:20.894	Graeme Obree (GB)	Hamar, Norway	19 Aug 1993
4 km team	4:03.840	Australia	Hamar, Norway	20 Aug 1993
		Brett Aitken, Stuart O'Grady, Tim O'Shaunessy, Billy Joe Shearsby		
1 hour (kms)	55.291	Tony Rominger (Switzerland)	Bordeaux, France	5 Nov 1994
Unpaced Flying Start				
200 metres	10.099	Vladimir Adamashvili (USSR)	Moscow, USSR	6 Aug 1990
500 metres	26.649	Aleksandr Kirichenko (USSR)	Moscow, USSR	29 Oct 1988

WOMEN

Distance	min:sec	Name and Country	Venue	Date
Unpaced Standing Start				
500 m	34.604	Felicia Ballanger (France)	Hyeres, France	3 Jul 1994
3 km	3:37.347	Rebecca Twigg (USA)	Hamar, Norway	20 Aug 1993
1 hour (kms)	47.112	Cathy Marsal (France)	Bordeaux, France	29 Apr 1995
Unpaced Flying Start				
200 metres	10.831	Olga Slyusareva (Russia)	Moscow, Russia	6 Aug 1990
500 metres	29.655	Erika Salumäe (USSR)	Moscow, USSR	6 Aug 1987

The Hour

The Hour is considered the most famous of cycling records and the first noted achievement for it was 25.508km *15.84 miles* by F. L. Dodds at the Cambridge University Ground on 25 March 1876. The first popularly regarded holder of the record, however, was Henri Desgrange (France), who had only learnt to ride a bicycle the previous year. Desgrange was later to organise the Tour de France and the great names in the history of the race, such as Anquetil, Merckx and Indurain, have all made their mark on the Hour. The table below show the progression of this record from Desgrange to its current best set by Tony Rominger.

The current women's best is 47.112km by Cathy Marsal (France) at Bordeaux, France on 29 Apr 1995.

Current holders of the one hour record, Tony Rominger (Switzerland) and Catherine Marsal (France).
(Photo: Allsport/Vandystadt/B. Bade and Y. Guichaoua)

Cyclist	Where	When	kms
Henri Destrange (France)	Paris, France	11 May 1893	35.525
Jules Dubois (France)	Paris	31 Oct 1894	38.220
Oscar van den Eynde (Belguim)	Paris	30 Jul 1897	39.240
Willie Hamilton (USA)	Denver, Colorado	9 Jul 1898	40.781
Lucien Petit-Breton (France)	Paris	24 Aug 1905	41.110
Marcel Berthet (France)	Paris	20 Jun 1907	41.520
Oscar Egg (Switzerland)	Paris	22 Aug 1912	42.360
Marcel Berthet (France)	Paris	7 Aug 1913	42.741
Oscar Egg (Switzerland)	Paris	21 Aug 1913	43.525
Marcel Berthet (France)	Paris	20 Sep 1913	43.775
Oscar Egg (Switzerland)	Paris	18 Aug 1914	44.247
Jan Van Hout (Netherlands)	Roermond, Netherlands	25 Aug 1933	44.588
Maurice Richard (France)	Milan, Italy	14 Oct 1935	44.777
Giuseppe Olmo (Italy)	Milan	31 Oct 1935	45.090
Maurice Richard (France)	Milan	14 Oct 1936	45.398
Frans Slaats (Netherlands)	Milan	29 Sep 1937	45.558
Fausto Coppi (Italy)	Milan	7 Nov 1942	45.871
Jacques Anquetil (France)	Milan	29 Jun 1956	46.159
Ercole Baldini (Italy)	Milan	19 Sep 1956	46.393
Roger Rivière (France)	Milan	18 Sep 1959	46.923
Roger Rivière (France)	Milan	23 Sep 1959	47.346
Jacques Anquetil (France)	Milan	27 Sep 1967	47.493
Ferdinand Bracke (Belgium)	Rome, Italy	30 Oct 1967	48.093
Ole Ritter (Denmark)	Mexico City	10 Oct 1968	48.653
Eddy Merckx (Belgium)	Mexico City	25 Oct 1972	49.431
Francesco Moser (Italy)	Mexico City	19 Jan 1984	50.808
Francesco Moser (Italy)	Mexico City	23 Jan 1984	51.151
Graeme Obree (GB)	Hamar, Norway	17 Jul 1993	51.596
Chris Boardman (GB)	Bordeaux, France	23 Jul 1993	52.270
Graeme Obree (GB)	Bordeaux	27 Apr 1994	52.713
Miguel Indurain (Spain)	Bordeaux	2 Sep 1994	53.040
Tony Rominger (Switzerland)	Bordeaux	22 Oct 1994	53.832
Tony Rominger (Switzerland)	Bordeaux	5 Nov 1994	55.291

Guess What?

Q. What is the greatest distance run in one hour?

A. See Page 224

365,000 km *226,800 miles* and visited 211 countries and territories to April 1995.

Cycle touring The greatest mileage amassed in a cycle tour was more than 646,960 km *402,000 miles* by the itinerant lecturer Walter Stolle (b. Sudetenland, 1926) from 24 Jan 1959 to 12 Dec 1976. He visited 159 countries starting from Romford, Essex. From 1922 to 25 Dec 1973 Tommy Chambers (1903–84) of Glasgow, rode a verified total of 1,286,517 km *799,405 miles*.

> Stephen Poulton cycled from sea level at Caernarvon, Gwynedd, via the Three Peaks of Snowdon, Scafell Pike and Ben Nevis, to sea level Fort William, Highland in 41hr 51min, from 1–2 Jul 1980.

Visiting every continent, John W. Hathaway (b. England, 13 Jan 1925) of Vancouver, Canada covered 81,430 km *50,600 miles* from 10 Nov 1974 to 6 Oct 1976. Veronica and Colin Scargill, of Bedford, travelled 29,000 km *18,020 miles* around the world on a tandem, 25 Feb 1974–27 Aug 1975.

The most participants in a bicycle tour are 31,678 in the 90 km *56 miles* London to Brighton Bike Ride on 19 Jun 1988. However, it is estimated that 45,000 cyclists took part in the 75 km *46 miles* Tour de l'Ile de Montréal, Canada on 7 Jun 1992. The most participants in a tour in an excess of 1000 km are 2037 (from 2157 starters) for the Australian Bicentennial Caltex Bike Ride from Melbourne to Sydney from 26 Nov–10 Dec 1988.

Cyclo-Cross

The greatest number of World Championships (instituted 1950) has been won by Eric De Vlaeminck (Belgium) (b. 23 Aug 1945) with the Amateur and Open in 1966 and six Professional titles in 1968–73.

British titles (instituted 1955) have been won most often by John Atkins (b. 7 Apr 1942) with five Amateur (1961–2, 1966–8), seven Professional (1969–75) and one Open title in 1977.

Highest altitude Canadians Bruce Bell, Philip Whelan and Suzanne MacFadyen cycled at an altitude of 6960 m *22,834 ft* on the peak of Mt Aconcagua, Argentina on 25 Jan 1991. This achievement was equalled by Mozart Hastenreiter Catão (Brazil) on 11 Mar 1993 and by Tim Sumner and Jonathon Green on 6 Jan 1994.

Cycle Speedway

The most British Senior Team Championships (instituted 1950) is nine by Poole, Dorset (1982, 1984, 1987–93).

The most individual titles is four by Derek Garnett (b. 16 Jul 1937) (1963, 1965, 1968 and 1972); he also won the inaugural British Veterans' Championship in 1987.

Dart Feat

The record time for going round the board clockwise in 'doubles' at arm's length is 9.2 sec by Dennis Gower at the Millers Arms, Hastings, E Sussex on 12 Oct 1975 and 14.5 sec in numerical order by Jim Pike (1903–60) at the Craven Club, Newmarket, Suffolk in March 1944.

The record for this feat at the 9ft *2.7 m* throwing distance, retrieving own darts, is 2 min 13 sec by Bill Duddy (b. 29 Sep 1932) at The Plough, Haringey, London on 29 Oct 1972.

Darts Scoring Records

24-Hour
MEN (8 players) 1,722,249 by Broken Hill Darts Club at Broken Hill, New South Wales, Australia on 28–29 Sep 1985. **WOMEN** (8 players) 744,439 by a team from the Lord Clyde, Leyton, London on 13–14 Oct 1990. **INDIVIDUAL** 566,175 by Russell Locke at Hugglescote Wornking Mens Club, Leics on 17–18 Sep 1993. **BULLS AND 25s** (8 players) 526,750 by a team at the George Inn, Morden, Surrey on 1–2 Jul 1994.

10-Hour
MOST TREBLES 3056 (from 7992 darts) by Paul Taylor at the Woodhouse Tavern, Leytonstone, London on 19 Oct 1985. **MOST DOUBLES** 3265 (from 8451 darts) by Paul Taylor at the Lord Brooke, Walthamstow, London on 5 Sep 1987. **HIGHEST SCORE** (retrieving own darts) 465,919 by Jon Archer and Neil Rankin at the Royal Oak, Cossington, Leics on 17 Nov 1990. **BULLS** (individual) 1320 by Jon Lowe at The Unicorn Tavern, Chesterfield, Derbys on 27 Oct 1994.

6-Hour
MEN 210,172 by Russell Locke at the Hugglescote Working Mens Club, Coalville, Leics on 10 Sep 1989. **WOMEN** 99,725 by Karen Knightly at the Lord Clydeon 17 Mar 1991.

Million and One Up
MEN (8 players) 36,583 darts by a team at the Buzzy's Pub and Grub, Lynn, Massachusetts, USA on 19–20 Oct 1991. **WOMEN** 70,019 darts by The Delinquents darts team at the Top George, Combe Martin, Devon on 11–13 Sep 1987.

Darts

Most titles Eric Bristow (b. 25 Apr 1957) has most wins in the World Masters Championship (instituted 1974) with five, 1977, 1979, 1981 and 1983–4, the World Professional Championship (instituted 1978) with five, 1980–81 and 1984–6, and the World Cup Singles (instituted 1977), four, 1983, 1985, 1987 and 1989.

John Lowe (b. 21 Jul 1945) is the only other man to have won each of the four major titles: World Masters, 1976 and 1980; World Professional, 1979, 1987 and 1993; World Cup Singles, 1981; and *News of the World*, 1981.

World Cup The first World Cup was held at the Wembley Conference Centre, London in 1977. England has a record seven wins at this biennial tournament. Eric Bristow and John Lowe played on all seven teams.

A biennial World Cup for women was instituted in 1983 and has been won three times by England.

Record prize John Lowe won £102,000 for achieving the first 501 scored with the minimum nine darts in a major event on 13 Oct 1984 at Slough in the quarter-finals of the World Match-play Championships. His darts were six successive treble 20s, treble 17, treble 18 and double 18.

Speed records The fastest time taken to complete three games of 301, finishing on doubles, is 1 min 38 sec by Ritchie Gardner on BBC TV's *Record Breakers* on 12 Sep 1989.

Least darts Scores of 201 in four darts, 301 in six darts, 401 in seven darts and 501 in nine darts, have been achieved on various occasions.

Roy Edwin Blowes (Canada) (b. 8 Oct 1930) was the first person to achieve a 501 in nine darts, 'double-on, double-off', at the Widgeons pub, Calgary, Canada at 9 Mar 1987. His scores were: bull, treble 20, treble 17, five treble 20s and a double 20 to finish.

The lowest number of darts thrown for a score of 1001 is 19 by: Cliff Inglis (b. 27 May 1935) (160, 180, 140, 180, 121, 180, 40) at the Bromfield Men's Club, Devon on 11 Nov 1975 and Jocky Wilson (b. 22 Mar 1950) (140, 140, 180, 180, 180, 131, Bull) at The London Pride, Bletchley, Bucks on 23 Mar 1989.

A score of 2001 in 52 darts was achieved by Alan Evans (b. 14 Jun 1949) at Ferndale, Mid Glam on 3 Sep 1976; 3001 in 73 darts was thrown by Tony Benson at the Plough Inn, Gorton, Manchester on 12 Jul 1986. Linda Batten (b. 26 Nov 1954) set a women's 3001 record of 117 darts at the Old Wheatsheaf, Enfield, London on 2 Apr 1986 and a total of 100,001 was achieved in 3579 darts by Chris Gray at the Dolphin, Cromer, Norfolk on 27 Apr 1993.

As well as being one of the most successful players in world darts and winner of the largest prize ever when completing a nine-dart 501, John Lowe has also set the best for one of the more unusual darts records in *The Guinness Book of Records*. The record in question is the most bulls in 10 hours; he hit 1320 bullseyes beating the previous record by 59.
(Photo: Allsport/H. Boylan)

Equestrian Sports

Show Jumping

Olympic Games The most Olympic gold medals is five by Hans Günter Winkler (West Germany) (b. 24 Jul 1926), four team in 1956, 1960, 1964 and 1972 and the individual Grand Prix in 1956. He also won team silver in 1976 and team bronze in 1968 for a record seven medals overall.

The most team wins in the Prix des Nations is six by Germany in 1936, 1956, 1960, 1964 and as West Germany in 1972 and 1988.

The lowest score obtained by a winner is no faults by Frantisek Ventura (Czechoslovakia) (1895–1969) on *Eliot*, 1928; Alwin Schockemöhle (West Germany) (b. 29 May 1937) on *Warwick Rex*, 1976 and Ludger Beerbaum (Germany) (b. 25 Aug 1963) on *Classic Touch*, 1992.

Pierre Jonquères d'Oriola (France) (b. 1 Feb 1920) uniquely won the individual gold medal twice, 1952 and 1964.

World Championships The men's World Championships (instituted 1953) have been won twice by Hans Günter Winkler (West Germany) (1954–5) and Raimondo d'Inzeo (Italy) (b. 8 Feb 1925) (1956 and 1960).

The women's title (1965–74) was won twice by Jane 'Janou' Tissot (*née* Lefebvre) (France) (b. Saigon, 14 May 1945) on *Rocket* (1970 and 1974).

A team competition was introduced in 1978 and the most wins is three by France, 1982, 1986 and 1990.

President's Cup Instituted in 1965 for Nations Cup teams, it has been won a record 14 times by Great Britain, 1965, 1967, 1970, 1972–4, 1977–9, 1983, 1985–6, 1989, 1991. David Broome (b. 1 Mar 1940) has represented Great Britain 106 times in Nations Cup events, 1959–94.

World Cup Instituted in 1979, double winners have been Conrad Homfeld (USA) (b. 25 Dec 1951), 1980 and 1985; Ian Millar (Canada) (b. 6 Jan 1947), 1988–9; and John Whitaker (GB) (b. 5 Aug 1955), 1990–91.

King George V Gold Cup and Queen Elizabeth II Cup David Broome has won the King George V Gold Cup (first held 1911) a record six times, 1960 on *Sunsalve*, 1966 on *Mister Softee*, 1972 on *Sportsman*, 1977 on *Philco*, 1981 on *Mr Ross* and 1991 on *Lannegan*.

The Queen Elizabeth II Cup (first held 1949), for women, has been won five times by his sister Elizabeth Edgar (b. 28 Apr 1943), 1977 on *Everest Wallaby*, 1979 on *Forever*, 1981 and 1982 on *Everest Forever*, 1986 on *Everest Rapier*.

The only horse to win both these trophies is *Sunsalve* in 1957 (with Elisabeth Anderson) and 1960.

Jumping records The official *Fédération Equestre Internationale* records are: high jump 2.47 m *8 ft 1¼ in* by *Huasó*, ridden by Capt. Alberto Larraguibel Morales (Chile) at Viña del Mar, Santiago, Chile on 5 Feb 1949; long jump over water 8.40 m *27 ft 6¾ in* by

Guess What?
Q. Who has grown the world's longest moustache?
A. See Page 62

Something, ridden by André Ferreira (South Africa) at Johannesburg, South Africa on 25 Apr 1975. The indoor high jump record is 2.40 m by *Optibeurs Leonardo* ridden by Franke Sloothaak (Germany) at Chaudefontaine, Switzerland on 9 Jun 1991.

The British high jump record is 2.32 m *7 ft 7¼ in* by the 16.2 hands *165 cm* grey gelding *Lastic* ridden by Nick Skelton (b. 30 Dec 1957) at Olympia, London on 16 Dec 1978.

Three-Day Event

Olympic Games and World Championships Charles Ferdinand Pahud de Mortanges (Netherlands) (1896–1971) won a record four Olympic gold medals, team 1924 and 1928, individual (riding *Marcroix*) 1928 and 1932, when he also won a team silver medal.

Bruce Oram Davidson (USA) (b. 13 Dec 1949) is the only rider to have won two world titles (instituted 1966), on *Irish Cap* in 1974 and *Might Tango* in 1978.

Richard John Hannay Meade (GB) (b. 4 Dec 1938) is the only British rider to win three Olympic gold medals—as an individual in 1972 with team titles in 1968 and 1972.

Badminton

The Badminton Three-Day Event (instituted 1949) has been won six times by Lucinda Jane Green (*née* Prior-Palmer) (b. 7 Nov 1953), in 1973 (on *Be Fair*), 1976 (*Wide Awake*), 1977 (*George*), 1979 (*Killaire*), 1983 (*Regal Realm*) and 1984 (*Beagle Bay*).

Dressage

Olympic Games and World Championships Germany (West Germany 1968–90) have won a record eight team gold medals, 1928, 1936, 1964, 1968, 1976, 1984, 1988 and 1992, and have most team wins, seven, at the World Championships (instituted 1966). Dr Reiner Klimke (West Germany) (b. 14 Jan 1936) has won a record six Olympic golds (team 1964–88, individual, 1984). He also won individual bronze in 1976 for a record seven medals overall and is the only rider to win two world titles, on *Mehmed* in 1974 and *Ahlerich* in 1982. Henri St Cyr (Sweden) (1904–79) won a record two individual Olympic gold medals, 1952 and 1956. This was equalled by Nicole Uphoff (Germany) in 1992, having previously won in 1988.

■ **George Bowman (left) (b. 14 Oct 1934) has won the British National Driving Championships a record 17 times to 1994.**
(Photo: Allsport/M. Cooper)

World Cup Instituted in 1986, the only double winner is Christine Stückelberger (Switzerland) (b. 22 May 1947) on *Gauguin de Lully*, 1987–8 and Monica Theodorescu (Greece) on *Ganimedes Tecrent*, 1993–4.

Carriage driving

World Championships were first held in 1972. Three team titles have been won by: Great Britain, 1972, 1974 and 1980; Hungary, 1976, 1978 and 1984; and the Netherlands, 1982, 1986 and 1988.

Two individual titles have been won by: György Bárdos (Hungary), 1978 and 1980; Tjeerd Velstra (Netherlands), 1982 and 1986; and Ijsbrand Chardon (Netherlands), 1988 and 1992.

British titles George Bowman (b. 14 Oct 1934) has won a record 17 Horse Teams titles at the National Driving Championships to 1994.

Fencing

Most titles *World* The greatest number of individual world titles won is five by Aleksandr Romankov (USSR) (b. 7 Nov 1953), at foil 1974, 1977, 1979, 1982 and 1983, but Christian d'Oriola (France) won four world foil titles, 1947, 1949, 1953–4 as well as two individual Olympic titles (1952 and 1956).

Four women foilists have won three world titles: Helene Mayer (Germany) (1910–53), 1929, 1931, 1937; Ilona Schacherer-Elek (Hungary) (1907–88), 1934–35, 1951; Ellen Müller–Preis (Austria) (b. 6 May 1912), 1947, 1949–50; and Cornelia Hanisch (West Germany) (b. 12 Jun 1952), 1979, 1981, 1985. Of these only Ilona Schacherer-Elek also won two individual Olympic titles (1936 and 1948). The longest span for winning an individual world or Olympic title is 20 years by Aladár Gerevich (Hungary) (b. 16 Mar 1910) at sabre, 1935–55.

Olympic The most individual Olympic gold medals won is three by Ramón Fonst (Cuba) (1883–1959) in 1900 and 1904 (two) and by Nedo Nadi (Italy) (1894–1952) in 1912 and 1920 (two). Nadi also won three team gold medals in 1920 making five gold medals at one celebration, the record for fencing and then a record for any sport. Aladár Gerevich (Hungary) won seven golds, one individual and six team, 1932–60; a span of 28 years, an Olympic record.

Edoardo Mangiarotti (Italy) (b. 7 Apr 1919) with six gold, five silver and two bronze, holds the record of 13 Olympic medals. He won them for foil and épée from 1936 to 1960.

The most gold medals by a woman is four (one individual, three team) by Yelena Dmitryevna Novikova (*née* Belova) (USSR) (b. 28 Jul 1947) from 1968 to 1976, and the record for all medals is seven (two gold, three silver, two bronze) by Ildikó Sági (formerly Ujlaki, *née* Retjö) (Hungary) (b. 11 May 1937) from 1960 to 1976.

British Three British fencers have won individual world titles: Gwen Neligan (1906–72) at foil in 1933; Henry William Furze 'Bill' Hoskyns (b. 19 Mar 1931) at épée in 1958; and Allan Louis Neville Jay (b. 30 Jun 1931) at foil in 1959, when he also won silver in épée. The only British fencer to win an Olympic gold medal is Gillian Mary Sheen (now Donaldson) (b. 21 Aug 1928) in the 1956 foil.

A record three Olympic medals were won by Edgar Isaac Seligman (1867–1958) with silver medals in the épée team event in 1906, 1908 and 1912.

Bill Hoskyns has competed most often for Great Britain with six Olympic appearances, 1956–76.

Amateur Fencing Association titles
The most won at one weapon is ten at women's foil by Gillian Sheen, 1949, 1951–8, 1960. The men's records are: foil, 7 by John Emyrs Lloyd (1908–1987) 1928, 1930–3, 1937–8; épée, 6 by Edward Owen 'Teddy' Bourne (b. 30 Sep 1948) 1966, 1972, 1974, 1976–8 and William Ralph Johnson (b. 3 Jun 1948) 1968, 1982, 1984–5, 1987, 1990; and sabre, 6 by Dr Roger F. Tredgold (1912–75) 1937, 1939, 1947–9, 1955.

Field Sports

Hunting

Pack *Largest* The pack with the greatest number of hounds has been the Duke of Beaufort's hounds maintained at Badminton, Avon since 1786. At times hunting six days a week, this pack once had 120 couples of hounds. It now meets four days a week.

Longest mastership The 10th Duke of Beaufort (1900–84) was Master of Foxhounds from 1924 until his death in 1984 and hunted his hounds on 3895 days from 1920–67.

Longest hunt The longest recorded hunt was one held by Squire Sandys which ran from

Between 1969 and 1992, John N. P. Watson (b. 18 Jun 1927) (right), hunting correspondent to *Country Life*, hunted with 283 different packs of foxhounds, staghounds and harehounds in Britain, Ireland, USA and Europe.
(Photo: Brian Moody)

Holmbank, northern Lancs to Ulpha, Cumbria, a total of nearly 80 miles *128km* in reputedly only 6 hours, in January or February 1743.

The longest duration hunt was one of 10hr 5min by Charlton Hunt of W Sussex, which ran from East Dean Wood at 7:45a.m. to a kill over 57¼ miles *92km* away at 5:50p.m. on 26 Jan 1738.

Beagling The longest mastership of a pack was by Jean Bethel 'Betty' McKeever (*née* Dawes) (1901–90), who was Master of the Blean Beagles in Kent from 1909 until her death in 1990. She was given her first pack by her father at the age of eight and remained the sole Master.

Guess What?
Q. What is the most expensive board game?
A. See Page 236

Game Shooting

Largest tally to a single sportsman A record 556,813 head of game fell to the guns of the 2nd Marquess of Ripon (1852–1923) between 1867 and when he dropped dead on a grouse moor after shooting his 52nd bird on the morning of 22 Sep 1923. This figure included 241,234 pheasants, 124,193 partridge and 31,900 hares. (His game books are held by the gunmakers James Purdey and Sons.)

Thomas, 6th Baron Walsingham (1843–1919), bagged 1070 grouse, a one-day record for a single gun, in Yorkshire on 30 Aug 1888.

Fives

Eton Fives

Most titles One pair has won the amateur championship (Kinnaird Cup) ten times—Brian C. Matthews (b. 15 Aug 1957) and John P. Reynolds (b. 9 Aug 1961), 1981–90. John Reynolds won an eleventh title with Manuel de Souza-Girao (b. 20 Aug 1970) in 1991.

Rugby Fives

Most titles The greatest number of Amateur Singles Championships (instituted 1932) ever won is 21 by Wayne Enstone (b. 12 Jun 1951) in 1973–8 and 1980–94.

The record for the Amateur Doubles Championship (instituted 1925) is 10 by David John Hebden (b. 30 Jun 1948) and Ian Paul Fuller (b. 25 May 1953) in 1980–85 and 1987–90, although Wayne Enstone has won the title 11 times with three different partners, 1975–9 (John East), 1986 (Steve Ashton) and 1991–5 (Neil Roberts).

International Football Competitions

Title (instituted)	Most Wins	Highest score (single game)
National level		
Olympic Games (1896)	3 Great Britain 1900, 08, 12	17–1 Denmark *v.* France 'A', 1908
(*unofficial until 1908*)	3 Hungary, 1952, 64, 68	
S. American Championships (1910)	15 Argentina, 1910, 21, 25, 27, 29,	
(*Copa America since 1975*)	37, 41, 45–7, 55, 57, 59, 91, 93	12–0 Argentina *v.* Ecuador, 1942
Asian Cup (1956)	3 Iran, 1968, 72, 76	10–1 China *v.* Brunei, 1976
African Cup of Nations (1957)	4 Ghana, 1963, 65, 78, 82	9–1 Ghana *v.* Niger, 1969
European Championships (1958)	2 West Germany, 1972, 80	12–1 Spain *v.* Malta, 1983
Club level		
World Club Championship (1960)	3 Peñarol (Uruguay), 1961, 66, 82	5–1 Real Madrid (Spain) *v.* Penarol, 1960
(*between winners of European*	3 Nacional (Uruguay), 1971, 80, 88	5–0 Peñarol *v.* Benfica (Portugal), 1961
Cup and Copa Libertadores)	3 Milan (Italy), 1969, 89, 90	
Europe		
UEFA Cup (1955)	3 Barcelona (Spain), 1958, 60, 66	14–0 Ajax (Netherlands) *v.* Red Boys (Luxembourg), 1984
European Cup (1956)	6 Real Madrid, 1956–60, 66	12–2 Feyenoord (Netherlands) *v.* KR Reykjavik (Iceland), 1969
Cup Winners Cup (1960)	3 Barcelona, 1979, 82, 89	16–1 Sporting Club Portugal *v.* Apoel Nicosia (Cyprus), 1963
South America		
Copa Libertadores (1960)	7 Independiente (Argentina), 1964–5, 72–5, 84	11–2 Peñarol *v.* Valencia (Venezuela), 1970
Africa		
Cup of Champion Clubs (1964)	3 Canon Yaoundé (Cameroon), 1971, 78, 80	9–0 Kambe Warriors (Zambia) *v.* Manjantja Maseru (Lesotho), 1972
	3 Hafia FC Conakry (Guinea), 1972, 75, 77	
	3 Zamalek (Eygpt), 1984, 86, 93	
Cup Winners Cup (1975)	4 Al Ahly Cairo (Eygpt), 1984–6, 93	12–1 SC Pamba (Tanzania) *v.* Anse Boileau (Seychelles), 1990

Football (Association)

The FIFA World Cup

The *Fédération Internationale de Football Association* (FIFA), which was founded on 21 May 1904, instituted the first World Cup on 13 Jul 1930, in Montevideo, Uruguay. It is held quadrennially.

Team records

Most wins Brazil has won four times, 1958, 1962, 1970 and 1994.

Appearances Brazil, uniquely, have taken part in all 15 finals tournaments. Only two other nations have entered all World Cup competitions, France and the USA although the USA withdrew in 1938 without playing.

Most goals *Game* This occurred in a qualifying match in Auckland on 15 Aug 1981 when New Zealand beat Fiji 13–0. The highest score during the final stages is 10, scored by Hungary in a 10–1 win over El Salvador at Elche, Spain on 15 Jun 1982. The highest match aggregate in the finals tournament is 12, when Austria beat Switzerland, 7–5, at Lausanne, Switzerland on 26 Jun 1954.

Tournament The greatest number in a single finals tournament is 27 (five games) by Hungary in 1954. Not surprisingly, Brazil have scored the most overall, 159 in 73 matches.

Individual records

Appearances Antonio Carbajal (Mexico) (b. 7 Jun 1929) is the only player to have appeared in five World Cup finals tournaments, keeping goal for Mexico in 1950, 1954, 1958, 1962 and 1966, playing 11 games in all. The most games in finals tournaments is 21 by: Uwe Seeler (West Germany) (b. 5 Nov 1936), 1958–70; Wladyslaw Zmuda (Poland) (b. 6 Jun 1954), 1974–86; Diego Armando Maradona (Argentina) (b. 30 Oct 1960), 1982–94; and Lothar Matthäus (Germany) (b. 21 Mar 1961), 1982–94.

Pelé (Brazil) is the only player to have been with three World Cup–winning teams, in 1958, 1962 and 1970.

The youngest ever to play in a finals match is Norman Whiteside, who played for Northern Ireland *v.* Yugoslavia aged 17 years 41 days on 17 Jun 1982. The oldest is Albert Roger Milla (b. 20 May 1952) for Cameroon *v.* Russia on 28 Jun 1994, aged 42 yr 39 days.

Most goals *Game* Oleg Salenko scored five goals in Russia's 6–1 win against Cameroon at Palo Alto, California, USA on 28 June 1994. Nine players have scored four goals in a single match and of these, three have also scored one of the 34 hat-tricks to have occured in finals matches; Sándor Kocsis (Hungary) (1929–79), Just Fontaine (France) (b. Marrakech, Morocco, 18 Aug 1933) and Gerd Müller (West Germany) (b. 3 Nov 1945).

Tournament Just Fontaine scored 13 goals in six matches in the final stages of the 1958 competition in Sweden. Fontaine, Jaïrzinho (Brazil) (b. 25 Dec 1944) and Alcide Ghiggia (Uruguay) are the only three players to have scored in every match in a final series. Jaïrzinho scored seven in six games in 1970 and Ghiggia, four in four games in 1950.

Overall Gerd Müller scored ten goals in 1970 and four in 1974 for the highest aggregate of 14 goals.

First-class Team Records

Goal scoring

Match The highest score recorded in a first-class match is 36. This occurred in the Scottish Cup match between Arbroath and Bon Accord on 5 Sep 1885, when Arbroath won 36–0 on their home ground. But for the lack of nets and the consequent waste of retrieval time the score must have been even higher. Seven further goals were disallowed for off-side.

The highest margin recorded in an international match is 17, when England beat Australia 17–0 at Sydney on 30 Jun 1951. This match is not listed by England as a *full* international. The highest in the British Isles was when England beat Ireland 13–0 at Belfast on 18 Feb 1882.

The highest score between English clubs in any major competition is 26, when Preston North End beat Hyde 26–0 in an FA Cup tie at Deepdale, Lancs on 15 Oct 1887. The highest score by one side in a Football League (First Division) match is 12 goals when West Bromwich Albion beat Darwen 12–0 at West Bromwich, W Mids on 4 Apr 1892; when Nottingham Forest beat Leicester Fosse by the same score at Nottingham on 21 Apr 1909; and when Aston Villa beat Accrington 12–2 at Perry Barr, W Mids on 12 Mar 1892.

The highest aggregate in League Football was 17 goals when Tranmere Rovers beat Oldham Athletic 13–4 in a Third Division (North) match at Prenton Park, Merseyside, on Boxing Day, 1935. The record margin in a League match has been 13 in the Newcastle United 13, Newport County 0 (Second Division) match on 5 Oct 1946 and in the Stockport County 13, Halifax Town 0 (Third Division (North)) match on 6 Jan 1934.

Season The highest number of goals by any British team in a professional league in a season is 142 in 34 matches by Raith Rovers (Scottish Second Division) in the 1937/8 season. The English League record is 134 in 46 matches by Peterborough United (Fourth Division) in 1960/61.

League Championships

The record number of successive national league championships is nine by: Celtic (Scotland) 1966–74; CSKA, Sofia (Bulgaria) 1954–62; and MTK Budapest (Hungary) 1917–25. The Sofia club holds a European post–war record of 26 league titles, including two under the name CFKA Sredets (re-named CSKA).

English The greatest number of League Championships (First Division) is 18 by Liverpool in 1901, 1906, 1922–3, 1947, 1964, 1966, 1973, 1976–7, 1979–80, 1982–4, 1986, 1988 and 1990. The record number of wins in a season is 33 from 42 matches by Doncaster Rovers in Third Division (North) in 1946/7. The First Division record is 31 wins from 42 matches by Tottenham Hotspur in 1960/1. In 1893/4 Liverpool won 22 and drew 6 in 28 Second Division games. They also won the promotion match. The most points in a season under the current scoring system is 102 from 46 matches by Swindon in the Fourth Division in 1985/6. Under the new system the First Division record would have been Liverpool's 98 in 1978/9, when they won 30 and drew 8 of their 42 matches.

'Double' The only FA Cup and League Championship 'doubles' are those of Preston North End in 1889, Aston Villa in 1897, Tottenham Hotspur in 1961, Arsenal in 1971, Liverpool in 1986 and Manchester United in 1994. Preston won the League without losing a match and the Cup without having a goal scored against them throughout the whole competition.

Closest win In 1923/4 Huddersfield won the First Division Championship over Cardiff by 0.02 of a goal with a goal average of 1.81. The 1988/9 League Championship was decided by the fact that Arsenal had scored more goals (73 to 65) than Liverpool, after both teams finished level on points and goal difference.

Scottish Glasgow Rangers have won the Scottish League Championship 45 times (including one shared 1891) between 1891 and 1995. Their 76 points in the Scottish First Division in 1920/1 (from a possible 84) represents a record in any division. However a better percentage was achieved by Rangers in 1898/9

League Cups

The Football League Cup (instituted 1960/1) has been won five times by Liverpool 1981–4 and 1995.

For the Scottish League Cup (instituted 1946/7) the most wins is 19 by Rangers between 1947 and 1993. Derek Johnstone (Rangers) (b. 4 Nov 1953) was 16 years 11 months old when he played in the Scottish League Cup final against Celtic on 24 Oct 1970.

World Cup

The most goals scored in a final is three by Geoffrey Charles Hurst (b. 8 Dec 1941) for England v. West Germany on 30 Jul 1966. Three players have scored in two finals: Vava (real name Edevaldo Izito Neto) (Brazil) (b. 12 Nov 1934) in 1958 and 1962, Pelé in 1958 and 1970; and Paul Breitner (West Germany) (b. 5 Sep 1951) in 1974 and 1982.

■ **Liverpool have won a record five League Cups and Ian Rush has uniquely been a member of each winning side.**
(Photo: Allsport/G. Chadwick)

when they gained the maximum of 36 by winning all their 18 matches.

Cup Competitions

FA Cup The greatest number of wins is eight by: Tottenham Hotspur, 1901, 1921, 1961, 1962, 1967, 1981, 1982 and 1991; and Manchester United, 1909, 1948, 1963, 1977, 1983, 1985, 1990 and 1994. The most appearances in the final is 13 by Manchester United. The most goals in a final is seven; when Blackburn Rovers beat Sheffield Wednesday 6–1 in 1890 and when Blackpool beat Bolton Wanderers 4–3 in 1953. The biggest victory is six when Bury beat Derby County 6–0 in 1903, in which year Bury did not concede a single goal in their five Cup matches.

Scottish FA Cup The greatest number of wins is 30 by Celtic in 1892, 1899, 1900, 1904, 1907–8, 1911–12, 1914, 1923, 1925, 1927, 1931, 1933, 1937, 1951, 1954, 1965, 1967, 1969, 1971–2, 1974–5, 1977, 1980, 1985, 1988–9 and 1995.

Longest unbeaten run Nottingham Forest were undefeated in 42 consecutive First Division matches from 20 Nov 1977 to 9 Dec 1978. In Scottish Football Glasgow Celtic were undefeated in 62 matches (49 won, 13 drawn), 13 Nov 1915–21 April 1917.

Individual Records

Goal scoring

Match The most scored by one player in a first-class match is 16 by Stephan Stanis (né Stanikowski, b. Poland, 15 Jul 1913) for Racing Club de Lens v. Aubry-Asturies, in Lens, France, in a wartime French Cup game on 13 Dec 1942.

The record number of

Guess What?

Q. How loud is the loudest scream?

A. See Page 63

goals scored by one player in an international match is ten by Sofus Nielsen (1888–1963) for Denmark v. France (17–1) in the 1908 Olympics and by Gottfried Fuchs (1889–1972) for Germany who beat Russia 16–0 in the 1912 Olympic tournament (consolation event) in Sweden.

Season The most goals in a League season is 60 in 39 games by William Ralph 'Dixie' Dean (1907–80) for Everton (First Division) in 1927/8 and 66 in 38 games by James Smith (1902–76) for Ayr United (Scottish Second Division) in the same season. With three more in Cup ties and 19 in representative matches Dean's total was 82.

British Goal-Scoring Records

Scottish Cup 13
John Petrie, Arbroath v. Bon Accord, 5 Sep 1885.

Football League 10
Joe Payne (1914–77), Luton Town v. Bristol Rovers (Div 3S) at Luton on 13 Apr 1936.

Football League Division One 7
Ted Drake (1912–95), Arsenal v. Aston Villa at Birmingham on 14 Dec 1935
James David Ross, Preston North End v. Stoke at Preston on 6 Oct 1888.

Football League Cup 6
Frankie Bunn (b. 6 Oct 1962), Oldham Athletic v. Scarborough at Oldham on 25 Oct 1989.

FA Cup (Preliminary Round) 10
Chris Marron for South Shields v. Radcliffe at South Shields on 20 Sep 1947.

FA Cup 9
Edward 'Ted' MacDougall (b. 8 Jan 1947) for Bournemouth v. Margate (first round) at Bournemouth on 20 Nov 1971.

Scottish League 8
James Edward McGrory (1904–82) for Celtic v. Dunfermline (Div 1) at Celtic Park, Glasgow on 14 Jan 1928.

Home International 6
Joe Bambrick (b. 3 Nov 1905) for Ireland v. Wales at Belfast on 1 Feb 1930.

Career Artur Friedenreich (Brazil) (1892–1969) scored an undocumented 1329 goals in a 26 year first-class football career, 1909–35. The most goals scored in a specified period is 1279 by Edson Arantes do Nascimento (Brazil) (b. 23 Oct 1940), known as Pelé, from 7 Sep 1956 to 1 Oct 1977 in 1363 games. His best year was 1959 with 126, and the *Milesimo* (1000th) came from a penalty for his club Santos in the Maracanã Stadium, Rio de Janeiro on 19 Nov 1969 when playing his 909th first-class match. He later added two more goals in special appearances. Franz 'Bimbo' Binder (b. 1 Dec 1911) scored 1006 goals in 756 games in Austria and Germany between 1930 and 1950.

The international career record for England is 49 goals by Robert 'Bobby' Charlton (b. 11 Oct 1937). His first was v. Scotland on 19 Apr 1958 and his last on 20 May 1970 v. Colombia.

The greatest number of goals scored in British first-class football is 550 (410 in Scottish League matches) by James McGrory of Glasgow Celtic (1922–38). The most scored in League matches is 434, for West Bromwich Albion, Fulham, Leicester City and Shrewsbury Town, by George Arthur Rowley (b. 21 Apr 1926) between 1946 and April 1965. Rowley also scored 32 goals in the FA Cup and one for England 'B'.

Fastest goals The fastest Football League goals on record were scored in 6 seconds by Albert E. Mundy (b. 12 May 1926) (Aldershot) in a Fourth Division match v. Hartlepool United at Victoria Ground, Hartlepool, Cleveland on 25 Oct 1958, by Barrie Jones (b. 31 Oct 1938) (Notts County) in a Third Division match v. Torquay United on 31 Mar 1962, and by Keith Smith (b. 15 Sep 1940) (Crystal Palace) in a Second Division match v. Derby County at the Baseball Ground, Derby on 12 Dec 1964.

The fastest confirmed hat-trick is in 2½ minutes by Ephraim 'Jock' Dodds (b. 7 Sep 1915) for Blackpool v. Tranmere Rovers on 28 Feb 1942, and Jimmy Scarth (b. 26 Aug 1920) for Gillingham v. Leyton Orient in Third Division (Southern) on 1 Nov 1952. Tommy Bryce scored for Queen of the South in the 9th, 10th and 11th minute of their game against Arbroath on 18 Dec 1993. A hat-trick in 1 min 50 sec is claimed for Maglioni of Independiente v. Gimnasia y Escrima de la Plata in Argentina on 18 Mar 1973. John McIntyre (Blackburn Rovers) scored four goals in 5 min v. Everton at Ewood Park, Blackburn, Lancs on 16 Sep 1922. William 'Ginger' Richardson (West Bromwich Albion) scored four goals in 5 min utes from the kick-off against West Ham United at Upton Park on 7 Nov 1931. Frank Keetley scored six goals in 21 min in the second half of the Lincoln City v.

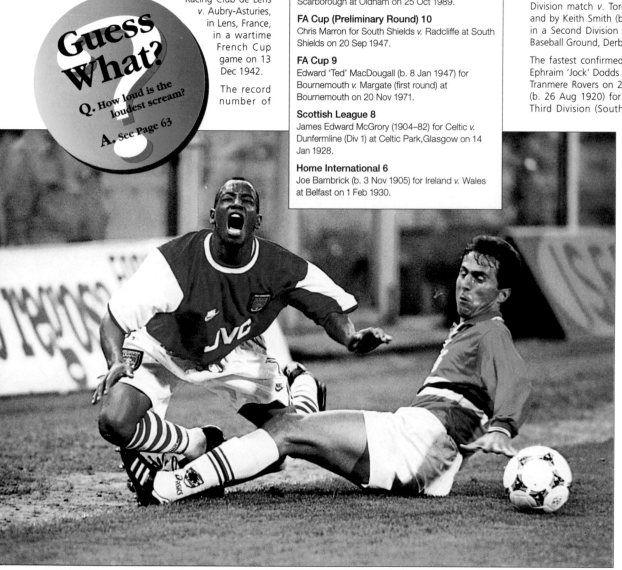

■ **Ian Wright of Arsenal became the first player in European club competitions to score in each leg of each round for a side that reached the final. He failed, however, to score in the final with Arsenal losing the Eurpopean Cup Winners' Cup to Real Zaragoza.**
(Photo: Allsport/B. Radford)

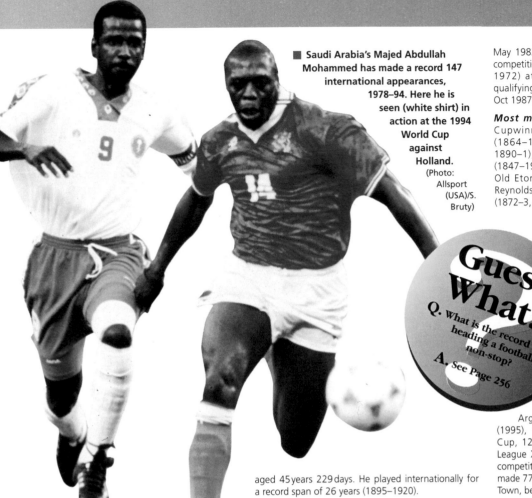

■ Saudi Arabia's Majed Abdullah Mohammed has made a record 147 international appearances, 1978–94. Here he is seen (white shirt) in action at the 1994 World Cup against Holland. (Photo: Allsport (USA)/S. Bruty)

Halifax Town league match on 16 Jan 1932. The international record is three goals in 3½ min by George William Hall (Tottenham Hotspur) for England against Ireland on 16 Nov 1938 at Old Trafford, Greater Manchester.

Fastest own goal Torquay United's Pat Kruse (b. 30 Nov 1953) equalled the fastest goal on record when he headed the ball into his own net only 6 seconds after kick-off *v.* Cambridge United on 3 Jan 1977.

Goalkeeping

The longest that any goalkeeper has succeeded in preventing any goals being scored past him in top-class competition is 1275 minutes by Abel Resino of Athletico Madrid to 17 Mar 1991. The record in international matches is 1142 minutes for Dino Zoff (Italy) (b. 22 Feb 1942), from September 1972 to June 1974.

The British club record in all competitive matches is 1196 minutes by Chris Woods (b. 14 Nov 1959) for Glasgow Rangers from 26 Nov 1986 to 31 Jan 1987.

International Caps

Oldest The oldest international has been William Henry 'Billy' Meredith (1874–1958) (Manchester City and United) who played outside right for Wales *v.* England at Highbury, London on 15 Mar 1920 when

aged 45 years 229 days. He played internationally for a record span of 26 years (1895–1920).

Youngest The youngest British international was Norman Whiteside, who played for Northern Ireland *v.* Yugoslavia at 17 yr 41 days on 17 Jun 1982.

England's youngest international was James Frederick McLeod Prinsep (1861–95) (Clapham Rovers) *v.* Scotland at Kennington Oval, London on 5 Apr 1879, at 17 yr 252 days. The youngest Welsh cap was Ryan Giggs (b. 29 Nov 1973) (Manchester United), *v.* Germany at Nuremburg, Germany on 16 Oct 1991, aged 17 yr 321 days. Scotland's youngest international has been John Alexander Lambie (1868–1923) (Queen's Park), at 17 yr 92 days *v.* Ireland on 20 Mar 1886. The youngest for the Republic of Ireland was James Holmes (b. 11 Nov 1953) (Coventry City), at 17 yr 200 days *v.* Austria in Dublin on 30 May 1971.

Most international appearances The greatest number of appearances for a national team is 147 by Majed Abdullah Mohammed (Saudi Arabia) from 1978 to 1994. The British record is Peter Shilton of England with 125.

The most international appearances by a woman for England is 85 by Gillian Coulthard to June 1995.

British International Appearances

ENGLAND 125, Peter Leslie Shilton (b. 18 Sep 1949) (Leicester City, Stoke City, Nottingham Forest, Southampton, Derby County) 1970–90.

NORTHERN IRELAND 119, Patrick Anthony Jennings (b. 12 Jun 1945) (Watford, Tottenham Hotspur, Arsenal) 1964–86

SCOTLAND 102, Kenneth Mathieson Dalglish (b. 4 Mar 1951) (Celtic, Liverpool) 1971–86

WALES 81, Neville Southall (b. 16 Sep 1958) (Everton) 1981–95

REPUBLIC OF IRELAND 77, Pat Bonner (b. 25 May 1960) (Celtic) 1981–94

Cup competitions

Youngest player The youngest player in an FA Cup final was James Prinsep (1861–95) for Clapham Rovers *v.* Old Etonians on 29 Mar 1879, aged 17 years 245 days. The youngest goal scorer in the FA Cup final was Norman Whiteside (b. 7 May 1965) for Manchester United *v.* Brighton at 18 yr 19 days on 26

May 1983. The youngest player ever in the FA Cup competition was full back Andrew Awford (b. 14 Jul 1972) at 15 yr 88 days for Worcester City in a qualifying round tie at Borehamwood, Herts on 10 Oct 1987.

Most medals Three players have won five FA Cupwinners' medals: James Henry Forrest (1864–1925) with Blackburn Rovers (1884–6, 1890–1); the Hon. Sir Arthur Fitzgerald Kinnaird (1847–1923) with Wanderers (1873, 1877–8) and Old Etonians (1879, 1882); and Charles Harold Reynolds Wollaston (1849–1926) with Wanderers (1872–3, 1876–8).

The most Scottish Cupwinners' medals won is eight by Charles Campbell (d. 1927) (Queen's Park) in 1874–6, 1880–82, 1884 and 1886.

Guess What?

Q. What is the record for heading a football non-stop?

A. See Page 256

Players

Most durable Peter Leslie Shilton (b. 18 Sep 1949) made a record 1380 senior UK appearances, including a record 996 League appearances, 286 for Leicester City (1966–74), 110 for Stoke City (1974–7), 202 for Nottingham Forest (1977–82), 188 for Southampton (1982–7), 175 for Derby County (1987–92), 34 for Plymouth Argyle (1992–4) and 1 for Bolton Wanderers (1995), 1 League play-off, 86 FA Cup, 102 League Cup, 125 internationals, 13 Under-23, 4 Football League XI and 53 various European and other club competitons. Norman John Trollope (b. 14 Jun 1943) made 770 League appearances for one club, Swindon Town, between 1960 and 1980.

Heaviest goalkeeper The biggest goalkeeper in representative football was the England international Willie Henry 'Fatty' Foulke (1874–1916), who stood 1.90 m *6 ft 3 in* and weighed 141 kg *22 st 3 lb*. His last games were for Bradford City, by which time he was 165 kg *26 st.* He once stopped a game by snapping the cross bar.

Fees

The highest transfer fee quoted for a player is a reported £13 million for Gianluigi Lentini (Italy), from Torino to AC Milan in June 1992.

The highest transfer fee for a British player is an estimated £8.5 million paid by Liverpool to Nottingham Forest for Stan Collymore (b. 22 Jan 1971) on 17 June 1995. This bettered by £1.5 million the previous record paid by Manchester Utd to Newcastle Utd for Andy Cole on 10 Jan 1995.

Attendances

Greatest crowds The greatest recorded crowd at any football match was 199,589 for the Brazil *v.* Uruguay World Cup match in the Maracanã Municipal Stadium, Rio de Janeiro, Brazil on 16 Jul 1950. The record attendance for a European Cup match is 136,505 at the semi-final between Glasgow Celtic and Leeds United at Hampden Park, Glasgow on 15 Apr 1970.

The British record paid attendance is 149,547 at the Scotland *v.* England international at Hampden Park, Glasgow on 17 Apr 1937. It is, however, probable that this total was exceeded (estimated 160,000) at the FA Cup final between Bolton Wanderers and West Ham United at Wembley Stadium on 28 Apr

1923, when the crowd spilled onto the pitch and the start was delayed 40 minutes until it was cleared. The counted admissions were 126,047.

The Scottish Cup record attendance is 146,433 when Celtic played Aberdeen at Hampden Park on 24 Apr 1937. The record attendance for a League match in Britain is 118,567 for Rangers v. Celtic at Ibrox Park, Glasgow on 2 Jan 1939.

The highest attendance at an amateur match has been 120,000 in Senayan Stadium, Jakarta, Indonesia on 26 Feb 1976 for the Pre-Olympic Group II final, North Korea v. Indonesia.

Smallest crowd The smallest crowd at a full home international was 2315 for Wales v. Northern Ireland on 27 May 1982 at the Racecourse Ground, Wrexham, Clwyd. The smallest paying attendance at a Football League fixture was for the Stockport County v. Leicester City match at Old Trafford, Manchester on 7 May 1921. Stockport's own ground was under suspension and the 'crowd' numbered 13 but an estimated 2000 gained free admission. When West Ham beat Castilla of Spain (5–1) in the European Cup Winners' Cup at Upton Park, Greater London on 1 Oct 1980 and when Aston Villa beat Besiktas of Turkey (3–1) in the European Cup at Villa Park, Birmingham on 15 Sep 1982, there were no paying spectators due to disciplinary action by the European Football Union.

> **Ken Ferris of Redbridge, Essex watched a League match at all the League grounds in England and Wales (including Berwick Rangers) in just 237 days, 10 Sep 1994- 6 May 1995. He began at Carlisle Utd and finished at Everton.**

Other Records (Non first-class games)

Highest scores *Teams* Drayton Grange Colts beat Eldon Sports Reserves 49–0 in a Daventry and District Sunday League match at Grange Estate, Northants on 13 Nov 1988. Every member of the side including the goalkeeper scored at least one goal.

In an Under-14 League match between Midas FC and Courage Colts, in Kent, on 11 Apr 1976, the full-time score after 70 minutes play was 59–1. Top scorer for Midas was Kevin Graham with 17 goals. Courage had scored the first goal.

Needing to improve their goal 'difference' to gain promotion in 1979, Ilinden FC of Yugoslavia, with the collusion of the opposition, Mladost, and the referee, won their final game of the season 134–1. Their rivals for promotion won their match, under similar circumstances, 88–0.

Individual Dean Goodliff scored 26 goals for Deleford Colts v. Iver Minors in the Slough Boys Soccer Combination Under-14 League at Iver, Bucks in his team's 33–0 win on 22 Dec 1985. The women's record is 22 goals by Linda Curl of Norwich Ladies in a 40–0 league victory over Milton Keynes Reserves at Norwich on 25 Sep 1983.

Season The greatest number of goals in a season reported for an individual player in junior professional league football is 96 by Tom Duffy (b. 7 Jan 1937), for Ardeer Thistle FC, Strathclyde in 1960/61. Paul Anthony Moulden (b. 6 Sep 1967) scored 289 goals in 40 games for Bolton Lads Club in Bolton Boys Federation intermediate league and cup matches in 1981/2. An additional 51 goals scored in other tour-

> **Goalkeeper Craig Manktelow (b. 5 Mar 1967) of Kawerau Electrical Services in New Zealand played 15 matches without conceding a goal, a total of 1350 min, from 6 May–19 Aug 1989.**

naments brought his total to 340, the highest season figure reported in any class of competitive football for an individual. He made his Football League debut for Manchester City on 1 Jan 1986 and has played for the England Youth team.

Fastest goals *Individual* Goals scored in 3 seconds and under after the kick-off have been achieved by a number of players. Damian Corcoran (b. 25 Nov 1976) scored three goals within a minute for 7th Fulwood Cubs v. 4th Fulwood Cubs on 1 Feb 1987.

Own goal The fastest own goal on record has been in 4 sec 'scored' by Richard Nash of Newick v. Burgess Hill Reserves at Newick, E Sussex on 8 Feb 1992.

Team The shortest time for a semi-professional team to score three goals from the start of a game is 122 sec by Burton Albion v. Redditch United in a Beazer Homes League Premier Division match on 2 Jan 1989.

Largest tournament The Metropolitan Police 5-a-side Youth Competition in 1981 attracted an entry of 7008 teams, a record for an FA sanctioned competition.

Most and least successful teams Winlaton West End FC, Tyne & Wear, completed a run of 95 league games without defeat between 1976 and 1980. Penlake Junior Football Club remained unbeaten for 153 games (winning 152 including 85 in succession) in the Warrington Hilden Friendly League from 1981 until defeated in 1986. Stockport United FC, of the Stockport Football League, lost 39 consecutive League and Cup matches, September 1976 to 18 Feb 1978.

Most indisciplined In the local cup match between Tongham Youth Club, Surrey and Hawley, Hants, on 3 Nov 1969, the referee booked all 22 players including one who went to hospital, and one of the linesmen. The match, won by Tongham 2–0, was described by a player as 'a good, hard game'.

In a Gancia Cup match at Waltham Abbey, Essex on 23 Dec 1973, the referee, Michael J. Woodhams, sent off the entire Juventus-Cross team and some club officials. Glencraig United, Faifley, near Clydebank, had all 11 team members and two substitutes for their 2–2 draw against Goldenhill Boys' Club on 2 Feb 1975 booked in the dressing room before a ball was kicked. The referee, Mr Tarbet of Bearsden, took exception to the chant which greeted his arrival. It was not his first meeting with Glencraig.

It was reported on 1 Jun 1993 that in a league match between Sportivo Ameliano and General Caballero in Paraguay, referee William Weiler sent off 20 players. Trouble flared after two Sportivo players were sent off, a ten-minute fight ensued and Weiler then dismissed a further 18 players, including the rest of the Sportivo team. Not suprisingly the match was abandonded.

Ball control Ricardinho Neves (Brazil) juggled a regulation soccer ball for 19 hr 5 min 31 sec nonstop with feet, legs and head without the ball ever touching the ground at the Los Angeles Convention Center, California, USA on 15–16 Jul 1994. The heading record is 7 hr 16 min by Tomas Lundman (Sweden) Valsta Centrum, Märsta, Sweden on 26 Nov 1994.

Jan Skorkovsky of Prague, Czechoslovakia kept a football up while he travelled a distance of 42.195 km 26.219 miles for the Prague City Marathon in 7 hr 18 min 55 sec on 8 Jul 1990.

Gaelic Football

All-Ireland Championships The greatest number of All-Ireland Championships won by one team is 30 by Ciarraidhe (Kerry) between 1903 and 1986. The greatest number of successive wins is four by Wexford (1915–18) and Kerry twice (1929–32, 1978–81).

The most finals contested by an individual is ten, including eight wins by the Kerry players Pat Spillane, Paudie O'Shea and Denis Moran, 1975–76, 1978–82, 1984–86.

The highest team score in a final was when Dublin, 27 (5 goals, 12 points) beat Armagh, 15 (3 goals, 6 points) on 25 Sep 1977. The highest combined score was 45 points when Cork (26) beat Galway (19) in 1973. A goal equals three points.

The highest individual score in an All-Ireland final has been 2 goals, 6 points by Jimmy Keaveney (Dublin) v. Armagh in 1977, and by Michael Sheehy (Kerry) v. Dublin in 1979.

Largest crowd The record crowd is 90,556 for the Down v. Offaly final at Croke Park, Dublin in 1961.

Gambling

Bingo

Largest house The largest 'house' in Bingo sessions was 15,756 at the Canadian National Exhibition, Toronto on 19 Aug 1983. Staged by the Variety Club of Ontario Tent Number 28, there was total prize money of $C250,000 with a record one-game payout of $C100,000.

Big win

The biggest individual gambling win is $111,240,463.10 by Leslie Robbins and Colleen DeVries of Fond du Lac, Wisconsin for the Powerball lottery drawn on 7 Jul 1993.

GB The largest prize won in any competition in Britain is £22,590,829 won by Mark Gardiner and Paul Maddison of Hastings, E Sussex on the National Lottery for the draw made on 10 Jun 1995.

Earliest and latest Full House A 'Full House' call occurred on the 15th number by Norman A. Wilson at Guide Post Working Men's Club, Bedlington, Northumberland on 22 Jun 1978, by Anne Wintle of Bryncethin, Mid Glam, on a coach trip to Bath on 17 Aug 1982 and by Shirley Lord at Kahibah Bowling Club, New South Wales, Australia on 24 Oct 1983.

'House' was not called until the 86th number at the Hillsborough Working Men's Club, Sheffield, S Yorks on 11 Jan 1982. There were 32 winners.

Football Pools

The winning dividend paid out by Littlewoods Pools in their first week in February 1923 was £2 12s 0d. In

Guess What?
Q. What is the largest crowd for a sports event?
A. See Page 220

World & British Gliding Single-Seater Records

Category	Distance	Name	Location	Date
Straight Distance	1460.8km *907.7miles*	Hans-Werner Grosse (West Germany)	Lübeck, Germany to Biarritz, France	25 Apr 1972
(British)	949.70km *590.1miles*	Karla Karel	Australia	20 Jan 1980
Declared Goal Distance	1254.26km *779.36miles*	Bruce Lindsey Drake (New Zealand)	Te Anau to Te Araroa, New Zealand	14 Jan 1978
		David Napier Speight (New Zealand)	Te Anau to Te Araroa, New Zealand	14 Jan 1978
		Sholto Hamilton 'Dick' Georgeson (New Zealand)	Te Anau to Te Araroa, New Zealand	14 Jan 1978
(British)	859.2km *534miles*	M. T. Alan Sands	Ridge soaring to Chilhowee, Va, USA	23 Apr 1986
Goal and Return	1646.68km *1023.20miles*	Thomas L. Knauff (USA)	Gliderport to Williamsport, Pa, USA	25 Apr 1983
(British)	1127.68km *700.72miles*	M. T. Alan Sands	Lock Haven, Pa to Bluefield, Va, USA	7 May 1985
Absolute Altitude	14,938m *49,009ft*	Robert R. Harris (USA)	California, USA	17 Feb 1986
(British)	11,500m *37,729ft*	H. C. Nicholas Goodhart	California, USA ..1	2 May 1955
Height Gain	12,894m *42,303ft*	Paul F. Bikle (USA)	Mojave, Lancaster, California, USA	25 Feb 1961
(British)	10,065m *33,022ft*	David Benton	Portmoak, Scotland	18 Apr 1980

SPEED OVER TRIANGULAR COURSE

Distance	km/h	mph	Name	Location	Date
100km	195.3	*121.35*	Ingo Renner (Australia)	Tocumwal, Australia	14 Dec 1982
(British)	166.38	*103.38*	Bruce Cooper	Australia	4 Jan 1991
300km	169.50	*105.32*	Jean-Paul Castel (France)	Bitterwasser, Namibia	15 Nov 1986
(British)	146.8	*91.2*	Edward Pearson	S. W. Africa (now Namibia)	30 Nov 1976
500km	170.06	*105.67*	Beat Bünzli (Switzerland)	Bitterwasser, Namibia	9 Jan 1988
(British)	141.3	*87.8*	Bradley James Grant Pearson	South Africa	28 Dec 1982
750km	158.41	*98.43*	Hans-Werner Grosse (West Germany)	Alice Springs, Australia	8 Jan 1985
(British)	109.8	*68.2*	Michael R. Carlton	South Africa	5 Jan 1975
1000km	145.33	*90.30*	Hans-Werner Grosse (West Germany)	Alice Springs, Australia	3 Jan 1979
(British)	112.15	*69.68*	George Lee	Australia	25 Jan 1989
1250km	133.24	*82.79*	Hans-Werner Grosse (West Germany)	Alice Springs, Australia	9 Dec 1980
(British)	109.01	*67.73*	Robert L. Robertson	USA	2 May 1986

1992/3 the three British Pools companies which comprise the Pool Promoters Association (Littlewoods, Vernons and Zetters) had a total record turnover of £963,753,000, of which Littlewoods contributed over 70 per cent.

Biggest win *British* The record individual payout is £2,924,622.60 paid by Littlewoods Pools to a syndicate at the Yew Tree Inn, Worsley, Greater Manchester for matches played on 19 Nov 1994.

The record total payout in a single week is £4,457,671 by Littlewoods for matches on 12 Mar 1994.

The greatest number of First Dividend wins by an individual is 832 by A.W.E. Summons of Haverfordwest, Powys, totalling £382,667, 1962–95.

Horse Racing

Highest ever odds The highest secured odds were 3,072,887 to 1 by an unnamed woman from Nottingham. For a 5p accumulator on five horses on 2 May 1995, she won £153,644.40 paid by Ladbrokes.

Edward Hodson of Wolverhampton, W Mids landed a 3,956,748 to 1 bet for a 55p stake on 11 Feb 1984, but his bookmaker had a £3000 payout limit.

The world record odds on a 'double' are 31,793 to 1 paid by the New Zealand Totalisator Agency Board on a five shilling tote ticket on *Red Emperor* and *Maida Dillon* at Addington, Christchurch in 1951.

Greatest payout Anthony A. Speelman and Nicholas John Cowan (both Great Britain) won $1,627,084.40, after federal income tax of $406,768.00 was withheld, on a $64 nine-horse accumulator at Santa Anita racecourse, California, USA on 19 Apr 1987. Their first seven selections won and the payout was for a jackpot, accumulated over 24 days.

The largest payout by a British bookmaker is £567,066.25 by Ladbrokes, paid to Dick Mussell of Havant, Hants for a combination of an accumulator, trebles, doubles and singles on five horses at Cheltenham on 12 Mar 1992.

Biggest tote win The best recorded tote win was one of £341 2s 6d to 2s representing odds of 3410¼

to 1, by Catharine Unsworth of Blundellsands, Liverpool, Merseyside at Haydock Park on a race won by *Coole* on 30 Nov 1929. The highest odds in Irish tote history were £289.64 for a 10p unit on *Gene's Rogue* at Limerick on 28 Dec 1981.

Largest bookmaker The world's largest bookmaker is Ladbrokes with a peak turnover from gambling in 1988 of £2107 million and the largest chain of betting shops, over 1900 in Great Britain and the Republic of Ireland at 1 Jul 1993, as well as outlets in Germany and Belgium.

Topmost tipster The only recorded instance of a racing correspondent forecasting ten out of ten winners on a race card was at Delaware Park, Wilmington, Delaware, USA on 28 Jul 1974 by Charles Lamb of the *Baltimore News American*.

The best performance by a British correspondent is seven out of seven winners at a meeting at Wolverhampton on 22 Mar 1982 by Bob Butchers of the *Daily Mirror*. This was repeated by Fred Shawcross of the *Today* newspaper at York on 12 May 1988. In greyhound racing the best performance is 12 out of 12 by Mark Sullivan of the *Sporting Life* for a meeting at Wimbledon on 21 Dec 1990.

Slot machines The biggest beating handed to a 'one-armed bandit' was $9,357,489.41 by Delores Adams, 60, at the Harrah's Reno Casino-Hotel, Nevada, USA on 30 May 1992.

Gliding

Most titles The most World Individual Championships (instituted 1937) won is four by Ingo Renner (Australia) in 1976 (Standard class), 1983, 1985 and 1987 (Open).

British The British National Championship (instituted 1939) has been won eight times by Ralph Jones (b. 29 Mar 1936). The first woman to win this title was

Anne Burns (b. 23 Nov. 1915) of Farnham, Surrey on 30 May 1966.

Women's altitude records The women's single-seater world record for absolute altitude is 12,637m *41,460ft* by Sabrina Jackintell (USA) in an Astir GS on 14 Feb 1979.

The height gain record is 10,212m *33,504ft* by Yvonne Loader (New Zealand) at Omarama, New Zealand on 12 Jan 1988.

The British single-seater absolute altitude record is 10,550m *34,612ft* by Anne Burns in a Skylark 3B over South Africa on 13 Jan 1961, when she set a then world record and still a British record for height gain of 9119m *29,918ft*.

Hang Gliding

World Championships The World Team Championships (officially instituted 1976) have been won most often by Great Britain (1981, 1985, 1989 and 1991).

World records The *Fédération Aéronautique Internationale* recognizes world records for rigid-wing, flexwing and multi-place flexwing. These records are the greatest in each category.

Men Greatest distance in straight line and declared goal distance: 488.2km *303.3miles* Larry Tudor (USA), Hobbs Airpark, New Mexico to Elkhart, Kansas, 3 Jul 1990. Height gain: 4343m *14,250ft* Larry Tudor (USA), Owens Valley, California, 4 Aug 1985.

Out and return distance: 310.3km *192.8miles* Larry Tudor (USA) and Geoffrey Loyns (GB), Owens Valley, 26 Jun 1988. Triangular course distance: 196.1km *121.79miles* James Lee (USA), Wild Horse Mesa, Colorado, 4 Jul 1991.

Women Greatest distance: 335.8km *208.6miles* Kari Castle (USA), Owens Valley, 22 Jul 1991. Height gain:

Guess What?
Q. Who were the last persons to be hung in Britain?
A. See Page 190

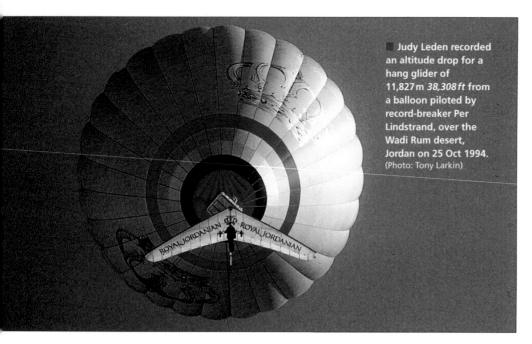

■ Judy Leden recorded an altitude drop for a hang glider of 11,827 m *38,308 ft* from a balloon piloted by record-breaker Per Lindstrand, over the Wadi Rum desert, Jordan on 25 Oct 1994. (Photo: Tony Larkin)

3970 m *13,025 ft* Judy Leden (GB) Kuruman, South Africa, 1 Dec 1992.

Out and return distance via single turn: 292.1 km *181.5 miles* Kari Castle (USA), Hobbs Airpark, 1 Jul 1990. Declared goal distance: 212.50 km *132.04 miles* Liavan Mallin (Ireland), Owens Valley, 13 Jul 1989.

Triangular course distance: Judy Leden (GB), 114.1 km *70.9 miles*, Kössen, Austria, 22 Jun 1991.

British The British record for distance is held by Geoffrey Loyns, 312.864 km *194.41 miles*, in Flagstaff, Arizona, USA on 11 Jun 1988. The best in Britain is 244 km *151.62 miles* by Gordon Rigg from Lords Seat to Witham Friary, Somerset on 4 Jun 1989.

Golf

Oldest club The oldest club of which there is written evidence is the Gentlemen Golfers (now the Honourable Company of Edinburgh Golfers) formed in March 1744 – ten years prior to the institution of the Royal and Ancient Club of St Andrews, Fife. However, the Royal Burgess Golfing Society of Edinburgh claims to have been founded in 1735.

Longest hole The longest hole in the world is the 7th hole (par-7) of the Satsuki GC, Sano, Japan, which measures 964 yd *881 m*.

The longest hole in Great Britain is the second at Gedney Hill, Lincs, which stretches 613 m *671 yd*.

Largest green Probably the largest green in the world is that of the par-6 635 m *695 yd* fifth hole at International GC, Bolton, Massachusetts, USA, with an area greater than 2600 m² *28,000 ft²*.

Highest shot on Earth Gerald Williams (USA) played a shot from the summit of Mt Aconcagua (6960 m *22,834 ft*), Argentina on 22 Jan 1989.

Biggest bunker The world's biggest bunker (called a trap in the USA) is Hell's Half Acre on the 535 m *585 yd* seventh hole of the Pine Valley course,

Clementon, New Jersey, USA, built in 1912 and generally regarded as the world's most trying course.

Longest course The world's longest course is the par-77 7612 m *8325 yd* International GC, Bolton, Massachussetts, USA, from the 'Tiger' tees, remodelled in 1969 by Robert Trent Jones.

Floyd Satterlee Rood used the United States as a course, when he played from the Pacific surf to the Atlantic surf from 14 Sep 1963 to 3 Oct 1964 in 114,737 strokes. He lost 3511 balls on the 5468 km *3397.7 mile* 'fairway'.

Golf Club

Golf club A Scottish iron golf club of *c.* 1700 sold for £92,400 at Sotheby's sale of golfing memorabilia at Loretto School, Musselburgh, Lothian, held on 13 Jul 1992 to coincide with the 121st Open Championship. It was bought by Titus Kendall on behalf of the Valderamma Golf Club in Sotte Grande, Spain.

Golf ball On 14 Jul 1992 Titus Kendall also paid a record £19,250 at Phillips, Edinburgh for a gutta (latex-type) golf ball made by Scot Allan Robertson in 1849.

Longest drives The greatest recorded drive on an ordinary course is one of 471 m *515 yd* by Michael Hoke Austin (b. 17 Feb 1910) of Los Angeles, California, USA, in the US National Seniors Open Championship at Las Vegas, Nevada on 25 Sep 1974. Austin, 1.88 m *6 ft 2 in* tall and weighing 92 kg *203 lb*, drove the ball to within a yard of the green on the par-4 412 m *450 yd* fifth hole of the Winterwood Course and it rolled 59 m *65 yd* past the flagstick. He was aided by an estimated 56 km/h *35 mph* tailwind.

Longest putt The longest recorded holed putt in a major tournament is 110 ft by; Jack Nicklaus (b. 21 Jan 1940) in the 1964 Tournament of Champions; and Nick Price in the 1992 United States PGA.

Robert Tyre 'Bobby' Jones Jr, (1902–71) was reputed to have holed a putt in excess of 30 m *100 ft* at the fifth green in the first round of the 1927 Open at St Andrews.

Bob Cook (USA) sank a putt measured at 42.74 m *140 ft 2¾ in* on the 18th at St Andrews in the International Fourball Pro Am Tournament on 1 Oct 1976.

Scores

Lowest 9 holes Nine holes in 25 (4, 3, 3, 2, 3, 3, 1, 4, 2) was recorded by A. J. 'Bill' Burke in a round of 57 (32+25) on the 5842 m *6389 yd* par-71

Normandie course at St Louis, Missouri, USA on 20 May 1970.

The tournament record is 27 by Mike Souchak (USA) (b. 10 May 1927) for the second nine (par-35), first round of the 1955 Texas Open (<> 72 holes); Andy North (USA) (b. 9 Mar 1950) second nine (par-34), first round, 1975 BC Open at En-Joie GC, Endicott, New York; José Maria Canizares (Spain) (b. 18 Feb 1947), first nine, third round, in the 1978 Swiss Open on the 6228 m *6811 yd* Crans GC, Crans-sur-Seine; and Robert Lee (GB) (b. 12 Oct 1961) first nine, first round, in the Monte Carlo Open on the 5714 m *6249 yd* Mont Agel course on 28 Jun 1985.

Lowest 18 holes *Men* At least four players have played a long course (over 6000 m *6561 yd*) in a score of 58, most recently Monte Carlo Money (USA) (b. 3 Dec 1954) at the par-72, 6041 m *6607 yd* Las Vegas Municipal GC, Nevada, USA on 11 Mar 1981.

Alfred Edward Smith (1903–85) achieved an 18-hole score of 55 (15 under par 70) on his home course of 3884 m *4248 yd*, scoring 4, 2, 3, 4, 2, 4, 3, 4, 3=29 out, and 2, 3, 3, 3, 3, 2, 5, 4, 1=26 in, on 1 Jan 1936.

The United States PGA Tournament record for 18 holes is 59 by Al Geiberger (b. 1 Sep 1937) (30+29) in the second round of the Danny Thomas Classic, on the 72-par 6628 m *7249 yd* Colonial GC course, Memphis, Tennessee on 10 Jun 1977; and by Chip Beck in the third round of the Las Vegas Invitational, on the 72-par 6381 m *6979 yd* Sunrise GC course, Las Vegas, Nevada on 11 Oct 1991.

Other golfers to have recorded 59 over 18 holes in major non-PGA tournaments include: Samuel Jackson 'Sam' Snead (b. 27 May 1912) in the third round of the Sam Snead Festival at White Sulphur Springs, West Virginia, USA on 16 May 1959; Gary Player (South Africa) (b. 1 Nov 1935) in the second round of the Brazilian Open in Rio de Janeiro on 29 Nov 1974; David Jagger (GB) (b. 9 Jun 1949) in a Pro-Am tournament prior to the 1973 Nigerian Open at Ikoyi GC, Lagos; and Miguel Martin (Spain) in the Argentine Southern Championship at Mar de Plata on 27 Feb 1987.

Women The lowest recorded score on an 18-hole course (over 5120 m *5600 yd*) for a woman is 62 (30+32) by Mary 'Mickey' Kathryn Wright (USA) (b. 14 Feb 1935) on the Hogan Park Course (par-71, 5747 m *6286 yd*) at Midland, Texas, USA, in November 1964, Janice Arnold (New Zealand) (31+31) at the Coventry Golf Club, W Mids (5317 m *5815 yd*) on 24 Sep 1990, Laura Davies (GB) (b. 5 Oct 1963) (32+30) at the Rail Golf Club, Springfield, Illinois, USA on 31 Aug 1991, and Hollis Stacy (b. 16 Mar 1954) at Meridian Valley, Seattle, Washington, USA on 18 Sep 1994.

Wanda Morgan (b. 22 Mar 1910) recorded a score of 60 (31+29) on the Westgate and Birchington GC course, Kent, over 18 holes (4573 m *5002 yd*) on 11 Jul 1929.

Great Britain The lowest score recorded in a professional tournament on a course of more than 5490 m *6000 yd* in Great Britain is 60 by: Paul Curry in the second round of the Bell's Scottish Open on the King's course (5899 m *6452 yd*), Gleneagles, Tayside on 9 Jul 1992; and Keith MacDonald in the third round of the Barratt Golf Mid Kent Classic at Mid Kent (5675 m *6206 yd*) GC, Gravesend, Kent on 6 Aug 1993.

Lowest 36 holes The record for 36 holes is 122 (59+63) by Sam Snead in the 1959 Sam Snead Festival on 16–17 May 1959.

Horton Smith (1908–63), twice US Masters

Guess What?

Q. What is the lowest 36-hole score in the US Open?

A. See Page 260

Most Major Golf Titles

The Open	Harry Vardon (1870–1937)	6	1896, 1898–9, 1903, 11, 14
The Amateur	John Ball (1861–1940)	8	1888, 90, 92, 94, 99, 1907, 10, 12
US Open	William 'Willie' Anderson (1880–1910)	4	1901, 03–05
	Robert Tyre 'Bobby' Jones Jr (1902–71)	4	1923, 26, 29–30
	William Benjamin Hogan (b. 13 Aug 1912)	4	1948, 50–51, 53
	Jack William Nicklaus (b. 21 Jan 1940)	4	1962, 67, 72, 80
US Amateur	Robert Tyre Jones Jr	5	1924–25, 27–8, 30
US PGA	Walter Charles Hagan (1892–1969)	5	1921, 24–7
	Jack William Nicklaus	5	1963, 71, 73, 75, 80
US Masters	Jack William Nicklaus	6	1963, 65–6, 72, 75, 86
US Women's Open	Elizabeth 'Betsy' Earle-Rawls (b. 4 May 1928)	4	1951, 53, 57, 60
	'Mickey' Wright (b. 14 Feb 1935)	4	1958–59, 61, 64
US Women's Amateur	Glenna Collett Vare (née Collett) (1903–89)	6	1922, 25, 28–30, 35
British Women's	Charlotte Cecilia Pitcairn Leitch (1891–1977)	4	1914, 20–21, 26
	Joyce Wethered (b. 17 Nov 1901) (Now Lady Heathcoat-Amory)	4	1922, 24–5, 29

Note: Nicklaus is the only golfer to have won 5 different major titles (The Open, US Open, Masters, PGA and US Amateur titles) twice and a record 20 all told (1959–86). In 1930 Bobby Jones achieved a unique 'Grand Slam' of the US and British Open and Amateur titles.

Champion, scored 121 (63+58) on a short course on 21 Dec 1928 (⇔ 72 holes).

The lowest score by a British golfer has been 124 (61+63) by Alexander Walter Barr 'Sandy' Lyle (b. 9 Feb 1958) in the Nigerian Open at the 5508 m *6024 yd* (par-71) Ikoyi GC, Lagos in 1978.

Lowest 72 holes The lowest recorded score on a first-class course is 255 (29 under par) by Leonard Peter Tupling (GB) (b. 6 Apr 1950) in the Nigerian Open at Ikoyi GC, Lagos in February 1981, made up of 63, 66, 62 and 64 (average 63.75 per round).

The lowest 72 holes in a US professional event is 257 (60, 68, 64, 65) by Mike Souchak in the 1955 Texas Open at San Antonio.

The 72 holes record on the European tour is 258 (64, 69, 60, 65) by David Llewellyn (b. 18 Nov 1951) in the Biarritz Open on 1–3 Apr 1988. This was equalled by Ian Woosnam (Wales) (b. 2 Mar 1958) (66, 67, 65, 60) in the Monte Carlo Open on 4–7 Jul 1990.

The lowest 72 holes in an open championship in Europe is 262 (67, 66, 66, 63) by Percy Alliss (GB) (1897–1975) in the 1932 Italian Open at San Remo, and by Lu Liang Huan (Taiwan) (b. 10 Dec 1935) in the 1971 French Open at Biarritz.

The lowest for four rounds in a British first-class tournament is 262 (66, 63, 66, 67) by Bernard Hunt in the Piccadilly Tournament on the par-68 5655 m *6184 yd* Wentworth East course, Virginia Water, Surrey on 4–5 Oct 1966.

The lowest four round total in a US LPGA Championship event is 267 (68, 66, 67, 66) by Betsy King (USA) (b. 13 Aug 1955) in the Mazda LPGA Championship on the par-71 5735 m *6272 yd* Bethesda Contry Club course, Bethesda, Maryland, USA on 14–17 May 1992. She won by 11 strokes and was 17 under-par, both LPGA Championship records.

Trish Johnson (b. 17 Jan 1966) scored 242 (64, 60, 60, 58) (21 under par) in the Bloor Homes Eastleigh Classic at the Fleming Park Course (4025 m *4402 yd*) at Eastleigh, Hants on 22–25 Jul 1987.

Horton Smith scored 245 (63, 58, 61 and 63) for 72 holes on the 4297 m *4700 yd* course (par-64) at Catalina Country Club, California, USA, to win the Catalina Open on 21–23 Dec 1928.

Most Shots

Most shots for one hole The highest score for a single hole in the British Open is 21 by a player in the inaugural meeting at Prestwick in 1860.

Double figures have been recorded on the card of the winner only once, when Willie Fernie (1851–1924) scored a ten at Musselburgh, Lothian in 1883.

World one-club record Thad Daber (USA), with a 6-iron, played the 5520 m *6037 yd* Lochmore GC, Cary, North Carolina, USA in 70 to win the 1987 World One-club Championship.

Throwing the golf ball The lowest recorded score for throwing a golf ball round 18 holes (over 5490 m *6000 yd*) is 82 by Joe Flynn (USA), 21, at the 5695 m *6228 yd* Port Royal course, Bermuda on 27 Mar 1975.

The longest throw is 120.24 m by Stefan Uhr (Sweden) at Prästholmen, Mora, Sweden on 20 Aug 1992.

Fastest rounds *Individual* With such variations in lengths of courses, speed records, even for rounds under par, are of little comparative value. The fastest round played when the golf ball comes to rest before each new stroke is 27 min 9 sec by James Carvill (b. 13 Oct 1965) at Warrenpoint Golf Course, Co. Down (18 holes, 5628 m *6154 yd*) on 18 Jun 1987.

Most Holes

Most holes played in a week Steve Hylton played 1128 holes at the Mason Rudolph GC (5541 m *6060 yd*), Clarksville, Tennessee, USA from 25–31 Aug 1980. Using a buggy for transport, Colin Young completed 1260 holes at Patshull Park GC (5863 m *6412 yd*), Pattingham, Shropshire from 2–9 Jul 1988.

Team The 35 members of the Team Balls Out Diving completed the 18-hole 5516 m *6033 yd* John E. Clark course at Point Micu, California, USA in 9 min 39 sec on 16 Nov 1992. They scored 71!

Most holes in 12/24 hours *On foot* Ian Colston, 35, played 22 rounds and five holes (401 holes) at Bendigo GC, Victoria, Australia (par-73, 5542 m *6061 yd*) on 27–28 Nov 1971.

The British record is 360 holes by Antony J. Clark at Childwall GC, Liverpool on 18 Jul 1983.

David Brett of Stockport played 218 holes in 12 hours at Didsbury GC, Greater Manchester (par-70, 5696 m *6230 yd*) on 22 Jun 1990.

Using golf carts David Cavalier played 846 holes at Arrowhead Country Club, North Canton, Ohio, USA (9-hole course, 2755 m *3013 yd*) on 6–7 Aug 1990. The best by a women is 509 by Cyndy Lent (USA) at Twin Lakes Country Club, Wisconsin on 7–8 Aug 1994.

Most balls hit in one hour The most balls driven in one hour, over 100 yards and into a target area, is 1536 by Noel Hunt at Shrigley Hall, Pott Shrigley, Cheshire on 2 May 1990.

Championship Records

The Open (inaugurated 1860, Prestwick, Strathclyde) *Any round* 63 by: Mark Stephen Hayes (USA) (b. 12 Jul 1949) at Turnberry, Strathclyde on 7 Jul 1977; Isao Aoki (Japan) (b. 31 Aug 1942) at Muirfield, Lothian on 19 Jul 1980; Gregory John Norman (Australia) (b. 10 Feb 1955) at Turnberry on 18 Jul 1986; Paul Broadhurst (GB) (b. 14 Aug 1965) at St Andrews, Fife on 21 Jul 1990; Joseph Martin 'Jodie' Mudd (USA) (b. 23 Apr 1960) at Royal Birkdale on 21 Jul 1991; Nicholas Alexander 'Nick' Faldo (GB) (b. 18 Jul 1957) on 16 July and William Payne Stewart (USA) (b. 30 Jan 1957) on 18 July, both at Royal St George's, Sandwich, Kent in 1993.

First 36 holes Nick Faldo completed the first 36 holes at Muirfield, Lothian in 130 strokes (66, 64) on 16–17 Jul 1992. (Faldo added a third round of 69 to equal the 54-hole record of 199 which he had set at St Andrews in 1990 (67, 65, 67)).

■ Jack Nicklaus is the only golfer to have won each of golf's four Majors at least three times. Only three other golfers have won all the Majors; Gene Sarazen, Gary Player and Ben Hogan but none have also matched Nicklaus' achievement of winning the US Amateur twice as well.
(Photo: Allsport (USA)/G. Newkirk)

■ Britain's Laura Davies is currently the world's number one lady golfer. In 1994 she became the first European golfer to head the money list for the LPGA tour in the USA and worldwide she won eight tournaments uniquely on five tours: 3 in the USA, 2 in Europe, 1 in Japan, 1 in Asia (Thailand) and 1 in Australia.
(Photo: Allsport/D. Cannon)

Total aggregate 267 (66, 68, 69, 64) by Greg Norman (Australia) at Royal St George's, 15–18 Jul 1993.

US Open (inaugurated in 1895) *Any round* 63 by: Johnny Miller (b. 29 Apr 1947) on the 6328 m *6921 yd* par-71 Oakmont Country Club course, Pennsylvania on 17 Jun 1973; by Jack Nicklaus and Tom Weiskopf (USA) (b. 9 Nov 1942) at Baltusrol Country Club (6414 m *7015 yd*), Springfield, New Jersey, both on 12 Jun 1980.

First 36 holes 134 by: Jack Nicklaus (63, 71) at Baltusrol, 12–13 Jun 1980; Chen Tze-Chung (Taiwan) (65, 69) at Oakland Hills, Birmingham, Michigan in 1985; and Lee Janzen (USA) (b. 28 Aug 1964) (67, 67) at Baltusrol, 17–18 Jun 1993.

Total aggregate 272 by: Jack Nicklaus (63, 71, 70, 68) at Baltusrol, 12–15 Jun 1980; and by Lee Janzen (67, 67, 69, 69) at Baltusrol, 17–20 Jun 1993.

US Masters (played on the 6382 m *6980 yd* Augusta National Golf Course, Georgia, first in 1934) *Any round* 63 by Nicholas Raymond Leige Price (Zimbabwe) (b. 28 Jan 1957) in 1986.

First 36 holes 131 (65, 66) by Raymond Loran Floyd (b. 4 Sep 1942) in 1976.

Total aggregate 271 by: Jack Nicklaus (67, 71, 64, 69) in 1965 and Raymond Floyd (65, 66, 70, 70) in 1976.

■ Americans Fred Couples and Davis Love III celebrate winning golf's World Cup at Dorado, Puerto Rico from 10–13 Nov 1994. It was the USA's record 20th success and the third in succession for Couples and Love, who also set the record for the lowest aggregate score with 536 (Couples individual record of 265).
(Photo: Allsport/S. Munday)

Team Competitons

World Cup (formerly Canada Cup) The World Cup (instituted as the Canada Cup in 1953) has been won most often by the USA with 20 victories between 1955 and 1994.

The only men to have been on six winning teams have been Arnold Palmer (b. 10 Sep 1929) (1960, 1962–4, 1966–7) and Jack Nicklaus (1963–4, 1966–7, 1971 and 1973). Only Nicklaus has taken the individual title three times (1963–4, 1971).

Ryder Cup

The biennial Ryder Cup professional match between the USA and Europe (British Isles or Great Britain prior to 1979) was instituted in 1927. The USA has won 23 to 5 (with 2 draws) to 1993.

Arnold Palmer has the record of winning most Ryder Cup matches with 22 from 32 played, with two halved and 8 lost. Christy O'Connor Sr (Ireland) (b. 21 Dec 1924) played in ten contests, 1955–73.

The lowest aggregate score for 144 holes is 536 by the USA, Fredrick Stephen Couples (b. 3 Oct 1959) and Davis Love III, at Dorado, Puerto Rico from 10–13 Nov 1994. Couples total of 265 is an individual record.

Walker Cup The series was instituted in 1921 (for the Walker Cup since 1922 and now held biennially). The USA have won 30, Great Britain & Ireland 3 (in 1938, 1971 and 1989) and the 1965 match was tied.

Jay Sigel (USA) (b. 13 Nov 1943) has won a record 18 matches, with five halved and ten lost, 1977–93. Joseph Boynton Carr (GB & I) (b. 18 Feb 1922) played in ten contests, 1947–67.

Curtis Cup The biennial ladies' Curtis Cup match between the USA and Great Britain and Ireland was first held in 1932. The USA have won 20 to 1994, GB & I five (1952, 1956, 1986, 1988 and 1992) and three matches have been tied.

Mary McKenna (GB & I) (b. 29 Apr 1949) played in a record ninth match in 1986, when for the first time she was on the winning team. Carole Semple Thompson (USA) has won a record 15 matches in 8 contests, 1974–94.

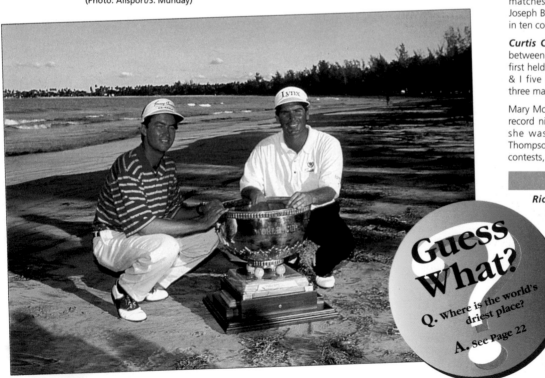

Individual Records

Richest prize The greatest first place prize money ever won is $1,000,000 awarded annually from 1987 to 1991 to the winners of the Sun City Challenge, Bophuthatswana, South Africa; Ian Woosnam (Wales) was the first winner in 1987.

The greatest total prize money is $2,700,000 (including $550,000 first prize) for the Johnnie Walker World Championship at Tryall GC, Montego Bay, Jamaica in 1992, 1993 and 1994.

Highest earnings US PGA and LPGA circuits The all-time career earnings record

Guess What?
Q. Where is the world's driest place?
A. See Page 22

on the US PGA circuit is held by Tom Kite (USA) (b. 9 Dec 1949) with $9,261,125, 1982–4 June 1995. Nick Price (Zimbabwe) won a season's record $1,499,927 in 1994. Greg Norman (Australia) has won a record $14,618,816 worldwide, 1976–June 1995.

The record career earnings for a woman is by Betsy King with $5,027,628 to 26 May 1995. The season's record is $863,578 by Elizabeth Ann 'Beth' Daniel (b. 14 Oct 1956) in 1990.

European circuit Colin Stuart Montgomerie (b. 23 Jun 1963) won a season's record £762,719 in European Order of Merit tournaments in 1994. Nick Faldo won a record £1,558,978 worldwide in 1992. He also holds the tour career earnings record with £3,988,568 (28 tour victories), 1976–1994.

Most tournament wins John Byron Nelson (USA) (b. 4 Feb 1912) won a record 18 tournaments (plus one unofficial) in one year, including a record 11 consecutively from 8 Mar to 4 Aug 1945.

Sam Snead from turning professional in 1934 won 84 official US PGA tour events, 1936–65. The ladies' PGA record is 88 by Kathy Whitworth (b. 27 Sep 1939) from 1959 to 1991. The most career victories in European Order of Merit tournaments is 55 by Severiano Ballesteros (Spain) (b. 9 Apr 1957), 1974–95.

Biggest winning margin The greatest margin of victory in a major tournament is 21 strokes by Jerry Pate (USA) (b. 16 Sep 1953), who won the Colombian Open with 262 from 10–13 Dec 1981.

Charlotte Cecilia Pitcairn Leitch (1891–1973) won the Canadian Ladies' Open Championship in 1921 by the biggest margin for a major title, 17 up and 15 to play.

Youngest and oldest champions The youngest winner of The Open was Tom Morris Jr (1851–75) at Prestwick, Strathclyde in 1868 aged 17 years 249 days.

The oldest Open champion was 'Old Tom' Morris (1821–1908), aged 46 yr 99 days when he won at Prestwick in 1867. Oldest this century has been the 1967 champion, Roberto de Vincenzo, at 44 yr 93 days.

The oldest US Open champion was Hale Irwin (USA) (b. 3 Jun 1945) at 45 yr 15 days on 18 Jun 1990.

Most club championships Helen Gray has been ladies champion at Todmorden GC, Lancs 38 times between 1952 and 1993.

The men's record is 37 (consecutive) by Richard John Fewster (b. 5 Jul 1935) at Bandee Golf Club, Merredin, Australia, 1956–92.

Patricia Shepherd (b. 7 Jan 1940) won 30 consecutive championships at Turriff GC, Grampian, 1959–88.

Largest tournament The Volkswagen Grand Prix Open Amateur Championship in the United Kingdom attracted a record 321,778 (206,820 men and 114,958 women) competitors in 1984.

Holes-in-One

Longest The longest straight hole ever holed in one shot was, appropriately, the tenth (408 m *447 yd*) at Miracle Hills GC, Omaha, Nebraska, USA by Robert Mitera (b. 1944) on 7 Oct 1965. Mitera stood 1.68 m *5 ft 6 in* tall and weighed 75 kg *165 lb* (11 st 11 lb). He

was a two handicap player who normally drove 224 m *245 yd*. A 80 km/h *50 mph* gust carried his shot over a 265 m *290 yd* drop-off.

The longest 'dog-leg' hole achieved in one is the 439 m *480 yd* fifth at Hope Country Club, Arkansas, USA by L. Bruce on 15 Nov 1962.

The women's record is 359 m *393 yd* by Marie Robie on the first hole of the Furnace Brook GC, Wollaston, Massachusetts, USA on 4 Sep 1949.

The longest hole in one performed in the British Isles is the seventh (par-4, 359 m *393 yd*) at West Lancashire GC by Peter Richard Parkinson (b. 26 Aug 1947) on 6 Jun 1972.

Consecutive There are at least 20 cases of 'aces' being achieved in two consecutive holes, of which the greatest was Norman L. Manley's unique 'double albatross' on the par-4 301 m *330 yd* seventh and par-4 265 m *290 yd* eighth holes on the Del Valle Country Club course, Saugus, California, USA on 2 Sep 1964.

The first woman to record consecutive 'aces' was Sue Prell, on the 13th and 14th holes at Chatswood GC, Sydney, Australia on 29 May 1977.

The closest to achieving three consecutive holes in one were Dr Joseph Boydstone on the 3rd, 4th and 9th at Bakersfield GC, California, USA, on 10 Oct 1962 and Rev. Harold Snider (b. 4 Jul 1900) who aced the 8th, 13th and 14th holes of the par-3 Ironwood course, Arizona, USA on 9 Jun 1976.

Youngest and oldest The youngest golfer recorded to have shot a hole-in-one is Coby Orr (5 years) of Littleton, Colorado on the 94 m *103 yd* fifth at the Riverside Golf Course, San Antonio, Texas, USA in 1975. The youngest girl is Nicola Mylonas, aged 10 years 64 days, on the 122 m *133 yd* 1st at South Course, Nudgee, Australia on 18 Sep 1993.

The British record was set by Luke Trayfoot, aged 6 yr 170 days, on the 99 m *106 yd* first at Moore Place, Esher, Surrey on 2 Jul 1994. The youngest girl to score an ace is Nicola Hammond, aged 10 yr 204 days on the 98 m *107 yd* third at Dereham GC, Norfolk on 17 June 1990.

The oldest golfers to have performed this feat are: (men) 99 yr 244 days Otto Bucher (Switzerland) (b. 12 May 1885) on the 119 m *130 yd* 12th at La Manga GC, Spain on 13 Jan 1985; (women) 95 yr 257 days Erna Ross (b. 9 Sep 1890) on the 102 m *112 yd* 17th at The Everglades Club, Palm Beach, Florida, USA on 23 Apr 1986.

The British records: (men) 92 yr 169 days Samuel Richard Walker (b. 6 Jan 1892) at the 143 m *156 yd* 8th at West Hove GC, E Sussex on 23 Jun 1984; (women) 90 yr 236 days Dorothy Huntley-Flindt (b. 19 Jun 1898) at the 102 m *112 yd* 13th at Barton-on-Sea GC, Hants on 10 Feb 1989.

The oldest player to score his age is C. Arthur Thompson (1869–1975) of Victoria, British Columbia, Canada, who scored 103 on the Uplands course of 5682 m *6215 yd* in 1973.

Young & Old

Youngest and oldest national champions Thuashni Selvaratnam (b. 9 Jun 1976) won the 1989 Sri Lankan Ladies Amateur Open Golf Championship, aged 12 years 324 days, at Nuwara Eliya GC on 29 Apr 1989. Maria Teresa 'Isa' Goldschmid (*née* Bevione) (b. 15 Oct 1925) won the Italian Women's Championship, aged 50 yr 200 days, at Oligata, Rome on 2 May 1976.

Lang Martin balanced seven golf balls vertically without adhesive at Charlotte, North Carolina, USA on 9 Feb 1980.

Greyhound Racing

Derby Two greyhounds have won the English Greyhound Derby (instituted 1927 at White City, London over 525 yd, now over 480 m at Wimbledon) twice: *Mick the Miller* on 25 Jul 1929, when owned by Albert H. Williams, and on 28 Jun 1930 when owned by Mrs Arundel H. Kempton, and *Patricia's Hope* on 24 Jun 1972 when owned by Gordon and Basil Marks and Brian Stanley and 23 Jun 1973 when owned by G. & B. Marks and J. O'Connor.

Guess What?
Q. Which horse has won the Grand National most often?
A. See Page 267

The highest prize was £40,000 to *Slippy Blue* for the Derby on 23 Jun 1990.

Grand National The only greyhound to have won the Grand National (instituted 1927 over 525 yd then 500 m at White City, now 474 m at Hall Green, Birmingham) three times is *Sherry's Prince* (1967–78) owned by Mrs Joyce Mathews of Sanderstead, Surrey, in 1970–72.

Derby 'triple' The only greyhounds to win the English, Scottish and Welsh Derby 'triple' are *Trev's Perfection*, owned by Fred Trevillion, in 1947, *Mile Bush Pride*, owned by Noel W. Purvis, in 1959, and *Patricia's Hope* in 1972.

Fastest greyhound The highest speed at which any greyhound has been timed is 67.32 km/h *41.83 mph* (366 m *400 yd* in 19.57 sec) by *Star Title* on the straightaway track at Wyong, New South Wales, Australia on 5 Mar 1994.

The highest speed recorded for a greyhound in Great Britain is 62.97 km/h *39.13 mph* by *Beef Cutlet*, when covering a straight course of 457 m *500 yd* in 26.13 sec at Blackpool, Lancs, on 13 May 1933.

The fastest automatically timed speed recorded for a full four-bend race is 62.59 km/h *38.89 mph* at Brighton, E Sussex by *Glen Miner* on 4 May 1982 with a time of 29.62 sec for 515 m *563 yd*.

The fastest over hurdles is 60.58 km/h *37.64 mph* at Brighton by *Wotchit Buster* on 22 Aug 1978.

Most wins The most career wins is 143 by the American greyhound, *JR's Ripper* in 1982–6.

The most consecutive victories is 37 by JJ Doc Richard, owned by Jack Boyd, at Mobile, Alabama, USA to the 29 May 1995. The run ended with a fourth place on 10 June. The British best is 32 by *Ballyregan Bob*, owned by Cliff Kevern and trained by George Curtis from 25 Aug 1984 to 9 Dec 1986, including 16 track record times. His race wins were by an average of more than nine lengths.

Highest earnings The career earnings record is held by *Homespun Rowdy* with $297,000 in the USA, 1984–7.

The richest first prize for a greyhound race is $125,000 won by *Ben G Speedboat* in the Great Greyhound Race of Champions at Seabrook, New Hampshire, USA on 23 Aug 1986.

Longest odds *Apollo Prince* won at odds of 250–1 at Sandown GRC, Springvale, Victoria, Australia on 14 Nov 1968.

Gymnastics ▶▶ ▶▶

Gymnastics

World Championships Women The greatest number of titles won in the World Championships (including Olympic Games) is 12 individual wins and six team by Larisa Semyonovna Latynina (née Diriy) (b. 27 Dec 1934) of the USSR, between 1954 and 1964.

The USSR won the team title on 21 occasions (11 world and 10 Olympics).

Men The most individual titles is 11 by Vitaliy Scherbo (Belarus) (b. 13 Jan 1972) between 1992 and 1994; he also won a team gold in 1992. Boris Anfiyanovich Shakhlin (USSR) (b. 27 Jan 1932) won ten individual titles between 1954 and 1964 but also had three team wins.

The USSR won the team title a record 13 times (eight World Championships, five Olympics) between 1952 and 1992.

Youngest champions Aurelia Dobre (Romania) (b. 6 Nov 1972) won the women's overall world title at 14 years 352 days at Rotterdam, Netherlands on 23 Oct 1987. Daniela Silivas (Romania) revealed in 1990 that she was born on 9 May 1971, a year later than previously claimed, so that she was 14 yr 185 days when she won the gold medal for balance beam on 10 Nov 1985.

The youngest male world champion was Dmitriy Bilozerchev (USSR) (b. 17 Dec 1966) at 16 yr 315 days at Budapest, Hungary on 28 Oct 1983.

Olympics The men's team title has been won a record five times by Japan (1960, 1964, 1968, 1972 and 1976) and the USSR (1952, 1956, 1980, 1988 and 1992). The USSR won the women's title ten times (1952–80, 1988 and 1992). Note the successes in 1992 were by the Unified team from the republics of the former USSR.

The most men's individual gold medals is six by: Boris Shakhlin (USSR), one in 1956, four (two shared) in 1960 and one in 1964; and Nikolay Yefimovich Andrianov (USSR) (b. 14 Oct 1952), one in 1972, four in 1976 and one in 1980.

■ **Shannon Miller (USA), at just 17, has won more World and Olympic titles than any other American gymnast. With five individual world titles she is just one short of the all-time record, six by Daniela Silivas (Romania).**
(Photo: Allsport/Vandystadt/Y. Guichaoua)

Exercises Speed & Stamina

Records are accepted for the most repetitions of the following activities within the given time span.

Press-Ups (Push-Ups)—24 Hours
46,001 Charles Servizio at Fontana City Hall, Fontana, California, USA on 24–25 Apr 1993.

Press-Ups (One Arm)—5 Hours
8151, Alan Rumbell at the Gym 'N' Slym, St Albans, Herts on 26 Jun 1993.

Press-Ups (Finger Tip)—5 Hours
7011 Kim Yang-ki at the Swiss Grand Hotel, Seoul, South Korea on 30 Aug 1990.

Press-Ups (One Finger)—Consecutive
124 Paul Lynch at the Hippodrome, Leicester Square, London on 21 Apr 1992.

Squat Thrusts—1 Hour
3552 Paul Wai Man Chung at the Yee Gin Kung Fu of Chung Sze Health (HK) Association, Kowloon, Hong Kong on 21 Aug 1992.

Burpees—1 Hour
1822 Paddy Doyle at The Irish Centre, Digbeth, Birmingham on 6 Feb 1993.

Double leg circles (pommel horse)
97 Tyler Farstad (Canada) at Surrey Gymnastic Society, Surrey, British Columbia, Canada on 27 Nov 1993.

Vera Caslavska-Odlozil (b. 3 May 1942) (Czechoslovakia) has won most individual gold medals with seven, three in 1964 and four (one shared) in 1968.

Larisa Latynina won six individual gold medals and was in three winning teams from 1956–64, making nine gold medals. She also won five silver and four bronze making 18 in all—an Olympic record.

The most medals for a male gymnast is 15 by Nikolay Andrianov (USSR), seven gold, five silver and three bronze from 1972–80.

Aleksandr Nikolayevich Dityatin (USSR) (b. 7 Aug 1957) is the only man to win a medal in all eight categories in the same Games, with three gold, four silver and one bronze at Moscow in 1980.

Youngest international

Pasakevi 'Voula' Kouna (b. 6 Dec 1971) was aged 9 years 299 days at the start of the Balkan Games at Serres, Greece on 1 Oct 1981, when she represented Greece.

British Championships The British Gymnastic Championship was won ten times by Arthur John Whitford (b. 2 Jul 1908) in 1928–36 and 1939. He was also in four winning teams. Wray 'Nik' Stuart (b. 20 Jul 1927) equalled the record of nine successive wins, 1956–64.

The women's record is eight by Mary Patricia Hirst (b. 18 Nov 1918) (1947, 1949–50 and 1952–6). Jackie Brady (b. 12 Dec 1975) uniquely won all apparatus titles and overall title in the same year, 1993.

The most overall titles in Modern Rhythmic Gymnastics is by Sharon Taylor with five successive, 1977–81.

World Cup Gymnasts who have won two World Cup (instituted 1975) overall titles are three men: Nikolay Andrianov (USSR), Aleksandr Dityatin (USSR) and Li Ning (China) (b. 8 Sep 1963), and one woman: Maria Yevgenyevna Filatova (USSR) (b. 19 Jul 1961).

Modern Rhythmic Gymnastics The most overall individual world titles in Modern Rhythmic Gymnastics is three by Maria Gigova (Bulgaria) in 1969, 1971 and 1973 (shared).

Bulgaria has a record eight team titles 1969, 1971, 1981, 1983, 1985, 1987, 1989 (shared) and 1993. Bianka Panova (Bulgaria) (b. 27 May 1960) won all four apparatus gold medals all with maximum scores, and won a team gold in 1987.

At the 1988 Olympic Games Marina Lobach (USSR) (b. 26 Jun 1970) won the rhythmic gymnastic title with perfect scores in all six disciplines.

Somersaults Ashrita Furman performed 8341 forward rolls in 10 hr 30 min over 19.67 km *12 miles 390 yards* from Lexington to Charleston, Massachusetts, USA on 30 Apr 1986.

Shigeru Iwasaki (b. 1960) backwards somersaulted 50 m *54.68 yd* in 10.8 sec at Tokyo, Japan on 30 Mar 1980.

Static wall 'sit' (or Samson's Chair) Rajkumar Chakraborty (India) stayed in an unsupported sitting position against a wall for 11 hr 5 min at Panposh Sports Hostel, Rourkela, India on 22 Apr 1994.

Handball

Most championships Olympic The USSR won five titles—men 1976, 1988 and 1992 (by the Unified Team from the republics of the ex-USSR), women 1976 and 1980. South Korea has also won two women's titles, in 1988 and 1992.

World Championships (instituted 1938) For the now predominant version of the game, indoors, the most men's titles is four by Romania, 1961, 1964, 1970 and 1974. However, Germany/West Germany won the outdoor title five times, 1938–66 and have won the indoor title twice, 1938 and 1978. Three women's titles have been won by (all indoor unless stated): Romania, 1956, 1960 (both outdoor) and 1962; the GDR 1971, 1975 and 1978; and the USSR 1982, 1986 and 1990.

European Champions' Cup Spartak of Kiev, USSR won 13 women's titles between 1970 and 1988.

Vfl Gummersbach, West Germany have won a record five men's titles, 1967, 1970–71, 1974, 1983. They are also the only club team to win all three European trophies; European Champions' Cup, European Cup Winners' Cup and IHF Cup.

High Score

Hans Eugster (Switzerland) (b. 27 Mar 1929) scored a perfect 10.00 in the compulsory parallel bars at the 1950 World Championships. Nadia Comaneci (Romania) (b. 12 Nov 1961) was the first to achieve a perfect score (10.00) in the Olympics, and achieved seven in all at Montreal, Canada in July 1976.

Britain *Most titles* The most men's national championship titles is seven by Brentwood '72 (British Championship, 1974; English National League, 1979–83; British League, 1985).

The most women's titles is eight by Wakefield Metros (English National League, 1982–7; British League, 1988, 1990).

Highest score The highest score in a men's league match is by Glasgow University, who beat Claremont, 69–5 at Glasgow, Strathclyde in March 1984.

The women's record is Wakefield Metros 47–13 defeat of Ruslip Eagles at Featherstone, W Yorks on 25 Feb 1990.

Highest score by an individual Graham Hammond scored 29 for Wakefield (39) against Hull Universty (13) at Eccles Recreation Centre in November 1990.

The women's record is 15 by Donna Hankinson (b. 24 Mar 1972) for Manchester United SSS (26) against Arcton (9) at Kirkby on 12 Nov 1989, Julie Wells (b. 9 Jan 1963) for Wakefield Metros (47) against Ruislip Eagles (13) at Featherstone, W Yorks on 25 Feb 1990, and by Catherine Densmore for Halewood Town (23) against Ruislip Eagles (17) at Bristol, Avon on 25 May 1991.

Harness Racing

Most successful driver In North American harness racing history has been Hervé Filion (b. 1 Feb 1940) of Québec, Canada, who had achieved 14,685 wins to 17 May 1995 including a then record 814 wins in a year (1989). The most wins in a year is 843 by Walter Case (USA) in 1992.

John D. Campbell (USA) (b. 8 Apr 1955) has the highest career earnings of $130,945,655 to 17 May 1995. This includes a year record of $11,620,878 in 1990 when he won 543 races.

Highest price The most expensive pacer is *Nihilator* who was syndicated by Wall Street Stable and Almahurst Stud Farm for $19.2 million in 1984.

The highest for a trotter is $6 million for *Mack Lobell* by John Erik Magnusson of Vislanda, Sweden in 1988.

Greatest winnings For any harness horse is $4,907,307 by the trotter *Peace Corps*, 1988–92. The greatest amount won by a pacer is $3,225,653 by *Nihilator*, who won 35 of 38 races in 1984–5.

The single season records are $2,264,714 by pacer *Cam's Card Shark* in 1994 and $1,878,798 by trotter *Mack Lobell* in 1987.

The largest ever purse was $2,161,000 for the Woodrow Wilson two-year-old race over 1 mile at the Meadowlands, New Jersey, USA on 16 Aug 1984. Of this sum a record $1,080,500 went to the winner *Nihilator*, driven by William O'Donnell (b. 4 May 1948).

Hockey

Most Olympic medals India was Olympic champion from the re-introduction of Olympic hockey in 1928 until 1960, when Pakistan beat them 1–0 at Rome. They had their eighth win in 1980. Of the six Indians who have won three Olympic team gold medals, two have also won a silver medal—Leslie Walter Claudius (b. 25 Mar 1927), in 1948, 1952, 1956 and 1960 (silver), and Udham Singh (b. 4 Aug 1928), in 1952, 1956, 1964 and 1960 (silver).

> The highest score in a handball international match was recorded when the USSR beat Afghanistan 86–2 in the 'Friendly Army Tournament' at Miskolc, Hungary in August 1981.

A women's tournament was added in 1980, and there have been four separate winners.

World Cup The FIH World Cup for men was first held in 1971, and for women in 1974. The most wins are, (men) four by Pakistan, 1971, 1978, 1982 and 1994; (women) five by the Netherlands, 1974, 1978, 1983, 1986 and 1990.

Champions' Trophy First held in 1978 and contested annually since 1980 by the top six men's teams in the world; the most wins is six, by Australia, 1983–5, 1989–90 and 1993. The first women's Champions' Trophy was held in 1987, Australia has won twice, 1991 and 1993.

> ## Guess What?
> Q. What is the record for international appearances in football?
> A. See Page 255

A. See Page 255

Men

Most international appearances Heiner Dopp (b. 27 Jun 1956) represented West Germany 286 times between 1975 and 1989, indoors and out.

The most by a player from the British Isles is 234 by Jonathon Nicholas Mark Potter (b. 19 Nov 1963), 106 for England and 128 for Great Britain, 1983–94. The most for Ireland is 135 by William David Robert McConnell (b. 19 Apr 1956) 1979–93, and Stephen Alexander Martin (b. 13 Apr 1959) 1980–93. The most indoor caps is 85 by Richard Clarke (England) (b. 3 Apr 1952), 1976–87.

Hockey umpire Graham Dennis Nash (b. 15 Mar 1943) umpired in five successive Olympics, 1976–92, and retired after Barcelona having officiated in a record 144 international matches.

International

In international hockey the highest score was when India defeated the USA 24–1 at Los Angeles, California, USA in the 1932 Olympic Games.

The greatest number of goals in an international in Britain was when England defeated France 16–0 at Beckenham, Kent on 25 Mar 1922.

Greatest scoring feats The greatest number of goals scored in international hockey is 267 by Paul Litjens (Netherlands) (b. 9 Nov 1947) in 177 games.

M. C. Marckx (Bowdon 2nd XI) scored 19 goals against Brooklands 2nd XI (score 23–0) on 31 Dec 1910. He was selected for England in March 1912 but declined due to business priorities. David Ashman has scored a record 2128 goals having played for Hampshire, Southampton, Southampton Kestrals and Hamble Old Boys (for whom he has scored 1969 goals, a record for one club), 1958–95.

Fastest goal in an international John French scored 7 seconds after the bully-off for England v. West Germany at Nottingham on 25 Apr 1971.

> **Greatest goalkeeping** Richard James Allen (India) (b. 4 Jun 1902) did not concede a goal during the 1928 Olympic tournament and a total of only three in 1936.

Women

Most international appearances Alison Ramsay has made a record 250 international appearances, 143 for Scotland and 107 for Great Britain, 1982–June 1995.

Highest scores The highest score in an international match was when England beat France 23–0 at Merton, Greater London on 3 Feb 1923.

In club hockey, Ross Ladies beat Wyeside, at Ross-on-Wye, Herefordshire 40–0 on 24 Jan 1929, when Edna Mary Blakelock (1904–89) scored a record 21 goals.

Highest attendance The highest attendance was 65,165 for the match between England and the USA at Wembley, London on 11 Mar 1978.

Horse Racing

Largest prizes The highest prize money for a day's racing is $10 million for the Breeders' Cup series of seven races staged annually in the USA since 1984. Included each year is a record $3 million for the Breeders' Cup Classic.

> The most horses in a race has been 66 in the Grand National on 22 Mar 1929. The record for the Flat is 58 in the Lincolnshire Handicap at Lincoln on 13 Mar 1948.

Horses

Most successful The horse with the best win-loss record was *Kincsem*, a Hungarian mare foaled in 1874, who was unbeaten in 54 races (1876–79) throughout Europe, including the Goodwood Cup of 1878.

Longest winning sequence Camarero, foaled in 1951, was undefeated in 56 races in Puerto Rico from 19 Apr 1953 to his first defeat on 17 Aug 1955 (in his career to 1956, he won 73 of 77 races).

Career Chorisbar (foaled 1935) won 197 of her 324 races in Puerto Rico, 1937–47. *Lenoxbar* (foaled 1935) won 46 races in one year, 1940, in Puerto Rico from 56 starts.

Same race Doctor Syntax (foaled 1811) won the Preston Gold Cup on seven successive occasions, 1815–21.

Triple Crown winners The English Triple Crown (2000 Guineas, Derby, St Leger) has been won 15 times, most recently by *Nijinsky* in 1970. The fillies'

High Price

Enormous valuations placed on potential stallions may be determined from sales of a minority holding, but such valuations would, perhaps, not be reached on the open market. The most paid for a yearling is $13.1m on 23 Jul 1985 at Keeneland, Kentucky, USA by Robert Sangster and partners for *Seattle Dancer*.

equivalent (1000 Guineas, Oaks, St Leger) has been won nine times, most recently by *Oh So Sharp* in 1985. Two of these fillies also won the 2000 Guineas: *Formosa* (in a dead-heat) in 1868 and *Sceptre* in 1902. The American Triple Crown (Kentucky Derby, Preakness Stakes, Belmont Stakes) has been achieved 11 times, most recently by *Affirmed* in 1978.

Greatest winnings The career earnings record is $6,679,242 by the 1987 Kentucky Derby winner *Alysheba* (foaled 1984) from 1986–8. The most prize money earned in a year is $4,578,454 by *Sunday Silence* (foaled 1986) in the USA in 1989. His total included $1,350,000 from the Breeders' Cup Classic and a $1 million bonus for the best record in the Triple Crown races: he won the Kentucky Derby and Preakness Stakes and was second in the Belmont Stakes. The leading money-winning filly or mare is *Dance Smartly* (foaled 1988) with $3,263,836 in North America, 1990–92. The one-race record is $2.6 million by *Spend A Buck* (foaled 1982) for the Jersey Derby, Garden State Park, New Jersey, USA on 27

Major Race Records

FLAT

Race (Instituted)	Record Time	Most Wins Jockey	Trainer	Owner	Largest Field
Derby (1780) 1m 4f 10yd *2423m* Epsom, Surrey	2min 32.31sec *Lammtarra* 1995	9–Lester Piggott 1954, 57, 60, 68, 70, 72, 76, 77, 83	7–Robert Robson 1793, 1802, 09, 10, 15, 17, 23 7–John Porter 1868, 82, 83, 86, 90, 91, 99 7–Fred Darling 1922, 25, 26, 31, 38, 40, 41	5–3rd Earl of Egremont 1782, 1804, 05, 07, 26 5–HH Aga Khan III 1930, 35, 36, 48, 52	34 (1862)
2000 Guineas (1809) 1 mile *1609m* Newmarket, Suffolk	1min 35.08sec *Mister Baileys* 1994	9–Jem Robinson 1825, 28, 31, 33, 34, 35, 36, 47, 48	7–John Scott 1842, 43, 49, 53, 56, 60, 62	5–4th Duke of Grafton 1820, 21, 22, 26, 27 5–5th Earl of Jersey 1831, 34, 35, 36, 37	28 (1930)
1000 Guineas (1814) 1 mile *1609m* Newmarket	1min 36.71sec *Las Meninas* 1994	7–George Fordham 1859, 61, 65, 68, 69, 81, 83	9–Robert Robson 1818, 19, 20, 21, 22, 23, 25, 26, 27	8–4th Duke of Grafton 1819, 20, 21, 22, 23, 25, 26, 27	29 (1926)
Oaks (1779) 1m 4f 10yd *2423m* Epsom	2min 34.19sec *Intrepidity* 1993	9–Frank Buckle 1797, 98, 99, 1802, 03, 05, 17, 18, 23	12–Robert Robson 1802, 04, 05, 07, 08, 09, 13, 15, 18, 22, 23, 25	6–4th Duke of Grafton 1813, 15, 22, 23, 28, 31	26 (1848)
St Leger (1776) 1m 6f 132yd *2937m* Doncaster, South Yorkshire	3min 01.6sec *Coronach* 1926 *Windsor Lad* 1934	9–Bill Scott 1821, 25, 28, 29, 38, 39, 40, 41, 46	16–John Scott 1827, 28, 29, 32, 34, 38, 39, 40, 41, 45, 51, 53, 56, 57, 59, 62	7–9th Duke of Hamilton 1786, 87, 88, 92, 1808, 09, 14	30 (1825)
King George VI and Queen Elizabeth Diamond Stakes (1951) 1½ miles *2414m* Ascot, Berkshire	2min 26.98sec *Grundy* 1975	7–Lester Piggott 1965, 66, 69, 70, 74, 77, 84	5–Dick Hern 1972, 79, 80, 85, 89	3–Sheikh Mohammed 1990, 93, 94	19 (1951)
Prix de l'Arc de Triomphe (1920) 2400 metres *1 mile 864yd* Longchamp, Paris, France	2min 26.3sec *Trempolino* 1987	4–Jacques Doyasbère 1942, 44, 50, 51 4–Frédéric Head 1966, 72, 76, 79 4–Yves Saint-Martin 1970, 74, 82, 84 4–Pat Eddery 1980, 85, 86, 87	4–Charles Semblat 1942, 44, 46, 49 4–Alec Head 1952, 59, 76, 81 4–François Mathet 1950, 51, 70, 82	6–Marcel Boussac 1936, 37, 42, 44, 46, 49	30 (1967)
VRC Melbourne Cup (1861) 3200 metres *1 mile 1739yd* Flemington, Victoria, Australia	3min 16.3sec *Kingston Rule* 1990	4–Bobby Lewis 1902, 15, 19, 27 4–Harry White 1974, 75, 78, 79	9–Bart Cummings 1965, 66, 67, 74, 75, 77, 79, 90, 91	4–Etienne de Mestre 1861, 62, 67, 78	39 (1890)
Kentucky Derby (1875) 1¼ miles *2012m* Churchill Downs, Louisville, USA	1min 59.4sec *Secretariat* 1973	5–Eddie Arcaro 1938, 41, 45, 48, 52 5–Bill Hartack 1957, 60, 62, 64, 69	6–Ben Jones 1938, 41, 44, 48, 49, 52	8–Calumet Farm 1941, 44, 48, 49, 52, 57, 58, 68	23 (1974)
Irish Derby (1866) 1½ miles *2414m* The Curragh, Co. Kildare	2 min 25.60 sec *St Jovite* 1992	6–Morny Wing 1921, 23, 30, 38, 42, 46	6–Vincent O'Brien 1953, 57, 70, 77, 84, 85	5–HH Aga Khan III 1925, 32, 40, 48, 49	24 (1962)
JUMPING					
Grand National (1839) 4½ miles *7242m* Aintree, Liverpool, Merseyside	8min 47.8sec *Mr Frisk* 1990	5–George Stevens 1856, 63, 64, 69, 70	4–Fred Rimell 1956, 61, 70, 76	3–James Machell 1873, 74, 76 3–Sir Charles Assheton-Smith 1893, 1912, 13 3–Noel Le Mare 1973, 74, 77	66 (1929)
Cheltenham Gold Cup (1924) 3m 2f 110yd *5230m* Cheltenham, Gloucestershire	6 min 23.4 sec *Silver Fame* 1951	4–Pat Taaffe 1964, 65, 66, 68	5–Tom Dreaper 1946, 64, 65, 66, 68	7–Dorothy Paget 1932, 33, 34, 35, 36, 40, 52	22 (1982)
Champion Hurdle (1927) 2m 110yd *3218m* Cheltenham	3 min 50.7 sec *Kribensis* 1990	4–Tim Molony 1951, 52, 53, 54	5–Peter Easterby 1967, 76, 77, 80, 81	4–Dorothy Paget 1932, 33, 40, 46	24 (1964) 24 (1991)

■ Michael Kinane (b. 22 Jun 1959) has been Irish champion jockey a record 10 times between 1984 and 1994 with a record 115 winners in 1993. He is also the only jockey from the British Isles to have ridden the winner in Australia's premier race, the Melbourne Cup, when *Vintage Crop* became the first European-trained winner of the race.

(Photo: Allsport/C. Cole)

Guess What?

Q. How old is the oldest ever horse?

A. See page 30

May 1985, of which $2 million was a bonus for having previously won the Kentucky Derby and two preparatory races at Garden State Park.

World speed records The highest race speed recorded is 69.62 km/h *43.26 mph*, 20.8 sec for ¼ mile *402 m*, by *Big Racket* at Mexico City, Mexico on 5 Feb 1945 and *Onion Roll* at Thistledown, Cleveland, Ohio, USA on 27 Sep 1993. The record for 1½ miles *2414 m* is 60.86 km/h *37.82 mph* by 3-year-old *Hawkster* (carrying 54.9 kg *121 lb*) at Santa Anita Park, Arcadia, California, USA on 14 Oct 1989 with a time of 2 min 22.8 sec.

Biggest weight The biggest weight ever carried is 190.5 kg *30 stone* by both Mr Maynard's mare and Mr Baker's horse in a match won by the former over a mile at York on 21 May 1788.

Oldest winners The oldest horses to win on the Flat have been the 18-year-olds *Revenge* at Shrewsbury on 23 Sep 1790, *Marksman* at Ashford, Kent on 4 Sep 1826 and *Jorrocks* at Bathurst, Australia on 28 Feb 1851. At the same age *Wild Aster* won three hurdle races in six days in March 1919 and *Sonny Somers* won two steeplechases in February 1980.

Jockeys

Most successful Billie Lee 'Bill' Shoemaker (USA) (b. weighing 1.1 kg *2½ lb*, 19 Aug 1931), whose racing weight was 44 kg *97 lb* at 1.50 m *4 ft 11 in*, rode a record 8833 winners from 40,350 mounts from his first ride on 19 Mar 1949 and first winner on 20 Apr 1949 to his retirement on 3 Feb 1990. Laffit Pincay (b. 29 Dec 1946, Panama City) has earned a career record $186,267,029 from 1964 to 1 May 1995.

The most races won by a jockey in a year is 598 from 2312 rides by Kent Jason Desormeaux (b. 27 Feb 1970) in 1989. The greatest amount won in a year is 3,133,742,000 yen (approximately $28.4 million) by Yutaka Take (b. 15 Mar 1969) in Japan in 1993.

Wins The most winners ridden in one day is nine by Chris Wiley Antley (USA) (b. 6 Jan 1966) on 31 Oct 1987. They consisted of four in the afternoon at Aqueduct, New York, USA and five in the evening at The Meadowlands, New Jersey, USA.

■ The most successful horse in terms of money won in a year is *Sunday Silence* in the USA in 1989. Seen here winning the Kentucky Derby (yellow jockey), he also won the Preakness Stakes and was second in the Belmont Stakes and, in all, won over $4.5 million in the year.

(Photo: Bob Thomas/Joyner)

Consecutive The longest winning streak is 12 by: Sir Gordon Richards (1904–86) (one race at Nottingham on 3 Oct, six out of six at Chepstow on 4 Oct and the first five races next day at Chepstow) in 1933; and by Pieter Stroebel at Bulawayo, Southern Rhodesia (now Zimbabwe), 7 Jun–7 Jul 1958.

> **One card**
> The most winners ridden on one card is eight by six riders, most recently (and from fewest rides) by Patrick Alan Day (b. 13 Oct 1953) from nine rides at Arlington International, Illinois, USA on 13 Sep 1989.

Trainers

Jack Charles Van Berg (USA) (b. 7 Jun 1936) has the greatest number of wins in a year, 496 in 1976. The career record is 6362 by Dale Baird (USA) (b. 17 Apr 1935) from 1962 to end of 1993. The greatest amount won in a year is $17,842,358 by Darrell Wayne Lukas (USA) (b. 2 Sep 1935) in 1988 and he has won a record $140,024,750 in his career.

The only trainer to saddle the first five finishers in a championship race is Michael William Dickinson (b. 3 Feb 1950) of Dunkeswick, W Yorks, in the Cheltenham Gold Cup on 17 Mar 1983; he won a record 12 races in one day, 27 Dec 1982.

Owners

The most lifetime wins by an owner is 4775 by Marion H. Van Berg (1895–1971) in North America in 35 years. The most wins in a year is 494 by Dan R. Lasater (USA) in 1974. The greatest amount won in a year is $6,881,902 by Sam-Son Farm in North America in 1991.

British Turf Records:

Flat Racing

Most successful horses *Eclipse* (foaled 1764) still has the best win-loss record, being unbeaten in a career of 18 races between May 1769 and October 1770. The longest winning sequence is 21 races by *Meteor* (foaled 1783) between 1786 and 1788. The most races won in a season is 23 (from 34 starts) by three-year-old *Fisherman* in 1856. *Catherina* (foaled 1830) won a career record 79 out of 176 races, 1832–41. The most successful sire was *Stockwell* (foaled 1849) whose progeny won 1153 races (1858–76) and who in 1866 set a record of 132 races won.

The greatest amount ever won by an British-trained horse is £1,283,794 by *Snurge* (foaled 1987), 1989–94. In 1985 the 4-year-old filly *Pebbles* won a record £1,012,611 in one season, including the Breeders' Cup Turf at Aqueduct, New York, USA.

The biggest winning margin in a Classic is 20 lengths by *Mayonaise* in the 1000 Guineas on 12 May 1859.

Since the introduction of the Pattern-race system in 1971, the most prolific British-trained winner of such races has been *Brigadier Gerard* (foaled 1968) with 13 wins, 1971–2.

Since the introduction in 1977 of official ratings in the International Classifications, the highest-rated horse has been *Dancing Brave* (foaled 1983) on 141 in 1986.

■ **Walter Swinburn celebrates winning the 1995 Derby in record time.** *Lammtarra*'s **time beat the 59-year record of** *Mahmoud* **by over a second.**
(Photo: Allsport/P. Cole)

The only horse to win two Horse of the Year awards (instituted 1959) is the filly *Dahlia* (foaled 1970) in 1973–4.

Longest odds The longest winning odds recorded in British horse racing is 250–1 when *Equinoctial* won at Kelso on 21 Nov 1990. Owner-trainer Norman Miller was not surprised by his horse's success despite being beaten in his previous race by 62 lengths.

Most successful jockeys Sir Gordon Richards won 4870 races from 21,815 mounts from his first mount at Lingfield Park, Surrey on 16 Oct 1920 to his last at Sandown Park, Surrey on 10 Jul 1954. His first win was on 31 Mar 1921. In 1953, at his 28th and final attempt, he won the Derby, six days after his knighthood. He was champion jockey 26 times between 1925 and 1953 and won a record 269 races (from 835 rides) in 1947. Lester Keith Piggott (b. 5 Nov 1935) won 4493 races in Great Britain, 1948 to June 1995, but his global total exceeds 5300. The most prize-money won in a year is £2,903,976 by William Fisher Hunter Carson (b. 16 Nov 1942) in 1990. The most wins in a day is seven by Patrick James John Eddery (b. 18 Mar 1952) at Newmarket and Newcastle on 26 Jun 1992.

The most Classic races won by a jockey is 30 by Lester Piggott from his first on *Never Say Die* in the 1954 Derby to the 1992 2000 Guineas on *Rodrigo de Triano*. (Derby—9, St Leger—8, Oaks—6, 2000 Guineas—5, 1000 Guineas—2.)

Most successful trainers The most wins in a season is 182 (from 1215 starts) by Richard Michael Hannon (b. 30 May 1945) of East Everleigh, Wilts in 1993. The record prize money earned in a season is £2,000,330 by Michael Ronald Stoute (b. 22 Oct 1945) of Newmarket in 1989; he set a record for worldwide earnings of £2,778,405 in 1986. The most Classics

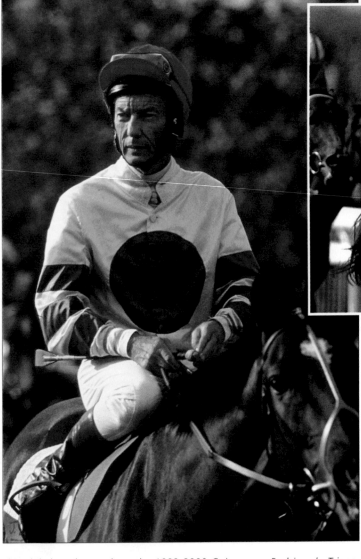

Guess What?

Q. How long is the longest whip ever 'cracked'?

A. See Page 210

The beginning of the 1995 Flat season brought the retirement of the great Lester Piggott. During a superlative career in which he rode over 5300 winners worldwide, one of his most notable achievement is having ridden 30 Classic winners over five decades. He is seen here on his last Classic success, *Rodrigo de Triano*, in the 1992 2000 Guineas.
(Photos: Allsport/C. Cole & S. Bruty)

won is 40 by John Scott (1794–1871) of Malton, Yorkshire between 1827 and 1863. James Croft (1787–1828) of Middleham, Yorkshire trained the first four horses in the St Leger on 16 Sep 1822. Alexander Taylor (1862–1943) of Manton, Wiltshire, was champion trainer in money won a record 12 times between 1907 and 1925. Henry Richard Amherst Cecil (b. 11 Jan 1943) of Newmarket has been champion in races won a record nine times, 1978–89.

Most successful owners H H Aga Khan III (1877–1957) was leading owner a record 13 times between 1924 and 1952. The record prize money won in a season was £2,666,730 by Sheikh Mohammed bin Rashid al Maktoum of Dubai (b. 1949) in 1994. His horses won a record 185 races in 1992. The most Classics won is 20 by George Fitzroy, 4th Duke of Grafton (1760–1844) between 1813 and 1831 and by Edward Stanley, 17th Earl of Derby (1865–1948) between 1910 and 1945.

The Derby The greatest of England's five Classics is the Derby Stakes, inaugurated on 4 May 1780, and named after Edward Stanley, 12th Earl of Derby (1752–1834). The distance was increased in 1784 from a mile to 1½ miles *2.414 km* (now officially described as 1 mile 4 furlongs 10 yd). The race has been run at Epsom Downs, Surrey, except for the two war periods, when it was run at Newmarket, Cambs, and is for three-year-olds only. Since 1884 the weights have been: colts 57.2 kg *9st*, fillies 54.9 kg *8st 9lb*. Geldings were eligible until 1906.

Largest and smallest winning margins Shergar won the Derby by a record 10 lengths in 1981. There have been two dead-heats: in 1828 when *Cadland* beat *The Colonel* in the run-off, and in 1884 between *St Gatien* and *Harvester* (stakes divided).

Largest prize The richest prize on the British Turf is £504,500 for the Derby won by *Lammtarra* on 10 Jun 1995.

Longest and shortest odds in the Derby Three winners have been returned at odds of 100–1: *Jeddah* (1898), *Signorinetta* (1908) and *Aboyeur* (1913). The shortest-priced winner was *Ladas* (1894) at 2–9 and the hottest losing favourite was *Surefoot*, fourth at 40–95 in 1890.

Jumping

Most successful horses *Sir Ken* (foaled 1947), who won the Champion Hurdle in 1952–4, won a record 16 hurdle races in succession, April 1951 to March 1953. Three other horses have also won a record three Champion Hurdles; *Hatton's Grace* (foaled 1940) 1949–51; *Persian War* (foaled 1963) 1968–70; *See You Then* (foaled 1980) 1985–7. The greatest number of Cheltenham Gold Cup wins is five by *Golden Miller* (foaled 1927), 1932–6. The mare *Dawn Run* (foaled 1978) uniquely won both the Champion Hurdle (1984) and Cheltenham Gold Cup (1986).

The greatest number of Horse of the Year awards (instituted 1959) is four by *Desert Orchid* (foaled 1979), 1987–90. The greatest amount earned by a British jumper is £652,802 by *Desert Orchid*, 1983–91.

The richest prize won over jumps in Britain is £122,540 by *Master Oats* in the Cheltenham Gold Cup on 16 Mar 1995.

Most successful jockeys Peter Michael Scudamore (b. 13 Jun 1958) won a career record 1678 races over jumps (from 7521 mounts) from 1978 to 7 Apr 1993.

The most wins in a season is 221 (from 663 rides) by Peter Scudamore in 1988/9. The greatest prize money won in a season is £1,235,170 by Norman Williamson (b. 16 Jan 1969) in 1994/5. The most wins in a day is six by two amateurs: Edward Potter Wilson (1846–1918) at Crewkerne, Somerset on 19 Mar 1878 and Charles James Cunningham (1849–1906) at Rugby, Warks on 29 Mar 1881. The record number of successive wins is ten by: John Alnham Gilbert (1920–93), 8–30 Sep 1959; and by Philip Charles Tuck (b. 10 Jul 1956), 23 Aug–3 Sep 1986. The record number of championships is eight (one shared) by Peter Scudamore in 1982, 1986–92.

Most successful trainers Martin Charles Pipe (b. 29 May 1945) won £1,203,014 in prize money in 1990/91, when his horses won a record 230 races from 782 starts. Frederick Thomas Winter (b. 20 Sep 1926) of Lambourn, Berks, was champion trainer in money won a record eight times between 1971 and 1985. William Arthur Stephenson (1920–92) of Leasingthorne, Co. Durham, won 2644 races over jumps, plus 344 on the Flat, a record total of 2988 in Britain, 1946–92. He was champion trainer in races won a record ten times between 1966 and 1977, a record equalled by Martin Pipe, 1989–95.

Grand National The first Grand National Steeple Chase may be regarded as the Grand Liverpool Steeple Chase of 26 Feb 1839 though the race was not given its present name until 1847. It

became a handicap in 1843. Except for 1916–18 and 1941–5, the race has been run at Aintree, near Liverpool, over 30 fences.

Most wins The only horse to win three times is *Red Rum* (foaled 1965) in 1973, 1974 and 1977, from five runs. He came second in 1975 and 1976. *Manifesto* (foaled 1888) ran a record eight times (1895–1904). He won in 1897 and 1899, came third three times and fourth once.

Heaviest weight The highest weight ever carried to victory in the Grand National is 79.4 kg *12st 7lb* by *Cloister* (1893), *Manifesto* (1899), *Jerry M.* (1912) and *Poethlyn* (1919).

Hurling

Most titles *All-Ireland* The greatest number of All-Ireland Championships won by one team is 27 by Cork between 1890 and 1990. The greatest number of successive wins is four by Cork (1941–4).

Most appearances The most appearances in All-Ireland finals is ten shared by Christy Ring (Cork and Munster) and John Doyle (Tipperary). They also share the record of All-Ireland medals won with eight each. Ring's appearances on the winning side were in 1941–4, 1946 and 1952–4, while Doyle's were in 1949–51, 1958, 1961–2 and 1964–5. Ring also played in a record 22 inter-provincial finals (1942–63) and was on the winning side 18 times.

Highest and lowest scores The highest score in an All-Ireland final was in 1989 when Tipperary 41 (4 goals, 29 points) beat Antrim (3 goals, 9 points). The record aggregate score was when Cork 39 (6 goals, 21 points) defeated Wexford 25 (5 goals, 10 points) in the 80-minute final of 1970. A goal equals three points. The highest recorded individual score was by Nick Rackard (Wexford), who scored 7 goals and 7 points against Antrim in the 1954 All-Ireland semi-final. The lowest score in an All-Ireland final was when Tipperary (1 goal, 1 point) beat Galway (nil) in the first championship at Birr in 1887.

> **The largest crowd for a hurling match was 84,865 for the All-Ireland final between Cork and Wexford at Croke Park, Dublin in 1954.**

Longest hit The greatest distance for a 'lift and stroke' is one of 118 m *129 yd* credited to Tom Murphy of Three Castles, Kilkenny, in a 'long puck' contest in 1906.

Ice Hockey

World Championships and Olympic Games World Championships were first held for amateurs in 1920 in conjunction with the Olympic Games, which were also considered as world championships up to 1968. From 1976 World Championships have been open to professionals. The USSR won 22 world titles between 1954 and 1990 (and Russia won in 1993), including the Olympic titles of 1956, 1964 and 1968. They have a record eight Olympic titles with a further five, 1972, 1976, 1984, 1988 and 1992 (as the CIS, with all players Russians). The longest Olympic career is that of Richard Torriani (Switzerland) (1911–88) from 1928 to 1948. The most gold medals won by any player is three, achieved by Soviet players Vitaliy Semyenovich Davydov, Anatoliy Vasilyevich Firsov,

> **The first three women's ice hockey world championships have been won by Canada, 1990, 1992 and 1994.**

Ice Skating ▶ ▶ ▶▶

Guess What?
Q. Where would you find the world's longest train?
A. See Page 122

Viktor Grigoryevich Kuzkin and Aleksandr Pavlovich Ragulin in 1964, 1968 and 1972, and by Vladislav Aleksandrovich Tretyak in 1972, 1976 and 1984.

NHL Records

Stanley Cup The Stanley Cup was first presented in 1893 (original cost $48.67) by Lord Stanley of Preston, then Governor-General of Canada. From 1894 it was contested by amateur teams for the Canadian Championship. From 1910 it became the award for the winners of the professional league play-offs. It has been won most often by the Montreal Canadiens with 24 wins in 1916, 1924, 1930–31, 1944, 1946, 1953, 1956–60, 1965–6, 1968–9, 1971, 1973, 1976–9, 1986, 1993, from a record 32 finals. Joseph Henri Richard (b. 29 Feb 1936) played on a record 11 winning teams for the Canadiens between 1956 and 1973.

Scoring records Wayne Gretzky (Edmonton and Los Angeles) has scored 346 points in Stanley Cup games, 110 goals and 236 assists, all are records. Gretzky scored a season's record 47 points (16 goals and a record 31 assists) in 1985. The most goals in a season is 19 by Reginald Joseph Leach (b. 23 Apr 1950) for Philadelphia in 1976 and Jari Kurri (Finland) (b. 18 May 1960) for Edmonton in 1985.

Five goals in a Stanley Cup game were scored by Maurice Richard (b. 4 Aug 1921) in Montreal's 5–1 win over Toronto on 23 Mar 1944, by Darryl Glen Sittler for Toronto (8) v. Philadelphia (5) on 22 Apr 1976, by Reggie Leach for Philadelphia (6) v. Boston (3) on 6 May 1976, and by Mario Lemieux (b. 5 Oct 1965) for Pittsburgh (10) v. Philadelphia (7) on 25 Apr 1989. A record six assists in a game were achieved by Mikko Leinonen (b. 15 Jul 1955) for New York Rangers (7) v. Philadelphia (3) on 8 Apr 1982 and by Wayne Gretzky for Edmonton (13) v. Los Angeles (3) on 9 Apr 1987, when his team set a Stanley Cup game record of 13 goals. The most points in a game is eight by Patrik Sundström (Sweden) (b. 14 Dec 1961), three goals and five assists, for New Jersey (10) v. Washington (4) on 22 Apr 1988 and by Mario Lemieux, five goals and three assists, for Pittsburgh v. Philadelphia.

Most games played Gordon 'Gordie' Howe (Canada) (b. 31 Mar 1928) played in a record 1767 regular season games (and 157 play-off games) over a record 26 seasons, from 1946 to 1971 for the Detroit Red Wings and in 1979/80 for the Hartford Whalers. He also played 419 games (and 78 play-off games) for the Houston Aeros and for the New England Whalers in the World Hockey Association (WHA) from 1973 to 1979, and a grand total of 2421 major league games.

Most goals and points *Career & season* Wayne Gretzky (Edmonton Oilers/Los Angeles Kings) holds the NHL scoring records for the regular season as well as for play-off games (⇔ above). He has scored 814 goals, 1692 assists for a record 2506 points from 1173 games. He has scored the most goals in a season, 92 for the Edmonton Oilers, 1981/2. He scored a record 215 points, including a record 163 assists in 1985/6. In 1981/2 in all games, adding Stanley Cup play-offs and for Canada in the World Championship, he scored 238 points (103 goals, 135 assists).

The North American career record for goals is 1071 by Gordie Howe in 32 seasons, 1946–80. He took 2204 games to achieve the 1000th goal, but Robert Marvin 'Bobby' Hull (b. 3 Jan 1939) (Chicago Black Hawks and Winnipeg Jets) scored his 1000th in his 1600th game on 12 Mar 1978.

Game The North American major league record for most points scored in one game is ten by Jim Harrison (b. 9 Jul 1947) (three goals, seven assists) for Alberta, later Edmonton Oilers in a WHA match at Edmonton on 30 Jan 1973, and by Darryl Sittler (b. 18 Sep 1950) (six goals, four assists) for Toronto Maple Leafs v. Boston Bruins in an NHL match at Toronto on 7 Feb 1976.

The most goals in a game is seven by Joe Malone in Québec's 10–6 win over Toronto St. Patricks at Québec City on 31 Jan 1920. The most assists is seven by Billy Taylor for Detroit v. Chicago on 16 Mar 1947 and three times by Wayne Gretzky for Edmonton, v. Washington on 15 Feb 1980, v. Chicago on 11 Dec 1985, and v. Québec on 14 Feb 1986.

Fastest goal From the opening whistle, the fastest is 5 seconds by Doug Smail (b. 2 Sep 1957) (Winnipeg Jets) v. St Louis Blues at Winnipeg on 20 Dec 1981, and by Bryan John Trottier (b. 17 Jul 1956) (New York Islanders) v. Boston Bruins at Boston on 22 Mar 1984. Bill Mosienko (b. 2 Nov 1921) (Chicago Black Hawks) scored three goals in 21 seconds v. New York Rangers on 23 Mar 1952.

Goaltending Terry Sawchuk (1929–70) played a record 971 games as a goaltender, for Detroit, Boston, Toronto, Los Angeles and New York Rangers from 1950 to 1970. He achieved a record 435 wins (to 337 losses, and 188 ties) and had a record 103 career shutouts. Jacques Plante (1929–86), with 434 NHL wins surpassed Sawchuk's figure by adding 15 wins in his one season in the WHA for a senior league total of 449 from 868 games. Bernie Parent (b. 3 Apr 1945) achieved a record 47 wins in a season, with 13 losses and 12 ties, for Philadelphia in 1973/4.

Gerry Cheevers (b. 2 Dec 1940) (Boston Bruins) went a record 32 successive games without a defeat in 1971–2.

Team records Montreal Canadiens won a record 60 games and 132 points (with 12 ties) from 80 games played in 1976/7; their eight losses was also the least ever in a season of 70 or more games. The highest percentage of wins in a season was .875% achieved by the Boston Bruins with 30 wins in 44 games in 1929/30. The longest undefeated run during a season, 35 games (25 wins and ten ties), was established by the Philadelphia Flyers from 14 Oct 1979 to 6 Jan 1980. The most goals scored in a season is 446 by the Edmonton Oilers in 1983/4, when they also achieved a record 1182 scoring points.

Game The highest aggregate score is 21 when Montreal Canadiens beat Toronto St Patrick's, 14–7, at Montreal on 10 Jan 1920, and Edmonton Oilers beat Chicago Black Hawks, 12–9, at Chicago on 11 Dec 1985. The single team record is 16 by Montreal Canadiens v. Québec Bulldogs (3), at Québec City on 3 Nov 1920.

The longest match was 2 hr 56 min 30 sec (playing time) when Detroit Red Wings beat Montreal Maroons 1–0 in the sixth period of overtime at the Forum, Montreal, at 2:25 a.m. on 25 Mar 1936. Norm Smith, the Red Wings goaltender, turned aside 92 shots for the NHL's longest single shutout.

Other Records

British competitions The English (later British) League Championship (instituted 1934) has been won by Streatham (later Redskins) five times, 1935, 1950, 1953, 1960 and 1982. Murrayfield Racers have won the Northern League (instituted 1966) seven times, 1970–72, 1976, 1979–80 and 1985. The Icy Smith Cup (first held 1966), the premier British club competition until 1981, was won by Murrayfield Racers nine times, 1966, 1969–72, 1975 and 1979–81. The British Championship (instituted 1982) has been won a record four times by Durham Wasps, 1987–8 and 1991–2. The British League title has been won five times by Durham Wasps, 1985, 1988–9 and 1991–2. The 'Grand Slam' of Autumn Cup (now Benson & Hedges Cup), British League and British Championships has been won by Dundee Rockets (1983/4), Durham Wasps (1990/91) and Cardiff Devils (1992/3).

Most goals *Team* The greatest number of goals recorded in a world championship match was when Australia beat New Zealand 58–0 at Perth on 15 Mar 1987.

British The highest score and aggregate in a British League match was set when Medway Bears beat Richmond Raiders 48–1 at Gillingham in a Second Division fixture on 1 Dec 1985, when Kevin MacNaught (Canada) (b. 23 Jul 1960) scored a record 25 points from seven goals and 18 assists.

The most individual goals scored in a senior game is 18 by Rick Smith (Canada) (b. 28 Aug 1964) in a 27–2 win for Chelmsford Chieftains against Sheffield Sabres in an English League match on 3 Mar 1991. Steve Moria (Canada) (b. 1960) achieved the highest number of assists, 13, for Fife Flyers at Cleveland on 28 Mar 1987. Rick Fera (Canada) (b. 1964) set British season's records of 165 g   318 points for Murrayfield Racers in 48   in 1986/7. Tim Salmon (Canada) (b   1964) achieved a season's record 183 assis   games for Ayr Bruins in 1985/6. The highest care   points for the Heineken League is 2136 (875 goals, 1281 assists) by Tony Hand (GB) (b. 15 Aug 1967) in 449 games to end of the 1994/5 season.

Fastest scoring In minor leagues, Per Olsen scored 2 seconds after the start of the match for Rungsted against Odense in the Danish First Division at Hørsholm, Denmark on 14 Jan 1990. Three goals in 10 seconds was achieved by Jørgen Palmgren Erichsen for Frisk v. Holmen in a junior league match in Norway on 17 Mar 1991. The Vernon Cougars scored five goals in 56 seconds against Salmon Arm Aces at Vernon, BC, Canada on 6 Aug 1982. The Kamloops Knights of Columbus scored seven goals in 2 min 22 sec v. Prince George Vikings on 25 Jan 1980.

Great Britain The fastest goal in the British League was scored by Stephen Johnson for Durham Wasps after four seconds v. Ayr Bruins at Ayr, Strathclyde on 6 Nov 1983. Mark Salisbury (GB) (b. 4 Dec 1970) scored a hat-trick in 19 seconds for Basingstoke Beavers v. Telford Tigers on 26 Jan 1991.

In an English Junior League (under-16) game Jonathan Lumbis scored a hat-trick in 13 seconds for Nottingham Cougars v. Peterborough Jets on 4 Nov 1984.

Ice Skating

Figure Skating

Most titles *Olympic* The most Olympic gold medals won by a figure skater is three by: Gillis Grafström (Sweden) (1893–1938) in 1920, 1924 and 1928 (also silver medal in 1932); Sonja Henie (Norway) (1912–69) in 1928, 1932 and 1936; and Irina Konstantinovna Rodnina (USSR) (b. 12 Sep 1949) with two different partners in the Pairs in 1972, 1976 and 1980.

World The greatest number of men's individual world figure skating titles (instituted 1896) is ten by Ulrich Salchow (Sweden) (1877–1949) in 1901–5 and 1907–11. The women's record (instituted 1906) is also ten individual titles by Sonja Henie between 1927 and 1936. Irina Rodnina won ten pairs titles

Guess What?

Q. What record does Stanley Wood hold?

A. See Page 130

■ Bonnie Blair is the current holder of the 500 m speed skating world record. She has won this event at the last three Olympic Games.
(Photos: Allsport (USA)/S. Bruty)

Distance Robin John Cousins (GB) (b. 17 Aug 1957) achieved 5.81 m *19 ft 1 in* in an axel jump and 5.48 m *18 ft* with a back flip at Richmond Ice Rink, Surrey on 16 Nov 1983.

Most mid-air rotations Kurt Browning (Canada) (b. 18 Jun 1966) was the first to achieve a quadruple jump in competition—a toe loop in the World Championships at Budapest, Hungary on 25 Mar 1988. The first woman to do so was Suruaya Bonaly (France) (b. 15 Dec 1973) in the World Championships at Munich, Germany on 16 Mar 1991.

> The world's largest indoor ice rink is in the Moscow Olympic arena which has an ice area of 8064 m² *86,800 ft²*. The five rinks at Fujikyu Highland Skating Centre, Japan total 26,500 m² *285,243 ft²*.

Speed Skating

Most titles *Olympic* The most Olympic gold medals won in speed skating is six by Lidiya Pavlovna Skoblikova (USSR) (b. 8 Mar 1939) in 1960 (two) and 1964 (four). The male record is five by: Clas Thunberg (Finland) (1893–1973) (including one tied) in 1924 and 1928; and Eric Arthur Heiden (USA) (b. 14 Jun 1958), uniquely at one Games at Lake Placid, New York, USA in 1980. The most medals is seven by: Clas Thunberg, who additionally won one silver and one tied bronze; and Ivar Ballangrud (1904–69) (Norway), four gold, two silver and a bronze, 1928–36.

World The greatest number of world overall titles (instituted 1893) won by any skater is five; by Oscar Mathisen (Norway) (1888–1954) in 1908–9 and 1912–14; and by Clas Thunberg in 1923, 1925, 1928–9 and 1931. The most titles won in the women's events (instituted 1936) is five by Karin Kania (*née* Enke) (GDR) (b. 20 Jun 1961) in 1982, 1984, 1986–8. Kania also won a record six overall titles at the World Sprint Championships 1980–81, 1983–4, 1986–7. A record six men's sprint overall titles have been won by Igor Zhelezovskiy (USSR/Belarus), 1985–6, 1989 and 1991–3.

The record score achieved for the world overall title is 156.201 points by Rintje Ritsma (Netherlands) at Hamar, Norway on 7–9 Jan 1994. The record low women's score is 164.658 points by Emese Hunyady (Austria) at Calgary, Canada on 26–27 Mar 1994.

World Short-track Championships The most successful skater in these championships (instituted 1978) has been Sylvia Daigle (Canada) (b. 1 Dec 1962) women's overall champion in 1979, 1983 and 1989–90.

The first British skater to win the world title was Wilfred John O'Reilly (b. 22 Aug 1964) at Sydney, Australia on 24 Mar 1991.

Longest race The 'Elfstedentocht' ('Tour of the Eleven Towns'), which originated in the 17th century, was held in the Netherlands from 1909–63, and again in 1985 and 1986, covering 200 km *124 miles 483 yd*. As the weather does not permit an annual race in the Netherlands, alternative 'Elfstedentocht' take place at suitable venues. These venues have included Lake Vesijärvi, near Lahti, Finland; Ottawa River, Canada and Lake Weissensee, Austria. The record time for 200 km is: men, 5 hr 40 min 37 sec by Dries van Wijhe (Netherlands); and women, 5 hr

(instituted 1908), four with Aleksey Nikolayevich Ulanov (b. 4 Nov 1947), 1969–72, and six with her husband Aleksandr Gennadyevich Zaitsev (b. 16 Jun 1952), 1973–8. The most ice dance titles (instituted 1952) won is six by Lyudmila Alekseyevna Pakhomova (1946–86) and her husband Aleksandr Georgiyevich Gorshkov (USSR) (b. 8 Oct 1946), 1970–74 and 1976. They also won the first ever Olympic ice dance title in 1976.

British The most individual British titles are: (men) 11 by Jack Ferguson Page (1900–47) (Manchester SC) in 1922–31 and 1933; and (women) six by Magdalena Cecilia Colledge (b. 28 Nov 1920) (Park Lane FSC, London) in 1935–6, 1937 (two), 1938 and 1946, and by Joanne Conway (b. 11 Mar 1971) between 1985 and 1991. Page and Ethel Muckelt (1885–1953) won nine pairs titles, 1923–31. The most by an ice dance couple is seven by Jayne Torvill (b. 7 Oct 1957) and Christopher Colin Dean (b. 27 Jul 1958), 1978–83, 1994.

Triple Crown Karl Schäfer (Austria) (1909–76) and Sonja Henie achieved double 'Grand Slams', both in the years 1932 and 1936. This feat was repeated by Katarina Witt (GDR) (b. 3 Dec 1965) in 1984 and 1988. The only British skaters to win the 'Grand Slam'

> **Guess What?**
> Q. Where was the largest iceberg sighted?
> A. See Page 12

of World, Olympic and European titles in the same year are John Anthony Curry (1949–94) in 1976 and the ice dancers Jayne Torvill and Christopher Dean in 1984.

Highest marks The highest tally of maximum six marks awarded in an international championship was 29 to Jayne Torvill and Christopher Dean (GB) in the World Ice Dance Championships at Ottawa, Canada on 22–24 Mar 1984. This comprised seven in the compulsory dances, a perfect set of nine for presentation in the set pattern dance and 13 in the free dance, including another perfect set from all nine judges for artistic presentation. They previously gained a perfect set of nine sixes for artistic presentation in the free dance at the 1983 World Championships in Helsinki, Finland and at the 1984 Winter Olympic Games in Sarajevo, Yugoslavia.

The most by a soloist is seven: by Donald George Jackson (Canada) (b. 2 Apr 1940) in the World Men's Championship at Prague, Czechoslovakia in 1962; and by Midori Ito (Japan) (b. 13 Aug 1969) in the World Women's Championships at Paris, France in 1989.

Speed Skating

WORLD RECORDS

MEN

Distance (m)min:sec	Name (Country)	Venue	Date
500 ....35.76	Dan Jansen (USA)	Calgary, Canada	30 Jan 1994
1000 ......1:12.43	Dan Jansen (USA)	Hamar, Norway	18 Feb 1994
1:12.05Au	Nick Thometz (USA)	Medeo, USSR	26 Mar 1987
1500 ......1:51.29	Johann Olav Koss (Norway)	Hamar, Norway	16 Feb 1994
3000 ......3:56.16	Thomas Bos (Netherlands)	Calgary, Canada	3 Mar 1992
5000 ......6:34.96	Johann Olav Koss (Norway)	Hamar, Norway	13 Feb 1994
10,000 ....13:30.55	Johann Olav Koss (Norway)	Hamar, Norway	20 Feb 1994

u unofficial. A set at high altitude.

WOMEN

500 ....38.69	Bonnie Blair (USA)	Calgary, Canada	12 Feb 1995
1000 ......1:17.65	Christa Rothenburger (now Luding) (GDR)	Calgary, Canada	26 Feb 1988
1500 ......1:59.30A	Karin Kania (*née* Enke) (GDR)	Medeo, USSR	22 Mar 1986
3000 ......4:09.32	Gunda Niemann (*née* Kleeman) (Germany)	Calgary, Canada	25 Mar 1994
5000 ......7:03.26	Gunda Niemann (*née* Kleeman) (Germany)	Calgary, Canada	26 Mar 1994
10,000* 15:25.25	Yvonne van Gennip (Netherlands)	Heerenveen, Netherlands	19 Mar 1988

* Record not officially recognized for this distance.

WORLD RECORDS – SHORT TRACK

MEN

500 ....42.99	Mirko Vuillermin (Italy)	Graz, Austria	21 Jan 1995
1000 ......1:28.47	Michael McMillen (New Zealand)	Denver, Colorado, USA	4 Apr 1992
1500 ......2:22.36	Eric Flaim (USA)	Beijing, China	21 Mar 1993
3000 ......5:00.83	Chae Ji-hoon (South Korea)	Lake Placid, USA	16 Jan 1993
5000 relay 7:10.95	New Zealand	Beijing, China	28 Mar 1993

(Michael McMillen, Chris Nicholson, Andrew Nicholson, Matthew Briggs)

WOMEN

500 ....45.60	Zhang Yanmei (China)	Beijing, China	27 Mar 1993
1000 ......1:34.07	Nathalie Lambert (Canada)	Hamar, Norway	7 Nov 1994
1500 ......2:27.38	Chun Lee-Kyung (South Korea)	Jaca, Spain	23 Feb 1995
3000 ......5:18.33	Mariarosa Candido (Italy)	Budapest, Hungary	17 Jan 1988
3000 relay 4:26.56	Canada	Beijing, China	28 Mar 1993

(Nathalie Lambert, Angela Cutrone, Isabelle Charest, Christine Boudrias)

BRITISH RECORDS – SHORT TRACK

MEN

500 ....43.19	Nicholas Gooch	Graz, Austria	20 Jan 1995
1000 ......1:31.32	Nicholas Gooch	Gyovick, Norway	18 Mar 1995
1500 ......2:18.84	Nicholas Gooch	Guildford	7 Mar 1995
3000 ......4:59.01	Nicholas Gooch	Humberside	6 Mar 1994
5000 relay 7:18.78	Great Britain	Hamar, Norway	9 Nov 1993

(Wilfred O'Reilly, Nicholas Gooch, Matthew Jasper, Jamie Fearn)

WOMEN

500 ....47.37	Debbie Palmer	Gyovick, Norway	18 Mar 1995
1000 ......1:41.25	Debbie Palmer	Bormio, Italy	27 Nov 1994
1500 ......2:38.13	Debbie Palmer	Brugge, Belgium	15 Jan 1994
3000 ......5:34.81	Debbie Palmer	Graz, Austria	21 Jan 1995
3000 relay 5:05.04	Great Britain	Budapest, Hungary	17 Jan 1988

(Caron New, Alyson Birch, Nicky Bell, Alea Hopcroft)

48 min 8 sec by Alida Pasveer (Netherlands), both at Lake Weissensee (altitude 1100 m *3609 ft*), Austria on 11 Feb 1989. Jan-Roelof Kruithof (Netherlands) won the race nine times, 1974, 1976–7, 1979–84. An estimated 16,000 skaters took part in 1986.

24 hours Martinus Kuiper (Netherlands) skated 546.65 km *339.67 miles* in 24 hours at Alkmaar, Netherlands on 12–13 Dec 1988.

Barrel jumping on ice skates The official distance record is 8.97 m *29 ft 5 in* over 18 barrels, by Yvon Jolin at Terrebonne, Québec, Canada on 25 Jan 1981. The women's record is 6.84 m *22 ft 5¼ in* over 13 barrels, by Marie-Josée Houle at Lasalle, Québec, Canada on 1 Mar 1987.

Judo

Most titles *World and Olympic* World Championships were inaugurated in Tokyo, Japan in 1956. Women's championships were first held in 1980 in New York, USA. Yasuhiro Yamashita (b. 1 Jun 1957), who won nine consecutive Japanese titles 1977–85, won five world and Olympic titles; Over 95 kg 1979, 1981 and 1983, Open 1981, and the Olympic Open category in 1984. He retired undefeated after 203 successive wins, 1977–85. Two other men have won four world titles, Shozo Fujii (Japan) (b. 12 May 1950), Under 80 kg 1971, 1973 and 1975, Under 78 kg 1979, and Naoya Ogawa (Japan), Open 1987, 1989, 1991 and Over 95 kg 1989. The only men to have won two Olympic gold medals are Wilhelm Ruska (Netherlands) (b. 29 Aug 1940), Over 93 kg and Open in 1972;

Peter Seisenbacher (Austria) (b. 25 Mar 1960), 86 kg 1984 and 1988; Hitoshi Saito (Japan) (b. 2 Jan 1961), Over 95 kg 1984 and 1988; and Waldemar Legien (Poland), 78 kg 1988 and 86 kg 1992. Ingrid Berghmans (Belgium) (b. 24 Aug 1961) has won a record six women's world titles (first held 1980): Open 1980, 1982, 1984 and 1986 and Under 72 kg in 1984 and 1989. She has also won four silver medals and a bronze. She won the Olympic 72 kg title in 1988, when women's judo was introduced as a demonstration sport.

Karen Briggs (b. 11 Apr 1963) is the most successful British player, with four women's world titles, Under 48 kg in 1982, 1984, 1986 and 1989.

British The greatest number of titles (instituted 1966) won is nine by David Colin Starbrook (b. 9 Aug 1945) (6th dan): Middleweight 1969–70, Light-heavyweight 1971–5 and the Open division 1970–71. Karen Briggs has won a women's record seven titles (instituted 1971), Open 1981–2, 1986–7, 1989–90 and 1992. Adrian Neil Adams (b. 27 Sep 1958) has the most successful international record of any British male player. He won two junior (1974 and 1977) and five senior (1979–80, 1983–5) European titles; four World Championships medals (one gold, one silver, two bronze) and two Olympic silver medals. He also won eight British senior titles.

10 hours Brian Woodward and David Norman completed 33,681 judo throwing techniques in a ten-hour period at the Whybridge Parent's Association Children Club, Rainham, Essex on 10 Apr 1994.

Jiu-Jitsu The World Council of Jiu-Jitsu Organization has staged World Championships biennially since 1984. The Canadian team has been the team winners on each occasion.

Karate

World Championships Great Britain have won a record six world titles (instituted 1970) at the Kumite team event, 1975, 1982, 1984, 1986, 1988 and 1990. Two men's individual kumite titles have been won by: Pat McKay (GB) at Under 80 kg, 1982 and 1984; Emmanuel Pinda (France) at Open, 1984 and Over 80 kg, 1988; Theirry Masci (France) at Under 70 kg, 1986 and 1988 and José Manuel Egea (Spain) at Under 80 kg, 1990 and 1992. Four women's kumite titles have been won by Guus van Mourik (Netherlands) at Over 60 kg, 1982, 1984, 1986 and 1988. Three individual kata titles have been won by men: Tsuguo Sakumoto (Japan) 1984, 1986 and 1988; women: Mie Nakayama (Japan) 1982, 1984 and 1986: Yuki Mimura (Japan) 1988, 1990 and 1992.

Top exponents The leading exponents among karateka are a number of 10th dans in Japan. The leading exponents in the United Kingdom are 8th dans: Tatsuo Suzuki (*Wado-ryu*) (b. 27 Apr 1928), Steve Arneil (*Kyokushinkai*), Keinosuke Enoeda and Shiro Asano (both *Shotokan*).

Lacrosse

Men

Most titles *World* The USA has won six of the seven World Championships, in 1967, 1974, 1982, 1986, 1990 and 1994. Canada won the other world title in 1978 beating the USA 17–16 after extra time—this was the first drawn international match.

English The English Club Championship (Iroquois Cup instituted 1890), has been won most often by Stockport with 17 wins between 1897 and 1989. The record score in a final is 33 by Stockport *v.* London University (4) on 9 May 1987.

Guess What?

Q. What is the fastest time to roll a barrel one mile?

A. See Page 206

Marbles

Most championships The British Championship (established 1926) has been won most often by the Toucan Terribles with 20 consecutive titles (1956–75). Three founder members, Len Smith, Jack and Charlie Dempsey, played in every title win. They were finally beaten in 1976 by the Pernod Rams, captained by Len Smith's son, Paul. Len Smith (1917–90) won the individual title 15 times (1957–64, 1966, 1968–73) but lost in 1974 to his son Alan.

> **Fastest time**
> The record for clearing the ring (between 1.75 and 1.9 m *5¾–6¼ ft* in diameter) of 49 marbles is 2 min 56 sec by the Black Dog Boozers of Crawley, W Sussex at BBC Television Centre, London for *Record Breakers* on 14 Sep 1987.

Most international appearances The record number of international representations is 42 by Peter Daniel Roden (Mellor) (b. 8 Nov 1954) from 1976–90.

Highest scores The highest score in an international match is Scotland's 34–3 win over Germany at Greater Manchester on 25 Jul 1994.

Women

World Championships/World Cup The first World Cup was held in 1982, replacing the World Championships which had been held three times since 1969. The USA have won four times, 1974, 1982, 1989 and 1993.

Most international appearances Vivien Jones played in 86 internationals (74 for Wales, 9 for the Celts and 3 for Great Britain), 1977–94. Caro Macintosh (b. 18 Feb 1932) played in 56 internationals (52 for Scotland and four for Great Britain).

Highest score The highest score by an international team was by Great Britain and Ireland with their 40–0 defeat of Long Island during their 1967 tour of the USA.

Microlighting

The *Fédération Aéronautique Internationale* accepts records for thee sub classes of microlights (R 1-2-4), and the following are a selection of the overall best (all in R1 sub-class).

World records Distance in a straight line: 1369 km *850 miles* Bernard d'Otreppe (Belgium), Fréjus La Palud, France, 6 Sep 1988.

Distance in a closed circuit: 1071.2 km *665.6 miles* Michel Serane (France), Besançon-Thise, France, 5 Aug 1991.

Altitude: 9720 m *31,890 ft* Serge Zin (France), Saint Auban, France, 18 Sep 1994.

Speed over a 15/25 km closed circuit: 194.5 km/h *120.8 mph* Phillippe Zen and Patrick Durand (France), Belley-Peyrieu, France, 1 Jun 1994.

Endurance Eve Jackson flew from Biggin Hill, Kent to Sydney, Australia from 26 Apr 1986 to 1 Aug 1987. The flight took 279 hr 55 min and covered 21,950 km *13,639 miles*. From 1 Dec 1987 to 29 Jan 1988, Brian Milton (GB) flew from London to Sydney with a flying time of 241 hr 20 min and covered 21,968 km *13,650 miles*. Vijaypat Singhania (India) flew from Biggin Hill to Delhi, India, a distance of 8724 km *5420 miles* in 87 hr 55 min, from 18 Aug to 10 Sep 1988.

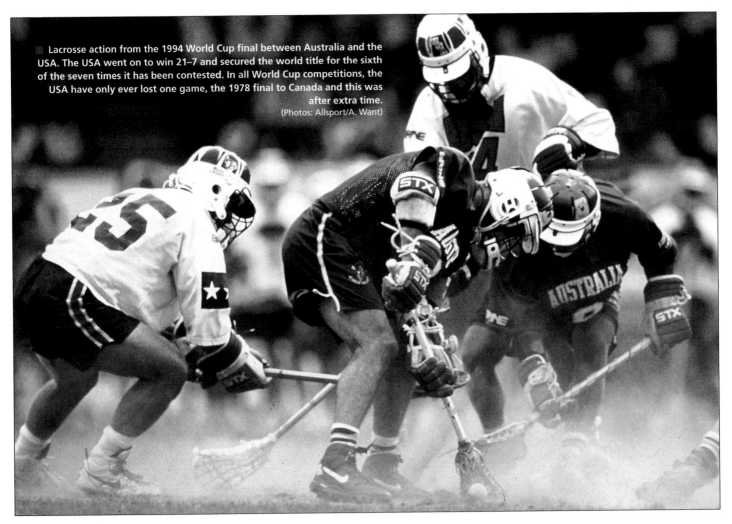

Lacrosse action from the 1994 World Cup final between Australia and the USA. The USA went on to win 21–7 and secured the world title for the sixth of the seven times it has been contested. In all World Cup competitions, the USA have only ever lost one game, the 1978 final to Canada and this was after extra time.
(Photos: Allsport/A. Want)

Modern Pentathlon & Biathlon

Points scored in riding, fencing, cross country and hence overall scores have no comparative value between one competition and another. In shooting and swimming (300 m) the scores are of record significance.

Modern Pentathlon

Most titles *World* András Balczó (Hungary) (b. 16 Aug 1938) won a record number of world titles (instituted 1949), six individual and seven team. He won the world individual title in 1963, 1965–7 and 1969 and the Olympic title in 1972. His seven team titles (1960–70) comprised five world and two Olympic. The USSR has won a record 14 world and four Olympic team titles. Hungary has also won a record four Olympic team titles (and ten world titles).

Women's World Championships were first held in 1981, replacing the World Cup which began in 1978. Poland have won a record five women's world team titles: 1985, 1988–91; Great Britain won three world titles, 1981–3, and three World Cups, 1978–80. Eva Fjellerup (Denmark) (b. 30 Apr 1962) has won the individual title three times, 1990–91, 1993.

Olympic (first held 1912) The greatest number of Olympic gold medals won is three, by András Balczó, a member of the winning team in 1960 and 1968 and the 1972 individual champion. Lars Hall (Sweden) (b. 30 Apr 1927) has uniquely won two individual championships (1952 and 1956). Pavel Serafimovich Lednyev (USSR) (b. 25 Mar 1943) won a record seven medals (two team gold, one team silver, one individual silver, three individual bronze), 1968–80.

The best British performance is the team gold medal in 1976 by Jim Fox, Adrian Philip Parker and Daniel Nightingale. The best individual placing is fourth by Jeremy Robert 'Jim' Fox (b. 19 Sep 1941) in 1972 and Richard Lawson Phelps (b. 19 Apr 1961) in 1984.

Probably the greatest margin of victory was by William Oscar Guernsey Grut (Sweden) (b. 17 Sep 1914) in the 1948 Games, when he won three events and was placed fifth and eighth in the other two.

British The most British titles is eleven by Richard Phelps, 1979, 1981–4, 1986, 1988, 1990–91, 1993 and 1995. Wendy Norman won a record seven women's titles, 1978–80, 1982, 1986–8.

Biathlon

Most titles *Olympic (first held 1960)* Two men's Olympic individual titles have been won by: Magnar Solberg (Norway) (b. 4 Feb 1937), in 1968 and 1972; and by Frank-Peter Rötsch (GDR) (b. 19 Apr 1964) at both 10 km and 20 km in 1988. Aleksandr Ivanovich Tikhonov (b. 2 Jan 1947) won four relay golds, 1968–80 and also won a silver in the 1968 20 km. A women's competition was introduced in 1992. The most titles is two by: Anfissa Restzova (Russia) (b. 16 Dec 1964), 7.5 km 1992, 4 × 7.5 km 1994; and Myriam Bédard (Canada) (b. 22 Dec 1969), 7.5 km, 15 km 1994.

World (instituted 1958) Frank Ullrich (GDR) (b. 24 Jan 1958) has won a record six individual world titles, four at 10 km, 1978–81, including the 1980 Olympics, and two at 20 km, 1982–3. Aleksandr Tikhonov was in ten winning Soviet relay teams, 1968–80 and won four individual titles.

The Biathlon World Cup (instituted 1979) was won four times by Frank Ullrich, 1978 and 1980–82; and Franz Peter Rötsch (GDR), 1984–5 and 1987–8.

Women The first World Championships were held in 1984. The most individual titles is three by Anne-Elinor Elvebakk (Norway), 10 km 1988, 7.5 km 1989–90. Kaya Parve (USSR) has won six titles, two individual and four relay, 1984–6, 1988. A women's World Cup began in 1988.

Motorcycle Racing

Oldest race The oldest annually contested motorcycle races in the world are the Auto-Cycle Union Tourist Trophy (TT) series, first held on the 25.44 km *15.81 mile* 'Peel' (St John's) course in the Isle of Man on 28 May 1907, and still run in the island on the 'Mountain' circuit.

Fastest circuits The highest average lap speed attained on any closed circuit is 257.958 km/h *160.288 mph* by Yvon du Hamel (Canada) (b. 1941) on a modified 903 cc four-cylinder Kawasaki Z1 at the 31-degree banked 4.02 km *2.5 mile* Daytona International Speedway, Florida, USA in March 1973. His lap time was 56.149 sec.

The fastest road circuit used to be Francorchamps circuit near Spa, Belgium, then 14.12 km *8.77 miles* in length. It was lapped in 3 min 50.3 sec (average speed 220.721 km/h *137.150 mph*) by Barry Stephen Frank Sheene (GB) (b. 11 Sep 1950) on a 495 cc 4-cylinder Suzuki during the Belgian Grand Prix on 3 Jul 1977. On that occasion he set a record time for this ten-lap (141.20 km *87.74 mile*) race of 38 min 58.5 sec (average speed 217.370 km/h *135.068 mph*).

Guess What?

Q. What are the three sports of a triathlon?

A. See Page 299

United Kingdom The lap record for the outer circuit (4.453 km *2.767 miles*) at the Brooklands Motor Course, near Weybridge, Surrey (open between 1907 and 1939) was 80 seconds (average speed 200.37 km/h *124.51 mph*) by Noel Baddow 'Bill' Pope (later Major) (GB) (1909–71) on a Brough Superior powered by a supercharged 996 cc V-twin '8-80' JAP engine developing 110 bhp, on 4 Jul 1939.

The fastest circuit in current use is that over public roads at Dundrod, Co. Antrim for the Ulster Grand Prix. Jason Griffiths (Wales) set a lap record of 202.94 km/h *126.10 mph* on 12 Aug 1994 and Steve Hislop (Scotland) (b. 11 Jan 1962) set an overall average speed of 195.48 km/h *121.46 mph* for the 'King of the Road' race on 11 Aug 1990.

Longest circuit The 60.72 km *37.73 mile* 'Mountain' circuit on the Isle of Man, over which the principal TT races have been run since 1911 (with minor amendments in 1920), has 264 curves and corners and is the longest used for any motorcycle race.

Most successful riders *World Championships* The most World Championship titles (instituted by the *Fédération Internationale Motocycliste* in 1949) won is 15 by Giacomo Agostini (Italy) (b. 16 Jun 1942), seven at 350 cc, 1968–74, and eight at 500 cc in 1966–72, 1975. He is the only man to win two World Championships in five consecutive years (350 cc and 500 cc titles 1968–72).

318.331 km/h in a Ford Thunderbird. Al Unser Jr (b. 19 Apr 1962) set the world record for a 500 mile 805 km race on 9 Aug 1990 when he won the Michigan 500A at an average speed of 189.7 mph 305.2 km/h.

World Championship Grand

Prix Motor Racing

Most successful drivers The World Drivers' Championship, inaugurated in 1950, has been won a record five times by Juan-Manuel Fangio (Argentina) (b. 24 Jun 1911) in 1951 and 1954–57. He retired in 1958, after having won 24 Grand Prix races (two shared) from 51 starts.

Alain Prost (France) (b. 24 Feb 1955) holds the records for both the most Grand Prix points in a career, 798.5 and the most Grand Prix victories, 51 from 199 races, 1980–93. The most Grand Prix victories in a year is nine by Nigel Mansell (GB) (b. 8 Aug 1953) in 1992. The most Grand Prix starts is 256 by Ricardo Patrese (Italy) (b. 17 Apr 1954) from 1977–93. The greatest number of pole positions is 65 by Ayrton Senna (Brazil) (1960–94) from 161 races (41 wins), 1985–94.

■ **Carl Fogarty, holder of the lap record for the Isle of Man TT course, won the 1994 World Superbike Championships, the first British solo rider to win a world title since Barry Sheene in 1977. He won 10 races in the season including the first at Donington Park, as seen here.**
(Photos: Allsport/M. Hewitt)

Angel Roldan Nieto (Spain) (b. 25 Jan 1947) won a record seven 125 cc titles, 1971–2, 1979, 1981–4 and he also won a record six titles at 50 cc, 1969–70, 1972, 1975–7. Phil Read (GB) (b. 1 Jan 1934) won a record four 250 cc titles, 1964–5, 1968, 1971. Rolf Biland (Switzerland) (b. 1 Apr 1951) won seven world side-car titles, 1978–9, 1981, 1983, 1992–4.

Agostini won 122 races (68 at 500 cc, 54 at 350 cc) in the World Championship series between 24 Apr 1965 and 25 Sep 1977, including a record 19 in 1970, a season's total also achieved by Mike Hailwood in 1966. The record number of career wins for any one class is 75 by Rolf Biland at side-car.

Most successful machines Japanese Yamaha machines won 45 World Championships between 1964 and 1992.

Tourist Trophy The record number of victories in the Isle of Man TT races is 19 by William Joseph Dunlop (Ireland) (b. 25 Feb 1952), 1977–95. The first man to win three consecutive TT titles in two events was James A. Redman (Rhodesia) (b. 8 Nov 1931). He won the 250 cc and 350 cc events in 1963–5. Stanley Michael Bailey Hailwood (1940–81) won three events in one year, in 1961 and 1967, and this feat was repeated by Joey Dunlop in 1985 and 1988; and by Steve Hislop in 1989 and 1991.

The Isle of Man TT circuit speed record is 198.92 km/h 123.61 mph by Carl George Fogarty (b. 1 Jul 1965) on 12 Jun 1992. On the same occasion Steve Hislop set the race speed record, 1 hr 51 min 59.6 sec for an average speed of 195.17 km/h 121.28 mph to win the

■ **Michael Doohan became the fifth Australian to win a motorcycling world championship when he won the 1994 500 cc title. He won nine races in the year including record six in succession, breaking the record set by the great Giacomo Agostini in 1972.**
(Photo: Allsport/M. Cooper)

1992 Senior TT on a Norton. The fastest woman around the 'Mountain' circuit is Sandra Barnett (GB) who achieved a speed of 179.86 km/h 111.76 mph in the 1995 Senior TT on 9 June.

Trials A record six World Trials Championships have been won by Jordi Tarrès (Spain) (b. 10 Sep 1966), 1987, 1989–91, 1993–4.

Moto-cross Joël Robert (Belgium) (b. 11 Nov 1943) won six 250 cc Moto-cross World Championships (1964, 1968–72). . Between 25 Apr 1964 and 18 Jun 1972 he won a record fifty 250 cc Grand Prix. The youngest moto-cross world champion was Dave Strijbos (Netherlands) (b. 9 Nov 1968), who won the 125 cc title aged 18 yr 296 days on 31 Aug 1986. Eric Geboers (Belgium) has uniquely won all three categories of the Moto-Cross World Championships, at 125 cc in 1982 and 1983, 250 cc in 1987 and 500 cc in 1988 and 1990.

Youngest and oldest world champions Loris Capirossi (Italy) (b. 4 Apr 1973) is the youngest to win a World Championship. He was 17 yr 165 days when he won the 125 cc title on 16 Sep 1990. The oldest was Hermann-Peter Müller (1909–76) of West Germany, who won the 250 cc title in 1955 aged 46.

Motor Racing

Fastest circuits The highest average lap speed attained on any closed circuit is 403.878 km/h 250.958 mph in a trial by Dr Hans Liebold (Germany) (b. 12 Oct 1926) who lapped the 12.64 km 7.85 mile high-speed track at Nardo, Italy in 1 min 52.67 sec in a Mercedes-Benz C111-IV experimental coupé on 5 May 1979. It was powered by a V8 engine with two KKK turbochargers, with an output of 500 hp at 6200 rpm.

Fastest race The fastest race is the Busch Clash at Daytona, Florida, USA over 50 miles 80.5 km on a 2½ mile 4 km 31-degree banked track. In 1987 Bill Elliott (b. 8 Oct 1955) averaged 197.802 mph

Oldest Race

The oldest race in the world still regularly run, is the RAC Tourist Trophy, first staged on 14 Sep 1905, in the Isle of Man. The oldest continental race is the French Grand Prix, first held on 26–27 Jun 1906. The Coppa Florio, in Sicily, has been held irregularly since 1906.

Guess What?

Q. What is the longest trial in British justice?

A. See Page 186

Oldest and youngest The youngest world champion was Emerson Fittipaldi (Brazil) (b. 12 Dec 1946) who won his first World Championship on 10 Sep 1972 aged 25 years 273 days. The oldest world champion was Juan-Manuel Fangio who won his last World Championship on 4 Aug 1957 aged 46 yr 41 days.

The youngest Grand Prix winner was Bruce Leslie McLaren (1937–70) of New Zealand, who won the United States Grand Prix at Sebring, Florida on 12 Dec 1959, aged 22 yr 104 days. Troy Ruttman (USA) was 22 yr 80 days when he won the Indianapolis 500 on 30 May 1952, which was part of the World Championships at the time. The oldest Grand Prix winner (in pre-World Championship days) was Tazio Giorgio Nuvolari (Italy) (1892–1953), who won the Albi Grand Prix at Albi, France on 14 Jul 1946, aged 53 yr 240 days. The oldest Grand Prix driver was Louis Alexandre Chiron (Monaco) (1899–1979), who finished sixth in the Monaco Grand Prix on 22 May 1955, aged 55 yr 292 days. The youngest driver to qualify for a Grand Prix was Michael Christopher Thackwell (New Zealand) (b. 30 Mar 1961) at the Canadian GP on 28 Sep 1980, aged 19 yr 182 days.

Manufacturers Ferrari have won a record eight manufacturers' World Championships, 1961, 1964, 1975–77, 1979, 1982–83. The most race wins is 105 by Ferrari to June 1995.

The greatest dominance by one team since the Constructor's Championship was instituted in 1958 was by McLaren in 1988 when they won 15 of the 16 Grands Prix. Ayrton Senna had eight wins and three seconds, Alain Prost had seven wins and seven seconds. The McLarens, powered by Honda engines, amassed over three times the points of their nearest rivals, Ferrari. Excluding the Indianapolis 500 race, then included in the World Drivers' Championship, Ferrari won all seven races in 1952 and the first eight (of nine) in 1953.

■ Gerhard Berger celebrates in typical fashion having won the 1994 German Grand Prix. It was a notable success for his team, Ferrari, as it was their first win in over four years and equalled the record of most wins for a manufacturer, 104, held by McLaren.
(Photos: Allsport/M. Hewitt and R. Rondeau)

Fastest race The fastest overall average speed for a Grand Prix race on a circuit in current use is 235.421 km/h *146.284 mph* by Nigel Mansell (GB) in a Williams-Honda at Zeltweg in the Austrian Grand Prix on 16 Aug 1987. The qualifying lap record was set by Keke Rosberg (Finland) at 1 min 05.59 sec, an average speed of 258.802 km/h *160.817 mph*, in a Williams-Honda at Silverstone in the British Grand Prix on 20 Jul 1985.

Closest finish The closest finish to a World Championship race was when Ayrton Senna (Brazil) in a Lotus beat Nigel Mansell (GB) in a Williams by 0.014 sec in the Spanish Grand Prix at Jerez de la Frontera on 13 Apr 1986. In the Italian Grand Prix at Monza on 5 Sep 1971, 0.61 sec separated winner Peter Gethin (GB) from the fifth placed driver.

British Grand Prix

First held in 1926 as the RAC Grand Prix, and held annually with the above name since 1949. The venues have been Aintree, Merseyside; Brands Hatch, Kent; Brooklands, Surrey; Donington, Leics and Silverstone, Northants.

Most wins The most wins by a driver is five by Jim Clark, 1962–5 and 1967, all in Lotus cars. Jim Clark and Jack Brabham (Australia) (b. 2 Apr 1926) have both won the race on three different circuits; Brands Hatch, Silverstone and Aintree. The most wins by a manufacturer is ten by Ferrari, 1951–4, 1956, 1958, 1961, 1976, 1978 and 1990.

> The fastest race time for the British Grand Prix is 1 hr 18 min 10.436 sec, average speed 235.405 km/h *146.274 mph*, when Alain Prost won in a McLaren at Silverstone on 21 Jul 1985.

Le Mans

The greatest distance ever covered in the 24-hour *Grand Prix d'Endurance* (first held on 26–27 May 1923) on the old Sarthe circuit at Le Mans, France is 5335.302 km *3315.203 miles* by Dr Helmut Marko (Austria) (b. 27 Apr 1943) and Gijs van Lennep (Netherlands) (b. 16 Mar 1942) in a 4907-cc flat-12

Porsche 917K Group 5 sports car, on 12–13 Jun 1971. The record for the greatest distance ever covered for the current circuit is 5331.998 km *3313.150 miles* (average speed 222.166 km/h *138.047 mph*) by Jan Lammers (Holland), Johnny Dumfries and Andy Wallace (both GB) in a Jaguar XJR9 on 11–12 Jun 1988.

The race lap record (now 13.536 km *8.411 mile* lap) is 3 min 21.27 sec (average speed 242.093 km/h *150.429 mph*) by Alain Ferté (France) in a Jaguar XRJ-9 on 10 Jun 1989. Hans Stück (West Germany) set the practice lap speed record of 251.664 km/h *156.377 mph* on 14 Jun 1985.

Most wins The race has been won by Porsche cars 13 times, in 1970–71, 1976–7, 1979, 1981–7, 1993. The most wins by one man is six by Jacques Bernard 'Jacky' Ickx (Belgium) (b. 1 Jan 1945), 1969, 1975–7 and 1981–2.

Indianapolis 500

The Indianapolis 500 mile *804 km* race (200 laps) was inaugurated in the USA on 30 May 1911. Three drivers have four wins: Anthony Joseph 'A.J.' Foyt Jr (USA) (b. 16 Jan 1935) in 1961, 1964, 1967 and 1977; Al Unser Sr (USA) (b. 29 May 1939) in 1970–71, 1978 and 1987; and Rick Ravon Mears (USA) (b. 3 Dec 1951) in

1979, 1984, 1988 and 1991. The record time is 2 hr 41 min 18.404 sec (299.307 km/h *185.981 mph*) by Arie Luyendyk (Netherlands) driving a Lola-Chevrolet on 27 May 1990. The record average speed for four-laps qualifying is 374.143 km/h *232.482 mph* by Roberto Guerrero (Colombia) in a Lola-Buick (including a one-lap record of 374.362 km/h *232.618 mph*) on 9 May 1992. The track record is 376.758 km/h *234.107 mph* by Arie Luyendyk (Netherlands) on 9 May 1995. A. J. Foyt Jr started in a record 35 races, 1958–92 and Rick Mears has started from pole position a record six times, 1979, 1982, 1986, 1988–89 and 1991. The record prize fund is $8,028,247 in 1995 and the individual prize record is $1,373,813 by Al Unser Jr in 1994.

Rallying

The earliest long rally was promoted by the Parisian daily *Le Matin* in 1907 from Peking (now Beijing), China to Paris over about 12,000 km *7500 miles* on 10 June. The winner, Prince Scipione Borghese (1872–1927) of Italy, arrived in Paris on 10 Aug 1907 in his 40-hp Itala accompanied by his chauffeur, Ettore, and Luigi Barzini.

Longest The longest ever rally was the *Singapore Airlines* London–Sydney Rally over 31,107 km *19,329 miles* from Covent Garden, London on 14 Aug 1977 to Sydney Opera House, won on 28 Sep 1977 by Andrew Cowan, Colin Malkin and Michael Broad in a Mercedes 280E. The longest held annually is the Safari Rally (first run in 1953 as the Coronation Rally, through Kenya, Tanzania and Uganda, but now restricted to Kenya). The race has covered up to 6234 km *3874 miles*, as in the 17th Safari held from 8–12 Apr 1971. It has been won a record five times by Shekhar Mehta (b. Kenya, 20 Jun 1945) in 1973, 1979–82.

Monte Carlo

The Monte Carlo Rally (first run 1911) has been won a record four times by: Sandro Munari (Italy) (b. 27 Mar 1940) in 1972, 1975, 1976 and 1977; and Walter Röhrl (West Germany) (b. 7 Mar 1947) (with co-driver Christian Geistdorfer) in 1980, 1982–4, each time in a different car. The smallest car to win was an 851-cc Saab driven by Erik Carlsson (Sweden) (b. 5 Mar 1929) and Gunnar Häggbom (Sweden) (b. 7 Dec 1935) on 25 Jan 1962, and by Carlsson and Gunnar Palm on 24 Jan 1963.

The Paris–Cape Town rally in January 1992 was scheduled to be raced over about 12,700 km *7890 miles* from Paris to Cape Town passing through twelve countries—France, Libya, Niger, Chad, Central African Republic, Cameroon, Gabon, Congo, Angola, Namibia and South Africa. However due to civil war, flooding and enviromental concerns, certain stages were cancelled or shortened and the rally covered just over 9500 km *5900 miles*.

Britain The RAC Rally (first held 1932) has been recognized by the FIA since 1957. Hannu Mikkola (Finland) (b. 24 May 1942) (with co-driver Arne Hertz (Sweden)) has a record four wins, in a Ford Escort, 1978–9 and an Audi Quattro, 1981–2. Hertz was also co-driver for Stig Blomqvist (Sweden) when he won in 1971.

World Championship The World Drivers' Championships (instituted 1979) has been won by Juha Kankkunen (Finland) (b. 2 Apr 1959) on a record four occasions, 1986–7, 1991 and 1993. The most wins in World Championship races is 21 by Juha Kankkunen (Finland). The most wins in a season is six by Didier Auriol (France) (b. 18 Aug 1958) in 1992. Lancia have won a record eleven manufacturers' World Championships between 1972 and 1992.

Drag Racing

Piston engined (NHRA events) The lowest elapsed time recorded by a piston-engined dragster from a standing start for 440 yd *402 m* is 4.718 sec by Shelly Anderson (USA), and the highest terminal velocity at the end of a 440 yd run is 314.46 mph *506.07 km/h* by Kenny Bernstein (USA) both at Pomona, California on 27 and 30 Oct 1994, respectively. For a petrol-driven piston-engined car the lowest elapsed time is 6.988 sec by Kurt Johnson (USA) at Englishtown, New Jersey on 21 May 1994, and the highest terminal velocity is 197.80 mph *318.32 km/h* by Darrell Alderman (USA) at Somona, California on 27 Jul 1994. The lowest elapsed time for a petrol-driven piston-engined motorcycle is 7.532 sec and the highest terminal velocity is 292.66 km/h *181.85 mph* by David Schultz (USA) at Reading, Pennsylvania on 18 Sep 1994 and 19 Sep 1993, respectively.

■ **The greatest terminal velocity over 440 yd by a go-kart is 78.01 mph *125.54 km/h* set by Dan Bozich (USA), in a kart constructed by Gail Westfall and Bozich, at Portland, Oregon, USA on 23 May 1992.**
(Photos: Allan's Photos)

■ **Santosh Yadav of India (right) raises her national flag in celebration of reaching the summit of Everest, for a second time, on 10 May 1993. It was on this day that a record 40 people reached the summit.**

Mountaineering

Mt Everest Everest (8848 m *29,029 ft*) was first climbed at 11:30 a.m. on 29 May 1953, when the summit was reached by Edmund Percival Hillary (b. 20 Jul 1919), of New Zealand, and Sherpa Tenzing Norgay (1914–86, formerly called Tenzing Khumjung Bhutia). The successful expedition was led by Col. (later Hon. Brigadier) Henry Cecil John Hunt (b. 22 Jun 1910).

Most conquests Ang Rita Sherpa (b. 1947), with ascents in 1983, 1984, 1985, 1987, 1988, 1990, 1992, 1993 and 1995 has scaled Everest nine times and all without the use of bottled oxygen.

Solo Reinhold Messner (Italy) (b. 17 Sep 1944) was the first to make the entire climb solo on 20 Aug 1980. Also Messner, with Peter Habeler (Austria) (b. 22 Jul 1942), made the first entirely oxygen-less ascent on 8 May 1978.

First Britons Douglas Scott (b. 29 May 1941) and Dougal Haston (1940–77) successfully completed the climb on 24 Sep 1975. The first British woman to succeed was Rebecca Stephens (b. 3 Oct 1961) on 17 May 1993.

First woman Junko Tabei (Japan) (b. 22 Sep 1939) reached the summit on 16 May 1975.

■ **Reinhold Messner (left) is considered the most accomplished mountaineer ever, having completed, among many superlative achievements, the first solo and oxygen-less ascents of Everest.**
(Photo: Gamma/Paul Hanny)

Oldest Ramon Blanco (Spain) (b. 30 Apr 1933) was aged 60 years 160 days when he reached the summit on 7 Oct 1993.

Most successful expedition The Mount Everest International Peace Climb, a team of American, Soviet and Chinese climbers, led by James W. Whittaker (USA), in 1990 succeeded in putting the greatest number of people on the summit, 20, from 7–10 May 1990.

Most in a day On 10 May 1993, 40 climbers (32 men and 8 women) from the USA, Canada, Australia, Great Britain, Russia, New Zealand, Finland, Lithuania, India and Nepal, from nine separate expeditions, reached the summit.

Mountaineer Reinhold Messner was the first person to successfully scale all 14 of the world's mountains of over 8000 m *26,250 ft*, all without oxygen. With his ascent of Kanchenjunga in 1982, he was the first to climb the world's three highest mountains, having earlier reached the summits of Everest and K2.

Greatest walls The highest final stage in any wall climb is that on the south face of Annapurna I

(8091 m *26,545ft*). It was climbed by the British expedition led by Christian John Storey Bonington (b. 6 Aug 1934) when from 2 Apr to 27 May 1970, using 5500 m *18,000ft* of rope, Donald Whillans (1933–85) and Dougal Haston scaled to the summit. The longest wall climb is on the Rupal-Flank from the base camp at 3560 m *11,680ft* to the South Point 8042 m *26,384ft* of Nanga Parbat, a vertical ascent of 4482 m *14,704ft*. This was scaled by the Austro-German-Italian expedition led by Dr Karl Maria Herrligkoffer (b. 13 Jun 1916) in April 1970.

The most demanding free climbs in the world are those rated at 5.13, the premier location for these being in the Yosemite Valley, California, USA.

The top routes in Britain are graded E7.7b, which relates closely to 5.13.

Highest bivouac Mark Whetu (New Zealand) (b. 27 Oct 1959) and Michael Anthony Rheinberger (Australia) (1940–94) reached the summit of Everest on 26 May 1994 and bivouacked just 20 m below the summit that night. Sadly a very weak Rheinberger died the next day during the descent.

Mountain Racing

Mount Cameroon Reginald Esuke (Cameroon) descended from the summit 4095 m *13,435ft* to Buea Stadium at 915 m *3002ft* in 1 hr 2 min 15 sec on 24 Jan 1988, achieving a vertical rate of 51 m *167.5ft* per min. Timothy Leku Lekunze (Cameroon) set the record for the race to the summit and back of 3 hr 46 min 34 sec on 25 Jan 1987, when the temperature varied from 35°C at the start to 0°C at the summit. The record time for the ascent is 2 hr 25 min 20 sec by Jack Maitland (GB) in 1988. The women's record for the race is 4 hr 42 min 31 sec by Fabiola Rueda (Colombia) (b. 26 Mar 1963) in 1989.

Ben Nevis

The record time for the race from Fort William Town park to the summit of Ben Nevis (1347 m *4418ft*) and return is 1 hr 25 min 34 sec by Kenneth Stuart and the women's record is 1 hr 43 min 25 sec by Pauline Haworth, both on 1 Sep 1984.

Snowdon The record from Llanberis to the summit of Snowdon (1085 m *3560ft*) is 1 hr 2 min 29 sec by Kenneth Stuart in 1985 and the women's record is 1 hr 12 min 48 sec in 1993.

Mountain Endurance Running

Lakeland 24-hour The record is 76 peaks achieved by Mark McDermott (Macclesfield Harriers), covering 140 km *87 miles* and 11,900 m *39,000ft* of ascents and descents, starting from Braithwaite, Cumbria on 19–20 Jun 1988.

Scottish 24-hour The record is 28 Munros (mountains over 3000 ft *914 m*) from Cluanie Inn, with 35,000 ft *10,668 m* of ascents and descents achieved by Jon Broxap on 30–31 Jul 1988.

Bob Graham The record for the round of 42 lakeland peaks covering a total distance of 62 miles *99 km* and 26,000 ft *7900 m* of ascent and descent, is 13 hr 54 min by William Bland, 34, on 19 Jun 1982. Ernest Roger Baumeister (b. 17 Dec 1941) (Dark Peak Fell Runners Club) ran the double Bob Graham Round in 46 hr

34½ min on 30 Jun–1 Jul 1979. The women's single round record is 18 hr 49 min by Anne Stentiford (Macclesfield Harriers) on 21 Sep 1991.

Scottish 4000ft peaks The record for traversing all eight 4000 ft *1219 m* peaks, a 85 mile *136 km* cross-country route from Glen Nevis to Glen More is 21 hr 39 min by Martin Stone on 4 Jul 1987.

Scottish 3000ft peaks The Munros record for climbing and linking the 277 peaks (over 3000ft *914m*) entirely on foot is 66 days 22 hr by Hugh Symonds (b. 1 Feb 1953). He covered 1374 miles *2211km* and climbed 422,000ft *128,600m* between Ben Hope and Ben Lomond, 19 Apr–25 Jun 1990. He rowed to Skye, sailed to Mull and ran between all the other peaks. He continued on foot through England, Wales and Ireland, climbing the remaining 26 3000ft peaks in a total of 97 days.

Welsh 3000ft peaks The record for traversing the 15 Welsh peaks is 4 hr 19 min 56 sec, from Snowdon Summit to Foel Fras by Colin Donnelly on 11 Jun 1988. The women's record is 5 hr 28 min 41 sec by Angela Carson on 5 Aug 1989.

English 3000ft peaks The record for a circuit of the four English peaks from Keswick, Cumbria is 7 hr 35 min by William Bland on 15 Jun 1979.

Everest Base Camp to Kathmandu The record is 3 days 10 hr 8 min by Hélène Diamantides and Alison Wright from 8–10 Oct 1987. They covered 288km *180 miles*, climbed 9800 m *32,000 ft* and descended 14,000 m *46,000 ft*.

British Three Peaks record The Three Peaks route from sea level at Fort William, Highland, to sea level at Caernarvon, via the summits of Ben Nevis, Scafell Pike and Snowdon, was walked by Arthur Eddleston (1939–84) (Cambridge H) in 5 days 23 hr 37 min from 11–17 May 1980. The women's walking record is 7 days 31 min by Ann Sayer from 8–15 Sep 1979. Peter and David Ford, David Robinson, Kevin Duggan and John O'Callaghan, of Luton and Dunstable, ran the distance in relay in 54 hr 39 min 14 sec from 7–9 Aug 1981.

Abseiling (or Rappelling) A team of four Royal Marines set an overall distance record of 1105.5 m *3627ft*, by each abseiling down the Boulby Potash Mine, Cleveland from 7.6 m *25ft* below ground level to the shaft bottom on 2 Nov 1993.

The longest descent down the side of a building is one of 446.5 m *1465 ft*, by two teams of twelve, representing the Royal Marines from Great Britain and the Canadian School of Rescue Training. All twenty-four people abseiled from the Space Deck of the CN Tower in Toronto, Canada to the ground on 1 Jul 1992. Two ropes were used, the first member of each team reaching the ground at exactly the same time.

The greatest distance abseiled by a team of ten in an eight-hour period is 72.42 km *45.00 miles*, by Royal Marines from the Commando Training Centre at Lympstone, Devon. They achieved the record by abseiling 1382 times down the side of the Civic Centre at Plymouth, Devon on 22 May 1993.

Guess What?
Q. Where is the world's largest lake?
A. See Page 17

Netball

Most titles *World* Australia has won the World Championships (instituted 1963) a record six times, 1963, 1971, 1975, 1979, 1983 and 1991.

English The National Club's Championships (instituted 1966) have been won seven times by Sudbury Netball Club (1968–69, 1970 (shared), 1971, 1973, 1984–5). Surrey has won the County Championships (instituted 1932) a record 21 times (1949–64, 1966, 1981, 1991, 1992: 1969 and 1986 (both shared)).

The record number of international appearances in netball is 118 by Kendra Slawinski (b. 11 Nov 1962) of England, 1981–95.

Highest scores On 9 Jul 1991, during the World Championships at Sydney, Australia, the Cook Islands beat Vanuatu 120–38. The record number of goals in the World Championship by an individual is 402 by Judith Heath (England) (b. 1942) in 1971.

Orienteering

Most titles *World* The men's relay has been won a record seven times by Norway, 1970, 1978, 1981, 1983, 1985, 1987 and 1989. Sweden have won the women's relay ten times, 1966, 1970, 1974, 1976, 1981, 1983, 1985, 1989, 1991 and 1993. Three women's individual titles have been won by Annichen Kringstad (Sweden) (b. 15 Jul 1960), 1981, 1983 and 1985. The men's title has been won twice by: Åge Hadler (Norway) (b. 14 Aug 1944), in 1966 and 1972; Egil Johansen (Norway) (b. 18 Aug 1954), 1976 and 1978; and Øyvin Thon (Norway) (b. 25 Mar 1958), in 1979 and 1981.

The best British performance was in 1993 when Yvette Hague (b. 14 Jul 1967) was third in the women's individual and the men's relay team finished in second place.

Ski (instituted 1975) Sweden have won the men's relay title five times, 1977, 1980, 1982, 1984 and 1990. Finland have won the women's relay five times, 1975, 1977, 1980, 1988 and 1990. The most individual titles is four by Ragnhild Bratberg (Norway), Classic 1986, 1990, Sprint 1988, 1990. The men's record is three by Anssi Juutilainen (Finland) Classic 1984, 1988, Sprint 1992.

British Carol McNeill (b. 20 Feb 1944) won the women's title six times, 1967, 1969, 1972–6. Geoffrey Peck (b. 27 Sep 1949) won the men's individual title a record five times, 1971, 1973, 1976–7 and 1979.

Terry Dooris (b. 22 Sep 1926) of Southern Navigators has competed in all 29 British individual championships, 1967–95.

Human Fly

The longest climb achieved on the vertical face of a building occurred on 25 May 1981 when Daniel Goodwin, 25, of California, USA climbed a record 443.2 m *1454ft* up the outside of the Sears Tower in Chicago, USA, using suction cups and metal clips for support.

Most competitors
The most competitors at an event in one day is 38,000 for the Ruf des Herbstes at Sibiu, Romania in 1982. The largest event is the five-day Swedish O-Ringen at Småland, which attracted 120,000 in July 1983.

Paragliding

The greatest distance flown is 283.9 km *176.4 miles* by Alex François Louw (South Africa) from Kuruman, South Africa on 31 Dec 1992. The women's record is 128.5 km *79.8 miles* by Judy Leden (GB) from Vryburg, South Africa on 9 Dec 1992. The height gain record is 4526 m *14,849 ft* by Robby Whittal (GB) at Brandvlei, South Africa on 6 Jan 1993 and the women's best is 2971 m *9747 ft* by Verena Mühr (Germany) at Bitterwasser, Namibia on 13 Dec 1991. All these records were tow launched.

British The greatest distance flown is 253 km *157 miles* by Robby Whittal at Kuruman on 22 Jan 1993. The greatest distance flown within Britain is 175.4 km *108.9 miles* from Long Mynd, Shrops to Pulloxhill, Beds by Steve Ham on 19 May 1994 (foot-launched).

Pelota Vasca (Jaï Alaï)

World Championships The *Federación Internacional de Pelota Vasca* stage World Championships every four years (first in 1952). The most successful pair have been Roberto Elias (Argentina) (b. 15 Dec 1918) and Juan Labat (Argentina) (b. 10 Jan 1912), who won the *Trinquete Share* four times, 1952, 1958, 1962 and 1966. Labat won a record seven world titles in all between 1952 and 1966. Riccardo Bizzozero (Argentina) (b. 25 Nov 1948) also won seven world titles in various *Trinquete* and *Frontón corto* events, 1970–82. The most wins in the long court game *Cesta Punta* is three by José Hamuy (Mexico) (1934–83), with two different partners, 1958, 1962 and 1966.

Pétanque

World Championships Winner of the most World Championships (instituted 1959) has been France with 14 titles to 1994. The women's World Championships (instituted 1988) have been won twice by Thailand, 1988 and 1990, and France 1992 and 1994.

Highest score The highest score in 24 hours is by Chris Walker (b. 16 Jan 1942) and his son Richard (b. 26 Dec 1966) who scored a record 2109 points in 24 hours (172 games) at the Gin Trap, Ringstead, Norfolk on 24–25 Jun 1988.

Pigeon Racing

Longest flights The official British duration record (into Great Britain) is 1887 km *1173 miles* in 15 days by *C.S.O.*, owned by Rosie and Bruce of Wick, in the 1976 Palamos Race. In the 1975 Palamos Race, *The*

Conqueror, owned by Alan Raeside, homed to Irvine, Strathclyde, 1625 km *1010 miles*, in 43 hr 56 min. The greatest number of flights over 1000 miles flown by one pigeon is that of *Dunning Independence*, owned by D. Smith, which annually flew from Palamos to Dunning, Perthshire, 1672 km *1039 miles*, between 1978 and 1981.

The greatest claimed homing flight by a pigeon was for one owned by the 1st Duke of Wellington (1769 – 1852). Released from a sailing ship off the Ichabo Islands, West Africa on 8 April, it dropped dead a mile from its loft at Nine Elms, Wandsworth, Greater London on 1 Jun 1845, 55 days later, having apparently flown an airline route of 8700 km *5400 miles*, but possibly a distance of 11,250 km *7000 miles* to avoid the Sahara Desert. In 1990 it was reported that a pigeon, owned by David Lloyd and George Workman of Nantyffyllon, Mid Glam, had completed a flight of 10,860 km *6750 miles* from its release at Lerwick, Shetland to Shanghai, China, possibly the longest non-homing flight ever. In both cases, however, the lack of constant surveillance makes it difficult to confirm that the pigeons completed the distances unaided.

Highest speeds In level flight in windless conditions it is very doubtful if any pigeon can exceed 96 km/h *60 mph*. The highest race speed recorded is one of 2952 m *3229 yd* per min (177.14 km/h *110.07 mph*) in the East Anglian Federation race from East Croydon, Surrey on 8 May 1965 when the 1428 birds were backed by a powerful south - south - west wind. The winner was owned by A. Vigeon & Son, Wickford, Essex.

The highest race speed recorded over a distance of more than 1000 km *621.37 miles* is 2224.5 m *2432.7 yd* per min (133.46 km/h *82.93 mph*) by a hen in the Central Cumberland Combine race over 1099.316 km *683 miles 147 yd* from Murray Bridge, South Australia to North Ryde, Sydney on 2 Oct 1971.

Career records The greatest competitive distance flown is 32,318 km *20,082 miles* by *Nunnies*, a chequer cock owned by Terry Haley of Abbot's Langley, Herts.

Highest-priced The highest sum paid is £110,.800 to Jan Herman of Waalre, Netherlands in July 1992 by Louella Pigeon World of Markfield, Leics for a four-year old cock bird, winner of the 1992 Barcelona International race, and subsequently named *Invincible Spirit*.

Polo

Most titles The British Open Championship for the Cowdray Park Gold Cup (instituted 1956) has been won five times by, Stowell Park, 1973–4, 1976, 1978 and 1980, and Tramontana, 1986–9, 1991.

Highest handicap The highest handicap based on six 7½ min 'chukkas' is ten goals introduced in the USA in 1891 and in the UK and in Argentina in 1910. A total of 56 players have received ten-goal handi-

caps and for the 1995 season there are seven playing in Britain, six Argentinians a and one Mexican. The last (of six) ten-goal handicap players from the UK was Gerald Matthew Balding (1903–57) in 1939.

The highest handicaps of current UK players is eight by Howard Hipwood (b. 24 Mar 1950) who, however had a handicap of nine in 1992. Claire J. Tomlinson of Gloucestershire attained a handicap of five, the highest ever by a woman, in 1986.

A match of two 40-goal teams has been staged on three occasions at Palermo, Buenos Aires, Argentina in 1975, in the USA in 1990 and Australia in 1991.

Most chukkas The greatest number of chukkas played on one ground in a day is 43. This was achieved by the Pony Club on the Number 3 Ground at Kirtlington Park, Oxon on 31 Jul 1991.

The highest aggregate number of goals scored in an international polo match is 30, when Argentina beat the USA 21–9 at Meadowbrook, Long Island, New York, USA in September 1936.

Pool

Pool or championship pocket billiards with numbered balls began to become standardized c. 1890. The greatest exponents were Ralph Greenleaf (USA) (1899–1950), who won the 'world' professional title 19 times (1919–37), and William Mosconi (USA) (1913–93), who dominated the game from 1941 to 1956.

The longest consecutive run in an American straight pool match is 625 balls by Michael Eufemia at Logan's Billiard Academy, Brooklyn, New York, USA on 2 Feb 1960, although this was not officially recognized. The official best is 526 by Willie Mosconi at Springfield, Ohio, USA in March 1954. The greatest number of balls pocketed in 24 hours is 16,497 by Paul Sullivan (GB) at the Abbey Leisure Centre, Selby, N Yorks on 16–17 Apr 1993.

Fly Away

The largest ever simultaneous release of pigeons was at Orleans, France in August 1988 when over 215,000 pigeons were released for a Dutch national race. In Great Britain the largest liberation was at Beachy Head near Eastbourne, E Sussex on 11 May 1991 when 42,500 birds were released for the Save The Children Fund Eastbourne Classic.

Potty

The record times for potting all 15 balls are: (men) 35.4 sec by Dave Pearson at the 701 Club, Failsworth, Oldham, Greater Manchester on 9 Dec 1993 and (women) 42.28 sec by Susan Thompson at the Ferry Inn, Holmsgarth, Lerwick, Shetland Isles on 28 Jan 1995.

Powerboat Racing

APBA Gold Cup The American Power Boat Association (APBA) was formed in 1903 and held its first Gold Cup on the Hudson River, New York, USA in 1904. The most wins is nine Chip Hanauer (USA), 1982–8, 1992–3. The highest average speed for the race is 146.269 mph *235.397 km/h* by Mark Tate (USA), piloting *Smokin' Joe's* in June 1994.

Cowes to Torquay This race was instituted in 1961 and at first was run from Cowes to Torquay, but from 1968 included the return journey, for a distance of 320.4 km *199 miles*. The most wins is four by Renato della Valle (Italy), 1982–5. The highest average speed is 138.24 km/h *85.89 mph* by Fabio Fuzzi (Italy), piloting *Cesa* in 1988.

Guess What?

Q. What is the highest speed achieved on water?

A. See Page 111

■ Guido Capellini (Italy) (left), winner of the powerboating Formula One World title in 1993 and 1994, in action at Abu Dhabi during the 1993 Championships.
(Photos: Allsport/P. Rondeau)

Cow pat tossing The record distances in the country sport of throwing dried cow pats or 'chips' depend on whether or not the projectile may be 'moulded into a spherical shape'. The greatest distance achieved under the 'non-sphericalisation and 100 per cent organic' rule (established in 1970) is 81.1m *266ft*, by Steve Urner at the Mountain Festival, Tehachapi, California, USA on 14 Aug 1981.

Longest races The longest offshore race has been the Port Richborough London to Monte Carlo Marathon Offshore international event. The race extended over 4742km *2947 miles* in 14 stages from 10–25 Jun 1972. It was won by *H.T.S.* (GB) driven by Mike Bellamy, Eddie Chater and Jim Brooker in 71hr 35min 56sec for an average of 66.24km/h *41.15mph*. The longest circuit race is the 24-hour race held annually since 1962 on the River Seine at Rouen, France.

Transatlantic crossing The fastest crossing from Ambrose Light Tower, New Jersey/New York, USA to Bishop Rock Light, Isles of Scilly, Cornwall is 2 days 14hr 7min 47seconds by *Gentry Eagle*, skippered by Tom Gentry (USA) on 24–27 Jul 1989.

Projectiles

Throwing The longest independently authenticated throw of any inert object heavier than air is 385.80m *1265ft 9in*, in the case of a lead weight with a long string tail attached, which was thrown by David Engvall at El Mirage, California, USA on 17 Oct 1993. The record for an object without any velocity-aiding feature is 383.13m *1257ft* by Scott Zimmerman, with a flying ring on 8 Jul 1986 at Fort Funston, California, USA.

Boomerang throwing The greatest number of consecutive two-handed catches is 817, by Michael Girvin (USA) on 17 Jul 1994 at Oakland, California, USA.

The longest out-and-return distance is one of 149.12m *489ft 3in*, by Michel Dufayard (France) on 5 Jul 1992 at Shrewsbury, Shrops.

The longest flight duration (with self-catch) is one of 2min 59.94sec by Dennis Joyce (USA) at Bethlehem, Pennsylvania, USA on 25 Jun 1987.

Robert Parkins (USA) caught 75 boomerang throws in 5 minutes at Amherst, Massachusetts, USA on 9 Aug 1992.

The juggling record—the number of consecutive catches with two boomerangs, keeping at least one boomerang aloft at all times—is 502, by Chet Snouffer (USA) at Geneva, Switzerland on 22 Aug 1992.

Flying disc throwing (formerly Frisbee) The World Flying Disc Federation distance records are: (men) 197.38m *647ft 7in*, by Niclas Bergehamn (Sweden) on 11 Aug 1993 at Linköping, Sweden; (women) 130.09m *426ft 10in*, by Amy Bekken (US) on 25 Jun 1990 at La Habra, California, USA.

The throw, run and catch records are: (men) 92.64m *303ft 11in*, by Hiroshi Oshima (Japan) on 20 Jul 1988 at San Francisco, California, USA; (women) 60.02m *196ft 11in*, by Judy Horowitz (US) on 29 Jun 1985 at La Mirada, California, USA.

The 24-hour distance records for a pair are: (men) 592.15km *367.94miles*, by Conrad Damon and Pete Fust (US) on 24–25 Apr 1993 at San Marino, California, USA; (women) 186.12km *115.65miles*, by Jo Cahow and Amy Berard (US) on 30–31 Dec 1979 at Pasadena, California, USA.

The records for maximum time aloft are: (men) 16.72sec, by Don Cain (US) on 26 May 1984 at Philadelphia, Pennsylvania, USA; (women) 11.81sec, by Amy Bekken (US) on 1 Aug 1991 at Santa Cruz, California, USA.

Racketball

World Championships Instituted in 1981, held biennially since 1984 and based on the US version of the game (racquetball), the USA has won all seven team titles, 1981, 1984, 1986 (tie with Canada), 1988, 1990, 1992 and 1994. The most singles titles won is two by: (men) Egan Inoue (USA), 1986 and 1990, and; (women) Cindy Baxter (USA), 1981 and 1986, Heather Stupp (Canada), 1988 and 1990, and Michelle Gould (USA), 1992 and 1994.

Britain The British Racketball Association was formed and staged inaugural British National Championships in 1984. Six titles have been won in the women's event by Elizabeth 'Bett' Dryhurst (b. 26 Nov 1945), 1985–8 (1988 shared), 1989 and 1991. The men's record is three by Nathan Dugan, 1993–5.

Rackets

World Championships Of the 22 world champions since 1820, the longest reign is by Geoffrey Willoughby Thomas Atkins (b. 20 Jan 1927) who gained the title by beating the professional James Dear (1910–81) in 1954, and held it until retiring, after defending it four times, in April 1972.

Most Amateur titles Since the Amateur Singles Championship was instituted in 1888 the most titles won by an individual is nine by: Edgar Maximilian Baerlein (1879–1971) between 1903 and 1923; and William Robin Boone (b. 12 Jul 1950) between 1976 and 1993. Since the institution of the Amateur Doubles Championship in 1890 the most shares in titles has been 12 by William Boone between 1975 and 1994. The most by one pair is 10 by David Sumner Milford (1905–84) and John Ross Thompson (b. 10 May 1918) between 1948 and 1959.

Greatest distances achieved with miscellaneous objects:

Brick 44.54m *146ft 1in*
   (standard 2.27kg *5lb* building brick)
Geoff Capes at Braybrook School, Orton Goldhay, Cambs on 19 Jul 1978.

Egg (fresh hen's) 98.51m *323ft 2½in*
   (without breaking it)
Johnny Dell Foley to Keith Thomas at Jewett, Texas, USA on 12 Nov 1978.

Haggis 55.11m *180ft 10in*
   (minimum weight 680g *1lb 8oz*)
Alan Pettigrew at Inchmurrin, Loch Lomond, Strathclyde on 24 May 1984.

Gumboot ('Wellie wanging', using a size 8 Challenger Dunlop boot)
Men 56.70m *186ft 0in*
Olav Jensen at Fagernes, Norway on 10 Jul 1988.
Women 40.70m *133ft 6in*
Mette Bergmann at Fagernes, Norway on 10 Jul 1988.

UK Men 52.73m *173ft 0in*
Tony Rodgers at London on 9 Sep 1978.
UK Women 39.60m *129ft 11in*
Rosemary Payne at Birmingham, W Mids on 21 Jun 1975.

Rolling pin 53.47m *175ft 5in*
   (907g *2lb*)
Lori La Deane Adams at Iowa State Fair, Iowa, USA on 21 Aug 1979.

Real/Royal Tennis

Most titles *World* The first recorded world tennis champion was Clergé (France) *c.* 1740. Jacques Edmond Barre (France) (1802–73) held the title for a record 33 years from 1829 to 1862. Pierre Etchebaster (1893–1980), a Basque, holds the record for the greatest number of successful defences of the title with eight between 1928 and 1952.

The Women's World Championships (instituted 1985) has been won three times by Penny Lumley (*née* Fellows) (GB), 1989, 1991 and 1995.

British The Amateur Championship of the British Isles (instituted 1888) has been won 16 times by Howard Rea Angus (b. 25 Jun 1944) 1966–80 and 1982. He also won eight Amateur Doubles Championships with David Warburg (1923–1987), 1967–70, 1972–4 and 1976, and was world champion 1976–81.

Oldest court The oldest of the surviving active courts in Great Britain is that at Falkland Palace, Fife built by King James V of Scotland in 1539.

Rodeo

The largest rodeo in the world is the National Finals Rodeo, organized by the Professional Rodeo Cowboys Association (PRCA) and the Women's Professional Rodeo Association (WPRA). The 1991 Finals had a paid attendance of 171,414 for ten performances. In 1991 a record $2.6 million in prize money was offered for the event, staged in Las Vegas.

Most world titles The record number of all-around titles (awarded to the leading money winner in a single season in two or more events) in the PRCA World Championships is six by: Larry Mahan (USA) (b. 21 Nov 1943), 1966–70 and 1973; by Tom Ferguson (b. 20 Dec 1950), 1974–9; and Ty Murray (b. 11 Oct 1969), 1989–94. Roy Cooper (b. 13 Nov 1955) has record career earnings of $1,510,795, 1975–94. Jim Shoulders (b. 13 May 1928) of Henrietta, Texas won a record 16 World Championships at four events between 1949 and 1959.

The record figure for prize money in a single season is $297,896 by Ty Murray in 1993.

Youngest champions The youngest winner of a world title is Anne Lewis (b. 1 Sep 1958), who won the WPRA barrel racing title in 1968, at 10 years old. Ty Murray is the youngest cowboy to win the PRCA All-Around Champion title, aged 20, in 1989.

Bull riding The highest score in bull riding was 100 points out of a possible 100 by Wade Leslie on Wolfman Skoal at Central Point, Oregon, USA in 1991.

Saddle bronc riding The highest scored saddle bronc ride is 95 out of a possible 100 by Doug Vold on *Transport* at Meadow Lake, Saskatchewan, Canada in 1979.

Bareback riding Joe Alexander of Cora, Wyoming, scored 93 out of a possible 100 on *Marlboro* at Cheyenne, Wyoming in 1974.

Roller Skating

Most titles *Speed* The most world speed titles won is 18 by two women: Alberta Vianello (Italy), eight track and ten road 1953–65; and Annie Lambrechts (Belgium), one track and 17 road 1964–81, at distances from 500 m to 10,000 m.

The most British national individual men's titles have been won by John Edward Fry (b. 21 Feb 1949) with 18 in 1967–86. Chloe Ronaldson (b. 30 Nov 1939) won 40 individual and 14 team women's senior titles from 1958 to 1985.

Figure The records for figure titles are: (men) five by Karl Heinz Losch (West Germany), 1958–9, 1961–2 and 1966; and Sandro Guerra (Italy), 1987–9 and 1991–2; (women) five by Rafaella del Vinaccio (Italy), 1988–92. The most world pair titles is six by Tammy Jeru (USA), 1983–6 (with John Arishita), 1990–91 (with Larry McGrew).

Speed skating The fastest speed put up in an official world record is 44.20 km/h *27.46 mph* when Luca Antoniel (Italy) (b. 12 Feb 1968) recorded 24.678 sec for 300 m on a road at Bello, Colombia on 15 Nov 1990. The women's record is 40.30 km/h *25.04 mph* by Marisa Canofoglia (Italy) (b. 30 Sep 1965) for 300 m on the road at Grenoble, France on 27 Aug 1987. The world records for 10,000 m on a road or track are: (men) 14 min 55.64 sec, Giuseppe De Persio (Italy) (b. 3 Jun 1959) at Gujan-Mestras, France on 1 Aug 1988; (women) 15 min 58.022 sec, Marisa Canofoglia (Italy) at Grenoble, France on 30 Aug 1987.

Largest rink The greatest indoor rink ever to operate was located in the Grand Hall, Olympia, London. Opened in 1890 and closed in 1912; it had an actual skating area of 6300 m² *68,000 ft²*. The current largest is the main arena of 3250 m² *34,981 ft²* at Guptill Roll-Arena, Boght Corner, New York, USA. The total rink area is 3844 m² *41,380 ft²*.

Bucking Bull

The top bucking bull *Red Rock* dislodged 312 riders, 1980–88, and was finally ridden to the eight-second bell by Lane Frost (1963–89) (world champion bull rider 1987) on 20 May 1988. *Red Rock* had retired at the end of the 1987 season but still continued to make guest appearances.

Land's End to John o' Groats Damian Magee roller skated the distance in 9 days 5 hr 23 min from 19–28 Jun 1992. The fastest time by a woman was 12 days 4 hr 15 min by Cheryl Fisher, 17, from 19 Sep–1 Oct 1987.

Skateboarding World championships have been staged intermittently since 1966. Eleftherios Argiropoulos covered 436.6 km *271.3 miles* in 36 hr 33 min 17 sec at Ekali, Greece on 4–5 Nov 1993.

The highest speed recorded on a skateboard is 126.12 km/h *78.37 mph* in a prone position by Roger Hickey, 32, on a course near Los Angeles, California, USA on 15 Mar 1990.

The stand-up record is 89.20 km/h *55.43 mph*, also achieved by Roger Hickey, at San Demas, California, USA on 3 Jul 1990.

Tony Alva, 19, set a long jump record of 5.18 m *17 ft* in clearing 17 barrels at the World Professional Skateboard Championships held at Long Beach, also in California, on 25 Sep 1977.

The high-jump record is 1.67 m *5 ft 5¾ in* by Trevor Baxter (b. 1 Oct 1962) of Burgess Hill, E Sussex at Grenoble, France on 14 Sep 1982.

Roller Hockey

England won the first World Championships, 1936–9, since when Portugal has won most titles with 14 between 1947 and 1993. Portugal has also won a record 18 European (instituted 1926) titles between 1947 and 1994.

Rowing

The earliest established sculling race is the Doggett's Coat and Badge, which was first rowed on 1 Aug 1716 from London Bridge to Chelsea as a race for apprentices, and is still contested annually.

Most Olympic medals Seven oarsmen have won three gold medals: John Brenden Kelly (USA) (1889–1960), father of the late HSH Princess Grace of Monaco, single sculls (1920) and double sculls (1920 and 1924); his cousin Paul Vincent Costello (USA) (1894–1986), double sculls (1920, 1924 and 1928); Jack Beresford Jr (GB) (1899–1977), single sculls (1924), coxless fours (1932) and double sculls (1936), Vyacheslav Nikolayevich Ivanov (USSR) (b. 30 Jul 1938), single sculls (1956, 1960 and 1964); Siegfried Brietzke (GDR) (b. 12 Jun 1952), coxless pairs (1972) and coxless fours (1976, 1980); Pertti Karppinen (Finland) (b. 17 Feb 1953), single sculls (1976, 1980 and 1984); and Steven Geoffrey Redgrave (GB) (b. 23 Mar 1962), coxed fours (1984), coxless pairs (1988 and 1992).

World Championships World rowing championships distinct from the Olympic Games were first held in 1962, at first four yearly, but from 1974 annually, except in Olympic years.

The most gold medals won at World Championships and Olympic Games is nine at coxed pairs by the Italian brothers Giuseppe (b. 24 Jul 1959) and Carmine (b. 5 Jan 1962) Abbagnale, World 1981–2, 1985, 1987, 1989–91, Olympics 1984 and 1988. Francesco Esposito (Italy) has won nine titles at lightweight events, coxless pairs, 1980–84, 1988, 1994 and coxless fours, 1990, 1992. At women's events Yelena Tereshina (b. 6 Feb 1959) has won a record seven golds, all eights for the USSR, 1978–9, 1981–3 and 1985–6.

The most wins at single sculls is five by: Peter-Michael Kolbe (West Germany) (b. 2 Aug 1953), 1975, 1978, 1981, 1983 and 1986; Pertti Karppinen, 1979 and 1985 with his three Olympic wins (above); Thomas Lange (GDR/Germany) (b. 27 Feb 1964), 1987, 1989 and 1991 and two Olympics 1988 and 1992; and in the women's events by Christine Hahn (*née* Scheiblich) (GDR) (b. 31 Dec 1954), 1974–5, 1977–8 (and the 1976 Olympic title).

Boat Race The earliest University Boat Race, which Oxford won, was from Hambledon Lock to Henley Bridge on 10 Jun 1829. Outrigged eights were first used in 1846. In the 141 races to 1995, Cambridge won 72 times, Oxford 68 times and there was a dead heat on 24 Mar 1877.

The race record time for the course of 6.779 km *4 miles 374 yd* (Putney to Mortlake) is 16 min 45 sec by Oxford on 18 Mar 1984. This represents an average speed of 24.28 km/h *15.09 mph*. The smallest winning margin has been by a canvas by Oxford in 1952 and 1980. The greatest margin (apart from sinking) was Cambridge's win by 20 lengths in 1900.

Boris Rankov (Oxford, 1978–83) rowed in a record six winning boats. Susan Brown (b. 29 Jun 1958), the first woman to take part, coxed the winning Oxford boats in 1981 and 1982. Daniel Topolski (b. 4 Jun 1945) coached Oxford to ten successive victories, 1976–85.

Big Blue

The tallest man ever to row in a University boat has been Gavin Stewart (Wadham, Oxford) (b. 25 Feb 1963) at 2.04 m *6 ft 8½ in* in 1987–8. The heaviest was Christopher Heathcote (b. March 1963), the Oxford No. 6, who weighed 110 kg *243 lb* in 1990.

The youngest 'blue' ever was Matthew John Brittin (Cambridge) (b. 1 Sep 1968) at 18 years 208 days, in 1986.

Head of the River A processional race for eights instituted in 1926, the Head has an entry limit of 420 crews (3780 competitors). The record for the course Mortlake–Putney (the reverse of the Boat Race) is 16 min 37 sec by the ARA National Squad in 1987.

Longest race The longest annual rowing race is the annual Tour du Lac Leman, Geneva, Switzerland for coxed fours (the five-man crew taking turns as cox) over 160 km *99 miles*. The record winning time is 12 hr 52 min by LAGA Delft, Netherlands on 3 Oct 1982.

Henley Royal Regatta The annual regatta at Henley-on-Thames, Oxon was inaugurated on 26 Mar 1839. Since then the course, except in 1923, has been about 2112 m *1 mile 550 yd*, varying slightly according to the length of boat. In 1967 the shorter craft were 'drawn up' so all bows start level.

The most wins in the Diamond Challenge Sculls (instituted 1844) is six by Guy Nickalls (GB) (1866–1935), 1888–91, 1893–4 and consecutively by Stuart Alexander Mackenzie (Australia and GB) (b. 5 Apr 1937), 1957–62. The record time is 7 min 23 sec by Vaclav Chalupa (Czechoslovakia) (b. 7 Dec 1967) on 2 Jul 1989. The record time for the Grand Challenge Cup (instituted 1839) event is 5 min 58 sec by Hansa Dortmund, West Germany on 2 Jul 1989.

Highest speed The record time for 2000 m *2187 yd* on non-tidal water is 5 min 24.28 sec (22.20 km/h *13.79 mph*) by an eight from Hansa Dortmund (Germany) at Essen, Germany on 17 May 1992. The women's record is 5 min 59.26 sec by Romania at Lake Barrington, Tasmania, Australia in November 1990. The single sculls record is 6 min 38.97 sec (18.04 km/h *11.21 mph*) by Xeno Müller (Switzerland) at Lucerne, Switzerland on 17 Jul 1994. On the same occasion, Silken Laumann (Canada) set a women's record of 7 min 17.09 sec.

Cross-Channel Arne Lindström (Norway) sculled across the English Channel in a record 3 hr 35 min on 14 Jul 1994.

River Thames Five members of the Lower Thames Rowing Club, Gravesend rowed the navigable length of the Thames, 299.14 km *185.88 miles*, from Lechlade Bridge, Glos to Southend Pier, Essex in 38 hr 43 min 20 sec from 8–9 May 1993. The fastest time from Folly Bridge, Oxford to Westminster Bridge, London (180 km *112 miles*) is 14 hr 25 min 15 sec by an eight from Kingston Rowing Club on 1 Feb 1986.

Walking on water Rémy Bricka of Paris, France 'walked' across the Atlantic Ocean on skis 4.2 m *13 ft 9 in* long in 1988. Leaving Tenerife, Canary Islands on 2 Apr 1988, he covered 5636 km *3502 miles*, arriving at Trinidad on 31 May 1988.

He also set a speed record of 7 min 7.41 sec for 1 km *1094 yd* on the Olympic pool in Montréal, Canada on 2 Aug 1989. He 'walks on water' by having ski-floats attached to his feet and by moving in the same way as in cross-country skiing, using a double-headed paddle instead of ski-poles.

International Dragon Boat Races Instituted in 1975 and held annually in Hong Kong, the fastest time achieved for the 640 metres *700 yd* course is 2 min 27.45 sec by the Chinese Shun De team on 30 Jun 1985. The best time for a British team was 2 min 36.40 sec by the Kingston Royals crew on 3 Jun 1990. Teams have 28 members—26 rowers, one steersman and one drummer.

> **The greatest distance rowed in 24 hours (upstream and downstream) is 227.33 km *141.26 miles* by six members of Dittons Skiff & Punting Club on the River Thames between Hampton Court and Teddington, Greater London on 3–4 Jun 1994.**

Rugby League

Records are based on the scoring system in use at the time.

World Cup There have been nine World Cup Competitions. Australia have most wins, with six, 1957, 1968, 1970, 1977, 1988 and 1992 as well as a win in the International Championship of 1975.

Most titles The Northern Rugby League was formed in 1901. The word 'Northern' was dropped in 1980. Wigan have won the League Championship a record 16 times (1909, 1922, 1926, 1934, 1946–7, 1950, 1952, 1960, 1987, 1990–95).

The Rugby League Challenge Cup (inaugurated 1896/7 season) has been won a record 16 times by Wigan, 1924, 1929, 1948, 1951, 1958–9, 1965, 1985, 1988–95.

There are four major competitions for RL clubs: Challenge Cup, League Championship, Premiership and Regal Trophy (formerly John Player Special Trophy). In 1990 these were officially called the 'Grand Slam' and Wigan won all four in the 1994/5 season.

Three other clubs have won all possible major Rugby League trophies in one season: Hunslet, 1907/8 season, Huddersfield, 1914/15 and Swinton, 1927/8, all won the Challenge Cup, League Championship, County Cup and County League (last two now defunct).

Highest Scores

Senior match The highest aggregate score in a game where a senior club has been concerned was 146 points, when Huddersfield beat Blackpool Gladiators, 142–4, at Huddersfield, W Yorks, in the first round of the Regal Trophy on 26 Nov 1994. The highest score in League football is 104 points by Keighley Cougars *v.* Highfield (4) on 23 Apr 1995. St Helens beat Carlisle 112–0 in the Lancashire Cup on 14 Sep 1986. In the Yorkshire Cup Hull Kingston Rovers beat Nottingham City 100–6 on 19 Aug 1990. The highest score in the First Division is 90 points by Leeds *v.* Barrow (nil) on 11 Feb 1990. The highest scoring draw is 46–46 between Sheffield Eagles and Leeds on 10 Apr 1994.

Challenge Cup Final The highest score in a Challenge Cup final is 38 points (8 tries, 7 goals) by Wakefield Trinity *v.* Hull (5) at Wembley, London on 14 May 1960. The record aggregate is 52 points when Wigan beat Hull 28–24 at Wembley on 4 May 1985. The greatest winning margin was 34 points when Huddersfield beat St Helens 37–3 at Oldham, Greater Manchester on 1 May 1915.

International match The highest score in an international match is Australia's 74–0 defeat of France at Béziers, France on 4 Dec 1994. Great Britain's highest score is 72 against France (6) in a Test match at Headingley, Leeds, W Yorks on 2 Apr 1993.

Touring teams The record score for a British team touring Australasia is 101 points by England *v.* South Australia (nil) at Adelaide in May 1914. The record for a touring team in Britain is 92 (10 goals, 24 tries) by Australia against Bramley 7 (2 goals and 1 try) at the Barley Mow Ground, Bramley, near Leeds on 9 Nov 1921.

■ **The Boat Race was won for a 71st time by Cambridge (right) in 1995. Here is part of the flotilla of supporters and officials that follow the crews, approaching Hammersmith Bridge.**
(Photo: Allsport/S. Miles)

Rodeo, Roller Skating

Most points Leigh scored a record 1436 points (258 tries, 199 goals, 6 drop goals) in the 1985/6 season, playing in 43 Cup and League games.

Highest Individual Scores

Most points, goals and tries in a game George Henry 'Tich' West (1882–1927) scored 53 points (10 goals and a record 11 tries) for Hull Kingston Rovers (73) in a Challenge Cup tie v. Brookland Rovers (5) on 4 Mar 1905.

The record points for a League match is 42 (4 tries, 13 goals) by Dean John Marwood (b. 22 Feb 1970) in Workington Town's 78–0 win over Highfield on 1 Nov 1992.

The most goals in a Cup match is 22 kicked by James 'Jim' Sullivan (1903–77) for Wigan v. Flimby and Fothergill on 14 Feb 1925. The most goals in a League match is 15 by Michael Stacey (b. 9 Feb 1953) for Leigh v. Doncaster on 28 Mar 1976. The most tries in a League match is ten by Lionel Cooper (b. Australia, 1922–87) for Huddersfield v. Keighley on 17 Nov 1951.

Most points *Season and career* The record number of points in a season was 496 by Benjamin Lewis Jones (Leeds) (b. 11 Apr 1931), 194 goals, 36 tries, in 1956/7.

Neil Fox (b. 4 May 1939) scored 6220 points (2575 goals including 4 drop goals, 358 tries) in a senior Rugby League career from 10 Apr 1956 to 19 Aug 1979, consisting of 4488 for Wakefield Trinity, 1089 for five other clubs, 228 for Great Britain, 147 for Yorkshire and 268 in other representative games.

Most tries *Season and career* Albert Aaron Rosenfeld (1885–1970) (Huddersfield), an Australian-born wing-threequarter, scored 80 tries in 42 matches in the 1913/14 season.

Brian Bevan (Australia) (1924–91), a wing-threequarter, scored 796 tries in 18 seasons (16 with Warrington, two with Blackpool Borough) from 1945 to 1964. He scored 740 for Warrington, 17 for Blackpool and 39 in representative matches.

Most goals *Season and career* The record number of goals in a season is 221, in 47 matches, by David Watkins (b. 5 Mar 1942) (Salford) in the 1972/3 season.

Jim Sullivan (Wigan) kicked 2867 goals in his club and representative career, 1921–46.

Individual international records Jim Sullivan (Wigan) played in most internationals (60 for Wales and Great Britain, 1921–39), kicked most goals (160) and scored most points (329).

Michael Sullivan (no kin) (b. 12 Jan 1934) of Huddersfield, Wigan, St Helens, York and Dewsbury played in 51 international games for England and Great Britain and scored a record 45 tries, 1954–63.

Michael O'Connor (b. 30 Nov 1960) scored a record 30 points (4 tries, 7 goals) for Australia v. Papua New Guinea at Wagga Wagga, Australia on 20 Jul 1988.

Longest kicks Arthur Atkinson (1908–63) (Castleford) kicked a penalty from his own 25-yard line, a distance of 75 yd *68 m* in a League game at St Helens on 26 Oct 1929.

The longest drop goal is 61 yd *56 m* by Joseph Paul 'Joe' Lydon (b. 22 Nov 1963) for Wigan against Warrington in a Challenge Cup semi-final at Maine Road, Manchester on 25 Mar 1989.

> David Watkins (Salford) played and scored in every club game during seasons 1972/3 and 1973/4, contributing 41 tries and 403 goals—a total of 929 points, in 92 games.

Fastest Try

Lee Jackson scored a try after nine seconds for Hull against Sheffield Eagles in a Yorkshire Cup semi-final at Don Valley Stadium, Sheffield, S Yorks on 6 Oct 1992. The fastest in an international match is 15 seconds by Bobby Fulton (b. 1 Dec 1947, Warrington, Lancs) for Australia against France at Odsal Stadium, Bradford, W Yorks on 1 Nov 1970.

Most Challenge Cup finals The most appearances is ten by Shaun Edwards (b. 17 Oct 1966), Wigan, 1984–5, 1988–95. He was on the winning side nine times (all but 1984). During his career at Wigan, 1983–95, Edwards has received 37 winners' or runners-up medals in major competitions

Youngest and oldest players Harold Spencer Edmondson (1903–82) played his first League game for Bramley at 15 years 81 days. The youngest representative player was Harold Wagstaff (1891–1939) who played for Yorkshire at 17 yr 141 days, and for England at 17 yr 228 days.

The youngest player in a Cup final was Francis Cummins (b. 12 Oct 1976) at 17 yr 200 days for Leeds when they lost 16–26 to Wigan at Wembley on 30 Apr 1994.

The youngest Great Britain international is Paul Newlove (b. 10 Aug 1971) who played in the first Test v. New Zealand on 21 Oct 1989 at Old Trafford, Greater Manchester, aged 18 yr 72 days. The oldest player for Great Britain was Jeffrey Grayshon (b. 4 Mar 1949) at 36 yr 250 days v. New Zealand at Elland Road, Leeds on 9 Nov 1985.

Most durable player The most appearances for one club is 774 by Jim Sullivan for Wigan, 1921–46. He played a record 928 first-class games in all. The longest continuous playing career is that of Augustus John 'Gus' Risman (1911–94), who played his first game for Salford on 31 Aug 1929 and his last for Batley on 27 Dec 1954.

Keith Elwell (b. 12 Feb 1950) played in 239 consecutive games for Widnes from 5 May 1977 to 5 Sep 1982.

Most and least successful teams Wigan won 31 consecutive league games from February 1970 to February 1971. Huddersfield were undefeated for 40 league and cup games in 1913/14. Hull is the only club to win all League games in a season, 26 in Division II 1978/9. Runcorn Highfield holds the record of losing 55 consecutive League games from 29 Jan 1989 to 27 Jan 1991. The run was ended with a 12–12 draw with Carlisle on 3 Feb 1991.

Record transfer fee Martin Offiah (b. 29 Dec 1966) became the costliest transferred player on 3 Jan 1992 when Wigan paid Widnes a fee of £440,000.

Great Crowd

The greatest attendance at any Rugby League match is 102,569 for the Warrington v. Halifax Challenge Cup final replay at Odsal Stadium, Bradford on 5 May 1954.

The record attendance for any international match is 73,631 for the World Cup Final between Australia and Great Britain at Wembley Stadium, London on 24 Oct 1992.

Amateur Rugby League

National Cup Pilkington Recreation (St Helens, Merseyside) have won the National Cup four times (1975, 1979, 1980, 1982). John McCabe (b. 26 Jan 1952) has played in a record five National Cup finals, winning on each occasion. He played for Pilkington Recreation in each of their four successes and captained Thatto Heath (St Helens, Merseyside) to victory in 1987.

Highest score Ngati Pikiao of Rotorua beat Tokoroa United 148–0 in a Bay of Plenty Rugby League under 17's league match at Pikiao, New Zealand on 10 Jul 1994.

Humberside beat Carlisle by 138 points to nil in the second round of the National Inter-league Competition on 20 Oct 1984.

Most tries Simon Haughton (b. 10 Nov 1975) scored 130 tries, including nine in one game, from the prop-forward position for the Bingley under-14 side, W Yorks in the 1989/90 season.

Rugby Union World Cup

Prior to the 1995 competition in South Africa, the first major sporting event to be staged there since their reintroduction to world sport, the World Cup had been held on two occasions, 1987 (in Australia and New Zealand) and 1991 (in the British Isles and France), with the winners being New Zealand and Australia respectively.

The 1995 World Cup was a superlative event in many respects as the tables clearly illustrate below.

In the competitions history overall, the team which has scored the most points is New Zealand with 768 and this includes a record 103 tries. The most points conceded is 462 in nine games by Japan.

The leading scorer in the tournament is Gavin Hastings (Scotland) with 227 points and the most in a single tournament is 126 by Grant Fox (New Zealand) in 1987. Hastings holds the overall record for penalties, 36, and conversions, 39. The leading try scorer is Rory Underwood (England) with 11, and Rob Andrew (England) has scored a record five drop goals. The most individual appearances is 17 by Sean Fitzpatrick of New Zealand.

■ **Left: The Webb Ellis Cup, rugby's ultimate prize. Right: Nelson Mandela officially opens the 1995 tournament.** (Photos: Allsport/Mike Hewitt and John Gichigi)

Individual Match Records (Team)

Highest score	145	New Zealand v. Japan (17).........Bloemfontein, 4 Jun 1995
Lowest score	0	Ivory Coast v. Scotland (89) ....Rustenberg, 26 May 1995
		Canada v. South Africa (20).......Port Elizabeth, 3 Jun 1995
Highest aggregate	.162	145–17 New Zealand v. Japan ...Bloemfontein, 4 Jun 1995
Lowest aggregate	12	9–3 Australia v. Western Samoa .....Pontypool, 9 Oct 1991
Tries	21	New Zealand v. Japan.................Bloemfontein, 4 Jun 1995
Conversions	20	New Zealand v. Japan.................Bloemfontein, 4 Jun 1995
Penalties	8	Scotland v. Tonga...........................Pretoria, 30 May 1995
		France v. Ireland...............................Durban, 10 Jun 1995
Drop goals	3	Fiji v. Romania ....Brive, 12 Oct 1991

Individual Match Records (Individual)

Points	45	Simon Culhane (New Zealand) v. Japan ...Bloemfontein, 4 Jun 1995
Tries	6	Marc Ellis (New Zealand) v. Japan ....Bloemfontein, 4 Jun 1995
Conversions	.20	Simon Culhane (New Zealand) v. Japan ...Bloemfontein, 4 Jun 1995
Penalties	8	Gavin Hastings (Scotland) v. Tonga................Pretoria, 30 May 1995
		Thierry Lacroix (France) v. Ireland ....Durban, 10 Jun 1995
Drop goals	2	Jonathan Davies (Wales) v. Ireland............Wellington, 25 May 1987
		Lisandro Arbizu (Argentina) v. Australia ....Llanelli, 4 Oct 1991
		Tomasi Rabaka (Fiji) v. Romania...........................Brive, 12 Oct 1991
		Rob Andrew (England) v. Argentina...............Durban, 27 May 1995
		Joel Stransky (S. Africa) v. N. Zealand ....Johannesburg, 24 Jun 1995

■ **South Africa's captain Francois Pienaar, holds aloft the Webb Ellis Cup and his team mates celebrate their historic 15–12 victory over New Zealand in the final at Johannesburg. The attendance of 65,000 is the largest for any World Cup game.** (Photo: Allsport/S. Botterill)

Guess What?
Q. Who made his 111th international appearance during the World Cup?
A. See Page 284

Pool A	p	w	l	f	a	pts
South Africa	3	3	0	68	26	9
Australia	3	2	1	87	41	7
Canada	3	1	2	45	50	5
Romania	3	0	3	14	97	3

Pool B	p	w	l	f	a	pts
England	3	3	0	95	60	9
Western Samoa	3	2	1	96	88	7
Italy	3	1	2	69	94	5
Argentina	3	0	3	69	87	3

Pool C	p	w	l	f	a	pts
New Zealand	3	3	0	222	45	9
Ireland	3	2	1	93	94	7
Wales	3	1	2	89	68	5
Japan	3	0	3	55	252	3

Pool D	p	w	l	f	a	pts
France	3	3	0	114	47	9
Scotland	3	2	1	149	27	7
Tonga	3	1	2	44	90	5
Ivory Coast	3	0	3	29	172	3

p=played, w=won, l=lost, f =points for, a=points against

Pool Results

A

South Africa v. Australia 27–18
Canada v. Romania....................34–3
South Africa v. Romania 21–8
Australia v. Canada 27–11
Australia v. Romania 42–3
South Africa v. Canada.............20–0

C

Wales v. Japan 57–10
New Zealand v. Ireland 43–19
Ireland v. Japan 50–28
New Zealand v. Wales 34–9
New Zealand v. Japan 145–17
Ireland v. Wales 24–23

B

Western Samoa v. Italy...............42–18
England v. Argentina 24–18
Western Samoa v. Argentina 32–26
England v. Italy 27–20
Italy v. Argentina.......................31–25
England v. Western Samoa 44–22

D

Scotland v. Ivory Coast 89–0
France v. Tonga 38–10
France v. Ivory Coast...................54–18
Scotland v. Tonga 41–5
Tonga v. Ivory Coast 29–11
France v. Scotland.......................22–19

Quarter Finals

France v. Ireland.............................36–12
England v. Australia......................25–22
South Africa v. Western Samoa....41–14
New Zealand v. Scotland 48–30

Semi Finals

South Africa v. France...................19–15
New Zealand v. England...............45–29

Third place play-off

France v. England....................19–9

Final

South Africa v. New Zealand........15–12

The knockout stages of the competition provided some of the most exciting rugby seen during the tournament with some close finishes, most notably Rob Andrew's last gasp drop goal winner in the quarter-final against Australia.

The final itself was the first ever World Cup game to require extra time and this was also won by virtue of a drop goal, six minutes from time, from South Africa's Joel Stransky. If the score had remained level, New Zealand would have won due to South Africa having players sent off earlier in the tournament.

■ Above: Scotland's Gavin Hastings takes a high ball under pressure during the decisive Pool D match against France. Hastings retired from international rugby at the end of the tournament on a high note. He had set records for points scored and penalties and conversions kicked in the World Cup competition.

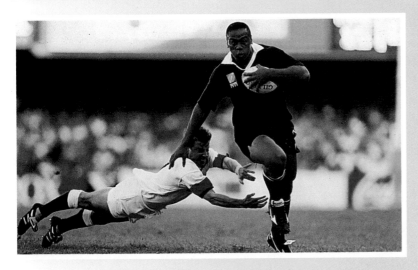

Left: Jonah Lomu of New Zealand evades the tackle of England's Rob Andrew in the semi-final. It was during this match that Lomu scored four tries bringing his tournament total to seven, an overall World Cup record he shares with his team mate Marc Ellis.
(Photos: Allsport/S. Bruty)

Most International Appearances

FRANCE	111	Philippe Sella (b. 14 Feb 1962)	1982–95
AUSTRALIA	91	David Ian Campese (b. 21 Oct 1962)	1982–95
ENGLAND	79	Rory Underwood (b. 19 Jun 1963)	1984–95
IRELAND	69	Cameron Michael Henderson Gibson (b. 3 Dec 1942)	1964–79
NEW ZEALAND	68	Sean Brian Thomas Fitzpatrick (b. 4 Jun 1963)	1986–95
SCOTLAND	62	Andrew Gavin Hastings (b. 3 Jan 1962)	1986–95
WALES	55	John Peter Rhys 'JPR' Williams (b. 2 Mar 1949)	1969–81
SOUTH AFRICA	38	Frederick Christoffel Hendrick Du Preez (b. 28 Nov 1935)	1960–71
	38	Jan Hendrik Ellis (b. 5 Jan 1943)	1965–76

Note: The criteria used to decide which games are classed as full internationals vary between countries.

Rugby Union

Records are based on the scoring system in use at the time.

International Championship

The International Championship was first contested by England, Ireland, Scotland and Wales in 1884. France first played in 1910.

Wales has won a record 22 times outright and tied for first a further 11 times to 1994. The most Grand Slams, winning all four matches, is 11 by England 1913–14, 1921, 1923–4, 1928, 1957, 1980, 1991–2 and 1995.

Highest team score The highest score in an International Championship match was set at Swansea on 1 Jan 1910 when Wales beat France 49–14 (8 goals, 1 penalty goal, 2 tries, to 1 goal, 2 penalty goals, 1 try).

Season's scoring Jonathan Mark Webb (b. 24 Aug 1963) scored a record 67 points (3 tries, 11 penalty goals, 11 conversions) in the four games of an International Championship series in 1992 (England scored a record 118 points during these four games).

Individual match records John 'Jack' Bancroft (1879–1942) kicked a record nine goals (8 conversions and 1 penalty goal) for Wales v. France at Swansea on 1 Jan 1910. Simon Hodgkinson kicked a Championship record seven penalty goals for England v. Wales at Cardiff on 19 Jan 1991.

Highest Team Scores

Internationals The highest score in any full international is when Hong Kong beat Singapore, 164–13 in a World Cup qualifying match at Kuala Lumpur, Malaysia on 27 Oct 1994.

The highest aggregate score for any international match between the Four Home Unions is 82 when England beat Wales by 82 points (7 goals, 1 drop goal and 6 tries) to nil at Blackheath, London on 19 Feb 1881. (Note: there was no point scoring in 1881.) The highest aggregate score under the modern points system between two of the eight major nations is 79,

when Australia beat France 48–31 at Ballymore, Brisbane, Australia on 24 Jun 1990.

The highest score by any overseas side in an international in the British Isles is 51 points by New Zealand against Scotland (15) at Murrayfield, Edinburgh on 20 Nov 1993.

Match In Denmark, Comet beat Lindo by 194–0 on 17 Nov 1973. The highest British score is 174–0 by 7th Signal Regiment v. 4th Armoured Workshop, REME, on 5 Nov 1980 at Herford, Germany. Scores of over 200 points have been recorded in school matches. The highest score in the Courage Clubs Championship is 146–0 by Billingham against Hartlepool Athletic in a Durham /Northumberland Division 3 match at Billingham, Co. Durham on 3 Oct 1987.

Highest Individual Scores

Internationals In the World Cup qualifying match between Hong Kong and Singapore at Kuala Lumpur, Malaysia on 27 Oct 1994 (see above), Hong Kong's Ashley Billington scored 50 points (10 tries). The most points by a British player is 44 by Andrew Gavin Hastings (b. 3 Jan 1962) (4 tries, 9 conversions, 2 penalties) for Scotland v. Ivory Coast at Rustenberg, South Africa on 26 May 1995. The highest individual points score in any match between the major nations is 27 by Christopher Robert Andrew (b. 18 Feb 1963) (1 try, 2 conversions, 5 penalty goals and a drop goal) for England against South Africa at Pretoria on 4 Jun 1994.

The highest number of points accumulated in a season by a club is 1917 points (including a record 345 tries) in 47 games by Neath, West Glamorgan in 1988/9.

The most tries in an international match between the major nations is five by George Campbell Lindsay (1863–1905) for Scotland v. Wales on 26 Feb 1887, and by Douglas 'Daniel' Lambert (1883–1915) for England v. France on 5 Jan 1907. Ian Scott Smith (Scotland) (1903–72) scored a record six consecutive international tries in 1925, comprising the last three v. France and two weeks later, the first three v. Wales.

The most penalty goals kicked in a match is eight by: Mark Andrew Wyatt (Canada) (b. 12 Apr 1961) v. Scotland at St John, New Brunswick, Canada on 25 May 1991; Neil Roger Jenkins (Wales) (b. 8 Jul 1971) v. Canada at Cardiff, S Glam on 10 Nov 1993, Santiago Meson (Argentina) (b. 25 Jan 1968) v. Canada at Buenos Aries, Argentina on 12 Mar 1995, Gavin Hastings (Scotland) v. Tonga at Pretoria, South Africa on 30 May 1995 and Thierry Lacroix (France) v. Ireland at Durban, South Africa on 10 Jun 1995.

Career In all internationals Michael Patrick Lynagh (b. 25 Oct 1963) scored a record 911 points in 72 matches for Australia, 1984–95. The most by a British player is 755 by Gavin Hastings, 689 for Scotland and 66 for the British Isles, 1986–95. The most tries is 63 by David Campese (b. 21 Oct 1962) in 91 internationals for Australia, 1982–95. The most by a British player is 47 by Rory Underwood (b. 18 Jun 1963) in 85 internationals for England and the British Isles, 1984–95

Season The first-class season scoring record is 581 points by Samuel Arthur Doble (1944–77) of Moseley, in 52 matches in 1971/2. He also scored 47 points for England in South Africa out of season.

Andy Higgin (b. 4 Mar 1963) scored a record 28 drop goals in a season in first-class rugby, for the Vale of Lune in 1986/7.

Career William Henry 'Dusty' Hare (b. 29 Nov 1952) scored 7337 points in first-class games from 1971–89, comprising 1800 for Nottingham, 4427 for Leicester, 240 for England, 88 for the British Isles and 782 in other representative matches.

Most tries Alan John Morley (b. 25 Jun 1950) scored 473 tries in senior rugby in 1968–86 including 378 for Bristol, a record for one club. John Huins scored 85 tries in 1953–4, 73 for St Luke's College, Exeter and 12 more for Neath and in trial games.

Match Jannie van der Westhuizen scored 80 points (14 tries, 9 conversions, 1 dropped goal, 1 penalty

Guess What?
Q. What is the highest score in a rugby league match?
A. See Page 281

In the 1995 International Championship, England completed a Grand Slam for a record 11th time. Here, Scotland's Kenny Logan, Doddie Weir and Peter Wright attempt to stop the England captain, Will Carling. Carling has captained England a record 53 times which includes 44 successive matches, also a record.
(Photos: Allsport/D. Rogers)

goal) for Carnarvon (88) v. Williston (12) at North West Cape, South Africa on 11 March 1972.

In a junior house match in February 1967 at William Ellis School, Edgware, Greater London, between Cumberland and Nunn, 12-year-old Thanos Morphitis (b. 5 Mar 1954) contributed 90 points (13 tries and 19 conversions) (77) to Cumberland's winning score.

Most international appearances Philippe Sella (France) b. 14 Feb 1962) has played in 111 internationals for France, 1982–95. The most by a British player is 85 by Rory Underwood, 79 for England and 6 for the British Isles, 1984–95. William James 'Willie John' McBride (b. 6 Jun 1940) made a record 17 appearances for the British Isles, as well as 63 for Ireland.

The most consecutive appearances is 63 by Sean Brian Thomas Fitzpatrick (New Zealand) (b. 4 Jun 1963), 1986–95. The British best is 53 by Willie John McBride for Ireland, 1964–75, and by Gareth Owen Edwards (b. 12 Jul 1947) who never missed a match throughout his career for Wales, 1967–78.

Youngest international Edinburgh Academy pupils Ninian Jamieson Finlay (1858–1936) and Charles Reid (1864–1909) were both 17 years 36 days old when they played for Scotland v. England in 1875 and 1881 respectively. However, as Finlay had one less leap year in his lifetime up to his first cap, the outright record must be credited to him. Semi Hekasilau Spec Taupeaafe played in a Test for Tonga against Western Samoa in 1989, aged 16.

> The County Championships (instituted 1889) have been won a record 16 times by Lancashire (between 1891 and 1993). The most individual appearances is 104 by Richard Trickey (Sale) (b. 6 Mar 1945) for Lancashire between 1964 and 1978.

Club Championships The most outright wins in the RFU Club Competition (John Player Cup, 1971–87, now Pilkington Cup) is nine by Bath, 1984–7, 1989–90, 1992, 1994–5. The highest team score (and aggregate) in the final is for Bath's 48–6 win over Gloucester in 1990. The Courage Clubs Championship (formerly the National Merit Tables and founded in 1985) has been won six times by Bath, 1987, 1989, 1991–4.

The most wins in the Welsh Rugby Union Challenge Cup now Swalec Cup (from 1992/3) is nine by Llanelli, 1973–6, 1985, 1988 and 1991–3. The highest team score in the final is 30 by Llanelli against Cardiff (7) in 1973. The highest aggregate is when Cardiff beat Newport 28–21 in 1986. Llanelli achieved the first league and cup double in Wales in 1993.

The most wins in the Scottish League Division One (instituted 1973/4) is ten by Hawick between 1973 and 1986.

Greatest crowd The record paying attendance is 104,000 for Scotland's 12–10 win over Wales at Murrayfield, Edinburgh on 1 Mar 1975.

> The Hong Kong Sevens, the world's most prestigious international tournament for seven-a-side teams, was first held in 1976. The record of seven wins is held by Fiji, 1977–8, 1980, 1984, 1990–92.

> The Middlesex Seven-a-sides were inaugurated in 1926 and have been won a record 13 times by Harlequins, 1926–9, 1933, 1935, 1967, 1978, 1986–90.

Longest kicks The longest recorded successful drop goal is 82 m *90 yd* by Gerald Hamilton 'Gerry' Brand (b. 8 Oct 1906) for South Africa v. England at Twickenham, Greater London, on 2 Jan 1932. This was taken 6 m *7 yd* inside the England 'half', 50 m *55 yd* from the posts, and dropped over the dead ball line.

The place kick record is reputed to be 91 m *100 yd* at Richmond Athletic Ground, London, by Douglas Francis Theodore Morkel (1886–1950) in an unsuccessful penalty for South Africa v. Surrey on 19 Dec 1906. This was not measured until 1932. In the match Bridlington School 1st XV v. an Army XV at Bridlington, Humberside on 29 Jan 1944, Ernie Cooper (b. 21 May 1926), captaining the school, landed a penalty from a measured 74 m *81 yd* from the post with a kick which carried over the dead ball line. The record in an international was set at 64.22 m *70 yd 8½ in* by Paul Huw Thorburn (b. 24 Nov 1962) for Wales v. Scotland on 1 Feb 1986.

All-rounder Canadian international Barrie Burnham scored all possible ways — try, conversion, penalty goal, drop goal, goal from mark — for Meralomas v. Georgians (20–11) at Vancouver, BC on 26 Feb 1966.

Fastest try The fastest try in an international game was when Herbert Leo 'Bart' Price (1899–1943) scored for England v. Wales at Twickenham on 20 Jan 1923 less than 10 sec after kick-off. The fastest try in any game was scored in 8 sec by Andrew Brown for Widden Old Boys v. Old Ashtonians at Gloucester on 22 Nov 1990.

Highest posts The world's highest rugby union goal posts are 33.54 m *110 ft ½ in* high at the Roan Antelope Rugby Union Club, Luanshya, Zambia. The posts at Old Halesonines RFC, Stourbridge, W Mids are 22.16 m *72 ft 8½ in*.

Most appearances Roy Evans of Banbury played a record 1193 games of rugby union all of which were played in the front row at tight head prop. His total includes 1007 played for Osterley from 12 Sep 1950–29 Apr 1989, a record for one club.

Most successful team The Feilding senior 4ths of New Zealand played 108 successive games without defeat from 1984–9. The Chiltern mini rugby side, from their formation as an Under-8 side, played 213 games without defeat, 29 Sep 1985–8 Apr 1990.

Women's Rugby

The women's World Cup has been contested twice (1991 and 1994) and the USA and England have reached the final on both occasions. The USA won in 1991 and England in 1994.

Sand & Ice Yachting

Highest speeds The highest speed officially recorded is 230 km/h *143 mph* by John D. Buckstaff in a Class A stern-steerer on Lake Winnebago, Wisconsin, USA in 1938. Such a speed is possible in a wind of 115 km/h *72 mph*.

Sand The official world record for a sand yacht is 107 km/h *66.48 mph* set by Christian-Yves Nau (France) (b. 1944) in *Mobil* at Le Touquet, France on 22 Mar 1981, when the wind speed reached 120 km/h *75 mph*. A speed of 142.26 km/h *88.4 mph* was attained by Nord Embroden (USA) in *Midnight at the Oasis* at Superior Dry Lake, California, USA on 15 Apr 1976.

Largest yacht The largest ice yacht was *Icicle*, built for Commodore John E. Roosevelt for racing on the Hudson River, New York in 1869. It was 21 m *68 ft 11 in* long and carried 99 m² *1070 ft²* of canvas.

■ The combination of wind, sand and sail in the sport of sand yachting can achieve speeds in excess of 80 km/h *50 mph*. The highest speed recorded is 142.2 km/h *88.4 mph*.
(Photo: Allsport/B. Martin)

Shinty

Most titles Newtonmore, Highland has won the Camanachd Association Challenge Cup (instituted 1896) a record 28 times, 1907–86. David Ritchie (b. 9 Jun 1944) and Hugh Chisholm (b. 14 Oct 1949) of Newtonmore, have won a record 12 winners' medals. In 1923 the Furnace Club, Argyll won the cup without conceding a goal throughout the competition.

In 1984 Kingussie Camanachd Club won all five senior competitions, including the Camanachd Cup final. This feat was equalled by Newtonmore in 1985.

Highest scores The highest Scottish Cup final score was in 1909 when Newtonmore beat Furnace 11–3 at Glasgow, Dr Johnnie Cattanach scoring eight hails or goals. In 1938 John Macmillan Mactaggart scored ten hails for Mid-Argyll in a Camanachd Cup match.

Shooting

Most Olympic medals Carl Townsend Osburn (USA) (1884–1966), in 1912, 1920 and 1924, won a record 11, five gold, four silver and two bronze. Six other marksmen have won five gold medals. The only marksman to win three individual gold medals has been Gudbrand Gudbrandsönn Skatteboe (Norway) (1875–1965) in 1906. Separate events for women were first held in 1984.

Bisley The National Rifle Association was instituted in 1859. The Queen's (King's) Prize has been shot since 1860 and has only once been won by a woman, Marjorie Elaine Foster (1894–1974) (score 280) on 19 Jul 1930. Arthur George Fulton (1887–1972) won three times (1912, 1926, 1931). Both his father and his son also won the Prize.

The highest score (possible 300) for the final of the Queen's Prize is 295. This was achieved by Lindsay

Peden (Scotland) (b. 12 Oct 1952) on 24 Jul 1982 and also, but on targets with a smaller bullseye, by Colin Brook (London & Middlesex RA) on 24 Jul 1993.

Clay pigeon Most world titles have been won by Susan Nattrass (Canada) (b. 5 Nov 1950) with six, 1974–5, 1977–9, 1981.

> The British individual small-bore rifle record for 60 shots prone is 597/600, by: Philip Scanlan (b. 4 Feb 1951), Alister Allan (b. 28 Jan 1944), John Booker (b. 19 Jul 1940), William Murray (b. 30 Oct 1956) and Willam Brown (b. 1 Feb 1952).

Bench rest shooting The smallest group on record at 1000 yd *914 m* is 3.960 in *10.058 cm* by Frank Weber (USA) with a .308 Baer at Williamsport, Pennsylvania, USA on 14 Nov 1993. The smallest at 500 m *546 yd* is 1.5 in *3.81 cm* by Ross Hicks (Australia) using a rifle of his own design at Canberra, Australia on 12 Mar 1994.

Skiing

Most titles *World/Olympic Championships—Alpine* The World Alpine Championships were inaugurated at Mürren, Switzerland, in 1931. The greatest number of titles won has been by Christl Cranz (b. 1 Jul 1914) of Germany, with seven individual—four slalom (1934, 1937–9) and three downhill (1935, 1937, 1939), and five combined (1934–5, 1937–9). She also won the gold medal for the Combined in the 1936 Olympics. The most won by a man is seven by Anton 'Toni' Sailer (Austria) (b. 17 Nov 1935), who won all four in 1956 (giant slalom, slalom, downhill and the non-Olympic Alpine combination) and the downhill, giant slalom and combined in 1958.

World/Olympic Championships — Nordic The first World Nordic Championships were those of the 1924

Shooting–Individual World Records

In 1986, the International Shooting Union (UIT) introduced new regulations for determining major championships and world records. Now the leading competitors undertake an additional round with a target sub-divided to tenths of a point for rifle and pistol shooting, and an extra 25,40 or 50 (depending on category) shots for trap and skeet. Harder targets have since been introduced and the table below shows the world records, as recognised by the UIT at the end of 1994, for the 15 Olympic shooting disciplines to be contested at Atlanta in 1996, giving in brackets the score for the number of shots specified plus the score in the additional round.

MEN

EVENT	Score		Name and Country	Venue	Date
FREE RIFLE 50m 3×40 shots	1287.9	(1186+101.9)	Rajmond Debevec (Slovenia)	Munich, Germany	29 Aug 1992
FREE RIFLE 50m 60 Shots Prone	703.5	(599+104.5)	Jens Harskov (Denmark)	Zürich, Switzerland	6 Jun 1991
AIR RIFLE 10m 60 shots	699.4	(596+103.4)	Rajmond Debevec (Yugoslavia)	Zürich, Switzerland	7 Jun 1990
FREE PISTOL 50m 60 shots	672.5	(575+97.5)	Sergey Pyzhyanov (Russia)	Milan, Italy	16 Jun 1993
RAPID-FIRE PISTOL 25m 60 shots	699.7	(596+107.5)	Ralf Schumann (Germany)	Barcelona, Spain	8 Jun 1994
AIR PISTOL 10m 60 shots	695.1	(593+102.1)	Sergey Pyzhyanov (USSR)	Munich, Germany	13 Oct 1989
RUNNING TARGET 10m 30/30 shots	678.8	(579+99.8)	Jens Zimmermann (Germany)	Milan, Italy	31 May 1994
SKEET 125 targets	149	(124+25)	Dean Clark (USA)	Barcelona, Spain	20 Jun 1993
	149	(124+25)	Andrea Benelli (Italy)	Fagnano, Italy	29 May 1994
	149	(124+25)	Andrea Benelli (Italy)	Lisbon, Portugal	5 Jun 1994
TRAP 125 targets	149	(125+24)	Giovanni Pellielo (Italy)	Nicosia, Cyprus	1 Apr 1994
	149	(124+25)	Marco Venturini (Italy)	Munich, Germany	10 Sep 1994
DOUBLE TRAP 150 targets	191	(143+48)	Joshua Lakatos (USA)	Barcelona, Spain	15 Jun 1993

WOMEN

EVENT	Score		Name and Country	Venue	Date
STANDARD RIFLE 50m 3×20 shots	689.3	(590+99.3)	Vessela Letcheva (Bulgaria)	Munich, Germany	28 Aug 1992
AIR RIFLE 10m 40 shots	500.8	(399+101.8)	Valentina Cherkasova (USSR)	Los Angeles, USA	23 Mar 1991
SPORT PISTOL 25m 60 shots	696.2	(594+102.2)	Diana Jorgova (Bulgaria)	Milan, Italy	31 May 1994
AIR PISTOL 10m 40 shots	492.4	(392+100.4)	Lieselotte Breker (West Germany)	Zagreb, Yugoslavia	18 May 1989
DOUBLE TRAP 120 targets	147	(112+35)	Deborah Gelisio (Italy)	Nicosia, Cyprus	3 Apr 1994

■ The successful Russian relay team— winners of the 4×5km gold at the 1994 Olympics. The team includes two of the most successful Nordic skiers ever, Lyubov Yegorova (far left) winner of a record six Olympic golds and Yelena Välbe (second left) winner of a record four World Cup titles.
(Photo: Allsport/S. Botterill)..

Winter Olympics in Chamonix, France. The greatest number of titles won is 11 by Gunde Svan (Sweden) (b. 12 Jan 1962), seven individual; 15km 1989, 30km 1985 and 1991, 50km 1985 and 1989, and Olympics, 15km 1984, 50km 1988: and four relays; 4 × 10km, 1987 and 1989, and Olympics, 1984 and 1988. The most titles won by a woman is 11 by Yelena Välbe (Russia) (née Trubizinina) (b. 24 Feb 1968), six individual and five relay, 1989–95. The most medals is 23 by Raisa Petrovna Smetanina (USSR) (b. 29 Feb 1952) including seven gold, 1974–92. Ulrich Wehling (GDR) (b. 8 Jul 1952) with the Nordic combined in 1972, 1976 and 1980, is the only skier to win the same event at three successive Olympics. The most titles won by a jumper is five by Birger Ruud (b. 23 Aug 1911) of Norway, in 1931–2 and 1935–7. Ruud is the only person to win Olympic events in each of the dissimilar Alpine and Nordic disciplines. In 1936 he won the Ski-jumping and the Alpine downhill (which was not then a separate event, but only a segment of the Combined event).

World Cup The World Cup was introduced for Alpine events in 1967. The most individual event wins is 86 (46 giant slalom, 40 slalom from a total of 287 races) by Ingemar Stenmark (Sweden) (b. 18 Mar 1956) in 1974–89, including a men's record 13 in one season in 1978/9, of which 10 were part of a record 14 successive giant slalom wins from 18 Mar 1978, his 22nd birthday, to 21 Jan 1980. Franz Klammer (Austria) (b. 3 Dec 1953) won a record 25 downhill races, 1974–84. Annemarie Moser (née Pröll) (Austria) (b. 27 Mar 1953) won a women's record 62 individual event wins, 1970–79. She had a record 11 consecutive downhill wins from Dec 1972 to Jan 1974. Vreni Schneider (Switzerland) (b. 26 Nov 1964) won a record 13 events (and a combined) including all seven slalom events in the 1988/9 season.

The Nations' Cup, awarded on the combined results of the men and women in the World Cup, has been won a record 16 times by Austria 1969, 1973–80, 1982, 1990–95.

Highest speed The official world record, as recognized by the International Ski Federation for a skier, is 241.448km/h *150.028mph* by Jeffrey Hamilton (USA) and the fastest by a woman is 225.000 km/h *139.808 mph* by Karine Dubouchet (France) both at Vars, France on 14 Apr 1995.

Most Olympic Skiing Titles

MEN

ALPINE.....3 Anton 'Toni' Sailer (Austria) (b. 17 Nov 1935) .....Downhill, slalom, giant slalom, 1956
3 Jean-Claude Killy (France) (b. 30 Aug 1943) ......Downhill, slalom, giant slalom 1968
3 Alberto Tomba (Italy) (b. 19 Dec 1966) *..............Slalom, giant slalom, 1988; giant slalom, 1992
NORDIC ...5 Bjørn Dæhlie (Norway) (b. 19 Jun 1967) ....15km, 50km, 4×10km 1992; 10km, 15km 1994
Jumping ...4 Matti Nykänen (Finland) (b. 17 Jul 1963) ....70m hill 1988; 90m hill 1984, 1988; Team 1988

WOMEN

ALPINE.....3 Vreni Schneider (Switzerland) (b. 26 Nov 1964)*.Giant slalom, slalom 1988; slalom 1994
NORDIC ...6 Lyubov Yegorova (Russia) (b. 5 May 1966) ....10km, 15km 4×5km 1992; 5km, 10km, 4×5km 1994

*Most medals

10 (women), Raisa Smetanina (USSR/CIS) (b. 29 Feb 1952), four gold, five silver and one bronze in Nordic events, 1976-92.
9 (men), Sixten Jernberg (Sweden) (b. 6 Feb 1929), four golds, three silver and two bronze in Nordic events, 1956-64.
In Alpine skiing, the record is five: Alberto Tomba won silver in the 1992 and 1994 slalom; Vreni Schneider won silver in the combined and bronze in the giant slalom in 1994; and Kjetil André Aamodt (Norway) (b. 2 Sep 1971) won one gold (super giant slalom 1992), two silver (downhill, combined 1994) and two bronze (giant slalom 1992, super giant slalom 1994).

■ This picture of the world's fastest skier Jeffrey Hamilton (USA), shows some of the aerodynamic equipment necessary, note the helmet and glove cones, to attain speeds in excess of 150mph *240km/h*.
(Photo: Allsport/Vandystadt/Zoom)

Ski Jump

The longest ski-jump ever recorded is one of 194m *636ft* by Piotr Fijas (Poland) at Planica, Yugoslavia on 14 Mar 1987. The women's record is 112m *367ft* by Eva Ganster (Austria) at Bischofshofen, Austria on 7 Jan 1994. The longest dry ski-jump is 92m *302ft* by Hubert Schwarz (West Germany) at Berchtesgarten, Germany on 30 Jun 1981.

Most World Cup Titles

ALPINE SKIING (instituted 1967)

MEN

OVERALL ....5 .....Marc Girardelli (Luxembourg) (b. 18 Jul 1963)...............1985–6, 1989, 1991, 1993
DOWNHILL ....5 .....Franz Klammer (Austria) (b. 3 Oct 1953)......................1975–8, 1983
SLALOM ....8 .....Ingemar Stenmark (Sweden) (b. 18 Mar 1956).............1975–81, 1983
GIANT SLALOM ....7 .....Ingemar Stenmark (Sweden)...................................1975–6, 1978–81, 1984
SUPER GIANT SLALOM ...4 .....Pirmin Zurbriggen (Switzerland) (b. 4 Feb 1963) 1987–90
Two men have won four titles in one year: Jean-Claude Killy (France) (b. 30 Aug 1943) won all four possible disciplines (downhill, slalom, giant slalom and overall) in 1967; and Pirmin Zurbriggen (Switzerland) (b. 4 Feb 1963) won four of the five possible disciplines (downhill, giant slalom, super giant slalom (added 1986) and overall) in 1987.

WOMEN

OVERALL ....6 .....Annemarie Moser-Pröll (Austria) (b. 27 Mar 1953).........1971–5, 1979
DOWNHILL ....7 .....Annemarie Moser-Pröll 1971–5, 1978–9
SLALOM ....6 .....Vreni Schneider (Switzerland) (b. 26 Nov 1964) 1989–90, 1992–5
GIANT SLALOM ....5 .....Vreni Schneider (Switzerland) 1986–7, 1989, 1991, 1995
SUPER GIANT SLALOM ...4 .....Carole Merle (France) (b. 24 Jan 1964) 1989–92

NORDIC SKIING (instituted 1981)

MEN

JUMPING ....4 .....Matti Nykänen (Finland) (b. 17 Jul 1963) 1983, 1985–6, 1988
CROSS-COUNTRY ....5 .....Gunde Svan (Sweden) (b. 12 Jan 1962) 1984–6, 1988–9

WOMEN

CROSS-COUNTRY ....4 .....Yelena Välbe (USSR/Russia) (b. 24 Feb 1968)..............1989, 1991–2, 1995

On 16 Apr 1988 at Les Arcs, France, Graham Wilkie (GB) (b. 21 Sep 1959) set a British men's record of 219.914 km/h *136.648 mph* and Patrick Knaff (France) set a one-legged record of 185.567 km/h *115.306 mph*. On 21 Apr 1993, a British women's record was set by Divina Galica (b. 13 Aug 1944) at 200.667 km/h *124.689 mph*, also at Les Arcs, France.

The highest average speed in the Olympic downhill race was 104.53 km/h *64.95 mph* by William D. Johnson (USA) (b. 30 Mar 1960) at Sarajevo, Yugoslavia on 16 Feb 1984. The fastest in a World Cup downhill is 112.4 km/h *69.8 mph* by Armin Assinger (Austria) at Sierra Nevada, Spain on 15 Mar 1993.

Highest speed—cross-country The record time for a 50 km race in a major championship is 1 hr 54 min 46 sec by Aleksey Prokurorov (Russia) at Thunder Bay, Canada on 19 Mar 1994, an average speed of 26.14 km/h *16.24 mph*.

Longest races The world's greatest Nordic ski race is the Vasaloppet, which commemorates an event of 1521 when Gustav Vasa (1496–1560), later King Gustavus Eriksson, fled 85.8 km *53.3 miles* from Mora to Sälen, Sweden. He was overtaken by loyal, speedy scouts on skis, who persuaded him to return eastwards to Mora to lead a rebellion and become the king of Sweden. The re-enactment of this return journey is now an annual event at 89 km *55.3 miles*. There were a record 10,934 starters on 6 Mar 1977 and a record 10,650 finishers on 4 Mar 1979. The fastest time is 3 hr 48 min 55 sec, by Bengt Hassis (Sweden) on 2 Mar 1986.

The Finlandia Ski Race, 75 km *46.6 miles* from Hämeenlinna to Lahti, on 26 Feb 1984 had a record 13,226 starters and 12,909 finishers.

Longest run The longest all-downhill ski run in the world is the Weissfluhjoch-Küblis Parsenn course,

■ In the calender year, 1994, Lucy Dicker and Arnie Wilson (both GB) skied everyday in a round-the- world expedition. In total they skied 5919 km *3678 miles*, 143,880 vertical metres *472,050 ft* at 237 resorts in 13 countries on 5 continents.

The first person to ski on all seven continents was Tom Hayes (USA) and the first women was Norma Rowlerson (GB).

near Davos, Switzerland, which measures 12.23 km *7.6 miles*.

Long-distance *Nordic* In 24 hours Seppo-Juhani Savolainen covered 415.5 km *258.2 miles* at Saariselkä, Finland on 8–9 Apr 1988. The women's record is 330 km *205.05 miles* by Sisko Kainulaisen at Jyväskylä, Finland on 23–24 Mar 1985.

In 48 hours Bjørn Løkken (Norway) (b. 27 Nov 1937) covered 513.568 km *319 miles 205 yd* on 11–13 Mar 1982.

Freestyle The first World Championships were held at Tignes, France in 1986, titles being awarded in ballet, moguls, aerials and combined. Edgar Grospiron (France) (b. 17 Mar 1969) has won a record three titles, moguls 1989 and aerials, 1991 and 1995. He has also won an Olympic title, 1992. The most Overall titles in the World Cup (instituted 1980) is ten by Connie Kissling (Switzerland) (b. 18 Jul 1961), 1983–92. The men's record is five by Eric Laboureix (France) (b. 12 Apr 1962), 1986–8, 1990–1.

Longest lift The longest gondola ski lift is 6239 m *3.88 miles* long at Grindelwald-Männlichen, Switzerland

(in two sections, but one gondola). The longest chair lift in the world was the Alpine Way to Kosciusko Chalet lift above Thredbo, near the Snowy Mountains, New South Wales, Australia. It took from 45 to 75 min to ascend the 5.6 km *3.5 miles*, according to the weather. It has now collapsed. The highest is at Chacaltaya, Bolivia, rising to 5029 m *16,500 ft*.

Ski-bob *Origins* The ski-bob was the invention of J. C. Stevenson of Hartford, Connecticut, USA in 1891, and patented (No. 47334) on 19 Apr 1892 as a 'bicycle with ski-runners'. The *Fédération Internationale de Skibob* was founded on 14 Jan 1961 in Innsbruck, Austria and the first World Championships were held at Bad Hofgastein, Austria in 1967.

The highest speed attained is 166 km/h *103.1 mph* by Erich Brenter (Austria) (b. 1940) at Cervinia, Italy in 1964.

World Championships The most individual combined titles is four by Petra Tschach-Wlezcek (Austria), 1988–91. The most titles by a man is three by Walter Kronseil (Austria), 1988–90.

Grass Skiing

World Championships (now awarded for Super-G, giant slalom, slalom and combined) have been held biennially from 1979. The most titles won is 14 by Ingrid Hirschhofer (Austria) 1979–93. The most by a man is seven by: Erwin Gansner (Switzerland), 1981–7; and Rainer Grossmann, 1985–93.

The feat of winning all four titles in one year has been achieved by: (men) Erwin Gansner, 1987 and Rainer Grossmann, 1991; and (women) Katja Krey (West Germany), 1989 and Ingrid Hirschhofer, 1993.

Downhill

The longest downhill race is the *Inferno* in Switzerland, 15.8 km *9.8 miles* from the top of the Schilthorn to Lauterbrunnen. The record entry was 1401 in 1981 and the record time 13 min 53.40 sec by Urs von Allmen (Switzerland) in 1991.

The speed record is 92.07 km/h *57.21 mph* by Klaus Spinka (Austria) at Waldsassen, Germany on 24 Sep 1989. Laurence Beck set a British record of 79.49 km/h *49.39 mph* at Owen, Germany on 8 Sep 1985.

Snow shoeing

The IASSRF (International Amateur SnowShoe Racing Federation) record for covering 1 mile *1.6 km* is 5 min 56.7 sec by Nick Akers of Edmonton, Alberta, Canada on 3 Feb 1991. The 100 m record is 14.07 sec by Jeremy Badeau at Canaseraga, New York, USA on 31 May 1991.

Skipping

10 Mile skip-run Vadivelu Karunakaren (India) skipped 10 miles *16 km* in 58 min at Madras, India, 1 Feb 1990.

Most turns *One hour* 14,628 by Park Bong-tae (South Korea) at Pusan, South Korea, 2 Jul 1989.

On a single rope, team of 90 196 by students from the Ino Elementary School, Toyama, Japan, 21 Aug 1994.

Most on a rope (minimum 12 turns obligatory) 220 by a team at the International Rope Skipping Competition, Greeley, Colorado, USA, 28 Jun 1990.

Guess What?

Q. How many sovereign countries are there in the world?

A. See Page 175

■ Stephen Hendry, winner of the 1995 World Championship, made a 147 break during his semi-final win over Jimmy White. He is only the third person to achieve this during the championships history.
(Photos: Allsport/M. Cooper)

Skittles

The highest score at West Country skittles by a team of eight is 99,051 by the 'Alkies' Skittles team at Courtlands Holiday Inn, Torquay, Devon on 4–5 Apr 1987; they reset the skittles after every ball. The highest hood skittle score in 24 hours is 144,648 pins by 12 players from the Semilong Working Mens Club, Northampton on 13–14 Jun 1992. The highest long alley score is 94,151 by a team from the Carpenters Arms, Leigh, Dorset on 10–11 Mar 1995. The highest table skittle score in 24 hours is 116,047 skittles by 12 players at the Castle Mona, Newcastle, Staffs on 15–16 Apr 1990.

Sled Dog Racing

Oldest The oldest established sled dog trail is the 1688 km *1049 mile* Iditarod Trail from Anchorage to Nome, Alaska, USA, which has existed since 1910 and has been the course of an annual race since 1967. The fastest time was set by Doug Swingley (USA), 9 days 2 hr 42 min 19 sec in 1995.

Longest The longest race is the 2000 km *1243 miles* Berengia Trail from Esso to Markovo, Russia, which started as a 250 km *155 miles* route in April 1990. Now established as an annual event, the 1991 race was won by Pavel Lazarev in 10 days 18 hr 17 min 56 sec.

Snooker

Most world titles The World Professional Championship (instituted 1927) was won a record 15 times by Joe Davis, on the first 15 occasions it was contested, 1927–40 and 1946. The most wins in the Amateur Championships (instituted 1963) have been two by: Gary Owen (England) in 1963 and 1966; Ray Edmonds (England) 1972 and 1974; and Paul Mifsud (Malta) 1985–6. Allison Fisher (b. 24 Feb 1968) has won seven women's World Championships, 1985–6, 1988–9, 1991–3.

Maureen Baynton (*née* Barrett) won a record eight Women's Amateur Championships between 1954 and 1968, as well as seven at billiards.

World Championships *Youngest* The youngest man to win a world title is Stephen O'Connor (Ireland) (b. 16 Oct 1972), who was 18 years 40 days when he won the World Amateur Snooker Championship in Colombo, Sri Lanka on 25 Nov 1990. Stephen Hendry (Scotland) (b. 13 Jan 1969) became the youngest World Professional champion, at 21 yr 106 days on 29 Apr 1990.

Stacey Hillyard (GB) (b. 5 Sep 1969) won the Women's World Amateur Championship in October 1984 at the age of 15.

Highest breaks The first to achieve the 'maximum' break of 147 was E. J. 'Murt' O'Donoghue (New Zealand) (1901–94) at Griffiths, New South Wales, Australia on 26 Sep 1934. The first officially ratified 147 was by Joe Davis against Willie Smith at Leicester Square Hall, London on 22 Jan 1955. The first achieved in a major tournament were by John Spencer (b. 18 Sep 1935) at Slough, Berks on 13 Jan 1979, but the table had oversized pockets, and by Steve Davis (b. 22 Aug 1957), who had a ratified break of 147 against John Spencer in the Lada Classic at Oldham, Greater Manchester on 11 Jan 1982. The youngest to score a competitive maximum was Ronnie O'Sullivan (b. 5 Dec 1975) at 15 years 98 days during the English Amateur Championship (Southern Area) at Aldershot, Hants on 13 Mar 1991. Cliff Thorburn (Canada) (b. 16 Jan 1948) was first to make two tournament 147 breaks on 23 Apr 1983 (the first in the World Professional Championships) and on 8 Mar 1989. Peter Ebdon (b. 27 Aug 1970), James Wattana (Thailand) (b. 17 Jan 1970) and Stephen Hendry (b. 13 Jan 1969) have also achieved this feat.

Steve Duggan (b. 10 Apr 1958) made a break of 148 in a witnessed practice frame in Doncaster, S Yorks on 27 Apr 1988 and Tony Drago (b. 22 Sep 1965) made a break of 149 in similar circumstances at West Norwood, Greater London on 1 Feb 1995. The break involved a free ball, which therefore created an 'extra' red, when all 15 reds were still on the table. In these very exceptional circumstances, the maximum break is 155. The only '16 red' clearance ever completed in a tournament was by Steve James (b. 2 May 1961) who made 135 against Alex Higgins (b. 18 Mar 1949) in the World Professional Championships at Sheffield, S Yorks on 14 Apr 1990.

The world amateur record break is 147 by Geet Sethi (India) in the Indian Amateur Championships on 21 Feb 1988.

The highest break by a woman is 137 by Stacey Hillyard in the General Portfolio Women's Classic at Aylesbury, Bucks on 23 Feb 1992.

Three consecutive century breaks were first compiled in a major tournament by Steve Davis: 108, 101 and 104 at Stoke-on-Trent, Staffs on 10 Sep 1988. Doug Mountjoy (b. 8 Jun 1942) equalled the feat: 131, 106 and 124 at Preston, Lancs on 27 Nov 1988. Four century breaks in five frames has been achieved by Peter Ebdon in the European Open qualifying competition at Blackpool on 6 Sep 1992 and by Stephen Hendry in the UK Championship final on 27 Nov 1994.

Longest unbeaten run From 17 Mar 1990 to his defeat by Jimmy White (b. 2 May 1962) on 13 Jan 1991, Stephen Hendry won five successive titles and 36 consecutive matches in ranking tournaments. During the summer of 1992, Ronnie O'Sullivan won 38 consecutive matches but these were in qualifying competitions.

Softball

Most titles The USA has won the men's world championship (instituted 1966) five times, 1966, 1968, 1976 (shared), 1980 and 1988, and the women's title (instituted 1965) four times in 1974, 1978, 1986 and 1990. The world's first slow-pitch championships for men's teams was held in Oklahoma City, USA in 1987, when the winners were the USA.

Speedway

World Championships The World Speedway Championship was inaugurated at Wembley, London on 10 Sep 1936. The most wins has been six by Ivan Gerald Mauger (New Zealand) (b. 4 Oct 1939) in 1968–70, 1972, 1977 and 1979. Barry Briggs (New Zealand) (b. 30 Dec 1934) made a record 18 appearances in the finals (1954–70, 1972), won the world title in 1957–8, 1964 and 1966 and scored a record 201 points from 87 races.

Ivan Mauger also won four World Team Cups (three for GB), two World Pairs (including one unofficial) and three world long track titles. Ove Fundin (Sweden) (b. 23 May 1933) won 12 world titles: five individual, one Pairs, and six World Team Cup medals in 1956–70. In 1985 Erik Gundersen (Denmark) became the first man to hold world titles at individual, pairs, team and long-track events simultaneously.

The World Pairs Championships (instituted unofficially 1968, officially 1970) have been won a record eight times by Denmark, 1979, 1985–91. The most successful individual in the World Pairs has been Hans Hollen Nielsen (b. 26 Dec 1959) with seven wins for Denmark. His partners were Ole Olsen, 1979, Erik Gundersen, 1986–9, and Jan O. Pedersen, 1990–91. Maximum points (then 30) were scored in the World Pairs Championship by: Jerzy Szczakiel (b. 28 Jan 1949) and Andrzej Wyglenda (Poland) at Rybnik, Poland in 1971; and Arthur Dennis Sigalos (b. 16 Aug

■ The Soviet Union and now Russia have dominated the ice speedway world championships since these began in 1966. They have won 25 of 29 individual competitions and 15 of 16 team titles which started in 1979.
(Photos: Allsport/C. Brunskill)

Most titles *Open Championship* The most wins in the Open Championship held annually in Britain, is ten by Jahangir Khan, in successive years, 1982–91. Hashim Khan (Pakistan) (b. 1915) won seven times, 1950–55 and 1957, and also won the Vintage title six times in 1978–83.

The most British Open women's titles is 16 by Heather Pamela McKay (née Blundell) (Australia) (b. 31 Jul 1941) from 1961 to 1977. She also won the World Open title in 1976 and 1979.

Amateur Championship The most wins in the Amateur Championship is six by Abdelfattah Amr Bey (Egypt) (b. 14 Feb 1910), who won in 1931–3 and 1935–7. Norman Francis Borrett (b. 1 Oct 1917) of England won in 1946–50.

Unbeaten sequences Heather McKay was unbeaten from 1962 to 1980. Jahangir Khan was unbeaten from his loss to Geoff Hunt at the British Open on 10 Apr 1981 until Ross Norman (New Zealand) ended his sequence in the World Open final on 11 Nov 1986.

Longest and shortest championship matches The longest recorded competitive match was one of 2 hr 45 min when Jahangir Khan beat Gamal Awad (Egypt) (b. 8 Sep 1955) 9–10, 9–5, 9–7, 9–2, the first game lasting a record 1 hr 11 min, in the final of the Patrick International Festival at Chichester, W Sussex on 30 Mar 1983. Philip Kenyon (England) (b. 9 May 1956) beat Salah Nadi (Egypt) (b. 11 Jan 1956) in just 6 min 37 sec (9–0, 9–0, 9–0) in the British Open at Lamb's Squash Club, London on 9 Apr 1992.

Most international appearances The men's record is 122 by David Gotto (b. 25 Dec 1948) for Ireland. The women's record is 119 by Rebecca O'Callaghan (née Best) (b. 18 Jun 1964) for Ireland.

1959) and Robert Benjamin 'Bobby' Schwartz (USA) (b. 10 Aug 1956) at Liverpool, New South Wales, Australia on 11 Dec 1982. The World Team Cup (instituted 1960) has been won a record nine times by: England/Great Britain (Great Britain 1968, 1971–3; England 1974–5, 1977, 1980, 1989); and Denmark 1978, 1981, 1983–8, 1991. Hans Nielsen (Denmark) has ridden in a record eight Team wins.

The only rider to have scored maximum points in every match of a Test series was Arthur 'Bluey' Wilkinson (1911–40) in five matches for Australia v. England in Sydney in 1937/8.

British championships
League racing was introduced to British speedway in 1929 and consisted of a Southern League and Northern Dirt Track League, the National League was formulated in 1932 and continued to 1964. The Wembley Lions who won in 1932, 1946–7, 1949–53, had a record eight victories. In 1965 it was replaced by the British League which Belle Vue (who had six National League wins, 1933–6, 1939 and 1963) have won five times, including three times in succession (1970–72).

In league racing the highest score recorded was when Berwick beat Exeter 78–18 in the 16-heat formula for the National League on 27 May 1989. A maximum possible score was achieved by Bristol when they defeated Glasgow (White City) 70–14 on 7 Oct 1949 in the National League Division Two. Oxford set a record of 28 successive wins in the British League in 1986. The highest number of League points scored by an individual in a season was 563 by Hans Nielsen for Oxford in the British League in 1988. The League career record is 6471 points by Nigel Boocock (b. 17 Sep 1937), 1955–80.

Belle Vue (Manchester) had a record nine victories (1933–7, 1946–7, 1949 and 1958) in the National Trophy Knock-out Competition (held 1931–64). This was replaced in 1965 by the Knock–Out Cup, which has been won eight times (one shared) by Cradley Heath. The highest recorded score in this competition is 81–25, when Hull beat Sheffield in 1979.

The British League Riders' Championship was instituted in 1965 and is an annual event contested by the top scorers from each team. Ivan Mauger holds the records for appearances, 15 and points scored, 146, 1965–79. The most wins is six by Barry Briggs, 1965–70.

Leicester are the only team to have used the same seven riders in a complete League programme. This was in 1969 when the same seven riders rode in all of the 36 matches.

Squash Rackets

World Championships Jahangir Khan (Pakistan) (b. 10 Dec 1963) won six World Open (instituted 1976) titles, 1981–5 and 1988, and the International Squash Rackets Federation world individual title (formerly World Amateur, instituted 1967) in 1979, 1983 and 1985. Jansher Khan (Pakistan) (b. 15 Jun 1969) has also won six World Opens 1987, 1989–90, 1992–4. Geoffrey B. Hunt (Australia) (b. 11 Mar 1947) won four World Open titles, 1976–7 and 1979–80 and three World Amateur, 1967, 1969 and 1971. The most women's World Open titles is five by Susan Devoy (New Zealand) (b. 4 Jan 1964), 1985, 1987, 1990–92.

The most men's world team titles is six by: Australia 1967, 1969, 1971, 1973, 1989 and 1991; and Pakistan 1977, 1981, 1983, 1985, 1987 and 1993. England won the women's title in 1985, 1987, 1989 and 1990, following Great Britain's win in 1979.

Guess What?

Q. What is the record weight for a squash?

A. See Page 48

Surfing

Most titles World Amateur Championships were inaugurated in May 1964 at Sydney, Australia. The most titles is three by Michael Novakov (Australia) who won the Kneeboard event in 1982, 1984 and 1986. A World Professional series was started in 1975. The men's title has been won five times by Mark Richards (Australia), 1975 and 1979–82 and the women's title (instituted 1979) four times by: Frieda Zamba (USA), 1984–6, 1988; and Wendy Botha (Australia, formerly South Africa), 1987, 1989, 1991–2.

Highest waves ridden Waimea Bay, Hawaii reputedly provides the most consistently high waves, often reaching the ridable limit of 9–11 m *30–35 ft*. The highest wave ever ridden was the *tsunami* of 'perhaps 50 ft', which struck Minole, Hawaii on 3 Apr 1868, and was ridden to save his life by a Hawaiian named Holua.

Longest sea wave ride About four to six times each year rideable surfing waves break in Matanchen Bay near San Blas, Nayarit, Mexico which makes rides of c. 1700 m *5700 ft* possible.

Longest ride *River bore* The longest recorded rides on a river bore have been set on the Severn bore, England. The official British Surfing Association record for riding a surfboard in a standing position is 4 km *2.5 mile* by David Lawson from Lower Rea to Lower Parting on 27 Sep 1988. The longest ride on a surfboard standing or lying down is 4.73 km *2.94 miles* by Colin Kerr Wilson (b. 23 Jun 1954) on 23 May 1982.

Highest speed In tests at Wimbledon Squash and Badminton Club in January 1988, Roy Buckland hit a squash ball by an overhead service at a measured speed of 232.7 km/h *144.6 mph* over the distance to the front wall. This is equivalent to an initial speed at the racket of 242.6 km/h *150.8 mph*.

Largest crowd and tournament The finals of the ICI World Team Championships at the Royal Albert Hall, London had a record attendance for squash of 3526 on 30 Oct 1987.

The InterCity National Squash Challenge was contested by 9588 players in 1988, a knock-out tournament record.

Swimming

Largest pools The largest swimming pool in the world is the seawater Orthlieb Pool in Casablanca, Morocco. It is 480 m *1574 ft* long and 75 m *246 ft* wide, and has an area of 3.6 ha *8.9 acres*. The largest land-locked swimming pool with heated water was the Fleishhacker Pool on Sloat Boulevard, near Great Highway, San Francisco, California, USA. It measured 305×46 m *1000×150 ft* and up to 4.26 m *14 ft* deep and contained 28,390 hectolitres *6,245,050 US gal* of heated water. It was opened on 2 May 1925 but has now been abandoned. The largest land-locked pool in current use is Willow Lake at Warren, Ohio, USA. It measures 183 m×46 m *600×150 ft*. The greatest spectator accommodation is 13,614 at Osaka, Japan. The largest in use in the United Kingdom is the Royal Commonwealth Pool, Edinburgh, completed in 1970 with 2000 permanent seats, but the covered over and unused pool at Earls Court, London (opened 1937) could seat some 12,000 spectators.

Swimming World Records (set in 50 m pools)

MEN

Event	min:sec	Name and Country	Venue	Date
FREESTYLE				
50 m	21.81	Tom Jager (USA) (b. 6 Oct 1964)	Nashville, TN, USA	24 Mar 1990
100 m	48.21	Aleksandr Popov (Russia) (b. 16 Nov 1971)	Monte Carlo	18 Jun 1994
200 m	1:46.69	Giorgio Lamberti (Italy) (b. 28 Jan 1969)	Bonn, Germany	15 Aug 1989
400 m	3:43.80	Kieren John Perkins (Australia) (b. 14 Aug 1973)	Rome, Italy	9 Sep 1994
800 m	7:46.00	Kieren John Perkins (Australia)	Victoria, Canada	24 Aug 1994
1500 m	14:41.66	Kieren John Perkins (Australia)	Victoria, Canada	24 Aug 1994
4×100 m	3:16.53	USA (Christopher Jacobs, Troy Dalbey, Tom Jager, Matthew Nicholas Biondi)	Seoul, South Korea	23 Sep 1988
4×200 m	7:11.95	CIS (Dmitriy Lepikov, Vladimir Pyechenko, Venyamin Tayanovich, Yevgeniy Sadovyi)	Barcelona, Spain	27 Jul 1992
BREASTSTROKE				
100 m	1:00.95	Károly Güttler (Hungary) (b. 15 Jun 1968)	Sheffield, S Yorks	3 Aug 1993
200 m	2:10.16	Michael Ray Barrowman (USA) (b. 4 Dec 1968)	Barcelona, Spain	29 Jul 1992
BUTTERFLY				
100 m	52.84	Pedro Pablo Morales (USA) (b. 5 Dec 1964)	Orlando, FL, USA	23 Jun 1986
200 m	1:55.22	Denis Pankratov (Russia)	Paris, France	14 Jun 1995
BACKSTROKE				
100 m	53.86	Jeff Rouse (USA) (b. 6 Feb 1970) (relay leg)	Barcelona, Spain	31 Jul 1992
200 m	1:56.57	Martin López-Zubero (Spain) (b. 23 Apr 1964)	Tuscaloosa, AL, USA	23 Nov 1991
MEDLEY				
200 m	1:58.16	Jani Nikanor Sievinen (Finland) (b. 31 Nov 1974)	Rome, Italy	11 Sep 1994
400 m	4:12.30	Tom Dolan (USA)	Rome, Italy	6 Sep 1994
4×100 m	3:36.93	USA (David Berkoff, Richard Schroeder, Matthew Nicholas Biondi, Christopher Jacobs)	Seoul, South Korea	25 Sep 1988
	3:36.93	USA (Jeff Rouse, Nelson Diebel, Pablo Morales, Jon Olsen)	Barcelona, Spain	31 Jul 1992

WOMEN

Event	min:sec	Name and Country	Venue	Date
FREESTYLE				
50 m	24.51	Le Jingyi (China)	Rome, Italy	11 Sep 1994
100 m	54.01	Le Jingyi (China)	Rome, Italy	5 Sep 1994
200 m	1:56.78	Franziska van Almsick (Germany) (b. 5 Apr 1978)	Rome, Italy	6 Sep 1994
400 m	4:03.85	Janet B Evans (USA) (b. 28 Aug 1971)	Seoul, South Korea	22 Sep 1988
800 m	8:16.22	Janet Evans (USA)	Tokyo, Japan	20 Aug 1989
1500 m	15:52.10	Janet Evans (USA)	Orlando, FL, USA	26 Mar 1988
4×100 m	3:37.91	China (Le Jingyi, Shan Ying, Le Ying, Lu Bin)	Rome, Italy	7 Sep 1994
4×200 m	7:55.47	GDR (Manuela Stellmach, Astrid Strauss, Anke Möhring, Heike Friedrich)	Strasbourg, France	18 Aug 1987
BREASTSTROKE				
100 m	1:07.69	Samantha Linette Riley (Australia) (b. 13 Nov 1973)	Rome, Italy	9 Sep 1994
200 m	2:24.76	Rebecca Brown (Australia) (b. 8 May 1977)	Brisbane, Australia	16 Mar 1994
BUTTERFLY				
100 m	57.93	Mary Terstegge Meagher (USA) (b. 27 Oct 1964)	Brown Deer, WI, USA	16 Aug 1981
200 m	2:05.96	Mary Terstegge Meagher (USA)	Brown Deer, WI, USA	13 Aug 1981
BACKSTROKE				
100 m	1:00.16	He Cihong (China)	Rome, Italy	11 Sep 1994
200 m	2:06.62	Krisztina Egerszegi (Hungary) (b. 16 Aug 1974)	Athens, Greece	25 Aug 1991
MEDLEY				
200 m	2:11.57	Lu Bin (China)	Hiroshima, Japan	7 Oct 1994
400 m	4:36.10	Petra Schneider (GDR) (b. 11 Jan 1963)	Guayaquil, Ecuador	1 Aug 1982
4×100 m	4:01.67	China (He Cihong, Dai Guohong, Liu Limin, Le Jingyi)	Rome, Italy	11 Sep 1994

Quick Dip

In a 25-yd pool, Tom Jager (USA) (b. 6 Oct 1964) achieved an average speed of 8.64 km/h *5.37 mph* for 50 yards in 19.05 sec at Nashville, Tennessee, USA on 23 Mar 1990. The women's fastest is 7.34 km/h *4.56 mph* by Le Jingyi (China) in her 50 m world record (⊳ World Record table).

Most world records Men: 32, Arne Borg (Sweden) (1901–87), 1921–9. Women: 42, Ragnhild Hveger (Denmark) (b. 10 Dec 1920), 1936–42. For currently recognized events (only metric distances in 50 m pools) the most is 26 by Mark Andrew Spitz (USA) (b. 10 Feb 1950), 1967–72, and 23 by Kornelia Ender (GDR) (b. 25 Oct 1958), 1973–6.

The most world records set in a single pool is 86 in the North Sydney pool, Australia between 1955 and 1978. This total includes 48 imperial distance records which ceased to be recognized in 1969. The pool, which was built in 1936, was originally 55 yards long but was shortened to 50 metres in 1964.

(Photos: Allsport (USA)/V. Caviatio)

Short-Course Swimming World Bests
(set in 25 m pools)

MEN

Event	min:sec	Name and country	Venue		Date
FREESTYLE					
50 m	21.50	Aleksandr Popov (Russia) (b. 16 Nov 1971)	Desenzano, Italy	13 Mar	1994
100 m	46.74	Aleksandr Popov (Russia)	Gelsenkirchen, Germany	19 Mar	1994
200 m	1:43.64	Giorgio Lamberti (Italy) (b. 28 Jan 1969)	Bonn, Germany	11 Feb	1990
400 m	3:40.46	Danyon Loader (New Zealand) ()	Sheffield, S Yorks	11 Feb	1995
800 m	7:34.90	Kieren Perkins (Australia) (b. 14 Aug 1973)	Sydney, Australia	25 Jul	1993
1500 m	14:26.52	Kieren Perkins (Australia)	Auckland, New Zealand	15 Jul	1993
4×50 m	1:27.62	Sweden	Stavanger, Norway	2 Dec	1994
4×100 m	3:12.11	Brazil	Palma de Mallorca, Spain	5 Dec	1993
4×200 m	7:05.17	West Germany	Bonn, Germany	9 Feb	1986
BACKSTROKE					
50 m	24.37	Jeff Rouse (USA) (b. 6 Feb 1970)	Sheffield, S Yorks	12 Feb	1995
100 m	51.43	Jeff Rouse (USA)	Sheffield, S Yorks	12 Apr	1993
200 m	1:52.51	Martin Lopez-Zubero (Spain)	Gainesville, FL, USA	11 Apr	1991
BREASTSTROKE					
50 m	27.00	Mark Warnecke (Germany)	Gelsenkirchen, Germany	18 Feb	1995
100 m	59.07	Philip John Rogers (Australia) (b. 24 Apr 1971)	Melbourne, Australia	29 Aug	1993
200 m	2:07.80	Philip John Rogers (Australia)	Melbourne, Australia	28 Aug	1993
BUTTERFLY					
50 m	23.55	Mark Andrew Foster (GB) (b. 12 May 1970)	Sheffield, S Yorks	11 Feb	1995
100 m	52.07	Marcel Gery (Canada) (b. 15 Mar 1965)	Leicester	23 Feb	1990
200 m	1:53.05	Franck Esposito (France) (b. 13 Apr 1971)	Paris, France	26 Mar	1994
MEDLEY					
100 m	53.78	Jani Nikanor Sievinen (Finland) (b. 31 Nov 1974)	Espoo, Finland	21 Nov	1992
200 m	1:54.65	Jani Sievinen (Finland)	Kuopio, Finland	21 Jan	1994
400 m	4:07.10	Jani Sievinen (Finland)	Malmö, Sweden	9 Feb	1993
4×50 m	1:38.01	Germany	Stavanger, Norway	3 Dec	1994
4×100 m	3:32.57	USA	Palma de Mallorca, Spain	2 Dec	1993

WOMEN

Event	min:sec	Name and country	Venue		Date
FREESTYLE					
50 m	24.23	Le Jingyi (China) (b. 19 Mar 1975)	Palma de Mallorca, Spain	3 Dec	1993
100 m	53.01	Le Jingyi (China)	Palma de Mallorca, Spain	2 Dec	1993
200 m	1:55.84	Franziska van Almsick (Germany) (b. 5 Apr 1978)	Beijing, China	9 Jan	1993
400 m	4:02.05	Astrid Strauss (GDR) (b. 24 Dec 1968)	Bonn, Germany	8 Feb	1987
800 m	8:15.34	Astrid Strauss (GDR)	Bonn, Germany	6 Feb	1987
1500 m	15:43.31	Petra Schneider (GDR) (b. 11 Jan 1963)	Gainesville, FL, USA	10 Jan	1982
4×50 m	1:40.63	Germany	Espoo, Finland	22 Nov	1992
4×100 m	3:35.97	China	Palma de Mallorca, Spain	4 Dec	1993
4×200 m	7:52.45	China	Palma de Mallorca, Spain	2 Dec	1993
BACKSTROKE					
50 m	27.64	Bai Xiuyu (China)	Desenzano, Italy	12 Mar	1994
100 m	58.50	Angel Martino (USA) (b. 27 Apr 1967)	Palma de Mallorca, Spain	3 Dec	1993
200 m	2:06.09	He Cihong (China)	Palma de Mallorca, Spain	5 Dec	1993
BREASTSTROKE					
50 m	31.19	Louise Karlsson (Sweden)	Espoo, Finland	21 Nov	1992
100 m	1:06.58	Dai Guohong (China)	Palma de Mallorca, Spain	4 Dec	1993
200 m	2:21.99	Dai Guohong (China)	Palma de Mallorca, Spain	3 Dec	1993
BUTTERFLY					
50 m	26.56	Angela Kennedy (Australia)	Sheffield, S Yorks	12 Feb	1995
100 m **	58.77	Angela Kennedy (Australia)	Gelsenkirchen, Germany	18 Feb	1995
200 m	2:05.65	Mary Terstegge Meagher (USA) (b. 27 Aug 1964)	Gainesville, FL, USA	2 Jan	1981
MEDLEY					
100 m	1:01.03	Louise Karlsson (Sweden) (b. 26 Apr 1974)	Espoo, Finland	22 Nov	1992
200 m	2:07.79	Allison Wagner (USA)	Palma de Mallorca, Spain	5 Dec	1993
400 m	4:29.00	Dai Gouhong (China)	Palma de Mallorca, Spain	2 Dec	1993
4×50 m	1:52.44	Germany	Espoo, Finland	21 Nov	1992
4×100 m	3:57.73	China	Palma de Mallorca, Spain	5 Dec	1993

* hand timed for first leg. ** slower than long-course best.

Most world titles In the World Championships (instituted 1973) the most medals won is 13 by Michael Gross (West Germany) (b. 17 Jun 1964), five gold, five silver and three bronze, 1982–90. The most by a woman is ten by Kornelia Ender with eight gold and two silver in 1973 and 1975. The most gold medals is six (two individual and four relay) by James Paul Montgomery (USA) (b. 24 Jan 1955) in 1973 and 1975. The most medals at a single championship is seven by Matthew Nicholas Biondi (USA) (b. 8 Oct 1965), three gold, one silver, three bronze, in 1986.

Olympic Records

Most medals *Men* The greatest number of Olympic gold medals won is nine by Mark Spitz (USA): 100 m and 200 m freestyle 1972; 100 m and 200 m butterfly 1972; 4×100 m freestyle 1968 and 1972; 4×200 m freestyle 1968 and 1972; 4×100 m medley 1972. *All but one of these performances (the 4×200 m freestyle of 1968) were also new world records.* He also won a silver (100 m butterfly) and a bronze (100 m freestyle) in 1968 for a record 11 medals. His record seven medals at one Games in 1972 was equalled by Matt Biondi (USA) who took five gold, one silver and one bronze in 1988. Biondi has also won a record 11 medals in total, winning a gold in 1984, and two golds and a silver in 1992.

Women The record number of gold medals won by a woman is six by Kristin Otto (GDR) (b. 7 Feb 1966) at Seoul in 1988: 100 m freestyle, backstroke and butterfly, 50 m freestyle, 4×100 m freestyle and 4×100 m medley. Dawn Fraser (Australia) (b. 4 Sep 1937) is the only swimmer to win the same event, the 100 m freestyle, on three successive occasions (1956, 1960 and 1964).

The most medals won by a woman is eight by: Dawn Fraser, four golds and four silvers 1956–64; Kornelia Ender, four golds and four silvers 1972–6; and Shirley Babashoff (USA) (b. 3 Jan 1957), two golds and six silvers 1972–6.

Most individual gold medals The record number of individual gold medals won is four by: Charles Meldrum Daniels (USA) (1884–1973) (100 m freestyle 1906 and 1908, 220 yd freestyle 1904, 440 yd freestyle 1904); Roland Matthes (GDR) (b. 17 Nov 1950) with 100 m and 200 m backstroke 1968 and 1972; Mark Spitz and Kristin Otto, and the divers Pat McCormick and Greg Louganis (⇔ Diving).

Most medals *British* The record number of gold medals won by a British swimmer (excluding water polo, *q.v.*) is four by Henry Taylor (1885–1951) in the mile freestyle (1906), 400 m freestyle (1908), 1500 m freestyle (1908) and 4×200 m freestyle (1908).

Henry Taylor won a record eight medals in all, with a further silver and three bronzes, 1906–20. The most medals by a British woman is four by Margaret Joyce

■ Martin Harris has set 38 British backstroke records from 1990 to 1995. (Photo: Allsport/A. Want)

Guess What?
Q. What is the record for running 100m backwards?
A. See Page 230

■ Jani Sievinen is the current holder of all short-course individual medley records, setting two in his home country, Finland.
(Photo: Allsport/S. Bruty)

Cooper (now Badcock) (b. 18 Apr 1909) with one silver and three bronze, 1928–32.

Diving

Most Olympic medals The most medals won by a diver is five by: Klaus Dibiasi (b. Austria, 6 Oct 1947) (Italy) (three gold, two silver), 1964–76; and Gregory Efthimios Louganis (USA) (b. 29 Jan 1960) (four golds, one silver), 1976, 1984, 1988. Dibiasi is the only diver to win the same event (highboard) at three successive Games (1968, 1972 and 1976). Two divers have won the highboard and springboard doubles at two Games: Patricia Joan McCormick (*née* Keller) (USA) (b. 12 May 1930), 1952 and 1956 and Louganis, 1984 and 1988.

British The highest placing by a Briton has been the silver medal by Beatrice Eileen Armstrong (later Purdy) (1894–1981) in the 1920 highboard event. The best placings by male divers are the bronze medals by Harold Clarke (b. 1888) (plain high diving, 1924) and Brian Eric Phelps (b. 21 Apr 1944) (highboard, 1960).

Most world titles Greg Louganis (USA) won a record five world titles, highboard in 1978, and both highboard and springboard in 1982 and 1986, as well as four Olympic gold medals in 1984 and 1988. Three gold medals at one event have also been won by Philip George Boggs (USA) (1949–90), springboard 1973, 1975 and 1978.

Highest scores Greg Louganis achieved record scores at the 1984 Olympic Games in Los Angeles, California, USA with 754.41 points for the 11-dive springboard event and 710.91 for the highboard. At the world championships in Guayaquil, Ecuador in 1984 he was awarded a perfect score of 10.0 by all seven judges for his highboard inward 1½ somersault in the pike position.

The first diver to be awarded a score of 10.0 by all seven judges was Michael Holman Finneran (b. 21 Sep 1948) in the 1972 US Olympic Trials, in Chicago, Illinois, for a backward 1½ somersault, 2½ twist, from the 10m board.

High diving The highest regularly performed head-first dives are those of professional divers from La Quebrada ('the break in the rocks') at Acapulco, Mexico, a height of 26.7m *87½ft*. The base rocks, 6.4m *21ft* out from the take-off, necessitate a leap of 8.22m *27ft* out. The water is 3.65m *12ft* deep.

The world record high dive from a diving board is 53.9m *176ft 10in,*by Olivier Favre (Switzerland) at Villers-le-Lac, France on 30 Aug 1987. The women's record is 36.80m *120ft 9in,* by Lucy Wardle (US) at Ocean Park, Hong Kong on 6 Apr 1985. The highest witnessed in Britain is one of 32.9m *108ft* into 2.43m *8ft* of water at the Aqua Show at Earl's Court, London on 22 Feb 1948 by Roy Fransen (1915–85).

Guess What?
Q. What is the deepest dive by a submarine?
A. See Page 106

Swimming (British National Records)

MEN

Event min:sec	Name	Venue	Date
FREESTYLE			
50 m 22.43	Mark Andrew Foster (b. 12 May 1970) ....Sheffield, S Yorks ....24 May 1992		
100 m 50.24	Michael Wenham Fibbens (b. 31 May 1968)............Sheffield, S Yorks ....22 May 1992		
200 m 1:48.84	Paul Rory Palmer (b. 18 Oct 1974)........................Sheffield, S Yorks ....3 Aug 1993		
400 m 3:48.14	Paul Palmer ....Sheffield, S Yorks ....6 Aug 1993		
800 m 8:00.63	Ian Wilson (b. 19 Dec 1970) ....Athens, Greece ....25 Aug 1991		
1500 m 15:03.72	Ian Wilson ....Athens, Greece ....25 Aug 1991		
4×100 m 3:21.41	GB (Michael Wenham Fibbens, Mark Andrew Foster, Paul Howe, Roland Lee) ....Barcelona, Spain ....29 Jul 1992		
4×200 m 7:22.57	GB (Paul Palmer, Steven Mellor, Stephen Akers, Paul Howe)...Barcelona, Spain ....27 Jul 1992		
BREASTSTROKE			
100 m 1:01.33	Nicholas Gillingham (b. 22 Jan 1967) ....Sheffield, S Yorks ....21 May 1992		
200 m 2:11.29	Nicholas Gillingham ....Barcelona, Spain ....29 Jul 1992		
BUTTERFLY			
100 m 53.30	Andrew David Jameson (b. 19 Feb 1965)................Seoul, South Korea..............21 Sep 1988		
200 m 2:00.21	Philip Hubble (b. 19 Jul 1960) ....Split, Yugoslavia ....11 Sep 1981		
BACKSTROKE			
100 m 55.00	Martin Clifford Harris (b. 21 May 1969) ....Sheffield, S Yorks ....22 Apr 1995		
200 m............1:59.52	Adam Ruckwood (b. 13 Sep 1974) ....Sheffield, S Yorks ....23 Apr 1995		
MEDLEY			
200 m 2:03.20	Neil Cochran (b. 12 Apr 1965)...............................Orlando, FL, USA ....25 Mar 1988		
400 m 4:24.20	John Philip Davey (b. 29 Dec 1964) ....Crystal Palace, London.........1 Aug 1987		
4×100 m 3:41.66	GB (Martin Harris, Nick Gillingham, Mike Fibbens, Mark Foster)..Sheffield, S Yorks ....8 Aug 1993		

WOMEN

Event min:sec	Name	Venue	Date
FREESTYLE			
50 m 26.01	Caroline Woodcock (b. 23 Aug 1972) ....Bonn, Germany...................20 Aug 1989		
100 m 55.79	Karen Pickering (b. 19 Dec 1971) ....Rome , Italy.........................5 Sep 1994		
200 m 1:59.74	June Alexandra Croft (b. 17 Jun 1963) ....Brisbane, Australia ....4 Oct 1982		
400 m 4:07.68	Sarah Hardcastle (b. 9 April 1969) ....Edinburgh, Lothian ....27 Jul 1986		
800 m 8:24.77	Sarah Hardcastle..Edinburgh, Lothian ....29 Jul 1986		
1500 m 16:39.46	Sarah Hardcastle..Edinburgh, Lothian ....31 Mar 1994		
4×100 m 3:45.52	GB (Susan Rolph, Alex Bennett, Claire Huddart, Karen Pickering)..............................Rome, Italy..........................7 Sep 1994		
4×200 m 8:09.62	England (Sarah Hardcastle, Claire Huddart, Alex Bennett, Karen Pickering) ....Victoria, Canada ....19 Aug 1994		
BREASTSTROKE			
100 m 1:10.39	Susannah 'Suki' Brownsdon (b. 16 Oct 1965)..........Strasbourg, France..............21 Aug 1987		
200 m 2:30.63	Marie Hardiman (b. 21 Jul 1975) ....Crystal Palace, London.......31 Jul 1994		
BUTTERFLY			
100 m 1:01.33	Madeleine Scarborough (b. 18 Aug 1964) ....Auckland, New Zealand .....28 Jan 1990		
200 m 2:11.97	Samantha Paula Purvis (b. 24 Jun 1967) ....Los Angeles, CA, USA ....4 Aug 1984		
BACKSTROKE			
100 m 1:03.27	Katharine Osher (*née* Read) (b. 30 Jun 1969).........Victoria, Canada ....21 Aug 1994		
200 m 2:13.91	Joanne Deakins (b. 20 Nov 1972)...........................Barcelona, Spain ....31 Jul 1992		
MEDLEY			
200 m 2:17.21	Jean Cameron Hill (b. 15 Jul 1964) ....Edinburgh, Lothian ....28 Jul 1986		
400 m 4:46.83	Sharron Davies (b. 1 Nov 1962)..............................Moscow, USSR....................26 Jul 1980		
4×100 m 4:11.88	England (Joanne Deakins, Susannah 'Suki' Brownsdon, Madeleine Scarborough, Karen Pickering) ....Auckland, New Zealand .....29 Jan 1990		

■ Veerabadran Kutraleeshwaran of India completed six ocean swims in 1994: Palk Straits, India–Sri Lanka; English Channel; Zannone–Cicero, Italy; Straits of Messina, Italy; Rottnest Channel, Australia and Andamans, India.

Channel Swimming

The first to swim the English Channel from shore to shore (without a life jacket) was the Merchant Navy captain Matthew Webb (1848–83) who swam an estimated 61 km *38 miles* to make the 33 km *21 mile* crossing from Dover, England to Calais Sands, France, in 21 hr 45 min from 12:56 p.m. to 10:41 a.m., 24–25 Aug 1875. Paul Boyton (USA) had swum from Cap Gris-Nez to the South Foreland in his patent life-saving suit in 23 hr 30 min on 28–29 May 1875. There is good evidence that Jean-Marie Saletti, a French soldier, escaped from a British prison hulk off Dover by swimming to Boulogne in July or August 1815.

The first crossing from France to England was made by Enrico Tiraboschi, a wealthy Italian living in Argentina, in 16 hr 33 min on 12 Aug 1923, to win the *Daily Sketch* prize of £1000.

The first woman to succeed was Gertrude Caroline Ederle (USA) (b. 23 Oct 1906) who swam from Cap Gris-Nez, France to Deal, England on 6 Aug 1926, in the then overall record time of 14 hr 39 min.

Fastest The official Channel Swimming Association (founded 1927) record is 7 hr 17 min by Chad Hundeby (b. 15 Feb 1971) of California, USA, from Shakespeare Beach, Dover to Cap Gris-Nez, France on 27 Sep 1994.

The fastest France–England time is 8 hr 5 min by Richard Davey (b. 23 Jun 1965) in 1988.

The fastest crossing by a relay team is 6 hr 52 min (England to France) by the US National Swim Team on 1 Aug 1990. They went on to complete the fastest two-way relay in 14 hr 18 min.

Earliest and latest The earliest date in the year on which the Channel has been swum is 30 May by Kevin Murphy (GB) (b. 23 Jan 1949) in 1990 in a time of 13 hr 16 min and with the water at a temperature of 12 °C *54 °F*. The latest is 28 October by Michael Peter Read (GB) (b. 9 Jun 1941) in 1979 in 17 hr 55 min.

Double crossing The first double crossing was by Antonio Abertondo (Argentina) (b. 1919), in 43 hr 10 min on 20–22 Sep 1961. The fastest double crossing was in 16 hr 10 min by Philip Rush (New Zealand) (b. 6 Nov 1963) on 17 Aug 1987 and he went on to complete the fastest ever triple crossing in 28 hr 21 min on 17–18 Aug 1987. The women's double crossing record is 17 hr 14 min by Susie Maroney (Australia) (b. 15 Nov 1974) on 23 Jul 1991.

Triple crossing The first triple crossing was by Jon Erikson (USA) (b. 6 Sep 1954) in 38 hr 27 min on 11–12 Aug 1981. The first by a woman was by Alison Streeter (GB) (b. 29 Aug 1964) in 34 hr 40 min on 2–3 Aug 1990. For the fastest by an individual, ⇨Double crossing.

Most conquests The greatest number of Channel conquests is 31 by Michael Read (GB) from 24 Aug 1969 to 19 Aug 1984. The most by a woman is 27 by Alison Streeter from 1982 to the end of 1994 (including a record seven in one year, 1992).

Oldest swimmer The oldest conqueror has been Bertram Clifford Batt (b. 22 Dec 1919), of Australia at 67 years 241 days when he swam from Cap Gris-Nez to Dover in 18 hr 37 min from 19–20 Aug 1987. The oldest woman was Susan Fraenkel (South Africa) (b. 22 Apr 1948) aged 46 years 103 days when she did the swim in 12 hr 5 min on 24 Jul 1994.

Guess What?

Q. Which two places are joined by the Channel Tunnel?

A. See Page 99

As of May 1995, there had been 6333 attempts to swim the Channel by 4363 people. Of these, 467 individuals (310 men and 157 women) from 47 countries have made 732 successful crossings; 683 solo, 20 double and 3 triple.

■ Alison Streeter has completed a record 27 crossings of the English Channel. Here she comes ashore on Shakespeare Beach, Dover and celebrates equalling the previous women's record of 19, on 22 Aug 1992. This was one of a record seven crossings in 1992.
(Photos: Mike Griggs)

Long-Distance Swimming

Longest swims The greatest recorded distance ever swum is 2938 km *1826 miles* down the Mississippi River, USA between Ford Dam near Minneapolis, Minnesota and Carrollton Ave, New Orleans, Louisiana, by Fred P. Newton, (b. 1903) of Clinton, Oklahoma from 6 Jul to 29 Dec 1930. He was 742 hours in the water.

In 1966 Mihir Sen of Calcutta, India uniquely swam the Palk Strait from Sri Lanka to India (in 25 hr 36 min on 5–6 April); the Straits of Gibraltar (in 8 hr 1 min on 24 August); the length of the Dardanelles (in 13 hr 55 min on 12 September); the Bosphorus (in 4 hr on 21 September), and the length of the Panama Canal (in 34 hr 15 min on 29–31 October).

> Merv Sharp of Weymouth, Dorset, has completed a crossing over (by plane), on (by ferry), in (swam seven times) and under (by train) the English Channel.

Irish Channel The swimming of the 37 km *23 mile* wide North Channel from Donaghadee, Northern Ireland to Portpatrick, Scotland was first accomplished by Tom Blower of Nottingham in 15 hr 26 min in 1947. A record time of 9 hr 53 min 42 sec was set by Alison Streeter on 22 Aug 1988. She was also the first person to complete the crossing from Scotland to Northern Ireland, in 10 hr 4 min on 25 Aug 1989.

Lake swims The fastest time for swimming the 36.5 km *22.7 mile* long Loch Ness is 9 hr 57 min by David Trevor Morgan (b. 25 Sep 1963) on 31 Jul 1983. David Morgan achieved a double crossing of Loch Ness in 23 hr 4 min on 1 Aug 1983. In 1988 he also uniquely swam Loch Ness in 11 hr 9 min on 16 Jul, Loch Lomond 34.6 km *21.5 miles* in 11 hr 48 min on 18 Jul and the English Channel in 11 hr 35 min on 20–21 Jul. The fastest time for swimming Lake Windermere, 16.9 km *10.5 miles* from Fellfoot to Waterhead, is 3 hr 49 min 12 sec by Justin Palfrey (b. 16 Jul 1971) on 7 Sep 1991.

24 hours Anders Forvass (Sweden) swam 101.9 km *63.3 miles* at the 25-metre Linköping public swimming pool, Sweden on 28–29 Oct 1989. In a 50 metre pool, Evan Barry (Australia) swam 96.7 km *60.08 miles*, at the Valley Pool, Brisbane, Australia on 19–20 Dec 1987.

The women's record is 93.625 km *58.17 miles* by Susie Maroney (Australia) at Carss Park, Sydney, Australia on 21–22 Apr 1995.

Long-distance relays The New Zealand national relay team of 20 swimmers swam a record 182.807 km *113.59 miles* in Lower Hutt, New Zealand in 24 hours, passing 160 km *100 miles* in 20 hr 47 min 13 sec on 9–10 Dec 1983. The 24 hours club record by a team of five is 162.52 km *100.99 miles* by the Portsmouth Northsea SC at the Victoria Swimming Centre, Portsmouth, Hants on 4–5 Mar 1993. The women's record is 143.11 km *88.93 miles* by the City of Newcastle ASC on 16–17 Dec 1986. The most participants in a one-day swim relay is 2375, each swimming a length, at Liverpool High School, Liverpool, New York, USA on 20–21 May 1994.

Sponsored swimming The greatest amount of money collected in a charity swim was £122,983.19 in 'Splash '92' organized by the Royal Bank of Scotland Swimming Club and was held at the Royal Commonwealth Pool, Edinburgh, Lothian on 25–26

Jan 1992 with 3218 participants. The record for an event staged at several pools was £548,006.14 by 'Penguin Swimathon '88', when 5482 swimmers participated at 43 pools throughout London on 26–28 Feb 1988.

Underwater swimming Paul Cryne (GB) and Samir Sawan al Awami of Qatar swam 78.92 km *49.04 miles* in a 24 hour-period from Doha, Qatar to Umm Said and back on 21–22 Feb 1985 using sub–aqua equipment. They were swimming underwater for 95.5 per cent of the time. A relay team of six swam 151.987 km *94.44 miles* in a swimming pool at Olomouc, Czechoslovakia on 17–18 Oct 1987.

Table Tennis

Most titles *World (instituted 1926)* G. Viktor Barna (1911–72) (b. Hungary, Gyözö Braun) won a record five singles, 1930, 1932–5 and eight men's doubles, 1929–35, 1939. Angelica Rozeanu (Romania) (b. 15 Oct 1921) won a record six women's singles, 1950–55, and Mária Mednyánszky (Hungary) (1901–79) won seven women's doubles, 1928, 1930–35. With two more at mixed doubles and seven team, Viktor Barna had 22 world titles in all, while 18 were won by Mária Mednyánszky. With the staging of the championships now biennial, the breaking of the above records would be very difficult.

The most men's team titles (Swaythling Cup) is 12 by: Hungary, 1927–31, 1933–5, 1938, 1949, 1952 and 1979; and China, 1961, 1963, 1965, 1971, 1975, 1977, 1981, 1983, 1987, 1993 and 1995. The women's record (Marcel Corbillon Cup) is 11 by China, 1965, eight successive 1975–89 (biennially), 1993 and 1995.

English Open (instituted 1921) Richard Bergmann (Austria, then GB) (1918–70) won a record six singles, 1939–40, 1948, 1950, 1952, 1954 and Viktor Barna won seven men's doubles, 1931, 1933–5, 1938–9, 1949. The women's singles record is six by Maria Alexandru (Romania) (b. 1941), 1963–4, 1970–72, 1974 and Diane Rowe (now Scholer) (b. 14 Apr 1933), won 12 women's doubles titles, 1950–56, 1960, 1962–5. Viktor Barna won 20 titles in all, and Diane Rowe 17.

Ping Pong

Counter hitting The record number of hits in 60 seconds is 173 by Jackie Bellinger (b. 9 Sep 1964) and Lisa Lomas (née Bellinger) (b. 9 Mar 1967) at the Northgate Sports Centre, Ipswich, Suffolk on 7 Feb 1993. With a bat in each hand, Gary D. Fisher of Olympia, Washington, USA completed 5000 consecutive volleys over the net in 44 min 28 sec on 25 Jun 1975.

English Closed The most titles won is 26 by Desmond Hugh Douglas (b. 20 Jul 1955), a record 11 men's singles, 1976, 1979–87 and 1990, 11 men's doubles and 4 mixed doubles. A record seven women's singles were won by Jill Patricia Hammersley (now Parker, née Shirley) (b. 6 Dec 1951) in 1973–6, 1978–9, 1981.

Internationals Joy Foster was aged 8 when she represented Jamaica in the West Indies Championships at Port of Spain, Trinidad in August 1958. The youngest ever to play for England was Nicola Deaton (b. 29 Oct 1976), aged 13 years 336 days, against Sweden at Burton on Trent, Staffs on 30 Sep 1990.

Jill Parker played for England on a record 413 occasions, 1967–83.

Taekwondo

The first World Taekwondo Championships were organized by the Korean Taekwondo Association and were held at Seoul in 1973. The World Taekwondo Federation was then formed and has organized biennial championships and women's events were first contested in 1987.

Most titles The most world titles won is four by Chung Kook-hyun (South Korea), light-middleweight 1982–3, welterweight 1985, 1987. Taekwondo was included as a demonstration sport at the 1988 Olympic Games.

Tennis (Lawn)

Grand Slam The first man to have won all four of the world's major championship singles: Wimbledon, US, Australian and French Open championships was Frederick John Perry (GB) (1909–95) when he won the French title in 1935. The first man to hold all four championships simultaneously was John Donald Budge (USA) (b. 13 Jun 1915) in 1938, and with Wimbledon and US in 1937, he won six successive grand slam tournaments. The first man to achieve the grand slam twice was Rodney George Laver (Australia) (b. 9 Aug 1938) as an amateur in 1962 and again in 1969 when the titles were open to professionals.

> **Guess What?**
> Q. What is a Grand Slam in rugby union?
> A. See page 284

Four women have achieved the grand slam and the first three won six successive grand slam tournaments: Maureen Catherine Connolly (USA) (1934–69), in 1953; Margaret Jean Court (née Smith) (Australia) (b. 16 Jul 1942) in 1970; and Martina Navrátilová (USA) (b. 18 Oct 1956) in 1983–4. The fourth was Stefanie Maria 'Steffi' Graf (West Germany) (b. 14 Jun 1969) in 1988, when she also won the women's singles Olympic gold medal. Pamela Howard Shriver (USA) (b. 4 Jul 1962) with Navrátilová won a record eight successive grand slam tournament women's doubles titles and 109 successive matches in all events from April 1983 to July 1985.

The first doubles pair to win the grand slam were the Australians Frank Allan Sedgeman (b. 29 Oct 1927) and Kenneth Bruce McGregor (b. 2 Jun 1929) in 1951.

The most singles championships won in grand slam tournaments is 24 by Margaret Court (11 Australian, 5 USA, 5 French, 3 Wimbledon), 1960–73. She also won the US Amateur in 1969 and 1970 when this was held as well as the US Open. The men's record is 12 by Roy Stanley Emerson (Australia) (b. 3 Nov 1936) (6 Australian, 2 each French, USA, Wimbledon), 1961–7.

The most grand slam tournament wins by a doubles partnership is 20 by Althea Louise Brough (USA) (b. 11 Mar 1923) and Margaret Evelyn Du Pont (née Osborne) (USA) (b. 4 Mar 1918), (12 US, 5 Wimbledon, 3 French), 1942–57; and by Martina Navrátilová and Pam Shriver, (7 Australian, 5 Wimbledon, 4 French, 4 USA), 1981–9.

Guess What?

Q. Name the three other women players to have won a Grand Slam

A. See Page 295

■ Martina Navrátilová considered by many to be the greatest women tennis player ever retired from singles competition at the end of the 1994 season. In a career that spanned three decades, Navrátilová won a world record 167 singles tournaments and 165 doubles titles.
(Photo: Allsport/G. Prior)

United States Championships

Most wins Margaret Evelyn du Pont (*née* Osborne) won a record 25 titles between 1941 and 1960. She won a record 13 women's doubles (12 with Althea Louise Brough), nine mixed doubles and three singles. The men's record is 16 by William Tatem Tilden, including seven men's singles, 1920–25, 1929—a record for singles shared with: Richard Dudley Sears (1861–1943), 1881–7; William A. Larned (1872–1926), 1901–2, 1907–11, and at women's singles by: Molla Mallory (*née* Bjurstedt) (1884–1959), 1915–16, 1918, 1920–22, 1926; and Helen Newington Moody (*née* Wills) (USA) (b. 6 Oct 1905), 1923–5, 1927–9, 1931.

Youngest and oldest The youngest champion was Vincent Richards (1903–59), who was 15 years 139 days when he won the men's doubles with Bill Tilden in 1918. The youngest singles champion was Tracy Ann Austin (b. 12 Dec 1962) who was 16 yr 271 days when she won the women's singles in 1979. The youngest men's champion was Pete Sampras (b. 12 Aug 1971) who was 19 yr 28 days when he won in 1990. The oldest champion was Margaret du Pont who won the mixed doubles at 42 yr 166 days in 1960. The oldest singles champion was William Larned at 38 yr 242 days in 1911.

French Championships

Most wins (from international status 1925) Margaret Court won a record 13 titles, five singles, four women's doubles and four mixed doubles, 1962–73. The men's record is nine by Henri Cochet (France) (1901–87), four singles, three men's doubles and two mixed doubles, 1926–30. The singles record is seven by Chris Evert, 1974–5, 1979–80, 1983, 1985–6. Björn Borg won a record six men's singles, 1974–5, 1978–81.

Youngest and oldest The youngest doubles champions were the 1981 mixed doubles winners, Andrea Jaeger (b. 4 Jun 1965) at 15 years 339 days and Jimmy Arias (b. 16 Aug 1964) at 16 yr 296 days. The youngest singles winners have been: Monica Seles (Yugoslavia) (b. 2 Dec 1973) who won the 1990 women's title at 16 yr 169 days and Michael Chang (USA) (b. 22 Feb 1972) the men's at 17 yr 109 days in 1989. The oldest champion was Elizabeth Ryan who won the 1934 women's doubles with Simone Mathieu (France) at 42 yr 88 days. The oldest singles champion was Andrés Gimeno (Spain) (b. 3 Aug 1937) in 1972 at 34 yr 301 days.

Old Champ

Oldest champions The oldest champion was Margaret Evelyn du Pont (*née* Osborne) at 44 years 125 days when she won the mixed doubles in 1962 with Neale Fraser (Australia). The oldest singles champion was Arthur Gore (GB) in 1909 at 41 yr 182 days.

Wimbledon Championships

Most wins *Women* Billie-Jean King (USA) (*née* Moffitt) (b. 22 Nov 1943) won a record 20 titles between 1961 and 1979, six singles, ten women's doubles and four mixed doubles. Elizabeth Montague Ryan (USA) (1892–1979) won a record 19 doubles (12 women's, 7 mixed) titles from 1914 to 1934.

Men The greatest number of titles by a man has been 13 by Hugh Laurence Doherty (GB) (1875–1919) with five singles titles (1902–6) and a record eight men's doubles (1897–1901, 1903–5) partnered by his brother Reginald Frank (1872–1910).

Singles Martina Navrátilová has won a record nine titles, 1978–9, 1982–7 and 1990. The most men's singles wins since the Challenge Round was abolished in 1922 is five consecutively, by Björn Rune Borg (Sweden) (b. 6 Jun 1956) in 1976–80. William Charles Renshaw (GB) (1861–1904) won seven singles in 1881–6 and 1889.

Mixed doubles The male record is four titles shared by: Elias Victor Seixas (USA) (b. 30 Aug 1923) in 1953–6; Kenneth Norman Fletcher (Australia) (b. 15 Jun 1940) in 1963, 1965–6, 1968; and Owen Keir Davidson (Australia) (b. 4 Oct 1943) in 1967, 1971,

Greatest crowd
The record crowd for one day was 39,813 on 26 Jun 1986. The record for the whole championship was 403,706 in 1989.

1973–4. The female record is seven by Elizabeth Ryan (USA) from 1919 to 1932.

Most appearances Arthur William Charles 'Wentworth' Gore (1868–1928) (GB) made a record 36 appearances at Wimbledon between 1888 and 1927. In 1964, Jean Borotra (France) (1898–1994) made his 35th appearances in the men's singles, 1922–64, and then played in the Veterans' Doubles to 1977 when he was 78.

Youngest champions The youngest champion was Charlotte 'Lottie' Dod (1871–1960), who was 15 years 285 days when she won in 1887. The youngest male champion was Boris Becker (West Germany) (b. 22 Nov 1967) who won the men's singles title in 1985 at 17 yr 227 days. The youngest ever player at Wimbledon was reputedly Mita Klima (Austria) who was 13 yr in the 1907 singles competition. The youngest seed was Jennifer Capriati (USA) (b. 29 Mar 1976) at 14 yr 89 days for her first match on 26 Jun 1990. She won this match, making her the youngest ever winner at Wimbledon.

Australian Championships

Most wins Margaret Jean Court (*née* Smith) (b. 16 Jul 1942) won the women's singles 11 times (1960–66, 1969–71 and 1973) as well as eight women's doubles and two mixed doubles, for a record total of 21 titles. A record six men's singles were won by Roy Stanley Emerson (Qld) (b. 3 Nov 1936), 1961 and 1963–7. Thelma Dorothy Long (*née* Coyne) (b. 30 May 1918) won a record 12 women's doubles and four mixed doubles for a record total of 16 doubles titles. Adrian Karl Quist (b. 4 Aug 1913) won ten consecutive men's doubles from 1936 to 1950 (the last eight with John Bromwich) and three men's singles.

Longest span, oldest and youngest Thelma Long won her first (1936) and last (1958) titles 22 years apart. Kenneth Robert Rosewall (b. 2 Nov 1934) won the singles in 1953 and in 1972 was, 19 years later, at 37 years 62 days, the oldest singles winner. The oldest champion was (Sir) Norman Everard Brookes (1877–1968), who was 46 yr 2 months when he won the 1924 men's doubles. The youngest champions were Rodney W. Heath, aged 17, when he won the men's singles in 1905, and Monica Seles, who won the women's singles at 17 yr 55 days in 1991.

Grand Prix Masters

The first Grand Prix Masters Championships were staged in Tokyo, Japan in 1970. They were held in New York, USA annually from 1977 to 1989 with qualification by relative success in the preceding year's Grand Prix tournaments. The event was replaced from 1990 by the ATP Tour Championship, held in Frankfurt, Germany. A record five titles have been won by Ivan Lendl, 1982–3, two in 1986 (January and December) and 1987. He appeared in nine successive finals, 1980–88. James Scott Connors (USA) (b. 2 Sep 1952) uniquely qualified for 14 consecutive years, 1972–85. He chose not to play in 1975, 1976 and 1985, and won in 1977. He qualified again in 1987 and 1988, but did not play in 1988.

A record seven doubles titles were won by John Patrick McEnroe (b. 16 Feb 1959) and Peter Fleming (b. 21 Jan 1955) (both USA), 1978–84.

Virginia Slims Championship The women's tour finishes with the Virginia Slims Championship, first contested in 1971. The Virginia Slims final is the one women's match played over the best of five sets (since 1983). Martina Navrátilová has a record six singles wins, between 1978 and 1986. She also has a record nine doubles wins, one with Billie-Jean King in 1980, and eight with Pam Shriver to 1991.

International Team

Davis Cup (instituted 1900) The most wins in the Davis Cup, the men's international team championship, has been 30 by the USA between 1900 and 1992. The most appearances for Cup winners is eight by Roy Emerson (Australia), 1959–62, 1964–7. Bill Tilden (USA) played in a record 28 matches in the final, winning a record 21, 17 out of 22 singles and 4 out of 6 doubles. He was in seven winning sides, 1920–26 and then four losing sides, 1927–30.

The British Isles/Great Britain have won nine times, in 1903–6, 1912, 1933–6.

Nicola Pietrangeli (Italy) (b. 11 Sep 1933) played a record 163 rubbers (66 ties), 1954 to 1972, winning 120. He played 109 singles (winning 78) and 54 doubles (winning 42).

The record number of rubbers by a British player is 65 (winning 43) by Michael John Sangster (b. 9 Sep 1940), 1960–68; the most wins is 45 from 52 rubbers by Fred Perry, including 34 of 38 singles, 1931–6.

Wightman Cup (instituted 1923) The annual women's match was won 51 times by the United States and 10 times by Great Britain. The contest was suspended from 1990 after a series of whitewashes by the US team. Sarah Virginia Wade (GB) (b. 10 Jul 1945) played in a record 21 ties and 56 rubbers, 1965–85, with a British record 19 wins. Christine Marie Evert (USA) (b. 21 Dec 1954) won all 26 of her singles matches, 1971 to 1985 and including doubles achieved a record 34 wins from 38 rubbers played. Jennifer Capriati became, at 13 years 168 days, the youngest ever Wightman Cup player when she beat Clare Wood (GB) 6–0, 6–0 at Williamsburg, Virginia, USA on 14 Sep 1989.

Federation Cup (instituted 1963) The most wins in the Federation Cup (known as the Fed Cup from 1995), the women's international team championship, is 14 by the USA between 1963 and 1990. Virginia Wade (GB) played each year from 1967 to 1983, in a record 57 ties, playing 100 rubbers, including 56 singles (winning 36) and 44 doubles (winning 30). Chris Evert won her first 29 singles matches, 1977–86. Her overall record, 1977–89 was 40 wins in 42 singles and 16 wins in 18 doubles matches.

Olympic Games Tennis was re-introduced to the Olympic Games in 1988, having originally been included at the Games from 1896 to 1924. It was also a demonstration sport in 1968 and 1984.

A record four gold medals as well as a silver and a bronze, were won by Max Decugis (France) (1882–1978), 1900–20. A women's record five medals (one gold, two silver, two bronze) were won by Kitty McKane (later Mrs Godfree) (GB) (1897–1992) in 1920 and 1924.

Longest span as national champion Keith Gledhill (b. 17 Feb 1911) won the US National Boys' Doubles Championship with Sidney Wood in August 1926. Sixty-one years later he won the US National 75 and over Men's Doubles Championship with Elbert Lewis at Goleta, California, USA in August 1987.

Ace

The fastest service timed with modern equipment is 222 km/h *138 mph* by Steve Denton (USA) (b. 5 Sep 1956) at Beaver Creek, Colorado, USA on 29 Jul 1984. The women's best is 185 km/h *115 mph* by Brenda Schultz (Netherlands) (b. 28 Dec 1970) and Jana Novotna (Czech Republic) (b. 2 Oct 1968), both at the 1993 Wimbledon Championships, on 25 June and 1 July respectively.

Dorothy May Bundy-Cheney (USA) (b. September 1916) won 180 US titles at various age groups from 1941 to March 1988.

International contest ***Longest span*** Jean Borotra played in every one of the twice yearly contests between the International Club of France and the I.C. of Great Britain from the first in 1929 until October 1993, a total of 116 consecutive matches. On the occasion of the 100th match at Wimbledon on 1–3 Nov 1985, he played a mixed doubles against Kitty Godfree (GB). Both were former Wimbledon singles champions, and aged 87 and 88 respectively.

Guess What?

Q. Who was the first player to win the Grand Slam?

A. See Page 295

■ **For the 1994 season, Arantxa Sánchez Vicario (Spain) won a women's record $2,943,665, winning two of the major tournaments, the French and US Opens.**
(Photo: Allsport/C. Brunskill)

Highest earnings Pete Sampras (USA) won a men's season's record of $4,857,812 and Arantxa Sánchez Vicario (Spain) a women's record of $2,943,665 both in 1994. The career earnings records are: (men) $20,512,417 by Ivan Lendl (Czechoslovakia, now USA) (b. 7 Mar 1960); (women) $20,065,290 by Martina Navrátilová both to the end of 1994. Navrátilová won a world record 167 singles tournaments and 165 doubles titles. Earnings from special restricted events and team tennis are not included.

The greatest first-place prize money ever won is $2 million by Pete Sampras when he won the Grand Slam Cup at Munich, Germany on 16 Dec 1990. In the final he beat Brad Gilbert (USA) (b. 9 Aug 1961) 6–3, 6–4, 6–2. Gilbert received $1 million, also well in excess of the previous figure. The highest total prize money for a tournament is $9,022,000 for the 1993 US Open Championships.

Greatest crowd A record 30,472 people were at the Astrodome, Houston, Texas, USA for the 'Battle of the Sexes' on 20 Sep 1973, when Billie-Jean King beat Robert Larimore Riggs (USA) (b. 25 Feb 1918). The record for an orthodox tennis match is 25,578 at Sydney, New South Wales, Australia on 27 Dec 1954 in the Davis Cup Challenge Round (first day) Australia v. USA.

Longest game The longest known singles game was one of 37 deuces (80 points) between Anthony Fawcett (Rhodesia) and Keith Glass (GB) in the first round of the Surrey Championships at Surbiton on 26 May 1975. It lasted 31 min. Noëlle van Lottum and Sandra Begijn played a game lasting 52 min in the semi-finals of the Dutch Indoor Championships at Ede, Gelderland on 12 Feb 1984.

The longest tiebreak was 26–24 for the fourth and decisive set of a first round men's doubles at the Wimbledon Championships on 1 Jul 1985. Jan Gunnarsson (Sweden) and Michael Mortensen (Denmark) defeated John Frawley (Australia) and Victor Pecci (Paraguay) 6–3, 6–4, 3–6, 7–6.

> The longest match in a grand slam tournament is 5 hr 26 min between Stefan Edberg (Sweden) and Michael Chang (USA) for the semi-final of the US Championships on 12–13 Sep 1992. Edberg won 6–7, 7–5, 7–6, 5–7, 6–4.

Tiddlywinks

World Championships Larry Kahn (USA) (b. 6 Dec 1953) has won the singles title 14 times, 1983–95. Geoff Meyers (b. 13 Aug 1968) and Andy Purvis (b. 12 May 1967) have won a record seven pairs titles, 1991–5.

National Championships Alan Dean (b. 22 Jul 1949) won the singles title six times, 1971–3, 1976, 1978 and 1986, and the pairs title six times. Jonathan Mapley (b. 1947) won the pairs title seven times, 1972, 1975, 1977, 1980, 1983–4 and 1987.

Potting records The record for potting 24 winks from 18 in *45 cm* is 21.8 sec by Stephen Williams

Tug of War

Most titles World Championships were held annually 1975–86 and biennially since, with a women's event introduced in 1986. The most successful team at the World Championships has been England, who have won 16 titles in all categories, 1975–93. Sweden have won the 520 kg category three times and the 560 kg at all five women's World Championships, 1986–94.

The Wood Treatment team (formerly the Bosley Farmers) of Cheshire won 20 consecutive AAA Catchweight Championships 1959–78, two world titles (1975–6) and ten European titles at 720 kg. Hilary Brown (b. 13 Apr 1934) was in every team. Trevor Brian Thomas (b. 1943) of British Aircraft Corporation Club is the only holder of three winners' medals in the European Open club competitions and added a world gold medal in 1988.

Longest pulls *Duration* The longest recorded pull (prior to the introduction of AAA rules) is one of 2 hr 41 min when 'H' Company beat 'E' Company of the 2nd Battalion of the Sherwood Foresters (Derbyshire Regiment) at Jubbulpore, India on 12 Aug 1889. The longest recorded pull under AAA rules (in which lying on the ground or entrenching the feet is not permitted) is one of 24 min 45 sec for the first pull between the Republic of Ireland and England during the world championships (640 kg class) at Malmö, Sweden on 18 Sep 1988.

Distance The record distance for a tug of war contest is 3623 m *3962 yd*, between Freedom Square and Independence Square at Lódź, Poland on 28 May 1994.

■ The record distance for a tug of war contest is 3623 m *3962 yd*, between Freedom Square and Independence Square at Lódź, Poland on 28 May 1994. Above one of the teams of twenty put their back into inching the rope their way.

(Altrincham Grammar School) in May 1966. Allen R. Astles (University of Wales) potted 10,000 winks in 3 hr 51 min 46 sec at Aberystwyth, Dyfed in February 1966.

The record for potting winks in relay is 41 in three minutes by Patrick Barrie, Nick Inglis, Geoff Myers and Andy Purvis, members of the Cambridge University Tiddlywinks Club at Queens' College, Cambridge on 21 Oct 1989 and 14 Jan 1995.

The long jump record is 9.52 m *31 ft 3 in* by Ben Soares (St Andrews Tiddlywinks Society) on 14 Jan 1995 and the high jump record is 3.49 m *11 ft 5 in* by Adrian Jones, David Smith and Ed Wynn (Cambridge University Tiddlywinks Club), all on 21 Oct 1989.

Trampolining

Most titles World Championships were instituted in 1964 and held biennially since 1968. The most titles won is nine by Judy Wills (USA) (b. 1948), a record five individual 1964–8, two pairs 1966–7 and two tumbling 1965–6. The men's record is five by Aleksandr Moskalenko (Russia), three individual 1990–4 and two pairs 1992–4. Brett Austine (Australia) won three individual titles at double mini, 1982–6.

A record nine United Kingdom titles have been won by Sue Challis (*née Shotton*) (b. 18 Oct 1965) (1980–82, 1984–5, 1987 (shared), 1990, 1992–3). The most by a man has been five by Stewart Matthews (b. 19 Feb 1962) (1976–80).

Youngest international *British* Andrea Holmes (b. 2 Jan 1970) competed for Britain at 12 years 131 days in the World Championships at Montana, USA on 13 May 1982.

Somersaults Christopher Gibson performed 3025 consecutive somersaults at Shipley Park, Derbys on 17 Nov 1989.

The most complete somersaults in one minute is 75 by Richard Cobbing of Lightwater, Surrey, at BBC Television Centre, London for *Record Breakers* on 8 Nov 1989. The most baranis in a minute is 78 by Zoe Finn of Chatham, Kent at BBC Television Centre, London for *Blue Peter* on 25 Jan 1988.

Triathlon

The triathlon combines long-distance swimming, cycling and running. Distances for each of the phases can vary, but for the best established event, the Hawaii Ironman (instituted 1978), competitors first swim 3.8 km *2.4 miles*, then cycle 180 km *112 miles*, and finally run a full marathon of 42.195 km *26 miles 385 yards*. Record times for the Hawaii Ironman are: (men) 8 hr 7 min 45 sec Mark Allen (USA) in 1993; (women) 8 hr 55 min 28 sec Paula Newby-Fraser (Zimbabwe) (b. 2 Jun 1962) in 1992. Dave Scott (USA) (b. 4 Jan 1959) has won a record six races, 1980, 1982–84 and 1986–87. Paula Newby-Fraser has won the women's race seven times, 1986, 1988–9 and 1991–4. The fastest time recorded over the Ironman distances is 8 hr 1 min 32 sec by Dave Scott at Lake Biwa, Japan on 30 Jul 1989. The women's record is 8 hr 55 min by Paula Newby-Fraser at Roth, Germany on 12 Jul 1992.

The fastest time recorded by a Briton for the Ironman distances is 8 hr 37 min 19 sec by Alan Ingarfield at Roth, Germany on 11 Jul 1992.

World Championships After earlier abortive efforts a world governing body *L'Union Internationale de Triathlon* (UIT) was founded at Avignon, France on 1 Apr 1989, staging the first official World Championships over the internationally recognised distances (1500 m swim, 40 km cycle, 10 km run) in August 1989. The annual race has been won twice by (men) Spencer Smith (GB), 1993–4 and (women) Michelle Jones (Australia), 1992–3.

A 'World Championship' race has been held annually in Nice, France from 1982; the distances 3200 m, 120 km and 32 km respectively, with the swim increased to 4000 m from 1988. Mark Allen (USA) has won ten times, 1982–86, 1989–93. Paula Newby-Fraser has a record four women's wins, 1989–92. Record times: men, Mark Allen 5 hr 46 min 10 sec in 1986; women, Erin Baker (New Zealand) (b. 23 May 1961) 6 hr 27 min 6 sec in 1988.

Volleyball

Most world titles World Championships were instituted in 1949 for men and 1952 for women. The USSR won six men's titles (1949, 1952, 1960, 1962, 1978 and 1982) and five women's (1952, 1956, 1960, 1970 and 1990)

Most Olympic titles The sport was introduced to the Olympic Games for both men and women in 1964. The USSR has won a record three men's (1964, 1968 and 1980) and four women's (1968, 1972, 1980 and 1988) titles. The only player to win four medals is Inna Valeryevna Ryskal (USSR) (b. 15 Jun 1944), who won women's silver medals in 1964 and 1976 and golds in 1968 and 1972. The record for men is held by Yuriy Mikhailovich Poyarkov (USSR) (b. 10 Feb 1937) who won gold medals in 1964 and 1968 and a bronze in 1972, and by Katsutoshi Nekoda (Japan) (b. 1 Feb 1944) who won gold in 1972, silver in 1968 and bronze in 1964.

Most internationals *Great Britain* Ucal Ashman (b. 10 Nov 1957) made a record 153 men's international appearances for England, 1976–86. The women's record is 171 by Ann Jarvis (b. 3 Jun 1955) for England, 1974–87.

Water Polo

Most Olympic titles Hungary has won the Olympic tournament most often with six wins in 1932, 1936, 1952, 1956, 1964 and 1976. Great Britain won in 1900, 1908, 1912 and 1920.

Five players share the record of three gold medals; Britons George Wilkinson (1879–1946) in 1900, 1908, 1912; Paulo 'Paul' Radmilovic (1886–1968), and Charles Sidney Smith (1879–1951) in 1908, 1912, 1920; and Hungarians Deszö Gyarmati (b. 23 Oct 1927) and György Kárpáti (b. 23 Jun 1935) in 1952, 1956, 1964. Paul Radmilovic also won a gold medal for the 4 × 200 m freestyle swimming in 1908.

World Championships First held at the World Swimming Championships in 1973. The most wins is two by the USSR 1975, 1982, Yugoslavia 1986, 1991, and Italy 1978, 1994. A women's competition was introduced in 1986, when it was won by Australia. The Netherlands won in 1991 and Hungary in 1994.

Most goals The greatest number of goals scored by an individual in an international is 13 by Debbie Handley (Australia) *v.* Canada at Guayaquil, Ecuador in 1982.

The greatest number of international appearances at water polo is 412 by Aleksey Stepanovich Barkalov (USSR) (b. 18 Feb 1946), 1965–80. The British record is 126 by Martyn Thomas, of Cheltenham, Glos, 1964–78.

Water Skiing Records

WORLD

Slalom

MEN: 4 buoys on a 10.25 m line, Andrew Mapple (GB) (b. 3 Nov 1958) at Charleston, South Carolina, USA on 4 Sep 1994.
WOMEN: 2.25 buoys on a 10.75 m line, Susi Graham (Canada) at Santa Rosa, Florida, USA on 25 Sep 1994.

Tricks

MEN: 11,590 points, Aymeric Benet (France) at West Palm Beach, Florida, USA on 30 Oct 1994.
WOMEN: 8580 points, Tawn Larsen (USA) at Groveland, Florida, USA on 4 Jul 1992.

Jumping

MEN: 67.1 m *220 ft*, Sammy Duvall (USA) at Santa Rosa Beach, Florida, USA 0n 10 Oct 1993.
WOMEN: 47.5 m *156 ft*, Deena Mapple (USA) (b. 2 Mar 1960) at Charlotte, Michigan, USA on 9 Jul 1988.

BRITISH

Slalom

MEN: (see World Listing)
WOMEN: 2 buoys at 11.25 m, Philippa Roberts, Cirencester, Glos, 1990.

Tricks

MEN: 8650 points, John Battleday (b. 1 Feb 1957) at Lyon, France on 5 Aug 1984.
WOMEN: 6820 points, Nicola Rasey (b. 6 Jun 1966) at Martigues, France on 27 Oct 1984.

Jumping

MEN: 61.9 m *203 ft* Michael Hazelwood at Birmingham, Alabama, USA on 30 Jun 1986.
WOMEN: 44.9 m *147 ft*, Kathy Hulme (b. 11 Feb 1959) at Kirtons Farm, Reading, Berkshire on 1 Aug 1982.

Water Skiing

Most titles World Overall Championships (instituted 1949) have been won four times by Samuel E. 'Sammy' Duvall III (USA) (b. 9 Aug 1962) in 1981, 1983, 1985 and 1987 and three times by two women, Willa McGuire (*née Worthington*) (USA) (b. 1928) in 1949–50 and 1955 and Elizabeth 'Liz' Allan-Shetter (USA) (b. 12 Jul 1947) in 1965, 1969 and 1975. Liz Allan-Shetter has won a record eight individual championship events and is the only person to win all four titles—slalom, jumping, tricks and overall in one year, at Copenhagen, Denmark in 1969. Patrice Martin (France) (b. 24 May 1964) has won a men's record seven titles. The USA have won the team championship on 17 successive occasions, 1957–89.

The most British Overall titles (instituted 1953) won by a man is seven by Michael Hazelwood (b. 14 Apr 1958) in 1974, 1976–9, 1981, 1983; the most by a woman is eleven by Philippa Mary Elizabeth Roberts (b. 11 Apr 1960), 1977, 1982, 1985–92, 1994. In barefoot skiing Richard Mainwaring has won ten men's titles, 1984–90, 1992–4 and the women's best is nine by Michelle Nutt (*née Doherty*), 1984–92.

Highest speed The fastest water skiing speed recorded is 230.26 km/h *143.08 mph* by Christopher Michael Massey (Australia) on the Hawkesbury River, Windsor, New South Wales, Australia on 6 Mar 1983. His drag boat driver was Stanley Charles Sainty. Donna Patterson Brice (b. 1953) set a feminine record of 178.8 km/h *111.11 mph* at Long Beach, California, USA on 21 Aug 1977.

The fastest recorded speed by a British skier over a measured kilometre is 154.38 km/h *95.93 mph* (average) on Lake Windermere, Cumbria on 16 Oct 1989 by Darren Kirkland. The fastest speed recorded by a British woman is 141.050 km/h *87.647 mph* by Nikki Carpenter on Lake Windermere, Cumbria on 18 Oct 1988.

Barefoot

World Championships (instituted 1978) The most Overall titles is four by Kim Lampard (Australia) 1980, 1982, 1985, 1986 and the men's record is three by Brett Wing (Australia) 1978, 1980, 1982. The team title has been won five times by Australia, 1978, 1980, 1982, 1985 and 1986.

■ Turkish lifter Halil Mutlu is holder of all three world records in the 54 kg weight category. Here he is seen in action in the then 52 kg weight category at the 1992 Olympics where he failed to win a medal.
(Photo: Allsport/D. Leah)

Guess What?

Q. What is the jumping record with skis?

A. See Page 299

Highest speed The official barefoot speed record is 218.44 km/h *135.74 mph* by Scott Michael Pellaton (b. 8 Oct 1956) over a quarter-mile course at Chandler, Arizona, California, USA in November 1989. The fastest by a woman is 118.56 km/h *73.67 mph* by Karen Toms (Australia) on the Hawkesbury River, Windsor, New South Wales on 31 Mar 1984.

The British records are: (men) 114.86 km/h *71.37 mph* by Richard Mainwaring (b. 4 Jun 1953) at Holme Pierrepont, Notts on 2 Dec 1978; (women) 80.25 km/h *49.86 mph* by Michelle Doherty (now Nutt) (b. 28 May 1964) (also 71.54 km/h *44.45 mph* backwards), both at Witney, Oxon on 18 Oct 1986.

Jumping The records are: (men) 27.5 m *90 ft 3 in* by Richard Mainwaring (GB) at Thurrock, Essex on 20 Aug 1994; (women) 16.6 m *54 ft 5 in* by Sharon Stekelenberg (Australia) in 1991.

The British women's record is 15.1 m *49 ft 6 in* by Kim Harding at Cirencester, Glos in August 1992.

Weightlifting

The first championships entitled 'world' were staged at the Café Monico, Piccadilly, London on 28 Mar 1891 and then in Vienna, Austria on 19–20 Jul 1898, subsequently recognized by the IWF. The *Fédération Internationale Haltérophile et Culturiste*, now the International Weightlifting Federation (IWF), was established in 1905, and its first official championships were held in Tallinn, Estonia on 29–30 Apr 1922.

Most titles *World* The most world title wins, including Olympic Games, is eight by: John Henry Davis (USA) (1921–84), 1938, 1946–52; Tommy Kono (USA) (b. 27 Jun 1930), 1952–9; Vasiliy Alekseyev (USSR) (b. 7 Jan 1942), 1970–77; and Naim Suleymanoğlü (Turkey) (b. 23 Jan 1967) (previously Neum Shalamanov (Bulgaria)), 1985–6, 1988–9, 1991–4.

Norbert Schemansky (USA) (b. 30 May 1924) won a record four Olympic weightlifting medals: gold, middle-heavyweight 1952; silver, heavyweight 1948; bronze, heavyweight 1960 and 1964.

Youngest and oldest world record holder Naim Suleimanov (later Neum Shalamanov) (Bulgaria) (b. 23 Jan 1967) (now Naim Suleymanoğlü of Turkey) set 56 kg world records for clean and jerk (160 kg) and total (285 kg) at 16 years 62 days at Allentown, New Jersey, USA on 26 Mar 1983. The oldest is Norbert Schemansky (USA) who snatched 362 lb 164.2 kg in the then unlimited heavyweight class, aged 37 yr 333 days, at Detroit, Michigan, USA on 28 Apr 1962.

Most successful British lifter The only British lifter to win an Olympic title has been Launceston Elliot

■ Briton Richard Mainwaring, holder of the world barefoot jumping record, launches himself off the end of the ramp, showing the technique needed for successful jumping.

World Weightlifting Records

From 1 Jan 1993, the International Weightlifting Federation (IWF) introduced modified weight categories thereby making the then world records redundant. This is the current list for the new weight categoriest.

Bodyweight	Lift	kg	lb	Name and Country	Place	Date
54 kg 119 lb	Snatch	130.5	287½	Halil Mutlu (Turkey)	Warsaw, Poland	3 May 1995
	Jerk	160	352¾	Halil Mutlu (Turkey)	Istanbul, Turkey	18 Nov 1994
	Total	290	639¼	Halil Mutlu (Turkey)	Istanbul, Turkey	18 Nov 1994
59 kg 130 lb	Snatch	140	308½	Hafiz Suleymanoğlü (Turkey)	Warsaw, Poland	3 May 1995
	Jerk	170	370¼	Nikolai Pershalov (Bulgaria)	Warsaw, Poland	3 May 1995
	Total	305	672¼	Nikolai Pershalov (Bulgaria)	Melbourne, Australia	13 Nov 1993
64 kg 141 lb	Snatch	147.5	325	Naim Suleymanoğlü (Turkey)*	Istanbul, Turkey	20 Nov 1994
	Jerk	182.5	402¼	Naim Suleymanoğlü (Turkey)*	Istanbul, Turkey	20 Nov 1994
	Total	330	727½	Naim Suleymanoğlü (Turkey)*	Istanbul, Turkey	20 Nov 1994
70 kg 154¼lb	Snatch	160	352¾	Fedail Guler (Turkey)	Istanbul, Turkey	21 Nov 1994
	Jerk	192.5	424¼	Yoto Yotov (Bulgaria)	Sokolov, Czech Republic	5 May 1994
	Total	350	771½	Fedail Guler (Turkey)	Istanbul, Turkey	21 Nov 1994
76 kg 167½ lb	Snatch	170	374¾	Ruslan Savchenko (Ukraine)	Melbourne, Australia	16 Nov 1993
	Jerk	207.5	457½	Pablo Lara (Cuba)	Mar del Plata, Argentina	14 Mar 1995
	Total	370	815¾	Ruslan Savchenko (Ukraine)	Melbourne, Australia	16 Nov 1993
83kg 183lb	Snatch	175.5	387	Sergo Chakhoyan (Armenia)	Istanbul, Turkey	23 Nov 1994
	Jerk	210.5	464	Sunay Bolut (Turkey)	Istanbul, Turkey	23 Nov 1994
	Total	382.5	843¼	Marc Huster (Germany)	Istanbul, Turkey	23 Nov 1994
91 kg 200½ lb	Snatch	186	410	Aleksey Petrov (Russia)	Istanbul, Turkey	24 Nov 1994
	Jerk	228	502½	Aleksey Petrov (Russia)	Istanbul, Turkey	24 Nov 1994
	Total	412.5	909¼	Aleksey Petrov (Russia)	Sokolov, Czech Republic	7 May 1994
99 kg 218½ lb	Snatch	192.5	424¼	Sergey Syrtsov (Russia)	Istanbul, Turkey	25 Nov 1994
	Jerk	225.5	497	Sergey Syrtsov (Russia)	Istanbul, Turkey	25 Nov 1994
	Total	417.5	920¼	Sergey Syrtsov (Russia)	Istanbul, Turkey	25 Nov 1994
108 kg 238lb	Snatch	200	441	Timour Taimazov (Ukraine)	Istanbul, Turkey	26 Nov 1994
	Jerk	235.5	519	Timour Taimazov (Ukraine)	Istanbul, Turkey	26 Nov 1994
	Total	435	959	Timour Taimazov (Ukraine)	Istanbul, Turkey	26 Nov 1994
Over 108 kg	Snatch	205	452	Aleksandr Kurlovich (Belarus)	Istanbul, Turkey	27 Nov 1994
	Jerk	253	557¾	Aleksandr Kurlovich (Belarus)	Istanbul, Turkey	27 Nov 1994
	Total	457.5	1008½	Aleksandr Kurlovich (Belarus)	Istanbul, Turkey	27 Nov 1994

*Formerly Naim Suleimanov or Neum Shalamanov of Bulgaria

Women's Weightlifting Records

Bodyweight	Lift	kg	lb	Name and Country	Place	Date
46 kg 101¼ lb	Snatch	80.5	177¼	Yun Yanhong (China)	Istanbul, Turkey	18 Nov 1994
	Jerk	102.5	226	Guang Hong (China)	Hiroshima, Japan	3 Oct 1994
	Total	182.5	402¼	Guang Hong (China)	Hiroshima, Japan	3 Oct 1994
50 kg 110¼ lb	Snatch	87.5	193	Liu Xiuhia (China)	Hiroshima, Japan	3 Oct 1994
	Jerk	110.5	243½	Liu Xiuhia (China)	Hiroshima, Japan	3 Oct 1994
	Total	197.5	435¼	Liu Xiuhia (China)	Hiroshima, Japan	3 Oct 1994
54 kg 119 lb	Snatch	92.5	204	Zhang Juhua (China)	Hiroshima, Japan	3 Oct 1994
	Jerk	112.5	248	Long Yuiling (China)	Shilong, China	16 Dec 1993
	Total	202.5	446¼	Zhang Juhua (China)	Hiroshima, Japan	3 Oct 1994
59 kg 130 lb	Snatch	98.5	217	Zou Feie (China)	Istanbul, Turkey	21 Nov 1994
	Jerk	123.5	272¼	Zou Feie (China)	Istanbul, Turkey	21 Nov 1994
	Total	220	485	Chen Xiaomin (China)	Hiroshima, Japan	4 Oct 1994
64 kg 141 lb	Snatch	105	231½	Li Hongyun (China)	Istanbul, Turkey	22 Nov 1994
	Jerk	130	286½	Li Hongyun (China)	Istanbul, Turkey	22 Nov 1994
	Total	235	518	Li Hongyun (China)	Istanbul, Turkey	22 Nov 1994
70 kg 154¼ lb	Snatch	102.5	226	Tang Weifang (China)	Hiroshima, Japan	4 Oct 1994
	Jerk	128.5	281	Zhou Meihong (China)	Istanbul, Turkey	23 Nov 1994
	Total	230	507	Tang Weifang (China)	Hiroshima, Japan	4 Oct 1994
76 kg 167¼ lb	Snatch	105.5	232½	Hua Ju (China)	Hiroshima, Japan	5 Oct 1994
	Jerk	140	308½	Zhang Guimei (China)	Shilong, China	18 Dec 1993
	Total	235	518	Zhang Guimei (China)	Shilong, China	18 Dec 1993
83kg 183 lb	Snatch	108	238	Zhang Xiaoli (China)	Hiroshima, Japan	5 Oct 1994
	Jerk	132.5	292	Maria Urrutia (Colombia)	Istanbul, Turkey	25 Nov 1994
	Total	237.5	523½	Zhang Xiaoli (China)	Hiroshima, Japan	5 Oct 1994
+83 kg	Snatch	105.5	232½	Li Yajuan (China)	Hiroshima, Japan	5 Oct 1994
	Jerk	155	341½	Li Yajuan (China)	Melbourne, Australia	20 Nov 1993
	Total	260	573	Li Yajuan (China)	Melbourne, Australia	20 Nov 1993

first woman to clean and jerk more than two times her own bodyweight was Cheng Jinling (China), who lifted 90kg 198 lb in the 44kg class of the World Championships at Jakarta, Indonesia in December 1988.

Women's World Championships These are held annually, first at Daytona Beach, Florida in October 1987. Women's world records have been ratified for the best marks at these championships. The most gold medals is 12 by Peng Liping (China), 52kg class, 1988–9 and 1991–2; and Milena Trendafilova (Bulgaria), 67.5 kg/70 kg/75 kg classes, 1989–93.

Powerlifting

The sport of powerlifting was first contested at national level in Great Britain in 1958. The first US Championships were held in 1964. The International Powerlifting Federation was founded in 1972, a year after the first, unofficial world championships were held. Official championships have been held annually for men from 1973 and for women from 1980. The three standard lifts are squat, bench press and dead lift, the totals from the three lifts determining results.

Most titles *World* The winner of the most world titles is Hideaki Inaba (Japan) with 17, at 52kg 1974–83, 1985–91. The most by a women is six by Beverley Francis (Australia) (b. 15 Feb 1955) at 75kg 1980, 1982; 82.5kg 1981, 1983–5; and Sisi Dolman (Netherlands) at 52 kg 1985–6, 1988–91. The most by a British lifter is seven by Ron Collins: 75kg 1972–4, 82kg 1975–7 and 1979.

British Edward John Pengelly (1949–94) won a record 14 consecutive national titles, 60kg 1976–9, 67½ kg 1980–89. He also won four world titles, 60kg 1976–7, 1979, 67½ kg 1985, and a record ten European titles, 60kg 1978–9, 67½kg 1981, 1983–9.

Most successful woman powerlifter Cathy Millen (New Zealand) currently holds 8 world records spread over two bodyweight categories, 16 British Commonwealth and 20 New Zealand records spread over five bodyweight categories. She has also won five world championships and 1994 total (682.5kg) is the highest ever recorded by a woman.

Powerlifting feats Lamar Gant (USA) was the first man to deadlift five times his own bodyweight, lifting 299.5 kg 661 lb when 59.5 kg 131 lb in 1985. Cammie Lynn Lusko (USA) (b. 5 Apr 1958) became the first woman to lift more than her bodyweight with one arm, with 59.5 kg 131 lb at a bodyweight of 58.3 kg 128.5 lb, at Milwaukee, Wisconsin, USA on 21 May 1983.

(1874–1930), the open one-handed lift champion in 1896 at Athens. Louis George Martin (b. Jamaica, 11 Nov 1936) won four world and European mid-heavyweight titles in 1959, 1962–3, 1965. He won an Olympic silver medal in 1964 and a bronze in 1960 and three Commonwealth gold medals in 1962, 1966, 1970. His total of British titles was 12.

Heaviest lift to bodyweight The first man to clean and jerk more than three times his bodyweight was Stefan Topurov (Bulgaria) (b. 11 Aug 1964), who lifted 180kg 396¾ lb at Moscow, USSR on 24 Oct 1983. The first man to snatch two-and-a-half times his own bodyweight was Naim Suleymanoğlü (Turkey), who lifted 150kg 330½ lb at Cardiff, S Glam on 27 Apr 1988. The

Guess What?

Q. What is the longest time stuck in a lift?

A. See Page 76

World Powerlifting Records (All weights in kilograms)

MEN

Class	Squat		Bench Press		Deadlift		Total	
52 kg	270	Andrzej Stanashek (Pol) 1994	177.5	Andrzej Stanashek 1994	256	E S Bhaskaran (Ind) 1993	587.5	Hideaki Inaba (Jap) 1987
56 kg	260	Magnus Karlsson (Swe) 1994	175	Magnus Karlsson 1993	289.5	Lamar Gant (USA) 1982	625	Lamar Gant 1982
60 kg	295.5	Magnus Karlsson 1994	180.5	Magnus Karlsson 1994	310	Lamar Gant 1988	707.5	Joe Bradley 1982
67.5 kg	300	Jessie Jackson (USA) 1987	200	Kristoffer Hulecki (Swe) 1985	316	Daniel Austin (USA) 1991	762.5	Daniel Austin 1989
75 kg	328	Ausby Alexander (USA) 1989	217.5	James Rouse (USA) 1980	337.5	Daniel Austin 1994	850	Rick Gaugler (USA) 1982
82.5 kg	379.5	Mike Bridges (USA) 1982	240	Mike Bridges 1981	357.5	Veli Kumpuniemi (Fin) 1980	952.5	Mike Bridges 1982
90 kg	375	Fred Hatfield (USA) 1980	255	Mike MacDonald (USA) 1980	372.5	Walter Thomas (USA) 1982	937.5	Mike Bridges 1980
100 kg	423	Ed Coan (USA) 1994	261.5	Mike MacDonald 1977	390	Ed Coan 1993	1035	Ed Coan 1994
110 kg	415	Kirk Karwoski (USA) 1994	270	Jeffrey Magruder (USA) 1982	395	John Kuc (USA) 1980	1000	John Kuc 1980
125 kg	440	Kirk Karwoski 1993	278.5	Tom Hardman (USA) 1982	387.5	Lars Norén (Swe) 1987	1005	Ernie Hackett (USA) 1982
125+ kg	447.5	Shane Hamman (USA) 1994	310	Antony Clark (USA) 1994	406	Lars Norén 1988	1100	Bill Kazmaier 1981

WOMEN

Class	Squat		Bench Press		Deadlift		Total	
44 kg	156	Raija Koskinen (Fin) 1995	82.5	Irina Krylova (Rus) 1993	165	Nancy Belliveau (USA) 1985	365	Jacquline Janot (Fra) 1993
48 kg	160.5	Raija Koskinen 1994	93	Isuko Watanabe (Jap) 1994	182.5	Majik Jones (USA) 1984	400	Elena Yamkich (Rus) 1994
52 kg	175.5	Mary Jeffrey (USA) (née Ryan) 1991	105	Mary Jeffrey 1991	197.5	Diana Rowell (USA) 1984	452.5	Mary Jeffrey 1991
56 kg	191	Mary Jeffrey 1989	115	Mary Jeffrey 1988	220.5	Carrie Boudreau (USA) 1995	517.5	Carrie Boudreau 1995
60 kg	210	Beate Amdahl (Nor) 1993	115	Eriko Himeno (Jap) 1995	213	Ruthi Shafer 1983	502.5	Vicki Steenrod (USA) 1985
67.5 kg	230	Ruthi Shafer 1984	120	Vicki Steenrod 1990	244	Ruthi Shafer 1984	565	Ruthi Shafer 1984
75 kg	240.5	Yelena Sukhoruk (Ukr) 1995	142.5	Liz Odendaal (Neth) 1989	252.5	Yelena Sukhoruk 1995	605	Yelena Sukhoruk 1995
82.5 kg	240	Cathy Millen (NZ) 1991	150.5	Cathy Millen 1993	257.5	Cathy Millen 1993	637.5	Cathy Millen 1993
90 kg	260	Cathy Millen 1994	160	Cathy Millen 1994	260	Cathy Millen 1994	682.5	Cathy Millen 1994
90+kg	277.5	Juanita Trujillo (USA) 1993	157.5	Ulrike Herchenhein (Ger) 1994	240	Ulrike Herchenhein 1994	640	Juanita Trujillo 1994

British Powerlifting Records (All weights in kilograms)

MEN

Class	Squat		Bench Press		Deadlift		Total	
52 kg	223.5	Peter Kemp 1995	130	Phil Stringer 1981	225	John Maxwell 1988	530	Phil Stringer 1982
56 kg	235	Phil Stringer 1982	137.5	Phil Stringer 1983	229	Precious McKenzie 1973	577.5	Gary Simes 1991
60 kg	247.5	Tony Galvez 1981	145	Gary Symes 1994	275	Eddy Pengelly 1977	645	Eddy Pengelly 1979
67.5 kg	290	Rodney Hypolite 1994	165.5	Mick McCrohon 1994	295	Eddy Pengelly 1982	722.5	Rodney Hypolite 1994
75 kg	302.5	John Howells 1979	185	Peter Fiore 1981	310	Robert Limerick 1984	760	Steve Alexander 1983
82.5 kg	337.5	Mike Duffy 1984	210	Mike Duffy 1981	355	Ron Collins 1980	855	Ron Collins 1980
90 kg	347.5	David Caldwell 1985	227.5	Jeff Chandler 1985	350.5	Ron Collins 1980	870	David Caldwell 1985
100 kg	380	Tony Stevens 1984	225.5	Brian Reynolds 1992	362.5	Tony Stevens 1984	955	Tony Stevens 1984
110 kg	372.5	Tony Stevens 1984	250	John Neighbour 1990	380	Arthur White 1982	940	John Neighbour 1987
125 kg	390	John Neighbour 1990	250	John Neighbour 1990	373	David Cullen 1992	957.5	Steven Zetolofsky 1984
125+kg	380	Steven Zetolofsky 1979	258	Terry Purdoe 1971	377.5	Andy Kerr 1982	982.5	Andy Kerr 1983

WOMEN

Class	Squat		Bench Press		Deadlift		Total	
44 kg	130	Helen Wolsey 1991	68	Helen Wolsey 1991	152.5	Helen Wolsey 1990	350	Helen Wolsey 1991
48 kg	132.5	Helen Wolsey 1990	75	Suzanne Smith 1985	155	Helen Wolsey 1990	355	Helen Wolsey 1990
52 kg	143	Jenny Hunter 1988	82	Jenny Hunter 1988	173.5	Jenny Hunter 1988	395	Jenny Hunter 1988
56 kg	158	Jenny Hunter 1988	88.5	Tony Hollis 1995	182.5	Jenny Hunter 1988	420	Jenny Hunter 1988
60 kg	163	Rita Bass 1988	92.5	Mandy Wadsworth 1992	192.5	Jackie Blasbery 1994	425	Jessica Kattan 1994
67.5 kg	175	Debbie Thomas 1988	102.5	Sandra Berry 1992	198	Sandra Berry 1992	460	Sandra Berry 1992
75 kg	202.5	Judith Oakes 1989	115	Judith Oakes 1989	215	Judith Oakes 1989	532.5	Judith Oakes 1989
82.5 kg	215	Judith Oakes 1988	122.5	Joanne Williams 1990	217.5	Judith Oakes 1989	542.5	Judith Oakes 1988
90 kg	200	Beverley Martin 1989	115	Joanne Williams 1989	215	Beverley Martin 1990	495	Beverley Martin 1989
90+kg	221	Beverley Martin 1995	137.5	Myrtle Augee 1989	230	Myrtle Augee 1989	587.5	Myrtle Augee 1989

Timed lifts *24 hours* A deadlifting record of 2,703,700 kg *5,960,631 lb* was set by a team of ten from HM Prison Wayland, Thetford, Norfolk on 10–11 May 1993. The deadlift record by an individual is 371,094 kg *818,121 lb* by Anthony Wright at HM Prison Featherstone, Wolverhampton, W Mids on 31 Aug–1 Sep 1990. A bench press record of 4,025,120 kg *8,873,860 lb* was set by a nine-man team from the Forum Health Club, Chelmsleywood, W Mids on 19–20 Mar 1994. A squat record of 2,168,625 kg *4,780,994 lb* was set by a ten-man team from St Albans Weightlifting Club and Ware Boys Club, Herts on 20–21 Jul 1986. A record 137,531 arm-curling repetitions using three 22 kg *48½ lb* weightlifting bars and dumb-bells was achieved by a team of nine from Pontefract Squash and Leisure Centre at Pontefract, W Yorks on 15–16 Apr 1995.

12 hours An individual bench press record of 535,835 kg *1,181,312 lb* was set by Chris Lawton at the Waterside Wine Bar, Solihull, W Mids on 3 Jun 1994.

Strandpulling

The International Steel Strandpullers' Association was founded by Gavin Pearson (Scotland) in 1940. The greatest ratified poundage to date is a super-heavyweight right-arm push of 815 lb *369.5 kg* by Malcolm Bartlett (b. 9 Jun 1955) of Oldham, Greater Manchester. The record for the back press anyhow is 650 lb *295 kg* by Paul Anderson, at Hull, Humberside on 29 Mar 1992. A record 22 British Open titles have been won by Ian Storton (b. 2 Feb 1951) of Morecambe, Lancs, 1974–88.

Wrestling

Most titles *Olympic* Three Olympic titles have been won by: Carl Westergren (Sweden) (1895–1958) in 1920, 1924 and 1932; Ivar Johansson (Sweden) (1903–79) in 1932 (two) and 1936; and Aleksandr Vasilyevich Medved (USSR) (b. 16 Sep 1937) in 1964, 1968 and 1972. Four Olympic medals were won by: Eino Leino (Finland) (1891–1986) at freestyle 1920–32; and by Imre Polyák (Hungary) (b. 16 Apr 1932) at Greco-Roman in 1952–64.

World The freestyler Aleksandr Medved

Guess What?
Q. what is the greatest weight lifted by hydraulic jacks?
A. See Page 75

(USSR) won a record ten World Championships, 1962–4, 1966–72 at three weight categories. Three wrestlers have won the same title in seven successive years: Valeriy Rezantsev (USSR) 1970–76, Makharbek Khdartsev (USSR) 1986–92 and Aleksandr Karelin (Russia) 1988–94.

Most titles and longest span *British* The most British titles won in one weight class is 14 by welterweight Fitzlloyd Walker (b. 7 Mar 1957), 1979–92. The longest span for BAWA titles is 24 years by George Mackenzie (1890–1957) between 1909 and 1933. He represented Great Britain in five successive Olympiads, 1908 to 1928.

Most wins In international competition, Osamu Watanabe (b. 21 Oct 1940), of Japan, the 1964 Olympic freestyle 63 kg champion, was unbeaten and did not concede a score in 189 consecutive matches. Outside of FILA sanctioned competition, Wade Schalles (USA) won 821 bouts from 1964 to 1984, with 530 of these victories by pin.

Longest bout The longest recorded bout was one of 11 hr 40 min when Martin Klein (Estonia representing Russia) (1885–1947) beat Alfred Asikáinen (Finland) (1888–1942) for the Greco-Roman 75 kg 'A' event silver medal in the 1912 Olympic Games in Stockholm, Sweden.

Heavy Weight

The heaviest wrestler in Olympic history is Chris Taylor (1950–79), bronze medallist in the super-heavyweight class in 1972, who stood 1.96 m *6 ft 5 in* tall and weighed over 190 kg *420 lb*. FILA introduced an upper weight limit of 130 kg *286 lb* for international competition in 1985.

Sumo Wrestling

The sport's origins in Japan date from c. 23 BC. The most successful wrestlers have been *yokozuna* Sadji Akiyoshi (b. 1912), alias Futabayama who set the all-time record of 69 consecutive wins (1937–9), *yokozuna* Koki Naya (b. 1940), alias Taiho ('Great Bird'), who won the Emperor's Cup 32 times up to his retirement in 1971 and the *ozeki* Tameemon Torokichi, alias Raiden (1767–1825), who in 21 years (1789–1810) won 254 bouts and lost only ten for the highest ever winning percentage of 96.2.

Yokozuna Mitsugu Akimoto (b. 1 Jun 1955), alias Chiyonofuji, set a record for domination of one of the six annual tournaments by winning the Kyushu Basho for eight successive years, 1981–88. He also holds the record for the most career wins, 1045 and *Makunouchi* (top division) wins, 807. Toshimitsu Ogata (b. 16 May 1953), alias Kitanoumi, set a record in 1978 winning 82 of the 90 bouts that top *rikishi* fight annually. He is youngest of the 65 men to have attained the rank of *yokozuna* (grand champion), aged 21 years and two months in July 1974.

Hawaiian-born Jesse Kuhaulua (b. 16 Jun 1944), alias Takamiyama, was the first non-Japanese to win an official top-division tournament, in July 1972 and in September 1981 he set a record of 1231 consecutive top-division bouts. In all six divisions, the most consecutive bouts is 1631 by Yukio Shoji (b. 14 Nov 1948), alias Aobajo, 1964–86. The most bouts in a career is 1891 by Kenji Hatano (b. 4 Jan 1948), alias Oshio, 1962–88.

Hawaiian-born Chad Rowan (b. 8 May 1969), alias Akebono, became the first foreign *rikishi* to be promoted to the top rank of *yokozuna* in January 1993. He is the tallest (204 cm *6 ft 8 in*) and heaviest (227 kg *501 lb*) *yokozuna* in sumo history. The heaviest ever *rikishi* is Samoan-American Salevaa Fuali Atisanoe alias Konishiki, of Hawaii, who weighed in at 267 kg *589 lb* at Tokyo's Ryogoku Kokugikan on 3 Jan 1994. Weight is amassed by over-alimentation with a high-protein stew called *chankonabe*.

Yachting

Olympic titles The first sportsman ever to win individual gold medals in four successive Olympic Games was Paul B. Elvstrøm (Denmark) (b. 25 Feb 1928) in the Firefly class in 1948 and the Finn class in 1952, 1956 and 1960. He also won eight other world titles in a total of six classes. The lowest number of penalty points by the winner of any class in an Olympic regatta is three points (five wins, one disqualified and one second in seven starts) by *Superdocious* of the Flying Dutchman class (Lt Rodney Stuart Pattisson, RN (b. 5 Aug 1943) and Iain Somerled Macdonald-Smith (b. 3 Jul 1945)) at Acapulco Bay, Mexico in October 1968.

British The only British yachtsman to win in two Olympic regattas is Rodney Pattisson in 1968 and again with *Superdoso* crewed by Christopher Davies (b. 29 Jun 1946) at Kiel, Germany in 1972. He gained a silver medal in 1976 with Julian Brooke Houghton (b. 16 Dec 1946).

Admiral's Cup and ocean racing The ocean racing team series which has had the most participating nations (three boats allowed to each nation) is the Admiral's Cup organized by the Royal Ocean Racing Club. A record 19 nations competed in 1975, 1977 and 1979. Britain has a record nine wins.

Modern ocean racing (in moderate or small sailing yachts, rather than professionally manned sailing ships) began with a race from Brooklyn, New York, USA to Bermuda, 630 nautical miles *1166 km* organized by Thomas Fleming Day, editor of the magazine *The Rudder* in June 1906. The race is still held today in every even numbered year, though the course is now Newport, Rhode Island, USA to Bermuda.

The race still regularly run with the earliest foundation, for any type of craft and either kind of water (fresh or salt), is the Chicago to Mackinac race on Lakes Michigan and Huron, first sailed in 1898. It was held again in 1904, then annually until the present day, except for 1917–20. The record for the course (333 nautical miles *616 km*) is 1 day 1 hr 50 min (average speed 12.89 knots *23.84 km/h*) by the sloop *Pied Piper*, owned by Dick Jennings (USA) in 1987.

The current record holder of the elapsed time records for both the premier American and British ocean races (the Newport, Rhode Island, to Bermuda race and the Fastnet race) is the sloop *Nirvana*, owned by Marvin Green (USA). The record for the Bermuda race, 635 nautical miles *1176 km*, is 2 days 14 hr 29 min in 1982 and for the Fastnet race, 605 nautical miles *1120 km*, is 2 days 12 hr 41 min in 1985, an average speed of 10.16 knots *18.81 km/h* and 9.97 knots *18.45 km/h* respectively.

Longest race The world's longest sailing race is the Vendée Globe Challenge, the first of which started from Les Sables d'Olonne, France on 26 Nov 1989. The distance circumnavigated without stopping was 22,500 nautical miles *41,652 km*. The race is for

Large Yacht

The largest yacht to have competed in the America's Cup was the 1903 defender, the gaff rigged cutter *Reliance*, designed by Nathanael Herreshoff (1848–1938), with an overall length of 43.89 m *144 ft*, a record sail area of 1501 m² *16,160 ft²* and a rig 53.3 m *175 ft* high.

boats between 50 and 60 ft, sailed single-handed. The record time on the course is 109 days 8 hr 48 min 50 sec by Titouan Lamazou (France) (b. 1955) in the sloop *Ecureuil d'Aquitaine* which finished at Les Sables on 19 Mar 1990.

The oldest regular sailing race around the world is the quadrennial Whitbread Round the World race (instituted August 1973) originally organized by the Royal Naval Sailing Association. It starts in England and the course around the world and the number of legs with stops at specified ports is varied from race to race. The distance for 1993–4 was 32,000 nautical miles *59,239 km* from Southampton and return, with stops and re-starts at Punta del Este, Uruguay; Fremantle, Australia; Auckland, New Zealand; Punta del Este, Uruguay and Fort Lauderdale, Florida, USA.

> ## Guess What?
> Q. Who was the first person, by boat, to circumnavigate the globe solo?
> A. See Page 112

America's Cup The Cup was originally won as an outright prize (with no special name) by the schooner *America* from 14 British yachts at Cowes on 22 Aug 1851. It was offered in 1857 by the winners, John C. Stevens, commodore of the New York Yacht Club and syndicate, as a perpetual challenge trophy 'for friendly competiton between countries'.

There have been 29 challenges since 8 Aug 1870, with the USA winning on every occasion except 1983 (to Australia) and 1995 (to New Zealand). In individual races sailed, American boats have won 81 races and foreign challengers have won 13.

Dennis Walter Conner (USA) (b. 16 Sep 1942) has been in more cup races as a member of the afterguard than any other sailor, six times since 1974, when he was starting helmsman with Ted Hood as skipper. He was winning skipper/helmsman in 1980, 1987 and 1989. He was losing skipper in 1983 and 1995. Charlie Barr (USA) (1864–1911) who defended in 1899, 1901 and 1903 and Harold S. Vanderbilt (USA) (1884–1970) in 1930, 1934 and 1937, each steered the successful winner three times in succession.

The closest finish in a race for the cup was on 4 Oct 1901, when *Shamrock II* (GB) finished 2 seconds ahead of the American *Columbia*.

Yacht and dinghy classes The oldest racing class still sailing is the Water Wag class of Dublin, formed in 1887. The design of the boat was changed in 1900 to that which is still used today. The oldest classes in Britain, both established in 1898 and both still racing in the same design of boat are the Seabird Half Rater, centreboard sailing dinghy of Abersoch and other north-west ports, and the Yorkshire One-design keel boat. The latter races from the Royal Yorkshire Yacht Club at Bridlington, Humberside.

The first international class for racing dinghies was the 14-foot International, whose principal trophy in Britain is the Prince of Wales Cup which has been contested annually since 1927 (except 1940–45). The most wins is 12 by Stewart Harold Morris between 1932 and 1965.

■ The America's Cup was contested for the 29th time in 1995 and for only the second time the USA were defeated. The successful team were *Black Magic* from New Zealand, a syndicate headed by record-breaking yachtsman Peter Blake (knighted in June 1995). Far right, he lifts the cup in celebration of a 5–0 whitewash of the American boat, *Young America*.
(Photos: Allsport (USA)/S. Dunn)

Guess What?

Q. How far is the Sun from Earth?

A. See Page 7

Highest speeds The highest speed reached under sail on water by any craft over a 500-metre timed run is 46.52 knots *86.21 km/h* by trifoiler *Yellow Pages Endeavour* piloted by Simon McKeon and Tim Daddo, both of Australia, at Sandy Point near Melbourne, Australia on 26 Oct 1993. The women's record is by boardsailer Babethe Coquelle (France) who achieved 40.05 knots *74.22 km/h* at Tarifa, Spain in July 1993.

The fastest for a boardsailer overall is 45.34 knots *83.95 km/h* by Thierry Bielak (France) at Saintes Maries de-la-Mer canal, Camargue, France on 24 Apr 1993.

British The records are (men) 41.22 knots *76.33 km/h* by Nick Luget and (women) 34.61 knots *64.09 km/h* by Samantha Harrison, both at Saintes Maries de-la-Mer on 22 Mar 1991.

Most competitors The most boats ever to start in a single race was 2072 in the Round Zeeland (Denmark) race on 21 Jun 1984, over a course of 235 nautical miles *435 km*. The greatest number to start in a race in Britain was 1781 keeled yachts and multihulls on 17 Jun 1989 from Cowes in the Annual Round-the-Island Race. The fastest time achieved in this annual event is 3 hr 55 min 28 sec by the trimaran *Paragon*, owned and sailed by Michael Whipp on 31 May 1986.

The largest trans-oceanic race was the ARC (Atlantic Rally for Cruisers), when 204 boats of the 209 starters from 24 nations completed the race from Las Palmas de Gran Canaria (Canary Islands) to Barbados in 1989.

Oldest club The oldest club in the world is the Royal Cork Yacht Club which claims descent from the Cork Harbour Water Club, established in Ireland by 1720.

The oldest active club in Britain is the Starcross Yacht Club at Powderham Point, Devon. Its first regatta was held in 1772. The oldest existing club to have been truly formed as a yacht club is the Royal Yacht Squadron, Cowes, Isle of Wight, instituted as 'The Yacht Club' at a meeting at the Thatched House Tavern, St James's Street, London on 1 Jun 1815.

Boardsailing

World Championships were first held in 1973 and the sport was added to the Olympic Games in 1984 when the winner was Stephan van den Berg (Netherlands) (b. 20 Feb 1962), who also won five world titles 1979–83.

Longest sailboard The longest 'snake' of boardsails was set by 70 windsurfers in tandem at the 'Sailboard Show '89' event at Narrabeen Lakes, Manly, Australia on 21 Oct 1989.

The world's longest sail board, 50.2 m *165 ft*, was constructed at Fredrikstad, Norway, and first sailed on 28 Jun 1986.

Guess What? Q. Where is the world's largest switchboard? A. See Page 80

■ The trifoiler *Yellow Pages Endeavour* piloted by Simon McKeon and Tim Daddo, both of Australia, which achieved the highest speed on water by any sailed-craft.

Olympic Games

Baron de Coubertin, instigator of the modern Olympic Games, which celebrates its centenary in 1996 when the Games will be held in Atlanta, Georgia, USA.
(Photos: Allsport)

The earliest celebration of the ancient Olympic Games of which there is a certain record is that of July 776 BC, when Coroibos, a cook from Elis, won the foot race, though their origin dates from perhaps as early as c. 1370 BC. The ancient Games were terminated by an order issued in Milan in AD 393 by Theodosius I, 'the Great' (c. 346–95), Emperor of Rome. At the instigation of Pierre de Fredi, Baron de Coubertin (1863–1937), the Olympic Games of the modern era were inaugurated in Athens on 6 Apr 1896.

Ever present Five countries have never failed to be represented at the 23 Summer Games that have been held (1896–1992): Australia, France, Greece, Great Britain and Switzerland (only contested the Equestrian events, held in Stockholm, Sweden, in 1956 and did not attend the Games in Melbourne). Of these only France, Great Britain and Switzerland have been present at all Winter celebrations (1924–94) as well.

Most participants The greatest number of competitors at a Summer Games celebration is 9369 (6659 men, 2710 women), who represented a record 169 nations, at Barcelona, Spain in 1992. The greatest number at the Winter Games is 1737 (1216 men, 521 women) representing 67 countries, at Lillehammer, Norway in 1994.

Largest crowd The largest crowd at any Olympic site was 104,102 at the 1952 ski-jumping at the Holmenkøllen, outside Oslo, Norway. Estimates of the number of spectators of the marathon race through Tokyo, Japan on 21 Oct 1964 ranged from 500,000 to 1,500,000. The total spectator attendance at Los Angeles in 1984 was given as 5,797,923 (⇔ General Records).

Olympic Torch relay The longest journey of the torch within one country, was for the XV Olympic Winter Games in Canada in 1988. The torch arrived from Greece at St John's, Newfoundland on 17 Nov 1987 and was transported 18,060 km *11,222 miles* (8188 km *5088 miles* by foot, 7111 km *4419 miles* by aircraft/ferry, 2756 km *1712 miles* by snowmobile and 5 km *3 miles* by dogsled) until its arrival at Calgary on 13 Feb 1988.

Most medals In ancient Olympic Games victors were given a chaplet of wild olive leaves. Leonidas of

Rhodos won 12 running titles 164–152 BC. The most individual gold medals won by a male competitor in the modern Games is ten by Raymond Clarence Ewry (USA) (1873–1937) (⇔ Athletics). The female record is seven by Vera Caslavska-Odlozil (Czechoslovakia) (⇔ Gymnastics).

The most gold medals won by a British competitor is four by: Paul Radmilovic (1886–1968) in water polo, 1908, 1912 and 1920 and 4 × 200 m freestyle relay in 1908; and swimmer Henry Taylor (1885–1951) in 1906 and 1908. The Australian swimmer Iain Murray Rose, who won four gold medals, was born in Birmingham, W Mids on 6 Jan 1939.

The only Olympian to win four consecutive individual titles in the same event has been Alfred Adolph Oerter (USA) (b. 19 Sep 1936), who won the discus, in 1956–68. However, Raymond Clarence Ewry (USA) won both the standing long jump and the standing high jump at four games in succession, 1900, 1904, 1906 and 1908. This is if the Intercalated Games of 1906, which were staged officially by the International Olympic Committee, are included. Also Paul Bert Elvstrøm (Denmark) (b. 25 Feb 1928) won four successive gold medals at monotype yachting events, 1948–60, but there was a class change (1948 Firefly class, 1952–60 Finn class).

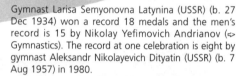

Swimmer Mark Andrew Spitz (USA) (b. 10 Feb 1950) won a record seven golds at one celebration, at Munich in 1972, including three in relays. The most won in individual events at one celebration is five by speed skater, Eric Arthur Heiden (USA) (b. 14 Jun 1958) at Lake Placid, New York, USA in 1980.

The only man to win a gold medal in both the Summer and Winter Games is Edward Patrick Francis Eagan (USA) (1898–1967) who won the 1920 light-heavyweight boxing title and was a member of the winning four-man bob in 1932. Christa Luding (*née* Rothenburger) (GDR) (b. 4 Dec 1959) became the first woman to win a medal at both the Summer and Winter Games when she won a silver in the cycling sprint event in 1988. She had previously won medals for speed skating, 500 m gold in 1984, and 1000 m gold and 500 m silver in 1988.

Gymnast Larisa Semyonovna Latynina (USSR) (b. 27 Dec 1934) won a record 18 medals and the men's record is 15 by Nikolay Yefimovich Andrianov (⇔ Gymnastics). The record at one celebration is eight by gymnast Aleksandr Nikolayevich Dityatin (USSR) (b. 7 Aug 1957) in 1980.

Youngest and oldest gold medallist The youngest ever winner was a French boy (whose name is not recorded) who coxed the Netherlands pair in 1900. He was 7–10 years old and he substituted for Dr Hermanus Gerhardus Brockmann (1871–?), who coxed in the heats but proved too heavy. The youngest ever female champion was Kim Yoon-mi (South Korea) (b. 1 Dec 1980), aged 13 years 85 days, in the 1994 women's 3000 m short-track speedskating relay event. Oscar Swahn was in the winning Running Deer shooting team in 1912 aged 64 yr 258 days and in this event was the oldest medallist, silver, at 72 yr 280 days in 1920.

Youngest and oldest British competitor The youngest competitor to represent Britain in the Olympic Games was Magdalena Cecilia Colledge (b. 28 Nov 1920), aged 11 years 73 days when she skated in the 1932 Games. The oldest was Hilda Lorna Johnstone (1902–90), aged 70 yr 5 days, in the equestrian dressage in the 1972 Games.

Longest span The longest span of an Olympic competitor is 40 years by: Dr Ivan Joseph Martin Osiier (Denmark) (1888–1965) in fencing, 1908–32 and 1948; Magnus Andreas Thulstrup Clasen Konow (Norway) (1887–1972) in yachting, 1908–20, 1928 and 1936–48; Paul Elvstrøm (Denmark) in yachting, 1948–60, 1968–72 and 1984–88; and Durward Randolph Knowles (Great Britain 1948, then Bahamas) (b. 2 Nov 1917) in yachting, 1948–72 and 1988. Brothers Piero (b. 4 Mar 1923) and Raimondo d'Inzeo (b. 8 Feb 1925) competed for Italy at a record eight celebrations from 1948–76. Raimondo won one gold, two silver and three bronze medals in equestrian events and Piero won two silver and four bronze medals at show jumping. This feat was equalled by Paul Elvstrøm and Durward Knowles in 1988 and yachtsman Hubert Raudaschl (Austria) (b. 26 Aug 1942), 1964–92 (went to Rome, 1960 but did not compete). The longest feminine span is 28 years by Anne Jessica Ransehousen (née Newberry) (USA) (b. 14 Oct 1938) 1960, 1964 and 1988 and Christilot Hanson-Boylen (Canada) 1964–76, 1984, 1992, both dressage. Fencer Kerstin Palm (Sweden) (b. 5 Feb 1946) competed in a women's record seven celebrations, 1964–88.

The longest span of any British competitor is 32 years by Enoch Jenkins (1892–1984) who competed in clay pigeon shooting in 1920, 1924 and 1952. The record number of appearances is six by swimmer and water polo player Paul Radmilovic, 1906–28 and fencer Bill Hoskyns, 1956–76. David Broome, who competed in show jumping in 1960, 1964, 1968, 1972 and 1988, was a member of the British team that travelled to Barcelona in 1992. He was, however, not selected to compete.

The greatest number of appearances for Great Britain by a woman is five by javelin thrower Tessa Ione Sanderson (b. 14 Mar 1956), 1976–92. The longest feminine span is 20 years by Dorothy Jennifer Beatrice Tyler (née Odam) (b. 14 Mar 1920) who high-jumped from 1936–56. However, Davina Mary Galicia (b. 13 Aug 1944) who competed in alpine skiing, 1964–72, took part in speed skiing which was a demonstration sport in 1992, therefore completing a span of 28 years.

Summer

	Year	Venue	Nations	Participants
I	1896	Athens Greece	13	311
II	1900	Paris, France	22	1330
III	1904	St Louis, USA	13	625
†	1906	Athens, Greece	20	884
IV	1908	London, Great Britain	22	2056
V	1912	Stockholm, Sweden	28	2546
VI	1916	Berlin, Germany*	-	-
VII	1920	Antwerp, Belgium	29	2692
VIII	1924	Paris, France	44	3092
IX	1928	Amsterdam, Netherlands	46	3014
X	1932	Los Angeles, USA	37	1408
XI	1936	Berlin, Germany	49	4066
XII	1940	Tokyo, Japan then Helsinki, Finland*	-	-
XIII	1944	London, Great Britain*	-	-
XIV	1948	London, Great BritainF	59	4099
XV	1952	Helsinki, Finland	69	4925
XVI	1956	Melbourne, Australia‡	67	3184
XVII	1960	Rome, Italy	83	5346
XVIII	1964	Tokyo, Japan	93	5140
XIX	1968	Mexico City, Mexico	112	5530
XX	1972	Munich, West Germany	122	7156
XXI	1976	Montreal, Canada	92	6085
XXII	1980	Moscow, USSR	81	5326
XXIII	1984	Los Angeles, USA	140	7078
XXIV	1988	Seoul, South Korea	159	8465
XXV	1992	Barcelona, Spain	169	9369
XXVI	1996	Atlanta, USA	-	-
XXVII	2000	Sydney, Australia	-	-

† This celebration is officially intercalated but not numbered

* Not held due to war

‡ Equestrian events were held in Stockholm, Sweden due to Australia's quarantine laws and there were 158 competitors from 29 nations.

Winter

	Year	Venue	Nations	Participants
I	1924	Chamonix, France	16	294
II	1928	St Moritz, Switzerland	25	495
III	1932	Lake Placid, USA	17	306
IV	1936	Garmisch-Partenkirchen, Germany	28	755
	1940	Sapporo, Japan then St Moritz, then Garmisch-Partenkirchen*	-	-
	1944	Cortina d'Ampezzo, Italy*	-	-
V	1948	St Moritz, Switzerland	28	713
VI	1952	Oslo, Norway	30	732
VII	1956	Cortina d'Ampezzo, Italy	32	819
VIII	1960	Squaw Valley, USA	30	665
IX	1964	Innsbruck, Austria	36	1186
X	1968	Grenoble, France	37	1293
XI	1972	Sapporo, Japan	35	1232
XII	1976	Innsbruck, Austria	37	1128
XIII	1980	Lake Placid, USA	37	1067
XIV	1984	Sarajevo, Yugoslavia	49	1278
XV	1988	Calgary, Canada	57	1428
XVI	1992	Albertville, France	64	1719
XVII	1994	Lillehammer, Norway	67	1737
XVIII	1998	Nagano, Japan	-	-

* Not held due to war

Most Medals

The total medals, for leading nations, for all Olympic events (including those now discontinued).

SUMMER GAMES (1896–92)

	Gold	Silver	Bronze	Total
USA	789	603	518	1910
USSR[1]	442	361	333	1136
Germany[2]	186	227	236	649
Great Britain	177	224	218	619
France	161	175	191	527
Sweden	133	149	171	453
GDR[3]	154	131	126	411
Italy	153	126	131	410
Hungary	136	124	144	404
Finland	98	77	112	287
Japan	90	83	93	266
Australia	78	76	98	252
Romania	59	70	90	219
Poland	43	62	105	210
Canada	46	66	80	192
Netherlands	45	52	72	169
Switzerland	42	63	58	163
Bulgaria	38	69	55	162
Czechoslovakia[4]	49	50	50	149
Denmark	26	51	53	130

Excludes medals won in Official Art competitions in 1912–48.

WINTER GAMES (1924–94)

	Gold	Silver	Bronze	Total
USSR[1]	99	71	71	241
Norway	73	77	64	214
USA	53	55	39	147
Austria	36	48	44	128
Germany[2]	45	43	37	125
Finland	36	45	42	123
GDR[3]	39	36	35	110
Sweden	39	26	34	99
Switzerland	27	29	29	85
Italy	25	21	21	67
Canada	19	21	24	64
France	16	16	21	53
Netherlands	14	19	17	50
Czechoslovakia[4]	2	8	16	26
Great Britain	7	4	12	23

[1] Includes Czarist Russia to 1912, CIS 1992, Russia 1994
[2] Germany 1896–1964 and 1992, West Germany 1968–88
[3] GDR (East Germany) 1968–88
[4] Includes Bohemia

■ Fulton County Stadium, one of the venues for the 1996 Olympic Games in Atlanta.
(Photo: Allsport USA)

Olympic Athletics Records

Men–Track Events	Time	Name	Year
100 m	9.92	Carl Lewis (USA)	1988
200 m	19.73	Mike Marsh (USA)	1992
400 m	43.50	Quincy Watts (USA)	1992
800 m	1:43.00	Joaquim Cruz (Brazil)	1984
1500 m	3:32.53	Sebastian Coe (Great Britain)	1984
5000 m	13:05.59	Said Aouita (Morocco)	1984
10,000 m	27:21.46	Brahim Boutayeb (Morocco)	1988
Marathon	2:09.21.	Carlos Lopes (Portugal)	1984
110 m hurdles	12.98	Roger Kingdom (USA)	1988
400 m hurdles	46.78	Kevin Young (USA)	1992
3000 m s'chase	8:05.51	Julius Kariuki (Kenya)	1988
20km walk	1:19:57	Jozef Priibilinec (Czechoslovakia)	1988
50km walk	3:38:29	Vyacheslav Ivanenko (USSR)	1988
4×100 m	37.40	USA	1992
4×400 m	2:55.74	USA	1992

Field Events	m		
High Jump	2.38	Gennadiy Avdeyenko (USSR)	1988
Pole Vault	5.90	Sergey Bubka (USSR)	1988
Long Jump	8.90	Bob Beamon (USA)	1968
Triple Jump*	17.63	Mike Conley (USA)*	1992
Shot	22.47	Ulf Timmermann (GDR)	1988
Discus	68.82	Jürgen Schult (GDR)	1988
Hammer	84.80	Sergey Litivinov (USSR)	1988
Javelin	89.66	Jan Zelezny (Czechoslovakia)	1992
Decathlon	8847 points	Daley Thompson (Great Britain)	1984

* Also 18.17m wind-assisted

Women–Track Events			
100 m*	10.62	Florence Griffith-Joyner (USA) *	1988
200 m	21.34	Florence Griffith-Joyner (USA)	1988
400 m	48.65	Olga Bryzgina (USSR)	1988
800 m	1:53.43	Nadyezda Olizarenko (USSR)	1980
1500 m	3:53.96	Paula Ivan (Romania)	1988
3000 m	8:26.53	Tatyana Samolenko (USSR)	1988
10,000 m	31:05.21	Olga Bondarenko (USSR)	1988
Marathon	2:24:52.	Joan Benoit (USA)	1984
100 m hurdles	12.38	Yordanka Donkova (Bulgaria)	1988
400 m hurdles	53.17	Debbie Flintoff-King (Australia)	1988
10km walk	44:32	Chen Yueling (China)	1992
4×100 m	41.60	GDR	1980
4×400 m	3:15.17	USSR	1988

* Also 10.54 wind-assisted in heat

Field Events	m		
High Jump	2.03	Louise Ritter (USA)	1988
Long Jump	7.40	Jackie Joyner-Kersee (USA)	1988
Shot	22.41	Ilona Slupianek (GDR)	1980
Discus	72.30	Martina Hellmann (GDR)	1988
Javelin	74.68	Petra Felke (GDR)	1988
Heptathlon	7291 points	Jackie Joyner-Kersee (USA)	1988

Olympic Sports In 1896 there were nine sports contested in the Olympic programme and this number has grown to the 1996 Games, where a record 27 sports will take place. The following list is of the sports to be contested with the original nine marked with an asterisk (*):

Archery, Athletics*, Badminton, Baseball, Basketball, Boxing, Canoeing, Cycling*, Equestrianism, Fencing*, Football, Gymnastics*, Handball, Hockey, Judo, Modern Pentathlon, Rowing, Shooting*, Softball, Swimming* (including Synchronised Swimming and Diving), Table Tennis, Tennis*, Volleyball (including Beach Volleyball), Water Polo, Weightlifting*, Wrestling*, Yachting

In contrast to the Summer Games, there has been little change in the sports contested from the first Winter Games in 1924. The following is a list of the sports which took place at the 1994 Games:

Skiing (Alpine/Freestyle/Nordic), Bobsleigh, Lugeing, Speed Skating, Figure Skating, Ice Hockey.

It should be noted of these, only Lugeing, Alpine and Freestyle Skiing were *not* a part of the first celebration.

The Guinness Book of Olympic Facts and Feats by Stan Greenberg which will be published in May 1996 provides an informative and in-depth analysis of all Olympic Games celebrations (Summer and Winter) since the first in 1896. Listing all medal winners and records, the book will be an invaluable guide for the Games in Atlanta in 1996.

Olympic Swimming Records

Freestyle	Time	Name	Year
50 m	21.91	Aleksandr Popov (CIS)	1992
100 m	48.83	Matt Biondi (USA)	1988
200 m	1:46.70	Yevgeniy Sadovyi (CIS)	1992
400 m	3:45.00	Yevgeniy Sadovyi (CIS)	1992
1500 m	14:43.48	Kieren Perkins (Australia)	1992
4×100 m	3:16.53	USA	1988
4×200 m	7:11.95	CIS	1992

Breaststroke			
100 m	1:01.50	Nelson Diebel (USA)	1992
200 m	2:10.16	Mike Barrowman (USA)	1992

Backstroke			
100 m	53.86	Jeff Rouse (USA)	1992
200 m	1:58.47	Martin López-Zubero (Spain)	1992

Butterfly			
100 m	53.00	Anthony Nesty (Surinam)	1988
200 m	1:56.26	Melvin Stewart (USA)	1992

Medley			
200 m	2:00.17	Támas Darnyi (Hungary)	1988
400 m	4:14.23	Támas Darnyi (Hungary)	1992
4×100 m	3:36.93	USA	1992

Women Freestyle			
50 m	24.79	Yang Wenyi (China)	1992
100 m	54.64	Zhuang Yong (China)	1992
200 m	1:57.65	Heike Friedrich (USA)	1988
400 m	4:03.85	Janet Evans (USA)	1988
800 m	8:20.20	Janet Evans (USA)	1988
4×100 m	3:39.46	USA	1992

Breaststroke			
100 m	1:07.95	Tania Dangalakova (Bulgaria)	1988
200 m	2:26.65	Kyoko Iwasaki (Japan)	1992

Backstroke			
100 m	1:00.68	Krisztina Egerszegi (Hungary)	1992
200 m	2:07.06	Krisztina Egerszegi (Hungary)	1992

Butterfly			
100 m	58.62	Qian Hong (China)	1992
200 m	2:06.90	Mary T. Meagher (USA)	1984

Medley			
200 m	2:11.65	Li Lin (China)	1992
400 m	4:36.29	Petra Schneider (GDR)	1980
4×100 m	4:02.54	USA	1992

Earth and Space

Highest-priced diamond (p. 23) $16,548,750 (£10,507,143) for a 100.10 carat pear-shaped 'D' Flawless diamond. It was sold at Sotheby's, Geneva, Switzerland on 17 May 1995, and was purchased by Sheikh Ahmed Fitaihi, who obtained it for his chain of jewellery shops in Saudi Arabia.

Animal Kingdom

Guide dogs (p. 31) Donna, the hearing guide dog with a record 18 years of active service behind her, died of a heart attack on 6 May 1995 aged 20 yr 2 months.

Snail racing (p. 43) A snail named Archie, owned by 6-year-old Carl Bramham of Pott Row, Norfolk, reportedly beat the world record in July 1995, covering the 13-inch course in 2 minutes.

Rarest bird (p. 43) It was reported in July 1995 that a female Spix's macaw, released in the Brazilian forest in March, has finally become friendly with the lone male Spix's macaw who has been unable to find a mate until now. The female specimen was identified through genetic screening as the most suitable of the 30 birds in private collections, thus minimizing the chances of inbreeding.

Largest undivided leaf (p. 49) A specimen of the water lily *Victoria amazonica* (Longwood hybrid) growing in the Princess of Wales Conservatory of the Royal Botanical Gardens, Kew, Surrey, measured 2.6m *8ft 6½in* in July 1995.

Tree planting (p. 51) The most trees planted by no more than 300 volunteers is 2589, when 218 pupils from Peel Hall Primary School and Joseph Eastham High planted the saplings at New Madamswood, Little Hulton, Greater Manchester on 14 Mar 1995.

Largest recorded tree fungus (p. 52) In 1995, the bracket fungus *Rigidoporus ulmarius* in the grounds of the International Mycological Institute at Kew, Surrey, measured 163 × 140cm *64 × 55in* with a circumference of 480cm *189in*. In 1992 it was growing at a rate of 22.5cm *9in* per year but this has now slowed to around 3.5cm *1.3in* per year.

Human Being

Memorizing pi (p. 62) Hiroyuki Goto, 21, of Tokyo, Japan recited pi to 42,195 places at the NHK Broadcasting Centre, Tokyo on 18 Feb 1995.

Science and Technology

Coal shovelling (p. 77) The record for filling a ½ ton *508kg* hopper with coal is 26.59 sec, by Wayne Miller of Fingal, Tasmania, Australia at Wonthaggi, Victoria, Australia on 17 Apr 1995.

Longest and shortest manned spaceflight (p. 84) The longest flight by a US spaceperson was one of 115 days 8 hr 44 min by Norman Thagard, who was launched to the *Mir* space station aboard *Soyuz TM21* on 14 Mar 1995 and landed aboard the US space shuttle STS 71 *Atlantis* on 7 Jul 1995. As a result he became the most experienced US space traveller.

Buildings and Structures

Brick carrying (p. 87) The greatest distance achieved for carrying a brick weighing 9lb *4.08kg* in a nominated ungloved hand in an uncradled downward pincher grip is 114.30 km *71.03 miles*, by Ashrita Furman of Jamaica, New York, USA on 3–4 Jun 1995.

Tallest lego tower (p. 90) A Lego tower measuring 22.41m *73 ft 6 in* high was built in Madrid, Spain on 7–10 Oct 1994.

■ The Troll platform, the tallest concrete structure ever to be moved across the earth, is towed to its place in Europe's largest offshore gas field, Troll, in the North Sea. It measures 472 m *1548 ft* from the top of the flare boom to the bottom of the skirts. The skirts of the concrete gravity base were pressed 36 m *118 ft* into the seabed to provide a sturdy foundation for a long life in rough weather. The tow took place in June 1995.

Stop Press

■ Water lilies growing at the Royal Botanical Gardens, Kew, where the UK's largest undivided leaf was grown this year. (Photo: Royal Botanic Gardens, Kew)

Restaurateurs (p. 93) The world's largest restaurant company is PepsiCo of Purchase, New York, USA—operator of Pizza Hut, Taco Bell and KFC—with 27,000 outlets around the world. Assets in 1994 were $24,792 million, with profits for that year of $1,752 million and with employees numbering 471,000 worldwide (⇨Human Achievements, Soft drinks)

Advertising signs (p. 100) The largest advertisement on a building measured 4402 m² *47,385 ft²* and was erected to promote the international airline Gulf Air. It was located by the M4 motorway, near Chiswick, London, and was displayed during May and June 1995.

Bonfire (p. 100) The photograph was taken by Richard Graham.

Snow and ice constructions—Snowman (p. 103) The tallest was 29.43 m *96 ft 7 in* high and was made by a team of local residents at Ohkura Village, Yamagata, Japan. It took 10 days and nights to build the snowman, which was completed on 10 Mar 1995.

Transport

Land speed (p. 117) The highest speed achieved in Britain is 446.69 km/h *277.56 mph* by Liv Berstad (Norway) at Santa Pod Raceway, Beds on 31 May 1993.

Highest mileage (p. 117) As of 10 Jul 1995 Albert Klein's VW Beetle has travelled 1,579,040 miles *2,541,218 km*.

Oldest driver (p. 118) It was reported that Edward Newsom of Brighton, E Sussex was still driving on 22 Jul 1995, his 104th birthday. Since he bought his first car in 1914, a Ford Model T, he has never made an insurance claim.

Model cars (p. 120) Under BSCRA rules, the greatest distance achieved in 24 hours by a 1:64 scale car is 320.029 km *198.857 miles* set by a team of four at the Rolls Royce Sports Hall, Derby on 1–2 Oct 1994.

Plane pulling (p. 126) A team of 60 people pulled a British Airways Boeing 747 weighing 205 tonnes a distance of 100 metres in 61.0 sec at Heathrow airport, near London on 25 May 1995.

Round the world—antipodal points (p. 127) David Sole, the former Scottish rugby union captain, travelled round the world on scheduled flights, taking in exact antipodal points, in a time of 64 hr 2 min from 2–5 May 1995. Leaving from London he flew to Madrid, Spain and then to Napier in New Zealand via Heathrow again, Singapore and Auckland. From Napier he went by helicopter to Ti Tree Point, on Highway 52 (the point exactly opposite Madrid airport on the other side of the world). Returning via Los Angeles his journey took him a total distance of 41,709 km *25,917 miles*.

Largest paper aircraft (p. 132) The largest flying paper aeroplane, with a wing span of 13.97 m *45 ft 10 in*, was constructed by a team of students from the Faculty of Aerospace Engineering at Delft University of Technology, Netherlands and flown on 16 May 1995. It was launched indoors and flew a distance of 34.80 m *114 ft 2 in*.

Parachuting records (p. 132) Total sport parachuting descents, Woman: Cheryl Stearns (USA), 10,100, mainly over the USA, up to 2 Aug 1995.

24-hour total, Man: Jay Stokes (USA), 331 (in accordance with United States Parachute Association rules), Raeford, North Carolina, USA, 30–31 May 1995.

Arts and Entertainment

Largest painting (p. 133) A painting of Elvis Presley measuring 7127.8 m² *76,726 ft²* was completed by students of Savannah College of Art and Design and members of the local community on Tybee Island, Georgia, USA on 8 Apr 1995.

Highest prices table (p. 134) The highest price achieved for a 20th-Century painting is FF 315 m (£33.123 m), paid for Picasso's *Les Noces de Pierette*. It was sold by Binoche et Godeau, Paris on 30 Nov 1989.

Largest mural (p. 134) The Pueblo Levee Project in Colorado, USA has produced the largest mural in the world, at 16,554.8 m² *178,200 ft²*.

Who's Who (p. 140) The longest entry in the book's current wider format, that of Dame Barbara Cartland, was allocated 223 lines in the 1996 edition.

Longest kept diary in the UK (p. 141) Lady Dorothy Longley of Crawley, Sussex, has written an entry in her diary every day since 1 Jan 1917—apart from one missing entry in July 1917 and a break between 19 Oct 1919 and 26 Dec 1919, when she vainly attempted to give up the habit—a total of 78½ years. She started the diary in 1916 at the age of twelve, but did not write every day for the first year.

Oldest author (p. 142) Sarah Louise Delany's second book, *The Delany Sisters' Book of Everyday Wisdom*, was published by Kodansha America in October 1994, when she was 105 years old. Her sister and co-author, A. Elizabeth Delany, was 103.

Highest printings (p. 143) The highest order for an initial print-run of a work of fiction is 2.8 million, ordered by US publisher Doubleday for John Grisham's sixth novel, *The Rainmaker*. Grisham's novels are reported to have sold 55 million copies to date, and worldwide box-office takings for three films made from his books (*The Firm, The Pelican Brief, The Client*) have reached $572 million.

Most syndicated cartoon strip (p. 143) 'Garfield' by Jim Davis currently appears in 2547 newspapers in 83 countries and 26 languages. It was first published on 19 Jun 1978.

Fastest drumming (p. 146) Rory Blackwell of Starcross, Devon played 400 separate drums in 16.2 seconds at Finlake Leisure Park, near Chudleigh, Devon on 29 May 1995.

Oldest opera singer (p. 148) The Ukrainian bass Mark Reizen (b. 3 Jul 1895) sang the substantial role of Prince Gremin in Tchaikovsky's *Eugene Onegin* at the Bolshoi Theatre in Moscow on his 90th birthday.

'Mastermind' records (p. 153) Civil servant Kevin Ashman scored a record 41 points in his heat of 'Mastermind', transmitted on 21 May 1995. He went on to win the 1995 title.

Dancing dragon (p. 158) The longest dancing dragon measured 1691.64 m *5550 ft 0 in* from the end of its nose to the tip of its tail. A total of 610 people brought the dragon to life on 19 May 1995, making it dance for more than 5 minutes at Tiantan (Temple of Heaven), Beijing, China.

Skipping (p. 160) Walfer Guerrero (Colombia) achieved 521 consecutive turns skipping on a tightrope at Circus Carré in Haarlem, Netherlands on 1 Jun 1995.

Business World

Highest office rents feature (p. 163) Equivalent figures from *Richard Ellis* dated June 1995 show that Bombay now has the highest rental levels, with a net rent in £ per square foot per annum of £107.26. Inner Central Tokyo takes second place.

Highest salary (p. 166) Thomas Lee earned at least $170 million in 1994, according to *Financial World*'s list of the highest-paid individuals on Wall Street.

Human World

United Kingdom Electoral Records—Most elections contested (p. 185) Screaming Lord Sutch of the Official Monster Raving Loony Party has contested 37 general elections or by-elections since 1963, losing his deposit on each occasion.

Greatest damages—Sexual harassment (p. 187) The record award in a sexual harassment case was $50 million (£32 million) to Peggy Kimzey, a former employee of Wal-Mart, the largest retail chain in the United States. She had worked at the branch in Warsaw, Missouri. The award of punitive damages was made by a jury at Jefferson City, Missouri on 28 Jun 1995. The jury also awarded her $35,000 (£22,000) for humiliation and mental anguish and $1 (63p) in lost wages. Wal-Mart said it would appeal.

Human Achievements

Most travelled—Around the World Together (p. 202) Dr Robert and Carmen Becker have visited all 192 sovereign countries and all but nine of the 65 non-sovereign or other territories.

Deep-diving records (p. 203) The record depth for the *ill-advised* and dangerous activity of breath-held diving is 127 m *417 ft* by Francisco 'Pipin' Ferreras (Cuba) off Key Largo, Florida, USA on 17 Dec 1994. He was under water for 2 min 22 sec.

Party-giving (p. 205) The largest teddy bears' picnic ever staged was attended by 33,573 bears together with their owners at Dublin Zoo, Republic of Ireland on 24 Jun 1995.

Brick lifting (p. 206) The greatest weight of bricks lifted was by Fred Burton of Cheadle, Staffs, who held 20 bricks weighing a total of 91.17 kg *201 lb 0 oz* for more than three seconds on 22 Jul 1995.

Bubble (p. 206) Alan McKay of Wellington, New Zealand created a bubble 17.2 m *56 ft 5 in* long on 25 Jul 1995. He made it using a bubble wand, washing-up liquid, glycerine and water.

Footbag (p. 207) The greatest number of kicks in five minutes is 956 by Andy Linder (USA) at Malta, Illinois, USA on 5 May 1995.

Spear throwing (p. 210) The record distance achieved throwing a spear (using an atlatl or hand-held device which fits onto it) is 258.63m *848ft 6½in* by David Engvall at Aurora, Colorado, USA on 15 Jul 1995.

Step-ups (p. 210) Fred Burton of Cheadle, Staffs completed 2469 step-ups in an hour on 8 Jul 1995 using a 38.1cm *15in* high exercise bench.

Window cleaning (p. 210) Lee Kelly of Weston-super-Mare, Avon cleaned three standard 1079 × 1194mm *42½ × 47in* office windows with a 300mm *11¾in* long squeegee and 9litres *2gal* of water in 8.4 seconds at Coney Beach Leisure, Porthcawl, Mid Glam on 1 Jul 1995.

Biscuit (p. 212) The largest biscuit ever made was an oatmeal chocolate chip cookie with an area of 185.8 m² *2000 ft²*, measuring 15.24 × 12.19 m *50 × 40ft*, made at Peterborough, Ontario, Canada on 20 May 1995. It was decorated with Italian buttercream icing and covered with chocolate chips and toasted coconut.

Can pyramid (p. 215) Ten science students at University College Dublin built a pyramid of 5525 empty cans in 30 minutes at Belfield on 14 Feb 1995.

Fan (p. 216) A hand-painted fan made of chinz and wood measuring 8 m *26ft 3in* when unfolded and 4.5m *14ft 8in* high was made by Victor Troyas Oses of Peralta, Spain in October 1994.

Beer label collection (p. 218) Jan Solberg of Oslo, Norway has amassed 424,868 different beer labels from around the world to June 1995.

Button collection Students and teacher Ellen Dambach of Rolling Hills Primary School, Vernon, New Jersey, USA, collected 1,000,000 clothing buttons between January and June 1995.

Cigarette card collection (p. 218) Edward Wharton-Tigar, owner of the world's largest cigarette card collection, died on 14 Jun 1995 aged 82. The collection has been bequeathed to the British Museum.

Credit card collection (p. 218) Walter Cavanagh's collection has now reached 1394, worth an aggregate total of more than $1.65 million in credit. His wallet now weighs 17.49kg *38lb 8oz*.

Sports and Games

Archery (p. 223) FITA Round (men) 50m 348 Han Seuong-hoon (South Korea) 1994. (Women) 60m 349 He Ying (China) 1995.

Athletics (p. 224) World records (Men) 1500 m 3:27.37 Noureddine Morceli (Algeria) at Nice, France on 12 Jul 1995.

■ Miguel Induráin dominated the Tour de France in July 1995 winning for a record fifth time.
(Photo: Allsport)

2000m 4:47.88 Noureddine Morceli (Algeria) at Paris, France on 3 Jul 1995.

Long jump 8.96m *29ft 4¾in* Iván Pedroso (Cuba) (b. 17 Dec 1972) at Sestriere, Italy on 29 Jul 1995.

Triple jump 18.29m *60ft ¼in* Jonathan Edwards (GB) at Gothenburg, Sweden on 7 Aug 1995.

(p. 225) World Records (Women) 5000m 14:36.45 Fernanda Ribeiro (Portugal) (b. 23 Jun 1969) at Hechtel, Belgium on 22 Jul 1995.

Pole vault 4.17m *13ft 8in* Daniela Bártová (Czech Republic) at Gisingen, Austria on 15 Jul 1995.

(p. 227) British records (men) Pole vault 5.70m *18ft 8¼in* Nick Buckfield at Sheffield, S Yorks on 23 Jul 1995.

Judy Oakes won a 35th national title when she won the AAA shot title in July 1995.

(p. 228) British records (women)

1000 m 2:32.82 Kelly Holmes (b. 4 Apr 1970) at Sheffield, S Yorks on 23 Jul 1995.

Pole vault 3.80 m *12 ft 5½ in* Kate Staples at Gateshead, Tyne & Wear on 2 Jul 1995.

Husband and wife, Richard and Sandra Brown (GB), set records for the fastest time to run between Land's End and John O' Groats in May 1995. They both set off from Land's End on 5 May and Richard completed the trip on 15 May with a time of 10 days 2 hr 25 min. Sandra arrived at John O' Groats three days later, 18 May, setting a new best of 13 days 10 hr 1 min.

Ann Sayer (GB), holder of the Land's End to John O' Groats walking record, became Britain's oldest women international when she competed in the 200km International Walk at Bazencourt, France on 2–3 Apr 1994, aged 57 years 169 days.

(p. 229) As of 1 Jul 1995, Norm Frank had completed 565 marathons.

Domino stacking (p. 235) Aleksandr Bendikov of Mogilev, Belarus successfully stacked 522 dominoes on a single supporting domino on 21 Sep 1994.

Cricket (p. 241) Dickie Bird stood in his 63rd Test in July 1995.

■ Jonathan Edwards has taken the records for triple jump to a new level during the 1995 season. Having set a wind-assisted leap of 18.43m *60ft 5½in* in July, he became the first person to officially jump over 60ft when he won the world title.
(Photo: Allsport)

(p. 245) Lancashire won a record-equalling third Benson and Hedges Cup on 15 Jul 1995, having previously won in 1984 and 1990.

Cycling (p. 248) Miguel Induráin won the Tour de France for a record-equalling fifth time in 1995, having previously won 1991–94.

Yvonne McGregor (GB) (b. 9 Apr 1961) cycled 47.411km *29.459miles* in one hour at Manchester on 17 Jun 1995.

Darts (p. 250) Steve Draper (GB) achieved a 'double-on, double-off' 501 at the Ex-Serviceman's Club, Wellingborough, Northants on 10 Nov 1994. His scores were: double 20, six treble 20s, treble 17 and bull.

Gambling (p. 257) A.W.E Summons won a First Dividend, his 833rd, for matches played on 27 May 1995.

Golf (p. 258) On 16 Jul at Edinburgh, a feathery golf ball was sold for £19,995 to Jaime Ortiz Patino (Spain) from the Valderrama course in Spain, venue for the 1997 Ryder Cup.

(p. 259) Laura Davies set European Tour scoring records when she won the 1995 Guardian Irish Holidays Open at St Margaret's GC, Dublin on 27–30 July. Her total of 267 (67, 66, 66, 68) was 25-under-par and she won by 16 strokes, all records.

Sean Murphy of Vancouver, Canada drove 2146 balls over 100yd and into a target area at Swifts Practice Range, Carlisle, Cumbria on 30 Jun 1995.

Motor Cycling (p. 273) In July, Rolf Biland won his 76th and 77th side-car Grand Prix races, winning the French and British races.

Motor Racing (p. 273) Juan-Manuel Fangio died on 17 Jul 1995.

(p. 275) The lowest elapsed time for a piston-engined dragster is 4.445sec by Larry Dixon (USA) at Englishtown, New Jersey on 19 May 1995.

Abseiling (or Rappelling) (p. 276) The greatest distance abseiled by ten people in an eight-hour period is 108.92 km *67.68 miles*, by a team from 10th (Volunteer) Batallion, The Parachute Regiment. They achieved the record by abseiling 1427 times down the side of Barclays Bank in Fenchurch Street, London on 6 May 1995.

Netball (p. 276) Australia won their seventh world title on 29 Jul 1995. During the championships, Irene van Dyk (South Africa) scored a record 543 goals and Kendra Slawinski made her 122nd appearance for England.

Flying disc throwing (p. 278) The World Flying Disc Federation distance records are: (men) 200.01 m *656ft 2in*, by Scott Stokely (US) on 14 May 1995 at Fort Collins, Colorado, USA; (women) 136.31m *447ft 3in*, by Anni Kreml (US) on 21 Aug 1994, also at Fort Collins, Colorado, USA.

Rugby Union (p. 284/285) Sean Fitzpatrick made his 70th international appearance for New Zealand on 29 Jul 1995. In the same match David Campese made his 92nd appearance for Australia.

Water Skiing (p. 299) Philippa Roberts won the British overall title for the 12th time in July 1995.

Weightlifting (p. 302) A team of ten deadlifted 2,747,520 kg *6,057,237 lb* in 24 hours at HMP Belmarsh, Thamesmead, Greater London on 25–26 Jun 1995.

Dear Guinness book of Records.

We received around 10,000 record claims and suggestions from all over the world in 1994. Of those, only about 30 of them made there way into the book as completely new categories. That's a considerable proportion of negatives. Our reasons for turning them down vary: sometimes the achievement is just too specialised; sometimes we are simply strapped for space. In any case, many more of the letters we receive deserve recognition, and so, for the second year running, we are giving you a small taste of the record-breakers and would-be record-breakers that didn't quite make it into the main listings of the book.

■ Schoolchildren from Gettysburg Elementary School in Clovis, California, USA really stretched themselves making the world's longest rubber band; after tying thousands of bands together, they painstakingly measured it with the help of their teacher, Mr Jeff Ogas. The result was a rubber band over 30.5 km *19 miles* long.

■ We tend to be rather averse to firsts, preferring those records that are *beatable*. This one we couldn't resist. Mel Lastman, mayor of the town of North York in Ontario, Canada, was so determined to surmount any sales challenge put to him that he set out to become the first person to have sold a refrigerator to an Inuit. He did it in March 1965 as part of a publicity stunt for his burgeoning appliance business, Bad Boy Appliances and Furniture Limited.

■ Harrod Blank, a film-maker and car-artist from El Cerrito, California, USA, made a 'Camera Van' by covering a van with 1705 cameras. Of these, 10 actually function and take pictures and 40 can flash simultaneously; the look of amazement on people's faces as they set eyes on the creation for the first time makes for some excellent snaps. It took Mr Blank one year and $10,000 to make.

■ A giant tape-measure 40 m *131 ft* long was made by IMAX and displayed at the V & A Waterfront in Cape Town, South Africa on 11 Dec 1994.

■ This bandy stick, 10.6 m *34 ft 9 in* long and weighing 360 kg *793 lb*, was made by students and teacher Kent Eriksson (all pictured) of the Wood Technology Programme at *Ovanaker Sweden* college in Trov, Sweden, between Autumn 1993 and Spring 1994.

VÄXJÖ
11/11-1994
HELLO GUINNESS BOOK OF RECORDS
IF YOU DON'T PUBLISH THIS LETTER IN THE BOOK OF RECORDS FOR THE
SILLIEST BLACKMAIL LETTER I'AM GOING TELL MUM.
BYE BYE IN THE MUSHROOM WOOD FROM
JOHAN RAGNARSSON

■ Mary Jane Sorgel of Mequon, Wisconsin, USA can twirl a baton, cheerleader-style, whilst her dog Muffy sits unaided on her head. In 1994 she performed the balancing act on a 747 jet aeroplane at an altitude of 7620 m *25,000 ft*, all on live TV.

■ Although we receive queries about fruit displays from time to time, we'd never received an apple-chain claim before. This one took place in Litoměřice, Czech Republic, and included 2986 apples, all from different trees and grown by different individuals. It was created as part of a local tradefair and each one was an entrant in the 'Apple of the Year' award.

The Six Golden Rules of Record-Breaking

1. Choose to beat a record that is in the current edition.

2. Remember that if the record you want to try and beat is not in the book, your chances of it being introduced are slim. You might improve those chances by ensuring that your record activity is a measurable one with plenty of popular appeal.

3. Check with us around *two months* before you proceed. The record you have in mind could easily have changed since publication.

4. Follow the general or specific guidelines that we can provide for your record attempt.

5. Produce documentation at all stages. It is not possible to sent out invigilators, so we need all the proof you can gather.

6. Please be patient. Regrettably, it can take four to six weeks for us to get back to you, longer if it requires further research on our part.

Write to us at: Guinness Publishing, 33 London Road, Enfield, Middlesex, EN2 6DJ, England.

■ Eleanor and Daniel Campanaro of Bangor, Pennsylvania, USA wrote to us after pressure from their friends, who thought that their particular perennial tradition deserved recognition. Eleanor and Daniel have their photograph taken in their wedding clothes every year on their anniversary. This picture was taken on their latest — their 44th.

Index

Note: References to superlatives (e.g. largest, heaviest etc) are not included as they apply to almost all entries.

A

A levels 198
abbreviations 138
abseiling* 276
absorbency 69
accidents 178, 179, 180, 220
accountants 162
acids 68
acoustics 69
acronyms 138–9
actors 152, 153, 155, 157
adders 37
addresses 169
advances: literature 141; music 149; theatre 159
advertising* 99–100, 143, 153
aerial acts 160
aerobatics 220
aeroflora 52
aeroplanes* 33, 125–32, 179, 180
AGM attendance 167
agriculture 170–4
AIDS 64
air: forces 195; passengers 130; speed 125–8; tickets 127
aircraft* 33, 125–32, 179, 180
aircraft carriers 106
airlines 130
airports 128, 129
airships 131
albatrosses 33, 35
albums 148, 149–52
alcohol consumption 214
alcoholics 61
alder 51
alkalis 68
alligators 35, 46
allotments 164
alphabets 137
alpine skiing 286–8
amaryllis 47
amber 24
ambulances 119
American football 220–1
America's Cup 303
amphibians 37, 43
amphitheatres 157
amusement resorts 91–2
anaesthesia 66
anagrams 138
angling 221–2
animals 25–46, 170, 171–4, 179; circus 160
annual general meetings 167
annual prizes 193
Antarctic crossings 203
antelopes 27, 30
anthems 144
antiques 97, 136
antipodal points* 127
anti-submarine successes 196
antlers 30, 46
aphid 25
applause 148

apple: peeling 49; picking 49
apple pies 211
apples 48
aquaria 52
aqueducts 97
archery* 223
arches 19, 96, 102
archipelagos 14
Arctic crossings 203
armadillos 27
armed forces 195
armies 195
armour 106, 194, 210
army drill 195
arrests (criminal) 192
art 133–5, 136; galleries 134, 135; robbery 189
arteries 61
artists 133–5
ascendants 58
ash 51
aspidistras 47
assassinations 188
assets 162
Association football 253–6
asteroids 8–9
astronauts 83–4
astronomy 5–11
athletics* 223–30
Atlantic crossings 110, 111, 112, 125, 128, 130, 131
atlases 141
atolls 15
atom bombs 179, 196
auctions 134, 136, 154, 171, 215
audiences: cinema 157; circus 160; concerts 147; radio 152; television 153; theatre 159
authors* 141–2
autographs 141
autogyros 131
avalanches 20, 179, 180
avenues 51
aviation* 125–32, 179, 180
avocados 49
axes 215

B

babies 57–8
bacteria 52
badgers 28
badminton 230
Badminton 251
bail 187
balance of payments 164–5
balancing: bricks 206; cigar boxes 206; coins 168; glass 207; golf balls 261; milk bottles 208; milk crates 208; on one foot 64
ball: control 256; spinning 206
ballet 148
balloon: releases 205, 206; sculptures 206
ballooning 131–2
ballot papers 184
ballroom dancing 160
bamboo 46, 49, 50
banana splits 211
bands 146–7, 149–52
bank fraud 190
bank rates 165
bank robberies 189
banknote forgery 190
banknotes 167

bankruptcies 162
banks 162
banquets 205
banyan 50
bar billiards 234
barbecues 211–12
barges 108
barley 170
barometers 70
barometric pressure 23, 70
barrel: jumping 270; rolling 206
barrows: pushing 206; racing 206
bars (public) 94
baseball 231–2
basins 16–17
basketball 232–4; dribbling 234; spinning 234
baskets 215; hanging 49
bath tub racing 206
baton twirling 206
bats 27, 29
batteries 74
battery-powered vehicles 118
battles 194
battleships 106
bays 11
BBC: radio 152; television 152–3
beaches 91
beagling 252
beans 48
beards 62
bears 28, 160; teddy* 136, 205
bed: making 206; pushing 206; racing 206
beech 51
beer 214; cans 218; keg lifting 206; labels* 218; mat flipping 206; mats 218; stein carrying 206; tankards 206
bees 41
beetles 25, 40, 41
beetroot 48
beheadings 190–1
bell ringing 145
bells 145
bequests 31, 166
best man 205
best-sellers: books 142; records 149–52
betting 257
biathlon 272
Bible 142
biceps 62
bicycles* 113–14, 248–50
Big Ben 79, 145
big wheels 92
billiards 234
billionaires 165–6
bills (birds) 34
bingo 256
bins (litter) 217
biographies 142
biplanes 126, 128
birch 51
birds* 32–5, 43, 46; talking 32–3
birds of prey 32, 33, 34
bird-watching 34, 35
birth rates 177
birth weights: humans 57; livestock 172, 174
birthday parties 205
births 57–8
biscuits* 212
bishops 200
bites 25, 37

bivouacs 276
Black Death 64, 179, 180
blackbirds 33
black-outs 74
blankets 215
blasphemy 192
blast furnaces 75
blood 61
blooms 46–9
Blue Riband 111
blue tits 33
blue whales 25, 27
board games* 235–6
boardsailing 113, 305
boas 37, 43
Boat Race 279–80
boats 105–13
bobsledding 236
body temperature 62, 65
boiling to death 190
boiling/melting points 68
bombers 126
bombs 179, 180, 196
bones 44, 46, 61
bonfires* 100
bonsai 50
bonspiel 247
bookmakers 257
books 140–4
bookshops 143
boomerang throwing 278
borders 175–6
bores: drilling 77; rivers 17, 290; shooting 286
bottle caps 215, 218
bottles 70, 214, 218; collections 218; message in 111; orchestra 146
boules 277
boundaries 175–6
bowling (tenpin) 236–7
bowls 237
box office grosses 154, 155, 156
boxing 237–40
brains* 44, 62
brass instruments 146
brasses 200
bread 213
breakwaters 100
breeding 25, 28, 31, 32, 35, 38, 172, 173, 174
brewing 214
bricks: balancing 206; carrying* 87; laying 87; lifting* 206; throwing 278
bridegrooms 204
brides 204
bridge (contract) 241
bridge: building 97; sale 97
bridges 95–7
brightness: planets 8; stars 6–7
broadcasts 145, 152–3
broadsheets 141
Broadway 159
broccoli 48
brushes 134
bubble-gum blowing 206
bubbles* 206
bucket chain 206
Buddha 103, 193
budgerigars 32, 33
budgets 165
buffalo 30
building contractors 90
building societies 162
buildings: for leisure 52, 90–4, 134, 135, 143, 147, 148, 157, 160;

for living 85–9; for working 89–90
bull riding 279
bulls 171, 172
bunkers (golf) 258
burning 190
burpees 262
buses 119
busy lizzies 47
butterfat 173
butterflies 25, 41
by-elections* 185

C

cabbages 25, 48
cable cars 76, 77, 179, 288
cables 76; bridges 95; telephones 79
cacti 47
cagebirds 32, 33
caged pets 31, 32, 33
cakes 212
calderas 20
calves 172
cameras 153–4
camping out 86
canals 97–8
canal-tunnels 99
cannabis 32, 190
cannons 197
canoeing 108, 240
canonization 200
cans* 215, 218
canyons 19
capital punishment 190–1
capitals 176, 180, 181
captains 196
car: ferries 108, 109; parks 120; wrecking 120
caravans 119
cardiac arrests 64
cardiopulmonary resuscitation 65
cards: Christmas 141; cigarette* 218, 232; collections 218; credit* 218; games 241; greeting 141; holding 241; house of 88; memorizing 62; playing 62, 136; telephone 80; throwing 241
careers 155
cargo: movements 127; vessels 108
caricatures 135
carillons 145
carnivores 28
carpets 136
carriage driving 113, 251
carrots 48
cars 115–20
cartoons* 143
carvings 134–5
casinos 88
cassettes 149
casting (angling) 222
castles 85; sand 86
catalytic crackers 74
catapulting 206
cathedrals 199, 200
Catherine wheels 216
cats 28, 31, 32
cattle 171, 172, 173; station 170
caves 15
caviar 38
caving 15
CD-ROMs 140, 143
cedar 51
celery 48

cellars 171
'cellos 145, 146
cells 60
cemeteries 100
centenarians 58
centipedes 25; human 207
centrifuges 70
ceramics 136, 217
champagne: cork flight 214;
    fountains 214
chandeliers 215
Channel crossings:
    ferries 111; flying 125;
    hovercraft 110;
    parachuting 132;
    rowing 280; sailing 113;
    swimming 294; tunnel 99
Channel swimming 294
Channel tunnel 99
charity fund-raising
    149, 169
charts (music) 148, 149–52
checkers 235
cheese 173, 212
cheetahs 27
chelonians 35–6
chemical warfare 195
chemicals 68–9, 179
chemist shops 162
chemistry 68–9
chemists 162
cheques 215, 167–8
cherry pies 212
chess 235
chestnuts 50, 51
chests 62
chicken plucking 173
chickens 34, 173
children 57–8
chimneys 87, 100
chimpanzees 29
chips: computer 73;
    fish and 94
chocolate models 212
choirs 147
choristers 200
chorus lines 159
Christian names 139
Christmas: cards 141;
    crackers 215;
    puddings 211, 212;
    trees 50; white 23
chrysanthemums 47
church 199–200;
    personnel 200
cigar box balancing 206
cigarette: cards* 218, 232;
    lighters 218; packets 218
cigars 215
cinema 154–7
cinemas 157
circulation: banknotes 167;
    newspapers 144;
    periodicals 144
circumnavigation:
    aeroplanes 125, 127;
    cycling 248, 250;
    driving 118;
    pole to pole 125, 203;
    sailing 112, 303;
    walking 201;
    yachting 112, 303
circus* 160
cities 89, 176, 180–1
civilian gallantry 193
clams 27, 42
clapping 148, 206
claws 44
clay pigeon shooting 286
clergy 200
cliffs 19
climbing 32, 275–6

clocks 79, 145
clones 46
clouds 23
clovers 49
coaching 113
coal: carrying 206–7;
    cutting 77; mines 77;
    shovelling* 77
coastlines 176
cocaine 32, 189–90
cockatoos 33
cockroaches 41
cocktails 214
coconuts 49
coffee mornings 205
coins 167–9; balancing 168;
    collections 168;
    column of 168;
    line of 169; pile of 169;
    snatching 168
collections* 218;
    art 134, 135;
    banknotes 167; coins 168
collisions 106
colonies: animals 26;
    countries 175
columnists 143–4
columns 100, 102
coma 65
comedy 159
comets 9–10
comic strips* 143
commerce 161–4
commercials 143, 153
common cold 64
community gardens 170
companies 78, 161–4,
    166, 167
compensation 187
compilers 144
composers 147–8
composite numbers 72
computation 62, 73
computers 73; human 62
concerts 147
concrete 98
conductors: lightning 23;
    orchestral 147
confectionery 213
conga 160
conjunctions (planetary) 8
conkers 50
conscientious objectors
    195–6
conscripts 195
consonants 137
constants 73
constellations 7
construction projects 89
consultation fees 166
container ships 108
continents 12–14
contract bridge 241
contracts: literature 141;
    television 153
conveyor belts 75
cooling towers 100
copper 77
coppice 50
coral 27
corks 214
corn cobs 48
correspondence 141
corridors 103
coryza 64
cosmonauts 83–4
costs (legal) 188
costumes 155
cotton 170
counters (post office) 169
countries 175–7
country dancing 160

coups 184
courgette 48
cow pat tossing 278
cow sheds 170
cows 171, 172, 173
CPR 65
crabs 39
crackers: catalytic 74;
    Christmas 215
cranes: birds 33;
    machinery 75
crate climbing 207
craters: lunar 9;
    meteoric 11; volcanic 20
crawfish 39
crawlers 119
crawling 207
crayfish 39
credit cards* 218
crematoria 100
Cresta Run 236
cribbage 241
cricket* 241–6
crime 188–90;
    prevention 189
criminal organizations 188
crochet 174
crocodiles 35
crop producers 170
crops 170
croquet 247
cross-Channel: ferries 111;
    flying 125; hovercraft 110;
    parachuting 132;
    rowing 280; sailing 113;
    swimming 294; tunnel 99
cross-country: running 247;
    skiing 286–8
crosswords 144
crowds 147, 200, 220
Crufts 31
crustaceans 39
cucumbers 48, 49; slicing 49
curling 247
currents: electric 38, 69;
    ocean 12
curtain calls 148
cuts: canal 98; scientific 70
cycle speedway 250
cycles 113–14
cycleway 97
cycling* 248–50
cyclo-cross 250
cypress 50, 51
cysts 66

D

daffodils 47
dagobas 200
dahlias 47
daisy chains 47
damages (legal)* 187
dams 98, 179, 180
dancing 148, 158, 159–60
dancing dragon* 158–9
darts* 250
Davis Cup 297
death rates 177
death row 190
death sentences 190
death slides 209
debating 137
debt 164
decaplets 58
decathlon 224, 227
decorations 192–4
deep diving* 203–4
deer 27, 28, 30
defamation 187
defence 194–5

defence spending 195
degrees 193, 197
deltas 17
demolition 87
demonstrations 179
density: compounds 69;
    elements 68; planets 8;
    population 176–7;
    traffic 121
dentists 179
dentition 63
dentures 63
department stores 162
depressions 15
Derby (horse racing)
    264, 267
descendants 58
deserts 18
destroyers 106
dialects 137
dialysis 66
diamonds* 23–4, 136, 215,
    216, 217
diaries* 141
dictionaries 140
diesel engines 74, 117
dieting 56
dining out 205
dinosaurs 44–6
diplodocus 44
directors: company 161;
    film 155
directorships 161
disasters 178, 179, 180, 220
discus 224, 225, 227, 228
diseases 25, 64, 179, 180
dishes (radio) 80–1
Disney 91, 152, 157
disputes 164
distilling 214
diving: animals 27, 30,
    34, 36; endeavours* 203–4,
    207; sport 293;
    submarines 106
divisions 183, 184
divorce 177, 187, 205
divorce settlements 187
DJ challenge 149
DNA 45
docks 113
doctorates 197
doctors 178–9
dog shows 31
dog sleds 203, 289
dogs* 26, 30–2
dolphins 43
domes 100–1
domestication 30, 32–3
dominoes: stacking* 235;
    toppling 235
doors 101
double bass 146
doughnuts 212
Dow Jones 167
dowries 166
drag racing* 275
dragon boat races 280
dragon dancing* 158–9
dragonflies 41
dragsters* 275
draughts 235
drawings 134
dreams 65
dredgers 108
dressage 251
dresses 155–6, 215
drilling 77–9
drills (military) 195
drink 214–15
drivers 118, 119
drives (golf) 258
driving* 117–19

drought 22
drug: hauls 189–90;
    sniffing 32
drumming* 146
drums 146
dry docks 113
ducks 33, 174
ducks and drakes 210
ductility 68
dumper trucks 119
dunes 18
dwarfs 55–6

E

eagles 35
earnings: economics 165;
    entertainment 152,
    153, 155
earrings 136, 218
ears 32
Earth 11
earthmovers 75
earthquakes 20, 179, 180
earthworks 101
earthworms 42
Easter eggs 212–13
eating 65
eating out 205
echos 69
eclipses 9
economics 164–5
editors 141, 143
education 197–8
eels 38
egg: and spoon racing 207;
    dropping 173; laying 173;
    shelling 173; throwing 278
eggs 34, 35, 41, 174
elections* 183–6
electric: cars 117;
    currents 38, 69; eels 38
electricity 69, 73–4
electromagnets 70
elements 67–8
elephants 27, 28, 30
elevators 75–6, 179
elm 46
embassies 90
emeralds 24
emigration 177
employers 161
employment 164
employment agencies 164
encores 148
encyclopedias 140
endangered species* 42–3
endowments 135, 198
engagements 204
engineering 74–5
engines: car 116, 117;
    diesel 74, 117; jet 125;
    railway 122, 125;
    rocket 82, 117; steam 73,
    105, 110, 117, 122, 125
English language 136–9
equestrian sports 251
equities 161
escalators 75; riding 75
escapes: parachute 132;
    prison 192;
    underwater 204
escapology 207
Eskimo rolls 240
Esperanto 137
estate 87
estuaries 17
Eton fives 252
eucalyptus 50, 51
European Parliament 184
evacuations 194

Index

Everest 15, 131, 275
executioners 191
exhibition centres 90
expenditure 165, 195
explosions 10–11, 20, 87, 179, 180
extinct animals 44–6
extras: cricket 245; film 155
extra-terrestrial vehicles 84
eyes 26
eyesight 34, 63

F

FA Cup 254, 255
facsimiles 80
fairs 92
falcons 33
false teeth 63
families: graduates 197; lineage 139; medical 178–9; names 139; wealthy 166
family businesses 161
family trees 58
famine 179, 180
fangs 37
fans* 216
fares (taxi) 119
farms 170
fashion: models 159; shows 159
fax machines 80
feasts 194, 205
feathers 34
fees: consultation 166; lecture 166
feet 64
felines 28, 31, 32, 160
fences 101
fencing 251–2
ferrets 31
ferries: car 108, 109; rail 109
ferris wheels 92
festivals: attendance 147; music 147
fibre optics 80
fiction 140, 142, 143
field gun pull 197
field sports 252
fields: magnetic 70; oil 78
figure skating: ice 268–9; roller 279
filling stations 120
films 152, 154–7
fines 190
fingernails 64
fingerprints 190
fingers 64
fir 50, 51
fire engines 119
fire pumping 119
fireballs 11
fires* 100, 179, 180
fireworks 179, 216
fiscal surplus 165
fish 37–8, 43, 46
fish and chip shops 94
fisheries 221
fishing 221–2
fives 252
fjords 11
flagpoles 101
flags 216
flamenco 160
flames 69
flares 79
flat racing 263–7
flats 87

fleas 41
fleece 174
fleets 110
flexible pole 160
flies 41
flight shooting 223
floodlights 101
floods 22–3, 179, 180
flotations (Stock Exchange) 167
flow: lava 20; rivers 17
flowers 46–9
'flu 179, 180
fly fishing 222
flying trapeze 160
flying-boats 125
flying-disc throwing* 278
fog 23, 179, 180
food* 205, 211–13; companies 213
footbag* 206, 207
football: American 220–1; Association 253–6; Gaelic 256; rugby* 280–5
football pools* 256–7
football stadia 91
footprints 44
fords 121
foreign aid 164
foreign debt 164
forests 50–1
forgery 190
forging 75
fork-lift trucks 75
forts 86
fossils 45, 46
fountains 101; champagne 214
fowl 34, 35, 173–4
foxhunting 252
fraud 187, 190
free-falling 132
freestyle skiing 288
freeze 22
French knitting 207
frequency 69
freshwater: angling 221–2; crustaceans 39; fish 38; islands 14; lakes 18
friction 69
Frisbee* 278
frogs 37, 43; poisonous 25
frontiers 175–6
fruit 47, 48–9, 211, 212, 213
FT-SE 100 index 166–7
fuschia 47
fuel: consumption 118; range 118
fumigation 101
fund-raising 149, 169
funerals 200
fungi* 52
furnaces 75
furniture 136, 217
fusion power 74

G

g force 34, 41, 65
Gaelic football 256
galaxies 5
gall bladders 66
galleries 134, 135
gallstones 66
gambling* 256–7
game: reserves 52; shooting 252
gaol breaks 192
garages 120
garbage dumps 103
garlic 48

gas deposits 79
gas flare 78
gases 68
gasholders 101
gastropods 25–6, 42
gauges 123
GCSEs 198
geese 33, 173
gems* 23–4, 136
general elections 183–6
generators 74
genocide 179–80
George Cross 192
gerbils 31, 32
gestation: animals 28; literature 140
geysers 20–2
giants 54–5
gin 146–7, 214
gingivitis 64
gingko 51
glaciers 19
gladioli 47
glass 70, 104, 200; balancing 207; blowing 70
gliders 132
gliding 257–8
globes 101
GNP 164
goats 171, 173
go-karts 119
gold 24, 68, 77, 165, 200
goldcrest 35
golden: discs 149; handshakes 166; weddings 204–5
goldfish 37
goldmining 77, 179
golf* 258–61
golf ball: balancing 261; throwing 259
goods yards 124
gooseberries 48
gorges 18–19
gorillas 29
goods yards 124
government expenditure 165
gradients 122, 123
graduates 197
grain elevators 101
Grammy awards 149
Grand National 264, 267
grape catching 49
grapefruit 48
grapes 48, 49
grass 46
grass skiing 288
grasshopper 40
grave digging 100
gravel mounds 103
Great Barrier Reef 15, 27
great-grandparents 58
Greco-Roman wrestling 302–3
green beans 48
greens (golf) 258
greeting cards 141
greyhound racing 261
greyhounds 31, 261
gross national product 164
ground figures 135
groups (music) 146–7, 148, 149–52
growth 27
guide dogs* 31
guillotinings 190
guinea pigs 31, 32
guitars 146
gulfs 11
gum disease 64
gumboot throwing 278

guns 106, 197
gurning 207
gushers 78
gymnastics 262
gyroplanes 131

H

habitations 85
hadrons 67
haemodialysis 66
haggis 213; hurling 278
hail 23, 179
hair 62–3; splitting 62
halites 16
Halley's Comet 9
hamburgers 213
Hamlet's soliloquy 63
hammer 224, 225, 227, 228
hamsters 31
handball 262–3
handpumping (railcars) 124
hands 64
handshakes (golden) 166
handshaking 184
hang gliding 257–8
hangars 90, 128
hanging baskets 49
hangings 190–1
hangmen 190–1
harbours 111, 113
hardness 68
hares 32
harness racing 263
hashish 190
headmasters 198
heads of state 181–2, 184
hearing* 29, 31
hearings 186–7
heart attacks 64
hearts 64, 66
heat 69
heat-resistance 69
hedges 51; laying 51; mazes 102
height: animals 27, 33, 44; buildings 87, 88, 90, 92–3, 94–5; humans 54–6, 235, 239; mountains 15; plants 47, 48, 50, 51
helicopters 128, 130–1, 179, 180
heliports 128
hemlock 51
henges 102
hens 173
heptathlon 225, 226, 228
herbs 47
herds 28
hibernation 30
hiccoughing 65
high diving: endeavours 207; sport 293
high jump 224, 225, 226, 227, 228
high wire 160
higher education 197
hill figures 134–5
hitch-hiking 207
hoardings 100
hoards 168
hockey 263; ice 267–8; roller 279
hod carrying 207
holes 69, 77
holes in one 261
holly 51
hominids 53

hominoids 53
Homo erectus/sapiens 53
honorary degrees 193
honours 192–4
hop farms 170
hop-scotch 207
horns 30, 43
horror films 156
horse racing 263–7
horseback riding: circus 160; travel 201
horse-chestnuts 50–1
horses 27, 30, 160, 171; equestrian sports 251; racing 263–7
hospital stay 65
hospitals 178
hot-air balloons 131–2
hotels 88, 89, 179
house of cards 88
House of Lords 183, 184
houses 86–7, 148, 178
hovercraft 110
HPVs 106, 114, 130
human: cannonball 160; centipede 207; computer 62; fly 276; logos 207; power 106, 114, 130; pyramid 160; survival 65, 203
human beings* 53–66
human-powered vehicles 106, 114, 130
hummingbirds 33, 35
hunting 252
hurdling 224, 225, 226, 227, 228
hurling 267
hurricanes 179
hydrofoils 108
hymns 144
hyperacuity 63
hypothermia 62

I

ice 19; constructions 103
ice hockey 267–8
ice lollies 213
ice skating 268–70
ice yachting 285
icebergs 12
icebreakers 108, 109
ice-core drilling 77
ice-cream sundaes 213
illnesses 64, 179, 180
immigration 177
income tax 165
incomes 166
incubation 35
index 69
Indianapolis 500 274
industry 161–4
infant mortality 177
inflation: economics 165; lung power 65
inflorescence 47
influenza 179, 180
injections 65
inland seas 17
insects 25, 40–1
instability (political) 184
instruments: musical 145–6; scientific 70–2
insular mountains 15
insurance 162
interchanges 121
internal combustion 116
Internet 73

*DENOTES A FURTHER ENTRY IN STOP PRESS

invasions 194
invertebrates 42
iron 77
iron lungs 65
irrigation 97, 99
islands 14–15
isolation 84
isotopes 65, 67–8

J

jade 24
jaï alaï 277
jails 191, 192
javelin 224, 225, 227, 228
jelly 213
jellyfish 43
jet aces 196
jets 125–8
jetties 91, 101
jewels* 23–4, 136, 189, 215, 216, 217
jigsaw puzzles 216
jiu-jitsu 270
jockeys 265–6, 267
joggling 211
John o' Groats to Land's End: backwards running 230; battery-powered vehicle 118; cycling 248; flying 127; pedal car 119; penny-farthing 113; roller-skating 279; running* 228; unicycling 114; walking 230
joke cracking 207
judges 188
judiciary 186–92
judo 270
juggling 211
jumble sales 162
jumping: animals 30, 31, 37, 41; over barrels 270; pogo stick 208; ramp 115, 118; sports* 224, 225, 226, 227, 228, 251, 287
junks 110
Jupiter 7, 8

K

kangaroos 30
karate 270
karting 119
kebabs 213
kettle 216
kidnappings 189
kidneys 66
killings (mass) 179–80
kings 181, 182
kiss of life 65
kissing 208
kitchens 101
kites 208
kittens 31, 32
knights 194
knitting 174, 207, 208
knives 217
knot-tying 208
krill 39

L

labels: beer 218; matchbox 218
labology 218
labour 164
labour camps 192

labour disputes 164
lacrosse 270–1
lactation 173
ladder climbing 208
lagoons 18
lakes 17–18, 98–9
lambs 174
lamps 69–70
land 12, 15, 164, 170
land rowing 208
land speed* 117
landing fields 128
landings (aircraft) 106
landowners 164
Land's End to John o'Groats: backwards running 230; battery-powered vehicle 118; cycling 248; flying 127; pedal car 119; penny-farthing 113; roller-skating 279; running* 228; unicycling 114; walking 230
landslides 179, 180
language 136–9
larch 51
lark 35
larva 26
lasagne 213
lasers 70
lava 20
law 186–92; firms 188
lawn mowers 119
lawn tennis 295–8
lawyers 188
Le Mans 274
lead mining 77
leap-frogging 208
leases 188
leaves* 49, 50, 51
lecture fees 166
leeks 48
legacies 31, 166
legislation* 186–8
legislators 182
legislatures* 182–6
Lego* 90
legs 27
lemmings 28
lemons 48
lemur 29
lending rates 165
lenses 154
lepidoptera 25, 41
leptons 67
letters: alphabet 137; autographs 141; mail 141, 169; to editor 141
levees 98
libel 187
libraries 143
lice 41
licence plates 116
lichen 46
life: assurance 162; expectancy 177–8; saving 179, 193
lifeboat medals 193
lifting and pulling with teeth 63
lifts: passenger 75–6, 179; ski 179, 288
lighters (cigarette) 218
lighthouses 101–2
lightning 23, 179, 180
lights 69
light-years 5, 6, 7
lilies* 46, 49
limbo 160; on roller skates 160
lime 51
liners 106

lines of sight 16
linguists 137
lions 28; taming 160
liquid range 68
literature 140–4
literary lunches 142
litigation* 186–8
litter: bins 217; collecting 208
litters (animals) 28, 172, 173, 174
liver transplants 66
livestock 170, 171–4
lizards 35, 46
loads 75, 120, 122, 126, 127, 131
loaves 213
lobby 89
lobster 39
local government 186
lochs 11, 17, 18, 99
locks 97–8
locomotives 122, 125
locusts 26
log rolling 208
logos 207
lollipops 213
long jump* 224, 225, 226, 227, 228
longevity: humans 58–60; pets 32
long-range attacks 196
loops (aerial) 220
lorries 120
losses: film 155; financial 162, 167; theatre 159; weight 27, 56
lotteries 256
lugeing 236
lunar conquests 84
lungs 65
lupins 47

M

machinery 70
Mafia 188
magazines 144
magicians 208
magnetic fields 70
magnets 69, 70
magnitude of stars 6
mail 141, 169
maize 170
majorities 183, 184, 185
malaria 25
malls 91
mambas 37
mammals 27–32, 43, 46
Man 28, 53
man-eaters 179
mantle of bees 41
manufactured articles 215–18
manuscripts 141
maps 140–1
marathons* 229–30
marbles 271
marches 147, 196
marching bands 147
marquees 102
marriage 177, 204–5
marrows 48
Mars 8
marsupials 30
martial arts 270
martyrs 200
mass: arrests 192; killings 179–80; poisoning 189; suicide 179
Mastermind* 153
masts 94–5, 110

matchbox labels 218
matchstick models 217
mathematics 72–3
mathematicians 72, 73
mayoralties 186
mayors 186
maypoles 102
mazes 102
measures 73
meat pies 213
medals (decorations) 192–3
medical families 178–9
melons 48
melting/boiling points 68
members of parliament 183, 185–6
memory* 62
menhirs 102
mental health 179
menus 205
merchant shipping 110
mercury 68
Mercury 8
message in a bottle 111
meteorites 10–11
meteorological balloon inflation 65
meteorology 22–3
meteors 10–11
metros 99, 124, 180
metsequoia 51
mice 30, 31, 32
microbes 52
microlighting 271
microphones 70
microprocessors 73
microscopes 74
microwriting 208
migration: animals 26, 33, 41; people 177
mileage* 117, 120
milestones 122
military and defence 194–7
milk: bottle balancing 208; crate balancing 208; shakes 215; yields 172–3
milking 37, 172–3
millionaires 165–6
mills: water 74; wind 73–4
minarets 200
mince pies 213
mines 77–9, 179, 180
mining 77–9; accidents 179, 180
mints 168
mirages 18
mirrors 80
misers 166
misprints 143
moats 86
models: aircraft 132; boats 110; cars* 120; fashion 159; railways 124–5; soldiers 136
modern pentathlon 272
molluscs 26, 27, 42–3
monarchy 181–2
money 167–9
monkey puzzles 51
monkeys 25, 29
monoliths 13, 102, 103
monuments 102–3
Moon 9, 82, 84
moons 8
moose 30
Morse code 80
mortality 177
mortars 197
mosaics 135
mosques 200
mosquitoes 25
motherhood 57–8
moths 26–7, 41

motionlessness 64
moto-cross 273
motor racing* 274–5
motorcars* 115–20
motorcycle racing* 273–4
motorcycles 114–15
motorways 121; exits 121
mounds 103
mountaineering 179, 180, 275–6
mountains 9, 11, 15–16
mousing 32
moustaches 62–3
movies 152, 154–7
MPs 183, 185–6
mules 30
mummies 53
Munchausen's syndrome 66
murals* 134
murderers 187, 188–9, 190, 191–2
muscles 61–2
museums 134, 135, 143
mushrooms* 52, 170
music 144–52
musical: chairs 208; instruments 145–6; manuscripts 141; marches 147; scales 144; shows 159
musicians 144, 145, 146, 147–8, 149–52
mutiny 195

N

names: company 167; personal 139; place 139; pub 94; scientific 138; trade unions 164
narcotics 32, 189–90
national: anthems 144; debt 164; wealth 164
natural gas: deposits 79; pipelines 78; production 79
natural phenomena 20–2
naturist resorts 92
naval battles 194
navies 195
necklaces 136
necks 64
needle threading 208
needlework: crochet 174; knitting 174, 208; quilting 217
negatives 154
neon signs 100
nerve gases 68
nerves 60
nests 35
netball* 276
new towns 180
newspapers 141, 143–4
newts 37
nightclubs 93
Nobel prizes 193
noise 25, 63
nonuplets 58
noodles 208
nordic skiing 286–8
notes 144
novels 140, 142, 143
nuclear: accidents 179, 180; power stations 74; reactors 74, 179, 180; waste 179; weapons 196
nudist camps 92
numbers 71–2
numismatics 168–9
nuts (engineering) 74

O

O levels 198
oak 51
oats 170
obelisks 102, 103
observatories 81
ocean drilling 77
oceans 11, 203
octopuses 42
offices* 90, 162–3
oil: companies 78, 161, 167;
    fields 78, 162;
    pipelines 77, 78;
    platforms 78, 179, 180;
    production 78; refineries 78;
    spills 78, 162;
    tankers 78, 108, 162
Olympic Games 306–8
omelettes 213
one-man bands 147
onions 48
opals 24
opera* 148
opera houses 148
operations 66
opossums 28
optical: fibres 80; prisms 70
optics 63
orchestras 146–7
orchids 47, 50
Order of Merit 193
orders 192
ore/oil carriers 108
organs: human 62, 64, 66;
    musical 145–6
orienteering 276
origins of Man 53
Oscars 157
ostriches 32, 33, 34
overdue books 143
oysters 42
ozone 22

P

Pacific crossings 111, 112,
    125, 131
pacing 263
paddle boats 105
paella 213
pagodas 200
paint brushes 134
painter 133
painting* 133–5
palaces 86
palindromes 138
palms 49
pancakes 213; tossing 213
pandemic 64, 179, 180
panic 179, 180
papacy 200
paper: aircraft* 132;
    chains 208; money 167;
    news 141, 143–4
parachuting* 132
paragliding 277
parasites 25, 41, 46, 50
parish: priests 200;
    registers 200
parking meters 120
parks 52
parliamentary divisions
    183, 184
parliaments 182–6
parrots 32
parsnips 48
particle accelerators 70, 71
particles 67, 68

parties: political 183–6;
    social* 205
party giving* 205
pass the parcel 208
passenger ships 106–8
pastry 213
patents 186, 187
patients 66
patrols 106
payouts 162, 256–7
peacocks 205
peals 145
pearls 24
pedal cars 119
pedal-boating 208
pedigree 139
peerage 193
peers 184, 193
pelicans 34
pelota vasca 277
pendulums 79
penguins 33
peninsulas 14
penknives 217
penny-farthings 113
pens 216, 217
pensions 164
pentathlon 226, 272
perfect numbers 72–3
periodicals 144
permafrost 19
personal wealth 165–6
petals 47
pétanque 277
petitions 182
petrol: consumption 118;
    filling stations 120
pets 30–3, 37
petunias 47
philately 169
philodendrons 47
phone-ins 152
phonographic
    identification 149
photographs 153, 154
photography 153–4
physical extremes 69–71
physicians 178–9
physics 69–71
pi* 62, 73
pianists 145, 147
pianos 145
picnics (teddy bears)* 205
piers 91–2, 101
pies 211, 212, 213
pigeons: clay shooting 286;
    racing 277
piggery 171
piggy banks 168
piglets 173
pigs 171, 173
pika 28
pillar boxes 169
pills 65
pilots 130
pine 50, 51
pineapples 48
pinnacles 14–15
pinnipeds 29–30
pipelines 77, 78
piranhas 38, 39
pistols (shooting) 286
piston-engines 117, 128
pizzas 213
place-names 139
plague 64, 179, 180
plane pulling* 126
planes: aircraft* 125–32;
    trees 50, 51
planetaria 81
planets 7–8
plants 46–52

plateaux 16
plates: juggling 211;
    spinning 160
platforms: oil 78, 179, 180;
    railway 124
platinum 24, 77
playing cards: antique 136;
    games 241; holding 241;
    memorizing 62;
    throwing 241
pleasure beaches 91
pleasure piers 91–2
plucking: chicken 173;
    turkey 173
Pluto 7
Poet Laureate 142
poetry 142
pogo stick jumping 208
poisons 68, 189; animals 25,
    38, 40, 43; fungi 52
polar bears 28, 160
polar conquests 202–3
polders 99
pole sitting 87
pole to pole
    circumnavigation 125, 203
pole vault* 224, 225, 226,
    227, 228
policies (insurance) 162
political divisions 175,
    183, 184
political office
    holders 184–6
politics 182–6
polo 277; water 299
polydactylism 64
ponies 30, 171
pool 277
pools: football* 256–7;
    swimming 291
pop: festivals 147;
    groups 147, 148, 149–52;
    music 147, 148, 149–52
popcorn 212
Popes 52, 200
poplars 51
poppies 46
populations 175–7, 180–1;
    prison 192
porcupines 30
porifera 26, 43
porpoises 28
ports 111, 113
post 141, 169
post offices 169
postage stamps 169
postal: addresses 169;
    services 169
posters 134
post-nominal: letters 193;
    numbers 181
potatoes 48; peeling 49
pottery 217
poultry 173–4
power 70, 73–4, 75;
    failure 74; lines 74;
    plants 74; stations 74
powerboat racing 277–8
powerlifting* 301–2
pram pushing 208–10, 230
precious stones* 23–4, 136
predators 25, 46
pregnancy 57–8
prehistoric animals 44–6
presidents 181, 182
press (forging) 75
press-ups 262
pressure 69;
    barometric 23, 70
priests 200
primates 29, 46, 53

Prime Ministers 183,
    184, 185
prime numbers 72
printers (literature) 142
printing* 142–3
prints 133, 134
prism 70
prison sentences 191–2
prisons 191–2
prizes: annual 193;
    mathematics 72; media 149,
    152, 157; Nobel 193
professors 197
profits 162
programmes: radio 152;
    television 153
projectiles 278
promenades 103
proofs 73
propellers 106, 126, 128
property 85–90, 162–4
props 155
protozoa 52
pseudonyms 141
psychiatrists 179
psychologists 179
public houses 94
publications 140–4
publishers 142
pubs 94
pulsars 7
pumpkins 48, 49
puppies 31
push-ups 262
puzzles: crossword 144;
    jigsaw 216;
    mathematical 73;
    monkey 51
pyramids: bottle caps 215;
    can* 215; human 160;
    motorcycle 115;
    structures 103
pythons 36

Q

quadruplets 57, 58, 60
quanta 67
quarks 67
quarries 77
quasars 6
queens 181, 182
quilts 217
quindecaplets 58
quintuplets 58
quizzes 142, 152, 153

R

rabbits 31, 32
racehorses 27, 30, 263–7
racketball 278
rackets 278
radar installations 74
radiation 179
radio 152; audiences 152;
    dishes 80–1; masts 94;
    stations 152
radishes 48
rafts 203, 241
railways 122–5;
    accidents 179, 180;
    bridges 95, 96; ferries 109;
    model 124–5;
    stations 123–4; tickets 124;
    travelling 124; tunnels 99;
    viaducts 97
rainbows 22
rainfall 22
rallying 274–5

ramp jumping 115, 118
ransoms 189
rappelling* 276
rapping 149
rats 26, 30, 32
ratting 31
rattlesnakes 37
reactors 74
real estate 85–90, 162–4
real tennis 279
reclamation plants 103
recorded sound 148,
    149–52
recorder 146
records 148, 149–52
redwoods 50, 51
reefs 15, 27
refineries 78
reflectors 80
refractories 69
refractors 80
refuelling 126
refuse tips 103
regattas 280
regeneration: animal 26;
    urban 89
registration numbers 116
reigns 181, 182
reincarnation 25–6
religion 199–200
rents* 90, 163
reproduction 52
reproductivity 57–8
reptiles 35–7, 43, 46
reserves (gold) 165
reservoirs 98–9
residences 86–7
resorts 91–2
restaurants 93
restaurateurs* 93
resuscitation 65
retailers 162
return of cash 166
revues 157
rhinoceroses 43
rhododendrons 47, 49
rhubarb 48
rhythmic gymnastics 262
rice 170, 208
riding in armour 210
rights: film 154;
    stock issue 167;
    television 153
ring roads 121
rinks 247, 269, 279
riots 179, 180
river: barriers 104;
    basins 16–17; bores 17, 290
rivers 16–17
riveting 109
roads 120–2;
    accidents 179, 180;
    loads 120
robberies 189
robins 33
rock: concerts 147;
    festivals 147;
    groups 147, 148, 149–52;
    pinnacles 14–15;
    stick of 213
rocket-powered
    vehicles 117
rockets 82
rocks 12, 13, 14–15
rodents 26, 30, 32
rodeo 279
roller coasters 92–3
roller cycling 248
roller hockey 279
roller skating 279
rolling: barrel 206; log 208
rolling pins 278

roofs 91
roots 46
rope slides 209
ropes 76
ropeways 76
roses 49
rowing 108, 111, 112, 279–80
Royal Academy 133, 134
Royal Society 193
royal tennis 279
royalty 181–2
rubbish dumps 103
rubies 24, 136
rugby: fives 252; league 280–1; union* 282–5
rugs 136
rulers (heads of state) 181–2
running 223–30, 247; backwards 230
runways 128
Ryder Cup 260

S

sacred objects 200
saddle bronc riding 279
sailboards 113, 305
sailfish 37, 222
sailing 110, 111, 112, 113, 303–5; accidents 179, 180
sails 110
St Swithin's Day 23
saints 200
salamanders 37, 43
salami 213
salary 166
sales 134, 136, 154, 159, 161–2, 171
salvage 204
Samson's chair 262
sand: castles 86; dunes 18; sculptures 135
sand yachting 285
sapphires 24
satellites: artificial 83; natural 8, 9
Saturn 8
sausages 213
scaffolding 103; erecting 103
scales: measuring 70; musical 144
Scalextric 120
scarecrows 103
scarves 217
schools 197–8; Sunday 200
science and technology* 67–84
scientific instruments 70–2
scorpions 40
Scrabble 235–6
screaming 63
screens 157
scriptwriters 153
scuba diving 203–4
sculling 279–80
sculptures 134–5; balloon 206; sand 135; scrap metal 135; snow and ice 103
sea: lochs 11; mounts 11; snakes 37; waves 12
seabirds 33, 34
sea-lions 29–30
seals 29–30
searchlights 69
seas 11, 12
seaways 97
seaweed 50

securities 167
seeds 49–50
seismology 20
sentences (judicial) 191–2
separation (of twins) 57, 58
septuplets 58
sequoias 50, 51
serials: film 155; radio 152; television 153
service stations 120
Seven Wonders 102
sewage: tunnels 99; works 103
sex ratio 177
sexual harassment* 187
Shakespeare 63
shares 166–7
sharks 25, 37, 38, 222
shaving 63
shearing 174
sheep 171, 174
sheep stations 171
sheep to shoulder 174
shellfish 42, 43
shells 42, 43
shinty 286
shipbuilding 110
ships 105–13, 179, 180, 189
shipwrecks 106
shoes 64, 217
shooting 286
shopping centres 91
shops 91, 94, 162
shorthand 210
shot put 224, 225, 226, 227, 228
shouting 63
show jumping 251
shows: comedy 159; fashion 159; musical 159; radio 152; television 153
shrews 27, 29
shuttles 83–4, 128
Siamese twins 58
sieges 195
sight 34, 63
signatures 141
signs* 99–100; of the Zodiac 7
silence 147–8
silver 217
singing* 144, 147, 148, 149–52, 200
singles 149–52
sittings (parliamentary) 183
skateboarding 279
skating: ice 268–70; roller 279
skeletons 44
ski orienteering 276
ski-bob 288
skid marks 117
skiing: alpine 286–8; freestyle 288; grass 288; nordic 286–8; North Pole 203; water* 299–300
ski-jumping 287
ski-lifts 179, 288
skipping* 160, 288
skittles 289
skulls 44, 53, 62
sledges 203, 289
sleep 28, 65
sleeplessness 65
slimming 56
slinging 210
slot cars 120
slot machines 257
sloths 28
slow worms 35
smell 26, 68

smog 179, 180
snail-racing 43
snails 25–6, 42, 43
snakebites 37
snakes 36–7, 43, 46
sneezing 65
snooker 279
snoring 65
snow 23; constructions 103; men* 103; plough blades 75; shoeing 288
snowmobiles 119
snowstorms 23
soaring 257–8
soccer 253–6
soft drinks 215
softball 279
solar power 74, 119
solar-powered vehicles 119, 132
solar system 5–11
soldiers 136, 195
solicitors 188
solitaire 236
somersaults 160, 262, 299
songs 144, 147, 148, 149–52
songwriters 144
sounds 63, 137, 144, 147, 148, 149–52
soundtracks 149
space: fatalities 84, 179; flights* 83–4; shuttles 83–4, 128; suits 84; telescopes 80; walks 83, 84
spans: bridges 95–6; life expectancy 177–8; political office 183, 184, 185, 186
spas 92
spear throwing* 210
spear-fishing 222
specialized structures* 99–104
speeches 183
speed marching 196
speed skating: ice 269–70; roller 279
speedway 289–90
spelling 139
spices 213
spiders 25, 39–40
spike driving 122
spills 78, 162
spinning: basketball 234; plate 160; top 210; wool 174
spires 200
spirits 214
spitting 210
spoil dumps 77
sponges 26, 43
sports* 219–308
springbok 28
spruce 50, 51
squares (streets) 122
squash (vegetable) 48
squash rackets 290
squat thrusts 262
squids 26, 42
squirrels 30
stadia 90, 91, 147
stages: film 155; theatrical 157
stained glass 104, 200
stair climbing 210
stairs 103
stalactites 15
stalagmites 15
stamp licking 169
stamps 169
standing 64; on one leg 64

Stanley Cup 268
starfish 38–9
stars 6–7
stately homes 85–6
states 175–7
statesmen 184
static wall 'sit' 262
stations: radio 152; railway 123–4
statues 103–4, 134–5, 193
statutes 186
steam: engines 73, 105, 110, 117, 122, 125; locomotives 122, 125; ships 105
steel 75
steeplechasing 263–7
step-ups* 210
stick of rock 213
stick-insects 40
stilt-walking 160, 210
Stock Exchanges 166–7
stonefish 38
stone skipping 210
storms 23, 179, 180
straits 12
strandpulling 302
strawberries 48, 49, 213
streets 121–2
stretcher bearing 210
strikes 164
string balls 210
stringed instruments 145, 146
structures 27, 85–104
studios 155
stuffed toys 217
stupas 200
sturgeon 38, 222
submarine: canyons 19; depressions 15; rivers 16
submarines 106, 107, 196; accidents 179, 180; captains 196
submergence 27, 30, 34, 36, 37, 106, 107, 203, 204
subways 99, 124, 180
suffrage 183, 184, 185
suggestion boxes 124
suicide 177, 179
suits 84
sumo wrestling 303
Sun 7
sundaes 213
Sunday schools 200
sundials 79
sunflowers 47
sunshine 22
sunspots 7
Super Bowl 221
superconductivity 69
supernovae 7
supersonic flight 125
surfing 290
surgery 66
surnames 139
surveyors 162
survival: animal 174; human 65, 203
suspension: bridges 95, 96; cables 76
swallowing 65
swamps 17
swans 32, 34
swarm 26
swede 48
sweetness 69
sweets 213
swifts 33, 34
swimming: animals 27, 29, 30, 34, 36, 37, 38; sport 291–5;

swimming pools 291
swings 104
switchbacks 92–3
switchboards 80
sycamore 51
symphonies 147
synagogues 199–200
synonyms 137, 138

T

table tennis 295
taekwondo 295
tailoring 174
take-overs 162
talking 63, 136–7, 183; birds 32–3
tandems 113
tankards 206
tankers 78, 108, 162
tanks 196–7; oil 78
tap dancing 160
tapes 149
tattoos 66
tax demands 166
taxation 165
taxis 119
teachers 198
teddy bears 136; picnic* 205
teeter boards 160
teeth 63; lifting and pulling with 63
tegestology 218
telecommunications 79–80
telegrams 80
telephones 79; cables 79; cards 80; exchanges 80; switchboards 80
telescopes 80–1
television 152–3; masts 94–5
temperature: climatic 7, 9, 22; human body 62, 65; physical extremes 69; superconducting 69
temples 86, 199
tennis: lawn 295–8; real/royal 279; table 295
tenpin bowling 236–7
tensile strength 68
tents 102
term of office 184, 185, 186
terns 33
terrorism 179, 180
text books 141
theatre 157, 159
theatre-goers 159
theorems 72
thermal expansion 68
thermometers 70
thermonuclear bombs 196
thoroughbreds 27, 30
Three Peaks 250, 276
three-day event 251
three-legged race 230
throwing* 210, 241, 246, 259, 278
thunder-days 23
tickets: air 127; train 124
tidal: barriers 104; waves 12, 290
tiddlywinks 298–9
tides 12
tigers 28, 160, 179
tightrope walking 160, 210
time: measures 73; pieces 79, 145, 153
tipsters 257
toads 37
toadstools 52
tobogganing 236

toes 62
tomatoes 48
tombs 104
top sellers: books 142; records 149–52
top spinning 210
tornadoes 23, 178, 179, 180
tortoises 35–6
totem poles 104
touch 64
Tour de France* 248
tourism 177
Tourist Trophy (TT) races 273
tours 147
towers 94–5, 104; Lego* 90
towing 120
town criers 63
towns 180–1
toxicity 68
toy shops 162
toys 136, 217
tracheostomies 66
tracking 31
tracks 122
trackways: footprints 44; roads 120
trade unions 164
traffic: jams 121; lights 121; volume 121
train spotting 123
trains 122–5; robbery 189
trampolining 160, 299
trams 119–20
transfer fees: football 255; rugby league 281
transformers 74
transmission lines 74
transmissions 74
transplants 66
transport* 105–32
trapeze 160
travelators 75
travelling: EU countries 128; world* 201, 202
treaties 183
tree: climbing 51; planting* 51; sitting 51; topping 51
trees 46, 50–1; family 58
triads 188
trials: criminal 186–7; motorcycling 273

triathlon 299
tricycles 248
trifles 213
trilithons 102
triple jump* 224, 225, 226, 227, 228
triplets 57, 58, 60
trolleybuses 120
trotting 263
trucks 118, 120
tsunami 12, 290
TT races 273
tubes 70
tug of war 298
tugs 108
tumours 66
tungsten 68
tunnelling 99, 179
tunnels 99, 123
turbines 74, 105
turkeys 173
turtles 35–6
tusks 30
TV 152–3; masts 94–5
twins 55, 56, 57, 58, 60
twitchers 34, 35
typewriting 210
typing 210
Tyrannosaurus Rex 44
tyre supporting 120
tyres 120

U

U-boats 196
UN speeches 183
undergraduates 197
undergrounds 99, 124, 180
underwater: caves 15; escapes 204; swimming 295
unemployment 164
unicycles 114
unions 164
United Nations 183
universe 5–11
universities 197
unsupported circles 210
uranium 77
urban settlements 89, 176, 180–1

V

vacuums 70
valleys 19
vases 217
vats 104
vegetables 47, 48–9
vehicles 84, 105–32
veins 61
velocity 69, 82, 84
venom: animals 25, 36–7, 38, 39, 40, 43; chemicals 68; fungi 52
Venus 8
verbs 137
viaducts 96, 97, 121
Victoria Cross 192, 193
video-tapes 152
viewers 153
villages 180–1
vines 170
vineyards 170
vintners 214
violins 146
violoncellos 145, 146
vipers 37
viruses 64
vision: bird 34; human 63
vitamins 49
vocabulary (bird) 32–3
voice 63, 144
volcanoes 8, 20, 21, 179
volleyball 299
voltages 70, 74
votes 183, 184, 185
vowels 137
vultures 32, 33

W

waists 64
waiting rooms 124
walking 201–2, 230; in space 83, 84; on hands 230; on stilts 160, 210; on water 280
wall of death 115
wallets 217
walls 104
walnut 51
wars 194–5
warships 106, 110

wasps 40
watches 79, 153
water: lilies* 46, 49; melon 48; mills 74; speed 111; spouts 23; supply tunnels 99; towers 104; wells 79
water polo 299
water skiing* 299–300
waterfalls 16, 104
watermelons 48
waterwheels 104
waves 12, 290
wealth 165–6
weasels 28
weather 22–3
wedding: dresses 215; trains 215
weddings 204–5
weeds 50
weight: humans 56; livestock 171–2, 173, 174; measures of 73
weight gaining 56
weight loss 27, 56
weightlifting* 300–2
wellie wanging 278
wellingtonia 49
wells: oil 78; water 79
whale factory 109
whales 25, 27, 28, 37
wheat 170
wheelchairs 201
wheelies: bicycles 114; motorcycles 115
whip cracking 210
whisky 214
whistling 63
white Christmas 23
Who's Who* 140
willow 51
wills 31, 166, 188
wind 23; generators 74; tunnels 73–4
windmills 73–4
windows 104; cleaning* 210; stained glass 104, 200
windsurfing 113, 305
wine 214–15; casks 104; cellars 171
wing walking 125
wingbeats 33, 41
wingspans: aircraft 125; animals 29, 33, 41

winkling 43
wire ropes 76
wireless 152
witchcraft 190
wolfram 68
wonders of the world 102
woodcocks 33, 34
wood-cutting 52
wooden ships 105
wooden structures 86, 90
woodpeckers 34
woods 50–1
wool 174
words 136–9
working: career 164; week 164
World Series 231
worms 27, 42; charming 42
worship 199–200
wreckers 120
wrecks 106
wrens 33
wrestling 302–3
wrist watches 79, 153
writing 140, 141–2; minuscule 208

Y

yachting 110, 111, 112, 113, 303–5; accidents 179, 180; ice 285; sand 285
yachts 107, 110
yaks 28
yakuza 188
yard of ale 214
yew 51
yodelling 63
yolks 173
Yorkshire puddings 213
yo-yos 210, 217

Z

ziggurats 104
zip-fasteners 217
Zodiac 7
zoos 52

*DENOTES A FURTHER ENTRY IN STOP PRESS

Acknowledgments

The Editor of *The Guinness Book of Records* wishes to thank: Amanda Brooks, Debbie Collings, Ann Collins, Dawn Gratton, Nicholas Heath-Brown, Christine Heilman, Muriel Ling, Sarah Llewellyn-Jones, Stewart Newport, Alex Reid, David Roberts, Sarah Silvé, Amanda Ward.

PICTURE RESEARCH James Clift, Alex Goldberg
PHOTOGRAPHIC AND DUPING SERVICES Avart Design Consultants
ARTWORK, MAPS AND DIAGRAMS Frances Button, Pat Gibbon, Peter Harper, Matthew Hillier S.W.L.A., Dick Millington, Sarah Silvé
COVER DESIGN Pentagram
COVER PICTURE Spectrum Colour Library
PRESS AND PUBLIC RELATIONS Cathy Brooks, Carole Jones

CONTRIBUTORS Alan Adler, Andrew Adams, John Arblaster, Bill Ashton, Brian Bailey, Richard Balkwill, Howard Bass, Michael Benton, Dennis Bird, Richard Braddish, Peter Brierley, Robert Brooke, Ian Buchanan, Bob Burton, Henry Button, Clive Carpenter, Mark Carwardine, Chris Cavey, Andy Chipling, Graham Coates, Graham Coombs, Caleb Crain, Alan Dawson, Andrew Duncan, Graham Dymott, Colin Dyson, Clive Everton, Archibald Fletcher, John Flynn, Brian Ford, Paulette Foyle, Bill Frindall, Tim Furniss, Clyde Gilmour, Ian Goold, Stan Greenberg, Liz Hawley, Robert Headland, Ron Hildebrant, Rick Hogben, Gordon Hull, Sir Peter Johnson, Ove Karlsson, Gary Krebs, Bernard Lavery, Peter Lunn, Tessa McWhirter, John Marshall, T. W. Mermel, Carol Michaelson, Andy Milroy, Michael Minges, Ray Mitchell, John Moody, Patrick Moore, Bill Morris, Ron Moulton, Barry Norman, Enzo Paci, Greg Parkinson, Geoff Pearse, John Randall, Elfan ap Rees, Chris Rhys, Jonathan Rice, Patrick Robertson, Dan Roddick, Peter Rowan, Joshua Rozenberg, Shin Saikyo, Steven Salberg, Irvin Saxton, Victoria Schilling, Alexander Schwartz, Colin Smith, Ian Smith, William Smith, Phoebe Snetsinger, Graham Snowdon, Martin Stone, John Tamplin, Juhani Virola, Tony Waltham, Ray Waterman, David Wells, Rick Wilson, Karen Romano Young.

Grateful acknowledgment is also made to the governing bodies and organizations who have helped in our researches.

BOOKS THAT STAND

GUINNESS PUBLISH

40 YEARS OF THE GUINNESS BOOK OF RECORDS

In 1759 Arthur Guinness founded the Guinness Brewery at St James' Gate, Dublin and by 1833, the brewery was the largest in Ireland. Arthur Guinness Son & Co Ltd became a limited liability company in London in 1886 and by the 1930s Guinness had two breweries in Britain producing its special porter stout. The slogans "Guinness is good for you", "Guinness for strength" and "My Goodness, My Guinness" appeared everywhere. Guinness was in a unique position in the brewing trade in Britain in that it was the only beer on sale in every public house yet Guinness did not actually own any of the pubs - except for the Castle Inn on its hop farms at Bodiam, Sussex. Thus the company was always on the look-out for promotional ideas.

Whilst at a shooting party in Co Wexford, Ireland, in 1951, Sir Hugh Beaver, the company's managing director, was involved in a dispute as to whether the golden plover was Europe's fastest game bird. In his host's library at Castlebridge House, Sir Hugh could not confirm the answer in any of the reference books. Again in 1954, an argument arose as to whether grouse were faster than golden plover. Sir Hugh realised that such questions could arise amongst people in pubs and that a book which answered these questions would be helpful to licensees.

Chris Chataway, the record-breaking athlete, was then an underbrewer at Guinness' Park Royal Brewery. When he heard of Sir Hugh's idea, he recommended the ideal people to produce the book - the twins Norris and Ross McWhirter, whom he had met through athletics events, both having won their Blues for sprinting at Oxford. The McWhirters were running a fact-finding agency in Fleet Street and so impressed the Board that they were immediately commissioned to compile what was to become The Guinness Book of Records.

After a busy year of research, the first copy of the 198-page Guinness Book of Records was bound by printers on 27 August, 1955. It was an instantaneous success and became Britain's No 1 best-seller before Christmas.

The British success was soon replicated elsewhere. The Guinness Book of Records English edition is now published in 40 different countries with another 37 editions in foreign languages. Total sales of all editions passed 50 million in 1984, 75 million in 1994 and will reach the 100 million mark early in the next millennium. Other language editions include world records and national records for the producing country.

Records are constantly changing and few survive from the first edition in 1955. In various places throughout this edition we show - in our 40-year panels - the extent of change from 1955 to 1995. As in 1955, our hope remains that this book can assist in resolving enquiries on facts, and may turn the heat of argument into the light of knowledge.

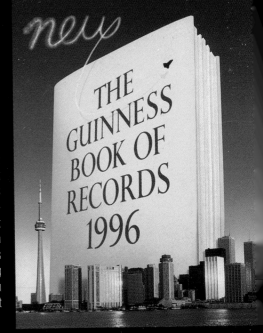

immediately opposite the Round Glass house that Sir Hugh Beaver had the debate with his
nness Book of Records originated. *2*. **Sir Hugh Beaver**. *3*. **Arthur Guinness** (1725-
:away in Oxford on 6 May 1954, when Bannister leapt into the record books by running
uinness Brewery at Park Royal, London, England, as it was in the 1950s. *6*. **Norris** and
ld. *7*. **The First Edition**. *8*. **Norris** and **Ross McWhirter** when the first edition was
es' Gate, Dublin.

THE GUINNESS BOOK OF RECORDS